This Is Who We Were:
A Companion to the 1940 Census

This Is Who We Were: A Companion to the 1940 Census

by

Scott Derks

Grey House Publishing

PUBLISHER: Leslie Mackenzie
EDITORIAL DIRECTOR: Laura Mars
ASSOCIATE EDITOR: Diana Delgado
PRODUCTION MANAGER: Kristen Thatcher
MARKETING DIRECTOR: Jessica Moody
AUTHOR: Scott Derks
COMPOSITION: David Garoogian

Grey House Publishing, Inc.
4919 Route 22
Amenia, NY 12501
518.789.8700
FAX 845.373.6390
www.greyhouse.com
e-mail: books @greyhouse.com

Publisher's Cataloging-In-Publication Data
(Prepared by The Donohue Group, Inc.)

Derks, Scott.

This is who we were : a companion to the 1940 Census / by Scott Derks.

p. : ill. ; cm.

Includes materials from the 1940 U.S. Census.
Includes index.
ISBN: 978-1-61925-007-9

1. United States—Economic conditions—1918-1945. 2. United States—Social conditions—1933-1945. 3. United States—Civilization—1918-1945. 4. Nineteen thirties. I. Title. II. Title: Census of the United States (1940)

HC106.3 .D47 2012
330.973

TABLE OF CONTENTS

Section Two: Historical Snapshots

This section includes lists of important "firsts" for America, from technical advances and political events to new products and top selling books. Combining serious American history with fun facts, these snapshots present, in chronological categories, an easy-to-read overview of what happened in the decade leading up to 1940.

Section Three: Economy of the Times

This section looks at a wide range of economic data, including food, clothing, transportation, housing and other selected prices, with reprints of actual advertisements for products and services of the time. It is arranged chronologically, year by year, and brings to life the economic engine that drove our country into the 1940s.

Section Four: All Around Us—What We Saw, Wrote, Read & Listened To

This section includes reprints of newspaper and magazine articles, letters, posters, and others items designed to help the reader focus on what was on the minds of Americans in the decade prior to the 1940 Census. As they move from 1930 to 1940, these printed pieces show how popular opinion may have formed, and changed, by the time Americans responded to the 1940 Census.

Section Five: 1940 Census Summary & Comparison Data

This section includes actual 1940 Census material, including a comprehensive U.S. report that summarizes individual responses, and twenty-six data tables that compare the 92 principal cities (plus the five boroughs of New York City) in 1940—those with 100,000 population or more.

Index

Dedicated to the courageous Americans of 1940, especially those who met the challenges of the Great Depression and defended America on the battlefield, in factories, and in the classroom.

INTRODUCTION

Upon hearing that the U.S. Census Bureau was releasing original data from the 1940 Census, we immediately envisioned *This is Who We Were: A Companion to the 1940 Census*. Drawing on our proven ability to find not only value, but "aha moments" from otherwise dry statistics, we went to work developing the story of America in 1940, using real lives of real people. What were Americans doing and thinking when the census taker knocked on their door? What job did they arrive home from? What food was on the dinner table? What family discussion was interrupted?

This is Who We Were describes 26 families who lived in the decade leading up to 1940, from housemaid in Harlem to heiress in Hawaii. In five sections that are detailed below, this new edition covers not only lifestyles, but history, economics, and current events of the years leading up to 1940. Using original material from the 1940 Census, first hand interviews, government data and dozens of images, *This is Who We Were* provides a unique way to study a unique time in America, as well as a fascinating comparison of 1940 America to 2010 America.

Front Matter

Media Response: Carefully selected from the years right before and right after the 1940 Census took place, the articles that follow this Introduction cover such topics as survey questions, degree of accuracy of the census, and how the census changed the political landscape. These articles from *The New York Times, San Antonio Press, The Racine Journal,* and *The Gallup Independent* take you behind the scenes of the 1940 Census.

Ranking Tables: Compiled by editors at Grey House Publishing, these tables compare and rank each state by sixteen topics, including population, age, educational attainment, home ownership, home value, rent, and houses with plumbing! Each table gives data from both the 1940 and the 2010 Census, and then ranks each state.

Section One: Profiles

Read about 26 Americans whose lives were sandwiched between the Great Depression and World War II, undeniably a fascinating time in America's history. Each profile provides a personal look into the different ways Americans coped, survived, and succeeded, written in an easy-to-read bulleted format and peppered with images. The 26 profiles represent dozens of occupations, working, middle and upper class Americans, and 17 states from all corners of the country. The detailed Table of Contents gives specifics: job, city and state, and a story headline.

Starting with a short introduction that emphasizes its relevance to 1940, each profile is arranged in specific categories—Life at Home, Life at Work, Life in the Community. When possible, profiles include original tables from the 1940 Census. For example, the story of an autoworker in Detroit, Michigan includes nine original tables from the 1940 Census, specific to Detroit in 1940. These tables are reprinted exactly as they appeared 73 years ago, and provide population statistics about Detroit's citizens, including age, education, country of birth, and employment.

Section Two: Historical Snapshots

Section two is made up of four long, bulleted lists—and what significant lists they are! In chronological order—Early 1930s, Mid 1930s, Late 1930s, and 1940—these include an amazing range of "firsts" and "turning points." These *Historical Snapshots* bring to mind when Hostess Twinkies made their debut (early 30s), when Social Security checks were first distributed (late 1930s), when McDonald's first opened (1940), and hundreds more facts that help paint a picture of America in the years leading up to, thus influencing, results of the 1940 Census.

Section Three: Economy of the Times

One of the most interesting things about researching an earlier time is learning how much things cost and what people were paid. This section of *This is Who We Were* offers this information in spades. Arranged by year, this data encompasses the entire decade that led up to 1940.

Economy of the Times, with Average Annual Income of Standard Jobs, Selected Prices, and National Consumer Expenditures, shows that public school teachers made $1,455 in 1930, a Polar Air refrigerator cost $22.98 in 1937, and the average utility bill in 1939 was $23.66 A YEAR!

Also included is a *Value of a Dollar Index* that compares the buying power of $1.00 in 2010 to the buying power of $1.00 in every year prior, back to 1860, helping to put the economic data in *This is Who We Were* into context. You'll discover that $1.00 in 2010 could buy $15.58 worth of goods in 1940. For example, the pound of coffee that cost $.33 in 1940 would cost $5.14 in 2010; a copper tea kettle that cost $3.49 in 1940 would cost $54.37 in 2010.

Section Four: All Around Us—What We Saw, Wrote, Read & Listened To

There is no better way to put your finger on the pulse of a country than to read its magazines and newspapers. This section offers over 50 original pieces—articles, comic strips, advertisements, and book excerpts—that influenced the Americans who made up the 1940 Census.

From "The Endless Chain of Credit" in the *Oberlin News Tribune* to "Food from Everywhere" in *Household Magazine* to "Pay-As-You-Listen is a Riddle of the Age" in *The New York Times,* this section offers a fascinating look at the current trends and issues facing the average American family from 1930–1940.

Section Five: 1940 Census Summary & Comparison Data

Here you will find two original elements from the 1940 Census—*United States Summary* and *Comparison of Principal Cities.*

The Summary explains how the 1940 Census data was collected and compiled, and compares its results with data as early as 1790—the year of the first U.S. Census. In 65 original pages, supported by maps, charts and tables, this document provides not only a look at America in 1940, but compares its findings to earlier enumerations.

The Comparison of Principal Cities includes those cities with populations of 100,000 or more in 1940, of which there were 92 (compared with 275 incorporated cities reported in the 2010 Census). These 92 cities are compared in 49 tables that detail population characteristics, like Minor Races, Male to Female Ratio, Age by Race, Age by Sex, Females in the Voting Population, Nonwhite Males and Females by Employment Status, Major Occupation Group for Female Workers, and more.

Index

Ending with a comprehensive Index, *This is Who We Were: A Companion to the 1940 Census* is sure to be of value as both a serious research tool for students of American history as well as an intriguing climb up America's family tree for all of us.

PREFACE

Shortly after sending out a tweet earlier this year announcing that the 1940 Census data was available, the U.S. National Archives website received so many hits that they nearly paralyzed the site.

The enthusiastic interest in who we were was fueled by the prospect of finding detailed information about our own family's past—including access to names, addresses, income, employment information and other personal details—plus seeing how the U.S. has changed in 72 years.

When a treasure trove of intriguing data is exposed to the sunlight, the first tendency is to wallow in the numbers as excited as a pig in extra fine slop. But person-kind can not live by statistics alone. The first step toward recovery is a recognition that people—regular, live-next-door-families—are at the core of the numbers. And it's these people who are at the core of *This is Who We Were: A Companion to the 1940 Census.*

This edition breathes life into 26 people and families who demonstrated the resilience of a nation that survived a Depression with sufficient moxie to transform America's manufacturing infrastructure into an aggressive war material machine.

This is Who We Were examines, up close and personal, the era that spawned the "Greatest Generation," made headlines with the conviction of the Scottsboro Boys, and was home to the kind of innovations that resulted in television, high-speed boats and portable foods.

What Has Changed

In addition to the personal details, the material released in the 1940 Census taught us much about how America has changed.

- The 1940 Census cost $1 billion (in 2010 dollars) verses $12.4 billion for the 2010 Census, even though the number of questions were cut by a third. In 1940, respondents had to answer 34 questions, compared to only 10 in 2010.
- America's population has more than doubled since 1940, from 132 million, to 308 million in 2010. The most populous state was New York then, is California now, and New York City is still the most populated city. In 1940, occupations included salesman, laborer, shipyard worker and farmer, compared to 2010 jobs—laboratory technician, Internet publisher, air transportation worker and human resources manager.
- The mean salary for men in 1940 (adjusted for inflation) was under $15,000 and for women, just over $9,000. Median income for men now is more than $33,000 and for women, $24,000. In 1940 only 5% of Americans had a bachelor's degree or higher and by 2010 that number was up to 28%.
- From 1790 to 1940 the proportion of people living in cities of 2,500 or more increased from 5.1% to 56.5%. In 2010, 82% of the population were living in urban areas.
- The decade between 1930 and 1940 was the first decade in American history in which immigration was not a factor in population growth.
- Partly as a result of the Great Depression, spanning most of the 1930s, women in the workplace rose; in 1940 25% of all women over the age of 14 were in the workforce compared to 22% in 1930 and 21% in 1920.

- In 1940 infant deaths among African Americans was 77.9 children per 1000 births, compared to white baby deaths of 47.1 per 1000. In 2010 the African American infant death ration was 13.3 per 1000 compared to 6.7 per 1000 in the general population.
- Life expectancy has greatly improved since 1940, when it was 62.9. In 2010, life expectancy had risen to 78.7.
- In 1940, the average cost to build a new single family home was $3,920. This cost rose to $222,511 by 2010.

This is Who We Were: A Companion to the 1940 Census provides a critical link to America's history. These stories of the men, women and children who actually took pen to paper and responded to the 1940 Census questions will encourage readers to focus on this particular time in U.S. history long enough to learn the whole story, not just for the few minutes it takes to scan down a list of numbers or names.

—Scott Derks

MEDIA RESPONSE

Despite the tremendous strides we have made since 1940, some things have remained the same. For example, Americans are still fascinated in what were called "statistical oddities" in 1940, we still debate what our government should be allowed to know about us, and we still report on the inequality of both women's earning power and congressional districts. The following articles, reprinted in their entirety, prove these points.

An Official View of Proposed Questions for 1940 Census

Director Explains Bureau's Position on Controversial Inquiries, Taking Exception to The Times Articles Which Are Defended by the Writer

The following letters from the Director of the Census and THE TIMES *chief Washington correspondent relate to a series of articles by the latter on the subject of the 1940 census, which will begin April 1. The background of the controversy is covered in an article on Page 6 of this section.*

TO THE EDITOR OF THE NEW YORK TIMES:

Arthur Krock's discussion of the coming decennial census in your issues of Feb. 22 and 23 contains misstatements of fact and improper inferences in the following particulars:

1. That the President has power, by executive order, to make confidential census information available to other branches of the government;

2. That Congress in its enactment of 1929, under which authority the 1940 census is being taken (this enactment approved and signed by President Hoover), specifically limited the population schedule of 1940 to twenty-one questions;

3. That the question in the housing schedule calling for information on home mortgages is new;

4. That the specific questions included in the 1940 schedules were selected with the approval of the President;

5. That the "income" question in the population schedule is not authorized by law and is not "germane" to the subject of unemployment;

6. That the determination of the specific questions resulted from the pressure of New Deal agencies;

7. That the questions in the supplementary census, to be asked of each twentieth person, involve discrimination, and that they have to do with subject-matter not heretofore employed in census taking and not of vital public interest.

Secrecy Specified

As to the right of the President or any governmental agency to publish or make use of any confidential information collected by the census, I quote from the Census Act of 1929:

"Section 11. That the information furnished under the provisions of this act shall be used only for the statistical purposes for which it is supplied. No publication shall be made by the census office whereby the data furnished by any particular establishment or individual can be identified, nor shall the director of the census permit any other than the sworn employes of the census office to examine the individual reports."

Again quoting from Section 18 of the same act:

"That in no case shall information furnished under the authority of this act be used to the detriment of the person or persons to whom such information relates."

The same enactment fixes the penalties applicable to the public (all persons 18 years of age and over) for refusal to answer the census inquiries and for intentionally giving wrong information.

The same enactment provides penalties of fine and imprisonment up to $2,000 or five years in prison or both for any census employe "if he shall, without the authority of the director of the census, publish or communicate any information coming into his possession by reason of his employment under the provisions of this act."

That it is within the power of the President, by executive order, as Mr. Krock contends, to set aside an act of Congress or to compel sworn census employes to commit felonies is a new theory in government.

The Population Schedule

As to Mr. Krock's statement that the Congressional enactment of 1929, which is the authority for the present census, specifically limited the questions on the population schedule to twenty-one, I quote from the law:

"Section 4. That the fifteenth (1930) and subsequent decennial censuses shall be restricted to inquiries relating to population, to agriculture, to irrigation, to drainage, to distribution, to unemployment and to mines. The number, form and subdivision of the inquiries in the schedules used to take the census shall be determined by the director of the census, with the approval of the Secretary of Commerce."

As to Mr. Krock's charge that the question in the housing schedule calling for facts on home mortgages is new and to his statement that "the American people have heretofore taken the view that none of this is a census taker's business," I call attention to the following, quoted verbatim from the census law under which the census of 1890 was taken (this law was approved and signed by President Benjamin Harrison):

"That it shall be the duty of the superintendent of census, in addition to the duties now required of him by law, to ascertain the number of persons who live on and cultivate their own farms and who live in their own homes, and the number who hire their farms and homes, and the number of farms and homes which are under mortgage, the amount of mortgage debt, and the value of the property mortgaged. He shall also ascertain whether such farms and homes have been mortgaged for the whole or part of the purchase money for the same, or for other purposes, and the rates of interest paid upon mortgage loans."

Housing Questions

The census of 1900 taken during the Administration of President McKinley, the census of 1910 during the Administration of President Taft, the census of 1920 during the Administration of President Wilson, all included questions on home ownership or rental, and if owned, free or mortgaged. The census of 1930 under President Hoover called for information on home owned or rented, value of home if owned, or monthly rental if rented, and likewise called for information as to whether or not there was a radio set in the home.

I should like to call Mr. Krock's attention to the census of 1850, which required all persons to report the value of real estate owned, and to the census of 1860, which required all persons to report the value of real estate owned together with the value of their personal estates. In the census of 1860 Abraham Lincoln reported the value of his real estate and the value of his personal estate as did all other persons.

Those who charge that the questions in the 1940 census violate privacy should know that they will not be called upon to give an appraisal of their personal property as in the census of 1860.

As to Mr. Krock's intimation that the questions in the 1940 census schedules were selected under approval or suggestion of the President, I should like to say that, to my knowledge, the President has not seen these questions and to assert that no indication nor intimation as to the selection of questions come from the White House.

If Mr. Krock jumped to the conclusion that the President favored these individual questions because of his formal proclamation calling upon the public to cooperate in the 1940 census, he should know that each President since 1900 has, prior to decennial censuses, issued such formal proclamations; that the draft of this message was prepared by census bureau employes, in line with the contents of previous Presidential proclamations, and then submitted to the Bureau of the Budget and to the Department of Justice for their approval before going to the White House.

The implication that this proclamation was issued in response to criticisms of the contents of the schedules will not stand up in view of the fact that the draft of this formal proclamation was prepared many weeks ago, before any objection to the questions had been registered.

The Income Inquiry

As to Mr. Krock's charge that the "income" inquiry in the population schedule is not in line with the precedent of Congressional enactment and that it is not "germane" to the subject of unemployment, I should like to call his attention to the Congressional enactment calling for the unemployment census of 1937. That law stated that its purpose was to provide information about persons "partially employed or unemployed and their dependents and income." The subsequent census of unemployment contained the question on annual income as required by that law.

Questions on income have been an important part of the census of agriculture for twenty years and the information yielded as to income from sale and use of farm products has been vital in legislative consideration of the farm problem. The 1930 census of agriculture showed that approximately 3,000,000 farms—nearly one-half of all farms—had incomes from the sale and use of products amounting to $1,000 a year and less.

Aid to Business Seen

As to Mr. Krock's contention that income is not "germane" to the subject of population and unemployment, I should like to say that wage-income is a question relating in a very vital sense both to population and to unemployment. While the returns from this question will be of great service in the form of totals to be used in computing national income, the greatest value appears when they are used as a basis for classifying the population. Business organizations can plan their marketing

continued on next page

activities much more effectively if they know in what areas high-income families are to be found, and in what areas low-income families, and also something about the other population characteristics which are found in combination with high and low income.

In other respects the relation between population and income is even more vital and fundamental. The annual increase in the population is now far smaller than it was a few years ago, and the number of children is rather rapidly declining. It has been frequently stated that a disproportionate fraction of these children are growing up in homes with very low incomes and thus receiving inadequate preparation for the duties of citizenship.

Education a Factor

Income data in the census will show to what extent this condition actually prevails. The income figures tabulated in combination with education will show the extent to which low income might be due to lack of education. Income tabulated in combination with age will show to what extent individual members of the American people are improving their economic status with increasing age; and also to what extent those approaching old age are compelled to get along on lower incomes.

The income question relates directly to unemployment. Under present conditions any statistics on employment which are to be of real use must go farther than giving simply the number of those who have no employment whatever.

It is necessary in addition to have some measure of the extent of employment of those not strictly unemployed but nevertheless very inadequately employed. The best possible measure of the adequacy of employment is the amount of income which the person receives from it; and when the amount of wage income is tabulated in combination with age, occupation, industry and other characteristics shown in the population census, it becomes one of the most important of all factors available for the analysis of the unemployment situation.

Mr. Krock's inference that certain questions on the 1940 schedule were included as a result of the pressure of New Deal agencies is devoid of all basis of fact. On the contrary, the very questions to which he registers objection were urged upon the census bureau by conservative business men and business organizations.

Business men, trade associations, chambers of commerce, advertising agencies and marketing experts have long urged the inclusion of the question on income. Business has always wanted information on wages and salaries to determine the extent of national, regional and local mass buying power in the field of consumer goods. The value of these statistics is self-evident to all engaged in marketing goods. The fact is that the question on income in the 1940 census does not call for total income. It merely asks how much the person received in wages or salary, including commissions, last year, up to $5,000. If he made more, he merely answers "over $5,000."

The construction of this question, with its $5,000 ceiling, makes it perfectly evident that its intention is to measure purchasing power for consumer goods and designate zones of high and low purchasing power. Anybody knows that salaries and wages below $5,000 are expended largely for consumer goods and that income above $5,000 is not so expended. The very nature of the question therefore explains its purpose.

A year ago a large group of people prominent in business and economics was called to Washington to examine proposed census questions. This conference expressed particular satisfaction with the questions relating to migration, employment, unemployment and economic status.

Letters and resolutions calling for statistics on earnings of the American people are in the files of the census bureau from many organizations. One of these came from a conference sponsored by the National Bureau of Economic Research, which includes directors from such groups as the American Engineering Council, the American Management Association, the National Publishers Association and the American Federation of Labor.

Committee Approval

It should also be remembered that this income question was approved unanimously by the advisory committee of the census bureau composed of non-governmental people and including Dr. Robert E. Chaddock of Columbia University, Dr. J. Frederick Dewhurst of the Twentieth Century Fund, Paul T. Cherington, market analyst; Dr. William F. Ogburn of the University of Chicago, Dr. Murray R. Benedict of the University of California and Dr. Willard R. Thorp of Dun & Bradstreet.

Demand for the housing census likewise came from business. The organizations and individuals which expressed their desire and need for a housing census included the National Retail Lumber Dealers Association, the National Sand and Gravel Association, the Structural Clay Products Institute, the Metal Window Institute, the National Lime Association, the National Paint, Varnish and Lacquer Association and others. The National Association of Real Estate Boards passed a resolution requesting Congress to authorize census questions on housing, home ownership and home finance. The National Association of Housing officials also petitioned Congress, as did the Housing Boards of New York State and Pennsylvania. William Green, president of the American Federation of Labor, called the housing census "a matter in which labor is particularly concerned." Hundreds of regional organizations have likewise expressed their interest.

As to the charge that the supplementary questions, to be asked of each twentieth person, involve discrimination and that they deal with subjects not heretofore employed in census taking, I should like to say that the very questions which Mr. Krock regards as invading privacy—requiring women to reveal marital status, number times married and number of children ever born—have been used in varying ways since 1880 and that the censuses of 1890, 1900 and 1910 called for much the same information.

Federation of Labor, called the housing census "a matter in which labor is particularly concerned." Hundreds of regional organizations have likewise expressed their interest.

As to the charge that the supplementary questions, to be asked of each twentieth person, involve discrimination and that they deal with subjects not heretofore employed in census taking, I should like to say that the very questions which Mr. Krock regards as invading privacy—requiring women to reveal marital status, number times married and number of children ever born—have been used in varying ways since 1880 and that the censuses of 1890, 1900 and 1910 called for much the same information.

One other query in the supplementary census calling for information as to whether or not a veteran was employed in the 1930 census and has been included at the suggestion of the Veterans' Administration and the American Legion.

Social Security Data

The only absolutely new question in the supplementary census is that asking whether the person has a social security number and the range of deductions made from salaries or wages for social security. As a matter of fact, the real reason for asking these supplementary questions of only 5 per cent of the population is that most of the questions on it are old and a sample involving between six and seven million will be sufficient to continue appraisal of the trends previously shown, and we are thus sparing 95 per cent of the people the time required to answer these questions. Rather than being a step involving discrimination, it is a step in favor of public convenience.

The censuses of the United States, through 150 years, have made available the most complete and accurate statistical record possessed by any nation. At every decennial census there has been some resistance to new questions, introduced to obtain information called for by the increasing complexity of American life. Fortunately, the public generally appreciates the value of census statistics and cooperates willingly. This is evident from the fact that in all these years it has rarely been necessary to resort to compulsion.

If Mr. Krock fears that the census violates the guarantees of the Bill of Rights, he should remember that the nation's founders also wrote the provision for decennial censuses in the Constitution and it was they who provided for compulsion in the answering of census inquiries.

W. L. Austin,
Director of the Census.

Washington, Feb. 27, 1940.

continued on next page

Mr. Krock Answers Charges

TO THE EDITOR OF THE NEW YORK TIMES:

The only statements in either of my census articles which may have conveyed an inaccurate impression were that "the law organizing the 1940 census restricted the population inquiry to twenty-one questions," and that Question 32 demands "money, wages and salary received." Many lawyers assure me that the first statement is correct "in effect" (the legal argument is too long to review here), but I should have written "in effect." There is no comma after the word "money" in Question 32, which represents, however, merely a difference between a completely intimate inquiry and a less complete one.

Mr. Austin's other charges of "direct misstatements" and "gross injustices" derive from heat, not light. Taking up the remainder:

1. The President's power to make the census information available to Congressional committees, etc., has been proved in the matter of other confidential data very recently. The Executive is the sole judge of whether the purpose of a law is served by disclosure.
2. Answered above.
3. The whole housing schedule is new.
4. Of course the President approved the questions; he issued a proclamation stressing the penalties for not answering.
5. The income of the "employed" is not germane to a census of the "unemployed." It is something else.
6. Observation here for a number of years makes me certain of this: Mr. Austin is welcome to a contrary opinion.
7. It is discriminatory because only 5 per cent are put to these questions. That's what I wrote originally.

General Observations

There is no space to answer Mr. Austin point by point, even though I took (as he has) three times as much for a reply. But these general observations may be submitted:

In the housing schedule, since "value" is not "tenure," and "rent" is not an incumbrance, the questions are probably unlawful.

The inquiry as to "race" is impertinent and, except in clear cases of color difference, not possible to answer accurately in most instances.

Mr. Austin's schedules were printed with Questions 32 and 33 as follows: "Amount of money wages and salary received, including commissions?" "Did this person receive income of $50 or more from sources other than money, wages or salary?" He now says enumerators have been instructed to seek such data up to $5,000 only; "over $5,000" will be considered a sufficient answer. (1) If the director can modify his own questions thus, he can expand them as he chooses, which is bureau legislation and a further invasion of individual rights. (2) Why should those who get less than $5,000 have to make detailed answers, and those above be excused? More discrimination.

The director argues that the census follows a familiar groove. Why then did he twice testify before a Congressional committee in 1939 that "there are great additional demands and need for new information," etc.? If he does not consider certain new questions out of order, because in previous censuses other impertinent questions were asked, how does he explain why those previous questions were discontinued?

The Matter of Penalties

Until 1919 a fine of $30 was imposed for refusal, negligence or falsity in answering. In that year the maximum fine was made $100. The 1929 act under which the 1940 census is being taken added a jail sentence, sixty days for refusal or neglect, and a year plus a $500 fine for falsity.

In its various census acts Congress has always been careful and specific concerning questions. It has never delegated discretion, including a director's right to modify the schedules under fire. The subject of inquiry has always been carefully prescribed by Congress—i.e., an "unemployment," not "employment," census being specifically authorized in the present instance. And in 1879 Congress struck out a question prescribed in 1873—"value or real estate owned." The 1940 inquiry is a reversion to a discredited piece of prying.

My opinion continues to be that some of the census questions are illegal by statute; others an invasion of constitutional right and not germane to the inquiry as authorized; that the New Deal planners inspired several of them, and that the machinery of enumeration does not provide proper protection even up to the time the Executive may by order remove these. In other words, I have nothing to retract. ARTHUR KROCK.

Washington, Feb. 28, 1940.

Mr. Austin Again Dissents

TO THE EDITOR OF THE NEW YORK TIMES:

I protest the continued misstatement of fact in the third article by Arthur Krock published Feb. 28, regarding the 1940 census. In this article Mr. Krock presents three more misstatements as follows:

First, that the penalties covering refusals to answer in the 1940 census are unlike those employed in the 1930 census;

Second, that the 1930 census did not contain an inquiry concerning race, and

Third, that the mimeographed instructions to enumerators concerning the interpretation and limitations placed on the inquiry of wages and salaries represents a recent change in policy and a modification through a regulation by the Director of the Census.

The actual facts are as follows:

First, there has been no change in the decennial census act adopted by Congress in 1929 fixing penalties for the 1930 census and all subsequent censuses including 1940. The only new decennial census legislation since June, 1929, was the census of housing, act of Aug. 11, 1939, which specifically provides that the penalties provided in the act of 1929 shall be applicable to the housing census;

Second, inquiries concerning race have been included in every census since 1850. The race items in the 1940 census are identical with those of the 1930 census except for a change in the definition of the term "Mexican";

Third, the Director of the Census has not modified by regulation the original intent of the question on money wages or salary as evidenced by the fact that the same basic instructions to enumerators covering interpretations and limitations were used in the trial census in two Indiana counties last August. Mr. Krock alleges that these were conceived in January this year.

Only minor modifications were made since the test census for the purpose of more sharply clarifying the definition of wages and salaries.

W. L. AUSTIN,
Director of the Census.

Washington, Feb. 29, 1940.

Mr. Krock Stands Ground

TO THE EDITOR OF THE NEW YORK TIMES:

Replying to the second letter of the Director of the Census:

1. I did not say that the 1940 penalties are different from those of 1930. I said they were extended to cover new questions—those on income—and that is correct.
2. In his own bulletin headed "Factual Record of Census Inquiries for 150 Years," etc., the "race" question is not included in his own digest. Why should I go beyond that? I have the document here.
3. I said these instructions to enumerators, mimeographed, were dated January, 1940, before the outcry, and they are. I have the document here. Whether or not they were used in a sample test, they are a modification of the question; I didn't say they were "conceived" this January. ARTHUR KROCK.

Washington, Feb. 29, 1940.

Source: *The New York Times*, March 3, 1940. © W.L. Austin.

HEADS WILL FALL FOLLOWING NEW NOSE-COUNT

By MORGAN M. BEATTY
AP Feature Service Writer

WASHINGTON—Political heads will roll in the 1940 battle of the census!

How many heads is problematical. It depends on:

How fast southern mothers produced children during the last 10 years.

How many *Joad families* swapped misery in Oklahoma for misery in California.

How many southern lads and lassies chose the old homestead for their port in the storm of the depression, instead of the big cities in the north.

Moreover, congressmen must decide what to do about the decennial man-under-the-bed — REAPPORTIONMENT!

If you take (1) the latest mathematical doodles of the Census Bureau, put 'em on a slide rule, and (2) assume the automatic reapportionment law of 1929 will survive the battle of the census, then you find at the end of your trial a gibbet for six congressmen.

At least six legislators from the northeastern and midwestern states will lose their $10,000-a-year jobs. And six congressmen from the south and far west will grow where no congressmen have sprouted since 1910.

That means a gain of at least 12 votes in the house of representatives for the south and far west by 1942. They'll pick up six actual votes, and benefit also by the death of six northern votes.

You can find plenty of statisticians who figure the northeastern states may lose more seats than that. Some say 10 or even 12 seats, instead of six. But the mathematical wizards who figured out reapportionment for me took the conservative side of the street.

Always A Struggle

The decennial battle of the census is as old as the nation.

As regular as death and taxes, one of these struggles has rolled around every 10 years for 150 years running. Most of the fights have been settled behind the locked doors of congressional committee rooms, without the public shedding of political blood.

But the last two! Whew! And right out in the open, where anybody could get a ringside seat.

Roughly speaking, these battles were miniature Civil wars—the south vs. the north. The men from down under defied the Constitution and the Founding Fathers in 1920. They blocked any reapportionment at all, and thereby saved themselves from losing seats to the growing north.

In 1929, the struggle was even harder, and dirtier. The south tried to bar aliens from the reapportionment count given to congress by the census bureau. The east has several million aliens. The north retaliated by trying to bar Negroes. Both amendments to the reapportionment law passed. It took three days of sizzling conferences to kill both.

Today, the same old struggle is brewing, only the shoe's on the other foot most of the time. The south's depression-damned emigrants and high birthrate, and the west's migrations, should give the southerners and westerners six more seats—if everything goes according to Hoyle.

Enter Senator Tobey

But that's where Senator Charles William Tobey's sideshow on the income questions comes in. For if enough citizens respond to the senator's excitement—and excitement over one's private affairs is a pretty contagious kind—then the regular census might conceivably suffer from errors and slammed doors.

Some congressmen might take the same view as Congressman Daniel Reed of upstate New York, when he says:

"The census bureau has had the respect and confidence of the people of this country for 150 years. . . . However, just as sure as no action is taken by congress to stop this snooping program into income, outside the census law, it is going to end in such a way that the value of this regular census is going to be destroyed!"

The congressman from New York did not go into details. But suppose the representatives who hail from all the sections liable to lose members in the 1940 census should take the same stand. There are 274 of these fellows, enough to block a new reapportionment law, the same way the south blocked it in 1920.

Another Detail

Then there's that "lame duck" technicality. By a fluke, the lame duck amendment makes the president report the census to the wrong congress.

Under the 1929 law, the president is directed to report the 1940 census to the second regular session of the 76th Congress. That's the congress now holding forth on Capitol Hill. But the census will hardly be begun before that session is history.

The census will be ready for the first session of the 77th Congress, however, and the president will doubtless report to that congress. But a technically-minded house with a mind to blocking reapportionment possibly could tell the house clerk to ignore the president's report because he made it to the wrong congress, i. e., contrary to law. And since the house clerk is the man who tells the states how many representatives they are en-

continued on next page

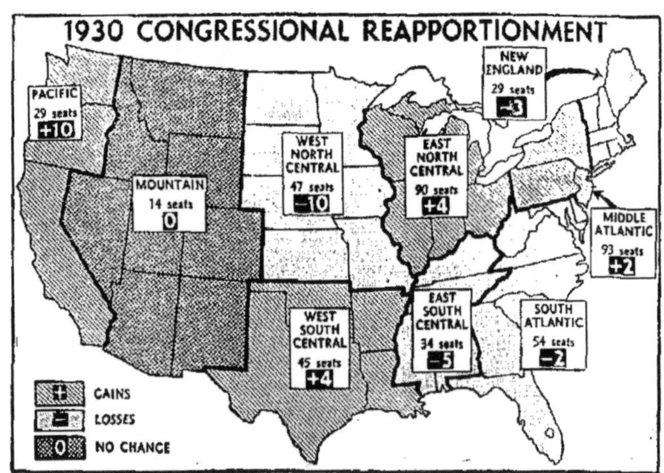

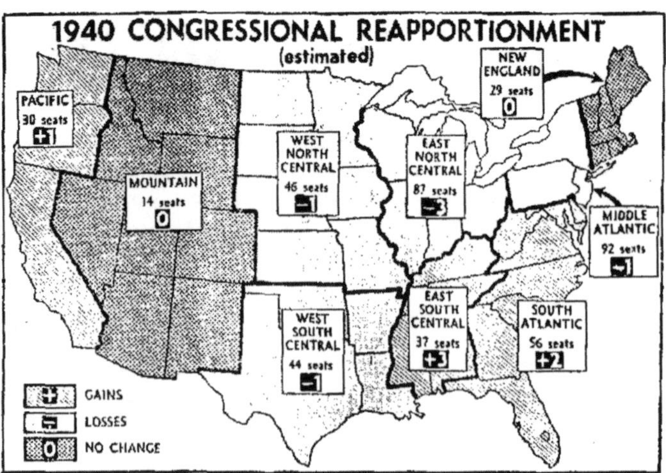

WILL THE PENDULUM SWING BACK? These maps show how the Congressional representation changed are based on the 1929 law and an estimate of what the 1940 census will show. Note that some sections that after the 1930 census, and how it may change after this year's. Figures on the forthcoming reapportionment lost ten years ago will probably gain this time.

titled to under the census, that trick could block automatic reapportionment based on the 1940 census.

Senator Vandenberg and President Roosevelt and the house census committee are trying to keep this *technicality from muddying* the reapportionment waters through an amendment to the 1929 law. But that movement isn't so all-fired popular with lots of members of the house of representatives. So some of them tacked that old bar-to-aliens amendment onto the senator's amendment.

Moreover, many a member of the house resents that 1929 reapportionment law. It came from the senate, *remember, Senator Arthur Vandenberg*, to be exact, and they don't like the senate keeping the house's house in order. Not a bit of it. Besides, that law would freeze the house of representatives at 435 members.

Your Worry, Too

But, goodness knows, if house members try to put any more seats in their crowded chamber they're going to run into trouble. Doubtless some of the new congressmen would find themselves out in the capitol corridors, competing against historical art for the tourist trade.

No. That's not practical either, so the whole thing adds up to the census battle of the century either on the floor, or behind closed doors, or both.

You and I could say pish and tush, and forget it if it weren't for the fact that your representation in congress is at stake.

Wyoming's seven state fish hatcheries produced more than 9,000,000 game fish for streams and lakes in 1939.

Source: *The Gallup Independent*, April 5, 1940.

1940 Census Uncovers Statistical Oddities

One motor - vehicle accident death occurs approximately every 15 minutes of each day during the year.

The annual diphtheria death rate has been decreased from 43 per 100,000 population in 1900 to 1.5 in 1939.

The trend in the death rate from respiratory diseases is steadily declining.

The census bureau says that almost twice as many people die from motor-vehicle accidents as from the following causes of death put together: typhoid and paratyphoid fever, measles, scarlet fever, whooping cough, diphtheria, epidemic cerebro-spinal meningitis, and malaria.

The states which showed the greatest percentage of increase in population in the 1940 census were Florida, New Mexico, California, Nevada, and Idaho. The District of Columbia, however, exceeded the percentage increase of these states.

Although it was third among the states in percentage of population increase in the 1940 census, California recorded the greatest absolute increase. Its increase was nearly 1,200 as compared with nearly 800,000 in New York state.

The Pacific division—California, Oregon and Washington—showed the largest percentage of increase of any of the regional divisions in the 1940 census. The increase in these states was 18.8 per cent. The South Atlantic division was second with 12.9 per cent. New England was the smallest with 3.3 per cent.

Only one geographic division—the Mountain states—showed a greater increase in population between 1930 and 1940 than between 1920 and 1930.

From 1790 to 1940 the proportion of people living in cities of 2,500 or more increased from 5.1 per cent to 56.5 per cent.

The 1940 census showed 412 cities of 25,000 or more, as compared with 376 such cities ten years previous. The number of people living in these cities of 25,000 or more was 52,535,767, as compared with 50,016,533 in 1930.

Cities of 25,000 and more showed a total population increase of only five per cent during the last decade, considerably below the seven per cent increase for the country as a whole.

The 1940 census reveals that the decade between 1930 and 1940 was the first decade in American history in which immigration was not a factor in population changes. It was an excess of emigration over immigration.

Nearly 52 per cent of all Negro births are supervised by midwives. Less than 23 per cent occur in hospitals. Among the white births only 3.4 per cent are attended by midwives and 55 per cent occur in hospitals.

The death rate of Negro babies under one year of age has declined from 192 per 1,000 births in 1916 to 77.9 in 1938. During the same period the death rate of white babies under one year has declined from 98 to 47.1.

The average of white mothers at the time of their first birth is 23 years, while the average age of Negro mothers at first birth is 20.

Death rates of Negro mothers because of pregnancy and childbirth have declined from 139 per 10,000 births in 1918 to 85 in 1938. During the same period deaths of white mothers from the same causes have declined from 89 to 38.

Births of Negro babies have increased from 240,683 in 1928 to 270,060 in 1939. During the same eleven years, births of white babies increased only from 1,982,246 to 1,982,671.

Census bureau records show that diseases of the heart are responsible for 26.6 per cent of all white deaths and only 17.4 per cent of Negro deaths.

Tuberculosis in all its forms is responsible for 9.4 per cent of all Negro deaths, while among whites it is responsible for only 3.8 per cent of all deaths.

Cancer and other malignant tumors are responsible for 11.7 per cent of deaths among whites and only 5.1 per cent of all deaths among Negroes.

Influenza and pneumonia combined cause 10.2 per cent of all deaths among Negroes, while they were responsible for only 7.1 per cent of all deaths among whites.

Production of bar toilet soap exceeds 400,000,000 pounds annually and white and yellow bar laundry soap exceeds 1,200,000,000 pounds.

Shaving soap to the value of $8,500,000 is made annually in the U. S. Of this, stick, powder, and cake shaving soap exceeds 5,600,000 pounds and shaving cream with soap base exceeds 7,611,000 pounds.

Production of waffle irons and griddles for home use approximates 750,000 per year.

Production of oleomargarine, butterine, nut margarene, and similar products showed a 23.5 per cent decline between 1937 and 1939. Annual production now amounts to about $35,000,000. Over 300,000,000 pounds of oleomargarine are made.

The average number of children ever born to Negro mothers is 3.5 as compared with 2.7 for white mothers.

Out of a total of 44,113,147 births recorded by the census bureau in the past 23 years, male births exceed bemale births by 1,200,575.

The census bureau has recorded 500,175 cases of twin births in 23 years. Accordihg to census figures, the odds are 88 to one in favor of a single birth as opposed to twins.

RAF Bombs Tripoli as Army Pounds Italian African Bases

(By The United Press)

The royal air force smashed hard at Tripoli, 550 miles west of Derna, as land forces pound at remaining Italian strongholds in Africa.

The RAF raid on Tripoli was directed at ships in the harbor, seaplanes and docks at the waterside. It was believed that the attack was designed to hamper or prevent reinforcement of Italian forces in Africa, possibly by the German Luftwaffe.

On land the British were pounding closer and closer to Benghazi, remaining fascist base in eastern Libya.

One substantial Italian garrison in the southern desert still holds out. This is that at Giarrabub, south of Bardia. It was believed that surrender of this garrison is only a matter of time as it is cut off from all contact with the rest of Graziani's troops except by air.

Source: *The Racine Journal-Times Sunday Bulletin*, February 2, 1941

Women Earners Up 20 Per Cent In Ten Years

Census Bureau's Preliminary Figures Indicate Over 2,000,000 Increase

By ANNE PETERSEN

The rapid increase in the number of working women in this country during the past ten years has been brought to light in preliminary figures issued by the Bureau of the Census. In statistical tables for occupations by sex, which have been based on a tabulation of a 5 per cent sample of the returns for 1940, the number is estimated at 12,846,565, or 25 per cent of all women in the country over 14 years of age.

Beginning with the depression years numbers of women who had never felt the necessity for seeking employment before entered the ranks of workers to become self-supporting or to help with family budgets. Many of these have stayed on the job, these figures would indicate. The totals are expected to climb still higher as the production activities of defense industries expand. The results of this increase are not reflected, however, in the census figures released, for these are based on the count taken in March, 1940.

The picture of a rapidly growing employed section of American women, as sketched in the bureau's early estimates, is interpreted by the Women's Bureau of the United States Department of Labor through a comparison of these totals with those compiled in 1930 for the census of occupations reported in that year.

Rose 20 Per Cent in Decade

An article in the current bulletin of the bureau, whose director is Miss Mary Anderson, states:

"It is no surprise that the number of women workers has increased markedly since 1930. The 10,750,000 women in gainful work in 1930 were considered an important number, but there are now more than 12,750,000 women in the labor market, an increase in the last ten years of about 20 per cent, though the woman population of fourteen years and over has increased by only 14 per cent."

The number of women in this age group today is estimated in the most recent census at approximately 50,357,892, with the number of men in this class computed at 50,614,304. Preliminary tables indicate that 79 per cent of the male population 14 years of age and over are in the labor force, as compared with 25.5 per cent of the nation's female population.

The newest figures also show that the proportion of women in the total number of employed persons in this country has been steadily growing in the past decade, although it was virtually stationary in the decade before the World War, according to the Women's Bureau:

"Women show a significant increase in the proportion they comprise of all persons in the labor market," the bureau says, "constituting 24 per cent, or practically one-fourth of the total in 1940, as compared with 22 per cent in 1930, and about 21 per cent in 1910 and 1920.

90 Per cent Employed

"The figures show that 90 per cent of the women as well as of the men reported in the labor market in 1940 have jobs, about 86 per cent of them in private industry."

These comparisons are presented as indicating a general trend, it is pointed out, both because the figures are offered by the Census Bureau as preliminary to the final count, and because the basis of reporting the two periods differs in two respects.

First, the 1940 totals include persons in the whole labor market, which is meant to include those unemployed but seeking work, as well as both inexperienced and new workers who had not previously been employed. The 1930 census reported those "gainfully employed," and enumerators were instructed to include in this category those out of work only if they were normally employed. At that time, also, there were no large public emergency agencies, such as the WPA, the NYA and the CCC.

Second, there is a difference in the age classification. The 1940 figures report persons 14 years and over, while the 1930 figures covered those of 10 years and over. This variation will not affect the final totals to any extent, it is pointed out, because there are today relatively few children 10 to 13 years of age who are at work.

Of women not classified in the employed group, the figures released by the Census Bureau show that more than twenty-eight million were engaged in home housework.

The New York Times
Published: March 23, 1941

Check of Census Shows Fewer Than 1 to 100 Missed By Enumerators

Sample of 13,590 Persons Indicates High Degree Of Accuracy; Comparison With Earlier Figures Impossible; Probably 1,250,000 in U. S. Missed

By DR. GEORGE GALLUP
Director, American Institute of Public Opinion

PRINCETON, N. J., May 17.—For the first time in the history of the United States an independent nation-wide audit has been made of the accuracy of the census in including the entire American population in its decennial count. The results of this check-up show that the national census of 1940, conducted under the dierction of W. L. Austin and Dr. Vergil Reed, achieved a degree of accuracy in its enumeration far above expectations of research men.

It is impossible, of course, to compare the accuracy of the 1940 census with earlier ones. Claims have been made that as many as 10 to 15 per cent of the population have been missed by the census enumerators. A careful check, however, by the American Institute of Public Opinion on the basis of the adult population, indicates that only about 1 per cent of the population was overlooked in the 1940 census. In statistical terms, the range of error in the census lies somewhere between 0.72 per cent and 1.23 per cent, with the most likely figure being about 1 per cent.

Interpreted in terms of population, this error would indicate that only about 1,250,000 persons were actually missed, out of a total of 131,669,275. That figure applies only to the whole national count. In any one community the percentage of error could be larger or smaller.

In checking up on the 1940 census, the Institute used the "sampling" process which is assuming great importance in research in the various social sciences and in business.

In fact, the sampling procedure was used by the Bureau of Census itself in connection with various phases of the 1940 enumeration. It obtained special data relating to population by interviewing every 20th person in the census, or, in other words, a sample of 1-20th of the population.

Most research men agree that the scope and usefulness of the census can be enormously expanded through further use of such sampling procedures.

Because of the growing importance of the process, the basic principles of sampling are receiving wide attention and study. They are set forth briefly in the following paragraphs, together with a description of how sampling was used by the Institute to check up on the census.

Basic Principles of Sampling Are Cited.

In simplest terms the basic principle of sampling is that the opinions or characteristics of the whole population can be determined by studying a relatively small sample or cross-section, proportionate to the various important population groups and properly distributed by sections of the country.

The secret of such sampling does not lie in large numbers. Statisticians have repeatedly demonstrated that a few thousand persons correctly selected will faithfully reflect the views of many millions. The secret is in the cross-section—in the selection of persons who compose the sample.

To be reliable, the cross-section must include the proper number of old and young, rich and poor, urban and rural population, etc., for every section of the country. For example, if 15 per cent

continued on next page

of the voters of any given State are on relief, then 15 per cent of the sample from that State must be made up of persons on relief. Similarly, if 50 per cent of the voters of a State live on farms, then the sample for that State must be divided betwen urban and rural in that same proportion. Thus the sample is, in effect, a miniature public, containing within itself all the elements of the whole public, in proper proportion.

Process for Checking Accuracy of the Census.

In checking up on the census, the Institute used a sample of 13,590 persons, selected to represent a true cross-section according to the principles set forth above. The objective was to interview this group carefully to find any individuals who claimed that they had not been enumerated by the census takers in the 1940 count.

Interviewers personally talked to the 13,590 persons in this cross-section, and took down the names and addresses of all who said they had not been included in the census. A second call was made some days later on those individuals who were uncertain as to whether the census had counted them. Upon completion of this recheck, it was found that a total of 349 persons—out of the original 13,590—claimed they had not been included in the census count.

The names and addresses of these 349 persons were then sent by the Institute to the Bureau of the Census in Washington, where they were checked against the official files.

This check showed that more than half had actually been enumerated—either at a previous address, or through some other member of the family, or by some other means.

This left only 128 persons out of the total of 13,590 in the Institute's sample who had not been included in the census. That is approximately 1 per cent, or, to be exact, 0.94 per cent, and some of these may have been enumerated at an address other than that reported to the interviewers.

How Size of Sample May Be Determined.

At this point the question naturally arises: How is it possible to determine the accuracy of a census of 131 million people by polling only 13,590?

On the basis of a representative sample of 13,590, the laws of probability indicate that the chances are 997 in 1,000 that the results would not have varied by more than 0.29 per cent above or 0.22 per cent below the figure of 0.94 per cent even if all the adult population had been interviewed in place of 13,590.

Actually, the statistical chances are 95 in 100 that the result would not have varied by more than 0.21 per cent above or 0.15 per cent below the figure 0.94 per cent of all adults had been interviewed.

The Institute's sample of 13,590 persons was divided into two groups of approximately 7,000 each. It is interesting to note that in the first group of 7,000 62 persons were found who had not been enumerated by the census, and in the second group of 7,000, it was found that 66 persons had been missed by the census.

This fact furnishes a good illustration of how the addition of thousands of cases does not appreciably alter the results found from the first few thousands. In short, if only 7,000 persons had been interviewed, the results would have shown virtually no difference.

continued on next page

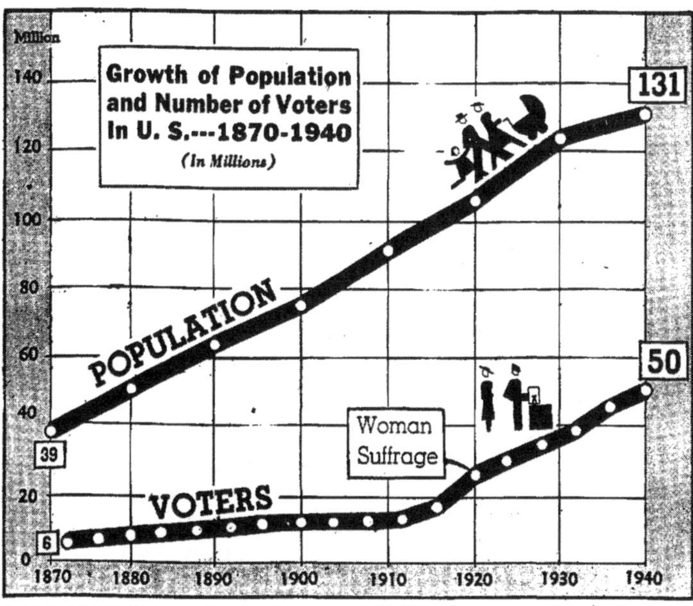

The trend of United States population growth, as shown by the United States census, and the number of votes cast in presidential elections since 1872. Note that whereas the population increased by about 3½ times between 1870 and 1940, the number of voters increased nearly eight-fold. Part of the voting increase came, of course when woman's suffrage was adopted in the summer of 1920.

Questions Most Frequently Asked About Gallup Poll

By American Institute of Public Opinion

Why Haven't I Been Interviewed?—This question is one which comes up frequently. The old-fashioned "straw" polls of the type conducted by the Literary Digest are largely responsible for the confusion in the minds of many people regarding the number of persons included in the modern public opinion surveys.

Straw polls relied almost entirely for their accuracy on reaching millions of voters. Modern "sampling" polls of the type conducted by the Institute rely for their accuracy on an entirely different principle—the careful selection of people interviewed.

In this respect, the modern surveys merely apply to public opinion research well-established procedures which have been used for years in the fields of medicine, education and all the social sciences.

The number of persons included in any Institute survey varies from 3,000 to 5,000, depending entirely upon the number of breakdowns and the statistical requirements. Assuming that year in and year out the Institute were to interview 10,000 people a week, it would take 150 years to get around to all the eligible voters in the nation.

What Is the Margin of Error?—The laws of probability, first set out in 1713, give the exact range of error which can be expected with samples of any size, be they large or small.

In samples of from 3,000 to 50,000, the statistical chances are 997 in 1,000 that error due solely to the number of persons included will not, under any normal circumstances, exceed 3 per cent.

Besides purely statistical error due to size of sample, allowance must be made for error due to flaws or faults in the cross-section, which can never be absolutely perfect. Using over 100 elections as a test of accuracy, the record shows that the Institute's error from all sources—from cross-section and size of sample combined—has averaged under 4 per cent for the six years since the organization was founded.

In the 1941 presidential election, the average state-by-state error was 2.5 per cent.

Who Is Interviewed?—Every survey includes a carefully-selected cross-section which embraces all the major population groups of the country in proper proportion. It includes the proper number of persons in families earning less than $20 a week, between $20 and $50 a week, and $50 a week and over.

It includes the old and the young, men and women, Democrats, Republicans, and independent party voters, the proper number of persons living in rural areas, in small towns, and in cities of all sizes.

When a cross-section is selected with statistical skill, the voters in the cross-section or miniature electorate will divide into opinion blocs in virtually the same way as all the 50,000,000 voters of the country would divide if their views were canvassed.

Are the Same People Interviewed Each Time?—No. Interviewers are instructed never to poll the same person more than once in any year. While the individuals interviewed in each survey are different, the types of persons interviewed are the same, since each cross-section includes all types in the population.

Who Are the Interviewers?—The majority of interviewers are college graduates who work part time on the surveys. New interviewers must submit character references from prominent business or civic leaders in their communities. At present the interviewers number approximately 1,100.

Who Pays for the Gallup Polls?—The entire cost is paid by a group of more than 100 daily newspapers who have exclusive right to publish the results in their communities. The Institute has no other sources of income.

Are These Newspapers All of One Political Party? No. About one-third are Democratic in their editorial leanings, one-third Republican, while the rest list themselves as independent.

What Is the Purpose of the Poll?—The Institute is a fact-finding organization. Its role is one of strict impartiality. It measures public opinion on vital political and social issues of the day, and reports the facts for the benefit of all.

Just as the Associated Press, United Press, and other great news services report what people do, the Institute reports what people think.

The Institute believes that in making the mass of voters articulate through the sampling referendum it is providing a worthwhile advance in the art of democratic government.

Source: *San Antonio Express*, May 18, 1941

Nearly 4,000 Tell Census They Are Centenarians

By The Associated Press.

WASHINGTON, June 22—Census figures showed today nearly 4,000 centenarians in the country, but even the Census Bureau did not believe it.

Commenting on the 1940 canvass which showed 3,679 persons at that time who said they were 100 or older, the bureau said the data "undoubtedly exaggerates the number of centenarians.' Very old people, officials suggested, frequently forget their real age.

The same report confirmed estimates that slightly more than 1,000,000 boys reach the draft age of 18 each year, but added that the number would decline a few thousand in each of the next five years, then turn slowly upward. This trend was based on the ages of boys in the 1940 census.

Another census report showed that there were more males than females in 1940 at each year of age up to 18 and between 41 and 64. Females were in the majority between 20 and 33 and above 67.

The New York Times

Published: June 23, 1943

1940 AND 2010 CENSUS DATA: STATE BY STATE COMPARISONS & RANKINGS

These 16 state-by-state tables were developed with census data from 1940 and 2010. Each table includes the data in three ways: alphabetical by state, ranked by 1940 numbers, and ranked by 2010 numbers, making it easy to see how things have changed in 70 years.*

**When reviewing the ranking columns, be aware that the District of Columbia is included in the list of states, as determined by both the 1940 and 2010 Census.*

Total Population

Area	Population		1940 Census		2010 Census	
	1940 Census	2010 Census	Area	Rank	Area	Rank
Alabama	2,832,961	4,779,736	New York	1	California	1
Alaska	n/a	710,231	Pennsylvania	2	Texas	2
Arizona	499,261	6,392,017	Illinois	3	New York	3
Arkansas	1,949,387	2,915,918	Ohio	4	Florida	4
California	6,907,387	37,253,956	California	5	Illinois	5
Colorado	1,123,296	5,029,196	Texas	6	Pennsylvania	6
Connecticut	1,709,242	3,574,097	Michigan	7	Ohio	7
Delaware	266,505	897,934	Massachusetts	8	Michigan	8
District of Columbia	663,091	601,723	New Jersey	9	Georgia	9
Florida	1,897,414	18,801,310	Missouri	10	North Carolina	10
Georgia	3,123,723	9,687,653	North Carolina	11	New Jersey	11
Hawaii	n/a	1,360,301	Indiana	12	Virginia	12
Idaho	524,873	1,567,582	Wisconsin	13	Washington	13
Illinois	7,897,241	12,830,632	Georgia	14	Massachusetts	14
Indiana	3,427,796	6,483,802	Tennessee	15	Indiana	15
Iowa	2,538,268	3,046,355	Kentucky	16	Arizona	16
Kansas	1,801,028	2,853,118	Alabama	17	Tennessee	17
Kentucky	2,845,627	4,339,367	Minnesota	18	Missouri	18
Louisiana	2,363,880	4,533,372	Virginia	19	Maryland	19
Maine	847,226	1,328,361	Iowa	20	Wisconsin	20
Maryland	1,821,244	5,773,552	Louisiana	21	Minnesota	21
Massachusetts	4,316,721	6,547,629	Oklahoma	22	Colorado	22
Michigan	5,256,106	9,883,640	Mississippi	23	Alabama	23
Minnesota	2,792,300	5,303,925	Arkansas	24	South Carolina	24
Mississippi	2,183,796	2,967,297	West Virginia	25	Louisiana	25
Missouri	3,784,664	5,988,927	South Carolina	26	Kentucky	26
Montana	559,456	989,415	Florida	27	Oregon	27
Nebraska	1,315,834	1,826,341	Maryland	28	Oklahoma	28
Nevada	110,247	2,700,551	Kansas	29	Connecticut	29
New Hampshire	491,524	1,316,470	Washington	30	Iowa	30
New Jersey	4,160,165	8,791,894	Connecticut	31	Mississippi	31
New Mexico	531,818	2,059,179	Nebraska	32	Arkansas	32
New York	13,479,142	19,378,102	Colorado	33	Kansas	33
North Carolina	3,571,623	9,535,483	Oregon	34	Utah	34
North Dakota	641,935	672,591	Maine	35	Nevada	35
Ohio	6,907,612	11,536,504	Rhode Island	36	New Mexico	36
Oklahoma	2,336,434	3,751,351	District of Columbia	37	West Virginia	37
Oregon	1,089,684	3,831,074	South Dakota	38	Nebraska	38
Pennsylvania	9,900,180	12,702,379	North Dakota	39	Idaho	39
Rhode Island	713,346	1,052,567	Montana	40	Hawaii	40
South Carolina	1,899,804	4,625,364	Utah	41	Maine	41
South Dakota	642,961	814,180	New Mexico	42	New Hampshire	42
Tennessee	2,915,841	6,346,105	Idaho	43	Rhode Island	43
Texas	6,414,824	25,145,561	Arizona	44	Montana	44
Utah	550,310	2,763,885	New Hampshire	45	Delaware	45
Vermont	359,231	625,741	Vermont	46	South Dakota	46
Virginia	2,677,773	8,001,024	Delaware	47	Alaska	47
Washington	1,736,191	6,724,540	Wyoming	48	North Dakota	48
West Virginia	1,901,974	1,852,994	Nevada	49	Vermont	49
Wisconsin	3,137,587	5,686,986	Alaska	n/a	District of Columbia	50
Wyoming	250,742	563,626	Hawaii	n/a	Wyoming	51
United States	131,669,275	308,745,538	United States	–	United States	–

Source: U.S. Census Bureau, 1940 Census of Population; U.S. Census Bureau, Census 2010

White Population

Area	Percent of Population		1940 Census		2010 Census	
	1940 Census	2010 Census	Area	Rank	Area	Rank
Alabama	65.3	68.5	New Hampshire	1	Vermont	1
Alaska	n/a	66.7	Vermont	1	Maine	2
Arizona	85.5	73.0	Maine	3	New Hampshire	3
Arkansas	75.2	77.0	Iowa	4	West Virginia	3
California	95.5	57.6	Minnesota	5	Iowa	5
Colorado	98.5	81.3	Wisconsin	5	Wyoming	6
Connecticut	98.0	77.6	Idaho	7	North Dakota	7
Delaware	86.5	68.9	Oregon	8	Montana	8
District of Columbia	71.5	38.5	Utah	8	Idaho	9
Florida	72.8	75.0	Massachusetts	10	Kentucky	10
Georgia	65.3	59.7	Nebraska	10	Wisconsin	11
Hawaii	n/a	24.7	Colorado	12	Nebraska	12
Idaho	98.9	89.1	North Dakota	13	Utah	12
Illinois	95.0	71.5	Rhode Island	13	South Dakota	14
Indiana	96.4	84.3	Wyoming	13	Minnesota	15
Iowa	99.3	91.3	Connecticut	16	Indiana	16
Kansas	96.3	83.8	Washington	17	Kansas	17
Kentucky	92.5	87.8	Montana	18	Oregon	18
Louisiana	64.0	62.6	Indiana	19	Missouri	19
Maine	99.7	95.2	Kansas	20	Ohio	20
Maryland	83.4	58.2	South Dakota	20	Pennsylvania	21
Massachusetts	98.6	80.4	Michigan	22	Rhode Island	22
Michigan	95.9	78.9	New York	23	Colorado	23
Minnesota	99.2	85.3	California	24	Massachusetts	24
Mississippi	50.7	59.1	Pennsylvania	25	Michigan	25
Missouri	93.5	82.8	Ohio	26	Connecticut	26
Montana	96.6	89.4	Illinois	27	Tennessee	26
Nebraska	98.6	86.1	New Jersey	28	Washington	28
Nevada	94.4	66.2	Nevada	29	Arkansas	29
New Hampshire	99.9	93.9	West Virginia	30	Florida	30
New Jersey	94.5	68.6	Missouri	31	Arizona	31
New Mexico	92.6	68.4	New Mexico	32	Oklahoma	32
New York	95.6	65.7	Kentucky	33	Illinois	33
North Carolina	71.9	68.5	Oklahoma	34	Texas	34
North Dakota	98.4	90.0	Delaware	35	Delaware	35
Ohio	95.1	82.7	Arizona	36	New Jersey	36
Oklahoma	90.1	72.2	Texas	36	Virginia	36
Oregon	98.7	83.6	Maryland	38	Alabama	38
Pennsylvania	95.2	81.9	Tennessee	39	North Carolina	38
Rhode Island	98.4	81.4	Virginia	40	New Mexico	40
South Carolina	57.1	66.2	Arkansas	41	Alaska	41
South Dakota	96.3	85.9	Florida	42	Nevada	42
Tennessee	82.6	77.6	North Carolina	43	South Carolina	42
Texas	85.5	70.4	District of Columbia	44	New York	44
Utah	98.7	86.1	Alabama	45	Louisiana	45
Vermont	99.9	95.3	Georgia	45	Georgia	46
Virginia	75.3	68.6	Louisiana	47	Mississippi	47
Washington	97.8	77.3	South Carolina	48	Maryland	48
West Virginia	93.8	93.9	Mississippi	49	California	49
Wisconsin	99.2	86.2	Alaska	n/a	District of Columbia	50
Wyoming	98.4	90.7	Hawaii	n/a	Hawaii	51
United States	89.8	72.4	United States	–	United States	–

Source: U.S. Census Bureau, 1940 Census of Population; U.S. Census Bureau, Census 2010

Black Population

Area	Percent of Population		1940 Census		2010 Census	
	1940 Census	2010 Census	Area	Rank	Area	Rank
Alabama	34.7	26.2	Mississippi	1	District of Columbia	1
Alaska	n/a	3.3	South Carolina	2	Mississippi	2
Arizona	3.0	4.1	Louisiana	3	Louisiana	3
Arkansas	24.8	15.4	Alabama	4	Georgia	4
California	1.8	6.2	Georgia	4	Maryland	5
Colorado	1.1	4.0	District of Columbia	6	South Carolina	6
Connecticut	1.9	10.1	North Carolina	7	Alabama	7
Delaware	13.5	21.4	Florida	8	North Carolina	8
District of Columbia	28.2	50.7	Arkansas	9	Delaware	9
Florida	27.1	16.0	Virginia	10	Virginia	10
Georgia	34.7	30.5	Tennessee	11	Tennessee	11
Hawaii	n/a	1.6	Maryland	12	Florida	12
Idaho	0.1	0.6	Texas	13	New York	13
Illinois	4.9	14.5	Delaware	14	Arkansas	14
Indiana	3.6	9.1	Kentucky	15	Illinois	15
Iowa	0.7	2.9	Oklahoma	16	Michigan	16
Kansas	3.6	5.9	Missouri	17	New Jersey	17
Kentucky	7.5	7.8	West Virginia	18	Ohio	18
Louisiana	35.9	32.0	New Jersey	19	Texas	19
Maine	0.2	1.2	Illinois	20	Missouri	20
Maryland	16.6	29.4	Ohio	20	Pennsylvania	21
Massachusetts	1.3	6.6	Pennsylvania	22	Connecticut	22
Michigan	4.0	14.2	New York	23	Indiana	23
Minnesota	0.4	5.2	Michigan	24	Nevada	24
Mississippi	49.2	37.0	Indiana	25	Kentucky	25
Missouri	6.5	11.6	Kansas	25	Oklahoma	26
Montana	0.2	0.4	Arizona	27	Massachusetts	27
Nebraska	1.1	4.5	Connecticut	28	Wisconsin	28
Nevada	0.6	8.1	California	29	California	29
New Hampshire	0.1	1.1	Rhode Island	30	Kansas	30
New Jersey	5.5	13.7	Massachusetts	31	Rhode Island	31
New Mexico	0.9	2.1	Colorado	32	Minnesota	32
New York	4.2	15.9	Nebraska	32	Nebraska	33
North Carolina	27.5	21.5	New Mexico	34	Arizona	34
North Dakota	0.0	1.2	Iowa	35	Colorado	35
Ohio	4.9	12.2	Nevada	36	Washington	36
Oklahoma	7.2	7.4	Minnesota	37	West Virginia	37
Oregon	0.2	1.8	Washington	37	Alaska	38
Pennsylvania	4.8	10.8	Wisconsin	37	Iowa	39
Rhode Island	1.6	5.7	Wyoming	37	New Mexico	40
South Carolina	42.9	27.9	Maine	41	Oregon	41
South Dakota	0.1	1.3	Montana	41	Hawaii	42
Tennessee	17.5	16.7	Oregon	41	South Dakota	43
Texas	14.4	11.8	Utah	41	Maine	44
Utah	0.2	1.1	Idaho	45	North Dakota	44
Vermont	0.1	1.0	New Hampshire	45	New Hampshire	46
Virginia	24.7	19.4	South Dakota	45	Utah	46
Washington	0.4	3.6	Vermont	45	Vermont	48
West Virginia	6.2	3.4	North Dakota	49	Wyoming	49
Wisconsin	0.4	6.3	Alaska	n/a	Idaho	50
Wyoming	0.4	0.8	Hawaii	n/a	Montana	51
United States	9.8	12.6	United States	–	United States	–

Source: U.S. Census Bureau, 1940 Census of Population; U.S. Census Bureau, Census 2010

American Indian/Alaska Native Population

Area	Percent of Population		1940 Census		2010 Census	
	1940 Census	2010 Census	Area	Rank	Area	Rank
Alabama	0.0	0.6	Arizona	1	Alaska	1
Alaska	n/a	14.8	New Mexico	2	New Mexico	2
Arizona	11.0	4.6	Nevada	3	South Dakota	3
Arkansas	0.0	0.8	South Dakota	4	Oklahoma	4
California	0.3	1.0	Montana	5	Montana	5
Colorado	0.1	1.1	Oklahoma	6	North Dakota	6
Connecticut	0.0	0.3	North Dakota	7	Arizona	7
Delaware	0.0	0.5	Wyoming	8	Wyoming	8
District of Columbia	0.0	0.3	Idaho	9	Washington	9
Florida	0.0	0.4	Utah	9	Idaho	10
Georgia	0.0	0.3	Washington	9	Oregon	10
Hawaii	n/a	0.3	North Carolina	12	North Carolina	12
Idaho	0.7	1.4	Minnesota	13	Nevada	13
Illinois	0.0	0.3	Oregon	14	Utah	13
Indiana	0.0	0.3	Wisconsin	14	Colorado	15
Iowa	0.0	0.4	California	16	Minnesota	15
Kansas	0.1	1.0	Nebraska	16	California	17
Kentucky	0.0	0.2	Maine	18	Kansas	17
Louisiana	0.1	0.7	Colorado	19	Nebraska	17
Maine	0.2	0.6	Kansas	19	Wisconsin	17
Maryland	0.0	0.4	Louisiana	19	Arkansas	21
Massachusetts	0.0	0.3	Michigan	19	Louisiana	22
Michigan	0.1	0.6	Mississippi	19	Texas	22
Minnesota	0.5	1.1	New York	19	Alabama	24
Mississippi	0.1	0.5	South Carolina	19	Maine	24
Missouri	0.0	0.5	Alabama	26	Michigan	24
Montana	3.0	6.3	Arkansas	26	New York	24
Nebraska	0.3	1.0	Connecticut	26	Rhode Island	24
Nevada	4.3	1.2	Delaware	26	Delaware	29
New Hampshire	0.0	0.2	District of Columbia	26	Mississippi	29
New Jersey	0.0	0.3	Florida	26	Missouri	29
New Mexico	6.5	9.4	Georgia	26	Florida	32
New York	0.1	0.6	Illinois	26	Iowa	32
North Carolina	0.6	1.3	Indiana	26	Maryland	32
North Dakota	1.6	5.4	Iowa	26	South Carolina	32
Ohio	0.0	0.2	Kentucky	26	Vermont	32
Oklahoma	2.7	8.6	Maryland	26	Virginia	32
Oregon	0.4	1.4	Massachusetts	26	Connecticut	38
Pennsylvania	0.0	0.2	Missouri	26	District of Columbia	38
Rhode Island	0.0	0.6	New Hampshire	26	Georgia	38
South Carolina	0.1	0.4	New Jersey	26	Hawaii	38
South Dakota	3.6	8.8	Ohio	26	Illinois	38
Tennessee	0.0	0.3	Pennsylvania	26	Indiana	38
Texas	0.0	0.7	Rhode Island	26	Massachusetts	38
Utah	0.7	1.2	Tennessee	26	New Jersey	38
Vermont	0.0	0.4	Texas	26	Tennessee	38
Virginia	0.0	0.4	Vermont	26	Kentucky	47
Washington	0.7	1.5	Virginia	26	New Hampshire	47
West Virginia	0.0	0.2	West Virginia	26	Ohio	47
Wisconsin	0.4	1.0	Alaska	n/a	Pennsylvania	47
Wyoming	0.9	2.4	Hawaii	n/a	West Virginia	47
United States	0.3	0.9	United States	–	United States	–

Note: (1) Excludes Alaska natives.
Source: U.S. Census Bureau, 1940 Census of Population; U.S. Census Bureau, Census 2010

Asian Population

Area	Percent of Population		1940 Census		2010 Census	
	1940 Census	2010 Census	Area	Rank	Area	Rank
Alabama	0.0	1.1	California	1	Hawaii	1
Alaska	n/a	5.4	Washington	2	California	2
Arizona	0.5	2.8	Nevada	3	New Jersey	3
Arkansas	0.0	1.2	Oregon	4	New York	4
California	2.4	13.0	Arizona	5	Nevada	5
Colorado	0.3	2.8	Utah	5	Washington	5
Connecticut	0.0	3.8	Colorado	7	Maryland	7
Delaware	0.0	3.2	Idaho	7	Virginia	7
District of Columbia	0.2	3.5	Wyoming	7	Alaska	9
Florida	0.0	2.4	District of Columbia	10	Massachusetts	10
Georgia	0.0	3.2	Montana	10	Illinois	11
Hawaii	n/a	38.6	New York	10	Minnesota	12
Idaho	0.3	1.2	Illinois	13	Connecticut	13
Illinois	0.1	4.6	Massachusetts	13	Texas	13
Indiana	0.0	1.6	Nebraska	13	Oregon	15
Iowa	0.0	1.7	New Jersey	13	District of Columbia	16
Kansas	0.0	2.4	New Mexico	13	Delaware	17
Kentucky	0.0	1.1	Alabama	18	Georgia	17
Louisiana	0.0	1.5	Arkansas	18	Rhode Island	19
Maine	0.0	1.0	Connecticut	18	Arizona	20
Maryland	0.0	5.5	Delaware	18	Colorado	20
Massachusetts	0.1	5.3	Florida	18	Pennsylvania	22
Michigan	0.0	2.4	Georgia	18	Florida	23
Minnesota	0.0	4.0	Indiana	18	Kansas	23
Mississippi	0.0	0.9	Iowa	18	Michigan	23
Missouri	0.0	1.6	Kansas	18	Wisconsin	26
Montana	0.2	0.6	Kentucky	18	New Hampshire	27
Nebraska	0.1	1.8	Louisiana	18	North Carolina	27
Nevada	0.7	7.2	Maine	18	Utah	29
New Hampshire	0.0	2.2	Maryland	18	Nebraska	30
New Jersey	0.1	8.3	Michigan	18	Iowa	31
New Mexico	0.1	1.4	Minnesota	18	Ohio	31
New York	0.2	7.3	Mississippi	18	Oklahoma	31
North Carolina	0.0	2.2	Missouri	18	Indiana	34
North Dakota	0.0	1.0	New Hampshire	18	Missouri	34
Ohio	0.0	1.7	North Carolina	18	Louisiana	36
Oklahoma	0.0	1.7	North Dakota	18	New Mexico	37
Oregon	0.6	3.7	Ohio	18	Tennessee	37
Pennsylvania	0.0	2.7	Oklahoma	18	South Carolina	39
Rhode Island	0.0	2.9	Pennsylvania	18	Vermont	39
South Carolina	0.0	1.3	Rhode Island	18	Arkansas	41
South Dakota	0.0	0.9	South Carolina	18	Idaho	41
Tennessee	0.0	1.4	South Dakota	18	Alabama	43
Texas	0.0	3.8	Tennessee	18	Kentucky	43
Utah	0.5	2.0	Texas	18	Maine	45
Vermont	0.0	1.3	Vermont	18	North Dakota	45
Virginia	0.0	5.5	Virginia	18	Mississippi	47
Washington	1.1	7.2	West Virginia	18	South Dakota	47
West Virginia	0.0	0.7	Wisconsin	18	Wyoming	49
Wisconsin	0.0	2.3	Alaska	n/a	West Virginia	50
Wyoming	0.3	0.8	Hawaii	n/a	Montana	51
United States	0.2	4.8	United States	–	United States	–

Source: U.S. Census Bureau, 1940 Census of Population; U.S. Census Bureau, Census 2010

Hispanic or Latino Population

Area	Percent of Population		1940 Census		2010 Census	
	1940 Census	2010 Census	Area	Rank	Area	Rank
Alabama	0.0	3.9	New Mexico	1	New Mexico	1
Alaska	n/a	5.5	Arizona	2	California	2
Arizona	20.4	29.6	Texas	3	Texas	2
Arkansas	0.0	6.4	Colorado	4	Arizona	4
California	6.0	37.6	California	5	Nevada	5
Colorado	8.2	20.7	Nevada	6	Florida	6
Connecticut	0.1	13.4	Wyoming	7	Colorado	7
Delaware	0.1	8.2	Florida	8	New Jersey	8
District of Columbia	0.1	9.1	New York	9	New York	9
Florida	1.3	22.5	Kansas	10	Illinois	10
Georgia	0.0	8.8	Idaho	11	Connecticut	11
Hawaii	n/a	8.9	Utah	11	Utah	12
Idaho	0.5	11.2	Montana	13	Rhode Island	13
Illinois	0.3	15.8	Nebraska	13	Oregon	14
Indiana	0.2	6.0	Illinois	15	Idaho	15
Iowa	0.1	5.0	Indiana	16	Washington	15
Kansas	0.7	10.5	Louisiana	16	Kansas	17
Kentucky	0.0	3.1	Michigan	16	Massachusetts	18
Louisiana	0.2	4.2	New Jersey	16	Nebraska	19
Maine	0.0	1.3	Oklahoma	16	District of Columbia	20
Maryland	0.0	8.2	Vermont	16	Hawaii	21
Massachusetts	0.1	9.6	Connecticut	22	Oklahoma	21
Michigan	0.2	4.4	Delaware	22	Wyoming	21
Minnesota	0.1	4.7	District of Columbia	22	Georgia	24
Mississippi	0.0	2.7	Iowa	22	North Carolina	25
Missouri	0.1	3.5	Massachusetts	22	Delaware	26
Montana	0.4	2.9	Minnesota	22	Maryland	26
Nebraska	0.4	9.2	Missouri	22	Virginia	28
Nevada	2.8	26.5	Ohio	22	Arkansas	29
New Hampshire	0.0	2.8	Oregon	22	Indiana	30
New Jersey	0.2	17.7	Pennsylvania	22	Wisconsin	31
New Mexico	41.7	46.3	Rhode Island	22	Pennsylvania	32
New York	1.0	17.6	South Dakota	22	Alaska	33
North Carolina	0.0	8.4	Washington	22	South Carolina	34
North Dakota	0.0	2.0	West Virginia	22	Iowa	35
Ohio	0.1	3.1	Wisconsin	22	Minnesota	36
Oklahoma	0.2	8.9	Alabama	37	Tennessee	37
Oregon	0.1	11.7	Arkansas	37	Michigan	38
Pennsylvania	0.1	5.7	Georgia	37	Louisiana	39
Rhode Island	0.1	12.4	Kentucky	37	Alabama	40
South Carolina	0.0	5.1	Maine	37	Missouri	41
South Dakota	0.1	2.7	Maryland	37	Kentucky	42
Tennessee	0.0	4.6	Mississippi	37	Ohio	42
Texas	11.5	37.6	New Hampshire	37	Montana	44
Utah	0.5	13.0	North Carolina	37	New Hampshire	45
Vermont	0.2	1.5	North Dakota	37	Mississippi	46
Virginia	0.0	7.9	South Carolina	37	South Dakota	46
Washington	0.1	11.2	Tennessee	37	North Dakota	48
West Virginia	0.1	1.2	Virginia	37	Vermont	49
Wisconsin	0.1	5.9	Alaska	n/a	Maine	50
Wyoming	2.4	8.9	Hawaii	n/a	West Virginia	51
United States	1.4	16.3	United States	–	United States	–

Note: (1) Based on the percentage of Spanish-speaking population.
Source: U.S. Census Bureau, 1940 Census of Population; U.S. Census Bureau, Census 2010

Foreign-Born Population

Area	Percent of Population		1940 Census		2010 Census	
	1940 Census	2010 Census	Area	Rank	Area	Rank
Alabama	0.4	3.4	New York	1	California	1
Alaska	n/a	7.2	Massachusetts	2	New York	2
Arizona	7.8	14.2	Rhode Island	3	New Jersey	3
Arkansas	0.4	4.3	Connecticut	4	Nevada	4
California	13.4	27.2	New Jersey	5	Florida	5
Colorado	6.4	9.8	New Hampshire	6	Hawaii	6
Connecticut	19.3	13.2	California	7	Texas	7
Delaware	5.6	8.2	Michigan	8	Massachusetts	8
District of Columbia	5.3	13.0	Illinois	9	Arizona	9
Florida	4.1	19.2	Washington	10	Illinois	10
Georgia	0.4	9.6	North Dakota	11	Connecticut	11
Hawaii	n/a	17.7	Minnesota	12	Maryland	11
Idaho	4.7	5.9	Montana	13	District of Columbia	13
Illinois	12.3	13.6	Nevada	14	Washington	14
Indiana	3.2	4.4	Maine	15	Rhode Island	15
Iowa	4.6	4.1	Pennsylvania	15	Virginia	16
Kansas	2.9	6.3	Wisconsin	17	Colorado	17
Kentucky	0.6	3.1	Vermont	18	New Mexico	18
Louisiana	1.2	3.6	Oregon	19	Oregon	18
Maine	9.9	3.3	Arizona	20	Georgia	20
Maryland	4.5	13.2	Ohio	21	Delaware	21
Massachusetts	19.9	14.5	South Dakota	22	Utah	21
Michigan	13.1	5.9	Wyoming	23	North Carolina	23
Minnesota	10.6	7.0	Colorado	24	Alaska	24
Mississippi	0.3	2.2	Nebraska	25	Minnesota	25
Missouri	3.0	3.7	Utah	26	Kansas	26
Montana	10.1	2.0	Delaware	27	Idaho	27
Nebraska	6.2	5.9	District of Columbia	28	Michigan	27
Nevada	10.0	19.3	Idaho	29	Nebraska	27
New Hampshire	13.9	5.3	Iowa	30	Pennsylvania	30
New Jersey	16.8	20.3	Maryland	31	New Hampshire	31
New Mexico	2.9	9.7	Florida	32	Oklahoma	32
New York	21.6	21.7	Texas	33	South Carolina	33
North Carolina	0.3	7.4	Indiana	34	Wisconsin	34
North Dakota	11.6	2.4	Missouri	35	Indiana	35
Ohio	7.5	3.8	Kansas	36	Tennessee	35
Oklahoma	0.9	5.2	New Mexico	36	Arkansas	37
Oregon	8.3	9.7	West Virginia	38	Iowa	38
Pennsylvania	9.9	5.6	Louisiana	39	Vermont	39
Rhode Island	19.5	12.6	Oklahoma	40	Ohio	40
South Carolina	0.3	4.7	Virginia	40	Missouri	41
South Dakota	6.9	2.3	Kentucky	42	Louisiana	42
Tennessee	0.4	4.4	Alabama	43	Alabama	43
Texas	3.7	16.1	Arkansas	43	Maine	44
Utah	6.1	8.2	Georgia	43	Kentucky	45
Vermont	8.8	4.0	Tennessee	43	Wyoming	45
Virginia	0.9	10.8	Mississippi	47	North Dakota	47
Washington	12.1	12.7	North Carolina	47	South Dakota	48
West Virginia	2.2	1.3	South Carolina	47	Mississippi	49
Wisconsin	9.2	4.6	Alaska	n/a	Montana	50
Wyoming	6.8	3.1	Hawaii	n/a	West Virginia	51
United States	8.8	12.7	United States	–	United States	–

Source: U.S. Census Bureau, 1940 Census of Population; U.S. Census Bureau, American Community Survey, 2006-2010 Five-Year Estimate

Males per 100 Females

Area	Males per 100 Females		1940 Census		2010 Census	
	1940 Census	2010 Census	Area	Rank	Area	Rank
Alabama	97.7	94.3	Nevada	1	Alaska	1
Alaska	n/a	108.5	Wyoming	2	Wyoming	2
Arizona	107.1	98.7	Montana	3	North Dakota	3
Arkansas	101.7	96.5	Idaho	4	Nevada	4
California	103.7	98.8	North Dakota	5	Utah	5
Colorado	102.6	100.5	Washington	6	Montana	6
Connecticut	98.9	94.8	Arizona	7	Colorado	7
Delaware	101.6	93.9	South Dakota	7	Idaho	8
District of Columbia	91.9	89.5	Oregon	9	Hawaii	9
Florida	98.8	95.6	Michigan	10	South Dakota	10
Georgia	96.6	95.4	Minnesota	11	Washington	11
Hawaii	n/a	100.3	New Mexico	11	California	12
Idaho	111.4	100.4	Wisconsin	13	Arizona	13
Illinois	100.4	96.2	West Virginia	14	Minnesota	14
Indiana	101.3	96.8	California	15	Nebraska	14
Iowa	101.8	98.1	Vermont	16	Wisconsin	14
Kansas	101.3	98.4	Colorado	17	Kansas	17
Kentucky	101.8	96.8	Utah	17	Texas	17
Louisiana	98.4	95.9	Nebraska	19	Iowa	19
Maine	101.0	95.8	Oklahoma	19	Oklahoma	20
Maryland	101.0	93.6	Iowa	21	Oregon	20
Massachusetts	95.0	93.7	Kentucky	21	New Mexico	22
Michigan	105.2	96.3	Arkansas	23	New Hampshire	23
Minnesota	104.6	98.5	Delaware	24	West Virginia	23
Mississippi	98.7	94.4	Virginia	25	Vermont	25
Missouri	98.8	96.0	Indiana	26	Indiana	26
Montana	114.8	100.8	Kansas	26	Kentucky	26
Nebraska	102.4	98.5	Maine	28	Arkansas	28
Nevada	125.4	102.0	Maryland	28	Michigan	29
New Hampshire	99.3	97.3	Texas	30	Virginia	29
New Jersey	99.0	94.8	Illinois	31	Illinois	31
New Mexico	104.6	97.7	Ohio	31	Missouri	32
New York	98.5	93.8	Pennsylvania	33	Louisiana	33
North Carolina	98.6	95.0	New Hampshire	34	Maine	34
North Dakota	109.4	102.1	New Jersey	35	Florida	35
Ohio	100.4	95.4	Connecticut	36	Georgia	36
Oklahoma	102.4	98.0	Florida	37	Ohio	36
Oregon	106.8	98.0	Missouri	37	Pennsylvania	38
Pennsylvania	100.0	95.1	Mississippi	39	Tennessee	38
Rhode Island	96.0	93.4	North Carolina	40	North Carolina	40
South Carolina	97.6	94.7	New York	41	Connecticut	41
South Dakota	107.1	100.1	Louisiana	42	New Jersey	41
Tennessee	98.4	95.1	Tennessee	42	South Carolina	43
Texas	100.9	98.4	Alabama	44	Mississippi	44
Utah	102.6	100.9	South Carolina	45	Alabama	45
Vermont	102.9	97.1	Georgia	46	Delaware	46
Virginia	101.5	96.3	Rhode Island	47	New York	47
Washington	109.1	99.3	Massachusetts	48	Massachusetts	48
West Virginia	103.8	97.3	District of Columbia	49	Maryland	49
Wisconsin	104.1	98.5	Alaska	n/a	Rhode Island	50
Wyoming	116.7	104.1	Hawaii	n/a	District of Columbia	51
United States	100.7	96.7	United States	–	United States	–

Source: U.S. Census Bureau, 1940 Census of Population; U.S. Census Bureau, Census 2010

Median Age

Area	Years		1940 Census		2010 Census	
	1940 Census	2010 Census	Area	Rank	Area	Rank
Alabama	23.8	37.9	California	1	Maine	1
Alaska	n/a	33.8	Oregon	2	Vermont	2
Arizona	25.4	35.9	New York	3	West Virginia	3
Arkansas	24.8	37.4	Washington	3	New Hampshire	4
California	33.0	35.2	District of Columbia	5	Florida	5
Colorado	29.2	36.1	Massachusetts	6	Pennsylvania	6
Connecticut	31.1	40.0	New Hampshire	7	Connecticut	7
Delaware	30.5	38.8	Illinois	8	Montana	8
District of Columbia	31.9	33.8	New Jersey	9	Rhode Island	9
Florida	28.9	40.7	Connecticut	10	Massachusetts	10
Georgia	24.5	35.3	Missouri	10	New Jersey	11
Hawaii	n/a	38.6	Nevada	10	Michigan	12
Idaho	26.4	34.6	Ohio	13	Delaware	13
Illinois	31.5	36.6	Rhode Island	14	Ohio	13
Indiana	30.3	37.0	Delaware	15	Hawaii	15
Iowa	30.2	38.1	Kansas	16	Wisconsin	16
Kansas	30.4	36.0	Indiana	17	Oregon	17
Kentucky	25.4	38.1	Iowa	18	Iowa	18
Louisiana	25.5	35.8	Vermont	19	Kentucky	18
Maine	29.6	42.7	Wisconsin	20	Maryland	20
Maryland	29.6	38.0	Nebraska	21	New York	20
Massachusetts	31.8	39.1	Maine	22	Tennessee	20
Michigan	29.3	38.9	Maryland	22	Alabama	23
Minnesota	29.5	37.4	Minnesota	24	Missouri	23
Mississippi	23.8	36.0	Michigan	25	South Carolina	23
Missouri	31.1	37.9	Colorado	26	Virginia	26
Montana	28.8	39.8	Pennsylvania	27	Arkansas	27
Nebraska	29.7	36.2	Florida	28	Minnesota	27
Nevada	31.1	36.3	Montana	29	North Carolina	27
New Hampshire	31.6	41.1	Wyoming	30	Washington	30
New Jersey	31.3	39.0	South Dakota	31	Indiana	31
New Mexico	23.0	36.7	Texas	32	North Dakota	31
New York	32.2	38.0	Idaho	33	South Dakota	33
North Carolina	23.1	37.4	Oklahoma	34	Wyoming	34
North Dakota	25.7	37.0	Tennessee	35	New Mexico	35
Ohio	30.8	38.8	Virginia	35	Illinois	36
Oklahoma	26.2	36.2	North Dakota	37	Nevada	37
Oregon	32.4	38.4	Louisiana	38	Nebraska	38
Pennsylvania	29.1	40.1	Arizona	39	Oklahoma	38
Rhode Island	30.7	39.4	Kentucky	39	Colorado	40
South Carolina	22.2	37.9	Arkansas	41	Kansas	41
South Dakota	27.4	36.9	Georgia	42	Mississippi	41
Tennessee	25.8	38.0	Utah	43	Arizona	43
Texas	26.8	33.6	West Virginia	43	Louisiana	44
Utah	24.3	29.2	Alabama	45	Georgia	45
Vermont	29.9	41.5	Mississippi	45	California	46
Virginia	25.8	37.5	North Carolina	47	Idaho	47
Washington	32.2	37.3	New Mexico	48	Alaska	48
West Virginia	24.3	41.3	South Carolina	49	District of Columbia	48
Wisconsin	29.8	38.5	Alaska	n/a	Texas	50
Wyoming	27.6	36.8	Hawaii	n/a	Utah	51
United States	29.0	37.2	United States	–	United States	–

Source: U.S. Census Bureau, 1940 Census of Population; U.S. Census Bureau, Census 2010

High School Graduation Rate

Area	Percent		1940 Census		2010 Census	
	1940 Census	2010 Census	Area	Rank	Area	Rank
Alabama	15.7	82.1	District of Columbia	1	Wyoming	1
Alaska	n/a	91.0	California	2	Minnesota	2
Arizona	29.0	85.6	Utah	3	Montana	3
Arkansas	14.9	82.9	Nevada	4	New Hampshire	4
California	36.9	80.7	Washington	5	Alaska	5
Colorado	31.7	89.7	Oregon	6	Vermont	5
Connecticut	24.5	88.6	Wyoming	6	Iowa	7
Delaware	23.4	87.7	Colorado	8	Utah	7
District of Columbia	40.7	87.4	Massachusetts	9	Nebraska	9
Florida	26.2	85.5	Idaho	10	Maine	10
Georgia	17.2	84.3	Montana	11	North Dakota	10
Hawaii	n/a	89.9	Arizona	12	Wisconsin	12
Idaho	30.1	88.3	Nebraska	13	Hawaii	13
Illinois	24.1	86.9	Iowa	14	Washington	14
Indiana	24.5	87.0	Maine	14	Colorado	15
Iowa	28.5	90.6	Kansas	16	South Dakota	16
Kansas	28.2	89.2	Vermont	17	Kansas	17
Kentucky	15.5	81.9	New Hampshire	18	Massachusetts	18
Louisiana	17.5	81.9	Florida	19	Oregon	19
Maine	28.5	90.3	Ohio	20	Michigan	20
Maryland	20.6	88.1	South Dakota	21	Connecticut	21
Massachusetts	30.4	89.1	Minnesota	22	Pennsylvania	22
Michigan	24.5	88.7	Connecticut	23	Idaho	23
Minnesota	24.8	91.8	Indiana	23	Maryland	24
Mississippi	15.9	81.0	Michigan	23	Ohio	24
Missouri	22.0	86.9	Texas	23	New Jersey	26
Montana	29.1	91.7	Oklahoma	27	Delaware	27
Nebraska	28.7	90.4	Illinois	28	District of Columbia	28
Nevada	34.8	84.7	Delaware	29	Indiana	29
New Hampshire	26.5	91.5	New Mexico	30	Illinois	30
New Jersey	22.5	88.0	New York	31	Missouri	30
New Mexico	23.3	83.3	New Jersey	32	Virginia	32
New York	22.9	84.9	North Dakota	33	Oklahoma	33
North Carolina	18.7	84.7	Wisconsin	34	Arizona	34
North Dakota	22.3	90.3	Missouri	35	Florida	35
Ohio	25.4	88.1	Virginia	36	New York	36
Oklahoma	24.2	86.2	Pennsylvania	37	Nevada	37
Oregon	32.7	88.8	Rhode Island	37	North Carolina	37
Pennsylvania	20.9	88.4	Maryland	39	Georgia	39
Rhode Island	20.9	83.5	North Carolina	40	South Carolina	40
South Carolina	18.2	84.1	South Carolina	41	Tennessee	41
South Dakota	24.9	89.6	Tennessee	42	Rhode Island	42
Tennessee	17.9	83.6	West Virginia	43	New Mexico	43
Texas	24.5	80.7	Louisiana	44	West Virginia	44
Utah	36.6	90.6	Georgia	45	Arkansas	45
Vermont	27.6	91.0	Mississippi	46	Alabama	46
Virginia	21.3	86.5	Alabama	47	Kentucky	47
Washington	33.3	89.8	Kentucky	48	Louisiana	47
West Virginia	17.6	83.2	Arkansas	49	Mississippi	49
Wisconsin	22.1	90.1	Alaska	n/a	California	50
Wyoming	32.7	92.3	Hawaii	n/a	Texas	50
United States	24.1	85.6	United States	–	United States	–

Note: Figures cover the population 25 years old and over.
Source: U.S. Census Bureau, 1940 Census of Population; U.S. Census Bureau, American Community Survey, 2010 One-Year Estimate

College Graduation Rate

Area	Percent		1940 Census		2010 Census	
	1940 Census	2010 Census	Area	Rank	Area	Rank
Alabama	2.9	21.9	District of Columbia	1	District of Columbia	1
Alaska	n/a	27.9	California	2	Massachusetts	2
Arizona	6.2	25.9	Nevada	3	Colorado	3
Arkansas	2.2	19.5	Arizona	4	Maryland	4
California	6.7	30.1	Utah	5	Connecticut	5
Colorado	5.9	36.4	Colorado	6	New Jersey	6
Connecticut	4.8	35.5	New York	7	Virginia	7
Delaware	5.2	27.8	Washington	7	Vermont	8
District of Columbia	11.0	50.1	Massachusetts	9	New Hampshire	9
Florida	4.9	25.8	Oregon	9	New York	10
Georgia	3.3	27.3	Delaware	11	Minnesota	11
Hawaii	n/a	29.5	Wyoming	12	Washington	12
Idaho	4.4	24.4	New Jersey	13	Illinois	13
Illinois	4.5	30.8	Florida	14	Rhode Island	14
Indiana	3.8	22.7	Connecticut	15	California	15
Iowa	4.1	24.9	Maryland	15	Kansas	16
Kansas	4.6	29.8	Montana	15	Hawaii	17
Kentucky	2.9	20.5	Oklahoma	18	Utah	18
Louisiana	3.5	21.4	South Carolina	18	Montana	19
Maine	3.3	26.8	Kansas	20	Oregon	19
Maryland	4.8	36.1	Illinois	21	Nebraska	21
Massachusetts	5.4	39.0	Rhode Island	21	Alaska	22
Michigan	4.0	25.2	Idaho	23	Delaware	23
Minnesota	4.2	31.8	New Mexico	23	North Dakota	24
Mississippi	3.0	19.5	Ohio	23	Georgia	25
Missouri	3.9	25.6	Texas	23	Pennsylvania	26
Montana	4.8	28.8	Virginia	23	Maine	27
Nebraska	4.3	28.6	Nebraska	28	North Carolina	28
Nevada	6.5	21.7	New Hampshire	28	South Dakota	29
New Hampshire	4.3	32.8	Minnesota	30	Wisconsin	29
New Jersey	5.0	35.4	Pennsylvania	30	Arizona	31
New Mexico	4.4	25.0	Iowa	32	Texas	31
New York	5.5	32.5	North Carolina	32	Florida	33
North Carolina	4.1	26.5	Vermont	32	Missouri	34
North Dakota	3.5	27.6	Michigan	35	Michigan	35
Ohio	4.4	24.6	Missouri	36	New Mexico	36
Oklahoma	4.7	22.9	Wisconsin	36	Iowa	37
Oregon	5.4	28.8	Indiana	38	Ohio	38
Pennsylvania	4.2	27.1	South Dakota	38	South Carolina	39
Rhode Island	4.5	30.2	Louisiana	40	Idaho	40
South Carolina	4.7	24.5	North Dakota	40	Wyoming	41
South Dakota	3.8	26.3	West Virginia	42	Tennessee	42
Tennessee	3.1	23.1	Georgia	43	Oklahoma	43
Texas	4.4	25.9	Maine	43	Indiana	44
Utah	6.1	29.3	Tennessee	45	Alabama	45
Vermont	4.1	33.6	Mississippi	46	Nevada	46
Virginia	4.4	34.2	Alabama	47	Louisiana	47
Washington	5.5	31.1	Kentucky	47	Kentucky	48
West Virginia	3.4	17.5	Arkansas	49	Arkansas	49
Wisconsin	3.9	26.3	Alaska	n/a	Mississippi	49
Wyoming	5.1	24.1	Hawaii	n/a	West Virginia	51
United States	4.6	28.2	United States	–	United States	–

Note: Figures cover the population 25 years old and over.
Source: U.S. Census Bureau, 1940 Census of Population; U.S. Census Bureau, American Community Survey, 2010 One-Year Estimate

One-Person Households

Area	Percent		1940 Census		2010 Census	
	1940 Census	2010 Census	Area	Rank	Area	Rank
Alabama	5.2	27.4	Nevada	1	District of Columbia	1
Alaska	n/a	25.6	Montana	2	North Dakota	2
Arizona	11.5	26.1	Washington	3	Montana	3
Arkansas	6.3	27.1	California	4	Rhode Island	4
California	13.5	23.3	Oregon	5	South Dakota	5
Colorado	11.5	27.9	Wyoming	6	New York	6
Connecticut	6.0	27.3	Arizona	7	Ohio	7
Delaware	7.2	25.6	Colorado	7	Massachusetts	8
District of Columbia	9.9	44.0	Idaho	9	Nebraska	8
Florida	9.6	27.2	District of Columbia	10	Maine	10
Georgia	5.6	25.4	Florida	11	Pennsylvania	10
Hawaii	n/a	23.3	New Hampshire	12	Iowa	12
Idaho	10.3	23.8	Kansas	13	West Virginia	12
Illinois	7.6	27.8	South Dakota	14	Missouri	14
Indiana	7.5	26.9	Nebraska	15	Vermont	15
Iowa	8.1	28.4	New Mexico	16	Wisconsin	15
Kansas	9.1	27.8	Maine	17	Minnesota	17
Kentucky	5.7	27.5	Missouri	17	New Mexico	17
Louisiana	7.0	26.9	Minnesota	19	Wyoming	17
Maine	8.3	28.6	Iowa	20	Colorado	20
Maryland	6.8	26.1	Vermont	21	Michigan	20
Massachusetts	7.2	28.7	North Dakota	22	Illinois	22
Michigan	6.5	27.9	Utah	22	Kansas	22
Minnesota	8.2	28.0	Illinois	24	Kentucky	24
Mississippi	6.3	26.3	New York	24	Oklahoma	24
Missouri	8.3	28.3	Indiana	26	Alabama	26
Montana	15.1	29.7	Oklahoma	27	Oregon	26
Nebraska	8.7	28.7	Rhode Island	27	Connecticut	28
Nevada	17.7	25.7	Ohio	29	Florida	29
New Hampshire	9.2	25.6	Delaware	30	Washington	29
New Jersey	5.7	25.2	Massachusetts	30	Arkansas	31
New Mexico	8.4	28.0	Louisiana	32	North Carolina	32
New York	7.6	29.1	Wisconsin	32	Indiana	33
North Carolina	4.0	27.0	Maryland	34	Louisiana	33
North Dakota	7.9	31.5	Texas	34	Tennessee	33
Ohio	7.3	28.9	Michigan	36	South Carolina	36
Oklahoma	7.4	27.5	Pennsylvania	37	Mississippi	37
Oregon	13.2	27.4	Arkansas	38	Arizona	38
Pennsylvania	6.4	28.6	Mississippi	38	Maryland	38
Rhode Island	7.4	29.6	Connecticut	40	Virginia	40
South Carolina	5.8	26.5	South Carolina	41	Nevada	41
South Dakota	8.8	29.4	Kentucky	42	Alaska	42
Tennessee	5.1	26.9	New Jersey	42	Delaware	42
Texas	6.8	24.2	Georgia	44	New Hampshire	42
Utah	7.9	18.7	Virginia	44	Georgia	45
Vermont	8.0	28.2	Alabama	46	New Jersey	46
Virginia	5.6	26.0	Tennessee	47	Texas	47
Washington	14.9	27.2	West Virginia	47	Idaho	48
West Virginia	5.1	28.4	North Carolina	49	California	49
Wisconsin	7.0	28.2	Alaska	n/a	Hawaii	49
Wyoming	12.8	28.0	Hawaii	n/a	Utah	51
United States	7.7	26.7	United States	–	United States	–

Source: U.S. Census Bureau, 1940 Census of Population; U.S. Census Bureau, Census 2010

Homeownership Rate

Area	Percent		1940 Census		2010 Census	
	1940 Census	2010 Census	Area	Rank	Area	Rank
Alabama	33.6	69.7	Utah	1	West Virginia	1
Alaska	n/a	63.1	Idaho	2	Minnesota	2
Arizona	47.9	66.0	Maine	3	Iowa	3
Arkansas	39.7	66.9	New Mexico	3	Michigan	3
California	43.4	56.0	Washington	5	Delaware	5
Colorado	46.3	65.5	Vermont	6	Maine	6
Connecticut	40.5	67.5	Michigan	7	New Hampshire	7
Delaware	47.1	72.0	Oregon	7	Vermont	8
District of Columbia	29.9	42.0	Minnesota	9	Utah	9
Florida	43.6	67.3	Wisconsin	10	Idaho	10
Georgia	30.8	65.7	Indiana	11	Indiana	11
Hawaii	n/a	57.7	Montana	12	Alabama	12
Idaho	57.9	69.9	New Hampshire	13	Mississippi	13
Illinois	40.3	67.4	Iowa	14	Pennsylvania	13
Indiana	53.1	69.8	Kansas	15	South Carolina	15
Iowa	51.5	72.1	Ohio	16	Wyoming	15
Kansas	51.0	67.7	North Dakota	17	Missouri	17
Kentucky	48.0	68.7	Virginia	18	Kentucky	18
Louisiana	36.9	67.3	Wyoming	19	New Mexico	19
Maine	57.3	71.3	Kentucky	20	Tennessee	20
Maryland	47.4	67.5	Arizona	21	South Dakota	21
Massachusetts	38.1	62.3	Maryland	22	Wisconsin	21
Michigan	55.4	72.1	Delaware	23	Montana	23
Minnesota	55.2	73.1	Nebraska	23	Kansas	24
Mississippi	33.3	69.6	Colorado	25	Ohio	25
Missouri	44.3	68.8	Nevada	26	Connecticut	26
Montana	52.0	68.0	Pennsylvania	27	Maryland	26
Nebraska	47.1	67.2	South Dakota	28	Illinois	28
Nevada	46.1	58.8	Missouri	29	Florida	29
New Hampshire	51.7	70.9	Tennessee	30	Louisiana	29
New Jersey	39.4	65.4	West Virginia	31	Oklahoma	29
New Mexico	57.3	68.5	Florida	32	Nebraska	32
New York	30.3	53.3	California	33	Virginia	32
North Carolina	42.4	66.7	Oklahoma	34	Arkansas	34
North Dakota	49.8	65.4	Texas	34	North Carolina	35
Ohio	50.0	67.6	North Carolina	36	Arizona	36
Oklahoma	42.8	67.3	Connecticut	37	Georgia	37
Oregon	55.4	62.1	Illinois	38	Colorado	38
Pennsylvania	45.9	69.6	Arkansas	39	New Jersey	39
Rhode Island	37.4	60.7	New Jersey	40	North Dakota	39
South Carolina	30.6	69.3	Massachusetts	41	Washington	41
South Dakota	45.0	68.1	Rhode Island	42	Texas	42
Tennessee	44.1	68.2	Louisiana	43	Alaska	43
Texas	42.8	63.7	Alabama	44	Massachusetts	44
Utah	61.1	70.5	Mississippi	45	Oregon	45
Vermont	55.9	70.7	Georgia	46	Rhode Island	46
Virginia	48.9	67.2	South Carolina	47	Nevada	47
Washington	57.0	63.9	New York	48	Hawaii	48
West Virginia	43.7	73.4	District of Columbia	49	California	49
Wisconsin	54.4	68.1	Alaska	n/a	New York	50
Wyoming	48.6	69.3	Hawaii	n/a	District of Columbia	51
United States	43.6	65.1	United States	–	United States	–

Source: U.S. Census Bureau, 1940 Census of Population; U.S. Census Bureau, Census 2010

Median Home Value

Area	Dollars		1940 Census		2010 Census	
	1940 Census	2010 Census	Area	Rank	Area	Rank
Alabama	1,610	123,900	District of Columbia	1	Hawaii	1
Alaska	n/a	241,400	Connecticut	2	District of Columbia	2
Arizona	1,400	168,800	New Jersey	3	California	3
Arkansas	1,100	106,300	New York	4	New Jersey	4
California	3,527	370,900	Delaware	5	Massachusetts	5
Colorado	2,091	236,600	Rhode Island	6	Maryland	6
Connecticut	4,615	288,800	Massachusetts	7	New York	7
Delaware	4,159	243,600	California	8	Connecticut	8
District of Columbia	7,568	426,900	Ohio	9	Washington	9
Florida	2,218	164,200	Illinois	10	Rhode Island	10
Georgia	1,957	156,200	Wisconsin	11	Virginia	11
Hawaii	n/a	525,400	Pennsylvania	12	Oregon	12
Idaho	1,600	165,100	Maryland	13	Delaware	13
Illinois	3,277	191,800	Minnesota	14	New Hampshire	14
Indiana	2,406	123,300	Michigan	15	Alaska	15
Iowa	2,253	123,400	Vermont	16	Colorado	16
Kansas	1,733	127,300	Virginia	17	Utah	17
Kentucky	2,074	121,600	New Hampshire	18	Vermont	18
Louisiana	1,414	137,500	Indiana	19	Minnesota	19
Maine	2,008	179,100	Missouri	20	Illinois	20
Maryland	3,031	301,400	Washington	21	Montana	21
Massachusetts	3,837	334,100	West Virginia	22	Wyoming	22
Michigan	2,863	123,300	Oregon	23	Maine	23
Minnesota	3,024	194,300	Utah	24	Nevada	24
Mississippi	1,189	100,100	Iowa	25	Wisconsin	25
Missouri	2,392	139,000	Florida	26	Arizona	26
Montana	1,651	181,200	Wyoming	27	Pennsylvania	27
Nebraska	2,156	127,600	Nebraska	28	Idaho	28
Nevada	1,987	174,800	South Carolina	29	Florida	29
New Hampshire	2,505	243,000	Colorado	30	New Mexico	30
New Jersey	4,528	339,200	Kentucky	31	Georgia	31
New Mexico	656	161,200	Maine	32	North Carolina	32
New York	4,389	296,500	Nevada	33	Missouri	33
North Carolina	1,802	154,200	Georgia	34	Tennessee	33
North Dakota	1,626	123,000	Tennessee	35	South Carolina	35
Ohio	3,415	134,400	North Carolina	36	Louisiana	36
Oklahoma	1,293	111,400	Kansas	37	Ohio	37
Oregon	2,343	244,500	Texas	38	South Dakota	38
Pennsylvania	3,205	165,500	Montana	39	Texas	39
Rhode Island	3,848	254,500	North Dakota	40	Nebraska	40
South Carolina	2,145	138,100	South Dakota	41	Kansas	41
South Dakota	1,618	129,700	Alabama	42	Alabama	42
Tennessee	1,826	139,000	Idaho	43	Iowa	43
Texas	1,693	128,100	Louisiana	44	Indiana	44
Utah	2,320	217,200	Arizona	45	Michigan	44
Vermont	2,836	216,800	Oklahoma	46	North Dakota	46
Virginia	2,633	249,100	Mississippi	47	Kentucky	47
Washington	2,359	271,800	Arkansas	48	Oklahoma	48
West Virginia	2,350	95,100	New Mexico	49	Arkansas	49
Wisconsin	3,232	169,400	Alaska	n/a	Mississippi	50
Wyoming	2,174	180,100	Hawaii	n/a	West Virginia	51
United States	2,938	179,900	United States	–	United States	–

Source: U.S. Census Bureau, 1940 Census of Population; U.S. Census Bureau, American Community Survey, 2010 One-Year Estimate

Median Gross Rent

Area	Dollars		1940 Census		2010 Census	
	1940 Census	2010 Census	Area	Rank	Area	Rank
Alabama	12	667	District of Columbia	1	Hawaii	1
Alaska	n/a	981	New York	2	District of Columbia	2
Arizona	18	844	New Jersey	3	California	3
Arkansas	12	638	Connecticut	4	Maryland	4
California	27	1,163	Massachusetts	4	New Jersey	5
Colorado	22	863	Illinois	6	New York	6
Connecticut	34	992	Michigan	6	Virginia	7
Delaware	30	952	Wisconsin	8	Massachusetts	8
District of Columbia	45	1,198	Delaware	9	Connecticut	9
Florida	16	947	Minnesota	10	Alaska	10
Georgia	13	819	Ohio	10	Delaware	11
Hawaii	n/a	1,291	Rhode Island	10	Nevada	11
Idaho	21	683	California	13	New Hampshire	13
Illinois	33	848	Maryland	13	Florida	14
Indiana	24	683	Pennsylvania	13	Washington	15
Iowa	23	629	Nevada	16	Rhode Island	16
Kansas	19	682	New Hampshire	16	Colorado	17
Kentucky	16	613	Maine	18	Illinois	18
Louisiana	15	736	Indiana	19	Arizona	19
Maine	25	707	Vermont	19	Vermont	20
Maryland	27	1,131	Iowa	21	Georgia	21
Massachusetts	34	1,009	Montana	21	Oregon	22
Michigan	33	730	Utah	21	Texas	23
Minnesota	28	764	Colorado	24	Utah	24
Mississippi	11	672	Missouri	24	Minnesota	25
Missouri	22	682	Nebraska	24	Pennsylvania	26
Montana	23	642	Washington	24	Louisiana	27
Nebraska	22	669	Wyoming	24	North Carolina	28
Nevada	26	952	Idaho	29	Michigan	29
New Hampshire	26	951	North Dakota	29	South Carolina	30
New Jersey	36	1,114	Oregon	29	Wisconsin	31
New Mexico	17	699	South Dakota	29	Maine	32
New York	39	1,020	Kansas	33	New Mexico	33
North Carolina	14	731	Virginia	33	Tennessee	34
North Dakota	21	583	Arizona	35	Wyoming	35
Ohio	28	685	New Mexico	36	Ohio	36
Oklahoma	16	659	Texas	36	Idaho	37
Oregon	21	816	West Virginia	36	Indiana	37
Pennsylvania	27	763	Florida	39	Kansas	39
Rhode Island	28	868	Kentucky	39	Missouri	39
South Carolina	12	728	Oklahoma	39	Mississippi	41
South Dakota	21	591	Louisiana	42	Nebraska	42
Tennessee	15	697	Tennessee	42	Alabama	43
Texas	17	801	North Carolina	44	Oklahoma	44
Utah	23	796	Georgia	45	Montana	45
Vermont	24	823	Alabama	46	Arkansas	46
Virginia	19	1,019	Arkansas	46	Iowa	47
Washington	22	908	South Carolina	46	Kentucky	48
West Virginia	17	571	Mississippi	49	South Dakota	49
Wisconsin	31	715	Alaska	n/a	North Dakota	50
Wyoming	22	693	Hawaii	n/a	West Virginia	51
United States	27	855	United States	–	United States	–

Source: U.S. Census Bureau, 1940 Census of Population; U.S. Census Bureau, American Community Survey, 2010 One-Year Estimate

Households Lacking Complete Plumbing

Area	Percent		1940 Census		2010 Census	
	1940 Census	2010 Census	Area	Rank	Area	Rank
Alabama	80.3	3.6	Mississippi	1	Alaska	1
Alaska	n/a	11.9	Arkansas	2	West Virginia	2
Arizona	53.5	2.3	North Dakota	3	Maine	3
Arkansas	83.5	4.3	Alabama	4	New Mexico	4
California	16.6	1.1	South Carolina	5	Arkansas	5
Colorado	53.7	1.3	Georgia	6	Mississippi	5
Connecticut	18.8	1.1	North Carolina	6	Montana	7
Delaware	40.3	1.6	Tennessee	8	Louisiana	8
District of Columbia	17.7	2.2	South Dakota	9	Alabama	9
Florida	46.2	1.4	Kentucky	10	Kentucky	10
Georgia	76.3	2.2	New Mexico	11	Oklahoma	11
Hawaii	n/a	1.5	Louisiana	12	Indiana	12
Idaho	61.6	1.6	Oklahoma	12	Michigan	12
Illinois	36.2	2.1	West Virginia	14	Missouri	12
Indiana	54.4	3.1	Virginia	15	South Dakota	12
Iowa	58.2	1.7	Montana	16	Pennsylvania	16
Kansas	60.1	2.3	Texas	17	South Carolina	17
Kentucky	73.8	3.5	Idaho	18	Texas	17
Louisiana	67.2	3.9	Kansas	19	Vermont	17
Maine	55.0	4.7	Wyoming	20	North Carolina	20
Maryland	39.5	1.5	Iowa	21	North Dakota	21
Massachusetts	17.3	1.0	Nebraska	22	Tennessee	21
Michigan	37.5	3.1	Missouri	23	Arizona	23
Minnesota	54.5	2.1	Maine	24	Kansas	23
Mississippi	86.0	4.3	Minnesota	25	Ohio	23
Missouri	57.0	3.1	Indiana	26	District of Columbia	26
Montana	63.1	4.1	Colorado	27	Georgia	26
Nebraska	57.7	2.2	Arizona	28	Nebraska	26
Nevada	43.7	1.2	Wisconsin	29	Illinois	29
New Hampshire	39.2	1.6	Florida	30	Minnesota	29
New Jersey	18.6	1.2	Nevada	31	Virginia	31
New Mexico	72.7	4.6	Vermont	32	Rhode Island	32
New York	17.8	1.6	Delaware	33	Wisconsin	34
North Carolina	76.3	2.5	Maryland	34	Iowa	35
North Dakota	80.4	2.4	Utah	35	Delaware	36
Ohio	38.1	2.3	New Hampshire	36	Idaho	36
Oklahoma	67.2	3.2	Oregon	37	New Hampshire	36
Oregon	38.8	1.3	Ohio	38	New York	36
Pennsylvania	37.2	2.7	Michigan	39	Hawaii	40
Rhode Island	23.8	1.9	Pennsylvania	40	Maryland	40
South Carolina	78.8	2.6	Illinois	41	Washington	40
South Dakota	74.6	3.1	Washington	42	Florida	43
Tennessee	75.6	2.4	Rhode Island	43	Colorado	44
Texas	62.1	2.6	Connecticut	44	Oregon	44
Utah	39.3	1.2	New Jersey	45	Nevada	46
Vermont	41.4	2.6	New York	46	New Jersey	46
Virginia	64.9	2.0	District of Columbia	47	Utah	46
Washington	35.5	1.5	Massachusetts	48	California	49
West Virginia	65.6	5.2	California	49	Connecticut	49
Wisconsin	48.7	1.8	Alaska	n/a	Massachusetts	51
Wyoming	59.1	1.9	Hawaii	n/a	Wyoming	32
United States	45.3	2.2	United States	–	United States	–

Note: Complete plumbing facilities are defined as hot and cold piped water, a bath- tub or shower, and a flush toilet. In earlier censuses, these facilities must have been for exclusive use of a housing unit's inhabitants; this requirement was dropped in 1990.
Source: U.S. Census Bureau, 1940 Census of Population; U.S. Census Bureau, American Community Survey, 2010 One-Year Estimate

SECTION ONE: PROFILES

Family of Four Depend on Ford Motor Company Job

The decade leading up to the 1940s, certainly a roller coaster for so many Americans, was less so for those who depended on automobile factory jobs. No matter the economy, many Americans were unwilling to give up the luxury afforded by an automobile, and the lifestyle of families like the Broos family was typical throughout the decade.

Life at Home

- The Broos family—mother, father and two daughters, 10 and 15 years old—lived in Detroit, Michigan, where Pete Broos worked for Ford Motor Company.
- The family lived in a five-room flat with three bedrooms, two common rooms, and a bathroom. Hot water was available from the tap in both the kitchen and bathroom, and running water was available in the yard.
- The flat also included a sink and a sewer connection.
- Peter and his wife Miriam thought about purchasing a home but were afraid to make the commitment of buying a house with its increased costs.
- Also, most mortgage lenders required a 30 percent down payment on a house, and most mortgage loans were for 10 years, which sometimes included a balloon payment, putting the payments out of reach.
- Peter and Mary were both third-generation Dutch, and prided themselves on controlling their expenses and living within their means.
- When the Depression began, Ford actually increased hourly wages, but rumors of layoffs persisted.
- Food was the family's greatest expense—about 32 percent of Peter's income.
- Eating out was too expensive for the family; only Peter ate lunches out.
- They used ice in the summer for the icebox; and the coolness of the cellar in the winter.
- Beef roast and apples and oranges were a few of the family's favorite things to eat.
- Popular vegetables at the Broos' table were potatoes, tomatoes and cabbage, and their food budget included some liquor and beer.
- Mary bought some fashionable knee high skirts, but wore them sparingly only in the summer, because Peter didn't approve.
- Peter's two suits and Mary's three dresses were worn only on special occasions, due to the high cost of having them cleaned.

Peter Broos worked for Ford Motor Company.

- The Broos family home had central heating, not uncommon, but still a luxury for a majority of families who worked in the factory.
- They also had a washing machine, which was purchased on an installment plan.
- Mary had time to be involved in a number of church groups, due largely to the time saved by devices like the washing machine.

- Daughters Alice and Ann convinced their parents to buy a radio, and they were devoted fans of the extremely popular *Amos and Andy* show.
- This 15-minute show was one of the first nationally syndicated radio shows in the country.
- Peter listened to religious programming on Sundays; the preaching against communism, international bankers, and the gold standard struck a cord with Detroit's auto workers.
- Medical expenses for the Broos included general checkups for the family and eyeglasses for Peter and Ann, the couple's 10-year-old.
- Alice and Ann attended public school, and their parents paid for their schoolbooks.
- The Broos family contributed $15.00 to the Dutch Congregationalist Church annually.
- The family went to about 30 movies a year, mostly in the afternoon when the tickets are cheaper.
- Their favorite film star was Charlie Chaplin in his guise as the little Tramp, and they heard that a talkie, *The Jazz Singer* with Al Jolson, exists, but have never seen it.
- In addition to movies, Alice and Ann enjoyed clipping the cartoons each day from the newspaper and compiled the story of "Why Mothers Get Gray" into scrapbooks covering years of cartoons.
- The "family telephone" was located at the corner down the street and cost $0.05 per call. It was used exclusively for calling the doctor or relatives on special occasions.

Life at Work

- Peter made $7.00 a day.
- Ford Motor Company, unlike most of the other automobile companies, did not pay for piecework, but hourly.
- Many manufacturers believed that the more money a worker can earn, the harder he will work, a philosophy that gave employees an incentive to work but also saved the company money when machinery breaks and the workers are unable to produce.

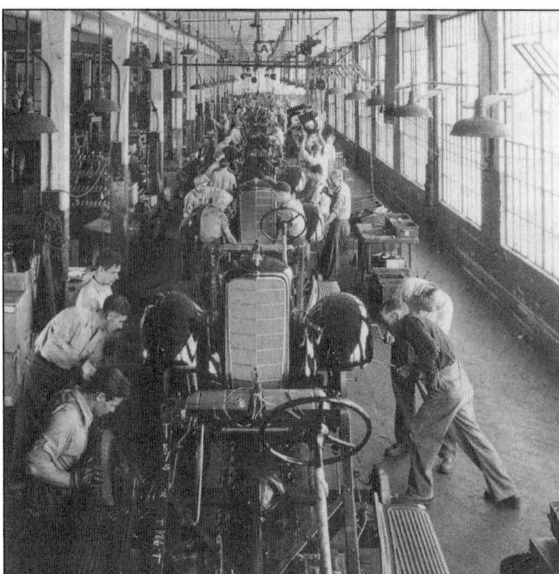

Ford Motor workers were paid by the hour.

- Ford instituted an eight-hour day, although workers were expected to get to work 15 to 20 minutes early to gather his tools and set up, and were not paid for 15- to 20-minute lunch breaks, or the time it took at the end of each day to put their tools up.
- The factory produced the Model A, which sold very well.
- The Model A had four cylinders, balloon tires, and a reliable electrical system, including a self-starter; it has a cruising speed of 55 miles per hour.
- It cost $495.00, approximately $100.00 less than the equivalent Chevrolet, Ford's primary competitor.

Life in the Community: Detroit, Michigan

- Before the automobile industry, Detroit was a Great Lakes' center for food processing, copper smelting, and iron making.
- The construction of Henry Ford's huge plants at the satellite industrial centers of Highland Park and River Rouge, allowed Detroit to grow, with at population just shy of one million.

- The urban transformation was driven by European immigrants and rural American immigrants, both seeking a better life.
- The Model T was not only a part of American material life but also a large part of its cultural life—the Temple Theater Building, Detroit's largest vaudeville theatre, had the city's first electric sign-a car with spinning wheels in lights that read "Watch the Fords Go By."
- During the 1930s, retailing, long thought to be a refuge for the small entrepreneur, gave way to big corporations establishing chains of retail outlets, and Americans bought more than one-fourth of their food and clothing (and much of their tobacco) from "chain stores."
- The early 1930s saw lines for city soup kitchens extend for blocks, and include thousands of children.

The nine tables that follow are reprinted from the actual 1940 census, for the city of Detroit. They include actual data on race, percentage of voting population, school attendance, number of school years completed, foreign born, and employment of workers 14 years and older by job, industry and race. In addition to being incredibly fascinating, these facts help to strengthen and visualize the actual environment in which Peter Broos lived and worked.

Table A-35.—AGE, BY RACE AND SEX, FOR THE CITY OF DETROIT: 1940 AND 1930

[Figures for white population in 1930 revised to include Mexicans classified with "Other races" in the 1930 reports. Percent not shown where less than 0.1 or where base is less than 100]

AGE AND CENSUS YEAR	ALL CLASSES			NATIVE WHITE			FOREIGN-BORN WHITE			NEGRO			OTHER RACES		
	Total	Male	Female	Total	Male	Female	Total	Male	Female	Total	Male	Female	Total	Male	Female
All ages: 1940	1,623,452	827,499	795,953	1,151,998	579,520	572,478	320,664	172,297	148,367	149,119	74,485	74,634	1,671	1,197	474
Under 5 years	117,389	60,002	57,387	105,558	54,019	51,539	288	138	150	11,383	5,760	5,623	160	85	75
5 to 9 years	114,346	57,893	56,453	101,600	51,498	50,102	991	521	470	11,618	5,795	5,823	137	79	58
10 to 14 years	134,054	67,765	66,289	118,998	60,401	58,597	2,593	1,311	1,282	12,326	5,978	6,348	137	75	62
15 to 19 years	141,002	69,444	71,558	121,219	59,769	61,450	7,993	4,010	3,983	11,673	5,593	6,080	117	72	45
20 to 24 years	149,667	71,223	78,444	127,669	61,311	66,358	9,772	4,555	5,217	12,141	5,295	6,846	85	62	23
25 to 29 years	148,548	71,984	76,564	116,792	57,426	59,366	16,842	7,700	9,142	14,796	6,770	8,026	118	88	30
30 to 34 years	141,495	69,910	71,585	100,143	50,158	49,985	25,866	12,355	13,511	15,292	7,241	8,051	194	156	38
35 to 39 years	144,723	75,057	69,666	89,143	46,429	42,714	37,830	19,612	18,218	17,522	8,831	8,691	228	185	43
40 to 44 years	135,595	72,537	63,058	76,129	40,002	36,127	44,678	24,395	20,283	14,618	8,003	6,615	170	137	33
45 to 49 years	125,560	69,526	56,034	64,579	34,203	30,376	50,121	29,160	20,961	10,733	6,061	4,672	127	102	25
50 to 54 years	97,879	54,937	42,942	47,540	24,879	22,661	43,540	26,115	17,425	6,699	3,861	2,838	100	82	18
55 to 59 years	64,982	35,584	29,398	31,101	15,844	15,257	29,698	17,407	12,291	4,144	2,304	1,840	39	29	10
60 to 64 years	43,601	22,305	21,296	20,914	10,149	10,765	20,250	10,847	9,403	2,407	1,285	1,122	30	24	6
65 to 69 years	29,256	13,917	15,339	14,344	6,613	7,731	12,900	6,341	6,559	1,995	949	1,046	17	14	3
70 to 74 years	18,105	8,187	9,918	8,575	3,762	4,813	8,572	4,011	4,561	950	408	542	8	6	2
75 years and over	17,250	7,228	10,022	7,694	3,057	4,637	8,730	3,819	4,911	822	351	471	4	1	3
Under 1 year	23,478	12,022	11,456	21,042	10,784	10,258	21	12	9	2,375	1,211	1,164	40	15	25
5 years	22,514	11,431	11,083	20,039	10,149	9,890	132	78	54	2,309	1,184	1,125	34	20	14
14 years	27,481	13,883	13,598	24,171	12,276	11,895	763	381	382	2,519	1,210	1,309	28	16	12
15 years	27,860	13,994	13,866	24,512	12,348	12,164	856	451	405	2,469	1,183	1,286	23	12	11
16 and 17 years	54,603	27,250	27,353	47,173	23,568	23,605	2,863	1,443	1,420	4,516	2,203	2,313	51	36	15
21 years and over	1,088,739	559,292	529,447	681,108	342,696	338,412	306,656	165,315	141,343	99,870	50,408	49,462	1,103	873	230
All ages: 1930	1,568,662	821,920	746,742	1,042,935	533,485	509,450	403,721	224,631	179,090	120,066	62,239	57,827	1,940	1,565	375
Under 5 years	146,610	74,639	71,971	133,390	68,024	65,366	2,449	1,225	1,224	10,618	5,314	5,304	153	76	77
5 to 9 years	148,173	74,956	73,217	129,323	65,331	63,992	8,547	4,427	4,120	10,201	5,146	5,055	102	52	50
10 to 14 years	133,280	66,409	66,871	116,082	57,987	58,095	9,399	4,658	4,741	7,728	3,719	4,009	71	45	26
15 to 19 years	123,082	59,216	63,866	99,629	48,023	51,606	15,901	7,712	8,189	7,454	3,409	4,045	98	72	26
20 to 24 years	151,642	75,248	76,394	108,300	53,629	54,671	29,967	15,272	14,695	13,078	6,088	6,990	297	259	38
25 to 29 years	170,272	89,944	80,328	104,863	55,363	49,500	46,518	24,989	21,529	18,473	9,221	9,252	418	371	47
30 to 34 years	160,573	87,439	73,134	90,986	48,571	42,415	53,205	29,949	23,256	16,116	8,686	7,430	266	233	33
35 to 39 years	156,526	88,222	68,304	80,340	43,386	36,954	61,962	36,821	25,141	14,035	7,854	6,181	189	161	28
40 to 44 years	119,148	68,655	50,493	57,599	31,028	26,571	52,917	32,490	20,427	8,515	5,036	3,479	117	101	16
45 to 49 years	86,582	49,322	37,260	40,709	21,656	19,053	39,690	23,990	15,700	6,095	3,601	2,494	88	75	13
50 to 54 years	60,275	32,695	27,580	29,003	14,991	14,012	27,807	15,671	12,136	3,402	1,980	1,422	63	53	10
55 to 59 years	40,251	20,878	19,373	20,100	10,150	9,950	18,303	9,683	8,620	1,817	1,017	800	31	28	3
60 to 64 years	28,891	14,271	14,620	13,636	6,691	6,945	14,197	7,045	7,152	1,030	508	522	28	27	1
65 to 69 years	19,878	9,401	10,477	8,846	4,175	4,671	10,460	4,966	5,494	560	252	308	12	8	4
70 to 74 years	12,155	5,568	6,587	5,443	2,421	3,022	6,398	3,023	3,375	311	123	188	3	1	2
75 years and over	10,283	4,400	5,883	4,081	1,641	2,380	5,859	2,613	3,246	400	143	257	3	3	-
Not reported	1,041	657	384	665	418	247	142	97	45	233	142	91	1	-	1
Under 1 year	28,523	14,516	14,007	26,276	13,374	12,902	160	83	77	2,062	1,046	1,016	25	13	12
5 years	30,727	15,687	15,040	27,495	14,050	13,445	975	518	457	2,231	1,103	1,128	26	16	10
14 years	25,409	12,693	12,716	21,908	10,933	10,975	1,986	998	988	1,499	752	747	16	10	6
15 years	24,510	12,255	12,255	20,999	10,495	10,504	2,208	1,125	1,083	1,293	628	665	10	7	3
16 and 17 years	47,542	23,116	24,426	38,838	18,911	19,927	5,841	2,877	2,964	2,825	1,306	1,519	38	22	16
21 years and over	991,100	534,313	456,787	544,827	284,893	259,934	362,832	204,357	158,475	81,968	43,783	38,185	1,473	1,280	193
Percent: 1940	100.0	100.0	100.0	100.0	100.0	100.0	100.0	100.0	100.0	100.0	100.0	100.0	100.0	100.0	100.0
Under 5 years	7.2	7.3	7.2	9.2	9.3	9.0	0.1	0.1	0.1	7.6	7.7	7.5	9.6	7.1	15.8
5 to 9 years	7.0	7.0	7.1	8.8	8.9	8.8	0.3	0.3	0.3	7.8	7.8	7.8	8.2	6.6	12.2
10 to 14 years	8.3	8.2	8.3	10.3	10.4	10.2	0.8	0.8	0.9	8.3	8.0	8.5	8.2	6.3	13.1
15 to 19 years	8.7	8.4	9.0	10.5	10.3	10.7	2.5	2.3	2.7	7.8	7.5	8.1	7.0	6.0	9.5
20 to 24 years	9.2	8.6	9.9	11.1	10.6	11.6	3.0	2.6	3.5	8.1	7.1	9.2	5.1	5.2	4.9
25 to 29 years	9.2	8.7	9.6	10.1	9.9	10.4	5.3	4.5	6.2	9.9	9.1	10.8	7.1	7.4	6.3
30 to 34 years	8.7	8.4	9.0	8.7	8.7	8.7	8.1	7.2	9.1	10.3	9.7	10.8	11.6	13.0	8.0
35 to 39 years	8.9	9.1	8.8	7.7	8.0	7.5	11.8	11.4	12.3	11.8	11.9	11.6	13.6	15.5	9.1
40 to 44 years	8.4	8.8	7.9	6.6	6.9	6.3	13.9	14.2	13.7	9.8	10.7	8.9	10.2	11.4	7.0
45 to 49 years	7.7	8.4	7.0	5.6	5.9	5.3	15.6	16.9	14.1	7.2	8.1	6.3	7.6	8.5	5.3
50 to 54 years	6.0	6.6	5.4	4.1	4.3	4.0	13.6	15.2	11.7	4.5	5.2	3.8	6.0	6.9	3.8
55 to 59 years	4.0	4.3	3.7	2.7	2.7	2.7	9.3	10.1	8.3	2.8	3.1	2.5	2.3	2.4	2.1
60 to 64 years	2.7	2.7	2.7	1.8	1.8	1.9	6.3	6.3	6.3	1.6	1.7	1.5	1.8	2.0	1.3
65 to 69 years	1.8	1.7	1.9	1.2	1.1	1.4	4.0	3.7	4.4	1.3	1.3	1.4	1.0	1.2	0.6
70 to 74 years	1.1	1.0	1.2	0.7	0.6	0.8	2.7	2.3	3.1	0.6	0.5	0.7	0.5	0.5	0.4
75 years and over	1.1	0.9	1.3	0.7	0.5	0.8	2.7	2.2	3.3	0.6	0.5	0.6	0.2	0.1	0.6
Under 1 year	1.4	1.5	1.4	1.8	1.9	1.8	-	-	-	1.6	1.6	1.6	2.4	1.3	5.3
5 years	1.4	1.4	1.4	1.7	1.8	1.7	-	-	-	1.5	1.6	1.5	2.0	1.7	3.0
14 years	1.7	1.7	1.7	2.1	2.1	2.1	0.2	0.2	0.3	1.7	1.6	1.8	1.7	1.3	2.5
15 years	1.7	1.7	1.7	2.1	2.1	2.1	0.3	0.3	0.3	1.7	1.6	1.7	1.4	1.0	2.3
16 and 17 years	3.4	3.3	3.4	4.1	4.1	4.1	0.9	0.8	1.0	3.0	3.0	3.1	3.1	3.0	3.2
21 years and over	67.1	67.6	66.5	59.1	59.1	59.1	95.6	95.9	95.3	67.0	67.7	66.3	66.0	72.9	48.5
Percent: 1930	100.0	100.0	100.0	100.0	100.0	100.0	100.0	100.0	100.0	100.0	100.0	100.0	100.0	100.0	100.0
Under 5 years	9.3	9.1	9.6	12.8	12.8	12.8	0.6	0.5	0.7	8.8	8.5	9.2	7.9	4.9	20.5
5 to 9 years	9.4	9.1	9.8	12.4	12.2	12.6	2.1	2.0	2.3	8.5	8.3	8.7	5.3	3.3	13.3
10 to 14 years	8.5	8.1	9.0	11.1	10.9	11.4	2.3	2.1	2.6	6.4	6.0	6.9	3.7	2.9	6.9
15 to 19 years	7.8	7.2	8.6	9.6	9.0	10.1	3.9	3.4	4.6	6.2	5.5	7.0	5.1	4.6	6.9
20 to 24 years	9.7	9.2	10.2	10.4	10.1	10.7	7.4	6.8	8.2	10.9	9.8	12.1	15.3	16.5	10.1
25 to 29 years	10.9	10.9	10.8	10.1	10.4	9.7	11.5	11.1	12.0	15.4	14.8	16.0	21.5	23.7	12.5
30 to 34 years	10.2	10.6	9.8	8.7	9.1	8.3	13.2	13.3	13.0	13.4	14.0	12.8	13.7	14.9	8.8
35 to 39 years	10.0	10.7	9.1	7.7	8.1	7.3	15.3	16.4	14.0	11.7	12.6	10.7	9.7	10.3	7.5
40 to 44 years	7.6	8.4	6.8	5.5	5.8	5.2	13.1	14.5	11.4	7.1	8.1	6.0	6.0	6.5	4.3
45 to 49 years	5.5	6.0	5.0	3.9	4.1	3.7	9.8	10.7	8.8	5.1	5.8	4.3	4.5	4.8	3.5
50 to 54 years	3.8	4.0	3.7	2.8	2.8	2.8	6.9	7.0	6.8	2.8	3.2	2.5	3.2	3.4	2.7
55 to 59 years	2.6	2.5	2.6	1.9	1.9	2.0	4.5	4.3	4.8	1.5	1.6	1.4	1.6	1.8	0.8
60 to 64 years	1.8	1.7	2.0	1.3	1.3	1.4	3.5	3.1	4.0	0.9	0.8	0.9	1.4	1.7	0.3
65 to 69 years	1.3	1.1	1.4	0.8	0.8	0.9	2.6	2.2	3.1	0.5	0.4	0.5	0.6	0.5	1.1
70 to 74 years	0.8	0.7	0.9	0.5	0.5	0.6	1.6	1.3	1.9	0.3	0.2	0.3	0.2	0.1	0.5
75 years and over	0.7	0.5	0.8	0.4	0.3	0.5	1.5	1.2	1.8	0.3	0.2	0.4	0.2	0.2	-
Not reported	0.1	0.1	0.1	0.1	0.1	-	-	-	-	0.2	0.2	0.2	0.1	-	0.3
Under 1 year	1.8	1.8	1.9	2.5	2.5	2.5	-	-	-	1.7	1.7	1.8	1.3	0.8	3.2
5 years	2.0	1.9	2.0	2.6	2.6	2.6	0.2	0.2	0.3	1.9	1.8	2.0	1.3	1.0	2.7
14 years	1.6	1.5	1.7	2.1	2.0	2.2	0.5	0.4	0.6	1.2	1.2	1.3	0.8	0.6	1.6
15 years	1.6	1.5	1.6	2.0	2.0	2.1	0.5	0.5	0.6	1.1	1.0	1.1	0.5	0.4	0.8
16 and 17 years	3.0	2.8	3.3	3.7	3.5	3.9	1.4	1.3	1.7	2.4	2.1	2.6	2.0	1.4	4.3
21 years and over	63.2	65.0	61.2	52.2	53.4	51.0	89.9	91.0	88.5	68.3	70.3	66.0	75.9	81.8	51.5

Table A-36.—RACE, BY NATIVITY AND SEX, FOR THE CITY OF DETROIT: 1940 AND 1930

[Figures for white population in 1930 have been revised to include Mexicans who were classified with "Other races" in the 1930 reports. Percent not shown where less than 0.1 or where base is less than 100. Sex ratio not shown where number of females is less than 100]

SEX, NATIVITY, AND CENSUS YEAR	All classes	White	Negro	Other races	OTHER RACES				PERCENT BY RACE				PERCENT BY NATIVITY					
					Indian	Chinese	Japanese	All other	All classes	White	Negro	Other races	All classes	White	Negro	Indian	Chinese	Japanese
TOTAL																		
1940	1,623,452	1,472,662	149,119	1,671	434	583	63	591	100.0	90.7	9.2	0.1	100.0	100.0	100.0	100.0	100.0	-
Native	1,300,764	1,151,998	147,682	1,084	269	273	25	517	100.0	88.6	11.4	0.1	80.1	78.2	99.0	62.0	46.8	-
Foreign born	322,688	320,664	1,437	587	165	310	38	74	100.0	99.4	0.4	0.2	19.9	21.8	1.0	38.0	53.2	-
1930	1,568,662	1,446,656	120,066	1,940	350	710	103	777	100.0	92.2	7.7	0.1	100.0	100.0	100.0	100.0	100.0	100.0
Native	1,162,780	1,042,935	118,621	1,224	265	273	43	643	100.0	89.7	10.2	0.1	74.1	72.1	98.8	75.7	38.5	41.7
Foreign born	405,882	403,721	1,445	716	85	437	60	134	100.0	99.5	0.4	0.2	25.9	27.9	1.2	24.3	61.5	58.3
MALE																		
1940	827,499	751,817	74,485	1,197	244	442	47	464	100.0	90.9	9.0	0.1	100.0	100.0	100.0	100.0	100.0	-
Native	653,994	579,520	73,729	745	156	175	14	400	100.0	88.6	11.3	0.1	79.0	77.1	99.0	63.9	39.6	-
Foreign born	173,505	172,297	756	452	88	267	33	64	100.0	99.3	0.4	0.3	21.0	22.9	1.0	36.1	60.4	-
1930	821,920	758,116	62,239	1,565	187	586	83	709	100.0	92.2	7.6	0.2	100.0	100.0	100.0	100.0	100.0	-
Native	595,885	533,485	61,443	957	147	195	31	584	100.0	89.5	10.3	0.2	72.5	70.4	98.7	78.6	33.3	-
Foreign born	226,035	224,631	796	608	40	391	52	125	100.0	99.4	0.4	0.3	27.5	29.6	1.3	21.4	66.7	-
FEMALE																		
1940	795,953	720,845	74,634	474	190	141	16	127	100.0	90.6	9.4	0.1	100.0	100.0	100.0	100.0	100.0	-
Native	646,770	572,478	73,953	339	113	98	11	117	100.0	88.5	11.4	0.1	81.3	79.4	99.1	59.5	69.5	-
Foreign born	149,183	148,367	681	135	77	43	5	10	100.0	99.5	0.5	0.1	18.7	20.6	0.9	40.5	30.5	-
1930	746,742	668,540	57,827	375	163	124	20	68	100.0	92.2	7.7	0.1	100.0	100.0	100.0	100.0	100.0	-
Native	566,895	509,450	57,178	267	118	78	12	59	100.0	89.9	10.1	-	75.9	74.0	98.9	72.4	62.9	-
Foreign born	179,847	179,090	649	108	45	46	8	9	100.0	99.6	0.4	0.1	24.1	26.0	1.1	27.6	37.1	-
MALES PER 100 FEMALES																		
1940	104.0	104.3	99.8	252.5	128.4	313.5	-	365.4	-	-	-	-	-	-	-	-	-	-
Native	101.1	101.2	99.7	219.8	138.1	-	-	341.9	-	-	-	-	-	-	-	-	-	-
Foreign born	116.3	116.1	111.0	334.8	-	-	-	-	-	-	-	-	-	-	-	-	-	-
1930	110.1	110.1	107.6	417.3	114.7	472.6	-	-	-	-	-	-	-	-	-	-	-	-
Native	105.1	104.7	107.5	358.4	124.6	-	-	-	-	-	-	-	-	-	-	-	-	-
Foreign born	125.7	125.4	122.7	563.0	-	-	-	-	-	-	-	-	-	-	-	-	-	-

Table A-37.—POTENTIAL VOTING POPULATION, BY CITIZENSHIP, RACE, NATIVITY, AND SEX, FOR THE CITY OF DETROIT: 1940 AND 1930

[Figures for white population in 1930 have been revised to include Mexicans who were classified with "Other races" in the 1930 reports. Percent not shown where less than 0.1]

CITIZENSHIP, RACE, AND NATIVITY	TOTAL POPULATION (ALL AGES)								POPULATION 21 YEARS OLD AND OVER							
	Total number		Percent		Male		Female		Total number		Percent		Male		Female	
	1940	1930	1940	1930	1940	1930	1940	1930	1940	1930	1940	1930	1940	1930	1940	1930
Total	1,623,452	1,568,662	100.0	100.0	827,499	821,920	795,953	746,742	1,088,739	991,100	100.0	100.0	559,292	534,313	529,447	456,787
Percent citizen	-	-	92.3	85.2	-	-	-	-	-	-	89.2	79.7	-	-	-	-
Percent alien and citiz. not rptd.	-	-	7.7	14.8	-	-	-	-	-	-	10.8	20.3	-	-	-	-
Citizen	1,498,555	1,336,020	100.0	100.0	775,011	695,858	723,544	640,162	971,801	789,618	100.0	100.0	510,475	423,772	460,826	365,846
White—Native	1,151,998	1,042,935	76.9	78.1	579,520	533,485	572,478	509,450	681,108	544,827	70.1	69.0	342,696	284,893	338,412	259,934
Naturalized	197,046	172,657	13.1	12.9	120,614	99,682	76,432	72,975	190,397	162,772	19.6	20.6	117,235	94,837	73,162	67,935
Negro—Native	147,682	118,621	10.0	8.9	73,729	61,443	73,953	57,178	98,492	80,626	10.1	10.2	49,678	43,027	48,814	37,599
Naturalized	745	583	-	-	403	291	342	292	720	553	0.1	0.1	392	277	328	276
Other races—Native	1,084	1,224	0.1	0.1	745	957	339	267	584	840	0.1	0.1	474	738	110	102
Indian	269	265	-	-	156	147	113	118	128	151	-	-	75	87	53	64
Chinese	273	273	-	-	175	195	98	78	115	139	-	-	94	125	21	14
Japanese	25	43	-	-	14	31	11	12	10	13	-	-	8	12	2	1
Filipino	435	605	-	-	354	568	81	37	300	527	-	0.1	278	510	22	17
Hindu	50	20	-	-	30	10	20	10	20	3	-	-	11	2	9	1
All other	32	18	-	-	16	6	16	12	11	7	-	-	8	2	3	5
Alien	115,788	225,029	100.0	100.0	48,218	122,454	67,570	102,575	109,028	194,585	100.0	100.0	44,878	107,245	64,150	87,340
White—First papers	36,031	86,567	31.1	38.5	24,639	69,262	11,392	17,305	35,428	84,114	32.5	43.2	24,316	67,894	11,112	16,220
No papers	78,648	137,057	67.9	60.9	22,857	52,184	55,791	84,873	72,583	109,203	66.6	56.1	19,903	38,427	52,680	70,776
Negro—First papers	173	204	0.1	0.1	114	164	59	40	168	204	0.2	0.1	112	164	56	40
No papers	349	485	0.3	0.2	156	236	193	249	330	431	0.3	0.2	148	218	182	213
Other races—Foreign born	587	716	0.5	0.3	452	608	135	108	519	633	0.5	0.3	399	542	120	91
Indian	165	85	0.1	-	88	40	77	45	136	65	0.1	-	72	32	64	33
Chinese	310	437	0.3	0.2	267	391	43	46	271	376	0.2	0.2	230	334	41	42
Japanese	38	60	-	-	33	52	5	8	38	59	-	-	33	51	5	8
Filipino	-	-	-	-	-	-	-	-	-	-	-	-	-	-	-	-
Hindu	44	117	-	0.1	43	114	1	3	44	117	-	0.1	43	114	1	3
All other	30	17	-	-	21	11	9	6	30	16	-	-	21	11	9	5
Citizenship not reported	9,109	7,613	100.0	100.0	4,270	3,608	4,839	4,005	8,410	6,897	100.0	100.0	3,939	3,296	4,471	3,601
White	8,939	7,440	98.1	97.7	4,187	3,503	4,752	3,937	8,250	6,743	98.1	97.8	3,861	3,199	4,389	3,544
Negro	170	173	1.9	2.3	83	105	87	68	160	154	1.9	2.2	78	97	82	57

Table A-38.—SCHOOL ATTENDANCE, BY AGE, RACE, AND SEX, FOR THE CITY OF DETROIT: 1940 AND 1930

[Figures for white population in 1930 revised to include Mexicans classified with "Other races" in the 1930 reports. Percent not shown where less than 0.1 or where base is less than 100]

AGE, SEX, AND CENSUS YEAR	ALL CLASSES			NATIVE WHITE			FOREIGN-BORN WHITE			NEGRO			OTHER RACES		
	Total number	Attending school		Total number	Attending school		Total number	Attending school		Total number	Attending school		Total number	Attending school	
		Number	Percent		Number	Percent		Number	Percent		Number	Percent		Number	Percent
1940															
Total, 5 to 24 years	539,069	323,891	60.1	469,486	286,351	61.0	21,349	8,194	38.4	47,758	29,008	60.7	476	338	71.0
5 years	22,514	12,510	55.6	20,039	11,068	55.2	132	62	47.0	2,309	1,363	59.0	34	17	-
6 years	20,738	18,720	90.3	18,265	16,450	90.1	172	148	86.0	2,279	2,102	92.2	22	20	-
7 to 9 years	71,094	69,363	97.6	63,296	61,850	97.7	687	671	97.7	7,030	6,764	96.2	81	78	-
10 to 13 years	106,573	104,473	98.0	94,827	93,105	98.2	1,830	1,792	97.9	9,607	9,471	96.6	109	105	96.3
14 years	27,481	26,786	97.5	24,171	23,608	97.7	763	741	97.1	2,519	2,410	95.7	28	27	-
15 years	27,860	26,797	96.2	24,512	23,633	96.4	856	832	97.2	2,469	2,311	93.6	23	21	-
16 and 17 years	54,603	41,099	75.3	47,173	35,806	75.9	2,863	2,155	75.3	4,516	3,095	68.5	51	43	-
18 and 19 years	58,539	15,429	26.4	49,534	13,128	26.5	4,274	1,204	28.2	4,688	1,083	23.1	43	14	-
20 years	27,922	2,929	10.5	23,515	2,553	10.9	2,141	221	10.3	2,249	149	6.6	17	6	-
21 to 24 years	121,745	5,785	4.8	104,154	5,150	4.9	7,631	368	4.8	9,892	260	2.6	68	7	-
Male, 5 to 24 years	266,325	165,594	62.2	232,979	146,817	63.0	10,397	4,335	41.7	22,661	14,240	62.8	288	202	70.1
5 years	11,431	6,197	54.2	10,149	5,465	53.8	78	27	-	1,184	695	58.7	20	10	-
6 years	10,601	9,518	89.8	9,356	8,382	89.6	93	79	-	1,140	1,046	91.8	12	11	-
7 to 9 years	35,861	3,5001	97.6	31,993	31,256	97.7	350	344	98.3	3,471	3,355	96.7	47	46	-
10 to 13 years	53,882	52,841	98.1	48,125	47,263	98.2	930	910	97.8	4,768	4,612	96.7	59	56	-
14 years	13,883	13,515	97.3	12,276	11,971	97.5	381	365	95.8	1,210	1,164	96.2	16	15	-
15 years	13,994	13,485	96.4	12,348	11,922	96.6	451	438	97.1	1,183	1,115	94.3	12	10	-
16 and 17 years	27,250	20,721	76.0	23,568	18,076	76.7	1,443	1,108	76.8	2,203	1,506	68.4	36	31	-
18 and 19 years	28,200	8,670	30.7	23,853	7,433	31.2	2,116	689	32.6	2,207	538	24.4	24	10	-
20 years	13,103	1,732	13.2	11,137	1,525	13.7	1,002	126	12.6	951	75	7.9	13	6	-
21 to 24 years	58,120	3,914	6.7	50,174	3,524	7.0	3,553	249	7.0	4,344	134	3.1	49	7	-
Female, 5 to 24 years	272,744	158,297	58.0	236,507	139,534	59.0	10,952	3,859	35.2	25,097	14,768	58.8	188	136	72.3
5 years	11,083	6,313	57.0	9,890	5,608	56.7	54	35	-	1,125	668	59.4	14	7	-
6 years	10,137	9,202	90.8	8,909	8,068	90.6	79	69	-	1,139	1,056	92.7	10	9	-
7 to 9 years	35,233	34,362	97.5	31,303	30,594	97.7	337	327	97.0	3,559	3,409	95.8	34	32	-
10 to 13 years	52,691	51,632	98.0	46,702	45,842	98.2	900	882	98.0	5,039	4,859	96.4	50	49	-
14 years	13,598	13,271	97.6	11,895	11,637	97.8	382	375	98.4	1,309	1,246	95.2	12	12	-
15 years	13,866	13,312	96.0	12,164	11,711	96.3	405	394	97.3	1,286	1,196	93.0	11	11	-
16 and 17 years	27,353	20,378	74.5	23,605	17,730	75.1	1,420	1,047	73.7	2,313	1,589	68.7	15	12	-
18 and 19 years	30,339	6,759	22.3	25,681	5,695	22.2	2,158	515	23.9	2,481	545	22.0	19	4	-
20 years	14,819	1,197	8.1	12,378	1,028	8.3	1,139	95	8.3	1,298	74	5.7	4	-	-
21 to 24 years	63,625	1,871	2.9	53,980	1,626	3.0	4,078	119	2.9	5,548	126	2.3	19	-	-
1930															
Total, 5 to 24 years	556,177	327,782	58.9	453,334	281,689	62.1	63,814	25,912	40.6	38,461	19,929	51.8	568	252	44.4
5 years	30,727	13,627	44.3	27,495	12,044	43.8	975	395	40.5	2,231	1,179	52.8	26	9	-
6 years	29,309	23,882	81.5	25,951	20,990	80.9	1,263	1,090	86.3	2,066	1,782	86.3	29	20	-
7 to 9 years	88,137	85,232	96.7	75,877	73,447	96.8	6,309	6,069	96.2	5,904	5,672	96.1	47	44	-
10 to 13 years	107,871	106,821	99.0	94,174	93,309	99.1	7,413	7,317	98.7	6,229	6,141	98.6	55	54	-
14 years	25,409	25,069	98.7	21,908	21,629	98.7	1,986	1,959	98.6	1,499	1,466	97.8	16	15	-
15 years	24,510	23,314	95.1	20,999	20,002	95.3	2,208	2,113	95.7	1,293	1,189	92.0	10	10	-
16 and 17 years	47,542	29,804	62.7	38,838	24,537	63.2	5,841	3,579	61.3	2,825	1,664	58.9	38	24	-
18 and 19 years	51,030	10,464	20.5	39,792	8,402	21.1	7,852	1,552	19.8	3,336	495	14.8	50	15	-
20 years	26,417	2,806	10.6	19,684	2,211	11.2	4,593	485	10.6	2,097	98	4.7	43	12	-
21 to 24 years	125,225	6,763	5.4	88,616	5,118	5.8	25,374	1,353	5.3	10,981	243	2.2	254	49	19.3
Male, 5 to 24 years	275,829	167,113	60.6	224,970	143,320	63.7	32,069	13,746	42.9	18,362	9,875	53.8	428	172	40.2
5 years	15,687	6,849	43.7	14,050	6,082	43.3	518	211	40.7	1,103	553	50.1	16	8	-
6 years	14,818	11,986	80.9	13,127	10,525	80.2	640	550	85.9	1,038	903	87.0	13	8	-
7 to 9 years	44,451	43,023	96.8	38,154	36,961	96.9	3,269	3,153	96.5	3,005	2,887	96.1	23	22	-
10 to 13 years	53,716	53,221	99.1	47,054	46,646	99.1	3,660	3,614	98.7	2,967	2,927	98.7	35	34	-
14 years	12,693	12,544	98.8	10,933	10,809	98.9	998	985	98.7	752	740	98.4	10	10	-
15 years	12,255	11,772	96.1	10,495	10,097	96.2	1,125	1,082	96.2	628	586	93.3	7	7	-
16 and 17 years	23,116	15,521	67.1	18,911	12,761	67.5	2,877	1,936	67.3	1,306	806	61.7	22	18	-
18 and 19 years	23,845	5,962	25.0	18,617	4,746	25.5	3,710	926	25.0	1,475	277	18.8	43	13	-
20 years	12,387	1,728	14.0	9,227	1,344	14.6	2,252	320	14.2	868	52	6.0	40	12	-
21 to 24 years	62,861	4,507	7.2	44,402	3,349	7.5	13,020	969	7.4	5,220	144	2.8	219	45	20.5
Female, 5 to 24 years	280,348	160,669	57.3	228,364	138,369	60.6	31,745	12,166	38.3	20,099	10,054	50.0	140	80	57.1
5 years	15,040	6,778	45.1	13,445	5,962	44.3	457	184	40.3	1,128	626	55.5	10	6	-
6 years	14,491	11,896	82.1	12,824	10,465	81.6	623	540	86.7	1,028	879	85.5	16	12	-
7 to 9 years	43,686	42,209	96.6	37,723	36,486	96.7	3,040	2,916	95.9	2,899	2,785	96.1	24	22	-
10 to 13 years	54,155	53,600	99.0	47,120	46,663	99.0	3,753	3,703	98.7	3,262	3,214	98.5	20	20	-
14 years	12,716	12,525	98.5	10,975	10,820	98.6	988	974	98.6	747	726	97.2	6	5	-
15 years	12,255	11,542	94.2	10,504	9,905	94.3	1,083	1,031	95.2	665	603	90.7	3	3	-
16 and 17 years	24,426	14,283	58.5	19,927	11,776	59.1	2,964	1,643	55.4	1,519	858	56.5	16	6	-
18 and 19 years	27,185	4,502	16.6	21,175	3,656	17.3	4,142	626	15.1	1,861	218	11.7	7	2	-
20 years	14,080	1,078	7.7	10,457	867	8.3	2,341	165	7.0	1,229	46	3.7	3	-	-
21 to 24 years	62,364	2,256	3.6	44,214	1,769	4.0	12,354	384	3.1	5,761	99	1.7	35	4	-

Table A-39.—PERSONS 25 YEARS OLD AND OVER, BY YEARS OF SCHOOL COMPLETED, RACE, AND SEX, FOR THE CITY OF DETROIT: 1940

[Percent not shown where less than 0.1; median and percent not shown where base is less than 100]

YEARS OF SCHOOL COMPLETED	ALL CLASSES			NATIVE WHITE			FOREIGN-BORN WHITE			NEGRO			OTHER RACES		
	Total	Male	Female	Total	Male	Female	Total	Male	Female	Total	Male	Female	Total	Male	Female
Persons 25 years old and over	966,994	501,172	465,822	576,954	292,522	284,432	299,027	161,762	137,265	89,978	46,064	43,914	1,035	824	211
No school years completed	30,424	14,803	15,621	2,385	1,257	1,128	24,588	11,576	13,012	3,355	1,895	1,460	96	75	21
Grade school: 1 to 4 years	86,226	47,301	38,925	18,541	9,388	9,153	52,044	28,869	23,175	15,486	8,922	6,564	155	122	33
5 or 6 years	102,645	53,975	48,670	41,810	20,853	20,957	42,721	23,422	19,299	17,986	9,595	8,391	128	105	23
7 or 8 years	314,020	166,094	147,926	190,068	99,388	90,680	97,562	53,354	44,208	26,156	13,174	12,982	234	178	56
High school: 1 to 3 years	182,265	90,662	91,603	132,984	66,300	66,684	34,263	17,688	16,575	14,880	6,565	8,315	138	109	29
4 years	160,046	74,373	85,673	119,085	53,930	65,155	33,297	17,011	16,286	7,517	3,320	4,197	147	112	35
College: 1 to 3 years	46,310	24,952	21,358	36,488	19,082	17,406	7,012	4,348	2,664	2,730	1,450	1,280	80	72	8
4 years or more	41,230	26,785	14,445	33,547	21,161	12,386	6,202	4,705	1,497	1,426	869	557	55	50	5
Not reported	3,828	2,227	1,601	2,046	1,163	883	1,338	789	549	442	274	168	2	1	1
Median school years completed	8.7	8.6	8.7	9.8	9.7	9.9	7.6	7.6	7.6	7.6	7.4	7.8	8.2	8.2	8.0
Percent less than 5 years completed	12.1	12.4	11.7	3.6	3.6	3.6	25.6	25.0	26.4	20.9	23.5	18.3	24.3	23.9	25.6
PERCENT DISTRIBUTION															
Persons 25 years old and over	100.0	100.0	100.0	100.0	100.0	100.0	100.0	100.0	100.0	100.0	100.0	100.0	100.0	100.0	100.0
No school years completed	3.1	3.0	3.4	0.4	0.4	0.4	8.2	7.2	9.5	3.7	4.1	3.3	9.3	9.1	10.0
Grade school: 1 to 4 years	8.9	9.4	8.4	3.2	3.2	3.2	17.4	17.8	16.9	17.2	19.4	14.9	15.0	14.8	15.6
5 or 6 years	10.6	10.8	10.4	7.2	7.1	7.4	14.3	14.5	14.1	20.0	20.8	19.1	12.4	12.7	10.9
7 or 8 years	32.5	33.1	31.8	32.9	34.0	31.9	32.6	33.0	32.2	29.1	28.6	29.6	22.6	21.6	26.5
High school: 1 to 3 years	18.8	18.1	19.7	23.0	22.7	23.4	11.5	10.9	12.1	16.5	14.3	18.9	13.3	13.2	13.7
4 years	16.6	14.8	18.4	20.6	18.4	22.9	11.1	10.5	11.9	8.4	7.2	9.6	14.2	13.6	16.6
College: 1 to 3 years	4.8	5.0	4.6	6.3	6.5	6.1	2.3	2.7	1.9	3.0	3.1	2.9	7.7	8.7	3.8
4 years or more	4.3	5.3	3.1	5.8	7.2	4.4	2.1	2.9	1.1	1.6	1.9	1.3	5.3	6.1	2.4
Not reported	0.4	0.4	0.3	0.4	0.4	0.3	0.4	0.5	0.4	0.5	0.6	0.4	0.2	0.1	0.5

Table A-40.—FOREIGN-BORN WHITE, BY COUNTRY OF BIRTH, BY SEX, FOR THE CITY OF DETROIT: 1940 AND 1930

[Figures for white population in 1930 revised to include Mexicans classified with "Other races" in the 1930 reports. Percent not shown where less than 0.1 or where base is less than 100]

COUNTRY OF BIRTH	BOTH SEXES		PERCENT		MALE		FEMALE	
	1940	1930	1940	1930	1940	1930	1940	1930
All countries	320,664	403,721	100.0	100.0	172,297	224,631	148,367	179,090
England	21,049	28,636	6.6	7.1	11,063	15,333	9,986	13,303
Scotland	17,061	23,546	5.3	5.8	8,829	12,632	8,232	10,914
Wales	691	1,260	0.2	0.3	405	751	286	509
Northern Ireland	2,211	3,524	0.7	0.9	1,176	1,966	1,035	1,558
Irish Free State (Eire)	4,760	6,293	1.5	1.6	2,570	3,524	2,190	2,769
Norway	1,137	1,596	0.4	0.4	679	1,003	458	593
Sweden	3,185	4,318	1.0	1.1	2,003	2,785	1,182	1,533
Denmark	1,510	1,930	0.5	0.5	985	1,288	525	642
Netherlands	1,711	2,092	0.5	0.5	1,036	1,250	675	842
Belgium	6,890	8,969	2.1	2.2	3,665	4,872	3,225	4,097
Luxemburg	58	75	-	-	29	50	29	25
Switzerland	776	1,048	0.2	0.3	450	634	326	414
France	1,639	2,333	0.5	0.6	761	1,136	878	1,197
Germany	23,785	32,716	7.4	8.1	12,208	16,992	11,577	15,724
Poland	52,235	66,113	16.3	16.4	28,490	37,134	23,745	28,979
Czechoslovakia	4,080	6,291	1.3	1.6	2,176	3,488	1,904	2,803
Austria	7,992	5,898	2.5	1.5	4,209	3,234	3,783	2,664
Hungary	11,382	11,162	3.5	2.8	5,954	6,020	5,428	5,142
Yugoslavia	6,278	9,014	2.0	2.2	3,773	5,554	2,505	3,460
Russia (U. S. S. R.)	20,252	21,781	6.3	5.4	11,236	12,284	9,016	9,497
Lithuania	4,142	4,879	1.3	1.2	2,380	2,940	1,762	1,939
Latvia	421	399	0.1	0.1	230	212	191	187

COUNTRY OF BIRTH	BOTH SEXES		PERCENT		MALE		FEMALE	
	1940	1930	1940	1930	1940	1930	1940	1930
Finland	1,944	2,811	0.6	0.7	872	1,394	1,072	1,417
Rumania	5,109	7,576	1.6	1.9	2,916	4,402	2,193	3,174
Bulgaria	702	818	0.2	0.2	520	670	182	148
Turkey in Europe	29	140	-	-	20	80	9	60
Greece	5,476	6,385	1.7	1.6	4,077	5,043	1,399	1,342
Italy	26,277	28,581	8.2	7.1	16,024	18,350	10,253	10,231
Spain	585	951	0.2	0.2	429	719	156	232
Portugal	50	68	-	-	41	55	9	13
Other Europe	2,412	3,152	0.8	0.8	1,695	2,336	717	816
Palestine and Syria	2,927	3,224	0.9	0.8	1,722	1,941	1,205	1,283
Turkey in Asia	2,813	2,343	0.9	0.6	1,683	1,500	1,130	843
Other Asia	1,864	2,698	0.6	0.7	1,188	1,801	676	897
Canada—French	9,699	12,477	3.0	3.1	4,715	6,547	4,984	5,930
Canada—Other	64,438	81,811	20.1	20.3	30,171	40,163	34,267	41,648
Newfoundland	488	720	0.2	0.2	268	393	220	327
Mexico	1,565	4,886	0.5	1.2	1,009	3,401	556	1,485
Cuba and other West Indies	202	219	0.1	0.1	129	142	73	77
Central and South America	396	472	0.1	0.1	253	324	143	148
Australia	131	167	-	-	68	97	63	70
Azores	3	6	-	-	-	3	3	3
All other and not reported	309	343	0.1	0.1	190	188	119	155

Table A-41.--PERSONS 14 YEARS OLD AND OVER, BY EMPLOYMENT STATUS, CLASS OF WORKER, RACE, AND SEX, FOR THE CITY OF DETROIT: 1940

[Percent not shown where less than 0.1 or where base is less than 100]

EMPLOYMENT STATUS	ALL CLASSES			NATIVE WHITE			FOREIGN-BORN WHITE			NEGRO			OTHER RACES		
	Total	Male	Female	Total	Male	Female	Total	Male	Female	Total	Male	Female	Total	Male	Female
Total population (all ages)	1,623,452	827,499	795,953	1,151,998	579,520	572,478	320,664	172,297	148,367	149,119	74,485	74,634	1,671	1,197	474
Persons 14 years old and over	1,285,144	655,722	629,422	850,013	425,878	424,135	317,555	170,708	146,847	116,311	58,162	58,149	1,265	974	291
In labor force	733,632	555,539	178,093	487,424	354,564	132,860	178,613	150,886	27,727	66,658	49,240	17,418	937	849	88
Not in labor force	551,512	100,183	451,329	362,589	71,314	291,275	138,942	19,822	119,120	49,653	8,922	40,731	328	125	203
Engaged in own home housew'k	360,893	3,502	357,391	225,500	2,176	223,324	105,925	975	104,950	29,313	347	28,966	155	4	151
In school	110,488	56,510	53,978	96,191	49,426	46,765	5,071	2,608	2,463	9,106	4,392	4,714	120	84	36
Unable to work	50,853	26,052	24,801	22,347	11,158	11,189	20,687	12,001	8,686	7,790	2,873	4,917	29	20	9
In institutions	1,785	899	886	1,097	519	578	512	244	268	176	136	40	-	-	-
Other and not reported	27,493	13,220	14,273	17,454	8,035	9,419	6,747	3,994	2,753	3,268	1,174	2,094	24	17	7
LABOR FORCE BY EMPLOYMENT STATUS															
In labor force	733,632	555,539	178,093	487,424	354,564	132,860	178,613	150,886	27,727	66,658	49,240	17,418	937	849	88
Employed (exc. public emerg. work)	625,456	474,250	151,206	420,738	307,280	113,458	158,764	133,388	25,376	45,137	32,846	12,291	817	736	81
At work	606,951	463,077	143,874	407,413	299,985	107,428	154,493	130,095	24,398	44,243	32,271	11,972	802	726	76
With a job	18,505	11,173	7,332	13,325	7,295	6,030	4,271	3,293	978	894	575	319	15	10	5
On public emerg. work (WPA, etc.)	29,458	24,102	5,356	14,374	11,125	3,249	4,825	4,471	354	10,219	8,469	1,750	40	37	3
Seeking work	78,718	57,187	21,531	52,312	36,159	16,153	15,024	13,027	1,997	11,302	7,925	3,377	80	76	4
Experienced workers	61,404	47,192	14,212	38,123	28,084	10,039	13,912	12,392	1,520	9,294	6,644	2,650	75	72	3
New workers	17,314	9,995	7,319	14,189	8,075	6,114	1,112	635	477	2,008	1,281	727	5	4	1
PERCENT BY SEX															
In labor force	100.0	75.7	24.3	100.0	72.7	27.3	100.0	84.5	15.5	100.0	73.9	26.1	100.0	90.6	9.4
Employed (exc. public emerg.)	100.0	75.8	24.2	100.0	73.0	27.0	100.0	84.0	16.0	100.0	72.8	27.2	100.0	90.1	9.9
On pub. emerg. work (WPA, etc.)	100.0	81.8	18.2	100.0	77.4	22.6	100.0	92.7	7.3	100.0	82.9	17.1	-	-	-
Seeking work	100.0	72.6	27.4	100.0	69.1	30.9	100.0	86.7	13.3	100.0	70.1	29.9	-	-	-
Not in labor force	100.0	18.2	81.8	100.0	19.7	80.3	100.0	14.3	85.7	100.0	18.0	82.0	100.0	38.1	61.9
Engaged in own home housew'k	100.0	1.0	99.0	100.0	1.0	99.0	100.0	0.9	99.1	100.0	1.2	98.8	100.0	2.6	97.4
In school	100.0	51.1	48.9	100.0	51.4	48.6	100.0	51.4	48.6	100.0	48.2	51.8	100.0	70.0	30.0
Unable to work	100.0	51.2	48.8	100.0	49.9	50.1	100.0	58.0	42.0	100.0	36.9	63.1	-	-	-
In institutions	100.0	50.4	49.6	100.0	47.3	52.7	100.0	47.7	52.3	100.0	77.3	22.7	-	-	-
Other and not reported	100.0	48.1	51.9	100.0	46.0	54.0	100.0	59.2	40.8	100.0	35.9	64.1	-	-	-
EMPLOYED WORKERS BY CLASS OF WORKER															
Employed (exc. public emerg.)	625,456	474,250	151,206	420,738	307,280	113,458	158,764	133,388	25,376	45,137	32,846	12,291	817	736	81
Wage and salary workers	565,246	426,414	138,832	388,606	282,315	106,291	134,285	112,732	21,553	41,755	30,827	10,928	600	540	60
Employers and own-account workers	54,292	45,695	8,597	28,379	23,377	5,002	22,634	20,237	2,397	3,079	1,891	1,188	200	190	10
Unpaid family workers	3,950	982	2,968	2,377	798	1,579	1,413	144	1,269	147	37	110	13	3	10
Class of worker not reported	1,968	1,159	809	1,376	790	586	432	275	157	156	91	65	4	3	1
At work	606,951	463,077	143,874	407,413	299,985	107,428	154,493	130,095	24,398	44,243	32,271	11,972	802	726	76
Wage and salary workers	550,000	417,816	132,184	377,095	276,376	100,719	131,268	110,522	20,746	41,045	30,383	10,662	592	535	57
Employers and own-account workers	51,434	43,309	8,125	26,868	22,166	4,702	21,460	19,187	2,273	2,912	1,771	1,141	194	185	9
Unpaid family workers	3,802	934	2,868	2,268	756	1,512	1,379	141	1,238	143	34	109	12	3	9
Class of worker not reported	1,715	1,018	697	1,182	687	495	386	245	141	143	83	60	4	3	1
With a job	18,505	11,173	7,332	18,325	7,295	6,030	4,271	3,293	978	894	575	319	15	10	5
Wage and salary workers	15,246	8,598	6,648	11,511	5,939	5,572	3,017	2,210	807	710	444	266	8	5	3
Employers and own-account workers	2,858	2,386	472	1,511	1,211	300	1,174	1,050	124	167	120	47	6	5	1
Unpaid family workers	148	48	100	109	42	67	34	3	31	4	3	1	1	-	1
Class of worker not reported	253	141	112	194	103	91	46	30	16	13	8	5	-	-	-
PERCENT DISTRIBUTION															
Persons 14 years old and over	100.0	100.0	100.0	100.0	100.0	100.0	100.0	100.0	100.0	100.0	100.0	100.0	100.0	100.0	100.0
In labor force	57.1	84.7	28.3	57.3	83.3	31.3	56.2	88.4	18.9	57.3	84.7	30.0	74.1	87.2	30.2
Not in labor force	42.9	15.3	71.7	42.7	16.7	68.7	43.8	11.6	81.1	42.7	15.3	70.0	25.9	12.8	69.8
Engaged in own home housew'k	28.1	0.5	56.8	26.5	0.5	52.7	33.4	0.6	71.5	25.2	0.6	49.8	12.3	0.4	51.9
In school	8.6	8.6	8.6	11.3	11.6	11.0	1.6	1.5	1.7	7.8	7.6	8.1	9.5	8.6	12.4
Unable to work	4.0	4.0	3.9	2.6	2.6	2.6	6.5	7.0	5.9	6.7	4.9	8.5	2.3	2.1	3.1
In institutions	0.1	0.1	0.1	0.1	0.1	0.1	0.2	0.1	0.2	0.2	0.2	0.1	-	-	-
Other and not reported	2.1	2.0	2.3	2.1	1.9	2.3	2.1	2.3	1.9	2.8	2.0	3.6	1.9	1.7	2.4
LABOR FORCE BY EMPLOYMENT STATUS															
In labor force	100.0	100.0	100.0	100.0	100.0	100.0	100.0	100.0	100.0	100.0	100.0	100.0	100.0	100.0	-
Employed (exc. public emerg. work)	85.3	85.4	84.9	86.3	86.7	85.4	88.9	88.4	91.5	67.7	66.7	70.6	87.2	86.7	-
At work	82.7	83.4	80.8	83.6	84.6	80.9	86.5	86.2	88.0	66.4	65.5	68.7	85.6	85.5	-
With a job	2.5	2.0	4.1	2.7	2.1	4.5	2.4	2.2	3.5	1.3	1.2	1.8	1.6	1.2	-
On public emerg. work (WPA, etc.)	4.0	4.3	3.0	2.9	3.1	2.4	2.7	3.0	1.3	15.3	17.2	10.0	4.3	4.4	-
Seeking work	10.7	10.3	12.1	10.7	10.2	12.2	8.4	8.6	7.2	17.0	16.1	19.4	8.5	9.0	-
Experienced workers	8.4	8.5	8.0	7.8	7.9	7.6	7.8	8.2	5.5	13.9	13.5	15.2	8.0	8.5	-
New workers	2.4	1.8	4.1	2.9	2.3	4.6	0.6	0.4	1.7	3.0	2.6	4.2	0.5	0.5	-
EMPLOYED WORKERS BY CLASS OF WORKER															
Employed (exc. public emerg.)	100.0	100.0	100.0	100.0	100.0	100.0	100.0	100.0	100.0	100.0	100.0	100.0	100.0	100.0	-
Wage and salary workers	90.4	89.9	91.8	92.4	91.9	93.7	84.6	84.5	84.9	92.5	93.9	88.9	73.4	73.4	-
Employers and own-account workers	8.7	9.6	5.7	6.7	7.6	4.4	14.3	15.2	9.4	6.8	5.8	9.7	24.5	25.8	-
Unpaid family workers	0.6	0.2	2.0	0.6	0.3	1.4	0.9	0.1	5.0	0.3	0.1	0.9	1.6	0.4	-
Class of worker not reported	0.3	0.2	0.5	0.3	0.3	0.5	0.5	0.2	0.6	0.3	0.3	0.5	0.5	0.4	-
At work	100.0	100.0	100.0	100.0	100.0	100.0	100.0	100.0	100.0	100.0	100.0	100.0	100.0	100.0	-
Wage and salary workers	90.6	90.2	91.9	92.6	92.1	93.8	85.0	85.0	85.0	92.8	94.1	89.1	73.8	73.7	-
Employers and own-account workers	8.5	9.4	5.6	6.6	7.4	4.4	13.9	14.7	9.3	6.6	5.5	9.5	24.2	25.5	-
Unpaid family workers	0.6	0.2	2.0	0.6	0.3	1.4	0.9	0.1	5.1	0.3	0.1	0.9	1.5	0.4	-
Class of worker not reported	0.3	0.2	0.5	0.3	0.2	0.5	0.2	0.2	0.6	0.3	0.3	0.5	0.5	0.4	-
With a job	100.0	100.0	100.0	100.0	100.0	100.0	100.0	100.0	100.0	100.0	100.0	100.0	-	-	-
Wage and salary workers	82.4	77.0	90.7	86.4	81.4	92.4	70.6	67.1	82.5	79.4	77.2	83.4	-	-	-
Employers and own-account workers	15.4	21.4	6.4	11.3	16.6	5.0	27.5	31.9	12.7	18.7	20.9	14.7	-	-	-
Unpaid family workers	0.8	0.4	1.4	0.8	0.6	1.1	0.8	0.1	3.2	0.4	0.5	0.3	-	-	-
Class of worker not reported	1.4	1.3	1.5	1.5	1.4	1.5	1.1	0.9	1.6	1.5	1.4	1.6	-	-	-

Table A-42.—EMPLOYED WORKERS 14 YEARS OLD AND OVER, BY MAJOR OCCUPATION GROUP, INDUSTRY GROUP, AND SEX, FOR THE CITY OF DETROIT: 1940

[Percent not shown where less than 0.1 or where base is less than 100]

MAJOR OCCUPATION GROUP AND INDUSTRY GROUP	Total	Male	Female	PERCENT BY OCCUPATION AND INDUSTRY			PERCENT BY SEX	
				Total	Male	Female	Male	Female
Total population (all ages)	1,623,452	827,499	795,953	-	-	-	51.0	49.0
All persons 14 years old and over	1,285,144	655,722	629,422	-	-	-	51.0	49.0
In labor force	733,632	555,539	178,093	100.0	100.0	100.0	75.7	24.3
Employed workers (except on public emergency work)	625,456	474,250	151,206	85.3	85.4	84.9	75.8	24.2
MAJOR OCCUPATION GROUP								
Employed (except on public emergency work)	625,456	474,250	151,206	100.0	100.0	100.0	75.8	24.2
Professional workers	36,704	21,219	15,485	5.9	4.5	10.2	57.8	42.2
Semiprofessional workers	9,267	7,619	1,648	1.5	1.6	1.1	82.2	17.8
Farmers and farm managers	128	114	14	-	-	-	89.1	10.9
Proprietors, managers, and officials, except farm	46,185	41,346	4,839	7.4	8.7	3.2	89.5	10.5
Clerical, sales, and kindred workers	135,559	77,910	57,649	21.7	16.4	38.1	57.5	42.5
Craftsmen, foremen, and kindred workers	109,149	106,854	2,295	17.5	22.5	1.5	97.9	2.1
Operatives and kindred workers	167,532	141,926	25,606	26.8	29.9	16.9	84.7	15.3
Domestic service workers	18,699	708	17,991	3.0	0.1	11.9	3.8	96.2
Service workers, except domestic	58,744	35,903	22,841	9.4	7.6	15.1	61.1	38.9
Farm laborers (wage workers) and farm foremen	241	234	7	-	-	-	97.1	2.9
Farm laborers, unpaid family workers	24	23	1	-	-	-	-	-
Laborers, except farm	39,223	37,543	1,680	6.3	7.9	1.1	95.7	4.3
Occupation not reported	4,001	2,851	1,150	0.6	0.6	0.8	71.3	28.7
INDUSTRY GROUP								
Employed (except on public emergency work)	625,456	474,250	151,206	100.0	100.0	100.0	75.8	24.2
Agriculture, forestry, and fishery	852	793	59	0.1	0.2	-	93.1	6.9
Agriculture	799	745	54	0.1	0.2	-	93.2	6.8
Forestry (except logging) and fishery	53	48	5	-	-	-	-	-
Mining	218	198	20	-	-	-	90.8	9.2
Coal mining	20	17	3	-	-	-	-	-
Crude petroleum and natural gas production	25	25	-	-	-	-	-	-
Other mines and quarries	173	156	17	-	-	-	90.2	9.8
Construction	24,099	23,497	602	3.9	5.0	0.4	97.5	2.5
Manufacturing	295,123	260,132	34,991	47.2	54.9	23.1	88.1	11.9
Food and kindred products	14,259	11,594	2,665	2.3	2.4	1.8	81.3	18.7
Textile-mill products	1,047	718	329	0.2	0.2	0.2	68.6	31.4
Apparel and other fabricated textile products	2,422	893	1,529	0.4	0.2	1.0	36.9	63.1
Logging	18	18	-	-	-	-	-	-
Sawmills and planing mills	548	520	28	0.1	0.1	-	94.9	5.1
Furniture, store fixtures, and miscellaneous wooden goods	2,533	2,034	499	0.4	0.4	0.3	80.3	19.7
Paper and allied products	1,777	1,274	503	0.3	0.3	0.3	71.7	28.3
Printing, publishing, and allied industries	10,335	8,188	2,147	1.7	1.7	1.4	79.2	20.8
Chemicals and allied products	5,915	4,375	1,540	0.9	0.9	1.0	74.0	26.0
Petroleum and coal products	1,103	972	131	0.2	0.2	0.1	88.1	11.9
Leather and leather products	550	367	183	0.1	0.1	0.1	66.7	33.3
Stone, clay, and glass products	2,786	2,361	425	0.4	0.5	0.3	84.7	15.3
Iron and steel and their products	19,500	17,254	2,246	3.1	3.6	1.5	88.5	11.5
Nonferrous metals and their products	5,978	5,363	615	1.0	1.1	0.4	89.7	10.3
Machinery	24,287	20,617	3,670	3.9	4.3	2.4	84.9	15.1
Automobiles and automobile equipment	187,528	171,988	15,540	30.0	36.3	10.3	91.7	8.3
Transportation equipment, except automobile	1,701	1,620	81	0.3	0.3	0.1	95.2	4.8
Other and not specified manufacturing industries	12,838	9,978	2,860	2.1	2.1	1.9	77.7	22.3
Transportation, communication, and other public utilities	36,321	31,176	5,145	5.8	6.6	3.4	85.8	14.2
Railroads (including railroad repair shops) and railway express service	8,476	7,515	961	1.4	1.6	0.6	88.7	11.3
Trucking service	5,655	5,352	303	0.9	1.1	0.2	94.6	5.4
Other transportation	8,910	8,416	494	1.4	1.8	0.3	94.5	5.5
Communication	4,777	2,450	2,327	0.8	0.5	1.5	51.3	48.7
Utilities	8,503	7,443	1,060	1.4	1.6	0.7	87.5	12.5
Wholesale and retail trade	116,730	78,960	37,770	18.7	16.6	25.0	67.6	32.4
Wholesale trade	16,474	13,667	2,807	2.6	2.9	1.9	83.0	17.0
Food and dairy products stores, and milk retailing	23,149	17,031	6,118	3.7	3.6	4.0	73.6	26.4
Eating and drinking places	20,043	11,565	8,478	3.2	2.4	5.6	57.7	42.3
Motor vehicles and accessories retailing, and filling stations	9,422	8,827	595	1.5	1.9	0.4	93.7	6.3
Other retail trade	47,642	27,870	19,772	7.6	5.9	13.1	58.5	41.5
Finance, insurance, and real estate	23,229	14,707	8,522	3.7	3.1	5.6	63.3	36.7
Business and repair services	12,674	10,644	2,030	2.0	2.2	1.3	84.0	16.0
Automobile storage, rental, and repair services	5,172	5,003	169	0.8	1.1	0.1	96.7	3.3
Business and repair services, except automobile	7,502	5,641	1,861	1.2	1.2	1.2	75.2	24.8
Personal services	46,970	14,392	32,578	7.5	3.0	21.5	30.6	69.4
Domestic service	20,125	1,476	18,649	3.2	0.3	12.3	7.3	92.7
Hotels and lodging places	8,536	3,696	4,840	1.4	0.8	3.2	43.3	56.7
Laundering, cleaning, and dyeing services	8,199	3,974	4,225	1.3	0.8	2.8	48.5	51.5
Miscellaneous personal services	10,110	5,246	4,864	1.6	1.1	3.2	51.9	48.1
Amusement, recreation, and related services	6,227	4,759	1,468	1.0	1.0	1.0	76.4	23.6
Professional and related services	37,422	16,017	21,405	6.0	3.4	14.2	42.8	57.2
Government	19,617	15,640	3,977	3.1	3.3	2.6	79.7	20.3
Industry not reported	5,974	3,335	2,639	1.0	0.7	1.7	55.8	44.2

Table A-43.—PERSONS 14 YEARS OLD AND OVER IN THE LABOR FORCE, 1940, AND GAINFUL WORKERS 14 YEARS OLD AND OVER, 1930, BY RACE AND SEX, FOR THE CITY OF DETROIT

[Totals for population and gainful workers for 1930 include "Unknown age." Figures for white population in 1930 have been revised to include Mexicans who were classified with "Other races" in the 1930 reports. Percent not shown where less than 0.1 or where base is less than 100]

CENSUS YEAR AND RACE	TOTAL					MALE					FEMALE				
	Population		Persons in the labor force, and gainful workers,[1] 14 years old and over			Population		Persons in the labor force, and gainful workers,[1] 14 years old and over			Population		Persons in the labor force, and gainful workers,[1] 14 years old and over		
	Total (all ages)	14 years old and over	Number	Per-cent of total popu-lation	Per-cent of popu-lation 14 yrs. and over	Total (all ages)	14 years old and over	Number	Per-cent of total popu-lation	Per-cent of popu-lation 14 yrs. and over	Total (all ages)	14 years old and over	Number	Per-cent of total popu-lation	Per-cent of popu-lation 14 yrs. and over
1940	1,623,452	1,285,144	733,632	45.2	57.1	827,499	655,722	555,539	67.1	84.7	795,953	629,422	178,093	22.4	28.3
White	1,472,662	1,167,568	666,037	45.2	57.0	751,817	596,586	505,450	67.2	84.7	720,845	570,982	160,587	22.3	28.1
Negro	149,119	116,311	66,658	44.7	57.3	74,485	58,162	49,240	66.1	84.7	74,634	58,149	17,418	23.3	30.0
Other races	1,671	1,265	937	56.1	74.1	1,197	974	849	70.9	87.2	474	291	88	18.6	30.2
1930	1,568,662	1,166,008	689,197	43.9	59.1	821,920	618,609	548,371	66.7	88.6	746,742	547,399	140,826	18.9	25.7
White	1,446,656	1,071,360	627,549	43.4	58.6	758,116	568,395	502,158	66.2	88.3	688,540	502,965	125,391	18.2	24.9
Negro	120,066	93,018	60,274	50.2	64.8	62,239	48,812	44,902	72.1	92.0	57,827	44,206	15,372	26.6	34.8
Other races	1,940	1,630	1,374	70.8	84.3	1,565	1,402	1,311	33.8	93.5	375	228	63	16.8	27.6

[1] Data for 1930 represent gainful workers 14 years old and over.

Ford Motor Company

- Ford was one of the leading names in automobile manufacturing during the 1920s, but lost popularity when it failed to upgrade its Model T, and lost millions later in the decade during the conversion from a Model T to a Model A.
- By 1929 the popularity of the Model A was tremendous; Ford produced $1.5 million in automobile sales, a market share of 34 percent and profits of $90 million.
- Owner Henry Ford despised systematic organization and believed in keeping his executives, including his son, constantly in conflict with each other; which often led to mismanagement of production and sales.
- Generally, the auto industry's anti-unionism was a model for United States industrial leaders.
- Company spies, blacklists, private disciplinary forces, and the simple refusal to talk to collective bodies of workers was part of the industry.
- Ford Motor Company had a department to oversee the behavior of its workers; their office periodically would speak to relatives, visit workers' homes, oversee their living conditions and habits, and offer advice as to how money should be spent. This behavior was justified by Ford as a way to teach immigrants how to adapt to American ways, saying "a well-regulated home life makes for a well-regulated work life."
- Between 1929 and 1932 the annual production of cars declined 75 percent but motor vehicle registrations dropped only 10 percent; Americans, no matter the state of the economy, were unwilling to give up the luxury afforded by an automobile.

Henry Ford (right) and son, Edsel, introduced the Model A in 1927.

American Automobile Workers, 1900-1933, Stan Coulthard, a Chrysler worker talks about getting a job

"I didn't know what a milling machine was; in fact I'd never worked in a machine shop before. I was taken on in the morning and told to report for the night shift the same day. As soon as I got in I was asked where were my tools? I lied by saying that I'd had no time to go home to get them. I got to the milling machine and didn't even know how to switch it on. I mucked about for a while pretending to be busy until the foreman had gone. Then I told the feller next to me that I'd just got in from Boston, that I didn't know one end of the machine from the other, that I needed a job and could he help me? He said he came from Boston, too, and showed me what to do. After a while he said that the stock I was making was scrap, that there was some good stuff in a pan behind me and to let on that I'd produced it. When the foreman came round to check and he passed it all right! I went on like that for two or three days until I'd got the hang of things. They got it out of my hide before I'd finished so I had no qualms whatever about cheating them."

American Automobile Workers, 1900-1933, a Ford Motor Company worker commenting on lunch breaks

"To transfer this to the stomach in 15 minutes without choking, and still have time to wipe the crumbs from one's mouth before the production bell sounds again, is an exact science made possible only by the application of Ford production principles."

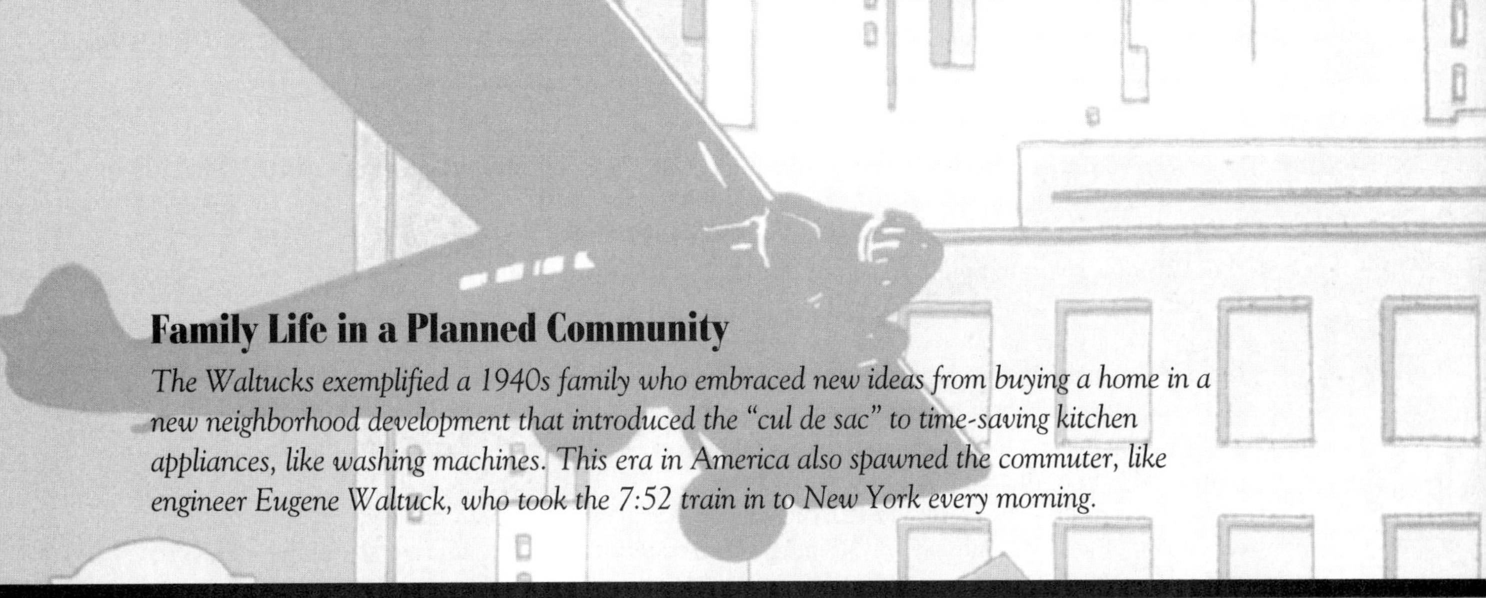

Family Life in a Planned Community

The Waltucks exemplified a 1940s family who embraced new ideas from buying a home in a new neighborhood development that introduced the "cul de sac" to time-saving kitchen appliances, like washing machines. This era in America also spawned the commuter, like engineer Eugene Waltuck, who took the 7:52 train in to New York every morning.

Life at Home

- The Waltuck family of four was one of the first to move from the bustle of New York City to the newly created, fully planned community of Radburn, New Jersey, marketed as a city designed around children.
- Designed for 25,000-30,000 residents, highly promoted Radburn was advertised as "the town for the motor age."
- The community featured 24 acres of parkland, sometimes called "green spaces," two swimming pools, four tennis courts, four ball fields, three playgrounds, five basketball courts and an archery plaza.
- Nine-year old Eugene Waltuck loved the parks, his friends and his secret nickname, Rocko.
- During its first year, 202 families comprising 587 people bought homes in the town, prompting *The New York Times* to comment: "If Radburn hasn't already received the Census Bureau's prize for the fastest-growing community, it ought to be awarded it without further delay."
- *Business Week* reported that the town appeared to be immune from the Depression, since the dismal state of the economy has "had practically no effect upon" the community's growth.
- John and his wife Donna Waltuck moved from New York City so that Eugene and his younger sister Vera could grow up in a healthy atmosphere.
- Donna was pregnant, and insisted that only the letters "PG" be used around the children
- She believed that Radburn provided a type of environment not possible in New York.
- Eugene loved the park near his home where, with so few cars around, his mother left him alone to play with his gang of six friends, who built a secret blood-brother fort near the overpass.
- The Waltuck home had all the modern conveniences, including ash chutes, underground garbage containers, accessible coal bins, modern bathrooms, up-to-date kitchens and spacious basements.
- Appliances included the no-wringer Easy Washer that cut laundry time in half, and the Hotpoint Electric Cookery, with its high-speed, calrod-element burner.

Eugene Waltuck's secret nickname is Rocko.

- Donna loved the fact that "everything is new and clean," and that the house was close to the school so that she can help out.
- John Waltuck, an engineer, walked from their house to catch the 7:52 commuter train to his New York City office each morning; seven out of 10 men in Radburn commuted to the city.
- Radburn "superblocks" were 1,200 by 1,800 feet long, free of automobile traffic, and edged by cul-de-sacs of 10 to 18 houses, creating a ratio of seven houses to an acre.
- More traditional suburban layouts were designed in a checkerboard pattern with blocks that were 200 by 600 feet and fewer houses per acre.
- By clustering homes close together, Radburn set aside 15 percent of the total area for green space that was shared by the entire community.
- Unlike conventional American houses, the interior design of Radburn's homes evolved from the outside in; rooms for family use and sleeping, which traditionally front the street, faced the walkways and parks, while kitchens overlooked the noisier cul-de-sacs instead of backyards.
- *The New York Times* editorialized that the Radburn plan was "the first deliberate attempt to harmonize the rights of the pedestrian and of the motorist."

Life at School

- The town's school superintendent believed in promoting good values, and every month a new poster from the "Hope of a Nation" poster series was hung in Eugene's classroom.
- The September poster read: "What will your job be out in the great, wide world when school days are over? Make it a BIG job!"

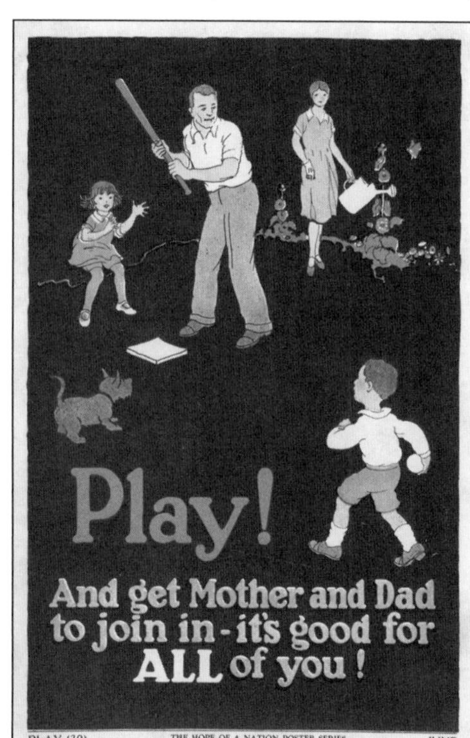

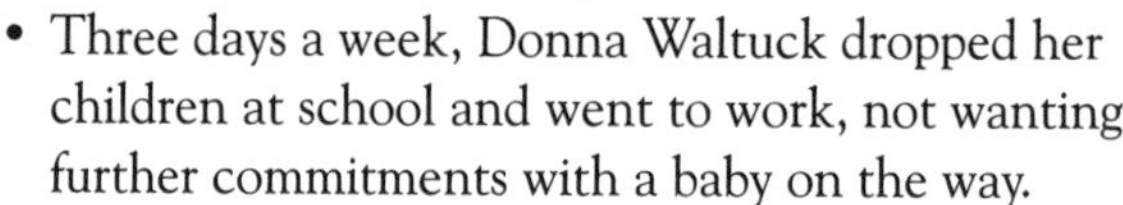

- Three days a week, Donna Waltuck dropped her children at school and went to work, not wanting further commitments with a baby on the way.

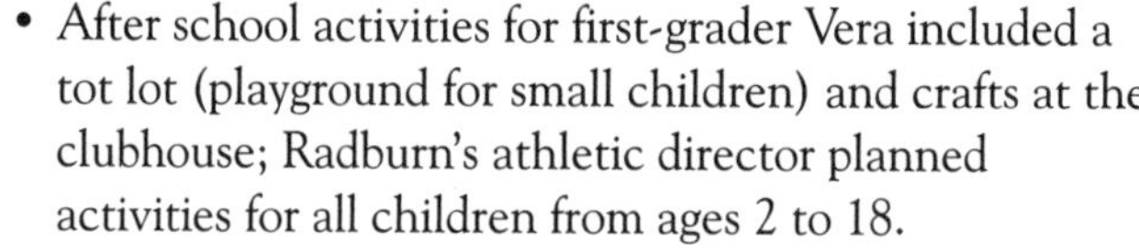

- After school activities for first-grader Vera included a tot lot (playground for small children) and crafts at the clubhouse; Radburn's athletic director planned activities for all children from ages 2 to 18.
- After school Eugene played basketball, baseball and learned tennis, and Vera also took ballet.
- During the summer, Eugene attended the town's summer camp, which was managed by a professional staff.
- Summer should also be a time for learning, not just for resting, according to the Teachers' College in New York, so Donna encouraged both children to start a hobby during summer vacation.
- For adults, Radburn schools offered courses in psychology, music appreciation, current events and American literature, in addition to amateur theater, bridge tournaments and craft lessons.
- Donna took conversational French; even though she dropped out of college in her sophomore year to marry, she still dreamed of finishing her education and spending a week in Paris.
- For Eugene's birthday, he and three friends played miniature golf—the national rage.
- He got a hole-in-one on the ninth hole, and the best score, although there was some disagreement about his math, and afterwards, everyone got to eat ice cream.
- He also got his birthday wish—a game of "Sorry."

- He drove his parents crazy with his newest saying, "So long…until tomorrow," heard nightly by radio announcer Lowell Thomas.
- Eugene's favorite radio shows were "Amos 'n' Andy" and "The Lone Ranger," whose opening line he also knew by heart: "A fiery horse with the speed of light, a cloud of dust, and a hearty 'Hi-yo, Silver!' The Lone Ranger rides again!"

Roads are designed to separate children and cars.

Life in the Community: Radburn, New Jersey

- Radburn was hailed as a town for children and America's first garden community, and it captured the imagination of hundreds of families.
- Most of the residents were young married couples with children, and Protestant; a dozen were Jewish and one practiced both Judaism and Catholicism.
- "The Radburn idea," according to one of its planners, "seeks to answer the enigma of how to live with the auto," or more precisely, how to live in spite of it.
- Advertisements for the community emphasized the role of its parks, saying, "To be complete, and provide fully for family life and growth, a home must be more than four walls. And no matter how attractive a house may be, it will fall short of present-day requirements if its location does not offer recreation and play facilities for children and adults."
- The town was designed with winding cul-de-sacs that followed the contours of the land; in the words of one developer: "At Radburn, everything is planned."
- The Radburn idea had five key elements: the superblock, specialized roads, separation of pedestrian and automobile traffic, houses turned to front the parks, and the park as the backbone of the neighborhood.
- Executives of the City Housing Corporation canvassed 27 sites throughout the Northeast before selecting rural land in Fair Lawn, New Jersey, 16 miles from New York.
- Two square miles of land, 1,300 acres, were purchased for $3.4 million, the price based on the town's proximity to New York City.
- Early plans called for a variety of houses that appealed to all income levels, but as planner Clarence Stein lamented, "If the poorly paid workers were admitted to the garden city, the industry that used them would have to subsidize the workers' houses and advance their wages."
- The typical house in Radburn cost between $7,900 and $18,200, approximately twice the average price of an American house.

By clustering the houses, space was created for parks and bike paths.

- The unique nature of the community was not only attractive, but the clustered housing and expansive parks reduced the cost of building the infrastructure, including roads and waterlines, by 25 percent.
- Radburn was the most visible product of the Regional Planning Association of America, an innovative planning group whose members included social critics such as Lewis Mumford, architects Clarence Stein and Henry Wright, as well as naturalist Benton MacKaye and economist Stuart Chase.

"Now We Have a Real Motortown, There Are Automobile Streets and Pedestrian Streets in Radburn, New Jersey, and It's a Safe Paradise for Children," by Harold F. Podhaski, Motor, January 1930

If there exists a paradise on earth for automobile owners, one may find it at Radburn, New Jersey, a dozen miles or so as the crow flies from New York City.

For here indeed has science constructed what may be fittingly described as a model town for this motor age, the only town of its kind, in fact, in the world today.

A town where one may roll the car along at as merry a clip as the heart desires without the fear that some careless youngster may dart suddenly across the way.

A town without street crossings, where traffic boulevards have no sidewalks, where jaywalkers are practically unknown.

In fact, a town where science has done virtually everything that it is possible to do to create a community safe and sane for motorist and pedestrian alike, yet has combined with these elements beauty and charm, and the utmost in modern efficiency.

Two years ago, on the site where now stands the town of Radburn, rolling green fields stretched far and wide, with but an occasional house or farm building here and there in silhouette against the horizon. Since then, ingenuity has transformed this scene into one of the most unique residential communities of the world. Unique for the present at least, though it is hardly likely to remain so because of the popularity the idea has won since the very outset, a popularity that may bring about the development of the motortown idea in other sections adjacent to the more congested metropolitan areas.

As our children are our greatest jewels, and their safety is one of the greatest of our cares, it is perhaps fitting that this story of Radburn and its building should begin with a description of the safety features primarily considered by the owners of this property when they planned their town, designed their houses and inaugurated their building program.

We realize full well in these days when nearly everyone owns an automobile, and many driver s are not as careful as they might be, that the crossing of a street has become a hazardous undertaking for children. The creation of a town where it would not be necessary for children-or anyone else for that matter-to cross the traffic boulevards, was decided upon as one of the main objectives.

At first thought, one might be inclined to consider this virtually a physical impossibility, without the erection of an underpass or overpass at every street crossing, obviously not to be thought of because of the cost involved. But it is possible and has been done at Radburn, which has been so designed and so constructed that there is not a single street crossing for pedestrians, not a traffic boulevard skirted by sidewalks, and only a single underpass. Yet, it is a good-sized town covering some 15 average blocks, or an area of nearly a square mile. . . .

Think of what this means to mothers! In the ordinary town or city, automobile traffic is a never-failing cause of worry to parents, for when the youngster is packed off to school in the morning there are usually streets that must be crossed en route with the ever-present danger of accident. The developers truthfully advertise that, "You can buy safety from traffic accidents for your whole family, and particularly for your children, when you buy a home in Radburn." If you want to own a lot of spacious private property, then Radburn isn't the answer. But if you like a place which is at the same time busy and safe for children, where you don't have to spend all your time driving around, and where you have beautiful parks and great public amenities, then it's a dandy. It's a town turned outside in-without any backdoors. A town where roads and parks fit together like the fingers on your right and left hands. A town in which children need never dodge motor trucks on their way to school.

Farmer Finds Second Career Creating Insurance Just for Farmers

There were few times in American history when ingenuity paid off more than in the decade leading up to the 1940s. Struggling farmers like George Mecherle found his second career when effects of the depression forced him to find a way to combine his experience with what many Americans needed—a better kind of automobile insurance for farmers.

Life at Home

- Insurance executive George J. Mecherle grew up on a farm in the prarieland of Illinois.
- Between his cherished *McGuffey Readers*, the mainstay of educational textbooks in the Midwest, and his ability to understand the moods and needs of farmers, George used his personal experience to reinvent the field of car insurance.
- The son of a German Lutheran immigrant and a devout Quaker mother, George spent his first 40 years farming and raising children.
- Gregarious, extroverted and talkative, he walked, talked and acted like a farmer, and was never happier than when discussing farming problems with his fellow farmers.
- Determined to maximize his yield and share his knowledge, he studied the most advanced scientific farm literature, such as *The Prairie Farmer* .
- But the poor health of his wife, Mae, worried the entire family, and George decided to give up on farming and move to Florida, where he hoped the climate would improve Mae's health.
- The couple got good money for their premier stock of shorthorn cattle, Poland China hogs, and their collection of latest farming equipment.
- They leased their 480 acres of productive land to a neighbor.
- The family discovered the joys of living at the ocean, surf fishing and the warm climate, but Mae's progressive rheumatism was undeterred by the change of location.
- After two years in Florida, they returned to Illinois and purchased a home near Bloomington, near the center of the state.
- At 42, George was not ready to retire, and worked selling insurance policies for the Union Automobile Indemnity Association of Bloomington, which wrote liability, property damage, fire, theft, and collision insurance on automobiles.
- He also became a regular at the card room of the Bloomington Club where he mingled with the merchants, storekeepers, thinkers, and professional men in the community, as well as the retired farmers.

George Mecherle sold insurance at the lowest price possible.

- He was an excellent salesman, but after a falling out with the owners of the insurance company, George signed on with the Illinois Tractor Company.
- There he was responsible finding customers amongst his farmers friends for the gasoline-powered contrivances that were becoming standard equipment on any farm.
- The Illinois Tractor Company was a minor player and did not lack for competition.
- Henry Ford's company controlled three-quarters of the tractor market in the United States and was engaged in a bitter rivalry with International Harvesters and General Motors for control.
- However, with his farming background and his ability to speak the farmers' language, George quickly became the top salesman, selling tractors faster than the company could deliver them.
- Despite his success, however, he again became dissatisfied with his bosses and quit.
- He was still intrigued with selling, however, especially selling insurance to farmers whose needs he fully understood as they continued to struggle with post-Depression uncertainty.
- Also during this time, Henry Ford was producing cars at the rate of one a minute, and automobiles, that needed reasonably priced insurance, were becoming a major force in the American economy.

George preferred working for himself.

Life at Work

- George Mecherle had slowly come to realize that the only person he liked working for was himself.
- After quitting two jobs following disputes with his boss, George's plan was to establish a farmer automobile insurance company on a statewide basis which would sell good insurance at the lowest possible price.
- Open only to farmers in the state of Illinois, it would be called State Farm Insurance and be headquartered in Bloomington, Illinois.
- George was convinced the insurance rates charged to farmers were too high because they included the risks of city drivers as well; farmers drove less—around fewer cars—and had fewer accidents.
- Moreover, after 20 years of suffering through the vagaries of the farm economy, it was time that somebody took care of the farmers.
- State Farm was founded as a mutual automobile insurance company owned by its policyholders.
- The concept of a "farmers' mutual" was a well-established, democratic form of insurance whose origins dated to the second decade of the nineteenth century.
- Every state in the Midwest had its full share of farmers' mutuals; in Illinois alone there were 216 mutuals that insured 35 percent of the state's farm property.
- George was 45 years old when he launched his new insurance company; there would be few second chances if he failed.
- Using the cardboard insert that supported his starched shirts to write on, George calculated he could insure an automobile for $1.00 per $100 of the physical valuation of the car.
- The prevailing rate was $1.00 per $40 of value.
- He also believed he could overcome the problems that many farm mutuals had experienced with automobile insurance, which included high overhead and no organization for the recovery of stolen vehicles.
- George wanted his insurance plan to be as distinct and new "as sunshine is from shadow."

Farmers desperately needed car insurance.

- All members were required to be men of property, and applications would be accepted only from Farm Bureau members and their immediate families.
- George believed that the stability of any insurance company depended on the character of the men and women it insured.
- George told his governing body "you will carry your insurance in a company in which all members are of the same stamp of men as yourself."
- He believed that farmers were a good risk, even if none of the city-oriented, large stock companies, which often treated farmers scornfully, agreed.
- Policies provided insurance protection against loss or damage to an automobile by fire, theft, or by collision with a movable object.
- George believed that anyone who hit a stationary object shouldn't be driving a car.
- Under the terms of the theft and collision policy lurked another new concept: policyholders would bear the first costs, up to $10, the remainder to be paid by State Farm.
- George believed that if the farmer had to pay for minor repairs, he would be more careful with his automobile; besides, the creation of a small deductible would prevent a flood of petty claims each time a member scraped a fender or dented a mudguard.
- Full coverage cost $15 for a life membership fee and $19 for the premium; initially, salesman had to convince farmers to buy a product that cost $34.
- Insurance was a tough sell—farm prices were down and few states required it—but George and his salesmen believed they were offering something that farmers could appreciate.
- Even the influential *Prairie Farmer* magazine agreed to accept advertising from the upstart company after subjecting George to a stern grilling.
- Initially, State Farm contacted the managers of each of the local farmer's mutuals and convinced them to take the State Farm man on a tour.
- The goals were simple: sell automobile insurance policies to farmers and train the farm mutual representative as a permanent agent once the initial sales drive was over.
- Within six months there were 1,300 policies in force and the hard-charging George and his team had gained an intimate knowledge of the best and worst restaurants and bed-and-breakfasts in rural Illinois.
- After the first year, the company placed policies in 46 counties through 90 mutual companies; the gross income totaled $45,000 with losses and adjustments of only $8,000.
- Expenses for the year included salaries of $1,600, rent for $520, and a $25,000 certificate of deposit as required by the state of Illinois.
- But early on, the young company became embroiled in a controversy concerning how to value the automobiles it was insuring.
- On the road, George and his sales team, anxious to please a prospective customer, said the valuation of the farmer's vehicle should be 80 percent of the cost of the car; the policy team back at the home office thought 80 percent of the list price was a more accurate valuation.

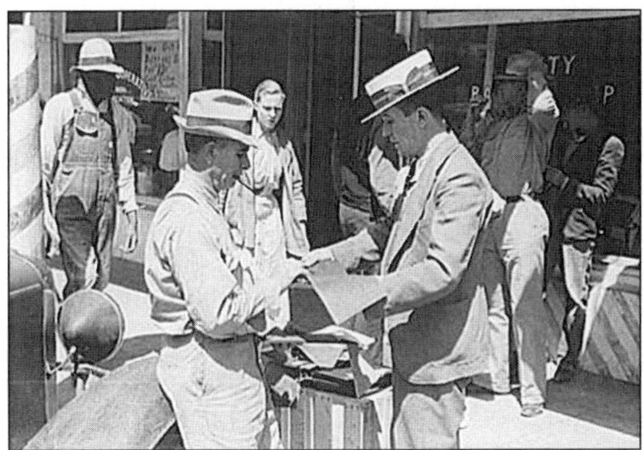
George was a natural salesperson.

George recruited high school principals as salespersons.

- Disagreement over this issue resulted in the resignation of one key employee and several of the founding board members.
- After several years, State Farm began insuring accidents involving stationary objects, and its policies included features such as wind coverage, loaned car protection and insurance for buses or private cars used for transporting children to school.
- Growth was tremendous, and to secure the right kind of sales force-men who were more than "order takers"—George began recruiting high school principals in small towns—they often needed additional income, had a keen knowledge of potential customers and often, the integrity George demanded.
- As State Farm's insurance business grew, so did the demand for the company to write policies for city dwellers and small-town merchants.
- A subsidiary was created to meet the needs of those who were not eligible as farmers; the company also accepted an invitation to begin selling policies in neighboring Indiana.
- State Farm invested $55,000 in a tract of land in downtown Bloomington to build its headquarters; the eight-story building cost a little more than $400,000 and was quickly fully occupied by the expanding insurance company.
- On the company's tenth anniversary, income reached $7.5 million, assets were $6.6 million, with a surplus of $5.6 million.
- The company had 370,045 policies in force, with 334 employees.
- Although competitors were baffled, George was not.
- Most other insurance companies required the full payment annually, paying an average 25 percent of cash premiums in commissioned wages-keeping the cost of sales high; because new policies were issued annually, the agent received his 25 percent commission every year.
- George developed semi-annual premiums-instead of yearly-an important selling point for farmers, who needed their payments to coincide with harvest time, when they could afford to pay.
- In addition, State Farm issued policies from its home office instead of the field office, saving the company the cost of clerical staffing in multiple offices.
- The home office was also responsible for billing and collecting renewal premiums, allowing the salesman in the field to focus on new sales and relieve the company of compensating him for collections; these measures resulted in cost savings that were passed on to customers.
- The most unique feature of the State Farm plan was its membership fee system; any person who joined State Farm did so for life as long as they remained "a good risk."
- While many other companies included the cost of acquiring customers in their fee structure, State Farm charged a fee only once, reducing the overall cost of the policy every year that it was renewed.
- During its first 10 years, State Farm performed at nearly 40 percent less than the stock companies.
- Even the decision to expand beyond the borders of Illinois had been successful; America was a big country with many more cities to conquer.

Life in the Community: Bloomington, Illinois

- As a steady stream of Germans flowed toward Wisconsin and southern Ohio in the mid- 1800s, thousands more, including George's parents, sought the comparative emptiness of Illinois.
- Miraculously, they had been able to run unscathed through the gauntlet of runners, ticket agents, boarding house scams and outright thieves who lived to strip new immigrants of their every possession the minute they arrived onshore.

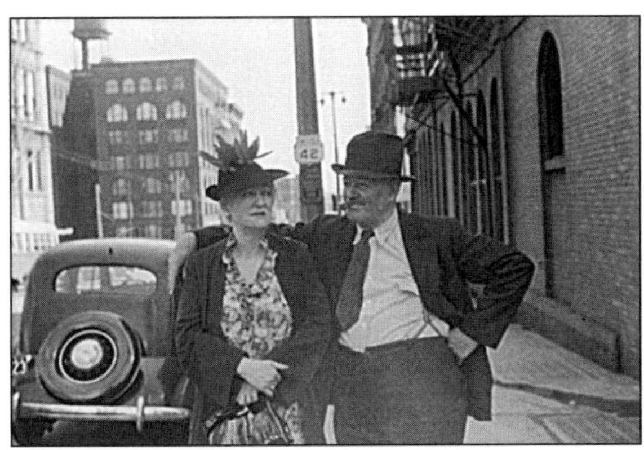
Some immigrants were skeptical about life in America.

- After five years of wandering, the couple settled near Bloomington, Illinois, a growing spot in the prairie, thanks to the Illinois Central Railway.
- Their decision coincided with the development of an improved plow that was designed to cut the prairie sod in great swaths.
- It was so large, 16 to 30 oxen were needed to pull it through the rich swampland, rendering the prairie useful for agriculture.
- People came from all over to trade and do business at the town's center, known today as Downtown Bloomington, including Abraham Lincoln, who was working as a lawyer in nearby Springfield.
- In 1900, a fire destroyed the majority of the downtown, especially the areas north and east of the courthouse, but quickly rebuilt from the designs of local architects George Miller, Paul O. Moratz, and A.L. Pillsbury.
- During the first three decades of the twentieth century, Bloomington continued to grow.
- Agriculture, the construction of highways and railroads, and the growth of the insurance business—mainly State Farm Insurance—all influenced the growth of Bloomington and its downtown area.

"States Still Experimenting With Automobile Insurance," C. L. Mosher, *The New York Times,* January 4, 1931

If the authorities of the various states throughout the country advocated compulsory automobile insurance-or, as they are called, "fiscal responsibility laws"-in the belief that the enactment of such legislation would decrease the number of motor car accidents, their hope has undoubtedly been banished by the ever increasing number of the fatalities and injuries in almost every state of the union.

The joy riders and the jaywalkers, like the poor, we have always with us. Insurance does palliate but it has not cured; it does, however, make it easier for everyone after the crash has occurred, but no one yet has put forth a method which legislators can adopt to prevent, or even curb, the number of unnecessary or avoidable motor car mishaps.

But the lawmakers have not been idle during the past three or four years; their efforts to improve road conditions have been earnest and frequent. Many theories have been and are being tried out, and new ones are now proposed, but of them all there is no one measure in sight which promises to be conspicuously better than the measures now in force....

In the New York legislature were introduced 11 bills for resolutions for the adoption of, or for commissions to consider, compulsory compensation insurance in connection with motor car accident. Bills for the creation of "state funds" were introduced in Massachusetts and New York. Bills for the adoption of indiscriminate "compulsory liability insurance" on the Massachusetts plan...were induced in New York, Rhode Island and Virginia; and bills along the line of the "AAA Bill" in whole or in part were introduced in Kentucky, Massachusetts, South Carolina and Virginia.

In addition to these, there were many proposed resolutions and a few exceptional proposals. The federal government, too, did not permit the year to pass without its contribution to interest in motor car protection, with the result that there are pending in Congress, for the District of Columbia, a measure following closely the lines of the "AAA Bill" and one for compulsory compensation insurance in a "state fund."

Family Wiped Out by Stock Market Crash

1940 was a defining year for so many Americans who struggled through the effects of the Depression. The Chappels were typical of a family for whom "living within their means" took on new meaning, as they sold furniture from their mansion-like home, and cancelled reservations at the Ritz-Carlton in New York for their daughter's debutante party.

Life at Home

- The Chappel family, who were heavily invested in the future of airplane travel, was devastated by the stock market crash of 1929 and forced to dramatically change their lifestyle .
- Quentin, along with his wife Edna and daughter Pauline, sold the family home in Oberlin, Ohio, which had more than 24,000 square feet of living space, and was thought to be the largest private residence in the city.
- Quentin inherited the house, with 35 rooms and 24 fireplaces, from Edna's father and had it redecorated by Louis Comfort Tiffany in 1910.
- Over the main staircase, the domed ceiling rose 75 feet high, paneled with alternating strips of walnut and satinwood; sliding pocket windows giving access to a three level side piazza, and the library had built-in black walnut bookcases and mahogany crown moldings.
- Their daughter Pauline was devastated that her débutante party could not be held at the Ritz-Carlton in New York, where the ballroom rental was $1,500, the minimum meal $3.00 per person, and the orchestra $1,000-extra if the party lasted past 2 a.m.
- She was also forced to postpone plans for a tour of Europe next year-something she dreamt about for years.
- During good times, Quentin was convinced that air travel represented the future, and the family often took luxury trips in airplanes styled after the finest trains, offering room for pool games, a beauty salon, and elaborate sleeping quarters—all at 125 miles per hour.
- On a lark, they even took a trip to New York one weekend to see comedian Will Rogers perform, with Quentin bringing along his secretary so he could keep up with business.
- He spent a lot of his time reading economic journals to determine his next financial decisions, and magazines like *Life*, to lift his spirits.

Before the Depression the Chappels often traveled in style.

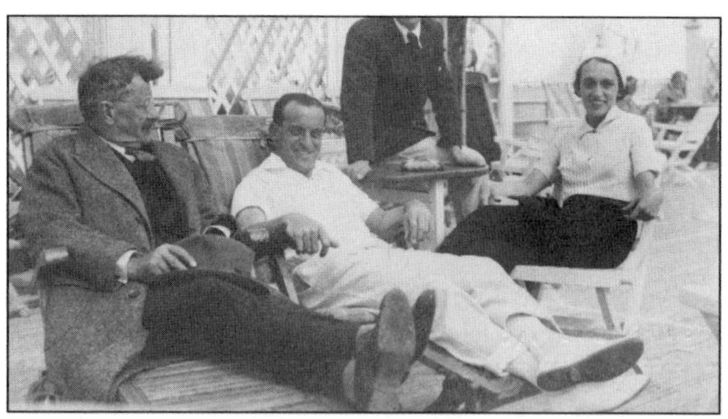

Quentin married well, investing his father-in-law's money in railroads and real estate.

Life at Work

- Quentin invested his father-in-law's considerable fortune in railroads and real estate, and made millions in the market.
- He was especially bullish on Seaboard Air Line, traditionally considered a railroad stock, because the company appeared to be positioned as a great aviation stock; he thought it had tremendous growth potential.
- He also believed in buying stock in big companies, such as United States Steel Corporation, International Harvester, International Nickel and American Tobacco, and those who moved toward centralized management, like Montgomery Ward and Woolworth, for example.
- Following his dramatic losses during the stock market crash, Quentin supported his family by selling pieces of their home's furniture and fixtures.
- He sold the Minton tile from 22 of the 24 fireplaces, but held on to a favorite one, which depicts 17 scenes of plays by William Shakespeare.
- As both an avid golfer and a man desperate to see the stock market get back on track, he kept in his office a cartoon from the *Oberlin News Tribune* showing Uncle Sam hitting a golf ball down the economic fairway.
- At the very least, he was pleased that America is preparing to repeal the Eighteenth Amendment outlawing alcohol sales, so that he can drown his misery legally.

Life in the Community: Oberlin, Ohio

- Oberlin, Ohio, is the home of Oberlin College, the first in the nation to provide coeducational classes.
- A third of the college's 1,400 students were employed to defray the cost of college; of the 475 working students, half have dormitory board jobs, while the rest worked in private homes firing furnaces, mowing lawns and caring for children.
- The Oberlin Village council set the annual salaries of its key officials as follows: city manager at $4,200, night policemen at $1,200, and fire chief at $1000; they also declared that "labor shall be paid at a rate not to exceed $0.85 per hour."
- The council also completed construction of the new water line from the dam in Kimpton to provide Oberlin with "plenty of water in years to come so there will be no shortages in dry seasons."
- Since the police began providing 24-hour service, they made 101 arrests, impounded 10 dogs, found 63 doors unlocked, investigated three stolen autos (recovering all) and seven stolen bicycles (recovering five), and replaced seven traffic signal bulbs.
- Oberlin's volunteer fire department answered 37 calls, nine in response to sparks on the roof of a home, six for chimney fires, and one for an electric iron catching fire.
- The community spent a total of $87,000 annually on municipal services.

Pauline has been forced to postpone her plans for touring Europe.

- At the H. G. Klermund Ford dealer, a DeLuxe Roadster was $475, a price cut of $45, and a Sport Coupe was $500, down from $525.
- Oberlin, like many communities throughout the nation, observed the eleventh anniversary of the passage of the Eighteenth Amendment, prohibiting the sale of alcohol.
- According to the *Oberlin News Tribune*, the prohibition of liquor sales "increased the national purchasing power by $6 billion a year by diverting a major portion of the old saloon keepers' receipts to more useful channels."
- The "useful channels" listed by the newspaper include, (1) it has reduced poverty from drink to a negligible minimum; (2) it has given at least three million boys and girls a chance to attend high school from homes that could not have afforded it in the saloon era; (3) it has added hundreds of millions of dollars of value to the great dairy industry and has aided agriculture generally; (4) it has bettered the condition of the army of workers by doing away with "Blue Monday," which was a regular bugbear of the manufacturers of the old days, decreasing quality and quantity once a week because of Saturday night carousals that lasted over until Tuesday.

John Kenneth Galbraith, "In Goldman Sachs We Trust," The Great Crash, 1929

"Knowledge, manipulative skill, or financial genius were not the only magic of the investment trust. There was also leverage. By the summer of 1929, one no longer spoke of investment trusts as such. One referred to high-leverage trusts, low-leverage trusts, or trusts without any leverage at all.

The principle of leverage is the same for an investment trust as in the game of crack-the whip. By the application of well-known physical laws, a modest movement near the point of origin is translated into a major jolt on the extreme periphery. In an investment trust, leverage was achieved by issuing bonds and preferred stock, as well as common stock to purchase, more or less exclusively, a portfolio of common stocks. When the common stock so purchased rose in value, a tendency which was always assumed, the value of bonds and preferred stock of the trust was largely unaffected. These securities had a fixed value derived from a specified return. Most or all of the gain from rising portfolio values was concentrated on the common stock of the investment trust which, as a result, rose marvelously.

Consider, by way of illustration, the case of an investment trust organized in early 1929 with a capital of $150 million-a plausible size by then. Let it be assumed, further, that a third of the capital was realized from the sale of bonds, a third from preferred stock, and the rest from the sale of common stock. If this $150 million were invested, and if the securities so purchased showed a normal appreciation, the portfolio value would have increased by midsummer by about 50 percent. The assets would be worth $255 million. The bonds and preferred stock would still be worth only $100 million; their earnings would not have increased, and they could claim no greater share of the assets in the hypothetical event of a liquidation of the company. The remaining $125 million, therefore, would underlie the value of the common stock of the trust. The latter, in other words, would have increased in asset value from $50 million to $125 million, or by 150 percent, and as the result of an increase of only 50 percent in the value of the assets of the trust as a whole.

This was the magic of leverage, but this was not all of it. Were the common stock of the trust, which had so miraculously increased in value, held by still another trust with similar leverage, the common stock of that trust would get an increase of between 700 and 800 percent from the original 50-percent advance. And so forth. In 1929 the discovery of the wonders of the geometric series struck Wall Street with a force comparable to the invention of the wheel."

The Depression

- During the decade of the 1920s, the sale of automobiles, electrical appliances, radios, refrigerators and other durable goods skyrocketed.
- This higher standard of living was made possible through the efficiency of the machine age, which brought prices down, and by the extended use of credit, which made immediate purchases based on future earnings possible.
- To make as many sales as possible, merchants made installment credit easier and easier to obtain; as a result, debt accumulated faster than wealth expanded.
- By 1930, the debt of the country had increased to one third of its wealth; in addition, millions of Americans who had become familiar with the procedure of investment through their purchase of Liberty Loan bonds during World War I were more comfortable buying stocks.
- Spurred by visions of dazzling gains, millions poured into the stock market.
- From 1927 to 1929, prices on the stock exchange soared; the Dow Jones high in 1926 was 162, while the high in 1929 was 381.
- Preceding the crash of 1929 were several key events, including the collapse of the Florida land speculation boom in 1926, the failure of 6,000 (or one fifth) of the nation's banks (many in rural areas), and the severe problems of several vital industries, including agriculture.
- To further exacerbate the problem, in 1927 the Federal Reserve system began an easy money policy by reducing discount rates, partly to aid business and to help foreign nations; the policy encouraged increased speculation.
- The Federal Reserve Board attempted to correct the situation by raising the discount rate; by December 1928 the call-loan rate reached 8.6 percent, but speculation continued.
- When the crash came on October 29, 1929, more than 16 million shares changed hands.
- The stock of General Electric Company dropped 47 points, American Telephone and Telegraph fell 34 points, and Westinghouse Electric and Manufacturing Company went down 35 points.
- By the end of 1929, stockholders had lost $40 billion in paper values, or more than the total cost of World War I, to the United States.
- The stock market crash began the impoverishment of millions of Americans, the demoralization of business and the growth of unemployment.
- Other nations experienced the misery and suffering at approximately the same time, largely as a result of the policies enacted following World War I; by 1930, the depression was worldwide.
- Throughout the United States, factories closed down, an increasing number of banks failed, prices of commodities sank, foreign trade languished, railroad loadings declined and railways became insolvent.
- By 1930, more than three million workers were unemployed, and by 1932, the figure stood at more than 12 million; during the same two years, 5,102 banks failed, setting a new record.
- Congress rejected President Herbert Hoover's proposal to save money by reducing the salaries of government officials, and opposed a general sales tax.
- Instead Congress sought to solve the problem by increasing income tax rates, raising postage rates and taxing items such as amusements, bank checks, stock sales, automobiles, gasoline, oil, tires, matches and refrigerators.

America Repatriates its Own Citizens to Mexico

As the U.S. desperately struggled to reverse the impact of the depression in the years leading up to 1940 by reserving jobs for "real Americans," American-born Maria Azuela and her children are swept up in the expulsion of 400,000 Mexicans. The 27-year-old American citizen of Mexican descent was subjected to a harrowing journey from Los Angeles to Mexico, where she had never lived.

Life at Home

- Maria Azuela was 27 was living outside Los Angeles when her husband died suddenly, leaving her alone with three young children.
- As a stone mason, Mario worked hard and made good money, and the couple were planning to buy a house, when he died violently in a job-related accident that his company said deserved no compensation.
- Maria's youngest, three-year-old Rigo, asked about his father nightly for weeks after he died.
- Three weeks after the funeral, Los Angeles authorities arrived at the three-room apartment and ordered her and her American-born children to leave the country.
- They told her that America was in the midst of a serious Depression, unemployment was on the rise, and room must be made for U.S. workers.
- To get Americans working again, President Herbert Hoover had backed a policy to repatriate hundreds of thousands of Mexican workers.
- In public announcements, Latinos were accused of taking jobs and government services from "real Americans."
- One federal official declared, "We need their jobs for needy citizens."
- The County Board of Supervisors and the Chamber of Commerce proclaimed "repatriation" of Mexicans to be a humane and utilitarian solution.
- The Mexican government supported the purge, touting the current development of agriculture colonies and irrigation projects in Mexico that would provide work for the displaced compatriots from the north.
- Approximately one million people of Mexican ancestry were relocated, more than half of whom were American citizens—400,000 men, women and children were expelled from the state of California alone.
- As frightened as Maria was when the officials told her she must leave, she laughed out loud.

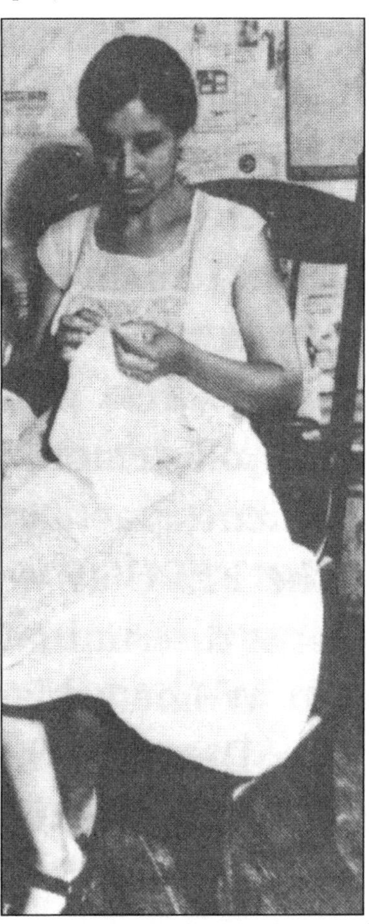

An American citizen of Mexican descent, Maria was sent back to Mexico when her husband died suddenly.

Maria and her children were forced to board a train to Guadalajara, Mexico.

- "I don't even speak Spanish very well," she told them, "and the children have never been to Mexico. They don't speak Spanish at all."
- He showed no interest in her American birth certificate or those of her children.
- They presented her with papers certifying that she was unemployed and thus a potential ward of the state and not welcome to return.
- Within a week she and her three children were driven to the depot and forced to board a train to Guadalajara, Mexico
- They were four of 400 frightened people shipped south that day, to the music of a mariachi band, hired to keep spirits high.
- 50,000 persons of Mexican ancestry were expelled from Los Angeles alone during a 6-month period.
- The forced immigration process of Maria and her children took 23 hours aboard a train that stopped often but carried little food; Rigo became dehydrated and developed a fever.
- When the train's porter finally came to check on the family, he ordered Maria to silence her son's crying-the other passengers were complaining.
- He didn't know where she could find clean drinking water and scolded her for not better preparing for the long trip.
- This was only her second trip to Mexico, the first to attend her grandmother's funeral a decade earlier.
- The Mexico of her grandmother was so foreign and desperate that she refused to go back, even to visit her husband's mother.
- America was her home and she had no desire to live anywhere else.
- Her father, Raymond, and pregnant mother had emigrated from near the Chihuahuan Desert in 1903.
- Revolution was in the air then, and they just wanted out.
- Raymond had been raised on a farm and knew hard work, knew how to work from "dark to dark."
- He heard that farmers in America were desperate for pickers who would stay in the fields all day and not quit on them.
- In America, he believed, his family could find peace and prosperity.

Life at Work

- Maria Azuela was frozen with fear when the conductor ordered her off the train in Guadalajara.
- A month earlier she was a happily married American citizen, who spent her days raising three children and waiting for her husband to return from work at sunset.
- Their apartment was neat, fully furnished and clean, its décor influenced by their Mexican past, their Catholic upbringing and their love of American culture.
- Her dream life disappeared beneath an accidental rock slide at her husband's work site, her subsequent

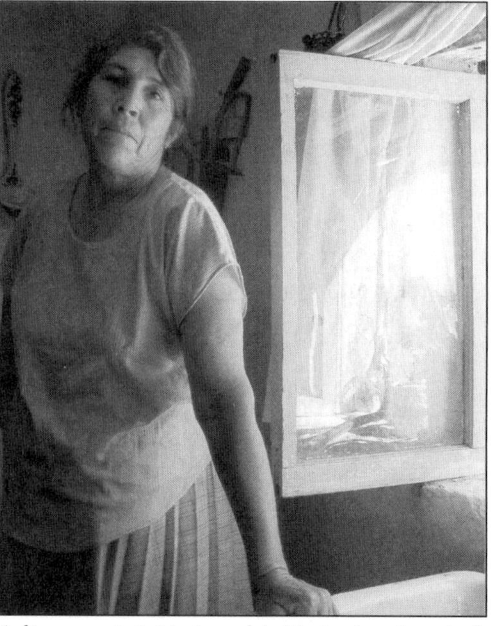
A distant cousin in Mexico took in Maria when she arrived.

expulsion by county officials eager to keep Mexicans off the welfare rolls, a long, exhausting train ride and the persistent cough of her youngest child.
- For two days after they left the train, she and her children slept on the depot benches and ate scraps left by other travelers.
- She had money in her dress pocket, but was terrified to spend any and then find herself destitute.
- On the third day she was roused from sleep and ordered to leave by police officials who were frustrated by her inability to speak Spanish.

Cheap, Mexican labor was in demand.

- Finally, they decided to ship the family by train to Chihuahua, where they wandered for days searching for a distant cousin she had met a decade earlier at her grandmother's funeral.
- When Maria arrived at her cousin's doorstep, she was told that if she wanted to stay, she would need to work raising chickens and collecting eggs.
- Her primary task was guarding the free ranging chickens from hawks, foxes, dogs and ten-fingered chicken thieves.
- She immediately ordered an English-language book on chicken farming, and enrolled the children in school.
- Having finished the eighth grade herself, Maria knew the only path back to America was through education.
- Four months after her arrival, she learned from newly arriving refugees that everything in her apartment had been stolen two days after she left and that another family was now living in her home.
- Returning to America was her goal, not to Los Angeles, but to Chicago, where she was told was a friendly-albeit cold-place to raise a family.
- She also learned that keeping chickens and hawks apart was a monumental task, and was whipped twice by her cousin for losing a chicken.
- When she decided to leave for Chicago someone helped her and her children across the border.
- After that her American birth certificate would keep her safe.

Life in the Community: Los Angeles, California

- Most Mexicans entered the United States through Arizona or Texas, with El Paso serving as the port of entry for close to 60 percent of all immigrants who eventually settled in Los Angeles.
- Opposition to Mexican labor began to grow and several national magazines, including *The Saturday Evening Post,* editorialized against the "Mexicanization" of America.
- Mexican immigrants clustered in Los Angeles because it already contained a large Latino community with a longstanding tradition of immigrants from Mexico.
- Los Angeles life and culture was completely transformed in the face of rapid Mexican settlement and urbanization.
- In almost every section of Los Angeles where Mexicans lived, they "shared" neighborhoods with other ethnic groups.
- The English language prevailed in the daily commerce and business world of the city, and despite the many familiarities to their homeland, Los Angeles was a strange environment to the immigrants and in stark contrast with their rural and beloved Mexico.

The nine tables that follow are reprinted from the actual 1940 census, for the city of Los Angeles. They include actual data on race, percentage of voting population, school attendance, number of school years completed, foreign born, and employment of workers 14 years and older by job, industry and race. In addition to being incredibly fascinating, these facts help to strengthen and visualize the actual environment in which Maria Azuela lived before the government forced her to leave.

Table B-35.—AGE, BY RACE AND SEX, FOR THE CITY OF LOS ANGELES: 1940 AND 1930

[Figures for white population in 1930 revised to include Mexicans classified with "Other races" in the 1930 reports. Percent not shown where less than 0.1 or where base is less than 100]

AGE AND CENSUS YEAR	ALL CLASSES			NATIVE WHITE			FOREIGN-BORN WHITE			NEGRO			OTHER RACES		
	Total	Male	Female	Total	Male	Female	Total	Male	Female	Total	Male	Female	Total	Male	Female
All ages: 1940	1,504,277	734,135	770,142	1,191,182	575,597	615,585	215,248	107,478	107,770	63,774	29,906	33,868	34,073	21,154	12,919
Under 5 years	83,973	42,929	41,044	77,478	39,607	37,871	245	125	120	3,784	1,926	1,858	2,466	1,271	1,195
5 to 9 years	80,162	40,197	39,965	73,590	36,953	36,637	480	226	254	3,744	1,813	1,931	2,348	1,205	1,143
10 to 14 years	90,088	45,455	44,633	82,139	41,376	40,763	1,156	579	577	3,876	1,958	1,918	2,917	1,542	1,375
15 to 19 years	104,139	51,135	53,004	92,135	45,119	47,016	3,956	1,917	2,039	4,310	2,136	2,174	3,738	1,963	1,775
20 to 24 years	124,750	61,182	63,568	108,611	53,442	55,169	7,086	3,301	3,785	5,257	2,409	2,848	3,796	2,030	1,766
25 to 29 years	141,813	70,315	71,498	119,196	59,254	59,942	12,120	5,569	6,551	7,066	3,249	3,817	3,431	2,243	1,188
30 to 34 years	134,451	66,962	67,489	108,201	53,755	54,446	16,339	7,838	8,501	6,839	3,062	3,777	3,072	2,307	765
35 to 39 years	131,273	65,571	65,702	98,929	49,297	49,632	22,591	11,203	11,388	6,676	2,958	3,718	3,077	2,113	964
40 to 44 years	121,214	60,554	60,660	89,259	44,172	45,087	23,823	12,106	11,717	5,524	2,633	2,891	2,608	1,643	965
45 to 49 years	111,092	54,736	56,356	79,174	38,100	41,074	25,398	13,344	12,054	4,745	2,262	2,483	1,775	1,030	745
50 to 54 years	100,990	49,638	51,352	69,236	32,348	36,888	26,082	14,034	12,048	3,775	1,825	1,950	1,897	1,431	466
55 to 59 years	83,794	40,266	43,528	56,698	25,826	30,872	23,058	12,142	10,916	2,720	1,247	1,473	1,318	1,051	267
60 to 64 years	69,084	31,488	37,596	47,734	20,709	27,025	18,428	9,089	9,339	2,001	932	1,069	921	758	163
65 to 69 years	53,888	23,202	30,686	37,816	15,549	22,267	13,901	6,566	7,335	1,781	777	1,004	390	310	80
70 to 74 years	36,461	15,456	21,005	25,300	10,240	15,060	10,113	4,679	5,434	855	377	478	193	160	33
75 years and over	37,105	15,049	22,056	25,686	9,850	15,836	10,472	4,760	5,712	821	342	479	126	97	29
Under 1 year	17,488	9,018	8,470	16,190	8,381	7,809	9	5	4	766	379	387	523	253	270
5 years	15,972	8,130	7,842	14,699	7,492	7,207	84	45	39	745	372	373	444	221	223
14 years	19,245	9,744	9,501	17,413	8,808	8,605	360	179	181	795	416	379	677	341	336
15 years	19,902	10,026	9,876	17,967	9,003	8,964	370	203	167	840	444	396	725	376	349
16 and 17 years	39,485	19,375	20,110	35,012	17,193	17,819	1,367	628	739	1,637	774	863	1,469	780	689
21 years and over	1,123,485	543,610	579,875	846,508	403,206	443,302	208,135	104,022	104,113	47,086	21,636	25,450	21,756	14,746	7,010
All ages: 1930	1,238,048	610,678	627,370	937,826	452,902	484,924	232,874	120,975	111,899	38,894	18,349	20,545	28,454	18,452	10,002
Under 5 years	78,799	40,206	38,593	72,687	37,067	35,620	712	353	359	2,435	1,220	1,215	2,965	1,566	1,399
5 to 9 years	86,569	43,375	43,194	76,727	38,430	38,297	3,449	1,716	1,733	2,808	1,420	1,388	3,585	1,809	1,776
10 to 14 years	77,634	38,819	38,815	66,999	33,553	33,446	5,960	2,954	3,006	2,505	1,208	1,297	2,170	1,104	1,066
15 to 19 years	84,516	40,698	43,818	70,456	33,765	36,691	9,818	4,756	5,062	2,643	1,211	1,432	1,599	956	633
20 to 24 years	109,221	53,055	56,166	86,865	41,443	45,422	16,307	8,157	8,150	3,455	1,488	1,967	2,594	1,967	627
25 to 29 years	122,836	61,529	61,307	92,050	45,198	46,852	23,183	12,134	11,049	4,326	1,926	2,400	3,277	2,271	1,006
30 to 34 years	116,783	58,782	58,001	86,473	42,792	43,681	23,255	12,287	10,968	4,145	1,966	2,179	2,910	1,737	1,173
35 to 39 years	114,695	57,399	57,296	81,610	39,737	41,873	26,259	14,306	11,953	4,563	2,083	2,480	2,263	1,273	990
40 to 44 years	101,434	51,952	49,482	69,126	33,799	35,327	26,400	14,544	11,856	3,455	1,739	1,716	2,453	1,870	583
45 to 49 years	89,528	45,328	44,200	59,548	28,698	30,850	24,967	13,540	11,427	2,995	1,445	1,550	2,018	1,645	373
50 to 54 years	75,022	36,845	38,177	51,133	23,947	27,186	20,374	10,655	9,719	2,107	1,060	1,047	1,408	1,183	225
55 to 59 years	57,188	27,051	30,137	39,749	18,100	21,649	15,553	7,772	7,781	1,257	635	622	629	544	85
60 to 64 years	45,603	20,786	24,817	30,871	13,575	17,296	13,526	6,523	7,003	883	394	489	323	294	29
65 to 69 years	33,493	15,013	18,480	22,488	9,601	12,887	10,297	5,070	5,227	564	218	346	144	124	20
70 to 74 years	22,724	10,339	12,385	15,972	6,975	8,997	6,352	3,147	3,205	336	160	176	64	57	7
75 years and over	21,306	9,145	12,161	14,534	5,959	8,575	6,357	3,003	3,354	381	155	226	34	28	6
Not reported	697	356	341	538	263	275	105	58	47	36	21	15	18	14	4
Under 1 year	15,103	7,718	7,385	14,153	7,229	6,924	28	12	16	461	225	236	461	252	209
5 years	17,756	9,063	8,693	16,076	8,225	7,851	320	163	157	582	299	283	778	376	402
14 years	15,604	7,885	7,719	13,325	6,745	6,580	1,396	706	690	530	247	283	353	187	166
15 years	15,603	7,698	7,905	13,315	6,516	6,799	1,518	776	742	456	226	230	314	180	134
16 and 17 years	31,997	15,566	16,431	26,845	13,076	13,769	3,551	1,709	1,842	1,025	455	570	576	326	250
21 years and over	891,136	438,491	452,645	635,336	302,846	332,490	210,238	109,949	100,289	27,905	13,043	14,862	17,657	12,653	5,004
Percent: 1940	100.0	100.0	100.0	100.0	100.0	100.0	100.0	100.0	100.0	100.0	100.0	100.0	100.0	100.0	100.0
Under 5 years	5.6	5.8	5.3	6.5	6.9	6.2	0.1	0.1	0.1	5.9	6.4	5.5	7.2	6.0	9.2
5 to 9 years	5.3	5.5	5.2	6.2	6.4	6.0	0.2	0.2	0.2	5.9	6.1	5.7	6.9	5.7	8.8
10 to 14 years	6.0	6.2	5.8	6.9	7.2	6.6	0.5	0.5	0.5	6.1	6.5	5.7	8.6	7.3	10.6
15 to 19 years	6.9	7.0	6.9	7.7	7.8	7.6	1.8	1.8	1.9	6.8	7.1	6.4	11.0	9.3	13.7
20 to 24 years	8.3	8.3	8.3	9.1	9.3	9.0	3.3	3.1	3.5	8.2	8.1	8.4	11.1	9.6	13.7
25 to 29 years	9.4	9.6	9.3	10.0	10.3	9.7	5.6	5.2	6.1	11.1	10.9	11.3	10.1	10.6	9.2
30 to 34 years	8.9	9.1	8.8	9.1	9.3	8.8	7.6	7.3	7.9	10.7	10.2	11.2	9.0	10.9	5.9
35 to 39 years	8.7	8.9	8.5	8.3	8.6	8.1	10.5	10.4	10.6	10.5	9.9	11.0	9.0	10.0	7.5
40 to 44 years	8.1	8.2	7.9	7.5	7.7	7.3	11.1	11.3	10.9	8.7	8.8	8.5	7.7	7.8	7.5
45 to 49 years	7.4	7.5	7.3	6.6	6.6	6.7	11.8	12.4	11.2	7.4	7.6	7.3	5.2	4.9	5.8
50 to 54 years	6.7	6.8	6.7	5.8	5.6	6.0	12.1	13.1	11.2	5.9	6.1	5.8	5.6	6.8	3.6
55 to 59 years	5.6	5.5	5.7	4.8	4.5	5.0	10.7	11.3	10.1	4.3	4.2	4.3	3.9	5.0	2.1
60 to 64 years	4.6	4.3	4.9	4.0	3.6	4.4	8.6	8.5	8.7	3.1	3.1	3.2	2.7	3.6	1.3
65 to 69 years	3.6	3.2	4.0	3.2	2.7	3.6	6.5	6.1	6.8	2.8	2.6	3.0	1.1	1.5	0.6
70 to 74 years	2.4	2.1	2.7	2.1	1.8	2.4	4.7	4.4	5.0	1.3	1.3	1.4	0.6	0.8	0.3
75 years and over	2.5	2.0	2.9	2.2	1.7	2.6	4.9	4.4	5.3	1.3	1.1	1.4	0.4	0.5	0.2
Under 1 year	1.2	1.2	1.1	1.4	1.5	1.3	-	-	-	1.2	1.3	1.1	1.5	1.2	2.1
5 years	1.1	1.1	1.0	1.2	1.3	1.2	-	-	-	1.2	1.2	1.1	1.3	1.0	1.7
14 years	1.3	1.3	1.2	1.5	1.5	1.4	0.2	0.2	0.2	1.2	1.4	1.1	2.0	1.6	2.6
15 years	1.3	1.4	1.3	1.5	1.6	1.5	0.2	0.2	0.2	1.3	1.5	1.2	2.1	1.8	2.7
16 and 17 years	2.6	2.6	2.6	2.9	3.0	2.9	0.6	0.6	0.7	2.6	2.6	2.5	4.3	3.7	5.3
21 years and over	74.7	74.0	75.3	71.1	70.1	72.0	96.7	96.8	96.6	73.8	72.3	75.1	63.9	69.7	54.3
Percent: 1930	100.0	100.0	100.0	100.0	100.0	100.0	100.0	100.0	100.0	100.0	100.0	100.0	100.0	100.0	100.0
Under 5 years	6.4	6.6	6.2	7.8	8.2	7.3	0.3	0.3	0.3	6.3	6.6	5.9	10.4	8.5	14.0
5 to 9 years	7.0	7.1	6.9	8.2	8.5	7.9	1.5	1.4	1.5	7.2	7.7	6.8	12.6	9.8	17.8
10 to 14 years	6.3	6.4	6.2	7.1	7.4	6.9	2.6	2.4	2.7	6.4	6.6	6.3	7.6	6.0	10.7
15 to 19 years	6.8	6.7	7.0	7.5	7.5	7.6	4.2	3.9	4.5	6.8	6.6	7.0	5.6	5.2	6.3
20 to 24 years	8.8	8.7	9.0	9.3	9.2	9.4	7.0	6.7	7.3	8.9	8.1	9.6	9.1	10.7	6.3
25 to 29 years	9.9	10.1	9.8	9.8	10.0	9.7	10.0	10.0	9.9	11.1	10.5	11.7	11.5	12.3	10.1
30 to 34 years	9.4	9.6	9.2	9.2	9.4	9.0	10.0	10.2	9.8	10.7	10.7	10.6	10.2	9.4	11.7
35 to 39 years	9.3	9.4	9.1	8.7	8.8	8.6	11.3	11.8	10.7	11.7	11.4	12.1	8.0	6.9	9.9
40 to 44 years	8.2	8.5	7.9	7.4	7.5	7.3	11.3	12.0	10.6	8.9	9.5	8.4	8.6	10.1	5.8
45 to 49 years	7.2	7.4	7.0	6.3	6.3	6.4	10.7	11.2	10.2	7.7	7.9	7.5	7.1	8.9	3.7
50 to 54 years	6.1	6.0	6.1	5.5	5.3	5.6	8.7	8.8	8.7	5.4	5.8	5.1	4.9	6.4	2.2
55 to 59 years	4.6	4.4	4.8	4.2	4.0	4.5	6.7	6.4	7.0	3.2	3.5	3.0	2.2	2.9	0.8
60 to 64 years	3.7	3.4	4.0	3.3	3.0	3.6	5.8	5.4	6.3	2.3	2.1	2.4	1.1	1.6	0.3
65 to 69 years	2.7	2.5	2.9	2.4	2.1	2.7	4.4	4.2	4.7	1.5	1.2	1.7	0.5	0.7	0.2
70 to 74 years	1.8	1.7	2.0	1.7	1.5	1.9	2.7	2.6	2.9	0.9	0.9	0.9	0.2	0.3	0.1
75 years and over	1.7	1.5	1.9	1.5	1.3	1.8	2.7	2.5	3.0	1.0	0.8	1.1	0.1	0.2	0.1
Not reported	0.1	0.1	0.1	0.1	0.1	0.1	-	-	-	0.1	0.1	0.1	0.1	0.1	-
Under 1 year	1.2	1.3	1.2	1.5	1.6	1.4	-	-	-	1.2	1.2	1.1	1.6	1.4	2.1
5 years	1.4	1.5	1.4	1.7	1.8	1.6	0.1	0.1	0.1	1.5	1.6	1.4	2.7	2.0	4.0
14 years	1.3	1.3	1.2	1.4	1.5	1.4	0.6	0.6	0.6	1.4	1.3	1.4	1.2	1.0	1.7
15 years	1.3	1.3	1.3	1.4	1.4	1.4	0.7	0.6	0.7	1.2	1.2	1.1	1.1	1.0	1.3
16 and 17 years	2.6	2.5	2.6	2.9	2.9	2.8	1.5	1.4	1.6	2.6	2.5	2.8	2.0	1.8	2.5
21 years and over	72.0	71.8	72.1	67.7	66.9	68.6	90.3	90.9	89.6	71.7	71.1	72.3	62.1	68.6	50.0

Table B-36.—RACE, BY NATIVITY AND SEX, FOR THE CITY OF LOS ANGELES: 1940 AND 1930

[Figures for white population in 1930 have been revised to include Mexicans who were classified with "Other races" in the 1930 reports. Percent not shown where less than 0.1 or where base is less than 100. Sex ratio not shown where number of females is less than 100]

SEX, NATIVITY, AND CENSUS YEAR	All classes	White	Negro	Other races	OTHER RACES				PERCENT BY RACE				PERCENT BY NATIVITY					
					Indian	Chinese	Japanese	All other	All classes	White	Negro	Other races	All classes	White	Negro	Indian	Chinese	Japanese
TOTAL																		
1940	1,504,277	1,406,430	63,774	34,073	862	4,736	23,321	5,154	100.0	93.5	4.2	2.3	100.0	100.0	100.0	100.0	100.0	100.0
Native	1,277,240	1,191,182	63,294	22,764	769	2,540	14,595	4,860	100.0	93.3	5.0	1.8	84.9	84.7	99.2	89.2	53.6	62.6
Foreign born	227,037	215,248	480	11,309	93	2,196	8,726	294	100.0	94.8	0.2	5.0	15.1	15.3	0.8	10.8	46.4	37.4
1930	1,238,048	1,170,700	38,894	28,454	616	3,009	21,081	3,748	100.0	94.6	3.1	2.3	100.0	100.0	100.0	100.0	100.0	100.0
Native	990,913	937,826	38,369	14,718	594	1,421	9,216	3,487	100.0	94.6	3.9	1.5	80.0	80.1	98.7	96.4	47.2	43.7
Foreign born	247,135	232,874	525	13,736	22	1,588	11,865	261	100.0	94.2	0.2	5.6	20.0	19.9	1.3	3.6	52.8	56.3
MALE																		
1940	734,135	683,075	29,906	21,154	435	3,311	13,073	4,335	100.0	93.0	4.1	2.9	100.0	100.0	100.0	100.0	100.0	100.0
Native	618,994	575,597	29,653	13,744	385	1,539	7,689	4,131	100.0	93.0	4.8	2.2	84.3	84.3	99.2	88.5	46.5	58.8
Foreign born	115,141	107,478	253	7,410	50	1,772	5,384	204	100.0	93.3	0.2	6.4	15.7	15.7	0.8	11.5	53.5	41.2
1930	610,678	573,877	18,349	18,452	287	2,228	12,597	3,340	100.0	94.0	3.0	3.0	100.0	100.0	100.0	100.0	100.0	100.0
Native	480,138	452,902	18,049	9,187	277	881	4,873	3,156	100.0	94.3	3.8	1.9	78.6	78.9	98.4	96.5	39.5	38.7
Foreign born	130,540	120,975	300	9,265	10	1,347	7,724	184	100.0	92.7	0.2	7.1	21.4	21.1	1.6	3.5	60.5	61.3
FEMALE																		
1940	770,142	723,355	33,868	12,919	427	1,425	10,248	819	100.0	93.9	4.4	1.7	100.0	100.0	100.0	100.0	100.0	100.0
Native	658,246	615,585	33,641	9,020	384	1,001	6,906	729	100.0	93.5	5.1	1.4	85.5	85.1	99.3	89.9	70.2	67.4
Foreign born	111,896	107,770	227	3,899	43	424	3,342	90	100.0	96.3	0.2	3.5	14.5	14.9	0.7	10.1	29.8	32.6
1930	627,370	596,823	20,545	10,002	329	781	8,484	408	100.0	95.1	3.3	1.6	100.0	100.0	100.0	100.0	100.0	100.0
Native	510,775	484,924	20,320	5,531	317	540	4,343	331	100.0	94.9	4.0	1.1	81.4	81.3	98.9	96.4	69.1	51.2
Foreign born	116,595	111,899	225	4,471	12	241	4,141	77	100.0	96.0	0.2	3.8	18.6	18.7	1.1	3.6	30.9	48.8
MALES PER 100 FEMALES																		
1940	95.3	94.4	88.3	163.7	101.9	232.4	127.6	529.3	-	-	-	-	-	-	-	-	-	-
Native	94.0	93.5	88.1	152.4	100.3	153.7	111.3	566.7	-	-	-	-	-	-	-	-	-	-
Foreign born	102.9	99.7	111.5	190.0	-	417.9	161.1	-	-	-	-	-	-	-	-	-	-	-
1930	97.3	96.2	89.3	184.5	87.2	285.3	148.5	818.6	-	-	-	-	-	-	-	-	-	-
Native	94.0	93.4	88.8	166.1	87.4	163.1	112.2	953.5	-	-	-	-	-	-	-	-	-	-
Foreign born	112.0	108.1	133.3	207.2	-	558.9	186.5	-	-	-	-	-	-	-	-	-	-	-

Table B-37.—POTENTIAL VOTING POPULATION, BY CITIZENSHIP, RACE, NATIVITY, AND SEX, FOR THE CITY OF LOS ANGELES: 1940 AND 1930

[Figures for white population in 1930 have been revised to include Mexicans who were classified with "Other races" in the 1930 reports. Percent not shown where less than 0.1]

CITIZENSHIP, RACE, AND NATIVITY	TOTAL POPULATION (ALL AGES)								POPULATION 21 YEARS OLD AND OVER							
	Total number		Percent		Male		Female		Total number		Percent		Male		Female	
	1940	1930	1940	1930	1940	1930	1940	1930	1940	1930	1940	1930	1940	1930	1940	1930
Total	1,504,277	1,238,048	100.0	100.0	734,135	610,678	770,142	627,370	1,123,485	891,136	100.0	100.0	543,610	438,491	579,875	452,645
Percent citizen	-	-	93.1	88.4	-	-	-	-	-	-	91.3	86.1	-	-	-	-
Percent alien and citiz. not rptd.	-	-	6.9	11.6	-	-	-	-	-	-	8.7	13.9	-	-	-	-
Citizen	1,400,979	1,094,847	100.0	100.0	684,280	534,179	716,699	560,668	1,025,708	767,614	100.0	100.0	496,506	371,717	529,202	395,897
White—Native	1,191,182	937,826	85.0	85.7	575,597	452,902	615,585	484,924	846,508	635,336	82.5	82.8	403,206	302,846	443,302	332,490
Naturalized	123,520	103,788	8.8	9.5	65,175	53,957	58,345	49,831	121,515	100,244	11.8	13.1	64,188	52,279	57,327	47,965
Negro—Native	63,294	38,369	4.5	3.5	29,653	18,049	33,641	20,320	46,621	27,424	4.5	3.6	21,392	12,765	25,229	14,659
Naturalized	219	146	-	-	111	84	108	62	214	140	-	-	110	83	104	57
Other races—Native	22,764	14,718	1.6	1.3	13,744	9,187	9,020	5,531	10,850	4,470	1.1	0.6	7,610	3,744	3,240	726
Indian	769	594	0.1	0.1	385	277	384	317	500	374	-	-	259	189	241	185
Chinese	2,540	1,421	0.2	0.1	1,539	881	1,001	540	1,149	573	0.1	0.1	826	439	323	134
Japanese	14,595	9,216	1.0	0.8	7,689	4,873	6,906	4,343	5,399	806	0.5	0.1	2,972	531	2,427	275
Filipino	4,465	3,231	0.3	0.3	3,909	3,014	556	217	3,620	2,640	0.4	0.3	3,449	2,534	171	106
Hindu	15	9	-	-	10	5	5	4	8	1	-	-	6	-	2	1
All other	380	247	-	-	212	137	168	110	174	76	-	-	98	51	76	25
Alien	95,322	138,667	100.0	100.0	45,991	74,500	49,331	64,167	90,305	119,328	100.0	100.0	43,497	64,899	46,808	54,429
White—First papers	21,405	21,834	22.5	15.7	12,557	15,708	8,848	6,126	20,951	21,216	23.2	17.8	12,314	15,395	8,637	5,821
No papers	62,419	102,766	65.5	74.1	25,922	49,341	36,497	53,425	58,264	84,630	64.5	70.9	23,949	40,430	34,315	44,200
Negro—First papers	43	40	-	-	25	32	18	8	43	39	-	-	25	32	18	7
No papers	146	291	0.2	0.2	77	154	69	137	141	256	0.2	0.2	73	133	68	123
Other races—Foreign born	11,309	13,736	11.9	9.9	7,410	9,265	3,899	4,471	10,906	13,187	12.1	11.1	7,136	8,909	3,770	4,276
Indian	93	22	0.1	-	50	10	43	12	87	17	0.1	-	45	[illegible]	42	9
Chinese	2,196	1,588	2.3	1.1	1,772	1,347	424	241	1,930	1,387	2.1	2.1	1,564	1,173	366	214
Japanese	8,726	11,865	9.2	8.6	5,384	7,724	3,342	4,141	8,612	11,534	9.5	9.7	5,330	7,547	3,282	3,987
Filipino	33	14	-	-	16	7	17	7	24	13	-	-	14	7	10	6
Hindu	45	68	-	-	42	64	3	4	44	66	-	0.1	41	62	3	4
All other	216	179	0.2	0.1	146	118	70	66	209	170	0.2	0.1	142	112	67	58
Citizenship not reported	7,976	4,534	100.0	100.0	3,864	1,999	4,112	2,535	7,472	4,194	100.0	100.0	3,607	1,875	3,865	2,319
White	7,904	4,486	99.1	98.9	3,824	1,969	4,080	2,517	7,405	4,148	99.1	98.9	3,571	1,845	3,834	2,303
Negro	72	48	0.9	1.1	40	30	32	18	67	46	0.9	1.1	36	30	31	16

Table B-38.—SCHOOL ATTENDANCE, BY AGE, RACE, AND SEX, FOR THE CITY OF LOS ANGELES: 1940 AND 1930

[Figures for white population in 1930 revised to include Mexicans classified with "Other races" in the 1930 reports. Percent not shown where less than 0.1 or where base is less than 100]

AGE, SEX, AND CENSUS YEAR	ALL CLASSES			NATIVE WHITE			FOREIGN-BORN WHITE			NEGRO			OTHER RACES		
	Total number	Attending school: Number	Attending school: Percent	Total number	Attending school: Number	Attending school: Percent	Total number	Attending school: Number	Attending school: Percent	Total number	Attending school: Number	Attending school: Percent	Total number	Attending school: Number	Attending school: Percent
1940															
Total, 5 to 24 years	399,139	244,024	61.1	356,475	220,259	61.8	12,678	4,641	36.6	17,187	10,500	61.1	12,799	8,624	67.4
5 years	15,972	8,580	53.7	14,699	7,802	53.1	84	33	-	745	471	63.2	444	274	61.7
6 years	15,329	14,065	91.8	14,016	12,835	91.6	85	69	-	753	714	94.8	475	447	94.1
7 to 9 years	48,861	47,673	97.6	44,875	43,789	97.6	311	298	95.8	2,246	2,194	97.7	1,429	1,392	97.4
10 to 13 years	70,843	69,431	98.0	64,726	63,461	98.0	796	768	96.5	3,081	3,014	97.8	2,240	2,188	97.7
14 years	19,245	18,775	97.6	17,413	16,990	97.6	360	349	96.9	795	774	97.4	677	662	97.8
15 years	19,902	19,284	96.9	17,967	17,412	96.9	370	359	97.0	840	807	96.1	725	706	97.4
16 and 17 years	39,485	35,065	88.8	35,012	31,074	88.8	1,367	1,183	86.5	1,637	1,417	86.6	1,469	1,391	94.7
18 and 19 years	44,752	18,073	40.4	39,156	15,535	39.7	2,219	874	39.4	1,833	760	41.5	1,544	904	58.5
20 years	22,430	4,424	19.7	19,332	3,804	19.7	1,276	228	17.9	974	135	13.9	848	257	30.3
21 to 24 years	102,320	8,654	8.5	89,279	7,557	8.5	5,810	480	8.3	4,283	214	5.0	2,948	403	13.7
Male, 5 to 24 years	197,969	124,862	63.1	176,890	112,511	63.6	6,023	2,491	41.4	8,316	5,230	62.9	6,740	4,630	68.7
5 years	8,130	4,340	53.4	7,492	3,955	52.8	45	21	-	372	232	62.4	221	132	59.7
6 years	7,596	6,957	91.6	6,947	6,344	91.3	32	27	-	367	347	94.6	250	239	95.6
7 to 9 years	24,471	23,858	97.5	22,514	21,951	97.5	149	143	96.0	1,074	1,046	97.4	734	718	97.8
10 to 13 years	35,711	34,989	98.0	32,568	31,908	98.0	400	392	98.0	1,542	1,514	98.2	1,201	1,175	97.8
14 years	9,744	9,508	97.6	8,808	8,595	97.6	179	172	96.1	416	407	97.8	341	334	97.9
15 years	10,026	9,715	96.9	9,003	8,724	96.9	203	195	96.1	444	430	96.8	376	366	97.3
16 and 17 years	19,375	17,432	90.0	17,193	15,473	90.0	628	550	87.6	774	670	86.6	780	739	94.7
18 and 19 years	21,734	9,724	44.7	18,923	8,306	43.9	1,086	505	46.5	918	406	44.2	807	507	62.8
20 years	10,809	2,580	23.9	9,336	2,216	23.7	609	146	24.0	437	68	15.6	427	150	35.1
21 to 24 years	50,373	5,759	11.4	44,106	5,039	11.4	2,692	340	12.6	1,972	110	5.6	1,603	270	16.8
Female, 5 to 24 years	201,170	119,162	59.2	179,585	107,748	60.0	6,655	2,150	32.3	8,871	5,270	59.4	6,059	3,994	65.9
5 years	7,842	4,240	54.1	7,207	3,847	53.4	39	12	-	373	239	64.1	223	142	63.7
6 years	7,733	7,108	91.9	7,069	6,491	91.8	53	42	-	386	367	95.1	225	208	92.4
7 to 9 years	24,390	23,815	97.6	22,361	21,838	97.7	162	155	95.7	1,172	1,148	98.0	695	674	97.0
10 to 13 years	35.132	34,442	98.0	32,158	31,553	98.1	396	376	94.9	1,539	1,500	97.5	1,039	1,013	97.5
14 years	9,501	9,267	97.5	8,605	8,395	97.6	181	177	97.8	379	367	96.8	336	328	97.6
15 years	9,876	9,569	96.9	8,964	8,688	96.9	167	164	98.2	396	377	95.2	349	340	97.4
16 and 17 years	20,110	17,633	87.7	17,819	15,601	87.6	739	633	85.7	863	747	86.6	689	652	94.6
18 and 19 years	23,018	8,349	36.3	20,233	7,229	35.7	1,133	369	32.6	915	354	38.7	737	397	53.9
20 years	11,621	1,844	15.9	9,996	1,588	15.9	667	82	12.3	537	67	12.5	421	107	25.4
21 to 24 years	51,947	2,895	5.6	45,173	2,518	5.6	3,118	140	4.5	2,311	104	4.5	1,345	133	9.9
1930															
Total, 5 to 24 years	357,940	223,854	62.5	301,047	193,441	64.3	35,534	16,526	46.5	11,411	6,931	60.7	9,948	6,956	69.9
5 years	17,756	9,767	55.0	16,076	8,792	54.7	320	139	43.4	582	361	62.0	778	475	61.1
6 years	17,337	15,361	88.6	15,610	13,827	88.6	452	391	86.5	540	481	89.1	735	662	90.1
7 to 9 years	51,476	49,472	96.1	45,041	43,305	96.1	2,677	2,562	95.7	1,686	1,610	95.5	2,072	1,995	96.3
10 to 13 years	62,030	61,382	99.0	53,674	53,129	99.0	4,564	4,506	98.7	1,975	1,949	98.7	1,817	1,798	99.0
14 years	15,604	15,415	98.8	13,325	13,176	98.9	1,396	1,371	98.2	530	521	98.3	353	347	98.3
15 years	15,603	15,257	97.8	13,315	13,050	98.0	1,518	1,469	96.8	456	436	95.6	314	302	96.2
16 and 17 years	31,997	27,688	86.5	26,845	23,461	87.4	3,551	2,830	79.7	1,025	886	86.4	576	511	88.7
18 and 19 years	36,916	14,800	40.1	30,296	12,466	41.1	4,749	1,545	32.5	1,162	442	38.0	709	347	48.9
20 years	19,394	4,393	22.7	15,621	3,752	24.0	2,697	429	15.9	598	87	14.5	478	125	26.2
21 to 24 years	89,827	10,319	11.5	71,244	8,483	11.9	13,610	1,284	9.4	2,857	158	5.5	2,116	394	18.6
Male, 5 to 24 years	175,947	113,010	64.2	147,191	97,318	66.1	17,583	8,522	48.5	5,327	3,374	63.3	5,846	3,796	64.9
5 years	9,063	4,939	54.5	8,225	4,459	54.2	163	75	46.0	299	178	59.5	376	227	60.4
6 years	8,845	7,824	88.5	7,957	7,035	88.4	224	192	85.7	284	253	89.1	380	344	90.5
7 to 9 years	25,467	24,474	96.1	22,248	21,395	96.2	1,329	1,272	95.7	837	794	94.9	1,053	1,013	96.2
10 to 13 years	30,934	30,615	99.0	26,808	26,542	99.0	2,248	2,217	98.6	961	948	98.6	917	908	99.0
14 years	7,885	7,795	98.9	6,745	6,674	98.9	706	696	98.6	247	241	97.6	187	184	98.4
15 years	7,698	7,568	98.3	6,516	6,421	98.5	776	754	97.2	226	220	97.3	180	173	96.1
16 and 17 years	15,566	13,862	89.1	13,076	11,727	89.7	1,709	1,429	83.6	455	409	89.9	326	297	91.1
18 and 19 years	17,434	7,609	43.6	14,173	6,326	44.6	2,271	845	37.2	530	214	40.4	460	224	48.7
20 years	9,089	2,345	25.8	7,241	1,975	27.3	1,247	233	18.7	247	41	16.6	354	96	27.1
21 to 24 years	43,966	5,979	13.6	34,202	4,764	13.9	6,910	809	11.7	1,241	76	6.1	1,613	330	20.5
Female, 5 to 24 years	181,993	110,844	60.9	153,856	96,123	62.5	17,951	8,004	44.6	6,084	3,557	58.5	4,102	3,160	77.0
5 years	8,693	4,828	55.5	7,851	4,333	55.2	157	64	40.8	283	183	64.7	402	248	61.7
6 years	8,492	7,537	88.8	7,653	6,798	88.7	228	199	87.3	256	228	89.1	355	318	89.6
7 to 9 years	26,009	24,998	96.1	22,793	21,910	96.1	1,348	1,290	95.7	849	816	96.1	1,019	982	96.4
10 to 13 years	31,096	30,767	98.9	26,866	26,587	99.0	2,316	2,289	98.8	1,014	1,001	98.7	900	890	98.9
14 years	7,719	7,620	98.7	6,580	6,502	98.8	690	675	97.8	283	280	98.9	166	163	98.2
15 years	7,905	7,689	97.3	6,799	6,629	97.5	742	715	96.4	230	216	93.9	134	129	96.3
16 and 17 years	16,431	13,826	84.1	13,769	11,734	85.2	1,842	1,401	76.1	570	477	83.7	250	214	85.6
18 and 19 years	19,482	7,191	36.9	16,123	6,140	38.1	2,478	700	28.2	632	228	36.1	249	123	49.4
20 years	10,305	2,048	19.9	8,380	1,777	21.2	1,450	196	13.5	351	46	13.1	124	29	23.4
21 to 24 years	45,861	4,340	9.5	37,042	3,719	10.0	6,700	475	7.1	1,616	82	5.1	503	64	12.7

Table B-39.—PERSONS 25 YEARS OLD AND OVER, BY YEARS OF SCHOOL COMPLETED, RACE, AND SEX, FOR THE CITY OF LOS ANGELES: 1940

[Percent not shown where less than 0.1; median and percent not shown where base is less than 100]

YEARS OF SCHOOL COMPLETED	ALL CLASSES			NATIVE WHITE			FOREIGN-BORN WHITE			NEGRO			OTHER RACES		
	Total	Male	Female	Total	Male	Female	Total	Male	Female	Total	Male	Female	Total	Male	Female
Persons 25 years old and over	1,021,165	493,237	527,928	757,229	359,100	398,129	202,325	101,330	100,995	42,803	19,664	23,139	18,808	13,143	5,665
No school years completed	22,115	10,495	11,620	3,718	1,934	1,784	16,034	7,272	8,762	1,253	609	644	1,110	680	430
Grade school: 1 to 4 years	47,466	24,820	22,646	18,116	10,057	8,059	23,559	11,571	11,988	4,087	1,947	2,140	1,704	1,245	459
5 or 6 years	66,712	34,305	32,407	35,041	18,067	16,974	24,200	12,220	11,9[illegible]0	5,[illegible]26	2,626	2,900	1,945	1,392	553
7 or 8 years	265,375	131,719	133,656	185,495	91,402	94,093	63,691	31,611	32,080	11,[illegible]09	5,378	6,031	4,780	3,328	1,452
High school: 1 to 3 years	186,113	86,121	99,992	152,981	70,171	82,810	21,582	10,191	11,391	[illegible],826	3,778	5,048	2,724	1,981	743
4 years	255,666	108,806	146,860	210,844	87,357	123,487	33,234	15,563	17,671	7,194	3,085	4,109	4,394	2,801	1,593
College: 1 to 3 years	95,417	47,614	47,803	82,921	40,359	42,562	8,858	5,223	3,635	2,577	1,196	1,381	1,061	836	225
4 years or more	72,648	42,780	29,868	61,041	34,827	26,214	9,367	6,557	2,810	1,324	653	671	916	743	173
Not reported	9,653	6,577	3,076	7,072	4,926	2,146	1,800	1,122	678	607	392	215	174	137	37
Median school years completed	10.7	10.5	10.9	11.6	11.4	11.8	8.1	8.2	8.1	8.8	8.7	8.9	8.9	8.9	8.9
Percent less than 5 years completed	6.8	7.2	6.5	2.9	3.3	2.5	19.6	18.6	20.5	12.5	13.0	12.0	15.0	14.6	15.7
PERCENT DISTRIBUTION															
Persons 25 years old and over	100.0	100.0	100.0	100.0	100.0	100.0	100.0	100.0	100.0	100.0	100.0	100.0	100.0	100.0	100.0
No school years completed	2.2	2.1	2.2	0.5	0.5	0.4	7.9	7.2	8.7	2.9	3.1	2.8	5.9	5.2	7.6
Grade school: 1 to 4 years	4.6	5.0	4.3	2.4	2.8	2.0	11.6	11.4	11.9	9.5	9.9	9.2	9.1	9.5	8.1
5 or 6 years	6.5	7.0	6.1	4.6	5.0	4.3	12.0	12.1	11.9	12.9	13.4	12.5	10.3	10.6	9.8
7 or 8 years	26.0	26.7	25.3	24.5	25.5	23.6	31.5	31.2	31.8	26.7	27.3	26.1	25.4	25.3	25.6
High school: 1 to 3 years	18.2	17.5	18.9	20.2	19.5	20.8	10.7	10.1	11.3	20.6	19.2	21.8	14.5	15.1	13.1
4 years	25.0	22.1	27.8	27.8	24.3	31.0	16.4	15.4	17.5	16.8	15.7	17.8	23.4	21.3	28.1
College: 1 to 3 years	9.3	9.7	9.1	11.0	11.2	10.7	4.4	5.2	3.6	6.0	6.1	6.0	5.6	6.4	4.0
4 years or more	7.1	8.7	5.7	8.1	9.7	6.6	4.6	6.5	2.8	3.1	3.3	2.9	4.9	5.7	3.1
Not reported	0.9	1.3	0.6	0.9	1.4	0.5	0.9	1.1	0.7	1.4	2.0	0.9	0.9	1.0	0.7

Table B-40.—FOREIGN-BORN WHITE, BY COUNTRY OF BIRTH, BY SEX, FOR THE CITY OF LOS ANGELES: 1940 AND 1930

[Figures for white population in 1930 revised to include Mexicans classified with "Other races" in the 1930 reports. Percent not shown where less than 0.1 or where base is less than 100]

COUNTRY OF BIRTH	BOTH SEXES		PERCENT		MALE		FEMALE	
	1940	1930	1940	1930	1940	1930	1940	1930
All countries	215,248	232,874	100.0	100.0	107,478	120,975	107,770	111,899
England	19,713	22,258	9.2	9.6	9,478	11,073	10,235	11,185
Scotland	5,980	6,898	2.8	3.0	2,928	3,557	3,052	3,341
Wales	741	1,084	0.3	0.5	402	601	339	483
Northern Ireland	1,646	2,212	0.8	0.9	794	1,054	852	1,158
Irish Free State (Eire)	4,194	5,000	1.9	2.1	1,953	2,390	2,241	2,610
Norway	3,435	3,747	1.6	1.6	1,703	1,942	1,732	1,805
Sweden	7,844	8,917	3.6	3.8	3,799	4,479	4,045	4,438
Denmark	3,138	3,536	1.5	1.5	1,766	2,037	1,372	1,499
Netherlands	2,013	1,892	0.9	0.8	1,155	1,085	858	807
Belgium	816	796	0.4	0.3	394	402	422	394
Luxemburg	95	107	-	-	50	61	45	46
Switzerland	1,940	2,150	0.9	0.9	1,082	1,220	858	930
France	3,196	3,482	1.5	1.5	1,368	1,548	1,828	1,934
Germany	17,528	18,094	8.1	7.8	8,835	9,347	8,693	8,747
Poland	7,448	6,895	3.5	3.0	3,962	3,750	3,486	3,145
Czechoslovakia	1,536	1,872	0.7	0.8	793	980	743	892
Austria	5,389	3,885	2.5	1.7	2,743	2,136	2,646	1,749
Hungary	3,978	3,055	1.8	1.3	1,917	1,593	2,061	1,462
Yugoslavia	3,441	3,290	1.6	1.4	2,179	2,149	1,262	1,141
Russia (U. S. S. R.)	25,595	19,744	11.9	8.5	12,955	10,243	12,640	9,501
Lithuania	1,158	952	0.5	0.4	634	569	524	383
Latvia	527	452	0.2	0.2	283	267	244	185
Finland	1,049	1,011	0,5	0.4	501	525	548	486
Rumania	2,750	2,481	1.3	1.1	1,418	1,300	1,332	1,181
Bulgaria	221	127	0.1	0.1	154	94	67	33
Turkey in Europe	17	65	-	-	5	39	12	26
Greece	1,905	1,848	0.9	0.8	1,526	1,533	379	315
Italy	13,256	12,685	6.2	5.4	7,955	7,746	5,301	4,939
Spain	1,154	1,421	0.5	0.6	711	888	443	533
Portugal	197	217	0.1	0.1	114	138	83	79
Other Europe	253	280	0.1	0.1	148	174	105	106
Palestine and Syria	1,066	872	0.5	0.4	597	514	469	358
Turkey in Asia	1,931	1,350	0.9	0.6	1,079	790	852	560
Other Asia	1,685	2,238	0.8	1.0	957	1,260	728	978
Canada—French	2,159	2,439	1.0	1.0	998	1,211	1,161	1,228
Canada—Other	25,596	28,305	11.9	12.2	11,177	12,949	14,419	15,356
Newfoundland	141	163	0.1	0.1	65	80	76	83
Mexico	36,840	53,573	17.1	23.0	17,129	27,374	19,711	26,199
Cuba and other West Indies	436	426	0.2	0.2	196	218	240	208
Central and South America	1,450	1,243	0.7	0.5	706	703	744	540
Australia	849	931	0.4	0.4	387	475	462	456
Azores	31	56	-	-	16	38	15	18
All other and not reported	911	825	0.4	0.4	466	443	445	382

Table B-41.—PERSONS 14 YEARS OLD AND OVER, BY EMPLOYMENT STATUS, CLASS OF WORKER, RACE, AND SEX, FOR THE CITY OF LOS ANGELES: 1940

[Percent not shown where less than 0.1 or where base is less than 100]

EMPLOYMENT STATUS	ALL CLASSES			NATIVE WHITE			FOREIGN-BORN WHITE			NEGRO			OTHER RACES		
	Total	Male	Female	Total	Male	Female	Total	Male	Female	Total	Male	Female	Total	Male	Female
Total population (all ages)	1,504,277	734,135	770,142	1,191,182	575,597	615,585	215,248	107,478	107,770	63,774	29,906	33,868	34,073	21,154	12,919
Persons 14 years old and over	1,269,299	615,298	654,001	975,388	466,469	508,919	213,727	106,727	107,000	53,165	24,625	28,540	27,019	17,477	9,542
In labor force	686,756	480,184	206,572	526,558	363,116	163,442	110,571	83,659	26,912	32,260	19,460	12,800	17,367	13,949	3,418
Not in labor force	582,543	135,114	447,429	448,830	103,353	345,477	103,156	23,068	80,088	20,905	5,165	15,740	9,652	3,528	6,124
Engaged in own home housew'k	334,979	2,693	332,286	255,529	1,973	253,556	65,245	570	64,675	10,314	109	10,205	3,891	41	3,850
In school	98,521	50,794	47,727	87,060	44,708	42,352	3,441	1,844	1,597	3,884	1,963	1,921	4,136	2,279	1,857
Unable to work	72,946	38,406	34,540	49,029	25,391	23,638	19,004	10,760	8,244	4,186	1,688	2,498	727	567	160
In institutions	6,771	5,027	1,744	5,156	3,842	1,314	1,030	685	345	440	379	61	145	121	24
Other and not reported	69,326	38,194	31,132	52,056	27,439	24,617	14,436	9,209	5,227	2,081	1,026	1,055	753	520	233
LABOR FORCE BY EMPLOYMENT STATUS															
In labor force	686,756	480,184	206,572	526,558	363,116	163,442	110,571	83,659	26,912	32,260	19,460	12,800	17,367	13,949	3,418
Employed (exc. public emerg. work)	586,897	407,425	179,472	451,564	309,374	142,190	95,589	71,437	24,152	23,678	13,800	9,878	16,066	12,814	3,252
At work	568,702	394,677	174,025	438,513	300,525	137,988	91,957	68,658	23,299	23,240	13,515	9,725	14,992	11,979	3,013
With a job	18,195	12,748	5,447	13,051	8,849	4,202	3,632	2,779	853	438	285	153	1,074	835	239
On public emerg. work (WPA, etc.)	13,551	14,402	4,149	14,009	10,736	3,273	1,717	1,490	227	2,733	2,093	640	92	83	9
Seeking work	81,308	58,357	22,951	60,985	43,006	17,979	13,265	10,732	2,533	5,849	3,567	2,282	1,209	1,052	157
Experienced workers	75,035	55,187	19,848	55,626	40,334	15,292	12,896	10,559	2,337	5,381	3,287	2,094	1,132	1,007	125
New workers	6,273	3,170	3,103	5,359	2,672	2,687	369	173	196	468	280	188	77	45	32
PERCENT BY SEX															
In labor force	100.0	69.9	30.1	100.0	69.0	31.0	100.0	75.7	24.3	100.0	60.3	39.7	100.0	80.3	19.7
Employed (exc. public emerg.)	100.0	69.4	30.6	100.0	68.5	31.5	100.0	74.7	25.3	100.0	58.3	41.7	100.0	79.8	20.2
On pub. emerg. work (WPA, etc.)	100.0	77.6	22.4	100.0	76.6	23.4	100.0	86.8	13.2	100.0	76.6	23.4	-	-	-
Seeking work	100.0	71.8	28.2	100.0	70.5	29.5	100.0	80.9	19.1	100.0	61.0	39.0	100.0	87.0	13.0
Not in labor force	100.0	23.2	76.8	100.0	23.0	77.0	100.0	22.4	77.6	100.0	24.7	75.3	100.0	36.6	63.4
Engaged in own home housew'k	100.0	0.8	99.2	100.0	0.8	99.2	100.0	0.9	99.1	100.0	1.1	98.9	100.0	1.1	98.9
In school	100.0	51.6	48.4	100.0	51.4	48.6	100.0	53.6	46.4	100.0	50.5	49.5	100.0	55.1	44.9
Unable to work	100.0	52.6	47.4	100.0	51.8	48.2	100.0	56.6	43.4	100.0	40.3	59.7	100.0	78.0	22.0
In institutions	100.0	74.2	25.8	100.0	74.5	25.5	100.0	66.5	33.5	100.0	86.1	13.9	100.0	83.4	16.6
Other and not reported	100.0	55.1	44.9	100.0	52.7	47.3	100.0	63.8	36.2	100.0	49.3	50.7	100.0	69.1	30.9
EMPLOYED WORKERS BY CLASS OF WORKER															
Employed (exc. public emerg.)	586,897	407,425	179,472	451,564	309,374	142,190	95,589	71,437	24,152	23,678	13,800	9,878	16,066	12,814	3,252
Wage and salary workers	487,137	330,701	156,436	384,247	258,570	125,677	70,515	50,959	19,556	21,396	12,308	9,088	10,979	8,864	2,115
Employers and own-account workers	91,603	74,408	17,195	61,953	49,128	12,825	23,423	20,189	3,234	2,102	1,433	669	4,125	3,658	467
Unpaid family workers	6,017	1,056	4,961	3,680	670	3,010	1,335	106	1,229	91	22	69	911	258	653
Class of worker not reported	2,140	1,260	880	1,684	1,006	678	316	183	133	89	37	52	51	34	17
At work	568,702	394,677	174,025	438,513	300,525	137,988	91,957	68,658	23,299	23,240	13,515	9,725	14,992	11,979	3,013
Wage and salary workers	475,925	323,303	152,622	375,818	253,135	122,683	68,736	49,712	19,024	21,136	12,147	8,989	10,235	8,309	1,926
Employers and own-account workers	85,184	69,307	15,877	57,732	45,900	11,832	21,682	18,691	2,991	1,940	1,318	622	3,830	3,398	432
Unpaid family workers	5,789	1,011	4,778	3,541	642	2,899	1,274	102	1,172	85	19	66	889	248	641
Class of worker not reported	1,804	1,056	748	1,422	848	574	265	153	112	79	31	48	38	24	14
With a job	18,195	12,748	5,447	13,051	8,849	4,202	3,632	2,779	853	438	285	153	1,074	835	239
Wage and salary workers	11,212	7,398	3,814	8,429	5,435	2,994	1,779	1,247	532	260	161	99	744	555	189
Employers and own-account workers	6,419	5,101	1,318	4,221	3,228	993	1,741	1,498	243	162	115	47	295	260	35
Unpaid family workers	228	45	183	139	28	111	61	4	57	6	3	3	22	10	12
Class of worker not reported	336	204	132	262	158	104	51	30	21	10	6	4	13	10	3
PERCENT DISTRIBUTION															
Persons 14 years old and over	100.0	100.0	100.0	100.0	100.0	100.0	100.0	100.0	100.0	100.0	100.0	100.0	100.0	100.0	100.0
In labor force	54.1	78.0	31.6	54.0	77.8	32.1	51.7	78.4	25.2	60.7	79.0	44.8	64.3	79.8	35.8
Not in labor force	45.9	22.0	68.4	46.0	22.2	67.9	48.3	21.6	74.8	39.3	21.0	55.2	35.7	20.2	64.2
Engaged in own home housew'k	26.4	0.4	50.8	26.2	0.4	49.8	30.5	0.5	60.4	19.4	0.4	35.8	14.4	0.2	40.3
In school	7.8	8.3	7.3	8.9	9.6	8.3	1.6	1.7	1.5	7.3	8.0	6.7	15.3	13.0	19.5
Unable to work	5.7	6.2	5.3	5.0	5.4	4.6	8.9	10.1	7.7	7.9	6.9	8.8	2.7	3.2	1.7
In institutions	0.5	0.8	0.3	0.5	0.8	0.3	0.5	0.6	0.3	0.8	1.5	0.2	0.5	0.7	0.3
Other and not reported	5.5	6.2	4.8	5.3	5.9	4.8	6.8	8.6	4.9	3.9	4.2	3.7	2.8	3.0	2.4
LABOR FORCE BY EMPLOYMENT STATUS															
In labor force	100.0	100.0	100.0	100.0	100.0	100.0	100.0	100.0	100.0	100.0	100.0	100.0	100.0	100.0	100.0
Employed (exc. public emerg. work)	85.5	84.8	86.9	85.8	85.2	87.0	86.5	85.4	89.7	73.4	70.9	77.2	92.5	91.9	95.1
At work	82.8	82.2	84.2	83.3	82.8	84.4	83.2	82.1	86.6	72.0	69.5	76.0	86.3	85.9	88.2
With a job	2.6	2.7	2.6	2.5	2.4	2.6	3.3	3.3	3.2	1.4	1.5	1.2	6.2	6.0	7.0
On public emerg. work (WPA, etc.)	2.7	3.0	2.0	2.7	3.0	2.0	1.6	1.8	0.8	8.5	10.8	5.0	0.5	0.6	0.3
Seeking work	11.8	12.2	11.1	11.6	11.8	11.0	12.0	12.8	9.4	18.1	18.3	17.8	7.0	7.5	4.6
Experienced workers	10.9	11.5	9.6	10.6	11.1	9.4	11.7	12.6	8.7	16.7	16.9	16.4	6.5	7.2	3.7
New workers	0.9	0.7	1.5	1.0	0.7	1.6	0.3	0.2	0.7	1.5	1.4	1.5	0.4	0.3	0.9
EMPLOYED WORKERS BY CLASS OF WORKER															
Employed (exc. public emerg.)	100.0	100.0	100.0	100.0	100.0	100.0	100.0	100.0	100.0	100.0	100.0	100.0	100.0	100.0	100.0
Wage and salary workers	83.0	81.2	87.2	85.1	83.6	88.4	73.8	71.3	81.0	90.4	89.2	92.0	68.3	69.2	65.0
Employers and own-account workers	15.6	18.3	9.6	13.7	15.9	9.0	24.5	28.3	13.4	8.9	10.4	6.8	25.7	28.5	14.4
Unpaid family workers	1.0	0.3	2.8	0.8	0.2	2.1	1.4	0.1	5.1	0.4	0.2	0.7	5.7	2.0	20.1
Class of worker not reported	0.4	0.3	0.5	0.4	0.3	0.5	0.3	0.3	0.6	0.4	0.3	0.5	0.3	0.3	0.5
At work	100.0	100.0	100.0	100.0	100.0	100.0	100.0	100.0	100.0	100.0	100.0	100.0	100.0	100.0	100.0
Wage and salary workers	83.7	81.9	87.7	85.7	84.2	88.9	74.7	72.4	81.7	90.9	89.9	92.4	68.3	69.4	63.9
Employers and own-account workers	15.0	17.6	9.1	13.2	15.3	8.6	23.6	27.2	12.8	8.3	9.8	6.4	25.5	28.4	14.3
Unpaid family workers	1.0	0.3	2.7	0.8	0.2	2.1	1.4	0.1	5.0	0.4	0.1	0.7	5.9	2.1	21.3
Class of worker not reported	0.3	0.3	0.4	0.3	0.3	0.4	0.3	0.2	0.5	0.3	0.2	0.5	0.3	0.2	0.5
With a job	100.0	100.0	100.0	100.0	100.0	100.0	100.0	100.0	100.0	100.0	100.0	100.0	100.0	100.0	.0.0
Wage and salary workers	61.6	58.0	70.0	64.6	61.4	71.3	49.0	44.9	62.4	59.4	56.5	64.7	69.3	66.5	79.1
Employers and own-account workers	35.3	40.0	24.2	32.3	36.5	23.6	47.9	53.9	28.5	37.0	40.4	30.7	27.5	31.1	14.6
Unpaid family workers	1.3	0.4	3.4	1.1	0.8	2.6	1.7	0.1	6.7	1.4	1.1	2.0	2.0	1.2	5.0
Class of worker not reported	1.8	1.6	2.4	2.0	1.8	2.5	1.4	1.1	2.5	2.3	2.1	2.6	1.2	1.2	1.3

Table B-42.—EMPLOYED WORKERS 14 YEARS OLD AND OVER, BY MAJOR OCCUPATION GROUP, INDUSTRY GROUP, AND SEX, FOR THE CITY OF LOS ANGELES: 1940

[Percent not shown where less than 0.1 or where base is less than 100]

MAJOR OCCUPATION GROUP AND INDUSTRY GROUP	Total	Male	Female	PERCENT BY OCCUPATION AND INDUSTRY			PERCENT BY SEX	
				Total	Male	Female	Male	Female
Total population (all ages)	1,504,277	734,135	770,142	-	-	-	48.8	51.2
All persons 14 years old and over	1,269,299	615,298	654,001	-	-	-	48.5	51.5
In labor force	686,755	480,184	206,572	100.0	100.0	100.0	69.9	30.1
Employed workers (except on public emergency work)	586,897	407,425	179,472	85.5	84.8	86.9	69.4	30.6
MAJOR OCCUPATION GROUP								
Employed (except on public emergency work)	586,897	407,425	179,472	100.0	100.0	100.0	69.4	30.6
Professional workers	53,010	31,166	21,844	9.0	7.6	12.2	58.8	41.2
Semiprofessional workers	13,006	9,772	3,234	2.2	2.4	1.8	75.1	24.9
Farmers and farm managers	2,275	2,073	202	0.4	0.5	0.1	91.1	8.9
Proprietors, managers, and officials, except farm	69,492	57,056	12,436	11.8	14.0	6.9	82.1	17.9
Clerical, sales, and kindred workers	150,452	86,096	64,356	25.6	21.1	35.9	57.2	42.8
Craftsmen, foremen, and kindred workers	75,806	73,761	2,045	12.9	18.1	1.1	97.3	2.7
Operatives and kindred workers	93,619	68,554	25,065	16.0	16.8	14.0	73.2	26.8
Domestic service workers	24,552	2,416	22,136	4.2	0.6	12.3	9.8	90.2
Service workers, except domestic	68,260	42,254	26,006	11.6	10.4	14.5	61.9	38.1
Farm laborers (wage workers) and farm foremen	3,392	3,231	161	0.6	0.8	0.1	95.3	4.7
Farm laborers, unpaid family workers	382	163	219	0.1	-	0.1	42.7	57.3
Laborers, except farm	29,307	28,672	635	5.0	7.0	0.4	97.8	2.2
Occupation not reported	3,344	2,211	1,133	0.6	0.5	0.6	66.1	33.9
INDUSTRY GROUP								
Employed (except on public emergency work)	586,897	407,425	179,472	100.0	100.0	100.0	69.4	30.6
Agriculture, forestry, and fishery	11,564	10,821	743	2.0	2.7	0.4	93.6	6.4
Agriculture	9,534	8,822	712	1.6	2.2	0.4	92.5	7.5
Forestry (except logging) and fishery	2,030	1,999	31	0.3	0.5	-	98.5	1.5
Mining	2,920	2,645	275	0.5	0.6	0.2	90.6	9.4
Coal mining	23	23	-	-	-	-	-	-
Crude petroleum and natural gas production	1,933	1,696	237	0.3	0.4	0.1	87.7	12.3
Other mines and quarries	964	926	38	0.2	0.2	-	96.1	3.9
Construction	33,719	32,899	820	5.7	8.1	0.5	97.6	2.4
Manufacturing	106,614	82,671	23,943	18.2	20.3	13.3	77.5	22.5
Food and kindred products	15,589	11,708	3,881	2.7	2.9	2.2	75.1	24.9
Textile-mill products	2,355	1,286	1,069	0.4	0.3	0.6	54.6	45.4
Apparel and other fabricated textile products	13,434	3,994	9,440	2.3	1.0	5.3	29.7	70.3
Logging	28	27	1	-	-	-	-	-
Sawmills and planing mills	1,039	981	58	0.2	0.2	-	94.4	5.6
Furniture, store fixtures, and miscellaneous wooden goods	6,370	5,737	633	1.1	1.4	0.4	90.1	9.9
Paper and allied products	1,990	1,460	530	0.3	0.4	0.3	73.4	26.6
Printing, publishing, and allied industries	11,537	9,385	2,152	2.0	2.3	1.2	81.3	18.7
Chemicals and allied products	3,681	2,828	853	0.6	0.7	0.5	76.8	23.2
Petroleum and coal products	3,454	2,860	594	0.6	0.7	0.3	82.8	17.2
Leather and leather products	1,313	891	422	0.2	0.2	0.2	67.9	32.1
Stone, clay, and glass products	2,967	2,553	414	0.5	0.6	0.2	86.0	14.0
Iron and steel and their products	7,171	6,707	464	1.2	1.6	0.3	93.5	6.5
Nonferrous metals and their products	2,818	2,593	225	0.5	0.6	0.1	92.0	8.0
Machinery	8,745	7,894	851	1.5	1.9	0.5	90.3	9.7
Automobiles and automobile equipment	3,016	2,790	226	0.5	0.7	0.1	92.5	7.5
Transportation equipment, except automobile	14,123	13,572	551	2.4	3.3	0.3	96.1	3.9
Other and not specified manufacturing industries	6,984	5,405	1,579	1.2	1.3	0.9	77.4	22.6
Transportation, communication, and other public utilities	44,463	37,882	6,581	7.6	9.3	3.7	85.2	14.8
Railroads (including railroad repair shops) and railway express service	9,068	8,728	340	1.5	2.1	0.2	96.3	3.7
Trucking service	4,704	4,500	204	0.8	1.1	0.1	95.7	4.3
Other transportation	12,419	11,765	654	2.1	2.9	0.4	94.7	5.3
Communication	8,249	3,970	4,279	1.4	1.0	2.4	48.1	51.9
Utilities	10,023	8,919	1,104	1.7	2.2	0.6	89.0	11.0
Wholesale and retail trade	149,108	104,191	44,917	25.4	25.6	25.0	69.9	30.1
Wholesale trade	27,808	22,233	5,575	4.7	5.5	3.1	80.0	20.0
Food and dairy products stores, and milk retailing	22,758	18,257	4,501	3.9	4.5	2.5	80.2	19.8
Eating and drinking places	27,308	16,185	11,123	4.7	4.0	6.2	59.3	40.7
Motor vehicles and accessories retailing, and filling stations	14,302	13,355	947	2.4	3.3	0.5	93.4	6.6
Other retail trade	56,932	34,161	22,771	9.7	8.4	12.7	60.0	40.0
Finance, insurance, and real estate	37,473	23,301	14,172	6.4	5.7	7.9	62.2	37.8
Business and repair services	18,645	16,353	2,292	3.2	4.0	1.3	87.7	12.3
Automobile storage, rental, and repair services	8,668	8,477	191	1.5	2.1	0.1	97.8	2.2
Business and repair services, except automobile	9,977	7,876	2,101	1.7	1.9	1.2	78.9	21.1
Personal services	66,186	23,607	42,579	11.3	5.8	23.7	35.7	64.3
Domestic service	30,857	6,235	24,622	5.3	1.5	13.7	20.2	79.8
Hotels and lodging places	11,271	5,578	5,693	1.9	1.4	3.2	49.5	50.5
Laundering, cleaning, and dyeing services	10,487	5,652	4,835	1.8	1.4	2.7	53.9	46.1
Miscellaneous personal services	13,571	6,142	7,429	2.3	1.5	4.1	45.3	54.7
Amusement, recreation, and related services	30,714	24,238	6,476	5.2	5.9	3.6	78.9	21.1
Professional and related services	52,878	24,687	28,191	9.0	6.1	15.7	46.7	53.3
Government	26,502	20,443	6,059	4.5	5.0	3.4	77.1	22.9
Industry not reported	6,111	3,687	2,424	1.0	0.9	1.4	60.3	39.7

Table B-43.—PERSONS 14 YEARS OLD AND OVER IN THE LABOR FORCE, 1940, AND GAINFUL WORKERS 14 YEARS OLD AND OVER, 1930, BY RACE AND SEX, FOR THE CITY OF LOS ANGELES

[Totals for population and gainful workers for 1930 include "Unknown age." Figures for white population in 1930 have been revised to include Mexicans who were classified with "Other races" in the 1930 reports. Percent not shown where less than 0.1 or where base is less than 100]

CENSUS YEAR AND RACE	TOTAL					MALE					FEMALE				
	Population		Persons in the labor force, and gainful workers,[1] 14 years old and over			Population		Persons in the labor force, and gainful workers,[1] 14 years old and over			Population		Persons in the labor force, and gainful workers,[1] 14 years old and over		
	Total (all ages)	14 years old and over	Number	Per-cent of total popu-lation	Per-cent of popu-lation 14 yrs. and over	Total (all ages)	14 years old and over	Number	Per-cent of total popu-lation	Per-cent of popu-lation 14 yrs. and over	Total (all ages)	14 years old and over	Number	Per-cent of total popu-lation	Per-cent of popu-lation 14 yrs. and over
1940	1,504,277	1,269,299	686,756	45.7	54.1	734,135	615,298	480,184	65.4	78.0	770,142	654,001	206,572	26.8	31.6
White	1,406,430	1,189,115	637,129	45.3	53.6	683,075	573,196	446,775	65.4	77.9	723,355	615,919	190,354	26.3	30.9
Negro	63,774	53,165	32,260	50.6	60.7	29,906	24,625	19,460	65.1	79.0	33,868	28,540	12,800	37.8	44.8
Other races	34,073	27,019	17,367	51.0	64.3	21,154	17,477	13,949	65.9	79.8	12,919	9,542	3,418	26.5	35.8
1930	1,238,048	1,010,650	580,409	46.9	57.4	610,678	496,163	417,067	68.3	84.1	627,370	514,487	163,342	26.0	31.7
White	1,170,700	958,887	544,967	46.6	56.8	573,877	467,255	391,524	68.2	83.8	596,823	491,632	153,443	25.7	31.2
Negro	38,894	31,676	21,350	54.9	67.4	18,349	14,748	12,900	70.3	87.5	20,545	16,928	8,450	41.1	49.9
Other races	28,454	20,087	14,092	49.5	70.2	18,452	14,160	12,643	68.5	89.3	10,002	5,927	1,449	14.5	24.4

[1] Data for 1930 represent gainful workers 14 years old and over.

> Visit the barrios of Los Angeles and you will see endless streets crowded with the shacks of the illiterate, diseased, pauperized Mexicans, taking no interest whatever in the community, living constantly on the ragged edge of starvation, bringing countless numbers of American citizens into the world with the reckless prodigality of rabbits.
>
> —Kenneth L. Roberts, *The Saturday Evening Post*

> Never again is there to be an unlimited influx of cheap alien labor; a numerical limitation of labor is here to stay, and there must be careful selection of our immigrants within the fixed limits...On the whole, immigrants from northwestern Europe furnish us the best material for American citizenship and the future of the building of the American race. They have higher living standards than the bulk of the immigrants from other lands; average higher intelligence, are better educated, more skilled, and are, on the whole, better to understand, appreciate and support our form of government...If our future population is to be prevented from deteriorating, physically and mentally, higher physical standards must be required of all immigrants. In addition, no alien should be admitted who has not an intellectual capacity superior to the American average...Further, aliens whose family history indicates that they come of unsound stock should be debarred.
>
> —Irving Fisher, professor at Yale university and chairman of the Eugenics Committee, in a statement to the Committee on Selective Immigration of the United States, January 6, 1924

Mexican Immigration Timeline

1900–1909: Mexican immigration increased dramatically; thousands of Mexicans were recruited to work on American railroads and farms.

1910–1917: Thousands fled to the United States to escape violence brought on by the Mexican Revolution; immigrants included wealthy businessmen, poor farmers, soldiers and political refugees.

1914: World War I erupted in Europe; Mexico was accused of collaborating with Germany.

1916: In a raid led by Pancho Villa across the U.S. border, U.S. citizens were killed in Columbus, New Mexico.

1917: The Mexican Revolution ended; Los Angeles officials, aroused by a growing anti-Mexican sentiment, sought to deport Mexican immigrants.

1918: Faced with labor shortages caused by America's entrance into WWI, labor leaders persuaded the federal government to drop the $8.00 tax and literacy test required of Mexican immigrants; Mexicans and Mexican-Americans comprised the largest group of agricultural workers in Imperial Valley, California.

1919: More than 650,000 Mexican-Americans lived in the American Southwest.

1920–1929: A strong U.S. economy attracted nearly a half million Mexicans to migrate for work.

1924: The United States established the border patrol to stop illegal immigration from Mexico-with little success.

1925: Chicago's Mexican population topped 20,000, the largest clustering of Hispanic Americans outside the Southwest.

1929–1932: The Great Depression caused factories to close and wages to fall; one third of all U.S. workers were unemployed.

1931: President Herbert Hoover initiated a plan to repatriate Mexicans; illegal immigrants, legal immigrants without papers and U.S. citizens of Mexican descent were all swept up in the massive effort to free up jobs for "real Americans."

> We left with just one trunk full of belongings. No furniture. A few metal cooking utensils. A small ceramic pitcher, because it reminded me of my mother...and very little clothing. We took blankets, only the very essentials.
>
> —Emilia Castaneda, deported in 1935

> The ideal farm worker is "a class of people who have not the ability to rise, who have not the initiative, who are children, who do not want to own land, who can be directed by men in the upper stratum of society.
>
> —Texas Congressman John C. Box during a House Immigration Committee meeting on Mexican Immigration

African American Couple Emigrate from Rural South to Urban North

The building of a black middle class played a critical role in the opportunities available to African Americans in the 1940 era, evidenced by this African American couple. After migrating to Harlem, New York from the deep South, they are building a future together thanks to the regularity of the railroad paycheck.

Life at Home

- Sam and Edna Whitley, like thousands of other Southern Blacks, moved to Harlem, New York from rural South Carolina to escape the poverty of the sharecropper system.
- Sam found work as a Pullman Porter and Edna worked as a domestic, when employment is available; they had no children.
- Living as sharecroppers in South Carolina, they lost hope of ever being free from constant debt to buy their own land.
- When the Whitleys first arrived in New York, they refused government relief; Sam had too much pride to consider taking charity from the government.
- They were each 18 when they married eight years ago.
- Sam had little formal education though his mother taught him the rudiments of reading and writing using the family Bible.
- He dropped out of school in the third grade to support his mother; he does not remember ever meeting his father.
- Edna was a preacher's daughter; she could both read and write.
- She left school after the sixth grade, when she was forced to work in the cotton fields full-time.
- The couple wanted children, but were uncertain about their jobs.
- They lived in a three-room tenement house that included one bedroom, high ceilings and faulty plumbing and wiring, and no refrigerator.
- Their landlord was unresponsive, but the Whitleys could not find a better living situation because the demand for housing in Harlem was so great.
- Sam and Edna decided to improve the looks of their home a bit by buying a new bedspread from Montgomery Ward for $1.94.

Sam Whitley worked as a Pullman Porter on the railroad.

Life at Work: The Pullman Company

- Sam worked as a Pullman Porter, serving the first class passengers who travelled with a sleeper.
- He often made the long trip from New York to Miami working up to 18 hours at a stretch.
- When he got the job, Sam went through a short training program, then worked for six months on probation before being hired.
- He was taught to be courteous, efficient, and to do whatever it took to make their first class travelers comfortable.
- Sam also made up berths, kept the cars in order, handled luggage, and saw that the washrooms were clean and adequately supplied with towels.
- In addition to coping with the long hours of being on call—to meet every whim of the passenger—Sam was often subjected to the abuse of passengers with very little recourse.
- Sam had seen other Pullman Porters fired for slight infractions, including drinking on the job—even when the porter in question didn't drink.
- He eventually had enough experience to bid for a "port-in-charge" position, but did not have the reading and writing skills to complete the paperwork and keep appropriate records.
- Sam worried about rumors that the declining first class traffic will reduce the number of weeks he could work.
- A large percentage of Sam's income was from customers' tips, and his base salary was not adequate.
- Sam knew that for the Pullman Company saw African Americans as perfect employees for its sleeping cars, first because of their skills as former slaves and second because they were happy with much less money than their White counterparts.
- Many Americans still preserved their antebellum attitudes toward the former slaves, and gave Pullman a ready market for their services; even the common man, for the price of a Pullman ticket, was waited upon in all the comfort of a Southern gentleman.

Life in the Community: Harlem, New York

- Harlem was known as a slum, and real estate was dominated by Whites, so even though people in Harlem paid higher rent, very few repairs were made.
- Rent parties were a common sight among residents of Harlem. As the name suggests, they were primarily used to raise enough money to pay the rent. The typical entrance fee was $0.25, and inside one finds live music and the opportunity to buy refreshments (including liquor much of the time), dance, etc.
- Bandleader Count Basie was creating a revolution in jazz; the Basie piano style de-emphasizes the left hand while promoting the use of the high-hat cymbal and the relaxed style of the saxophone.
- The density of people in Harlem was 336 per acre, while the density of people in Manhattan was 223 per acre; many Black families take in borders to supplement their incomes.
- The Afro-American Realty Company told clients that it doesn't matter how many people lived in the house as long as the rent was paid up.
- Unemployment was 20.3 percent.
- As jobs grew scarce and African-American migration increased, many workers in Harlem were grossly over-qualified for the positions they held; a doctor of medicine might be a janitor in a hospital or a man with a master's in business might work in a factory with no hope of ever being promoted to management.
- The passage of the National Labor Relations Act, also known as the Wagner Act, established a mandate for industry to bargain with unions—the first time in American history the national government had placed its weight behind the principle of unionism.
- Harlem was in an uproar over the riots, started when a young African-American boy was caught stealing and word spread that the boy had been beaten and killed by the shop owner; the Young Liberators and the Young Communist League fanned the flames of the riot with fliers that alleged brutality.
- Following the riots, New York Mayor La Guardia created a committee to investigate conditions in Harlem that led to the riot, including housing, playgrounds, discrimination in employment, education, and relief agencies.
- A nationwide government study of working class families showed some improvement in living conditions.
- Basic food needs were met more fully, milk consumption had increased, housing was more comfortable, with plumbing and electricity the norm rather than the exception.
- In addition, radios were commonplace, most working class homes switch from cooking with coal or wood to gas and use of machines was common.

The nine tables that follow are reprinted from the actual 1940 census, for the city of New York City. They include actual data on race, percentage of voting population, school attendance, number of school years completed, foreign born, and employment of workers 14 years and older by job, industry and race. In addition to being incredibly fascinating, these facts help to strengthen and visualize the actual environment in which Sam and Edna Whitley lived and worked.

Table C-35.—AGE, BY RACE AND SEX, FOR THE CITY OF NEW YORK: 1940 AND 1930

[Figures for white population in 1930 revised to include Mexicans classified with "Other races" in the 1930 reports. Percent not shown where less than 0.1 or where base is less than 100]

AGE AND CENSUS YEAR	ALL CLASSES			NATIVE WHITE			FOREIGN-BORN WHITE			NEGRO			OTHER RACES		
	Total	Male	Female	Total	Male	Female	Total	Male	Female	Total	Male	Female	Total	Male	Female
All ages: 1940	7,454,995	3,676,293	3,778,702	4,897,481	2,397,164	2,500,317	2,080,020	1,057,839	1,022,181	458,444	205,727	252,717	19,050	15,563	3,487
Under 5 years	433,894	221,415	212,479	400,656	204,900	195,756	2,583	1,310	1,273	29,691	14,706	14,985	964	499	465
5 to 9 years	470,556	238,798	231,758	430,383	218,849	211,534	6,101	3,038	3,063	33,134	16,442	16,692	938	469	469
10 to 14 years	561,108	283,453	277,655	510,778	258,847	251,931	13,642	6,832	6,810	35,848	17,294	18,554	840	480	360
15 to 19 years	606,942	300,717	306,225	536,926	267,425	269,501	34,486	17,163	17,323	34,678	15,574	19,104	852	555	297
20 to 24 years	649,153	304,862	344,291	566,019	270,434	295,585	41,165	18,615	22,550	41,099	15,251	25,848	870	562	308
25 to 29 years	697,153	322,558	374,595	547,673	259,948	287,725	96,917	41,380	55,537	50,978	20,008	30,970	1,585	1,222	363
30 to 34 years	691,027	331,782	359,245	464,272	226,078	238,194	173,415	81,972	91,443	51,180	21,924	29,256	2,160	1,808	352
35 to 39 years	669,421	330,950	338,471	362,781	178,358	184,423	251,438	126,448	124,990	52,186	23,418	28,768	3,016	2,726	290
40 to 44 years	628,714	317,471	311,243	302,549	149,293	153,256	281,569	145,301	136,268	41,789	20,299	21,490	2,807	2,578	229
45 to 49 years	550,743	282,769	267,974	233,673	115,648	118,025	284,754	150,517	134,237	30,381	14,802	15,579	1,935	1,802	133
50 to 54 years	467,020	243,321	223,699	173,898	84,449	89,449	270,272	147,338	122,934	21,468	10,251	11,217	1,382	1,283	99
55 to 59 years	346,871	178,162	168,709	120,929	57,354	63,575	210,936	113,428	97,508	14,251	6,675	7,576	755	705	50
60 to 64 years	267,974	132,668	135,306	95,411	43,605	51,806	162,750	84,260	78,490	9,285	4,311	4,974	528	492	36
65 to 69 years	190,439	89,275	101,164	69,641	29,909	39,732	114,028	56,461	57,567	6,521	2,676	3,845	249	229	20
70 to 74 years	120,675	54,474	66,201	43,812	17,959	25,853	73,558	35,194	38,364	3,197	1,219	1,978	108	102	6
75 years and over	103,305	43,618	59,687	38,080	14,108	23,972	62,406	28,582	33,824	2,758	877	1,881	61	51	10
Under 1 year	81,889	41,795	40,094	76,006	38,897	37,109	123	57	66	5,576	2,748	2,828	184	93	91
5 years	88,368	44,847	43,521	80,891	41,165	39,726	980	474	506	6,323	3,120	3,203	174	88	86
14 years	113,310	56,949	56,361	102,350	51,621	50,729	3,732	1,851	1,881	7,065	3,376	3,689	163	101	62
15 years	114,889	57,734	57,155	103,876	52,455	51,421	3,936	1,935	2,001	6,910	3,234	3,676	167	110	57
16 and 17 years	238,386	118,975	119,411	212,614	106,441	106,173	11,953	6,056	5,897	13,474	6,261	7,213	345	217	128
21 years and over	5,254,633	2,570,647	2,683,986	2,908,645	1,393,545	1,515,100	2,013,349	1,024,793	988,556	317,355	138,864	178,491	15,284	13,445	1,839
All ages: 1930	6,930,446	3,472,956	3,457,490	4,294,196	2,123,577	2,170,619	2,295,181	1,180,947	1,114,234	327,706	156,968	170,738	13,363	11,464	1,899
Under 5 years	535,600	272,438	263,162	502,444	255,839	246,605	5,573	2,817	2,756	26,920	13,431	13,489	663	351	312
5 to 9 years	577,284	291,782	285,502	530,497	268,571	261,926	21,884	11,051	10,833	24,365	11,894	12,471	538	266	272
10 to 14 years	575,300	290,263	285,037	531,036	268,341	262,695	25,309	12,780	12,529	18,662	8,987	9,675	293	155	138
15 to 19 years	599,286	293,740	305,546	510,342	252,903	257,439	67,431	31,397	36,034	21,120	9,169	11,951	393	271	122
20 to 24 years	687,417	327,734	359,683	485,070	235,085	249,985	162,618	75,099	87,519	38,658	16,664	21,994	1,071	886	185
25 to 29 years	695,984	341,448	354,536	393,504	191,999	201,505	251,671	124,777	126,894	48,661	22,779	25,882	2,148	1,893	255
30 to 34 years	649,576	327,685	321,891	329,596	162,429	167,167	277,079	142,987	134,092	40,533	20,121	20,412	2,368	2,148	220
35 to 39 years	621,248	319,859	301,389	272,926	135,538	137,388	309,408	163,942	145,466	36,924	18,539	18,385	1,990	1,840	150
40 to 44 years	518,588	272,868	245,720	199,377	98,857	100,520	292,075	159,583	132,492	25,515	12,909	12,606	1,621	1,519	102
45 to 49 years	422,063	219,600	202,463	151,843	74,032	77,811	250,204	135,056	115,148	19,057	9,607	9,450	959	905	54
50 to 54 years	340,807	175,346	165,461	126,094	61,130	64,964	202,176	107,610	94,566	11,922	6,032	5,890	615	574	41
55 to 59 years	246,277	123,128	123,149	93,257	44,458	48,799	146,325	75,200	71,125	6,365	3,155	3,210	330	315	15
60 to 64 years	190,527	92,494	98,033	69,444	31,886	37,558	117,138	58,732	58,406	3,767	1,708	2,059	178	168	10
65 to 69 years	127,356	60,451	66,905	45,149	20,131	25,018	79,787	39,351	40,436	2,331	891	1,440	89	78	11
70 to 74 years	77,327	35,866	41,461	28,853	12,401	16,452	47,205	22,986	24,219	1,236	448	788	33	31	2
75 years and over	59,819	25,243	34,576	20,918	8,109	12,809	37,703	16,721	20,982	1,184	400	784	14	13	1
Not reported	5,987	3,011	2,976	3,846	1,868	1,978	1,595	858	737	486	234	252	60	51	9
Under 1 year	100,398	51,178	49,220	94,819	48,409	46,410	251	125	126	5,176	2,569	2,607	152	75	77
5 years	112,108	56,813	55,295	104,372	53,003	51,369	2,257	1,125	1,132	5,340	2,606	2,734	139	79	60
14 years	112,112	56,347	55,765	103,303	51,952	51,351	5,242	2,647	2,595	3,518	1,719	1,799	49	29	20
15 years	112,305	56,540	55,765	102,155	51,562	50,593	6,771	3,375	3,396	3,325	1,572	1,753	54	31	23
16 and 17 years	232,443	114,770	117,673	202,327	100,571	101,756	22,683	10,823	11,860	7,319	3,308	4,011	114	68	46
21 years and over	4,511,021	2,262,581	2,248,440	2,120,168	1,029,912	1,090,256	2,149,455	1,111,448	1,038,007	230,069	110,911	119,158	11,329	10,310	1,019
Percent: 1940	100.0	100.0	100.0	100.0	100.0	100.0	100.0	100.0	100.0	100.0	100.0	100.0	100.0	100.0	100.0
Under 5 years	5.8	6.0	5.6	8.2	8.5	7.8	0.1	0.1	0.1	6.5	7.1	5.9	5.1	3.2	13.3
5 to 9 years	6.3	6.5	6.1	8.8	9.1	8.5	0.3	0.3	0.3	7.2	8.0	6.6	4.9	3.0	13.4
10 to 14 years	7.5	7.7	7.3	10.4	10.8	10.1	0.7	0.6	0.7	7.8	8.4	7.3	4.4	3.1	10.3
15 to 19 years	8.1	8.2	8.1	11.0	11.2	10.8	1.7	1.6	1.7	7.6	7.6	7.6	4.5	3.6	8.5
20 to 24 years	8.7	8.3	9.1	11.6	11.3	11.8	2.0	1.8	2.2	9.0	7.4	10.2	4.6	3.6	8.8
25 to 29 years	9.4	8.8	9.9	11.2	10.8	11.5	4.7	3.9	5.4	11.1	9.7	12.3	8.3	7.9	10.4
30 to 34 years	9.3	9.0	9.5	9.5	9.4	9.5	8.3	7.7	8.9	11.2	10.7	11.6	11.3	11.6	10.1
35 to 39 years	9.0	9.0	9.0	7.4	7.4	7.4	12.1	12.0	12.2	11.4	11.4	11.4	15.8	17.5	8.3
40 to 44 years	8.4	8.6	8.2	6.2	6.2	6.1	13.5	13.7	13.3	9.1	9.9	8.5	14.7	16.6	6.6
45 to 49 years	7.4	7.7	7.1	4.8	4.8	4.7	13.7	14.2	13.1	6.6	7.2	6.2	10.2	11.6	3.8
50 to 54 years	6.3	6.6	5.9	3.6	3.5	3.6	13.0	13.9	12.0	4.7	5.0	4.4	7.3	8.2	2.8
55 to 59 years	4.7	4.8	4.5	2.5	2.4	2.5	10.1	10.7	9.5	3.1	3.2	3.0	4.0	4.5	1.4
60 to 64 years	3.6	3.6	3.6	1.9	1.8	2.1	7.8	8.0	7.7	2.0	2.1	2.0	2.8	3.2	1.0
65 to 69 years	2.6	2.4	2.7	1.4	1.2	1.6	5.5	5.3	5.6	1.4	1.3	1.5	1.3	1.5	0.6
70 to 74 years	1.6	1.5	1.8	0.9	0.7	1.0	3.5	3.3	3.8	0.7	0.6	0.8	0.6	0.7	0.2
75 years and over	1.4	1.2	1.6	0.8	0.6	1.0	3.0	2.7	3.3	0.6	0.4	0.7	0.3	0.3	0.3
Under 1 year	1.1	1.1	1.1	1.6	1.6	1.5	-	-	-	1.2	1.3	1.1	1.0	0.6	2.6
5 years	1.2	1.2	1.2	1.7	1.7	1.6	-	-	-	1.4	1.5	1.3	0.9	0.6	2.5
14 years	1.5	1.5	1.5	2.1	2.2	2.0	0.2	0.2	0.2	1.5	1.6	1.5	0.9	0.6	1.8
15 years	1.5	1.6	1.5	2.1	2.2	2.1	0.2	0.2	0.2	1.5	1.6	1.5	0.9	0.7	1.6
16 and 17 years	3.2	3.2	3.2	4.3	4.4	4.2	0.6	0.6	0.6	2.9	3.0	2.9	1.8	1.4	3.7
21 years and over	70.5	69.9	71.0	59.4	58.1	60.6	96.8	96.9	96.7	69.2	67.5	70.6	80.2	86.4	52.7
Percent: 1930	100.0	100.0	100.0	100.0	100.0	100.0	100.0	100.0	100.0	100.0	100.0	100.0	100.0	100.0	100.0
Under 5 years	7.7	7.8	7.6	11.7	12.0	11.4	0.2	0.2	0.2	8.2	8.6	7.9	5.0	3.1	16.4
5 to 9 years	8.3	8.4	8.3	12.4	12.6	12.1	1.0	0.9	1.0	7.4	7.6	7.3	4.0	2.3	14.3
10 to 14 years	8.3	8.4	8.2	12.4	12.6	12.1	1.1	1.1	1.1	5.7	5.7	5.7	2.2	1.4	7.3
15 to 19 years	8.6	8.5	8.8	11.9	11.9	11.9	2.9	2.7	3.2	6.4	5.8	7.0	2.9	2.4	6.4
20 to 24 years	9.9	9.4	10.4	11.3	11.1	11.5	7.1	6.4	7.9	11.8	10.6	12.9	8.0	7.7	9.7
25 to 29 years	10.0	9.8	10.3	9.2	9.0	9.3	11.0	10.6	11.4	14.8	14.5	15.2	16.1	16.5	13.4
30 to 34 years	9.4	9.4	9.3	7.7	7.6	7.7	12.1	12.1	12.0	12.4	12.8	12.0	17.7	18.7	11.6
35 to 39 years	9.0	9.2	8.7	6.4	6.4	6.3	13.5	13.9	13.1	11.3	11.8	10.8	14.9	16.1	7.9
40 to 44 years	7.5	7.9	7.1	4.6	4.7	4.6	12.7	13.5	11.9	7.8	8.2	7.4	12.1	13.3	5.4
45 to 49 years	6.1	6.3	5.9	3.5	3.5	3.6	10.9	11.4	10.3	5.8	6.1	5.5	7.2	7.9	2.8
50 to 54 years	4.9	5.0	4.8	2.9	2.9	3.0	8.8	9.1	8.5	3.6	3.8	3.4	4.6	5.0	2.2
55 to 59 years	3.6	3.5	3.6	2.2	2.1	2.2	6.4	6.4	6.4	1.9	2.0	1.9	2.5	2.7	0.8
60 to 64 years	2.7	2.7	2.8	1.6	1.5	1.7	5.1	5.0	5.2	1.1	1.1	1.2	1.3	1.5	0.5
65 to 69 years	1.8	1.7	1.9	1.1	0.9	1.2	3.5	3.3	3.6	0.7	0.6	0.8	0.7	0.7	0.6
70 to 74 years	1.1	1.0	1.2	0.7	0.6	0.8	2.1	1.9	2.2	0.4	0.3	0.5	0.2	0.3	0.1
75 years and over	0.9	0.7	1.0	0.5	0.4	0.6	1.6	1.4	1.9	0.4	0.3	0.5	0.1	0.1	0.1
Not reported	0.1	0.1	0.1	0.1	0.1	0.1	0.1	0.1	0.1	0.1	0.1	0.1	0.4	0.4	0.5
Under 1 year	1.4	1.5	1.4	2.2	2.3	2.1	-	-	-	1.6	1.6	1.5	1.1	0.7	4.1
5 years	1.6	1.6	1.6	2.4	2.5	2.4	0.1	0.1	0.1	1.6	1.7	1.6	1.0	0.7	3.2
14 years	1.6	1.6	1.6	2.4	2.4	2.4	0.2	0.2	0.2	1.1	1.1	1.1	0.4	0.3	1.1
15 years	1.6	1.6	1.6	2.4	2.4	2.3	0.3	0.3	0.3	1.0	1.0	1.0	0.4	0.3	1.2
16 and 17 years	3.4	3.3	3.4	4.7	4.7	4.7	1.0	0.9	1.1	2.2	2.1	2.3	0.9	0.6	2.4
21 years and over	65.1	65.1	65.0	49.4	48.5	50.2	93.7	94.1	93.2	70.2	70.7	69.8	84.8	89.9	53.7

Table C-36.—RACE, BY NATIVITY AND SEX, FOR THE CITY OF NEW YORK: 1940 AND 1930

[Figures for white population in 1930 have been revised to include Mexicans who were classified with "Other races" in the 1930 reports. Percent not shown where less than 0.1 or where base is less than 100. Sex ratio not shown where number of females is less than 100]

SEX, NATIVITY, AND CENSUS YEAR	All classes	White	Negro	Other races	OTHER RACES				PERCENT BY RACE				PERCENT BY NATIVITY					
					Indian	Chinese	Japanese	All other	All classes	White	Negro	Other races	All classes	White	Negro	Indian	Chinese	Japanese
TOTAL																		
1940	7,454,995	6,977,501	458,444	19,050	1,064	12,753	2,087	3,146	100.0	93.6	6.1	0.3	100.0	100.0	100.0	100.0	100.0	100.0
Native	5,316,338	4,897,481	410,026	8,831	638	4,745	631	2,817	100.0	92.1	7.7	0.2	71.3	70.2	89.4	60.0	37.2	30.2
Foreign born	2,138,657	2,080,020	48,418	10,219	426	8,008	1,456	329	100.0	97.3	2.3	0.5	28.7	29.8	10.6	40.0	62.8	69.8
1930	6,930,446	6,589,377	327,706	13,363	391	8,414	2,356	2,202	100.0	95.1	4.7	0.2	100.0	100.0	100.0	100.0	100.0	100.0
Native	4,571,760	4,294,196	272,952	4,612	294	1,926	536	1,856	100.0	93.9	6.0	0.1	66.0	65.2	83.3	75.2	22.9	22.8
Foreign born	2,358,686	2,295,181	54,754	8,751	97	6,488	1,820	346	100.0	97.3	2.3	0.4	34.0	34.8	16.7	24.8	77.1	77.2
MALE																		
1940	3,676,293	3,455,003	205,727	15,563	590	10,967	1,470	2,536	100.0	94.0	5.6	0.4	100.0	100.0	100.0	100.0	100.0	100.0
Native	2,585,482	2,397,164	181,870	6,448	321	3,547	325	2,255	100.0	92.7	7.0	0.2	70.3	69.4	88.4	54.4	32.3	22.1
Foreign born	1,090,811	1,057,839	23,857	9,115	269	7,420	1,145	281	100.0	97.0	2.2	0.8	29.7	30.6	11.6	45.6	67.7	77.9
1930	3,472,956	3,304,524	156,968	11,464	212	7,549	1,748	1,955	100.0	95.2	4.5	0.3	100.0	100.0	100.0	100.0	100.0	100.0
Native	2,255,955	2,123,577	128,891	3,487	152	1,414	275	1,646	100.0	94.1	5.7	0.2	65.0	64.3	82.1	71.7	18.7	15.7
Foreign born	1,217,001	1,180,947	28,077	7,977	60	6,135	1,473	309	100.0	97.0	2.3	0.7	35.0	35.7	17.9	28.3	81.3	84.3
FEMALE																		
1940	3,778,702	3,522,498	252,717	3,487	474	1,786	617	610	100.0	93.2	6.7	0.1	100.0	100.0	100.0	100.0	100.0	100.0
Native	2,730,856	2,500,317	228,156	2,383	317	1,198	306	562	100.0	91.6	8.4	0.1	72.3	71.0	90.3	66.9	67.1	49.6
Foreign born	1,047,846	1,022,181	24,561	1,104	157	588	311	48	100.0	97.6	2.3	0.1	27.7	29.0	9.7	33.1	32.9	50.4
1930	3,457,490	3,284,853	170,738	1,899	179	865	608	247	100.0	95.0	4.9	0.1	100.0	100.0	100.0	100.0	100.0	100.0
Native	2,315,805	2,170,619	144,061	1,125	142	512	261	210	100.0	93.7	6.2	-	67.0	66.1	84.4	79.3	59.2	42.9
Foreign born	1,141,685	1,114,234	26,677	774	37	353	347	37	100.0	97.6	2.3	0.1	33.0	33.9	15.6	20.7	40.8	57.1
MALES PER 100 FEMALES																		
1940	97.3	98.1	81.4	446.3	124.5	614.1	238.2	415.7	-	-	-	-	-	-	-	-	-	-
Native	94.7	95.9	79.7	270.6	101.3	296.1	106.2	401.2	-	-	-	-	-	-	-	-	-	-
Foreign born	104.1	103.5	97.1	825.6	171.3	1,261.9	368.2	-	-	-	-	-	-	-	-	-	-	-
1930	100.4	100.6	91.9	603.7	118.4	872.7	287.5	791.5	-	-	-	-	-	-	-	-	-	-
Native	97.4	97.8	89.5	310.0	107.0	276.2	105.4	783.8	-	-	-	-	-	-	-	-	-	-
Foreign born	106.6	106.0	105.2	1,030.6	-	1,738.0	424.5	-	-	-	-	-	-	-	-	-	-	-

Table C-37.—POTENTIAL VOTING POPULATION, BY CITIZENSHIP, RACE, NATIVITY, AND SEX, FOR THE CITY OF NEW YORK: 1940 AND 1930

[Figures for white population in 1930 have been revised to include Mexicans who were classified with "Other races" in the 1930 reports. Percent not shown where less than 0.1]

CITIZENSHIP, RACE, AND NATIVITY	TOTAL POPULATION (ALL AGES)								POPULATION 21 YEARS OLD AND OVER							
	Total number		Percent		Male		Female		Total number		Percent		Male		Female	
	1940	1930	1940	1930	1940	1930	1940	1930	1940	1930	1940	1930	1940	1930	1940	1930
Total	7,454,995	6,930,446	100.0	100.0	3,676,293	3,472,956	3,778,702	3,457,490	5,254,633	4,511,021	100.0	100.0	2,570,647	2,262,581	2,683,986	2,248,440
Percent citizen	-	-	89.0	83.7	-	-	-	-	-	-	85.2	77.2	-	-	-	-
Percent alien and citiz. not rptd.	-	-	11.0	16.3	-	-	-	-	-	-	14.8	22.8	-	-	-	-
Citizen	6,632,398	5,802,229	100.0	100.0	3,334,268	2,944,082	3,298,130	2,858,147	4,474,689	3,488,111	100.0	100.0	2,249,729	1,780,797	2,224,960	1,702,314
White—Native	4,897,481	4,294,196	73.8	74.0	2,397,164	2,123,577	2,500,317	2,170,619	2,908,645	2,120,168	65.0	60.9	1,393,545	1,029,912	1,515,100	1,090,256
Naturalized	1,298,360	1,217,790	19.6	21.0	738,635	680,388	559,725	537,402	1,272,872	1,168,689	28.4	33.6	725,888	656,236	546,984	512,453
Negro—Native	410,026	272,952	6.2	4.7	181,870	128,891	228,156	144,061	270,140	179,483	6.0	5.2	115,520	84,692	154,620	94,791
Naturalized	17,700	12,679	0.3	0.2	10,151	7,739	7,549	4,940	17,388	11,810	0.4	0.3	10,011	7,340	7,377	4,470
Other races—Native	8,831	4,612	0.1	0.1	6,448	3,487	2,383	1,125	5,644	2,961	0.1	0.1	4,765	2,617	879	344
Indian	638	294	-	-	321	152	317	142	377	205	-	-	191	108	186	97
Chinese	4,745	1,926	0.1	-	3,547	1,414	1,198	512	2,935	1,093	0.1	-	2,548	971	387	122
Japanese	631	536	-	-	325	275	306	261	250	91	-	-	133	60	117	31
Filipino	2,659	1,760	-	-	2,160	1,575	499	185	2,003	1,515	-	-	1,836	1,428	167	87
Hindu	58	19	-	-	28	8	30	11	17	3	-	-	7	1	10	2
All other	100	77	-	-	67	63	33	14	63	54	-	-	50	49	12	5
Alien	705,916	1,046,105	100.0	100.0	290,885	495,428	415,031	550,677	670,141	951,350	100.0	100.0	273,111	450,696	397,030	500,654
White—First papers	187,454	230,748	26.6	22.1	105,690	164,058	81,764	66,690	182,999	225,327	27.3	23.7	103,416	161,042	79,583	64,285
No papers	481,687	768,502	68.2	73.5	164,367	305,010	317,320	463,492	451,617	682,458	67.4	71.7	149,589	264,848	302,028	417,610
Negro—First papers	7,080	6,732	1.0	0.6	3,891	4,427	3,189	2,305	7,023	6,651	1.0	0.7	3,872	4,396	3,151	2,255
No papers	19,476	31,372	2.8	3.0	7,822	13,956	11,654	17,416	18,862	28,546	2.8	3.0	7,554	12,717	11,308	15,829
Other races—Foreign born	10,219	8,751	1.4	0.8	9,115	7,977	1,104	774	9,640	8,368	1.4	0.9	8,680	7,693	960	675
Indian	426	97	0.1	-	269	60	157	37	355	78	0.1	-	230	50	125	28
Chinese	8,008	6,488	1.1	0.6	7,420	6,135	588	353	7,624	6,222	1.1	0.7	7,097	5,906	527	316
Japanese	1,456	1,820	0.2	0.2	1,145	1,473	311	347	1,345	1,728	0.2	0.2	1,079	1,429	266	299
Filipino	68	37	-	-	45	24	23	13	61	34	-	-	43	24	18	10
Hindu	155	221	-	-	141	203	14	18	150	218	-	-	137	202	13	16
All other	106	88	-	-	95	82	11	6	105	88	-	-	94	82	11	6
Citizenship not reported	116,681	82,112	100.0	100.0	51,140	33,446	65,541	48,666	109,808	76,560	100.0	100.0	47,807	31,088	61,996	45,472
White	112,519	78,141	96.4	95.2	49,147	31,491	63,372	46,650	105,861	72,981	96.4	95.3	45,900	29,322	59,961	43,659
Negro	4,162	3,971	3.6	4.8	1,993	1,955	2,169	2,016	3,942	3,579	3.6	4.7	1,907	1,766	2,085	1,813

Table C-38.—SCHOOL ATTENDANCE, BY AGE, RACE, AND SEX, FOR THE CITY OF NEW YORK: 1940 AND 1930

[Figures for white population in 1930 revised to include Mexicans classified with "Other races" in the 1930 reports. Percent not shown where less than 0.1 or where base is less than 100]

AGE, SEX, AND CENSUS YEAR	ALL CLASSES			NATIVE WHITE			FOREIGN-BORN WHITE			NEGRO			OTHER RACES		
	Total number	Attending school		Total number	Attending school		Total number	Attending school		Total number	Attending school		Total number	Attending school	
		Number	Percent		Number	Percent		Number	Percent		Number	Percent		Number	Percent
1940															
Total, 5 to 24 years	2,287,759	1,350,041	59.0	2,044,106	1,223,732	59.9	95,394	38,961	40.8	144,759	85,048	58.8	3,500	2,300	65.7
5 years	88,368	25,836	29.2	80,891	23,845	29.5	980	314	32.0	6,323	1,608	25.4	174	69	39.7
6 years	88,718	77,089	86.9	81,065	70,723	87.2	1,077	872	81.0	6,383	5,335	83.6	193	159	82.4
7 to 9 years	293,470	283,447	96.6	268,427	259,433	96.6	4,044	3,780	93.5	20,428	19,694	96.4	571	540	94.6
10 to 13 years	447,798	434,889	97.1	408,428	396,885	97.2	9,910	9,466	95.5	28,783	27,884	96.9	677	654	96.6
14 years	113,310	109,423	96.6	102,350	98,948	96.7	3,732	3,543	94.9	7,065	6,776	95.9	163	156	95.7
15 years	114,889	110,459	96.1	103,876	99,957	96.2	3,936	3,749	95.2	6,910	6,590	95.4	167	163	97.6
16 and 17 years	238,386	185,098	77.6	212,614	165,326	77.8	11,953	8,926	74.7	13,474	10,571	78.5	345	275	79.7
18 and 19 years	253,667	74,066	29.2	220,436	64,290	29.2	18,597	5,175	27.8	14,294	4,458	31.2	340	143	42.1
20 years	127,862	17,480	13.7	110,093	15,419	14.0	9,859	1,176	11.9	7,738	836	10.8	172	49	28.5
21 to 24 years	521,291	32,254	6.2	455,926	28,906	6.3	31,306	1,960	6.3	33,361	1,296	3.9	698	92	13.2
Male, 5 to 24 years	1,127,830	695,356	61.7	1,015,555	632,536	62.3	45,648	20,542	45.0	64,561	40,934	63.4	2,066	1,344	65.1
5 years	44,847	12,940	28.9	41,165	11,993	29.1	474	145	30.6	3,120	766	24.6	88	36	-
6 years	45,142	39,217	86.9	41,313	36,059	87.3	557	456	81.9	3,175	2,619	82.5	97	83	-
7 to 9 years	148,809	143,700	96.6	136,371	131,755	96.6	2,007	1,884	93.9	10,147	9,793	96.5	284	268	94.4
10 to 13 years	226,504	220,075	97.2	207,226	201,486	97.2	4,981	4,751	95.4	13,918	13,475	96.8	379	363	95.8
14 years	56,949	54,998	96.6	51,621	49,891	96.6	1,851	1,757	94.9	3,376	3,252	96.3	101	98	97.0
15 years	57,734	55,606	96.3	52,455	50,547	96.4	1,935	1,846	95.4	3,234	3,106	96.0	110	107	97.3
16 and 17 years	118,975	94,205	79.2	106,441	84,400	79.3	6,056	4,655	76.9	6,261	4,975	79.5	217	175	80.6
18 and 19 years	124,008	41,999	33.9	108,529	36,815	33.9	9,172	3,027	33.0	6,079	2,052	33.8	228	105	46.1
20 years	61,263	10,830	17.7	53,598	9,657	18.0	4,703	778	16.5	2,847	359	12.6	115	36	31.3
21 to 24 years	243,599	21,786	8.9	216,836	19,933	9.2	13,912	1,243	8.9	12,404	537	4.3	447	73	16.3
Female, 5 to 24 years	1,159,929	654,685	56.4	1,028,551	591,196	57.5	49,746	18,419	37.0	80,198	44,114	55.0	1,434	956	66.7
5 years	43,521	12,896	29.6	39,726	11,852	29.8	506	169	33.4	3,203	842	26.3	86	33	-
6 years	43,576	37,872	86.9	39,752	34,664	87.2	520	416	80.0	3,208	2,716	84.7	96	76	-
7 to 9 years	144,661	139,747	96.6	132,056	127,678	96.7	2,037	1,896	93.1	10,281	9,901	96.3	287	272	94.8
10 to 13 years	221,294	214,814	97.1	201,202	195,399	97.1	4,929	4,715	95.7	14,865	14,409	96.9	298	291	97.7
14 years	56,361	54,425	96.6	50,729	49,057	96.7	1,881	1,786	94.9	3,689	3,524	95.5	62	58	-
15 years	57,155	54,853	96.0	51,421	49,410	96.1	2,001	1,903	95.1	3,676	3,484	94.8	57	56	-
16 and 17 years	119,411	90,893	76.1	106,173	80,926	76.2	5,897	4,271	72.4	7,213	5,596	77.6	128	100	78.1
18 and 19 years	129,659	32,067	24.7	111,907	27,475	24.6	9,425	2,148	22.8	8,215	2,406	29.3	112	38	33.9
20 years	66,599	6,650	10.0	56,495	5,762	10.2	5,156	398	7.7	4,891	477	9.8	57	13	-
21 to 24 years	277,692	10,468	3.8	239,090	8,973	3.8	17,394	717	4.1	20,957	759	3.6	251	19	7.6
1930															
Total, 5 to 24 years	2,439,287	1,362,751	55.9	2,056,945	1,237,685	60.2	277,242	77,432	27.9	102,805	46,617	45.3	2,295	1,017	44.3
5 years	112,108	28,632	25.5	104,372	26,823	25.7	2,257	504	22.3	5,340	1,268	23.7	139	42	30.2
6 years	115,242	92,352	80.1	107,000	86,052	80.4	3,108	2,394	77.0	5,018	3,815	76.1	121	91	75.2
7 to 9 years	349,934	338,303	96.7	319,125	308,879	96.8	16,519	15,870	96.1	14,012	13,293	94.9	278	261	93.9
10 to 13 years	463,188	456,204	98.5	427,733	421,470	98.5	20,067	19,680	98.1	15,144	14,818	97.8	244	236	96.7
14 years	112,112	108,723	97.0	103,303	100,227	97.0	5,242	5,052	96.4	3,518	3,396	96.5	49	48	-
15 years	112,305	101,860	90.3	102,155	92,164	90.2	6,771	6,133	90.6	3,325	3,020	90.8	54	43	-
16 and 17 years	232,443	132,712	57.1	202,327	116,559	57.6	22,683	11,933	52.6	7,319	4,156	56.8	114	64	56.1
18 and 19 years	254,538	53,524	21.0	205,860	45,266	22.0	37,977	6,628	17.5	10,476	1,570	15.0	225	60	26.7
20 years	131,955	16,667	12.6	99,709	13,766	13.8	25,529	2,496	9.8	6,570	381	5.8	147	24	16.3
21 to 24 years	555,462	34,274	6.2	385,361	26,479	6.9	137,089	6,742	4.9	32,088	905	2.8	924	148	16.0
Male, 5 to 24 years	1,203,519	702,126	58.3	1,024,900	637,812	62.2	130,327	41,371	31.7	46,714	22,359	47.9	1,578	584	37.0
5 years	56,813	14,449	25.4	53,003	13,563	25.6	1,125	254	22.6	2,606	609	23.4	79	23	-
6 years	58,294	46,618	80.0	54,183	43,489	80.3	1,613	1,244	77.1	2,444	1,843	75.4	54	42	-
7 to 9 years	176,675	170,727	96.6	161,385	156,112	96.7	8,313	7,998	96.2	6,844	6,491	94.8	133	126	94.7
10 to 13 years	233,916	230,415	98.5	216,389	213,233	98.5	10,133	9,943	98.1	7,268	7,119	97.9	126	120	95.2
14 years	56,347	54,756	97.2	51,952	50,499	97.2	2,647	2,560	96.7	1,719	1,669	97.1	29	28	-
15 years	56,540	51,345	90.8	51,562	46,747	90.7	3,375	3,118	92.4	1,572	1,455	92.6	31	25	-
16 and 17 years	114,770	69,016	60.1	100,571	60,834	60.5	10,823	6,205	57.3	3,306	1,940	58.6	68	37	-
18 and 19 years	122,430	31,344	25.6	100,770	26,637	26.4	17,199	3,979	23.1	4,289	684	15.9	172	44	25.6
20 years	62,152	10,397	16.7	48,011	8,643	18.0	11,454	1,578	13.8	2,576	160	6.2	111	16	14.4
21 to 24 years	265,582	23,059	8.7	187,074	18,055	9.7	63,645	4,492	7.1	14,088	389	2.8	775	123	15.9
Female, 5 to 24 years	1,235,768	660,625	53.5	1,032,045	599,873	58.1	146,915	36,061	24.5	56,091	24,258	43.2	717	433	60.4
5 years	55,295	14,183	25.6	51,369	13,260	25.8	1,132	250	22.1	2,734	654	23.9	60	19	-
6 years	56,948	45,734	80.3	52,817	42,563	80.6	1,495	1,150	76.9	2,569	1,972	76.8	67	49	-
7 to 9 years	173,259	167,576	96.7	157,740	152,767	96.8	8,206	7,872	95.9	7,168	6,802	94.9	145	135	93.1
10 to 13 years	229,272	225,789	98.5	211,344	208,237	98.5	9,934	9,737	98.0	7,876	7,599	[illegible]	118	116	98.3
14 years	55,765	53,967	96.8	51,351	49,728	96.8	2,595	2,492	96.0	1,799	1,727	96.0	20	20	-
15 years	55,765	50,015	89.7	50,593	45,417	89.8	3,396	3,015	88.8	1,753	1,565	89.3	23	18	-
16 and 17 years	117,673	63,696	54.1	101,756	55,725	54.8	11,860	5,728	48.3	4,011	2,216	55.2	46	27	-
18 and 19 years	132,108	22,180	16.8	105,090	18,629	17.7	20,778	2,649	12.7	6,187	886	14.3	53	16	-
20 years	69,803	6,270	9.0	51,698	5,123	9.9	14,075	918	6.5	3,994	221	5.5	36	8	-
21 to 24 years	289,880	11,215	3.9	198,287	8,424	4.2	73,444	2,250	3.1	18,000	516	2.9	149	25	16.8

Table C-39.—PERSONS 25 YEARS OLD AND OVER, BY YEARS OF SCHOOL COMPLETED, RACE, AND SEX, FOR THE CITY OF NEW YORK: 1940

[Percent not shown where less than 0.1; median and percent not shown where base is less than 100]

YEARS OF SCHOOL COMPLETED	ALL CLASSES			NATIVE WHITE			FOREIGN-BORN WHITE			NEGRO			OTHER RACES		
	Total	Male	Female	Total	Male	Female	Total	Male	Female	Total	Male	Female	Total	Male	Female
Persons 25 years old and over	4,733,342	2,327,048	2,406,294	2,452,719	1,176,709	1,276,010	1,982,043	1,010,881	971,162	283,994	126,460	157,534	14,586	12,998	1,588
No school years completed	361,184	168,413	192,771	21,613	9,787	11,826	325,905	150,661	175,244	9,778	4,414	5,364	3,888	3,551	337
Grade school: 1 to 4 years	340,551	171,962	168,589	47,904	23,248	24,656	253,517	129,707	123,810	36,215	16,228	19,987	2,915	2,779	136
5 or 6 years	367,288	183,754	183,534	108,791	52,733	56,058	208,431	108,206	100,225	48,372	21,250	27,122	1,694	1,565	129
7 or 8 years	1,934,829	939,513	995,316	1,059,451	503,256	556,195	771,640	389,004	382,636	101,145	45,007	56,138	2,593	2,246	347
High school: 1 to 3 years	600,541	289,124	311,417	429,601	203,919	225,682	128,331	66,773	61,558	41,738	17,700	24,038	871	732	139
4 years	585,923	249,407	336,516	418,943	168,634	250,309	138,772	68,710	70,062	27,284	11,392	15,892	924	671	253
College: 1 to 3 years	174,912	97,789	77,123	131,156	70,465	60,691	34,426	22,485	11,941	8,875	4,470	4,405	455	369	86
4 years or more	266,091	174,510	91,581	202,872	127,586	75,286	56,643	42,963	13,680	5,840	3,353	2,487	736	608	128
Not reported	102,023	52,576	49,447	32,388	17,081	15,307	64,378	32,372	32,006	4,747	2,646	2,101	510	477	33
Median school years completed	8.3	8.3	8.3	8.9	9.0	8.9	7.4	7.5	7.4	7.9	7.9	7.9	5.3	4.9	8.0
Percent less than 5 years completed	14.8	14.6	15.0	2.8	2.8	2.9	29.2	27.7	30.8	16.2	16.3	16.1	46.6	48.7	29.8
PERCENT DISTRIBUTION															
Persons 25 years old and over	100.0	100.0	100.0	100.0	100.0	100.0	100.0	100.0	100.0	100.0	100.0	100.0	100.0	100.0	100.0
No school years completed	7.6	7.2	8.0	0.9	0.8	0.9	16.4	14.9	18.0	3.4	3.5	3.4	26.7	27.3	21.2
Grade school: 1 to 4 years	7.2	7.4	7.0	2.0	2.0	1.9	12.8	12.8	12.7	12.8	12.8	12.7	20.0	21.4	8.6
5 or 6 years	7.8	7.9	7.6	4.4	4.5	4.4	10.5	10.7	10.3	17.0	16.8	17.2	11.6	12.0	8.1
7 or 8 years	40.9	40.4	41.4	43.2	42.8	43.6	38.9	38.5	39.4	35.6	35.6	35.6	17.8	17.3	21.9
High school: 1 to 3 years	12.7	12.4	12.9	17.5	17.3	17.7	6.5	6.6	6.3	14.7	14.0	15.3	6.0	5.6	8.8
4 years	12.4	10.7	14.0	17.1	14.3	19.6	7.0	6.8	7.2	9.6	9.0	10.1	6.3	5.2	15.9
College: 1 to 3 years	3.7	4.2	3.2	5.3	6.0	4.8	1.7	2.2	1.2	3.1	3.5	2.8	3.1	2.8	5.4
4 years or more	5.6	7.5	3.8	8.3	10.8	5.9	2.9	4.3	1.4	2.1	2.7	1.6	5.0	4.7	8.1
Not reported	2.2	2.3	2.1	1.3	1.5	1.2	3.2	3.2	3.3	1.7	2.1	1.3	3.5	3.7	2.1

Table C-40.—FOREIGN-BORN WHITE, BY COUNTRY OF BIRTH, BY SEX, FOR THE CITY OF NEW YORK: 1940 AND 1930

[Figures for white population in 1930 revised to include Mexicans classified with "Other races" in the 1930 reports. Percent not shown where less than 0.1 or where base is less than 100]

COUNTRY OF BIRTH	BOTH SEXES		PERCENT		MALE		FEMALE	
	1940	1930	1940	1930	1940	1930	1940	1930
All countries	2,080,020	2,295,181	100.0	100.0	1,057,839	1,180,947	1,022,181	1,114,234
England	63,115	78,003	3.0	3.4	30,411	38,538	32,704	39,465
Scotland	33,292	38,535	1.6	1.7	15,758	19,018	17,534	19,517
Wales	1,296	1,903	0.1	0.1	667	988	629	915
Northern Ireland	21,501	27,821	1.0	1.2	9,384	12,169	12,117	15,652
Irish Free State (Eire)	160,325	192,810	7.7	8.4	69,988	85,746	90,337	107,064
Norway	30,750	38,130	1.5	1.7	16,471	21,171	14,279	16,959
Sweden	28,881	37,267	1.4	1.6	14,674	19,357	14,207	17,910
Denmark	8,845	11,096	0.4	0.5	5,425	6,946	3,420	4,150
Netherlands	5,608	5,335	0.3	0.2	3,704	3,619	1,904	1,716
Belgium	3,888	3,854	0.2	0.2	1,993	1,952	1,895	1,902
Luxemburg	340	323	-	-	175	174	165	149
Switzerland	8,551	9,895	0.4	0.4	4,412	5,147	4,139	4,748
France	19,696	23,288	0.9	1.0	8,397	10,263	11,299	13,025
Germany	224,749	237,588	10.8	10.4	112,916	121,590	111,833	115,998
Poland	194,163	238,339	9.3	10.4	97,816	120,318	96,347	118,021
Czechoslovakia	26,884	35,318	1.3	1.5	12,042	15,964	14,842	19,354
Austria	145,106	127,169	7.0	5.5	70,537	62,587	74,569	64,582
Hungary	62,588	59,883	3.0	2.6	28,557	27,444	34,031	32,439
Yugoslavia	6,475	6,450	0.3	0.3	3,712	3,638	2,763	2,812
Russia (U. S. S. R.)	395,696	442,431	19.0	19.3	200,663	227,120	195,033	215,311
Lithuania	15,089	15,005	0.7	0.7	7,944	8,162	7,145	6,843
Latvia	5,317	5,172	0.3	0.2	2,785	2,692	2,532	2,480
Finland	11,245	13,224	0.5	0.6	4,563	5,833	6,682	7,391
Rumania	40,655	46,750	2.0	2.0	20,316	23,377	20,339	23,373
Bulgaria	670	578	-	-	394	342	276	236
Turkey in Europe	265	747	-	-	146	383	119	364
Greece	28,593	27,182	1.4	1.2	19,304	18,567	9,289	8,615
Italy	409,489	440,250	19.7	19.2	227,084	246,088	182,405	194,162
Spain	13,583	14,000	0.7	0.6	9,504	10,153	4,079	3,847
Portugal	2,676	2,231	0.1	0.1	2,008	1,756	668	475
Other Europe	5,757	4,844	0.3	0.2	3,691	3,160	2,066	1,684
Palestine and Syria	8,598	8,696	0.4	0.4	4,545	4,578	4,053	4,118
Turkey in Asia	17,398	14,368	0.8	0.6	9,645	8,050	7,753	6,318
Other Asia	5,107	5,621	0.2	0.2	3,293	3,514	1,814	2,107
Canada—French	6,270	6,863	0.3	0.3	2,753	3,308	3,517	3,555
Canada—Other	29,237	32,760	1.4	1.4	11,768	14,038	17,469	18,722
Newfoundland	4,838	5,303	0.2	0.2	2,171	2,555	2,667	2,748
Mexico	2,973	4,163	0.1	0.2	1,708	2,559	1,265	1,604
Cuba and other West Indies	13,344	13,046	0.6	0.6	7,136	7,303	6,208	5,743
Central and South America	12,429	14,298	0.6	0.6	6,807	8,202	5,622	6,096
Australia	987	1,164	-	0.1	513	650	474	514
Azores	69	95	-	-	35	66	34	29
All other and not reported	3,682	3,383	0.2	0.1	2,024	1,862	1,658	1,521

Table C-41.—PERSONS 14 YEARS OLD AND OVER, BY EMPLOYMENT STATUS, CLASS OF WORKER, RACE, AND SEX, FOR THE CITY OF NEW YORK: 1940

[Percent not shown where less than 0.1 or where base is less than 100]

EMPLOYMENT STATUS	ALL CLASSES			NATIVE WHITE			FOREIGN-BORN WHITE			NEGRO			OTHER RACES		
	Total	Male	Female	Total	Male	Female	Total	Male	Female	Total	Male	Female	Total	Male	Female
Total population (all ages)	7,454,995	3,676,293	3,778,702	4,897,481	2,397,164	2,500,317	2,080,020	1,057,839	1,022,181	458,444	205,727	252,717	19,050	15,563	3,487
Persons 14 years old and over	6,102,747	2,989,576	3,113,171	3,658,014	1,766,189	1,891,825	2,061,426	1,048,510	1,012,916	366,836	160,661	206,175	16,471	14,216	2,255
In labor force	3,474,760	2,424,740	1,050,020	2,113,054	1,403,145	709,909	1,114,459	879,446	235,013	234,336	129,853	104,483	12,911	12,296	615
Not in labor force	2,627,987	564,836	2,063,151	1,544,960	363,044	1,181,916	946,967	169,064	777,903	132,500	30,808	101,692	3,560	1,920	1,640
Engaged in own home housew'k	1,592,195	20,265	1,571,930	852,525	10,247	842,278	675,850	8,973	666,877	62,563	991	61,572	1,257	54	1,203
In school	474,543	248,124	226,419	422,821	222,304	200,517	22,889	11,998	10,891	27,902	13,183	14,719	931	639	292
Unable to work	293,980	162,619	131,361	105,263	53,804	51,459	159,113	98,217	60,896	28,901	9,958	18,943	703	640	63
In institutions	34,202	18,746	15,456	16,802	9,200	7,602	14,490	7,549	6,941	2,704	1,797	907	206	200	6
Other and not reported	233,067	115,082	117,985	147,549	67,489	80,060	74,625	42,327	32,298	10,430	4,879	5,551	463	387	76
LABOR FORCE BY EMPLOYMENT STATUS															
In labor force	3,474,760	2,424,740	1,050,020	2,113,054	1,403,145	709,909	1,114,459	879,446	235,013	234,336	129,853	104,483	12,911	12,296	615
Employed (exc. public emerg. work)	2,839,366	1,964,346	875,020	1,711,638	1,127,160	584,478	946,938	738,020	208,918	169,497	88,386	81,111	11,293	10,780	513
At work	2,765,695	1,917,928	847,767	1,669,669	1,104,589	565,080	918,934	716,249	202,685	166,185	86,681	79,504	10,907	10,409	498
With a job	73,671	46,418	27,253	41,969	22,571	19,398	28,004	21,771	6,233	3,312	1,705	1,607	386	371	15
On public emerg. work (WPA, etc.)	103,386	86,845	16,541	61,920	51,403	10,517	21,415	19,911	1,504	19,936	15,428	4,508	115	103	12
Seeking work	532,008	373,549	158,459	339,496	224,582	114,914	146,106	121,515	24,591	44,903	26,039	18,864	1,503	1,413	90
Experienced workers	459,422	335,922	123,500	276,438	191,793	84,645	141,561	119,197	22,364	39,995	23,565	16,430	1,428	1,367	61
New workers	72,586	37,627	34,959	63,056	32,789	30,269	4,545	2,318	2,227	4,908	2,474	2,434	75	46	29
PERCENT BY SEX															
In labor force	100.0	69.8	30.2	100.0	66.4	33.6	100.0	78.9	21.1	100.0	55.4	44.6	100.0	95.2	4.8
Employed (exc. public emerg.)	100.0	69.2	30.8	100.0	65.9	34.1	100.0	77.9	22.1	100.0	52.1	47.9	100.0	95.5	4.5
On pub. emerg. work (WPA, etc.)	100.0	84.0	16.0	100.0	83.0	17.0	100.0	93.0	7.0	100.0	77.4	22.6	100.0	89.6	10.4
Seeking work	100.0	70.2	29.8	100.0	66.2	33.8	100.0	83.2	16.8	100.0	58.0	42.0	100.0	94.0	6.0
Not in labor force	100.0	21.5	78.5	100.0	23.5	76.5	100.0	17.9	82.1	100.0	23.3	76.7	100.0	53.9	46.1
Engaged in own home housew'k	100.0	1.3	98.7	100.0	1.2	98.8	100.0	1.3	98.7	100.0	1.6	98.4	100.0	4.3	95.7
In school	100.0	52.3	47.7	100.0	52.6	47.4	100.0	52.4	47.6	100.0	47.2	52.8	100.0	68.6	31.4
Unable to work	100.0	55.3	44.7	100.0	51.1	48.9	100.0	61.7	38.3	100.0	34.5	65.5	100.0	91.0	9.0
In institutions	100.0	54.8	45.2	100.0	54.8	45.2	100.0	52.1	47.9	100.0	66.5	33.5	100.0	97.1	2.9
Other and not reported	100.0	49.4	50.6	100.0	45.7	54.3	100.0	56.7	43.3	100.0	46.8	53.2	100.0	83.6	16.4
EMPLOYED WORKERS BY CLASS OF WORKER															
Employed (exc. public emerg.)	2,839,366	1,964,346	875,020	1,711,638	1,127,160	584,478	946,938	738,020	208,918	169,497	88,386	81,111	11,293	10,780	513
Wage and salary workers	2,459,880	1,647,274	812,606	1,548,333	992,373	555,960	743,765	564,074	179,691	159,008	82,450	76,558	8,774	8,377	397
Employers and own-account workers	347,006	303,310	43,696	144,706	124,915	19,791	190,344	170,526	19,818	9,560	5,541	4,019	2,396	2,328	68
Unpaid family workers	18,091	5,652	12,439	9,303	4,688	4,615	8,514	875	7,639	196	51	145	78	38	40
Class of worker not reported	14,389	8,110	6,279	9,296	5,184	4,112	4,315	2,545	1,770	733	344	389	45	37	8
At work	2,765,695	1,917,928	847,767	1,669,669	1,104,589	565,080	918,934	716,249	202,685	166,185	86,681	79,504	10,907	10,409	498
Wage and salary workers	2,404,444	1,615,540	788,904	1,514,554	976,011	538,543	724,845	550,085	174,760	156,373	81,159	75,214	8,672	8,285	387
Employers and own-account workers	331,238	289,936	41,302	138,100	119,549	18,551	182,031	163,148	18,883	8,987	5,184	3,803	2,120	2,055	65
Unpaid family workers	17,599	5,454	12,145	9,005	4,527	4,478	8,332	843	7,489	189	49	140	73	35	38
Class of worker not reported	12,414	6,998	5,416	8,010	4,502	3,508	3,726	2,173	1,553	636	289	347	42	34	8
With a job	73,671	46,418	27,253	41,969	22,571	19,398	28,004	21,771	6,233	3,312	1,705	1,607	386	371	15
Wage and salary workers	55,486	31,734	23,702	33,779	16,362	17,417	18,920	13,989	4,931	2,635	1,291	1,344	102	92	10
Employers and own-account workers	15,768	13,374	2,394	6,606	5,366	1,240	8,313	7,378	935	573	357	216	276	273	3
Unpaid family workers	492	198	294	298	161	137	182	32	150	7	2	5	5	3	2
Class of worker not reported	1,975	1,112	863	1,286	682	604	589	372	217	97	55	42	3	3	-
PERCENT DISTRIBUTION															
Persons 14 years old and over	100.0	100.0	100.0	100.0	100.0	100.0	100.0	100.0	100.0	100.0	100.0	100.0	100.0	100.0	100.0
In labor force	56.9	81.1	33.7	57.8	79.4	37.5	54.1	83.9	23.2	63.9	80.8	50.7	78.4	86.5	27.3
Not in labor force	43.1	18.9	66.3	42.2	20.6	62.5	45.9	16.1	76.8	36.1	19.2	49.3	21.6	13.5	72.7
Engaged in own home housew'k	26.1	0.7	50.5	23.3	0.6	44.5	32.8	0.9	65.8	17.1	0.6	29.9	7.6	0.4	53.3
In school	7.8	8.3	7.3	11.6	12.6	10.6	1.1	1.1	1.1	7.6	8.2	7.1	5.7	4.5	12.9
Unable to work	4.8	5.4	4.2	2.9	3.0	2.7	7.7	9.4	6.0	7.9	6.2	9.2	4.3	4.5	2.8
In institutions	0.6	0.6	0.5	0.5	0.5	0.4	0.7	0.7	0.7	0.7	1.1	0.4	1.3	1.4	0.3
Other and not reported	3.8	3.8	3.8	4.0	3.8	4.2	3.6	4.0	3.2	2.8	3.0	2.7	2.8	2.7	3.4
LABOR FORCE BY EMPLOYMENT STATUS															
In labor force	100.0	100.0	100.0	100.0	100.0	100.0	100.0	100.0	100.0	100.0	100.0	100.0	100.0	100.0	100.0
Employed (exc. public emerg. work)	81.7	81.0	83.3	81.0	80.3	82.3	85.0	83.9	88.9	72.3	68.1	77.6	87.5	87.7	83.4
At work	79.6	79.1	80.7	79.0	78.7	79.6	82.5	81.4	86.2	70.9	66.8	76.1	84.5	84.7	81.0
With a job	2.1	1.9	2.6	2.0	1.6	2.7	2.5	2.5	2.7	1.4	1.3	1.5	3.0	3.0	2.4
On public emerg. work (WPA, etc.)	3.0	3.6	1.6	2.9	3.7	1.5	1.9	2.3	0.6	8.5	11.9	4.3	0.9	0.8	2.0
Seeking work	15.3	15.4	15.1	16.1	16.0	16.2	13.1	13.8	10.5	19.2	20.1	18.1	11.6	11.5	14.6
Experienced workers	13.2	13.9	11.8	13.1	13.7	11.9	12.7	13.6	9.5	17.1	18.1	15.7	11.1	11.1	9.9
New workers	2.1	1.6	3.3	3.0	2.3	4.3	0.4	0.3	0.9	2.1	1.9	2.3	0.6	0.4	4.7
EMPLOYED WORKERS BY CLASS OF WORKER															
Employed (exc. public emerg.)	100.0	100.0	100.0	100.0	100.0	100.0	100.0	100.0	100.0	100.0	100.0	100.0	100.0	100.0	100.0
Wage and salary workers	86.6	83.9	92.9	90.5	88.0	95.1	78.5	76.4	86.0	93.8	93.3	94.4	77.7	77.7	77.4
Employers and own-account workers	12.2	15.4	5.0	8.5	11.1	3.4	20.1	23.1	9.5	5.6	6.3	5.0	21.2	21.6	13.3
Unpaid family workers	0.6	0.3	1.4	0.5	0.4	0.8	0.9	0.1	3.7	0.1	0.1	0.2	0.7	0.4	7.8
Class of worker not reported	0.5	0.4	0.7	0.5	0.5	0.7	0.5	0.3	0.8	0.4	0.4	0.5	0.4	0.3	1.6
At work	100.0	100.0	100.0	100.0	100.0	100.0	100.0	100.0	100.0	100.0	100.0	100.0	100.0	100.0	100.0
Wage and salary workers	86.9	84.2	93.1	90.7	88.4	95.3	78.9	76.8	86.2	94.1	93.6	94.6	79.5	79.6	77.7
Employers and own-account workers	12.0	15.1	4.9	8.3	10.8	3.3	19.8	22.8	9.3	5.4	6.0	4.8	19.4	19.7	13.1
Unpaid family workers	0.6	0.3	1.4	0.5	0.4	0.8	0.9	0.1	3.7	0.1	0.1	0.2	0.7	0.3	7.6
Class of worker not reported	0.4	0.4	0.6	0.5	0.4	0.6	0.4	0.3	0.8	0.4	0.3	0.4	0.4	0.3	1.6
With a job	100.0	100.0	100.0	100.0	100.0	100.0	100.0	100.0	100.0	100.0	100.0	100.0	100.0	100.0	-
Wage and salary workers	75.2	68.4	87.0	80.5	72.5	89.8	67.6	64.3	79.1	79.6	75.7	83.6	26.4	24.8	-
Employers and own-account workers	21.4	28.8	8.8	15.7	23.8	6.4	29.7	33.9	15.0	17.3	20.9	13.4	71.5	73.6	-
Unpaid family workers	0.7	0.4	1.1	0.7	0.7	0.7	0.6	0.1	2.4	0.2	0.1	0.3	1.3	0.8	-
Class of worker not reported	2.7	2.4	3.2	3.1	3.0	3.1	2.1	1.7	3.5	2.9	3.2	2.6	0.8	0.8	-

Table C-42.—EMPLOYED WORKERS 14 YEARS OLD AND OVER, BY MAJOR OCCUPATION GROUP, INDUSTRY GROUP, AND SEX, FOR THE CITY OF NEW YORK: 1940

[Percent not shown where less than 0.1 or where base is less than 100]

MAJOR OCCUPATION GROUP AND INDUSTRY GROUP	Total	Male	Female	PERCENT BY OCCUPATION AND INDUSTRY			PERCENT BY SEX	
				Total	Male	Female	Male	Female
Total population (all ages)	7,454,995	3,676,293	3,778,702	-	-	-	49.3	50.7
All persons 14 years old and over	6,102,747	2,989,576	3,113,171	-	-	-	49.0	51.0
In labor force	3,474,760	2,424,740	1,050,020	100.0	100.0	100.0	69.8	30.2
Employed workers (except on public emergency work)	2,839,366	1,964,346	875,020	81.7	81.0	83.3	69.2	30.8
MAJOR OCCUPATION GROUP								
Employed (except on public emergency work)	2,839,366	1,964,346	875,020	100.0	100.0	100.0	69.2	30.8
Professional workers	217,032	126,887	90,145	7.6	6.5	10.3	58.5	41.5
Semiprofessional workers	42,198	30,052	12,146	1.5	1.5	1.4	71.2	28.8
Farmers and farm managers	558	519	39	-	-	-	93.0	7.0
Proprietors, managers, and officials, except farm	288,152	259,075	29,077	10.1	13.2	3.3	89.9	10.1
Clerical, sales, and kindred workers	770,804	446,199	324,605	27.1	22.7	37.1	57.9	42.1
Craftsmen, foremen, and kindred workers	329,479	319,308	10,171	11.6	16.3	1.2	96.9	3.1
Operatives and kindred workers	580,053	388,788	191,265	20.4	19.8	21.9	67.0	33.0
Domestic service workers	123,202	6,976	116,226	4.3	0.4	13.3	5.7	94.3
Service workers, except domestic	346,264	256,696	89,568	12.2	13.1	10.2	74.1	25.9
Farm laborers (wage workers) and farm foremen	960	914	46	-	-	-	95.2	4.8
Farm laborers, unpaid family workers	60	50	10	-	-	-	-	-
Laborers, except farm	114,168	111,567	2,601	4.0	5.7	0.3	97.7	2.3
Occupation not reported	26,436	17,315	9,121	0.9	0.9	1.0	65.5	34.5
INDUSTRY GROUP								
Employed (except on public emergency work)	2,839,366	1,964,346	875,020	100.0	100.0	100.0	69.2	30.8
Agriculture, forestry, and fishery	3,468	3,229	239	0.1	0.2	-	93.1	6.9
Agriculture	2,813	2,599	214	0.1	0.1	-	92.4	7.6
Forestry (except logging) and fishery	655	630	25	-	-	-	96.2	3.8
Mining	996	822	174	-	-	-	82.5	17.5
Coal mining	93	82	11	-	-	-	-	-
Crude petroleum and natural gas production	78	66	12	-	-	-	-	-
Other mines and quarries	825	674	151	-	-	-	81.7	18.3
Construction	131,599	127,880	3,719	4.6	6.5	0.4	97.2	2.8
Manufacturing	746,466	504,413	242,053	26.3	25.7	27.7	67.6	32.4
Food and kindred products	67,648	54,260	13,388	2.4	2.8	1.5	80.2	19.8
Textile-mill products	42,081	26,440	15,641	1.5	1.3	1.8	62.8	37.2
Apparel and other fabricated textile products	236,604	121,618	114,986	8.3	6.2	13.1	51.4	48.6
Logging	50	44	6	-	-	-	-	-
Sawmills and planing mills	1,407	1,291	116	-	0.1	-	91.8	8.2
Furniture, store fixtures, and miscellaneous wooden goods	21,104	18,415	2,689	0.7	0.9	0.3	87.3	12.7
Paper and allied products	20,049	12,610	7,439	0.7	0.6	0.9	62.9	37.1
Printing, publishing, and allied industries	81,528	62,074	19,454	2.9	3.2	2.2	76.1	23.9
Chemicals and allied products	30,400	19,973	10,427	1.1	1.0	1.2	65.7	34.3
Petroleum and coal products	8,074	6,371	1,703	0.3	0.3	0.2	78.9	21.1
Leather and leather products	26,702	18,936	7,766	0.9	1.0	0.9	70.9	29.1
Stone, clay, and glass products	8,366	6,960	1,406	0.3	0.4	0.2	83.2	16.8
Iron and steel and their products	24,332	20,387	3,945	0.9	1.0	0.5	83.8	16.2
Nonferrous metals and their products	21,099	17,314	3,785	0.7	0.9	0.4	82.1	17.9
Machinery	44,459	36,106	8,353	1.6	1.8	1.0	81.2	18.8
Automobiles and automobile equipment	5,256	4,421	835	0.2	0.2	0.1	84.1	15.9
Transportation equipment, except automobile	21,985	21,163	822	0.8	1.1	0.1	96.3	3.7
Other and not specified manufacturing industries	85,322	56,030	29,292	3.0	2.9	3.3	65.7	34.3
Transportation, communication, and other public utilities	251,416	220,359	31,057	8.9	11.2	3.5	87.6	12.4
Railroads (including railroad repair shops) and railway express service	32,779	31,130	1,649	1.2	1.6	0.2	95.0	5.0
Trucking service	28,347	27,352	995	1.0	1.4	0.1	96.5	3.5
Other transportation	102,686	98,192	4,494	3.6	5.0	0.5	95.6	4.4
Communication	36,407	18,340	18,067	1.3	0.9	2.1	50.4	49.6
Utilities	51,197	45,345	5,852	1.8	2.3	0.7	88.6	11.4
Wholesale and retail trade	621,757	470,614	151,143	21.9	24.0	17.3	75.7	24.3
Wholesale trade	99,660	79,079	20,581	3.5	4.0	2.4	79.3	20.7
Food and dairy products stores, and milk retailing	133,741	114,878	18,863	4.7	5.8	2.2	85.9	14.1
Eating and drinking places	112,822	86,611	26,211	4.0	4.4	3.0	76.8	23.2
Motor vehicles and accessories retailing, and filling stations	17,299	15,837	1,462	0.6	0.8	0.2	91.5	8.5
Other retail trade	258,235	174,209	84,026	9.1	8.9	9.6	67.5	32.5
Finance, insurance, and real estate	224,460	162,199	62,261	7.9	8.3	7.1	72.3	27.7
Business and repair services	74,133	61,177	12,956	2.6	3.1	1.5	82.5	17.5
Automobile storage, rental, and repair services	25,738	25,214	524	0.9	1.3	0.1	98.0	2.0
Business and repair services, except automobile	48,395	35,963	12,432	1.7	1.8	1.4	74.3	25.7
Personal services	293,887	109,819	184,068	10.4	5.6	21.0	37.4	62.6
Domestic service	135,788	13,752	122,036	4.8	0.7	13.9	10.1	89.9
Hotels and lodging places	55,832	31,981	23,851	2.0	1.6	2.7	57.3	42.7
Laundering, cleaning, and dyeing services	45,141	28,394	16,747	1.6	1.4	1.9	62.9	37.1
Miscellaneous personal services	57,126	35,692	21,434	2.0	1.8	2.4	62.5	37.5
Amusement, recreation, and related services	42,996	31,610	11,386	1.5	1.6	1.3	73.5	26.5
Professional and related services	247,816	122,769	125,047	8.7	6.2	14.3	49.5	50.5
Government	126,733	108,811	17,922	4.5	5.5	2.0	85.9	14.1
Industry not reported	73,639	40,644	32,995	2.6	2.1	3.8	55.2	44.8

Table C-43.—PERSONS 14 YEARS OLD AND OVER IN THE LABOR FORCE, 1940, AND GAINFUL WORKERS 14 YEARS OLD AND OVER, 1930, BY RACE AND SEX, FOR THE CITY OF NEW YORK

[Totals for population and gainful workers for 1930 include "Unknown age." Figures for white population in 1930 have been revised to include Mexicans who were classified with "Other races" in the 1930 reports. Percent not shown where less than 0.1 or where base is less than 100]

CENSUS YEAR AND RACE	TOTAL					MALE					FEMALE				
	Population		Persons in the labor force, and gainful workers,[1] 14 years old and over			Population		Persons in the labor force, and gainful workers,[1] 14 years old and over			Population		Persons in the labor force, and gainful workers,[1] 14 years old and over		
	Total (all ages)	14 years old and over	Number	Per-cent of total popu-lation	Per-cent of popu-lation 14 yrs. and over	Total (all ages)	14 years old and over	Number	Per-cent of total popu-lation	Per-cent of popu-lation 14 yrs. and over	Total (all ages)	14 years old and over	Number	Per-cent of total popu-lation	Per-cent of popu-lation 14 yrs. and over
1940	7,454,995	6,102,747	3,474,760	46.6	56.9	3,676,293	2,989,576	2,424,740	66.0	81.1	3,778,702	3,113,171	1,050,020	27.8	33.7
White	6,977,501	5,719,440	3,227,513	46.3	56.4	3,455,003	2,814,699	2,282,591	66.1	81.1	3,522,498	2,904,741	944,922	26.8	32.5
Negro	458,444	366,836	234,336	51.1	63.9	205,727	160,661	129,853	63.1	80.8	252,717	206,175	104,483	41.3	50.7
Other races	19,050	16,471	12,911	67.8	78.4	15,563	14,216	12,296	79.0	86.5	3,487	2,255	615	17.6	27.3
1930	6,930,446	5,354,374	3,186,958	46.0	59.5	3,472,956	2,674,820	2,324,296	66.9	86.9	3,457,490	2,679,554	862,662	25.0	32.2
White	6,589,377	5,081,179	2,982,779	45.3	58.7	3,304,524	2,539,724	2,199,622	66.6	86.6	3,284,853	2,541,455	783,157	23.8	30.8
Negro	327,706	261,277	193,730	59.1	74.1	156,968	124,375	114,535	73.0	92.1	170,738	136,902	79,195	46.4	57.8
Other races	13,363	11,918	10,449	78.2	87.7	11,464	10,721	10,139	88.4	94.6	1,899	1,197	310	16.3	25.9

[1] Data for 1930 represent gainful workers 14 years old and over.

Those Pullman Blues, quoting Malcolm X, speaking of his days as a food seller on the coaches for New Haven

"We were in that world between Black train employees and White passengers: We were in that world of Negroes who are both servants and psychologists, aware that White people are so obsessed with their own importance that they will pay liberally, even dearly, for the impression of being catered to and entertained."

Those Pullman Blues, quoting Norman Bookman

"One time a man was riding with us on the Lark. He was talking and they were discussing politics, and they were saying, 'Well, there's so many niggers in San Francisco and so many niggers in L.A.,' and so on. The woman with him looked up at me-I didn't say anything till the next morning. [The train] came in, and she was with him. They were not together. And I said, 'Pardon me, I'd like to ask a question if I may. What did I do wrong last night? I've been up all night wondering what was done wrong. I thought I was giving fair service.'

Then he started apologizing for having made the mistake in saying those words, and he wanted to give me a little piece of change for it. I said, 'Oh, no, you don't owe me nothing.' But now, you see, I could have put it another way or jumped in that night. They're all drinking, and it could have been an embarrassing thing, or he could have gotten angry, or maybe I got angry and cussed him out, or something else. So you learn how to handle these things this way."

The Sharecropper System

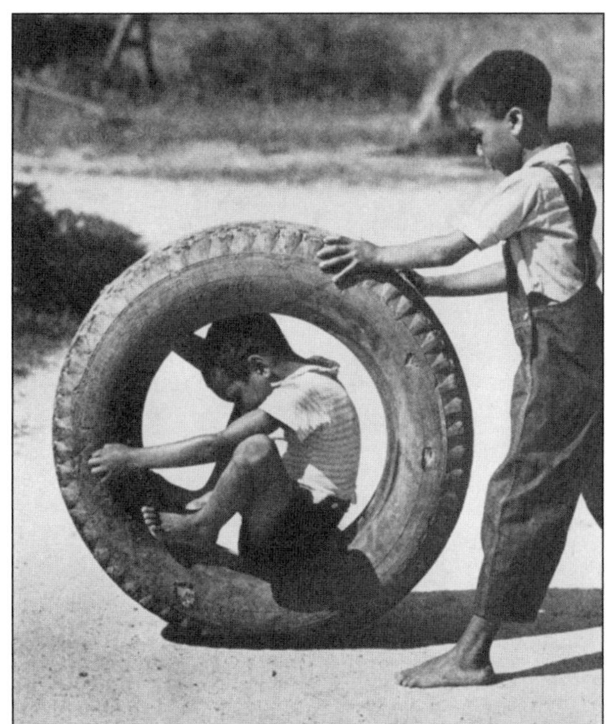
Poverty was a constant companion under the sharecropper system.

- By moving to New York, the couple broke the cycle of poverty inherent in the sharecropper system.
- In general, the tenant farmer borrowed everything he needed to work with-seed, plow, mule, etc.-from the landowner, who was paid back with a portion of the crops.
- This system came into play after the Civil War, according to some "so that plantation owners could pretend that the Emancipation Proclamation had never occurred."
- This system normally imprisoned the tenant farmer; rarely could enough "good years" equal the cost of the goods "borrowed" so the sharecropper could purchase land.
- Their decision was reinforced by the boll weevil invasion of 1923, which wiped out entire cotton fields, and caused a general depression in the South. They moved North to see if what they had heard about freedom was true.
- They were not alone; in 1920, 85 percent of all Blacks lived south of the Mason-Dixon line compared with 92 percent at the time of the Civil War; by 1940 the percentage would drop to 76 percent.
- The couple did not engage in any practices such as illegal liquor distilling to supplement their income, despite the temptation; they needed the money but after a neighbor was taken to jail for manipulating the gas meter, the husband decided that it was better for him not to engage in those activities.

Tennessee Farmer Finds Success as Welder for TVA

The Tennessee Valley Authority brought electricity to the rural South and prosperity to thousands of TVA workers in the years surrounding 1940. The Danielsons earned about five times their farming earnings, enough to buy a radio, a refrigerator, and save for a car. The TVA's massive, multi-faceted enterprise also honed America's war mobilization skills that were critical in the days of World War II.

Life at Home

- Timothy Danielson worked for the Tennessee Valley Authority (TVA) building dams and during the past four years, his income rose almost five times.
- As a farmer, he rarely made more than $350.00 a year, electricity was unavailable, he did not own a radio or an icebox refrigerator.
- When he, his wife, Martha and their three children moved to the TVA-created community of Norris, they had electricity, a radio, refrigerator, and were able to save for a car.
- The town of Norris was created by the Tennessee Valley Authority to house the workers who constructed the Norris Dam.
- Unlike many "textile towns," which stacked row after row of houses together on a street, Norris' neighborhoods followed the undulating grade of the natural land and thousands of trees were left standing to beautify the homes.
- The houses in Norris used the traditional Southern "dog-trot" or "shotgun" design (meaning a shotgun could blast through the house from one end to the other without hitting a thing) with a hall or breezeway in the middle and rooms on each side.
- Norris had 291 single-family homes, 10 duplexes, five apartment houses, a park, a playground, and a town common, built to the edge of a lake.
- Beer was not sold in Norris because most TVA projects are dry.
- Norris was set up more like a technical college than a construction site, and Timothy took woodworking classes and mathematics.
- Other classes included technical subjects for dam builders and even a "discussion group" on the history of public ownership and labor problems in America.
- TVA's concept of rebuilding the Tennessee Valley included helping the entire family.

The Tennessee Valley Project improved the lives of poor tenant farmers and their families.

Construction crew in the cafeteria at Cherokee Dam.

- Cooking and decorating classes were available for the woman, which Martha enjoyed.
- The Authority offered free educational movies in Norris, and the commercial theater featured curly-headed moppet Shirley Temple.
- Workers enjoyed electrical appliances for the first time.
- The Norris Dam's construction required that an entire graveyard be moved, including the remains of Martha's grandparents, where they have been buried near Hogskin Creek.
- At Caryville, where Timothy's family originated, 73 houses, a nine-room brick school and the Baptist church were moved to make way for the lake.
- The Danielson's diet and cash flow is supplemented by work on a farm owned by Martha's brother, possible due to the TVA's 33-hour work week.

Life at Work: The TVA

- When the dam-building project began, 40,000 people applied for jobs, which were estimated to last for four years, but the project was completed 18 months ahead of schedule.
- Timothy started for the TVA doing construction and graduated to welder, a job he enjoyed.
- He also kept a small farm with his brother-in-law.
- To provide the maximum number of jobs, the project had four shifts and a 33-hour week.
- The Norris Dam was 265 feet high, 1,872 feet long, and 204 feet thick at its base. The reservoir area covered 34,200 acres.
- After gaining experience in construction and welding, Timothy was allowed to rotate jobs every five weeks to gain experience in different kinds of jobs, including foreman.
- At construction camps meals cost $0.35 for all you can eat, $0.30 if you are a regular boarder. In Norris the standard price was $0.25 per meal.
- Meals included fruit, cereals, and salads, "with so much to eat you can be a Yankee and have dinner at night, or a Southerner and have supper in the evening."
- Nearly all dam-builders were craft unionists, and the office worker's union had CIO affiliation.

- Hourly wages paid by the TVA included: carpenter, $1.10; rigger, $1.25; accounting clerk, $1.50; rigger foreman, $1.50; shovel operator, $1.50, set by the government's definition of "prevailing" wages with "due regard" for rates secured through collective agreement.
- The Knoxville paper reported, "It is no news that the number of employees in the Authority who are unhappy over the conditions of their work is increasing. To a large extent this fact merely results from the growing maturity of the Authority and it's a reaction from the possibly excessive enthusiasm of the organization days."
- The TVA introduced fertilizers, and new farming methods brought back the soil of the region—terracing, contour farming, strip cropping, and soil surveys.
- In exchange for free fertilizer, Martha's brother agreed to follow the advice of the agricultural experts, keep records of yields, and conduct farm tours.
- Eventually, 15,000 demonstration farms such as this are established throughout the TVA.
- A nursery was set up at Norris with tree seedlings for wind breaks, erosion control, and fruit to the Danielson's and other farming families.
- The TVA electrical rates were below the prevailing rates in the area and one man saw his bill drop from $2.30 a month to $0.75.
- Many homeowners used more electricity because of its affordability.
- Norris was a totally planned community, conceived by the Tennessee Valley Authority as a modern, almost Utopian, town that included education, socialization, and adult education.
- The houses are of board-and-batten construction, and built by local carpenters and masons who were paid a union wage.
- Norris included a tract of woodland of community forest and land was provided for community gardens and private yards.
- The school was in the center of town and "they backed it up against a hill so the children on the second floor could walk out without having to use stairs."

Installation of a rotor in the Norris Dam powerhouse.

- The school's technology included a "trick electric eye" that turned on the lights in cloudy weather.
- The children did not carry books home, but studied in the library from an array of books
- The library was also made available to "grown people in the town" who were permitted to use the school auditorium and woodworking shop at the school.
- Instead of report cards, teachers wrote letters to the parents concerning their child's progress; "they put down grades only in case some child might be transferred."
- The school created a business to deliver the town's news bulletins; in return the town contributed a five-acre plot of ground. "So they organized the Norris School Produce company to raise vegetables.

When they needed capital, they raised $50.00 by selling 500 $0.10 bonds, paying three percent interest. Stock in the company, though, was obtainable only by work-eight hours for one share."

- The Norris community also decided by a 99 percent vote to have a "Religious Fellowship" for all denominations and meet in the school auditorium.
- This decision led to rumors that the TVA town of Norris is "churchless," even though services were held each Sunday.

Knoxville News, "TVA Head's Wife Leads WCTU-like Campaign," April 23, 1937

"NORRIS—This is the modern, up-to-date-some call it Utopian-town of the modern, farthest reaching arm of the New Deal. People have come from all over the world to see it and the scientific, esthetic, and social developments it represents.

Yet on Tuesday the people here will go to the polls like those of any other American country town to vote on whether they want beer sold in the town and if so, how.

The pre-referendum campaign is much like the old-fashioned temperance rows that have split less modern American villages for 100 years. Norris, child of the New Deal though it may be, is uninfluenced by the fact that it was the New Deal that brought prohibition repeal to America as the very first of its accomplishments. It seems to be anybody's guess as to the outcome of the beer fight.

The pre-election campaign so far has been featured by the circulation of a petition opposing the sale of beer in Norris. It was signed by 128 persons, mostly women. The importance of the petition lies not so much in the number of persons who signed it as the fact that it was circulated by Mrs. A.E. Morgan, wife of the TVA Chairman..."

Creation of the TVA

- In 1933, when Roosevelt came to office, 13 million people were out of work, a third of the work force, and a third more people than the year before.
- The sum of all goods and services produced by the country had fallen by half since 1929.
- Farm prices, marriages, and birth rates were all down.
- No matter how desperate conditions were nationally, they were worse in the Tennessee Valley.
- In 1933 the annual per capita income in the Valley was $168.00.
- Malaria affected up to 30 percent of the population of some areas.
- More than half the region's three million people lived on farms; half of those lived on farms they did not own.
- Only three farms in 100 had electricity.
- Unchecked fires burned 10 percent of the region's woodlands yearly.
- The answer, President Franklin Roosevelt declared, was the Tennessee Valley Authority, a development envisioned to help flood control, prevent soil erosion, improve soil, and promote better economic diversification through industry.
- The bill creating the TVA was signed May 18, 1933.
- Less than three months after the TVA Act was signed, construction began on the first hydroelectric dam located on the Clinch River in northeast Tennessee.
- This required the digging of a 650-mile navigable waterway from Knoxville, to the upper reaches of the Tennessee River system, to Paducah on the Ohio to promote conservation and the development of recreational facilities, and to attract new industries to the region.
- When Roosevelt was asked, "What are you going to say when they ask you the political philosophy behind the TVA?"

- "I'll tell them it's neither fish nor fowl," Roosevelt answered, "but, whatever it is, it will taste awfully good to the people of the Tennessee Valley."
- By 1939 five hydroelectric facilities were in operation and five others were under construction.
- The TVA and electricity became synonymous to the farmers of the Tennessee Valley; a roadside sign in rural Tennessee read, "Farm for Sale. Have TVA."
- Electricity supplied farmers with pumps, washing machines, and other labor-saving devices; one Mississippi farmer reported that his ability to own a refrigerator in 1936 allowed him to sell butter, cream, and milk, providing an extra $30.00 a month in income.
- Seven of 12 million acres needed erosion control in 1933, and one million acres were eroded to the point of abandonment.
- During the war effort, TVA power was used by the Aluminum Company of America to manufacture aluminum for airplanes and by the secret "Manhattan Project" in Oak Ridge, Tennessee, where the atomic bomb was being developed.

A History of the Tennessee Valley Authority: "One day in the early 1940s a TVA land buyer was driving on a country road at dusk when he saw the farmer of a newly electrified farm, sitting on a little knoll overlooking his farm. Below him the house, the barn, and smokehouse were ablaze with light. And on the hill sat this farmer enthralled by a special wonder.About a week later the TVA man attended a church to which this farmer belongs. During the service, the farmer got up to express his spiritual condition: 'Brothers and sisters, I want to tell you this. The greatest thing on earth is to have the love of God in your heart, and the next greatest thing is to have electricity in your house.' "

The Fight for Equality and Civil Rights is Vibrant

In a high profile civil rights case that paved the way for racial equality and the emergence of America's black middle class in the 1940s, Alabama courts falsely convicted nine black youths of raping two white women. Northern aristocrat Penelope Vertrees took up the cause of the accused Scottsboro Boys.

Life at Home

- Penelope Vertrees was delighted with herself the first time she wrote a check to help the Scottsboro boys.
- Significantly, it was the tenth anniversary of her husband's death when she used his money-$100-to support the Negroes of Scottsboro, Alabama, for the first time.
- She knew without equivocation that Henry would never have approved; giving money at church was one thing, he would have said, but supporting causes you didn't know anything about was another kettle of fish.
- Penelope's involvement with the Scottsboro boys started because her maid Lucinda's cousin was the mother of one of the boys accused of raping two white women in Alabama.
- Lucinda had been working for Penelope since they were both teenagers, so when Lucinda lingered at the dining room door after bringing in a bowl of breakfast grits, Penelope knew something was on her mind.
- After being invited to speak up, Lucinda told the story of the nine black youths who had been arrested and tried in Scottsboro, Alabama, for raping two white hobo women on a train.
- Four of the accused were from Chattanooga, Tennessee, including Lucinda's cousin's son.
- The trouble had started when the Chattanooga-to-Memphis freight train was stopped in Paint Rock, Alabama, by a sheriff's posse investigating a fight between white and black youths on the train.
- In all, nine Negro youths aged 14 to 20 were removed from the train, even though several were not involved in the fight and most of the hobo travelers did not know each other.
- As they were taken from the train, two white women, Victoria Price and Ruby Bates, accused the men of rape.
- Physical evidence of a rape was scanty, and the reputation of both women tawdry at best.

Penelope Vertrees quietly supported the Scottsboro boys.

- A grand jury indicted the nine for rape, based on the women's testimony.
- Trials for the boys took place almost immediately to thwart efforts to lynch them.
- Of the six members of the Jackson County, Alabama bar appointed to defend the boys, only the aging Milo Moody and Chattanooga attorney Stephen Roddy spoke for the Scottsboro boys at the trial.
- Stephen R. Roddy was retained by Chattanooga's Interdenominational Colored Ministers' Alliance.
- When they learned four of the boys were from Chattanooga, the Alliance decided to become involved, raising $50.08 and approaching Stephen Roddy about taking the case.

Nine black youths were arrested in Scottsboro,Arizona,for raping two white women.

- The Chattanooga attorney agreed to defend the nine for $120.
- The grand jury formally indicted the nine boys and set the trial date.
- In Scottsboro, the first Monday of each month was known as "Fair Day," and people from as far away as 50 miles came to town to meet friends, attend county court trials, sell produce and buy supplies.
- On this first Monday, several thousand people pushed their way past the National Guard picket lines, who had been ordered by the governor to maintain order.
- Rooftops became crowded as people climbed up for a better view of the courthouse.
- Stories circulated about the proper way to punish black youths who took liberties with white women.
- In the courtroom, attorney Stephen Roddy had already been drinking.
- He informed the judge that he was not there as counsel for the defense, but was a representative for interested parties.
- He would not clearly define his position, except to say that he had not prepared for the case.
- When Milo Moody stepped up and agreed to help Roddy, the case was able to proceed on schedule.
- Roddy's petition for a change of venue was quickly dismissed, and defendants Clarence Norris and Charley Weems were tried together.

Victoria Price,one of the two accusers,on the witness stand.

- The first trial lasted a day and a half, and within an hour of their case going to the jury, defendant Haywood Patterson went on trial.
- In the middle of Patterson's trial, the first jury returned a verdict of guilty and sentenced Norris and Weems to death.
- The crowd's roar of approval was heard by the Patterson jury.
- The trial of Haywood Patterson took the afternoon of April 7 and the morning of April 8.
- The jury went into deliberations by 11:00 a.m.
- They reached a decision within 25 minutes, but by that time the trial of Ozie Powell, Willie Roberson, Andy Wright, Eugene Williams, and Olen Montgomery was already underway.
- Haywood Patterson was also found guilty and sentenced to death.

The Scottsboro boys and their attorney.

- The crowd controlled its response to this verdict under threat from the judge.
- The third case went to the jury at 4:20 p.m.
- Roy Wright was only 14 years old, and under Alabama law could only be tried in juvenile court.
- Solicitor H. G. Bailey offered Wright life imprisonment in return for a guilty plea in an effort to complete the trials quickly.
- Roddy would not agree, as a guilty plea would prevent an appeal.
- On Thursday morning, the fourth day of trials, the five were declared guilty and given the death sentence.

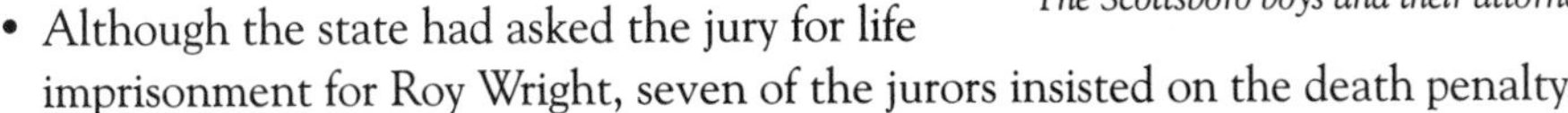

- Although the state had asked the jury for life imprisonment for Roy Wright, seven of the jurors insisted on the death penalty.

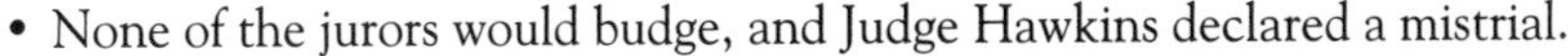

- None of the jurors would budge, and Judge Hawkins declared a mistrial.
- In just three days, all of the boys except Roy Wright were convicted and sentenced to death.
- Penelope listened, read the news accounts, kept her own counsel and became a supporter of the Scottsboro boys.
- Someone had to help them gain their freedom through the courts; besides, all the mass meetings in places like New York and Chicago were doing nothing but stirring up bad feelings throughout the South.
- The Scottsboro boys were innocent and did not deserve to be executed, but that didn't mean that women didn't need protection from the lustful ways of men of all colors and shades.

Life at Work

- For the past year, Penelope Vertrees had quietly but proudly supported the cause of the Scottsboro boys, so when her maid asked to talk this time, Penelope assumed more money was needed.
- Recently, she had celebrated with Lucinda the announcement that the U.S. Supreme Court had reversed the convictions of the Scottsboro boys.
- The high court ruled that Alabama had failed to provide adequate assistance of counsel as required by the due process clause of the Fourteenth Amendment.
- New trials were to be scheduled, she knew, and trials meant lawyers and lawyers equaled money.
- Even before the ruling and the need for another trial, Alabama's schools were on the edge of bankruptcy and capable of opening for only a few months.
- An expensive trial under the national spotlight would only exacerbate the problem.
- Besides, the people of Alabama were getting pretty tired of outsiders coming into the state telling them how to treat their Negroes and run their courts.
- Several deputies and scores of tenant farmers had been shot in race incidents stirred up by outside agitators; more trouble could be coming, and Penelope was unsure how she felt about that.
- As a member of both the Daughters of the American Revolution and the Colonial Dames, she did have a reputation to maintain.
- But this time Lucinda wanted more than money.
- She wanted Penelope to open her home to visitors from the North who were working on the defense of the Scottsboro boys.
- In a clear, quiet voice, Lucinda asked her to turn her home into a wayside motel for people doing research for the trial.
- The very idea was shocking.
- Although her financial support was well known in the black community of Chattanooga, no one on the altar guild of her church dreamed that she had been helping the Scottsboro boys for more than a year.

- Part of the strategy at the next trial was to insist that some Negroes be allowed on the jury.
- She had never seen a colored man serve on a jury and was unsure of how he might handle himself.
- Then, Penelope realized how much courage the request had required: no maid would even think she could determine the social calendar for the lady of the house.
- But now that a new trial was scheduled, there was no telling who might show up at the house.
- After the first trials, both the Central Committee of the Communist Party of the U.S. and the National Association for the Advancement of Colored People fought for control in the case.
- The more conservative NAACP had tried to remain uninvolved, not wanting to be associated with the incident unless they were sure the boys were innocent.
- The Communist Party, on the other hand, got involved as soon as convictions were issued and began a telegram campaign to court officials.
- The Communist Party believed the Negroes' problems were another phase of the capitalistic class exploitation.
- They felt that destruction of the existing economic order was the only way to solve the problem.
- The battle for power between the two groups made Penelope dizzy and more than occasionally suspicious about how her money was being spent.
- But she knew that the ministers who comprised the Interdenominational Colored Ministers' Alliance were honorable men who had the best interests of their race at heart.
- Lucinda reassured her of that often.

Life in the Community: Scottsboro, Alabama

- Scottsboro had a population of 3,500, a central waterworks system, a sewage plant that served the white sections of town, and two hosiery mills that employed 850 people.
- The seat of the largely agrarian Jackson County, Scottsboro served as the trade center for the surrounding farms.
- Along with the rest of the Tennessee Valley, Jackson County was hit hard by the stock market crash, and was suffering from two years of drought.
- Farmers were planting less cotton and concentrating efforts on subsistence crops, leaving less money to spend in town.

- They were equally distressed by the widespread publicity and negative images projected on the community by out-of-state press reports about the Scottsboro case.
- Huge rallies, which attracted thousands, had been staged in major cities across the nation and as far away as Berlin, where the inflamed crowd engaged in rock throwing.

- Equally distressing was the willingness of the mothers of the Scottsboro boys to tour the country whipping up racial unrest and raising money for the International Labor Defense.
- They had even heard that when the supply of mothers was inadequate, substitutes were found.
- And they hated the Communist-backed efforts to brand the convictions of the Scottsboro boys as an attempt by the white ruling classes to inflict "willful, cold-blooded and deliberate murder."
- These same rallies often resulted in petition drives and telegram campaigns for justice.
- The Scottsboro rallies had even spawned calls for other forms of freedom.
- The International Labor Defense used the upcoming trials as a springboard in nearby Birmingham to discuss freedom of speech for Negroes, repeal of vagrancy laws, abolition of the chain gang, elimination of poll taxes and an increase in welfare appropriations.

Scottsboro Boys Timeline

1931

March 25: The Scottsboro boys were arrested and charged with assault; rape charges were added against all nine boys based on the accusations made by Victoria Price and Ruby Bates.

March 26: The Alabama National Guard was called out to prevent the lynching of the nine at Scottsboro jail.

March 30: The grand jury indicted all the Scottsboro boys for rape.

April 6: Trials began before Judge A. E. Hawkins.

April 7: Clarence Norris, Charles Weems, Haywood Patterson, Olen Montgomery, Ozie Powell, Willie Robertson, Eugene Williams and Andy Wright were tried, convicted and sentenced to death; the trial of Roy Wright ended in a mistrial when some jurors held out for the death penalty even though the prosecution asked for life imprisonment.

June: Executions were halted pending an appeal to the Alabama Supreme Court.

April-December: The NAACP and the Communist-backed International Labor Defense fought for control of the appeal.

1932

January: Attorneys argued their appeal motions before the Alabama Supreme Court. The NAACP withdrew from the case; Ruby Bates denied in a letter to a friend that she was raped by the Scottsboro boys.

March: The Alabama Supreme Court affirmed the conviction of seven of the Scottsboro boys; the conviction of 14-yearold Roy Wright was reversed because he was a juvenile.

May: The U.S. Supreme Court agreed to review the Scottsboro convictions.

November: The U.S. Supreme Court reversed the convictions of the Scottsboro boys because Alabama failed to provide adequate counsel as required by the Fourteenth Amendment; a new trial was ordered.

Ruby Bates retracted her testimony against the Scottsboro boys, and led a parade of 3,000 before the White House to appeal for their freedom.

"Protest at Executions, Speakers Here Say Eight Negroes in Alabama Were 'Railroaded,'" *The New York Times,* June 29, 1931

Three thousand Negroes crowded yesterday afternoon into Salem Methodist Episcopal Church, at 129th Street and Seventh Avenue, to protest the execution, scheduled for July 10, in Scottsboro, Ala., of eight Negroes, all minors, for attacks on two white girls.

The speakers were Walter White, secretary of the Association for the Advancement of Colored People; William Pickens, field secretary of the association, and Bishop R. C. Lawson of the Pentecostal Church of Harlem, who presided.

White and Pickens, who went to Alabama to investigate, declared that the defendants, ranging in age from 14 to 20, were "railroaded." Only one attorney of six in the town of Scottsboro dared to accept the task of defending the youths, Pickens said, because Scottsboro, normally 1,400 in population, was thronged with a crowd of 10,000 during the trial.

The speakers deprecated the efforts of Communists on behalf of the condemned boys, saying they were harming the case more than helping it. Communists broke up a similar protest meeting recently in Chicago, Pickens said. Ten patrolmen were on duty at the church to prevent interference.

Anyone who tries to take an impartial attitude towards the conduct of the Scottsboro case is immediately branded a communist and a nigger-lover.

—Rabbi Benjamin Goldstein, who was given the option to sever all connection with the Scottsboro case or resign from Temple Beth Or, Montgomery, Alabama. Goldstein resigned.

"Negro Pastors Assail Labor Defense Body, Red Propaganda Is Real Aim of Scottsboro Moves, Chattanooga Alliance Charges," *The New York Times,* May 24, 1931

CHATTANOOGA, Tennessee—The City Interdenominational Ministers' Alliance of Negro Divines today broadcast a denunciation for the international labor defense for its activity on behalf of eight Negro youths under death sentence for a purported attack on two white girl hobos aboard a freight train near Scottsboro, Ala.

The statement of the ministers said the labor defense interest is "mainly for the purpose of drawing Negroes of the South into the Communist organization, and if the movement is successful it will tear the South asunder and destroy the peace and harmony existing for many years."

"13 Are Sentenced in Scottsboro Row, Each Gets $100 Fine or 60 Days in Jail for March on Capitol in Protest to High Court," *The New York Times,* November 11, 1932

WASHINGTON—Judge Isaac R. Hitt in police court today sentenced 13 participants in the Capitol Monday prior to the Supreme Court's decision in the Scottsboro case to a $100 fine or 60 days in jail.

The charge against all 13 was illegal parading and in six cases assaulting policemen.

The Scottsboro case is] a nauseating struggle between the Communist group and Negro society, not so much that justice may be done as that selfish interests may be advanced through the capitalization of the episode.

—George Fort Milton, chairman of the Southern Commission on the Study of Lynching, 1931

Free the Nine Scottsboro Boys!

Dear Fellow Worker

We, nine Negro boys, of Scottsboro, has been saved from the electric chair once more. We was saved because you and all the working-people heeded our cry to save us. You and all the working-people of the world followed the International Labor Defense to save us

We boys is innocent They framed us up down here only because we is children of working people, and because our skins is black For that they want to send us to the electric chair. But our lives is innocent They got no right to send us to the electric chair But they will if you give them the chance

Now even the Supreme Court has to give us a new trial But the boss men down here in Kilby prison, they sure still aiming to burn us We'll get you next time the prison guards tell us Only the I.L.D can save us. They saved us so far We ask all working people, black and white, to help the I L.D save us Don't let them kill us We innocent boys Only they want to kill us cause our skins is black and cause we is poor Help the I.L.D. save us

Willie Robinson
Haywood Patterson
Olen Montgomery X

Roy Wright
Andy Wright
Ozie Powell

Clarence Norris X
Charlie Weems X
Eugene Williams X

RESOLVED: We, Negro and white workers of the United States demand the immediate and unconditional release of these innocent Negro working class boys. They have been framed-up and sentenced to death in an attempt to split the growing unity of the white and Negro workers They have been sentenced to die because they represent a nation of enslaved Negro workers and poor farmers in the South, struggling for freedom. Their fight is our fight. As long as the Negro masses are doubly exploited, jim-crowed, lynched, the white workers will suffer from the great division in their workingclass ranks The fight to free the Scottsboro boys is the fight of the whole working class. "The 9 Negro Scottsboro boys must be freed!"

"Help the I. L. D. Save Us!"

NAME	ADDRESS
Inolee Gordon	11th St + East Spruce Ext
Mrs. Mary Helen Gordon	11th St & East Spruce Ext
Fatima Alley 23 St	Price McKinney
J. T. Simmins	R. 7. Box 152
Alice E Simmins	R 7 Box 152
Gladys Hall	
Mrs Elnora Crabtree	808 S. 4 St
Miss Fannie Thompson	808 S 4 St.
John A. Hall	401 No Front St
John Mierys	Yakima
Mike Mierys	Yakima
Ed Mierys	Wapato
John Finks	Wapato
Ed. Funk	Brownstown
J. F. Fink	Brownstown

THEY MUST BE FREED!

NINE INNOCENT LIVES FACE INSTANT MURDER

Judge Callaghan, member of Klu Klux Klan, has just denied a new trial to Heywood Patterson and Clarence Norris, two of the Scottsboro boys. Callaghan fiendishly orders that new briefs be filed by March 3rd.

By this move, he seeks to make it impossible for I. L. D. attorneys to file new briefs. This will enable him to have the Scottsboro boys executed by March 5th.

BUT HE WILL NOT SUCCEED!

The united protests of all workers, professionals and all sincere Scottsboro defenders will stop this bloody murder!

ATTEND THIS

SCOTTSBORO MASS MEETING

FRIDAY, MARCH 2, 8 p. m.

I. W. O. HALL, 415 LENOX AVENUE

NEW YORK DISTRICT INTERNATIONAL LABOR DEFENSE, 870 Broadway
HARLEM SECTION INTERNATIONAL LABOR DEFENSE, 326 Lenox Avenue

TEAR THIS OFF AND MAIL AT ONCE TO GOVERNOR MILLER

Governor Miller,
Montgomery, Alabama.

Scottsboro boys innocent of any crime. Demand their immediate, unconditional release.

Signed William Barfield

Address 59 W. 128 St.

Civil Unrest Sweeps Across America

In the decade leading up to 1940, various revolutionary groups gathered to cope with the devastation brought by the Depression. Often it was left to men like First Sgt. Clay Montgomery to sort out the complex political issues leading up to America's entry into World War II. This thirty year veteran was faced with the distasteful task of defending Washington DC from a ragtag army of World War I veterans seeking benefits.

Life at Work in Washington, DC

- First Sergeant Clay Montgomery was thinking about retirement after nearly 30 years in the army.
- He was assigned to a company of the 112th Infantry stationed in Fort Washington, Maryland, near the nation's capital, nearby to his daughter, her Department of Labor clerk husband and his grandchildren.
- Clay's duty was light, his captain was easy to please, and his soldiers were volunteers who respected discipline and knew the value of a steady paycheck.
- Nevertheless, his thoughts kept returning to his wife Eula's family land in North Carolina, where their oldest son farmed tobacco and was a church pastor.
- Across the nation, jobs were scarce, even for veterans who fought gallantly for their country during the Great War.
- These veterans were promised a bonus, from the federal government, to compensate them for the lower-than-market rates they received during their time in service.
- Congressman Wright Patman of Texas proposed legislation that would release these funds immediately, which gained approval in the House, but the Senate was slow to act.
- So, like good soldiers, this army of unemployed organized themselves into quasi-military units.
- Their goal was to march on Washington and force the federal government to support immediate payment of their bonus.
- Clay was appalled, feeling that serving one's country was a privilege, and the bonus a reward, not an entitlement to be demanded while the nation was struggling with lasting effects of the depression.
- Even worse, the governors of Indiana and Ohio supplied the bonus marchers with transportation, and food was donated by patriotic organizations.

Clay Montgomery has spent a lifetime in the army.

- As the Bonus Army, as they were called, approached Washington, Clay's battalion was ordered to receive intensive training in riot control.
- He realized the possibility of being asked to take up arms against his fellow Americans against the men who fought beside him in the Great War.
- As marchers, many of whom were unemployed, arrived from around the country, the government found vacant buildings where they could sleep and provided mobile kitchens and supplies to keep the Bonus Expeditionary Force alive.
- When the vacant buildings were filled, a camp was established across the river in Anacostia, growing to 20,000, including some wives and children, and city officials became concerned that epidemic disease might sweep the city.
- Most days, the Bonus Army would peacefully march to the capital in an orderly manner carrying placards, and those marchers with a different agenda, especially those espousing communism or radical ideas, were driven from the group.
- On several Sundays, Clay and his wife, Eula, visited the Anacostia camp to talk with the men.
- Disagreements arose when he told them they were wrong, but offered to pray for their souls.
- Eula always brought a basket of food for the children.
- In early June, despite the presence of men from across the nation camping nearby, the U.S. Senate soundly defeated the Bonus Army Bill.
- With nowhere to go and no backup strategy, the Bonus Army simply stayed in Washington and waited for a different result.
- Rumors flew that the men were planning a violent overthrow of the government, although Clay saw no evidence of a conspiracy-just desperate men with no leadership.
- District of Columbia policemen attempted to evict the marchers from the vacant buildings which set off a riot—the first major disturbance of the Bonus Army Movement.
- President Herbert Hoover was asked to provide assistance, an action Clay had been dreading.
- He was ordered to assemble the troops and load them into waiting trucks.
- In Washington, Clay and his troops found an assembled force of 600 consisting of a squadron of cavalry, a platoon of tanks and a battalion of the 12th Infantry under the direct command of Brigadier General Perry Miles, an officer with whom Clay had served, and overall command of General Douglas MacArthur.
- On the same day the riot had begun, Clay's troops led by the cavalry, followed by the tanks and supported by the infantry, moved in to disperse the rioters.
- Token resistance offered by the Bonus Army was put down with tear gas grenades, and the cavalry moved the marchers off government property.
- Thank God, thought Clay.
- As wrong as they may have been, he could not stomach the idea of harming a fellow war veteran in the shadow of the nation's Capitol Building.
- When the property was clear, the troops broke for dinner; no apparent injuries had taken place on either side of the lines.
- Later that evening, Clay was ordered to reform the units and evict the marchers from the Anacostia Camp, and worried that if violence was to occur, it would take place there.
- To keep their minds off the task ahead, his troops marched with a steady cadence toward the camp.
- As they approached, they were met by a man who claimed to be a leader, asking for one hour to evacuate the camp.
- General MacArthur agreed, and the troops set up camp for the night.
- The next morning, the troops that marched into the deserted Bonus Army Camp, found that approximately 20,000 members of the Bonus Army had left the city without a serious injury or a shot being fired.

The nine tables that follow are reprinted from the actual 1940 census, for the District of Columbia. They include actual data on race, percentage of voting population, school attendance, number of school years completed, foreign born, and employment of workers 14 years and older by job, industry and race. In addition to being incredibly fascinating, these facts help to strengthen and visualize the actual environment in which Sergeant Clay Montgomery worked.

Table 3.—AGE, BY RACE AND SEX, FOR THE DISTRICT OF COLUMBIA: 1940 AND 1930

[Figures for white population in 1930 revised to include Mexicans classified with "Other races" in the 1930 reports. Percent not shown where less than 0.1 or where base is less than 100]

AREA, AGE, AND CENSUS YEAR	ALL CLASSES			NATIVE WHITE			FOREIGN-BORN WHITE			NEGRO			OTHER RACES		
	Total	Male	Female	Total	Male	Female	Total	Male	Female	Total	Male	Female	Total	Male	Female
THE DISTRICT															
All ages: 1940	663,091	317,522	345,569	440,312	209,828	230,484	34,014	17,920	16,094	187,266	88,672	98,594	1,499	1,102	397
Under 5 years	39,851	20,054	19,797	25,501	12,850	12,651	36	19	17	14,193	7,126	7,067	121	59	62
5 to 9 years	37,245	18,643	18,602	23,278	11,713	11,565	94	54	40	13,783	6,824	6,959	90	52	38
10 to 14 years	41,089	20,549	20,540	26,828	13,460	13,368	170	82	88	14,013	6,963	7,050	78	44	34
15 to 19 years	48,680	23,588	25,092	33,236	16,444	16,792	516	266	250	14,849	6,835	8,014	79	43	36
20 to 24 years	65,483	31,247	34,236	46,659	23,256	23,403	796	407	389	17,935	7,542	10,393	93	42	51
25 to 29 years	74,346	35,783	38,563	50,428	24,846	25,582	1,719	809	910	22,031	10,004	12,027	168	124	44
30 to 34 years	65,768	31,826	33,942	43,176	20,916	22,260	2,627	1,268	1,359	19,764	9,471	10,293	201	171	30
35 to 39 years	58,348	28,183	30,165	36,480	17,471	19,009	3,787	1,899	1,888	17,895	8,652	9,243	186	161	25
40 to 44 years	53,889	25,853	28,036	35,080	16,331	18,749	4,476	2,416	2,060	14,169	6,967	7,202	164	139	25
45 to 49 years	46,641	22,630	24,011	30,546	14,389	16,157	4,639	2,594	2,045	11,345	5,559	5,786	111	88	23
50 to 54 years	37,918	18,268	19,650	24,908	11,496	13,412	4,369	2,540	1,829	8,567	4,168	4,399	74	64	10
55 to 59 years	28,870	13,436	15,434	19,157	8,508	10,649	3,412	1,890	1,522	6,251	2,996	3,255	50	42	8
60 to 64 years	23,757	10,772	12,985	16,280	7,041	9,239	2,699	1,430	1,269	4,735	2,265	2,470	43	36	7
65 to 69 years	18,309	7,730	10,579	12,522	5,050	7,472	1,985	966	1,019	3,781	1,694	2,087	21	20	1
70 to 74 years	11,651	4,777	6,874	8,340	3,245	5,095	1,331	655	676	1,974	871	1,103	6	6	-
75 years and over	11,246	4,183	7,063	7,893	2,812	5,081	1,358	625	733	1,981	735	1,246	14	11	3
Under 1 year	8,422	4,255	4,167	5,522	2,805	2,717	1	-	1	2,873	1,441	1,432	26	9	17
5 years	7,328	3,623	3,705	4,440	2,216	2,224	20	14	6	2,843	1,376	1,467	25	17	8
14 years	8,582	4,314	4,268	5,620	2,880	2,740	48	23	25	2,904	1,404	1,500	10	7	3
15 years	8,874	4,349	4,525	6,000	2,977	3,023	48	22	26	2,815	1,345	1,470	11	5	6
16 and 17 years	18,344	9,012	9,332	12,408	6,152	6,256	165	85	80	5,732	2,753	2,979	39	22	17
21 years and over	484,738	229,341	255,397	323,484	151,450	172,034	33,039	17,429	15,610	127,100	59,565	67,535	1,115	897	218
All ages: 1930	486,869	231,883	254,986	323,995	153,339	170,656	29,986	15,684	14,302	132,068	62,225	69,843	820	635	185
Under 5 years	32,304	16,398	15,906	22,185	11,312	10,873	56	26	30	10,006	5,036	4,970	57	24	33
5 to 9 years	35,624	17,797	17,827	24,508	12,350	12,158	219	102	117	10,838	5,314	5,524	59	31	28
10 to 14 years	32,712	16,015	16,697	22,911	11,424	11,487	277	138	139	9,484	4,432	5,052	40	21	19
15 to 19 years	35,806	16,899	18,907	24,434	11,803	12,631	658	311	347	10,675	4,757	5,918	39	28	11
20 to 24 years	48,387	22,909	25,478	32,282	15,591	16,691	1,588	757	831	14,406	6,472	7,934	111	89	22
25 to 29 years	48,120	23,401	24,719	30,415	15,035	15,380	2,586	1,259	1,327	14,989	6,994	7,995	130	113	17
30 to 34 years	45,095	21,411	23,684	29,494	13,814	15,680	3,127	1,612	1,515	12,360	5,889	6,471	114	96	18
35 to 39 years	43,587	20,724	22,863	27,633	12,849	14,784	3,703	1,998	1,705	12,154	5,797	6,357	97	80	17
40 to 44 years	36,326	17,314	19,012	23,014	10,701	12,313	3,700	2,079	1,621	9,563	4,493	5,070	49	41	8
45 to 49 years	32,574	15,277	17,297	20,312	9,219	11,093	3,303	1,777	1,526	8,920	4,247	4,673	39	34	5
50 to 54 years	28,732	13,653	15,079	18,804	8,606	10,198	2,962	1,593	1,369	6,944	3,433	3,511	22	21	1
55 to 59 years	21,609	10,038	11,571	15,247	6,804	8,443	2,331	1,241	1,090	4,001	1,966	2,035	30	27	3
60 to 64 years	16,958	7,761	9,197	12,252	5,476	6,776	1,909	1,000	909	2,785	1,274	1,511	12	11	1
65 to 69 years	11,712	5,194	6,518	8,267	3,540	4,727	1,491	794	697	1,942	849	1,093	12	11	1
70 to 74 years	7,694	3,297	4,397	5,668	2,332	3,336	898	452	446	1,123	508	615	5	5	-
75 years and over	7,847	2,980	4,867	5,514	2,024	3,490	1,105	511	594	1,226	444	782	2	1	1
Not reported	1,782	815	967	1,055	459	596	73	34	39	652	320	332	2	2	-
Under 1 year	6,136	3,136	3,000	4,272	2,208	2,064	4	-	4	1,847	921	926	13	7	6
5 years	7,115	3,626	3,489	4,886	2,511	2,375	16	7	9	2,200	1,101	1,099	13	7	6
14 years	6,331	3,118	3,213	4,413	2,217	2,196	58	22	36	1,848	873	975	12	6	6
15 years	6,403	3,095	3,308	4,472	2,193	2,279	97	45	52	1,823	846	977	11	11	-
16 and 17 years	13,365	6,487	6,878	9,076	4,523	4,553	233	116	117	4,040	1,841	2,199	16	7	9
21 years and over	341,465	160,809	180,656	223,938	103,713	120,225	28,533	14,994	13,539	88,388	41,584	46,804	606	518	88
Percent: 1940	100.0	100.0	100.0	100.0	100.0	100.0	100.0	100.0	100.0	100.0	100.0	100.0	100.0	100.0	100.0
Under 5 years	6.0	6.3	5.7	5.8	6.1	5.5	0.1	0.1	0.1	7.6	8.0	7.2	8.1	5.4	15.6
5 to 9 years	5.6	5.9	5.4	5.3	5.6	5.0	0.3	0.3	0.2	7.4	7.7	7.1	6.0	4.7	9.6
10 to 14 years	6.2	6.5	5.9	6.1	6.4	5.8	0.5	0.5	0.5	7.5	7.9	7.2	5.2	4.0	8.6
15 to 19 years	7.3	7.4	7.3	7.5	7.8	7.3	1.5	1.5	1.6	7.9	7.7	8.1	5.3	3.9	9.1
20 to 24 years	9.9	9.8	9.9	10.6	11.1	10.2	2.3	2.3	2.4	9.6	8.5	10.5	6.2	3.8	12.8
25 to 29 years	11.2	11.3	11.2	11.5	11.8	11.1	5.1	4.5	5.7	11.8	11.3	12.2	11.2	11.3	11.1
30 to 34 years	9.9	10.0	9.8	9.8	10.0	9.7	7.7	7.1	8.4	10.6	10.7	10.4	13.4	15.5	7.6
35 to 39 years	8.8	8.9	8.7	8.3	8.3	8.2	11.1	10.6	11.7	9.6	9.8	9.4	12.4	14.6	6.3
40 to 44 years	8.1	8.1	8.1	8.0	7.8	8.1	13.2	13.5	12.8	7.6	7.9	7.3	10.9	12.6	6.3
45 to 49 years	7.0	7.1	6.9	6.9	6.9	7.0	13.6	14.5	12.7	6.1	6.3	5.9	7.4	8.0	5.8
50 to 54 years	5.7	5.8	5.7	5.7	5.5	5.8	12.8	14.2	11.4	4.6	4.7	4.5	4.9	5.8	2.5
55 to 59 years	4.4	4.2	4.5	4.4	4.1	4.6	10.0	10.5	9.5	3.3	3.4	3.3	3.3	3.8	2.0
60 to 64 years	3.6	3.4	3.8	3.7	3.4	4.0	7.9	8.0	7.9	2.5	2.6	2.5	2.9	3.3	1.8
65 to 69 years	2.8	2.4	3.1	2.8	2.4	3.2	5.8	5.4	6.3	2.0	1.9	2.1	1.4	1.8	0.3
70 to 74 years	1.8	1.5	2.0	1.9	1.5	2.2	3.9	3.7	4.2	1.1	1.0	1.1	0.4	0.5	-
75 years and over	1.7	1.3	2.0	1.8	1.3	2.2	4.0	3.5	4.6	1.1	0.8	1.3	0.9	1.0	0.8
Under 1 year	1.3	1.3	1.2	1.3	1.3	1.2	-	-	-	1.5	1.6	1.5	1.7	0.8	4.3
5 years	1.1	1.1	1.1	1.0	1.1	1.0	0.1	0.1	-	1.5	1.6	1.5	1.7	1.5	2.0
14 years	1.3	1.4	1.2	1.3	1.4	1.2	0.1	0.1	0.2	1.6	1.6	1.5	0.7	0.6	0.8
15 years	1.3	1.4	1.3	1.4	1.4	1.3	0.1	0.1	0.2	1.5	1.5	1.5	0.7	0.5	1.5
16 and 17 years	2.8	2.8	2.7	2.8	2.9	2.7	0.5	0.5	0.5	3.1	3.1	3.0	2.6	2.0	4.3
21 years and over	73.1	72.2	73.9	73.5	72.2	74.6	97.1	97.3	97.0	67.9	67.2	68.5	74.4	81.4	54.9
Percent: 1930	100.0	100.0	100.0	100.0	100.0	100.0	100.0	100.0	100.0	100.0	100.0	100.0	100.0	100.0	100.0
Under 5 years	6.6	7.1	6.2	6.8	7.4	6.4	0.2	0.2	0.2	7.6	8.1	7.1	7.0	3.8	17.8
5 to 9 years	7.3	7.7	7.0	7.6	8.1	7.1	0.7	0.7	0.8	8.2	8.5	7.9	7.2	4.9	15.1
10 to 14 years	6.7	6.9	6.5	7.1	7.5	6.7	0.9	0.9	1.0	7.2	7.1	7.2	4.9	3.3	10.3
15 to 19 years	7.4	7.3	7.4	7.5	7.7	7.4	2.2	2.0	2.4	8.1	7.6	8.5	4.8	4.4	5.9
20 to 24 years	9.9	9.9	10.0	10.0	10.2	9.8	5.3	4.8	5.8	10.9	10.4	11.4	13.5	14.0	11.9
25 to 29 years	9.9	10.1	9.7	9.4	9.8	9.0	8.6	8.0	9.3	11.3	11.2	11.4	15.9	17.8	9.2
30 to 34 years	9.3	9.2	9.3	9.1	9.0	9.2	10.4	10.3	10.6	9.4	9.5	9.3	13.9	15.1	9.7
35 to 39 years	9.0	8.9	9.0	8.5	8.4	8.7	12.3	12.7	11.9	9.2	9.3	9.1	11.8	12.6	9.2
40 to 44 years	7.5	7.5	7.5	7.1	7.0	7.2	12.8	13.3	11.3	7.2	7.2	7.3	6.0	6.5	4.3
45 to 49 years	6.7	6.6	6.8	6.3	6.0	6.5	11.0	11.3	10.7	6.8	6.8	6.7	4.8	5.4	2.7
50 to 54 years	5.9	5.9	5.9	5.8	5.6	6.0	9.9	10.2	9.6	5.3	5.5	5.0	2.7	3.3	0.5
55 to 59 years	4.4	4.3	4.5	4.7	4.4	4.9	7.8	7.9	7.6	3.0	3.2	2.9	3.7	4.3	1.6
60 to 64 years	3.5	3.3	3.6	3.8	3.6	4.0	6.4	6.4	6.4	2.1	2.0	2.2	1.5	1.7	0.5
65 to 69 years	2.4	2.2	2.6	2.6	2.3	2.8	5.0	5.1	4.9	1.5	1.4	1.6	1.5	1.7	0.5
70 to 74 years	1.6	1.4	1.7	1.7	1.5	2.0	3.0	2.9	3.1	0.9	0.8	0.9	0.6	0.8	-
75 years and over	1.6	1.3	1.9	1.7	1.3	2.0	3.7	3.3	4.2	0.9	0.7	1.1	0.2	0.2	0.5
Not reported	0.4	0.4	0.4	0.3	0.3	0.3	0.2	0.2	0.3	0.5	0.5	0.5	0.2	0.3	-
Under 1 year	1.3	1.4	1.2	1.3	1.4	1.2	-	-	-	1.4	1.5	1.3	1.6	1.1	3.2
5 years	1.5	1.6	1.4	1.5	1.6	1.4	0.1	-	0.1	1.7	1.8	1.6	1.6	1.1	3.2
14 years	1.3	1.3	1.3	1.4	1.4	1.3	0.2	0.1	0.3	1.4	1.4	1.4	1.5	0.9	3.2
15 years	1.3	1.3	1.3	1.4	1.4	1.3	0.3	0.3	0.4	1.4	1.4	1.4	1.3	1.7	-
16 and 17 years	2.7	2.8	2.7	2.8	2.9	2.7	0.8	0.7	0.8	3.1	3.0	3.1	2.0	1.1	4.9
21 years and over	70.1	69.3	70.8	69.1	67.6	70.4	95.2	95.6	94.7	66.9	66.8	67.0	73.9	81.6	47.6

Table 4.—AGE, BY SEX, FOR THE DISTRICT OF COLUMBIA: 1870 TO 1940

[Percent not shown where less than 0.1]

AGE AND SEX	POPULATION								PERCENT BY AGE							
	1940	1930	1920	1910	1900	1890	1880	1870	1940	1930	1920	1910	1900	1890	1880	1870
Total, all ages	663,091	486,869	437,571	331,069	278,718	230,392	177,624	131,700	100.0	100.0	100.0	100.0	100.0	100.0	100.0	100.0
Under 5 years	39,851	32,304	30,436	26,669	23,150	20,303	20,635	17,778	6.0	6.6	7.0	8.1	8.3	8.8	11.6	13.5
5 to 9 years	37,245	35,624	29,840	25,312	23,731	21,522	20,082	13,469	5.6	7.3	6.8	7.6	8.5	9.3	11.3	10.2
10 to 14 years	41,089	32,712	29,816	24,649	22,734	22,852	18,405	14,336	6.2	6.7	6.8	7.4	8.2	9.9	10.4	10.9
15 to 19 years	48,680	35,806	33,526	28,112	24,814	24,260	16,108	13,010	7.3	7.4	7.7	8.5	8.9	10.5	9.1	9.9
20 to 24 years	65,483	48,387	51,055	34,424	31,510	26,131	18,316	13,001	9.9	9.9	11.7	10.4	11.3	11.3	10.3	9.9
25 to 29 years	74,346	48,120	49,997	35,113	29,755	20,681	15,684	12,674	11.2	9.9	11.4	10.6	10.7	9.0	8.8	9.6
30 to 34 years	65,768	45,095	39,924	31,029	24,768	17,652	12,844	10,538	9.9	9.3	9.1	9.4	8.9	7.7	7.2	8.0
35 to 39 years	58,348	43,587	38,629	29,662	21,881	16,479	14,213	9,706	8.8	9.0	8.8	9.0	7.9	7.2	8.0	7.4
40 to 44 years	53,889	36,326	32,535	23,572	17,934	13,788	11,199	7,307	8.1	7.5	7.4	7.1	6.4	6.0	6.3	5.5
45 to 49 years	46,641	32,574	29,518	18,565	14,626	13,154	8,574	5,746	7.0	6.7	6.7	5.6	5.2	5.7	4.8	4.4
50 to 54 years	37,918	28,732	22,672	15,511	13,299	10,821	7,462	4,995	5.7	5.9	5.2	4.7	4.8	4.7	4.2	3.8
55 to 59 years	28,870	21,609	14,584	10,751	10,286	6,792	4,537	2,895	4.4	4.4	3.3	3.2	3.7	2.9	2.6	2.2
60 to 64 years	23,757	16,958	12,515	9,448	8,201	5,877	3,963	2,450	3.6	3.5	2.9	2.9	2.9	2.6	2.2	1.9
65 to 69 years	18,309	11,712	8,114	7,668	5,035	3,683	2,312	1,519	2.8	2.4	1.9	2.3	1.8	1.6	1.3	1.2
70 to 74 years	11,651	7,694	6,010	4,928	3,440	2,499	1,627	1,128	1.8	1.6	1.4	1.5	1.2	1.1	0.9	0.9
75 years and over	11,246	7,847	6,511	4,421	3,259	2,397	1,663	1,148	1.7	1.6	1.5	1.3	1.2	1.0	0.9	0.9
Not reported	-	1,782	1,889	1,235	295	1,501	-	-	-	0.4	0.4	0.4	0.1	0.7	-	-
Male, all ages	317,522	231,883	203,543	158,050	132,004	109,584	83,578	62,192	100.0	100.0	100.0	100.0	100.0	100.0	100.0	100.0
Under 5 years	20,054	16,398	15,196	13,401	11,683	10,153	10,385	8,863	6.3	7.1	7.5	8.5	8.9	9.3	12.4	14.3
5 to 9 years	18,643	17,797	14,773	12,666	11,708	10,728	9,764	6,677	5.9	7.7	7.3	8.0	8.9	9.8	11.7	10.7
10 to 14 years	20,549	16,015	14,561	12,151	10,953	11,217	9,065	6,884	6.5	6.9	7.2	7.7	8.3	10.2	10.8	11.1
15 to 19 years	28,588	16,899	15,647	13,232	11,362	10,760	7,050	5,522	7.4	7.3	7.7	8.4	8.6	9.8	8.4	8.9
20 to 24 years	31,247	22,909	21,949	16,066	13,774	11,604	7,558	5,302	9.8	9.9	10.8	10.2	10.4	10.6	9.0	8.5
25 to 29 years	35,783	23,401	22,291	16,517	13,346	9,227	6,763	5,729	11.3	10.1	11.0	10.5	10.1	8.4	8.1	9.2
30 to 34 years	31,826	21,411	18,390	14,685	11,911	8,254	5,773	5,107	10.0	9.2	9.0	9.3	9.0	7.5	6.9	8.2
35 to 39 years	28,183	20,724	17,772	13,931	10,409	7,682	6,795	4,922	8.9	8.9	8.7	8.8	7.9	7.0	8.1	7.9
40 to 44 years	25,853	17,314	15,120	11,490	8,679	6,549	5,687	3,635	8.1	7.5	7.4	7.3	6.6	6.0	6.8	5.8
45 to 49 years	22,630	15,277	14,438	8,818	6,876	6,724	4,408	2,898	7.1	6.6	7.1	5.6	5.2	6.1	5.3	4.7
50 to 54 years	18,268	13,653	10,956	7,378	6,371	5,559	3,752	2,550	5.8	5.9	5.4	4.7	4.8	5.1	4.5	4.1
55 to 59 years	13,436	10,038	6,928	4,987	5,285	3,520	2,272	1,417	4.2	4.3	3.4	3.2	4.0	3.2	2.7	2.3
60 to 64 years	10,772	7,761	5,761	4,261	4,123	2,964	1,916	1,120	3.4	3.3	2.8	2.7	3.1	2.7	2.3	1.8
65 to 69 years	7,730	5,194	3,488	3,676	2,431	1,768	1,091	674	2.4	2.2	1.7	2.3	1.8	1.6	1.3	1.1
70 to 74 years	4,777	3,297	2,488	2,351	1,611	1,152	715	459	1.5	1.4	1.2	1.5	1.2	1.1	0.9	0.7
75 years and over	4,183	2,980	2,685	1,930	1,321	946	584	433	1.3	1.3	1.3	1.2	1.0	0.9	0.7	0.7
Not reported	-	815	1,100	510	162	767	-	-	-	0.4	0.5	0.3	0.1	0.7	-	-
Female, all ages	345,569	254,986	234,028	173,019	146,714	120,808	94,046	69,508	100.0	100.0	100.0	100.0	100.0	100.0	100.0	100.0
Under 5 years	19,797	15,906	15,240	13,268	11,467	10,150	10,250	8,915	5.7	6.2	6.5	7.7	7.8	8.4	10.9	12.8
5 to 9 years	18,602	17,827	15,067	12,646	12,028	10,794	10,318	6,792	5.4	7.0	6.4	7.3	8.2	8.9	11.0	9.8
10 to 14 years	20,540	16,697	15,255	12,498	11,781	11,635	9,340	7,452	5.9	6.5	6.5	7.2	8.0	9.6	9.9	10.7
15 to 19 years	25,092	18,907	17,879	14,880	13,452	13,500	9,058	7,488	7.3	7.4	7.6	8.6	9.2	11.2	9.6	10.8
20 to 24 years	34,236	25,478	29,106	18,358	17,786	14,527	10,758	7,699	9.9	10.0	12.4	10.6	12.1	12.0	11.4	11.1
25 to 29 years	38,563	24,719	27,706	18,596	16,410	11,454	8,921	6,945	11.2	9.7	11.8	10.7	11.2	9.5	9.5	10.0
30 to 34 years	33,942	23,684	21,534	16,344	12,857	9,398	7,071	5,431	9.8	9.3	9.2	9.4	8.8	7.8	7.5	7.8
35 to 39 years	30,165	22,863	20,857	15,731	11,472	8,797	7,418	4,784	8.7	9.0	8.9	9.1	7.8	7.3	7.9	6.9
40 to 44 years	28,036	19,012	17,415	12,082	9,255	7,239	5,512	3,672	8.1	7.5	7.4	7.0	6.3	6.0	5.9	5.3
45 to 49 years	24,011	17,297	15,080	9,747	7,750	6,430	4,166	2,848	6.9	6.8	6.4	5.6	5.3	5.3	4.4	4.1
50 to 54 years	19,650	15,079	11,716	8,133	6,928	5,262	3,710	2,445	5.7	5.9	5.0	4.7	4.7	4.4	3.9	3.5
55 to 59 years	15,434	11,571	7,656	5,764	5,001	3,272	2,265	1,478	4.5	4.5	3.3	3.3	3.4	2.7	2.4	2.1
60 to 64 years	12,985	9,197	6,754	5,187	4,078	2,913	2,047	1,330	3.8	3.6	2.9	3.0	2.8	2.4	2.2	1.9
65 to 69 years	10,579	6,518	4,626	3,992	2,604	1,915	1,221	845	3.1	2.6	2.0	2.3	1.8	1.6	1.3	1.2
70 to 74 years	6,874	4,397	3,522	2,577	1,829	1,337	912	669	2.0	1.7	1.5	1.5	1.2	1.1	1.0	1.0
75 years and over	7,063	4,867	3,826	2,491	1,938	1,451	1,079	715	2.0	1.9	1.6	1.4	1.3	1.2	1.1	1.0
Not reported	-	967	789	725	133	734	-	-	-	0.4	0.3	0.4	0.1	0.6	-	-

Table 4a.—AGE, BY SEX, OF THE WHITE AND NONWHITE POPULATION, FOR THE DISTRICT OF COLUMBIA: 1870 TO 1940

[Percent not shown where less than 0.1]

COLOR, AGE, AND SEX	POPULATION								PERCENT DISTRIBUTION							
	1940	1930	1920	1910	1900	1890	1880	1870	1940	1930	1920	1910	1900	1890	1880	1870
WHITE																
Male, all ages	227,748	169,023	152,031	115,001	93,197	75,753	57,320	42,980	100.0	100.0	100.0	100.0	100.0	100.0	100.0	100.0
Under 5 years	12,869	11,338	11,422	9,810	8,072	6,751	6,570	6,070	5.7	6.7	7.5	8.5	8.7	8.9	11.5	14.1
5 to 9 years	11,767	12,452	10,646	9,166	8,106	6,966	6,446	4,754	5.2	7.4	7.0	8.0	8.7	9.2	11.2	11.1
10 to 14 years	13,542	11,562	10,492	8,754	7,531	7,283	6,348	4,651	5.9	6.8	6.9	7.6	8.1	9.6	11.1	10.8
15 to 19 years	16,710	12,114	11,380	9,489	7,541	7,138	5,013	3,723	7.3	7.2	7.5	8.3	8.1	9.4	8.7	8.7
20 to 24 years	23,663	16,348	16,298	11,263	9,169	8,010	5,053	3,508	10.4	9.7	10.7	9.8	9.8	10.6	8.8	8.2
25 to 29 years	25,655	16,294	16,745	11,427	9,345	6,404	4,439	3,903	11.3	9.6	11.0	9.9	10.0	8.5	7.7	9.1
30 to 34 years	22,184	15,426	13,931	10,631	8,786	6,031	3,935	3,688	9.7	9.1	9.2	9.2	9.4	8.0	6.9	8.6
35 to 39 years	19,870	14,847	12,695	9,810	7,362	5,090	4,607	3,414	8.5	8.8	8.4	8.5	7.9	6.7	8.0	7.9
40 to 44 years	18,747	12,780	11,128	8,457	6,142	4,509	3,980	2,551	8.2	7.6	7.3	7.4	6.6	6.0	6.9	5.9
45 to 49 years	16,983	10,996	10,473	6,500	4,786	4,768	3,190	2,069	7.5	6.5	6.9	5.7	5.1	6.3	5.6	4.8
50 to 54 years	14,036	10,199	8,493	5,505	4,501	4,102	2,763	1,817	6.2	6.0	5.6	4.8	4.8	5.4	4.8	4.2
55 to 59 years	10,398	8,045	5,600	3,848	4,164	2,811	1,770	1,030	4.6	4.8	3.7	3.3	4.5	3.7	3.1	2.4
60 to 64 years	8,471	6,476	4,698	3,344	3,310	2,348	1,459	802	3.7	3.8	3.1	2.9	3.6	3.1	2.5	1.9
65 to 69 years	6,016	4,334	2,856	3,062	1,923	1,425	832	464	2.6	2.6	1.9	2.7	2.1	1.9	1.5	1.1
70 to 74 years	3,900	2,784	2,053	2,010	1,311	943	527	300	1.7	1.6	1.4	1.7	1.4	1.2	0.9	0.7
75 years and over	3,437	2,535	2,267	1,601	1,023	706	388	236	1.5	1.5	1.5	1.4	1.1	0.9	0.7	0.5
Not reported	-	493	854	324	125	468	-	-	-	0.3	0.6	0.3	0.1	0.6	-	-
Female, all ages	246,578	184,958	174,829	121,127	98,335	78,942	60,686	45,298	100.0	100.0	100.0	100.0	100.0	100.0	100.0	100.0
Under 5 years	12,668	10,903	11,210	9,551	7,790	6,549	6,386	5,996	5.1	5.9	6.4	7.9	7.9	8.3	10.5	13.2
5 to 9 years	11,605	12,275	10,769	8,943	8,141	6,903	6,732	4,838	4.7	6.6	6.2	7.4	8.3	8.7	11.1	10.7
10 to 14 years	13,456	11,626	10,879	8,664	7,895	7,349	6,322	4,878	5.5	6.3	6.2	7.2	8.0	9.3	10.4	10.8
15 to 19 years	17,042	12,978	12,405	9,975	8,291	8,485	6,018	4,570	6.9	7.0	7.1	8.2	8.4	10.7	9.9	10.1
20 to 24 years	23,792	17,522	22,096	11,783	10,666	9,062	6,449	4,673	9.6	9.5	12.6	9.7	10.8	11.5	10.6	10.3
25 to 29 years	26,492	16,707	21,058	12,063	10,671	7,339	5,244	4,427	10.7	9.0	12.0	10.0	10.9	9.3	8.6	9.8
30 to 34 years	23,619	17,195	16,158	11,386	9,023	6,264	4,609	3,663	9.6	9.3	9.2	9.4	9.2	7.9	7.6	8.1
35 to 39 years	20,897	16,489	14,823	10,869	7,640	5,486	4,767	3,086	8.5	8.9	8.5	9.0	7.8	6.9	7.9	6.8
40 to 44 years	20,809	13,934	12,845	8,718	6,246	4,891	3,726	2,503	8.4	7.5	7.3	7.2	6.4	6.2	6.1	5.5
45 to 49 years	18,202	12,619	11,339	6,972	5,238	4,463	2,832	1,924	7.4	6.8	6.5	5.8	5.3	5.7	4.7	4.2
50 to 54 years	15,241	11,567	9,128	5,901	4,864	3,821	2,493	1,602	6.2	6.3	5.2	4.9	4.9	4.8	4.1	3.5
55 to 59 years	12,171	9,533	6,244	4,410	3,875	2,421	1,628	968	4.9	5.2	3.6	3.6	3.9	3.1	2.7	2.1
60 to 64 years	10,508	7,685	5,442	4,079	3,144	2,158	1,401	873	4.3	4.2	3.1	3.4	3.2	2.7	2.3	1.9
65 to 69 years	8,491	5,424	3,814	3,285	2,008	1,404	858	517	3.4	2.9	2.2	2.7	2.0	1.8	1.4	1.1
70 to 74 years	5,771	3,782	2,878	2,105	1,388	982	615	400	2.3	2.0	1.6	1.7	1.4	1.2	1.0	0.9
75 years and over	5,814	4,084	3,185	1,988	1,368	966	606	380	2.4	2.2	1.8	1.6	1.4	1.2	1.0	0.8
Not reported	-	635	556	435	87	399	-	-	-	0.3	0.3	0.4	0.1	0.5	-	-
NONWHITE																
Male, all ages	89,774	62,860	51,512	43,049	38,807	33,831	26,258	19,212	100.0	100.0	100.0	100.0	100.0	100.0	100.0	100.0
Under 5 years	7,185	5,060	3,774	3,591	3,611	3,402	3,815	2,793	8.0	8.0	7.3	8.3	9.3	10.1	14.5	14.5
5 to 9 years	6,876	5,345	4,128	3,500	3,602	3,762	3,318	1,923	7.7	8.5	8.0	8.1	9.3	11.1	12.6	10.0
10 to 14 years	7,007	4,453	4,069	3,397	3,422	3,934	2,717	2,233	7.8	7.1	7.9	7.9	8.8	11.6	10.3	11.6
15 to 19 years	6,878	4,785	4,267	3,743	3,821	3,622	2,087	1,799	7.7	7.6	8.3	8.7	9.8	10.7	7.8	9.4
20 to 24 years	7,584	6,561	5,651	4,803	4,605	3,594	2,505	1,794	8.4	10.4	11.0	11.2	11.9	10.6	9.5	9.3
25 to 29 years	10,128	7,107	5,546	5,090	4,000	2,823	2,324	1,826	11.3	11.3	10.8	11.8	10.3	8.3	8.9	9.5
30 to 34 years	9,642	5,985	4,459	4,054	3,125	2,223	1,838	1,419	10.7	9.5	8.7	9.4	8.1	6.6	7.0	7.4
35 to 39 years	8,813	5,877	5,077	4,121	3,047	2,592	2,188	1,508	9.8	9.3	9.9	9.6	7.9	7.7	8.3	7.8
40 to 44 years	7,106	4,534	3,992	3,033	2,537	2,040	1,707	1,084	7.9	7.2	7.7	7.0	6.5	6.0	6.5	5.6
45 to 49 years	5,647	4,281	3,965	2,318	2,090	1,956	1,218	829	6.3	6.8	7.7	5.4	5.4	5.8	4.6	4.3
50 to 54 years	4,232	3,454	2,463	1,873	1,870	1,457	989	733	4.7	5.5	4.8	4.4	4.8	4.3	3.8	3.8
55 to 59 years	3,038	1,993	1,328	1,139	1,121	709	502	387	3.4	3.2	2.6	2.6	2.9	2.1	1.9	2.0
60 to 64 years	2,301	1,285	1,063	917	813	616	457	318	2.6	2.0	2.1	2.1	2.1	1.8	1.7	1.7
65 to 69 years	1,714	860	632	614	508	343	259	210	1.9	1.4	1.2	1.4	1.3	1.0	1.0	1.1
70 to 74 years	877	513	435	341	300	219	188	159	1.0	0.8	0.8	0.8	0.8	0.6	0.7	0.8
75 years and over	746	445	417	329	298	240	196	197	0.8	0.7	0.8	0.8	0.8	0.7	0.7	1.0
Not reported	-	322	246	186	37	299	-	-	-	0.5	0.5	0.4	0.1	0.9	-	-
Female, all ages	98,991	70,028	59,199	51,892	48,379	41,866	33,360	24,210	100.0	100.0	100.0	100.0	100.0	100.0	100.0	100.0
Under 5 years	7,129	5,003	4,030	3,717	3,677	3,601	3,864	2,919	7.2	7.1	6.8	7.2	7.6	8.6	11.6	12.1
5 to 9 years	6,997	5,552	4,298	3,703	3,882	3,891	3,586	1,954	7.1	7.9	7.3	7.1	8.0	9.3	10.7	8.1
10 to 14 years	7,084	5,071	4,376	3,834	3,886	4,286	3,018	2,574	7.2	7.2	7.4	7.4	8.0	10.2	9.0	10.6
15 to 19 years	8,050	5,929	5,474	4,905	5,161	5,015	3,040	2,918	8.1	8.5	9.2	9.5	10.7	12.0	9.1	12.1
20 to 24 years	10,444	7,956	7,010	6,575	7,070	5,465	4,309	3,026	10.6	11.4	11.8	12.7	14.6	13.1	12.9	12.5
25 to 29 years	12,071	8,012	6,648	6,533	5,739	4,115	3,677	2,518	12.2	11.4	11.2	12.6	11.9	9.8	11.0	10.4
30 to 34 years	10,323	6,489	5,376	4,958	3,834	3,134	2,462	1,768	10.4	9.3	9.1	9.6	7.9	7.5	7.4	7.3
35 to 39 years	9,268	6,374	6,034	4,862	3,832	3,311	2,651	1,698	9.4	9.1	10.2	9.4	7.9	7.9	7.9	7.0
40 to 44 years	7,227	5,078	4,570	3,364	3,009	2,348	1,786	1,169	7.3	7.3	7.7	6.5	6.2	5.6	5.4	4.8
45 to 49 years	5,809	4,678	3,741	2,775	2,512	1,967	1,334	924	5.9	6.7	6.3	5.3	5.2	4.7	4.0	3.8
50 to 54 years	4,409	3,512	2,588	2,282	2,064	1,441	1,217	843	4.5	5.0	4.4	4.3	4.3	3.4	3.6	3.5
55 to 59 years	3,263	2,038	1,412	1,354	1,126	851	637	510	3.3	2.9	2.4	2.6	2.3	2.0	1.9	2.1
60 to 64 years	2,477	1,512	1,312	1,108	934	755	646	457	2.5	2.2	2.2	2.1	1.9	1.8	1.9	1.9
65 to 69 years	2,088	1,094	812	707	596	511	363	328	2.1	1.6	1.4	1.4	1.2	1.2	1.1	1.4
70 to 74 years	1,103	615	644	472	441	355	297	269	1.1	0.9	1.1	0.9	0.9	0.8	0.9	1.1
75 years and over	1,249	783	541	503	570	485	473	335	1.3	1.1	1.1	1.0	1.2	1.2	1.4	1.4
Not reported	-	332	233	290	46	335	-	-	-	0.5	0.4	0.6	0.1	0.8	-	-

Table 5.—POTENTIAL VOTING POPULATION, BY CITIZENSHIP, RACE, NATIVITY, AND SEX, FOR THE DISTRICT OF COLUMBIA: 1940 AND 1930

[Figures for white population in 1930 have been revised to include Mexicans who were classified with "Other races" in the 1930 reports. Percent not shown where less than 0.1]

AREA, CITIZENSHIP, RACE, AND NATIVITY	TOTAL POPULATION (ALL AGES)								POPULATION 21 YEARS OLD AND OVER							
	Total number		Percent		Male		Female		Total number		Percent		Male		Female	
	1940	1930	1940	1930	1940	1930	1940	1930	1940	1930	1940	1930	1940	1930	1940	1930
Total	663,091	486,869	100.0	100.0	317,522	231,883	345,569	254,986	484,738	341,465	100.0	100.0	229,341	160,809	255,397	180,656
Percent citizen	-	-	98.4	97.6	-	-	-	-	-	-	97.9	96.9	-	-	-	-
Percent alien and citiz. not rptd.	-	-	1.6	2.4	-	-	-	-	-	-	2.1	3.1	-	-	-	-
Citizen	652,490	475,340	100.0	100.0	312,529	226,245	339,961	249,095	474,793	330,866	100.0	100.0	224,695	155,614	250,098	175,252
White—Native	440,312	323,995	67.5	68.2	209,828	153,339	230,484	170,656	323,484	223,938	68.1	67.7	151,450	103,713	172,034	120,225
Naturalized	24,090	19,047	3.7	4.0	13,434	10,483	10,656	8,564	23,733	18,477	5.0	5.6	13,263	10,202	10,470	8,275
Negro—Native	186,782	131,611	28.6	27.7	88,356	61,908	98,426	69,703	126,627	87,952	26.7	26.6	59,254	41,281	67,373	46,671
Naturalized	225	157	-	-	153	115	72	42	223	155	-	-	152	114	71	41
Other races—Native	1,081	530	0.2	0.1	758	400	323	130	726	344	0.2	0.1	576	304	150	40
Indian	183	37	-	-	97	17	86	20	158	22	-	-	89	10	69	12
Chinese	294	177	-	-	202	119	92	58	154	84	-	-	124	75	30	9
Japanese	35	22	-	-	16	9	19	13	22	4	-	-	10	1	12	3
Filipino	562	293	0.1	0.1	439	254	123	39	387	233	0.1	0.1	351	217	36	15
Hindu	-	-	-	-	-	-	-	-	-	-	-	-	-	-	-	-
All other	7	1	-	-	4	1	3	-	5	1	-	-	2	1	3	-
Alien	8,437	9,075	100.0	100.0	3,906	4,471	4,531	4,604	7,887	8,242	100.0	100.0	3,620	4,076	4,267	4,166
White—First papers	2,641	2,346	31.3	25.9	1,567	1,619	1,074	727	2,583	2,275	32.8	27.6	1,535	1,580	1,048	695
No papers	5,227	6,267	62.0	69.1	1,891	2,498	3,336	3,769	4,768	5,547	60.5	67.8	1,662	2,178	3,106	3,374
Negro—First papers	33	36	0.4	0.4	24	30	9	6	33	36	0.4	0.4	24	30	9	6
No papers	118	136	1.4	1.5	80	89	38	47	114	122	1.4	1.5	78	79	36	43
Other races—Foreign born	418	290	5.0	3.2	344	235	74	55	389	262	4.9	3.2	321	214	68	48
Indian	7	3	0.1	-	5	-	2	3	5	2	0.1	-	3	-	2	2
Chinese	362	221	4.3	2.4	304	186	58	35	338	198	4.3	2.4	284	166	54	32
Japanese	33	56	0.4	0.6	23	41	10	15	33	53	0.4	0.6	23	41	10	12
Filipino	5	1	0.1	-	4	1	1	-	4	1	0.1	-	3	1	1	-
Hindu	4	7	-	0.1	4	6	-	1	4	7	0.1	0.1	4	6	-	1
All other	7	2	0.1	-	4	1	3	1	5	1	0.1	-	4	-	1	1
Citizenship not reported	2,164	2,454	100.0	100.0	1,087	1,167	1,077	1,287	2,058	2,357	100.0	100.0	1,026	1,119	1,032	1,238
White	2,056	2,326	95.0	94.8	1,028	1,084	1,028	1,242	1,955	2,234	95.0	94.8	969	1,039	986	1,195
Negro	108	128	5.0	5.2	59	83	49	45	103	123	5.0	5.2	57	80	46	43

Table 6.—SCHOOL ATTENDANCE, BY AGE, RACE, AND SEX, FOR THE DISTRICT OF COLUMBIA: 1940 AND 1930

[Figures for white population in 1930 revised to include Mexicans classified with "Other races" in the 1930 reports. Percent not shown where less than 0.1 or where base is less than 100]

AREA, AGE, SEX, AND CENSUS YEAR	ALL CLASSES			NATIVE WHITE			FOREIGN-BORN WHITE			NEGRO			OTHER RACES		
	Total number	Attending school		Total number	Attending school		Total number	Attending school		Total number	Attending school		Total number	Attending school	
		Number	Percent		Number	Percent		Number	Percent		Number	Percent		Number	Percent
THE DISTRICT: 1940															
Total, 5 to 24 years	192,497	110,040	57.2	130,001	75,329	57.9	1,576	704	44.7	60,580	33,799	55.8	340	208	61.2
5 years	7,328	2,821	38.5	4,440	1,851	41.7	20	6	-	2,843	956	33.6	25	8	-
6 years	7,171	6,129	85.5	4,430	3,843	86.7	15	12	-	2,706	2,258	83.4	20	16	-
7 to 9 years	22,746	22,095	97.1	14,408	14,020	97.3	59	56	-	8,234	7,975	96.9	45	44	-
10 to 13 years	32,507	31,806	97.8	21,208	20,758	97.9	122	119	97.5	11,109	10,867	97.8	68	62	-
14 years	8,582	8,337	97.1	5,620	5,471	97.3	48	44	-	2,904	2,812	96.8	10	10	-
15 years	8,874	8,469	95.4	6,000	5,794	96.6	48	47	-	2,815	2,618	93.0	11	10	-
16 and 17 years	18,344	13,939	76.0	12,408	10,219	82.4	165	140	84.8	5,732	3,547	61.9	39	33	-
18 and 19 years	21,462	7,882	36.7	14,828	6,122	41.3	303	137	45.2	6,302	1,612	25.6	29	11	-
20 years	11,488	2,233	19.4	7,985	1,773	22.2	159	36	22.6	3,328	419	12.6	16	5	-
21 to 24 years	53,995	6,329	11.7	38,674	5,478	14.2	637	107	16.8	14,607	735	5.0	77	9	-
Male, 5 to 24 years	94,027	56,331	59.9	64,873	39,264	60.5	809	409	50.6	28,164	16,545	58.7	181	113	62.4
5 years	3,623	1,328	36.7	2,216	885	39.9	14	5	-	1,376	434	31.5	17	4	-
6 years	3,628	3,089	85.1	2,259	1,959	86.7	8	6	-	1,349	1,115	82.7	12	9	-
7 to 9 years	11,392	11,070	97.2	7,238	7,046	97.3	32	30	-	4,099	3,972	96.9	23	22	-
10 to 13 years	16,235	15,875	97.8	10,580	10,343	97.8	59	58	-	5,559	5,441	97.9	37	33	-
14 years	4,314	4,195	97.2	2,880	2,801	97.3	23	21	-	1,404	1,366	97.3	7	7	-
15 years	4,849	4,161	96.1	2,977	2,877	96.6	22	21	-	1,345	1,279	95.1	5	4	-
16 and 17 years	9,012	6,833	75.8	6,152	5,048	82.1	85	72	-	2,753	1,693	61.5	22	20	-
18 and 19 years	10,227	4,074	39.8	7,315	3,267	44.7	159	81	50.9	2,737	720	26.3	16	6	-
20 years	5,347	1,226	22.9	3,911	1,032	26.4	70	25	-	1,359	166	12.2	7	3	-
21 to 24 years	25,900	4,460	17.2	19,345	4,006	20.7	337	90	26.7	6,183	359	5.8	35	5	-
Female, 5 to 24 years	98,470	53,709	54.5	65,128	36,065	55.4	767	295	38.5	32,416	17,254	53.2	159	95	59.7
5 years	3,705	1,493	40.3	2,224	966	43.4	6	1	-	1,467	522	35.6	8	4	-
6 years	3,543	3,040	85.8	2,171	1,884	86.8	7	6	-	1,357	1,143	84.2	8	7	-
7 to 9 years	11,354	11,025	97.1	7,170	6,974	97.3	27	26	-	4,135	4,003	96.8	22	22	-
10 to 13 years	16,272	15,931	97.9	10,628	10,415	98.0	63	61	-	5,550	5,426	97.8	31	29	-
14 years	4,268	4,142	97.0	2,740	2,670	97.4	25	23	-	1,500	1,446	96.4	3	3	-
15 years	4,525	4,288	94.8	3,023	2,917	96.5	26	26	-	1,470	1,339	91.1	6	6	-
16 and 17 years	9,332	7,106	76.1	6,256	5,171	82.7	80	68	-	2,979	1,854	62.2	17	13	-
18 and 19 years	11,235	3,808	33.9	7,513	2,855	38.0	144	56	38.9	3,565	892	25.0	13	5	-
20 years	6,141	1,007	16.4	4,074	741	18.2	89	11	-	1,969	253	12.8	9	2	-
21 to 24 years	28,095	1,869	6.7	19,329	1,472	7.6	300	17	5.7	8,424	376	4.5	42	4	-

Table 6.—SCHOOL ATTENDANCE, BY AGE, RACE, AND SEX, FOR THE DISTRICT OF COLUMBIA: 1940 AND 1930—Continued

[Figures for white population in 1930 revised to include Mexicans classified with "Other races" in the 1930 reports. Percent not shown where less than 0.1 or where base is less than 100]

AREA, AGE, SEX, AND CENSUS YEAR	ALL CLASSES			NATIVE WHITE			FOREIGN-BORN WHITE			NEGRO			OTHER RACES		
	Total number	Attending school		Total number	Attending school		Total number	Attending school		Total number	Attending school		Total number	Attending school	
		Number	Percent		Number	Percent		Number	Percent		Number	Percent		Number	Percent
THE DISTRICT: 1930															
Total, 5 to 24 years	152,529	89,077	58.4	104,135	63,651	61.1	2,742	1,091	39.8	45,403	24,159	53.2	249	176	70.7
5 years	7,115	2,675	37.6	4,886	1,929	39.5	16	5	-	2,200	737	33.5	13	4	-
6 years	7,081	5,700	80.5	4,878	4,056	83.1	28	24	-	2,162	1,608	74.4	13	12	-
7 to 9 years	21,428	20,650	96.4	14,744	14,306	97.0	175	167	95.4	6,476	6,146	94.9	33	31	-
10 to 13 years	26,381	26,021	98.6	18,498	18,288	98.9	219	214	97.7	7,636	7,492	98.1	28	27	-
14 years	6,331	6,155	97.2	4,413	4,316	97.8	58	58	-	1,848	1,769	95.7	12	12	-
15 years	6,403	6,008	93.8	4,472	4,267	95.4	97	90	-	1,823	1,640	90.0	11	11	-
16 and 17 years	13,365	9,051	67.7	9,076	6,575	72.4	233	171	73.4	4,040	2,292	56.7	16	13	-
18 and 19 years	16,038	5,459	34.0	10,886	4,151	38.1	328	112	34.1	4,812	1,191	24.8	12	5	-
20 years	8,958	1,982	22.1	6,019	1,517	25.2	243	52	21.4	2,677	399	14.9	19	14	-
21 to 24 years	39,429	5,376	13.6	26,263	4,246	16.2	1,345	198	14.7	11,729	885	7.5	92	47	-
Male, 5 to 24 years	73,620	44,867	60.9	51,168	32,672	63.9	1,308	610	46.6	20,975	11,465	54.7	169	120	71.0
5 years	3,626	1,342	37.0	2,511	981	39.1	7	1	-	1,101	357	32.4	7	3	-
6 years	3,517	2,825	80.3	2,439	2,025	83.0	8	8	-	1,064	786	73.9	6	6	-
7 to 9 years	10,654	10,266	96.4	7,400	7,186	97.1	87	85	-	3,149	2,979	94.6	18	16	-
10 to 13 years	12,897	12,710	98.6	9,207	9,094	98.8	116	115	99.1	3,559	3,486	97.9	15	15	-
14 years	3,118	3,035	97.3	2,217	2,165	97.7	22	22	-	873	842	96.4	6	6	-
15 years	3,095	2,922	94.4	2,193	2,090	95.3	45	43	-	846	778	92.0	11	11	-
16 and 17 years	6,487	4,479	69.0	4,523	3,319	73.4	116	91	78.4	1,841	1,062	57.7	7	7	-
18 and 19 years	7,317	2,798	38.2	5,087	2,196	43.2	150	65	43.3	2,070	532	25.7	10	5	-
20 years	3,965	1,037	26.2	2,737	816	29.8	113	32	28.3	1,102	179	16.2	13	10	-
21 to 24 years	18,944	3,453	18.2	12,854	2,800	21.8	644	148	23.0	5,370	464	8.6	76	41	-
Female, 5 to 24 years	78,909	44,210	56.0	52,967	30,979	58.5	1,434	481	33.5	24,428	12,694	52.0	80	56	-
5 years	3,489	1,333	38.2	2,375	948	39.9	9	4	-	1,099	380	34.6	6	1	-
6 years	3,564	2,875	80.7	2,439	2,031	83.3	20	16	-	1,098	822	74.9	7	6	-
7 to 9 years	10,774	10,384	96.4	7,344	7,120	96.9	88	82	-	3,327	3,167	95.2	15	15	-
10 to 13 years	13,484	13,311	98.7	9,291	9,194	99.0	103	99	96.1	4,077	4,006	98.3	13	12	-
14 years	3,213	3,120	97.1	2,196	2,151	98.0	36	36	-	975	927	95.1	6	6	-
15 years	3,308	3,086	93.3	2,279	2,177	95.5	52	47	-	977	862	88.2	-	-	-
16 and 17 years	6,878	4,572	66.5	4,553	3,256	71.5	117	80	68.4	2,199	1,230	55.9	9	6	-
18 and 19 years	8,721	2,661	30.5	5,799	1,955	33.7	178	47	26.4	2,742	659	24.0	2	-	-
20 years	4,993	945	18.9	3,282	701	21.4	130	20	15.4	1,575	220	14.0	6	4	-
21 to 24 years	20,485	1,923	9.4	13,409	1,446	10.8	701	50	7.1	6,959	421	6.6	16	6	-

Table 7.—SCHOOL ATTENDANCE, BY AGE, RACE, AND SEX, FOR THE DISTRICT OF COLUMBIA: 1890 TO 1940

[Figures for white population in 1930 revised to include Mexicans classified with "Other races" in the 1930 reports. Percent not shown where less than 0.1 or where base is less than 100]

AREA, AGE, SEX, AND CENSUS YEAR	ALL CLASSES			NATIVE WHITE			FOREIGN-BORN WHITE		
	Total number	Attending school		Total number	Attending school		Total number	Attending school	
		Number	Percent		Number	Percent		Number	Percent
TOTAL									
1940: 5 to 20 years	138,502	103,711	74.9	91,327	69,851	76.5	939	597	63.6
5 to 9 years	37,245	31,045	83.4	23,278	19,714	84.7	94	74	-
10 to 14 years	41,089	40,143	97.7	26,828	26,229	97.8	170	163	95.9
15 to 20 years	60,168	32,523	54.1	41,221	23,908	58.0	675	360	53.3
1930: 5 to 20 years	113,100	83,701	74.0	77,872	59,405	76.3	1,397	893	63.9
5 to 9 years	35,624	29,025	81.5	24,508	20,291	82.8	219	196	89.5
10 to 14 years	32,712	32,176	98.4	22,911	22,604	98.7	277	272	98.2
15 to 20 years	44,764	22,500	50.3	30,453	16,510	54.2	901	425	47.2
1920: 5 to 20 years	101,880	64,475	63.3	70,928	46,105	65.0	2,120	1,088	51.3
5 to 9 years	29,840	22,650	75.9	21,210	15,968	75.3	204	159	77.9
10 to 14 years	29,816	28,187	94.5	20,855	19,890	95.4	516	482	93.4
15 to 20 years	42,224	13,638	32.3	28,863	10,247	35.5	1,400	447	31.9
1910: 5 to 20 years	84,491	52,124	61.7	57,216	36,634	64.0	2,124	1,032	48.6
5 to 9 years	25,312	17,062	67.4	17,652	12,049	68.3	457	307	67.2
10 to 14 years	24,649	22,978	93.2	16,893	15,941	94.4	525	489	93.1
15 to 20 years	34,530	12,084	35.0	22,671	8,644	38.1	1,142	236	20.7
1900: 5 to 20 years	77,291	39,027	50.5	49,945	27,381	54.8	1,267	469	37.0
5 to 9 years	23,731	10,651	44.9	16,089	7,722	48.0	158	82	51.9
10 to 14 years	22,734	19,898	87.5	15,102	13,758	91.1	324	258	79.6
15 to 20 years	30,826	8,478	27.5	18,754	5,901	31.5	785	129	16.4
1890: 5 to 19 years	68,634	35,570	51.8	43,074	24,358	56.5	1,050	442	42.1
5 to 9 years	21,522	9,253	43.0	13,669	6,438	47.1	200	118	56.5
10 to 14 years	22,852	19,248	84.2	14,316	12,785	89.3	316	250	79.1
15 to 19 years	24,260	7,069	29.1	15,089	5,135	34.0	534	79	14.8
MALE									
1940: 5 to 20 years	68,127	51,871	76.1	45,528	35,258	77.4	472	319	67.6
5 to 9 years	18,643	15,487	83.1	11,713	9,890	84.4	54	41	-
10 to 14 years	20,549	20,070	97.7	13,460	13,144	97.7	82	79	-
15 to 20 years	28,935	16,314	56.4	20,355	12,224	60.1	336	199	59.2
1930: 5 to 20 years	54,676	41,414	75.7	38,314	29,872	78.0	664	462	69.6
5 to 9 years	17,797	14,433	81.1	12,350	10,192	82.5	102	94	92.2
10 to 14 years	16,015	15,745	98.3	11,424	11,259	98.6	138	137	99.3
15 to 20 years	20,864	11,236	53.9	14,540	8,421	57.9	424	231	54.5
1920: 5 to 20 years	48,547	31,869	65.6	34,125	23,008	67.4	1,083	606	56.0
5 to 9 years	14,773	11,181	75.7	10,542	7,910	75.0	103	82	79.6
10 to 14 years	14,561	13,738	94.3	10,211	9,698	95.0	281	265	94.3
15 to 20 years	19,213	6,950	36.2	13,372	5,400	40.4	699	259	37.1
1910: 5 to 20 years	40,888	25,369	62.0	28,821	18,235	64.4	1,105	547	49.5
5 to 9 years	12,666	8,541	67.4	8,929	6,131	68.7	237	166	70.0
10 to 14 years	12,151	11,292	92.9	8,492	8,016	94.4	262	244	93.1
15 to 20 years	16,071	5,536	34.4	10,900	4,088	37.5	606	137	22.6
1900: 5 to 20 years	36,498	18,283	50.0	24,221	13,152	54.3	586	229	39.1
5 to 9 years	11,708	5,284	45.1	8,087	3,930	48.9	69	38	-
10 to 14 years	10,953	9,397	85.8	7,367	6,606	89.7	164	124	75.6
15 to 20 years	13,837	3,552	25.7	8,817	2,616	29.7	353	67	19.0
1890: 5 to 19 years	32,705	16,861	51.6	20,891	11,779	56.4	496	223	45.0
5 to 9 years	10,728	4,618	43.0	6,862	3,272	47.7	104	58	55.8
10 to 14 years	11,217	9,342	83.3	7,115	6,309	88.7	168	128	76.2
15 to 19 years	10,760	2,901	27.0	6,914	2,198	31.8	224	37	16.5
FEMALE									
1940: 5 to 20 years	70,375	51,840	73.7	45,799	34,593	75.5	467	278	59.5
5 to 9 years	18,602	15,558	83.6	11,565	9,824	84.9	40	33	-
10 to 14 years	20,540	20,073	97.7	13,368	13,085	97.9	88	84	-
15 to 20 years	31,233	16,209	51.9	20,866	11,684	56.0	339	161	47.5
1930: 5 to 20 years	58,424	42,287	72.4	39,558	29,533	74.7	733	431	58.8
5 to 9 years	17,827	14,592	81.9	12,158	10,099	83.1	117	102	87.2
10 to 14 years	16,697	16,431	98.4	11,487	11,345	98.8	139	135	97.1
15 to 20 years	23,900	11,264	47.1	15,913	8,089	50.8	477	194	40.7
1920: 5 to 20 years	53,333	32,606	61.1	36,803	23,097	62.8	1,037	482	46.5
5 to 9 years	15,067	11,469	76.1	10,668	8,058	75.5	101	77	76.2
10 to 14 years	15,255	14,449	94.7	10,644	10,192	95.8	235	217	92.3
15 to 20 years	23,011	6,688	29.1	15,491	4,847	31.3	701	188	26.8
1910: 5 to 20 years	43,603	26,755	61.4	28,895	18,399	63.7	1,019	485	47.6
5 to 9 years	12,646	8,521	67.4	8,723	5,918	67.8	220	141	64.1
10 to 14 years	12,498	11,686	93.5	8,401	7,925	94.3	263	245	93.2
15 to 20 years	18,459	6,548	35.5	11,771	4,556	38.7	536	99	18.5
1900: 5 to 20 years	40,793	20,794	51.0	25,724	14,229	55.3	681	240	35.2
5 to 9 years	12,023	5,367	44.6	8,052	3,792	47.1	89	44	-
10 to 14 years	11,781	10,501	89.1	7,785	7,152	92.5	160	134	83.8
15 to 20 years	16,989	4,926	29.0	9,937	3,285	33.1	432	62	14.4
1890: 5 to 19 years	35,929	18,709	52.1	22,183	12,579	56.7	554	219	39.5
5 to 9 years	10,794	4,635	42.9	6,807	3,166	46.5	96	55	-
10 to 14 years	11,635	9,906	85.1	7,201	6,475	89.9	148	122	82.4
15 to 19 years	13,500	4,168	30.9	8,175	2,937	35.9	310	42	13.5

AREA, AGE, SEX, AND CENSUS YEAR	NEGRO			OTHER RACES		
	Total number	Attending school		Total number	Attending school	
		Number	Percent		Number	Percent
TOTAL						
1940: 5 to 20 years	45,973	33,064	71.9	263	199	75.7
5 to 9 years	13,783	11,189	81.2	90	68	-
10 to 14 years	14,013	13,679	97.6	78	72	-
15 to 20 years	18,177	8,196	45.1	95	59	-
1930: 5 to 20 years	33,674	23,274	69.1	157	129	82.2
5 to 9 years	10,838	8,491	78.3	59	47	-
10 to 14 years	9,484	9,261	97.6	40	39	-
15 to 20 years	13,352	5,522	41.4	58	43	-
1920: 5 to 20 years	28,744	17,233	60.0	88	49	-
5 to 9 years	8,410	6,511	77.4	16	12	-
10 to 14 years	8,432	7,802	92.5	13	13	-
15 to 20 years	11,902	2,920	24.5	59	24	-
1910: 5 to 20 years	25,086	14,419	57.5	65	39	-
5 to 9 years	7,192	4,697	65.3	11	9	-
10 to 14 years	7,211	6,529	90.5	20	19	-
15 to 20 years	10,683	3,193	29.9	34	11	-
1900: 5 to 20 years	26,046	11,163	42.9	33	14	-
5 to 9 years	7,475	2,841	38.0	9	6	-
10 to 14 years	7,301	5,878	80.5	7	4	-
15 to 20 years	11,270	2,444	21.7	17	4	-
1890: 5 to 19 years	Figures for "Other races" for 1890 include Negroes.			24,510	10,770	43.9
5 to 9 years				7,653	2,702	35.3
10 to 14 years				8,220	6,213	75.6
15 to 19 years				8,637	1,855	21.5
MALE						
1940: 5 to 20 years	21,981	16,186	73.6	146	108	74.0
5 to 9 years	6,824	5,521	80.9	52	35	-
10 to 14 years	6,963	6,807	97.8	44	40	-
15 to 20 years	8,194	3,858	47.1	50	33	-
1930: 5 to 20 years	15,605	11,001	70.5	93	79	-
5 to 9 years	5,314	4,122	77.6	31	25	-
10 to 14 years	4,432	4,328	97.7	21	21	-
15 to 20 years	5,859	2,551	43.5	41	33	-
1920: 5 to 20 years	13,277	8,224	61.9	62	31	-
5 to 9 years	4,120	3,183	77.3	8	6	-
10 to 14 years	4,063	3,769	92.8	6	6	-
15 to 20 years	5,094	1,272	25.0	48	19	-
1910: 5 to 20 years	11,413	6,559	57.5	49	28	-
5 to 9 years	3,494	2,239	64.1	6	5	-
10 to 14 years	3,384	3,019	89.2	13	13	-
15 to 20 years	4,535	1,301	28.7	30	10	-
1900: 5 to 20 years	11,670	4,843	41.5	21	9	-
5 to 9 years	3,597	1,313	36.5	5	3	-
10 to 14 years	3,419	2,665	77.9	3	2	-
15 to 20 years	4,654	865	18.6	13	4	-
1890: 5 to 19 years	Figures for "Other races" for 1890 include Negroes.			11,318	4,859	42.9
5 to 9 years				3,762	1,288	34.2
10 to 14 years				3,934	2,905	73.8
15 to 19 years				3,622	666	18.4
FEMALE						
1940: 5 to 20 years	23,992	16,878	70.3	117	91	77.8
5 to 9 years	6,959	5,668	81.4	38	33	-
10 to 14 years	7,050	6,872	97.5	34	32	-
15 to 20 years	9,983	4,338	43.5	45	26	-
1930: 5 to 20 years	18,069	12,273	67.9	64	50	-
5 to 9 years	5,524	4,369	79.1	28	22	-
10 to 14 years	5,052	4,933	97.6	19	18	-
15 to 20 years	7,493	2,971	39.7	17	10	-
1920: 5 to 20 years	15,467	9,009	58.2	26	18	-
5 to 9 years	4,290	3,328	77.6	8	6	-
10 to 14 years	4,369	4,033	92.3	7	7	-
15 to 20 years	6,808	1,648	24.2	11	5	-
1910: 5 to 20 years	13,673	7,860	57.5	16	11	-
5 to 9 years	3,698	2,458	66.5	5	4	-
10 to 14 years	3,827	3,510	91.7	7	6	-
15 to 20 years	6,148	1,892	30.8	4	1	-
1900: 5 to 20 years	14,376	6,320	44.0	12	5	-
5 to 9 years	3,878	1,528	39.4	4	3	-
10 to 14 years	3,882	3,213	82.8	4	2	-
15 to 20 years	6,616	1,579	23.9	4	-	-
1890: 5 to 19 years	Figures for "Other races" for 1890 include Negroes.			13,192	5,911	44.8
5 to 9 years				3,891	1,414	36.3
10 to 14 years				4,286	3,306	77.2
15 to 19 years				5,015	1,189	23.7

Table 8.—PERSONS 25 YEARS OLD AND OVER, BY YEARS OF SCHOOL COMPLETED, RACE, AND SEX, FOR THE DISTRICT OF COLUMBIA: 1940

[Percent not shown where less than 0.1; median and percent not shown where base is less than 100]

YEARS OF SCHOOL COMPLETED	ALL CLASSES			NATIVE WHITE			FOREIGN-BORN WHITE			NEGRO			OTHER RACES		
	Total	Male	Female	Total	Male	Female	Total	Male	Female	Total	Male	Female	Total	Male	Female
Persons 25 years old and over	430,743	203,441	227,302	284,810	132,105	152,705	32,402	17,092	15,310	112,493	53,382	59,111	1,038	862	176
No school years completed	6,707	3,300	3,407	901	447	454	1,833	827	1,006	3,833	1,913	1,920	140	113	27
Grade school: 1 to 4 years	28,465	15,301	13,164	5,504	3,118	2,386	3,156	1,760	1,396	19,658	10,299	9,359	147	124	23
5 or 6 years	41,298	20,768	20,530	15,180	7,891	7,289	3,817	2,028	1,789	22,182	10,745	11,437	119	104	15
7 or 8 years	108,258	52,496	55,762	66,990	32,666	34,324	10,591	5,423	5,168	30,489	14,248	16,241	188	159	29
High school: 1 to 3 years	65,456	29,221	36,235	46,706	21,050	25,656	3,139	1,550	1,589	15,495	6,525	8,970	116	96	20
4 years	86,840	31,605	55,235	71,785	24,997	46,788	4,977	2,289	2,688	9,975	4,240	5,735	103	79	24
College: 1 to 3 years	41,065	17,815	23,250	34,636	14,715	19,921	1,601	880	721	4,750	2,152	2,598	78	68	10
4 years or more	47,252	30,029	17,223	40,046	25,599	14,447	2,699	2,015	684	4,389	2,320	2,069	118	95	23
Not reported	5,402	2,906	2,496	3,062	1,622	1,440	589	320	269	1,722	940	782	29	24	5
Median school years completed	10.3	9.9	10.6	12.1	12.0	12.1	8.3	8.4	8.3	7.6	7.5	7.8	8.0	8.0	8.4
Percent less than 5 years completed	8.2	9.1	7.3	2.2	2.7	1.9	15.4	15.1	15.7	20.9	22.9	19.1	27.6	27.5	28.4
PERCENT DISTRIBUTION															
Persons 25 years old and over	100.0	100.0	100.0	100.0	100.0	100.0	100.0	100.0	100.0	100.0	100.0	100.0	100.0	100.0	100.0
No school years completed	1.6	1.6	1.5	0.3	0.3	0.3	5.7	4.8	6.6	3.4	3.6	3.2	13.5	13.1	15.3
Grade school: 1 to 4 years	6.6	7.5	5.8	1.9	2.4	1.6	9.7	10.3	9.1	17.5	19.3	15.8	14.2	14.4	13.1
5 or 6 years	9.6	10.2	9.0	5.3	6.0	4.8	11.8	11.9	11.7	19.7	20.1	19.3	11.5	12.1	8.5
7 or 8 years	25.1	25.8	24.5	23.5	24.7	22.5	32.7	31.7	33.8	27.1	26.7	27.5	18.1	18.4	16.5
High school: 1 to 3 years	15.2	14.4	15.9	16.4	15.9	16.8	9.7	9.1	10.4	13.8	12.2	15.2	11.2	11.1	11.4
4 years	20.2	15.5	24.3	25.2	18.9	30.6	15.4	13.4	17.6	8.9	7.9	9.7	9.9	9.2	13.6
College: 1 to 3 years	9.5	8.8	10.2	12.2	11.1	13.0	4.9	5.1	4.7	4.2	4.0	4.4	7.5	7.9	5.7
4 years or more	11.0	14.8	7.6	14.1	19.4	9.5	8.3	11.8	4.5	3.9	4.3	3.5	11.4	11.0	13.1
Not reported	1.3	1.4	1.1	1.1	1.2	0.9	1.8	1.9	1.8	1.5	1.8	1.3	2.8	2.8	2.8

Table 9.—FOREIGN-BORN WHITE, BY COUNTRY OF BIRTH, BY SEX, FOR THE DISTRICT OF COLUMBIA: 1940 AND 1930

[Figures for white population in 1930 revised to include Mexicans classified with "Other races" in the 1930 reports. Percent not shown where less than 0.1 or where base is less than 100]

COUNTRY OF BIRTH	BOTH SEXES 1940	BOTH SEXES 1930	PERCENT 1940	PERCENT 1930	MALE 1940	MALE 1930	FEMALE 1940	FEMALE 1930
All countries	34,014	29,986	100.0	100.0	17,920	15,684	16,094	14,302
England	2,665	2,835	7.8	9.5	1,248	1,351	1,417	1,484
Scotland	942	884	2.8	2.9	448	403	494	481
Wales	71	116	0.2	0.4	34	63	37	53
Northern Ireland	432	493	1.3	1.6	191	203	241	290
Irish Free State (Eire)	2,326	3,026	6.8	10.1	967	1,261	1,359	1,765
Norway	264	228	0.8	0.8	132	113	132	115
Sweden	580	435	1.7	1.5	306	208	274	227
Denmark	259	229	0.8	0.8	157	153	102	76
Netherlands	203	151	0.6	0.5	124	93	79	58
Belgium	94	92	0.3	0.3	52	49	42	43
Luxemburg	17	8	-	-	10	4	7	4
Switzerland	349	360	1.0	1.2	173	184	176	176
France	719	708	2.1	2.4	280	298	439	410
Germany	3,390	3,411	10.0	11.4	1,678	1,728	1,712	1,683
Poland	2,019	1,562	5.9	5.2	1,122	879	897	683
Czechoslovakia	265	193	0.8	0.6	140	100	125	93
Austria	879	493	2.6	1.6	490	296	389	197
Hungary	412	228	1.2	0.8	200	129	212	99
Yugoslavia	91	55	0.3	0.2	68	40	23	15
Russia (U. S. S. R.)	6,038	4,914	17.8	16.4	3,167	2,606	2,871	2,308
Lithuania	523	256	1.5	0.9	281	147	242	109
Latvia	209	142	0.6	0.5	101	71	108	71
Finland	138	69	0.4	0.2	74	41	64	28
Rumania	299	160	0.9	0.5	161	82	138	78
Bulgaria	25	16	0.1	0.1	18	12	7	4
Turkey in Europe	9	25	-	0.1	6	15	3	10
Greece	1,863	1,347	5.5	4.5	1,299	918	564	429
Italy	4,913	4,330	14.4	14.4	2,988	2,626	1,925	1,704
Spain	167	148	0.5	0.5	117	104	50	44
Portugal	37	23	0.1	0.1	24	13	13	10
Other Europe	86	93	0.3	0.3	63	50	23	43
Palestine and Syria	362	305	1.1	1.0	221	166	141	139
Turkey in Asia	356	198	1.0	0.7	215	126	141	72
Other Asia	156	132	0.5	0.4	106	90	50	42
Canada—French	276	223	0.8	0.7	109	113	167	110
Canada—Other	1,748	1,458	5.1	4.9	728	615	1,020	843
Newfoundland	58	33	0.2	0.1	30	21	28	12
Mexico	94	113	0.3	0.4	42	62	52	51
Cuba and other West Indies	150	130	0.4	0.4	77	57	73	73
Central and South America	354	231	1.0	0.8	170	129	184	102
Australia	61	43	0.2	0.1	33	25	28	18
Azores	6	2	-	-	5	2	1	-
All other and not reported	109	88	0.3	0.3	65	38	44	50

Table 10.—FOREIGN-BORN WHITE, 1910 TO 1940, AND TOTAL FOREIGN BORN, 1850 TO 1900, BY COUNTRY OF BIRTH, FOR THE DISTRICT OF COLUMBIA

[Figures are given for each country for all census years since 1850 for which data are available. Figures for foreign-born white population in 1930 have been revised to include Mexicans who were classified with "Other races" in the 1930 reports. Percent not shown where less than 0.1]

COUNTRY OF BIRTH	FOREIGN-BORN WHITE				TOTAL FOREIGN BORN						PERCENT DISTRIBUTION									
	1940	1930	1920	1910	1900	1890	1880	1870	1860	1850	1940	1930	1920	1910	1900	1890	1880	1870	1860	1850
All countries	34,014	29,986	28,548	24,351	20,119	18,770	17,122	16,254	12,484	4,918	100.0	100.0	100.0	100.0	100.0	100.0	100.0	100.0	100.0	100.0
NORTH-WESTERN EUROPE																				
England	2,665	2,835	2,990	2,634	2,299	2,128	1,649	1,422	1,030	682	7.8	9.5	10.5	10.8	11.4	11.3	9.6	8.7	8.3	13.9
Scotland	942	884	793	705	574	578	495	352	258	142	2.8	2.9	2.8	2.9	2.9	3.1	2.9	2.2	2.1	2.9
Wales	71	116	106	86	82	71	56	29	28	20	0.2	0.4	0.4	0.4	0.4	0.4	0.3	0.2	0.2	0.4
Northern Ireland	432	493									1.3	1.6								
Irish Free State (Eire)	2,326	3,026	4,320	5,343	6,220	7,224	7,840	8,218	7,258	2,341	6.8	10.1	15.1	21.9	30.9	38.5	45.8	50.6	58.1	47.6
Norway	264	228	219	149	101	70	19	5	1	-	0.8	0.8	0.8	0.6	0.5	0.4	0.1	-	-	-
Sweden	580	435	481	358	234	128	51	22	16	5	1.7	1.5	1.7	1.5	1.2	0.7	0.3	0.1	0.1	0.1
Denmark	259	229									0.8	0.8								
Iceland	10	6	237	174	88	72	45	29	5	6	-	-	0.8	0.7	0.4	0.4	0.3	0.2	-	0.1
Netherlands[1]	203	151	127	64	42	32	71	23	12	4	0.6	0.5	0.4	0.3	0.2	0.2	0.4	0.1	0.1	0.1
Belgium	94	92	76	41	32	24	22	8	20	14	0.3	0.3	0.3	0.2	0.2	0.1	0.1	-	0.2	0.3
Luxemburg	17	8	13	2	-	-	-	1	-	-	-	-	-	-	-	-	-	-	-	-
Switzerland	349	360	358	281	244	211	196	175	97	36	1.0	1.2	1.3	1.2	1.2	1.1	1.1	1.1	0.8	0.7
France	719	708	687	510	389	385	293	233	160	80	2.1	2.4	2.4	2.1	1.9	2.1	1.7	1.4	1.3	1.6
CENTRAL EUROPE																				
Germany	3,390	3,411	3,382	[2]5,082	5,857	5,778	5,055	4,920	3,222	1,415	10.0	11.4	11.8	20.9	29.1	30.8	29.5	30.3	25.8	28.8
Poland	2,019	1,562	716	[2]563	132	65	116	49	30	-	5.9	5.2	2.5	2.3	0.7	0.3	0.7	0.3	0.2	-
Czechoslovakia	265	193	122	-	-	-	-	-	-	-	0.8	0.6	0.4	-	-	-	-	-	-	-
Austria	879	493	525	[2]417	199	140	91	35	32	3	2.6	1.6	1.8	1.7	1.0	0.7	0.5	0.2	0.3	0.1
Hungary	412	228	219	155	48	41	35	46	-	-	1.2	0.8	0.8	0.6	0.2	0.2	0.2	0.3	-	-
Yugoslavia	91	55	43	-	-	-	-	-	-	-	0.3	0.2	0.2	-	-	-	-	-	-	-
EASTERN EUROPE																				
Russia (U.S.S.R.)	6,038	4,914									17.8	16.4								
Latvia	209	142	5,181								0.6	0.5	18.1	12.2						
Estonia	16	2		[2]2,969	807	244	67	22	5	2	-	-			4.0	1.3	0.4	0.1	-	-
Lithuania	523	256	38								1.5	0.9	0.1							
Finland	138	69	104	21	14						0.4	0.2	0.4	0.1	0.1					
Rumania	299	160	86	41	2	-	-	-	-	-	0.9	0.5	0.3	0.2	-	-	-	-	-	-
Bulgaria	25	16	5	1	-	-	-	-	-	-	0.1	0.1	-	-	-	-	-	-	-	-
Turkey in Europe	9	25	72	41	[3]39	[3]7	[3]9	[3]1	[3]2	-	-	0.1	0.3	0.2	0.2	-	0.1	-	-	-
SOUTHERN EUROPE																				
Greece	1,863	1,347	1,207	342	34	5	5	4	2	-	5.5	4.5	4.2	1.4	0.2	-	-	-	-	-
Italy	4,913	4,330	3,764	2,761	930	457	244	182	97	74	14.4	14.4	13.2	11.3	4.6	2.5	1.4	1.1	0.8	1.5
Spain	167	148	108	48	31	44	35	37	57	20	0.5	0.5	0.4	0.2	0.2	0.2	0.2	0.2	0.5	0.4
Portugal	37	23	11	2	6	9	13	9	2	6	0.1	0.1	-	-	-	-	0.1	0.1	-	0.1
OTHER EUROPE	60	85	25	[4]20	7	25	6	13	10	-	0.2	0.3	0.1	0.1	-	0.1	-	0.1	0.1	-
ASIA																				
Palestine	81	46	19								0.2	0.2	0.1							
Syria	281	259	211	[5]139	([3])	([3])	([3])	([3])	([3])	-	0.8	0.9	0.7	0.6	-	-	-	-	-	-
Turkey in Asia	356	198	62								1.0	0.7	0.2							
Other Asia	156	132	90	21	469	135	42	11	2	5	0.5	0.4	0.3	0.1	2.3	0.7	0.2	0.1	-	0.1
AMERICA																				
Canada—French	276	223	147	109	97	32					0.8	0.7	0.5	0.4	0.5	0.2				
Canada—Other	1,748	1,458	1,541	1,014	809	623	447	286	59	32	5.1	4.9	5.4	4.2	4.0	3.3	2.6	1.8	0.5	0.7
Newfoundland	58	33	18	10	([6])	([6])	5	4			0.2	0.1	0.1	-	-	-	-	-		
Mexico	94	113	65	23	38	24	12	17	13	9	0.3	0.4	0.2	0.1	0.2	0.1	0.1	0.1	0.1	0.2
Cuba	96	80	64	53	43		22	11			0.3	0.3	0.2	0.2	0.2		0.1	0.1		
Other West Indies	54	50	50	31	91	102	84	42	24	15	0.2	0.2	0.2	0.1	0.5	0.5	0.5	0.3	0.2	0.3
Central America	70	56	51	32	32	16	3	3	2	-	0.2	0.2	0.2	0.1	0.2	0.1	-	-	-	-
South America	284	175	103	25	49	34	34	13	24	5	0.8	0.6	0.4	0.1	0.2	0.2	0.2	0.1	0.2	0.1
ALL OTHER																				
Australia	61	43	25	21	19	12	7	7	6	-	0.2	0.1	0.1	0.1	0.1	0.1	-	-	-	-
Azores	5	2	-								-	-	-							
Other Atlantic Islands	8	6	7	4	6	3	6	3	5	-	-	-	-	-	-	-	-	-	-	-
Born at sea	3	14	16	16	21	12	16	15	-	-	-	-	0.1	0.1	0.1	0.1	0.1	0.1	-	-
All other and not reported	98	68	64	43	34	29	31	7	5	2	0.3	0.2	0.2	0.2	0.2	0.2	0.2	-	-	-

[1] Listed as Holland prior to 1910.
[2] Persons reported in 1910 as of Polish mother tongue born in Austria, Germany, and Russia have been deducted from their respective countries and combined as Poland.
[3] Turkey in Asia included with Turkey in Europe prior to 1910.
[4] Includes 9 persons born in Serbia which became part of Yugoslavia in 1918.
[5] Turkey in Asia included Armenia, Palestine, and Syria in 1910. Subsequent to 1910 Armenia included with Other Asia.
[6] Newfoundland included with Canada in 1890 and 1900.

Table 11.—PERSONS 14 YEARS OLD AND OVER, BY EMPLOYMENT STATUS, CLASS OF WORKER, RACE, AND SEX, FOR THE DISTRICT OF COLUMBIA: 1940

[Percent not shown where less than 0.1 or where base is less than 100]

EMPLOYMENT STATUS	ALL CLASSES			NATIVE WHITE			FOREIGN-BORN WHITE			NEGRO			OTHER RACES		
	Total	Male	Female	Total	Male	Female	Total	Male	Female	Total	Male	Female	Total	Male	Female
Total population (all ages)	663,091	317,522	345,569	440,312	209,828	230,484	34,014	17,920	16,094	187,266	88,672	98,594	1,499	1,102	397
Persons 14 years old and over	553,488	262,590	290,898	370,325	174,685	195,640	33,762	17,788	15,974	148,181	69,163	79,018	1,220	954	266
In labor force	344,033	212,118	131,915	227,402	140,913	86,489	18,967	14,453	4,514	96,826	55,997	40,829	838	755	83
Not in labor force	209,455	50,472	158,983	142,923	33,772	109,151	14,795	3,335	11,460	51,355	13,166	38,189	382	199	183
Engaged in own home housew'k	111,620	771	110,849	78,709	506	78,203	9,536	63	9,473	23,273	199	23,074	102	3	99
In school	42,346	21,740	20,606	30,763	16,261	14,502	550	324	226	10,946	5,103	5,843	87	52	35
Unable to work	22,103	10,058	12,045	12,168	5,832	6,336	2,067	1,213	854	7,837	2,986	4,851	31	27	4
In institutions	9,516	5,894	3,622	5,430	3,311	2,119	942	662	280	3,029	1,844	1,185	115	77	38
Other and not reported	23,870	12,009	11,861	15,853	7,862	7,991	1,700	1,073	627	6,270	3,034	3,236	47	40	7
LABOR FORCE BY EMPLOYMENT STATUS															
In labor force	344,033	212,118	131,915	227,402	140,913	86,489	18,967	14,453	4,514	96,826	55,997	40,829	838	755	83
Employed (exc. public emerg. work)	308,900	189,587	119,313	210,546	130,135	80,411	17,710	13,453	4,257	79,860	45,292	34,568	784	707	77
At work	303,430	186,415	117,015	206,725	127,947	78,778	17,200	13,051	4,149	78,740	44,728	34,012	765	689	76
With a job	5,470	3,172	2,298	3,821	2,188	1,633	510	402	108	1,120	564	556	19	18	1
On public emerg. work (WPA, etc.)	10,417	7,492	2,925	4,005	2,503	1,502	237	187	50	6,171	4,798	1,373	4	4	-
Seeking work	24,716	15,039	9,677	12,851	8,275	4,576	1,020	813	207	10,795	5,907	4,888	50	44	6
Experienced workers	21,005	13,193	7,812	10,923	7,356	3,567	988	801	187	9,045	4,992	4,053	49	44	5
New workers	3,711	1,846	1,865	1,928	919	1,009	32	12	20	1,750	915	835	1	-	1
PERCENT BY SEX															
In labor force	100.0	61.7	38.3	100.0	62.0	38.0	100.0	76.2	23.8	100.0	57.8	42.2	100.0	90.1	9.9
Employed (exc. public emerg.)	100.0	61.4	38.6	100.0	61.8	38.2	100.0	76.0	24.0	100.0	56.7	43.3	100.0	90.2	9.8
On pub. emerg. work (WPA, etc.)	100.0	71.9	28.1	100.0	62.5	37.5	100.0	78.9	21.1	100.0	77.8	22.2	-	-	-
Seeking work	100.0	60.8	39.2	100.0	64.4	35.6	100.0	79.7	20.3	100.0	54.7	45.3	-	-	-
Not in labor force	100.0	24.1	75.9	100.0	23.6	76.4	100.0	22.5	77.5	100.0	25.6	74.4	100.0	52.1	47.9
Engaged in own home housew'k	100.0	0.7	99.3	100.0	0.6	99.4	100.0	0.7	99.3	100.0	0.9	99.1	100.0	2.9	97.1
In school	100.0	51.3	48.7	100.0	52.9	47.1	100.0	58.9	41.1	100.0	46.6	53.4	-	-	-
Unable to work	100.0	45.5	54.5	100.0	47.9	52.1	100.0	58.7	41.3	100.0	38.1	61.9	-	-	-
In institutions	100.0	61.9	38.1	100.0	61.0	39.0	100.0	70.3	29.7	100.0	60.9	39.1	100.0	67.0	33.0
Other and not reported	100.0	50.3	49.7	100.0	49.6	50.4	100.0	63.1	36.9	100.0	48.4	51.6	-	-	-
EMPLOYED WORKERS BY CLASS OF WORKER															
Employed (exc. public emerg.)	308,900	189,587	119,313	210,546	130,135	80,411	17,710	13,453	4,257	79,860	45,292	34,568	784	707	77
Wage and salary workers	281,602	169,815	111,787	193,905	117,801	76,104	12,178	8,990	3,188	74,999	42,558	32,441	520	466	54
Employers and own-account workers	25,114	18,976	6,138	15,380	11,818	3,562	5,009	4,377	632	4,477	2,543	1,934	248	238	10
Unpaid family workers	1,153	248	905	627	187	440	416	28	388	99	33	66	11	-	11
Class of worker not reported	1,031	548	483	634	329	305	107	58	49	285	158	127	5	3	2
At work	303,430	186,415	117,015	206,725	127,947	78,778	17,200	13,051	4,149	78,740	44,728	34,012	765	689	76
Wage and salary workers	277,561	167,650	109,911	190,996	116,232	74,764	11,957	8,823	3,134	74,097	42,138	31,959	511	457	54
Employers and own-account workers	23,836	18,024	5,812	14,575	11,237	3,338	4,738	4,148	590	4,284	2,410	1,874	239	229	10
Unpaid family workers	1,119	239	880	604	179	425	408	28	380	97	32	65	10	-	10
Class of worker not reported	914	502	412	550	299	251	97	52	45	262	148	114	5	3	2
With a job	5,470	3,172	2,298	3,821	2,188	1,633	510	402	108	1,120	564	556	19	18	1
Wage and salary workers	4,041	2,165	1,876	2,909	1,569	1,340	221	167	54	902	420	482	9	9	-
Employers and own-account workers	1,278	952	326	805	581	224	271	229	42	193	133	60	9	9	-
Unpaid family workers	34	9	25	23	8	15	8	-	8	2	1	1	1	-	1
Class of worker not reported	117	46	71	84	30	54	10	6	4	23	10	13	-	-	-
PERCENT DISTRIBUTION															
Persons 14 years old and over	100.0	100.0	100.0	100.0	100.0	100.0	100.0	100.0	100.0	100.0	100.0	100.0	100.0	100.0	100.0
In labor force	62.2	80.8	45.3	61.4	80.7	44.2	56.2	81.3	28.3	65.3	81.0	51.7	68.7	79.1	31.2
Not in labor force	37.8	19.2	54.7	38.6	19.3	55.8	43.8	18.7	71.7	34.7	19.0	48.3	31.3	20.9	68.8
Engaged in own home housew'k	20.2	0.3	38.1	21.3	0.3	40.0	28.2	0.4	59.3	15.7	0.3	29.2	8.4	0.3	37.2
In school	7.7	8.3	7.1	8.3	9.3	7.4	1.6	1.8	1.4	7.4	7.4	7.4	7.1	5.5	13.2
Unable to work	4.0	3.8	4.1	3.3	3.3	3.2	6.1	6.8	5.3	5.3	4.3	6.1	2.5	2.8	1.5
In institutions	1.7	2.2	1.2	1.5	1.9	1.1	2.8	3.7	1.8	2.0	2.7	1.5	9.4	8.1	14.3
Other and not reported	4.3	4.6	4.1	4.3	4.5	4.1	5.0	6.0	3.9	4.2	4.4	4.1	3.9	4.2	2.6
LABOR FORCE BY EMPLOYMENT STATUS															
In labor force	100.0	100.0	100.0	100.0	100.0	100.0	100.0	100.0	100.0	100.0	100.0	100.0	100.0	100.0	-
Employed (exc. public emerg. work)	89.8	89.4	90.4	92.6	92.4	93.0	93.4	93.1	94.3	82.5	80.9	84.7	93.6	93.6	-
At work	88.2	87.9	88.7	90.9	90.8	91.1	90.7	90.3	91.9	81.3	79.9	83.3	91.3	91.3	-
With a job	1.6	1.5	1.7	1.7	1.6	1.9	2.7	2.8	2.4	1.2	1.0	1.4	2.3	2.4	-
On public emerg. work (WPA, etc.)	3.0	3.5	2.2	1.8	1.8	1.7	1.2	1.3	1.1	6.4	8.6	3.4	0.5	0.5	-
Seeking work	7.2	7.1	7.3	5.7	5.9	5.3	5.4	5.6	4.6	11.1	10.5	12.0	6.0	5.8	-
Experienced workers	6.1	6.2	5.9	4.8	5.2	4.1	5.2	5.5	4.1	9.3	8.9	9.9	5.8	5.8	-
New workers	1.1	0.9	1.4	0.8	0.7	1.2	0.2	0.1	0.4	1.8	1.6	2.0	0.1	-	-
EMPLOYED WORKERS BY CLASS OF WORKER															
Employed (exc. public emerg.)	100.0	100.0	100.0	100.0	100.0	100.0	100.0	100.0	100.0	100.0	100.0	100.0	100.0	100.0	-
Wage and salary workers	91.2	89.6	93.7	92.1	90.5	94.6	68.8	66.8	74.9	93.9	94.0	93.8	66.3	65.9	-
Employers and own-account workers	8.1	10.0	5.1	7.3	9.1	4.4	28.3	32.5	14.8	5.6	5.6	5.6	31.6	33.7	-
Unpaid family workers	0.4	0.1	0.8	0.3	0.1	0.5	2.3	0.2	9.1	0.1	0.1	0.2	1.4	-	-
Class of worker not reported	0.3	0.3	0.4	0.3	0.3	0.4	0.6	0.4	1.2	0.4	0.3	0.4	0.6	0.4	-
At work	100.0	100.0	100.0	100.0	100.0	100.0	100.0	100.0	100.0	100.0	100.0	100.0	100.0	100.0	-
Wage and salary workers	91.5	89.9	93.9	92.4	90.8	94.9	69.5	67.6	75.5	94.1	94.2	94.0	66.8	66.3	-
Employers and own-account workers	7.9	9.7	5.0	7.1	8.8	4.2	27.5	31.8	14.2	5.4	5.4	5.5	31.2	33.2	-
Unpaid family workers	0.4	0.1	0.8	0.3	0.1	0.5	2.4	0.2	9.2	0.1	0.1	0.2	1.3	-	-
Class of worker not reported	0.3	0.3	0.4	0.3	0.2	0.3	0.6	0.4	1.1	0.3	0.3	0.3	0.7	0.4	-
With a job	100.0	100.0	100.0	100.0	100.0	100.0	100.0	100.0	100.0	100.0	100.0	100.0	-	-	-
Wage and salary workers	73.9	68.3	81.6	76.1	71.7	82.1	43.3	41.5	50.0	80.5	74.5	86.7	-	-	-
Employers and own-account workers	23.4	30.0	14.2	21.1	26.6	13.7	53.1	57.0	38.9	17.2	23.6	10.8	-	-	-
Unpaid family workers	0.6	0.3	1.1	0.6	0.4	0.9	1.6	-	7.4	0.2	0.2	0.2	-	-	-
Class of worker not reported	2.1	1.5	3.1	2.2	1.4	3.3	2.0	1.5	3.7	2.1	1.8	2.3	-	-	-

Table 12.—EMPLOYED WORKERS 14 YEARS OLD AND OVER, BY MAJOR OCCUPATION GROUP, INDUSTRY GROUP, AND SEX, FOR THE DISTRICT OF COLUMBIA: 1940

[Percent not shown where less than 0.1 or where base is less than 100]

MAJOR OCCUPATION GROUP AND INDUSTRY GROUP	Total	Male	Female	PERCENT BY OCCUPATION AND INDUSTRY			PERCENT BY SEX	
				Total	Male	Female	Male	Female
Total population (all ages)	663,091	317,522	345,569	-	-	-	47.9	52.1
All persons 14 years old and over	553,488	262,590	290,898	-	-	-	47.4	52.6
In labor force	344,033	212,118	131,915	100.0	100.0	100.0	61.7	38.3
Employed workers (except on public emergency work)	308,900	189,587	119,313	89.8	89.4	90.4	61.4	38.6
MAJOR OCCUPATION GROUP								
Employed (except on public emergency work)	308,900	189,587	119,313	100.0	100.0	100.0	61.4	38.6
Professional workers	30,194	19,078	11,116	9.8	10.1	9.3	63.2	36.8
Semiprofessional workers	4,706	3,797	909	1.5	2.0	0.8	80.7	19.3
Farmers and farm managers	64	60	4	-	-	-	-	-
Proprietors, managers, and officials, except farm	22,236	19,046	3,190	7.2	10.0	2.7	85.7	14.3
Clerical, sales, and kindred workers	103,992	47,637	56,355	33.7	25.1	47.2	45.8	54.2
Craftsmen, foremen, and kindred workers	29,178	28,547	631	9.4	15.1	0.5	97.8	2.2
Operatives and kindred workers	32,610	25,872	6,738	10.6	13.6	5.6	79.3	20.7
Domestic service workers	25,380	1,420	23,960	8.2	0.7	20.1	5.6	94.4
Service workers, except domestic	42,174	26,789	15,385	13.7	14.1	12.9	63.5	36.5
Farm laborers (wage workers) and farm foremen	188	186	2	0.1	0.1	-	98.9	1.1
Farm laborers, unpaid family workers	3	3	-	-	-	-	-	-
Laborers, except farm	16,389	16,077	312	5.3	8.5	0.3	98.1	1.9
Occupation not reported	1,786	1,075	711	0.6	0.6	0.6	60.2	39.8
INDUSTRY GROUP								
Employed (except on public emergency work)	308,900	189,587	119,313	100.0	100.0	100.0	61.4	38.6
Agriculture, forestry, and fishery	578	558	20	0.2	0.3	-	96.5	3.5
Agriculture	537	519	18	0.2	0.3	-	96.6	3.4
Forestry (except logging) and fishery	41	39	2	-	-	-	-	-
Mining	125	123	2	-	0.1	-	98.4	1.6
Coal mining	11	11	-	-	-	-	-	-
Crude petroleum and natural gas production	11	10	1	-	-	-	-	-
Other mines and quarries	103	102	1	-	0.1	-	99.0	1.0
Construction	19,730	19,379	351	6.4	10.2	0.3	98.2	1.8
Manufacturing	22,238	19,210	3,028	7.2	10.1	2.5	86.4	13.6
Food and kindred products	3,172	2,846	326	1.0	1.5	0.3	89.7	10.3
Textile-mill products	57	40	17	-	-	-	-	-
Apparel and other fabricated textile products	157	78	79	0.1	-	0.1	49.7	50.3
Logging	3	3	-	-	-	-	-	-
Sawmills and planing mills	122	109	13	-	0.1	-	89.3	10.7
Furniture, store fixtures, and miscellaneous wooden goods	267	241	26	0.1	0.1	-	90.3	9.7
Paper and allied products	316	208	108	0.1	0.1	0.1	65.8	34.2
Printing, publishing, and allied industries	9,501	7,560	1,941	3.1	4.0	1.6	79.6	20.4
Chemicals and allied products	322	258	64	0.1	0.1	0.1	80.1	19.9
Petroleum and coal products	62	59	3	-	-	-	-	-
Leather and leather products	45	31	14	-	-	-	-	-
Stone, clay, and glass products	574	542	32	0.2	0.3	-	94.4	5.6
Iron and steel and their products	6,099	5,880	219	2.0	3.1	0.2	96.4	3.6
Nonferrous metals and their products	227	207	20	0.1	0.1	-	91.2	8.8
Machinery	589	538	51	0.2	0.3	-	91.5	8.5
Automobiles and automobile equipment	92	84	8	-	-	-	-	-
Transportation equipment, except automobile	133	121	12	-	0.1	-	91.0	9.0
Other and not specified manufacturing industries	500	405	95	0.2	0.2	0.1	81.0	19.0
Transportation, communication, and other public utilities	21,132	17,798	3,334	6.8	9.4	2.8	84.2	15.8
Railroads (including railroad repair shops) and railway Express service	4,559	4,287	272	1.5	2.3	0.2	94.0	6.0
Trucking service	1,509	1,446	63	0.5	0.8	0.1	95.8	4.2
Other transportation	7,103	6,828	275	2.3	3.6	0.2	96.1	3.9
Communication	4,029	1,644	2,385	1.3	0.9	2.0	40.8	59.2
Utilities	3,932	3,593	339	1.3	1.9	0.3	86.3	13.7
Wholesale and retail trade	52,581	36,776	15,805	17.0	19.4	13.2	69.9	30.1
Wholesale trade	5,624	4,864	760	1.8	2.6	0.6	86.5	13.5
Food and dairy products stores, and milk retailing	8,645	7,269	1,376	2.8	3.8	1.2	84.1	15.9
Eating and drinking places	10,507	6,120	4,387	3.4	3.2	3.7	58.2	41.8
Motor vehicles and accessories retailing, and filling stations	3,949	3,700	249	1.3	2.0	0.2	93.7	6.3
Other retail trade	23,856	14,823	9,033	7.7	7.8	7.6	62.1	37.9
Finance, insurance, and real estate	14,620	9,558	5,062	4.7	5.0	4.2	65.4	34.6
Business and repair services	5,278	4,539	739	1.7	2.4	0.6	86.0	14.0
Automobile storage, rental, and repair services	2,651	2,596	55	0.9	1.4	-	97.9	2.1
Business and repair services, except automobile	2,627	1,943	684	0.9	1.0	0.6	74.0	26.0
Personal services	46,850	11,670	35,180	15.2	6.2	29.5	24.9	75.1
Domestic service	27,417	2,592	24,825	8.9	1.4	20.8	9.5	90.5
Hotels and lodging places	8,508	3,802	4,706	2.8	2.0	3.9	44.7	55.3
Laundering, cleaning, and dyeing services	5,502	2,608	2,894	1.8	1.4	2.4	47.4	52.6
Miscellaneous personal services	5,423	2,668	2,755	1.8	1.4	2.3	49.2	50.8
Amusement, recreation, and related services	2,710	2,066	644	0.9	1.1	0.5	76.2	23.8
Professional and related services	29,827	13,997	15,830	9.7	7.4	13.3	46.9	53.1
Government	89,499	51,677	37,822	29.0	27.3	31.7	57.7	42.3
Industry not reported	3,732	2,236	1,496	1.2	1.2	1.3	59.9	40.1

Table 12a.—WHITE EMPLOYED WORKERS 14 YEARS OLD AND OVER, BY MAJOR OCCUPATION GROUP, INDUSTRY GROUP, AND SEX, FOR THE DISTRICT OF COLUMBIA: 1940

[Percent not shown where less than 0.1 or where base is less than 100]

MAJOR OCCUPATION GROUP AND INDUSTRY GROUP	Total	Male	Female	PERCENT BY OCCUPATION AND INDUSTRY			PERCENT BY SEX	
				Total	Male	Female	Male	Female
Total (all ages)	474,326	227,748	246,578	-	-	-	48.0	52.0
All persons 14 years old and over	404,087	192,473	211,614	-	-	-	47.6	52.4
In labor force	246,369	155,366	91,003	100.0	100.0	100.0	63.1	36.9
Employed workers (except on public emergency work)	228,256	143,588	84,668	92.6	92.4	93.0	62.9	37.1
MAJOR OCCUPATION GROUP								
Employed (except on public emergency work)	228,256	143,588	84,668	100.0	100.0	100.0	62.9	37.1
Professional workers	27,367	17,901	9,466	12.0	12.5	11.2	65.4	34.6
Semiprofessional workers	4,429	3,589	840	1.9	2.5	1.0	81.0	19.0
Farmers and farm managers	57	54	3	-	-	-	-	-
Proprietors, managers, and officials, except farm	21,298	18,255	3,043	9.3	12.7	3.6	85.7	14.3
Clerical, sales, and kindred workers	98,472	43,216	55,256	43.1	30.1	65.3	43.9	56.1
Craftsmen, foremen, and kindred workers	26,221	25,679	542	11.5	17.9	0.6	97.9	2.1
Operatives and kindred workers	21,235	17,268	3,967	9.3	12.0	4.7	81.3	18.7
Domestic service workers	3,021	265	2,756	1.3	0.2	3.3	8.8	91.2
Service workers, except domestic	21,238	13,061	8,177	9.3	9.1	9.7	61.5	38.5
Farm laborers (wage workers) and farm foremen	134	132	2	0.1	0.1	-	98.5	1.5
Farm laborers, unpaid family workers	2	2	-	-	-	-	-	-
Laborers, except farm	3,476	3,397	79	1.5	2.4	0.1	97.7	2.3
Occupation not reported	1,306	769	537	0.6	0.5	0.6	58.9	41.1
INDUSTRY GROUP								
Employed (except on public emergency work)	228,256	143,588	84,668	100.0	100.0	100.0	62.9	37.1
Agriculture, forestry, and fishery	392	374	18	0.2	0.3	-	95.4	4.6
Agriculture	359	343	16	0.2	0.2	-	95.5	4.5
Forestry (except logging) and fishery	33	31	2	-	-	-	-	-
Mining	81	79	2	-	0.1	-	-	-
Coal mining	9	9	-	-	-	-	-	-
Crude petroleum and natural gas production	10	9	1	-	-	-	-	-
Other mines and quarries	62	61	1	-	-	-	-	-
Construction	12,747	12,440	307	5.6	8.7	0.4	97.6	2.4
Manufacturing	18,967	16,239	2,728	8.3	11.3	3.2	85.6	14.4
Food and kindred products	2,702	2,410	292	1.2	1.7	0.3	89.2	10.8
Textile-mill products	52	36	16	-	-	-	-	-
Apparel and other fabricated textile products	146	72	74	0.1	0.1	0.1	49.3	50.7
Logging	2	2	-	-	-	-	-	-
Sawmills and planing mills	94	81	13	-	0.1	-	-	-
Furniture, store fixtures, and miscellaneous wooden goods	231	205	26	0.1	0.1	-	88.7	11.3
Paper and allied products	243	159	84	0.1	0.1	0.1	65.4	34.6
Printing, publishing, and allied industries	8,182	6,453	1,729	3.6	4.5	2.0	78.9	21.1
Chemicals and allied products	287	226	61	0.1	0.2	0.1	78.7	21.3
Petroleum and coal products	56	53	3	-	-	-	-	-
Leather and leather products	42	28	14	-	-	-	-	-
Stone, clay, and glass products	280	250	30	0.1	0.2	-	89.3	10.7
Iron and steel and their products	5,185	4,980	205	2.3	3.5	0.2	96.0	4.0
Nonferrous metals and their products	211	191	20	0.1	0.1	-	90.5	9.5
Machinery	569	518	51	0.2	0.4	0.1	91.0	9.0
Automobiles and automobile equipment	85	77	8	-	0.1	-	-	-
Transportation equipment, except automobile	129	117	12	0.1	0.1	-	90.7	9.3
Other and not specified manufacturing industries	471	381	90	0.2	0.3	0.1	80.9	19.1
Transportation, communication, and other public utilities	15,858	12,624	3,234	6.9	8.8	3.8	79.6	20.4
Railroads (including railroad repair shops) and railway express service	2,825	2,594	231	1.2	1.8	0.3	91.8	8.2
Trucking service	662	605	57	0.3	0.4	0.1	91.4	8.6
Other transportation	5,977	5,720	257	2.6	4.0	0.3	95.7	4.3
Communication	3,906	1,530	2,376	1.7	1.1	2.8	39.2	60.8
Utilities	2,488	2,175	313	1.1	1.5	0.4	87.4	12.6
Wholesale and retail trade	41,632	27,603	14,029	18.2	19.2	16.6	66.3	33.7
Wholesale trade	4,741	4,013	728	2.1	2.8	0.9	84.6	15.4
Food and dairy products stores, and milk retailing	7,038	5,761	1,277	3.1	4.0	1.5	81.9	18.1
Eating and drinking places	6,297	3,121	3,176	2.8	2.2	3.8	49.6	50.4
Motor vehicles and accessories retailing, and filling stations	3,490	3,247	243	1.5	2.3	0.3	93.0	7.0
Other retail trade	20,066	11,461	8,605	8.8	8.0	10.2	57.1	42.9
Finance, insurance, and real estate	10,851	6,373	4,478	4.8	4.4	5.3	58.7	41.3
Business and repair services	4,201	3,493	708	1.8	2.4	0.8	83.1	16.9
Automobile storage, rental, and repair services	1,808	1,758	50	0.8	1.2	0.1	97.2	2.8
Business and repair services, except automobile	2,393	1,735	658	1.0	1.2	0.8	72.5	27.5
Personal services	14,799	5,712	9,087	6.5	4.0	10.7	38.6	61.4
Domestic service	4,052	604	3,448	1.8	0.4	4.1	14.9	85.1
Hotels and lodging places	4,599	1,992	2,607	2.0	1.4	3.1	43.3	56.7
Laundering, cleaning, and dyeing services	2,672	1,406	1,266	1.2	1.0	1.5	52.6	47.4
Miscellaneous personal services	3,476	1,710	1,766	1.5	1.2	2.1	49.2	50.8
Amusement, recreation, and related services	1,910	1,411	499	0.8	1.0	0.6	73.9	26.1
Professional and related services	24,144	11,073	13,071	10.6	7.7	15.4	45.9	54.1
Government	79,991	44,734	35,257	35.0	31.2	41.6	55.9	44.1
Industry not reported	2,683	1,433	1,250	1.2	1.0	1.5	53.4	46.6

Table 12b.—NONWHITE EMPLOYED WORKERS 14 YEARS OLD AND OVER, BY MAJOR OCCUPATION GROUP, INDUSTRY GROUP, AND SEX, FOR THE DISTRICT OF COLUMBIA: 1940

[Percent not shown where less than 0.1 or where base is less than 100]

MAJOR OCCUPATION GROUP AND INDUSTRY GROUP	Total	Male	Female	PERCENT BY OCCUPATION AND INDUSTRY			PERCENT BY SEX	
				Total	Male	Female	Male	Female
Total (all ages)	188,765	89,774	98,991	-	-	-	47.6	52.4
All persons 14 years old and over	149,401	70,117	79,284	-	-	-	46.9	53.1
In labor force	97,664	56,752	40,912	100.0	100.0	100.0	58.1	41.9
Employed workers (except on public emergency work)	80,644	45,999	34,645	82.6	81.1	84.7	57.0	43.0
MAJOR OCCUPATION GROUP								
Employed (except on public emergency work)	80,644	45,999	34,645	100.0	100.0	100.0	57.0	43.0
Professional workers	2,827	1,177	1,650	3.5	2.6	4.8	41.6	58.4
Semiprofessional workers	277	208	69	0.3	0.5	0.2	75.1	24.9
Farmers and farm managers	7	6	1	-	-	-	-	-
Proprietors, managers, and officials, except farm	938	791	147	1.2	1.7	0.4	84.3	15.7
Clerical, sales, and kindred workers	5,520	4,421	1,099	6.8	9.6	3.2	80.1	19.9
Craftsmen, foremen, and kindred workers	2,957	2,868	89	3.7	6.2	0.3	97.0	3.0
Operatives and kindred workers	11,375	8,604	2,771	14.1	18.7	8.0	75.6	24.4
Domestic service workers	22,359	1,155	21,204	27.7	2.5	61.2	5.2	94.8
Service workers, except domestic	20,936	13,728	7,208	26.0	29.8	20.8	65.6	34.4
Farm laborers (wage workers) and farm foremen	54	54	-	0.1	0.1	-	-	-
Farm laborers, unpaid family workers	1	1	-	-	-	-	-	-
Laborers, except farm	12,913	12,680	233	16.0	27.6	0.7	98.2	1.8
Occupation not reported	480	306	174	0.6	0.7	0.5	63.8	36.3
INDUSTRY GROUP								
Employed (except on public emergency work)	80,644	45,999	34,645	100.0	100.0	100.0	57.0	43.0
Agriculture, forestry, and fishery	186	184	2	0.2	0.4	-	98.9	1.1
Agriculture	178	176	2	0.2	0.4	-	98.9	1.1
Forestry (except logging) and fishery	8	8	-	-	-	-	-	-
Mining	44	44	-	0.1	0.1	-	-	-
Coal mining	2	2	-	-	-	-	-	-
Crude petroleum and natural gas production	1	1	-	-	-	-	-	-
Other mines and quarries	41	41	-	0.1	0.1	-	-	-
Construction	6,983	6,939	44	8.7	15.1	0.1	99.4	0.6
Manufacturing	3,271	2,971	300	4.1	6.5	0.9	90.8	9.2
Food and kindred products	470	436	34	0.6	0.9	0.1	92.8	7.2
Textile-mill products	5	4	1	-	-	-	-	-
Apparel and other fabricated textile products	11	6	5	-	-	-	-	-
Logging	1	1	-	-	-	-	-	-
Sawmills and planing mills	28	28	-	-	0.1	-	-	-
Furniture, store fixtures, and miscellaneous wooden goods	36	36	-	-	0.1	-	-	-
Paper and allied products	73	49	24	0.1	0.1	0.1	-	-
Printing, publishing, and allied industries	1,319	1,107	212	1.6	2.4	0.6	83.9	16.1
Chemicals and allied products	35	32	3	-	0.1	-	-	-
Petroleum and coal products	6	6	-	-	-	-	-	-
Leather and leather products	3	3	-	-	-	-	-	-
Stone, clay, and glass products	294	292	2	0.4	0.6	-	99.3	0.7
Iron and steel and their products	914	900	14	1.1	2.0	-	98.5	1.5
Nonferrous metals and their products	16	16	-	-	-	-	-	-
Machinery	20	20	-	-	-	-	-	-
Automobiles and automobile equipment	7	7	-	-	-	-	-	-
Transportation equipment, except automobile	4	4	-	-	-	-	-	-
Other and not specified manufacturing industries	29	24	5	-	0.1	-	-	-
Transportation, communication, and other public utilities	5,274	5,174	100	6.5	11.2	0.3	98.1	1.9
Railroads (including railroad repair shops) and railway express service	1,734	1,693	41	2.2	3.7	0.1	97.6	2.4
Trucking service	847	841	6	1.1	1.8	-	99.3	0.7
Other transportation	1,126	1,108	18	1.4	2.4	0.1	98.4	1.6
Communication	123	114	9	0.2	0.2	-	92.7	7.3
Utilities	1,444	1,418	26	1.8	3.1	0.1	98.2	1.8
Wholesale and retail trade	10,949	9,173	1,776	13.6	19.9	5.1	83.8	16.2
Wholesale trade	883	851	32	1.1	1.8	0.1	96.4	3.6
Food and dairy products stores, and milk retailing	1,607	1,508	99	2.0	3.3	0.3	93.8	6.2
Eating and drinking places	4,210	2,999	1,211	5.2	6.5	3.5	71.2	28.8
Motor vehicles and accessories retailing, and filling stations	459	453	6	0.6	1.0	-	98.7	1.3
Other retail trade	3,790	3,362	428	4.7	7.3	1.2	88.7	11.3
Finance, insurance, and real estate	3,769	3,185	584	4.7	6.9	1.7	84.5	15.5
Business and repair services	1,077	1,046	31	1.3	2.3	0.1	97.1	2.9
Automobile storage, rental, and repair services	843	838	5	1.0	1.8	-	99.4	0.6
Business and repair services, except automobile	234	208	26	0.3	0.5	0.1	88.9	11.1
Personal services	32,051	5,958	26,093	39.7	13.0	75.3	18.6	81.4
Domestic service	23,365	1,988	21,377	29.0	4.3	61.7	8.5	91.5
Hotels and lodging places	3,909	1,810	2,099	4.8	3.9	6.1	46.3	53.7
Laundering, cleaning, and dyeing services	2,830	1,202	1,628	3.5	2.6	4.7	42.5	57.5
Miscellaneous personal services	1,947	958	989	2.4	2.1	2.9	49.2	50.8
Amusement, recreation, and related services	800	655	145	1.0	1.4	0.4	81.9	18.1
Professional and related services	5,683	2,924	2,759	7.0	6.4	8.0	51.5	48.5
Government	9,508	6,943	2,565	11.8	15.1	7.4	73.0	27.0
Industry not reported	1,049	803	246	1.3	1.7	0.7	76.5	23.5

Table 13.—PERSONS 14 YEARS OLD AND OVER IN THE LABOR FORCE, 1940, AND GAINFUL WORKERS 14 YEARS OLD AND OVER, 1900 TO 1930, BY RACE AND SEX, FOR THE DISTRICT OF COLUMBIA

[Figures for persons and gainful workers 14 years old and over for 1900 to 1930 include unknown age. Figures for white population in 1930 have been revised to include Mexicans who were classified with "Other races" in the 1930 reports. Percent not shown where less than 0.1 or where base is less than 100]

CENSUS YEAR AND RACE	TOTAL					MALE					FEMALE				
	Population		Persons in the labor force, and gainful workers,[1] 14 years old and over			Population		Persons in the labor force, and gainful workers,[1] 14 years old and over			Population		Persons in the labor force, and gainful workers,[1] 14 years old and over		
	Total (all ages)	14 years old and over	Number	Percent of total population	Percent of population 14 yrs. and over	Total (all ages)	14 years old and over	Number	Percent of total population	Percent of population 14 yrs. and over	Total (all ages)	14 years old and over	Number	Percent of total population	Percent of population 14 yrs. and over
1940	663,091	553,488	344,033	51.9	62.2	317,522	262,590	212,118	66.8	80.8	345,569	290,898	131,915	38.2	45.3
White	474,326	404,087	246,369	51.9	61.0	227,748	192,473	155,366	68.2	80.7	246,578	211,614	91,003	36.9	43.0
Negro	187,266	148,181	96,826	51.7	65.3	88,672	69,163	55,997	63.2	81.0	98,594	79,018	40,829	41.4	51.7
Other races	1,499	1,220	838	55.9	68.7	1,102	954	755	68.5	79.1	397	266	83	20.9	31.2
1930	486,869	392,560	243,677	50.0	62.1	231,883	184,791	154,874	66.8	83.8	254,986	207,769	88,803	34.8	42.7
White	353,981	288,296	170,091	48.1	59.0	169,023	135,910	112,618	66.6	82.9	184,958	152,386	57,473	31.1	37.7
Negro	132,068	103,588	73,066	55.3	70.5	62,225	48,316	41,770	67.1	86.5	69,843	55,272	31,296	44.8	56.6
Other races	820	676	520	63.4	76.9	635	566	486	76.5	86.0	185	111	34	18.4	30.6
1920	437,571	353,521	235,768	53.9	66.7	203,543	161,967	143,205	70.4	88.4	234,028	191,554	92,563	39.6	48.3
White	326,860	265,676	170,871	52.3	64.3	152,031	121,553	106,866	70.3	87.9	174,829	144,123	64,005	36.6	44.4
Negro	109,966	87,158	64,333	58.5	73.8	50,855	39,789	35,794	70.4	90.0	59,111	47,369	28,539	48.3	60.2
Other races	745	687	564	75.7	82.1	657	625	545	83.0	87.2	88	62	19	-	-
1910	331,069	259,462	157,718	47.6	60.8	158,050	122,282	104,861	66.3	85.8	173,019	137,180	52,857	30.5	38.5
1900	278,718	213,677	126,448	45.4	59.2	132,004	99,831	85,477	64.8	85.6	146,714	113,846	40,971	27.9	36.0

[1] Figures for 1900 to 1930 represent gainful workers 14 years old and over.

PERCENT DISTRIBUTION OF PERSONS 14 YEARS OLD AND OVER, BY EMPLOYMENT STATUS AND SEX, FOR THE DISTRICT OF COLUMBIA: 1940

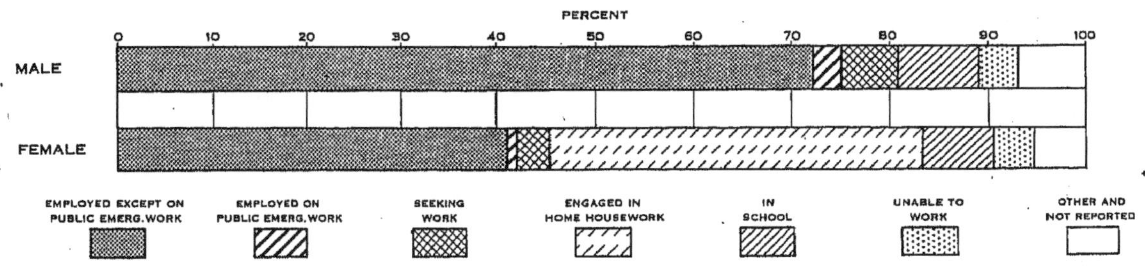

"On to Washington with the Bonus Hikers,"
***The Literary Digest*, June 11, 1932**

Mulligan, bread, and coffee-coffee, bread and beans-so it goes, ringing the changes. Three times a day on the road to Washington, when the people are kind, as they have been hitherto, and three times a day in Washington itself.

Men must eat, Washington argues. Somebody must feed them, even at a time when producing mulligan for a thousand or more men is harder than pulling rabbits out of a silk hat.

And yet, the general opinion seems to be that these gaunt, travel-stained veterans have created a most embarrassing situation for Congress by hitchhiking from the ends of the land to the national capital, under circumstances of piercing publicity-incidentally kidnapping a freight-train for a few hours while passing through Illinois-to make a seemingly impossible demand upon the nation.

Two billion dollars for ex-servicemen-immediately-in cash!

Nice news for a distracted Congress!

Rolling-kitchens and bed-sacks from the War Department for veterans barracked in vacant stores and a garage. Talk of pup-tents in open spaces near Bolling Field. "Bonus Camp."

One contingent all the way from Portland, Oregon, with the help of motor-trucks lent by the governors of various states. Other contingents reported "on the road" from New Orleans, Philadelphia, Cleveland, Albany, El Paso, and way off in Nevada, "waiting for a train over the desert."

"Isn't there some way of turning them back," twitters Washington…

The veterans' campaign was described by Representative Henry T. Rainey, Democratic House leader, as "useless." He said, "It is too bad these men were not advised against this useless journey. There isn't a chance for the bonus. If the bill passes, it will be vetoed. It can't get a two-thirds vote to pass over a veto. I never heard of a more useless trip than this being made to Washington."

"The Pension Racket," by Orland Kay Armstrong,
***The North American Review,* June 1931**

There is no better illustration of the rapid drift of our national government into the whirlpools of lawmaking at the demands of and for the benefit of organized minorities than legislation for the veterans of the World War.

Since the Armistice, that legislation has moved forward, gaining momentum with each session of Congress, and shifting its emphasis from the original efforts to pay, in some measure, the debt our nation owed the wounded and disabled, to a free-for-all fight to see who should head the procession in passing laws for "veterans' relief" of any kind and character, whatever the cost and however absurd the provisions by which the veterans are to be relieved.

"No pensions to follow this war!" was the announcement of the government while the war was in progress. A liberal war risk insurance was to take the place of the old-fashioned pensions that had followed in an endless and irksome train behind all past wars of the United States.

A war without pensioned soldiers? The history of America has been written in her pensions. Land grants for the soldiers of the Revolutionary War. Grants and money for the veterans of 1812 and the Indian Wars. Pensions for Civil War veterans, beginning at a $6-a-month minimum back in 1895 and growing to $100 for the survivors of the Union Army today, with widows' pensions to be paid on and on a generation from today. Pensions for Spanish-American veterans-but not in such amounts comparable to Civil War pensions. The war did not last so long and there were fewer troops, consequently, less organized pressure.

And now the World War, with its businesslike system of insurance. No more pension bills by congressmen for worthy and neglected constituents. No more heavy burden of taxation to go rolling on from the backs of one generation to another. Once the insurance obligations were taken off, and disabled veterans provided for, the task would be done.

Congress old at the business in those years just following 1918 must have smiled at all this. Nearly three and a half million veterans! No pensions? Some of them in service only a few weeks or months; only about half of them overseas; comparatively few in trench warfare longer than a few weeks; about 80 untouched by wounds of war to one wounded; but all veterans, nonetheless. An average of 8,000 to the congressional district. All voters with families and friends. *What? No Pensions?*

Through progressive steps, the foundation for a pensions system was laid from 1918 to the sessions of the Seventy-first Congress. And this Congress, which came to an end last March fourth, started the system off on its long journey down the years.

As a World War veteran, and one intensely interested in legislation for the benefit of veterans sick or disabled as a result of military or naval service, I have watched the efforts of Congress to swing veterans' relief into a channel where its flow can be an ever-increasing political asset, with amazement. I have been chagrined to see the appropriation of money for veterans reach the plane of a tremendous racket.

"Communications," *The Commonwealth,* November 16, 1932: To the Editor: May I suggest an argument in favor of the bonus payment which I have not seen advanced so far. Indeed, the argument is good for the payment of pensions to all veterans, widows of veterans, husbands of remarried widows of veterans, their children and grandchildren. The argument is this: The more we pay for the last war, the more likely we are to think twice before starting or being drawn into another war. Let's make war so burdensome for ourselves and the generations to come that it will become financially impossible.

And as for the immediate payment of the bonus, I think that a little inflation will be just the thing. The vast body of American debtors, cracking under the strain of debts incurred under inflated valuation, have a right to relief by being allowed to pay with inflated currency.

—A.R. Bandini, Crockett, California

"Facts about the Soldiers' Bonus" by General Frank T. Hines, Administrator of Veterans' Affairs, Review of Reviews and World's Work, December 1932

From the close of the Revolutionary War up to May 31, 1932, the government disbursed for veterans' relief approximately $14,346,962,000. Of this account, $8.618 billion represented the amount paid as pension to veterans of all wars prior to the World War, and to those soldiers of the regular establishment who have been pensioned for injuries or disease resulting in the line of duty in the regular army, navy or Marine Corps.

The net disbursements for direct monetary benefits to the World War veterans and their dependents, up to May 31, 1932, amounted to $4.17 billion. The balance of the disbursements on account of World War veterans, amounting to $1.559 billion, is because of indirect benefits such as hospitalization, domiciliary care, travel expenses to veterans, burials, etc., and administration costs.

It is well to review briefly the history of adjusted compensation. The question of legislating on this matter was before the Congress from 1920 to 1924. It was the desire of Congress to make some adjustment in the remuneration given to men who served in the army, navy, and Marine Corps, adjusting their wages to some extent to compare with those who labored at home...

The bill which finally became a law was passed over President Coolidge's veto. It provided that each veteran having held a rank below that of lieutenant-commander in the navy or major in the army should receive as adjusted compensation (after deduction for the first 60 days of service, for which a cash settlement had been made at the time of discharge) credit at the rate of $1 per day for service in the United States and $1.25 for service overseas...

As a concrete example: A veteran with 178 days' service in the United States and 176 days' service overseas, on the basis of $1 and $1.25 per day, secured an adjustment in a net amount of $398. To this adjusted service credit there was added 25 percent because of the deferred payment. Thus, the gross credit to be used as a net single premium amounted to $498, which was sufficient to procure an adjusted service certificate in the average case with an amount shown on the face thereof of $1,000...

Certainly, no reasonable person holding a 20-year endowment life insurance policy with a commercial insurance company would seriously press a claim for payment thereof before the policy could normally mature.

As I see it, there is no proposal which would stimulate business so much as the liquidation by the government of its obligation to the veterans in small amounts that were due 11 years ago. The money would be distributed in almost every channel of trade, mainly through the lower strata of society, and afford relief from what will be a continued depression if heroic measures are not taken to change the business methods now operating this country.

"The 'Ghost Parade' of the Bonus Seekers,"
***The Literary Digest*, June 18, 1932**

"They marched in the dark like ghosts out of the forgotten past."

That's how they looked to Floyd Gibbons, these worn and ragged World War veterans, as they staged their bonus parade through the streets of a nervous Washington.

But there was no disorder-welcome news to a nation which had half-expected some outbreak of violence among these thousands of men who had hitchhiked, walked, or ridden freight trains to the capital to demand a bonus.

This time there was no more disorder than that other time these men marched. Then, as Mr. Gibbons tells us in his sympathetic description-"In the light of day and the glory of youth, and with the prayers and hopes of the nation pinned above their khaki-clad breasts, they marched that same route between thousands of proud and admiring public officials and civilians."

But now, continues this copyrighted article for Universal Service, they marched like ghosts-

"Four abreast they marched-5,000 strong.

"Few uniforms tonight and those ragged and wear-worn.

"The grease-stained overalls of jobless factory workers.

"The frayed straw hats of unemployed farm hands.

"The shoddy, elbow-patched garments of idle clerks.

"All were down at the heel. All were slim and gaunt, and their eyes had a light in them. There were empty sleeves and limping men with canes.

"They were 5,000 hungry ghosts of the heroes of 1917. Not so young now. They came back triumphant from the smoke of battle in distant wars, only to go down in the battle of life with their own kind. Their own people. Their own Government. The Government they fought for.

"They did not march in the light of day. They marched in darkness. The moving-picture record of the march of the 5,000 ghosts will be dim and obscure, if any at all.

"That's why they marched at night, with their shoes worn thin and their boots run down at the heel. They marched without hats, many of them because they have no hats. Many were without coats.

"But they were clean-shaven, every man of them. And the shirts they wore, though patched and torn and thin and cheap, were clean from their own washing.

"And they marched, proud and unashamed, carrying the flag they fought for."

One hundred thousand watched this strange demonstration of the "Bonus Expeditionary Forces," whose members already had alarmed or angered many officials, legislators and editors by congregating at Washington, but also had won the plaudits of a few.

"First came the colors and pro-bonus banners of the massed units," writes the correspondent of *The New York Times,* "and after them, in a place of honor, the veterans who had received medals for heroism. There were scores of these."

And now the *Washington Post* gives us a glimpse of the parade:

"Gone was the jauntiness that everyone saw in these men when they marched away to the World War. Many of them limped, seemed tired, and the rigors of distress were written hard into their sunbaked faces.

"Their thoughts were written on the placards they carried: 'Remember 1917-1918-Pay the Bonus Now,' 'Pay the Bonus,' 'We Want the Bonus,' 'Here We Stay, till the Bonus They Pay,' 'Suppose the Kaiser Had Won the War? Would the Bonus Have Paid the Bill?'

"On and on the marchers stepped. More banners. 'Millions for War-Not One Cent for the Hungry Vets,' 'Remember November,' 'No Bonus-No Votes,' 'Who Won the War? We Haven't Won Anything.'

"Their leaders have harangued them throughout the day with the watchwords-'Every man walk who can, and carry those who can't.'

"Their leaders told them to help police should an outbreak occur."

For the police had received reports that communists were planning a fight. But nothing happened then.

The situation on the Washington "front" was complex and rapidly becoming more so. Over thousands of veterans were converging on the capital from all points of the compass. Here and there, state and local authorities helped them on their way. Those already on the ground were sleeping in hastily built shacks, or in the open, on the sun-baked mud flats of south Washington.

Divided into six regiments, they were maintaining military discipline, and the chief rules were: "No panhandling; no liquor; no radical talk; stay until we get paid."

Although the men were getting but two three-cent meals a day, the "army's" money was running out. Police had served notice that they must leave the city on a certain day, and that they would be given a 50-mile ride to start them back home. They had refused to go. Meanwhile, they were lobbying intensively, doing their utmost to win the bonus votes of congressmen.

But the payment of their 1945 adjusted compensation certificates now, involving the expenditure of $2.4 billion, would be disastrous, according to the Administration.

This bonus march is "a disgrace to the name of veteran," declares the *Sacramento Bee,* and "the country is in no mood to be coerced in this fashion." Agreeing, the *Springfield Union* asserts that "the country has not yet sunk to the level of mob rule."

"If disorder and bloodshed should ensue," says the *Washington Post,* "the responsibility will rest primarily upon the individuals in Congress who have deliberately misled the veterans."

"It requires no army to bring honest and fair legislation out of Washington," remarks the *Omaha World-Herald.* "If it did require an army, then free government would be lost, and we should live no longer by law, but by ukase."

A bonus, many papers point out, would be in the interest of a special class, while hundreds of thousands of others also are unemployed.

"Nothing is too good for the veteran actually disabled in the war," asserts the *Boston Herald,* "and for the dependents of those who gave 'the last full measure of devotion,' but this bonus is a malicious raid."

An interesting summary of what the United States has done for its veterans in comparison with other countries is provided by the *New Haven Register:*

"This year's American Relief Bill for ex-soldiers is $1,072,064,527. Great Britain, France, Italy, Canada, and Germany combined will spend on their veterans' relief $891,190,360. For the approximately 34 million men mobilized by all these countries, about 10 percent less is being spent than for the approximately four million men mobilized by the United States.

"This year's American Relief Bill for the ex-soldiers shakes down to about $223 for every man mobilized. Great Britain's bill averages down to about $26 per man. France's payments will be about $33 per man. And the most generous of the lot of those principal belligerents is Canada, which will give out about $98 per man on the basis of the number mobilized to fight in the allied forces.

"With such comparisons in mind, it is impossible to become much bothered about the serious grounds these bonus-hikers have for their demands for more cash. The comparisons are not absolutely parallel in all ways. Payments have taken different forms in the different countries; scales vary, and other considerations besides cash outlays enter in the question. But on the whole, such differences add to, not detract from, the impropriety of the American bonus-hikers' demands."

"Correspondence: It Is Not a Bonus," by F. W. Burgess,
***The Nation*, March 11, 1931**

To the Editor of *The Nation:*

Sir: I am much chagrined that *The Nation* should have published the two editorials, "Cash for the Veterans" and "The Bonus Raid."

In the first place, the word "bonus" is misleading for what has been properly and legislatively called adjusted compensation. The stipulated pay in the army was $30 per month and board. Qualified men within the age limits were compelled to enter the army regardless of their profession or earning capacity, and to take their chances of becoming cannon fodder or permanent inmates of hospitals. At the same time, common laborers were receiving from $4 to $6 a day and mechanics from $6 to $10, with nearly unlimited overtime, which was not allowed in the service. Let the profiteers be left out of the reckoning.

After five years, Congress enacted legislation providing compensation at the rate of $1 per day for service in this country and $1.25 per day for service overseas. But in spite of the fact that this compensation constituted wages for services rendered, and wages are recognized as having the first lien on capital in nearly all states of the Union, the federal government, on the advice of the greatest Secretary of the Treasury since Hamilton, evaded responsibility by issuing certificates of indebtedness to the veterans, now worth only 22.5 percent of their face value with interest computed at six percent. The face value, by the way, varies from $30 to $1,789, not $1,000 to $2,000 as stated in your editorial.

"Hard-headed" businessmen foresee economic disaster if the veterans are paid now. But how foresighted are they? It was they who recommended the reduction of super taxes to stimulate business. Yet general business went steadily down while stock brokerage went up until it was so topheavy, it fell of its own weight. As for the forecasts of our perennial Secretary of the Treasury, in spite of his annual predictions of a deficit, the government has paid off $3.5 billion of United States Bonds out of annual surpluses and returned to large corporations and wealthy individuals $1.25 billion in supposedly overpaid income taxes-although there is no doubt that the incomes were very carefully scrutinized by batteries of overpaid lawyers and underpaid accountants. Forecasts, in fact, have failed so repeatedly and completely that it would be safer to class them with dreams, mules, and weather predictions and go contrary.

Speedboat Champion Strives to Create the Ultimate Machine

This self-made millionaire gave other wealthy men of the 1940s quality speedboats, and the dream of capturing the world speed records from England and France. Inventor Ben Covington invested in his passion of speedboat racing, and poured millions into powerboat racing designs, determined that American speedboat racing would be the best and most innovative in the world.

Life at Home

- Benjamin Hamilton Woodley Covington VIII was the third oldest of 11.
- He often "worked" with his father, a ferryboat operator on Lake Osakis, and felt the exhilaration of speed on the water, while developing an aptitude for solving mechanical problems.
- Races between ferryboat operators would often occur which, since speed was good for business, were taken seriously.
- At 29 years old, Ben designed mechanical devices for unloading trucks efficiently.
- His patented invention was an immediate success and his startup company exploded with orders; to meet this demand, Ben invited his eight brothers to join him in business.
- They moved operations from St Paul, Minnesota, to Detroit, Michigan, where they established a manufacturing plant alongside other emerging giants Ford, Dodge and Chalmers.
- With his brothers' help and the opportunity afforded to those with new wealth, Ben felt free to explore his first love-speedboat racing.
- A truck was a truck, but a perfectly designed boat that cut through the water barely etching a perfect wake was poetry in its highest form.

Life at Work

- Ben Covington's mechanical genius came natural to him and his business success made him rich.
- But Ben's passion was boat racing.
- After buying the powerboat *Miss Detroit I* , and the company that built her, Ben began his quest to rob England and France of the bragging rights for the fastest boat in the world.
- He proceeded to break the speed record five times, with the fastest time of 124.860 mph.
- Ben not only challenged other boats, but trains as well, racing one of his boats against the Havana Special, 1,250 miles up the Atlantic coast from Miami to New York City and beating the train by 12 minutes.
- Ben won five straight powerboat Gold Cup Races, as well as the prestigious international Harmsworth Trophy twice.
- As a result, the rules governing the Gold Cup Races were changed dramatically by the American Powerboat Association, limiting

Ben Covington built boats that went faster than the competition.

After the stock market crash in 1929, powerboat racing was a hobby only the rich could afford.

engine size, length and configuration of hulls, claiming to encourage "Gentlemen's Runabouts" that could be used for family recreation as well as racing.

- The changes targeted racers like Ben, whose advanced technology and use of aircraft engines dominated the Gold Cup.
- Ben's response was to develop an entirely new boat, and his comfortable, safe runabout with a bottom that incorporated all of the characteristics of his Cup capturing boats was an immediate success.
- Some of America's wealthiest sportsmen-Edward Noble, William Randolph Hearst, John Dodge, Col. Vincent and P. K. Wrigley-were among the first to purchase the new design.
- What began as an attempt by the American Power Boat Association (APBA) to end Ben Covington's domination of the Gold Cup competition resulted in an entire new line of runabouts.
- Ben christened a new specialty boat factory designed to produce 1,200 custom, top-quality boats a year, as powerboat racing designed to establish world records became a millionaire's hobby.
- Even weekend waterbug racers began to drive boats built for competition, and engines were either Evinrude, Johnson, or Elto models with speeds ranging from 35 to 60 mph.
- Most drivers raced bareheaded, some wore a leather cap, and many ignored the requirement to wear life jackets in competition.
- Ben's assault on the world's speed records was built around his own runabout, powerful engines and a specialized hull.
- Ben often raced against his younger brother.
- During one race on the Detroit River between the brothers and English racing record-breaker Kaye Don, driving *Miss England II,* Don won the first heat before an estimated record crowd of over a million spectators.
- In the second heat, Ben was leading Don, when *Miss England II* suddenly flipped over rounding one of the turns, without injury to Don and his co-driver.
- Ben finished the race first, but both he and Don were disqualified because they had jumped the starter's gun by seven seconds.
- Ben's little brother completed the course without penalty and won the trophy.

Life in the Community: Detroit, Michigan

- Detroit, Michigan, began life as a small French trading post in the 1700s and the eventual development of the automobile industry-and boat manufacturing-led Detroit to flourish as a major industrial center.
- Poles made up the largest group of foreign-born workers and more than 66,000 Poles lived in the city.
- Once known as the "Paris of the Midwest" for its tree-shaded avenues, Detroit grew more blue-collar as its riverfront became lined with factories and grain silos.
- At the same time, Detroit's downtown flourished architecturally, largely under the leadership of Albert Kahn, who designed several dominating, Art Deco skyscrapers.

The nine tables that follow are reprinted from the actual 1940 census, for the city of Detroit. They include actual data on race, percentage of voting population, school attendance, number of school years completed, foreign born, and employment of workers 14 years and older by job, industry and race. In addition to being incredibly fascinating, these facts help to strengthen and visualize the actual environment in which Ben Hamilton lived and worked.

Table A-35.—AGE, BY RACE AND SEX, FOR THE CITY OF DETROIT: 1940 AND 1930

[Figures for white population in 1930 revised to include Mexicans classified with "Other races" in the 1930 reports. Percent not shown where less than 0.1 or where base is less than 100]

AGE AND CENSUS YEAR	ALL CLASSES			NATIVE WHITE			FOREIGN-BORN WHITE			NEGRO			OTHER RACES		
	Total	Male	Female	Total	Male	Female	Total	Male	Female	Total	Male	Female	Total	Male	Female
All ages: 1940	1,623,452	827,499	795,953	1,151,998	579,520	572,478	320,664	172,297	148,367	149,119	74,485	74,634	1,671	1,197	474
Under 5 years	117,389	60,002	57,387	105,558	54,019	51,539	288	138	150	11,383	5,760	5,623	160	85	75
5 to 9 years	114,346	57,893	56,453	101,600	51,498	50,102	991	521	470	11,618	5,795	5,823	137	79	58
10 to 14 years	134,054	67,765	66,289	118,998	60,401	58,597	2,593	1,311	1,282	12,326	5,978	6,348	137	75	62
15 to 19 years	141,002	69,444	71,558	121,219	59,769	61,450	7,993	4,010	3,983	11,673	5,593	6,080	117	72	45
20 to 24 years	149,667	71,223	78,444	127,669	61,311	66,358	9,772	4,555	5,217	12,141	5,295	6,846	85	62	23
25 to 29 years	148,548	71,984	76,564	116,792	57,426	59,366	16,842	7,700	9,142	14,796	6,770	8,026	118	88	30
30 to 34 years	141,495	69,910	71,585	100,143	50,158	49,985	25,866	12,355	13,511	15,292	7,241	8,051	194	156	38
35 to 39 years	144,723	75,057	69,666	89,143	46,429	42,714	37,830	19,612	18,218	17,522	8,831	8,691	228	185	43
40 to 44 years	135,595	72,537	63,058	76,129	40,002	36,127	44,678	24,395	20,283	14,618	8,003	6,615	170	137	33
45 to 49 years	125,560	69,526	56,034	64,579	34,203	30,376	50,121	29,160	20,961	10,733	6,061	4,672	127	102	25
50 to 54 years	97,879	54,937	42,942	47,540	24,879	22,661	43,540	26,115	17,425	6,699	3,861	2,838	100	82	18
55 to 59 years	64,982	35,584	29,398	31,101	15,844	15,257	29,698	17,407	12,291	4,144	2,304	1,840	39	29	10
60 to 64 years	43,601	22,305	21,296	20,914	10,149	10,765	20,250	10,847	9,403	2,407	1,285	1,122	30	24	6
65 to 69 years	29,256	13,917	15,339	14,344	6,613	7,731	12,900	6,341	6,559	1,995	949	1,046	17	14	3
70 to 74 years	18,105	8,187	9,918	8,575	3,762	4,813	8,572	4,011	4,561	950	408	542	8	6	2
75 years and over	17,250	7,228	10,022	7,694	3,057	4,637	8,730	3,819	4,911	822	351	471	4	1	3
Under 1 year	23,478	12,022	11,456	21,042	10,784	10,258	21	12	9	2,375	1,211	1,164	40	15	25
5 years	22,514	11,431	11,083	20,039	10,149	9,890	132	78	54	2,309	1,184	1,125	34	20	14
14 years	27,481	13,883	13,598	24,171	12,276	11,895	763	381	382	2,519	1,210	1,309	28	16	12
15 years	27,860	13,994	13,866	24,512	12,348	12,164	856	451	405	2,469	1,183	1,286	23	12	11
16 and 17 years	54,603	27,250	27,353	47,173	23,568	23,605	2,863	1,443	1,420	4,516	2,203	2,313	51	36	15
21 years and over	1,088,739	559,292	529,447	681,108	342,696	338,412	306,658	165,315	141,343	99,870	50,408	49,462	1,103	873	230
All ages: 1930	1,568,662	821,920	746,742	1,042,935	533,485	509,450	403,721	224,631	179,090	120,066	62,239	57,827	1,940	1,565	375
Under 5 years	146,610	74,639	71,971	133,390	68,024	65,366	2,449	1,225	1,224	10,618	5,314	5,304	153	76	77
5 to 9 years	148,173	74,956	73,217	129,323	65,331	63,992	8,547	4,427	4,120	10,201	5,146	5,055	102	52	50
10 to 14 years	133,280	66,409	66,871	116,082	57,987	58,095	9,399	4,658	4,741	7,728	3,719	4,009	71	45	26
15 to 19 years	123,082	59,216	63,866	99,629	48,023	51,606	15,901	7,712	8,189	7,454	3,409	4,045	98	72	26
20 to 24 years	151,642	75,248	76,394	108,300	53,629	54,671	29,967	15,272	14,695	13,078	6,088	6,990	297	259	38
25 to 29 years	170,272	89,944	80,328	104,863	55,363	49,500	46,518	24,989	21,529	18,473	9,221	9,252	418	371	47
30 to 34 years	160,573	87,439	73,134	90,986	48,571	42,415	53,205	29,949	23,256	16,116	8,686	7,430	266	233	33
35 to 39 years	156,526	88,222	68,304	80,340	43,386	36,954	61,962	36,821	25,141	14,035	7,854	6,181	189	161	28
40 to 44 years	119,148	68,655	50,493	57,599	31,028	26,571	52,917	32,490	20,427	8,515	5,036	3,479	117	101	16
45 to 49 years	86,582	49,322	37,260	40,709	21,656	19,053	39,690	23,990	15,700	6,095	3,601	2,494	88	75	13
50 to 54 years	60,275	32,695	27,580	29,003	14,991	14,012	27,807	15,671	12,136	3,402	1,980	1,422	63	53	10
55 to 59 years	40,251	20,878	19,373	20,100	10,150	9,950	18,303	9,683	8,620	1,817	1,017	800	31	28	3
60 to 64 years	28,891	14,271	14,620	13,636	6,691	6,945	14,197	7,045	7,152	1,030	508	522	28	27	1
65 to 69 years	19,878	9,401	10,477	8,846	4,175	4,671	10,460	4,966	5,494	560	252	308	12	8	4
70 to 74 years	12,155	5,568	6,587	5,443	2,421	3,022	6,398	3,023	3,375	311	123	188	3	1	2
75 years and over	10,283	4,400	5,883	4,021	1,641	2,380	5,859	2,613	3,246	400	143	257	3	3	-
Not reported	1,041	657	384	665	418	247	142	97	45	233	142	91	1	-	1
Under 1 year	28,523	14,516	14,007	26,276	13,374	12,902	160	83	77	2,062	1,046	1,016	25	13	12
5 years	30,727	15,687	15,040	27,495	14,050	13,445	975	518	457	2,231	1,103	1,128	26	16	10
14 years	25,409	12,693	12,716	21,908	10,933	10,975	1,986	998	988	1,499	752	747	16	10	6
15 years	24,510	12,255	12,255	20,999	10,495	10,504	2,208	1,125	1,083	1,293	628	665	10	7	3
16 and 17 years	47,542	23,116	24,426	38,838	18,911	19,927	5,841	2,877	2,964	2,825	1,306	1,519	38	22	16
21 years and over	991,100	534,313	456,787	544,827	284,893	259,934	362,832	204,357	158,475	81,968	43,783	38,185	1,473	1,280	193
Percent: 1940	100.0	100.0	100.0	100.0	100.0	100.0	100.0	100.0	100.0	100.0	100.0	100.0	100.0	100.0	100.0
Under 5 years	7.2	7.3	7.2	9.2	9.3	9.0	0.1	0.1	0.1	7.6	7.7	7.5	9.6	7.1	15.8
5 to 9 years	7.0	7.0	7.1	8.8	8.9	8.8	0.3	0.3	0.3	7.8	7.8	7.8	8.2	6.6	12.2
10 to 14 years	8.3	8.2	8.3	10.3	10.4	10.2	0.8	0.8	0.9	8.3	8.0	8.5	8.2	6.3	13.1
15 to 19 years	8.7	8.4	9.0	10.5	10.3	10.7	2.5	2.3	2.7	7.8	7.5	8.1	7.0	6.0	9.5
20 to 24 years	9.2	8.6	9.9	11.1	10.6	11.6	3.0	2.6	3.5	8.1	7.1	9.2	5.1	5.2	4.9
25 to 29 years	9.2	8.7	9.6	10.1	9.9	10.4	5.3	4.5	6.2	9.9	9.1	10.8	7.1	7.4	6.3
30 to 34 years	8.7	8.4	9.0	8.7	8.7	8.7	8.1	7.2	9.1	10.3	9.7	10.8	11.6	13.0	8.0
35 to 39 years	8.9	9.1	8.8	7.7	8.0	7.5	11.8	11.4	12.3	11.8	11.9	11.6	13.6	15.5	9.1
40 to 44 years	8.4	8.8	7.9	6.6	6.9	6.3	13.9	14.2	13.7	9.8	10.7	8.9	10.2	11.4	7.0
45 to 49 years	7.7	8.4	7.0	5.6	5.9	5.3	15.6	16.9	14.1	7.2	8.1	6.3	7.6	8.5	5.3
50 to 54 years	6.0	6.6	5.4	4.1	4.3	4.0	13.6	15.2	11.7	4.5	5.2	3.8	6.0	6.9	3.8
55 to 59 years	4.0	4.3	3.7	2.7	2.7	2.7	9.3	10.1	8.3	2.8	3.1	2.5	2.3	2.4	2.1
60 to 64 years	2.7	2.7	2.7	1.8	1.8	1.9	6.3	6.3	6.3	1.6	1.7	1.5	1.8	2.0	1.3
65 to 69 years	1.8	1.7	1.9	1.2	1.1	1.4	4.0	3.7	4.4	1.3	1.3	1.4	1.0	1.2	0.6
70 to 74 years	1.1	1.0	1.2	0.7	0.6	0.8	2.7	2.3	3.1	0.6	0.5	0.7	0.5	0.5	0.4
75 years and over	1.1	0.9	1.3	0.7	0.5	0.8	2.7	2.2	3.3	0.6	0.5	0.6	0.2	0.1	0.6
Under 1 year	1.4	1.5	1.4	1.8	1.9	1.8	-	-	-	1.6	1.6	1.6	2.4	1.3	5.3
5 years	1.4	1.4	1.4	1.7	1.8	1.7	-	-	-	1.5	1.6	1.5	2.0	1.7	3.0
14 years	1.7	1.7	1.7	2.1	2.1	2.1	0.2	0.2	0.3	1.7	1.6	1.8	1.7	1.3	2.5
15 years	1.7	1.7	1.7	2.1	2.1	2.1	0.3	0.3	0.3	1.7	1.6	1.7	1.4	1.0	2.3
16 and 17 years	3.4	3.3	3.4	4.1	4.1	4.1	0.9	0.8	1.0	3.0	3.0	3.1	3.1	3.0	3.2
21 years and over	67.1	67.6	66.5	59.1	59.1	59.1	95.6	95.9	95.3	67.0	67.7	66.3	66.0	72.9	48.5
Percent: 1930	100.0	100.0	100.0	100.0	100.0	100.0	100.0	100.0	100.0	100.0	100.0	100.0	100.0	100.0	100.0
Under 5 years	9.3	9.1	9.6	12.8	12.8	12.8	0.6	0.5	0.7	8.8	8.5	9.2	7.9	4.9	20.5
5 to 9 years	9.4	9.1	9.8	12.4	12.2	12.6	2.1	2.0	2.3	8.5	8.3	8.7	5.3	3.3	13.3
10 to 14 years	8.5	8.1	9.0	11.1	10.9	11.4	2.3	2.1	2.6	6.4	6.0	6.9	3.7	2.9	6.9
15 to 19 years	7.8	7.2	8.6	9.6	9.0	10.1	3.9	3.4	4.6	6.2	5.5	7.0	5.1	4.6	6.9
20 to 24 years	9.7	9.2	10.2	10.4	10.1	10.7	7.4	6.8	8.2	10.9	9.8	12.1	15.3	16.5	10.1
25 to 29 years	10.9	10.9	10.8	10.1	10.4	9.7	11.5	11.1	12.0	15.4	14.8	16.0	21.5	23.7	12.5
30 to 34 years	10.2	10.6	9.8	8.7	9.1	8.3	13.2	13.3	13.0	13.4	14.0	12.8	13.7	14.9	8.8
35 to 39 years	10.0	10.7	9.1	7.7	8.1	7.3	15.3	16.4	14.0	11.7	12.6	10.7	9.7	10.3	7.5
40 to 44 years	7.6	8.4	6.8	5.5	5.8	5.2	13.1	14.5	11.4	7.1	8.1	6.0	6.0	6.5	4.3
45 to 49 years	5.5	6.0	5.0	3.9	4.1	3.7	9.8	10.7	8.8	5.1	5.8	4.3	4.5	4.8	3.5
50 to 54 years	3.8	4.0	3.7	2.8	2.8	2.8	6.9	7.0	6.8	2.8	3.2	2.5	3.2	3.4	2.7
55 to 59 years	2.6	2.5	2.6	1.9	1.9	2.0	4.5	4.3	4.8	1.5	1.6	1.4	1.6	1.8	0.8
60 to 64 years	1.8	1.7	2.0	1.3	1.3	1.4	3.5	3.1	4.0	0.9	0.8	0.9	1.4	1.7	0.3
65 to 69 years	1.3	1.1	1.4	0.8	0.8	0.9	2.6	2.2	3.1	0.5	0.4	0.5	0.6	0.5	1.1
70 to 74 years	0.8	0.7	0.9	0.5	0.5	0.6	1.6	1.3	1.9	0.3	0.2	0.3	0.2	0.1	0.5
75 years and over	0.7	0.5	0.8	0.4	0.3	0.5	1.5	1.2	1.8	0.3	0.2	0.4	0.2	0.2	-
Not reported	0.1	0.1	0.1	0.1	0.1	-	-	-	-	0.2	0.2	0.2	0.1	-	0.3
Under 1 year	1.8	1.8	1.9	2.5	2.5	2.5	-	-	-	1.7	1.7	1.8	1.3	0.8	3.2
5 years	2.0	1.9	2.0	2.6	2.6	2.6	0.2	0.2	0.3	1.9	1.8	2.0	1.3	1.0	2.7
14 years	1.6	1.5	1.7	2.1	2.0	2.2	0.5	0.4	0.6	1.2	1.2	1.3	0.8	0.6	1.6
15 years	1.6	1.5	1.6	2.0	2.0	2.1	0.5	0.5	0.6	1.1	1.0	1.1	0.5	0.4	0.8
16 and 17 years	3.0	2.8	3.3	3.7	3.5	3.9	1.4	1.3	1.7	2.4	2.1	2.6	2.0	1.4	4.3
21 years and over	63.2	65.0	61.2	52.2	53.4	51.0	89.9	91.0	88.5	68.3	70.3	66.0	75.9	81.8	51.5

Table A-36.—RACE, BY NATIVITY AND SEX, FOR THE CITY OF DETROIT: 1940 AND 1930

[Figures for white population in 1930 have been revised to include Mexicans who were classified with "Other races" in the 1930 reports. Percent not shown where less than 0.1 or where base is less than 100. Sex ratio not shown where number of females is less than 100]

SEX, NATIVITY, AND CENSUS YEAR	All classes	White	Negro	Other races	OTHER RACES				PERCENT BY RACE				PERCENT BY NATIVITY					
					Indian	Chinese	Japanese	All other	All classes	White	Negro	Other races	All classes	White	Negro	Indian	Chinese	Japanese
TOTAL																		
1940	1,623,452	1,472,662	149,119	1,671	434	583	63	591	100.0	90.7	9.2	0.1	100.0	100.0	100.0	100.0	100.0	-
Native	1,300,764	1,151,998	147,682	1,084	269	273	25	517	100.0	88.6	11.4	0.1	80.1	78.2	99.0	62.0	46.8	-
Foreign born	322,688	320,664	1,437	587	165	310	38	74	100.0	99.4	0.4	0.2	19.9	21.8	1.0	38.0	53.2	-
1930	1,568,662	1,446,656	120,066	1,940	350	710	103	777	100.0	92.2	7.7	0.1	100.0	100.0	100.0	100.0	100.0	100.0
Native	1,162,780	1,042,935	118,621	1,224	265	273	43	643	100.0	89.7	10.2	0.1	74.1	72.1	98.8	75.7	38.5	41.7
Foreign born	405,882	403,721	1,445	716	85	437	60	134	100.0	99.5	0.4	0.2	25.9	27.9	1.2	24.3	61.5	58.3
MALE																		
1940	827,499	751,817	74,485	1,197	244	442	47	464	100.0	90.9	9.0	0.1	100.0	100.0	100.0	100.0	100.0	-
Native	653,994	579,520	73,729	745	156	175	14	400	100.0	88.6	11.3	0.1	79.0	77.1	99.0	63.9	39.6	-
Foreign born	173,505	172,297	756	452	88	267	33	64	100.0	99.3	0.4	0.3	21.0	22.9	1.0	36.1	60.4	-
1930	821,920	758,116	62,239	1,565	187	586	83	709	100.0	92.2	7.6	0.2	100.0	100.0	100.0	100.0	100.0	-
Native	595,885	533,485	61,443	957	147	195	31	584	100.0	89.5	10.3	0.2	72.5	70.4	98.7	78.6	33.3	-
Foreign born	226,035	224,631	796	608	40	391	52	125	100.0	99.4	0.4	0.3	27.5	29.6	1.3	21.4	66.7	-
FEMALE																		
1940	795,953	720,845	74,634	474	190	141	16	127	100.0	90.6	9.4	0.1	100.0	100.0	100.0	100.0	100.0	-
Native	646,770	572,478	73,953	339	113	98	11	117	100.0	88.5	11.4	0.1	81.3	79.4	99.1	59.5	69.5	-
Foreign born	149,183	148,367	681	135	77	43	5	10	100.0	99.5	0.5	0.1	18.7	20.6	0.9	40.5	30.5	-
1930	746,742	668,540	57,827	375	163	124	20	68	100.0	92.2	7.7	0.1	100.0	100.0	100.0	100.0	100.0	-
Native	566,895	509,450	57,178	267	118	78	12	59	100.0	89.9	10.1	-	75.9	74.0	98.9	72.4	62.9	-
Foreign born	179,847	179,090	649	108	45	46	8	9	100.0	99.6	0.4	0.1	24.1	26.0	1.1	27.6	37.1	-
MALES PER 100 FEMALES																		
1940	104.0	104.3	99.8	252.5	128.4	313.5	-	365.4	-	-	-	-	-	-	-	-	-	-
Native	101.1	101.2	99.7	219.8	138.1	-	-	341.9	-	-	-	-	-	-	-	-	-	-
Foreign born	116.3	116.1	111.0	334.8	-	-	-	-	-	-	-	-	-	-	-	-	-	-
1930	110.1	110.1	107.6	417.3	114.7	472.6	-	-	-	-	-	-	-	-	-	-	-	-
Native	105.1	104.7	107.5	358.4	124.6	-	-	-	-	-	-	-	-	-	-	-	-	-
Foreign born	125.7	125.4	122.7	563.0	-	-	-	-	-	-	-	-	-	-	-	-	-	-

Table A-37.—POTENTIAL VOTING POPULATION, BY CITIZENSHIP, RACE, NATIVITY, AND SEX, FOR THE CITY OF DETROIT: 1940 AND 1930

[Figures for white population in 1930 have been revised to include Mexicans who were classified with "Other races" in the 1930 reports. Percent not shown where less than 0.1]

CITIZENSHIP, RACE, AND NATIVITY	TOTAL POPULATION (ALL AGES)								POPULATION 21 YEARS OLD AND OVER							
	Total number		Percent		Male		Female		Total number		Percent		Male		Female	
	1940	1930	1940	1930	1940	1930	1940	1930	1940	1930	1940	1930	1940	1930	1940	1930
Total	1,623,452	1,568,662	100.0	100.0	827,499	821,920	795,953	746,742	1,088,739	991,100	100.0	100.0	559,292	534,313	529,447	456,787
Percent citizen	-	-	92.3	85.2	-	-	-	-	-	-	89.2	79.7	-	-	-	-
Percent alien and citiz. not rptd.	-	-	7.7	14.8	-	-	-	-	-	-	10.8	20.3	-	-	-	-
Citizen	1,498,555	1,336,020	100.0	100.0	775,011	695,858	723,544	640,162	971,301	789,618	100.0	100.0	510,475	423,772	460,826	365,846
White—Native	1,151,998	1,042,935	76.9	78.1	579,520	533,485	572,478	509,450	681,108	544,827	70.1	69.0	342,696	284,893	338,412	259,934
Naturalized	197,046	172,657	13.1	12.9	120,614	99,682	76,432	72,975	190,397	162,772	19.6	20.6	117,235	94,837	73,162	67,935
Negro—Native	147,682	118,621	10.0	8.9	73,729	61,443	73,953	57,178	98,492	80,626	10.1	10.2	49,678	43,027	48,814	37,599
Naturalized	745	583	-	-	403	291	342	292	720	553	0.1	0.1	392	277	328	276
Other races—Native	1,084	1,224	0.1	0.1	745	957	339	267	584	840	0.1	0.1	474	738	110	102
Indian	269	265	-	-	156	147	113	118	128	151	-	-	75	87	53	64
Chinese	273	273	-	-	175	195	98	78	115	139	-	-	94	125	21	14
Japanese	25	43	-	-	14	31	11	12	10	13	-	-	8	12	2	1
Filipino	435	605	-	-	354	568	81	37	300	527	-	0.1	278	510	22	17
Hindu	50	20	-	-	30	10	20	10	20	3	-	-	11	2	9	1
All other	32	18	-	-	16	6	16	12	11	7	-	-	8	2	3	5
Alien	115,788	225,029	100.0	100.0	48,218	122,454	67,570	102,575	109,028	194,585	100.0	100.0	44,878	107,245	64,150	87,340
White—First papers	36,031	86,567	31.1	38.5	24,639	69,262	11,392	17,305	35,428	84,114	32.5	43.2	24,316	67,894	11,112	16,220
No papers	78,648	137,057	67.9	60.9	22,857	52,184	55,791	84,873	72,583	109,203	66.6	56.1	19,903	38,427	52,680	70,776
Negro—First papers	173	204	0.1	0.1	114	164	59	40	168	204	0.2	0.1	112	164	56	40
No papers	349	485	0.3	0.2	156	236	193	249	330	431	0.3	0.2	148	218	182	213
Other races—Foreign born	587	716	0.5	0.3	452	608	135	108	519	633	0.5	0.3	399	542	120	91
Indian	165	85	0.1	-	88	40	77	45	136	65	0.1	-	72	32	64	33
Chinese	310	437	0.3	0.2	267	391	43	46	271	376	0.2	0.2	230	334	41	42
Japanese	38	60	-	-	33	52	5	8	38	59	-	-	33	51	5	8
Filipino	-	-	-	-	-	-	-	-	-	-	-	-	-	-	-	-
Hindu	44	117	-	0.1	43	114	1	3	44	117	-	0.1	43	114	1	3
All other	30	17	-	-	21	11	9	6	30	16	-	-	21	11	9	5
Citizenship not reported	9,109	7,613	100.0	100.0	4,270	3,608	4,839	4,005	8,410	6,897	100.0	100.0	3,939	3,296	4,471	3,601
White	8,939	7,440	98.1	97.7	4,187	3,503	4,752	3,937	8,250	6,743	98.1	97.8	3,861	3,199	4,389	3,544
Negro	170	173	1.9	2.3	83	105	87	68	160	154	1.9	2.2	78	97	82	57

Table A-38.—SCHOOL ATTENDANCE, BY AGE, RACE, AND SEX, FOR THE CITY OF DETROIT: 1940 AND 1930

[Figures for white population in 1930 revised to include Mexicans classified with "Other races" in the 1930 reports. Percent not shown where less than 0.1 or where base is less than 100]

AGE, SEX, AND CENSUS YEAR	ALL CLASSES			NATIVE WHITE			FOREIGN-BORN WHITE			NEGRO			OTHER RACES		
	Total number	Attending school: Number	Attending school: Percent	Total number	Attending school: Number	Attending school: Percent	Total number	Attending school: Number	Attending school: Percent	Total number	Attending school: Number	Attending school: Percent	Total number	Attending school: Number	Attending school: Percent
1940															
Total, 5 to 24 years	539,069	323,891	60.1	459,486	286,351	61.0	21,349	8,194	38.4	47,758	29,008	60.7	476	338	71.0
5 years	22,514	12,510	55.6	20,039	11,068	55.2	132	62	47.0	2,309	1,363	59.0	34	17	-
6 years	20,738	18,720	90.3	18,265	16,450	90.1	172	148	86.0	2,279	2,102	92.2	22	20	-
7 to 9 years	71,094	69,363	97.6	63,296	61,850	97.7	687	671	97.7	7,030	6,764	96.2	81	78	-
10 to 13 years	106,573	104,473	98.0	94,827	93,105	98.2	1,830	1,792	97.9	9,807	9,471	96.6	109	105	96.3
14 years	27,481	26,786	97.5	24,171	23,608	97.7	763	741	97.1	2,519	2,410	95.7	28	27	-
15 years	27,860	26,797	96.2	24,512	23,633	96.4	856	832	97.2	2,469	2,311	93.6	23	21	-
16 and 17 years	54,603	41,099	75.3	47,173	35,806	75.9	2,863	2,155	75.3	4,516	3,095	68.5	51	43	-
18 and 19 years	58,539	15,429	26.4	49,534	13,128	26.5	4,274	1,204	28.2	4,688	1,083	23.1	43	14	-
20 years	27,922	2,929	10.5	23,515	2,553	10.9	2,141	221	10.3	2,249	149	6.6	17	6	-
21 to 24 years	121,745	5,785	4.8	104,154	5,150	4.9	7,631	368	4.8	9,892	260	2.6	68	7	-
Male, 5 to 24 years	266,325	165,594	62.2	232,979	146,817	63.0	10,397	4,335	41.7	22,661	14,240	62.8	288	202	70.1
5 years	11,431	6,197	54.2	10,149	5,465	53.8	78	27	-	1,184	695	58.7	20	10	-
6 years	10,601	9,518	89.8	9,356	8,382	89.6	93	79	-	1,140	1,046	91.8	12	11	-
7 to 9 years	35,861	3,5001	97.6	31,998	31,256	97.7	350	344	98.3	3,471	3,355	96.7	47	46	-
10 to 13 years	53,882	52,841	98.1	48,125	47,263	98.2	930	910	97.8	4,768	4,612	96.7	59	56	-
14 years	13,883	13,515	97.3	12,276	11,971	97.5	381	365	95.8	1,210	1,164	96.2	16	15	-
15 years	13,994	13,485	96.4	12,348	11,922	96.5	451	438	97.1	1,183	1,115	94.3	12	10	-
16 and 17 years	27,250	20,721	76.0	23,568	18,076	76.7	1,443	1,108	76.8	2,203	1,506	68.4	36	31	-
18 and 19 years	28,200	8,670	30.7	23,853	7,433	31.2	2,116	689	32.6	2,207	538	24.4	24	10	-
20 years	13,103	1,732	13.2	11,137	1,525	13.7	1,002	126	12.6	951	75	7.9	13	6	-
21 to 24 years	58,120	3,914	6.7	50,174	3,524	7.0	3,553	249	7.0	4,344	134	3.1	49	7	-
Female, 5 to 24 years	272,744	158,297	58.0	236,507	139,534	59.0	10,952	3,859	35.2	25,097	14,768	58.8	188	136	72.3
5 years	11,083	6,313	57.0	9,890	5,603	56.7	54	35	-	1,125	668	59.4	14	7	-
6 years	10,137	9,202	90.8	8,909	8,068	90.6	79	69	-	1,139	1,056	92.7	10	9	-
7 to 9 years	35,233	34,362	97.5	31,303	30,594	97.7	337	327	97.0	3,559	3,409	95.8	34	32	-
10 to 13 years	52,691	51,632	98.0	46,702	45,842	98.2	900	882	98.0	5,039	4,859	96.4	50	49	-
14 years	13,598	13,271	97.6	11,895	11,637	97.8	382	376	98.4	1,309	1,246	95.2	12	12	-
15 years	13,866	13,312	96.0	12,164	11,711	96.3	405	394	97.3	1,286	1,196	93.0	11	11	-
16 and 17 years	27,353	20,378	74.5	23,605	17,730	75.1	1,420	1,047	73.7	2,313	1,589	68.7	15	12	-
18 and 19 years	30,339	6,759	22.3	25,681	5,695	22.2	2,158	515	23.9	2,481	545	22.0	19	4	-
20 years	14,819	1,197	8.1	12,378	1,028	8.3	1,139	95	8.3	1,298	74	5.7	4	-	-
21 to 24 years	63,625	1,871	2.9	53,980	1,626	3.0	4,078	119	2.9	5,548	126	2.3	19	-	-
1930															
Total, 5 to 24 years	556,177	327,782	58.9	453,334	281,689	62.1	63,814	25,912	40.6	38,461	19,929	51.8	568	252	44.4
5 years	30,727	13,627	44.3	27,495	12,044	43.8	975	395	40.5	2,231	1,179	52.8	26	9	-
6 years	29,309	23,882	81.5	25,951	20,990	80.9	1,263	1,090	86.3	2,066	1,782	86.3	29	20	-
7 to 9 years	88,137	85,232	96.7	75,877	73,447	96.8	6,309	6,069	96.2	5,904	5,672	96.1	47	44	-
10 to 13 years	107,871	106,821	99.0	94,174	93,309	99.1	7,413	7,317	98.7	6,229	6,141	98.6	55	54	-
14 years	25,409	25,069	98.7	21,908	21,629	98.7	1,986	1,959	98.6	1,499	1,466	97.8	16	15	-
15 years	24,510	23,314	95.1	20,999	20,002	95.3	2,208	2,113	95.7	1,293	1,189	92.0	10	10	-
16 and 17 years	47,542	29,804	62.7	38,838	24,537	63.2	5,841	3,579	61.3	2,825	1,664	58.9	38	24	-
18 and 19 years	51,030	10,464	20.5	39,792	8,402	21.1	7,852	1,552	19.8	3,336	495	14.8	50	15	-
20 years	26,417	2,806	10.6	19,684	2,211	11.2	4,593	485	10.6	2,097	98	4.7	43	12	-
21 to 24 years	125,225	6,763	5.4	88,616	5,118	5.8	25,374	1,353	5.3	10,981	243	2.2	254	49	19.3
Male, 5 to 24 years	275,829	167,113	60.6	224,970	143,320	63.7	32,069	13,746	42.9	18,362	9,875	53.8	428	172	40.2
5 years	15,687	6,849	43.7	14,050	6,082	43.3	518	211	40.7	1,103	553	50.1	16	8	-
6 years	14,818	11,986	80.9	13,127	10,525	80.2	640	550	85.9	1,038	903	87.0	13	8	-
7 to 9 years	44,451	43,023	96.8	38,154	36,961	96.9	3,269	3,153	96.5	3,005	2,887	96.1	23	22	-
10 to 13 years	53,716	53,221	99.1	47,054	46,646	99.1	3,660	3,614	98.7	2,967	2,927	98.7	35	34	-
14 years	12,693	12,544	98.8	10,938	10,809	98.9	998	985	98.7	752	740	98.4	10	10	-
15 years	12,255	11,772	96.1	10,495	10,097	96.2	1,125	1,082	96.2	628	586	93.3	7	7	-
16 and 17 years	23,116	15,521	67.1	18,911	12,761	67.5	2,877	1,936	67.3	1,306	806	61.7	22	18	-
18 and 19 years	23,845	5,962	25.0	18,617	4,746	25.5	3,710	926	25.0	1,475	277	18.8	43	13	-
20 years	12,387	1,728	14.0	9,227	1,344	14.6	2,252	320	14.2	868	52	6.0	40	12	-
21 to 24 years	62,861	4,507	7.2	44,402	3,349	7.5	13,020	969	7.4	5,220	144	2.8	219	45	20.5
Female, 5 to 24 years	280,348	160,669	57.3	228,364	138,369	60.6	31,745	12,166	38.3	20,099	10,054	50.0	140	80	57.1
5 years	15,040	6,778	45.1	13,445	5,962	44.3	457	184	40.3	1,128	626	55.5	10	6	-
6 years	14,491	11,896	82.1	12,824	10,465	81.6	623	540	86.7	1,028	879	85.5	16	12	-
7 to 9 years	43,686	42,209	96.6	37,723	36,486	96.7	3,040	2,916	95.9	2,899	2,785	96.1	24	22	-
10 to 13 years	54,155	53,600	99.0	47,120	46,663	99.0	3,753	3,703	98.7	3,262	3,214	98.5	20	20	-
14 years	12,716	12,525	98.5	10,975	10,820	98.6	988	974	98.6	747	726	97.2	6	5	-
15 years	12,255	11,542	94.2	10,504	9,905	94.3	1,083	1,031	95.2	665	603	90.7	3	3	-
16 and 17 years	24,426	14,283	58.5	19,927	11,776	59.1	2,964	1,643	55.4	1,519	858	56.5	16	6	-
18 and 19 years	27,185	4,502	16.6	21,175	3,656	17.3	4,142	626	15.1	1,861	218	11.7	7	2	-
20 years	14,080	1,078	7.7	10,457	867	8.3	2,341	165	7.0	1,229	46	3.7	3	-	-
21 to 24 years	62,364	2,256	3.6	44,214	1,769	4.0	12,354	384	3.1	5,761	99	1.7	35	4	-

Table A-39.—PERSONS 25 YEARS OLD AND OVER, BY YEARS OF SCHOOL COMPLETED, RACE, AND SEX, FOR THE CITY OF DETROIT: 1940

[Percent not shown where less than 0.1; median and percent not shown where base is less than 100]

YEARS OF SCHOOL COMPLETED	ALL CLASSES			NATIVE WHITE			FOREIGN-BORN WHITE			NEGRO			OTHER RACES		
	Total	Male	Female	Total	Male	Female	Total	Male	Female	Total	Male	Female	Total	Male	Female
Persons 25 years old and over	966,994	501,172	465,822	576,954	292,522	284,432	299,027	161,762	137,265	89,978	46,064	43,914	1,035	824	211
No school years completed	30,424	14,803	15,621	2,385	1,257	1,128	24,588	11,576	13,012	3,355	1,895	1,460	96	75	21
Grade school: 1 to 4 years	86,226	47,301	38,925	18,541	9,388	9,153	52,044	28,869	23,175	15,486	8,922	6,564	155	122	33
5 or 6 years	102,645	53,975	48,670	41,810	20,853	20,957	42,721	23,422	19,299	17,986	9,595	8,391	128	105	23
7 or 8 years	314,020	166,094	147,926	190,068	99,388	90,680	97,562	53,354	44,208	26,156	13,174	12,982	234	178	56
High school: 1 to 3 years	182,265	90,662	91,603	132,984	66,300	66,684	34,263	17,688	16,575	14,880	6,565	8,315	138	109	29
4 years	160,046	74,373	85,673	119,085	53,930	65,155	33,297	17,011	16,286	7,517	3,320	4,197	147	112	35
College: 1 to 3 years	46,310	24,952	21,358	36,488	19,082	17,406	7,012	4,348	2,664	2,730	1,450	1,280	80	72	8
4 years or more	41,230	26,785	14,445	33,547	21,161	12,386	6,202	4,705	1,497	1,426	869	557	55	50	5
Not reported	3,828	2,227	1,601	2,046	1,163	883	1,338	789	549	442	274	168	2	1	1
Median school years completed	8.7	8.6	8.7	9.8	9.7	9.9	7.6	7.6	7.6	7.6	7.4	7.8	8.2	8.2	8.0
Percent less than 5 years completed	12.1	12.4	11.7	3.6	3.6	3.6	25.6	25.0	26.4	20.9	23.5	18.3	24.3	23.9	25.6
PERCENT DISTRIBUTION															
Persons 25 years old and over	100.0	100.0	100.0	100.0	100.0	100.0	100.0	100.0	100.0	100.0	100.0	100.0	100.0	100.0	100.0
No school years completed	3.1	3.0	3.4	0.4	0.4	0.4	8.2	7.2	9.5	3.7	4.1	3.3	9.3	9.1	10.0
Grade school: 1 to 4 years	8.9	9.4	8.4	3.2	3.2	3.2	17.4	17.8	16.9	17.2	19.4	14.9	15.0	14.8	15.6
5 or 6 years	10.6	10.8	10.4	7.2	7.1	7.4	14.3	14.5	14.1	20.0	20.8	19.1	12.4	12.7	10.9
7 or 8 years	32.5	33.1	31.8	32.9	34.0	31.9	32.6	33.0	32.2	29.1	28.6	29.6	22.6	21.6	26.5
High school: 1 to 3 years	18.8	18.1	19.7	23.0	22.7	23.4	11.5	10.9	12.1	16.5	14.3	18.9	13.3	13.2	13.7
4 years	16.6	14.8	18.4	20.6	18.4	22.9	11.1	10.5	11.9	8.4	7.2	9.6	14.2	13.6	16.6
College: 1 to 3 years	4.8	5.0	4.6	6.3	6.5	6.1	2.3	2.7	1.9	3.0	3.1	2.9	7.7	8.7	3.8
4 years or more	4.3	5.3	3.1	5.8	7.2	4.4	2.1	2.9	1.1	1.6	1.9	1.3	5.3	6.1	2.4
Not reported	0.4	0.4	0.3	0.4	0.4	0.3	0.4	0.5	0.4	0.5	0.6	0.4	0.2	0.1	0.5

Table A-40.—FOREIGN-BORN WHITE, BY COUNTRY OF BIRTH, BY SEX, FOR THE CITY OF DETROIT: 1940 AND 1930

[Figures for white population in 1930 revised to include Mexicans classified with "Other races" in the 1930 reports. Percent not shown where less than 0.1 or where base is less than 100]

COUNTRY OF BIRTH	BOTH SEXES		PERCENT		MALE		FEMALE	
	1940	1930	1940	1930	1940	1930	1940	1930
All countries	320,664	403,721	100.0	100.0	172,297	224,631	148,367	179,090
England	21,049	28,636	6.6	7.1	11,063	15,333	9,986	13,303
Scotland	17,061	23,546	5.3	5.8	8,829	12,632	8,232	10,914
Wales	691	1,260	0.2	0.3	405	751	286	509
Northern Ireland	2,211	3,524	0.7	0.9	1,176	1,966	1,035	1,558
Irish Free State (Eire)	4,760	6,293	1.5	1.6	2,570	3,524	2,190	2,769
Norway	1,137	1,596	0.4	0.4	679	1,003	458	593
Sweden	3,185	4,318	1.0	1.1	2,003	2,785	1,182	1,533
Denmark	1,510	1,930	0.5	0.5	985	1,288	525	642
Netherlands	1,711	2,092	0.5	0.5	1,036	1,250	675	842
Belgium	6,890	8,969	2.1	2.2	3,665	4,872	3,225	4,097
Luxemburg	58	75	-	-	29	50	29	25
Switzerland	776	1,048	0.2	0.3	450	634	326	414
France	1,639	2,333	0.5	0.6	761	1,136	878	1,197
Germany	23,785	32,716	7.4	8.1	12,208	16,992	11,577	15,724
Poland	52,235	66,113	16.3	16.4	28,490	37,134	23,745	28,979
Czechoslovakia	4,080	6,291	1.3	1.6	2,176	3,488	1,904	2,803
Austria	7,992	5,898	2.5	1.5	4,209	3,234	3,783	2,664
Hungary	11,382	11,162	3.5	2.8	5,954	6,020	5,428	5,142
Yugoslavia	6,278	9,014	2.0	2.2	3,773	5,554	2,505	3,460
Russia (U. S. S. R.)	20,252	21,781	6.3	5.4	11,236	12,284	9,016	9,497
Lithuania	4,142	4,879	1.3	1.2	2,380	2,940	1,762	1,939
Latvia	421	399	0.1	0.1	230	212	191	187
Finland	1,944	2,811	0.6	0.7	872	1,394	1,072	1,417
Rumania	5,109	7,576	1.6	1.9	2,916	4,402	2,193	3,174
Bulgaria	702	818	0.2	0.2	520	670	182	148
Turkey in Europe	29	140	-	-	20	80	9	60
Greece	5,476	6,385	1.7	1.6	4,077	5,043	1,399	1,342
Italy	26,277	28,581	8.2	7.1	16,024	18,350	10,253	10,231
Spain	585	951	0.2	0.2	429	719	156	232
Portugal	50	68	-	-	41	55	9	13
Other Europe	2,412	3,152	0.8	0.8	1,695	2,336	717	816
Palestine and Syria	2,927	3,224	0.9	0.8	1,722	1,941	1,205	1,283
Turkey in Asia	2,813	2,343	0.9	0.6	1,683	1,500	1,130	843
Other Asia	1,864	2,698	0.6	0.7	1,188	1,801	676	897
Canada—French	9,699	12,477	3.0	3.1	4,715	6,547	4,984	5,930
Canada—Other	64,438	81,811	20.1	20.3	30,171	40,163	34,267	41,648
Newfoundland	488	720	0.2	0.2	268	393	220	327
Mexico	1,565	4,886	0.5	1.2	1,009	3,401	556	1,485
Cuba and other West Indies	202	219	0.1	0.1	129	142	73	77
Central and South America	396	472	0.1	0.1	253	324	143	148
Australia	131	167	-	-	68	97	63	70
Azores	3	6	-	-	-	3	3	3
All other and not reported	309	343	0.1	0.1	190	188	119	155

Table A-41.--PERSONS 14 YEARS OLD AND OVER, BY EMPLOYMENT STATUS, CLASS OF WORKER, RACE, AND SEX, FOR THE CITY OF DETROIT: 1940

[Percent not shown where less than 0.1 or where base is less than 100]

EMPLOYMENT STATUS	ALL CLASSES			NATIVE WHITE			FOREIGN-BORN WHITE			NEGRO			OTHER RACES		
	Total	Male	Female	Total	Male	Female	Total	Male	Female	Total	Male	Female	Total	Male	Female
Total population (all ages)	1,623,452	827,499	795,953	1,151,998	579,520	572,478	320,664	172,297	148,367	149,119	74,485	74,634	1,671	1,197	474
Persons 14 years old and over	1,285,144	655,722	629,422	850,013	425,878	424,135	317,555	170,708	146,847	116,311	58,162	58,149	1,265	974	291
In labor force	733,632	555,539	178,093	487,424	354,564	132,860	178,613	150,886	27,727	66,658	49,240	17,418	937	849	88
Not in labor force	551,512	100,183	451,329	362,589	71,314	291,275	138,942	19,822	119,120	49,653	8,922	40,731	328	125	203
Engaged in own home housew'k	360,893	3,502	357,391	225,500	2,176	223,324	105,925	975	104,950	29,313	347	28,966	155	4	151
In school	110,488	56,510	53,978	96,191	49,426	46,765	5,071	2,608	2,463	9,106	4,392	4,714	120	84	36
Unable to work	50,853	26,052	24,801	22,347	11,158	11,189	20,687	12,001	8,686	7,790	2,873	4,917	29	20	9
In institutions	1,785	899	886	1,097	519	578	512	244	268	176	136	40	-	-	-
Other and not reported	27,493	13,220	14,273	17,454	8,035	9,419	6,747	3,994	2,753	3,268	1,174	2,094	24	17	7
LABOR FORCE BY EMPLOYMENT STATUS															
In labor force	733,632	555,539	178,093	487,424	354,564	132,860	178,613	150,886	27,727	66,658	49,240	17,418	937	849	88
Employed (exc. public emerg. work)	625,456	474,250	151,206	420,738	307,280	113,458	158,764	133,388	25,376	45,137	32,846	12,291	817	736	81
At work	606,951	463,077	143,874	407,413	299,985	107,428	154,493	130,095	24,398	44,243	32,271	11,972	802	726	76
With a job	18,505	11,173	7,332	13,325	7,295	6,030	4,271	3,293	978	894	575	319	15	10	5
On public emerg. work (WPA, etc.)	29,458	24,102	5,356	14,874	11,125	3,249	4,825	4,471	354	10,219	8,469	1,750	40	37	3
Seeking work	78,718	57,187	21,531	52,312	36,159	16,153	15,024	13,027	1,997	11,302	7,925	3,377	80	76	4
Experienced workers	61,404	47,192	14,212	38,123	28,084	10,039	13,912	12,392	1,520	9,294	6,644	2,650	75	72	3
New workers	17,314	9,995	7,319	14,189	8,075	6,114	1,112	635	477	2,008	1,281	727	5	4	1
PERCENT BY SEX															
In labor force	100.0	75.7	24.3	100.0	72.7	27.3	100.0	84.5	15.5	100.0	73.9	26.1	100.0	90.6	9.4
Employed (exc. public emerg.)	100.0	75.8	24.2	100.0	73.0	27.0	100.0	84.0	16.0	100.0	72.8	27.2	100.0	90.1	9.9
On pub. emerg. work (WPA, etc.)	100.0	81.8	18.2	100.0	77.4	22.6	100.0	92.7	7.3	100.0	82.9	17.1	-	-	-
Seeking work	100.0	72.6	27.4	100.0	69.1	30.9	100.0	86.7	13.3	100.0	70.1	29.9	-	-	-
Not in labor force	100.0	18.2	81.8	100.0	19.7	80.3	100.0	14.3	85.7	100.0	18.0	82.0	100.0	38.1	61.9
Engaged in own home housew'k	100.0	1.0	99.0	100.0	1.0	99.0	100.0	0.9	99.1	100.0	1.2	98.8	100.0	2.6	97.4
In school	100.0	51.1	48.9	100.0	51.4	48.6	100.0	51.4	48.6	100.0	48.2	51.8	100.0	70.0	30.0
Unable to work	100.0	51.2	48.8	100.0	49.9	50.1	100.0	58.0	42.0	100.0	36.9	63.1	-	-	-
In institutions	100.0	50.4	49.6	100.0	47.3	52.7	100.0	47.7	52.3	100.0	77.3	22.7	-	-	-
Other and not reported	100.0	48.1	51.9	100.0	46.0	54.0	100.0	59.2	40.8	100.0	35.9	64.1	-	-	-
EMPLOYED WORKERS BY CLASS OF WORKER															
Employed (exc. public emerg.)	625,456	474,250	151,206	420,738	307,280	113,458	158,764	133,388	25,376	45,137	32,846	12,291	817	736	81
Wage and salary workers	565,246	426,414	138,832	388,606	282,315	106,291	134,285	112,732	21,553	41,755	30,827	10,928	600	540	60
Employers and own-account workers	54,292	45,695	8,597	28,379	23,377	5,002	22,634	20,237	2,397	3,079	1,891	1,188	200	190	10
Unpaid family workers	3,950	982	2,968	2,377	798	1,579	1,413	144	1,269	147	37	110	13	3	10
Class of worker not reported	1,968	1,159	809	1,376	790	586	432	275	157	156	91	65	4	3	1
At work	606,951	463,077	143,874	407,413	299,985	107,428	154,493	130,095	24,398	44,243	32,271	11,972	802	726	76
Wage and salary workers	550,000	417,816	132,184	377,095	276,376	100,719	131,268	110,522	20,746	41,045	30,383	10,662	592	535	57
Employers and own-account workers	51,434	43,309	8,125	26,868	22,166	4,702	21,460	19,187	2,273	2,912	1,771	1,141	194	185	9
Unpaid family workers	3,802	934	2,868	2,268	756	1,512	1,379	141	1,238	143	34	109	12	3	9
Class of worker not reported	1,715	1,018	697	1,182	687	495	386	245	141	143	83	60	4	3	1
With a job	18,505	11,173	7,332	13,325	7,295	6,030	4,271	3,293	978	894	575	319	15	10	5
Wage and salary workers	15,246	8,598	6,648	11,511	5,939	5,572	3,017	2,210	807	710	444	266	8	5	3
Employers and own-account workers	2,858	2,386	472	1,511	1,211	300	1,174	1,050	124	167	120	47	6	5	1
Unpaid family workers	148	48	100	109	42	67	34	3	31	4	3	1	1	-	1
Class of worker not reported	253	141	112	194	103	91	46	30	16	13	8	5	-	-	-
PERCENT DISTRIBUTION															
Persons 14 years old and over	100.0	100.0	100.0	100.0	100.0	100.0	100.0	100.0	100.0	100.0	100.0	100.0	100.0	100.0	100.0
In labor force	57.1	84.7	28.3	57.3	83.3	31.3	56.2	88.4	18.9	57.3	84.7	30.0	74.1	87.2	30.2
Not in labor force	42.9	15.3	71.7	42.7	16.7	68.7	43.8	11.6	81.1	42.7	15.3	70.0	25.9	12.8	69.8
Engaged in own home housew'k	28.1	0.5	56.8	26.5	0.5	52.7	33.4	0.6	71.5	25.2	0.6	49.8	12.3	0.4	51.9
In school	8.6	8.6	8.6	11.3	11.6	11.0	1.6	1.5	1.7	7.8	7.6	8.1	9.5	8.6	12.4
Unable to work	4.0	4.0	3.9	2.6	2.6	2.6	6.5	7.0	5.9	6.7	4.9	8.5	2.3	2.1	3.1
In institutions	0.1	0.1	0.1	0.1	0.1	0.1	0.2	0.1	0.2	0.2	0.2	0.1	-	-	-
Other and not reported	2.1	2.0	2.3	2.1	1.9	2.3	2.1	2.3	1.9	2.8	2.0	3.6	1.9	1.7	2.4
LABOR FORCE BY EMPLOYMENT STATUS															
In labor force	100.0	100.0	100.0	100.0	100.0	100.0	100.0	100.0	100.0	100.0	100.0	100.0	100.0	100.0	-
Employed (exc. public emerg. work)	85.3	85.4	84.9	86.3	86.7	85.4	88.9	88.4	91.5	67.7	66.7	70.6	87.2	86.7	-
At work	82.7	83.4	80.8	83.6	84.6	80.9	96.5	86.2	88.0	66.4	65.5	68.7	85.6	85.5	-
With a job	2.5	2.0	4.1	2.7	2.1	4.5	2.4	2.2	3.5	1.3	1.2	1.8	1.6	1.2	-
On public emerg. work (WPA, etc.)	4.0	4.3	3.0	2.9	3.1	2.4	2.7	3.0	1.3	15.3	17.2	10.0	4.3	4.4	-
Seeking work	10.7	10.3	12.1	10.7	10.2	12.2	8.4	8.6	7.2	17.0	16.1	19.4	8.5	9.0	-
Experienced workers	8.4	8.5	8.0	7.8	7.9	7.6	7.8	8.2	5.5	13.9	13.5	15.2	8.0	8.5	-
New workers	2.4	1.8	4.1	2.9	2.3	4.6	0.6	0.4	1.7	3.0	2.6	4.2	0.5	0.5	-
EMPLOYED WORKERS BY CLASS OF WORKER															
Employed (exc. public emerg.)	100.0	100.0	100.0	100.0	100.0	100.0	100.0	100.0	100.0	100.0	100.0	100.0	100.0	100.0	-
Wage and salary workers	90.4	89.9	91.8	92.4	91.9	93.7	84.6	84.5	84.9	92.5	93.9	88.9	73.4	73.4	-
Employers and own-account workers	8.7	9.6	5.7	6.7	7.6	4.4	14.3	15.2	9.4	6.8	5.8	9.7	24.5	25.8	-
Unpaid family workers	0.6	0.2	2.0	0.6	0.3	1.4	0.9	0.1	5.0	0.3	0.1	0.9	1.6	0.4	-
Class of worker not reported	0.3	0.2	0.5	0.3	0.3	0.5	0.5	0.2	0.6	0.3	0.3	0.5	0.5	0.4	-
At work	100.0	100.0	100.0	100.0	100.0	100.0	100.0	100.0	100.0	100.0	100.0	100.0	100.0	100.0	-
Wage and salary workers	90.6	90.2	91.9	92.6	92.1	93.8	85.0	85.0	85.0	92.8	94.1	89.1	73.8	73.7	-
Employers and own-account workers	8.5	9.4	5.6	6.6	7.4	4.4	13.9	14.7	9.3	6.6	5.5	9.5	24.2	25.5	-
Unpaid family workers	0.6	0.2	2.0	0.6	0.3	1.4	0.9	0.1	5.1	0.3	0.1	0.9	1.5	0.4	-
Class of worker not reported	0.3	0.2	0.5	0.3	0.2	0.5	0.2	0.2	0.6	0.3	0.3	0.5	0.5	0.4	-
With a job	100.0	100.0	100.0	100.0	100.0	100.0	100.0	100.0	100.0	100.0	100.0	100.0	-	-	-
Wage and salary workers	82.4	77.0	90.7	86.4	81.4	92.4	70.6	67.1	82.5	79.4	77.2	83.4	-	-	-
Employers and own-account workers	15.4	21.4	6.4	11.3	16.6	5.0	27.5	31.9	12.7	18.7	20.9	14.7	-	-	-
Unpaid family workers	0.8	0.4	1.4	0.8	0.6	1.1	0.8	0.1	3.2	0.4	0.5	0.3	-	-	-
Class of worker not reported	1.4	1.3	1.5	1.5	1.4	1.5	1.1	0.9	1.6	1.5	1.4	1.6	-	-	-

Table A-42.—EMPLOYED WORKERS 14 YEARS OLD AND OVER, BY MAJOR OCCUPATION GROUP, INDUSTRY GROUP, AND SEX, FOR THE CITY OF DETROIT: 1940

[Percent not shown where less than 0.1 or where base is less than 100]

MAJOR OCCUPATION GROUP AND INDUSTRY GROUP	Total	Male	Female	PERCENT BY OCCUPATION AND INDUSTRY			PERCENT BY SEX	
				Total	Male	Female	Male	Female
Total population (all ages)	1,623,452	827,499	795,953	-	-	-	51.0	49.0
All persons 14 years old and over	1,285,144	655,722	629,422	-	-	-	51.0	49.0
In labor force	733,632	555,539	178,093	100.0	100.0	100.0	75.7	24.3
Employed workers (except on public emergency work)	625,456	474,250	151,206	85.3	85.4	84.9	75.8	24.2
MAJOR OCCUPATION GROUP								
Employed (except on public emergency work)	625,456	474,250	151,206	100.0	100.0	100.0	75.8	24.2
Professional workers	36,704	21,219	15,485	5.9	4.5	10.2	57.8	42.2
Semiprofessional workers	9,267	7,619	1,648	1.5	1.6	1.1	82.2	17.8
Farmers and farm managers	128	114	14	-	-	-	89.1	10.9
Proprietors, managers, and officials, except farm	46,185	41,346	4,839	7.4	8.7	3.2	89.5	10.5
Clerical, sales, and kindred workers	135,559	77,910	57,649	21.7	16.4	38.1	57.5	42.5
Craftsmen, foremen, and kindred workers	109,149	106,854	2,295	17.5	22.5	1.5	97.9	2.1
Operatives and kindred workers	167,532	141,926	25,606	26.8	29.9	16.9	84.7	15.3
Domestic service workers	18,699	708	17,991	3.0	0.1	11.9	3.8	96.2
Service workers, except domestic	58,744	35,903	22,841	9.4	7.6	15.1	61.1	38.9
Farm laborers (wage workers) and farm foremen	241	234	7	-	-	-	97.1	2.9
Farm laborers, unpaid family workers	24	23	1	-	-	-	-	-
Laborers, except farm	39,223	37,543	1,680	6.3	7.9	1.1	95.7	4.3
Occupation not reported	4,001	2,851	1,150	0.6	0.6	0.8	71.3	28.7
INDUSTRY GROUP								
Employed (except on public emergency work)	625,456	474,250	151,206	100.0	100.0	100.0	75.8	24.2
Agriculture, forestry, and fishery	852	793	59	0.1	0.2	-	93.1	6.9
Agriculture	799	745	54	0.1	0.2	-	93.2	6.8
Forestry (except logging) and fishery	53	48	5	-	-	-	-	-
Mining	218	198	20	-	-	-	90.8	9.2
Coal mining	30	17	3	-	-	-	-	-
Crude petroleum and natural gas production	25	25	-	-	-	-	-	-
Other mines and quarries	173	156	17	-	-	-	90.2	9.8
Construction	24,099	23,497	602	3.9	5.0	0.4	97.5	2.5
Manufacturing	295,123	260,132	34,991	47.2	54.9	23.1	88.1	11.9
Food and kindred products	14,259	11,594	2,665	2.3	2.4	1.8	81.3	18.7
Textile-mill products	1,047	718	329	0.2	0.2	0.2	68.6	31.4
Apparel and other fabricated textile products	2,422	893	1,529	0.4	0.2	1.0	36.9	63.1
Logging	18	18	-	-	-	-	-	-
Sawmills and planing mills	548	520	28	0.1	0.1	-	94.9	5.1
Furniture, store fixtures, and miscellaneous wooden goods	2,533	2,034	499	0.4	0.4	0.3	80.3	19.7
Paper and allied products	1,777	1,274	503	0.3	0.3	0.3	71.7	28.3
Printing, publishing, and allied industries	10,335	8,188	2,147	1.7	1.7	1.4	79.2	20.8
Chemicals and allied products	5,915	4,375	1,540	0.9	0.9	1.0	74.0	26.0
Petroleum and coal products	1,103	972	131	0.2	0.2	0.1	88.1	11.9
Leather and leather products	550	367	183	0.1	0.1	0.1	66.7	33.3
Stone, clay, and glass products	2,786	2,361	425	0.4	0.5	0.3	84.7	15.3
Iron and steel and their products	19,500	17,254	2,246	3.1	3.6	1.5	88.5	11.5
Nonferrous metals and their products	5,978	5,362	615	1.0	1.1	0.4	89.7	10.3
Machinery	24,287	20,617	3,670	3.9	4.3	2.4	84.9	15.1
Automobiles and automobile equipment	187,528	171,988	15,540	30.0	36.3	10.3	91.7	8.3
Transportation equipment, except automobile	1,701	1,620	81	0.3	0.3	0.1	95.2	4.8
Other and not specified manufacturing industries	12,838	9,978	2,860	2.1	2.1	1.9	77.7	22.3
Transportation, communication, and other public utilities	36,321	31,176	5,145	5.8	6.6	3.4	85.8	14.2
Railroads (including railroad repair shops) and railway express service	8,476	7,515	961	1.4	1.6	0.6	88.7	11.3
Trucking service	5,655	5,352	303	0.9	1.1	0.2	94.6	5.4
Other transportation	8,910	8,416	494	1.4	1.8	0.3	94.5	5.5
Communication	4,777	2,450	2,327	0.8	0.5	1.5	51.3	48.7
Utilities	8,503	7,443	1,060	1.4	1.6	0.7	87.5	12.5
Wholesale and retail trade	116,730	78,960	37,770	18.7	16.6	25.0	67.6	32.4
Wholesale trade	16,474	13,667	2,807	2.6	2.9	1.9	83.0	17.0
Food and dairy products stores, and milk retailing	23,149	17,031	6,118	3.7	3.6	4.0	73.6	26.4
Eating and drinking places	20,043	11,565	8,478	3.2	2.4	5.6	57.7	42.3
Motor vehicles and accessories retailing, and filling stations	9,422	8,827	595	1.5	1.9	0.4	93.7	6.3
Other retail trade	47,642	27,870	19,772	7.6	5.9	13.1	58.5	41.5
Finance, insurance, and real estate	23,229	14,707	8,522	3.7	3.1	5.6	63.3	36.7
Business and repair services	12,674	10,644	2,030	2.0	2.2	1.3	84.0	16.0
Automobile storage, rental, and repair services	5,172	5,003	169	0.8	1.1	0.1	96.7	3.3
Business and repair services, except automobile	7,502	5,641	1,861	1.2	1.2	1.2	75.2	24.8
Personal services	46,970	14,392	32,578	7.5	3.0	21.5	30.6	69.4
Domestic service	20,125	1,476	18,649	3.2	0.3	12.3	7.3	92.7
Hotels and lodging places	8,536	3,696	4,840	1.4	0.8	3.2	43.3	56.7
Laundering, cleaning, and dyeing services	8,199	3,974	4,225	1.3	0.8	2.8	48.5	51.5
Miscellaneous personal services	10,110	5,246	4,864	1.6	1.1	3.2	51.9	48.1
Amusement, recreation, and related services	6,227	4,759	1,468	1.0	1.0	1.0	76.4	23.6
Professional and related services	37,422	16,017	21,405	6.0	3.4	14.2	42.8	57.2
Government	19,617	15,640	3,977	3.1	3.3	2.6	79.7	20.3
Industry not reported	5,974	3,335	2,639	1.0	0.7	1.7	55.8	44.2

Table A-43.—PERSONS 14 YEARS OLD AND OVER IN THE LABOR FORCE, 1940, AND GAINFUL WORKERS 14 YEARS OLD AND OVER, 1930, BY RACE AND SEX, FOR THE CITY OF DETROIT

[Totals for population and gainful workers for 1930 include "Unknown age." Figures for white population in 1930 have been revised to include Mexicans who were classified with "Other races" in the 1930 reports. Percent not shown where less than 0.1 or where base is less than 100]

CENSUS YEAR AND RACE	TOTAL					MALE					FEMALE				
	Population		Persons in the labor force, and gainful workers,[1] 14 years old and over			Population		Persons in the labor force, and gainful workers,[1] 14 years old and over			Population		Persons in the labor force, and gainful workers,[1] 14 years old and over		
	Total (all ages)	14 years old and over	Number	Per-cent of total popu-lation	Per-cent of popu-lation 14 yrs. and over	Total (all ages)	14 years old and over	Number	Per-cent of total popu-lation	Per-cent of popu-lation 14 yrs. and over	Total (all ages)	14 years old and over	Number	Per-cent of total popu-lation	Per-cent of popu-lation 14 yrs. and over
1940	1,623,452	1,285,144	733,632	45.2	57.1	827,499	655,722	555,539	67.1	84.7	795,953	629,422	178,093	22.4	28.3
White	1,472,662	1,167,568	666,037	45.2	57.0	751,817	596,586	505,450	67.2	84.7	720,845	570,982	160,587	22.3	28.1
Negro	149,119	116,311	66,658	44.7	57.3	74,485	58,162	49,240	66.1	84.7	74,634	58,149	17,418	23.3	30.0
Other races	1,671	1,265	937	56.1	74.1	1,197	974	849	70.9	87.2	474	291	88	18.6	30.2
1930	1,568,662	1,166,008	689,197	43.9	59.1	821,920	618,609	548,371	66.7	88.6	746,742	547,399	140,826	18.9	25.7
White	1,446,656	1,071,360	627,549	43.4	58.6	758,116	568,395	502,158	66.2	88.3	688,540	502,965	125,391	18.2	24.9
Negro	120,066	93,018	60,274	50.2	64.8	62,239	48,812	44,902	72.1	92.0	57,827	44,206	15,372	26.6	34.8
Other races	1,940	1,630	1,374	70.8	84.3	1,565	1,402	1,311	33.8	93.5	375	228	63	16.8	27.6

[1] Data for 1930 represent gainful workers 14 years old and over.

"California Ocean Classic in April," ***Syracuse Herald*** **(New York), March 1, 1930:** The second annual fall California long-distance powerboat ocean race will be staged on April 24 to 27, under the auspices of Long Beach Yacht Club, adjacent to Los Angeles. Eleven early entries are on hand for the event, which covers a nautical distance of 446.1 miles and is the longest powerboat race in the world. Besides the Long Beach Club, the St. Francis of San Francisco and Santa Barbara Yacht clubs are cooperating in staging the event. The race is open to cruisers and express cruisers less than 110 feet overall, owned and chartered by recognized yacht clubs.

"Former Local Man Is Cup Contender," *The New Castle News* (Pennsylvania), September 29, 1933

Newcastle people are looking to the President's Cup Race in the Pontiac River Friday and Saturday with more than ordinary interest this year. A former New Castle man, George C. Reis, is entered in the race and is considered the leading contender for the cup.

The race is for motor boats of 625 cubic inches displacement. When Calvin Coolidge was in the president's chair he donated a gold cup to be sought for each year. Mr. Reis won the cup two years ago, and tradition says no one wins it twice. That's a tradition he hopes to break. Mr. Reis has already won two major racing events of the year, the National Sweepstakes at Montauk, Long Island, and the Gold Cup Race in Detroit, which he won the same day Gar Wood kept America supreme in the motor boat racing.

"Wood Tunes Up His Boat," *The Raleigh Times* (North Carolina), April 11, 1931

Miami Beach, Florida—With his racing craft tuned to perfection, Gar Wood today was ready for his attempt to wrest the world speedboat crown from Kaye Don, of England.

Wood announced last night he would drive his twin motored *Miss America IX*over a measured mile course in Indian Creek here today in the hope of bettering the 103.49 miles an hour set by Don in Buenos Aires last week. The Detroit sportsman instructed his mechanics to be ready to put this boat on the course at noon unless strong crosswinds made the water too choppy for speed.

The weather forecast today was for gentle to moderate winds from the east and southeast. The course runs north and south.

Part of the electrical timing apparatus used in checking the exact speed over a measured mile was installed yesterday under the direction of Otis Porter, timer for the American Automobile Association. Porter said the device would be in working order before noon today.

Wood returned to his home in Indian Creek last Sunday to prepare his boat for his attempt to regain the record. He sent the craft roaring over the measured mile course of 102.56 miles an hour March 20 to better the mark established by the late Sir Henry O.D. Segrave on Lake Windermere, England.

Outboard Racing Timeline

1881: Gustav Trouv described his new electric, portable motor for boats and presented it to the French Academy of Sciences.

1898: The French Yachting Union organized boat races for launches powered by either steam, naphtha or petroleum engines mounted inboard.

1906: Cameron Waterman produced a single cylinder detachable marine motor with its flywheel enclosed in the crankcase called the Waterman Outboard Porto.

1907: The Cameron Waterman Company sold 3,000 outboards in America and Denmark.

1908: Ole Evinrude sold 25 of his single-cylinder, water-cooled outboard motors with 1.5 horsepower for $62 each.

1912: Swedish engineers created the first two-cylinder detachable motor capable of 2.5 horsepower.

1913: The Evinrude Company employed 300 workers to meet domestic and foreign demand.

1920: Thirty outboard motor companies had been created.

1922: The Johnson Brothers introduced at the New York Post Show the Johnson light twin and sold more than 3,000 motors in one year for $140 each.

1923: The Mississippi Valley Powerboat Association sanctioned the first three-mile outboard race to be contested in the United States; it was won by an Elto Twin pushing a displacement hull at an average speed of nine mph.

1924: The American Powerboat Association established a set of rules to apply to boats powered by detachable motors.

1925: The six-horsepower Johnson Big Twin, priced at $190, was introduced.

1926: A 71-mile outboard marathon boat race was staged in New York State; the winner took four hours, 46 minutes.

1927: Bigger engines produced more record-breaking speeds, topping 32 mph.

1928: The Elto outboard set a speed record of 41.7 mph and sold 10,000 units nationwide.

1929: Long 250-mile boat races gained in popularity, often requiring 14 hours on the water.

1930: Hull designs continued to improve speeds, led by the Century Boat Company in Milwaukee, Wisconsin.

Boxer Claims the Role of Villain to Achieve Success

Professional sports were on the rise as 1940 came into view and Americans searched for a diversion from tough economic times. Enter French Canadian Paul Lecomte, who excelled at fist fighting and schoolyard brawling. Emigrating to Bangor, Maine and the opportunity to box professionally before enthusiastic fans, he gladly played the outsider, giving his audience someone to cheer against, and him a much-needed paycheck.

Life at Home

- Born on a farm in Canada, Paul Lecomte's mother died months after giving birth to him, the last of nine children.
- A sickly infant, his siblings had little time for him, and shipped him from the farm to his grandmother's sprawling mansion in the city of Quebec at the age of two.
- There he was raised alongside the servants' children and often relegated to the servants' dining table; his boisterous ways often upset his grandmother.
- At his grandmother's insistence, he attended school, where he struggled with reading, handwriting, math and getting along with others.
- He excelled at fist-fighting, schoolyard brawling and long-distance spitting.
- His grandmother found little that was laudatory in his accomplishments.
- After he finished the sixth grade he ran away from home to work for his older brother, who was happy to have an additional hand on the farm.
- To tame his younger brother and get some return on his food investment, Paul's brother taught him how to box, and scheduled him every Friday night in the area's barn fights.
- Weighing in at just 120 pounds, Paul took on all sizes of fighters during the organized brawls; he even knocked out a few, thanks to a powerful right hand and a total lack of fear.
- He quickly became a crowd favorite, especially after he spat out a broken, bloody tooth and rallied to knock out his older, bigger opponent 11 rounds later.
- At 16, he took on a tall thin fighter, who had considerable military training in the high art of boxing.
- Paul lasted almost three rounds before collapsing in a pool of blood.
- After his anger died down, he realized, for the first time, the need to learn his opponent's tactics, including punch avoidance, using his

Paul Lecomte was brought up by his grandmother in Quebec.

feet to avoid damage and most of all the science of counter-attacking.
- His plan was to get across the border in the United States and seek proper training.
- America needed laborers, especially cheap, illegal foreign labor, and recruiters from textile mills in Maine often combed French-Canada in search of it.
- Paul could barely read French and certainly no English, but decided to run illegal liquor boxes across the United States line, which he'd done before, only this time remain in America.
- Within days of arriving in the United States, he had found a textile mill job, gotten in a fist fight, lost his job, and was invited to join the Saturday night fight circuit in Maine.

At 16-years-old, Paul was a crowd-pleasing boxer, taking on any opponent.

Life at Work

- Paul Lecomte became known as "Frenchie" in fighting circles.
- He envied the names of other fighters, such as "Hurricane Hank" or "Perpetual Motion" that brought the roaring crowd to its feet.
- Paul's nickname of Frenchie implied that he was a foreigner and always solicited "boo" and "go back home," especially after he would knock out the hometown favorite.
- He quickly took on the villain's role, and built a powerful reputation for savagery; encouraging local fans to bet against him.
- Paul kept the fight close and the betting lively to give everyone, especially the professional gamblers, their money's worth.
- Paul found a promoter who spoke French and was willing to train the 160-pound boxing machine, schedule three to five fights a month and, unlike some managers, not steal all his earnings.
- Slowly he learned to trust another man.
- Life in the United States was frustrating for him; why had no one bothered to learn French?
- After all, Americans shared a friendly border with Canada, where affluent French-speakers were important and the least, Paul thought, Americans could do was learn a little French.
- Paul's first fluency in English was a long string of curses and rude rebukes.
- Luckily, Bangor's legions of tough, self-sufficient lumbermen included a crop of French Canadians whose accents brought him great comfort.
- And more than a few American girls were willing to endure his halting English to spend time with the muscular fighter from French-Quebec.
- To supplement his income, Paul helped run illegal liquor across the border.
- Prohibition was dead—everyone knew that—but people still needed to drink their cares away while they waited for the laws to change.
- Paul was fascinated by President Franklin Roosevelt's "fireside chats" delivered over the radio, appreciating that the most powerful man in the country was willing to talk to him-an immigrant-personally about the future of the U.S.

- Through these radio broadcasts he learned of the Civilian Conservation Corps (CCC), designed to employ millions of young men between the ages of 17 and 27.
- This volunteer army would get paid to work in national forests, parks and federal lands in nine-month stints.
- Reasoning that young men with money loved to watch fights and gamble, Paul started a traveling boxing match, touring from camp to camp, accompanied by friends willing to take a few bets.
- In one night on the road, Paul battled his sparring partner to a convincing sixth-round knockout, then took on the camp's bravest brawler.
- The bets rolled in despite the depressed economy.
- Paul fought under two names: "Frenchie" in New England and "The Canadian Killer" in the CCC camps across the South and Midwest.

Life in the Community: Bangor, Maine

- The building of the first sawmill in Bangor in 1772 marked the beginning of a century of dominance by Bangor in the world lumber industry.
- In the mid 1830s, Bangor was home to more than 300 sawmills, earning the city the undisputed title "Lumber Capital of the World."
- Lumberjacks harvested the northern Maine woods and sent their logs down the Penobscot River where they were picked up by runners in Bangor.
- After the Bangor mills processed the lumber, some of the lumber was then sent farther down the Penobscot to Winterport and Belfast, where some of the world's finest schooners were built.
- Bangor's prosperity in the lumber industry began to fade in the late 1800s, replaced by the ice industry, with ice from the Penobscot River considered to be the finest in the world and shipped as far as India.
- The Depression did not hit Bangor as hard as some cities: only a few shops and no banks closed.
- French Canadians continued to emigrate from Canada to the United States through the 1940s.
- Paul Lecomte was sure that at least three of his older brothers and sisters lived the States, but wasn't sure of their location.

"Garden Planning Dramatic Policy Change; To End Regular Boxing, Wrestling Dates," by James P. Dawson, *The New York Times*, February 13, 1933

The days of professional boxing and wrestling, on the comprehensive scale on which these two sports events were promoted heretofore, are numbered at Madison Square Garden.

Unless all signs fail, boxing, which, as an entertainment in the old Garden under the late Tex Rickard, was primarily responsible for the present arena, will be relegated to the status of minor importance in the future activities in the Garden.

As far as can be determined, it is proposed, commencing next fall, to eliminate the regular weekly boxing day Friday on the Garden's calendar, and the custom of semi-monthly wrestling attractions. There will be substituted only important boxing and wrestling events when, and if, they develop. Amateur boxing, it is understood, will be encouraged. . . .

Hockey, circus, rodeo, bike races, track meets and various tradeshows all give a good account of themselves, according to reliable information, but boxing and wrestling are not so profitable. Therefore, the conclusion is reached that before long many of the regular Friday night boxing and Monday night wrestling dates will be eliminated, and will be replaced by other attractions which these new improvements are making available.

South Carolina Family Endures Death, Debts and Selling the Farm

The decade leading to 1940 saw a steady migration of families as they sought ways to survive. The Hope family from York, South Carolina was forced from their life on the farm to life in the city, where they learned new skills in a world that was increasingly urbanized and dependent on manufacturing.

Life at Home

- Robert Meek Hope raised cotton, like his father before him, but also kept an orchard of apples, grapes and peaches on his land in York, South Carolina to increase self-sufficiency.
- The family also ate the cows and chickens they raised.
- Robert took great pride in his looks and his farm, but his passion was his hunting dogs.
- Twelve-year old Martha loved to tell how her daddy was so smart and his dogs so good, he could tell which dog was closest to catching the quarry based on its howl.
- Robert traveled on weekends to demonstrate their hunting prowess in dog shows around the state.
- The dogs loved these trips and so did Martha and her little brother, Sonny, because their father always brought back an eight-inch stick of mint candy.
- When Robert died suddenly, the children were told it was pneumonia.
- Martha's mother Edna was offered a job at a dry cleaner's in town, so she moved her family to her great-uncle's house, where she will pay room and board.
- The house is big, but Martha worried the yard is too small to grow family's vegetables.
- When she found out the farm would be sold, Martha didn't even cry once-until her little brother Sonny started.
- Sonny was excited about the move to town, but wouldn't talk about his father's death.
- He told everyone he plans to be a salesman for Curtis Publishing Company and win lots of

Martha Hope prepared to leave the farm.

After the move into town, Sonny planned to be a super salesman.

prizes, and spent hours going through the book of prizes for top student salesmen
- His goal was a Columbia Motobike costing 800 brown vouchers.
- Sonny also thought he was the "kick-the-can" champion of the world, and practiced every day kicking an Esso oil can from the house to Uncle Ted's store down the road and back.
- They bought most of their supplies from Uncle Ted's store.
- Uncle Ted kept lots of food in stock, but doesn't allow credit, especially to relatives.
- Sometimes, though, he gave away little treats, especially Ritz Crackers, which were a new product by National Biscuit Company.
- Since her father's funeral, Martha had to take on more responsibility for the family.
- Her aunt told her, "You need to make sure your little brother knows that Santa Claus does not exist and won't be coming this year. There is no use pretending now."
- Martha did as she was told, because an adult said so, even though it never occurred to her that Santa Claus wasn't real.
- On the farm, the family cooked and heated their 900-square-foot house with a wood stove, sometimes sleeping in the kitchen for warmth during the coldest days of winter.
- It operated around the clock even in summer, and wood was cut weekly to keep it running, and it always had a skillet of cornbread on top.
- On cold mornings, the dogs fought over the chance to lie by the warm oven door.
- The house had no electricity, but the rural electrical cooperative promised hook up by the end of the year.
- On the farm, everyone had a job.
- Most fieldwork was done by her father and a sharecropper; Martha cut cane and chopped cotton, and every year after the weather cooled, her family and a neighbor together butchered three or four hogs.
- Once the hogs were killed, sausage was ground, liver pudding made, lard rendered, and hams hung for curing.
- In the garden, Martha grew turnips and string beans that were sold at the farmer's market.
- After her father died, she convinced her uncle to take her and her turnip crop to market, but lost out to refrigerated trucks from Florida that forced down the prices.
- She was hugely disappointed and couldn't buy anything, especially bananas, which she loved.
- To get the best possible price for their cotton crop, Martha carefully treated the cotton with a mixture of arsenic and molasses to kill the destructive boll weevils.
- Martha was careful not to get any on her hands or in her mouth, remembering that her friend Sarah was poisoned with arsenic and missed several weeks of school.
- Always good with numbers, Martha helped record the purchases when the farm was sold.
- For one whole day she watched her father's entire life being auctioned, for a total of $841.
- Most of the bidders were from nearby farms, especially aunts and uncles who thought that helping to buy out the farm was a fair thing to do for their brother.
- Uncle Neely spent the most, $561, primarily for the mules.
- Martha was angry with her uncle for spreading rumors of her father dying from a knife wound that he got in a bar fight, when everyone in the family knew he died of pneumonia.

- She was also angry that the relatives wanted her mother to turn Lucinda out in the streets when they moved to the city.
- Lucinda was a 13-year-old black girl who moved in with Martha and her family when her father tossed her out of the house for talking back.
- Martha and Lucinda did everything together, except go to school, although Martha helped her with her schoolwork at night.
- Edna told Martha that she had to think about what's best for the entire family.

Most of the family's supplies came from Uncle Ted's store.

Life at School and Work

- In preparation for the new school year, Martha poured over the Montgomery Ward catalog.
- Some people in the neighborhood were Sears fans, but this family liked Montgomery Ward better.
- Martha knew that no money will be available for new dresses this year, but looking at the wonderful pictures kept her hopes up.
- Sonny was starting the second grade, and hoped there are pictures on the wall like in his old classroom.
- In the first grade he learned to tie his shoes by looking at a detailed, step-by-step drawing on the wall; some days they even practiced in class.
- Like most farm boys, Sonny rarely wore shoes before he started school, except on Sunday, and those fastened with a buckle.
- His first-grade teacher, Miss Gaillard was not a high school graduate, and since she only attended school through grade six, was permitted only to teach through the fourth grade.
- When Miss Gaillard was sick or away, Martha taught Sonny's class because she was the best reader in the school.
- Martha's sixth-grade class included a commendation of George Washington's birthday, and an Easter pageant followed by an Easter egg hunt.
- Martha was proud to play the role of Martha at the tomb when the stone was rolled away.
- Her father came to both presentations, but didn't say much afterward-he rarely did.
- For her little brother's birthday, Martha and her mother made a stuffed character from his favorite storybook, *Where's Angus?* with an embroidered nose, mouth and eyes, and a red ribbon with little silver bells around its neck.
- After the farm was sold, Martha's Aunt Cora gave her a booklet called "How to Make Draperies" by the Singer Sewing Machine Company.

- Since she was a little girl, Martha enjoyed helping her mother pump the pedal on the family sewing machine, and wanted to learn to sew herself a dress to wear to the new school.
- On top of everything else, Martha is concerned that she will no longer be able to help the road grader man, with whom she rode in the truck that cleaned ditches and graded the road.
- At the end of each trip he said, "Thanks for your help; I don't know if I could have done it without you."

Life in the Community: York, South Carolina

- South Carolina's foreign-born population is only one percent, one of the lowest in the nation, and agriculture dominates the state's economy, with two thirds of the state's 166,000 farms operated by tenants who do not own the land they till.
- South Carolina's 110,000 manufacturing jobs have an average annual wage of $615.
- Two percent of the state's farms have electricity.
- South Carolina was one of six states without old-age pensions, one of 14 without assistance for the blind, and one of two with no aid for dependent children.
- The Works Progress Administration (WPA), administered by the federal government, slowly transformed the economic landscape by building roads, schools, bridges and dams.
- The newly-created Public Service Authority, known as Santee-Cooper, produced and sold electricity, developed inland navigation along three South Carolina rivers and reclaimed swamps and reforested watersheds.

Partial listing of the estate of Robert Meek Hope, sold at auction, York, South Carolina, December 22, 1934

Item	Price
Four Mules	561.00
Three Cows	72.00
Wagon	15.00
Wagon Harness	9.50
Horse Collars	1.75
Disc Harrow	8.50
Tractor Harrow	26.00
Four Side Harrows	8.20
Two Drag Harrows	2.25
Stalk Cutter	0.60
Mower	1.25
Seed Fork and Rake	1.00
Five Cotton Planters	14.50
Corn Planter	2.60
Guano Plow	1.00
Single Row Oat Drill	3.60
Three Row Oat Drills	4.70
Four Plow Sacks	0.70
Four Turn Plows	20.00
Middle Buster	1.75
Three Go-Devils	2.50
Shop Tools	6.50
Bellows	1.25
Blower	4.50
Corn Sheller	1.20
Grindstone	1.45
Mailbox	0.50
Farm Bell	1.00
Wheelbarrow	1.50
Wagon Wheels	0.60
Hack Saw	0.45
Pipe Wrench	0.75
Grain Cradle	0.75
Mowing Scythe	1.25
Pitch Fork	0.50
Two Shovels	0.55
Gears	3.80
Anvil	2.50
Hoses	4.40
Manure Spreader	1.00
Crosscut Saw	0.45
Dinner Bell	2.00
Icebox	2.50
Cabinet	3.00
Wardrobe	2.80
Table	2.10
Baby Bed	0.25
Two Beds and Springs	3.00
Bureau	5.75

Microphone Innovations Usher in Popular Crooners

"Romeo of Song" Russ Columbo established himself as a major talent based on the innovations underway within the 1940-era music industry, when radios were becoming a necessity in most homes. With improvements in the microphone and radio broadcasts, Columbo's crooning style charmed America.

Life at Home

- Russ Columbo insisted he was not a blues singer, a crooner, or a straight baritone, but a unique talent with a sound all his own.
- Born in Camden, New Jersey, on January 14, 1908, to Italian immigrants Nicolo, a stonemason and his wife Giulia, Columbo was the couple's twelfth child.
- His name was Ruggiero, but a childhood friend couldn't say it, so Russ stuck.
- Russ was considered a child prodigy, mastering the violin by age five.
- The family moved often, and finally settled in in Los Angeles when Russ was eight.
- The family paid $15 for his student violin, but eventually saved up $45 to purchase a standard instrument that he continued to improve on through his teenage years.
- Russ' humble family life, good looks, and musical talent made him a favorite among a diverse high school crowd.
- He played first violin in the school orchestra and stuck out with his winning smile.
- When he quit high school to tour as part of an orchestra, he also became involved in the motion picture industry and played his violin on the set of films to provide atmosphere.
- Russ had always been fascinated by the growing popularity of motion pictures.
- He fell in love for the first time with Pola Negri, who presented Russ with an opal ring that once belonged to the late actor Rudolf Valentino who said that the ring was cursed, and who died at age 31.
- Russ lived with his parents and kept only a few close friends, his best friend being photographer Lansing Brown.

Russ Columbo was a popular crooner, along with rival Bing Crosby, before being accidentally shot and killed at age 26.

CBS rushed to sign acts, including Bing Crosby, to meet the demand of radio listeners.

- While visiting Brown's home, and looking at a collection of antique dueling pistols, a shot suddenly discharged, ricocheted off the wall and caught Russ in the left eye.
- Brown called the police, who discovered that Russ was still alive, but he died later that night.
- Universal Studios makeup artist Jack Pierce, best known for his work on Boris Karloff in the movies *Frankenstein* and *The Mummy*, made up Russ for funeral viewing.
- Pallbearers included Zeppo Marx and singing rival Bing Crosby.
- His siblings tried to keep his death a secret from their mother, who was in the hospital with a heart ailment, by sending postcards "from Russ", playing records of his radio shows and carefully editing the newspapers she read.
- After Carole Lombard's death, the actress with whom Russ was to have dinner with the night of his death, rumors arose of her ghost being seen at her house wearing a red dress (the outfit for their dinner date), looking happily at a Russ Coumbo waiting for her.

Life at Work

- Russ Columbo sang in the vocal style known as "crooning."
- With the perfection of the microphone, singers could sing softer, more subtly and more intimate.
- The style suited Russ well, but the form was mocked because it made a man sound sensitive and overly romantic.
- Women loved the technique, and it became popular on radio and later as movies incorporated sound, which was an ideal style for the cinema.
- Rudy Vallee and Bing Crosby made an impact in both singing and acting, and Russ was joining their ranks.
- Cardinal O'Connell of Boston publicly denounced the new style, and *The New York Times* considered the style corruptive and said it needed to go.
- Russ hated the term "crooner" and took lessons in opera singing to try to shake the moniker.

- The jazzy background accompaniment to many of the crooner's tunes brought protests about the impact that people of color were having on white musicians.
- In addition, singers, once positioned off to the side while the band leader held center stage, became stars.
- In addition to singing, acting and playing the violin, Russ also tried his hand at songwriting, helping to pen the tunes "Prisoner of Love" and "You Call It Madness (But I Call It Love)."
- Songwriter Con Conrad heard Russ performing and encouraged him to move to New York City and try his hand at radio, just as Bing Crosby had recently done with great success.
- Russ was initially turned down, but NBC took him on for the 11:30 pm slot on Tuesday.
- He was so successful on radio, sponsors Maxwell House and later Listerine paid Russ $2,500-$3,000 per week.
- When Bing Crosby boasted some of the top recordings and was on his way to bigger things in movies, public relations men concocted a fake rivalry between him and Russ.
- Their phony story was aided by the fact that Crosby was a CBS radio personality, and Russ occupied a similar time slot on NBC.
- Known as the "Battle of the Baritones" the war was short-lived and shortly thereafter, he left NBC and began touring the country with his own orchestra.
- He wanted to move back to Los Angeles and give Hollywood another try.
- Days before his death, Russ returned to the recording studio for the first time in two years, leaving fans with one more hint of what he could have become.

Life in the Community: Camden, New Jersey

- Camden New Jersey lies on the banks of the Delaware River in the northern part of the state.
- It was home to one of the first commercial recording studios in the United States and hosted the first drive-in movie, the brainchild of Camden native Richard M. Hollingshead, Jr.
- A sales manager at his father's auto parts store, Hollingshead began experimenting with finding a wider theater seat more comfortable for larger people, mostly with his mother in mind.
- The first drive-in offered 500 slots with a 40x50-foot screen; the debut movie was *Wife Beware*.
- The advertising slogan was "The whole family is welcome, regardless of how noisy the children are"; the cost was $0.25 per person and $0.25 per car, with a maximum charge of $1.
- Camden was also the headquarters of Campbell's Soup.

The nine tables that follow are reprinted from the actual 1940 census, for the city of Camden. They include actual data on race, percentage of voting population, school attendance, number of school years completed, foreign born, and employment of workers 14 years and older by job, industry and race. In addition to being incredibly fascinating, these facts help to strengthen and visualize the actual environment in which Russ Columbo lived and worked.

Table A-35.—AGE, BY RACE AND SEX, FOR THE CITY OF CAMDEN: 1940 AND 1930

[Figures for white population in 1930 revised to include Mexicans classified with "Other races" in the 1930 reports. Percent not shown where less than 0.1 or where base is less than 100]

AGE AND CENSUS YEAR	ALL CLASSES			NATIVE WHITE			FOREIGN-BORN WHITE			NEGRO			OTHER RACES		
	Total	Male	Female	Total	Male	Female	Total	Male	Female	Total	Male	Female	Total	Male	Female
All ages: 1940	117,536	58,802	58,734	89,999	44,817	45,182	14,996	7,757	7,239	12,478	6,182	6,296	63	46	17
Under 5 years	7,965	4,100	3,865	6,838	3,544	3,294	4	1	3	1,121	554	567	2	1	1
5 to 9 years	8,189	4,185	4,004	7,039	3,586	3,453	16	6	10	1,132	592	540	2	1	1
10 to 14 years	10,078	5,045	5,033	8,766	4,378	4,388	56	32	24	1,251	632	619	5	3	2
15 to 19 years	11,158	5,537	5,621	9,825	4,873	4,952	184	92	92	1,140	565	575	9	7	2
20 to 24 years	11,795	5,693	6,102	10,526	5,097	5,429	211	113	98	1,055	481	574	3	2	1
25 to 29 years	10,563	5,244	5,319	9,124	4,568	4,556	447	212	235	987	461	526	5	3	2
30 to 34 years	8,872	4,484	4,388	7,184	3,691	3,493	761	364	397	921	423	498	6	6	-
35 to 39 years	8,188	3,971	4,217	5,912	2,897	3,015	1,176	542	634	1,098	530	568	2	2	-
40 to 44 years	8,315	4,117	4,198	5,445	2,703	2,742	1,887	937	950	970	471	499	13	6	7
45 to 49 years	8,441	4,326	4,115	5,043	2,523	2,520	2,555	1,360	1,195	840	441	399	3	2	1
50 to 54 years	7,197	3,783	3,414	4,165	2,107	2,058	2,407	1,336	1,071	616	331	285	9	9	-
55 to 59 years	5,357	2,790	2,567	3,054	1,482	1,572	1,838	1,049	789	463	257	206	2	2	-
60 to 64 years	4,300	2,200	2,100	2,641	1,314	1,327	1,330	705	625	329	181	148	-	-	-
65 to 69 years	3,145	1,500	1,645	1,949	914	1,035	917	468	449	277	116	161	2	2	-
70 to 74 years	2,053	962	1,091	1,268	580	688	650	307	343	135	75	60	-	-	-
75 years and over	1,920	865	1,055	1,220	560	660	557	233	324	143	72	71	-	-	-
Under 1 year	1,575	821	754	1,368	711	657	-	-	-	207	110	97	-	-	-
5 years	1,579	824	755	1,353	695	658	3	1	2	223	128	95	-	-	-
14 years	2,159	1,070	1,089	1,876	930	946	18	12	6	264	127	137	1	1	-
15 years	2,040	1,040	1,000	1,789	914	875	16	11	5	234	114	120	1	1	-
16 and 17 years	4,348	2,144	2,204	3,806	1,869	1,937	62	28	34	477	244	233	3	3	-
21 years and over	77,743	38,817	38,926	55,393	27,440	27,953	14,685	7,598	7,087	7,620	3,745	3,875	45	34	11
All ages: 1930	118,700	59,442	59,258	88,672	43,933	44,739	18,620	9,780	8,840	11,340	5,676	5,664	68	53	15
Under 5 years	10,090	5,010	5,080	8,904	4,422	4,482	44	25	19	1,139	562	577	3	1	2
5 to 9 years	11,723	5,891	5,832	10,391	5,226	5,165	152	79	73	1,175	583	592	5	3	2
10 to 14 years	12,146	6,088	6,058	10,980	5,517	5,463	182	94	88	978	475	503	6	2	4
15 to 19 years	11,370	5,471	5,899	9,963	4,759	5,204	464	248	216	939	462	477	4	2	2
20 to 24 years	10,335	5,031	5,304	8,512	4,189	4,323	805	388	417	1,016	452	564	2	2	-
25 to 29 years	9,340	4,630	4,710	6,923	3,461	3,462	1,259	593	666	1,151	570	581	7	6	1
30 to 34 years	9,211	4,571	4,640	6,165	3,064	3,101	2,019	1,008	1,011	1,018	490	528	9	9	-
35 to 39 years	9,941	5,143	4,798	5,918	2,965	2,953	2,908	1,579	1,329	1,107	593	514	8	6	2
40 to 44 years	8,467	4,438	4,029	4,902	2,459	2,443	2,699	1,528	1,171	862	447	415	4	4	-
45 to 49 years	7,039	3,683	3,356	4,000	2,001	1,999	2,381	1,329	1,052	650	346	304	8	7	1
50 to 54 years	5,787	2,988	2,799	3,535	1,759	1,776	1,769	960	809	482	268	214	1	1	-
55 to 59 years	4,413	2,233	2,180	2,781	1,390	1,391	1,295	668	627	333	172	161	4	3	1
60 to 64 years	3,479	1,709	1,770	2,193	1,066	1,127	1,074	522	552	208	117	91	4	4	-
65 to 69 years	2,437	1,198	1,239	1,566	770	796	741	368	373	127	57	70	3	3	-
70 to 74 years	1,543	741	802	1,044	486	558	433	214	219	66	41	25	-	-	-
75 years and over	1,331	593	738	862	381	481	392	176	216	77	36	41	-	-	-
Not reported	48	24	24	33	18	15	3	1	2	12	5	7	-	-	-
Under 1 year	1,877	927	950	1,645	817	828	1	-	1	231	110	121	-	-	-
5 years	2,256	1,151	1,105	1,975	1,008	967	11	7	4	268	135	133	2	1	1
14 years	2,394	1,254	1,140	2,171	1,144	1,027	35	15	20	188	95	93	-	-	-
15 years	2,277	1,106	1,171	2,040	976	1,064	54	28	26	182	102	80	1	-	1
16 and 17 years	4,603	2,242	2,361	4,079	1,982	2,097	165	89	76	357	170	187	2	1	1
21 years and over	71,286	36,030	35,256	46,678	23,210	23,468	17,637	9,260	8,377	6,921	3,515	3,406	50	45	5
Percent: 1940	100.0	100.0	100.0	100.0	100.0	100.0	100.0	100.0	100.0	100.0	100.0	100.0	-	-	-
Under 5 years	6.8	7.0	6.6	7.6	7.9	7.3	-	-	-	9.0	9.0	9.0	-	-	-
5 to 9 years	7.0	7.1	6.8	7.8	8.0	7.6	0.1	0.1	0.1	9.1	9.6	8.6	-	-	-
10 to 14 years	8.6	8.6	8.6	9.7	9.8	9.7	0.4	0.4	0.3	10.0	10.2	9.8	-	-	-
15 to 19 years	9.5	9.4	9.6	10.9	10.9	11.0	1.2	1.2	1.3	9.1	9.1	9.1	-	-	-
20 to 24 years	10.0	9.7	10.4	11.7	11.4	12.0	1.4	1.5	1.4	8.5	7.8	9.1	-	-	-
25 to 29 years	9.0	8.9	9.1	10.1	10.2	10.1	3.0	2.7	3.2	7.9	7.5	8.4	-	-	-
30 to 34 years	7.5	7.6	7.5	8.0	8.2	7.7	5.1	4.7	5.5	7.4	6.8	7.9	-	-	-
35 to 39 years	7.0	6.8	7.2	6.6	6.5	6.7	7.8	7.0	8.8	8.8	8.6	9.0	-	-	-
40 to 44 years	7.1	7.0	7.1	6.1	6.0	6.1	12.6	12.1	13.1	7.8	7.6	7.9	-	-	-
45 to 49 years	7.2	7.4	7.0	5.6	5.6	5.6	17.0	17.5	16.5	6.7	7.1	6.3	-	-	-
50 to 54 years	6.1	6.4	5.8	4.6	4.7	4.6	16.1	17.2	14.8	4.9	5.4	4.5	-	-	-
55 to 59 years	4.6	4.7	4.4	3.4	3.3	3.5	12.3	13.5	10.9	3.7	4.2	3.3	-	-	-
60 to 64 years	3.7	3.7	3.6	2.9	2.9	2.9	8.9	9.1	8.6	2.6	2.9	2.4	-	-	-
65 to 69 years	2.7	2.6	2.8	2.2	2.0	2.3	6.1	6.0	6.2	2.2	1.9	2.6	-	-	-
70 to 74 years	1.7	1.6	1.9	1.4	1.3	1.5	4.3	4.0	4.7	1.1	1.2	1.0	-	-	-
75 years and over	1.6	1.5	1.8	1.4	1.2	1.5	3.7	3.0	4.5	1.1	1.2	1.1	-	-	-
Under 1 year	1.3	1.4	1.3	1.5	1.6	1.5	-	-	-	1.7	1.8	1.5	-	-	-
5 years	1.3	1.4	1.3	1.5	1.6	1.5	-	-	-	1.8	2.1	1.5	-	-	-
14 years	1.8	1.8	1.9	2.1	2.1	2.1	0.1	0.2	0.1	2.1	2.1	2.2	-	-	-
15 years	1.7	1.8	1.7	2.0	2.0	1.9	0.1	0.1	0.1	1.9	1.8	1.9	-	-	-
16 and 17 years	3.7	3.6	3.8	4.2	4.2	4.3	0.4	0.4	0.5	3.8	3.9	3.7	-	-	-
21 years and over	66.1	66.0	66.3	61.5	61.2	61.9	97.9	98.0	97.9	61.1	60.6	61.5	-	-	-
Percent: 1930	100.0	100.0	100.0	100.0	100.0	100.0	100.0	100.0	100.0	100.0	100.0	100.0	-	-	-
Under 5 years	8.5	8.4	8.6	10.0	10.1	10.0	0.2	0.3	0.2	10.0	9.9	10.2	-	-	-
5 to 9 years	9.9	9.9	9.8	11.7	11.9	11.5	0.8	0.8	0.8	10.4	10.3	10.5	-	-	-
10 to 14 years	10.2	10.2	10.2	12.4	12.6	12.2	1.0	1.0	1.0	8.6	8.4	8.9	-	-	-
15 to 19 years	9.6	9.2	10.0	11.2	10.8	11.6	2.5	2.5	2.4	8.3	8.1	8.4	-	-	-
20 to 24 years	8.7	8.5	9.0	9.6	9.5	9.7	4.3	4.0	4.7	9.0	8.0	10.0	-	-	-
25 to 29 years	7.9	7.8	7.9	7.8	7.9	7.7	6.8	6.1	7.5	10.1	10.0	10.3	-	-	-
30 to 34 years	7.8	7.7	7.8	7.0	7.0	6.9	10.8	10.3	11.4	9.0	8.6	9.3	-	-	-
35 to 39 years	8.4	8.7	8.1	6.7	6.7	6.6	15.6	16.1	15.0	9.8	10.4	9.1	-	-	-
40 to 44 years	7.1	7.5	6.8	5.5	5.6	5.5	14.5	15.6	13.2	7.6	7.9	7.3	-	-	-
45 to 49 years	5.9	6.2	5.7	4.5	4.6	4.5	12.8	13.6	11.9	5.7	6.1	5.4	-	-	-
50 to 54 years	4.9	5.0	4.7	4.0	4.0	4.0	9.5	9.8	9.2	4.3	4.7	3.8	-	-	-
55 to 59 years	3.7	3.8	3.7	3.1	3.2	3.1	7.0	6.8	7.1	2.9	3.0	2.8	-	-	-
60 to 64 years	2.9	2.9	3.0	2.5	2.4	2.5	5.8	5.3	6.2	1.8	2.1	1.6	-	-	-
65 to 69 years	2.1	2.0	2.1	1.8	1.8	1.8	4.0	3.8	4.2	1.1	1.0	1.2	-	-	-
70 to 74 years	1.3	1.2	1.4	1.2	1.1	1.2	2.3	2.2	2.5	0.6	0.7	0.4	-	-	-
75 years and over	1.1	1.0	1.2	1.0	0.9	1.1	2.1	1.8	2.4	0.7	0.6	0.7	-	-	-
Not reported	-	-	-	-	-	-	-	-	-	0.1	0.1	0.1	-	-	-
Under 1 year	1.6	1.6	1.6	1.9	1.9	1.9	-	-	-	2.0	1.9	2.1	-	-	-
5 years	1.9	1.9	1.9	2.2	2.3	2.2	0.1	0.1	-	2.4	2.4	2.3	-	-	-
14 years	2.0	2.1	1.9	2.4	2.6	2.3	0.2	0.2	0.2	1.7	1.7	1.6	-	-	-
15 years	1.9	1.9	2.0	2.3	2.2	2.4	0.3	0.3	0.3	1.6	1.8	1.4	-	-	-
16 and 17 years	3.9	3.8	4.0	4.6	4.5	4.7	0.9	0.9	0.9	3.1	3.0	3.3	-	-	-
21 years and over	60.1	60.6	59.5	52.6	52.8	52.5	94.7	94.7	94.8	61.0	61.9	60.1	-	-	-

Table A-36.—RACE, BY NATIVITY AND SEX, FOR THE CITY OF CAMDEN: 1940 AND 1930

[Figures for white population in 1930 have been revised to include Mexicans who were classified with "Other races" in the 1930 reports. Percent not shown where less than 0.1 or where base is less than 100. Sex ratio not shown where number of females is less than 100. Nativity distribution for 1930 not available for individual "Other races"]

SEX, NATIVITY, AND CENSUS YEAR	All classes	White	Negro	Other races	OTHER RACES				PERCENT BY RACE				PERCENT BY NATIVITY					
					Indian	Chinese	Japanese	All other	All classes	White	Negro	Other races	All classes	White	Negro	Indian	Chinese	Japanese
TOTAL																		
1940	117,536	104,995	12,478	63	17	43	-	3	100.0	89.3	10.6	0.1	100.0	100.0	100.0	-	-	-
Native	102,471	89,999	12,433	39	15	23	-	1	100.0	87.8	12.1	-	87.2	85.7	99.6	-	-	-
Foreign born	15,065	14,996	45	24	2	20	-	2	100.0	99.5	0.3	0.2	12.8	14.3	0.4	-	-	-
1930	118,700	107,292	11,340	68	1	53	7	7	100.0	90.4	9.6	0.1	100.0	100.0	100.0	-	-	-
Native	99,984	88,672	11,274	38	-	-	-	-	100.0	88.7	11.3	-	84.2	82.6	99.4	-	-	-
Foreign born	18,716	18,620	66	30	-	-	-	-	100.0	99.5	0.4	0.2	15.8	17.4	0.6	-	-	-
MALE																		
1940	58,802	52,574	6,182	46	11	32	-	3	100.0	89.4	10.5	0.1	100.0	100.0	100.0	-	-	-
Native	50,989	44,817	6,148	24	10	13	-	1	100.0	87.9	12.1	-	86.7	85.2	99.5	-	-	-
Foreign born	7,813	7,757	34	22	1	19	-	2	100.0	99.3	0.4	0.3	13.3	14.8	0.5	-	-	-
1930	59,442	53,713	5,676	53	-	-	-	-	100.0	90.4	9.5	0.1	100.0	100.0	100.0	-	-	-
Native	49,594	43,933	5,635	26	-	-	-	-	100.0	88.6	11.4	0.1	83.4	81.8	99.3	-	-	-
Foreign born	9,848	9,780	41	27	-	-	-	-	100.0	99.3	0.4	0.3	16.6	18.2	0.7	-	-	-
FEMALE																		
1940	58,734	52,421	6,296	17	6	11	-	-	100.0	89.3	10.7	-	100.0	100.0	100.0	-	-	-
Native	51,482	45,182	6,285	15	5	10	-	-	100.0	87.8	12.2	-	87.7	86.2	99.8	-	-	-
Foreign born	7,252	7,239	11	2	1	1	-	-	100.0	99.8	0.2	-	12.3	13.8	0.2	-	-	-
1930	59,258	53,579	5,664	15	-	-	-	-	100.0	90.4	9.6	-	100.0	100.0	100.0	-	-	-
Native	50,390	44,739	5,639	12	-	-	-	-	100.0	88.8	11.2	-	85.0	83.5	99.6	-	-	-
Foreign born	8,868	8,840	25	3	-	-	-	-	100.0	99.7	0.3	-	15.0	16.5	0.4	-	-	-
MALES PER 100 FEMALES																		
1940	100.1	100.3	98.2	-	-	-	-	-	-	-	-	-	-	-	-	-	-	-
Native	99.0	99.2	97.8	-	-	-	-	-	-	-	-	-	-	-	-	-	-	-
Foreign born	107.7	107.2	-	-	-	-	-	-	-	-	-	-	-	-	-	-	-	-
1930	100.3	100.3	100.2	-	-	-	-	-	-	-	-	-	-	-	-	-	-	-
Native	98.4	98.2	99.9	-	-	-	-	-	-	-	-	-	-	-	-	-	-	-
Foreign born	111.1	110.6	-	-	-	-	-	-	-	-	-	-	-	-	-	-	-	-

Table A-37.—POTENTIAL VOTING POPULATION, BY CITIZENSHIP, RACE, NATIVITY, AND SEX, FOR THE CITY OF CAMDEN: 1940 AND 1930

[Figures for white population in 1930 have been revised to include Mexicans who were classified with "Other races" in the 1930 reports. Percent not shown where less than 0.1. Nativity distribution for 1930 not available for individual "Other races"]

CITIZENSHIP, RACE, AND NATIVITY	TOTAL POPULATION (ALL AGES)								POPULATION 21 YEARS OLD AND OVER							
	Total number		Percent		Male		Female		Total number		Percent		Male		Female	
	1940	1930	1940	1930	1940	1930	1940	1930	1940	1930	1940	1930	1940	1930	1940	1930
Total	117,536	118,700	100.0	100.0	58,802	59,442	58,734	59,258	77,743	71,286	100.0	100.0	38,817	36,030	38,926	35,256
Percent citizen	-	-	95.6	93.8	-	-	-	-	-	-	93.5	90.4	-	-	-	-
Percent alien and citiz. not rptd	-	-	4.4	6.2	-	-	-	-	-	-	6.5	9.6	-	-	-	-
Citizen	112,374	111,292	100.0	100.0	56,781	55,953	55,593	55,339	72,719	64,435	100.0	100.0	36,870	32,844	35,849	31,591
White—Native	89,999	88,672	80.1	79.7	44,817	43,933	45,182	44,739	55,393	46,678	76.2	72.4	27,440	23,210	27,953	23,468
Naturalized	9,877	11,284	8.8	10.1	5,772	6,342	4,105	4,942	9,702	10,850	13.3	16.8	5,685	6,121	4,017	4,729
Negro—Native	12,433	11,274	11.1	10.1	6,148	5,635	6,285	5,639	7,576	6,862	10.4	10.6	3,712	3,476	3,864	3,386
Naturalized	26	24	-	-	20	17	6	7	26	23	-	-	20	17	6	6
Other races—Native	39	38	-	-	24	26	15	12	22	22	-	-	13	20	9	2
Indian	15	-	-	-	10	-	5	-	9	-	-	-	5	-	4	-
Chinese	23	-	-	-	13	-	10	-	12	-	-	-	7	-	5	-
Japanese	-	-	-	-	-	-	-	-	-	-	-	-	-	-	-	-
Filipino	1	-	-	-	1	-	-	-	1	-	-	-	1	-	-	-
Hindu	-	-	-	-	-	-	-	-	-	-	-	-	-	-	-	-
All other	-	-	-	-	-	-	-	-	-	-	-	-	-	-	-	-
Alien	3,944	7,110	100.0	100.0	1,519	3,348	2,425	3,762	3,846	6,556	100.0	100.0	1,468	3,046	2,378	3,510
White—First papers	922	1,462	23.4	20.6	575	1,180	347	282	910	1,425	23.7	21.7	565	1,156	345	269
No papers	2,989	5,587	75.8	78.6	915	2,122	2,074	3,465	2,904	5,076	75.5	77.4	875	1,848	2,029	3,228
Negro—First papers	3	6	0.1	0.1	2	5	1	1	3	6	0.1	0.1	2	5	1	1
No papers	6	25	0.2	0.4	5	14	1	11	6	21	0.2	0.3	5	12	1	9
Other races—Foreign born	24	30	0.6	0.4	22	27	2	3	23	28	0.6	0.4	21	25	2	3
Indian	2	-	0.1	-	1	-	1	-	2	-	0.1	-	1	-	1	-
Chinese	20	-	0.5	-	19	-	1	-	19	-	0.5	-	18	-	1	-
Japanese	-	-	-	-	-	-	-	-	-	-	-	-	-	-	-	-
Filipino	1	-	-	-	1	-	-	-	1	-	-	-	1	-	-	-
Hindu	1	-	-	-	1	-	-	-	1	-	-	-	1	-	-	-
All other	-	-	-	-	-	-	-	-	-	-	-	-	-	-	-	-
Citizenship not reported	1,218	298	100.0	100.0	502	141	716	157	1,178	295	100.0	100.0	479	140	699	155
White	1,208	287	99.2	96.3	495	136	713	151	1,169	286	99.2	96.9	473	135	696	151
Negro	10	11	0.8	3.7	7	5	3	6	9	9	0.8	3.1	6	5	3	4

Table A-38.—SCHOOL ATTENDANCE, BY AGE, RACE, AND SEX, FOR THE CITY OF CAMDEN: 1940 AND 1930

[Figures for white population in 1930 revised to include Mexicans classified with "Other races" in the 1930 reports. Percent not shown where less than 0.1 or where base is less than 100]

AGE, SEX, AND CENSUS YEAR	ALL CLASSES			NATIVE WHITE			FOREIGN-BORN WHITE			NEGRO			OTHER RACES		
	Total number	Attending school		Total number	Attending school		Total number	Attending school		Total number	Attending school		Total number	Attending school	
		Number	Percent		Number	Percent		Number	Percent		Number	Percent		Number	Percent
1940															
Total, 5 to 24 years	41,220	21,745	52.8	36,156	18,895	52.3	467	129	27.6	4,578	2,711	59.2	19	10	-
5 years	1,579	343	21.7	1,353	283	20.9	3	1	-	223	59	26.5	-	-	-
6 years	1,476	1,127	76.4	1,254	956	76.2	2	1	-	219	170	77.6	1	-	-
7 to 9 years	5,134	4,922	95.9	4,432	4,247	95.8	11	11	-	690	663	96.1	1	1	-
10 to 13 years	7,919	7,627	96.3	6,890	6,628	96.2	38	34	-	987	961	97.4	4	4	-
14 years	2,159	2,076	96.2	1,876	1,803	96.1	18	17	-	264	255	96.6	1	1	-
15 years	2,040	1,923	94.3	1,789	1,696	94.8	16	14	-	234	212	90.6	1	1	-
16 and 17 years	4,348	2,559	58.9	3,806	2,236	58.7	62	35	-	477	287	60.2	3	1	-
18 and 19 years	4,770	766	16.1	4,230	685	16.2	106	12	11.3	429	67	15.6	5	2	-
20 years	2,403	131	5.5	2,138	115	5.4	51	3	-	214	13	6.1	-	-	-
21 to 24 years	9,392	271	2.9	8,388	246	2.9	160	1	0.6	841	24	2.9	3	-	-
Male, 5 to 24 years	20,460	11,117	54.3	17,934	9,662	53.9	243	72	29.6	2,270	1,377	60.7	13	6	-
5 years	824	174	21.1	695	141	20.3	1	-	-	128	33	25.8	-	-	-
6 years	781	583	74.6	671	503	75.0	-	-	-	109	80	73.4	1	-	-
7 to 9 years	2,580	2,467	95.6	2,220	2,120	95.5	5	5	-	355	342	96.3	-	-	-
10 to 13 years	3,975	3,827	96.3	3,448	3,319	96.3	20	17	-	505	489	96.8	2	2	-
14 years	1,070	1,030	96.3	930	894	96.1	12	11	-	127	124	97.6	1	1	-
15 years	1,040	981	94.3	914	869	95.1	11	9	-	114	102	89.5	1	1	-
16 and 17 years	2,144	1,319	61.5	1,869	1,146	61.3	28	19	-	244	153	62.7	3	1	-
18 and 19 years	2,353	478	20.3	2,090	429	20.5	53	7	-	207	41	19.8	3	1	-
20 years	1,118	75	6.7	996	68	6.8	28	3	-	94	4	-	-	-	-
21 to 24 years	4,575	183	4.0	4,101	173	4.2	85	1	-	387	9	2.3	2	-	-
Female, 5 to 24 years	20,760	10,628	51.2	18,222	9,233	50.7	224	57	25.4	2,308	1,334	57.8	6	4	-
5 years	755	169	22.4	658	142	21.6	2	1	-	95	26	-	-	-	-
6 years	695	544	78.3	583	453	77.7	2	1	-	110	90	81.8	-	-	-
7 to 9 years	2,554	2,455	96.1	2,212	2,127	96.2	6	6	-	335	321	95.8	1	1	-
10 to 13 years	3,944	3,800	96.3	3,442	3,309	96.1	18	17	-	482	472	97.9	2	2	-
14 years	1,089	1,046	96.1	946	909	96.1	6	6	-	137	131	95.6	-	-	-
15 years	1,000	942	94.2	875	827	94.5	5	5	-	120	110	91.7	-	-	-
16 and 17 years	2,204	1,240	56.3	1,937	1,090	56.3	34	16	-	233	134	57.5	-	-	-
18 and 19 years	2,417	288	11.9	2,140	256	12.0	53	5	-	222	26	11.7	2	1	-
20 years	1,285	56	4.4	1,142	47	4.1	23	-	-	120	9	7.5	-	-	-
21 to 24 years	4,817	88	1.8	4,287	73	1.7	75	-	-	454	15	3.3	1	-	-
1930															
Total, 5 to 24 years	45,574	25,931	56.9	39,846	23,308	58.5	1,603	503	31.4	4,108	2,109	51.3	17	11	-
5 years	2,256	508	22.5	1,975	445	22.5	11	-	-	268	63	23.5	2	-	-
6 years	2,283	1,699	74.4	2,020	1,519	75.2	18	13	-	245	167	68.2	-	-	-
7 to 9 years	7,184	6,877	95.7	6,396	6,175	96.5	123	119	96.7	662	580	87.6	3	3	-
10 to 13 years	9,752	9,580	98.2	8,809	8,692	98.7	147	141	95.9	790	741	93.8	6	6	-
14 years	2,394	2,303	96.2	2,171	2,099	96.7	35	34	-	188	170	90.4	-	-	-
15 years	2,277	2,047	89.9	2,040	1,853	90.8	54	46	-	182	147	80.8	1	1	-
16 and 17 years	4,603	1,807	39.3	4,079	1,588	38.9	165	73	44.2	357	145	40.6	2	1	-
18 and 19 years	4,490	594	13.2	3,844	512	13.3	245	31	12.7	400	51	12.8	1	-	-
20 years	2,085	156	7.5	1,756	130	7.4	141	14	9.9	188	12	6.4	-	-	-
21 to 24 years	8,250	360	4.4	6,756	295	4.4	664	32	4.8	828	33	4.0	2	-	-
Male, 5 to 24 years	22,481	13,227	58.8	19,691	11,893	60.4	809	275	34.0	1,972	1,055	53.5	9	4	-
5 years	1,151	266	23.1	1,008	239	23.7	7	-	-	135	27	20.0	1	-	-
6 years	1,149	873	76.0	1,016	780	76.8	8	5	-	125	88	70.4	-	-	-
7 to 9 years	3,591	3,443	95.9	3,202	3,089	96.5	64	63	-	323	289	89.5	2	2	-
10 to 13 years	4,834	4,754	98.3	4,373	4,317	98.7	79	76	-	380	359	94.5	2	2	-
14 years	1,254	1,213	96.7	1,144	1,110	97.0	15	15	-	95	88	-	-	-	-
15 years	1,106	1,018	92.0	976	909	93.1	28	23	-	102	86	84.3	-	-	-
16 and 17 years	2,242	974	43.4	1,982	865	43.6	89	45	-	170	64	37.6	1	-	-
18 and 19 years	2,123	356	16.8	1,801	302	16.8	131	23	17.6	190	31	16.3	1	-	-
20 years	952	88	9.2	799	72	9.0	74	10	-	79	6	-	-	-	-
21 to 24 years	4,079	242	5.9	3,390	210	6.2	314	15	4.8	373	17	4.6	2	-	-
Female, 5 to 24 years	23,093	12,704	55.0	20,155	11,415	56.6	794	228	28.7	2,136	1,054	49.3	8	7	-
5 years	1,105	242	21.9	967	206	21.3	4	-	-	133	36	27.1	1	-	-
6 years	1,134	826	72.8	1,004	739	73.6	10	8	-	120	79	65.8	-	-	-
7 to 9 years	3,593	3,434	95.6	3,194	3,086	96.6	59	56	-	339	291	85.8	1	1	-
10 to 13 years	4,918	4,826	98.1	4,436	4,375	98.6	68	65	-	410	382	93.2	4	4	-
14 years	1,140	1,090	95.6	1,027	989	96.3	20	19	-	93	82	-	-	-	-
15 years	1,171	1,029	87.9	1,064	944	88.7	26	23	-	80	61	-	1	1	-
16 and 17 years	2,361	833	35.3	2,097	723	34.5	76	28	-	187	81	43.3	1	1	-
18 and 19 years	2,367	238	10.1	2,043	210	10.3	114	8	7.0	210	20	9.5	-	-	-
20 years	1,133	68	6.0	957	58	6.1	67	4	-	109	6	5.5	-	-	-
21 to 24 years	4,171	118	2.8	3,366	85	2.5	350	17	4.9	455	16	3.5	-	-	-

Table A-39.—PERSONS 25 YEARS OLD AND OVER, BY YEARS OF SCHOOL COMPLETED, RACE, AND SEX, FOR THE CITY OF CAMDEN: 1940

[Percent not shown where less than 0.1; median and percent not shown where base is less than 100]

YEARS OF SCHOOL COMPLETED	ALL CLASSES			NATIVE WHITE			FOREIGN-BORN WHITE			NEGRO			OTHER RACES		
	Total	Male	Female	Total	Male	Female	Total	Male	Female	Total	Male	Female	Total	Male	Female
Persons 25 years old and over	68,351	34,242	34,109	47,005	23,339	23,666	14,525	7,513	7,012	6,779	3,358	3,421	42	32	10
No school years completed	3,981	1,979	2,002	462	238	224	3,067	1,490	1,577	443	243	200	9	8	1
Grade school: 1 to 4 years	8,156	4,173	3,983	3,165	1,544	1,621	3,499	1,820	1,679	1,488	805	683	4	4	-
5 or 6 years	11,527	5,756	5,771	7,604	3,719	3,885	2,318	1,221	1,097	1,602	815	787	3	1	2
7 or 8 years	26,074	12,879	13,195	20,522	10,122	10,400	3,644	1,864	1,780	1,897	885	1,012	11	8	3
High school: 1 to 3 years	9,161	4,537	4,624	7,706	3,821	3,885	690	384	306	763	331	432	2	1	1
4 years	5,300	2,446	2,854	4,555	2,059	2,496	491	270	221	250	115	135	4	2	2
College: 1 to 3 years	1,209	691	518	1,034	589	445	82	55	27	92	46	46	1	1	-
4 years or more	1,356	951	405	1,131	794	337	133	113	20	91	43	48	1	1	-
Not reported	1,587	830	757	826	453	373	601	296	305	153	75	78	7	6	1
Median school years completed	7.7	7.7	7.7	8.2	8.2	8.1	5.3	5.5	5.2	6.7	6.5	7.0	-	-	-
Percent less than 5 years completed	17.8	18.0	17.5	7.7	7.6	7.8	45.2	44.1	46.4	28.5	31.2	25.8	-	-	-
PERCENT DISTRIBUTION															
Persons 25 years old and over	100.0	100.0	100.0	100.0	100.0	100.0	100.0	100.0	100.0	100.0	100.0	100.0	-	-	-
No school years completed	5.8	5.8	5.9	1.0	1.0	0.9	21.1	19.8	22.5	6.5	7.2	5.8	-	-	-
Grade school: 1 to 4 years	11.9	12.2	11.7	6.7	6.6	6.8	24.1	24.2	23.9	21.9	24.0	20.0	-	-	-
5 or 6 years	16.9	16.8	16.9	16.2	15.9	16.4	16.0	16.3	15.6	23.6	24.3	23.0	-	-	-
7 or 8 years	38.1	37.6	38.7	43.7	43.4	43.9	25.1	24.8	25.4	28.0	26.4	29.6	-	-	-
High school: 1 to 3 years	13.4	13.2	13.6	16.4	16.4	16.4	4.8	5.1	4.4	11.3	9.9	12.6	-	-	-
4 years	7.8	7.1	8.4	9.7	8.8	10.5	3.4	3.6	3.2	3.7	3.4	3.9	-	-	-
College: 1 to 3 years	1.8	2.0	1.5	2.2	2.5	1.9	0.6	0.7	0.4	1.4	1.4	1.3	-	-	-
4 years or more	2.0	2.8	1.2	2.4	3.4	1.4	0.9	1.5	0.3	1.3	1.3	1.4	-	-	-
Not reported	2.3	2.4	2.2	1.8	1.9	1.6	4.1	3.9	4.3	2.3	2.2	2.3	-	-	-

Table A-40.—FOREIGN-BORN WHITE, BY COUNTRY OF BIRTH, BY SEX, FOR THE CITY OF CAMDEN: 1940 AND 1930

[Figures for white population in 1930 revised to include Mexicans classified with "Other races" in the 1930 reports. Percent not shown where less than 0.1 or where base is less than 100]

COUNTRY OF BIRTH	BOTH SEXES		PERCENT		MALE		FEMALE	
	1940	1930	1940	1930	1940	1930	1940	1930
All countries	14,996	18,620	100.0	100.0	7,757	9,780	7,239	8,840
England	963	1,379	6.4	7.4	465	677	498	702
Scotland	319	403	2.1	2.2	156	199	163	204
Wales	25	54	0.2	0.3	15	27	10	27
Northern Ireland	273	369	1.8	2.0	114	151	159	218
Irish Free State (Eire)	477	747	3.2	4.0	168	291	309	456
Norway	107	154	0.7	0.8	63	95	44	59
Sweden	101	162	0.7	0.9	61	95	40	67
Denmark	26	47	0.2	0.3	17	37	9	10
Netherlands	15	29	0.1	0.2	10	18	5	11
Belgium	20	27	0.1	0.1	12	14	8	13
Luxemburg	3	-	-	-	2	-	1	-
Switzerland	37	73	0.2	0.4	14	36	23	37
France	89	122	0.6	0.7	39	57	50	65
Germany	1,180	1,789	7.9	9.6	555	862	625	927
Poland	2,785	3,528	18.6	18.9	1,382	1,799	1,403	1,729
Czechoslovakia	77	191	0.5	1.0	35	91	42	100
Austria	529	371	3.5	2.0	261	193	268	178
Hungary	161	152	1.1	0.8	74	77	87	75
Yugoslavia	96	128	0.6	0.7	62	83	34	45
Russia (U. S. S. R.)	1,537	1,777	10.2	9.5	831	946	706	831
Lithuania	255	274	1.7	1.5	127	150	128	124
Latvia	18	15	0.1	0.1	8	10	10	5
Finland	50	74	0.3	0.4	20	40	30	34
Rumania	81	111	0.5	0.6	43	58	38	53
Bulgaria	6	5	-	-	2	3	4	2
Turkey in Europe	3	-	-	-	2	-	1	-
Greece	99	146	0.7	0.8	73	104	26	42
Italy	4,908	5,508	32.7	29.6	2,755	3,140	2,153	2,368
Spain	9	12	0.1	0.1	6	8	3	4
Portugal	7	7	-	-	6	6	1	1
Other Europe	16	47	0.1	0.3	10	32	6	15
Palestine and Syria	11	7	0.1	-	8	3	3	4
Turkey in Asia	95	151	0.6	0.8	50	86	45	65
Other Asia	66	45	0.4	0.2	42	25	24	20
Canada—French	29	36	0.2	0.2	13	21	16	15
Canada—Other	190	337	1.3	1.8	88	157	102	180
Newfoundland	227	222	1.5	1.2	113	119	114	103
Mexico	6	7	-	-	4	7	2	-
Cuba and other West Indies	15	13	0.1	0.1	6	9	9	4
Central and South America	54	63	0.4	0.3	29	33	25	30
Australia	19	16	0.1	0.1	10	10	9	6
Azores	-	-	-	-	-	-	-	-
All other and not reported	12	22	0.1	0.1	6	11	6	11

Table A-41.—PERSONS 14 YEARS OLD AND OVER, BY EMPLOYMENT STATUS, CLASS OF WORKER, RACE, AND SEX, FOR THE CITY OF CAMDEN: 1940

[Percent not shown where less than 0.1 or where base is less than 100]

EMPLOYMENT STATUS	ALL CLASSES			NATIVE WHITE			FOREIGN-BORN WHITE			NEGRO			OTHER RACES		
	Total	Male	Female	Total	Male	Female	Total	Male	Female	Total	Male	Female	Total	Male	Female
Total population (all ages)	117,536	58,802	58,734	89,999	44,817	45,182	14,996	7,757	7,239	12,478	6,182	6,296	63	46	17
Persons 14 years old and over	93,463	46,542	46,921	69,232	34,239	34,993	14,938	7,730	7,208	9,238	4,531	4,707	55	42	13
In labor force	54,105	38,306	15,799	40,420	28,027	12,393	8,241	6,620	1,621	5,403	3,622	1,781	41	37	4
Not in labor force	39,358	8,236	31,122	28,812	6,212	22,600	6,697	1,110	5,587	3,835	909	2,926	14	5	9
Engaged in own home housew'k	24,396	287	24,109	17,452	197	17,255	4,928	64	4,864	2,010	26	1,984	6	-	6
In school	7,576	4,014	3,562	6,621	3,522	3,099	88	54	34	862	434	428	5	4	1
Unable to work	5,301	2,804	2,497	3,129	1,648	1,481	1,413	811	602	757	344	413	2	1	1
In institutions	65	55	10	49	47	2	2	2	-	14	6	8	-	-	-
Other and not reported	2,020	1,076	944	1,561	798	763	266	179	87	192	99	93	1	-	1
LABOR FORCE BY EMPLOYMENT STATUS															
In labor force	54,105	38,306	15,799	40,420	28,027	12,393	8,241	6,620	1,621	5,403	3,622	1,781	41	37	4
Employed (exc. public emerg. work)	41,588	29,081	12,507	31,785	21,887	9,898	6,948	5,514	1,434	2,819	1,647	1,172	36	33	3
At work	40,436	28,311	12,125	30,966	21,381	9,585	6,667	5,284	1,383	2,770	1,616	1,154	33	30	3
With a job	1,152	770	382	819	506	313	281	230	51	49	31	18	3	3	-
On public emerg. work (WPA, etc.)	4,103	3,460	643	2,496	2,020	476	411	381	30	1,194	1,057	137	2	2	-
Seeking work	8,414	5,765	2,649	6,139	4,120	2,019	882	725	157	1,390	918	472	3	2	1
Experienced workers	6,350	4,572	1,778	4,457	3,158	1,299	834	701	133	1,058	712	346	1	1	-
New workers	2,064	1,193	871	1,682	962	720	48	24	24	332	206	126	2	1	1
PERCENT BY SEX															
In labor force	100.0	70.8	29.2	100.0	69.3	30.7	100.0	80.3	19.7	100.0	67.0	33.0	-	-	-
Employed (exc. public emerg.)	100.0	69.9	30.1	100.0	68.9	31.1	100.0	79.4	20.6	100.0	58.4	41.6	-	-	-
On pub. emerg. work (WPA, etc.)	100.0	84.3	15.7	100.0	80.9	19.1	100.0	92.7	7.3	100.0	88.5	11.5	-	-	-
Seeking work	100.0	68.5	31.5	100.0	67.1	32.9	100.0	82.2	17.8	100.0	66.0	34.0	-	-	-
Not in labor force	100.0	20.9	79.1	100.0	21.6	78.4	100.0	16.6	83.4	100.0	23.7	76.3	-	-	-
Engaged in own home housew'k	100.0	1.2	98.8	100.0	1.1	98.9	100.0	1.3	98.7	100.0	1.3	98.7	-	-	-
In school	100.0	53.0	47.0	100.0	53.2	46.8	-	-	-	100.0	50.3	49.7	-	-	-
Unable to work	100.0	52.9	47.1	100.0	52.7	47.3	100.0	57.4	42.6	100.0	45.4	54.6	-	-	-
In institutions	-	-	-	-	-	-	-	-	-	-	-	-	-	-	-
Other and not reported	100.0	53.3	46.7	100.0	51.1	48.9	100.0	67.3	32.7	100.0	51.6	48.4	-	-	-
EMPLOYED WORKERS BY CLASS OF WORKER															
Employed (exc. public emerg.)	41,588	29,081	12,507	31,785	21,887	9,898	6,948	5,514	1,434	2,819	1,647	1,172	36	33	3
Wage and salary workers	37,291	25,568	11,723	29,245	19,868	9,377	5,403	4,177	1,226	2,631	1,513	1,118	12	10	2
Employers and own-account workers	3,912	3,307	605	2,236	1,845	391	1,487	1,317	170	168	124	44	21	21	-
Unpaid family workers	203	102	101	163	95	68	36	5	31	1	-	1	3	2	1
Class of worker not reported	182	104	78	141	79	62	22	15	7	19	10	9	-	-	-
At work	40,436	28,311	12,125	30,966	21,381	9,585	6,667	5,284	1,383	2,770	1,616	1,154	33	30	3
Wage and salary workers	36,684	25,235	11,449	28,765	19,618	9,147	5,301	4,109	1,192	2,606	1,498	1,108	12	10	2
Employers and own-account workers	3,411	2,895	516	1,929	1,607	322	1,314	1,159	155	150	111	39	18	18	-
Unpaid family workers	197	100	97	157	93	64	36	5	31	1	-	1	3	2	1
Class of worker not reported	144	81	63	115	63	52	16	11	5	13	7	6	-	-	-
With a job	1,152	770	382	819	506	313	281	230	51	49	31	18	3	3	-
Wage and salary workers	607	333	274	480	250	230	102	68	34	25	15	10	-	-	-
Employers and own-account workers	501	412	89	307	238	69	173	158	15	18	13	5	3	3	-
Unpaid family workers	6	2	4	6	2	4	-	-	-	-	-	-	-	-	-
Class of worker not reported	38	23	15	26	16	10	6	4	2	6	3	3	-	-	-
PERCENT DISTRIBUTION															
Persons 14 years old and over	100.0	100.0	100.0	100.0	100.0	100.0	100.0	100.0	100.0	100.0	100.0	100.0	-	-	-
In labor force	57.9	82.3	33.7	58.4	81.9	35.4	55.2	85.6	22.5	58.5	79.9	37.8	-	-	-
Not in labor force	42.1	17.7	66.3	41.6	18.1	64.6	44.8	14.4	77.5	41.5	20.1	62.2	-	-	-
Engaged in own home housew'k	26.1	0.6	51.4	25.2	0.6	49.3	33.0	0.8	67.5	21.8	0.6	42.1	-	-	-
In school	8.1	8.6	7.6	9.6	10.3	8.9	0.6	0.7	0.5	9.3	9.6	9.1	-	-	-
Unable to work	5.7	6.0	5.3	4.5	4.8	4.2	9.5	10.5	8.4	8.2	7.6	8.8	-	-	-
In institutions	0.1	0.1	-	0.1	0.1	-	-	-	-	0.2	0.1	0.2	-	-	-
Other and not reported	2.2	2.3	2.0	2.3	2.3	2.2	1.8	2.3	1.2	2.1	2.2	2.0	-	-	-
LABOR FORCE BY EMPLOYMENT STATUS															
In labor force	100.0	100.0	100.0	100.0	100.0	100.0	100.0	100.0	100.0	100.0	100.0	100.0	-	-	-
Employed (exc. public emerg. work)	76.9	75.9	79.2	78.6	78.1	79.9	84.3	83.3	88.5	52.2	45.5	65.8	-	-	-
At work	74.7	73.9	76.7	76.6	76.3	77.3	80.9	79.8	85.3	51.3	44.6	64.8	-	-	-
With a job	2.1	2.0	2.4	2.0	1.8	2.5	3.4	3.5	3.1	0.9	0.9	1.0	-	-	-
On public emerg. work (WPA, etc.)	7.6	9.0	4.1	6.2	7.2	3.8	5.0	5.8	1.9	22.1	29.2	7.7	-	-	-
Seeking work	15.6	15.0	16.8	15.2	14.7	16.3	10.7	11.0	9.7	25.7	25.3	26.5	-	-	-
Experienced workers	11.7	11.9	11.3	11.0	11.3	10.5	10.1	10.6	8.2	19.6	19.7	19.4	-	-	-
New workers	3.8	3.1	5.5	4.2	3.4	5.8	0.6	0.4	1.5	6.1	5.7	7.1	-	-	-
EMPLOYED WORKERS BY CLASS OF WORKER															
Employed (exc. public emerg.)	100.0	100.0	100.0	100.0	100.0	100.0	100.0	100.0	100.0	100.0	100.0	100.0	-	-	-
Wage and salary workers	89.7	87.9	93.7	92.0	90.8	94.7	77.8	75.8	85.5	93.3	91.9	95.4	-	-	-
Employers and own-account workers	9.4	11.4	4.8	7.0	8.4	4.0	21.4	23.9	11.9	6.0	7.5	3.8	-	-	-
Unpaid family workers	0.5	0.4	0.8	0.5	0.4	0.7	0.5	0.1	2.2	-	-	0.1	-	-	-
Class of worker not reported	0.4	0.4	0.6	0.4	0.4	0.6	0.3	0.3	0.5	0.7	0.6	0.8	-	-	-
At work	100.0	100.0	100.0	100.0	100.0	100.0	100.0	100.0	100.0	100.0	100.0	100.0	-	-	-
Wage and salary workers	90.7	89.1	94.4	92.9	91.8	95.4	79.5	77.8	86.2	94.1	92.7	96.0	-	-	-
Employers and own-account workers	8.4	10.2	4.3	6.2	7.5	3.4	19.7	21.9	11.2	5.4	6.9	3.4	-	-	-
Unpaid family workers	0.5	0.4	0.8	0.5	0.4	0.7	0.5	0.1	2.2	-	-	0.1	-	-	-
Class of worker not reported	0.4	0.3	0.5	0.4	0.3	0.5	0.2	0.2	0.4	0.5	0.4	0.5	-	-	-
With a job	100.0	100.0	100.0	100.0	100.0	100.0	100.0	100.0	-	-	-	-	-	-	-
Wage and salary workers	52.7	43.2	71.7	58.6	49.4	73.5	36.3	29.6	-	-	-	-	-	-	-
Employers and own-account workers	43.5	53.5	23.3	37.5	47.0	22.0	61.6	68.7	-	-	-	-	-	-	-
Unpaid family workers	0.5	0.3	1.0	0.7	0.4	1.3	-	-	-	-	-	-	-	-	-
Class of worker not reported	3.3	3.0	3.9	3.2	3.2	3.2	2.1	1.7	-	-	-	-	-	-	-

Table A-42.—EMPLOYED WORKERS 14 YEARS OLD AND OVER, BY MAJOR OCCUPATION GROUP, INDUSTRY GROUP, AND SEX, FOR THE CITY OF CAMDEN: 1940

[Percent not shown where less than 0.1 or where base is less than 100]

MAJOR OCCUPATION GROUP AND INDUSTRY GROUP	Total	Male	Female	PERCENT BY OCCUPATION AND INDUSTRY			PERCENT BY SEX	
				Total	Male	Female	Male	Female
Total population (all ages)	117,536	58,802	58,734	-	-	-	50.0	50.0
All persons 14 years old and over	93,463	46,542	46,921	-	-	-	49.8	50.2
In labor force	54,105	38,306	15,799	100.0	100.0	100.0	70.8	29.2
Employed workers (except on public emergency work)	41,588	29,081	12,507	76.9	75.9	79.2	69.9	30.1
MAJOR OCCUPATION GROUP								
Employed (except on public emergency work)	41,588	29,081	12,507	100.0	100.0	100.0	69.9	30.1
Professional workers	1,903	897	1,006	4.6	3.1	8.0	47.1	52.9
Semiprofessional workers	468	384	84	1.1	1.3	0.7	82.1	17.9
Farmers and farm managers	9	9	-	-	-	-	-	-
Proprietors, managers, and officials, except farm	2,753	2,405	348	6.6	8.3	2.8	87.4	12.6
Clerical, sales, and kindred workers	7,097	4,048	3,049	17.1	13.9	24.4	57.0	43.0
Craftsmen, foremen, and kindred workers	7,293	7,098	195	17.5	24.4	1.6	97.3	2.7
Operatives and kindred workers	12,729	7,864	4,865	30.6	27.0	38.9	61.8	38.2
Domestic service workers	1,279	33	1,246	3.1	0.1	10.0	2.6	97.4
Service workers, except domestic	3,522	2,399	1,123	8.5	8.2	9.0	68.1	31.9
Farm laborers (wage workers) and farm foremen	21	21	-	0.1	0.1	-	-	-
Farm laborers, unpaid family workers	1	1	-	-	-	-	-	-
Laborers, except farm	4,077	3,635	442	9.8	12.5	3.5	89.2	10.8
Occupation not reported	436	287	149	1.0	1.0	1.2	65.8	34.2
INDUSTRY GROUP								
Employed (except on public emergency work)	41,588	29,081	12,507	100.0	100.0	100.0	69.9	30.1
Agriculture, forestry, and fishery	57	55	2	0.1	0.2	-	-	-
Agriculture	50	48	2	0.1	0.2	-	-	-
Forestry (except logging) and fishery	7	7	-	-	-	-	-	-
Mining	10	9	1	-	-	-	-	-
Coal mining	-	-	-	-	-	-	-	-
Crude petroleum and natural gas production	2	2	-	-	-	-	-	-
Other mines and quarries	8	7	1	-	-	-	-	-
Construction	1,843	1,809	34	4.4	6.2	0.3	98.2	1.8
Manufacturing	20,073	14,168	5,905	48.3	48.7	47.2	70.6	29.4
Food and kindred products	2,492	1,740	752	6.0	6.0	6.0	69.8	30.2
Textile-mill products	897	558	339	2.2	1.9	2.7	62.2	37.8
Apparel and other fabricated textile products	1,246	337	909	3.0	1.2	7.3	27.0	73.0
Logging	2	2	-	-	-	-	-	-
Sawmills and planing mills	20	19	1	-	0.1	-	-	-
Furniture, store fixtures, and miscellaneous wooden goods	428	389	39	1.0	1.3	0.3	90.9	9.1
Paper and allied products	563	489	74	1.4	1.7	0.6	86.9	13.1
Printing, publishing, and allied industries	1,190	939	251	2.9	3.2	2.0	78.9	21.1
Chemicals and allied products	725	606	119	1.7	2.1	1.0	83.6	16.4
Petroleum and coal products	411	401	10	1.0	1.4	0.1	97.6	2.4
Leather and leather products	964	791	173	2.3	2.7	1.4	82.1	17.9
Stone, clay, and glass products	194	184	10	0.5	0.6	0.1	94.8	5.2
Iron and steel and their products	843	749	94	2.0	2.6	0.8	88.8	11.2
Nonferrous metals and their products	112	96	16	0.3	0.3	0.1	85.7	14.3
Machinery	3,630	2,290	1,340	8.7	7.9	10.7	63.1	36.9
Automobiles and automobile equipment	191	166	25	0.5	0.6	0.2	86.9	13.1
Transportation equipment, except automobile	3,222	3,173	49	7.7	10.9	0.4	98.5	1.5
Other and not specified manufacturing industries	2,943	1,239	1,704	7.1	4.3	13.6	42.1	57.9
Transportation, communication, and other public utilities	2,921	2,638	283	7.0	9.1	2.3	90.3	9.7
Railroads (including railroad repair shops) and railway express service	988	962	26	2.4	3.3	0.2	97.4	2.6
Trucking service	278	273	5	0.7	0.9	-	98.2	1.8
Other transportation	813	793	20	2.0	2.7	0.2	97.5	2.5
Communication	335	124	211	0.8	0.4	1.7	37.0	63.0
Utilities	507	486	21	1.2	1.7	0.2	95.9	4.1
Wholesale and retail trade	7,116	5,290	1,826	17.1	18.2	14.6	74.3	25.7
Wholesale trade	793	693	100	1.9	2.4	0.8	87.4	12.6
Food and dairy products stores, and milk retailing	1,722	1,468	254	4.1	5.0	2.0	85.2	14.8
Eating and drinking places	1,239	752	487	3.0	2.6	3.9	60.7	39.3
Motor vehicles and accessories retailing, and filling stations	433	407	26	1.0	1.4	0.2	94.0	6.0
Other retail trade	2,929	1,970	959	7.0	6.8	7.7	67.3	32.7
Finance, insurance, and real estate	1,031	659	372	2.5	2.3	3.0	63.9	36.1
Business and repair services	780	693	87	1.9	2.4	0.7	88.8	11.2
Automobile storage, rental, and repair services	420	413	7	1.0	1.4	0.1	98.3	1.7
Business and repair services, except automobile	360	280	80	0.9	1.0	0.6	77.8	22.2
Personal services	2,855	960	1,895	6.9	3.3	15.2	33.6	66.4
Domestic service	1,359	72	1,287	3.3	0.2	10.3	5.3	94.7
Hotels and lodging places	317	155	162	0.8	0.5	1.3	48.9	51.1
Laundering, cleaning, and dyeing services	413	241	172	1.0	0.8	1.4	58.4	41.6
Miscellaneous personal services	766	492	274	1.8	1.7	2.2	64.2	35.8
Amusement, recreation, and related services	266	220	46	0.6	0.8	0.4	82.7	17.3
Professional and related services	2,301	926	1,375	5.5	3.2	11.0	40.2	59.8
Government	1,312	1,078	234	3.2	3.7	1.9	82.2	17.8
Industry not reported	1,023	576	447	2.5	2.0	3.6	56.3	43.7

Table A-43.—PERSONS 14 YEARS OLD AND OVER IN THE LABOR FORCE, 1940, AND GAINFUL WORKERS 14 YEARS OLD AND OVER, 1930, BY RACE AND SEX, FOR THE CITY OF CAMDEN

[Totals for population and gainful workers for 1930 include "Unknown age." Figures for white population in 1930 have been revised to include Mexicans who were classified with "Other races" in the 1930 reports. Percent not shown where less than 0.1 or where base is less than 100]

CENSUS YEAR AND RACE	TOTAL					MALE					FEMALE				
	Population		Persons in the labor force, and gainful workers,[1] 14 years old and over			Population		Persons in the labor force, and gainful workers,[1] 14 years old and over			Population		Persons in the labor force, and gainful workers,[1] 14 years old and over		
	Total (all ages)	14 years old and over	Number	Per-cent of total popu-lation	Per-cent of popu-lation 14 yrs. and over	Total (all ages)	14 years old and over	Number	Per-cent of total popu-lation	Per-cent of popu-lation 14 yrs. and over	Total (all ages)	14 years old and over	Number	Per-cent of total popu-lation	Per-cent of popu-lation 14 yrs. and over
1940	117,536	93,463	54,105	46.0	57.9	58,802	46,542	38,306	65.1	82.3	58,734	46,921	15,799	26.9	33.7
White	104,995	84,170	48,661	46.3	57.8	52,574	41,969	34,647	65.9	82.6	52.421	42,201	14,014	26.7	33.2
Negro	12,478	9,238	5,403	43.3	58.5	6,182	4,531	3,622	58.6	79.9	6,296	4,707	1,781	28.3	37.8
Other races	63	55	41	-	-	46	42	37	-	-	17	13	4	-	-
1930	118,700	87,135	50,118	42.2	57.5	59,442	43,707	37,460	63.0	85.7	59,258	43,428	12,658	21.4	29.1
White	107,292	78,845	44,723	41.7	56.7	53,713	39,509	33,797	62.9	85.5	53,579	39,336	10,926	20.4	27.8
Negro	11,340	8,236	5,349	47.2	64.9	5,676	4,151	3,618	63.7	87.2	5,664	4,085	1,731	30.6	42.4
Other races	68	54	46	-	-	53	47	45	-	-	15	7	1	-	-

[1] Data for 1930 represent gainful workers 14 years old and over.

"He's Thrilling Girls, This Russ Columbo," *Sandusky Star Journal* (Ohio), October 17, 1931

Russ Columbo came out of the west very reluctantly.

When a man is only 23 and is packing the cinema folk into his own nightclub, and when the same movie maestros are dangling contacts in front of the patrician nose, there is considerable trepidation involved in a decision to toss this aside and go to New York to crash the gates of broadcasting.

But friends finally persuaded Columbo that only the biggest time was good enough for his voice. So we said goodbye to the Club Pyramid, his band, his friends, the movies and thousands of women admirers who had petitioned him to remain in their ecstatic midst.

Now there are a lot of excellent singers in New York who are getting gray waiting for their chance in broadcasting. Some of them are almost as tall and dark and handsome as Russ Columbo.

However, after a few anxious days trying to identify himself as a Pacific Coast celebrity who really had something to sell, he was permitted to sidle up to an NBC microphone and warble "Body and Soul."

And already, scented stationery and daintily inscribed requests for photos are tumbling into the cubbyhole for the Columbo mail.

It is an exciting chapter in the life and times of a once-poor Italian-American boy who was christened Ruggiero. Columbo is his real name, incidentally.

He was born in San Francisco in 1908, began practicing on the violin at seven and got his first orchestra job at 17, in a Los Angeles high school.

Part of his money went to help support the family, and the rest went for violin lessons under a capable teacher.

In an emergency one night, he doubled for the orchestra's vocalist and kept on singing ever after.

He sang leading roles in a number of talkies, but only as a sideline.

He organized his own bright spot, The Club Pyramid, composed of a few seductive tunes, wrote a few lyrics, led his orchestra, sang winningly to the cash customers and grinned happily over the gate receipts.

Con Conrad, New York songwriter, was the one who really induced Columbo to try for radio fame. Columbo now is grateful.

"About my style of singing," said Russ. "I have a lot of trouble defining it. I'm not a crooner, or a blues singer, or a straight baritone. I've tried to make my phrasing different, and I take a lot of liberty with the music.

"One of the things they seem to like best is the voice obbligato on repeat choruses, very much as I used to do them on the violin.

"I like to lead an orchestra and try to work at different effects. I'm also composing a little. I write late at night mostly; I get some of my best ideas after I've gone to bed."

"Mae West Film at Granada Saturday," ***West Seattle Herald*** **December 12, 1934:** In *Belle of the Nineties*, showing four days starting Tuesday, Mae West traumatizes the strident days when men gambled with hearts, paid off with aces and fought for fun. She is cast as Ruby Carter, the center of a whirlpool of action that brings her down the river from a St. Louis burlesque show to one of the most famous gaming houses in the South. John Mack Brown and Roger Pryer support her, with Duke Ellington and his orchestra also featured. Russ Columbo, June Knight and Roger Pryor will share the bill in *Wake Up and Dream*, a gay comedy romance with music. "The Flying Mouse," Walt Disney's *Silly Symphonies*, will be a third sensation.

"You Call It Madness (But I Call It Love)"

(By Con Conrad, Gladys DuBois, Russ Columbo, Paul Gregory)

I can't forget the night I met you,
That's all I'm dreaming of.
Now you call it madness,
But I call it love.

You made a promise to be faithful
By all the stars above.
And now you call it madness,
But I call it love.

My heart is beating,
It keeps repeating for you constantly.
You're all I'm needing
And so I'm pleading,
Please come back to me.

You made a plaything out of romance,
What were you thinking of?
Now you call it madness,
But I call it love.

"Rudy Vallee," *Radio Album*, Spring 1935: Wistful, boyish, sophomoric Rudy Vallee crooned his way with a gay heigh-ho into Mrs. and Miss America's hearts back in 1928. No Gallup polls accounted for the whys of his whirlwind success, but as Whistler had his mother, Morgan her piano, so Rudy had a nasal twang that makes him the number one vagabond lover. Perhaps astrologists saw it in the stars, but in Island Pond, Vermont, on July 28, 1901, when Herbert Prior Vallee first graced the village druggist's nursery, no one predicted any spotlights for him. Young Herbert might still be delivering aspirin and jerking sodas if he hadn't heard Rudy Wiedoeft. Promptly, he borrowed a never-to-be-returned saxophone, inveigled a correspondence course out of Wiedoeft and for his teacher's and publicity's sakes changed Herbert to Rudy. Saxing his way into the University of Maine hall of incurable musicians, he put the "Stein Song" and S.A.E.'s "Violet" on the top of the campus hit parade. Leaving those careless hours and happy days, Rudy took up the baton at Yale, where his Connecticut Yankees roused slumbering Eli. Some Londoners heard about the boys and asked them over. For two years the gang stopped at the Savoy with nightly visits of the Prince of Wales, their best publicity. Again Rudy yenned for the New Haven quads in the Whiffenproof songs at Morey's and returned to a B.A. in romantic languages. Sunk in academic oblivion, he was down to his last pawn ticket when the Heigh-Ho Club put him on the air. He wowed the matinee listeners. In a fervor, Fleishman's yeast rose to snatch him up. This was Rudy's hour. Opening his eyes to new talent, he unearthed, among others, McCarthy, Bob Burns, Alice Faye, and Burns and Allen. As a maestro master of ceremonies, only he could think of using the many-wived, Hamlet-minded Barrymore as his stooge. Only Rudy could take it when, to his surprise, the great lover gets the last laugh. Women will always adore Rudy; men will always hate him.

Judge Takes the Road Less Travelled

Julia Stern grew up witnessing the dedication of her mother aiding in the adoption of children, especially hard-to-place Jews, leading Julia to attend Yale law school—one of the few open to both women and Jewish applicants around 1940. As a female judge appointed to the Domestic Relations Court in Manhattan, she felt she could handle the flood of divorce, desertion, adoptions and child abuse cases, and make a difference in the lives of unfortunate children.

Life at Home

- Julia Stern found her way into law and the legal bench as a judge through an unusual route-a textile mill.
- The daughter of a prominent Reform rabbi and an activist mother, Julia was born in 1901, and grew up secure in a nation invigorated by the possibilities of commerce and rapidly rising prestige abroad.
- Her mother's work with the poor focused on adopted children, especially the hard-to-place Jew, and Julia often worked alongside her mother on difficult cases and learned as a young girl about the complexities of family relationships.
- The experience shaped her life and, as a judge, successful adoptions brought her a special joy.
- Her father, too, led by example as a member of the National Association for the Advancement of Colored People.
- When a local minister told her father he couldn't be expected to sit down to dinner with a black artist also invited to the family's home for a meal, her father said, "Oh, I'm so sorry. May I take you downstairs and help you get your coat?"
- Her grandparents were staunch supporters of the need for a Jewish homeland in Palestine, having emigrated to America in 1888 from Galicia to promote the Zionist idea in the United States.
- Julia attended Bryn Mawr after being subjected to an hour-long grilling from the school president, who was determined to keep "undesirables" out of his college.
- After two years, she transferred to Radcliffe to take more economics courses.
- During the day she attended classes and taught foreign residents of Boston how to read, and at night she learned about economic conditions by working in a local factory.
- Disillusioned by the bluestocking atmosphere of Radcliffe, Julia finished at Barnard with a degree in economics.

Judge Julia Stern was concerned about the welfare of children.

- There, she published an article in the student newspaper calling on young people to "claim responsibility" for solving the social problems of their time.
- In a New Jersey mill, where she took employment under an assumed name, Julia witnessed legions of women arrive for the night shift exhausted and discouraged, and watched 14-year old children quit school and quickly grow old under the strain of working in the mills night after night.
- She came to understand the intimidation tactics of the owners determined to keep out the unions, and was eventually blacklisted from mills in the area.
- The experience pointed her to law school, an unusual path for a woman, and was encouraged by her father, especially since her goals included social justice.
- When she was told that only Yale University and the University of Chicago were open to both women and Jews, she chose Yale, where five of the 125 students were women.
- She was well accepted and popular until her second year, when she became heavily involved in the support of a group of striking textile workers.
- While encouraging a mass rally of workers to denounce the employers' "feudal tyranny" and their "octopus-like espionage system," she urged the workers to persist in their strike.
- Prominent members of her father's synagogue resigned the temple, and some Yale law students stopped speaking to her.
- Her activist role also attracted the attention of a young law professor, whom she eventually married, but who died of leukemia within five years.
- She wore his small gold Longines wrist watch as a constant reminder.
- Julia raised their son alone, who was four when his father died.
- She met a fellow attorney who shares her passionate devotion to children's causes-and the game of bridge.

Life at Work

- At 34 years old, Julia Stern was appointed to the Domestic Relations Court in Manhattan by Fiorello La Guardia, the first judicial appointment in New York State to elevate a woman above the rank of magistrate.
- She headed the city's Workman's Compensation Division, where she was able both to implement labor reforms and enrage the business community who have personally attacked her.
- She voted for Norman Thomas on the Socialist ticket for president and later toured Russia for three months, fueling the accusation she was a "red," or communist.
- When asked to be a judge, she hesitated, as her passion lay in the labor movement.
- Domestic Relations Court judges were reported to have little power but enormous workloads when presiding over what most called "poor people's court."
- A day in Domestic Relations Court watching case after tragic case helped convince her that she could make a difference as a judge.
- According to newspaper reports, a man who had appeared before Julia during one of her first days on the bench said his court appearance went well: "The judge wasn't there," he said, "but his wife treated me just fine."
- Divorce, desertion, adoptions and child abuse flooded her court on a daily basis.
- Her current salary is $10,000 a year, a raise of $6,500 over her previous position.
- She is concerned about the "vast chasm between our rhetoric of freedom, equality and charity, and what we are doing, or not doing, for poor people, especially children."
- Julia did everything possible to avoid identifying herself as a woman judge; merit, not gender, was all that mattered in court, she says.
- Adoptions were among the happiest events in Julia's courtroom, and she championed adoption's civic potential as well as its personal value; providing children with a family to love them would produce more law-abiding citizens.

Julia Stern loved working with children.

- Her goal was always the best interest of the child, she liked to say, which meant she was often in conflict with the teaching of the Catholic Church, which insisted that the children must always be awarded to the Catholic member of the couple.
- Julia liked to make her views known in and out of the courtroom, and regularly wrote letters to editors to complain about antiquated custody law or the "Oliver Twist treatment" provided by private child care agencies.

Life in the Community: New York City

- Second-generation East European Jewish women were well-represented in public colleges and universities, including New York's Hunter College, where many trained as teachers.
- According to one study, Jewish women constituted almost half of all New York City's teachers.
- Despite their academic achievements, "foreign students" were considered "raucous, gawkv, and afflicted with acne, halitosis and deplorable hairdo's."
- For many, the availability of public libraries was critical to their education; there, many immigrants and children of immigrants, including Jewish women, learned the English language and American ways.
- To receive a New York City teaching license, candidates faced both a written exam and a grueling oral interview where candidates were judged on their breeding, energy and alertness.
- A prospective teacher, especially a second-generation immigrant, was required to be audible, articulate, pleasant and well-modulated, without being nasal, high-pitched, monotonous, strident or noisy.
- The prospective teacher needed to speak without vulgarisms or foreignisms that might be imitated by students.

The nine tables that follow are reprinted from the actual 1940 census, for New York City. They include actual data on race, percentage of voting population, school attendance, number of school years completed, foreign born, and employment of workers 14 years and older by job, industry and race. In addition to being incredibly fascinating, these facts help to strengthen and visualize the actual environment in which Julia Stern lived and worked.

Table C-35.—AGE, BY RACE AND SEX, FOR THE CITY OF NEW YORK: 1940 AND 1930

[Figures for white population in 1930 revised to include Mexicans classified with "Other races" in the 1930 reports. Percent not shown where less than 0.1 or where base is less than 100]

AGE AND CENSUS YEAR	ALL CLASSES			NATIVE WHITE			FOREIGN-BORN WHITE			NEGRO			OTHER RACES		
	Total	Male	Female	Total	Male	Female	Total	Male	Female	Total	Male	Female	Total	Male	Female
All ages: 1940	7,454,995	3,676,293	3,778,702	4,897,481	2,397,164	2,500,317	2,080,020	1,057,839	1,022,181	458,444	205,727	252,717	19,050	15,563	3,487
Under 5 years	433,894	221,415	212,479	400,656	204,900	195,756	2,583	1,310	1,273	29,691	14,706	14,985	964	499	465
5 to 9 years	470,556	238,798	231,758	430,383	218,849	211,534	6,101	3,038	3,063	33,134	16,442	16,692	938	469	469
10 to 14 years	561,108	283,453	277,655	510,778	258,847	251,931	13,642	6,832	6,810	35,848	17,294	18,554	840	480	360
15 to 19 years	606,942	300,717	306,225	536,926	267,425	269,501	34,486	17,163	17,323	34,678	15,574	19,104	852	555	297
20 to 24 years	649,153	304,862	344,291	566,019	270,434	295,585	41,165	18,615	22,550	41,099	15,251	25,848	870	562	308
25 to 29 years	697,153	322,558	374,595	547,673	259,948	287,725	96,917	41,380	55,537	50,978	20,008	30,970	1,585	1,222	363
30 to 34 years	691,027	331,782	359,245	464,272	226,078	238,194	173,415	81,972	91,443	51,180	21,924	29,256	2,160	1,808	352
35 to 39 years	669,421	330,950	338,471	362,781	178,358	184,423	251,438	126,448	124,990	52,186	23,418	28,768	3,016	2,726	290
40 to 44 years	628,714	317,471	311,243	302,549	149,293	153,256	281,569	145,301	136,268	41,789	20,299	21,490	2,807	2,578	229
45 to 49 years	550,743	282,769	267,974	233,673	115,648	118,025	284,754	150,517	134,237	30,381	14,802	15,579	1,935	1,802	133
50 to 54 years	467,020	243,321	223,699	173,898	84,449	89,449	270,272	147,338	122,934	21,468	10,251	11,217	1,382	1,283	99
55 to 59 years	346,871	178,162	168,709	120,929	57,354	63,575	210,936	113,428	97,508	14,251	6,675	7,576	755	705	50
60 to 64 years	267,974	132,668	135,306	95,411	43,605	51,806	162,750	84,260	78,490	9,285	4,311	4,974	528	492	36
65 to 69 years	190,439	89,275	101,164	69,641	29,909	39,732	114,028	56,461	57,567	6,521	2,676	3,845	249	229	20
70 to 74 years	120,675	54,474	66,201	43,812	17,959	25,853	73,558	35,194	38,364	3,197	1,219	1,978	108	102	6
75 years and over	103,305	43,618	59,687	38,080	14,108	23,972	62,406	28,582	33,824	2,758	877	1,881	61	51	10
Under 1 year	81,889	41,795	40,094	76,006	38,897	37,109	123	57	66	5,576	2,748	2,828	184	93	91
5 years	88,368	44,847	43,521	80,891	41,165	39,726	980	474	506	6,323	3,120	3,203	174	88	86
14 years	113,310	56,949	56,361	102,350	51,621	50,729	3,732	1,851	1,881	7,065	3,376	3,689	163	101	62
15 years	114,889	57,734	57,155	103,876	52,455	51,421	3,936	1,935	2,001	6,910	3,234	3,676	167	110	57
16 and 17 years	238,386	118,975	119,411	212,614	106,441	106,173	11,953	6,056	5,897	13,474	6,261	7,213	345	217	128
21 years and over	5,254,633	2,570,647	2,683,986	2,908,645	1,393,545	1,515,100	2,013,349	1,024,793	988,556	317,355	138,864	178,491	15,284	13,445	1,839
All ages: 1930	6,930,446	3,472,956	3,457,490	4,294,196	2,123,577	2,170,619	2,295,181	1,180,947	1,114,234	327,706	156,968	170,738	13,363	11,464	1,899
Under 5 years	535,600	272,438	263,162	502,444	255,839	246,605	5,573	2,817	2,756	26,920	13,431	13,489	663	351	312
5 to 9 years	577,284	291,782	285,502	530,497	268,571	261,926	21,884	11,051	10,833	24,365	11,894	12,471	538	266	272
10 to 14 years	575,300	290,263	285,037	531,036	268,341	262,695	25,309	12,780	12,529	18,662	8,987	9,675	293	155	138
15 to 19 years	599,286	293,740	305,546	510,342	252,903	257,439	67,431	31,397	36,034	21,120	9,169	11,951	393	271	122
20 to 24 years	687,417	327,734	359,683	485,070	235,085	249,985	162,618	75,099	87,519	38,658	16,664	21,994	1,071	886	185
25 to 29 years	695,984	341,448	354,536	393,504	191,999	201,505	251,671	124,777	126,894	48,661	22,779	25,882	2,148	1,893	255
30 to 34 years	649,576	327,685	321,891	329,596	162,429	167,167	277,079	142,987	134,092	40,533	20,121	20,412	2,368	2,148	220
35 to 39 years	621,248	319,859	301,389	272,926	135,538	137,388	309,408	163,942	145,466	36,924	18,539	18,385	1,990	1,840	150
40 to 44 years	518,588	272,868	245,720	199,377	98,857	100,520	292,075	159,583	132,492	25,515	12,909	12,606	1,621	1,519	102
45 to 49 years	422,063	219,600	202,463	151,843	74,032	77,811	250,204	135,056	115,148	19,057	9,607	9,450	959	905	54
50 to 54 years	340,807	175,346	165,461	126,094	61,130	64,964	202,176	107,610	94,566	11,922	6,032	5,890	615	574	41
55 to 59 years	246,277	123,128	123,149	93,257	44,458	48,799	146,325	75,200	71,125	6,365	3,155	3,210	330	315	15
60 to 64 years	190,527	92,494	98,033	69,444	31,886	37,558	117,138	58,732	58,406	3,767	1,708	2,059	178	168	10
65 to 69 years	127,356	60,451	66,905	45,149	20,131	25,018	79,787	39,351	40,436	2,331	891	1,440	89	78	11
70 to 74 years	77,327	35,866	41,461	28,853	12,401	16,452	47,205	22,986	24,219	1,236	448	788	33	31	2
75 years and over	59,819	25,243	34,576	20,918	8,109	12,809	37,703	16,721	20,982	1,184	400	784	14	13	1
Not reported	5,987	3,011	2,976	3,846	1,868	1,978	1,595	858	737	486	234	252	60	51	9
Under 1 year	100,398	51,178	49,220	94,819	48,409	46,410	251	125	126	5,176	2,569	2,607	152	75	77
5 years	112,108	56,813	55,295	104,372	53,003	51,369	2,257	1,125	1,132	5,340	2,606	2,734	139	79	60
14 years	112,112	56,347	55,765	103,303	51,952	51,351	5,242	2,647	2,595	3,518	1,719	1,799	49	29	20
15 years	112,305	56,540	55,765	102,155	51,562	50,593	6,771	3,375	3,396	3,325	1,572	1,753	54	31	23
16 and 17 years	232,443	114,770	117,673	202,327	100,571	101,756	22,683	10,823	11,860	7,319	3,308	4,011	114	68	46
21 years and over	4,511,021	2,262,581	2,248,440	2,120,168	1,029,912	1,090,256	2,149,455	1,111,448	1,038,007	230,069	110,911	119,158	11,329	10,310	1,019
Percent: 1940	100.0	100.0	100.0	100.0	100.0	100.0	100.0	100.0	100.0	100.0	100.0	100.0	100.0	100.0	100.0
Under 5 years	5.8	6.0	5.6	8.2	8.5	7.8	0.1	0.1	0.1	6.5	7.1	5.9	5.1	3.2	13.3
5 to 9 years	6.3	6.5	6.1	8.8	9.1	8.5	0.3	0.3	0.3	7.2	8.0	6.6	4.9	3.0	13.4
10 to 14 years	7.5	7.7	7.3	10.4	10.8	10.1	0.7	0.6	0.7	7.8	8.4	7.3	4.4	3.1	10.3
15 to 19 years	8.1	8.2	8.1	11.0	11.2	10.8	1.7	1.6	1.7	7.6	7.6	7.6	4.5	3.6	8.5
20 to 24 years	8.7	8.3	9.1	11.6	11.3	11.8	2.0	1.8	2.2	9.0	7.4	10.2	4.6	3.6	8.8
25 to 29 years	9.4	8.8	9.9	11.2	10.8	11.5	4.7	3.9	5.4	11.1	9.7	12.3	8.3	7.9	10.4
30 to 34 years	9.3	9.0	9.5	9.5	9.4	9.5	8.3	7.7	8.9	11.2	10.7	11.6	11.3	11.6	10.1
35 to 39 years	9.0	9.0	9.0	7.4	7.4	7.4	12.1	12.0	12.2	11.4	11.4	11.4	15.8	17.5	8.3
40 to 44 years	8.4	8.6	8.2	6.2	6.2	6.1	13.5	13.7	13.3	9.1	9.9	8.5	14.7	16.6	6.6
45 to 49 years	7.4	7.7	7.1	4.8	4.8	4.7	13.7	14.2	13.1	6.6	7.2	6.2	10.2	11.6	3.8
50 to 54 years	6.3	6.6	5.9	3.6	3.5	3.6	13.0	13.9	12.0	4.7	5.0	4.4	7.3	8.2	2.8
55 to 59 years	4.7	4.8	4.5	2.5	2.4	2.5	10.1	10.7	9.5	3.1	3.2	3.0	4.0	4.5	1.4
60 to 64 years	3.6	3.6	3.6	1.9	1.8	2.1	7.8	8.0	7.7	2.0	2.1	2.0	2.8	3.2	1.0
65 to 69 years	2.6	2.4	2.7	1.4	1.2	1.6	5.5	5.3	5.6	1.4	1.3	1.5	1.3	1.5	0.6
70 to 74 years	1.6	1.5	1.8	0.9	0.7	1.0	3.5	3.3	3.8	0.7	0.6	0.8	0.6	0.7	0.2
75 years and over	1.4	1.2	1.6	0.8	0.6	1.0	3.0	2.7	3.3	0.6	0.4	0.7	0.3	0.3	0.3
Under 1 year	1.1	1.1	1.1	1.6	1.6	1.5	-	-	-	1.2	1.3	1.1	1.0	0.6	2.6
5 years	1.2	1.2	1.2	1.7	1.7	1.6	-	-	-	1.4	1.5	1.3	0.9	0.6	2.5
14 years	1.5	1.5	1.5	2.1	2.2	2.0	0.2	0.2	0.2	1.5	1.6	1.5	0.9	0.6	1.8
15 years	1.5	1.6	1.5	2.1	2.2	2.1	0.2	0.2	0.2	1.5	1.6	1.5	0.9	0.6	1.8
16 and 17 years	3.2	3.2	3.2	4.3	4.4	4.2	0.6	0.6	0.6	2.9	3.0	2.9	1.8	0.7	1.6
21 years and over	70.5	69.9	71.0	59.4	58.1	60.6	96.8	96.9	96.7	69.2	67.5	70.6	80.2	86.4	52.7
Percent: 1930	100.0	100.0	100.0	100.0	100.0	100.0	100.0	100.0	100.0	100.0	100.0	100.0	100.0	100.0	100.0
Under 5 years	7.7	7.8	7.6	11.7	12.0	11.4	0.2	0.2	0.2	8.2	8.6	7.9	5.0	3.1	16.4
5 to 9 years	8.3	8.4	8.3	12.4	12.6	12.1	1.0	0.9	1.0	7.4	7.6	7.3	4.0	2.3	14.3
10 to 14 years	8.3	8.4	8.2	12.4	12.6	12.1	1.1	1.1	1.1	5.7	5.7	5.7	2.2	1.4	7.3
15 to 19 years	8.6	8.5	8.8	11.9	11.9	11.9	2.9	2.7	3.2	6.4	5.8	7.0	2.9	2.4	6.4
20 to 24 years	9.9	9.4	10.4	11.3	11.1	11.5	7.1	6.4	7.9	11.8	10.6	12.9	8.0	7.7	9.7
25 to 29 years	10.0	9.8	10.3	9.2	9.0	9.3	11.0	10.6	11.4	14.8	14.5	15.2	16.1	16.5	13.4
30 to 34 years	9.4	9.4	9.3	7.7	7.6	7.7	12.1	12.1	12.0	12.4	12.8	12.0	17.7	18.7	11.6
35 to 39 years	9.0	9.2	8.7	6.4	6.4	6.3	13.5	13.9	13.1	11.3	11.8	10.8	14.9	16.1	7.9
40 to 44 years	7.5	7.9	7.1	4.6	4.7	4.6	12.7	13.5	11.9	7.8	8.2	7.4	12.1	13.3	5.4
45 to 49 years	6.1	6.3	5.9	3.5	3.5	3.6	10.9	11.4	10.3	5.8	6.1	5.5	7.2	7.9	2.8
50 to 54 years	4.9	5.0	4.8	2.9	2.9	3.0	8.8	9.1	8.5	3.6	3.8	3.4	4.6	5.0	2.2
55 to 59 years	3.6	3.5	3.6	2.2	2.1	2.2	6.4	6.4	6.4	1.9	2.0	1.9	2.5	2.7	0.8
60 to 64 years	2.7	2.7	2.8	1.6	1.5	1.7	5.1	5.0	5.2	1.1	1.1	1.2	1.3	1.5	0.5
65 to 69 years	1.8	1.7	1.9	1.1	0.9	1.2	3.5	3.3	3.6	0.7	0.6	0.8	0.7	0.7	0.6
70 to 74 years	1.1	1.0	1.2	0.7	0.6	0.8	2.1	1.9	2.2	0.4	0.3	0.5	0.2	0.3	0.1
75 years and over	0.9	0.7	1.0	0.5	0.4	0.6	1.6	1.4	1.9	0.4	0.3	0.5	0.1	0.1	0.1
Not reported	0.1	0.1	0.1	0.1	0.1	0.1	0.1	0.1	0.1	0.1	0.1	0.1	0.4	0.4	0.5
Under 1 year	1.4	1.5	1.4	2.2	2.3	2.1	-	-	-	1.6	1.6	1.5	1.1	0.7	4.1
5 years	1.6	1.6	1.6	2.4	2.5	2.4	0.1	0.1	0.1	1.6	1.7	1.6	1.0	0.7	3.2
14 years	1.6	1.6	1.6	2.4	2.4	2.4	0.2	0.2	0.2	1.1	1.1	1.1	0.4	0.3	1.1
15 years	1.6	1.6	1.6	2.4	2.4	2.3	0.3	0.3	0.3	1.0	1.0	1.0	0.4	0.3	1.2
16 and 17 years	3.4	3.3	3.4	4.7	4.7	4.7	1.0	0.9	1.1	2.2	2.1	2.3	0.9	0.6	2.4
21 years and over	65.1	65.1	65.0	49.4	48.5	50.2	93.7	94.1	93.2	70.2	70.7	69.8	84.8	89.9	53.7

Table C-36.—RACE, BY NATIVITY AND SEX, FOR THE CITY OF NEW YORK: 1940 AND 1930

[Figures for white population in 1930 have been revised to include Mexicans who were classified with "Other races" in the 1930 reports. Percent not shown where less than 0.1 or where base is less than 100. Sex ratio not shown where number of females is less than 100]

SEX, NATIVITY, AND CENSUS YEAR	All classes	White	Negro	Other races	OTHER RACES				PERCENT BY RACE				PERCENT BY NATIVITY					
					Indian	Chinese	Japanese	All other	All classes	White	Negro	Other races	All classes	White	Negro	Indian	Chinese	Japanese
TOTAL																		
1940	7,454,995	6,977,501	458,444	19,050	1,064	12,753	2,087	3,146	100.0	93.6	6.1	0.3	100.0	100.0	100.0	100.0	100.0	100.0
Native	5,316,338	4,897,481	410,026	8,831	638	4,745	631	2,817	100.0	92.1	7.7	0.2	71.3	70.2	89.4	60.0	37.2	30.2
Foreign born	2,138,657	2,080,020	48,418	10,219	426	8,008	1,456	329	100.0	97.3	2.3	0.5	28.7	29.8	10.6	40.0	62.8	69.8
1930	6,930,446	6,589,377	327,706	13,363	391	8,414	2,356	2,202	100.0	95.1	4.7	0.2	100.0	100.0	100.0	100.0	100.0	100.0
Native	4,571,760	4,294,196	272,952	4,612	294	1,926	536	1,856	100.0	93.9	6.0	0.1	66.0	65.2	83.3	75.2	22.9	22.8
Foreign born	2,358,686	2,295,181	54,754	8,751	97	6,488	1,820	346	100.0	97.3	2.3	0.4	34.0	34.8	16.7	24.8	77.1	77.2
MALE																		
1940	3,676,293	3,455,003	205,727	15,563	590	10,967	1,470	2,536	100.0	94.0	5.6	0.4	100.0	100.0	100.0	100.0	100.0	100.0
Native	2,585,482	2,397,164	181,870	6,448	321	3,547	325	2,255	100.0	92.7	7.0	0.2	70.3	69.4	88.4	54.4	32.3	22.1
Foreign born	1,090,811	1,057,839	23,857	9,115	269	7,420	1,145	281	100.0	97.0	2.2	0.8	29.7	30.6	11.6	45.6	67.7	77.9
1930	3,472,956	3,304,524	156,968	11,464	212	7,549	1,748	1,955	100.0	95.2	4.5	0.3	100.0	100.0	100.0	100.0	100.0	100.0
Native	2,255,955	2,123,577	128,891	3,487	152	1,414	275	1,646	100.0	94.1	5.7	0.2	65.0	64.3	82.1	71.7	18.7	15.7
Foreign born	1,217,001	1,180,947	28,077	7,977	60	6,135	1,473	309	100.0	97.0	2.3	0.7	35.0	35.7	17.9	28.3	81.3	84.3
FEMALE																		
1940	3,778,702	3,522,498	252,717	3,487	474	1,786	617	610	100.0	93.2	6.7	0.1	100.0	100.0	100.0	100.0	100.0	100.0
Native	2,730,856	2,500,317	228,156	2,383	317	1,198	306	562	100.0	91.6	8.4	0.1	72.3	71.0	90.3	66.9	67.1	49.6
Foreign born	1,047,846	1,022,181	24,561	1,104	157	588	311	48	100.0	97.6	2.3	0.1	27.7	29.0	9.7	33.1	32.9	50.4
1930	3,457,490	3,284,853	170,738	1,899	179	865	608	247	100.0	95.0	4.9	0.1	100.0	100.0	100.0	100.0	100.0	100.0
Native	2,315,805	2,170,619	144,061	1,125	142	512	261	210	100.0	93.7	6.2	-	67.0	66.1	84.4	79.3	59.2	42.9
Foreign born	1,141,685	1,114,234	26,677	774	37	353	347	37	100.0	97.6	2.3	0.1	33.0	33.9	15.6	20.7	40.8	57.1
MALES PER 100 FEMALES																		
1940	97.3	98.1	81.4	446.3	124.5	614.1	238.2	415.7	-	-	-	-	-	-	-	-	-	-
Native	94.7	95.9	79.7	270.6	101.3	296.1	106.2	401.2	-	-	-	-	-	-	-	-	-	-
Foreign born	104:1	103.5	97.1	825.6	171.3	1,261.9	368.2	-	-	-	-	-	-	-	-	-	-	-
1930	100.4	100.6	91.9	603.7	118.4	872.7	287.5	791.5	-	-	-	-	-	-	-	-	-	-
Native	97.4	97.8	89.5	310.0	107.0	276.2	105.4	783.8	-	-	-	-	-	-	-	-	-	-
Foreign born	106.6	106.0	105.2	1,030.6	-	1,738.0	424.5	-	-	-	-	-	-	-	-	-	-	-

Table C-37.—POTENTIAL VOTING POPULATION, BY CITIZENSHIP, RACE, NATIVITY, AND SEX, FOR THE CITY OF NEW YORK: 1940 AND 1930

[Figures for white population in 1930 have been revised to include Mexicans who were classified with "Other races" in the 1930 reports. Percent not shown where less than 0.1]

CITIZENSHIP, RACE, AND NATIVITY	TOTAL POPULATION (ALL AGES)								POPULATION 21 YEARS OLD AND OVER							
	Total number		Percent		Male		Female		Total number		Percent		Male		Female	
	1940	1930	1940	1930	1940	1930	1940	1930	1940	1930	1940	1930	1940	1930	1940	1930
Total	7,454,995	6,930,446	100.0	100.0	3,676,293	3,472,956	3,778,702	3,457,490	5,254,633	4,511,021	100.0	100.0	2,570,647	2,262,581	2,683,986	2,248,440
Percent citizen	-	-	89.0	83.7	-	-	-	-	-	-	85.2	77.2	-	-	-	-
Percent alien and citiz. not rptd.	-	-	11.0	16.3	-	-	-	-	-	-	14.8	22.8	-	-	-	-
Citizen	6,632,398	5,802,229	100.0	100.0	3,334,268	2,944,082	3,298,130	2,858,147	4,474,689	3,483,111	100.0	100.0	2,249,729	1,780,797	2,224,960	1,702,314
White—Native	4,897,481	4,294,196	73.8	74.0	2,397,164	2,123,577	2,500,317	2,170,619	2,908,645	2,120,158	65.0	60.9	1,393,545	1,029,912	1,515,100	1,090,256
Naturalized	1,298,360	1,217,790	19.6	21.0	738,635	680,388	559,725	537,402	1,272,872	1,168,689	28.4	33.6	725,888	656,236	546,984	512,453
Negro—Native	410,026	272,952	6.2	4.7	181,870	128,891	228,156	144,061	270,140	179,483	6.0	5.2	115,520	84,692	154,620	94,791
Naturalized	17,700	12,679	0.3	0.2	10,151	7,739	7,549	4,940	17,388	11,810	0.4	0.3	10,011	7,340	7,377	4,470
Other races—Native	8,831	4,612	0.1	0.1	6,448	3,487	2,383	1,125	5,644	2,961	0.1	0.1	4,765	2,617	879	344
Indian	638	294	-	-	321	152	317	142	377	205	-	-	191	108	186	97
Chinese	4,745	1,926	0.1	-	3,547	1,414	1,198	512	2,935	1,093	0.1	-	2,548	971	387	122
Japanese	631	536	-	-	325	275	306	261	250	91	-	-	133	60	117	31
Filipino	2,659	1,760	-	-	2,160	1,575	499	185	2,008	1,515	-	-	1,836	1,428	167	87
Hindu	58	19	-	-	28	8	30	11	17	3	-	-	7	1	10	2
All other	100	77	-	-	67	63	33	14	62	54	-	-	50	49	12	5
Alien	705,916	1,046,105	100.0	100.0	290,885	495,428	415,031	550,677	670,141	951,350	100.0	100.0	273,111	450,696	397,030	500,654
White—First papers	187,454	230,748	26.6	22.1	105,690	164,058	81,764	66,690	182,999	225,327	27.3	23.7	103,416	161,042	79,583	64,285
No papers	481,687	768,502	68.2	73.5	164,367	305,010	317,320	463,492	451,617	682,458	67.4	71.7	149,589	264,848	302,028	417,610
Negro—First papers	7,080	6,732	1.0	0.6	3,891	4,427	3,189	2,305	7,023	6,651	1.0	0.7	3,872	4,396	3,151	2,255
No papers	19,476	31,372	2.8	3.0	7,822	13,956	11,654	17,416	18,862	28,546	2.8	3.0	7,554	12,717	11,308	15,829
Other races—Foreign born	10,219	8,751	1.4	0.8	9,115	7,977	1,104	774	9,640	8,368	1.4	0.9	8,680	7,693	960	675
Indian	426	97	0.1	-	269	60	157	37	355	78	0.1	-	230	50	125	28
Chinese	8,008	6,488	1.1	0.6	7,420	6,135	588	353	7,624	6,222	1.1	0.7	7,097	5,906	527	316
Japanese	1,456	1,820	0.2	0.2	1,145	1,473	311	347	1,345	1,728	0.2	0.2	1,079	1,429	266	299
Filipino	68	37	-	-	45	24	23	13	61	34	-	-	43	24	18	10
Hindu	155	221	-	-	141	208	14	18	150	218	-	-	137	202	13	16
All other	106	88	-	-	95	82	11	6	105	88	-	-	94	82	11	6
Citizenship not reported	116,681	82,112	100.0	100.0	51,140	33,446	65,541	48,666	109,808	76,560	100.0	100.0	47,807	31,088	61,996	45,472
White	112,519	78,141	96.4	95.2	49,147	31,491	63,372	46,650	105,861	72,981	96.4	95.3	45,900	29,322	59,961	43,659
Negro	4,162	3,971	3.6	4.8	1,993	1,955	2,169	2,016	3,942	3,579	3.6	4.7	1,907	1,766	2,085	1,813

Table C-38.—SCHOOL ATTENDANCE, BY AGE, RACE, AND SEX, FOR THE CITY OF NEW YORK: 1940 AND 1930

[Figures for white population in 1930 revised to include Mexicans classified with "Other races" in the 1930 reports. Percent not shown where less than 0.1 or where base is less than 100]

AGE, SEX, AND CENSUS YEAR	ALL CLASSES			NATIVE WHITE			FOREIGN-BORN WHITE			NEGRO			OTHER RACES		
	Total number	Attending school		Total number	Attending school		Total number	Attending school		Total number	Attending school		Total number	Attending school	
		Number	Percent		Number	Percent		Number	Percent		Number	Percent		Number	Percent
1940															
Total, 5 to 24 years	2,287,759	1,350,041	59.0	2,044,106	1,223,732	59.9	95,394	38,961	40.8	144,759	85,048	58.8	3,500	2,300	65.7
5 years	88,368	25,836	29.2	80,891	23,845	29.5	980	314	32.0	6,323	1,608	25.4	174	69	39.7
6 years	88,718	77,089	86.9	81,065	70,723	87.2	1,077	872	81.0	6,383	5,335	83.6	193	159	82.4
7 to 9 years	293,470	283,447	96.6	268,427	259,433	96.6	4,044	3,780	93.5	20,428	19,694	96.4	571	540	94.6
10 to 13 years	447,798	434,889	97.1	408,428	396,885	97.2	9,910	9,466	95.5	28,783	27,884	96.9	677	654	96.6
14 years	113,310	109,423	96.6	102,350	98,948	96.7	3,732	3,543	94.9	7,065	6,776	95.9	163	156	95.7
15 years	114,889	110,459	96.1	103,876	99,957	96.2	3,936	3,749	95.2	6,910	6,590	95.4	167	163	97.6
16 and 17 years	238,386	185,098	77.6	212,614	165,326	77.8	11,953	8,926	74.7	13,474	10,571	78.5	345	275	79.7
18 and 19 years	253,667	74,066	29.2	220,436	64,290	29.2	18,597	5,175	27.8	14,294	4,458	31.2	340	143	42.1
20 years	127,862	17,480	13.7	110,098	15,419	14.0	9,859	1,176	11.9	7,738	836	10.8	172	49	28.5
21 to 24 years	521,291	32,254	6.2	455,926	28,906	6.3	31,306	1,960	6.3	33,361	1,296	3.9	698	92	13.2
Male, 5 to 24 years	1,127,830	695,356	61.7	1,015,555	632,536	62.3	45,648	20,542	45.0	64,561	40,934	63.4	2,066	1,344	65.1
5 years	44,847	12,940	28.9	41,165	11,993	29.1	474	145	30.6	3,120	766	24.6	88	36	-
6 years	45,142	39,217	86.9	41,313	36,059	87.3	557	456	81.9	3,175	2,619	82.5	97	83	-
7 to 9 years	148,809	143,700	96.6	136,371	131,755	96.6	2,007	1,884	93.9	10,147	9,793	96.5	284	268	94.4
10 to 13 years	226,504	220,075	97.2	207,226	201,486	97.2	4,981	4,751	95.4	13,918	13,475	96.8	379	363	95.8
14 years	56,949	54,998	96.6	51,621	49,891	96.6	1,851	1,757	94.9	3,376	3,252	96.3	101	98	97.0
15 years	57,734	55,606	96.3	52,455	50,547	96.4	1,935	1,846	95.4	3,234	3,106	96.0	110	107	97.3
16 and 17 years	118,975	94,205	79.2	106,441	84,400	79.3	6,056	4,655	76.9	6,261	4,975	79.5	217	175	80.6
18 and 19 years	124,006	41,999	33.9	108,529	36,815	33.9	9,172	3,027	33.0	6,079	2,052	33.8	228	105	46.1
20 years	61,263	10,830	17.7	53,598	9,657	18.0	4,703	778	16.5	2,847	359	12.6	115	36	31.3
21 to 24 years	243,599	21,786	8.9	216,836	19,933	9.2	13,912	1,243	8.9	12,404	537	4.3	447	73	16.3
Female, 5 to 24 years	1,159,929	654,685	56.4	1,028,551	591,196	57.5	49,746	18,419	37.0	80,198	44,114	55.0	1,434	956	66.7
5 years	43,521	12,896	29.6	39,726	11,852	29.8	506	169	33.4	3,203	842	26.3	86	33	-
6 years	43,576	37,872	86.9	39,752	34,664	87.2	520	416	80.0	3,208	2,716	84.7	96	76	-
7 to 9 years	144,661	139,747	96.6	132,056	127,678	96.7	2,037	1,896	93.1	10,281	9,901	96.3	287	272	94.8
10 to 13 years	221,294	214,814	97.1	201,202	195,399	97.1	4,929	4,715	95.7	14,865	14,409	96.9	298	291	97.7
14 years	56,361	54,425	96.6	50,729	49,057	96.7	1,881	1,786	94.9	3,689	3,524	95.5	62	58	-
15 years	57,155	54,853	96.0	51,421	49,410	96.1	2,001	1,903	95.1	3,676	3,484	94.8	57	56	-
16 and 17 years	119,411	90,893	76.1	106,173	80,926	76.2	5,897	4,271	72.4	7,213	5,596	77.6	128	100	78.1
18 and 19 years	129,659	32,067	24.7	111,907	27,475	24.6	9,425	2,148	22.8	8,215	2,406	29.3	112	38	33.9
20 years	66,599	6,650	10.0	56,495	5,762	10.2	5,156	398	7.7	4,891	477	9.8	57	13	-
21 to 24 years	277,692	10,468	3.8	239,090	8,973	3.8	17,394	717	4.1	20,957	759	3.6	251	19	7.6
1930															
Total, 5 to 24 years	2,439,287	1,362,751	55.9	2,056,945	1,237,685	60.2	277,242	77,432	27.9	102,805	46,617	45.3	2,295	1,017	44.3
5 years	112,108	28,632	25.5	104,372	26,823	25.7	2,257	504	22.3	5,340	1,263	23.7	139	42	30.2
6 years	115,242	92,352	80.1	107,000	86,052	80.4	3,108	2,394	77.0	5,013	3,815	76.1	121	91	75.2
7 to 9 years	349,934	338,303	96.7	319,125	308,879	96.8	16,519	15,870	96.1	14,012	13,293	94.9	278	261	93.9
10 to 13 years	463,188	456,204	98.5	427,733	421,470	98.5	20,067	19,680	98.1	15,144	14,818	97.8	244	236	96.7
14 years	112,112	108,728	97.0	103,303	100,227	97.0	5,242	5,052	96.4	3,518	3,396	96.5	49	48	-
15 years	112,305	101,360	90.3	102,155	92,164	90.2	6,771	6,133	90.6	3,325	3,020	90.8	54	43	-
16 and 17 years	232,443	132,712	57.1	202,327	116,559	57.6	22,683	11,933	52.6	7,319	4,156	56.8	114	64	56.1
18 and 19 years	254,538	53,524	21.0	205,860	45,266	22.0	37,977	6,628	17.5	10,476	1,570	15.0	225	60	26.7
20 years	131,955	16,667	12.6	99,709	13,766	13.8	25,529	2,496	9.8	6,570	381	5.8	147	24	16.3
21 to 24 years	555,462	34,274	6.2	385,361	26,479	6.9	137,089	6,742	4.9	32,088	905	2.8	924	148	16.0
Male, 5 to 24 years	1,203,519	702,126	58.3	1,024,900	637,812	62.2	130,327	41,371	31.7	46,714	22,359	47.9	1,578	584	37.0
5 years	56,813	14,449	25.4	53,003	13,563	25.6	1,125	254	22.6	2,606	609	23.4	79	23	-
6 years	58,294	46,618	80.0	54,183	43,489	80.3	1,613	1,244	77.1	2,444	1,843	75.4	54	42	-
7 to 9 years	176,675	170,727	96.6	161,385	156,112	96.7	8,313	7,998	96.2	6,844	6,491	94.8	133	126	94.7
10 to 13 years	233,916	230,415	98.5	216,389	213,233	98.5	10,133	9,943	98.1	7,268	7,119	97.9	126	120	95.2
14 years	56,347	54,756	97.2	51,952	50,499	97.2	2,647	2,560	96.7	1,719	1,669	97.1	29	28	-
15 years	56,540	51,345	90.8	51,562	46,747	90.7	3,375	3,118	92.4	1,572	1,455	92.6	31	25	-
16 and 17 years	114,770	69,016	60.1	100,571	60,834	60.5	10,823	6,205	57.3	3,308	1,940	58.6	68	37	-
18 and 19 years	122,430	31,344	25.6	100,770	26,637	26.4	17,199	3,979	23.1	4,289	684	15.9	172	44	25.6
20 years	62,152	10,397	16.7	48,011	8,643	18.0	11,454	1,578	13.8	2,576	160	6.2	111	16	14.4
21 to 24 years	265,582	23,059	8.7	187,074	18,055	9.7	63,645	4,492	7.1	14,088	389	2.8	775	123	15.9
Female, 5 to 24 years	1,235,768	660,625	53.5	1,032,045	599,873	58.1	146,915	36,061	24.5	56,091	24,258	43.2	717	433	60.4
5 years	55,295	14,183	25.6	51,369	13,260	25.8	1,132	250	22.1	2,734	654	23.9	60	19	-
6 years	56,948	45,734	80.3	52,817	42,563	80.6	1,495	1,150	76.9	2,569	1,972	76.8	67	49	-
7 to 9 years	173,259	167,576	96.7	157,740	152,767	96.8	8,206	7,872	95.9	7,168	6,802	94.9	145	135	93.1
10 to 13 years	229,272	225,789	98.5	211,344	208,237	98.5	9,934	9,737	98.0	7,876	7,699	97.8	118	116	98.3
14 years	55,765	53,967	96.8	51,351	49,728	96.8	2,595	2,492	96.0	1,799	1,727	96.0	20	20	-
15 years	55,765	50,015	89.7	50,593	45,417	89.8	3,396	3,015	88.8	1,753	1,565	89.3	23	18	-
16 and 17 years	117,673	63,696	54.1	101,756	55,725	54.8	11,860	5,728	48.3	4,011	2,216	55.2	46	27	-
18 and 19 years	132,108	22,180	16.8	105,090	18,629	17.7	20,778	2,649	12.7	6,187	886	14.3	53	16	-
20 years	69,803	6,270	9.0	51,698	5,123	9.9	14,075	918	6.5	3,994	221	5.5	36	8	-
21 to 24 years	289,880	11,215	3.9	198,287	8,424	4.2	73,444	2,250	3.1	18,000	516	2.9	149	25	16.8

Table C-39.—PERSONS 25 YEARS OLD AND OVER, BY YEARS OF SCHOOL COMPLETED, RACE, AND SEX, FOR THE CITY OF NEW YORK: 1940

[Percent not shown where less than 0.1; median and percent not shown where base is less than 100]

YEARS OF SCHOOL COMPLETED	ALL CLASSES			NATIVE WHITE			FOREIGN-BORN WHITE			NEGRO			OTHER RACES		
	Total	Male	Female	Total	Male	Female	Total	Male	Female	Total	Male	Female	Total	Male	Female
Persons 25 years old and over	4,733,342	2,327,048	2,406,294	2,452,719	1,176,709	1,276,010	1,982,043	1,010,881	971,162	283,994	126,460	157,534	14,586	12,998	1,588
No school years completed	361,184	168,418	192,771	21,613	9,787	11,826	325,905	150,661	175,244	9,778	4,414	5,364	3,888	3,551	337
Grade school: 1 to 4 years	340,551	171,962	168,589	47,904	23,248	24,656	253,517	129,707	123,810	36,215	16,228	19,987	2,915	2,779	136
5 or 6 years	367,288	183,754	183,534	108,791	52,733	56,058	208,431	108,206	100,225	48,372	21,250	27,122	1,694	1,565	129
7 or 8 years	1,934,829	939,513	995,316	1,059,451	503,256	556,195	771,640	389,004	382,636	101,145	45,007	56,138	2,593	2,246	347
High school: 1 to 3 years	600,541	289,124	311,417	429,601	203,919	225,682	128,331	66,773	61,558	41,738	17,700	24,038	871	732	139
4 years	585,923	249,407	336,516	418,943	168,634	250,309	138,772	68,710	70,062	27,284	11,392	15,892	924	671	253
College: 1 to 3 years	174,912	97,789	77,123	131,156	70,465	60,691	34,426	22,485	11,941	8,875	4,470	4,405	455	369	86
4 years or more	266,091	174,510	91,581	202,872	127,586	75,286	56,643	42,963	13,680	5,840	3,353	2,487	736	608	128
Not reported	102,023	52,576	49,447	32,388	17,081	15,307	64,378	32,372	32,006	4,747	2,646	2,101	510	477	33
Median school years completed	8.3	8.3	8.3	8.9	9.0	8.9	7.4	7.5	7.4	7.9	7.9	7.9	5.3	4.9	8.0
Percent less than 5 years completed	14.8	14.6	15.0	2.8	2.8	2.9	29.2	27.7	30.8	16.2	16.3	16.1	46.6	48.7	29.8
PERCENT DISTRIBUTION															
Persons 25 years old and over	100.0	100.0	100.0	100.0	100.0	100.0	100.0	100.0	100.0	100.0	100.0	100.0	100.0	100.0	100.0
No school years completed	7.6	7.2	8.0	0.9	0.8	0.9	16.4	14.9	18.0	3.4	3.5	3.4	26.7	27.3	21.2
Grade school: 1 to 4 years	7.2	7.4	7.0	2.0	2.0	1.9	12.8	12.8	12.7	12.8	12.8	12.7	20.0	21.4	8.6
5 or 6 years	7.8	7.9	7.6	4.4	4.5	4.4	10.5	10.7	10.3	17.0	16.8	17.2	11.6	12.0	8.1
7 or 8 years	40.9	40.4	41.4	43.2	42.8	43.6	38.9	38.5	39.4	35.6	35.6	35.6	17.8	17.3	21.9
High school: 1 to 3 years	12.7	12.4	12.9	17.5	17.3	17.7	6.5	6.6	6.3	14.7	14.0	15.3	6.0	5.6	8.8
4 years	12.4	10.7	14.0	17.1	14.3	19.6	7.0	6.8	7.2	9.6	9.0	10.1	6.3	5.2	15.9
College: 1 to 3 years	3.7	4.2	3.2	5.3	6.0	4.8	1.7	2.2	1.2	3.1	3.5	2.8	3.1	2.8	5.4
4 years or more	5.6	7.5	3.8	8.3	10.8	5.9	2.9	4.3	1.4	2.1	2.7	1.6	5.0	4.7	8.1
Not reported	2.2	2.3	2.1	1.3	1.5	1.2	3.2	3.2	3.3	1.7	2.1	1.3	3.5	3.7	2.1

Table C-40.—FOREIGN-BORN WHITE, BY COUNTRY OF BIRTH, BY SEX, FOR THE CITY OF NEW YORK: 1940 AND 1930

[Figures for white population in 1930 revised to include Mexicans classified with "Other races" in the 1930 reports. Percent not shown where less than 0.1 or where base is less than 100]

COUNTRY OF BIRTH	BOTH SEXES		PERCENT		MALE		FEMALE	
	1940	1930	1940	1930	1940	1930	1940	1930
All countries	2,080,020	2,295,181	100.0	100.0	1,057,839	1,180,947	1,022,181	1,114,234
England	63,115	78,003	3.0	3.4	30,411	38,538	32,704	39,465
Scotland	33,292	38,535	1.6	1.7	15,758	19,018	17,534	19,517
Wales	1,296	1,903	0.1	0.1	667	988	629	915
Northern Ireland	21,501	27,821	1.0	1.2	9,384	12,169	12,117	15,652
Irish Free State (Eire)	160,325	192,810	7.7	8.4	69,988	85,746	90,337	107,064
Norway	30,750	38,130	1.5	1.7	16,471	21,171	14,279	16,959
Sweden	28,881	37,267	1.4	1.6	14,674	19,357	14,207	17,910
Denmark	8,845	11,096	0.4	0.5	5,425	6,946	3,420	4,150
Netherlands	5,608	5,335	0.3	0.2	3,704	3,619	1,904	1,716
Belgium	3,888	3,854	0.2	0.2	1,993	1,952	1,895	1,902
Luxemburg	340	323	-	-	175	174	165	149
Switzerland	8,551	9,895	0.4	0.4	4,412	5,147	4,139	4,748
France	19,696	23,288	0.9	1.0	8,397	10,263	11,299	13,025
Germany	224,749	237,588	10.8	10.4	112,916	121,590	111,833	115,998
Poland	194,163	238,339	9.3	10.4	97,816	120,318	96,347	118,021
Czechoslovakia	26,884	35,318	1.3	1.5	12,042	15,964	14,842	19,354
Austria	145,106	127,169	7.0	5.5	70,537	62,587	74,569	64,582
Hungary	62,588	59,883	3.0	2.6	28,557	27,444	34,031	32,439
Yugoslavia	6,475	6,450	0.3	0.3	3,712	3,638	2,763	2,812
Russia (U. S. S. R.)	395,696	442,431	19.0	19.3	200,663	227,120	195,033	215,311
Lithuania	15,089	15,005	0.7	0.7	7,944	8,162	7,145	6,843
Latvia	5,317	5,172	0.3	0.2	2,785	2,692	2,532	2,480
Finland	11,245	13,224	0.5	0.6	4,563	5,833	6,682	7,391
Rumania	40,655	46,750	2.0	2.0	20,316	23,377	20,339	23,373
Bulgaria	670	578	-	-	394	342	276	236
Turkey in Europe	265	747	-	-	146	383	119	364
Greece	28,593	27,182	1.4	1.2	19,304	18,567	9,289	8,615
Italy	409,489	440,250	19.7	19.2	227,084	246,088	182,405	194,162
Spain	13,583	14,000	0.7	0.6	9,504	10,153	4,079	3,847
Portugal	2,676	2,231	0.1	0.1	2,008	1,756	668	475
Other Europe	5,757	4,844	0.3	0.2	3,691	3,160	2,066	1,684
Palestine and Syria	8,598	8,696	0.4	0.4	4,545	4,578	4,053	4,118
Turkey in Asia	17,398	14,368	0.8	0.6	9,645	8,050	7,753	6,318
Other Asia	5,107	5,621	0.2	0.2	3,293	3,514	1,814	2,107
Canada—French	6,270	6,863	0.3	0.3	2,753	3,308	3,517	3,555
Canada—Other	29,237	32,760	1.4	1.4	11,768	14,038	17,469	18,722
Newfoundland	4,838	5,303	0.2	0.2	2,171	2,555	2,667	2,748
Mexico	2,973	4,163	0.1	0.2	1,708	2,559	1,265	1,604
Cuba and other West Indies	13,344	13,046	0.6	0.6	7,136	7,303	6,208	5,743
Central and South America	12,429	14,298	0.6	0.6	6,807	8,202	5,622	6,096
Australia	987	1,164	-	0.1	513	650	474	514
Azores	69	95	-	-	35	66	34	29
All other and not reported	3,682	3,383	0.2	0.1	2,024	1,862	1,658	1,521

Table C-41.—PERSONS 14 YEARS OLD AND OVER, BY EMPLOYMENT STATUS, CLASS OF WORKER, RACE, AND SEX, FOR THE CITY OF NEW YORK: 1940

[Percent not shown where less than 0.1 or where base is less than 100]

EMPLOYMENT STATUS	ALL CLASSES			NATIVE WHITE			FOREIGN-BORN WHITE			NEGRO			OTHER RACES		
	Total	Male	Female	Total	Male	Female	Total	Male	Female	Total	Male	Female	Total	Male	Female
Total population (all ages)	7,454,995	3,676,293	3,778,702	4,897,481	2,397,164	2,500,317	2,080,020	1,057,839	1,022,181	458,444	205,727	252,717	19,050	15,563	3,487
Persons 14 years old and over	6,102,747	2,989,576	3,113,171	3,658,014	1,766,189	1,891,825	2,061,426	1,048,510	1,012,916	366,836	160,661	206,175	16,471	14,216	2,255
In labor force	3,474,760	2,424,740	1,050,020	2,113,054	1,403,145	709,909	1,114,459	879,446	235,013	234,336	129,853	104,483	12,911	12,296	615
Not in labor force	2,627,987	564,836	2,063,151	1,544,960	363,044	1,181,916	946,967	169,064	777,903	132,500	30,808	101,692	3,560	1,920	1,640
Engaged in own home housew'k	1,592,195	20,265	1,571,930	852,525	10,247	842,278	675,850	8,973	666,877	62,563	991	61,572	1,257	54	1,203
In school	474,543	248,124	226,419	422,821	222,304	200,517	22,889	11,998	10,891	27,902	13,183	14,719	931	639	292
Unable to work	293,980	162,619	131,361	105,263	53,804	51,459	159,113	98,217	60,896	28,901	9,958	18,943	703	640	63
In institutions	34,202	18,746	15,456	16,802	9,200	7,602	14,490	7,549	6,941	2,704	1,797	907	206	200	6
Other and not reported	238,067	115,082	117,985	147,549	67,489	80,060	74,625	42,327	32,298	10,430	4,879	5,551	463	387	76
LABOR FORCE BY EMPLOYMENT STATUS															
In labor force	3,474,760	2,424,740	1,050,020	2,113,054	1,403,145	709,909	1,114,459	879,446	235,013	234,336	129,853	104,483	12,911	12,296	615
Employed (exc. public emerg. work)	2,839,366	1,964,346	875,020	1,711,638	1,127,160	584,478	946,938	738,020	208,918	169,497	88,386	81,111	11,293	10,780	513
At work	2,765,695	1,917,928	847,767	1,669,669	1,104,589	565,080	918,934	716,249	202,685	166,185	86,681	79,504	10,907	10,409	498
With a job	73,671	46,418	27,253	41,969	22,571	19,398	28,004	21,771	6,233	3,312	1,705	1,607	386	371	15
On public emerg. work (WPA, etc.)	103,386	86,845	16,541	61,920	51,403	10,517	21,415	19,911	1,504	19,936	15,428	4,508	115	103	12
Seeking work	532,008	373,549	158,459	339,496	224,582	114,914	146,106	121,515	24,591	44,903	26,039	18,864	1,503	1,413	90
Experienced workers	459,422	335,922	123,500	276,438	191,793	84,645	141,561	119,197	22,364	39,995	23,565	16,430	1,428	1,367	61
New workers	72,586	37,627	34,959	63,058	32,789	30,269	4,545	2,318	2,227	4,908	2,474	2,434	75	46	29
PERCENT BY SEX															
In labor force	100.0	69.8	30.2	100.0	66.4	33.6	100.0	78.9	21.1	100.0	55.4	44.6	100.0	95.2	4.8
Employed (exc. public emerg.)	100.0	69.2	30.8	100.0	65.9	34.1	100.0	77.9	22.1	100.0	52.1	47.9	100.0	95.5	4.5
On pub. emerg. work (WPA, etc.)	100.0	84.0	16.0	100.0	83.0	17.0	100.0	93.0	7.0	100.0	77.4	22.6	100.0	89.6	10.4
Seeking work	100.0	70.2	29.8	100.0	66.2	33.8	100.0	83.2	16.8	100.0	58.0	42.0	100.0	94.0	6.0
Not in labor force	100.0	21.5	78.5	100.0	23.5	76.5	100.0	17.9	82.1	100.0	23.3	76.7	100.0	53.9	46.1
Engaged in own home housew'k	100.0	1.3	98.7	100.0	1.2	98.8	100.0	1.3	98.7	100.0	1.6	98.4	100.0	4.3	95.7
In school	100.0	52.3	47.7	100.0	52.6	47.4	100.0	52.4	47.6	100.0	47.2	52.8	100.0	68.6	31.4
Unable to work	100.0	55.3	44.7	100.0	51.1	48.9	100.0	61.7	38.3	100.0	34.5	65.5	100.0	91.0	9.0
In institutions	100.0	54.8	45.2	100.0	54.8	45.2	100.0	52.1	47.9	100.0	66.5	33.5	100.0	97.1	2.9
Other and not reported	100.0	49.4	50.6	100.0	45.7	54.3	100.0	56.7	43.3	100.0	46.8	53.2	100.0	83.6	16.4
EMPLOYED WORKERS BY CLASS OF WORKER															
Employed (exc. public emerg.)	2,839,366	1,964,346	875,020	1,711,638	1,127,160	584,478	946,938	738,020	208,918	169,497	88,386	81,111	11,293	10,780	513
Wage and salary workers	2,459,880	1,647,274	812,606	1,548,333	992,373	555,960	743,765	564,074	179,691	159,008	82,450	76,558	8,774	8,377	397
Employers and own-account workers	347,006	303,310	43,696	144,706	124,915	19,791	190,344	170,526	19,818	9,560	5,541	4,019	2,396	2,328	68
Unpaid family workers	18,091	5,652	12,439	9,308	4,688	4,615	8,514	875	7,639	196	51	145	78	38	40
Class of worker not reported	14,389	8,110	6,279	9,296	5,184	4,112	4,315	2,545	1,770	733	344	389	45	37	8
At work	2,765,695	1,917,928	847,767	1,669,669	1,104,589	565,080	918,934	716,249	202,685	166,185	86,681	79,504	10,907	10,409	498
Wage and salary workers	2,404,444	1,615,540	788,904	1,514,554	976,011	538,543	724,845	550,085	174,760	156,378	81,159	75,214	8,672	8,285	387
Employers and own-account workers	331,238	289,936	41,302	138,100	119,549	18,551	182,081	163,148	18,883	8,987	5,184	3,803	2,120	2,055	65
Unpaid family workers	17,599	5,454	12,145	9,005	4,527	4,478	8,332	843	7,489	189	49	140	73	35	38
Class of worker not reported	12,414	6,998	5,416	8,010	4,502	3,508	3,726	2,173	1,553	636	289	347	42	34	8
With a job	73,671	46,418	27,253	41,969	22,571	19,398	28,004	21,771	6,233	3,312	1,705	1,607	386	371	15
Wage and salary workers	55,436	31,734	23,702	33,779	16,362	17,417	18,920	13,989	4,931	2,635	1,291	1,344	102	92	10
Employers and own-account workers	15,768	13,374	2,394	6,606	5,366	1,240	8,313	7,378	935	573	357	216	276	273	3
Unpaid family workers	492	198	294	298	161	137	182	32	150	7	2	5	5	3	2
Class of worker not reported	1,975	1,112	863	1,286	682	604	589	372	217	97	55	42	3	3	-
PERCENT DISTRIBUTION															
Persons 14 years old and over	100.0	100.0	100.0	100.0	100.0	100.0	100.0	100.0	100.0	100.0	100.0	100.0	100.0	100.0	100.0
In labor force	56.9	81.1	33.7	57.8	79.4	37.5	54.1	83.9	23.2	63.9	80.8	50.7	78.4	86.5	27.3
Not in labor force	43.1	18.9	66.3	42.2	20.6	62.5	45.9	16.1	76.8	36.1	19.2	49.3	21.6	13.5	72.7
Engaged in own home housew'k	26.1	0.7	50.5	23.3	0.6	44.5	32.8	0.9	65.8	17.1	0.6	29.9	7.6	0.4	53.3
In school	7.8	8.3	7.3	11.6	12.6	10.6	1.1	1.1	1.1	7.6	8.2	7.1	5.7	4.5	12.9
Unable to work	4.8	5.4	4.2	2.9	3.0	2.7	7.7	9.4	6.0	7.9	6.2	9.2	4.3	4.5	2.8
In institutions	0.6	0.6	0.5	0.5	0.5	0.4	0.7	0.7	0.7	0.7	1.1	0.4	1.3	1.4	0.3
Other and not reported	3.8	3.8	3.8	4.0	3.8	4.2	3.6	4.0	3.2	2.8	3.0	2.7	2.8	2.7	3.4
LABOR FORCE BY EMPLOYMENT STATUS															
In labor force	100.0	100.0	100.0	100.0	100.0	100.0	100.0	100.0	100.0	100.0	100.0	100.0	100.0	100.0	100.0
Employed (exc. public emerg. work)	81.7	81.0	83.3	81.0	80.3	82.3	85.0	83.9	88.9	72.3	68.1	77.6	87.5	87.7	83.4
At work	79.6	79.1	80.7	79.0	78.7	79.6	82.5	81.4	86.2	70.9	66.8	76.1	84.5	84.7	81.0
With a job	2.1	1.9	2.6	2.0	1.6	2.7	2.5	2.5	2.7	1.4	1.3	1.5	3.0	3.0	2.4
On public emerg. work (WPA, etc.)	3.0	3.6	1.6	2.9	3.7	1.5	1.9	2.3	0.6	8.5	11.9	4.3	0.9	0.8	2.0
Seeking work	15.3	15.4	15.1	16.1	16.0	16.2	13.1	13.8	10.5	19.2	20.1	18.1	11.6	11.5	14.6
Experienced workers	13.2	13.9	11.8	13.1	13.7	11.9	12.7	13.6	9.5	17.1	18.1	15.7	11.1	11.1	9.9
New workers	2.1	1.6	3.3	3.0	2.3	4.3	0.4	0.3	0.9	2.1	1.9	2.3	0.6	0.4	4.7
EMPLOYED WORKERS BY CLASS OF WORKER															
Employed (exc. public emerg.)	100.0	100.0	100.0	100.0	100.0	100.0	100.0	100.0	100.0	100.0	100.0	100.0	100.0	100.0	100.0
Wage and salary workers	86.6	83.9	92.9	90.5	88.0	95.1	78.5	76.4	86.0	93.8	93.3	94.4	77.7	77.7	77.4
Employers and own-account workers	12.2	15.4	5.0	8.5	11.1	3.4	20.1	23.1	9.5	5.6	6.3	5.0	21.2	21.6	13.3
Unpaid family workers	0.6	0.3	1.4	0.5	0.4	0.8	0.9	0.1	3.7	0.1	0.1	0.2	0.7	0.4	7.8
Class of worker not reported	0.5	0.4	0.7	0.5	0.5	0.7	0.5	0.3	0.8	0.4	0.4	0.5	0.4	0.3	1.6
At work	100.0	100.0	100.0	100.0	100.0	100.0	100.0	100.0	100.0	100.0	100.0	100.0	100.0	100.0	100.0
Wage and salary workers	86.9	84.2	93.1	90.7	88.4	95.3	78.9	76.8	86.2	94.1	93.6	94.6	79.5	79.6	77.7
Employers and own-account workers	12.0	15.1	4.9	8.3	10.8	3.3	19.8	22.8	9.3	5.4	6.0	4.8	19.4	19.7	13.1
Unpaid family workers	0.6	0.3	1.4	0.5	0.4	0.8	0.9	0.1	3.7	0.1	0.1	0.2	0.7	0.3	7.6
Class of worker not reported	0.4	0.4	0.6	0.5	0.4	0.6	0.4	0.3	0.8	0.4	0.3	0.4	0.4	0.3	1.6
With a job	100.0	100.0	100.0	100.0	100.0	100.0	100.0	100.0	100.0	100.0	100.0	100.0	100.0	100.0	-
Wage and salary workers	75.2	68.4	87.0	80.5	72.5	89.8	67.6	64.3	79.1	79.6	75.7	83.6	26.4	24.8	-
Employers and own-account workers	21.4	28.8	8.8	15.7	23.8	6.4	29.7	33.9	15.0	17.3	20.9	13.4	71.5	73.6	-
Unpaid family workers	0.7	0.4	1.1	0.7	0.7	0.7	0.6	0.1	2.4	0.2	0.1	0.3	1.3	0.8	-
Class of worker not reported	2.7	2.4	3.2	3.1	3.0	3.1	2.1	1.7	3.5	2.9	3.2	2.6	0.8	0.8	-

Table C-42.—EMPLOYED WORKERS 14 YEARS OLD AND OVER, BY MAJOR OCCUPATION GROUP, INDUSTRY GROUP, AND SEX, FOR THE CITY OF NEW YORK: 1940

[Percent not shown where less than 0.1 or where base is less than 100]

MAJOR OCCUPATION GROUP AND INDUSTRY GROUP	Total	Male	Female	PERCENT BY OCCUPATION AND INDUSTRY			PERCENT BY SEX	
				Total	Male	Female	Male	Female
Total population (all ages)	7,454,995	3,676,293	3,778,702	-	-	-	49.3	50.7
All persons 14 years old and over	6,102,747	2,989,576	3,113,171	-	-	-	49.0	51.0
In labor force	3,474,760	2,424,740	1,050,020	100.0	100.0	100.0	69.8	30.2
Employed workers (except on public emergency work)	2,839,366	1,964,346	875,020	81.7	81.0	83.3	69.2	30.8
MAJOR OCCUPATION GROUP								
Employed (except on public emergency work)	2,839,366	1,964,346	875,020	100.0	100.0	100.0	69.2	30.8
Professional workers	217,032	126,887	90,145	7.6	6.5	10.3	58.5	41.5
Semiprofessional workers	42,198	30,052	12,146	1.5	1.5	1.4	71.2	28.8
Farmers and farm managers	558	519	39	-	-	-	93.0	7.0
Proprietors, managers, and officials, except farm	288,152	259,075	29,077	10.1	13.2	3.3	89.9	10.1
Clerical, sales, and kindred workers	770,804	446,199	324,605	27.1	22.7	37.1	37.9	42.1
Craftsmen, foremen, and kindred workers	329,479	319,308	10,171	11.6	16.3	1.2	96.9	3.1
Operatives and kindred workers	580,053	388,788	191,265	20.4	19.8	21.9	67.0	33.0
Domestic service workers	123,202	6,976	116,226	4.3	0.4	13.3	5.7	94.3
Service workers, except domestic	346,264	256,696	89,568	12.2	13.1	10.2	74.1	25.9
Farm laborers (wage workers) and farm foremen	960	914	46	-	-	-	95.2	4.8
Farm laborers, unpaid family workers	60	50	10	-	-	-	-	-
Laborers, except farm	114,168	111,567	2,601	4.0	5.7	0.3	97.7	2.3
Occupation not reported	26,436	17,315	9,121	0.9	0.9	1.0	65.5	34.5
INDUSTRY GROUP								
Employed (except on public emergency work)	2,839,366	1,964,346	875,020	100.0	100.0	100.0	69.2	30.8
Agriculture, forestry, and fishery	3,468	3,229	239	0.1	0.2	-	93.1	6.9
Agriculture	2,813	2,599	214	0.1	0.1	-	92.4	7.6
Forestry (except logging) and fishery	655	630	25	-	-	-	96.2	3.8
Mining	996	822	174	-	-	-	82.5	17.5
Coal mining	93	82	11	-	-	-	-	-
Crude petroleum and natural gas production	78	66	12	-	-	-	-	-
Other mines and quarries	825	674	151	-	-	-	81.7	18.3
Construction	131,599	127,880	3,719	4.6	6.5	0.4	97.2	2.8
Manufacturing	746,466	504,413	242,053	26.3	25.7	27.7	67.6	32.4
Food and kindred products	67,648	54,260	13,388	2.4	2.8	1.5	80.2	19.8
Textile-mill products	42,081	26,440	15,641	1.5	1.3	1.8	62.8	37.2
Apparel and other fabricated textile products	236,604	121,618	114,986	8.3	6.2	13.1	51.4	48.6
Logging	50	44	6	-	-	-	-	-
Sawmills and planing mills	1,407	1,291	116	-	0.1	-	91.8	8.2
Furniture, store fixtures, and miscellaneous wooden goods	21,104	18,415	2,689	0.7	0.9	0.3	87.3	12.7
Paper and allied products	20,049	12,610	7,439	0.7	0.6	0.9	62.9	37.1
Printing, publishing, and allied industries	81,528	62,074	19,454	2.9	3.2	2.2	76.1	23.9
Chemicals and allied products	30,400	19,973	10,427	1.1	1.0	1.2	65.7	34.3
Petroleum and coal products	8,074	6,371	1,703	0.3	0.3	0.2	78.9	21.1
Leather and leather products	26,702	18,936	7,766	0.9	1.0	0.9	70.9	29.1
Stone, clay, and glass products	8,366	6,960	1,406	0.3	0.4	0.2	83.2	16.8
Iron and steel and their products	24,332	20,387	3,945	0.9	1.0	0.5	83.8	16.2
Nonferrous metals and their products	21,099	17,314	3,785	0.7	0.9	0.4	82.1	17.9
Machinery	44,459	36,106	8,353	1.6	1.8	1.0	81.2	18.8
Automobiles and automobile equipment	5,256	4,421	835	0.2	0.2	0.1	84.1	15.9
Transportation equipment, except automobile	21,985	21,163	822	0.8	1.1	0.1	96.3	3.7
Other and not specified manufacturing industries	85,322	56,030	29,292	3.0	2.9	3.3	65.7	34.3
Transportation, communication, and other public utilities	251,416	220,359	31,057	8.9	11.2	3.5	87.6	12.4
Railroads (including railroad repair shops) and railway express service	32,779	31,130	1,649	1.2	1.6	0.2	95.0	5.0
Trucking service	28,347	27,352	995	1.0	1.4	0.1	96.5	3.5
Other transportation	102,686	98,192	4,494	3.6	5.0	0.5	95.6	4.4
Communication	36,407	18,340	18,067	1.3	0.9	2.1	50.4	49.6
Utilities	51,197	45,345	5,852	1.8	2.3	0.7	88.6	11.4
Wholesale and retail trade	621,757	470,614	151,143	21.9	24.0	17.3	75.7	24.3
Wholesale trade	99,660	79,079	20,581	3.5	4.0	2.4	79.3	20.7
Food and dairy products stores, and milk retailing	133,741	114,878	18,863	4.7	5.8	2.2	85.9	14.1
Eating and drinking places	112,822	86,611	26,211	4.0	4.4	3.0	76.8	23.2
Motor vehicles and accessories retailing, and filling stations	17,299	15,837	1,462	0.6	0.8	0.2	91.5	8.5
Other retail trade	258,235	174,209	84,026	9.1	8.9	9.6	67.5	32.5
Finance, insurance, and real estate	224,460	162,199	62,261	7.9	8.3	7.1	72.3	27.7
Business and repair services	74,133	61,177	12,956	2.6	3.1	1.5	82.5	17.5
Automobile storage, rental, and repair services	25,738	25,214	524	0.9	1.3	0.1	98.0	2.0
Business and repair services, except automobile	48,395	35,963	12,432	1.7	1.8	1.4	74.3	25.7
Personal services	293,887	109,819	184,068	10.4	5.6	21.0	37.4	62.6
Domestic service	135,788	13,752	122,036	4.8	0.7	13.9	10.1	89.9
Hotels and lodging places	55,832	31,981	23,851	2.0	1.6	2.7	57.3	42.7
Laundering, cleaning, and dyeing services	45,141	28,394	16,747	1.6	1.4	1.9	62.9	37.1
Miscellaneous personal services	57,126	35,692	21,434	2.0	1.8	2.4	62.5	37.5
Amusement, recreation, and related services	42,996	31,610	11,386	1.5	1.6	1.3	73.5	26.5
Professional and related services	247,816	122,769	125,047	8.7	6.2	14.3	49.5	50.5
Government	126,733	108,811	17,922	4.5	5.5	2.0	85.9	14.1
Industry not reported	73,639	40,644	32,995	2.6	2.1	3.8	55.2	44.8

Table C-43.—PERSONS 14 YEARS OLD AND OVER IN THE LABOR FORCE, 1940, AND GAINFUL WORKERS 14 YEARS OLD AND OVER, 1930, BY RACE AND SEX, FOR THE CITY OF NEW YORK

[Totals for population and gainful workers for 1930 include "Unknown age." Figures for white population in 1930 have been revised to include Mexicans who were classified with "Other races" in the 1930 reports. Percent not shown where less than 0.1 or where base is less than 100]

CENSUS YEAR AND RACE	TOTAL					MALE					FEMALE				
	Population		Persons in the labor force, and gainful workers,[1] 14 years old and over			Population		Persons in the labor force, and gainful workers,[1] 14 years old and over			Population		Persons in the labor force, and gainful workers,[1] 14 years old and over		
	Total (all ages)	14 years old and over	Number	Per-cent of total popu-lation	Per-cent of popu-lation 14 yrs. and over	Total (all ages)	14 years old and over	Number	Per-cent of total popu-lation	Per-cent of popu-lation 14 yrs. and over	Total (all ages)	14 years old and over	Number	Per-cent of total popu-lation	Per-cent of popu-lation 14 yrs. and over
1940	7,454,995	6,102,747	3,474,760	46.6	56.9	3,676,293	2,989,576	2,424,740	66.0	81.1	3,778,702	3,113,171	1,050,020	27.8	33.7
White	6,977,501	5,719,440	3,227,513	46.3	56.4	3,455,003	2,814,699	2,282,591	66.1	81.1	3,522,498	2,904,741	944,922	26.8	32.5
Negro	458,444	366,836	234,336	51.1	63.9	205,727	160,661	129,853	63.1	80.8	252,717	206,175	104,483	41.3	50.7
Other races	19,050	16,471	12,911	67.8	78.4	15,563	14,216	12,296	79.0	86.5	3,487	2,255	615	17.6	27.3
1930	6,930,446	5,354,374	3,186,958	46.0	59.5	3,472,956	2,674,820	2,324,296	66.9	86.9	3,457,490	2,679,554	862,662	25.0	32.2
White	6,589,377	5,081,179	2,982,779	45.3	58.7	3,304,524	2,539,724	2,199,622	66.6	86.6	3,284,853	2,541,455	783,157	23.8	30.8
Negro	327,706	261,277	193,730	59.1	74.1	156,968	124,375	114,535	73.0	92.1	170,738	136,902	79,195	46.4	57.8
Other races	13,363	11,918	10,449	78.2	87.7	11,464	10,721	10,139	88.4	94.6	1,899	1,197	310	16.3	25.9

[1] Data for 1930 represent gainful workers 14 years old and over.

Government Work Program Strengthens American Music Scene

Part of President Roosevelt's Public Works Project, the Federal Music Project hired 15,000 musicians to give 225,000 performances to millions of Americans. The initiative raised the musical IQ of every region of the country and accelerated the pace, creativity and depth of the music scene in the 1940s. When unemployed textile worker Mark Strahorn was hired to play his fiddle, it not only paid his bills, but renewed his passion for music.

Life at Home

- When the textile mill where Mark Strahorn worked in Winston-Salem, North Carolina closed abruptly, Mark's family went from living week to week to living minute to minute.
- The only money Mark could make in a community littered with unemployed textile workers was with his fiddle as a member of the Empty Road band.
- The Works Progress Administration was his salvation in these tough times.
- Mark stayed in school through the sixth grade before taking a job beside his cousin and uncles in the gray cloth mill run by the money men in Chicago.
- Mark and 631 workers were laid off, and alcohol did not cure the pain of losing his livelihood.
- President Franklin Roosevelt believed that public works jobs funded by the government such as building roads, laying out parks, constructing bridges and creating art were necessary.
- By paying the unemployed to work on government projects, they reinforced the idea that everyone was working together, which helped remove the social stigma of being on relief while stimulating both the individual self-worth of Americans and the national economy.
- The largest agency created by the Emergency Relief Appropriations Act was the Works Progress Administration, commonly called the WPA, headed by Harry Hopkins.
- The high-energy Hopkins was described as having "a mind like a razor, a tongue like a skinning knife, a temper like Tartar and a sufficient vocabulary of parlor profanity to make a mule skinner jealous."
- Even in a town populated by go-getters, the 42-year-old Hopkins stood out.
- The United States had mobilized 4.7 million soldiers, sailors, and marines to fight in World War I; Hopkins was determined to employ a

Mark Strahorn (center), unemployed father of three, played his fiddle in a band called Empty Road.

similar number-four million jobless men and women-as rapidly as possible to fight the Depression.

- The WPA hired more than three million people in its first year.
- Its mission was broad: to build one million miles of highway, nearly 100,000 bridges, and buildings as diverse as The Dock Street Theatre in Charleston, South Carolina, and Timberline Lodge on the slopes of Oregon's Mount Hood.
- Often, local political bosses determined who got the jobs, some of which came only after political donations, while others were meted out fairly.
- Worker advocates criticized the creation of federal work gangs, while conservatives lodged complaints about the "undeserving poor."
- The president's wife, Eleanor, pushed Hopkins to establish projects for thousands of artists, musicians, actors and writers.
- To those who complained, Hopkins replied, "Hell, they've got to eat just like other people."
- Hopkins believed that the Federal Project Number One, the collective name for a group of arts projects under the WPA, was an opportunity to rediscover and redefine American culture.
- Mark, who married at 16, was a father at 17, and unemployed at 28, applied for construction work, but heard that the search was on for touring musicians who were willing to entertain.
- Mark, who could play by ear by the time he was nine, preferred rubbing a fiddle to moving rock any day, especially in the heat of the Southern sun.

Life at Work

- The American music scene was alive with possibilities and variety when Mark Strahorn was hired by the Federal Music Project.
- Jazz was gaining momentum, thanks to the talent of Count Basie, Duke Ellington, and Louis Armstrong.
- Ragtime was evolving into swing as Big Bands led by popular entertainers such as Artie Shaw ignited a dance craze, and the ubiquity of radio permitted every home to be a concert hall.
- At the same time, talking pictures had eliminated the need for 22,000 theater musicians essential to the silent movie experience, while the emerging quality of phonographic records suppressed the public's desire for live performances.

Harry Hopkins, right, head of the Works Progress Administration.

- Even the New Jersey Funeral Directors Association promoted the cost-effective use of radio instead of live musicians.
- When Mark lost his textile job, 12,000 of the 15,000 members of the American Federation of Musicians in New York City were out of work.
- Russian-born conductor and violinist Nikolai Sokoloff was selected to head the Federal Music Project after 15 years of directing the Cleveland Symphony.
- At first, Sokoloff attempted to pay higher wages to musicians who could read music and had classical training, but advocates of "popular music" eventually convinced him that all performing musicians who had been on the relief roles should make $23.86 a week.
- Musicians' pay was nearly double the average WPA wage of $52 a month.
- Eager to promote "quality music," Sokoloff's Federal Music Project sponsored concerts in symphony halls and county parks-anywhere he could lift the musical IQ of Americans.

Many protested cutbacks in Federal Project Number One – which employed musicians and artists.

- In all, WPA's 15,000 musicians gave 225,000 performances, including free concerts at New York's Central Park.
- Millions of Americans flocked to the concerts and brought their children.
- Mark performed in his first concert in Raleigh, North Carolina, followed by Richmond, Virginia, and Washington, DC; no audience was too small, no event too unlikely.
- Initially, he was instructed to play the fiddle in a more cultured manner.
- Mark quickly learned that the difference in playing the violin was more than style: the goal of violin music was beauty and power, while the goal of fiddling was danceability.
- Mark worked hard to make the transition from fiddle to "fancy" music; the showdown came seven months into his job traveling from school to school playing "proper" music.
- The band arrived playing mountain music in a bus one late afternoon, knowing that, for the rest of the evening, they were expected to be an orchestra and play selections from three European composers.
- Only this time, a large crowd that had gathered in the parking lot heard the informal jam session.
- So that evening after the first movement of Bach was completed and the sweet sounds of the violin had died away, a tall, thin man in overalls rose from his seat and said, "Not to be ungrateful, but we were wanting some more bus music."
- After that, every concert opened with "quality music" and ended with a hoedown, energetically driven by Mark's fiddling.
- The WPA aggressively advertised the music project and charged $0.25-$0.50 per person when there was any cost at all; in the first nine months of 1936, 32 million Americans attended Federal Music Project performances.
- While the emphasis was on "quality music," meaning classical, over time the project embraced Texas fiddlers, Ohio jug bands, and Appalachian banjo pickers.

- American composers such as George Gershwin, Victor Herbert and John Philip Sousa were given wide exposure to avoid accusations of being un-American; Broadway style music, epitomized by Jerome Kern, Oscar Hammerstein and Irving Berlin, began to appear more regularly.
- The Federal Project Number One also celebrated the talent of artists, actors and writers, and resulted in hundreds of public murals, books about each of the 48 states, and thousands of photographs depicting the everyday life of Americans.
- President Roosevelt was determined to use any means of "disposing of surplus workers" during the deep economic downturn.
- He considered work relief, unemployment insurance, and old age pensions as part of a comprehensive package and pathway to sustainable economic stability.
- Mark's favorite concert was performing country music in Burlington, North Carolina.
- Taking the lead instrumental in the second song, he drove the crowd into a frenzy as the other musicians hustled to catch up.
- It wasn't classical that day, but it was fun.
- Mark also performed at dozens of school concerts across North Carolina and Virginia.
- After one week of touring schools, he told his wife, "I didn't know there were that many kids in the entire world."
- As a result, children came to him eager to learn how to play an instrument, and many telling their parents about what they had heard and why it stirred their souls.
- Electricity was just reaching many of the rural areas of North Carolina, bringing light to the night and radio music to the family for the first time.
- Thanks to the variety of sounds coming from the radio, musical tastes of working Americans grew more sophisticated, and a rural farm family could stay informed about world events.
- When the textile mills began reopening in Winston-Salem, Mark had a decision to make.
- Cutbacks in the Federal Project Number One told Mark he should return to textiles, but alive feeling he playing music was tough to turn his back on.

Life in the Community: Winston-Salem, North Carolina

- The R. J. Reynolds Tobacco Company dominated the economic heartbeat of Winston-Salem, and more than half of its workers were employed either for Reynolds or in the Hanes textile factories.
- The Reynolds company imported so much French cigarette paper and Turkish tobacco for Camel cigarettes that Winston-Salem was designated as an official port of entry for the United States.
- The Wesley Hanes's Shamrock Hosiery Mills in Winston-Salem, later renamed Hanesbrands, the company was responsible for textile innovations such as women's nylon hosiery.
- Malcolm Purcell McLean formed McLean Trucking Company, which benefited from the strong tobacco and textile industries headquartered in Winston-Salem.

Methodist Minister Tames Troubled Churches

The churches of West Virginia played a critical role in aiding the community during the unpredictable economic swings of the years surrounding 1940. James Merriwether was assigned to dozens of troubled churches in West Virginia since he left the newspaper business to enter the ministry. As a district superintendent, he travelled to preach, meet ministers and deal with the administrative affairs of the church.

Life at Home

- Born on January 1, 1873, the second of four children, James Merriwether grew up near Washington Crossing, New Jersey.
- He quit school in the third grade because of his father's financial misfortune, and was sent to live and work on a neighboring farm.
- As a teenager, James left the farm and went to Trenton, New Jersey, where he worked in a brickyard and later as a typesetter for the newspaper.
- When he was in his early twenties, he took a job writing for the Trenton newspaper, eventually becoming its city editor.
- While at the newspaper, he received "the call" and decided to attend seminary.
- He enrolled in Princeton University and bought a grocery store to support himself, which was later sold to the Redfronts chain.
- James met Edie at church, and they were engaged before he left for West Virginia to minister to men working in the coal mines.
- Shortly after their marriage, they moved to Monongalia County, West Virginia and had four children.
- James was district superintendent for the West Virginia Methodist Church, the Methodist church being the largest denomination in West Virginia.
- Often away from home traveling for the church, James sometimes woke up the entire family when he returned home to fix French toast and celebrate his return.
- Ever clever with words, before a meal he often told the children, "I don't know how I'm going to get outside of this"; after a meal he might remark, "I feel of fullness."

The Merriwethers' house was a parsonage provided by the Church.

- Edie was the disciplinarian in the family; at mealtimes she used a stick to whack the children if they misbehaved-the same stick she used to keep order when they rode in the car.
- Their house, a parsonage provided by the church, was a two-story cottage with three bedrooms upstairs and a living room, dining room, kitchen, and back porch downstairs.
- The living room was furnished with a piano, a couch called a divan, a rocking chair, and an overstuffed chair.
- Family sing-alongs around the piano were standard entertainment and included both religious ballads and popular secular songs.
- To assist Edie, a woman was been hired to help with the cleaning.
- Mondays were reserved for washing; Tuesdays were for ironing; Thursday was baking day and Saturday was for cleaning the house.
- On Wednesday nights, the family attended prayer meetings, and they attended church twice on Sundays.
- Since no work is done on Sundays, the afternoon meal was prepared on Saturday; the children did not play cards, nor did Edie use any electrical equipment, such as a vacuum cleaner, on that day.
- The family got little of its food from the store, though the children loved "store-bought bread."
- Edie and the girls made their own clothing, from the cotton shirtwaist tops they often wear, to three-piece suits.
- The boys wore three-piece suits to church.
- Going to the Anderson-Newcomb department store was a special treat for the family.
- The girls enjoyed collecting paper doll figures and dresses from the Sunday newspaper; they had dozens of dolls and doll dresses.

Games were popular in the Merriwether house.

- The boys loved to play a game called the "Flying Puzzle," based on an airplane trip from New York to Paris-two cities they have never seen.
- The constant presence of railroad cars in Huntington also brought hobos, and the family often fed the hungry men who appeared at their doorstep.
- Once in a while, the family attended the Keith-Albee Theater, considered a movie palace, where Will Rogers movies always drew big crowds.
- Much of the family's free time was spent at Ritter Park, which offered tennis courts, a baseball diamond, a skating rink, and swimming.

Life at Work

- After many years of "rescuing" troubled churches, James was named the district superintendent for eight counties in West Virginia.
- As district superintendent, he often traveled to different churches to preach, meet with ministers, and deal with administrative matters of the church.
- Often he was gone for four or five days at a time as he attempted to cover all the churches in his district, driving a Model A Ford.
- A typical work weekend included preaching on Sunday morning in Parkerburg, a conference with preachers in Clarksburg that afternoon, preaching an evening service in Charleston, and then an all-night drive to Cleveland to begin meetings there the next morning; his teenage son often helped with the driving.

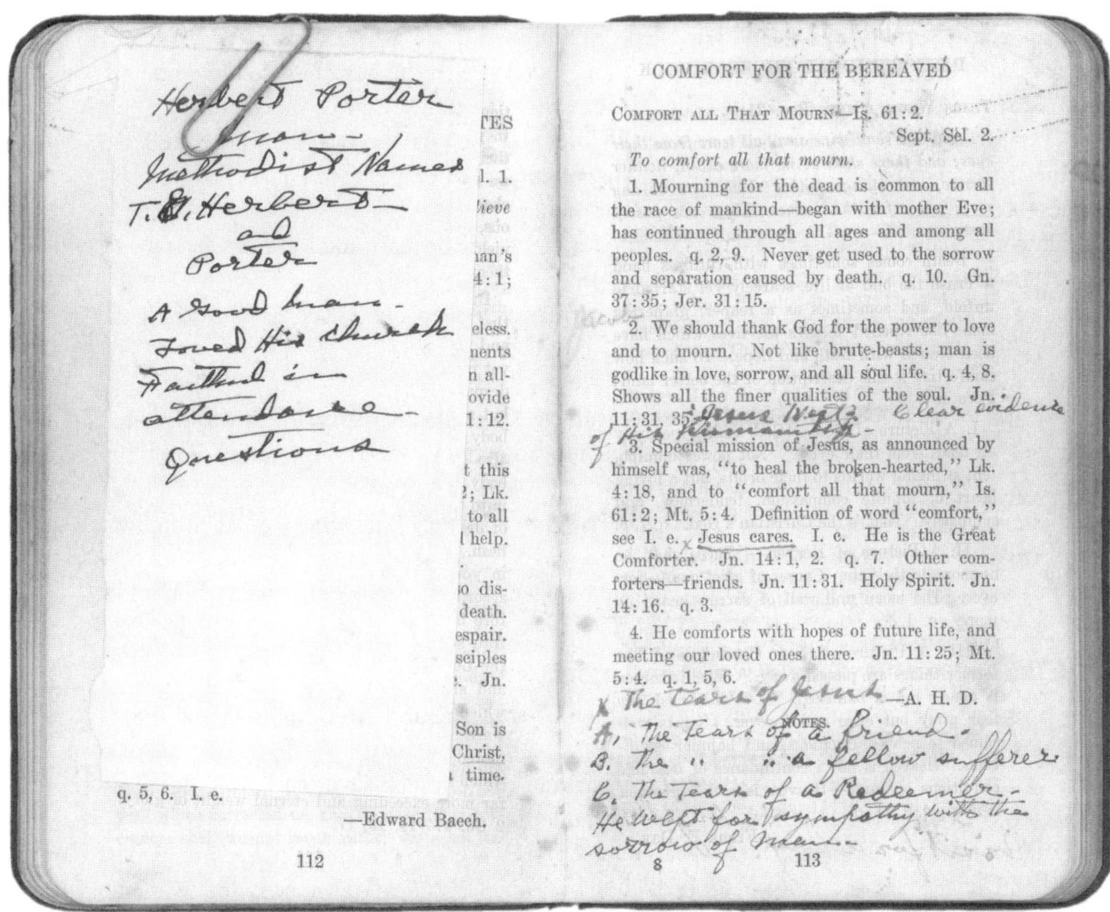

Herbert Porter
Sermon—
Methodist Names
T. H. Herbert—
and
Porter
A good man.
Loved His church
Faithful in
attendance—
Questions

q. 5, 6. I. e.

—Edward Baech.

112

COMFORT FOR THE BEREAVED

COMFORT ALL THAT MOURN—Is. 61:2.
Sept. Sel. 2.

To comfort all that mourn.

1. Mourning for the dead is common to all the race of mankind—began with mother Eve; has continued through all ages and among all peoples. q. 2, 9. Never get used to the sorrow and separation caused by death. q. 10. Gn. 37:35; Jer. 31:15.

2. We should thank God for the power to love and to mourn. Not like brute-beasts; man is godlike in love, sorrow, and all soul life. q. 4, 8. Shows all the finer qualities of the soul. Jn. 11:31, 35. Jesus wept. Clear evidence of His humanity.

3. Special mission of Jesus, as announced by himself was, "to heal the broken-hearted," Lk. 4:18, and to "comfort all that mourn," Is. 61:2; Mt. 5:4. Definition of word "comfort," see I. e. Jesus cares. I. e. He is the Great Comforter. Jn. 14:1, 2. q. 7. Other comforters—friends. Jn. 11:31. Holy Spirit. Jn. 14:16. q. 3.

4. He comforts with hopes of future life, and meeting our loved ones there. Jn. 11:25; Mt. 5:4. q. 1, 5, 6.

—A. H. D.

NOTES.

X The tears of Jesus
A. The tears of a friend.
B. The " " a fellow sufferer.
C. The tears of a Redeemer.
He wept for sympathy with the sorrow of man.

8 113

- He was known for his forceful presentation, often leaving the pulpit to walk around while he talks.
- Because he was also known for his ability to "raise troubled churches," the bishop assigned him to several churches that needed to increase enrollment, raise additional funds, or gain a more stable foundation.
- During some parts of his career, he and the family moved annually to assist churches, where congregations loved his deep, powerful voice.
- Although known as a dynamic speaker, around his family he was often silent; he and his son rarely spoke when driving to appointments across the state.
- While traveling, he often stopped at church members' homes where he has been invited to eat.
- Most of his church members were coal miners or connected to the mine.
- Services often included preaching and "witnessing," during which the men and women of the church told everyone "what the Lord has done for them that week."
- Music in the church often included old favorites such as "Rock of Ages" and "Amazing Grace," all sung from the *Cokesburg Hymn Book* .
- A typical Methodist church in his district had 100 members, but some large congregations reached 250 members, with the largest churches typically boasting a brick building with a steeple.
- As district superintendent, he was also responsible for coordinating the annual meeting, when pastors in his area gather to discuss changes in membership, giving, conversions, baptisms, and other church administrative matters.
- Many of the pastors within his district were circuit riders, traveling from one church to another on a typical weekend.
- James worked to establish a pension fund for ministers, who often had to live their final years on the unpredictable generosity of congregations.

- The telephone perplexed him, and he yelled, "Well, how's that?" when he answered it.
- He was known for his brief letters, often written on paper with the bottom torn off; while on one of his frequent trips, he recently wrote Edie, "I met two ladies today. One of them smiled."
- Edie often attended church conferences with James and she was also a leader in the Ladies' Aid, Women's Home Mission, Women's Foreign Mission, and the Temperance Union.
- James often told people, "I have everything but money."
- When congregations made special gifts to him for preaching or marrying a couple, he gave it to church missions funds.
- Congregations often gave him food, including corn and chickens, and even dress clothing in appreciation for his work.
- Many congregations had little to give
- The character of his congregations often changed based on the prosperity of the mning company that most of them worked for, and many miners moved every two to three years to search for better jobs.
- He believed that people should balance their lives, often saying; "Show me a good church worker, and I will show you a neglected family."
- He also believed in humor and encouraged the family to tell stories around the kitchen table.

Life in the Community: Huntington, West Virginia

- The economy of Huntington revolved around the Chesapeake and Ohio Railroad and the transportation of coal.
- Tons of coal passed through the city either by barge or the Chesapeake and Ohio Railroad.
- Jobs with the railroads were cherished positions, offering good, steady pay.
- International Nickel Company and West Virginia Steel were also critical to the economy of the area.
- Marshall College had a reputation for providing a quality education to the men and women of West Virginia, and it worked to shift its image from that of "primarily a teacher's college."
- The president of Marshall, James E. Allen, believed in the value of a liberal education and idealized the "universal man" as exemplified in the Italian Renaissance.
- The the college and community struggled to recover from a flood caused by the rampaging waters of the Ohio River; property losses were severe.
- The county high school, the only one in the area, operated on double shifts, since the county had too many students, too few buildings, and no ability to raise taxes.
- A highlight of the year was the annual band festival, when up to 50 high school bands came to Marshall College in Huntington to compete.
- Huntington was known as a "City of Churches," with most grouped downtown.
- City leaders were concerned about creeping immorality; some of the recent movies have shown kissing, and one newsstand sold a magazine called *Sexology, The Magazine of Sex Science* from under the counter.
- Skiing and ping-pong were popular, replacing the rage of miniature golf.
- West Virginia was one of the nation's largest suppliers of coal.
- Coal was not only plentiful; it was of very high quality.
- However, the coal seams in West Virginia were far from population centers, as 80 percent of West Virginia's miners lived in company-owned houses.
- Most were finished outside with weatherboard, usually nailed directly to the frame, with only paper for sheeting; only 38 percent were plastered, only 2.4 percent had tubs or showers, three percent had inside flush toilets, and 14 percent had running water.
- To maintain maximum control, most mines required their workers to rent company houses; those who chose to live outside the miners' camps were often the first to be laid off during the slow season.

- The company often owned everything in the camp; a popular saying was "The only thing the company don't own is God."
- Irregular employment, insecurity of job, lack of home ownership, frequent moving, payment in scrip, and high prices at the company store were considered part of the life of being a coal miner.
- Prices in the company-controlled stores were often two to three times higher than the prices charged by chain stores in town.
- The children of miners were often undernourished and many had pellagra and rickets; for many, milk was a special treat.
- Coal production peaked in 1918 at 523 million net tons, driven by war demands.
- Despite declining demand after World War I, West Virginia and Kentucky coal production continued to expand.
- Railroad profits were closely linked to coal production; in 1930, a quarter of railroad revenues were derived from coal transportation.
- Since the early 1920s, the West Virginia miners had been joining unions, often in large groups, to reduce the chance of company retaliation.
- Several major strikes were extremely bloody; newly unionized miners were murdered as a threat to other miners.
- By the late 1930s, many were discouraged; often the miners got fired by the company and received less support from the National Miner's Union than they had expected.

The Fight to Make America Liquor-Free Continues

Despite the passage of the Twenty-first Amendment, Christian Fundamentalists continued to work against the sale of intoxicating liquor. In the years leading up to 1940, Zachary Junger used radio technology and a Mexican station whose license extended into the heartland of America, to preach the story of alcohol abstinence.

Life at Home

- Zachary Junger was born in 1900, the third child of Nathan and Nannie Junger.
- Family lore recorded that his birth occurred in a dugout in the forks of the Tongue River three miles west of Paducah, Texas, but his pro-liquor enemies claimed that Zach was born on the dark side of the moon, weaned on dill pickle, and fed crabapples and green persimmons.
- Zach enjoyed saying that when the doctor held him by his ankles and spanked him to make him cry, he opened his lungs and mouth wide and found no reason to close them since.
- On nationwide radio broadcasts he was promoted as "the voice of temperance" and announced, "I have been protesting evil treatment from that day to this."
- His father deserted the family two months after he was born, so Zach's early years were spent in the home of his grandparents.
- West Texas was ranch country, composed mostly of cattle, coyotes, prairie dogs, rattlesnakes, horned frogs and dog owls.
- His mother took in washing to earn their keep.
- At the age of four, while on a trip with his aunt, Zach fell in love with a little cigar box cart and took it home with him as though it were his.
- When his theft was discovered, he had to return the toy and confess that he was a sinner and a sneak or get whipped "until his hide won't hold shucks."
- It was a seminal event that forever removed his temptation to steal anything, including the reputation of another.
- To help the family make ends meet, he and his siblings often walked the right-of-way of the railroad tracks in search of lumps of coal that had fallen from the railroad engines.
- Zach and his brother also picked up and delivered clothing for their mother to wash.
- Despite her hard life, his mother continued to believe in God, read her Bible daily, and regularly attended a primitive Baptist church.

Zachary Junger preached in churches and on the radio of the dangers of sinful alcohol.

- She sang hymns while she worked: "There Is a Great Day Coming" or "The Home Over There" or "When I Can Read My Title Clear."
- When Zach was nine, he got a job helping a blind local businessman who sold insurance and real estate.
- For $1.25 a week, before school each morning Zach would lead the man from his home to his office, and back home every evening, also fetching firewood, and running errands.
- When Zach was 12, his father returned and Zach's parents remarried and relocated to eastern Oklahoma near the Muddy Boggy River outside the town of Soper.
- There, Zach learned to work "like a grown-up," driving two yoke of oxen to haul logs or hewing ties for sale to the railroad.
- School and church disappeared from his life.
- The family moved frequently, living in shacks or tents.
- When Zach was 18, the family lived in Red River country and settled on a farm six miles north of Detroit, Texas.
- He rejoined the church and began his lifelong crusade to rid the world of alcohol.
- He also met a young woman who made her intentions clear, telling him, "If you don't intend to go to Sunday School and church and prayer meeting with me, you may as well take your hat and go home."
- Heeding the church teachings, Zach challenged the common practice of harvesting crops seven days a week, which violated the commandment to keep the Sabbath day holy.
- Shortly thereafter he was called to preach, which meant going back to school.
- With only a second-grade education, Zach went back to school "so green" he said, "I had to keep walking to keep from taking root and growing."
- He eventually attended Simmons College, also working odd jobs to pay bills and tuition.
- "We had beans and cornbread for dinner and at night we had cornbread and beans," he would tell his radio listeners; "If a doctor had tested our blood in those days, he would have found it at least 98 percent bean juice."
- While still in school, he took a pastorate call to Cuthbert, Texas, where once a month he led Sunday School, preached, sang and swept, and sometimes he was even paid.
- The First Baptist Church of Weatherford, Texas called him as he completed his degree in Bible study.
- While in Weatherford, he earned a master's degree from Brown University, and a disdain for modern theories that ridiculed the authority of the Bible or belief in blood atonement, bodily resurrection, or the second coming.

Life at Work

- Zachary Junger found a spiritual home in Stamford, Texas, where he took his wife, child, and newly-earned master's degree.
- With the First Baptist Church as his base, Zach fought "sin inside the church and outside it," opposing gambling, drinking, dancing, Sunday picture shows, and civic corruption of all kinds.
- He discovered the power of radio preaching, especially when the topic was liquor, and opened his own radio station, broadcasting only in Texas so an interstate radio license would not be required.
- His temperance work began in earnest when Al Smith ran for president, on a platform against national prohibition.
- A speech he gave to the Parker County Women's Christian Temperance Union (WCTU), was published in the local newspaper and as a pamphlet for national distribution, and earned him speaking requests from all corners of the state.
- Zach was called to a parish in Western Pennsylvania where the anti-drinking sentiment was strong and the range of the local radio station wide.
- He worked tirelessly to stop the passage of the Twenty-first Amendment to the Constitution, designed to nullify the passage of the Eighteenth Amendment.

President's Message

"WHAT DO YOU KNOW?"

Dear Comrades:

"What do you know?" "How much do you know?" These are questions asked recently by Ruth Cameron. This writer then discussed our thinking.

A daily newspaper that comes to our home carries each day a short quiz called "Horse Sense." I usually take time to check this to see if I do or do not see the ordinary things of life. Do I walk with my eyes open or half open? Do I think or day-dream?

It has been surprising to me how many ordinary questions I miss.

I wonder if this is not true regarding our knowledge of what the liquor traffic is, and what it is doing?

Do people realize that in Pennsylvania a licensee who accepts food, clothing, articles of any kind, in payment for liquor, is breaking the law?

The law states that liquor shall be sold for *cash*. Those who sell on time, and then cash relief or pay checks to pay for drinks already consumed are also breaking the law.

Do our taxpayers realize what it costs our state, in maintenance of institutions, to license liquor?

Do our Christian men and women know the amount spent for liquor in Pennsylvania last year?

Do they realize the increase in sales in 1939 over 1938?

Does the average automobile driver realize what one drink may mean to his driving?

Captain James Killip's $7,000 "Safety School on Wheels" is a scientific wonder. Your State President had the privilege, at the Tampa Fair, of testing her coördination, to prove whether she is or is not capable of driving a car.

"He that hath ears to hear, let him hear." May we take time to listen, especially to the words spoken to us in God's word.

"Give therefore thy servant an understanding heart." Solomon's request should be my request today.

What do I know? Not much.

Can I be helpful with what knowledge I have? Yes, if I am willing.

Yours for Pennsylvania homes,

ELLA B. BLACK,
State President.

- The Twentieth Amendment, which had given women the right to vote, also gave them the power to stop the "wets" by exercising their power at the ballot box.
- Using a public address system mounted on his car, Zach drove all across the western part of Pennsylvania preaching for prohibition and against sinful drunkenness.
- He spoke on public streets, in public parks, and on courthouse lawns.
- His favorite targets were the illegal liquor joints in the north of the town, just across the county line.

- Using his influence as a radio personality, he had these closed down.
- The city fathers and business leaders quickly appointed a committee to ask Zach to quiet down, and one pro-booze politician threatened to blow Zach's brains out.
- "Good prophets were put here to lead, not follow," he told himself. "They should be the creators of public opinion."
- Denounced as a troublemaker and a "political parson," Zach persisted, even when the church leadership declared that the liquor fight was a losing cause and should be avoided in the pulpit.
- With that, he abandoned the pulpit and took to the radio in earnest.
- In two daily 15-minute broadcasts, he spoke of the reasons that liquor should not be allowed back through the front door, highlighting the ways liquor unleashed domestic violence, infidelity, unemployment and poverty.
- He preached that the current failure of prohibition was not an endorsement of liquor, but the work of the devil.
- Zach prayed with his radio audience that politicians would reject the proposed Twenty-first Amendment to the Constitution-the first reversal of an amendment in history-so that America could remain dry forever.
- When the Twenty-first Amendment was ratified, Zach's time on the radio was curtailed-until he received a call from Mexico.
- A group of right-thinking Americans established a radio station with a strong, unregulated signal that could reach deep into the heartland of America, licensed by the Mexican Government according to the Havana Radio Treaty.
- Zach continued with his temperance talk to a nation who thought the prohibition issue had been settled.
- His voice reached most of the United States, Cuba, parts of South America and as far west as Hawaii, and mail poured in from all over the world.
- Based on the level of donations, many in the United States were not convinced the fight was over, and talk of another prohibition amendment was in the air, with many counties approving the halting alcohol sales in their communities.
- On the strength of his radio popularity, Zach the crusade, using his speaking circuit to tear the hide off John Barleycorn at every stop.

"The Curse of Strong Drink," The Booze Buster by Sam Morris

Strong drink caused Noah to commit the first sin following the flood.
Strong drink caused Lot to become the father of his own daughters' children.
Strong drink debauched and killed Nabal, the son of famous old Caleb.
Strong drink played a part in the story of David's sins of adultery and murder.
Strong drink was employed by Absolom when he killed his half-brother Amnon.
Strong drink caused the defeat of the Amalekites by David.
Strong drink led to the murder of Elah, King of Israel, by Zimri, who took the throne.
Strong drink caused the defeat of Ben-hadah by wicked old Ahab.
Strong drink caused the death of Belshazzar and the defeat and overthrow of mighty Babylon by Darius the Mede.
Strong drink is depicted in Proverbs as the instrument of the harlot when she wishes to entice men.
Too many people weep and wail about the awful booze conditions around them but never open their mouths in public against those conditions, and they never help the WCTU, the Anti-Saloon League, or the Prohibition Party. They vote for wet Parties and candidates, they trade where booze is sold, and they keep quiet "because they don't want to stir up trouble." They are dry in the mouth but wet every other way. They are prohibition scarecrows.

—Sam Morris, radio broadcast

"Repeal Clover Has Withered," by the Radio Evangel,
***The National Voice*, March 10, 1938**

It was the repeal of the dry laws that was to emancipate America from the economic dumps. It was going to help balance the budget for one thing; but it has, if anything, unbalanced the budget a whole lot worse than it was-during prohibition. Oh, we were going to be in clover just as soon as we got that terrible prohibition of legalized booze out of the way. Oh, yea!

And all we've gotten out of it is multiplied headaches, more relief, more misery, more hell, more lawlessness, more crime, more broken homes, more divorces, more sin, more whoopee. YES, and we were going to have liquor minus what they called the "old saloon." And what have we got? Well, we've got so many saloons now it would make Bathhouse John, Hinky, Dink and Joe Schmitzelheimer dizzy to try to count them. True, they have "dolled them up" to make them look like "what they ain't," but the sickening smell of booze clings to the taverns and inns just as it used to cling to the "old saloons." True, the lady bartender may have improved the atmosphere to some extent, but tell us, has it improved the thousands of girls that have been turned into bartenders?

The following statistics are from the *Christian Herald,* and should be of interest to our readers:

"We drank 15 gallons of liquor per capita in the U.S. in 1937. That means a liquor bill of about $5 billion.

"Out of the $5 billion, the government collected $0.12 on the dollar: a good stiff tax. But it wasn't enough; last year the government ran a deficit of $2,707,347,110.60!

"Taxes have not been reduced; they have been increased. Relief has remained practically stationary. The budget has not been balanced. The gross public debt has reached the highest point in the nation's history. "Add to that the cost of enforcing repeal, which is about the same cost of enforcing prohibition: $13 million.

Add also this: A billion dollars a year was diverted, during prohibition, to legitimate business channels; the relegalized traffic, in a 54-month period since 1932, has taken away from this legitimate business some $12,417,790,860. Add to that another $4 billion in costs of liquor-bred accidents, crime, destitution, disease and inefficiency. Add to that...

"You add it. I'm tired."

I would rather chase a hummingbird all over the field and never get in 10 feet of him than to chase a hornet three feet and grab him. Brother, when you vote for wet politicians you get stung every time.No politician can serve humanity and the liquor traffic at the same time. If the dry voters would oppose politicians who are wet, and refuse to wear wet party colors, we could lick the booze business to a frazzle.

—Sam Morris, radio broadcast, 1937

Pennsylvania Youth's Temperance Council, 27th Annual Convention and Leadership Training School, 1937

The purpose of the Youth's Temperance Council is to unite the Young People of the community, state and nation in a Christian Citizenship program, to build for total abstinence for the individual and sobriety for the nation.

PLEDGE

I promise, by the help of God, never to drink alcoholic liquors; never to use tobacco in any of its forms, and to use every means to fulfill the command: Keep thyself pure.

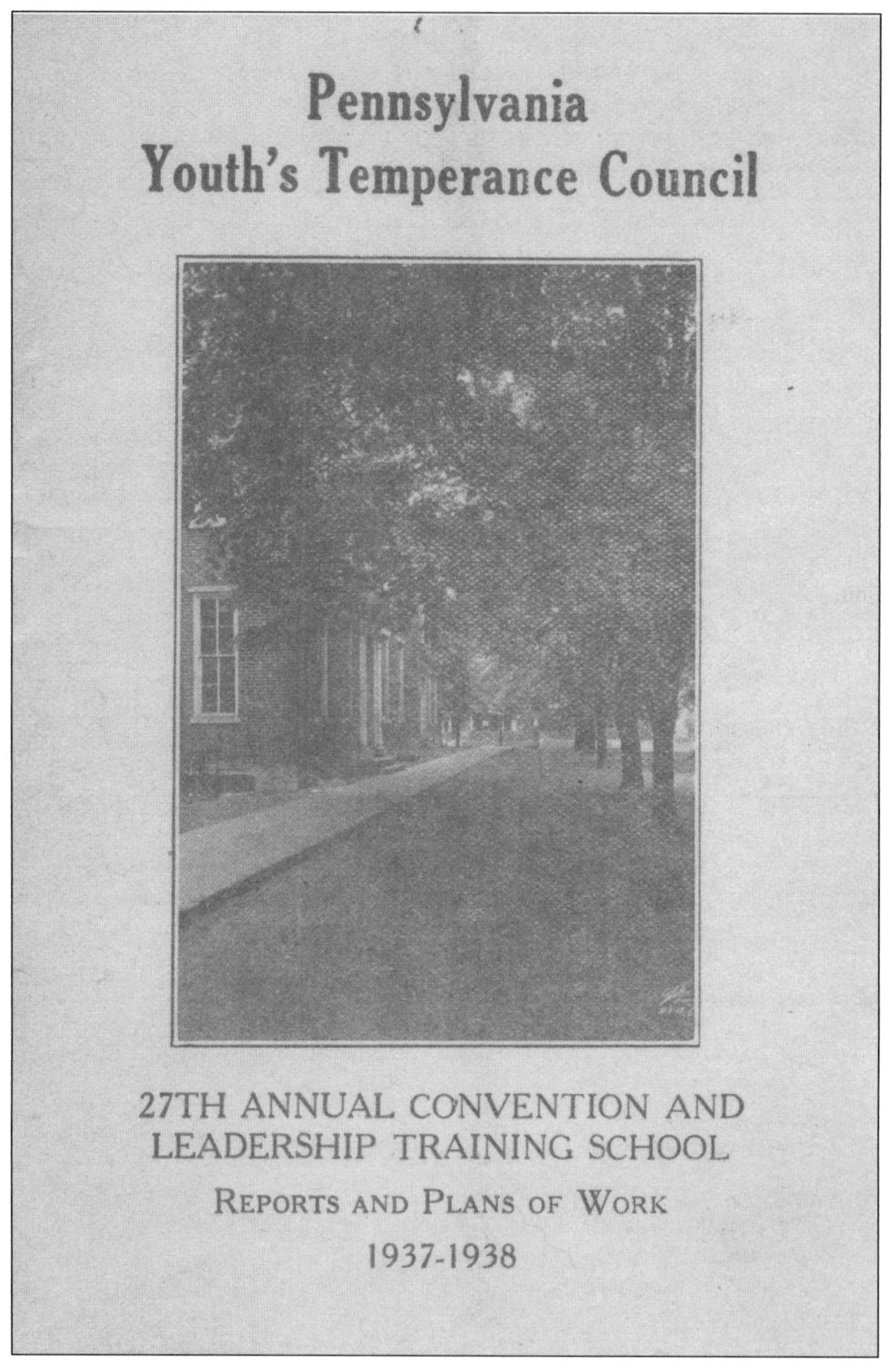
Pennsylvania
Youth's Temperance Council

27TH ANNUAL CONVENTION AND LEADERSHIP TRAINING SCHOOL

REPORTS AND PLANS OF WORK

1937-1938

The Man Who Made the Electric Light Bulb Affordable

William J. Woods' technological innovation transformed the light bulb from a luxury item to a household necessity by the year 1940. He was linked in history books to Thomas Alva Edison as the man who made Edison's invention affordable. When the war in Europe erupted, Woods' glassblowing technique was also used to manufacture Christmas ornaments, once the exclusive domain of German firms.

Life at Home

- William J. Woods arrived in Corning, New York to work as a glassblower at the Corning Glass Works.
- Raised in Martinsburg, Pennsylvania, his first job was as a boxer.
- Will learned the art of blowing glass at the Westinghouse Glass Works in western Pennsylvania, but wanted to work for the innovative Corning company.
- Corning Glass Works was the first company able to create a long-lasting glass bulb for Thomas Edison's amazing electric lamp.
- The factory's gaffers-glassblowers-mastered the technique, and the production of bulbs rose swiftly.
- Engineers developed a machine to speed bulb production and, with four bulb-blowing positions operating, the first "solid steel gaffer" produced 10 bulbs per minute.
- A second, fully automatic bulb-blowing machine ended the need for human assistants and produced 42 bulbs a minute.

Life at Work

William J. Woods' ribbon machine made electricity affordable.

- Will Woods was a Corning Glass Works production superintendent assigned to the Wellsboro, Pennsylvania, facility, with a restless, creative mind, and an idea for a new machine.
- The shovel he used to collect glass developed a hole in its blade, through which appeared a light-bulb shaped molten glob of glass.
- This sight inspired Will with the idea of blowing light bulb blanks through a hole in a metal plate.
- He reasoned that bulbs could be blown automatically by sagging a ribbon of glass through holes in a continuously moving belt of steel, then shape the glass with a puff of compressed air as molds came up from below.
- Like most ideas that contemplate radical change, his was met with skepticism and laughter by his fellow glassblowers.
- Working with the company's chief engineer in complete secrecy, Will obtained a piece of boiler plate with a hole in it from the machine shop.

- When company officials gathered to view the experiment, a glob of glass was spread over the hole and, as it sagged through, the blowhead and mold were applied and the bulb was formed.
- From a technical point of view, Will's idea was revolutionary.
- Bulbs and bottles had always been anchored by blowing rods or retaining rings as the hot glass took shape, and using gravity was a complete departure.

One of Corning's plants in Pennsylvania.

- Like human glassblowers, early machines had blown upward into the bubble to keep the top thin; Will's idea discarded the approach of imitating the gaffer.
- Will continued to work in secret in the company's Wellsboro plant, investing years of patient, inspired effort.
- By 1940, the ribbon machine that Will had conceived was popping out millions of bulbs annually.
- In a 10-year period, light bulbs moved from being a luxury item to a necessity.
- In another capacity, in 1940, the versatile ribbon machine at Corning made 300,000 crafted glass Christmas ornaments a day, typically supplied by glass craftsmen in Germany who were capable of producing 600 a day.
- Corning sent the Christmas ornament bulbs to several customers, the largest being Max Eckhart, who ran a company known as Shiny Brite, but plans to add silver inside the ornaments were shelved by wartime material shortages.
- America, on the brink of war, was still able to light the house, turn on the Christmas tree and savor the beauty of its ornaments, thanks to the ribbon machine.

Life in the Community: Corning, New York

- Corning, a business-oriented town, was named for Erastus Corning, an Albany, New York, financier and railroad executive who invested in the company that developed the community.
- The Corning area's first real industry was lumber.
- Corning Glass Works was originally founded in the Williamsburg section of Brooklyn, New York, but later moved its operations by barge to the city of Corning.
- Corning was one of several glass-cutting firms working in the area.

"Edison Memorial Bulb," *Northern Gazette*, Alberta Canada, December 10, 1937

The giant electric light bulb, 14 feet tall, which glows as a land beacon atop the $100,000 Edison Memorial Tower at Menlo Park, New Jersey, was completed by the Corning Glass Works.

It took a crew of expert glass workers eight months to complete this emblematic diadem for the tower, the task of laying the model out into curved "orange peel like" sections consuming the greater part of the elapsed time.

The 150-foot beacon will commemorate the invention of the incandescent electric light by Thomas Alva Edison, who in 1879 sent a rough sketch of his idea to Corning, asking that a bulb of glass of definite dimensions be blown.

This original glass bulb, enclosing Edison's carbon filament, became the world's first practical electric light. Corning's contribution to the Memorial commemorating the event is likewise notable since the 14-foot bulb is the first globular cast job in the history of the glass industry.

In preparing the bulb for shipment, more than 6,000 pounds of amber-tinted Pyrex glass were fitted over steel skeleton fashioned in a Bronx iron works and shipped to Corning. The bulb itself consists of 164 pieces of cast glass in a two-inch diamond pattern and is nine feet, six inches in diameter. The combined bulb and steel skeleton weighs six tons.

When finally set up, the giant bulb was transformed into a gleaming tower at night, casting its rays for miles about the surrounding Jersey countryside.

Electric Light Bulb Timeline

1809: Humphry Davy, an English chemist, invented the first electric light by connecting two wires to a battery and attaching a charcoal strip between the other ends of the wires; the charged carbon glowed, making the first arc lamp.

1820: Warren De la Rue enclosed a platinum coil in an evacuated tube and passed an electric current through it; the cost of the precious metal platinum made this innovation impractical for widespread use.

1835: James Bowman Lindsay demonstrated a constant electric lighting system using a prototype light bulb.

1850: Edward Shepard invented an electrical incandescent arc lamp using a charcoal filament; Joseph Wilson Swan started working with carbonized paper filaments the same year.

1854: Henricg Global, a German watchmaker, invented the first true light bulb using a carbonized bamboo filament placed inside a glass bulb.

1875: Herman Sprengel invented the mercury vacuum pump, making it possible to develop a practical electric light bulb; Henry Woodward and Matthew Evans patented a light bulb.

1878: Sir Joseph Wilson Swan, an English physicist, was the first person to invent a practical and longer-lasting electric light bulb (13.5 hours); Swan used a carbon fiber filament derived from cotton.

1879: Thomas Alva Edison invented a carbon filament that burned for 40 hours by placing his filament in an oxygenless bulb.

1880: Edison continued to improve his light bulb until it could last for over 1,200 hours using a bamboo-derived filament.

1903: Willis Whitney invented a metal-coated carbon filament that would not make the inside of a light bulb turn dark.

1906: The General Electric Company was the first to patent a method of making Tungsten filaments for use in incandescent light bulbs, though the filaments were costly.

1910: William David Coolidge invented an improved method of making Tungsten filaments, which outlasted all other types of filaments, and Coolidge made the cost practical.

1925: The first frosted light bulbs were produced.

1926: William Woods of Corning Glass Works invented the Ribbon Machine, which automated the process of creating a light bulb sleeve, dramatically reducing the cost of light bulbs.

1940: Corning Glass Works used the Ribbon Machine to create Christmas ornaments.

"Testimonial Dinner Given in Honor of Corning Glass Works," ***The Wellsboro Agitator*** **(Pennsylvania), September 18, 1940:** Wellsboro spokesmen expressed the appreciation of the community at a testimonial dinner of the Chamber of Commerce and service club members Monday evening at the Penn-Wells Hotel, "thanking" the Corning Glass Works for the establishment of its Christmas tree ornaments manufacturing department in Wellsboro, which has more than doubled the number of persons employed by the Wellsboro division.

Not since the height of the Tioga natural gas drilling at Moon Lake 10 years ago had a Chamber of Commerce meeting generated such enthusiasm in hundreds of persons gathered in the hotel dining room to hear the felicitations exchanged by Wellsboro citizens and Glass Works officials...

The Chamber of Commerce banquet was a "Christmas dinner," and the Corning Glass Works was "Santa Claus," Larry Woodin, official spokesman for the chamber, told the company officials. "Fourteen years ago," Mr. Woodin said, "when I came to Wellsboro, we had hundreds of people walking the streets, with no work, and wondering what they would do when Christmas time came. Now 1,000 people are working for Santa Claus, making Christmas ornaments; everybody has a job, and the town is booming. When Christmas comes around this year, it will be a real Christmas."

Corning Museum of Glass, Corning, New York.

Newspaper Sportswriter is Best Job in the World

In the erratic economy leading up to 1940, Americans coped by flocking to movie theaters and canonizing their sports heroes. Alan Miller had a ringside seat to some of the finest boxing, golf and tennis matches of the times, telling stories about victory and defeat to a sports-crazy nation on the brink of war.

Life at Home

- The son of an attorney and one of six children, Alan Miller was born in Pensacola, Florida.
- He dropped out of high school at age 16 and accepted a full-time sports writer's job at the *Pensacola Journal* newspaper, and served apprenticeships with the *Dallas Dispatch* and the *Minneapolis* News before turning 20 years old.
- After serving in the Army in Europe, he went to New York City and was hired by the *New York Daily Mail* as a sports reporter specializing in tennis.
- Tennis was capturing nationwide attention as America's men had begun challenging the best France and England had to offer.
- After a few years and an ownership change, the *Daily Mail* folded and Al returned to Europe with four weeks' pay and $500 savings.
- Once his $500 was gone, Al landed a job at the *New York Herald,* Paris edition.
- There he covered The International Lawn Tennis Challenge in Paris, Wimbledon in London, and watched America tennis greats "Big" Bill Tilden and "Little" Bill Johnston develop into international stars.
- The athletic Tilden brought a swashbuckling, masculine style to the game that helped erase its image as a sport for upper-class dilettantes.

Sportswriter Alan Miller and his wife Irene.

- At the *New York Herald* Al gained experience as a rewrite man, night editor, headline writer, reporter and copy reader.
- After nine years in Paris, he returned to the United States and joined the sports department of the *New York Herald Tribune*.
- Al loved the noisy clatter of a fully staffed newsroom and cherished the skill required to dictate the essence of a great fight or game to a rewrite man without missing a fact, adjective or comma.
- At the sport's desk, a deadline for one of the newspaper's multiple editions always lurked close by.
- While fans celebrated the latest victory, Al and his ilk were writing for the unseen readers, attempting to "take" them to the game and help them sense its excitement.
- Once his stories were in press, he hung out sipping whiskey, talking sports and waiting for the early edition to roll off the presses between 2:00 and 4:00 a.m.
- He typically reported to the office between lunch and 4 p.m.
- He and his wife Irene, an American-born pianist he met in Paris, lived in an apartment in upper Manhattan in New York City.

- The couple decorated their home in the art deco style which was born in Paris in the 1920s, exemplified by geometric shapes and patterns celebrating modern technology and industry.
- Telephones, housewares, furniture and even cars were created in the art deco style.
- Regular movies were the most popular leisure pastime for most Americans at the time, and Al and Irene were devoted to film.
- The couple was especially proud of their new Stewart Warner Concert Grand Sheridan model radio phonograph cabinet.
- Together they listened to Orson Welles's radio show of the "invasion" from Mars based on H. G. Wells's *War of the Worlds*, sounding so authentic, that people believed Martians had actually landed in New Jersey.

Life at Work

- Early in his career, Al Miller came to the conclusion that reporters were not born, but made by learning through trial and error.
- Getting the facts straight was just the beginning; getting the correct tone and color within the context of a story was the real goal.

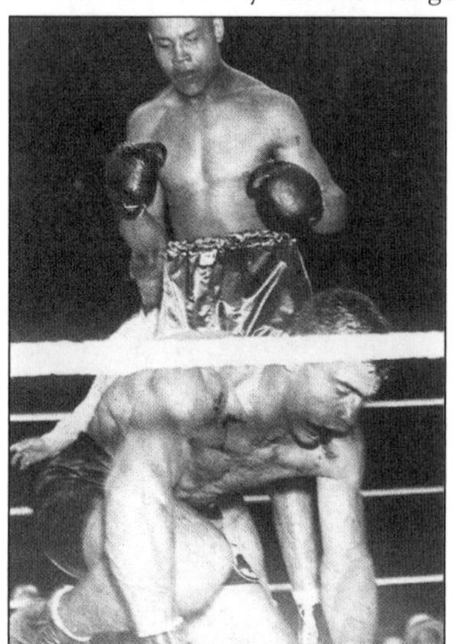

Al was spattered with blood…

- Sports writing was a special calling and Al fully understood that he lived in a Golden Age of sports and sportswriters.
- Ring Lardner, Grantland Rice, Damon Runyon, W. O. McGeehan, Paul Gallico, and Heywood Broun were all tough competitors in the daily sportswriters' game.
- These writers were given a great deal of leeway in terms of style and content, and some sportswriters wrote cynical, witty prose while others wrote "Gee Whiz" more romantic stories that celebrated an athlete's every move.
- At some papers, hero worship dominated sports journalism and Al hated it.
- The business was littered with drunks and hacks, and some sportswriters took money under the table to report only good news.
- He surmised that younger reporters suffered from a lack of supervision in the modern era of sports writing and tended to be more interested in the byline than the content of the story.
- His real awakening to good writing occurred when he discovered Bernard Darwin, the grandson of Charles Darwin, who wrote for the *London Times*.

…and threatened with a tennis racket.

- Although Darwin was a golf reporter, he possessed the ability to weave fascinating facts and historical footnotes into the tapestry of his writing.
- Bernard Darwin and Neville Carlos, who reported on cricket, provided high school dropout Al with his education in journalism.
- By relating events as they encountered them, Darwin and Carlos wrote what they thought, unlike the columnist, who attempted to tell the reader what to think.
- New York City was a daily sports extravaganza and thanks to his front seat as a reporter, Al was splattered with blood during prize fights,

soaked to the bone watching major league baseball in the rain, and threatened with a tennis racket by an athlete unappreciative of his writing style.

- Al briefly worked as a columnist with access to any event, but soon decided to direct his energy toward larger, more detailed pieces-especially concerning golf and tennis.
- He gained a reputation for being superbly prepared and capable of conducting in-depth interviews.
- He liked to think of himself as a "word gymnast," but told most people he was simply a "despoiler of good ink."
- After briefly covering hockey at Madison Square Garden, his editor suggested that he write about the forgotten athletes in retirement, which marked the turning point in his career.
- Al's features included retired athletes such as Olympic medalist Johnny Hayes, Giants' second baseman Larry Doyle, and miracle Braves' pitcher Dick Rudolph.
- When Al caught up with them, Hayes owned a tea and coffee shop in Manhattan and Dick Rudolph was an undertaker.
- Al's most popular story concerned Sam Langford, a black boxer who fought in the days before Jack Johnson.
- Langford, who was not allowed to vie for the title because of his race, was in a Harlem tenement, blind and living in squalor.
- The story, picked up by the Associated Press, was so moving that Langford received cash donations from all over the country, which he used to set up a fund for former fighters suffering from diabetes.

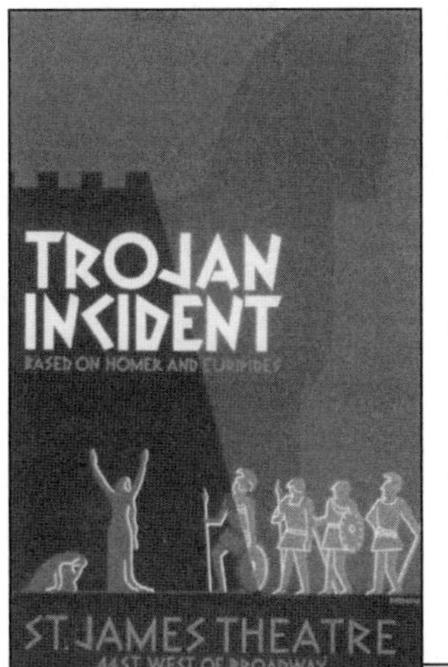

Life in the Community: New York, New York

- Al Miller loved a good game and a good conversation.
- While in Paris he met the up-and-coming Ernest Hemingway and attended parties at the house of Gertrude Stein.
- In New York he was given a window to the world of sports, a free pass to the greatest shows in a city that loved to show off.
- He watched Joe Louis regain the heavyweight championship of the world by knocking out Max Schmeling in the first round at Yankee Stadium on June 23, 1938.
- He attended the first National Invitational Basketball Tournament held at Madison Square Garden where Temple defeated Colorado 60-36.
- He was at the light heavyweight bout at Madison Square Garden when Henry Armstrong became the first man to hold three titles in three weight classes at once.
- He saw amateur Don Budge become the first player to complete the Grand Slam in tennis with titles of all four championships.
- Al witnessed professional football come of age as the New York Giants won the National Football League championship game against the Green Bay Packers 23-17 before 48,120 people in December 1938.
- Despite an ongoing economic depression, New York City was a Mecca for sports lovers: New York Yankees dominated baseball; Polo Grounds were regular hosts to National Football League championships; top-level tennis was regularly available; college basketball was coming into its own; and boat racing regularly demanded coverage.

New York City offered a variety of things to do.

The nine tables that follow are reprinted from the actual 1940 census, for the city of New York. They include actual data on race, percentage of voting population, school attendance, number of school years completed, foreign born, and employment of workers 14 years and older by job, industry and race. In addition to being incredibly fascinating, these facts help to strengthen and visualize the actual environment in which Alan Miller lived and worked.

Table C-35.—AGE, BY RACE AND SEX, FOR THE CITY OF NEW YORK: 1940 AND 1930

[Figures for white population in 1930 revised to include Mexicans classified with "Other races" in the 1930 reports. Percent not shown where less than 0.1 or where base is less than 100]

AGE AND CENSUS YEAR	ALL CLASSES			NATIVE WHITE			FOREIGN-BORN WHITE			NEGRO			OTHER RACES		
	Total	Male	Female	Total	Male	Female	Total	Male	Female	Total	Male	Female	Total	Male	Female
All ages: 1940	7,454,995	3,676,293	3,778,702	4,897,481	2,397,164	2,500,317	2,080,020	1,057,839	1,022,181	458,444	205,727	252,717	19,050	15,563	3,487
Under 5 years	433,894	221,415	212,479	400,656	204,900	195,756	2,583	1,310	1,273	29,691	14,706	14,985	964	499	465
5 to 9 years	470,556	238,798	231,758	430,383	218,849	211,534	6,101	3,038	3,063	33,134	16,442	16,692	938	469	469
10 to 14 years	561,108	283,453	277,655	510,778	258,847	251,931	13,642	6,832	6,810	35,848	17,294	18,554	840	480	360
15 to 19 years	606,942	300,717	306,225	536,926	267,425	269,501	34,486	17,163	17,323	34,678	15,574	19,104	852	555	297
20 to 24 years	649,153	304,862	344,291	566,019	270,434	295,585	41,165	18,615	22,550	41,099	15,251	25,848	870	562	308
25 to 29 years	697,153	322,558	374,595	547,673	259,948	287,725	96,917	41,380	55,537	50,978	20,008	30,970	1,585	1,222	363
30 to 34 years	691,027	331,782	359,245	464,272	226,078	238,194	173,415	81,972	91,443	51,180	21,924	29,256	2,160	1,808	352
35 to 39 years	669,421	330,950	338,471	362,781	178,358	184,423	251,438	126,448	124,990	52,186	23,418	28,768	3,016	2,726	290
40 to 44 years	628,714	317,471	311,243	302,549	149,293	153,256	281,569	145,301	136,268	41,789	20,299	21,490	2,807	2,578	229
45 to 49 years	550,743	282,769	267,974	233,673	115,648	118,025	284,754	150,517	134,237	30,381	14,802	15,579	1,935	1,802	133
50 to 54 years	467,020	243,321	223,699	173,898	84,449	89,449	270,272	147,338	122,934	21,468	10,251	11,217	1,382	1,283	99
55 to 59 years	346,871	178,162	168,709	120,929	57,354	63,575	210,936	113,428	97,508	14,251	6,675	7,576	755	705	50
60 to 64 years	267,974	132,668	135,306	95,411	43,605	51,806	162,750	84,260	78,490	9,285	4,311	4,974	528	492	36
65 to 69 years	190,439	89,275	101,164	69,641	29,909	39,732	114,028	56,461	57,567	6,521	2,676	3,845	249	229	20
70 to 74 years	120,675	54,474	66,201	43,812	17,959	25,853	73,558	35,194	38,364	3,197	1,219	1,978	108	102	6
75 years and over	103,305	43,618	59,687	38,080	14,108	23,972	62,406	28,582	33,824	2,758	877	1,881	61	51	10
Under 1 year	81,889	41,795	40,094	76,006	38,897	37,109	123	57	66	5,576	2,748	2,828	184	93	91
5 years	88,368	44,847	43,521	80,891	41,165	39,726	980	474	506	6,323	3,120	3,203	174	88	86
14 years	113,310	56,949	56,361	102,350	51,621	50,729	3,732	1,851	1,881	7,065	3,376	3,689	163	101	62
15 years	114,889	57,734	57,155	103,876	52,455	51,421	3,986	1,935	2,001	6,910	3,234	3,676	167	110	57
16 and 17 years	238,386	118,975	119,411	212,614	106,441	106,173	11,953	6,056	5,897	13,474	6,261	7,213	345	217	128
21 years and over	5,254,633	2,570,647	2,683,986	2,908,645	1,393,545	1,515,100	2,013,349	1,024,793	988,556	317,355	138,864	178,491	15,284	13,445	1,839
All ages: 1930	6,930,446	3,472,956	3,457,490	4,294,196	2,123,577	2,170,619	2,295,181	1,180,947	1,114,234	327,706	156,968	170,738	13,363	11,464	1,899
Under 5 years	535,600	272,438	263,162	502,444	255,839	246,605	5,573	2,817	2,756	26,920	13,431	13,489	663	351	312
5 to 9 years	577,284	291,782	285,502	530,497	268,571	261,926	21,884	11,051	10,833	24,365	11,894	12,471	538	266	272
10 to 14 years	575,300	290,263	285,037	531,036	268,341	262,695	25,309	12,780	12,529	18,662	8,987	9,675	293	155	138
15 to 19 years	599,286	293,740	305,546	510,342	252,903	257,439	67,431	31,397	36,034	21,120	9,169	11,951	393	271	122
20 to 24 years	687,417	327,734	359,683	485,070	235,085	249,985	162,618	75,099	87,519	38,658	16,664	21,994	1,071	886	185
25 to 29 years	695,984	341,448	354,536	393,504	191,999	201,505	251,671	124,777	126,894	48,661	22,779	25,882	2,148	1,893	255
30 to 34 years	649,576	327,685	321,891	329,596	162,429	167,167	277,079	142,987	134,092	40,533	20,121	20,412	2,368	2,148	220
35 to 39 years	621,248	319,859	301,389	272,926	135,538	137,388	309,408	163,942	145,466	36,924	18,539	18,385	1,990	1,840	150
40 to 44 years	518,588	272,868	245,720	199,377	98,857	100,520	292,075	159,583	132,492	25,515	12,909	12,606	1,621	1,519	102
45 to 49 years	422,063	219,600	202,463	151,843	74,032	77,811	250,204	135,056	115,148	19,057	9,607	9,450	959	905	54
50 to 54 years	340,807	175,346	165,461	126,094	61,130	64,964	202,176	107,610	94,566	11,922	6,032	5,890	615	574	41
55 to 59 years	246,277	123,128	123,149	93,257	44,458	48,799	146,325	75,200	71,125	6,365	3,155	3,210	330	315	15
60 to 64 years	190,527	92,494	98,033	69,444	31,886	37,558	117,138	58,732	58,406	3,767	1,708	2,059	178	168	10
65 to 69 years	127,356	60,451	66,905	45,149	20,131	25,018	79,787	39,351	40,436	2,331	891	1,440	89	78	11
70 to 74 years	77,327	35,866	41,461	28,853	12,401	16,452	47,205	22,986	24,219	1,236	448	788	33	31	2
75 years and over	59,819	25,243	34,576	20,918	8,109	12,809	37,703	16,721	20,982	1,184	400	784	14	13	1
Not reported	5,987	3,011	2,976	3,846	1,868	1,978	1,595	858	737	486	234	252	60	51	9
Under 1 year	100,398	51,178	49,220	94,819	48,409	46,410	251	125	126	5,176	2,569	2,607	152	75	77
5 years	112,108	56,813	55,295	104,372	53,003	51,369	2,257	1,125	1,132	5,340	2,606	2,734	139	79	60
14 years	112,112	56,347	55,765	103,303	51,952	51,351	5,242	2,647	2,595	3,518	1,719	1,799	49	29	20
15 years	112,305	56,540	55,765	102,155	51,562	50,593	6,771	3,375	3,396	3,325	1,572	1,753	54	31	23
16 and 17 years	232,443	114,770	117,673	202,327	100,571	101,756	22,683	10,823	11,860	7,319	3,308	4,011	114	68	46
21 years and over	4,511,021	2,262,581	2,248,440	2,120,168	1,029,912	1,090,256	2,149,455	1,111,448	1,038,007	230,069	110,911	119,158	11,329	10,310	1,019
Percent: 1940	100.0	100.0	100.0	100.0	100.0	100.0	100.0	100.0	100.0	100.0	100.0	100.0	100.0	100.0	100.0
Under 5 years	5.8	6.0	5.6	8.2	8.5	7.8	0.1	0.1	0.1	6.5	7.1	5.9	5.1	3.2	13.3
5 to 9 years	6.3	6.5	6.1	8.8	9.1	8.5	0.3	0.3	0.3	7.2	8.0	6.6	4.9	3.0	13.4
10 to 14 years	7.5	7.7	7.3	10.4	10.8	10.1	0.7	0.6	0.7	7.8	8.4	7.3	4.4	3.1	10.3
15 to 19 years	8.1	8.2	8.1	11.0	11.2	10.8	1.7	1.6	1.7	7.6	7.6	7.6	4.5	3.6	8.5
20 to 24 years	8.7	8.3	9.1	11.6	11.3	11.8	2.0	1.8	2.2	9.0	7.4	10.2	4.6	3.6	8.8
25 to 29 years	9.4	8.8	9.9	11.2	10.8	11.5	4.7	3.9	5.4	11.1	9.7	12.3	8.3	7.9	10.4
30 to 34 years	9.3	9.0	9.5	9.5	9.4	9.5	8.3	7.7	8.9	11.2	10.7	11.6	11.3	11.6	10.1
35 to 39 years	9.0	9.0	9.0	7.4	7.4	7.4	12.1	12.0	12.2	11.4	11.4	11.4	15.8	17.5	8.3
40 to 44 years	8.4	8.6	8.2	6.2	6.2	6.1	13.5	13.7	13.3	9.1	9.9	8.5	14.7	16.6	6.6
45 to 49 years	7.4	7.7	7.1	4.8	4.8	4.7	13.7	14.2	13.1	6.6	7.2	6.2	10.2	11.6	3.8
50 to 54 years	6.3	6.6	5.9	3.6	3.5	3.6	13.0	13.9	12.0	4.7	5.0	4.4	7.3	8.2	2.8
55 to 59 years	4.7	4.8	4.5	2.5	2.4	2.5	10.1	10.7	9.5	3.1	3.2	3.0	4.0	4.5	1.4
60 to 64 years	3.6	3.6	3.6	1.9	1.8	2.1	7.8	8.0	7.7	2.0	2.1	2.0	2.8	3.2	1.0
65 to 69 years	2.6	2.4	2.7	1.4	1.2	1.6	5.5	5.3	5.6	1.4	1.3	1.5	1.3	1.5	0.6
70 to 74 years	1.6	1.5	1.8	0.9	0.7	1.0	3.5	3.3	3.8	0.7	0.6	0.8	0.6	0.7	0.2
75 years and over	1.4	1.2	1.6	0.8	0.6	1.0	3.0	2.7	3.3	0.6	0.4	0.7	0.3	0.3	0.3
Under 1 year	1.1	1.1	1.1	1.6	1.6	1.5	-	-	-	1.2	1.3	1.1	1.0	0.6	2.6
5 years	1.2	1.2	1.2	1.7	1.7	1.6	-	-	-	1.4	1.5	1.3	0.9	0.6	2.5
14 years	1.5	1.5	1.5	2.1	2.2	2.0	0.2	0.2	0.2	1.5	1.6	1.5	0.9	0.6	1.8
15 years	1.5	1.6	1.5	2.1	2.2	2.1	0.2	0.2	0.2	1.5	1.6	1.5	0.9	0.7	1.6
16 and 17 years	3.2	3.2	3.2	4.3	4.4	4.2	0.6	0.6	0.6	2.9	3.0	2.9	1.8	1.4	3.7
21 years and over	70.5	69.9	71.0	59.4	58.1	60.6	96.8	96.9	96.7	69.2	67.5	70.6	80.2	86.4	52.7
Percent: 1930	100.0	100.0	100.0	100.0	100.0	100.0	100.0	100.0	100.0	100.0	100.0	100.0	100.0	100.0	100.0
Under 5 years	7.7	7.8	7.6	11.7	12.0	11.4	0.2	0.2	0.2	8.2	8.6	7.9	5.0	3.1	16.4
5 to 9 years	8.3	8.4	8.3	12.4	12.6	12.1	1.0	0.9	1.0	7.4	7.6	7.3	4.0	2.3	14.3
10 to 14 years	8.3	8.4	8.2	12.4	12.6	12.1	1.1	1.1	1.1	5.7	5.7	5.7	2.2	1.4	7.3
15 to 19 years	8.6	8.5	8.8	11.9	11.9	11.9	2.9	2.7	3.2	6.4	5.8	7.0	2.9	2.4	6.4
20 to 24 years	9.9	9.4	10.4	11.3	11.1	11.5	7.1	6.4	7.9	11.8	10.6	12.9	8.0	7.7	9.7
25 to 29 years	10.0	9.8	10.3	9.2	9.0	9.3	11.0	10.6	11.4	14.8	14.5	15.2	16.1	16.5	13.4
30 to 34 years	9.4	9.4	9.3	7.7	7.6	7.7	12.1	12.1	12.0	12.4	12.8	12.0	17.7	18.7	11.6
35 to 39 years	9.0	9.2	8.7	6.4	6.4	6.3	13.5	13.9	13.1	11.3	11.8	10.8	14.9	16.1	7.9
40 to 44 years	7.5	7.9	7.1	4.6	4.7	4.6	12.7	13.5	11.9	7.8	8.2	7.4	12.1	13.3	5.4
45 to 49 years	6.1	6.3	5.9	3.5	3.5	3.6	10.9	11.4	10.3	5.8	6.1	5.5	7.2	7.9	2.8
50 to 54 years	4.9	5.0	4.8	2.9	2.9	3.0	8.8	9.1	8.5	3.6	3.8	3.4	4.6	5.0	2.2
55 to 59 years	3.6	3.5	3.6	2.2	2.1	2.2	6.4	6.4	6.4	1.9	2.0	1.9	2.5	2.7	0.8
60 to 64 years	2.7	2.7	2.8	1.6	1.5	1.7	5.1	5.0	5.2	1.1	1.1	1.2	1.3	1.5	0.5
65 to 69 years	1.8	1.7	1.9	1.1	0.9	1.2	3.5	3.3	3.6	0.7	0.6	0.8	0.7	0.7	0.6
70 to 74 years	1.1	1.0	1.2	0.7	0.6	0.8	2.1	1.9	2.2	0.4	0.3	0.5	0.2	0.3	0.1
75 years and over	0.9	0.7	1.0	0.5	0.4	0.6	1.6	1.4	1.9	0.4	0.3	0.5	0.1	0.1	0.1
Not reported	0.1	0.1	0.1	0.1	0.1	0.1	0.1	0.1	0.1	0.1	0.1	0.1	0.4	0.4	0.5
Under 1 year	1.4	1.5	1.4	2.2	2.3	2.1	-	-	-	1.6	1.6	1.5	1.1	0.7	4.1
5 years	1.6	1.6	1.6	2.4	2.5	2.4	0.1	0.1	0.1	1.6	1.7	1.6	1.0	0.7	3.2
14 years	1.6	1.6	1.6	2.4	2.4	2.4	0.2	0.2	0.2	1.1	1.1	1.1	0.4	0.3	1.1
15 years	1.6	1.6	1.6	2.4	2.4	2.3	0.3	0.3	0.3	1.0	1.0	1.0	0.4	0.3	1.2
16 and 17 years	3.4	3.3	3.4	4.7	4.7	4.7	1.0	0.9	1.1	2.2	2.1	2.3	0.9	0.6	2.4
21 years and over	65.1	65.1	65.0	49.4	48.5	50.2	93.7	94.1	93.2	70.2	70.7	69.8	84.8	89.9	53.7

Table C-36.—RACE, BY NATIVITY AND SEX, FOR THE CITY OF NEW YORK: 1940 AND 1930

[Figures for white population in 1930 have been revised to include Mexicans who were classified with "Other races" in the 1930 reports. Percent not shown where less than 0.1 or where base is less than 100. Sex ratio not shown where number of females is less than 100]

SEX, NATIVITY, AND CENSUS YEAR	All classes	White	Negro	Other races	OTHER RACES: Indian	Chinese	Japanese	All other	PERCENT BY RACE: All classes	White	Negro	Other races	PERCENT BY NATIVITY: All classes	White	Negro	Indian	Chinese	Japanese
TOTAL																		
1940	7,454,995	6,977,501	458,444	19,050	1,064	12,758	2,087	3,146	100.0	93.6	6.1	0.3	100.0	100.0	100.0	100.0	100.0	100.0
Native	5,316,338	4,897,481	410,026	8,831	638	4,745	631	2,817	100.0	92.1	7.7	0.2	71.3	70.2	89.4	60.0	37.2	30.2
Foreign born	2,138,657	2,080,020	48,418	10,219	426	8,008	1,456	329	100.0	97.3	2.3	0.5	28.7	29.8	10.6	40.0	62.8	69.8
1930	6,930,446	6,589,377	327,706	13,363	391	8,414	2,356	2,202	100.0	95.1	4.7	0.2	100.0	100.0	100.0	100.0	100.0	100.0
Native	4,571,760	4,294,196	272,952	4,612	294	1,926	536	1,856	100.0	93.9	6.0	0.1	66.0	65.2	83.3	75.2	22.9	22.8
Foreign born	2,358,686	2,295,181	54,754	8,751	97	6,488	1,820	346	100.0	97.3	2.3	0.4	34.0	34.8	16.7	24.8	77.1	77.2
MALE																		
1940	3,676,293	3,455,003	205,727	15,563	590	10,967	1,470	2,536	100.0	94.0	5.6	0.4	100.0	100.0	100.0	100.0	100.0	100.0
Native	2,585,482	2,397,164	181,870	6,448	321	3,547	325	2,255	100.0	92.7	7.0	0.2	70.3	69.4	88.4	54.4	32.3	22.1
Foreign born	1,090,811	1,057,839	23,857	9,115	269	7,420	1,145	281	100.0	97.0	2.2	0.8	29.7	30.6	11.6	45.6	67.7	77.9
1930	3,472,956	3,304,524	156,968	11,464	212	7,549	1,748	1,955	100.0	95.2	4.5	0.3	100.0	100.0	100.0	100.0	100.0	100.0
Native	2,255,955	2,123,577	128,891	3,487	152	1,414	275	1,646	100.0	94.1	5.7	0.2	65.0	64.3	82.1	71.7	18.7	15.7
Foreign born	1,217,001	1,180,947	28,077	7,977	60	6,135	1,473	309	100.0	97.0	2.3	0.7	35.0	35.7	17.9	28.3	81.3	84.3
FEMALE																		
1940	3,778,702	3,522,498	252,717	3,487	474	1,786	617	610	100.0	93.2	6.7	0.1	100.0	100.0	100.0	100.0	100.0	100.0
Native	2,730,856	2,500,317	228,156	2,383	317	1,198	306	562	100.0	91.6	8.4	0.1	72.3	71.0	90.3	66.9	67.1	49.6
Foreign born	1,047,846	1,022,181	24,561	1,104	157	588	311	48	100.0	97.6	2.3	0.1	27.7	29.0	9.7	33.1	32.9	50.4
1930	3,457,490	3,284,853	170,738	1,899	179	865	608	247	100.0	95.0	4.9	0.1	100.0	100.0	100.0	100.0	100.0	100.0
Native	2,315,805	2,170,619	144,061	1,125	142	512	261	210	100.0	93.7	6.2	-	67.0	66.1	84.4	79.3	59.2	42.9
Foreign born	1,141,685	1,114,234	26,677	774	37	353	347	37	100.0	97.6	2.3	0.1	33.0	33.9	15.6	20.7	40.8	57.1
MALES PER 100 FEMALES																		
1940	97.3	98.1	81.4	446.3	124.5	614.1	238.2	415.7	-	-	-	-	-	-	-	-	-	-
Native	94.7	95.9	79.7	270.6	101.3	296.1	106.2	401.2	-	-	-	-	-	-	-	-	-	-
Foreign born	104:1	103.5	97.1	825.6	171.3	1,261.9	368.2	-	-	-	-	-	-	-	-	-	-	-
1930	100.4	100.6	91.9	603.7	118.4	872.7	287.5	791.5	-	-	-	-	-	-	-	-	-	-
Native	97.4	97.8	89.5	310.0	107.0	276.2	105.4	783.8	-	-	-	-	-	-	-	-	-	-
Foreign born	106.6	106.0	105.2	1,030.6	-	1,738.0	424.5	-	-	-	-	-	-	-	-	-	-	-

Table C-37.—POTENTIAL VOTING POPULATION, BY CITIZENSHIP, RACE, NATIVITY, AND SEX, FOR THE CITY OF NEW YORK: 1940 AND 1930

[Figures for white population in 1930 have been revised to include Mexicans who were classified with "Other races" in the 1930 reports. Percent not shown where less than 0.1]

CITIZENSHIP, RACE, AND NATIVITY	TOTAL POPULATION (ALL AGES): Total number 1940	Total number 1930	Percent 1940	Percent 1930	Male 1940	Male 1930	Female 1940	Female 1930	POPULATION 21 YEARS OLD AND OVER: Total number 1940	Total number 1930	Percent 1940	Percent 1930	Male 1940	Male 1930	Female 1940	Female 1930
Total	7,454,995	6,930,446	100.0	100.0	3,676,293	3,472,956	3,778,702	3,457,490	5,254,633	4,511,021	100.0	100.0	2,570,647	2,262,581	2,683,986	2,248,440
Percent citizen	-	-	89.0	83.7	-	-	-	-	-	-	85.2	77.2	-	-	-	-
Percent alien and citiz. not rptd.	-	-	11.0	16.3	-	-	-	-	-	-	14.8	22.8	-	-	-	-
Citizen	6,632,398	5,802,229	100.0	100.0	3,334,268	2,944,082	3,298,130	2,858,147	4,474,689	3,483,111	100.0	100.0	2,249,729	1,780,797	2,224,960	1,702,314
White—Native	4,897,481	4,294,196	73.8	74.0	2,397,164	2,123,577	2,500,317	2,170,619	2,908,645	2,120,158	65.0	60.9	1,393,545	1,029,912	1,515,100	1,090,256
Naturalized	1,298,360	1,217,790	19.6	21.0	738,635	680,388	559,725	537,402	1,272,872	1,168,689	28.4	33.6	725,888	656,236	546,984	512,453
Negro—Native	410,026	272,952	6.2	4.7	181,870	128,891	228,156	144,061	270,140	179,483	6.0	5.2	115,520	84,692	154,620	94,791
Naturalized	17,700	12,679	0.3	0.2	10,151	7,739	7,549	4,940	17,388	11,810	0.4	0.3	10,011	7,340	7,377	4,470
Other races—Native	8,831	4,612	0.1	0.1	6,448	3,487	2,383	1,125	5,644	2,961	0.1	0.1	4,765	2,617	879	344
Indian	638	294	-	-	321	152	317	142	377	205	-	-	191	108	186	97
Chinese	4,745	1,926	0.1	-	3,547	1,414	1,198	512	2,935	1,098	0.1	-	2,548	971	387	122
Japanese	631	536	-	-	325	275	306	261	250	91	-	-	133	60	117	31
Filipino	2,659	1,760	-	-	2,160	1,575	499	185	2,008	1,515	-	-	1,836	1,428	167	87
Hindu	58	19	-	-	28	8	30	11	17	3	-	-	7	1	10	2
All other	100	77	-	-	67	63	33	14	63	54	-	-	50	49	12	5
Alien	705,916	1,046,105	100.0	100.0	290,885	495,428	415,031	550,677	670,141	951,350	100.0	100.0	273,111	450,696	397,030	500,654
White—First papers	187,454	230,748	26.6	22.1	105,690	164,058	81,764	66,690	182,999	225,327	27.3	23.7	103,416	161,042	79,583	64,285
No papers	481,687	768,502	68.2	73.5	164,367	305,010	317,320	463,492	451,617	682,458	67.4	71.7	149,589	264,848	302,028	417,610
Negro—First papers	7,080	6,732	1.0	0.6	3,891	4,427	3,189	2,305	7,023	6,651	1.0	0.7	3,872	4,396	3,151	2,255
No papers	19,476	31,372	2.8	3.0	7,822	13,956	11,654	17,416	18,862	28,546	2.8	3.0	7,554	12,717	11,308	15,829
Other races—Foreign born	10,219	8,751	1.4	0.8	9,115	7,977	1,104	774	9,640	8,368	1.4	0.9	8,680	7,693	960	675
Indian	426	97	0.1	-	269	60	157	37	355	78	0.1	-	230	50	125	28
Chinese	8,008	6,488	1.1	0.6	7,420	6,135	588	353	7,624	6,222	1.1	0.7	7,097	5,906	527	316
Japanese	1,456	1,820	0.2	0.2	1,145	1,473	311	347	1,345	1,728	0.2	0.2	1,079	1,429	266	299
Filipino	68	37	-	-	45	24	23	13	61	34	-	-	43	24	18	10
Hindu	155	221	-	-	141	203	14	18	150	218	-	-	137	202	13	16
All other	106	88	-	-	95	82	11	6	105	88	-	-	94	82	11	6
Citizenship not reported	116,681	82,112	100.0	100.0	51,140	33,446	65,541	48,666	109,803	76,560	100.0	100.0	47,807	31,088	61,996	45,472
White	112,519	78,141	96.4	95.2	49,147	31,491	63,372	46,650	105,861	72,981	96.4	95.3	45,900	29,322	59,961	43,659
Negro	4,162	3,971	3.6	4.8	1,993	1,955	2,169	2,016	3,942	3,579	3.6	4.7	1,907	1,766	2,085	1,813

Table C-38.—SCHOOL ATTENDANCE, BY AGE, RACE, AND SEX, FOR THE CITY OF NEW YORK: 1940 AND 1930

[Figures for white population in 1930 revised to include Mexicans classified with "Other races" in the 1930 reports. Percent not shown where less than 0.1 or where base is less than 100]

AGE, SEX, AND CENSUS YEAR	ALL CLASSES			NATIVE WHITE			FOREIGN-BORN WHITE			NEGRO			OTHER RACES		
	Total number	Attending school		Total number	Attending school		Total number	Attending school		Total number	Attending school		Total number	Attending school	
		Number	Percent		Number	Percent		Number	Percent		Number	Percent		Number	Percent
1940															
Total, 5 to 24 years	2,287,759	1,350,041	59.0	2,044,106	1,223,732	59.9	95,394	38,961	40.8	144,759	85,048	58.8	3,500	2,300	65.7
5 years	88,368	25,836	29.2	80,891	23,845	29.5	980	314	32.0	6,323	1,608	25.4	174	69	39.7
6 years	88,718	77,089	86.9	81,065	70,723	87.2	1,077	872	81.0	6,383	5,335	83.6	193	159	82.4
7 to 9 years	293,470	283,447	96.6	268,427	259,433	96.6	4,044	3,780	93.5	20,428	19,694	96.4	571	540	94.6
10 to 13 years	447,798	434,889	97.1	408,428	396,885	97.2	9,910	9,466	95.5	28,783	27,884	96.9	677	654	96.6
14 years	113,310	109,423	96.6	102,350	98,948	96.7	3,732	3,543	94.9	7,065	6,776	95.9	163	156	95.7
15 years	114,889	110,459	96.1	103,876	99,957	96.2	3,936	3,749	95.2	6,910	6,590	95.4	167	163	97.6
16 and 17 years	238,386	185,098	77.6	212,614	165,326	77.8	11,953	8,926	74.7	13,474	10,571	78.5	345	275	79.7
18 and 19 years	253,667	74,066	29.2	220,436	64,290	29.2	18,597	5,175	27.8	14,294	4,458	31.2	340	143	42.1
20 years	127,862	17,480	13.7	110,093	15,419	14.0	9,859	1,176	11.9	7,738	836	10.8	172	49	28.5
21 to 24 years	521,291	32,254	6.2	455,926	28,906	6.3	31,306	1,960	6.3	33,361	1,296	3.9	698	92	13.2
Male, 5 to 24 years	1,127,830	695,356	61.7	1,015,555	632,536	62.3	45,648	20,542	45.0	64,561	40,934	63.4	2,066	1,344	65.1
5 years	44,847	12,940	28.9	41,165	11,993	29.1	474	145	30.6	3,120	766	24.6	88	36	-
6 years	45,142	39,217	86.9	41,313	36,059	87.3	557	456	81.9	3,175	2,619	82.5	97	83	-
7 to 9 years	148,809	143,700	96.6	136,371	131,755	96.6	2,007	1,884	93.9	10,147	9,793	96.5	284	268	94.4
10 to 13 years	226,504	220,075	97.2	207,226	201,486	97.2	4,981	4,751	95.4	13,918	13,475	96.8	379	363	95.8
14 years	56,949	54,998	96.6	51,621	49,891	96.6	1,851	1,757	94.9	3,376	3,252	96.3	101	98	97.0
15 years	57,734	55,606	96.3	52,455	50,547	96.4	1,935	1,846	95.4	3,234	3,106	96.0	110	107	97.3
16 and 17 years	118,975	94,205	79.2	106,441	84,400	79.3	6,056	4,655	76.9	6,261	4,975	79.5	217	175	80.6
18 and 19 years	124,008	41,999	33.9	108,529	36,815	33.9	9,172	3,027	33.0	6,079	2,052	33.8	228	105	46.1
20 years	61,263	10,830	17.7	53,598	9,657	18.0	4,703	778	16.5	2,847	359	12.6	115	36	31.3
21 to 24 years	243,599	21,786	8.9	216,836	19,933	9.2	13,912	1,243	8.9	12,404	537	4.3	447	73	16.3
Female, 5 to 24 years	1,159,929	654,685	56.4	1,028,551	591,196	57.5	49,746	18,419	37.0	80,198	44,114	55.0	1,434	956	66.7
5 years	43,521	12,896	29.6	39,726	11,852	29.8	506	169	33.4	3,203	842	26.3	86	33	-
6 years	43,576	37,872	86.9	39,752	34,664	87.2	520	416	80.0	3,208	2,716	84.7	96	76	-
7 to 9 years	144,661	139,747	96.6	132,056	127,678	96.7	2,037	1,896	93.1	10,281	9,901	96.3	287	272	94.8
10 to 13 years	221,294	214,814	97.1	201,202	195,399	97.1	4,929	4,715	95.7	14,865	14,409	96.9	298	291	97.7
14 years	56,361	54,425	96.6	50,729	49,057	96.7	1,881	1,786	94.9	3,689	3,524	95.5	62	58	-
15 years	57,155	54,853	96.0	51,421	49,410	96.1	2,001	1,903	95.1	3,676	3,484	94.8	57	56	-
16 and 17 years	119,411	90,893	76.1	106,173	80,926	76.2	5,897	4,271	72.4	7,213	5,596	77.6	128	100	78.1
18 and 19 years	129,659	32,067	24.7	111,907	27,475	24.6	9,425	2,148	22.8	8,215	2,406	29.3	112	38	33.9
20 years	66,599	6,650	10.0	56,495	5,762	10.2	5,156	398	7.7	4,891	477	9.8	57	13	-
21 to 24 years	277,692	10,468	3.8	239,090	8,973	3.8	17,394	717	4.1	20,957	759	3.6	251	19	7.6
1930															
Total, 5 to 24 years	2,439,287	1,362,751	55.9	2,056,945	1,237,685	60.2	277,242	77,432	27.9	102,805	46,617	45.3	2,295	1,017	44.3
5 years	112,108	28,632	25.5	104,372	26,823	25.7	2,257	504	22.3	5,340	1,268	23.7	139	42	30.2
6 years	115,242	92,352	80.1	107,000	86,052	80.4	3,108	2,394	77.0	5,018	3,815	76.1	121	91	75.2
7 to 9 years	349,934	338,303	96.7	319,125	308,879	96.8	16,519	15,870	96.1	14,012	13,293	94.9	278	261	93.9
10 to 13 years	463,188	456,204	98.5	427,733	421,470	98.5	20,067	19,680	98.1	15,144	14,818	97.8	244	236	96.7
14 years	112,112	108,723	97.0	103,303	100,227	97.0	5,242	5,052	96.4	3,518	3,396	96.5	49	48	-
15 years	112,305	101,360	90.3	102,155	92,164	90.2	6,771	6,133	90.6	3,325	3,020	90.8	54	43	-
16 and 17 years	232,443	132,712	57.1	202,327	116,559	57.6	22,683	11,933	52.6	7,319	4,156	56.8	114	64	56.1
18 and 19 years	254,538	53,524	21.0	205,860	45,266	22.0	37,977	6,628	17.5	10,476	1,570	15.0	225	60	26.7
20 years	131,955	16,667	12.6	99,709	13,766	13.8	25,529	2,496	9.8	6,570	381	5.8	147	24	16.3
21 to 24 years	555,462	34,274	6.2	385,361	26,479	6.9	137,089	6,742	4.9	32,088	905	2.8	924	148	16.0
Male, 5 to 24 years	1,203,519	702,126	58.3	1,024,900	637,812	62.2	130,327	41,371	31.7	46,714	22,359	47.9	1,578	584	37.0
5 years	56,813	14,449	25.4	53,008	13,563	25.6	1,125	254	22.6	2,606	609	23.4	79	23	-
6 years	58,294	46,618	80.0	54,183	43,489	80.3	1,613	1,244	77.1	2,444	1,843	75.4	54	42	-
7 to 9 years	176,675	170,727	96.6	161,385	156,112	96.7	8,313	7,998	96.2	6,844	6,491	94.8	133	126	94.7
10 to 13 years	233,916	230,415	98.5	216,389	213,233	98.5	10,133	9,943	98.1	7,268	7,119	97.9	126	120	95.2
14 years	56,347	54,756	97.2	51,952	50,499	97.2	2,647	2,560	96.7	1,719	1,669	97.1	29	28	-
15 years	56,540	51,345	90.8	51,562	46,747	90.7	3,375	3,118	92.4	1,572	1,455	92.6	31	25	-
16 and 17 years	114,770	69,016	60.1	100,571	60,834	60.5	10,823	6,205	57.3	3,308	1,940	58.6	68	37	-
18 and 19 years	122,430	31,344	25.6	100,770	26,637	26.4	17,199	3,979	23.1	4,289	684	15.9	172	44	25.6
20 years	62,152	10,397	16.7	48,011	8,643	18.0	11,454	1,578	13.8	2,576	160	6.2	111	16	14.4
21 to 24 years	265,582	23,059	8.7	187,074	18,055	9.7	63,645	4,492	7.1	14,088	389	2.8	775	123	15.9
Female, 5 to 24 years	1,235,768	660,625	53.5	1,032,045	599,873	58.1	146,915	36,061	24.5	56,091	24,258	43.2	717	433	60.4
5 years	55,295	14,183	25.6	51,369	13,260	25.8	1,132	250	22.1	2,734	654	23.9	60	19	-
6 years	56,948	45,734	80.3	52,817	42,563	80.6	1,495	1,150	76.9	2,569	1,972	76.8	67	49	-
7 to 9 years	173,259	167,576	96.7	157,740	152,767	96.8	8,206	7,872	95.9	7,168	6,802	94.9	145	135	93.1
10 to 13 years	229,272	225,789	98.5	211,344	208,237	98.5	9,984	9,737	98.0	7,876	7,699	97.8	118	116	98.3
14 years	55,765	53,967	96.8	51,351	49,728	96.8	2,595	2,492	96.0	1,799	1,727	96.0	20	20	-
15 years	55,765	50,015	89.7	50,593	45,417	89.8	3,396	3,015	88.8	1,753	1,565	89.3	23	18	-
16 and 17 years	117,673	63,696	54.1	101,756	55,725	54.8	11,860	5,728	48.3	4,011	2,216	55.2	46	27	-
18 and 19 years	132,108	22,180	16.8	105,090	18,629	17.7	20,778	2,649	12.7	6,187	886	14.3	53	16	-
20 years	69,803	6,270	9.0	51,698	5,123	9.9	14,075	918	6.5	3,994	221	5.5	36	8	-
21 to 24 years	289,880	11,215	3.9	198,287	8,424	4.2	73,444	2,250	3.1	18,000	516	2.9	149	25	16.8

Table C-39.—PERSONS 25 YEARS OLD AND OVER, BY YEARS OF SCHOOL COMPLETED, RACE, AND SEX, FOR THE CITY OF NEW YORK: 1940

[Percent not shown where less than 0.1; median and percent not shown where base is less than 100]

YEARS OF SCHOOL COMPLETED	ALL CLASSES			NATIVE WHITE			FOREIGN-BORN WHITE			NEGRO			OTHER RACES		
	Total	Male	Female	Total	Male	Female	Total	Male	Female	Total	Male	Female	Total	Male	Female
Persons 25 years old and over	4,733,342	2,327,048	2,406,294	2,452,719	1,176,709	1,276,010	1,982,043	1,010,881	971,162	283,994	126,460	157,534	14,586	12,998	1,588
No school years completed	361,184	168,413	192,771	21,613	9,787	11,826	325,905	150,661	175,244	9,778	4,414	5,364	3,888	3,551	337
Grade school: 1 to 4 years	340,551	171,962	168,589	47,904	23,248	24,656	253,517	129,707	123,810	36,215	16,228	19,987	2,915	2,779	136
5 or 6 years	367,288	183,754	183,534	108,791	52,733	56,058	208,431	108,206	100,225	48,372	21,250	27,122	1,694	1,565	129
7 or 8 years	1,934,829	939,513	995,316	1,059,451	503,256	556,195	771,640	389,004	382,636	101,145	45,007	56,138	2,593	2,246	347
High school: 1 to 3 years	600,541	289,124	311,417	429,601	203,919	225,682	128,331	66,773	61,558	41,738	17,700	24,038	871	732	139
4 years	585,923	249,407	336,516	418,943	168,634	250,309	138,772	68,710	70,062	27,284	11,392	15,892	924	671	253
College: 1 to 3 years	174,912	97,789	77,123	131,156	70,465	60,691	34,426	22,485	11,941	8,875	4,470	4,405	455	369	86
4 years or more	266,091	174,510	91,581	202,872	127,586	75,286	56,643	42,963	13,680	5,840	3,353	2,487	736	608	128
Not reported	102,023	52,576	49,447	32,388	17,081	15,307	64,378	32,372	32,006	4,747	2,646	2,101	510	477	33
Median school years completed	8.3	8.3	8.3	8.9	9.0	8.9	7.4	7.5	7.4	7.9	7.9	7.9	5.3	4.9	8.0
Percent less than 5 years completed	14.8	14.6	15.0	2.8	2.8	2.9	29.2	27.7	30.8	16.2	16.3	16.1	46.6	48.7	29.8
PERCENT DISTRIBUTION															
Persons 25 years old and over	100.0	100.0	100.0	100.0	100.0	100.0	100.0	100.0	100.0	100.0	100.0	100.0	100.0	100.0	100.0
No school years completed	7.6	7.2	8.0	0.9	0.8	0.9	16.4	14.9	18.0	3.4	3.5	3.4	26.7	27.3	21.2
Grade school: 1 to 4 years	7.2	7.4	7.0	2.0	2.0	1.9	12.8	12.8	12.7	12.8	12.8	12.7	20.0	21.4	8.6
5 or 6 years	7.8	7.9	7.6	4.4	4.5	4.4	10.5	10.7	10.3	17.0	16.8	17.2	11.6	12.0	8.1
7 or 8 years	40.9	40.4	41.4	43.2	42.8	43.6	38.9	38.5	39.4	35.6	35.6	35.6	17.8	17.3	21.9
High school: 1 to 3 years	12.7	12.4	12.9	17.5	17.3	17.7	6.5	6.6	6.3	14.7	14.0	15.3	6.0	5.6	8.8
4 years	12.4	10.7	14.0	17.1	14.3	19.6	7.0	6.8	7.2	9.6	9.0	10.1	6.3	5.2	15.9
College: 1 to 3 years	3.7	4.2	3.2	5.3	6.0	4.8	1.7	2.2	1.2	3.1	3.5	2.8	3.1	2.8	5.4
4 years or more	5.6	7.5	3.8	8.3	10.8	5.9	2.9	4.3	1.4	2.1	2.7	1.6	5.0	4.7	8.1
Not reported	2.2	2.3	2.1	1.3	1.5	1.2	3.2	3.2	3.3	1.7	2.1	1.3	3.5	3.7	2.1

Table C-40.—FOREIGN-BORN WHITE, BY COUNTRY OF BIRTH, BY SEX, FOR THE CITY OF NEW YORK: 1940 AND 1930

[Figures for white population in 1930 revised to include Mexicans classified with "Other races" in the 1930 reports. Percent not shown where less than 0.1 or where base is less than 100]

COUNTRY OF BIRTH	BOTH SEXES		PERCENT		MALE		FEMALE	
	1940	1930	1940	1930	1940	1930	1940	1930
All countries	2,080,020	2,295,181	100.0	100.0	1,057,839	1,180,947	1,022,181	1,114,234
England	63,115	78,003	3.0	3.4	30,411	38,538	32,704	39,465
Scotland	33,292	38,535	1.6	1.7	15,758	19,018	17,534	19,517
Wales	1,296	1,903	0.1	0.1	667	988	629	915
Northern Ireland	21,501	27,821	1.0	1.2	9,384	12,169	12,117	15,652
Irish Free State (Eire)	160,325	192,810	7.7	8.4	69,988	85,746	90,337	107,064
Norway	30,750	38,130	1.5	1.7	16,471	21,171	14,279	16,959
Sweden	28,881	37,267	1.4	1.6	14,674	19,357	14,207	17,920
Denmark	8,845	11,096	0.4	0.5	5,425	6,946	3,420	4,150
Netherlands	5,608	5,335	0.3	0.2	3,704	3,619	1,904	1,716
Belgium	3,888	3,854	0.2	0.2	1,993	1,952	1,895	1,902
Luxemburg	340	323	-	-	175	174	165	149
Switzerland	8,551	9,895	0.4	0.4	4,412	5,147	4,139	4,748
France	19,696	23,288	0.9	1.0	8,397	10,263	11,299	13,025
Germany	224,749	237,588	10.8	10.4	112,916	121,590	111,833	115,998
Poland	194,163	238,339	9.3	10.4	97,816	120,318	96,347	118,021
Czechoslovakia	26,884	35,318	1.3	1.5	12,042	15,964	14,842	19,354
Austria	145,106	127,169	7.0	5.5	70,537	62,587	74,569	64,582
Hungary	62,588	59,883	3.0	2.6	28,557	27,444	34,031	32,439
Yugoslavia	6,475	6,450	0.3	0.3	3,712	3,638	2,763	2,812
Russia (U. S. S. R.)	395,696	442,431	19.0	19.3	200,663	227,120	195,033	215,311
Lithuania	15,089	15,005	0.7	0.7	7,944	8,162	7,145	6,843
Latvia	5,317	5,172	0.3	0.2	2,785	2,692	2,532	2,480
Finland	11,245	13,224	0.5	0.6	4,563	5,833	6,682	7,391
Rumania	40,655	46,750	2.0	2.0	20,316	23,377	20,339	23,373
Bulgaria	670	578	-	-	394	342	276	236
Turkey in Europe	265	747	-	-	146	383	119	364
Greece	28,593	27,182	1.4	1.2	19,304	18,567	9,289	8,615
Italy	409,489	440,250	19.7	19.2	227,084	246,088	182,405	194,162
Spain	13,583	14,000	0.7	0.6	9,504	10,153	4,079	3,847
Portugal	2,676	2,231	0.1	0.1	2,008	1,756	668	475
Other Europe	5,757	4,844	0.3	0.2	3,691	3,160	2,066	1,684
Palestine and Syria	8,598	8,696	0.4	0.4	4,545	4,578	4,053	4,118
Turkey in Asia	17,398	14,368	0.8	0.6	9,645	8,050	7,753	6,318
Other Asia	5,107	5,621	0.2	0.2	3,293	3,514	1,814	2,107
Canada—French	6,270	6,863	0.3	0.3	2,753	3,308	3,517	3,555
Canada—Other	29,237	32,760	1.4	1.4	11,768	14,038	17,469	18,722
Newfoundland	4,838	5,303	0.2	0.2	2,171	2,555	2,667	2,748
Mexico	2,973	4,163	0.1	0.2	1,708	2,559	1,265	1,604
Cuba and other West Indies	13,344	13,046	0.6	0.6	7,136	7,303	6,208	5,743
Central and South America	12,429	14,298	0.6	0.6	6,807	8,202	5,622	6,096
Australia	987	1,164	-	0.1	513	650	474	514
Azores	69	95	-	-	35	66	34	29
All other and not reported	3,682	3,383	0.2	0.1	2,024	1,862	1,658	1,521

Table C-41.—PERSONS 14 YEARS OLD AND OVER, BY EMPLOYMENT STATUS, CLASS OF WORKER, RACE, AND SEX, FOR THE CITY OF NEW YORK: 1940

[Percent not shown where less than 0.1 or where base is less than 100]

EMPLOYMENT STATUS	ALL CLASSES			NATIVE WHITE			FOREIGN-BORN WHITE			NEGRO			OTHER RACES		
	Total	Male	Female	Total	Male	Female	Total	Male	Female	Total	Male	Female	Total	Male	Female
Total population (all ages)	7,454,995	3,676,293	3,778,702	4,897,481	2,397,164	2,500,317	2,080,020	1,057,839	1,022,181	458,444	205,727	252,717	19,050	15,563	3,487
Persons 14 years old and over	6,102,747	2,989,576	3,113,171	3,658,014	1,766,189	1,891,825	2,061,426	1,048,510	1,012,916	366,836	160,661	206,175	16,471	14,216	2,255
In labor force	3,474,760	2,424,740	1,050,020	2,113,054	1,403,145	709,909	1,114,459	879,446	235,013	234,336	129,853	104,483	12,911	12,296	615
Not in labor force	2,627,987	564,836	2,063,151	1,544,960	363,044	1,181,916	946,967	169,064	777,903	132,500	30,808	101,692	3,560	1,920	1,640
Engaged in own home housew'k	1,592,195	20,265	1,571,930	852,525	10,247	842,278	675,850	8,973	666,877	62,563	991	61,572	1,257	54	1,203
In school	474,543	248,124	226,419	422,821	222,304	200,517	22,889	11,998	10,891	27,902	13,183	14,719	931	639	292
Unable to work	293,980	162,619	131,361	105,263	53,804	51,459	159,113	98,217	60,896	28,901	9,958	18,943	703	640	63
In institutions	34,202	18,746	15,456	16,802	9,200	7,602	14,490	7,549	6,941	2,704	1,797	907	206	200	6
Other and not reported	233,067	115,082	117,985	147,549	67,489	80,060	74,625	42,327	32,298	10,430	4,879	5,551	463	387	76
LABOR FORCE BY EMPLOYMENT STATUS															
In labor force	3,474,760	2,424,740	1,050,020	2,113,054	1,403,145	709,909	1,114,459	879,446	235,013	234,336	129,853	104,483	12,911	12,296	615
Employed (exc. public emerg. work)	2,839,366	1,964,346	875,020	1,711,638	1,127,160	584,478	946,938	738,020	208,918	169,497	88,386	81,111	11,293	10,780	513
At work	2,765,695	1,917,928	847,767	1,669,669	1,104,589	565,080	918,934	716,249	202,685	166,185	86,681	79,504	10,907	10,409	498
With a job	73,671	46,418	27,253	41,969	22,571	19,398	28,004	21,771	6,233	3,312	1,705	1,607	386	371	15
On public emerg. work (WPA, etc.)	103,386	86,845	16,541	61,920	51,403	10,517	21,415	19,911	1,504	19,936	15,428	4,508	115	103	12
Seeking work	532,008	373,549	158,459	339,496	224,582	114,914	146,106	121,515	24,591	44,903	26,039	18,864	1,503	1,413	90
Experienced workers	459,422	335,922	123,500	276,438	191,793	84,645	141,561	119,197	22,364	39,995	23,565	16,430	1,428	1,367	61
New workers	72,586	37,627	34,959	63,058	32,789	30,269	4,545	2,318	2,227	4,908	2,474	2,434	75	46	29
PERCENT BY SEX															
In labor force	100.0	69.8	30.2	100.0	66.4	33.6	100.0	78.9	21.1	100.0	55.4	44.6	100.0	95.2	4.8
Employed (exc. public emerg.)	100.0	69.2	30.8	100.0	65.9	34.1	100.0	77.9	22.1	100.0	52.1	47.9	100.0	95.5	4.5
On pub. emerg. work (WPA, etc.)	100.0	84.0	16.0	100.0	83.0	17.0	100.0	93.0	7.0	100.0	77.4	22.6	100.0	89.6	10.4
Seeking work	100.0	70.2	29.8	100.0	66.2	33.8	100.0	83.2	16.8	100.0	58.0	42.0	100.0	94.0	6.0
Not in labor force	100.0	21.5	78.5	100.0	23.5	76.5	100.0	17.9	82.1	100.0	23.3	76.7	100.0	53.9	46.1
Engaged in own home housew'k	100.0	1.3	98.7	100.0	1.2	98.8	100.0	1.3	98.7	100.0	1.6	98.4	100.0	4.3	95.7
In school	100.0	52.3	47.7	100.0	52.6	47.4	100.0	52.4	47.6	100.0	47.2	52.8	100.0	68.6	31.4
Unable to work	100.0	55.3	44.7	100.0	51.1	48.9	100.0	61.7	38.3	100.0	34.5	65.5	100.0	91.0	9.0
In institutions	100.0	54.8	45.2	100.0	54.8	45.2	100.0	52.1	47.9	100.0	66.5	33.5	100.0	97.1	2.9
Other and not reported	100.0	49.4	50.6	100.0	45.7	54.3	100.0	56.7	43.3	100.0	46.8	53.2	100.0	83.6	16.4
EMPLOYED WORKERS BY CLASS OF WORKER															
Employed (exc. public emerg.)	2,839,366	1,964,346	875,020	1,711,638	1,127,160	584,478	946,938	738,020	208,918	169,497	88,386	81,111	11,293	10,780	513
Wage and salary workers	2,459,880	1,647,274	812,606	1,548,333	992,373	555,960	743,765	564,074	179,691	159,008	82,450	76,558	8,774	8,377	397
Employers and own-account workers	347,006	303,310	43,696	144,706	124,915	19,791	190,344	170,526	19,818	9,560	5,541	4,019	2,396	2,328	68
Unpaid family workers	18,091	5,652	12,439	9,308	4,688	4,615	8,514	875	7,639	196	51	145	78	38	40
Class of worker not reported	14,389	8,110	6,279	9,296	5,184	4,112	4,315	2,545	1,770	733	344	389	45	37	8
At work	2,765,695	1,917,928	847,767	1,669,669	1,104,589	565,080	918,934	716,249	202,685	166,185	86,681	79,504	10,907	10,409	498
Wage and salary workers	2,404,444	1,615,540	788,904	1,514,554	976,011	538,543	724,845	550,085	174,760	156,378	81,159	75,214	8,672	8,285	387
Employers and own-account workers	331,238	289,936	41,302	138,100	119,549	18,551	182,031	163,148	18,883	8,987	5,184	3,803	2,120	2,055	65
Unpaid family workers	17,599	5,454	12,145	9,005	4,527	4,478	8,332	843	7,489	189	49	140	73	35	38
Class of worker not reported	12,414	6,998	5,416	8,010	4,502	3,508	3,726	2,173	1,553	636	289	347	42	34	8
With a job	73,671	46,418	27,253	41,969	22,571	19,398	28,004	21,771	6,233	3,312	1,705	1,607	386	371	15
Wage and salary workers	55,486	31,734	23,702	33,779	16,362	17,417	18,920	13,989	4,931	2,635	1,291	1,344	102	92	10
Employers and own-account workers	15,768	13,374	2,394	6,606	5,366	1,240	8,313	7,378	935	573	357	216	276	273	3
Unpaid family workers	492	198	294	298	161	137	182	32	150	7	2	5	5	3	2
Class of worker not reported	1,975	1,112	863	1,286	682	604	589	372	217	97	55	42	3	3	-
PERCENT DISTRIBUTION															
Persons 14 years old and over	100.0	100.0	100.0	100.0	100.0	100.0	100.0	100.0	100.0	100.0	100.0	100.0	100.0	100.0	100.0
In labor force	56.9	81.1	33.7	57.8	79.4	37.5	54.1	83.9	23.2	63.9	80.8	50.7	78.4	86.5	27.3
Not in labor force	43.1	18.9	66.3	42.2	20.6	62.5	45.9	16.1	76.8	36.1	19.2	49.3	21.6	13.5	72.7
Engaged in own home housew'k	26.1	0.7	50.5	23.3	0.6	44.5	32.8	0.9	65.8	17.1	0.6	29.9	7.6	0.4	53.3
In school	7.8	8.3	7.3	11.6	12.6	10.6	1.1	1.1	1.1	7.6	8.2	7.1	5.7	4.5	12.9
Unable to work	4.8	5.4	4.2	2.9	3.0	2.7	7.7	9.4	6.0	7.9	6.2	9.2	4.3	4.5	2.8
In institutions	0.6	0.6	0.5	0.5	0.5	0.4	0.7	0.7	0.7	0.7	1.1	0.4	1.3	1.4	0.3
Other and not reported	3.8	3.8	3.8	4.0	3.8	4.2	3.6	4.0	3.2	2.8	3.0	2.7	2.8	2.7	3.4
LABOR FORCE BY EMPLOYMENT STATUS															
In labor force	100.0	100.0	100.0	100.0	100.0	100.0	100.0	100.0	100.0	100.0	100.0	100.0	100.0	100.0	100.0
Employed (exc. public emerg. work)	81.7	81.0	83.3	81.0	80.3	82.3	85.0	83.9	88.9	72.3	68.1	77.6	87.5	87.7	83.4
At work	79.6	79.1	80.7	79.0	78.7	79.6	82.5	81.4	86.2	70.9	66.8	76.1	84.5	84.7	81.0
With a job	2.1	1.9	2.6	2.0	1.6	2.7	2.5	2.5	2.7	1.4	1.3	1.5	3.0	3.0	2.4
On public emerg. work (WPA, etc.)	3.0	3.6	1.6	2.9	3.7	1.5	1.9	2.3	0.6	8.5	11.9	4.3	0.9	0.8	2.0
Seeking work	15.3	15.4	15.1	16.1	16.0	16.2	13.1	13.8	10.5	19.2	20.1	18.1	11.6	11.5	14.6
Experienced workers	13.2	13.9	11.8	13.1	13.7	11.9	12.7	13.6	9.5	17.1	18.1	15.7	11.1	11.1	9.9
New workers	2.1	1.6	3.3	3.0	2.3	4.3	0.4	0.3	0.9	2.1	1.9	2.3	0.6	0.4	4.7
EMPLOYED WORKERS BY CLASS OF WORKER															
Employed (exc. public emerg.)	100.0	100.0	100.0	100.0	100.0	100.0	100.0	100.0	100.0	100.0	100.0	100.0	100.0	100.0	100.0
Wage and salary workers	86.6	83.9	92.9	90.5	88.0	95.1	78.5	76.4	86.0	93.8	93.3	94.4	77.7	77.7	77.4
Employers and own-account workers	12.2	15.4	5.0	8.5	11.1	3.4	20.1	23.1	9.5	5.6	6.3	5.0	21.2	21.6	13.3
Unpaid family workers	0.6	0.3	1.4	0.5	0.4	0.8	0.9	0.1	3.7	0.1	0.1	0.2	0.7	0.4	7.8
Class of worker not reported	0.5	0.4	0.7	0.5	0.5	0.7	0.5	0.3	0.8	0.4	0.4	0.5	0.4	0.3	1.6
At work	100.0	100.0	100.0	100.0	100.0	100.0	100.0	100.0	100.0	100.0	100.0	100.0	100.0	100.0	100.0
Wage and salary workers	86.9	84.2	93.1	90.7	88.4	95.3	78.9	76.8	86.2	94.1	93.6	94.6	79.5	79.6	77.7
Employers and own-account workers	12.0	15.1	4.9	8.3	10.8	3.3	19.8	22.8	9.3	5.4	6.0	4.8	19.4	19.7	13.1
Unpaid family workers	0.6	0.3	1.4	0.5	0.4	0.8	0.9	0.1	3.7	0.1	0.1	0.2	0.7	0.3	7.6
Class of worker not reported	0.4	0.4	0.6	0.5	0.4	0.6	0.4	0.3	0.8	0.4	0.3	0.4	0.4	0.3	1.6
With a job	100.0	100.0	100.0	100.0	100.0	100.0	100.0	100.0	100.0	100.0	100.0	100.0	100.0	100.0	-
Wage and salary workers	75.2	68.4	87.0	80.5	72.5	89.8	67.6	64.3	79.1	79.6	75.7	83.6	26.4	24.8	-
Employers and own-account workers	21.4	28.8	8.8	15.7	23.8	6.4	29.7	33.9	15.0	17.3	20.9	13.4	71.5	73.6	-
Unpaid family workers	0.7	0.4	1.1	0.7	0.7	0.7	0.6	0.1	2.4	0.2	0.1	0.3	1.3	0.8	-
Class of worker not reported	2.7	2.4	3.2	3.1	3.0	3.1	2.1	1.7	3.5	2.9	3.2	2.6	0.8	0.8	-

Table C-42.—EMPLOYED WORKERS 14 YEARS OLD AND OVER, BY MAJOR OCCUPATION GROUP, INDUSTRY GROUP, AND SEX, FOR THE CITY OF NEW YORK: 1940

[Percent not shown where less than 0.1 or where base is less than 100]

MAJOR OCCUPATION GROUP AND INDUSTRY GROUP	Total	Male	Female	PERCENT BY OCCUPATION AND INDUSTRY			PERCENT BY SEX	
				Total	Male	Female	Male	Female
Total population (all ages)	7,454,995	3,676,293	3,778,702	-	-	-	49.3	50.7
All persons 14 years old and over	6,102,747	2,989,576	3,113,171	-	-	-	49.0	51.0
In labor force	3,474,760	2,424,740	1,050,020	100.0	100.0	100.0	69.8	30.2
Employed workers (except on public emergency work)	2,839,366	1,964,346	875,020	81.7	81.0	83.3	69.2	30.8
MAJOR OCCUPATION GROUP								
Employed (except on public emergency work)	2,839,366	1,964,346	875,020	100.0	100.0	100.0	69.2	30.8
Professional workers	217,032	126,887	90,145	7.6	6.5	10.3	58.5	41.5
Semiprofessional workers	42,198	30,052	12,146	1.5	1.5	1.4	71.2	28.8
Farmers and farm managers	558	519	39	-	-	-	93.0	7.0
Proprietors, managers, and officials, except farm	288,152	259,075	29,077	10.1	13.2	3.3	89.9	10.1
Clerical, sales, and kindred workers	770,804	446,199	324,605	27.1	22.7	37.1	37.9	42.1
Craftsmen, foremen, and kindred workers	329,479	319,308	10,171	11.6	16.3	1.2	96.9	3.1
Operatives and kindred workers	580,053	388,788	191,265	20.4	19.8	21.9	67.0	33.0
Domestic service workers	123,202	6,976	116,226	4.3	0.4	13.3	5.7	94.3
Service workers, except domestic	346,264	256,696	89,568	12.2	13.1	10.2	74.1	25.9
Farm laborers (wage workers) and farm foremen	960	914	46	-	-	-	95.2	4.8
Farm laborers, unpaid family workers	60	50	10	-	-	-	-	-
Laborers, except farm	114,168	111,567	2,601	4.0	5.7	0.3	97.7	2.3
Occupation not reported	26,436	17,315	9,121	0.9	0.9	1.0	65.5	34.5
INDUSTRY GROUP								
Employed (except on public emergency work)	2,839,366	1,964,346	875,020	100.0	100.0	100.0	69.2	30.8
Agriculture, forestry, and fishery	3,468	3,229	239	0.1	0.2	-	93.1	6.9
Agriculture	2,813	2,599	214	0.1	0.1	-	92.4	7.6
Forestry (except logging) and fishery	655	630	25	-	-	-	96.2	3.8
Mining	996	822	174	-	-	-	82.5	17.5
Coal mining	93	82	11	-	-	-	-	-
Crude petroleum and natural gas production	78	66	12	-	-	-	-	-
Other mines and quarries	825	674	151	-	-	-	81.7	18.3
Construction	131,599	127,880	3,719	4.6	6.5	0.4	97.2	2.8
Manufacturing	746,466	504,413	242,053	26.3	25.7	27.7	67.6	32.4
Food and kindred products	67,648	54,260	13,388	2.4	2.8	1.5	80.2	19.8
Textile-mill products	42,081	26,440	15,641	1.5	1.3	1.8	62.8	37.2
Apparel and other fabricated textile products	236,604	121,618	114,986	8.3	6.2	13.1	51.4	48.6
Logging	50	44	6	-	-	-	-	-
Sawmills and planing mills	1,407	1,291	116	-	0.1	-	91.8	8.2
Furniture, store fixtures, and miscellaneous wooden goods	21,104	18,415	2,689	0.7	0.9	0.3	87.3	12.7
Paper and allied products	20,049	12,610	7,439	0.7	0.6	0.9	62.9	37.1
Printing, publishing, and allied industries	81,528	62,074	19,454	2.9	3.2	2.2	76.1	23.9
Chemicals and allied products	30,400	19,973	10,427	1.1	1.0	1.2	65.7	34.3
Petroleum and coal products	8,074	6,371	1,703	0.3	0.3	0.2	78.9	21.1
Leather and leather products	26,702	18,936	7,766	0.9	1.0	0.9	70.9	29.1
Stone, clay, and glass products	8,366	6,960	1,406	0.3	0.4	0.2	83.2	16.8
Iron and steel and their products	24,332	20,387	3,945	0.9	1.0	0.5	83.8	16.2
Nonferrous metals and their products	21,099	17,314	3,785	0.7	0.9	0.4	82.1	17.9
Machinery	44,459	36,106	8,353	1.6	1.8	1.0	81.2	18.8
Automobiles and automobile equipment	5,256	4,421	835	0.2	0.2	0.1	84.1	15.9
Transportation equipment, except automobile	21,985	21,163	822	0.8	1.1	0.1	96.3	3.7
Other and not specified manufacturing industries	85,322	56,030	29,292	3.0	2.9	3.3	65.7	34.3
Transportation, communication, and other public utilities	251,416	220,359	31,057	8.9	11.2	3.5	87.6	12.4
Railroads (including railroad repair shops) and railway express service	32,779	31,130	1,649	1.2	1.6	0.2	95.0	5.0
Trucking service	28,347	27,352	995	1.0	1.4	0.1	96.5	3.5
Other transportation	102,686	98,192	4,494	3.6	5.0	0.5	95.6	4.4
Communication	36,407	18,340	18,067	1.3	0.9	2.1	50.4	49.6
Utilities	51,197	45,345	5,852	1.8	2.3	0.7	88.6	11.4
Wholesale and retail trade	621,757	470,614	151,143	21.9	24.0	17.3	75.7	24.3
Wholesale trade	99,660	79,079	20,581	3.5	4.0	2.4	79.3	20.7
Food and dairy products stores, and milk retailing	133,741	114,878	18,863	4.7	5.8	2.2	85.9	14.1
Eating and drinking places	112,822	86,611	26,211	4.0	4.4	3.0	76.8	23.2
Motor vehicles and accessories retailing, and filling stations	17,299	15,837	1,462	0.6	0.8	0.2	91.5	8.5
Other retail trade	258,235	174,209	84,026	9.1	8.9	9.6	67.5	32.5
Finance, insurance, and real estate	224,460	162,199	62,261	7.9	8.3	7.1	72.3	27.7
Business and repair services	74,133	61,177	12,956	2.6	3.1	1.5	82.5	17.5
Automobile storage, rental, and repair services	25,738	25,214	524	0.9	1.3	0.1	98.0	2.0
Business and repair services, except automobile	48,395	35,963	12,432	1.7	1.8	1.4	74.3	25.7
Personal services	293,887	109,819	184,068	10.4	5.6	21.0	37.4	62.6
Domestic service	135,788	13,752	122,036	4.8	0.7	13.9	10.1	89.9
Hotels and lodging places	55,832	31,981	23,851	2.0	1.6	2.7	57.3	42.7
Laundering, cleaning, and dyeing services	45,141	28,394	16,747	1.6	1.4	1.9	62.9	37.1
Miscellaneous personal services	57,126	35,692	21,434	2.0	1.8	2.4	62.5	37.5
Amusement, recreation, and related services	42,996	31,610	11,386	1.5	1.6	1.3	73.5	26.5
Professional and related services	247,816	122,769	125,047	8.7	6.2	14.3	49.5	50.5
Government	126,733	108,811	17,922	4.5	5.5	2.0	85.9	14.1
Industry not reported	73,639	40,644	32,995	2.6	2.1	3.8	55.2	44.8

Table C-43.—PERSONS 14 YEARS OLD AND OVER IN THE LABOR FORCE, 1940, AND GAINFUL WORKERS 14 YEARS OLD AND OVER, 1930, BY RACE AND SEX, FOR THE CITY OF NEW YORK

[Totals for population and gainful workers for 1930 include "Unknown age." Figures for white population in 1930 have been revised to include Mexicans who were classified with "Other races" in the 1930 reports. Percent not shown where less than 0.1 or where base is less than 100]

CENSUS YEAR AND RACE	TOTAL					MALE					FEMALE				
	Population		Persons in the labor force, and gainful workers,[1] 14 years old and over			Population		Persons in the labor force, and gainful workers,[1] 14 years old and over			Population		Persons in the labor force, and gainful workers,[1] 14 years old and over		
	Total (all ages)	14 years old and over	Number	Percent of total population	Percent of population 14 yrs. and over	Total (all ages)	14 years old and over	Number	Percent of total population	Percent of population 14 yrs. and over	Total (all ages)	14 years old and over	Number	Percent of total population	Percent of population 14 yrs. and over
1940	7,454,995	6,102,747	3,474,760	46.6	56.9	3,676,293	2,989,576	2,424,740	66.0	81.1	3,778,702	3,113,171	1,050,020	27.8	33.7
White	6,977,501	5,719,440	3,227,513	46.3	56.4	3,455,003	2,814,699	2,282,591	66.1	81.1	3,522,498	2,904,741	944,922	26.8	32.5
Negro	458,444	366,836	234,336	51.1	63.9	205,727	160,661	129,853	63.1	80.8	252,717	206,175	104,483	41.3	50.7
Other races	19,050	16,471	12,911	67.8	78.4	15,563	14,216	12,296	79.0	86.5	3,487	2,255	615	17.6	27.3
1930	6,930,446	5,354,374	3,186,958	46.0	59.5	3,472,956	2,674,820	2,324,296	66.9	86.9	3,457,490	2,679,554	862,662	25.0	32.2
White	6,589,377	5,081,179	2,982,779	45.3	58.7	3,304,524	2,539,724	2,199,622	66.6	86.6	3,284,853	2,541,455	783,157	23.8	30.8
Negro	327,706	261,277	193,730	59.1	74.1	156,968	124,375	114,535	73.0	92.1	170,738	136,902	79,195	46.4	57.8
Other races	13,363	11,918	10,449	78.2	87.7	11,464	10,721	10,139	88.4	94.6	1,899	1,197	310	16.3	25.9

[1] Data for 1930 represent gainful workers 14 years old and over.

Discovering the Power of Technicolor

Americans continued to fill movie theaters as 1940 approached, especially with improved movie sound and motion, and the introduction of color to the screen. After years of experimentation, Herbert Kalmus was responsible for perfecting—and naming—Technicolor, using his actress wife's red hair and blue eyes as the ultimate color match test.

Life at Home

- Herbert Thomas Kalmus was a serious student at Massachusetts Institute of Technology, determined to make himself an authority in the field of electrochemistry.
- After he received his bachelor's degree from MIT, he married Natalie, his college sweetheart, earned his doctorate at the University of Zurich, then taught physics, electrochemistry, and metallurgy at MIT and Queen's University, Kingston, Ontario, Canada.
- Herbert and fellow MIT graduate Daniel Comstock formed Kalmus, Comstock, and Wescott, an industrial research and development firm, with mechanic W. Burton Wescott.
- When the firm was hired to analyze an inventor's flicker-free motion picture system, they became intrigued with the art and science of filmmaking, particularly the color motion picture processes.
- Movie studios were starting to experiment with how to add splashes of color to their black-and-white feature films, but the technique was crude and cumbersome.
- Herbert and his partners continued to experiment with a device called Vanascope, using Natalie's red hair and blue eyes as the color standard for new dyes.
- When they hit on a satisfactory process, Herbert called it Technicolor-in honor of his alma mater, Massachusetts Institute of Technology.
- They built a complete photochemical laboratory on a railway car that could be rolled to anywhere a picture company was working, and deliver processed film on the spot.

Herbert Thomas Kalmus invented Technicolor.

- The railway car's only trip was to Florida to film the first Technicolor movie, *The Gulf Between*, in which Natalie played a leading role.
- But at the preview before a scientific gathering in New York, something went wrong and further showings were canceled.
- Three years later the Herbert and his partners tried again, with results so impressive that several movie magnates invested considerable capital in the future of Technicolor
- The screening of Nicholas Schenek's *The Toll of the Sea* brought enthusiastic approval, but the time it took to turn out enough prints to release the picture all over the country, seriously limited its profitability.

Cartoons came to life with the aid of color.

- Natalie and Herbert divorced, but continued to work together perfecting the color process, living in the same house for the next two decades.
- The success of films such as *Gold Diggers of Broadway* brought more Technicolor work than Herbert could handle

Life at Work

- Herbert Kalmus knew he was a success when he watched the final screening of *Gone With the Wind.*
- The movie world had finally discovered the power of color, Herbert owned all 30 Technicolor cameras in existence, and customary rental charge was $25,000.
- As protective as a new father, Herbert doled them out to the studios most likely to use his invention properly.
- The Walt Disney Studios was among the first to truly grasp Technicolor's potential, and the world watched *Snow White and the Seven Dwarfs* in color-Herbert's color.
- To ensure quality, Natalie followed the cameras onto the film set to see that color was not used simply to attract attention, but woven into the fabric of the picture show.
- A full-length motion picture in Technicolor cost from $100,000 to $250,000 extra to make.
- When Walt Disney used the new Technicolor film in his cartoon shorts, particularly the Oscar-winning *Flowers and Trees* in 1932 and *The Three Little Pigs* in 1933, other studios followed suit; producers, directors and writers incorporated the cost of color into their films.
- The first full-length picture shot in Technicolor was *Becky Sharp*, produced by Pioneer Pictures in association with Technicolor Corporation and released by RKO.
- The Technicolor plant was turning out three million feet of film per month.
- The use of dramatic color was bolstered by the production of *The Trail of the Lonesome Pine*, which featured rich scenes of natural scenery in full color.
- A wider adoption of Technicolor was slow in contrast to the acceptance of sound, which had pushed aside silent movies in under a decade.
- Herbert was so focused on color quality, that studios using his innovation were required to employ his technicians, Technicolor's makeup and Technicolor's processing.
- After a few moderate successes, Fox Studios embarked on a full slate of Technicolor films, featuring Westerns and musicals.
- The industry remained split: black-and-white was traditional and gritty; color was glossy and eye-popping and top stars such as Claudette Colbert and Joan Crawford were concerned they didn't photograph well in color.
- Then came a stream of spectacular Technicolor hits: *Snow White and the Seven Dwarfs*; *The Wizard of Oz;* and *Gone With the Wind.*
- The showing of *Gone With the Wind* in December 1939 starring Clark Gable, Vivien Leigh, Leslie Howard, Olivia de Havilland, and Hattie McDaniel, was a huge, widely anticipated event.

Hollywood managed to survive during the Depression.

Hollywood, California

Life in the Community: Hollywood, California

- Hollywood, California, was a neighborhood in Los Angeles, California-situated west-northwest of downtown Los Angeles.
- Thanks to its fame as the historical center of movie studios and movie stars, the word "Hollywood" was often used as a metonymy of American cinema.
- Earlier in the century, Hollywood officials, struggling to secure an adequate water supply, voted for Hollywood to be annexed into the City of Los Angeles, whose water system was piped down from the Owens River.
- That era also saw director D.W. Griffith sent by Biograph Company to the West Coast with his acting troupe - Blanche Sweet, Lillian Gish, Mary Pickford, Lionel Barrymore, etc.
- Griffith filmed the first Hollywood movie, *In Old California*, after which other movie-makers headed west to avoid the fees imposed by Thomas Edison, who owned patents on the movie-making process on the East Coast.
- When the depression hit and the bottom fell out of the global economy, Hollywood entered a Golden Age, as talking pictures provided a much-needed diversion for the American people.
- In the decade leading up to 1940, a nickel bought a movie ticket, which included a cartoon, a newsreel, a B-feature and the main film - four hours of entertainment.
- Columbia and Warner Brothers packed theaters across America with films packed with wronged heroes, like *I Am a Fugitive From a Chain Gang*, who seemed as overwhelmed by forces outside their control as the audience watching them.
- Also popular were films starring rogues who refused to be cowed by the Depression, like organized criminals Edward G. Robinson and James Cagney, and the mocking comedies of the Marx Brothers.
- After a few rough years of declining attendance, Hollywood recovered with the release of Walt Disney's *Snow White and the Seven Dwarfs* and MGM 's *Gone With the Wind*, which both used Technicolor to its best advantage.

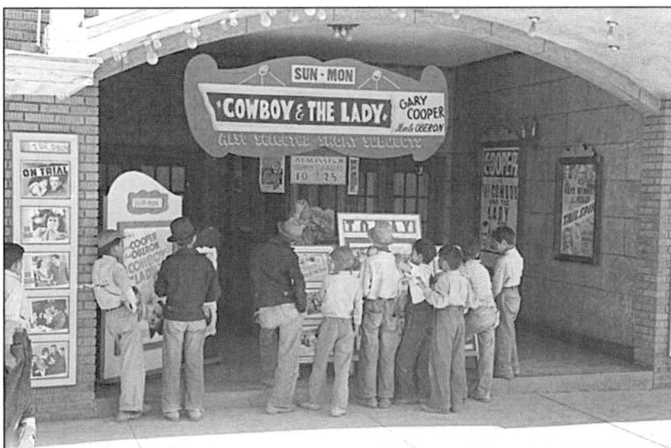

Millions of Americans went to the movies once a week.

Memorable Movies

- Gone With the Wind
- The Wizard of Oz
- Goodbye, Mr. Chips
- Stagecoach
- Wuthering Heights
- Midnight
- Gunga Din
- Ninotchka
- Mr. Smith Goes to Washington
- Dark Victory
- The Women
- The Old Maid

The nine tables that follow are reprinted from the actual 1940 census, for the city of Los Angeles. They include actual data on race, percentage of voting population, school attendance, number of school years completed, foreign born, and employment of workers 14 years and older by job, industry and race. In addition to being incredibly fascinating, these facts help to strengthen and visualize the actual environment in which Herbert Thomas Kalmus lived and worked.

Table B-35.—AGE, BY RACE AND SEX, FOR THE CITY OF LOS ANGELES: 1940 AND 1930

[Figures for white population in 1930 revised to include Mexicans classified with "Other races" in the 1930 reports. Percent not shown where less than 0.1 or where base is less than 100]

AGE AND CENSUS YEAR	ALL CLASSES			NATIVE WHITE			FOREIGN-BORN WHITE			NEGRO			OTHER RACES		
	Total	Male	Female	Total	Male	Female	Total	Male	Female	Total	Male	Female	Total	Male	Female
All ages: 1940	1,504,277	734,135	770,142	1,191,182	575,597	615,585	215,248	107,478	107,770	63,774	29,906	33,868	34,073	21,154	12,919
Under 5 years	83,973	42,929	41,044	77,478	39,607	37,871	245	125	120	3,784	1,926	1,858	2,466	1,271	1,195
5 to 9 years	80,162	40,197	39,965	73,590	36,953	36,637	480	226	254	3,744	1,813	1,931	2,348	1,205	1,143
10 to 14 years	90,088	45,455	44,633	82,139	41,376	40,763	1,156	579	577	3,876	1,958	1,918	2,917	1,542	1,375
15 to 19 years	104,139	51,135	53,004	92,135	45,119	47,016	3,956	1,917	2,039	4,310	2,136	2,174	3,738	1,963	1,775
20 to 24 years	124,750	61,182	63,568	108,611	53,442	55,169	7,086	3,301	3,785	5,257	2,409	2,848	3,796	2,030	1,766
25 to 29 years	141,813	70,315	71,498	119,196	59,254	59,942	12,120	5,569	6,551	7,066	3,249	3,817	3,431	2,243	1,188
30 to 34 years	134,451	66,962	67,489	108,201	53,755	54,446	16,339	7,838	8,501	6,839	3,062	3,777	3,072	2,307	765
35 to 39 years	131,273	65,571	65,702	98,929	49,297	49,632	22,591	11,203	11,388	6,676	2,958	3,718	3,077	2,113	964
40 to 44 years	121,214	60,554	60,660	89,259	44,172	45,087	23,823	12,106	11,717	5,524	2,633	2,891	2,608	1,643	965
45 to 49 years	111,092	54,736	56,356	79,174	38,100	41,074	25,398	13,344	12,054	4,745	2,262	2,483	1,775	1,030	745
50 to 54 years	100,990	49,638	51,352	69,236	32,348	36,888	26,082	14,034	12,048	3,775	1,825	1,950	1,897	1,431	466
55 to 59 years	83,794	40,266	43,528	56,698	25,826	30,872	23,058	12,142	10,916	2,720	1,247	1,473	1,318	1,051	267
60 to 64 years	69,084	31,488	37,596	47,734	20,709	27,025	18,428	9,089	9,339	2,001	932	1,069	921	758	163
65 to 69 years	53,888	23,202	30,686	37,816	15,549	22,267	13,901	6,566	7,335	1,781	777	1,004	390	310	80
70 to 74 years	36,461	15,456	21,005	25,300	10,240	15,060	10,113	4,679	5,434	855	377	478	193	160	33
75 years and over	37,105	15,049	22,056	25,686	9,850	15,836	10,472	4,760	5,712	821	342	479	126	97	29
Under 1 year	17,488	9,018	8,470	16,190	8,381	7,809	9	5	4	766	379	387	523	253	270
5 years	15,972	8,130	7,842	14,699	7,492	7,207	84	45	39	745	372	373	444	221	223
14 years	19,245	9,744	9,501	17,413	8,808	8,605	360	179	181	795	416	379	677	341	336
15 years	19,902	10,026	9,876	17,967	9,003	8,964	370	203	167	840	444	396	725	376	349
16 and 17 years	39,485	19,375	20,110	35,012	17,193	17,819	1,367	628	739	1,637	774	863	1,469	780	689
21 years and over	1,123,485	543,610	579,875	846,508	403,206	443,302	208,135	104,022	104,113	47,086	21,636	25,450	21,756	14,746	7,010
All ages: 1930	1,238,048	610,678	627,370	937,826	452,902	484,924	232,874	120,975	111,899	38,894	18,349	20,545	28,454	18,452	10,002
Under 5 years	78,799	40,206	38,593	72,687	37,067	35,620	712	353	359	2,435	1,220	1,215	2,965	1,566	1,399
5 to 9 years	86,569	43,375	43,194	76,727	38,430	38,297	3,449	1,716	1,733	2,808	1,420	1,388	3,585	1,809	1,776
10 to 14 years	77,634	38,819	38,815	66,999	33,553	33,446	5,960	2,954	3,006	2,505	1,208	1,297	2,170	1,104	1,066
15 to 19 years	84,516	40,698	43,818	70,456	33,765	36,691	9,818	4,756	5,062	2,643	1,211	1,432	1,599	966	633
20 to 24 years	109,221	53,055	56,166	86,865	41,443	45,422	16,307	8,157	8,150	3,455	1,488	1,967	2,594	1,967	627
25 to 29 years	122,836	61,529	61,307	92,050	45,198	46,852	23,183	12,134	11,049	4,326	1,926	2,400	3,277	2,271	1,006
30 to 34 years	116,783	58,782	58,001	86,473	42,792	43,681	23,255	12,287	10,968	4,145	1,966	2,179	2,910	1,737	1,173
35 to 39 years	114,695	57,399	57,296	81,610	39,737	41,873	26,259	14,306	11,953	4,563	2,083	2,480	2,263	1,273	990
40 to 44 years	101,434	51,952	49,482	69,126	33,799	35,327	26,400	14,544	11,856	3,455	1,739	1,716	2,453	1,870	583
45 to 49 years	89,528	45,328	44,200	59,548	28,698	30,850	24,967	13,540	11,427	2,995	1,445	1,550	2,018	1,645	373
50 to 54 years	75,022	36,845	38,177	51,133	23,947	27,186	20,374	10,655	9,719	2,107	1,060	1,047	1,408	1,183	225
55 to 59 years	57,188	27,051	30,137	39,749	18,100	21,649	15,553	7,772	7,781	1,257	635	622	629	544	85
60 to 64 years	45,603	20,786	24,817	30,871	13,575	17,296	13,526	6,523	7,003	883	394	489	323	294	29
65 to 69 years	33,493	15,013	18,480	22,488	9,601	12,887	10,297	5,070	5,227	564	218	346	144	124	20
70 to 74 years	22,724	10,339	12,385	15,972	6,975	8,997	6,352	3,147	3,205	336	160	176	64	57	7
75 years and over	21,306	9,145	12,161	14,534	5,959	8,575	6,357	3,003	3,354	381	155	226	34	28	6
Not reported	697	356	341	538	263	275	105	58	47	36	21	15	18	14	4
Under 1 year	15,103	7,718	7,385	14,153	7,229	6,924	28	12	16	461	225	236	461	252	209
5 years	17,756	9,063	8,693	16,076	8,225	7,851	320	163	157	582	299	283	778	376	402
14 years	15,604	7,885	7,719	13,325	6,745	6,580	1,396	706	690	530	247	283	353	187	166
15 years	15,603	7,698	7,905	13,315	6,516	6,799	1,518	776	742	456	226	230	314	180	134
16 and 17 years	31,997	15,566	16,431	26,845	13,076	13,769	3,551	1,709	1,842	1,025	455	570	576	326	250
21 years and over	891,136	438,491	452,645	635,336	302,846	332,490	210,238	109,949	100,289	27,905	13,043	14,862	17,657	12,653	5,004
Percent: 1940	100.0	100.0	100.0	100.0	100.0	100.0	100.0	100.0	100.0	100.0	100.0	100.0	100.0	100.0	100.0
Under 5 years	5.6	5.8	5.3	6.5	6.9	6.2	0.1	0.1	0.1	5.9	6.4	5.5	7.2	6.0	9.2
5 to 9 years	5.3	5.5	5.2	6.2	6.4	6.0	0.2	0.2	0.2	5.9	6.1	5.7	6.9	5.7	8.8
10 to 14 years	6.0	6.2	5.8	6.9	7.2	6.6	0.5	0.5	0.5	6.1	6.5	5.7	8.6	7.3	10.6
15 to 19 years	6.9	7.0	6.9	7.7	7.8	7.6	1.8	1.8	1.9	6.8	7.1	6.4	11.0	9.3	13.7
20 to 24 years	8.3	8.3	8.3	9.1	9.3	9.0	3.3	3.1	3.5	8.2	8.1	8.4	11.1	9.6	13.7
25 to 29 years	9.4	9.6	9.3	10.0	10.3	9.7	5.6	5.2	6.1	11.1	10.9	11.3	10.1	10.6	9.2
30 to 34 years	8.9	9.1	8.8	9.1	9.3	8.8	7.6	7.3	7.9	10.7	10.2	11.2	9.0	10.9	5.9
35 to 39 years	8.7	8.9	8.5	8.3	8.6	8.1	10.5	10.4	10.6	10.5	9.9	11.0	9.0	10.0	7.5
40 to 44 years	8.1	8.2	7.9	7.5	7.7	7.3	11.1	11.3	10.9	8.7	8.8	8.5	7.7	7.8	7.5
45 to 49 years	7.4	7.5	7.3	6.6	6.6	6.7	11.8	12.4	11.2	7.4	7.6	7.3	5.2	4.9	5.8
50 to 54 years	6.7	6.8	6.7	5.8	5.6	6.0	12.1	13.1	11.2	5.9	6.1	5.8	5.6	6.8	3.6
55 to 59 years	5.6	5.5	5.7	4.8	4.5	5.0	10.7	11.3	10.1	4.3	4.2	4.3	3.9	5.0	2.1
60 to 64 years	4.6	4.3	4.9	4.0	3.6	4.4	8.6	8.5	8.7	3.1	3.1	3.2	2.7	3.6	1.3
65 to 69 years	3.6	3.2	4.0	3.2	2.7	3.6	6.5	6.1	6.8	2.8	2.6	3.0	1.1	1.5	0.6
70 to 74 years	2.4	2.1	2.7	2.1	1.8	2.4	4.7	4.4	5.0	1.3	1.3	1.4	0.6	0.8	0.3
75 years and over	2.5	2.0	2.9	2.2	1.7	2.6	4.9	4.4	5.3	1.3	1.1	1.4	0.4	0.5	0.2
Under 1 year	1.2	1.2	1.1	1.4	1.5	1.3	-	-	-	1.2	1.3	1.1	1.5	1.2	2.1
5 years	1.1	1.1	1.0	1.2	1.3	1.2	-	-	-	1.2	1.2	1.1	1.3	1.0	1.7
14 years	1.3	1.3	1.2	1.5	1.5	1.4	0.2	0.2	0.2	1.2	1.4	1.1	2.0	1.6	2.6
15 years	1.3	1.4	1.3	1.5	1.6	1.5	0.2	0.2	0.2	1.3	1.5	1.2	2.1	1.8	2.7
16 and 17 years	2.6	2.6	2.6	2.9	3.0	2.9	0.6	0.6	0.7	2.6	2.6	2.5	4.3	3.7	5.3
21 years and over	74.7	74.0	75.3	71.1	70.1	72.0	96.7	96.8	96.6	73.8	72.3	75.1	63.9	69.7	54.3
Percent: 1930	100.0	100.0	100.0	100.0	100.0	100.0	100.0	100.0	100.0	100.0	100.0	100.0	100.0	100.0	100.0
Under 5 years	6.4	6.6	6.2	7.8	8.2	7.3	0.3	0.3	0.3	6.3	6.6	5.9	10.4	8.5	14.0
5 to 9 years	7.0	7.1	6.9	8.2	8.5	7.9	1.5	1.4	1.5	7.2	7.7	6.8	12.6	9.8	17.8
10 to 14 years	6.3	6.4	6.2	7.1	7.4	6.9	2.6	2.4	2.7	6.4	6.6	6.3	7.6	6.0	10.7
15 to 19 years	6.8	6.7	7.0	7.5	7.5	7.6	4.2	3.9	4.5	6.8	6.6	7.0	5.6	5.2	6.3
20 to 24 years	8.8	8.7	9.0	9.3	9.2	9.4	7.0	6.7	7.3	8.9	8.1	9.6	9.1	10.7	6.3
25 to 29 years	9.9	10.1	9.8	9.8	10.0	9.7	10.0	10.0	9.9	11.1	10.5	11.7	11.5	12.3	10.1
30 to 34 years	9.4	9.6	9.2	9.2	9.4	9.0	10.0	10.2	9.8	10.7	10.7	10.6	10.2	9.4	11.7
35 to 39 years	9.3	9.4	9.1	8.7	8.8	8.6	11.3	11.8	10.7	11.7	11.4	12.1	8.0	6.9	9.9
40 to 44 years	8.2	8.5	7.9	7.4	7.5	7.3	11.3	12.0	10.6	8.9	9.5	8.4	8.6	10.1	5.8
45 to 49 years	7.2	7.4	7.0	6.3	6.3	6.4	10.7	11.2	10.2	7.7	7.9	7.5	7.1	8.9	3.7
50 to 54 years	6.1	6.0	6.1	5.5	5.3	5.6	8.7	8.8	8.7	5.4	5.8	5.1	4.9	6.4	2.2
55 to 59 years	4.6	4.4	4.8	4.2	4.0	4.5	6.7	6.4	7.0	3.2	3.5	3.0	2.2	2.9	0.8
60 to 64 years	3.7	3.4	4.0	3.3	3.0	3.6	5.8	5.4	6.3	2.3	2.1	2.4	1.1	1.6	0.3
65 to 69 years	2.7	2.5	2.9	2.4	2.1	2.7	4.4	4.2	4.7	1.5	1.2	1.7	0.5	0.7	0.2
70 to 74 years	1.8	1.7	2.0	1.7	1.5	1.9	2.7	2.6	2.9	0.9	0.9	0.9	0.2	0.3	0.1
75 years and over	1.7	1.5	1.9	1.5	1.3	1.8	2.7	2.5	3.0	1.0	0.8	1.1	0.1	0.2	0.1
Not reported	0.1	0.1	0.1	0.1	0.1	0.1	-	-	-	0.1	0.1	0.1	0.1	0.1	-
Under 1 year	1.2	1.3	1.2	1.5	1.6	1.4	-	-	-	1.2	1.2	1.1	1.6	1.4	2.1
5 years	1.4	1.5	1.4	1.7	1.8	1.6	0.1	0.1	0.1	1.5	1.6	1.4	2.7	2.0	4.0
14 years	1.3	1.3	1.2	1.4	1.5	1.4	0.6	0.6	0.6	1.4	1.3	1.4	1.2	1.0	1.7
15 years	1.3	1.3	1.3	1.4	1.4	1.4	0.7	0.6	0.7	1.2	1.2	1.1	1.1	1.0	1.3
16 and 17 years	2.6	2.5	2.6	2.9	2.9	2.8	1.5	1.4	1.6	2.6	2.5	2.8	2.0	1.8	2.5
21 years and over	72.0	71.8	72.1	67.7	66.9	68.6	90.3	90.9	89.6	71.7	71.1	72.3	62.1	68.6	50.0

Table B-36.—RACE, BY NATIVITY AND SEX, FOR THE CITY OF LOS ANGELES: 1940 AND 1930

[Figures for white population in 1930 have been revised to include Mexicans who were classified with "Other races" in the 1930 reports. Percent not shown where less than 0.1 or where base is less than 100. Sex ratio not shown where number of females is less than 100]

SEX, NATIVITY, AND CENSUS YEAR	All classes	White	Negro	Other races	OTHER RACES				PERCENT BY RACE				PERCENT BY NATIVITY					
					Indian	Chinese	Japanese	All other	All classes	White	Negro	Other races	All classes	White	Negro	Indian	Chinese	Japanese
TOTAL																		
1940	1,504,277	1,406,430	63,774	34,073	862	4,736	23,321	5,154	100.0	93.5	4.2	2.3	100.0	100.0	100.0	100.0	100.0	100.0
Native	1,277,240	1,191,182	63,294	22,764	769	2,540	14,595	4,860	100.0	93.3	5.0	1.8	84.9	84.7	99.2	89.2	53.6	62.6
Foreign born	227,037	215,248	480	11,309	93	2,196	8,726	294	100.0	94.8	0.2	5.0	15.1	15.3	0.8	10.8	46.4	37.4
1930	1,238,048	1,170,700	38,894	28,454	616	3,009	21,081	3,748	100.0	94.6	3.1	2.3	100.0	100.0	100.0	100.0	100.0	100.0
Native	990,913	937,826	38,369	14,718	594	1,421	9,216	3,487	100.0	94.6	3.9	1.5	80.0	80.1	98.7	96.4	47.2	43.7
Foreign born	247,135	232,874	525	13,736	22	1,588	11,865	261	100.0	94.2	0.2	5.6	20.0	19.9	1.3	3.6	52.8	56.3
MALE																		
1940	734,135	683,075	29,906	21,154	435	3,311	13,073	4,335	100.0	93.0	4.1	2.9	100.0	100.0	100.0	100.0	100.0	100.0
Native	618,994	575,597	29,653	13,744	385	1,539	7,689	4,131	100.0	93.0	4.8	2.2	84.3	84.3	99.2	88.5	46.5	58.8
Foreign born	115,141	107,478	253	7,410	50	1,772	5,384	204	100.0	93.3	0.2	6.4	15.7	15.7	0.8	11.5	53.5	41.2
1930	610,678	573,877	18,349	18,452	287	2,228	12,597	3,340	100.0	94.0	3.0	3.0	100.0	100.0	100.0	100.0	100.0	100.0
Native	480,138	452,902	18,049	9,187	277	881	4,873	3,156	100.0	94.3	3.8	1.9	78.6	78.9	98.4	96.5	39.5	38.7
Foreign born	130,540	120,975	300	9,265	10	1,347	7,724	184	100.0	92.7	0.2	7.1	21.4	21.1	1.6	3.5	60.5	61.3
FEMALE																		
1940	770,142	723,355	33,868	12,919	427	1,425	10,248	819	100.0	93.9	4.4	1.7	100.0	100.0	100.0	100.0	100.0	100.0
Native	658,246	615,585	33,641	9,020	384	1,001	6,906	729	100.0	93.5	5.1	1.4	85.5	85.1	99.3	89.9	70.2	67.4
Foreign born	111,896	107,770	227	3,899	43	424	3,342	90	100.0	96.3	0.2	3.5	14.5	14.9	0.7	10.1	29.8	32.6
1930	627,370	596,823	20,545	10,002	329	781	8,484	408	100.0	95.1	3.3	1.6	100.0	100.0	100.0	100.0	100.0	100.0
Native	510,775	484,924	20,320	5,531	317	540	4,343	331	100.0	94.9	4.0	1.1	81.4	81.3	98.9	96.4	69.1	51.2
Foreign born	116,595	111,899	225	4,471	12	241	4,141	77	100.0	96.0	0.2	3.8	18.6	18.7	1.1	3.6	30.9	48.8
MALES PER 100 FEMALES																		
1940	95.3	94.4	88.3	163.7	101.9	232.4	127.6	529.3	-	-	-	-	-	-	-	-	-	-
Native	94.0	93.5	88.1	152.4	100.3	153.7	111.3	566.7	-	-	-	-	-	-	-	-	-	-
Foreign born	102.9	99.7	111.5	190.0	-	417.9	161.1	-	-	-	-	-	-	-	-	-	-	-
1930	97.3	96.2	89.3	184.5	87.2	285.3	148.5	818.6	-	-	-	-	-	-	-	-	-	-
Native	94.0	93.4	88.8	166.1	87.4	163.1	112.2	953.5	-	-	-	-	-	-	-	-	-	-
Foreign born	112.0	108.1	133.3	207.2	-	558.9	186.5	-	-	-	-	-	-	-	-	-	-	-

Table B-37.—POTENTIAL VOTING POPULATION, BY CITIZENSHIP, RACE, NATIVITY, AND SEX, FOR THE CITY OF LOS ANGELES: 1940 AND 1930

[Figures for white population in 1930 have been revised to include Mexicans who were classified with "Other races" in the 1930 reports. Percent not shown where less than 0.1]

CITIZENSHIP, RACE, AND NATIVITY	TOTAL POPULATION (ALL AGES)								POPULATION 21 YEARS OLD AND OVER							
	Total number		Percent		Male		Female		Total number		Percent		Male		Female	
	1940	1930	1940	1930	1940	1930	1940	1930	1940	1930	1940	1930	1940	1930	1940	1930
Total	1,504,277	1,238,048	100.0	100.0	734,135	610,678	770,142	627,370	1,123,485	891,136	100.0	100.0	543,610	438,491	579,875	452,645
Percent citizen	-	-	93.1	88.4	-	-	-	-	-	-	91.3	86.1	-	-	-	-
Percent alien and citiz. not rptd.	-	-	6.9	11.6	-	-	-	-	-	-	8.7	13.9	-	-	-	-
Citizen	1,400,979	1,094,847	100.0	100.0	684,280	534,179	716,699	560,668	1,025,708	767,614	100.0	100.0	496,506	371,717	529,202	395,897
White—Native	1,191,182	937,826	85.0	85.7	575,597	452,902	615,585	484,924	846,508	635,336	82.5	82.8	403,206	302,846	443,302	332,490
Naturalized	123,520	103,788	8.8	9.5	65,175	53,957	58,345	49,831	121,515	100,244	11.8	13.1	64,188	52,279	57,327	47,965
Negro—Native	63,294	38,369	4.5	3.5	29,653	18,049	33,641	20,320	46,621	27,424	4.5	3.6	21,392	12,765	25,229	14,659
Naturalized	219	146	-	-	111	84	108	62	214	140	-	-	110	83	104	57
Other races—Native	22,764	14,718	1.6	1.3	13,744	9,187	9,020	5,531	10,850	4,470	1.1	0.6	7,610	3,744	3,240	726
Indian	769	594	0.1	0.1	385	277	384	317	500	374	-	-	259	189	241	185
Chinese	2,540	1,421	0.2	0.1	1,539	881	1,001	540	1,149	573	0.1	0.1	826	439	323	134
Japanese	14,595	9,216	1.0	0.8	7,689	4,873	6,906	4,343	5,399	806	0.5	0.1	2,972	531	2,427	275
Filipino	4,465	3,231	0.3	0.3	3,909	3,014	556	217	3,620	2,640	0.4	0.3	3,449	2,534	171	106
Hindu	15	9	-	-	10	5	5	4	8	1	-	-	6	-	2	1
All other	380	247	-	-	212	137	168	110	174	76	-	-	98	51	76	25
Alien	95,322	138,667	100.0	100.0	45,991	74,500	49,331	64,167	90,305	119,328	100.0	100.0	43,497	64,899	46,808	54,429
White—First papers	21,405	21,834	22.5	15.7	12,557	15,708	8,848	6,126	20,951	21,216	23.2	17.8	12,314	15,395	8,637	5,821
No papers	62,419	102,766	65.5	74.1	25,922	49,341	36,497	53,425	58,264	84,630	64.5	70.9	23,949	40,430	34,315	44,200
Negro—First papers	43	40	-	-	25	32	18	8	43	39	-	-	25	32	18	7
No papers	146	291	0.2	0.2	77	154	69	137	141	256	0.2	0.2	73	133	68	123
Other races—Foreign born	11,309	13,736	11.9	9.9	7,410	9,265	3,899	4,471	10,906	13,167	12.1	11.1	7,136	8,909	3,770	4,276
Indian	93	22	0.1	-	50	10	43	12	87	17	0.1	-	45	[illegible]	42	9
Chinese	2,196	1,588	2.3	1.1	1,772	1,347	424	241	1,930	1,387	2.1	2.1	1,564	1,173	366	214
Japanese	8,726	11,865	9.2	8.6	5,384	7,724	3,342	4,141	8,612	11,534	9.5	9.7	5,330	7,547	3,282	3,987
Filipino	33	14	-	-	16	7	17	7	24	13	-	-	14	7	10	6
Hindu	45	68	-	-	42	64	3	4	44	66	-	0.1	41	62	3	4
All other	216	179	0.2	0.1	146	118	70	66	209	170	0.2	0.1	142	112	67	58
Citizenship not reported	7,976	4,534	100.0	100.0	3,864	1,999	4,112	2,535	7,472	4,194	100.0	100.0	3,607	1,875	3,865	2,319
White	7,904	4,486	99.1	98.9	3,824	1,969	4,080	2,517	7,405	4,148	99.1	98.9	3,571	1,845	3,834	2,303
Negro	72	48	0.9	1.1	40	30	32	18	67	46	0.9	1.1	36	30	31	16

Table B-38.—SCHOOL ATTENDANCE, BY AGE, RACE, AND SEX, FOR THE CITY OF LOS ANGELES: 1940 AND 1930

[Figures for white population in 1930 revised to include Mexicans classified with "Other races" in the 1930 reports. Percent not shown where less than 0.1 or where base is less than 100]

AGE, SEX, AND CENSUS YEAR	ALL CLASSES			NATIVE WHITE			FOREIGN-BORN WHITE			NEGRO			OTHER RACES		
	Total number	Attending school		Total number	Attending school		Total number	Attending school		Total number	Attending school		Total number	Attending school	
		Number	Percent		Number	Percent		Number	Percent		Number	Percent		Number	Percent
1940															
Total, 5 to 24 years	399,139	244,024	61.1	356,475	220,259	61.8	12,678	4,641	36.6	17,187	10,500	61.1	12,799	8,624	67.4
5 years	15,972	8,580	53.7	14,699	7,802	53.1	84	33	-	745	471	63.2	444	274	61.7
6 years	15,329	14,065	91.8	14,016	12,835	91.6	85	69	-	753	714	94.8	475	447	94.1
7 to 9 years	48,861	47,673	97.6	44,875	43,789	97.6	311	298	95.8	2,246	2,194	97.7	1,429	1,392	97.4
10 to 13 years	70,843	69,431	98.0	64,726	63,461	98.0	796	768	96.5	3,081	3,014	97.8	2,240	2,188	97.7
14 years	19,245	18,775	97.6	17,413	16,990	97.6	360	349	96.9	795	774	97.4	677	662	97.8
15 years	19,902	19,284	96.9	17,967	17,412	96.9	370	359	97.0	840	807	96.1	725	706	97.4
16 and 17 years	39,485	35,065	88.8	35,012	31,074	88.8	1,367	1,183	86.5	1,637	1,417	86.6	1,469	1,391	94.7
18 and 19 years	44,752	18,073	40.4	39,156	15,535	39.7	2,219	874	39.4	1,833	760	41.5	1,544	904	58.5
20 years	22,430	4,424	19.7	19,332	3,804	19.7	1,276	228	17.9	974	135	13.9	848	257	30.3
21 to 24 years	102,320	8,654	8.5	89,279	7,557	8.5	5,810	480	8.3	4,283	214	5.0	2,948	403	13.7
Male, 5 to 24 years	197,969	124,862	63.1	176,890	112,511	63.6	6,023	2,491	41.4	8,316	5,230	62.9	6,740	4,630	68.7
5 years	8,130	4,340	53.4	7,492	3,955	52.8	45	21	-	372	232	62.4	221	132	59.7
6 years	7,596	6,957	91.6	6,947	6,344	91.3	32	27	-	367	347	94.6	250	239	95.6
7 to 9 years	24,471	23,858	97.5	22,514	21,951	97.5	149	143	96.0	1,074	1,046	97.4	734	718	97.8
10 to 13 years	35,711	34,989	98.0	32,568	31,908	98.0	400	392	98.0	1,542	1,514	98.2	1,201	1,175	97.8
14 years	9,744	9,508	97.6	8,808	8,595	97.6	179	172	96.1	416	407	97.8	341	334	97.9
15 years	10,026	9,715	96.9	9,003	8,724	96.9	203	195	96.1	444	430	96.8	376	366	97.3
16 and 17 years	19,375	17,432	90.0	17,193	15,473	90.0	628	550	87.6	774	670	86.6	780	739	94.7
18 and 19 years	21,734	9,724	44.7	18,923	8,306	43.9	1,086	505	46.5	918	406	44.2	807	507	62.8
20 years	10,809	2,580	23.9	9,336	2,216	23.7	609	146	24.0	437	68	15.6	427	150	35.1
21 to 24 years	50,373	5,759	11.4	44,106	5,039	11.4	2,692	340	12.6	1,972	110	5.6	1,603	270	16.8
Female, 5 to 24 years	201,170	119,162	59.2	179,585	107,748	60.0	6,655	2,150	32.3	8,871	5,270	59.4	6,059	3,994	65.9
5 years	7,842	4,240	54.1	7,207	3,847	53.4	39	12	-	373	239	64.1	223	142	63.7
6 years	7,733	7;108	91.9	7,069	6,491	91.8	53	42	-	386	367	95.1	225	208	92.4
7 to 9 years	24,390	23,815	97.6	22,361	21,838	97.7	162	155	95.7	1,172	1,148	98.0	695	674	97.0
10 to 13 years	35.132	34,442	98.0	32,158	31,553	98.1	396	376	94.9	1,539	1,500	97.5	1,039	1,013	97.5
14 years	9,501	9,267	97.5	8,605	8,395	97.6	181	177	97.8	379	367	96.8	336	328	97.6
15 years	9,876	9,569	96.9	8,964	8,688	96.9	167	164	98.2	396	377	95.2	349	340	97.4
16 and 17 years	20,110	17,633	87.7	17,819	15,601	87.6	739	633	85.7	863	747	86.6	689	652	94.6
18 and 19 years	23,018	8,349	36.3	20,233	7,229	35.7	1,133	369	32.6	915	354	38.7	737	397	53.9
20 years	11,621	1,844	15.9	9,996	1,588	15.9	667	82	12.3	537	67	12.5	421	107	25.4
21 to 24 years	51,947	2,895	5.6	45,173	2,518	5.6	3,118	140	4.5	2,311	104	4.5	1,345	133	9.9
1930															
Total, 5 to 24 years	357,940	223,854	62.5	301,047	193,441	64.3	35,534	16,526	46.5	11,411	6,931	60.7	9,948	6,956	69.9
5 years	17,756	9,767	55.0	16,076	8,792	54.7	320	139	43.4	582	361	62.0	778	475	61.1
6 years	17,337	15,361	88.6	15,610	13,827	88.6	452	391	86.5	540	481	89.1	735	662	90.1
7 to 9 years	51,476	49,472	96.1	45,041	43,305	96.1	2,677	2,562	95.7	1,686	1,610	95.5	2,072	1,995	96.3
10 to 13 years	62,030	61,382	99.0	53,674	53,129	99.0	4,564	4,506	98.7	1,975	1,949	98.7	1,817	1,798	99.0
14 years	15,604	15,415	98.8	13,325	13,176	98.9	1,396	1,371	98.2	530	521	98.3	353	347	98.3
15 years	15,603	15,257	97.8	13,315	13,050	98.0	1,518	1,469	96.8	456	436	95.6	314	302	96.2
16 and 17 years	31,997	27,688	86.5	26,845	23,461	87.4	3,551	2,830	79.7	1,025	886	86.4	576	511	88.7
18 and 19 years	36,916	14,800	40.1	30,296	12,466	41.1	4,749	1,545	32.5	1,162	442	38.0	709	347	48.9
20 years	19,394	4,393	22.7	15,621	3,752	24.0	2,697	429	15.9	598	87	14.5	478	125	26.2
21 to 24 years	89,827	10,319	11.5	71,244	8,483	11.9	13,610	1,284	9.4	2,857	158	5.5	2,116	394	18.6
Male, 5 to 24 years	175,947	113,010	64.2	147,191	97,318	66.1	17,583	8,522	48.5	5,327	3,374	63.3	5,846	3,796	64.9
5 years	9,063	4,939	54.5	8,225	4,459	54.2	163	75	46.0	299	178	59.5	376	227	60.4
6 years	8,845	7,824	88.5	7,957	7,035	88.4	224	192	85.7	284	253	89.1	380	344	90.5
7 to 9 years	25,467	24,474	96.1	22,248	21,395	96.2	1,329	1,272	95.7	837	794	94.9	1,053	1,013	96.2
10 to 13 years	30,934	30,615	99.0	26,808	26,542	99.0	2,248	2,217	98.6	961	948	98.6	917	908	99.0
14 years	7,885	7,795	98.9	6,745	6,674	98.9	706	696	98.6	247	241	97.6	187	184	98.4
15 years	7,698	7,568	98.3	6,516	6,421	98.5	776	754	97.2	226	220	97.3	180	173	96.1
16 and 17 years	15,566	13,862	89.1	13,076	11,727	89.7	1,709	1,429	83.6	455	409	89.9	326	297	91.1
18 and 19 years	17,434	7,609	43.6	14,173	6,326	44.6	2,271	845	37.2	530	214	40.4	460	224	48.7
20 years	9,089	2,345	25.8	7,241	1,975	27.3	1,247	233	18.7	247	41	16.6	354	96	27.1
21 to 24 years	43,966	5,979	13.6	34,202	4,764	13.9	6,910	809	11.7	1,241	76	6.1	1,613	330	20.5
Female, 5 to 24 years	181,993	110,844	60.9	153,856	96,123	62.5	17,951	8,004	44.6	6,084	3,557	58.5	4,102	3,160	77.0
5 years	8,693	4,828	55.5	7,851	4,333	55.2	157	64	40.8	283	183	64.7	402	248	61.7
6 years	8,492	7,537	88.8	7,653	6,792	88.7	228	199	87.3	256	228	89.1	355	318	89.6
7 to 9 years	26,009	24,998	96.1	22,793	21,910	96.1	1,348	1,290	95.7	849	816	96.1	1,019	982	96.4
10 to 13 years	31,096	30,767	98.9	26,866	26,587	99.0	2,316	2,289	98.8	1,014	1,001	98.7	900	890	98.9
14 years	7,719	7,620	98.7	6,580	6,502	98.8	690	675	97.8	283	280	98.9	166	163	98.2
15 years	7,905	7,689	97.3	6,799	6,629	97.5	742	715	96.4	230	216	93.9	134	129	96.3
16 and 17 years	16,431	13,826	84.1	13,769	11,734	85.2	1,842	1,401	76.1	570	477	83.7	250	214	85.6
18 and 19 years	19,482	7,191	36.9	16,123	6,140	38.1	2,478	700	28.2	632	228	36.1	249	123	49.4
20 years	10,305	2,048	19.9	8,380	1,777	21.2	1,450	196	13.5	351	46	13.1	124	29	23.4
21 to 24 years	45,861	4,340	9.5	37,042	3,719	10.0	6,700	475	7.1	1,616	82	5.1	503	64	12.7

Table B-39.—PERSONS 25 YEARS OLD AND OVER, BY YEARS OF SCHOOL COMPLETED, RACE, AND SEX, FOR THE CITY OF LOS ANGELES: 1940

[Percent not shown where less than 0.1; median and percent not shown where base is less than 100]

YEARS OF SCHOOL COMPLETED	ALL CLASSES			NATIVE WHITE			FOREIGN-BORN WHITE			NEGRO			OTHER RACES		
	Total	Male	Female	Total	Male	Female	Total	Male	Female	Total	Male	Female	Total	Male	Female
Persons 25 years old and over	1,021,165	493,237	527,928	757,229	359,100	398,129	202,325	101,330	100,995	42,803	19,664	23,139	18,808	13,143	5,665
No school years completed	22,115	10,495	11,620	3,718	1,934	1,784	16,034	7,272	8,762	1,253	609	644	1,110	680	430
Grade school: 1 to 4 years	47,466	24,820	22,646	18,116	10,057	8,059	23,559	11,571	11,988	4 087	1,947	2,140	1,704	1,245	459
5 or 6 years	66,712	34,305	32,407	35,041	18,067	16,974	24,200	12,220	11,9[illegible]0	5,[illegible]26	2,626	2,900	1,945	1,392	553
7 or 8 years	265,375	131,719	133,656	185,495	91,402	94,093	63,691	31,611	32,080	11[illegible]09	5,378	6,031	4,780	3,328	1,452
High school: 1 to 3 years	186,113	86,121	99,992	152,981	70,171	82,810	21,582	10,191	11,391	[illegible],826	3,778	5,048	2,724	1,981	743
4 years	255,666	108,806	146,860	210,844	87,357	123,487	33,234	15,563	17,671	7,194	3,085	4,109	4,394	2,801	1,593
College: 1 to 3 years	95,417	47,614	47,803	82,921	40,359	42,562	8,858	5,223	3,635	2,577	1,196	1,381	1,061	836	225
4 years or more	72,648	42,780	29,868	61,041	34,827	26,214	9,367	6,557	2,810	1,324	653	671	916	743	173
Not reported	9,653	6,577	3,076	7,072	4,926	2,146	1,800	1,122	678	607	392	215	174	137	37
Median school years completed	10.7	10.5	10.9	11.6	11.4	11.8	8.1	8.2	8.1	8.8	8.7	8.9	8.9	8.9	8.9
Percent less than 5 years completed	6.8	7.2	6.5	2.9	3.3	2.5	19.6	18.6	20.5	12.5	13.0	12.0	15.0	14.6	15.7
PERCENT DISTRIBUTION															
Persons 25 years old and over	100.0	100.0	100.0	100.0	100.0	100.0	100.0	100.0	100.0	100.0	100.0	100.0	100.0	100.0	100.0
No school years completed	2.2	2.1	2.2	0.5	0.5	0.4	7.9	7.2	8.7	2.9	3.1	2.8	5.9	5.2	7.6
Grade school: 1 to 4 years	4.6	5.0	4.3	2.4	2.8	2.0	11.6	11.4	11.9	9.5	9.9	9.2	9.1	9.5	8.1
5 or 6 years	6.5	7.0	6.1	4.6	5.0	4.3	12.0	12.1	11.9	12.9	13.4	12.5	10.3	10.6	9.8
7 or 8 years	26.0	26.7	25.3	24.5	25.5	23.6	31.5	31.2	31.8	26.7	27.3	26.1	25.4	25.3	25.6
High school: 1 to 3 years	18.2	17.5	18.9	20.2	19.5	20.8	10.7	10.1	11.3	20.6	19.2	21.8	14.5	15.1	13.1
4 years	25.0	22.1	27.8	27.8	24.3	31.0	16.4	15.4	17.5	16.8	15.7	17.8	23.4	21.3	28.1
College: 1 to 3 years	9.3	9.7	9.1	11.0	11.2	10.7	4.4	5.2	3.6	6.0	6.1	6.0	5.6	6.4	4.0
4 years or more	7.1	8.7	5.7	8.1	9.7	6.6	4.6	6.5	2.8	3.1	3.3	2.9	4.9	5.7	3.1
Not reported	0.9	1.3	0.6	0.9	1.4	0.5	0.9	1.1	0.7	1.4	2.0	0.9	0.9	1.0	0.7

Table B-40.—FOREIGN-BORN WHITE, BY COUNTRY OF BIRTH, BY SEX, FOR THE CITY OF LOS ANGELES: 1940 AND 1930

[Figures for white population in 1930 revised to include Mexicans classified with "Other races" in the 1930 reports. Percent not shown where less than 0.1 or where base is less than 100]

COUNTRY OF BIRTH	BOTH SEXES		PERCENT		MALE		FEMALE	
	1940	1930	1940	1930	1940	1930	1940	1930
All countries	215,248	232,874	100.0	100.0	107,478	120,975	107,770	111,899
England	19,713	22,258	9.2	9.6	9,478	11,073	10,235	11,185
Scotland	5,980	6,898	2.8	3.0	2,928	3,557	3,052	3,341
Wales	741	1,084	0.3	0.5	402	601	339	483
Northern Ireland	1,646	2,212	0.8	0.9	794	1,054	852	1,158
Irish Free State (Eire)	4,194	5,000	1.9	2.1	1,953	2,390	2,241	2,610
Norway	3,435	3,747	1.6	1.6	1,703	1,942	1,732	1,805
Sweden	7,844	8,917	3.6	3.8	3,799	4,479	4,045	4,438
Denmark	3,138	3,536	1.5	1.5	1,766	2,037	1,372	1,499
Netherlands	2,013	1,892	0.9	0.8	1,155	1,085	858	807
Belgium	816	796	0.4	0.3	394	402	422	394
Luxemburg	95	107	-	-	50	61	45	46
Switzerland	1,940	2,150	0.9	0.9	1,082	1,220	858	930
France	3,196	3,482	1.5	1.5	1,368	1,548	1,828	1,934
Germany	17,528	18,094	8.1	7.8	8,835	9,347	8,693	8,747
Poland	7,448	6,895	3.5	3.0	3,962	3,750	3,486	3,145
Czechoslovakia	1,536	1,872	0.7	0.8	793	980	743	892
Austria	5,389	3,885	2.5	1.7	2,743	2,136	2,646	1,749
Hungary	3,978	3,055	1.8	1.3	1,917	1,593	2,061	1,462
Yugoslavia	3,441	3,290	1.6	1.4	2,179	2,149	1,262	1,141
Russia (U. S. S. R.)	25,595	19,744	11.9	8.5	12,955	10,243	12,640	9,501
Lithuania	1,158	952	0.5	0.4	634	569	524	383
Latvia	527	452	0.2	0.2	283	267	244	185
Finland	1,049	1,011	0,5	0.4	501	525	548	486
Rumania	2,750	2,481	1.3	1.1	1,418	1,300	1,332	1,181
Bulgaria	221	127	0.1	0.1	154	94	67	33
Turkey in Europe	17	65	-	-	5	39	12	26
Greece	1,905	1,848	0.9	0.8	1,526	1,533	379	315
Italy	13,256	12,685	6.2	5.4	7,955	7,746	5,301	4,939
Spain	1,154	1,421	0.5	0.6	711	888	443	533
Portugal	197	217	0.1	0.1	114	138	83	79
Other Europe	253	280	0.1	0.1	148	174	105	106
Palestine and Syria	1,066	872	0.5	0.4	597	514	469	358
Turkey in Asia	1,931	1,350	0.9	0.6	1,079	790	852	560
Other Asia	1,685	2,238	0.8	1.0	957	1,260	728	978
Canada—French	2,159	2,439	1.0	1.0	998	1,211	1,161	1,228
Canada—Other	25,596	28,305	11.9	12.2	11,177	12,949	14,419	15,356
Newfoundland	141	163	0.1	0.1	65	80	76	83
Mexico	36,840	53,573	17.1	23.0	17,129	27,374	19,711	26,199
Cuba and other West Indies	436	426	0.2	0.2	196	218	240	208
Central and South America	1,450	1,243	0.7	0.5	706	703	744	540
Australia	849	931	0.4	0.4	387	475	462	456
Azores	31	56	-	-	16	38	15	18
All other and not reported	911	825	0.4	0.4	466	443	445	382

Table B-41.—PERSONS 14 YEARS OLD AND OVER, BY EMPLOYMENT STATUS, CLASS OF WORKER, RACE, AND SEX, FOR THE CITY OF LOS ANGELES: 1940

[Percent not shown where less than 0.1 or where base is less than 100]

EMPLOYMENT STATUS	ALL CLASSES			NATIVE WHITE			FOREIGN-BORN WHITE			NEGRO			OTHER RACES		
	Total	Male	Female	Total	Male	Female	Total	Male	Female	Total	Male	Female	Total	Male	Female
Total population (all ages)	1,504,277	734,135	770,142	1,191,182	575,597	615,585	215,248	107,478	107,770	63,774	29,906	33,868	34,073	21,154	12,919
Persons 14 years old and over	1,269,299	615,298	654,001	975,388	466,469	508,919	213,727	106,727	107,000	53,165	24,625	28,540	27,019	17,477	9,542
In labor force	686,756	480,184	206,572	526,558	363,116	163,442	110,571	83,659	26,912	32,260	19,460	12,800	17,367	13,949	3,418
Not in labor force	582,543	135,114	447,429	448,830	103,353	345,477	103,156	23,068	80,088	20,905	5,165	15,740	9,652	3,528	6,124
Engaged in own home housew'k	334,979	2,693	332,286	255,529	1,973	253,556	65,245	570	64,675	10,314	109	10,205	3,891	41	3,850
In school	98,521	50,794	47,727	87,060	44,708	42,352	3,441	1,844	1,597	3,884	1,963	1,921	4,136	2,279	1,857
Unable to work	72,946	38,406	34,540	49,029	25,391	23,638	19,004	10,760	8,244	4,186	1,688	2,498	727	567	160
In institutions	6,771	5,027	1,744	5,156	3,842	1,314	1,030	685	345	440	379	61	145	121	24
Other and not reported	69,326	38,194	31,132	52,056	27,439	24,617	14,436	9,209	5,227	2,081	1,026	1,055	753	520	233
LABOR FORCE BY EMPLOYMENT STATUS															
In labor force	686,756	480,184	206,572	526,558	363,116	163,442	110,571	83,659	26,912	32,260	19,460	12,800	17,367	13,949	3,418
Employed (exc. public emerg. work)	586,897	407,425	179,472	451,564	309,374	142,190	95,589	71,437	24,152	23,678	13,800	9,878	16,066	12,814	3,252
At work	568,702	394,677	174,025	438,513	300,525	137,988	91,957	68,658	23,299	23,240	13,515	9,725	14,992	11,979	3,013
With a job	18,195	12,748	5,447	13,051	8,849	4,202	3,632	2,779	853	438	285	153	1,074	835	239
On public emerg. work (WPA, etc.)	13,551	14,402	4,149	14,009	10,736	3,273	1,717	1,490	227	2,733	2,093	640	92	83	9
Seeking work	81,308	58,357	22,951	60,985	43,006	17,979	13,265	10,732	2,533	5,849	3,567	2,282	1,209	1,052	157
Experienced workers	75,035	55,187	19,848	55,626	40,334	15,292	12,896	10,559	2,337	5,381	3,287	2,094	1,132	1,007	125
New workers	6,273	3,170	3,103	5,359	2,672	2,687	369	173	196	468	280	188	77	45	32
PERCENT BY SEX															
In labor force	100.0	69.9	30.1	100.0	69.0	31.0	100.0	75.7	24.3	100.0	60.3	39.7	100.0	80.3	19.7
Employed (exc. public emerg.)	100.0	69.4	30.6	100.0	68.5	31.5	100.0	74.7	25.3	100.0	58.3	41.7	100.0	79.8	20.2
On pub. emerg. work (WPA, etc.)	100.0	77.6	22.4	100.0	76.6	23.4	100.0	86.8	13.2	100.0	76.6	23.4	-	-	-
Seeking work	100.0	71.8	28.2	100.0	70.5	29.5	100.0	80.9	19.1	100.0	61.0	39.0	100.0	87.0	13.0
Not in labor force	100.0	23.2	76.8	100.0	23.0	77.0	100.0	22.4	77.6	100.0	24.7	75.3	100.0	36.6	63.4
Engaged in own home housew'k	100.0	0.8	99.2	100.0	0.8	99.2	100.0	0.9	99.1	100.0	1.1	98.9	100.0	1.1	98.9
In school	100.0	51.6	48.4	100.0	51.4	48.6	100.0	53.6	46.4	100.0	50.5	49.5	100.0	55.1	44.9
Unable to work	100.0	52.6	47.4	100.0	51.8	48.2	100.0	56.6	43.4	100.0	40.3	59.7	100.0	78.0	22.0
In institutions	100.0	74.2	25.8	100.0	74.5	25.5	100.0	66.5	33.5	100.0	86.1	13.9	100.0	83.4	16.6
Other and not reported	100.0	55.1	44.9	100.0	52.7	47.3	100.0	63.8	36.2	100.0	49.3	50.7	100.0	69.1	30.9
EMPLOYED WORKERS BY CLASS OF WORKER															
Employed (exc. public emerg.)	586,897	407,425	179,472	451,564	309,374	142,190	95,589	71,437	24,152	23,678	13,800	9,878	16,066	12,814	3,252
Wage and salary workers	487,137	330,701	156,436	384,247	258,570	125,677	70,515	50,959	19,556	21,396	12,308	9,088	10,979	8,864	2,115
Employers and own-account workers	91,603	74,408	17,195	61,953	49,128	12,825	23,423	20,189	3,234	2,102	1,433	669	4,125	3,658	467
Unpaid family workers	6,017	1,056	4,961	3,680	670	3,010	1,335	106	1,229	91	22	69	911	258	653
Class of worker not reported	2,140	1,260	880	1,684	1,006	678	316	183	133	89	37	52	51	34	17
At work	568,702	394,677	174,025	438,513	300,525	137,988	91,957	68,658	23,299	23,240	13,515	9,725	14,992	11,979	3,013
Wage and salary workers	475,925	323,303	152,622	375,818	253,135	122,683	68,736	49,712	19,024	21,136	12,147	8,989	10,235	8,309	1,926
Employers and own-account workers	85,184	69,307	15,877	57,732	45,900	11,832	21,682	18,691	2,991	1,940	1,318	622	3,830	3,398	432
Unpaid family workers	5,789	1,011	4,778	3,541	642	2,899	1,274	102	1,172	85	19	66	889	248	641
Class of worker not reported	1,804	1,056	748	1,422	848	574	265	153	112	79	31	48	38	24	14
With a job	18,195	12,748	5,447	13,051	8,849	4,202	3,632	2,779	853	438	285	153	1,074	835	239
Wage and salary workers	11,212	7,398	3,814	8,429	5,435	2,994	1,779	1,247	532	260	161	99	744	555	189
Employers and own-account workers	6,419	5,101	1,318	4,221	3,228	993	1,741	1,498	243	162	115	47	295	260	35
Unpaid family workers	228	45	183	139	28	111	61	4	57	6	3	3	22	10	12
Class of worker not reported	336	204	132	262	158	104	51	30	21	10	6	4	13	10	3
PERCENT DISTRIBUTION															
Persons 14 years old and over	100.0	100.0	100.0	100.0	100.0	100.0	100.0	100.0	100.0	100.0	100.0	100.0	100.0	100.0	100.0
In labor force	54.1	78.0	31.6	54.0	77.8	32.1	51.7	78.4	25.2	60.7	79.0	44.8	64.3	79.8	35.8
Not in labor force	45.9	22.0	68.4	46.0	22.2	67.9	48.3	21.6	74.8	39.3	21.0	55.2	35.7	20.2	64.2
Engaged in own home housew'k	26.4	0.4	50.8	26.2	0.4	49.8	30.5	0.5	60.4	19.4	0.4	35.8	14.4	0.2	40.3
In school	7.8	8.3	7.3	8.9	9.6	8.3	1.6	1.7	1.5	7.3	8.0	6.7	15.3	13.0	19.5
Unable to work	5.7	6.2	5.3	5.0	5.4	4.6	8.9	10.1	7.7	7.9	6.9	8.8	2.7	3.2	1.7
In institutions	0.5	0.8	0.3	0.5	0.8	0.3	0.5	0.6	0.3	0.8	1.5	0.2	0.5	0.7	0.3
Other and not reported	5.5	6.2	4.8	5.3	5.9	4.8	6.8	8.6	4.9	3.9	4.2	3.7	2.8	3.0	2.4
LABOR FORCE BY EMPLOYMENT STATUS															
In labor force	100.0	100.0	100.0	100.0	100.0	100.0	100.0	100.0	100.0	100.0	100.0	100.0	100.0	100.0	100.0
Employed (exc. public emerg. work)	85.5	84.8	86.9	85.8	85.2	87.0	86.5	85.4	89.7	73.4	70.9	77.2	92.5	91.9	95.1
At work	82.8	82.2	84.2	83.3	82.8	84.4	83.2	82.1	86.6	72.0	69.5	76.0	86.3	85.9	88.2
With a job	2.6	2.7	2.6	2.5	2.4	2.6	3.3	3.3	3.2	1.4	1.5	1.2	6.2	6.0	7.0
On public emerg. work (WPA, etc.)	2.7	3.0	2.0	2.7	3.0	2.0	1.6	1.8	0.8	8.5	10.8	5.0	0.5	0.6	0.3
Seeking work	11.8	12.2	11.1	11.6	11.8	11.0	12.0	12.8	9.4	18.1	18.3	17.8	7.0	7.5	4.6
Experienced workers	10.9	11.5	9.6	10.6	11.1	9.4	11.7	12.6	8.7	16.7	16.9	16.4	6.5	7.2	3.7
New workers	0.9	0.7	1.5	1.0	0.7	1.6	0.3	0.2	0.7	1.5	1.4	1.5	0.4	0.3	0.9
EMPLOYED WORKERS BY CLASS OF WORKER															
Employed (exc. public emerg.)	100.0	100.0	100.0	100.0	100.0	100.0	100.0	100.0	100.0	100.0	100.0	100.0	100.0	100.0	100.0
Wage and salary workers	83.0	81.2	87.2	85.1	83.6	88.4	73.8	71.3	81.0	90.4	89.2	92.0	68.3	69.2	65.0
Employers and own-account workers	15.6	18.3	9.6	13.7	15.9	9.0	24.5	28.3	13.4	8.9	10.4	6.8	25.7	28.5	14.4
Unpaid family workers	1.0	0.3	2.8	0.8	0.2	2.1	1.4	0.1	5.1	0.4	0.2	0.7	5.7	2.0	20.1
Class of worker not reported	0.4	0.3	0.5	0.4	0.3	0.5	0.3	0.3	0.6	0.4	0.3	0.5	0.3	0.3	0.5
At work	100.0	100.0	100.0	100.0	100.0	100.0	100.0	100.0	100.0	100.0	100.0	100.0	100.0	100.0	100.0
Wage and salary workers	83.7	81.9	87.7	85.7	84.2	88.9	74.7	72.4	81.7	90.9	89.9	92.4	68.3	69.4	63.9
Employers and own-account workers	15.0	17.6	9.1	13.2	15.3	8.6	23.6	27.2	12.8	8.3	9.8	6.4	25.5	28.4	14.3
Unpaid family workers	1.0	0.3	2.7	0.8	0.2	2.1	1.4	0.1	5.0	0.4	0.1	0.7	5.9	2.1	21.3
Class of worker not reported	0.3	0.3	0.4	0.3	0.3	0.4	0.3	0.2	0.5	0.3	0.2	0.5	0.3	0.2	0.5
With a job	100.0	100.0	100.0	100.0	100.0	100.0	100.0	100.0	100.0	100.0	100.0	100.0	100.0	100.0	.0.0
Wage and salary workers	61.6	58.0	70.0	64.6	61.4	71.3	49.0	44.9	62.4	59.4	56.5	64.7	69.3	66.5	79.1
Employers and own-account workers	35.3	40.0	24.2	32.3	36.5	23.6	47.9	53.9	28.5	37.0	40.4	30.7	27.5	31.1	14.6
Unpaid family workers	1.3	0.4	3.4	1.1	0.3	2.6	1.7	0.1	6.7	1.4	1.1	2.0	2.0	1.2	5.0
Class of worker not reported	1.8	1.6	2.4	2.0	1.8	2.5	1.4	1.1	2.5	2.3	2.1	2.6	1.2	1.2	1.3

Table B-42.—EMPLOYED WORKERS 14 YEARS OLD AND OVER, BY MAJOR OCCUPATION GROUP, INDUSTRY GROUP, AND SEX, FOR THE CITY OF LOS ANGELES: 1940

[Percent not shown where less than 0.1 or where base is less than 100]

MAJOR OCCUPATION GROUP AND INDUSTRY GROUP	Total	Male	Female	PERCENT BY OCCUPATION AND INDUSTRY			PERCENT BY SEX	
				Total	Male	Female	Male	Female
Total population (all ages)	1,504,277	734,135	770,142	-	-	-	48.8	51.2
All persons 14 years old and over	1,269,299	615,298	654,001	-	-	-	48.5	51.5
In labor force	686,756	480,184	206,572	100.0	100.0	100.0	69.9	30.1
Employed workers (except on public emergency work)	586,897	407,425	179,472	85.5	84.8	86.9	69.4	30.6
MAJOR OCCUPATION GROUP								
Employed (except on public emergency work)	586,897	407,425	179,472	100.0	100.0	100.0	69.4	30.6
Professional workers	53,010	31,166	21,844	9.0	7.6	12.2	58.8	41.2
Semiprofessional workers	13,006	9,772	3,234	2.2	2.4	1.8	75.1	24.9
Farmers and farm managers	2,275	2,073	202	0.4	0.5	0.1	91.1	8.9
Proprietors, managers, and officials, except farm	69,492	57,056	12,436	11.8	14.0	6.9	82.1	17.9
Clerical, sales, and kindred workers	150,452	86,096	64,356	25.6	21.1	35.9	57.2	42.8
Craftsmen, foremen, and kindred workers	75,806	73,761	2,045	12.9	18.1	1.1	97.3	2.7
Operatives and kindred workers	93,619	68,554	25,065	16.0	16.8	14.0	73.2	26.8
Domestic service workers	24,552	2,416	22,136	4.2	0.6	12.3	9.8	90.2
Service workers, except domestic	68,260	42,254	26,006	11.6	10.4	14.5	61.9	38.1
Farm laborers (wage workers) and farm foremen	3,392	3,231	161	0.6	0.8	0.1	95.3	4.7
Farm laborers, unpaid family workers	382	163	219	0.1	-	0.1	42.7	57.3
Laborers, except farm	29,307	28,672	635	5.0	7.0	0.4	97.8	2.2
Occupation not reported	3,344	2,211	1,133	0.6	0.5	0.6	66.1	33.9
INDUSTRY GROUP								
Employed (except on public emergency work)	586,897	407,425	179,472	100.0	100.0	100.0	69.4	30.6
Agriculture, forestry, and fishery	11,564	10,821	743	2.0	2.7	0.4	93.6	6.4
Agriculture	9,534	8,822	712	1.6	2.2	0.4	92.5	7.5
Forestry (except logging) and fishery	2,030	1,999	31	0.3	0.5	-	98.5	1.5
Mining	2,920	2,645	275	0.5	0.6	0.2	90.6	9.4
Coal mining	23	23	-	-	-	-	-	-
Crude petroleum and natural gas production	1,933	1,696	237	0.3	0.4	0.1	87.7	12.3
Other mines and quarries	964	926	38	0.2	0.2	-	96.1	3.9
Construction	33,719	32,899	820	5.7	8.1	0.5	97.6	2.4
Manufacturing	106,614	82,671	23,943	18.2	20.3	13.3	77.5	22.5
Food and kindred products	15,589	11,708	3,881	2.7	2.9	2.2	75.1	24.9
Textile-mill products	2,355	1,286	1,069	0.4	0.3	0.6	54.6	45.4
Apparel and other fabricated textile products	13,434	3,994	9,440	2.3	1.0	5.3	29.7	70.3
Logging	28	27	1	-	-	-	-	-
Sawmills and planing mills	1,039	981	58	0.2	0.2	-	94.4	5.6
Furniture, store fixtures, and miscellaneous wooden goods	6,370	5,737	633	1.1	1.4	0.4	90.1	9.9
Paper and allied products	1,990	1,460	530	0.3	0.4	0.3	73.4	26.6
Printing, publishing, and allied industries	11,537	9,385	2,152	2.0	2.3	1.2	81.3	18.7
Chemicals and allied products	3,681	2,828	853	0.6	0.7	0.5	76.8	23.2
Petroleum and coal products	3,454	2,860	594	0.6	0.7	0.3	82.8	17.2
Leather and leather products	1,313	891	422	0.2	0.2	0.2	67.9	32.1
Stone, clay, and glass products	2,967	2,553	414	0.5	0.6	0.2	86.0	14.0
Iron and steel and their products	7,171	6,707	464	1.2	1.6	0.3	93.5	6.5
Nonferrous metals and their products	2,818	2,593	225	0.5	0.6	0.1	92.0	8.0
Machinery	8,745	7,894	851	1.5	1.9	0.5	90.3	9.7
Automobiles and automobile equipment	3,016	2,790	226	0.5	0.7	0.1	92.5	7.5
Transportation equipment, except automobile	14,123	13,572	551	2.4	3.3	0.3	96.1	3.9
Other and not specified manufacturing industries	6,984	5,405	1,579	1.2	1.3	0.9	77.4	22.6
Transportation, communication, and other public utilities	44,463	37,882	6,581	7.6	9.3	3.7	85.2	14.8
Railroads (including railroad repair shops) and railway express service	9,068	8,728	340	1.5	2.1	0.2	96.3	3.7
Trucking service	4,704	4,500	204	0.8	1.1	0.1	95.7	4.3
Other transportation	12,419	11,765	654	2.1	2.9	0.4	94.7	5.3
Communication	8,249	3,970	4,279	1.4	1.0	2.4	48.1	51.9
Utilities	10,023	8,919	1,104	1.7	2.2	0.6	89.0	11.0
Wholesale and retail trade	149,108	104,191	44,917	25.4	25.6	25.0	69.9	30.1
Wholesale trade	27,808	22,233	5,575	4.7	5.5	3.1	80.0	20.0
Food and dairy products stores, and milk retailing	22,758	18,257	4,501	3.9	4.5	2.5	80.2	19.8
Eating and drinking places	27,308	16,185	11,123	4.7	4.0	6.2	59.3	40.7
Motor vehicles and accessories retailing, and filling stations	14,302	13,355	947	2.4	3.3	0.5	93.4	6.6
Other retail trade	56,932	34,161	22,771	9.7	8.4	12.7	60.0	40.0
Finance, insurance, and real estate	37,473	23,301	14,172	6.4	5.7	7.9	62.2	37.8
Business and repair services	18,645	16,353	2,292	3.2	4.0	1.3	87.7	12.3
Automobile storage, rental, and repair services	8,668	8,477	191	1.5	2.1	0.1	97.8	2.2
Business and repair services, except automobile	9,977	7,876	2,101	1.7	1.9	1.2	78.9	21.1
Personal services	66,186	23,607	42,579	11.3	5.8	23.7	35.7	64.3
Domestic service	30,857	6,235	24,622	5.3	1.5	13.7	20.2	79.8
Hotels and lodging places	11,271	5,578	5,693	1.9	1.4	3.2	49.5	50.5
Laundering, cleaning, and dyeing services	10,487	5,652	4,835	1.8	1.4	2.7	53.9	46.1
Miscellaneous personal services	13,571	6,142	7,429	2.3	1.5	4.1	45.3	54.7
Amusement, recreation, and related services	30,714	24,238	6,476	5.2	5.9	3.6	78.9	21.1
Professional and related services	52,878	24,687	28,191	9.0	6.1	15.7	46.7	53.3
Government	26,502	20,443	6,059	4.5	5.0	3.4	77.1	22.9
Industry not reported	6,111	3,687	2,424	1.0	0.9	1.4	60.3	39.7

Table B-43.—PERSONS 14 YEARS OLD AND OVER IN THE LABOR FORCE, 1940, AND GAINFUL WORKERS 14 YEARS OLD AND OVER, 1930, BY RACE AND SEX, FOR THE CITY OF LOS ANGELES

[Totals for population and gainful workers for 1930 include "Unknown age." Figures for white population in 1930 have been revised to include Mexicans who were classified with "Other races" in the 1930 reports. Percent not shown where less than 0.1 or where base is less than 100]

CENSUS YEAR AND RACE	TOTAL					MALE					FEMALE				
	Population		Persons in the labor force, and gainful workers,[1] 14 years old and over			Population		Persons in the labor force, and gainful workers,[1] 14 years old and over			Population		Persons in the labor force, and gainful workers,[1] 14 years old and over		
	Total (all ages)	14 years old and over	Number	Per-cent of total popu-lation	Per-cent of popu-lation 14 yrs. and over	Total (all ages)	14 years old and over	Number	Per-cent of total popu-lation	Per-cent of popu-lation 14 yrs. and over	Total (all ages)	14 years old and over	Number	Per-cent of total popu-lation	Per-cent of popu-lation 14 yrs. and over
1940	1,504,277	1,269,299	686,756	45.7	54.1	734,135	615,298	480,184	65.4	78.0	770,142	654,001	206,572	26.8	31.6
White	1,406,430	1,189,115	637,129	45.3	53.6	683,075	573,196	446,775	65.4	77.9	723,355	615,919	190,354	26.3	30.9
Negro	63,774	53,165	32,260	50.6	60.7	29,906	24,625	19,460	65.1	79.0	33,868	28,540	12,800	37.8	44.8
Other races	34,073	27,019	17,367	51.0	64.3	21,154	17,477	13,949	65.9	79.8	12,919	9,542	3,418	26.5	35.8
1930	1,238,048	1,010,650	580,409	46.9	57.4	610,678	496,163	417,067	68.3	84.1	627,370	514,487	163,342	26.0	31.7
White	1,170,700	958,887	544,967	46.6	56.8	573,877	467,255	391,524	68.2	83.8	596,823	491,632	153,443	25.7	31.2
Negro	38,894	31,676	21,350	54.9	67.4	18,349	14,748	12,900	70.3	87.5	20,545	16,928	8,450	41.1	49.9
Other races	28,454	20,087	14,092	49.5	70.2	18,452	14,160	12,643	68.5	89.3	10,002	5,927	1,449	14.5	24.4

[1] Data for 1930 represent gainful workers 14 years old and over.

"Becky Sharp in Color to Revolutionize Industry, Black-and-White Pictures to Be the Rarity in 10 Years," *The Charleston Gazette* (West Virginia), February 3, 1935

Jock Whitney's little excursion into the movies is being watched with eager eyes. *Becky Sharp*, the Whitney movie, is all in color. Miriam Hopkins' blonde hair will be as fair as it is in real life, and her deep blue eyes will have their natural tint. And Dr. Herbert Kalmus, as head of Technicolor, said *Becky Sharp* will be the forerunner of other all-color feature films, simply because it will be the first all-color drama.

"In 10 years," said Dr. Kalmus, "black-and-white pictures will be a rarity. Our three-color process has made it possible for every tint to be so distinct and beautiful that the motion picture stars will demand color. We feel that *Becky Sharp* will do for the feature-length pictures what Walter Disney did for cartoons.

"Up to the time Disney made his Silly Symphonies in color, we couldn't get a cartoonist to so much as consider color. Then came *The Three Little Pigs* and other Disney cartoons, which opened up new vistas to other cartoonists who suddenly realized that color was a decided asset to their product."

"Movie Shorts," *The San Diego Light*, February 22, 1937: Mickey Mouse is going to continue to lead the parade of film stars in Hollywood, and he will continue to be seen in Technicolor. Walt Disney, his proud papa, has just signed a contract with Dr. Herbert Kalmus for 18 shorts including Mickey, *Silly Symphonies,* and one feature. This feature is *Snow White and the Seven Dwarfs*, and Disney has been working on the famous fairytale for over a year. At the rate he turns out features, it is safe to promise that one will be all he can manage in 12 months.

"New Color Technique Marks Film Innovation, Hollywood Plans 13 Technicolor Features," *The Charleston Gazette* (West Virginia), March 1, 1936

Why is *The Trail of the Lonesome Pine* so much better than any color film yet produced?

At the Wanger Studios, they claim it was made without regard for the color technicians-that Henry Hathaway, the director, put his outdoor epic on the film just as he might have photographed a black-and-white spectacle, and paid no attention to the "dos" and "don'ts" laid down so emphatically in the past by the color experts.

Dr. Herbert Kalmus, just back from a trip abroad, says Walter Wanger is intelligent and that he did have technical advice, but that he didn't let it interfere with his own ideas....

If Technicolor is really as strongly entrenched as everyone says, and it must be since 13 pictures are planned in Hollywood as against the two made last year, then what will be the effect on the motion picture stars of today? Will color have the same effect as sound and eliminate certain favorites, or will it really help those who have facial defects and blemishes to overcome these?

Dr. Kalmus says that beauty of face, hair and character is intensified, and that lack of beauty will not suffer in the flattering tints which make an unattractive woman more attractive, and an ordinary male an Adonis.

"*The Wizard of Oz* Brings to Screen Something New," *Belton Journal* (Texas), October 12, 1939: Presenting what is heralded as the most ideal combination of color, music, dancing, spectacle, pageantry, laughs and thrills, *The Wizard of Oz* filmization of the celebrated story by L. Frank Baum comes Sunday and Monday and Tuesday to the Beltonian Theaters, as the most sensational musical to come out of the annals of Hollywood screen entertainment. Successfully combining for the first time adult and juvenile appeal in a motion picture, Technicolor is used for the first time on a sound psychological basis.

Photographic Film Timeline

1822: Nicéphore Niépce took the first fixed, permanent photograph, of an engraving of Pope Pius VII, using a non-lens contact-printing "heliographic process."

1826: Nicéphore Niépce took the first fixed, permanent photograph from nature, a landscape that required an eight-hour exposure.

1839: Louis Daguerre patented the daguerreotype; William Fox Talbot invented the positive/negative process widely used in photography.

1851: Frederick Scott Archer introduced the collodion process, which involved using wet plates.

1854: André-Adolphe-Eugène Disdéri was credited with the introduction of the *carte de visite*, a type of small photograph.

1861: James Clerk Maxwell showed the first color photograph, an additive projected image of a tartan ribbon.

1868: Louis Ducos du Hauron patented a method of subtractive color photography.

1871: Richard Maddox invented the gelatin emulsion.

1878: Eadweard Muybridge made a high-speed photographic demonstration of a moving horse, airborne during a trot, using a trip-wire system.

1887: The celluloid film base was introduced; Gabriel Lippmann invented a "method of reproducing colors photographically based on the phenomenon of interference."

1888: The Kodak No. 1 box camera was mass marketed as the first easy-to-use camera.

1891: Thomas Edison patented the "kinetoscopic camera" (motion pictures).

1895: Auguste and Louis Lumière invented the cinématographe.

1898: Kodak introduced the Folding Pocket Kodak.

1900: Kodak introduced the first Brownie.

1901: Kodak introduced the 120 film format.

1902: Arthur Korn devised a practical phototelegraphy technology used by national wire services.

1907: The Autochrome Lumière became the first color photography process marketed.

1908: Kinemacolor, a two-color process that was the first commercial "natural color" system for movies, was introduced.

1909: Kodak introduced a 35 mm "safety" motion picture film on an acetate base as an alternative to the highly flammable nitrate base. The motion picture industry discontinued its use after 1911 due to technical imperfections.

1912: The Vest Pocket Kodak used 127 film; Kodak introduced the 22 mm amateur motion picture format, a "safety" stock on acetate base.

1913: Kodak made 35 mm panchromatic motion picture film available on a bulk special order basis.

1914: Kodak introduced the Autographic film system; *The World, the Flesh and the Devil*, the first dramatic feature film in color (Kinemacolor), was released.

1920s: Yasujiro Niwa invented a device for phototelegraphic transmission through cable and later via radio.

1922: Kodak made 35 mm panchromatic motion picture film available as a regular stock; Kodak introduced 16 mm reversal film, on a cellulose acetate (safety) base.

1923: Doc Harold Edgerton invented the xenon flash lamp and strobe photography.

1925: Leica introduced the 35 mm format to still photography.

1926: Kodak introduced its 35 mm Motion Picture Duplicating Film for duplicate negatives. Previously, motion picture studios used a second camera alongside the primary camera to create a duplicate negative.

1932: Disney made the first full-color movie, the cartoon *Flowers and Trees*, in Technicolor; Kodak introduced the first 8 mm amateur motion-picture film, cameras, and projectors.

1934: The 135 film cartridge was introduced, making 35 mm easy to use.

1935: *Becky Sharp*, the first feature film made in full color (Technicolor), was released.

1936: IHAGEE introduced the Ihagee Kine Exakta 1, the first 35 mm single lens reflex camera; Kodachrome multi-layered reversal color film was developed.

1937: Agfacolor-Neu reversal color film was introduced.

1939: Agfacolor negative-positive color material, the first modern "print" film, was introduced; The View-Master stereo viewer was invented.

New York Bond Trader Sees a Rebounding Economy

Richard Hastings was increasingly optimistic about the economy as 1940 approached, and believed that the war in Europe would spark demand for American goods. He loved the research required for his job as a bond trader for Manufacturer's Trust and how it forced him to stay aware of the reasons behind the fluctuating economy.

Life at Home

- Richard and Helen Hastings and their three children lived in Mamaroneck, a suburb of New York City.
- Richard commuted daily to his office job the city, and enjoyed the physical work of maintaining the house and lawn.
- Helen was raised Catholic and Richard, Presbyterian, so they compromised by attending the Episcopal Church.
- They vacationed on a farm in Vermont, the trip taking all day in their late model Dodge.
- Richard's father was a heavy smoker, and died at the age of 41, leaving his estate to his oldest son, Robert.
- Robert studied economics at Columbia University, and worked on Wall Street.
- Richard followed his brother's footsteps, and strict orders, by majoring in economics at Columbia University.
- After college, Richard worked for a general contractor instead of pleasing his brother by going into banking.
- Helen graduated from Barnard and was an assistant researcher for the American Museum of Natural History before marrying Richard.
- Her work was published in *The Scientific Monthly* in an article titled, "Survey of the Life of Louis Agassiz, the Centenary of the Glacial Theory."
- Their two-story house had living room, dining room, and kitchen on the first floor, with a master bedroom, three other bedrooms, and a bath on the second floor; and a basement for storage.
- Richard spent considerable time working on his home, painting and fixing up, before Robert got him a job at Manufacturer's Trust, a well-respected Wall Street firm, as a bond trader.
- He shaved on the train into work, returning home at 7:30 p.m.
- The Hastings saved their money, unsure of the future.
- Richard loved to sail and often went with his friend, a local judge.
- He also loved working with his hands, and built a flat-bottom, straight-sided canoe that he named *Damnation*.
- Once a week, he attended a luncheon meeting of the Kiwanis Club, always amazed that so many men sang so badly, so consistently.

Richard Hastings worked in New York City and commuted to his home in the suburbs.

Stealing New York's Stuff

- The Hastings family at their biggest meal of the week at 4:30 each Sunday, which was usually roast beef, pork or lamp chops, and lots of fresh vegetables.
- Most nights, he played the piano for half an hour, largely classical pieces.
- Richard and Helen often invited friends over to listen to the radio, especially the *Chase and Sanborn Hour,* which featured a ventriloquist and his irreverent puppet, Charlie McCarthy.

Life at Work

- Richard Hasting's position at Manufacturer's Trust primarily involved investing bonds for hospitals, schools, and colleges.
- He loved the research that the job required-understanding the cash flows, predicting problems, and calculating risk.
- He especially enjoyed the ever-changing risks within his business; one minor change in Europe could have a major impact on the United States bond market.
- His business boomed, despite the recession, as the war in Europe drove the economy; and the demand for capital expansion was high.
- The war also caused gold to flow into the United States from Europe-up 80 percent from the previous year.
- This surplus of funds into the United States, and particularly into New York banks, drove interest rates down.
- The average bank rate on short-term loans in New York City was 1.8 percent, while the average rate among western states was 2.5 percent.
- Pundits declared that "the old stock market is dead; the new stock market is emerging," as a seat on the New York Stock Exchange cost approximately $80,000, and the Dow Jones Industrial Average hovered at 150.
- The fluctuating economy had Richard cautious, as he knew that business failures were at their highest in years.

Life in the Community: New York City

- New York and New Yorkers believed the city was at its zenith.
- The towering shaft of the RCA Building, the starkness of the new George Washington Bridge, the vivid colors of Radio City Music Hall, all made New York City a magical place.
- Mayor Fiorello La Guardia made the city work, believing that "to the victor belongs the responsibility for good government."
- Reflecting the diversity of New York, La Guardia, who was half Jewish, campaigned in English, Italian, and Yiddish.
- *Harper's Magazine* said, "New York City happens to be one of the communities in the United States where good government is measured by getting a great deal for your money."
- New York boasted the six tallest buildings in the country.
- Three major baseball teams and eight major daily newspapers called New York home.
- The World's Fair, developed in New York to chase away the recession, epitomized the big, bold and thrilling nature of the city in 1940.

- Built on a former garbage dump, the Fair covered 1,200 acres.
- New York reflected the old and the new, as blocks from the imposing Chrysler Building, herds of cattle could be seen on the sidewalk waiting to be butchered in "Blood Alley."
- Italian hand organs were heard on the streets next to Yiddish-language movie houses.
- *Gone with the Wind* took New York by storm, and was one of more than 500 feature films to appear in the year leading up to 1940.
- The New York World's Fair Music Festival featured Beethoven's *Ninth Symphony*, with tickets ranging from $1 to $2.50 and the Brooklyn Academy of Music featured Martha Graham and Company in *American Document*.

Richard occasionally attended large dinners with fellow bond traders and bankers.

New Yorkers believed that the city was at its zenith.

The nine tables that follow are reprinted from the actual 1940 census, for the city of New York City. They include actual data on race, percentage of voting population, school attendance, number of school years completed, foreign born, and employment of workers 14 years and older by job, industry and race. In addition to being incredibly fascinating, these facts help to strengthen and visualize the actual environment in which Richard Hastings lived and worked.

Table C-35.—AGE, BY RACE AND SEX, FOR THE CITY OF NEW YORK: 1940 AND 1930

[Figures for white population in 1930 revised to include Mexicans classified with "Other races" in the 1930 reports. Percent not shown where less than 0.1 or where base is less than 100]

AGE AND CENSUS YEAR	ALL CLASSES			NATIVE WHITE			FOREIGN-BORN WHITE			NEGRO			OTHER RACES		
	Total	Male	Female	Total	Male	Female	Total	Male	Female	Total	Male	Female	Total	Male	Female
All ages: 1940	7,454,995	3,676,293	3,778,702	4,897,481	2,397,164	2,500,317	2,080,020	1,057,839	1,022,181	458,444	205,727	252,717	19,050	15,563	3,487
Under 5 years	433,894	221,415	212,479	400,656	204,900	195,756	2,583	1,310	1,273	29,691	14,706	14,985	964	499	465
5 to 9 years	470,556	238,798	231,758	430,383	218,849	211,534	6,101	3,038	3,063	33,134	16,442	16,692	938	469	469
10 to 14 years	561,108	283,453	277,655	510,778	258,847	251,931	13,642	6,832	6,810	35,848	17,294	18,554	840	480	360
15 to 19 years	606,942	300,717	306,225	536,926	267,425	269,501	34,486	17,163	17,323	34,678	15,574	19,104	852	555	297
20 to 24 years	649,153	304,862	344,291	566,019	270,434	295,585	41,165	18,615	22,550	41,099	15,251	25,848	870	562	308
25 to 29 years	697,153	322,558	374,595	547,673	259,948	287,725	96,917	41,380	55,537	50,978	20,008	30,970	1,585	1,222	363
30 to 34 years	691,027	331,782	359,245	464,272	226,078	238,194	173,415	81,972	91,443	51,180	21,924	29,256	2,160	1,808	352
35 to 39 years	669,421	330,950	338,471	362,781	178,358	184,423	251,438	126,448	124,990	52,186	23,418	28,768	3,016	2,726	290
40 to 44 years	628,714	317,471	311,243	302,549	149,293	153,256	281,569	145,301	136,268	41,789	20,299	21,490	2,807	2,578	229
45 to 49 years	550,743	282,769	267,974	233,673	115,648	118,025	284,754	150,517	134,237	30,381	14,802	15,579	1,935	1,802	133
50 to 54 years	467,020	243,321	223,699	173,898	84,449	89,449	270,272	147,338	122,934	21,468	10,251	11,217	1,382	1,283	99
55 to 59 years	346,871	178,162	168,709	120,929	57,354	63,575	210,936	113,428	97,508	14,251	6,675	7,576	755	705	50
60 to 64 years	267,974	132,668	135,306	95,411	43,605	51,806	162,750	84,260	78,490	9,285	4,311	4,974	528	492	36
65 to 69 years	190,439	89,275	101,164	69,641	29,909	39,732	114,028	56,461	57,567	6,521	2,676	3,845	249	229	20
70 to 74 years	120,675	54,474	66,201	43,812	17,959	25,853	73,558	35,194	38,364	3,197	1,219	1,978	108	102	6
75 years and over	103,305	43,618	59,687	38,080	14,108	23,972	62,406	28,582	33,824	2,758	877	1,881	61	51	10
Under 1 year	81,889	41,795	40,094	76,006	38,897	37,109	123	57	66	5,576	2,748	2,828	184	93	91
5 years	88,368	44,847	43,521	80,891	41,165	39,726	980	474	506	6,323	3,120	3,203	174	88	86
14 years	113,310	56,949	56,361	102,350	51,621	50,729	3,732	1,851	1,881	7,065	3,376	3,689	163	101	62
15 years	114,889	57,734	57,155	103,876	52,455	51,421	3,986	1,935	2,001	6,910	3,234	3,676	167	110	57
16 and 17 years	238,386	118,975	119,411	212,614	106,441	106,173	11,953	6,056	5,897	13,474	6,261	7,213	345	217	128
21 years and over	5,254,633	2,570,647	2,683,986	2,908,645	1,393,545	1,515,100	2,013,349	1,024,793	988,556	317,355	138,864	178,491	15,284	13,445	1,839
All ages: 1930	6,930,446	3,472,956	3,457,490	4,294,196	2,123,577	2,170,619	2,295,181	1,180,947	1,114,234	327,706	156,968	170,738	13,363	11,464	1,899
Under 5 years	535,600	272,438	263,162	502,444	255,839	246,605	5,573	2,817	2,756	26,920	13,431	13,489	663	351	312
5 to 9 years	577,284	291,782	285,502	530,497	268,571	261,926	21,884	11,051	10,833	24,365	11,894	12,471	538	266	272
10 to 14 years	575,300	290,263	285,037	531,036	268,341	262,695	25,309	12,780	12,529	18,662	8,987	9,675	293	155	138
15 to 19 years	599,286	293,740	305,546	510,342	252,903	257,439	67,431	31,397	36,084	21,120	9,169	11,951	393	271	122
20 to 24 years	687,417	327,734	359,683	485,070	235,085	249,985	162,618	75,099	87,519	38,658	16,664	21,994	1,071	886	185
25 to 29 years	695,984	341,448	354,536	393,504	191,999	201,505	251,671	124,777	126,894	48,661	22,779	25,882	2,148	1,893	255
30 to 34 years	649,576	327,685	321,891	329,596	162,429	167,167	277,079	142,987	134,092	40,533	20,121	20,412	2,368	2,148	220
35 to 39 years	621,248	319,859	301,389	272,926	135,538	137,388	309,408	163,942	145,466	36,924	18,539	18,385	1,990	1,840	150
40 to 44 years	518,588	272,868	245,720	199,377	98,857	100,520	292,075	159,583	132,492	25,515	12,909	12,606	1,621	1,519	102
45 to 49 years	422,063	219,600	202,463	151,843	74,032	77,811	250,204	135,056	115,148	19,057	9,607	9,450	959	905	54
50 to 54 years	340,807	175,346	165,461	126,094	61,130	64,964	202,176	107,610	94,566	11,922	6,032	5,890	615	574	41
55 to 59 years	246,277	123,128	123,149	93,257	44,458	48,799	146,325	75,200	71,125	6,365	3,155	3,210	330	315	15
60 to 64 years	190,527	92,494	98,033	69,444	31,886	37,558	117,138	58,732	58,406	3,767	1,708	2,059	178	168	10
65 to 69 years	127,356	60,451	66,905	45,149	20,131	25,018	79,787	39,351	40,436	2,331	891	1,440	89	78	11
70 to 74 years	77,327	35,866	41,461	28,853	12,401	16,452	47,205	22,986	24,219	1,236	448	788	33	31	2
75 years and over	59,819	25,243	34,576	20,918	8,109	12,809	37,703	16,721	20,982	1,184	400	784	14	13	1
Not reported	5,987	3,011	2,976	3,846	1,868	1,978	1,595	858	737	486	234	252	60	51	9
Under 1 year	100,398	51,178	49,220	94,819	48,409	46,410	251	125	126	5,176	2,569	2,607	152	75	77
5 years	112,108	56,813	55,295	104,372	53,003	51,369	2,257	1,125	1,132	5,340	2,606	2,734	139	79	60
14 years	112,112	56,347	55,765	103,303	51,952	51,351	5,242	2,647	2,595	3,518	1,719	1,799	49	29	20
15 years	112,305	56,540	55,765	102,155	51,562	50,593	6,771	3,375	3,396	3,325	1,572	1,753	54	31	23
16 and 17 years	232,443	114,770	117,673	202,327	100,571	101,756	22,683	10,823	11,860	7,319	3,308	4,011	114	68	46
21 years and over	4,511,021	2,262,581	2,248,440	2,120,168	1,029,912	1,090,256	2,149,455	1,111,448	1,038,007	230,069	110,911	119,158	11,329	10,310	1,019
Percent: 1940	100.0	100.0	100.0	100.0	100.0	100.0	100.0	100.0	100.0	100.0	100.0	100.0	100.0	100.0	100.0
Under 5 years	5.8	6.0	5.6	8.2	8.5	7.8	0.1	0.1	0.1	6.5	7.1	5.9	5.1	3.2	13.3
5 to 9 years	6.3	6.5	6.1	8.8	9.1	8.5	0.3	0.3	0.3	7.2	8.0	6.6	4.9	3.0	13.4
10 to 14 years	7.5	7.7	7.3	10.4	10.8	10.1	0.7	0.6	0.7	7.8	8.4	7.3	4.4	3.1	10.3
15 to 19 years	8.1	8.2	8.1	11.0	11.2	10.8	1.7	1.6	1.7	7.6	7.6	7.6	4.5	3.6	8.5
20 to 24 years	8.7	8.3	9.1	11.6	11.3	11.8	2.0	1.8	2.2	9.0	7.4	10.2	4.6	3.6	8.8
25 to 29 years	9.4	8.8	9.9	11.2	10.8	11.5	4.7	3.9	5.4	11.1	9.7	12.3	8.3	7.9	10.4
30 to 34 years	9.3	9.0	9.5	9.5	9.4	9.5	8.3	7.7	8.9	11.2	10.7	11.6	11.3	11.6	10.1
35 to 39 years	9.0	9.0	9.0	7.4	7.4	7.4	12.1	12.0	12.2	11.4	11.4	11.4	15.8	17.5	8.3
40 to 44 years	8.4	8.6	8.2	6.2	6.2	6.1	13.5	13.7	13.3	9.1	9.9	8.5	14.7	16.6	6.6
45 to 49 years	7.4	7.7	7.1	4.8	4.8	4.7	13.7	14.2	13.1	6.6	7.2	6.2	10.2	11.6	3.8
50 to 54 years	6.3	6.6	5.9	3.6	3.5	3.6	13.0	13.9	12.0	4.7	5.0	4.4	7.3	8.2	2.8
55 to 59 years	4.7	4.8	4.5	2.5	2.4	2.5	10.1	10.7	9.5	3.1	3.2	3.0	4.0	4.5	1.4
60 to 64 years	3.6	3.6	3.6	1.9	1.8	2.1	7.8	8.0	7.7	2.0	2.1	2.0	2.8	3.2	1.0
65 to 69 years	2.6	2.4	2.7	1.4	1.2	1.6	5.5	5.3	5.6	1.4	1.3	1.5	1.3	1.5	0.6
70 to 74 years	1.6	1.5	1.8	0.9	0.7	1.0	3.5	3.3	3.8	0.7	0.6	0.8	0.6	0.7	0.2
75 years and over	1.4	1.2	1.6	0.8	0.6	1.0	3.0	2.7	3.3	0.6	0.4	0.7	0.3	0.3	0.3
Under 1 year	1.1	1.1	1.1	1.6	1.6	1.5	-	-	-	1.2	1.3	1.1	1.0	0.6	2.6
5 years	1.2	1.2	1.2	1.7	1.7	1.6	-	-	-	1.4	1.5	1.3	0.9	0.6	2.5
14 years	1.5	1.5	1.5	2.1	2.2	2.0	0.2	0.2	0.2	1.5	1.6	1.5	0.9	0.6	1.8
15 years	1.5	1.6	1.5	2.1	2.2	2.1	0.2	0.2	0.2	1.5	1.6	1.5	0.9	0.7	1.6
16 and 17 years	3.2	3.2	3.2	4.3	4.4	4.2	0.6	0.6	0.6	2.9	3.0	2.9	1.8	1.4	3.7
21 years and over	70.5	69.9	71.0	59.4	58.1	60.6	96.8	96.9	96.7	69.2	67.5	70.6	80.2	86.4	52.7
Percent: 1930	100.0	100.0	100.0	100.0	100.0	100.0	100.0	100.0	100.0	100.0	100.0	100.0	100.0	100.0	100.0
Under 5 years	7.7	7.8	7.6	11.7	12.0	11.4	0.2	0.2	0.2	8.2	8.6	7.9	5.0	3.1	16.4
5 to 9 years	8.3	8.4	8.3	12.4	12.6	12.1	1.0	0.9	1.0	7.4	7.6	7.3	4.0	2.3	14.3
10 to 14 years	8.3	8.4	8.2	12.4	12.6	12.1	1.1	1.1	1.1	5.7	5.7	5.7	2.2	1.4	7.3
15 to 19 years	8.6	8.5	8.8	11.9	11.9	11.9	2.9	2.7	3.2	6.4	5.8	7.0	2.9	2.4	6.4
20 to 24 years	9.9	9.4	10.4	11.3	11.1	11.5	7.1	6.4	7.9	11.8	10.6	12.9	8.0	7.7	9.7
25 to 29 years	10.0	9.8	10.3	9.2	9.0	9.3	11.0	10.6	11.4	14.8	14.5	15.2	16.1	16.5	13.4
30 to 34 years	9.4	9.4	9.3	7.7	7.6	7.7	12.1	12.1	12.0	12.4	12.8	12.0	17.7	18.7	11.6
35 to 39 years	9.0	9.2	8.7	6.4	6.4	6.3	13.5	13.9	13.1	11.3	11.8	10.8	14.9	16.1	7.9
40 to 44 years	7.5	7.9	7.1	4.6	4.7	4.6	12.7	13.5	11.9	7.8	8.2	7.4	12.1	13.3	5.4
45 to 49 years	6.1	6.3	5.9	3.5	3.5	3.6	10.9	11.4	10.3	5.8	6.1	5.5	7.2	7.9	2.8
50 to 54 years	4.9	5.0	4.8	2.9	2.9	3.0	8.8	9.1	8.5	3.6	3.8	3.4	4.6	5.0	2.2
55 to 59 years	3.6	3.5	3.6	2.2	2.1	2.2	6.4	6.4	6.4	1.9	2.0	1.9	2.5	2.7	0.8
60 to 64 years	2.7	2.7	2.8	1.6	1.5	1.7	5.1	5.0	5.2	1.1	1.1	1.2	1.3	1.5	0.5
65 to 69 years	1.8	1.7	1.9	1.1	0.9	1.2	3.5	3.3	3.6	0.7	0.6	0.8	0.7	0.7	0.6
70 to 74 years	1.1	1.0	1.2	0.7	0.6	0.8	2.1	1.9	2.2	0.4	0.3	0.5	0.2	0.3	0.1
75 years and over	0.9	0.7	1.0	0.5	0.4	0.6	1.6	1.4	1.9	0.4	0.3	0.5	0.1	0.1	0.1
Not reported	0.1	0.1	0.1	0.1	0.1	0.1	0.1	0.1	0.1	0.1	0.1	0.1	0.4	0.4	0.5
Under 1 year	1.4	1.5	1.4	2.2	2.3	2.1	-	-	-	1.6	1.6	1.5	1.1	0.7	4.1
5 years	1.6	1.6	1.6	2.4	2.5	2.4	0.1	0.1	0.1	1.6	1.7	1.6	1.0	0.7	3.2
14 years	1.6	1.6	1.6	2.4	2.4	2.4	0.2	0.2	0.2	1.1	1.1	1.1	0.4	0.3	1.1
15 years	1.6	1.6	1.6	2.4	2.4	2.3	0.3	0.3	0.3	1.0	1.0	1.0	0.4	0.3	1.2
16 and 17 years	3.4	3.3	3.4	4.7	4.7	4.7	1.0	0.9	1.1	2.2	2.1	2.3	0.9	0.6	2.4
21 years and over	65.1	65.1	65.0	49.4	48.5	50.2	93.7	94.1	93.2	70.2	70.7	69.8	84.8	89.9	53.7

Table C-36.—RACE, BY NATIVITY AND SEX, FOR THE CITY OF NEW YORK: 1940 AND 1930

[Figures for white population in 1930 have been revised to include Mexicans who were classified with "Other races" in the 1930 reports. Percent not shown where less than 0.1 or where base is less than 100. Sex ratio not shown where number of females is less than 100]

SEX, NATIVITY, AND CENSUS YEAR	All classes	White	Negro	Other races	OTHER RACES				PERCENT BY RACE				PERCENT BY NATIVITY					
					Indian	Chinese	Japanese	All other	All classes	White	Negro	Other races	All classes	White	Negro	Indian	Chinese	Japanese
TOTAL																		
1940	7,454,995	6,977,501	458,444	19,050	1,064	12,758	2,087	3,146	100.0	93.6	6.1	0.3	100.0	100.0	100.0	100.0	100.0	100.0
Native	5,316,338	4,897,481	410,026	8,831	638	4,745	631	2,817	100.0	92.1	7.7	0.2	71.3	70.2	89.4	60.0	37.2	30.2
Foreign born	2,138,657	2,080,020	48,418	10,219	426	8,008	1,456	329	100.0	97.3	2.3	0.5	28.7	29.8	10.6	40.0	62.8	69.8
1930	6,930,446	6,589,377	327,706	13,363	391	8,414	2,356	2,202	100.0	95.1	4.7	0.2	100.0	100.0	100.0	100.0	100.0	100.0
Native	4,571,760	4,294,196	272,952	4,612	294	1,926	536	1,856	100.0	93.9	6.0	0.1	66.0	65.2	83.3	75.2	22.9	22.8
Foreign born	2,358,686	2,295,181	54,754	8,751	97	6,488	1,820	346	100.0	97.3	2.3	0.4	34.0	34.8	16.7	24.8	77.1	77.2
MALE																		
1940	3,676,293	3,455,003	205,727	15,563	590	10,967	1,470	2,536	100.0	94.0	5.6	0.4	100.0	100.0	100.0	100.0	100.0	100.0
Native	2,585,482	2,397,164	181,870	6,448	321	3,547	325	2,255	100.0	92.7	7.0	0.2	70.3	69.4	88.4	54.4	32.3	22.1
Foreign born	1,090,811	1,057,839	23,857	9,115	269	7,420	1,145	281	100.0	97.0	2.2	0.8	29.7	30.6	11.6	45.6	67.7	77.9
1930	3,472,956	3,304,524	156,968	11,464	212	7,549	1,748	1,955	100.0	95.2	4.5	0.3	100.0	100.0	100.0	100.0	100.0	100.0
Native	2,255,955	2,123,577	128,891	3,487	152	1,414	275	1,646	100.0	94.1	5.7	0.2	65.0	64.3	82.1	71.7	18.7	15.7
Foreign born	1,217,001	1,180,947	28,077	7,977	60	6,135	1,473	309	100.0	97.0	2.3	0.7	35.0	35.7	17.9	28.3	81.3	84.3
FEMALE																		
1940	3,778,702	3,522,498	252,717	3,487	474	1,786	617	610	100.0	93.2	6.7	0.1	100.0	100.0	100.0	100.0	100.0	100.0
Native	2,730,856	2,500,317	228,156	2,383	317	1,198	306	562	100.0	91.6	8.4	0.1	72.3	71.0	90.3	66.9	67.1	49.6
Foreign born	1,047,846	1,022,181	24,561	1,104	157	588	311	48	100.0	97.6	2.3	0.1	27.7	29.0	9.7	33.1	32.9	50.4
1930	3,457,490	3,284,853	170,738	1,899	179	865	608	247	100.0	95.0	4.9	0.1	100.0	100.0	100.0	100.0	100.0	100.0
Native	2,315,805	2,170,619	144,061	1,125	142	512	261	210	100.0	93.7	6.2	-	67.0	66.1	84.4	79.3	59.2	42.9
Foreign born	1,141,685	1,114,234	26,677	774	37	353	347	37	100.0	97.6	2.3	0.1	33.0	33.9	15.6	20.7	40.8	57.1
MALES PER 100 FEMALES																		
1940	97.3	98.1	81.4	446.3	124.5	614.1	238.2	415.7	-	-	-	-	-	-	-	-	-	-
Native	94.7	95.9	79.7	270.6	101.3	296.1	106.2	401.2	-	-	-	-	-	-	-	-	-	-
Foreign born	104.1	103.5	97.1	825.6	171.3	1,261.9	368.2	-	-	-	-	-	-	-	-	-	-	-
1930	100.4	100.6	91.9	603.7	118.4	872.7	287.5	791.5	-	-	-	-	-	-	-	-	-	-
Native	97.4	97.8	89.5	310.0	107.0	276.2	105.4	783.8	-	-	-	-	-	-	-	-	-	-
Foreign born	106.6	106.0	105.2	1,030.6	-	1,738.0	424.5	-	-	-	-	-	-	-	-	-	-	-

Table C-37.—POTENTIAL VOTING POPULATION, BY CITIZENSHIP, RACE, NATIVITY, AND SEX, FOR THE CITY OF NEW YORK: 1940 AND 1930

[Figures for white population in 1930 have been revised to include Mexicans who were classified with "Other races" in the 1930 reports. Percent not shown where less than 0.1]

CITIZENSHIP, RACE, AND NATIVITY	TOTAL POPULATION (ALL AGES)								POPULATION 21 YEARS OLD AND OVER							
	Total number		Percent		Male		Female		Total number		Percent		Male		Female	
	1940	1930	1940	1930	1940	1930	1940	1930	1940	1930	1940	1930	1940	1930	1940	1930
Total	7,454,995	6,930,446	100.0	100.0	3,676,293	3,472,956	3,778,702	3,457,490	5,254,633	4,511,021	100.0	100.0	2,570,647	2,262,581	2,683,986	2,248,440
Percent citizen	-	-	89.0	83.7	-	-	-	-	-	-	85.2	77.2	-	-	-	-
Percent alien and citiz. not rptd.	-	-	11.0	16.3	-	-	-	-	-	-	14.8	22.8	-	-	-	-
Citizen	6,632,398	5,802,229	100.0	100.0	3,334,268	2,944,082	3,298,130	2,858,147	4,474,689	3,488,111	100.0	100.0	2,249,729	1,780,797	2,224,960	1,702,314
White—Native	4,897,481	4,294,196	73.8	74.0	2,397,164	2,123,577	2,500,317	2,170,619	2,908,645	2,120,168	65.0	60.9	1,393,545	1,029,912	1,515,100	1,090,256
Naturalized	1,298,360	1,217,790	19.6	21.0	738,635	680,388	559,725	537,402	1,272,872	1,168,689	28.4	33.6	725,888	656,236	546,984	512,453
Negro—Native	410,026	272,952	6.2	4.7	181,870	128,891	228,156	144,061	270,140	179,483	6.0	5.2	115,520	84,692	154,620	94,791
Naturalized	17,700	12,679	0.3	0.2	10,151	7,739	7,549	4,940	17,388	11,810	0.4	0.3	10,011	7,340	7,377	4,470
Other races—Native	8,831	4,612	0.1	0.1	6,448	3,487	2,383	1,125	5,644	2,961	0.1	0.1	4,765	2,617	879	344
Indian	638	294	-	-	321	152	317	142	377	205	-	-	191	108	186	97
Chinese	4,745	1,926	0.1	-	3,547	1,414	1,198	512	2,935	1,093	0.1	-	2,548	971	387	122
Japanese	631	536	-	-	325	275	306	261	250	91	-	-	133	60	117	31
Filipino	2,659	1,760	-	-	2,160	1,575	499	185	2,003	1,515	-	-	1,836	1,428	167	87
Hindu	58	19	-	-	28	8	30	11	17	3	-	-	7	1	10	2
All other	100	77	-	-	67	63	33	14	62	54	-	-	50	49	12	5
Alien	705,916	1,046,105	100.0	100.0	290,885	495,428	415,031	550,677	670,141	951,350	100.0	100.0	273,111	450,696	397,030	500,654
White—First papers	187,454	230,748	26.6	22.1	105,690	164,058	81,764	66,690	182,999	225,327	27.3	23.7	103,416	161,042	79,583	64,285
No papers	481,687	768,502	68.2	73.5	164,367	305,010	317,320	463,492	451,617	682,458	67.4	71.7	149,589	264,848	302,028	417,610
Negro—First papers	7,080	6,732	1.0	0.6	3,891	4,427	3,189	2,305	7,023	6,651	1.0	0.7	3,872	4,396	3,151	2,255
No papers	19,476	31,372	2.8	3.0	7,822	13,956	11,654	17,416	18,862	28,546	2.8	3.0	7,554	12,717	11,308	15,829
Other races—Foreign born	10,219	8,751	1.4	0.8	9,115	7,977	1,104	774	9,640	8,368	1.4	0.9	8,680	7,693	960	675
Indian	426	97	0.1	-	269	60	157	37	355	78	0.1	-	230	50	125	28
Chinese	8,008	6,488	1.1	0.6	7,420	6,135	588	353	7,624	6,222	1.1	0.7	7,097	5,906	527	316
Japanese	1,456	1,820	0.2	0.2	1,145	1,473	311	347	1,345	1,728	0.2	0.2	1,079	1,429	266	299
Filipino	68	37	-	-	45	24	23	13	61	34	-	-	43	24	18	10
Hindu	155	221	-	-	141	203	14	18	150	218	-	-	137	202	13	16
All other	106	88	-	-	95	82	11	6	105	88	-	-	94	82	11	6
Citizenship not reported	116,681	82,112	100.0	100.0	51,140	33,446	65,541	48,666	109,808	76,560	100.0	100.0	47,807	31,088	61,996	45,472
White	112,519	78,141	96.4	95.2	49,147	31,491	63,372	46,650	105,861	72,981	96.4	95.3	45,900	29,322	59,961	43,659
Negro	4,162	3,971	3.6	4.8	1,993	1,955	2,169	2,016	3,942	3,579	3.6	4.7	1,907	1,766	2,035	1,813

Table C-38.—SCHOOL ATTENDANCE, BY AGE, RACE, AND SEX, FOR THE CITY OF NEW YORK: 1940 AND 1930

[Figures for white population in 1930 revised to include Mexicans classified with "Other races" in the 1930 reports. Percent not shown where less than 0.1 or where base is less than 100]

AGE, SEX, AND CENSUS YEAR	ALL CLASSES			NATIVE WHITE			FOREIGN-BORN WHITE			NEGRO			OTHER RACES		
	Total number	Attending school: Number	Attending school: Percent	Total number	Attending school: Number	Attending school: Percent	Total number	Attending school: Number	Attending school: Percent	Total number	Attending school: Number	Attending school: Percent	Total number	Attending school: Number	Attending school: Percent
1940															
Total, 5 to 24 years	2,287,759	1,350,041	59.0	2,044,106	1,223,732	59.9	95,394	38,961	40.8	144,759	85,048	58.8	3,500	2,300	65.7
5 years	88,368	25,836	29.2	80,891	23,845	29.5	980	314	32.0	6,323	1,608	25.4	174	69	39.7
6 years	88,718	77,089	86.9	81,065	70,723	87.2	1,077	872	81.0	6,383	5,335	83.6	193	159	82.4
7 to 9 years	293,470	283,447	96.6	268,427	259,433	96.6	4,044	3,780	93.5	20,428	19,694	96.4	571	540	94.6
10 to 13 years	447,798	434,889	97.1	408,428	396,885	97.2	9,910	9,456	95.5	28,783	27,884	96.9	677	654	96.6
14 years	113,310	109,423	96.6	102,350	98,948	96.7	3,732	3,543	94.9	7,065	6,776	95.9	163	156	95.7
15 years	114,889	110,459	96.1	103,876	99,957	96.2	3,936	3,749	95.2	6,910	6,590	95.4	167	163	97.6
16 and 17 years	238,386	185,098	77.6	212,614	165,326	77.8	11,953	8,926	74.7	13,474	10,571	78.5	345	275	79.7
18 and 19 years	253,667	74,066	29.2	220,436	64,290	29.2	18,597	5,175	27.8	14,294	4,458	31.2	340	143	42.1
20 years	127,862	17,480	13.7	110,093	15,419	14.0	9,859	1,176	11.9	7,738	836	10.8	172	49	28.5
21 to 24 years	521,291	32,254	6.2	455,926	28,906	6.3	31,306	1,960	6.3	33,361	1,296	3.9	698	92	13.2
Male, 5 to 24 years	1,127,830	695,356	61.7	1,015,555	632,536	62.3	45,648	20,542	45.0	64,561	40,934	63.4	2,066	1,344	65.1
5 years	44,847	12,940	28.9	41,165	11,993	29.1	474	145	30.6	3,120	766	24.6	88	36	-
6 years	45,142	39,217	86.9	41,313	36,059	87.3	557	456	81.9	3,175	2,619	82.5	97	83	-
7 to 9 years	148,809	143,700	96.6	136,371	131,755	96.6	2,007	1,884	93.9	10,147	9,793	96.5	284	268	94.4
10 to 13 years	226,504	220,075	97.2	207,226	201,486	97.2	4,981	4,751	95.4	13,918	13,475	96.8	379	363	95.8
14 years	56,949	54,998	96.6	51,621	49,891	96.6	1,851	1,757	94.9	3,376	3,252	96.3	101	98	97.0
15 years	57,734	55,606	96.3	52,455	50,547	96.4	1,935	1,846	95.4	3,234	3,106	96.0	110	107	97.3
16 and 17 years	118,975	94,205	79.2	106,441	84,400	79.3	6,056	4,655	76.9	6,261	4,975	79.5	217	175	80.6
18 and 19 years	124,008	41,999	33.9	108,529	36,815	33.9	9,172	3,027	33.0	6,079	2,052	33.8	228	105	46.1
20 years	61,263	10,830	17.7	53,598	9,657	18.0	4,703	778	16.5	2,847	359	12.6	115	36	31.3
21 to 24 years	243,599	21,786	8.9	216,836	19,933	9.2	13,912	1,243	8.9	12,404	537	4.3	447	73	16.3
Female, 5 to 24 years	1,159,929	654,685	56.4	1,028,551	591,196	57.5	49,746	18,419	37.0	80,198	44,114	55.0	1,434	956	66.7
5 years	43,521	12,896	29.6	39,726	11,852	29.8	506	169	33.4	3,203	842	26.3	86	33	-
6 years	43,576	37,872	86.9	39,752	34,664	87.2	520	416	80.0	3,208	2,716	84.7	96	76	-
7 to 9 years	144,661	139,747	96.6	132,056	127,678	96.7	2,037	1,896	93.1	10,281	9,901	96.3	287	272	94.8
10 to 13 years	221,294	214,814	97.1	201,202	195,399	97.1	4,929	4,715	95.7	14,865	14,409	96.9	298	291	97.7
14 years	56,361	54,425	96.6	50,729	49,057	96.7	1,881	1,786	94.9	3,689	3,524	95.5	62	58	-
15 years	57,155	54,853	96.0	51,421	49,410	96.1	2,001	1,903	95.1	3,676	3,484	94.8	57	56	-
16 and 17 years	119,411	90,893	76.1	106,173	80,926	76.2	5,897	4,271	72.4	7,213	5,596	77.6	128	100	78.1
18 and 19 years	129,659	32,067	24.7	111,907	27,475	24.6	9,425	2,148	22.8	8,215	2,406	29.3	112	38	33.9
20 years	66,599	6,650	10.0	56,495	5,762	10.2	5,156	398	7.7	4,891	477	9.8	57	13	-
21 to 24 years	277,692	10,468	3.8	239,090	8,973	3.8	17,394	717	4.1	20,957	759	3.6	251	19	7.6
1930															
Total, 5 to 24 years	2,439,287	1,362,751	55.9	2,056,945	1,237,685	60.2	277,242	77,432	27.9	102,805	46,617	45.3	2,295	1,017	44.3
5 years	112,108	28,632	25.5	104,372	26,823	25.7	2,257	504	22.3	5,340	1,263	23.7	139	42	30.2
6 years	115,242	92,352	80.1	107,000	86,052	80.4	3,108	2,394	77.0	5,013	3,815	76.1	121	91	75.2
7 to 9 years	349,934	338,303	96.7	319,125	308,879	96.8	16,519	15,870	96.1	14,012	13,293	94.9	278	261	93.9
10 to 13 years	463,188	456,204	98.5	427,733	421,470	98.5	20,067	19,680	98.1	15,144	14,818	97.8	244	236	96.7
14 years	112,112	108,723	97.0	103,303	100,227	97.0	5,242	5,052	96.4	3,518	3,396	96.5	49	48	-
15 years	112,305	101,860	90.3	102,155	92,164	90.2	6,771	6,133	90.6	3,325	3,020	90.8	54	43	-
16 and 17 years	232,443	132,712	57.1	202,327	116,559	57.6	22,683	11,933	52.6	7,319	4,156	56.8	114	64	56.1
18 and 19 years	254,538	53,524	21.0	205,860	45,266	22.0	37,977	6,628	17.5	10,476	1,570	15.0	225	60	26.7
20 years	131,955	16,667	12.6	99,709	13,766	13.8	25,529	2,496	9.8	6,570	381	5.8	147	24	16.3
21 to 24 years	555,462	34,274	6.2	385,361	26,479	6.9	137,089	6,742	4.9	32,088	905	2.8	924	148	16.0
Male, 5 to 24 years	1,203,519	702,126	58.3	1,024,900	637,812	62.2	130,327	41,371	31.7	46,714	22,359	47.9	1,578	584	37.0
5 years	56,813	14,449	25.4	53,008	13,563	25.6	1,125	254	22.6	2,606	609	23.4	79	23	-
6 years	58,294	46,618	80.0	54,183	43,489	80.3	1,613	1,244	77.1	2,444	1,843	75.4	54	42	-
7 to 9 years	176,675	170,727	96.6	161,385	156,112	96.7	8,313	7,998	96.2	6,844	6,491	94.8	133	126	94.7
10 to 13 years	233,916	230,415	98.5	216,389	213,233	98.5	10,133	9,943	98.1	7,268	7,119	97.9	126	120	95.2
14 years	56,347	54,756	97.2	51,952	50,499	97.2	2,647	2,560	96.7	1,719	1,669	97.1	29	28	-
15 years	56,540	51,345	90.8	51,562	46,747	90.7	3,375	3,118	92.4	1,572	1,455	92.6	31	25	-
16 and 17 years	114,770	69,016	60.1	100,571	60,834	60.5	10,823	6,205	57.3	3,308	1,940	58.6	68	37	-
18 and 19 years	122,430	31,344	25.6	100,770	26,637	26.4	17,199	3,979	23.1	4,289	684	15.9	172	44	25.6
20 years	62,152	10,397	16.7	48,011	8,643	18.0	11,454	1,578	13.8	2,576	160	6.2	111	16	14.4
21 to 24 years	265,582	23,059	8.7	187,074	18,055	9.7	63,645	4,492	7.1	14,088	389	2.8	775	123	15.9
Female, 5 to 24 years	1,235,768	660,625	53.5	1,032,045	599,873	58.1	146,915	36,061	24.5	56,091	24,258	43.2	717	433	60.4
5 years	55,295	14,183	25.6	51,369	13,260	25.8	1,132	250	22.1	2,734	654	23.9	60	19	-
6 years	56,948	45,734	80.3	52,817	42,563	80.6	1,495	1,150	76.9	2,569	1,972	76.8	67	49	-
7 to 9 years	173,259	167,576	96.7	157,740	152,767	96.8	8,206	7,872	95.9	7,168	6,802	94.9	145	135	93.1
10 to 13 years	229,272	225,789	98.5	211,344	208,237	98.5	9,934	9,737	98.0	7,876	7,699	[illegible]	118	116	98.3
14 years	55,765	53,967	96.8	51,351	49,728	96.8	2,595	2,492	96.0	1,799	1,727	96.0	20	20	-
15 years	55,765	50,015	89.7	50,593	45,417	89.8	3,396	3,015	88.8	1,753	1,565	89.3	23	18	-
16 and 17 years	117,673	63,696	54.1	101,756	55,725	54.8	11,860	5,728	48.3	4,011	2,216	55.2	46	27	-
18 and 19 years	132,108	22,180	16.8	105,090	18,629	17.7	20,778	2,649	12.7	6,187	886	14.3	53	16	-
20 years	69,803	6,270	9.0	51,698	5,123	9.9	14,075	918	6.5	3,994	221	5.5	36	8	-
21 to 24 years	289,880	11,215	3.9	198,287	8,424	4.2	73,444	2,250	3.1	18,000	516	2.9	149	25	16.8

Table C-39.—PERSONS 25 YEARS OLD AND OVER, BY YEARS OF SCHOOL COMPLETED, RACE, AND SEX, FOR THE CITY OF NEW YORK: 1940

[Percent not shown where less than 0.1; median and percent not shown where base is less than 100]

YEARS OF SCHOOL COMPLETED	ALL CLASSES			NATIVE WHITE			FOREIGN-BORN WHITE			NEGRO			OTHER RACES		
	Total	Male	Female	Total	Male	Female	Total	Male	Female	Total	Male	Female	Total	Male	Female
Persons 25 years old and over	4,733,342	2,327,048	2,406,294	2,452,719	1,176,709	1,276,010	1,982,043	1,010,881	971,162	283,994	126,460	157,534	14,586	12,998	1,588
No school years completed	361,184	168,413	192,771	21,613	9,787	11,826	325,905	150,661	175,244	9,778	4,414	5,364	3,888	3,551	337
Grade school: 1 to 4 years	340,551	171,962	168,589	47,904	23,248	24,656	253,517	129,707	123,810	36,215	16,228	19,987	2,915	2,779	136
5 or 6 years	367,288	183,754	183,534	108,791	52,733	56,058	208,431	108,206	100,225	48,372	21,250	27,122	1,694	1,565	129
7 or 8 years	1,934,829	939,513	995,316	1,059,451	503,256	556,195	771,640	389,004	382,636	101,145	45,007	56,138	2,593	2,246	347
High school: 1 to 3 years	600,541	289,124	311,417	429,601	203,919	225,682	128,331	66,773	61,558	41,738	17,700	24,038	871	732	139
4 years	585,923	249,407	336,516	418,943	168,634	250,309	138,772	68,710	70,062	27,284	11,392	15,892	924	671	253
College: 1 to 3 years	174,912	97,789	77,123	131,156	70,465	60,691	34,426	22,485	11,941	8,875	4,470	4,405	455	369	86
4 years or more	266,091	174,510	91,581	202,872	127,586	75,286	56,643	42,963	13,680	5,840	3,353	2,487	736	608	128
Not reported	102,023	52,576	49,447	32,388	17,081	15,307	64,378	32,372	32,006	4,747	2,646	2,101	510	477	33
Median school years completed	8.3	8.3	8.3	8.9	9.0	8.9	7.4	7.5	7.4	7.9	7.9	7.9	5.3	4.9	8.0
Percent less than 5 years completed	14.8	14.6	15.0	2.8	2.8	2.9	29.2	27.7	30.8	16.2	16.3	16.1	46.6	48.7	29.8
PERCENT DISTRIBUTION															
Persons 25 years old and over	100.0	100.0	100.0	100.0	100.0	100.0	100.0	100.0	100.0	100.0	100.0	100.0	100.0	100.0	100.0
No school years completed	7.6	7.2	8.0	0.9	0.8	0.9	16.4	14.9	18.0	3.4	3.5	3.4	26.7	27.3	21.2
Grade school: 1 to 4 years	7.2	7.4	7.0	2.0	2.0	1.9	12.8	12.8	12.7	12.8	12.8	12.7	20.0	21.4	8.6
5 or 6 years	7.8	7.9	7.6	4.4	4.5	4.4	10.5	10.7	10.3	17.0	16.8	17.2	11.6	12.0	8.1
7 or 8 years	40.9	40.4	41.4	43.2	42.8	43.6	38.9	38.5	39.4	35.6	35.6	35.6	17.8	17.3	21.9
High school: 1 to 3 years	12.7	12.4	12.9	17.5	17.3	17.7	6.5	6.6	6.3	14.7	14.0	15.3	6.0	5.6	8.8
4 years	12.4	10.7	14.0	17.1	14.3	19.6	7.0	6.8	7.2	9.6	9.0	10.1	6.3	5.2	15.9
College: 1 to 3 years	3.7	4.2	3.2	5.3	6.0	4.8	1.7	2.2	1.2	3.1	3.5	2.8	3.1	2.8	5.4
4 years or more	5.6	7.5	3.8	8.3	10.8	5.9	2.9	4.3	1.4	2.1	2.7	1.6	5.0	4.7	8.1
Not reported	2.2	2.3	2.1	1.3	1.5	1.2	3.2	3.2	3.3	1.7	2.1	1.3	3.5	3.7	2.1

Table C-40.—FOREIGN-BORN WHITE, BY COUNTRY OF BIRTH, BY SEX, FOR THE CITY OF NEW YORK: 1940 AND 1930

[Figures for white population in 1930 revised to include Mexicans classified with "Other races" in the 1930 reports. Percent not shown where less than 0.1 or where base is less than 100]

COUNTRY OF BIRTH	BOTH SEXES		PERCENT		MALE		FEMALE	
	1940	1930	1940	1930	1940	1930	1940	1930
All countries	2,080,020	2,295,181	100.0	100.0	1,057,839	1,180,947	1,022,181	1,114,234
England	63,115	78,003	3.0	3.4	30,411	38,538	32,704	39,465
Scotland	33,292	38,535	1.6	1.7	15,758	19,018	17,534	19,517
Wales	1,296	1,903	0.1	0.1	667	988	629	915
Northern Ireland	21,501	27,821	1.0	1.2	9,384	12,169	12,117	15,652
Irish Free State (Eire)	160,325	192,810	7.7	8.4	69,988	85,746	90,337	107,064
Norway	30,750	38,130	1.5	1.7	16,471	21,171	14,279	16,959
Sweden	28,881	37,267	1.4	1.6	14,674	19,357	14,207	17,910
Denmark	8,845	11,096	0.4	0.5	5,425	6,946	3,420	4,150
Netherlands	5,608	5,335	0.3	0.2	3,704	3,619	1,904	1,716
Belgium	3,888	3,854	0.2	0.2	1,993	1,952	1,895	1,902
Luxemburg	340	323	-	-	175	174	165	149
Switzerland	8,551	9,895	0.4	0.4	4,412	5,147	4,139	4,748
France	19,696	23,288	0.9	1.0	8,397	10,263	11,299	13,025
Germany	224,749	237,588	10.8	10.4	112,916	121,590	111,833	115,998
Poland	194,163	238,339	9.3	10.4	97,816	120,318	96,347	118,021
Czechoslovakia	26,884	35,318	1.3	1.5	12,042	15,964	14,842	19,354
Austria	145,106	127,169	7.0	5.5	70,537	62,587	74,569	64,582
Hungary	62,588	59,883	3.0	2.6	28,557	27,444	34,031	32,439
Yugoslavia	6,475	6,450	0.3	0.3	3,712	3,638	2,763	2,812
Russia (U. S. S. R.)	395,696	442,431	19.0	19.3	200,663	227,120	195,033	215,311
Lithuania	15,089	15,005	0.7	0.7	7,944	8,162	7,145	6,843
Latvia	5,317	5,172	0.3	0.2	2,785	2,692	2,532	2,480
Finland	11,245	13,224	0.5	0.6	4,563	5,833	6,682	7,391
Rumania	40,655	46,750	2.0	2.0	20,316	23,377	20,339	23,373
Bulgaria	670	578	-	-	394	342	276	236
Turkey in Europe	265	747	-	-	146	383	119	364
Greece	28,593	27,182	1.4	1.2	19,304	18,567	9,289	8,615
Italy	409,489	440,250	19.7	19.2	227,084	246,088	182,405	194,162
Spain	13,583	14,000	0.7	0.6	9,504	10,153	4,079	3,847
Portugal	2,676	2,231	0.1	0.1	2,008	1,756	668	475
Other Europe	5,757	4,844	0.3	0.2	3,691	3,160	2,066	1,684
Palestine and Syria	8,598	8,696	0.4	0.4	4,545	4,578	4,053	4,118
Turkey in Asia	17,398	14,368	0.8	0.6	9,645	8,050	7,753	6,318
Other Asia	5,107	5,621	0.2	0.2	3,293	3,514	1,814	2,107
Canada—French	6,270	6,863	0.3	0.3	2,753	3,308	3,517	3,555
Canada—Other	29,237	32,760	1.4	1.4	11,768	14,038	17,469	18,722
Newfoundland	4,838	5,303	0.2	0.2	2,171	2,555	2,667	2,748
Mexico	2,973	4,163	0.1	0.2	1,708	2,559	1,265	1,604
Cuba and other West Indies	13,344	13,046	0.6	0.6	7,136	7,303	6,208	5,743
Central and South America	12,429	14,298	0.6	0.6	6,807	8,202	5,622	6,096
Australia	987	1,164	-	0.1	513	650	474	514
Azores	69	95	-	-	35	66	34	29
All other and not reported	3,682	3,383	0.2	0.1	2,024	1,862	1,658	1,521

Table C-41.—PERSONS 14 YEARS OLD AND OVER, BY EMPLOYMENT STATUS, CLASS OF WORKER, RACE, AND SEX, FOR THE CITY OF NEW YORK: 1940

[Percent not shown where less than 0.1 or where base is less than 100]

EMPLOYMENT STATUS	ALL CLASSES			NATIVE WHITE			FOREIGN-BORN WHITE			NEGRO			OTHER RACES		
	Total	Male	Female	Total	Male	Female	Total	Male	Female	Total	Male	Female	Total	Male	Female
Total population (all ages)	7,454,995	3,676,293	3,778,702	4,897,481	2,397,164	2,500,317	2,080,020	1,057,839	1,022,181	458,444	205,727	252,717	19,050	15,563	3,487
Persons 14 years old and over	6,102,747	2,989,576	3,113,171	3,658,014	1,766,189	1,891,825	2,061,426	1,048,510	1,012,916	366,836	160,661	206,175	16,471	14,216	2,255
In labor force	3,474,760	2,424,740	1,050,020	2,113,054	1,403,145	709,909	1,114,459	879,446	235,013	234,336	129,853	104,483	12,911	12,296	615
Not in labor force	2,627,987	564,836	2,063,151	1,544,960	363,044	1,181,916	946,967	169,064	777,903	132,500	30,808	101,692	3,560	1,920	1,640
Engaged in own home housew'k	1,592,195	20,265	1,571,930	852,525	10,247	842,278	675,850	8,973	666,877	62,563	991	61,572	1,257	54	1,203
In school	474,543	248,124	226,419	422,821	222,304	200,517	22,889	11,998	10,891	27,902	13,183	14,719	931	639	292
Unable to work	293,980	162,619	131,361	105,263	53,804	51,459	159,113	98,217	60,896	28,901	9,958	18,943	703	640	63
In institutions	34,202	18,746	15,456	16,802	9,200	7,602	14,490	7,549	6,941	2,704	1,797	907	206	200	6
Other and not reported	233,067	115,082	117,985	147,549	67,489	80,060	74,625	42,327	32,298	10,430	4,879	5,551	463	387	76
LABOR FORCE BY EMPLOYMENT STATUS															
In labor force	3,474,760	2,424,740	1,050,020	2,113,054	1,403,145	709,909	1,114,459	879,446	235,013	234,336	129,853	104,483	12,911	12,296	615
Employed (exc. public emerg. work)	2,839,366	1,964,346	875,020	1,711,638	1,127,160	584,478	946,938	738,020	208,918	169,497	88,386	81,111	11,293	10,780	513
At work	2,765,695	1,917,928	847,767	1,669,669	1,104,589	565,080	918,934	716,249	202,685	166,185	86,681	79,504	10,907	10,409	498
With a job	73,671	46,418	27,253	41,969	22,571	19,398	28,004	21,771	6,233	3,312	1,705	1,607	386	371	15
On public emerg. work (WPA, etc.)	103,386	86,845	16,541	61,920	51,403	10,517	21,415	19,911	1,504	19,936	15,428	4,508	115	103	12
Seeking work	532,008	373,549	158,459	339,496	224,582	114,914	146,106	121,515	24,591	44,903	26,039	18,864	1,503	1,413	90
Experienced workers	459,422	335,922	123,500	276,438	191,793	84,645	141,561	119,197	22,364	39,995	23,565	16,430	1,428	1,367	61
New workers	72,586	37,627	34,959	63,058	32,789	30,269	4,545	2,318	2,227	4,908	2,474	2,434	75	46	29
PERCENT BY SEX															
In labor force	100.0	69.8	30.2	100.0	66.4	33.6	100.0	78.9	21.1	100.0	55.4	44.6	100.0	95.2	4.8
Employed (exc. public emerg.)	100.0	69.2	30.8	100.0	65.9	34.1	100.0	77.9	22.1	100.0	52.1	47.9	100.0	95.5	4.5
On pub. emerg. work (WPA, etc.)	100.0	84.0	16.0	100.0	83.0	17.0	100.0	93.0	7.0	100.0	77.4	22.6	100.0	89.6	10.4
Seeking work	100.0	70.2	29.8	100.0	66.2	33.8	100.0	83.2	16.8	100.0	58.0	42.0	100.0	94.0	6.0
Not in labor force	100.0	21.5	78.5	100.0	23.5	76.5	100.0	17.9	82.1	100.0	23.3	76.7	100.0	53.9	46.1
Engaged in own home housew'k	100.0	1.3	98.7	100.0	1.2	98.8	100.0	1.3	98.7	100.0	1.6	98.4	100.0	4.3	95.7
In school	100.0	52.3	47.7	100.0	52.6	47.4	100.0	52.4	47.6	100.0	47.2	52.8	100.0	68.6	31.4
Unable to work	100.0	55.3	44.7	100.0	51.1	48.9	100.0	61.7	38.3	100.0	34.5	65.5	100.0	91.0	9.0
In institutions	100.0	54.8	45.2	100.0	54.8	45.2	100.0	52.1	47.9	100.0	66.5	33.5	100.0	97.1	2.9
Other and not reported	100.0	49.4	50.6	100.0	45.7	54.3	100.0	56.7	43.3	100.0	46.8	53.2	100.0	83.6	16.4
EMPLOYED WORKERS BY CLASS OF WORKER															
Employed (exc. public emerg.)	2,839,366	1,964,346	875,020	1,711,638	1,127,160	584,478	946,938	738,020	208,918	169,497	88,386	81,111	11,293	10,780	513
Wage and salary workers	2,459,880	1,647,274	812,606	1,548,333	992,373	555,960	743,765	564,074	179,691	159,008	82,450	76,558	8,774	8,377	397
Employers and own-account workers	347,006	303,310	43,696	144,706	124,915	19,791	190,344	170,526	19,818	9,560	5,541	4,019	2,396	2,328	68
Unpaid family workers	18,091	5,652	12,439	9,303	4,688	4,615	8,514	875	7,639	196	51	145	78	38	40
Class of worker not reported	14,389	8,110	6,279	9,296	5,184	4,112	4,315	2,545	1,770	733	344	389	45	37	8
At work	2,765,695	1,917,928	847,767	1,669,669	1,104,589	565,080	918,934	716,249	202,685	166,185	86,681	79,504	10,907	10,409	498
Wage and salary workers	2,404,444	1,615,540	788,904	1,514,554	976,011	538,543	724,845	550,085	174,760	156,373	81,159	75,214	8,672	8,285	387
Employers and own-account workers	331,238	289,936	41,302	138,100	119,549	18,551	182,031	163,148	18,883	8,987	5,184	3,803	2,120	2,055	65
Unpaid family workers	17,599	5,454	12,145	9,005	4,527	4,478	8,332	843	7,489	189	49	140	73	35	38
Class of worker not reported	12,414	6,998	5,416	8,010	4,502	3,508	3,726	2,173	1,553	636	289	347	42	34	8
With a job	73,671	46,418	27,253	41,969	22,571	19,398	28,004	21,771	6,233	3,312	1,705	1,607	386	371	15
Wage and salary workers	55,436	31,734	23,702	33,779	16,362	17,417	18,920	13,989	4,931	2,635	1,291	1,344	102	92	10
Employers and own-account workers	15,768	13,374	2,394	6,606	5,366	1,240	8,313	7,378	935	573	357	216	276	273	3
Unpaid family workers	492	198	294	298	161	137	182	32	150	7	2	5	5	3	2
Class of worker not reported	1,975	1,112	863	1,286	682	604	589	372	217	97	55	42	3	3	-
PERCENT DISTRIBUTION															
Persons 14 years old and over	100.0	100.0	100.0	100.0	100.0	100.0	100.0	100.0	100.0	100.0	100.0	100.0	100.0	100.0	100.0
In labor force	56.9	81.1	33.7	57.8	79.4	37.5	54.1	83.9	23.2	63.9	80.8	50.7	78.4	86.5	27.3
Not in labor force	43.1	18.9	66.3	42.2	20.6	62.5	45.9	16.1	76.8	36.1	19.2	49.3	21.6	13.5	72.7
Engaged in own home housew'k	26.1	0.7	50.5	23.3	0.6	44.5	32.8	0.9	65.8	17.1	0.6	29.9	7.6	0.4	53.3
In school	7.8	8.3	7.3	11.6	12.6	10.6	1.1	1.1	1.1	7.6	8.2	7.1	5.7	4.5	12.9
Unable to work	4.8	5.4	4.2	2.9	3.0	2.7	7.7	9.4	6.0	7.9	6.2	9.2	4.3	4.5	2.8
In institutions	0.6	0.6	0.5	0.5	0.5	0.4	0.7	0.7	0.7	0.7	1.1	0.4	1.3	1.4	0.3
Other and not reported	3.8	3.8	3.8	4.0	3.8	4.2	3.6	4.0	3.2	2.8	3.0	2.7	2.8	2.7	3.4
LABOR FORCE BY EMPLOYMENT STATUS															
In labor force	100.0	100.0	100.0	100.0	100.0	100.0	100.0	100.0	100.0	100.0	100.0	100.0	100.0	100.0	100.0
Employed (exc. public emerg. work)	81.7	81.0	83.3	81.0	80.3	82.3	85.0	83.9	88.9	72.3	68.1	77.6	87.5	87.7	83.4
At work	79.6	79.1	80.7	79.0	78.7	79.6	82.5	81.4	86.2	70.9	66.8	76.1	84.5	84.7	81.0
With a job	2.1	1.9	2.6	2.0	1.6	2.7	2.5	2.5	2.7	1.4	1.3	1.5	3.0	3.0	2.4
On public emerg. work (WPA, etc.)	3.0	3.6	1.6	2.9	3.7	1.5	1.9	2.3	0.6	8.5	11.9	4.3	0.9	0.8	2.0
Seeking work	15.3	15.4	15.1	16.1	16.0	16.2	13.1	13.8	10.5	19.2	20.1	18.1	11.6	11.5	14.6
Experienced workers	13.2	13.9	11.8	13.1	13.7	11.9	12.7	13.6	9.5	17.1	18.1	15.7	11.1	11.1	9.9
New workers	2.1	1.6	3.3	3.0	2.3	4.3	0.4	0.3	0.9	2.1	1.9	2.3	0.6	0.4	4.7
EMPLOYED WORKERS BY CLASS OF WORKER															
Employed (exc. public emerg.)	100.0	100.0	100.0	100.0	100.0	100.0	100.0	100.0	100.0	100.0	100.0	100.0	100.0	100.0	100.0
Wage and salary workers	86.6	83.9	92.9	90.5	88.0	95.1	78.5	76.4	86.0	93.8	93.3	94.4	77.7	77.7	77.4
Employers and own-account workers	12.2	15.4	5.0	8.5	11.1	3.4	20.1	23.1	9.5	5.6	6.3	5.0	21.2	21.6	13.3
Unpaid family workers	0.6	0.3	1.4	0.5	0.4	0.8	0.9	0.1	3.7	0.1	0.1	0.2	0.7	0.4	7.8
Class of worker not reported	0.5	0.4	0.7	0.5	0.5	0.7	0.5	0.3	0.8	0.4	0.4	0.5	0.4	0.3	1.6
At work	100.0	100.0	100.0	100.0	100.0	100.0	100.0	100.0	100.0	100.0	100.0	100.0	100.0	100.0	100.0
Wage and salary workers	86.9	84.2	93.1	90.7	88.4	95.3	78.9	76.8	86.2	94.1	93.6	94.6	79.5	79.6	77.7
Employers and own-account workers	12.0	15.1	4.9	8.3	10.8	3.3	19.8	22.8	9.3	5.4	6.0	4.8	19.4	19.7	13.1
Unpaid family workers	0.6	0.3	1.4	0.5	0.4	0.8	0.9	0.1	3.7	0.1	0.1	0.2	0.7	0.3	7.6
Class of worker not reported	0.4	0.4	0.6	0.5	0.4	0.6	0.4	0.3	0.8	0.4	0.3	0.4	0.4	0.3	1.6
With a job	100.0	100.0	100.0	100.0	100.0	100.0	100.0	100.0	100.0	100.0	100.0	100.0	100.0	100.0	-
Wage and salary workers	75.2	68.4	87.0	80.5	72.5	89.8	67.6	64.3	79.1	79.6	75.7	83.6	26.4	24.8	-
Employers and own-account workers	21.4	28.8	8.8	15.7	23.8	6.4	29.7	33.9	15.0	17.3	20.9	13.4	71.5	73.6	-
Unpaid family workers	0.7	0.4	1.1	0.7	0.7	0.7	0.6	0.1	2.4	0.2	0.1	0.3	1.3	0.8	-
Class of worker not reported	2.7	2.4	3.2	3.1	3.0	3.1	2.1	1.7	3.5	2.9	3.2	2.6	0.8	0.8	-

Table C-42.—EMPLOYED WORKERS 14 YEARS OLD AND OVER, BY MAJOR OCCUPATION GROUP, INDUSTRY GROUP, AND SEX, FOR THE CITY OF NEW YORK: 1940

[Percent not shown where less than 0.1 or where base is less than 100]

MAJOR OCCUPATION GROUP AND INDUSTRY GROUP	Total	Male	Female	PERCENT BY OCCUPATION AND INDUSTRY			PERCENT BY SEX	
				Total	Male	Female	Male	Female
Total population (all ages)	7,454,995	3,676,293	3,778,702	-	-	-	49.3	50.7
All persons 14 years old and over	6,102,747	2,989,576	3,113,171	-	-	-	49.0	51.0
In labor force	3,474,760	2,424,740	1,050,020	100.0	100.0	100.0	69.8	30.2
Employed workers (except on public emergency work)	2,839,366	1,964,346	875,020	81.7	81.0	83.3	69.2	30.8
MAJOR OCCUPATION GROUP								
Employed (except on public emergency work)	2,839,366	1,964,346	875,020	100.0	100.0	100.0	69.2	30.8
Professional workers	217,032	126,887	90,145	7.6	6.5	10.3	58.5	41.5
Semiprofessional workers	42,198	30,052	12,146	1.5	1.5	1.4	71.2	28.8
Farmers and farm managers	558	519	39	-	-	-	93.0	7.0
Proprietors, managers, and officials, except farm	288,152	259,075	29,077	10.1	13.2	3.3	89.9	10.1
Clerical, sales, and kindred workers	770,804	446,199	324,605	27.1	22.7	37.1	37.9	42.1
Craftsmen, foremen, and kindred workers	329,479	319,308	10,171	11.6	16.3	1.2	96.9	3.1
Operatives and kindred workers	580,053	388,788	191,265	20.4	19.8	21.9	67.0	33.0
Domestic service workers	123,202	6,976	116,226	4.3	0.4	13.3	5.7	94.3
Service workers, except domestic	346,264	256,696	89,568	12.2	13.1	10.2	74.1	25.9
Farm laborers (wage workers) and farm foremen	960	914	46	-	-	-	95.2	4.8
Farm laborers, unpaid family workers	60	50	10	-	-	-	-	-
Laborers, except farm	114,168	111,567	2,601	4.0	5.7	0.3	97.7	2.3
Occupation not reported	26,436	17,315	9,121	0.9	0.9	1.0	65.5	34.5
INDUSTRY GROUP								
Employed (except on public emergency work)	2,839,366	1,964,346	875,020	100.0	100.0	100.0	69.2	30.8
Agriculture, forestry, and fishery	3,468	3,229	239	0.1	0.2	-	93.1	6.9
Agriculture	2,813	2,599	214	0.1	0.1	-	92.4	7.6
Forestry (except logging) and fishery	655	630	25	-	-	-	96.2	3.8
Mining	996	822	174	-	-	-	82.5	17.5
Coal mining	93	82	11	-	-	-	-	-
Crude petroleum and natural gas production	78	66	12	-	-	-	-	-
Other mines and quarries	825	674	151	-	-	-	81.7	18.3
Construction	131,599	127,880	3,719	4.6	6.5	0.4	97.2	2.8
Manufacturing	746,466	504,413	242,053	26.3	25.7	27.7	67.6	32.4
Food and kindred products	67,648	54,260	13,388	2.4	2.8	1.5	80.2	19.8
Textile-mill products	42,081	26,440	15,641	1.5	1.3	1.8	62.8	37.2
Apparel and other fabricated textile products	236,604	121,618	114,986	8.3	6.2	13.1	51.4	48.6
Logging	50	44	6	-	-	-	-	-
Sawmills and planing mills	1,407	1,291	116	-	0.1	-	91.8	8.2
Furniture, store fixtures, and miscellaneous wooden goods	21,104	18,415	2,689	0.7	0.9	0.3	87.3	12.7
Paper and allied products	20,049	12,610	7,439	0.7	0.6	0.9	62.9	37.1
Printing, publishing, and allied industries	81,528	62,074	19,454	2.9	3.2	2.2	76.1	23.9
Chemicals and allied products	30,400	19,973	10,427	1.1	1.0	1.2	65.7	34.3
Petroleum and coal products	8,074	6,371	1,703	0.3	0.3	0.2	78.9	21.1
Leather and leather products	26,702	18,936	7,766	0.9	1.0	0.9	70.9	29.1
Stone, clay, and glass products	8,366	6,960	1,406	0.3	0.4	0.2	83.2	16.8
Iron and steel and their products	24,332	20,387	3,945	0.9	1.0	0.5	83.8	16.2
Nonferrous metals and their products	21,099	17,314	3,785	0.7	0.9	0.4	82.1	17.9
Machinery	44,459	36,106	8,353	1.6	1.8	1.0	81.2	18.8
Automobiles and automobile equipment	5,256	4,421	835	0.2	0.2	0.1	84.1	15.9
Transportation equipment, except automobile	21,985	21,163	822	0.8	1.1	0.1	96.3	3.7
Other and not specified manufacturing industries	85,322	56,030	29,292	3.0	2.9	3.3	65.7	34.3
Transportation, communication, and other public utilities	251,416	220,359	31,057	8.9	11.2	3.5	87.6	12.4
Railroads (including railroad repair shops) and railway express service	32,779	31,130	1,649	1.2	1.6	0.2	95.0	5.0
Trucking service	28,347	27,352	995	1.0	1.4	0.1	96.5	3.5
Other transportation	102,686	98,192	4,494	3.6	5.0	0.5	95.6	4.4
Communication	36,407	18,340	18,067	1.3	0.9	2.1	50.4	49.6
Utilities	51,197	45,345	5,852	1.8	2.3	0.7	88.6	11.4
Wholesale and retail trade	621,757	470,614	151,143	21.9	24.0	17.3	75.7	24.3
Wholesale trade	99,660	79,079	20,581	3.5	4.0	2.4	79.3	20.7
Food and dairy products stores, and milk retailing	133,741	114,878	18,863	4.7	5.8	2.2	85.9	14.1
Eating and drinking places	112,822	86,611	26,211	4.0	4.4	3.0	76.8	23.2
Motor vehicles and accessories retailing, and filling stations	17,299	15,837	1,462	0.6	0.8	0.2	91.5	8.5
Other retail trade	258,235	174,209	84,026	9.1	8.9	9.6	67.5	32.5
Finance, insurance, and real estate	224,460	162,199	62,261	7.9	8.3	7.1	72.3	27.7
Business and repair services	74,133	61,177	12,956	2.6	3.1	1.5	82.5	17.5
Automobile storage, rental, and repair services	25,738	25,214	524	0.9	1.3	0.1	98.0	2.0
Business and repair services, except automobile	48,395	35,963	12,432	1.7	1.8	1.4	74.3	25.7
Personal services	293,887	109,819	184,068	10.4	5.6	21.0	37.4	62.6
Domestic service	135,788	13,752	122,036	4.8	0.7	13.9	10.1	89.9
Hotels and lodging places	55,832	31,981	23,851	2.0	1.6	2.7	57.3	42.7
Laundering, cleaning, and dyeing services	45,141	28,394	16,747	1.6	1.4	1.9	62.9	37.1
Miscellaneous personal services	57,126	35,692	21,434	2.0	1.8	2.4	62.5	37.5
Amusement, recreation, and related services	42,996	31,610	11,386	1.5	1.6	1.3	73.5	26.5
Professional and related services	247,816	122,769	125,047	8.7	6.2	14.3	49.5	50.5
Government	126,733	108,811	17,922	4.5	5.5	2.0	85.9	14.1
Industry not reported	73,639	40,644	32,995	2.6	2.1	3.8	55.2	44.8

Table C-43.—PERSONS 14 YEARS OLD AND OVER IN THE LABOR FORCE, 1940, AND GAINFUL WORKERS 14 YEARS OLD AND OVER, 1930, BY RACE AND SEX, FOR THE CITY OF NEW YORK

[Totals for population and gainful workers for 1930 include "Unknown age." Figures for white population in 1930 have been revised to include Mexicans who were classified with "Other races" in the 1930 reports. Percent not shown where less than 0.1 or where base is less than 100]

CENSUS YEAR AND RACE	TOTAL					MALE					FEMALE				
	Population		Persons in the labor force, and gainful workers,[1] 14 years old and over			Population		Persons in the labor force, and gainful workers,[1] 14 years old and over			Population		Persons in the labor force, and gainful workers,[1] 14 years old and over		
	Total (all ages)	14 years old and over	Number	Percent of total population	Percent of population 14 yrs. and over	Total (all ages)	14 years old and over	Number	Percent of total population	Percent of population 14 yrs. and over	Total (all ages)	14 years old and over	Number	Percent of total population	Percent of population 14 yrs. and over
1940	7,454,995	6,102,747	3,474,760	46.6	56.9	3,676,293	2,989,576	2,424,740	66.0	81.1	3,778,702	3,113,171	1,050,020	27.8	33.7
White	6,977,501	5,719,440	3,227,513	46.3	56.4	3,455,003	2,814,699	2,282,591	66.1	81.1	3,522,498	2,904,741	944,922	26.8	32.5
Negro	458,444	366,836	234,336	51.1	63.9	205,727	160,661	129,853	63.1	80.8	252,717	206,175	104,483	41.3	50.7
Other races	19,050	16,471	12,911	67.8	78.4	15,563	14,216	12,296	79.0	86.5	3,487	2,255	615	17.6	27.3
1930	6,930,446	5,354,374	3,186,958	46.0	59.5	3,472,956	2,674,820	2,324,296	66.9	86.9	3,457,490	2,679,554	862,662	25.0	32.2
White	6,589,377	5,081,179	2,982,779	45.3	58.7	3,304,524	2,539,724	2,199,622	66.6	86.6	3,284,853	2,541,455	783,157	23.8	30.8
Negro	327,706	261,277	193,730	59.1	74.1	156,968	124,375	114,535	73.0	92.1	170,738	136,902	79,195	46.4	57.8
Other races	13,363	11,918	10,449	78.2	87.7	11,464	10,721	10,139	88.4	94.6	1,899	1,197	310	16.3	25.9

[1] Data for 1930 represent gainful workers 14 years old and over.

Keeping up With the "Swingingest Female Alive"

In 1940, Americans couldn't get enough of Kansas City jazz, the trademark of pianist and musical arranger Mary Lou Williams. Her smooth simplicity and extended solo riffs caught the ear of Benny Goodman and Tommy Dorsey, for whom she wrote and arranged countless hits. She played to packed houses with the band Clouds of Joy, and those who didn't see her live listened to her music from a new invention—the jukebox.

Life at Home

- Born Mary Elfreida Scruggs, Mary Lou was one of 11 children, and moved to Pittsburgh when she was five or six years old.
- Her mother played the organ, and Mary Lou began playing the piano for money when she was seven, sometimes earning $20 to $30 a day.
- When Mary Lou was 10, the Mellon family paid her $100 to play piano for a party and brought her to the event in a chauffeur-driven limousine.
- When she was 11, Mary was asked to substitute for the regular pianist on a touring show of the Earl Hines Band, *Hits and Bits,* and all the coaching she needed was a cast member simply humming the tunes for her on the day of the performance.
- For the next two summers, she traveled with the show, which brought her into contact with popular groups like McKinney's Cotton Pickers and Duke Ellington's Washingtonians.
- By the time she turned 13, she was a veteran musician with fans all along the East Coast.
- One of those fans was future husband and saxophonist John Williams, whose combo played with *Hits and Bit.*
- When Seymour and Jeanette, a top vaudeville team on the Orpheum circuit, proposed that John Williams could join their circuit, he insisted on taking Mary Lou along.
- "Cut her hair and put pants on her!" shouted Seymour in response. "We cannot have a girl in the outfit."
- After hearing her play the piano, however, Seymour changed his mind and she stayed with the act until it broke up a year later.
- When she was 15, and jamming with McKinney's Cotton Pickers at Harlem's Rhythm Club at 3 am, Louis Armstrong entered the room, paused to listen, then "Louis picked me up and kissed me."
- After they were married, John Williams and Mary Lou toured the South with her own small band until John joined *Clouds of Joy.*
- Soon after they moved to Kansas City, Missouri for a job at the Pla-Mor, one the city's top ballrooms, and worked in Kansas City for seven years.
- "Kaycee was really jumping," Mary Lou said. "So many great bands have sprung up there or moved in from over the river. It attracted musicians from all over the South and Southwest."

Mary Lou Williams was a jazz pianist with fans all along the East Coast–including Louis Armstrong–by the time she was 13 years old.

Louis Armstrong at the piano.

Life at Work

- Kansas City was a wide-open town, firmly under the control of political boss Tom Pendergast, who ignored the national Prohibition against alcohol sales, while promoting gambling and other vice in the city.
- "Naturally, work was plentiful for musicians," Mary Lou Williams said.
- Talented musicians flocked to the town-where the music never went to bed-to play in after-hours jam sessions with established musicians like Herschel Evans, Coleman Hawkins and Lester ("Prez") Young.
- "We didn't have closing hours in those spots," Mary Lou said. "We'd play all morning and half through the day if we wished, and, in fact, we often did. The music was so good we seldom got to bed before midday."
- Kansas City jazz was recognized as a unique sound with its preference for a 4/4 beat that made it more relaxed and fluid.
- New York had developed its own swinging jazz sound, Chicago was recognized as a center for its own jazz style, and the crossroads community of Kansas City owned its own distinctive sound.
- Extended soloing fueled by a culture whose goal was to "say something" with one's instrument also marked Kansas City jazz as distinctive.
- At times, one "song" could be performed for several hours, with the best musicians often soloing for dozens of choruses at a time.
- Constructed around a 12-bar blues structure, rather than the eight-bar jazz standard, the style left room for elaborate riffing by individuals or pairs.
- Since the big bands in Kansas City also played by memory, composing collectively rather than sight-reading, the KC style was often looser and more spontaneous.
- It was a sound that suited Mary Lou's musical skills.
- Critics wrote of Mary Lou, "If you shut your eyes, you would bet she was a man."
- *Time* magazine said she played "the solid, unpretentious, flesh-&-bone kind of jazz piano that is expected from such vigorous Negro masters as James P. Johnson."

Clouds of Joy's success was a direct result of the songs that Mary Lou wrote and arranged for them.

- For a decade, Andy Kirk's *Clouds of Joy* and Mary Lou were inseparable.
- She wrote most of its arrangements, and many, such as "Roll 'Em" and "Froggy Bottom" quickly became classics among jazz players.
- Writing up to 15 scores a week, she provided the *Clouds of Joy* with 200 arrangements, including "Walkin' and Swingin'," "Twinklin'," "Cloudy'," and "Little Joe from Chicago."
- During a recording trip to Chicago, Mary Lou recorded "Drag 'Em" and "Night Life" as piano solos.
- The records sold briskly, lifting Mary Lou to national prominence.
- She also began playing solo gigs and working as a freelance arranger for Earl Hines, Benny Goodman, and Tommy Dorsey.
- Mary Lou and the *Clouds of Joy* also scored another hit with "Until The Real Thing Comes Along," and suddenly, their sound was coming from every bar; when they played live to packed houses, and from the newly developed jukebox.
- Some nights they performed "Real Thing" half a dozen times because the demand was so great, despite the fact that its gloomy sound was a departure from KC swing.
- When she wrote *In the Groove* with Dick Wilson, Benny Goodman asked Mary Lou to write a blues number for his band.
- The result was "Roll 'Em," a boogie-woogie piece based on the blues, which followed her successful "Camel Hop," Goodman's theme song for his radio show sponsored by Camel cigarettes.
- Goodman wanted Mary Lou to write for him exclusively, but she refused, preferring to freelance and make her own path.

Life in the Community: Kansas City, Missouri

- Kansas City, Missouri straddles the border between Missouri and Kansas at the confluence of the Kansas and Missouri rivers.
- Incorporated in 1850 as Town of Kansas with a population of 1,500, it quickly became known for its famous Kansas City streak, and the Pendergast Era (1840-1940), when Democrat city bosses James Pendergast and Tom Pendergast, ushered in a colorful and influential era for the city.

The Chester?eld Club was one of many popular jazz clubs in Kansas City.

- The Pendergasts declared that national Prohibition was meaningless in Kansas City, and developed the Kansas City boulevard and park system.
- American aviator Charles Lindbergh helped convince the new Transcontinental & Western Airline (later TWA) to locate its corporate headquarters in Kansas City because of its central location, making Kansas City a hub of national aviation.
- Kansas City was also often a national crossroads of cultures as transcontinental flights and train journeys most times required a stop in the city.
- Jazz musicians associated with the style were born in other places but got caught up in the friendly musical competition among performers that could keep a single song being performed in variations for an entire night.
- Members of the Big Bands would perform at regular venues earlier in the evening, and go to the jazz clubs later to jam for the rest of the night.
- Clubs were scattered throughout the city, but the most fertile area was the inner city neighborhood of 18th Street and Vine.
- Among the clubs were the Amos 'n' Andy, Boulevard Lounge, Cherry Blossom, Chesterfield Club, Chocolate Bar, Dante's Inferno, Elk's Rest, Hawaiian Gardens, Hell's Kitchen, the Hi Hat, the Hey Hey, Lone Star, Old Kentucky Bar-B-Que, Paseo Ballroom, Pla-Mor Ballroom, Reno Club, Spinning Wheel, Street's Blue Room, Subway and Sunset.

> There was usually something worth hearing in town in those days, even if Pittsburgh was not one of the jazz centers. One Saturday night I went to the theater on Frenchtown Avenue where all the Negro shows were booked. But I hardly noticed any part of the show; my attention was focused on a lady pianist who worked there. She sat cross-legged on the piano, cigarette in her mouth, writing music with her right hand while accompanying the show with a swinging left! Impressed, I told myself, "Mary, you'll do that one day." And I did, traveling with Andy Kirk's band in the 1930s on one-nighters.
>
> -Mary Lou Williams

Recorded Popular Songs

"Over the Rainbow" - Judy Garland
"God Bless America" - Kate Smith
"Three Little Fishies" - Kay Kyser
"When the Saints Go Marching In" - Louis Armstrong
"Moonlight Serenade" - Glenn Miller
"Beer Barrel Polka" - Will Glahe
"Sunrise Serenade" - Glenn Miller
"Says My Heart" - Red Norvo
"Little Brown Jug" - Glenn Miller
"South of the Border (Down Mexico Way)" - Shep Fields
"Jeepers Creepers" - Al Donohue
"If I Didn't Care" - Ink Spots
"Wishing (Will Make It So)" - Glenn Miller
"And the Angels Sing" - Benny Goodman
"Deep Purple" - Larry Clinton
"Heaven Can Wait" - Glen Gray
"They Say" - Artie Shaw
"Stairway to the Stars" - Glenn Miller
"Scatter-Brain" - Frankie Masters
"At the Woodchopper's Ball" - Woody Herman

"Mary Lou Williams With Andy Kirk Band," *Cumberland Evening Times* (Maryland), July 13, 1937: Mary Lou Williams is featured with Andy Kirk's Orchestra Thursday evening at Crystal Park. She is known as "America's Sweetheart of the ivories," and the most talked about "swing" pianist in the orchestral world. She's the girl that swings the band. She makes the piano speak in a language to which every dance responds...an unusual personality...she's America's foremost femme stylist of the piano.

Mary Lou Williams is the gal that makes all of Benny Goodman, Lou Armstrong, and Bob Crosby's special swing numbers.

The nine tables that follow are reprinted from the actual 1940 census, for the city of Kansas City. They include actual data on race, percentage of voting population, school attendance, number of school years completed, foreign born, and employment of workers 14 years and older by job, industry and race. In addition to being incredibly fascinating, these facts help to strengthen and visualize the actual environment in which Mary Lou Williams lived and worked.

Table A-35.—AGE, BY RACE AND SEX, FOR KANSAS CITY: 1940 AND 1930

[Figures for white population in 1930 revised to include Mexicans classified with "Other races" in the 1930 reports. Percent not shown where less than 0.1 or where base is less than 100]

AGE AND CENSUS YEAR	ALL CLASSES			NATIVE WHITE			FOREIGN-BORN WHITE			NEGRO			OTHER RACES		
	Total	Male	Female	Total	Male	Female	Total	Male	Female	Total	Male	Female	Total	Male	Female
All ages: 1940	399,178	190,117	209,061	338,007	159,779	178,228	19,339	10,405	8,934	41,574	19,736	21,838	258	197	61
Under 5 years	23,123	11,805	11,318	20,633	10,571	10,062	20	12	8	2,450	1,211	1,239	20	11	9
5 to 9 years	23,147	11,701	11,446	20,605	10,417	10,188	30	12	18	2,495	1,266	1,229	17	6	11
10 to 14 years	25,333	12,666	12,667	22,711	11,376	11,335	66	39	27	2,553	1,249	1,304	3	2	1
15 to 19 years	30,063	14,205	15,858	27,074	12,829	14,245	195	100	95	2,789	1,275	1,514	5	1	4
20 to 24 years	33,883	14,873	19,010	30,527	13,498	17,029	258	124	134	3,086	1,245	1,841	12	6	6
25 to 29 years	35,720	16,309	19,411	31,395	14,407	16,988	638	279	359	3,652	1,593	2,059	35	30	5
30 to 34 years	35,117	16,152	18,965	30,271	13,927	16,344	1,115	559	556	3,690	1,628	2,062	41	38	3
35 to 39 years	35,073	16,285	18,788	29,205	13,557	15,648	1,676	888	788	4,151	1,806	2,345	41	34	7
40 to 44 years	32,510	15,651	16,859	26,583	12,691	13,892	1,899	1,011	888	3,998	1,924	2,074	30	25	5
45 to 49 years	30,375	14,928	15,447	24,205	11,674	12,531	2,338	1,320	1,018	3,823	1,926	1,897	9	8	1
50 to 54 years	26,235	13,129	13,106	20,828	10,105	10,723	2,542	1,511	1,031	2,851	1,503	1,348	14	10	4
55 to 59 years	21,035	10,466	10,569	16,599	8,007	8,592	2,286	1,298	988	2,136	1,151	985	14	10	4
60 to 64 years	16,220	7,875	8,345	12,870	6,049	6,821	1,915	1,052	863	1,430	770	660	5	4	1
65 to 69 years	12,988	5,988	7,000	10,178	4,562	5,616	1,632	847	785	1,174	575	599	4	4	-
70 to 74 years	8,823	4,045	4,778	6,954	3,073	3,881	1,202	630	572	662	337	325	5	5	-
75 years and over	9,533	4,039	5,494	7,369	3,036	4,333	1,527	723	804	634	277	357	3	3	-
Under 1 year	4,731	2,459	2,272	4,259	2,228	2,031	1	1	-	467	228	239	4	2	2
5 years	4,465	2,273	2,192	3,962	2,011	1,951	8	2	6	488	258	230	7	2	5
14 years	5,253	2,584	2,669	4,731	2,331	2,400	18	13	5	504	240	264	-	-	-
15 years	5,550	2,747	2,803	5,025	2,507	2,518	19	10	9	505	230	275	1	-	1
16 and 17 years	11,533	5,608	5,925	10,378	5,059	5,319	63	30	33	1,091	518	573	1	1	-
21 years and over	291,001	136,949	154,052	241,144	112,073	129,071	18,987	10,224	8,763	30,660	14,476	16,184	210	176	34
All ages: 1930	399,746	194,542	205,204	334,682	161,334	173,348	26,043	14,245	11,798	38,574	18,599	19,975	447	364	83
Under 5 years	26,128	13,202	12,926	23,903	12,083	11,820	49	21	28	2,154	1,086	1,068	22	12	10
5 to 9 years	29,029	14,568	14,461	26,379	13,250	13,129	163	75	88	2,475	1,237	1,238	12	6	6
10 to 14 years	26,920	13,304	13,616	24,567	12,208	12,359	230	118	112	2,113	974	1,139	10	4	6
15 to 19 years	29,776	13,862	15,914	26,589	12,389	14,200	649	314	335	2,484	1,115	1,369	54	44	10
20 to 24 years	38,439	17,045	21,394	33,645	15,008	18,637	1,344	648	696	3,351	1,308	2,043	99	81	18
25 to 29 years	39,911	18,446	21,465	33,612	15,510	18,102	1,891	969	922	4,318	1,894	2,424	90	73	17
30 to 34 years	37,426	18,001	19,425	31,237	15,011	16,226	2,066	1,095	971	4,077	1,852	2,225	46	43	3
35 to 39 years	37,774	18,641	19,133	30,240	14,722	15,518	2,851	1,626	1,225	4,654	2,265	2,389	29	28	1
40 to 44 years	32,180	16,319	15,861	25,274	12,523	12,751	3,061	1,815	1,246	3,818	1,957	1,861	27	24	3
45 to 49 years	27,703	14,148	13,555	21,318	10,505	10,813	2,973	1,744	1,229	3,394	1,884	1,510	18	15	3
50 to 54 years	22,374	11,324	11,050	17,340	8,554	8,786	2,647	1,467	1,180	2,368	1,287	1,081	19	16	3
55 to 59 years	16,945	8,618	8,327	13,453	6,673	6,780	2,203	1,227	976	1,283	714	569	6	4	2
60 to 64 years	12,968	6,490	6,478	10,214	5,015	5,199	1,932	1,046	886	811	419	392	11	10	1
65 to 69 years	9,623	4,729	4,894	7,449	3,591	3,858	1,667	891	776	505	245	260	2	2	-
70 to 74 years	6,256	3,070	3,186	4,864	2,321	2,543	1,088	597	491	304	152	152	-	-	-
75 years and over	5,886	2,563	3,323	4,340	1,835	2,505	1,209	580	629	336	147	189	1	1	-
Not reported	408	212	196	258	136	122	20	12	8	129	63	66	1	1	-
Under 1 year	5,008	2,526	2,482	4,621	2,327	2,294	3	1	2	382	197	185	2	1	1
5 years	5,730	2,902	2,828	5,274	2,683	2,591	16	8	8	437	210	227	3	1	2
14 years	5,518	2,753	2,765	5,020	2,536	2,484	58	29	29	439	187	252	1	1	-
15 years	5,327	2,560	2,767	4,833	2,335	2,498	69	33	36	423	191	232	2	1	1
16 and 17 years	11,589	5,600	5,989	10,364	4,997	5,367	232	118	114	974	470	504	19	15	4
21 years and over	280,895	136,599	144,296	227,114	108,741	118,373	24,715	13,613	11,102	28,736	13,962	14,774	330	283	47
Percent: 1940	100.0	100.0	100.0	100.0	100.0	100.0	100.0	100.0	100.0	100.0	100.0	100.0	100.0	100.0	-
Under 5 years	5.8	6.2	5.4	6.1	6.6	5.6	0.1	0.1	0.1	5.9	6.1	5.7	7.8	5.6	-
5 to 9 years	5.8	6.2	5.5	6.1	6.5	5.7	0.2	0.1	0.2	6.0	6.4	5.6	6.6	3.0	-
10 to 14 years	6.3	6.7	6.1	6.7	7.1	6.4	0.3	0.4	0.3	6.1	6.3	6.0	1.2	1.0	-
15 to 19 years	7.5	7.5	7.6	8.0	8.0	8.0	1.0	1.0	1.1	6.7	6.5	6.9	1.9	0.5	-
20 to 24 years	8.5	7.8	9.1	9.0	8.4	9.6	1.3	1.2	1.5	7.4	6.3	8.4	4.7	3.0	-
25 to 29 years	8.9	8.6	9.3	9.3	9.0	9.5	3.3	2.7	4.0	8.8	8.1	9.4	13.6	15.2	-
30 to 34 years	8.8	8.5	9.1	9.0	8.7	9.2	5.8	5.4	6.2	8.9	8.2	9.4	15.9	19.3	-
35 to 39 years	8.8	8.6	9.0	8.6	8.5	8.8	8.7	8.5	8.8	10.0	9.2	10.7	15.9	17.3	-
40 to 44 years	8.1	8.2	8.1	7.9	7.9	7.8	9.8	9.7	9.9	9.6	9.7	9.5	11.6	12.7	-
45 to 49 years	7.6	7.9	7.4	7.2	7.3	7.0	12.1	12.7	11.4	9.2	9.8	8.7	3.5	4.1	-
50 to 54 years	6.6	6.9	6.3	6.2	6.3	6.0	13.1	14.5	11.5	6.9	7.6	6.2	5.4	5.1	-
55 to 59 years	5.3	5.5	5.1	4.9	5.0	4.8	11.8	12.5	11.1	5.1	5.8	4.5	5.4	5.1	-
60 to 64 years	4.1	4.1	4.0	3.8	3.8	3.8	9.9	10.1	9.7	3.4	3.9	3.0	1.9	2.0	-
65 to 69 years	3.3	3.1	3.3	3.0	2.9	3.2	8.4	8.1	8.8	2.8	2.9	2.7	1.6	2.0	-
70 to 74 years	2.2	2.1	2.3	2.1	1.9	2.2	6.2	6.1	6.4	1.6	1.7	1.5	1.9	2.5	-
75 years and over	2.4	2.1	2.6	2.2	1.9	2.4	7.9	6.9	9.0	1.5	1.4	1.6	1.2	1.5	-
Under 1 year	1.2	1.3	1.1	1.3	1.4	1.1	-	-	-	1.1	1.2	1.1	1.6	1.0	-
5 years	1.1	1.2	1.0	1.2	1.3	1.1	-	-	0.1	1.2	1.3	1.1	2.7	1.0	-
14 years	1.3	1.4	1.3	1.4	1.5	1.3	0.1	0.1	0.1	1.2	1.2	1.2	-	-	-
15 years	1.4	1.4	1.3	1.5	1.6	1.4	0.1	0.1	0.1	1.2	1.2	1.3	0.4	-	-
16 and 17 years	2.9	2.9	2.8	3.1	3.2	3.0	0.3	0.3	0.4	2.6	2.6	2.6	0.4	0.5	-
21 years and over	72.9	72.0	73.7	71.3	70.1	72.4	98.2	98.3	98.1	73.7	73.3	74.1	81.4	89.3	-
Percent: 1930	100.0	100.0	100.0	100.0	100.0	100.0	100.0	100.0	100.0	100.0	100.0	100.0	100.0	100.0	-
Under 5 years	6.5	6.8	6.3	7.1	7.5	6.8	0.2	0.1	0.2	5.6	5.8	5.3	4.9	3.3	-
5 to 9 years	7.3	7.5	7.0	7.9	8.2	7.6	0.6	0.5	0.7	6.4	6.7	6.2	2.7	1.6	-
10 to 14 years	6.7	6.8	6.6	7.3	7.6	7.1	0.9	0.8	0.9	5.5	5.2	5.7	2.2	1.1	-
15 to 19 years	7.4	7.1	7.8	7.9	7.7	8.2	2.5	2.2	2.8	6.4	6.0	6.9	12.1	12.1	-
20 to 24 years	9.6	8.8	10.4	10.1	9.3	10.8	5.2	4.5	5.9	8.7	7.0	10.2	22.1	22.3	-
25 to 29 years	10.0	9.5	10.5	10.0	9.6	10.4	7.3	6.8	7.8	11.2	10.2	12.1	20.1	20.1	-
30 to 34 years	9.4	9.3	9.5	9.3	9.3	9.4	7.9	7.7	8.2	10.6	10.0	11.1	10.3	11.8	-
35 to 39 years	9.4	9.6	9.3	9.0	9.1	9.0	10.9	11.4	10.4	12.1	12.2	12.0	6.5	7.7	-
40 to 44 years	8.0	8.4	7.7	7.6	7.8	7.4	11.8	12.7	10.6	9.9	10.5	9.3	6.0	6.6	-
45 to 49 years	6.9	7.3	6.6	6.4	6.5	6.2	11.4	12.2	10.4	8.8	10.1	7.6	4.0	4.1	-
50 to 54 years	5.6	5.8	5.4	5.2	5.3	5.1	10.2	10.3	10.0	6.1	6.9	5.4	4.3	4.4	-
55 to 59 years	4.2	4.4	4.1	4.0	4.1	3.9	8.5	8.6	8.3	3.3	3.8	2.8	1.3	1.1	-
60 to 64 years	3.2	3.3	3.2	3.1	3.1	3.0	7.4	7.3	7.5	2.1	2.3	2.0	2.5	2.7	-
65 to 69 years	2.4	2.4	2.4	2.2	2.2	2.2	6.4	6.3	6.6	1.3	1.3	1.3	0.4	0.5	-
70 to 74 years	1.6	1.6	1.6	1.5	1.4	1.5	4.2	4.2	4.2	0.8	0.8	0.8	-	-	-
75 years and over	1.5	1.3	1.6	1.3	1.1	1.4	4.6	4.1	5.3	0.9	0.8	0.9	0.2	0.3	-
Not reported	0.1	0.1	0.1	0.1	0.1	0.1	0.1	0.1	0.1	0.3	0.3	0.3	0.2	0.3	-
Under 1 year	1.3	1.3	1.2	1.4	1.4	1.3	-	-	-	1.0	1.1	0.9	0.4	0.3	-
5 years	1.4	1.5	1.4	1.6	1.7	1.5	0.1	0.1	0.1	1.1	1.1	1.1	0.7	0.3	-
14 years	1.4	1.4	1.3	1.5	1.6	1.4	0.2	0.2	0.2	1.1	1.0	1.3	0.2	0.3	-
15 years	1.3	1.3	1.3	1.4	1.4	1.4	0.3	0.2	0.3	1.1	1.0	1.2	0.4	0.3	-
16 and 17 years	2.9	2.9	2.9	3.1	3.1	3.1	0.9	0.8	1.0	2.5	2.5	2.5	4.3	4.1	-
21 years and over	70.3	70.2	70.3	67.9	67.4	68.3	94.9	95.6	94.1	74.5	75.1	74.0	73.8	77.7	-

Table A-36.—RACE, BY NATIVITY AND SEX, FOR KANSAS CITY: 1940 AND 1930

[Figures for white population in 1930 have been revised to include Mexicans who were classified with "Other races" in the 1930 reports. Percent not shown where less than 0.1 or where base is less than 100. Sex ratio not shown where number of females is less than 100]

SEX, NATIVITY, AND CENSUS YEAR	All classes	White	Negro	Other races	OTHER RACES				PERCENT BY RACE				PERCENT BY NATIVITY					
					Indian	Chinese	Japanese	All other	All classes	White	Negro	Other races	All classes	White	Negro	Indian	Chinese	Japanese
TOTAL																		
1940	399,178	357,346	41,574	258	60	56	5	137	100.0	89.5	10.4	0.1	100.0	100.0	100.0	-	-	-
Native	379,758	338,007	41,541	210	59	17	1	133	100.0	89.0	10.9	0.1	95.1	94.6	99.9	-	-	-
Foreign born	19,420	19,339	33	48	1	39	4	4	100.0	99.6	0.2	0.2	4.9	5.4	0.1	-	-	-
1930	399,746	360,725	38,574	447	115	108	26	198	100.0	90.2	9.6	0.1	100.0	100.0	100.0	100.0	100.0	-
Native	373,548	334,682	38,516	350	115	37	7	191	100.0	89.6	10.3	0.1	93.4	92.8	99.8	100.0	34.3	-
Foreign born	26,198	26,043	58	97	-	71	19	7	100.0	99.4	0.2	0.4	6.6	7.2	0.2	-	65.7	-
MALE																		
1940	190,117	170,184	19,736	197	27	45	5	120	100.0	89.5	10.4	0.1	100.0	100.0	100.0	-	-	-
Native	179,651	159,779	19,717	155	27	11	1	116	100.0	88.9	11.0	0.1	94.5	93.9	99.9	-	-	-
Foreign born	10,466	10,405	19	42	-	34	4	4	100.0	99.4	0.2	0.4	5.5	6.1	0.1	-	-	-
1930	194,542	175,579	18,599	364	62	91	24	187	100.0	90.3	9.6	0.2	100.0	100.0	100.0	-	-	-
Native	180,167	161,334	18,557	276	62	28	6	180	100.0	89.5	10.3	0.2	92.6	91.9	99.8	-	-	-
Foreign born	14,375	14,245	42	88	-	63	18	7	100.0	99.1	0.3	0.6	7.4	8.1	0.2	-	-	-
FEMALE																		
1940	209,061	187,162	21,838	61	33	11	-	17	100.0	89.5	10.4	-	100.0	100.0	100.0	-	-	-
Native	200,107	178,228	21,824	55	32	6	-	17	100.0	89.1	10.9	-	95.7	95.2	99.9	-	-	-
Foreign born	8,954	8,934	14	6	1	5	-	-	100.0	99.8	0.2	0.1	4.3	4.8	0.1	-	-	-
1930	205,204	185,146	19,975	83	53	17	2	11	100.0	90.2	9.7	-	100.0	100.0	100.0	-	-	-
Native	193,381	173,348	19,959	74	53	9	1	11	100.0	89.6	10.3	-	94.2	93.6	99.9	-	-	-
Foreign born	11,823	11,798	16	9	-	8	1	-	100.0	99.8	0.1	0.1	5.8	6.4	0.1	-	-	-
MALES PER 100 FEMALES																		
1940	90.9	90.9	90.4	-	-	-	-	-	-	-	-	-	-	-	-	-	-	-
Native	89.8	89.6	90.3	-	-	-	-	-	-	-	-	-	-	-	-	-	-	-
Foreign born	116.9	116.5	-	-	-	-	-	-	-	-	-	-	-	-	-	-	-	-
1930	94.8	94.8	93.1	-	-	-	-	-	-	-	-	-	-	-	-	-	-	-
Native	93.2	93.1	93.0	-	-	-	-	-	-	-	-	-	-	-	-	-	-	-
Foreign born	121.6	120.7	-	-	-	-	-	-	-	-	-	-	-	-	-	-	-	-

Table A-37.—POTENTIAL VOTING POPULATION, BY CITIZENSHIP, RACE, NATIVITY, AND SEX, FOR KANSAS CITY: 1940 AND 1930

[Figures for white population in 1930 have been revised to include Mexicans who were classified with "Other races" in the 1930 reports. Percent not shown where less than 0.1]

CITIZENSHIP, RACE, AND NATIVITY	TOTAL POPULATION (ALL AGES)								POPULATION 21 YEARS OLD AND OVER							
	Total number		Percent		Male		Female		Total number		Percent		Male		Female	
	1940	1930	1940	1930	1940	1930	1940	1930	1940	1930	1940	1930	1940	1930	1940	1930
Total	399,178	399,746	100.0	100.0	190,117	194,542	209,061	205,204	291,001	280,895	100.0	100.0	136,949	136,599	154,052	144,296
Percent citizen	-	-	98.2	97.4	-	-	-	-	-	-	97.6	96.7	-	-	-	-
Percent alien and citiz. not rptd.	-	-	1.8	2.6	-	-	-	-	-	-	2.4	3.3	-	-	-	-
Citizen	391,801	389,530	100.0	100.0	186,426	188,973	205,375	200,557	283,888	271,640	100.0	100.0	133,387	131,512	150,501	140,128
White—Native	338,007	334,682	86.3	85.9	159,779	161,334	178,228	173,348	241,144	227,114	84.9	83.6	112,073	108,741	129,071	118,373
Naturalized	12,031	15,954	3.1	4.1	6,767	8,787	5,264	7,167	11,941	15,576	4.2	5.7	6,715	8,627	5,226	6,949
Negro—Native	41,541	38,516	10.6	9.9	19,717	18,557	21,824	19,959	30,630	28,679	10.8	10.6	14,458	13,921	16,172	14,758
Naturalized	12	28	-	-	8	19	4	9	11	27	-	-	7	18	4	9
Other races—Native	210	350	0.1	0.1	155	276	55	74	162	244	0.1	0.1	134	205	28	39
Indian	59	115	-	-	27	62	32	53	46	80	-	-	24	47	22	33
Chinese	17	37	-	-	11	28	6	9	10	19	-	-	8	19	2	-
Japanese	1	7	-	-	1	6	-	1	1	4	-	-	1	4	-	-
Filipino	133	189	-	-	116	179	17	10	105	140	-	0.1	101	134	4	6
Hindu	-	-	-	-	-	-	-	-	-	-	-	-	-	-	-	-
All other	-	2	-	-	-	1	-	1	-	1	-	-	-	1	-	-
Alien	5,565	9,000	100.0	100.0	2,822	4,900	2,743	4,100	5,351	8,104	100.0	100.0	2,717	4,443	2,634	3,661
White—First papers	1,764	1,949	31.7	21.7	1,203	1,469	561	480	1,735	1,904	32.4	23.5	1,191	1,443	544	461
No papers	3,745	6,941	67.3	77.1	1,571	3,332	2,174	3,609	3,561	6,101	66.5	75.3	1,478	2,911	2,083	3,190
Negro—First papers	1	5	-	0.1	1	5	-	-	1	5	-	0.1	1	5	-	-
No papers	7	8	0.1	0.1	5	6	2	2	6	8	0.1	0.1	5	6	1	2
Other races—Foreign born	48	97	0.9	1.1	42	88	6	9	48	86	0.9	1.1	42	78	6	8
Indian	1	-	-	-	-	-	1	-	1	-	-	-	-	-	1	-
Chinese	39	71	0.7	0.8	34	63	5	8	39	60	0.7	0.7	34	53	5	7
Japanese	4	19	0.1	0.2	4	18	-	1	4	19	0.1	0.2	4	18	-	1
Filipino	3	-	0.1	-	3	-	-	-	3	-	0.1	-	3	-	-	-
Hindu	1	3	-	-	1	3	-	-	1	3	-	-	1	3	-	-
All other	-	4	-	-	-	4	-	-	-	4	-	-	-	4	-	-
Citizenship not reported	1,812	1,216	100.0	100.0	869	669	943	547	1,762	1,151	100.0	100.0	845	644	917	507
White	1,799	1,199	99.3	98.6	864	657	935	542	1,750	1,134	99.3	98.5	840	632	910	502
Negro	13	17	0.7	1.4	5	12	8	5	12	17	0.7	1.5	5	12	7	5

Table A-38.—SCHOOL ATTENDANCE, BY AGE, RACE, AND SEX, FOR KANSAS CITY: 1940 AND 1930

[Figures for white population in 1930 revised to include Mexicans classified with "Other races" in the 1930 reports. Percent not shown where less than 0.1 or where base is less than 100]

AGE, SEX, AND CENSUS YEAR	ALL CLASSES			NATIVE WHITE			FOREIGN-BORN WHITE			NEGRO			OTHER RACES		
	Total number	Attending school		Total number	Attending school		Total number	Attending school		Total number	Attending school		Total number	Attending school	
		Number	Percent		Number	Percent		Number	Percent		Number	Percent		Number	Percent
1940															
Total, 5 to 24 years	112,426	63,980	56.9	100,917	57,817	57.3	549	208	37.9	10,923	5,931	54.3	37	24	-
5 years	4,465	2,448	54.8	3,962	2,206	55.7	8	4	-	488	233	47.7	7	5	-
6 years	4,400	4,039	91.8	3,882	3,568	91.9	8	7	-	508	463	91.1	2	1	-
7 to 9 years	14,282	13,879	97.2	12,761	12,416	97.3	14	13	-	1,499	1,442	96.2	8	8	-
10 to 13 years	20,080	19,564	97.4	17,980	17,534	97.5	48	44	-	2,049	1,983	96.8	3	3	-
14 years	5,253	5,043	96.0	4,731	4,567	96.5	18	16	-	504	460	91.3	-	-	-
15 years	5,550	5,171	93.2	5,025	4,703	93.6	19	19	-	505	448	88.7	1	1	-
16 and 17 years	11,533	8,079	70.1	10,378	7,412	71.4	63	44	-	1,091	622	57.0	1	1	-
18 and 19 years	12,980	3,605	27.8	11,671	3,357	28.8	113	41	36.3	1,193	206	17.3	3	1	-
20 years	6,511	858	13.2	5,840	815	14.0	41	3	-	627	38	6.1	3	2	-
21 to 24 years	27,372	1,294	4.7	24,687	1,239	5.0	217	17	7.8	2,459	36	1.5	9	2	-
Male, 5 to 24 years	53,445	32,527	60.9	48,120	29,490	61.3	275	117	42.5	5,035	2,910	57.8	15	10	-
5 years	2,273	1,263	55.6	2,011	1,134	56.4	2	-	-	258	127	49.2	2	2	-
6 years	2,259	2,076	91.9	1,986	1,829	92.1	3	3	-	269	243	90.3	1	1	-
7 to 9 years	7,169	6,963	97.1	6,420	6,249	97.3	7	6	-	739	705	95.4	3	3	-
10 to 13 years	10,082	9,805	97.3	9,045	8,810	97.4	26	23	-	1,009	970	96.1	2	2	-
14 years	2,584	2,480	96.0	2,331	2,254	96.7	13	12	-	240	214	89.2	-	-	-
15 years	2,747	2,576	93.8	2,507	2,361	94.2	10	10	-	230	205	89.1	-	-	-
16 and 17 years	5,608	4,033	71.9	5,059	3,704	73.2	30	23	-	518	305	58.9	1	1	-
18 and 19 years	5,850	1,966	33.6	5,263	1,845	35.1	60	26	-	527	95	18.0	-	-	-
20 years	2,791	486	17.4	2,513	461	18.3	18	1	-	259	23	8.9	1	1	-
21 to 24 years	12,082	879	7.3	10,985	843	7.7	106	13	12.3	986	23	2.3	5	-	-
Female, 5 to 24 years	58,981	31,453	53.3	52,797	28,327	53.7	274	91	33.2	5,888	3,021	51.3	22	14	-
5 years	2,192	1,185	54.1	1,951	1,072	54.9	6	4	-	230	106	46.1	5	3	-
6 years	2,141	1,963	91.7	1,896	1,739	91.7	5	4	-	239	220	92.1	1	-	-
7 to 9 years	7,113	6,916	97.2	6,341	6,167	97.3	7	7	-	760	737	97.0	5	5	-
10 to 13 years	9,998	9,759	97.6	8,935	8,724	97.6	22	21	-	1,040	1,013	97.4	1	1	-
14 years	2,669	2,563	96.0	2,400	2,313	96.4	5	4	-	264	246	93.2	-	-	-
15 years	2,803	2,595	92.6	2,518	2,342	93.0	9	9	-	275	243	88.4	1	1	-
16 and 17 years	5,925	4,046	68.3	5,319	3,708	69.7	33	21	-	573	317	55.3	-	-	-
18 and 19 years	7,130	1,639	23.0	6,408	1,512	23.6	53	15	-	666	111	16.7	3	1	-
20 years	3,720	372	10.0	3,327	354	10.6	23	2	-	368	15	4.1	2	1	-
21 to 24 years	15,290	415	2.7	13,702	396	2.9	111	4	3.6	1,473	13	0.9	4	2	-
1930															
Total, 5 to 24 years	124,164	70,047	56.4	111,180	63,979	57.5	2,386	736	30.8	10,423	5,272	50.6	175	60	34.3
5 years	5,730	3,073	53.6	5,274	2,877	54.6	16	4	-	437	192	43.9	3	-	-
6 years	5,783	5,190	89.7	5,273	4,788	90.8	23	19	-	485	382	78.8	2	1	-
7 to 9 years	17,516	16,995	97.0	15,832	15,419	97.4	124	119	96.0	1,553	1,450	93.4	7	7	-
10 to 13 years	21,402	21,054	98.4	19,547	19,263	98.5	172	169	98.3	1,674	1,613	96.4	9	9	-
14 years	5,518	5,310	96.2	5,020	4,855	96.7	58	54	-	439	400	91.1	1	1	-
15 years	5,327	4,852	91.1	4,833	4,430	91.7	69	61	-	423	359	84.9	2	2	-
16 and 17 years	11,589	7,176	61.9	10,364	6,514	62.9	232	128	55.2	974	524	53.8	19	10	-
18 and 19 years	12,860	3,454	26.9	11,392	3,153	27.7	348	87	25.0	1,087	205	18.9	33	9	-
20 years	6,998	982	14.0	6,130	908	14.8	237	20	8.4	612	50	8.2	19	4	-
21 to 24 years	31,441	1,961	6.2	27,515	1,772	6.4	1,107	75	6.8	2,739	97	3.5	80	17	-
Male, 5 to 24 years	58,779	34,962	59.5	52,855	32,044	60.6	1,155	380	32.9	4,634	2,495	53.8	135	43	31.9
5 years	2,902	1,547	53.3	2,683	1,460	54.4	8	2	-	210	85	40.5	1	-	-
6 years	2,896	2,576	89.0	2,669	2,393	89.7	10	8	-	217	175	80.6	-	-	-
7 to 9 years	8,770	8,497	96.9	7,898	7,689	97.4	57	55	-	810	748	92.3	5	5	-
10 to 13 years	10,551	10,390	98.5	9,672	9,545	98.7	89	88	-	787	754	95.8	3	3	-
14 years	2,753	2,658	96.5	2,536	2,465	97.2	29	25	-	187	167	89.3	1	1	-
15 years	2,560	2,346	91.6	2,335	2,156	92.3	33	26	-	191	163	85.3	1	1	-
16 and 17 years	5,600	3,559	63.6	4,997	3,226	64.6	118	65	55.1	470	261	55.5	15	7	-
18 and 19 years	5,702	1,804	31.6	5,057	1,647	32.6	163	57	35.0	454	93	20.5	28	7	-
20 years	3,007	511	17.0	2,663	481	18.1	104	10	9.6	225	17	7.6	15	3	-
21 to 24 years	14,038	1,074	7.7	12,345	982	8.0	544	44	8.1	1,083	32	3.0	66	16	-
Female, 5 to 24 years	65,385	35,085	53.7	58,325	31,935	54.8	1,231	356	28.9	5,789	2,777	48.0	40	17	-
5 years	2,828	1,526	54.0	2,591	1,417	54.7	8	2	-	227	107	47.1	2	-	-
6 years	2,887	2,614	90.5	2,604	2,395	92.0	13	11	-	268	207	77.2	2	1	-
7 to 9 years	8,746	8,498	97.2	7,934	7,730	97.4	67	64	-	743	702	94.5	2	2	-
10 to 13 years	10,851	10,664	98.3	9,875	9,718	98.4	83	81	-	887	859	96.8	6	6	-
14 years	2,765	2,652	95.9	2,484	2,390	96.2	29	29	-	252	233	92.5	-	-	-
15 years	2,767	2,506	90.6	2,498	2,274	91.0	36	35	-	232	196	84.5	1	1	-
16 and 17 years	5,989	3,617	60.4	5,367	3,288	61.3	114	63	55.3	504	263	52.2	4	3	-
18 and 19 years	7,158	1,650	23.1	6,335	1,506	23.8	185	30	16.2	633	112	17.7	5	2	-
20 years	3,991	471	11.8	3,467	427	12.3	133	10	7.5	387	33	8.5	4	1	-
21 to 24 years	17,403	887	5.1	15,170	790	5.2	563	31	5.5	1,656	65	3.9	14	1	-

Table A-39.—PERSONS 25 YEARS OLD AND OVER, BY YEARS OF SCHOOL COMPLETED, RACE, AND SEX, FOR KANSAS CITY: 1940

[Percent not shown where less than 0.1; median and percent not shown where base is less than 100]

YEARS OF SCHOOL COMPLETED	ALL CLASSES			NATIVE WHITE			FOREIGN-BORN WHITE			NEGRO			OTHER RACES		
	Total	Male	Female	Total	Male	Female	Total	Male	Female	Total	Male	Female	Total	Male	Female
Persons 25 years old and over	263,629	124,867	138,762	216,457	101,088	115,369	18,770	10,118	8,652	28,201	13,490	14,711	201	171	30
No school years completed	4,379	2,332	2,047	1,080	587	493	2,188	1,119	1,069	1,088	606	482	23	20	3
Grade school: 1 to 4 years	14,352	7,991	6,361	7,055	4,009	3,046	2,775	1,524	1,251	4,509	2,447	2,062	13	11	2
5 or 6 years	20,483	10,495	9,988	13,345	6,897	6,448	2,334	1,260	1,074	4,787	2,326	2,461	17	12	5
7 or 8 years	78,404	38,412	39,992	63,974	31,092	32,882	6,413	3,391	3,022	7,982	3,900	4,082	35	29	6
High school: 1 to 3 years	44,695	20,027	24,668	38,563	17,294	21,269	1,420	729	691	4,683	1,977	2,706	29	27	2
4 years	60,076	24,217	35,859	54,944	21,894	33,050	2,146	1,089	1,057	2,943	1,199	1,744	43	35	8
College: 1 to 3 years	23,112	10,623	12,489	21,268	9,713	11,555	574	369	205	1,247	521	726	23	20	3
4 years or more	15,947	9,596	6,351	14,679	8,794	5,885	609	473	136	647	318	329	12	11	1
Not reported	2,181	1,174	1,007	1,549	808	741	311	164	147	315	196	119	6	6	-
Median school years completed	9.9	9.4	10.3	10.7	10.3	11.0	7.6	7.6	7.6	7.9	7.7	8.1	10.0	10.2	-
Percent less than 5 years completed	7.1	8.3	6.1	3.8	4.5	3.1	26.4	26.1	26.8	19.8	22.6	17.3	17.9	18.1	-
PERCENT DISTRIBUTION															
Persons 25 years old and over	100.0	100.0	100.0	100.0	100.0	100.0	100.0	100.0	100.0	100.0	100.0	100.0	100.0	100.0	-
No school years completed	1.7	1.9	1.5	0.5	0.6	0.4	11.7	11.1	12.4	3.9	4.5	3.3	11.4	11.7	-
Grade school: 1 to 4 years	5.4	6.4	4.6	3.3	4.0	2.6	14.8	15.1	14.5	16.0	18.1	14.0	6.5	6.4	-
5 or 6 years	7.8	8.4	7.2	6.2	6.8	5.6	12.4	12.5	12.4	17.0	17.2	16.7	8.5	7.0	-
7 or 8 years	29.7	30.8	28.8	29.6	30.8	28.5	34.2	33.5	34.9	28.3	28.9	27.7	17.4	17.0	-
High school: 1 to 3 years	17.0	16.0	17.8	17.8	17.1	18.4	7.6	7.2	8.0	16.6	14.7	18.4	14.4	15.8	-
4 years	22.8	19.4	25.8	25.4	21.7	28.6	11.4	10.8	12.2	10.4	8.9	11.9	21.4	20.5	-
College: 1 to 3 years	8.8	8.5	9.0	9.8	9.6	10.0	3.1	3.6	2.4	4.4	3.9	4.9	11.4	11.7	-
4 years or more	6.0	7.7	4.6	6.8	8.7	5.1	3.2	4.7	1.6	2.3	2.4	2.2	6.0	6.4	-
Not reported	0.8	0.9	0.7	0.7	0.8	0.6	1.7	1.6	1.7	1.1	1.5	0.8	3.0	3.5	-

Table A-40.—FOREIGN-BORN WHITE, BY COUNTRY OF BIRTH, BY SEX, FOR KANSAS CITY: 1940 AND 1930

[Figures for white population in 1930 revised to include Mexicans classified with "Other races" in the 1930 reports. Percent not shown where less than 0.1 or where base is less than 100]

COUNTRY OF BIRTH	BOTH SEXES		PERCENT		MALE		FEMALE	
	1940	1930	1940	1930	1940	1930	1940	1930
All countries	19,339	26,043	100.0	100.0	10,405	14,245	8,934	11,798
England	1,067	1,627	5.5	6.2	533	846	534	781
Scotland	369	527	1.9	2.0	185	298	184	229
Wales	48	112	0.2	0.4	26	60	22	52
Northern Ireland	149	304	0.8	1.2	76	153	73	151
Irish Free State (Eire)	1,096	1,638	5.7	6.3	527	808	569	830
Norway	112	181	0.6	0.7	58	110	54	71
Sweden	1,124	1,650	5.8	6.3	562	872	562	778
Denmark	311	450	1.6	1.7	202	295	109	155
Netherlands	84	103	0.4	0.4	60	74	24	29
Belgium	266	286	1.4	1.1	148	161	118	125
Luxemburg	11	10	0.1	-	7	7	4	3
Switzerland	210	278	1.1	1.1	117	158	93	120
France	232	346	1.2	1.3	97	150	135	196
Germany	2,701	3,682	14.0	14.1	1,416	1,956	1,285	1,726
Poland	1,358	1,646	7.0	6.3	693	836	665	810
Czechoslovakia	125	198	0.6	0.8	71	109	54	89
Austria	585	722	3.0	2.8	318	375	267	347
Hungary	176	202	0.9	0.8	101	106	75	96
Yugoslavia	165	138	0.9	0.5	94	85	71	53
Russia (U. S. S. R.)	2,800	3,415	14.5	13.1	1,484	1,792	1,316	1,623
Lithuania	222	151	1.1	0.6	115	85	107	66
Latvia	36	72	0.2	0.3	17	40	19	32
Finland	28	39	0.1	0.1	17	21	11	18
Rumania	187	217	1.0	0.8	102	117	85	100
Bulgaria	16	35	0.1	0.1	15	34	1	1
Turkey in Europe	10	1	0.1	-	6	-	4	1
Greece	362	425	1.9	1.6	297	356	65	69
Italy	3,130	3,723	16.2	14.3	1,843	2,195	1,287	1,528
Spain	28	42	0.1	0.2	17	30	11	12
Portugal	2	5	-	-	2	2	-	3
Other Europe	17	61	0.1	0.2	6	29	11	32
Palestine and Syria	145	188	0.7	0.7	79	103	66	85
Turkey in Asia	20	33	0.1	0.1	12	24	8	9
Other Asia	28	39	0.1	0.1	19	29	9	10
Canada—French	73	159	0.4	0.6	27	73	46	86
Canada—Other	893	1,266	4.6	4.9	414	633	479	633
Newfoundland	7	9	-	-	5	5	2	4
Mexico	1,012	1,868	5.2	7.2	576	1,111	436	757
Cuba and other West Indies	21	33	0.1	0.1	7	19	14	14
Central and South America	57	60	0.3	0.2	24	21	33	39
Australia	25	46	0.1	0.2	13	32	12	14
Azores	-	-	-	-	-	-	-	-
All other and not reported	31	56	0.2	0.2	17	35	14	21

Table A-41.—PERSONS 14 YEARS OLD AND OVER, BY EMPLOYMENT STATUS, CLASS OF WORKER, RACE, AND SEX, FOR KANSAS CITY: 1940

[Percent not shown where less than 0.1 or where base is less than 100]

EMPLOYMENT STATUS	ALL CLASSES			NATIVE WHITE			FOREIGN-BORN WHITE			NEGRO			OTHER RACES		
	Total	Male	Female	Total	Male	Female	Total	Male	Female	Total	Male	Female	Total	Male	Female
Total population (all ages)	399,178	190,117	209,061	338,007	159,779	178,228	19,339	10,405	8,934	41,574	19,736	21,838	258	197	61
Persons 14 years old and over	332,828	156,529	176,299	278,789	129,746	149,043	19,241	10,355	8,886	34,580	16,250	18,330	218	178	40
In labor force	191,278	129,678	61,600	158,723	107,348	51,375	9,902	8,351	1,551	22,472	13,813	8,659	181	166	15
Not in labor force	141,550	26,851	114,699	120,066	22,398	97,668	9,339	2,004	7,335	12,108	2,437	9,671	37	12	25
Engaged in own home housew'k	88,765	613	88,152	76,120	512	75,608	6,042	47	5,995	6,589	54	6,535	14	-	14
In school	22,815	11,647	11,168	20,926	10,754	10,172	133	82	51	1,748	809	939	8	2	6
Unable to work	18,719	9,119	9,600	13,534	6,672	6,862	2,277	1,316	961	2,896	1,122	1,774	12	9	3
In institutions	897	411	486	653	254	399	144	79	65	99	78	21	1	-	1
Other and not reported	10,354	5,061	5,293	8,833	4,206	4,627	743	480	263	776	374	402	2	1	1
LABOR FORCE BY EMPLOYMENT STATUS															
In labor force	191,278	129,678	61,600	158,723	107,348	51,375	9,902	8,351	1,551	22,472	13,813	8,659	181	166	15
Employed (exc. public emerg. work)	160,944	108,099	52,845	136,753	91,636	45,117	8,616	7,226	1,390	15,408	9,084	6,324	167	153	14
At work	157,415	105,702	51,713	133,770	89,621	44,149	8,335	6,987	1,348	15,146	8,942	6,204	164	152	12
With a job	3,529	2,397	1,132	2,983	2,015	968	281	239	42	262	142	120	3	1	2
On public emerg. work (WPA, etc.)	10,542	8,170	2,372	7,260	5,531	1,729	302	260	42	2,978	2,377	601	2	2	-
Seeking work	19,792	13,409	6,383	14,710	10,181	4,529	984	865	119	4,086	2,352	1,734	12	11	1
Experienced workers	17,615	12,363	5,252	12,833	9,263	3,570	957	858	99	3,813	2,231	1,582	12	11	1
New workers	2,177	1,046	1,131	1,877	918	959	27	7	20	273	121	152	-	-	-
PERCENT BY SEX															
In labor force	100.0	67.8	32.2	100.0	67.6	32.4	100.0	84.3	15.7	100.0	61.5	38.5	100.0	91.7	8.3
Employed (exc. public emerg.)	100.0	67.2	32.8	100.0	67.0	33.0	100.0	83.9	16.1	100.0	59.0	41.0	100.0	91.6	8.4
On pub. emerg. work (WPA, etc.)	100.0	77.5	22.5	100.0	76.2	23.8	100.0	86.1	13.9	100.0	79.8	20.2	-	-	-
Seeking work	100.0	67.7	32.3	100.0	69.2	30.8	100.0	87.9	12.1	100.0	57.6	42.4	-	-	-
Not in labor force	100.0	19.0	81.0	100.0	18.7	81.3	100.0	21.5	78.5	100.0	20.1	79.9	-	-	-
Engaged in own home housew'k	100.0	0.7	99.3	100.0	0.7	99.3	100.0	0.8	99.2	100.0	0.8	99.2	-	-	-
In school	100.0	51.0	49.0	100.0	51.4	48.6	100.0	61.7	38.3	100.0	46.3	53.7	-	-	-
Unable to work	100.0	48.7	51.3	100.0	49.3	50.7	100.0	57.8	42.2	100.0	38.7	61.3	-	-	-
In institutions	100.0	45.8	54.2	100.0	38.9	61.1	100.0	54.9	45.1	-	-	-	-	-	-
Other and not reported	100.0	48.9	51.1	100.0	47.6	52.4	100.0	64.6	35.4	100.0	48.2	51.8	-	-	-
EMPLOYED WORKERS BY CLASS OF WORKER															
Employed (exc. public emerg.)	160,944	108,099	52,845	136,753	91,636	45,117	8,616	7,226	1,390	15,408	9,084	6,324	167	153	14
Wage and salary workers	139,903	92,034	47,869	119,659	78,709	40,950	5,852	4,773	1,079	14,260	8,427	5,833	132	125	7
Employers and own-account workers	19,457	15,547	3,910	15,752	12,471	3,281	2,622	2,426	196	1,048	622	426	35	28	7
Unpaid family workers	1,038	217	821	891	204	687	111	9	102	36	4	32	-	-	-
Class of worker not reported	546	301	245	451	252	199	31	18	13	64	31	33	-	-	-
At work	157,415	105,702	51,713	133,770	89,621	44,149	8,335	6,987	1,348	15,146	8,942	6,204	164	152	12
Wage and salary workers	137,731	90,654	47,077	117,774	77,507	40,267	5,742	4,688	1,054	14,084	8,334	5,750	131	125	6
Employers and own-account workers	18,218	14,584	3,634	14,756	11,707	3,049	2,460	2,274	186	969	576	393	33	27	6
Unpaid family workers	999	208	791	859	195	664	106	9	97	34	4	30	-	-	-
Class of worker not reported	467	256	211	381	212	169	27	16	11	59	28	31	-	-	-
With a job	3,529	2,397	1,132	2,983	2,015	968	281	239	42	262	142	120	3	1	2
Wage and salary workers	2,172	1,380	792	1,885	1,202	683	110	85	25	176	93	83	1	-	1
Employers and own-account workers	1,239	963	276	996	764	232	162	152	10	79	46	33	2	1	1
Unpaid family workers	39	9	30	32	9	23	5	-	5	2	-	2	-	-	-
Class of worker not reported	79	45	34	70	40	30	4	2	2	5	3	2	-	-	-
PERCENT DISTRIBUTION															
Persons 14 years old and over	100.0	100.0	100.0	100.0	100.0	100.0	100.0	100.0	100.0	100.0	100.0	100.0	100.0	100.0	-
In labor force	57.5	82.8	34.9	56.9	82.7	34.5	51.5	80.6	17.5	65.0	85.0	47.2	83.0	93.3	-
Not in labor force	42.5	17.2	65.1	43.1	17.3	65.5	48.5	19.4	82.5	35.0	15.0	52.8	17.0	6.7	-
Engaged in own home housew'k	26.7	0.4	50.0	27.3	0.4	50.7	31.4	0.5	67.5	19.1	0.3	35.7	6.4	-	-
In school	6.9	7.4	6.3	7.5	8.3	6.8	0.7	0.8	0.6	5.1	5.0	5.1	3.7	1.1	-
Unable to work	5.6	5.8	5.4	4.9	5.1	4.6	11.8	12.7	10.8	8.4	6.9	9.7	5.5	5.1	-
In institutions	0.3	0.3	0.3	0.2	0.2	0.3	0.7	0.8	0.7	0.3	0.5	0.1	0.5	-	-
Other and not reported	3.1	3.2	3.0	3.2	3.2	3.1	3.9	4.6	3.0	2.2	2.3	2.2	0.9	0.6	-
LABOR FORCE BY EMPLOYMENT STATUS															
In labor force	100.0	100.0	100.0	100.0	100.0	100.0	100.0	100.0	100.0	100.0	100.0	100.0	100.0	100.0	-
Employed (exc. public emerg. work)	84.1	83.4	85.8	86.2	85.4	87.8	87.0	86.5	89.6	68.6	65.8	73.0	92.3	92.2	-
At work	82.3	81.5	83.9	84.3	83.5	85.9	84.2	83.7	86.9	67.4	64.7	71.6	90.6	91.6	-
With a job	1.8	1.8	1.8	1.9	1.9	1.9	2.8	2.9	2.7	1.2	1.0	1.4	1.7	0.6	-
On public emerg. work (WPA, etc.)	5.5	6.3	3.9	4.6	5.2	3.4	3.0	3.1	2.7	13.3	17.2	6.9	1.1	1.2	-
Seeking work	10.3	10.3	10.4	9.3	9.5	8.8	9.9	10.4	7.7	18.2	17.0	20.0	6.6	6.6	-
Experienced workers	9.2	9.5	8.5	8.1	8.6	6.9	9.7	10.3	6.4	17.0	16.2	18.3	6.6	6.6	-
New workers	1.1	0.8	1.8	1.2	0.9	1.9	0.3	0.1	1.3	1.2	0.9	1.8	-	-	-
EMPLOYED WORKERS BY CLASS OF WORKER															
Employed (exc. public emerg.)	100.0	100.0	100.0	100.0	100.0	100.0	100.0	100.0	100.0	100.0	100.0	100.0	100.0	100.0	-
Wage and salary workers	86.9	85.1	90.6	87.5	85.9	90.8	67.9	66.1	77.6	92.5	92.8	92.2	79.0	81.7	-
Employers and own-account workers	12.1	14.4	7.4	11.5	13.6	7.3	30.4	33.6	14.1	6.8	6.8	6.7	21.0	18.3	-
Unpaid family workers	0.6	0.2	1.6	0.7	0.2	1.5	1.3	0.1	7.3	0.2	-	0.5	-	-	-
Class of worker not reported	0.3	0.3	0.5	0.3	0.3	0.4	0.4	0.2	0.9	0.4	0.3	0.5	-	-	-
At work	100.0	100.0	100.0	100.0	100.0	100.0	100.0	100.0	100.0	100.0	100.0	100.0	100.0	100.0	-
Wage and salary workers	87.5	85.8	91.0	88.0	86.5	91.2	68.9	67.1	78.2	93.0	93.2	92.7	79.9	82.2	-
Employers and own-account workers	11.6	13.8	7.0	11.0	13.1	6.9	29.5	32.5	13.8	6.4	6.4	6.3	20.1	17.8	-
Unpaid family workers	0.6	0.2	1.5	0.6	0.2	1.5	1.3	0.1	7.2	0.2	-	0.5	-	-	-
Class of worker not reported	0.3	0.2	0.4	0.3	0.2	0.4	0.3	0.2	0.8	0.4	0.3	0.5	-	-	-
With a job	100.0	100.0	100.0	100.0	100.0	100.0	100.0	100.0	-	100.0	100.0	100.0	-	-	-
Wage and salary workers	61.5	57.6	70.0	63.2	59.7	70.6	39.1	35.6	-	67.2	65.5	69.2	-	-	-
Employers and own-account workers	35.1	40.2	24.4	33.4	37.9	24.0	57.7	63.6	-	30.2	32.4	27.5	-	-	-
Unpaid family workers	1.1	0.4	2.7	1.1	0.4	2.4	1.8	-	-	0.8	-	1.7	-	-	-
Class of worker not reported	2.2	1.9	3.0	2.3	2.0	3.1	1.4	0.8	-	1.9	2.1	1.7	-	-	-

Table A-42.—EMPLOYED WORKERS 14 YEARS OLD AND OVER, BY MAJOR OCCUPATION GROUP, INDUSTRY GROUP, AND SEX, FOR KANSAS CITY: 1940

[Percent not shown where less than 0.1 or where base is less than 100]

MAJOR OCCUPATION GROUP AND INDUSTRY GROUP	Total	Male	Female	PERCENT BY OCCUPATION AND INDUSTRY			PERCENT BY SEX	
				Total	Male	Female	Male	Female
Total population (all ages)	399,178	190,117	209,061	-	-	-	47.6	52.4
All persons 14 years old and over	332,828	156,529	176,299	-	-	-	47.0	53.0
In labor force	191,278	129,678	61,600	100.0	100.0	100.0	67.8	32.2
Employed workers (except on public emergency work)	160,944	108,099	52,845	84.1	83.4	85.8	67.2	32.8
MAJOR OCCUPATION GROUP								
Employed (except on public emergency work)	160,944	108,099	52,845	100.0	100.0	100.0	67.2	32.8
Professional workers	11,543	6,461	5,082	7.2	6.0	9.6	56.0	44.0
Semiprofessional workers	2,174	1,451	723	1.4	1.3	1.4	66.7	33.3
Farmers and farm managers	162	151	11	0.1	0.1	-	93.2	6.8
Proprietors, managers, and officials, except farm	18,600	15,749	2,851	11.6	14.6	5.4	84.7	15.3
Clerical, sales, and kindred workers	49,063	28,336	20,727	30.5	26.2	39.2	57.8	42.2
Craftsmen, foremen, and kindred workers	17,719	17,053	666	11.0	15.8	1.3	96.2	3.8
Operatives and kindred workers	25,495	18,236	7,259	15.8	16.9	13.7	71.5	28.5
Domestic service workers	7,906	593	7,313	4.9	0.5	13.8	7.5	92.5
Service workers, except domestic	19,325	11,705	7,620	12.0	10.8	14.4	60.6	39.4
Farm laborers (wage workers) and farm foremen	249	237	12	0.2	0.2	-	95.2	4.8
Farm laborers, unpaid family workers	15	11	4	-	-	-	-	-
Laborers, except farm	7,694	7,497	197	4.8	6.9	0.4	97.4	2.6
Occupation not reported	999	619	380	0.6	0.6	0.7	62.0	38.0
INDUSTRY GROUP								
Employed (except on public emergency work)	160,944	108,099	52,845	100.0	100.0	100.0	67.2	32.8
Agriculture, forestry, and fishery	671	630	41	0.4	0.6	0.1	93.9	6.1
Agriculture	660	619	41	0.4	0.6	0.1	93.8	6.2
Forestry (except logging) and fishery	11	11	-	-	-	-	-	-
Mining	256	248	8	0.2	0.2	-	96.9	3.1
Coal mining	26	26	-	-	-	-	-	-
Crude petroleum and natural gas production	57	54	3	-	-	-	-	-
Other mines and quarries	173	168	5	0.1	0.2	-	97.1	2.9
Construction	6,814	6,591	223	4.2	6.1	0.4	96.7	3.3
Manufacturing	31,657	23,748	7,909	19.7	22.0	15.0	75.0	25.0
Food and kindred products	6,732	5,573	1,159	4.2	5.2	2.2	82.8	17.2
Textile-mill products	188	112	76	0.1	0.1	0.1	59.6	40.4
Apparel and other fabricated textile products	4,043	926	3,117	2.5	0.9	5.9	22.9	77.1
Logging	10	9	1	-	-	-	-	-
Sawmills and planing mills	313	283	30	0.2	0.3	0.1	90.4	9.6
Furniture, store fixtures, and miscellaneous wooden goods	934	801	133	0.6	0.7	0.3	85.8	14.2
Paper and allied products	819	557	262	0.5	0.5	0.5	68.0	32.0
Printing, publishing, and allied industries	4,276	3,152	1,124	2.7	2.9	2.1	73.7	26.3
Chemicals and allied products	1,857	1,327	530	1.2	1.2	1.0	71.5	28.5
Petroleum and coal products	986	799	187	0.6	0.7	0.4	81.0	19.0
Leather and leather products	245	176	69	0.2	0.2	0.1	71.8	28.2
Stone, clay, and glass products	480	416	64	0.3	0.4	0.1	86.7	13.3
Iron and steel and their products	3,472	3,214	258	2.2	3.0	0.5	92.6	7.4
Nonferrous metals and their products	505	478	27	0.3	0.4	0.1	94.7	5.3
Machinery	2,000	1,725	275	1.2	1.6	0.5	86.3	13.8
Automobiles and automobile equipment	3,058	2,892	166	1.9	2.7	0.3	94.6	5.4
Transportation equipment, except automobile	213	195	18	0.1	0.2	-	91.5	8.5
Other and not specified manufacturing industries	1,526	1,113	413	0.9	1.0	0.8	72.9	27.1
Transportation, communication, and other public utilities	17,295	15,238	2,057	10.7	14.1	3.9	88.1	11.9
Railroads (including railroad repair shops) and railway express service	6,347	6,077	270	3.9	5.6	0.5	95.7	4.3
Trucking service	2,463	2,325	138	1.5	2.2	0.3	94.4	5.6
Other transportation	3,799	3,410	389	2.4	3.2	0.7	89.8	10.2
Communication	2,084	1,198	886	1.3	1.1	1.7	57.5	42.5
Utilities	2,602	2,228	374	1.6	2.1	0.7	85.6	14.4
Wholesale and retail trade	44,728	30,318	14,410	27.8	28.0	27.3	67.8	32.2
Wholesale trade	10,138	7,983	2,155	6.3	7.4	4.1	78.7	21.3
Food and dairy products stores, and milk retailing	5,842	4,809	1,033	3.6	4.4	2.0	82.3	17.7
Eating and drinking places	6,514	3,395	3,119	4.0	3.1	5.9	52.1	47.9
Motor vehicles and accessories retailing, and filling stations	3,778	3,260	518	2.3	3.0	1.0	86.3	13.7
Other retail trade	18,456	10,871	7,585	11.5	10.1	14.4	58.9	41.1
Finance, insurance, and real estate	11,960	7,698	4,262	7.4	7.1	8.1	64.4	35.6
Business and repair services	4,384	3,775	609	2.7	3.5	1.2	86.1	13.9
Automobile storage, rental, and repair services	1,966	1,918	48	1.2	1.8	0.1	97.6	2.4
Business and repair services, except automobile	2,418	1,857	561	1.5	1.7	1.1	76.8	23.2
Personal services	19,696	6,142	13,554	12.2	5.7	25.6	31.2	68.8
Domestic service	8,687	934	7,753	5.4	0.9	14.7	10.8	89.2
Hotels and lodging places	3,965	1,930	2,035	2.5	1.8	3.9	48.7	51.3
Laundering, cleaning, and dyeing services	3,284	1,535	1,749	2.0	1.4	3.3	46.7	53.3
Miscellaneous personal services	3,760	1,743	2,017	2.3	1.6	3.8	46.4	53.6
Amusement, recreation, and related services	1,768	1,265	503	1.1	1.2	1.0	71.5	28.5
Professional and related services	13,346	5,897	7,449	8.3	5.5	14.1	44.2	55.8
Government	6,477	5,336	1,141	4.0	4.9	2.2	82.4	17.6
Industry not reported	1,892	1,213	679	1.2	1.1	1.3	64.1	35.9

Table A-43.—PERSONS 14 YEARS OLD AND OVER IN THE LABOR FORCE, 1940, AND GAINFUL WORKERS 14 YEARS OLD AND OVER, 1930, BY RACE AND SEX, FOR KANSAS CITY

[Totals for population and gainful workers for 1930 include "Unknown age." Figures for white population in 1930 have been revised to include Mexicans who were classified with "Other races" in the 1930 reports. Percent not shown where less than 0.1 or where base is less than 100]

CENSUS YEAR AND RACE	TOTAL					MALE					FEMALE				
	Population		Persons in the labor force, and gainful workers,[1] 14 years old and over			Population		Persons in the labor force, and gainful workers,[1] 14 years old and over			Population		Persons in the labor force, and gainful workers,[1] 14 years old and over		
	Total (all ages)	14 years old and over	Number	Per-cent of total popu-lation	Per-cent of popu-lation 14 yrs. and over	Total (all ages)	14 years old and over	Number	Per-cent of total popu-lation	Per-cent of popu-lation 14 yrs. and over	Total (all ages)	14 years old and over	Number	Per-cent of total popu-lation	Per-cent of popu-lation 14 yrs. and over
1940	399,178	332,828	191,278	47.9	57.5	190,117	156,529	129,678	68.2	82.8	209,061	176,299	61,600	29.5	34.9
White	357,346	298,030	168,625	47.2	56.6	170,184	140,101	115,699	68.0	82.6	187,162	157,929	52,926	28.3	33.5
Negro	41,574	34,580	22,472	54.1	65.0	19,736	16,250	13,813	70.0	85.0	21,838	18,330	8,659	39.7	47.2
Other races	258	218	181	70.2	83.0	197	178	166	84.3	93.3	61	40	15	-	-
1930	399,746	323,187	194,657	48.7	60.2	194,542	156,221	137,689	70.8	88.1	205,204	166,966	56,968	27.8	34.1
White	360,725	290,512	171,465	47.5	59.0	175,579	140,389	123,218	70.2	87.8	185,146	150,123	48,247	26.1	32.1
Negro	38,574	32,271	22,841	59.2	70.8	18,599	15,489	14,160	76.1	91.4	19,975	16,782	8,681	43.5	51.7
Other races	447	404	351	78.5	86.9	364	343	311	85.4	90.7	83	61	40	-	-

[1] Data for 1930 represent gainful workers 14 years old and over.

RCA-Victor Researcher Works in Secret on Inventing Television

America eagerly awaited to see who would be the first to develop a television with picture quality good enough to entice the average consumer, help sell products to a mass market, and fill a need in the business community. By 1940, RCA-Victor was the clear winner, and employee Kenneth Beltran the genius behind the screen.

Life at Home

- The Beltran family lived in Camden, New Jersey, where Kenneth works for RCA-Victor Company on developing television.
- Quiet by nature, he did not discuss his work, leading his wife, Celeste, to believe he was involved in improving the sound transmission of radio.
- He has been working on his current assignment for two years, and warned never to discuss it.
- RCA wanted to delay the introduction of television to the public until it perfected the receiver and controls the patents.
- RCA declared publicly that "television, as it stands today, cannot by the wildest stretch of the imagination be declared a public service for the benefit of the vast audience which radio broadcasting has won."
- Individual inventors and innovators outside RCA pushed for faster introduction, to meet public demand.
- Kenneth and Celeste lived in a cottage home with two bedrooms, but Kenneth decided the time is not right for children.
- Kenneth had little interest in yard work, baseball, fishing, or rides in the country; "Work is my recreation," he loved to say.
- Celeste was active in her church, and sponsored a tea at her home for Margaret Winslett, a missionary from China who is home on furlough.
- She also served on the membership committee of the Junior Service League, whose work focused on helping the children of men who are temporarily out of work due to the current economic downturn.
- To further her support, she bought clams for $0.25 a peck, from unemployed factory workers who are now digging clams to support their families.
- She noticed that many unemployed individuals and their families, spent considerable time at the new introduced double feature movies, and wondered if they are lazy or simply trying to escape.
- Many new films featured gangsters and monsters, hardly suitable for children.

Kenneth Beltran worked with Dr. Vladimir Zworykin.

Several companies, and inventors, were competing to control the patents on television.

Life at Work

- Kenneth worked with Dr. Vladimir Zworykin to perfect the cathode ray tube system of scanning for RCA-Victor Company.
- Patent rights for the new technology was worth millions to RCA-Victor.
- Many independent inventors worked on similar projects, including 24-year-old Philo Farnsworth in Los Angeles.
- The pressure to be first was intense, and secrecy was paramount while RCA worked on a plan to create a 400-line television screen that would provide better detail.
- All of the television equipment manufacturers prepared to sell stock, raise capital for expansion, and capture the current TV craze.
- Many believed the future of television would be defined by RCA when it introduced its long awaited television set.
- Television sets currently on the market, made by Shortwave and Television Corporation of Boston, the Jenkins Television Corporation of Passaic, New Jersey, and the Western Television Corporation of Chicago, sold for $125 to $300.
- Teams of engineers were employed by RCA-Victor on the project, and more than $500,000 was spent to develop television experimental broadcasting and receiving units.
- RCA and affiliates held experimental licenses to 11 of the 29 proposals.
- Lawsuits were also in vogue, and competitors filed damage suits against RCA-which dominated the radio field-totaling $48 million charging unfair competition.
- Radio, in its early days, passed through a similar phase.
- General James G. Harbord, chairman of the board of RCA, said television will play a role in business: "A great corporation whose directorate is scattered across the continent suddenly needs a meeting of its board of directors. Buzzers buzz, wires hum, and bells ring in a dozen distant cities. The call goes out. The hour is named. Switches are thrown and at the appointed time, say perhaps an hour after the call was issued, a quorum is assembled by electricity and called to order by the chairman."
- Under Harbord's vision, a television meeting required a television set in each man's office, and each could see and hear all of the other members of the group, and each would be able to affix their signatures, and facsimiles would be flashed back to the chairman before the board meeting adjourned.
- Another use of television was purchasing, where that "great stores" displayed their wares over the television and, using telephones, companies ordered what they needed instantly.
- This innovation eliminated salesmen's travel time and expense, and some believed that actors would become important to the television sales process.

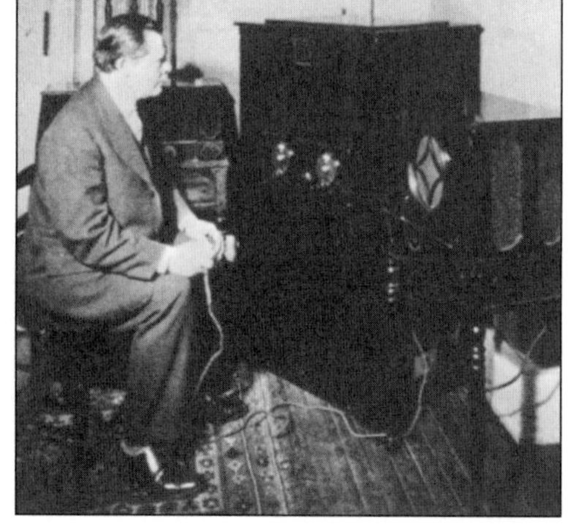

The nine tables that follow are reprinted from the actual 1940 census, for the city of Camden. They include actual data on race, percentage of voting population, school attendance, number of school years completed, foreign born, and employment of workers 14 years and older by job, industry and race. In addition to being incredibly fascinating, these facts help to strengthen and visualize the actual environment in which Kenneth Beltran lived and worked.

Table A-35.—AGE, BY RACE AND SEX, FOR THE CITY OF CAMDEN: 1940 AND 1930

[Figures for white population in 1930 revised to include Mexicans classified with "Other races" in the 1930 reports. Percent not shown where less than 0.1 or where base is less than 100]

AGE AND CENSUS YEAR	ALL CLASSES			NATIVE WHITE			FOREIGN-BORN WHITE			NEGRO			OTHER RACES		
	Total	Male	Female	Total	Male	Female	Total	Male	Female	Total	Male	Female	Total	Male	Female
All ages: 1940	117,536	58,802	58,734	89,999	44,817	45,182	14,996	7,757	7,239	12,478	6,182	6,296	63	46	17
Under 5 years	7,965	4,100	3,865	6,838	3,544	3,294	4	1	3	1,121	554	567	2	1	1
5 to 9 years	8,189	4,185	4,004	7,039	3,586	3,453	16	6	10	1,132	592	540	2	1	1
10 to 14 years	10,078	5,045	5,033	8,766	4,378	4,388	56	32	24	1,251	632	619	5	3	2
15 to 19 years	11,158	5,537	5,621	9,825	4,873	4,952	184	92	92	1,140	565	575	9	7	2
20 to 24 years	11,795	5,693	6,102	10,526	5,097	5,429	211	113	98	1,055	481	574	3	2	1
25 to 29 years	10,563	5,244	5,319	9,124	4,568	4,556	447	212	235	987	461	526	5	3	2
30 to 34 years	8,872	4,484	4,388	7,184	3,691	3,493	761	364	397	921	423	498	6	6	-
35 to 39 years	8,188	3,971	4,217	5,912	2,897	3,015	1,176	542	634	1,098	530	568	2	2	-
40 to 44 years	8,315	4,117	4,198	5,445	2,703	2,742	1,887	937	950	970	471	499	13	6	7
45 to 49 years	8,441	4,326	4,115	5,043	2,523	2,520	2,555	1,360	1,195	840	441	399	3	2	1
50 to 54 years	7,197	3,783	3,414	4,165	2,107	2,058	2,407	1,336	1,071	616	331	285	9	9	-
55 to 59 years	5,357	2,790	2,567	3,054	1,482	1,572	1,838	1,049	789	463	257	206	2	2	-
60 to 64 years	4,300	2,200	2,100	2,641	1,314	1,327	1,330	705	625	329	181	148	-	-	-
65 to 69 years	3,145	1,500	1,645	1,949	914	1,035	917	468	449	277	116	161	2	2	-
70 to 74 years	2,053	962	1,091	1,268	580	688	650	307	343	135	75	60	-	-	-
75 years and over	1,920	865	1,055	1,220	560	660	557	233	324	143	72	71	-	-	-
Under 1 year	1,575	821	754	1,368	711	657	-	-	-	207	110	97	-	-	-
5 years	1,579	824	755	1,353	695	658	3	1	2	223	128	95	-	-	-
14 years	2,159	1,070	1,089	1,876	930	946	18	12	6	264	127	137	1	1	-
15 years	2,040	1,040	1,000	1,789	914	875	16	11	5	234	114	120	1	1	-
16 and 17 years	4,348	2,144	2,204	3,806	1,869	1,937	62	28	34	477	244	233	3	3	-
21 years and over	77,743	38,817	38,926	55,393	27,440	27,953	14,685	7,598	7,087	7,620	3,745	3,875	45	34	11
All ages: 1930	118,700	59,442	59,258	88,672	43,933	44,739	18,620	9,780	8,840	11,340	5,676	5,664	68	53	15
Under 5 years	10,090	5,010	5,080	8,904	4,422	4,482	44	25	19	1,139	562	577	3	1	2
5 to 9 years	11,723	5,891	5,832	10,391	5,226	5,165	152	79	73	1,175	583	592	5	3	2
10 to 14 years	12,146	6,088	6,058	10,980	5,517	5,463	182	94	88	978	475	503	6	2	4
15 to 19 years	11,370	5,471	5,899	9,963	4,759	5,204	464	248	216	939	462	477	4	2	2
20 to 24 years	10,335	5,031	5,304	8,512	4,189	4,323	805	388	417	1,016	452	564	2	2	-
25 to 29 years	9,340	4,630	4,710	6,923	3,461	3,462	1,259	593	666	1,151	570	581	7	6	1
30 to 34 years	9,211	4,571	4,640	6,165	3,064	3,101	2,019	1,008	1,011	1,018	490	528	9	9	-
35 to 39 years	9,941	5,143	4,798	5,918	2,965	2,953	2,908	1,579	1,329	1,107	593	514	8	6	2
40 to 44 years	8,467	4,438	4,029	4,902	2,459	2,443	2,699	1,528	1,171	862	447	415	4	4	-
45 to 49 years	7,039	3,683	3,356	4,000	2,001	1,999	2,381	1,329	1,052	650	346	304	8	7	1
50 to 54 years	5,787	2,988	2,799	3,535	1,759	1,776	1,769	960	809	482	268	214	1	1	-
55 to 59 years	4,413	2,233	2,180	2,781	1,390	1,391	1,295	668	627	333	172	161	4	3	1
60 to 64 years	3,479	1,709	1,770	2,193	1,066	1,127	1,074	522	552	208	117	91	4	4	-
65 to 69 years	2,437	1,198	1,239	1,566	770	796	741	368	373	127	57	70	3	3	-
70 to 74 years	1,543	741	802	1,044	486	558	433	214	219	66	41	25	-	-	-
75 years and over	1,331	593	738	862	381	481	392	176	216	77	36	41	-	-	-
Not reported	48	24	24	33	18	15	3	1	2	12	5	7	-	-	-
Under 1 year	1,877	927	950	1,645	817	828	1	-	1	231	110	121	-	-	-
5 years	2,256	1,151	1,105	1,975	1,008	967	11	7	4	268	135	133	2	1	1
14 years	2,394	1,254	1,140	2,171	1,144	1,027	35	15	20	188	95	93	-	-	-
15 years	2,277	1,106	1,171	2,040	976	1,064	54	28	26	182	102	80	1	-	1
16 and 17 years	4,603	2,242	2,361	4,079	1,982	2,097	165	89	76	357	170	187	2	1	1
21 years and over	71,286	36,030	35,256	46,678	23,210	23,468	17,637	9,260	8,377	6,921	3,515	3,406	50	45	5
Percent: 1940	100.0	100.0	100.0	100.0	100.0	100.0	100.0	100.0	100.0	100.0	100.0	100.0	-	-	-
Under 5 years	6.8	7.0	6.6	7.6	7.9	7.3	-	-	-	9.0	9.0	9.0	-	-	-
5 to 9 years	7.0	7.1	6.8	7.8	8.0	7.6	0.1	0.1	0.1	9.1	9.6	8.6	-	-	-
10 to 14 years	8.6	8.6	8.6	9.7	9.8	9.7	0.4	0.4	0.3	10.0	10.2	9.8	-	-	-
15 to 19 years	9.5	9.4	9.6	10.9	10.9	11.0	1.2	1.2	1.3	9.1	9.1	9.1	-	-	-
20 to 24 years	10.0	9.7	10.4	11.7	11.4	12.0	1.4	1.5	1.4	8.5	7.8	9.1	-	-	-
25 to 29 years	9.0	8.9	9.1	10.1	10.2	10.1	3.0	2.7	3.2	7.9	7.5	8.4	-	-	-
30 to 34 years	7.5	7.6	7.5	8.0	8.2	7.7	5.1	4.7	5.5	7.4	6.8	7.9	-	-	-
35 to 39 years	7.0	6.8	7.2	6.6	6.5	6.7	7.8	7.0	8.8	8.8	8.6	9.0	-	-	-
40 to 44 years	7.1	7.0	7.1	6.1	6.0	6.1	12.6	12.1	13.1	7.8	7.6	7.9	-	-	-
45 to 49 years	7.2	7.4	7.0	5.6	5.6	5.6	17.0	17.5	16.5	6.7	7.1	6.3	-	-	-
50 to 54 years	6.1	6.4	5.8	4.6	4.7	4.6	16.1	17.2	14.8	4.9	5.4	4.5	-	-	-
55 to 59 years	4.6	4.7	4.4	3.4	3.3	3.5	12.3	13.5	10.9	3.7	4.2	3.3	-	-	-
60 to 64 years	3.7	3.7	3.6	2.9	2.9	2.9	8.9	9.1	8.6	2.6	2.9	2.4	-	-	-
65 to 69 years	2.7	2.6	2.8	2.2	2.0	2.3	6.1	6.0	6.2	2.2	1.9	2.6	-	-	-
70 to 74 years	1.7	1.6	1.9	1.4	1.3	1.5	4.3	4.0	4.7	1.1	1.2	1.0	-	-	-
75 years and over	1.6	1.5	1.8	1.4	1.2	1.5	3.7	3.0	4.5	1.1	1.2	1.1	-	-	-
Under 1 year	1.3	1.4	1.3	1.5	1.6	1.5	-	-	-	1.7	1.8	1.5	-	-	-
5 years	1.3	1.4	1.3	1.5	1.6	1.5	-	-	-	1.8	2.1	1.5	-	-	-
14 years	1.8	1.8	1.9	2.1	2.1	2.1	0.1	0.2	0.1	2.1	2.1	2.2	-	-	-
15 years	1.7	1.8	1.7	2.0	2.0	1.9	0.1	0.1	0.1	1.9	1.8	1.9	-	-	-
16 and 17 years	3.7	3.6	3.8	4.2	4.2	4.3	0.4	0.4	0.5	3.8	3.9	3.7	-	-	-
21 years and over	66.1	66.0	66.3	61.5	61.2	61.9	97.9	98.0	97.9	61.1	60.6	61.5	-	-	-
Percent: 1930	100.0	100.0	100.0	100.0	100.0	100.0	100.0	100.0	100.0	100.0	100.0	100.0	-	-	-
Under 5 years	8.5	8.4	8.6	10.0	10.1	10.0	0.2	0.3	0.2	10.0	9.9	10.2	-	-	-
5 to 9 years	9.9	9.9	9.8	11.7	11.9	11.5	0.8	0.8	0.8	10.4	10.3	10.5	-	-	-
10 to 14 years	10.2	10.2	10.2	12.4	12.6	12.2	1.0	1.0	1.0	8.6	8.4	8.9	-	-	-
15 to 19 years	9.6	9.2	10.0	11.2	10.8	11.6	2.5	2.5	2.4	8.3	8.1	8.4	-	-	-
20 to 24 years	8.7	8.5	9.0	9.6	9.5	9.7	4.3	4.0	4.7	9.0	8.0	10.0	-	-	-
25 to 29 years	7.9	7.8	7.9	7.8	7.9	7.7	6.8	6.1	7.5	10.1	10.0	10.3	-	-	-
30 to 34 years	7.8	7.7	7.8	7.0	7.0	6.9	10.8	10.3	11.4	9.0	8.6	9.3	-	-	-
35 to 39 years	8.4	8.7	8.1	6.7	6.7	6.6	15.6	16.1	15.0	9.8	10.4	9.1	-	-	-
40 to 44 years	7.1	7.5	6.8	5.5	5.6	5.5	14.5	15.6	13.2	7.6	7.9	7.3	-	-	-
45 to 49 years	5.9	6.2	5.7	4.5	4.6	4.5	12.8	13.6	11.9	5.7	6.1	5.4	-	-	-
50 to 54 years	4.9	5.0	4.7	4.0	4.0	4.0	9.5	9.8	9.2	4.3	4.7	3.8	-	-	-
55 to 59 years	3.7	3.8	3.7	3.1	3.2	3.1	7.0	6.8	7.1	2.9	3.0	2.8	-	-	-
60 to 64 years	2.9	2.9	3.0	2.5	2.4	2.5	5.8	5.3	6.2	1.8	2.1	1.6	-	-	-
65 to 69 years	2.1	2.0	2.1	1.8	1.8	1.8	4.0	3.8	4.2	1.1	1.0	1.2	-	-	-
70 to 74 years	1.3	1.2	1.4	1.2	1.1	1.2	2.3	2.2	2.5	0.6	0.7	0.4	-	-	-
75 years and over	1.1	1.0	1.2	1.0	0.9	1.1	2.1	1.8	2.4	0.7	0.6	0.7	-	-	-
Not reported	-	-	-	-	-	-	-	-	-	0.1	0.1	0.1	-	-	-
Under 1 year	1.6	1.6	1.6	1.9	1.9	1.9	-	-	-	2.0	1.9	2.1	-	-	-
5 years	1.9	1.9	1.9	2.2	2.3	2.2	0.1	0.1	-	2.4	2.4	2.3	-	-	-
14 years	2.0	2.1	1.9	2.4	2.6	2.3	0.2	0.2	0.2	1.7	1.7	1.6	-	-	-
15 years	1.9	1.9	2.0	2.3	2.2	2.4	0.3	0.3	0.3	1.6	1.8	1.4	-	-	-
16 and 17 years	3.9	3.8	4.0	4.6	4.5	4.7	0.9	0.9	0.9	3.1	3.0	3.3	-	-	-
21 years and over	60.1	60.6	59.5	52.6	52.8	52.5	94.7	94.7	94.8	61.0	61.9	60.1	-	-	-

Table A-36.—RACE, BY NATIVITY AND SEX, FOR THE CITY OF CAMDEN: 1940 AND 1930

[Figures for white population in 1930 have been revised to include Mexicans who were classified with "Other races" in the 1930 reports. Percent not shown where less than 0.1 or where base is less than 100. Sex ratio not shown where number of females is less than 100. Nativity distribution for 1930 not available for individual "Other races"]

SEX, NATIVITY, AND CENSUS YEAR	All classes	White	Negro	Other races	OTHER RACES				PERCENT BY RACE				PERCENT BY NATIVITY					
					Indian	Chinese	Japanese	All other	All classes	White	Negro	Other races	All classes	White	Negro	Indian	Chinese	Japanese
TOTAL																		
1940	117,536	104,995	12,478	63	17	43	-	3	100.0	89.3	10.6	0.1	100.0	100.0	100.0	-	-	-
Native	102,471	89,999	12,433	39	15	23	-	1	100.0	87.8	12.1	-	87.2	85.7	99.6	-	-	-
Foreign born	15,065	14,996	45	24	2	20	-	2	100.0	99.5	0.3	0.2	12.8	14.3	0.4	-	-	-
1930	118,700	107,292	11,340	68	1	53	7	7	100.0	90.4	9.6	0.1	100.0	100.0	100.0	-	-	-
Native	99,984	88,672	11,274	38	-	-	-	-	100.0	88.7	11.3	-	84.2	82.6	99.4	-	-	-
Foreign born	18,716	18,620	66	30	-	-	-	-	100.0	99.5	0.4	0.2	15.8	17.4	0.6	-	-	-
MALE																		
1940	58,802	52,574	6,182	46	11	32	-	3	100.0	89.4	10.5	0.1	100.0	100.0	100.0	-	-	-
Native	50,989	44,817	6,148	24	10	13	-	1	100.0	87.9	12.1	-	86.7	85.2	99.5	-	-	-
Foreign born	7,813	7,757	34	22	1	19	-	2	100.0	99.3	0.4	0.3	13.3	14.8	0.5	-	-	-
1930	59,442	53,713	5,676	53	-	-	-	-	100.0	90.4	9.5	0.1	100.0	100.0	100.0	-	-	-
Native	49,594	43,933	5,635	26	-	-	-	-	100.0	88.6	11.4	0.1	83.4	81.8	99.3	-	-	-
Foreign born	9,848	9,780	41	27	-	-	-	-	100.0	99.3	0.4	0.3	16.6	18.2	0.7	-	-	-
FEMALE																		
1940	58,734	52,421	6,296	17	6	11	-	-	100.0	89.3	10.7	-	100.0	100.0	100.0	-	-	-
Native	51,482	45,182	6,285	15	5	10	-	-	100.0	87.8	12.2	-	87.7	86.2	99.8	-	-	-
Foreign born	7,252	7,239	11	2	1	1	-	-	100.0	99.8	0.2	-	12.3	13.8	0.2	-	-	-
1930	59,258	53,579	5,664	15	-	-	-	-	100.0	90.4	9.6	-	100.0	100.0	100.0	-	-	-
Native	50,390	44,739	5,639	12	-	-	-	-	100.0	88.8	11.2	-	85.0	83.5	99.6	-	-	-
Foreign born	8,868	8,840	25	3	-	-	-	-	100.0	99.7	0.3	-	15.0	16.5	0.4	-	-	-
MALES PER 100 FEMALES																		
1940	100.1	100.3	98.2	-	-	-	-	-	-	-	-	-	-	-	-	-	-	-
Native	99.0	99.2	97.8	-	-	-	-	-	-	-	-	-	-	-	-	-	-	-
Foreign born	107.7	107.2	-	-	-	-	-	-	-	-	-	-	-	-	-	-	-	-
1930	100.3	100.3	100.2	-	-	-	-	-	-	-	-	-	-	-	-	-	-	-
Native	98.4	98.2	99.9	-	-	-	-	-	-	-	-	-	-	-	-	-	-	-
Foreign born	111.1	110.6	-	-	-	-	-	-	-	-	-	-	-	-	-	-	-	-

Table A-37.—POTENTIAL VOTING POPULATION, BY CITIZENSHIP, RACE, NATIVITY, AND SEX, FOR THE CITY OF CAMDEN: 1940 AND 1930

[Figures for white population in 1930 have been revised to include Mexicans who were classified with "Other races" in the 1930 reports. Percent not shown where less than 0.1. Nativity distribution for 1930 not available for individual "Other races"]

CITIZENSHIP, RACE, AND NATIVITY	TOTAL POPULATION (ALL AGES)								POPULATION 21 YEARS OLD AND OVER							
	Total number		Percent		Male		Female		Total number		Percent		Male		Female	
	1940	1930	1940	1930	1940	1930	1940	1930	1940	1930	1940	1930	1940	1930	1940	1930
Total	117,536	118,700	100.0	100.0	58,802	59,442	58,734	59,258	77,743	71,286	100.0	100.0	38,817	36,030	38,926	35,256
Percent citizen	-	-	95.6	93.8	-	-	-	-	-	-	93.5	90.4	-	-	-	-
Percent alien and citiz. not rptd.	-	-	4.4	6.2	-	-	-	-	-	-	6.5	9.6	-	-	-	-
Citizen	112,374	111,292	100.0	100.0	56,781	55,953	55,593	55,339	72,719	64,435	100.0	100.0	36,870	32,844	35,849	31,591
White—Native	89,999	88,672	80.1	79.7	44,817	43,933	45,182	44,739	55,393	46,678	76.2	72.4	27,440	23,210	27,953	23,468
Naturalized	9,877	11,284	8.8	10.1	5,772	6,342	4,105	4,942	9,702	10,850	13.3	16.8	5,685	6,121	4,017	4,729
Negro—Native	12,433	11,274	11.1	10.1	6,148	5,635	6,285	5,639	7,576	6,862	10.4	10.6	3,712	3,476	3,864	3,386
Naturalized	26	24	-	-	20	17	6	7	26	23	-	-	20	17	6	6
Other races—Native	39	38	-	-	24	26	15	12	22	22	-	-	13	20	9	2
Indian	15	-	-	-	10	-	5	-	9	-	-	-	5	-	4	-
Chinese	23	-	-	-	13	-	10	-	12	-	-	-	7	-	5	-
Japanese	-	-	-	-	-	-	-	-	-	-	-	-	-	-	-	-
Filipino	1	-	-	-	1	-	-	-	1	-	-	-	1	-	-	-
Hindu	-	-	-	-	-	-	-	-	-	-	-	-	-	-	-	-
All other	-	-	-	-	-	-	-	-	-	-	-	-	-	-	-	-
Alien	3,944	7,110	100.0	100.0	1,519	3,348	2,425	3,762	3,846	6,556	100.0	100.0	1,468	3,046	2,378	3,510
White—First papers	922	1,462	23.4	20.6	575	1,180	347	282	910	1,425	23.7	21.7	565	1,156	345	269
No papers	2,989	5,587	75.8	78.6	915	2,122	2,074	3,465	2,904	5,076	75.5	77.4	875	1,848	2,029	3,228
Negro—First papers	3	6	0.1	0.1	2	5	1	1	3	6	0.1	0.1	2	5	1	1
No papers	6	25	0.2	0.4	5	14	1	11	6	21	0.2	0.3	5	12	1	9
Other races—Foreign born	24	30	0.6	0.4	22	27	2	3	23	28	0.6	0.4	21	25	2	3
Indian	2	-	0.1	-	1	-	1	-	2	-	0.1	-	1	-	1	-
Chinese	20	-	0.5	-	19	-	1	-	19	-	0.5	-	18	-	1	-
Japanese	-	-	-	-	-	-	-	-	-	-	-	-	-	-	-	-
Filipino	1	-	-	-	1	-	-	-	1	-	-	-	1	-	-	-
Hindu	1	-	-	-	1	-	-	-	1	-	-	-	1	-	-	-
All other	-	-	-	-	-	-	-	-	-	-	-	-	-	-	-	-
Citizenship not reported	1,218	298	100.0	100.0	502	141	716	157	1,178	295	100.0	100.0	479	140	699	155
White	1,208	287	99.2	96.3	495	136	713	151	1,169	286	99.2	96.9	473	135	696	151
Negro	10	11	0.8	3.7	7	5	3	6	9	9	0.8	3.1	6	5	3	4

Table A-38.—SCHOOL ATTENDANCE, BY AGE, RACE, AND SEX, FOR THE CITY OF CAMDEN: 1940 AND 1930

[Figures for white population in 1930 revised to include Mexicans classified with "Other races" in the 1930 reports. Percent not shown where less than 0.1 or where base is less than 100]

AGE, SEX, AND CENSUS YEAR	ALL CLASSES			NATIVE WHITE			FOREIGN-BORN WHITE			NEGRO			OTHER RACES		
	Total number	Attending school		Total number	Attending school		Total number	Attending school		Total number	Attending school		Total number	Attending school	
		Number	Percent		Number	Percent		Number	Percent		Number	Percent		Number	Percent
1940															
Total, 5 to 24 years	41,220	21,745	52.8	36,156	18,895	52.3	467	129	27.6	4,578	2,711	59.2	19	10	-
5 years	1,579	343	21.7	1,353	288	20.9	3	1	-	223	59	26.5	-	-	-
6 years	1,476	1,127	76.4	1,254	956	76.2	2	1	-	219	170	77.6	1	-	-
7 to 9 years	5,134	4,922	95.9	4,432	4,247	95.8	11	11	-	690	663	96.1	1	1	-
10 to 13 years	7,919	7,627	96.3	6,890	6,628	96.2	38	34	-	987	961	97.4	4	4	-
14 years	2,159	2,076	96.2	1,875	1,803	96.1	18	17	-	264	255	96.6	1	1	-
15 years	2,040	1,923	94.3	1,789	1,696	94.8	16	14	-	234	212	90.6	1	1	-
16 and 17 years	4,348	2,559	58.9	3,806	2,236	58.7	62	35	-	477	287	60.2	3	1	-
18 and 19 years	4,770	766	16.1	4,230	685	16.2	106	12	11.3	429	67	15.6	5	2	-
20 years	2,403	131	5.5	2,138	115	5.4	51	3	-	214	13	6.1	-	-	-
21 to 24 years	9,392	271	2.9	8,388	246	2.9	160	1	0.6	841	24	2.9	3	-	-
Male, 5 to 24 years	20,460	11,117	54.3	17,934	9,662	53.9	243	72	29.6	2,270	1,377	60.7	13	6	-
5 years	824	174	21.1	695	141	20.3	1	-	-	128	33	25.8	-	-	-
6 years	781	583	74.6	671	503	75.0	-	-	-	109	80	73.4	1	-	-
7 to 9 years	2,580	2,467	95.6	2,220	2,120	95.5	5	5	-	355	342	96.3	-	-	-
10 to 13 years	3,975	3,827	96.3	3,448	3,319	96.3	20	17	-	505	489	96.8	2	2	-
14 years	1,070	1,030	96.3	930	894	96.1	12	11	-	127	124	97.6	1	1	-
15 years	1,040	981	94.3	914	869	95.1	11	9	-	114	102	89.5	1	1	-
16 and 17 years	2,144	1,319	61.5	1,869	1,146	61.3	28	19	-	244	153	62.7	3	1	-
18 and 19 years	2,353	478	20.3	2,090	429	20.5	53	7	-	207	41	19.8	3	1	-
20 years	1,118	75	6.7	996	68	6.8	28	3	-	94	4	-	-	-	-
21 to 24 years	4,575	183	4.0	4,101	173	4.2	85	1	-	387	9	2.3	2	-	-
Female, 5 to 24 years	20,760	10,628	51.2	18,222	9,233	50.7	224	57	25.4	2,308	1,334	57.8	6	4	-
5 years	755	169	22.4	658	142	21.6	2	1	-	95	26	-	-	-	-
6 years	695	544	78.3	583	453	77.7	2	1	-	110	90	81.8	-	-	-
7 to 9 years	2,554	2,455	96.1	2,212	2,127	96.2	6	6	-	335	321	95.8	1	1	-
10 to 13 years	3,944	3,800	96.3	3,442	3,309	96.1	18	17	-	482	472	97.9	2	2	-
14 years	1,089	1,046	96.1	946	909	96.1	6	6	-	137	131	95.6	-	-	-
15 years	1,000	942	94.2	875	827	94.5	5	5	-	120	110	91.7	-	-	-
16 and 17 years	2,204	1,240	56.3	1,937	1,090	56.3	34	16	-	233	134	57.5	-	-	-
18 and 19 years	2,417	288	11.9	2,140	256	12.0	53	5	-	222	26	11.7	2	1	-
20 years	1,285	56	4.4	1,142	47	4.1	23	-	-	120	9	7.5	-	-	-
21 to 24 years	4,817	88	1.8	4,287	73	1.7	75	-	-	454	15	3.3	1	-	-
1930															
Total, 5 to 24 years	45,574	25,931	56.9	39,846	23,308	58.5	1,603	503	31.4	4,108	2,109	51.3	17	11	-
5 years	2,256	508	22.5	1,975	445	22.5	11	-	-	268	63	23.5	2	-	-
6 years	2,283	1,699	74.4	2,020	1,519	75.2	18	13	-	245	167	68.2	-	-	-
7 to 9 years	7,184	6,877	95.7	6,396	6,175	96.5	123	119	96.7	662	580	87.6	3	3	-
10 to 13 years	9,752	9,580	98.2	8,809	8,692	98.7	147	141	95.9	790	741	93.8	6	6	-
14 years	2,394	2,303	96.2	2,171	2,099	96.7	35	34	-	188	170	90.4	-	-	-
15 years	2,277	2,047	89.9	2,040	1,853	90.8	54	46	-	182	147	80.8	1	1	-
16 and 17 years	4,603	1,807	39.3	4,079	1,588	38.9	165	73	44.2	357	145	40.6	2	1	-
18 and 19 years	4,490	594	13.2	3,844	512	13.3	245	31	12.7	400	51	12.8	1	-	-
20 years	2,085	156	7.5	1,756	130	7.4	141	14	9.9	188	12	6.4	-	-	-
21 to 24 years	8,250	360	4.4	6,756	295	4.4	664	32	4.8	828	33	4.0	2	-	-
Male, 5 to 24 years	22,481	13,227	58.8	19,691	11,893	60.4	809	275	34.0	1,972	1,055	53.5	9	4	-
5 years	1,151	266	23.1	1,008	239	23.7	7	-	-	135	27	20.0	1	-	-
6 years	1,149	873	76.0	1,016	780	76.8	8	5	-	125	88	70.4	-	-	-
7 to 9 years	3,591	3,443	95.9	3,202	3,089	96.5	64	63	-	323	289	89.5	2	2	-
10 to 13 years	4,834	4,754	98.3	4,373	4,317	98.7	79	76	-	380	359	94.5	2	2	-
14 years	1,254	1,213	96.7	1,144	1,110	97.0	15	15	-	95	88	-	-	-	-
15 years	1,106	1,018	92.0	976	909	93.1	28	23	-	102	86	84.3	-	-	-
16 and 17 years	2,242	974	43.4	1,982	865	43.6	89	45	-	170	64	37.6	1	-	-
18 and 19 years	2,123	356	16.8	1,801	302	16.8	131	23	17.6	190	31	16.3	1	-	-
20 years	952	88	9.2	799	72	9.0	74	10	-	79	6	-	-	-	-
21 to 24 years	4,079	242	5.9	3,390	210	6.2	314	15	4.8	373	17	4.6	2	-	-
Female, 5 to 24 years	23,093	12,704	55.0	20,155	11,415	56.6	794	228	28.7	2,136	1,054	49.3	8	7	-
5 years	1,105	242	21.9	967	206	21.3	4	-	-	133	36	27.1	1	-	-
6 years	1,134	826	72.8	1,004	739	73.6	10	8	-	120	79	65.8	-	-	-
7 to 9 years	3,593	3,434	95.6	3,194	3,086	96.6	59	56	-	339	291	85.8	1	1	-
10 to 13 years	4,918	4,826	98.1	4,436	4,375	98.6	68	65	-	410	382	93.2	4	4	-
14 years	1,140	1,090	95.6	1,027	989	96.3	20	19	-	93	82	-	-	-	-
15 years	1,171	1,029	87.9	1,064	944	88.7	26	23	-	80	61	-	1	1	-
16 and 17 years	2,361	833	35.3	2,097	723	34.5	76	28	-	187	81	43.3	1	1	-
18 and 19 years	2,367	238	10.1	2,043	210	10.3	114	8	7.0	210	20	9.5	-	-	-
20 years	1,133	68	6.0	957	58	6.1	67	4	-	109	6	5.5	-	-	-
21 to 24 years	4,171	118	2.8	3,366	85	2.5	350	17	4.9	455	16	3.5	-	-	-

Table A-39.—PERSONS 25 YEARS OLD AND OVER, BY YEARS OF SCHOOL COMPLETED, RACE, AND SEX, FOR THE CITY OF CAMDEN: 1940

[Percent not shown where less than 0.1; median and percent not shown where base is less than 100]

YEARS OF SCHOOL COMPLETED	ALL CLASSES			NATIVE WHITE			FOREIGN-BORN WHITE			NEGRO			OTHER RACES		
	Total	Male	Female	Total	Male	Female	Total	Male	Female	Total	Male	Female	Total	Male	Female
Persons 25 years old and over	68,351	34,242	34,109	47,005	23,339	23,666	14,525	7,513	7,012	6,779	3,358	3,421	42	32	10
No school years completed	3,981	1,979	2,002	462	238	224	3,067	1,490	1,577	443	243	200	9	8	1
Grade school: 1 to 4 years	8,156	4,173	3,983	3,165	1,544	1,621	3,499	1,820	1,679	1,488	805	683	4	4	-
5 or 6 years	11,527	5,756	5,771	7,604	3,719	3,885	2,318	1,221	1,097	1,602	815	787	3	1	2
7 or 8 years	26,074	12,879	13,195	20,522	10,122	10,400	3,644	1,864	1,780	1,897	885	1,012	11	8	3
High school: 1 to 3 years	9,161	4,537	4,624	7,706	3,821	3,885	690	384	306	763	331	432	2	1	1
4 years	5,300	2,446	2,854	4,555	2,059	2,496	491	270	221	250	115	135	4	2	2
College: 1 to 3 years	1,209	691	518	1,034	589	445	82	55	27	92	46	46	1	1	-
4 years or more	1,356	951	405	1,131	794	337	133	113	20	91	43	48	1	1	-
Not reported	1,587	830	757	826	453	373	601	296	305	153	75	78	7	6	1
Median school years completed	7.7	7.7	7.7	8.2	8.2	8.1	5.3	5.5	5.2	6.7	6.5	7.0	-	-	-
Percent less than 5 years completed	17.8	18.0	17.5	7.7	7.6	7.8	45.2	44.1	46.4	28.5	31.2	25.8	-	-	-
PERCENT DISTRIBUTION															
Persons 25 years old and over	100.0	100.0	100.0	100.0	100.0	100.0	100.0	100.0	100.0	100.0	100.0	100.0	-	-	-
No school years completed	5.8	5.8	5.9	1.0	1.0	0.9	21.1	19.8	22.5	6.5	7.2	5.8	-	-	-
Grade school: 1 to 4 years	11.9	12.2	11.7	6.7	6.6	6.8	24.1	24.2	23.9	21.9	24.0	20.0	-	-	-
5 or 6 years	16.9	16.8	16.9	16.2	15.9	16.4	16.0	16.3	15.6	23.6	24.3	23.0	-	-	-
7 or 8 years	38.1	37.6	38.7	43.7	43.4	43.9	25.1	24.8	25.4	28.0	26.4	29.6	-	-	-
High school: 1 to 3 years	13.4	13.2	13.6	16.4	16.4	16.4	4.8	5.1	4.4	11.3	9.9	12.6	-	-	-
4 years	7.8	7.1	8.4	9.7	8.8	10.5	3.4	3.6	3.2	3.7	3.4	3.9	-	-	-
College: 1 to 3 years	1.8	2.0	1.5	2.2	2.5	1.9	0.6	0.7	0.4	1.4	1.4	1.3	-	-	-
4 years or more	2.0	2.8	1.2	2.4	3.4	1.4	0.9	1.5	0.3	1.3	1.3	1.4	-	-	-
Not reported	2.3	2.4	2.2	1.8	1.9	1.6	4.1	3.9	4.3	2.3	2.2	2.3	-	-	-

Table A-40.—FOREIGN-BORN WHITE, BY COUNTRY OF BIRTH, BY SEX, FOR THE CITY OF CAMDEN: 1940 AND 1930

[Figures for white population in 1930 revised to include Mexicans classified with "Other races" in the 1930 reports. Percent not shown where less than 0.1 or where base is less than 100]

COUNTRY OF BIRTH	BOTH SEXES		PERCENT		MALE		FEMALE	
	1940	1930	1940	1930	1940	1930	1940	1930
All countries	14,996	18,620	100.0	100.0	7,757	9,780	7,239	8,840
England	963	1,379	6.4	7.4	465	677	498	702
Scotland	319	403	2.1	2.2	156	199	163	204
Wales	25	54	0.2	0.3	15	27	10	27
Northern Ireland	273	369	1.8	2.0	114	151	159	218
Irish Free State (Eire)	477	747	3.2	4.0	168	291	309	456
Norway	107	154	0.7	0.8	63	95	44	59
Sweden	101	162	0.7	0.9	61	95	40	67
Denmark	26	47	0.2	0.3	17	37	9	10
Netherlands	15	29	0.1	0.2	10	18	5	11
Belgium	20	27	0.1	0.1	12	14	8	13
Luxemburg	3	-	-	-	2	-	1	-
Switzerland	37	73	0.2	0.4	14	36	23	37
France	89	122	0.6	0.7	39	57	50	65
Germany	1,180	1,789	7.9	9.6	555	862	625	927
Poland	2,785	3,528	18.6	18.9	1,382	1,799	1,403	1,729
Czechoslovakia	77	191	0.5	1.0	35	91	42	100
Austria	529	371	3.5	2.0	261	193	268	178
Hungary	161	152	1.1	0.8	74	77	87	75
Yugoslavia	96	128	0.6	0.7	62	83	34	45
Russia (U. S. S. R.)	1,537	1,777	10.2	9.5	831	946	706	831
Lithuania	255	274	1.7	1.5	127	150	128	124
Latvia	18	15	0.1	0.1	8	10	10	5

COUNTRY OF BIRTH	BOTH SEXES		PERCENT		MALE		FEMALE	
	1940	1930	1940	1930	1940	1930	1940	1930
Finland	50	74	0.3	0.4	20	40	30	34
Rumania	81	111	0.5	0.6	43	58	38	53
Bulgaria	6	5	-	-	2	3	4	2
Turkey in Europe	3	-	-	-	2	-	1	-
Greece	99	146	0.7	0.8	73	104	26	42
Italy	4,908	5,508	32.7	29.6	2,755	3,140	2,153	2,368
Spain	9	12	0.1	0.1	6	8	3	4
Portugal	7	7	-	-	6	6	1	1
Other Europe	16	47	0.1	0.3	10	32	6	15
Palestine and Syria	11	7	0.1	-	8	3	3	4
Turkey in Asia	95	151	0.6	0.8	50	86	45	65
Other Asia	66	45	0.4	0.2	42	25	24	20
Canada—French	29	36	0.2	0.2	13	21	16	15
Canada—Other	190	337	1.3	1.8	88	157	102	180
Newfoundland	227	222	1.5	1.2	113	119	114	103
Mexico	6	7	-	-	4	7	2	-
Cuba and other West Indies	15	13	0.1	0.1	6	9	9	4
Central and South America	54	63	0.4	0.3	29	33	25	30
Australia	19	16	0.1	0.1	10	10	9	6
Azores	-	-	-	-	-	-	-	-
All other and not reported	12	22	0.1	0.1	6	11	6	11

Table A-41.—PERSONS 14 YEARS OLD AND OVER, BY EMPLOYMENT STATUS, CLASS OF WORKER, RACE, AND SEX, FOR THE CITY OF CAMDEN: 1940

[Percent not shown where less than 0.1 or where base is less than 100]

EMPLOYMENT STATUS	ALL CLASSES			NATIVE WHITE			FOREIGN-BORN WHITE			NEGRO			OTHER RACES		
	Total	Male	Female	Total	Male	Female	Total	Male	Female	Total	Male	Female	Total	Male	Female
Total population (all ages)	117,536	58,802	58,734	89,999	44,817	45,182	14,996	7,757	7,239	12,478	6,182	6,296	63	46	17
Persons 14 years old and over	93,463	46,542	46,921	69,232	34,239	34,993	14,938	7,730	7,208	9,238	4,531	4,707	55	42	13
In labor force	54,105	38,306	15,799	40,420	28,027	12,393	8,241	6,620	1,621	5,403	3,622	1,781	41	37	4
Not in labor force	39,358	8,236	31,122	28,812	6,212	22,600	6,697	1,110	5,587	3,835	909	2,926	14	5	9
Engaged in own home housew'k	24,396	287	24,109	17,452	197	17,255	4,928	64	4,864	2,010	26	1,984	6	-	6
In school	7,576	4,014	3,562	6,621	3,522	3,099	88	54	34	862	434	428	5	4	1
Unable to work	5,301	2,804	2,497	3,129	1,648	1,481	1,413	811	602	757	344	413	2	1	1
In institutions	65	55	10	49	47	2	2	2	-	14	6	8	-	-	-
Other and not reported	2,020	1,076	944	1,561	798	763	266	179	87	192	99	93	1	-	1
LABOR FORCE BY EMPLOYMENT STATUS															
In labor force	54,105	38,306	15,799	40,420	28,027	12,393	8,241	6,620	1,621	5,403	3,622	1,781	41	37	4
Employed (exc. public emerg. work)	41,588	29,081	12,507	31,785	21,887	9,898	6,948	5,514	1,434	2,819	1,647	1,172	36	33	3
At work	40,436	28,311	12,125	30,966	21,381	9,585	6,667	5,284	1,383	2,770	1,616	1,154	33	30	3
With a job	1,152	770	382	819	506	313	281	230	51	49	31	18	3	3	-
On public emerg. work (WPA, etc.)	4,103	3,460	643	2,496	2,020	476	411	381	30	1,194	1,057	137	2	2	-
Seeking work	8,414	5,765	2,649	6,139	4,120	2,019	882	725	157	1,390	918	472	3	2	1
Experienced workers	6,350	4,572	1,778	4,457	3,158	1,299	834	701	133	1,058	712	346	1	1	-
New workers	2,064	1,193	871	1,682	962	720	48	24	24	332	206	126	2	1	1
PERCENT BY SEX															
In labor force	100.0	70.8	29.2	100.0	69.3	30.7	100.0	80.3	19.7	100.0	67.0	33.0	-	-	-
Employed (exc. public emerg.)	100.0	69.9	30.1	100.0	68.9	31.1	100.0	79.4	20.6	100.0	58.4	41.6	-	-	-
On pub. emerg. work (WPA, etc.)	100.0	84.3	15.7	100.0	80.9	19.1	100.0	92.7	7.3	100.0	88.5	11.5	-	-	-
Seeking work	100.0	68.5	31.5	100.0	67.1	32.9	100.0	82.2	17.8	100.0	66.0	34.0	-	-	-
Not in labor force	100.0	20.9	79.1	100.0	21.6	78.4	100.0	16.6	83.4	100.0	23.7	76.3	-	-	-
Engaged in own home housew'k	100.0	1.2	98.8	100.0	1.1	98.9	100.0	1.3	98.7	100.0	1.3	98.7	-	-	-
In school	100.0	53.0	47.0	100.0	53.2	46.8	-	-	-	100.0	50.3	49.7	-	-	-
Unable to work	100.0	52.9	47.1	100.0	52.7	47.3	100.0	57.4	42.6	100.0	45.4	54.6	-	-	-
In institutions	-	-	-	-	-	-	-	-	-	-	-	-	-	-	-
Other and not reported	100.0	53.3	46.7	100.0	51.1	48.9	100.0	67.3	32.7	100.0	51.6	48.4	-	-	-
EMPLOYED WORKERS BY CLASS OF WORKER															
Employed (exc. public emerg.)	41,588	29,081	12,507	31,785	21,887	9,898	6,948	5,514	1,434	2,819	1,647	1,172	36	33	3
Wage and salary workers	37,291	25,568	11,723	29,245	19,868	9,377	5,403	4,177	1,226	2,631	1,513	1,118	12	10	2
Employers and own-account workers	3,912	3,307	605	2,236	1,845	391	1,487	1,317	170	168	124	44	21	21	-
Unpaid family workers	203	102	101	163	95	68	36	5	31	1	-	1	3	2	1
Class of worker not reported	182	104	78	141	79	62	22	15	7	19	10	9	-	-	-
At work	40,436	28,311	12,125	30,966	21,381	9,585	6,667	5,284	1,383	2,770	1,616	1,154	33	30	3
Wage and salary workers	36,684	25,235	11,449	28,765	19,618	9,147	5,301	4,109	1,192	2,606	1,498	1,108	12	10	2
Employers and own-account workers	3,411	2,895	516	1,929	1,607	322	1,314	1,159	155	150	111	39	18	18	-
Unpaid family workers	197	100	97	157	93	64	36	5	31	1	-	1	3	2	1
Class of worker not reported	144	81	63	115	63	52	16	11	5	13	7	6	-	-	-
With a job	1,152	770	382	819	506	313	281	230	51	49	31	18	3	3	-
Wage and salary workers	607	333	274	480	250	230	102	68	34	25	15	10	-	-	-
Employers and own-account workers	501	412	89	307	238	69	173	158	15	18	13	5	3	3	-
Unpaid family workers	6	2	4	6	2	4	-	-	-	-	-	-	-	-	-
Class of worker not reported	38	23	15	26	16	10	6	4	2	6	3	3	-	-	-
PERCENT DISTRIBUTION															
Persons 14 years old and over	100.0	100.0	100.0	100.0	100.0	100.0	100.0	100.0	100.0	100.0	100.0	100.0	-	-	-
In labor force	57.9	82.3	33.7	58.4	81.9	35.4	55.2	85.6	22.5	58.5	79.9	37.8	-	-	-
Not in labor force	42.1	17.7	66.3	41.6	18.1	64.6	44.8	14.4	77.5	41.5	20.1	62.2	-	-	-
Engaged in own home housew'k	26.1	0.6	51.4	25.2	0.6	49.3	33.0	0.8	67.5	21.8	0.6	42.1	-	-	-
In school	8.1	8.6	7.6	9.6	10.3	8.9	0.6	0.7	0.5	9.3	9.6	9.1	-	-	-
Unable to work	5.7	6.0	5.3	4.5	4.8	4.2	9.5	10.5	8.4	8.2	7.6	8.8	-	-	-
In institutions	0.1	0.1	-	0.1	0.1	-	-	-	-	0.2	0.1	0.2	-	-	-
Other and not reported	2.2	2.3	2.0	2.3	2.3	2.2	1.8	2.3	1.2	2.1	2.2	2.0	-	-	-
LABOR FORCE BY EMPLOYMENT STATUS															
In labor force	100.0	100.0	100.0	100.0	100.0	100.0	100.0	100.0	100.0	100.0	100.0	100.0	-	-	-
Employed (exc. public emerg. work)	76.9	75.9	79.2	78.6	78.1	79.9	84.3	83.3	88.5	52.2	45.5	65.8	-	-	-
At work	74.7	73.9	76.7	76.6	76.3	77.3	80.9	79.8	85.3	51.3	44.6	64.8	-	-	-
With a job	2.1	2.0	2.4	2.0	1.8	2.5	3.4	3.5	3.1	0.9	0.9	1.0	-	-	-
On public emerg. work (WPA, etc.)	7.6	9.0	4.1	6.2	7.2	3.8	5.0	5.8	1.9	22.1	29.2	7.7	-	-	-
Seeking work	15.6	15.0	16.8	15.2	14.7	16.3	10.7	11.0	9.7	25.7	25.3	26.5	-	-	-
Experienced workers	11.7	11.9	11.3	11.0	11.3	10.5	10.1	10.6	8.2	19.6	19.7	19.4	-	-	-
New workers	3.8	3.1	5.5	4.2	3.4	5.8	0.6	0.4	1.5	6.1	5.7	7.1	-	-	-
EMPLOYED WORKERS BY CLASS OF WORKER															
Employed (exc. public emerg.)	100.0	100.0	100.0	100.0	100.0	100.0	100.0	100.0	100.0	100.0	100.0	100.0	-	-	-
Wage and salary workers	89.7	87.9	93.7	92.0	90.8	94.7	77.8	75.6	85.5	93.3	91.9	95.4	-	-	-
Employers and own-account workers	9.4	11.4	4.8	7.0	8.4	4.0	21.4	23.9	11.9	6.0	7.5	3.8	-	-	-
Unpaid family workers	0.5	0.4	0.8	0.5	0.4	0.7	0.5	0.1	2.2	-	-	0.1	-	-	-
Class of worker not reported	0.4	0.4	0.6	0.4	0.4	0.6	0.3	0.3	0.5	0.7	0.6	0.8	-	-	-
At work	100.0	100.0	100.0	100.0	100.0	100.0	100.0	100.0	100.0	100.0	100.0	100.0	-	-	-
Wage and salary workers	90.7	89.1	94.4	92.9	91.8	95.4	79.5	77.8	86.2	94.1	92.7	96.0	-	-	-
Employers and own-account workers	8.4	10.2	4.3	6.2	7.5	3.4	19.7	21.9	11.2	5.4	6.9	3.4	-	-	-
Unpaid family workers	0.5	0.4	0.8	0.5	0.4	0.7	0.5	0.1	2.2	-	-	0.1	-	-	-
Class of worker not reported	0.4	0.3	0.5	0.4	0.3	0.5	0.2	0.2	0.4	0.5	0.4	0.5	-	-	-
With a job	100.0	100.0	100.0	100.0	100.0	100.0	100.0	100.0	-	-	-	-	-	-	-
Wage and salary workers	52.7	43.2	71.7	58.6	49.4	73.5	36.3	29.6	-	-	-	-	-	-	-
Employers and own-account workers	43.5	53.5	23.3	37.5	47.0	22.0	61.6	68.7	-	-	-	-	-	-	-
Unpaid family workers	0.5	0.3	1.0	0.7	0.4	1.3	-	-	-	-	-	-	-	-	-
Class of worker not reported	3.3	3.0	3.9	3.2	3.2	3.2	2.1	1.7	-	-	-	-	-	-	-

Table A-42.—EMPLOYED WORKERS 14 YEARS OLD AND OVER, BY MAJOR OCCUPATION GROUP, INDUSTRY GROUP, AND SEX, FOR THE CITY OF CAMDEN: 1940

[Percent not shown where less than 0.1 or where base is less than 100]

MAJOR OCCUPATION GROUP AND INDUSTRY GROUP	Total	Male	Female	PERCENT BY OCCUPATION AND INDUSTRY			PERCENT BY SEX	
				Total	Male	Female	Male	Female
Total population (all ages)	117,536	58,802	58,734	-	-	-	50.0	50.0
All persons 14 years old and over	93,463	46,542	46,921	-	-	-	49.8	50.2
In labor force	54,105	38,306	15,799	100.0	100.0	100.0	70.8	29.2
Employed workers (except on public emergency work)	41,588	29,081	12,507	76.9	75.9	79.2	69.9	30.1
MAJOR OCCUPATION GROUP								
Employed (except on public emergency work)	41,588	29,081	12,507	100.0	100.0	100.0	69.9	30.1
Professional workers	1,903	897	1,006	4.6	3.1	8.0	47.1	52.9
Semiprofessional workers	468	384	84	1.1	1.3	0.7	82.1	17.9
Farmers and farm managers	9	9	-	-	-	-	-	-
Proprietors, managers, and officials, except farm	2,753	2,405	348	6.6	8.3	2.8	87.4	12.6
Clerical, sales, and kindred workers	7,097	4,048	3,049	17.1	13.9	24.4	57.0	43.0
Craftsmen, foremen, and kindred workers	7,293	7,098	195	17.5	24.4	1.6	97.3	2.7
Operatives and kindred workers	12,729	7,864	4,865	30.6	27.0	38.9	61.8	38.2
Domestic service workers	1,279	33	1,246	3.1	0.1	10.0	2.6	97.4
Service workers, except domestic	3,522	2,399	1,123	8.5	8.2	9.0	68.1	31.9
Farm laborers (wage workers) and farm foremen	21	21	-	0.1	0.1	-	-	-
Farm laborers, unpaid family workers	1	1	-	-	-	-	-	-
Laborers, except farm	4,077	3,635	442	9.8	12.5	3.5	89.2	10.8
Occupation not reported	436	287	149	1.0	1.0	1.2	65.8	34.2
INDUSTRY GROUP								
Employed (except on public emergency work)	41,588	29,081	12,507	100.0	100.0	100.0	69.9	30.1
Agriculture, forestry, and fishery	57	55	2	0.1	0.2	-	-	-
Agriculture	50	48	2	0.1	0.2	-	-	-
Forestry (except logging) and fishery	7	7	-	-	-	-	-	-
Mining	10	9	1	-	-	-	-	-
Coal mining	-	-	-	-	-	-	-	-
Crude petroleum and natural gas production	2	2	-	-	-	-	-	-
Other mines and quarries	8	7	1	-	-	-	-	-
Construction	1,843	1,809	34	4.4	6.2	0.3	98.2	1.8
Manufacturing	20,073	14,168	5,905	48.3	48.7	47.2	70.6	29.4
Food and kindred products	2,492	1,740	752	6.0	6.0	6.0	69.8	30.2
Textile-mill products	897	558	339	2.2	1.9	2.7	62.2	37.8
Apparel and other fabricated textile products	1,246	337	909	3.0	1.2	7.3	27.0	73.0
Logging	2	2	-	-	-	-	-	-
Sawmills and planing mills	20	19	1	-	0.1	-	-	-
Furniture, store fixtures, and miscellaneous wooden goods	428	389	39	1.0	1.3	0.3	90.9	9.1
Paper and allied products	563	489	74	1.4	1.7	0.6	86.9	13.1
Printing, publishing, and allied industries	1,190	939	251	2.9	3.2	2.0	78.9	21.1
Chemicals and allied products	725	606	119	1.7	2.1	1.0	83.6	16.4
Petroleum and coal products	411	401	10	1.0	1.4	0.1	97.6	2.4
Leather and leather products	964	791	173	2.3	2.7	1.4	82.1	17.9
Stone, clay, and glass products	194	184	10	0.5	0.6	0.1	94.8	5.2
Iron and steel and their products	843	749	94	2.0	2.6	0.8	88.8	11.2
Nonferrous metals and their products	112	96	16	0.3	0.3	0.1	85.7	14.3
Machinery	3,630	2,290	1,340	8.7	7.9	10.7	63.1	36.9
Automobiles and automobile equipment	191	166	25	0.5	0.6	0.2	86.9	13.1
Transportation equipment, except automobile	3,222	3,173	49	7.7	10.9	0.4	98.5	1.5
Other and not specified manufacturing industries	2,943	1,239	1,704	7.1	4.3	13.6	42.1	57.9
Transportation, communication, and other public utilities	2,921	2,638	283	7.0	9.1	2.3	90.3	9.7
Railroads (including railroad repair shops) and railway express service	988	962	26	2.4	3.3	0.2	97.4	2.6
Trucking service	278	273	5	0.7	0.9	-	98.2	1.8
Other transportation	813	793	20	2.0	2.7	0.2	97.5	2.5
Communication	335	124	211	0.8	0.4	1.7	37.0	63.0
Utilities	507	486	21	1.2	1.7	0.2	95.9	4.1
Wholesale and retail trade	7,116	5,290	1,826	17.1	18.2	14.6	74.3	25.7
Wholesale trade	793	693	100	1.9	2.4	0.8	87.4	12.6
Food and dairy products stores, and milk retailing	1,722	1,468	254	4.1	5.0	2.0	85.2	14.8
Eating and drinking places	1,239	752	487	3.0	2.6	3.9	60.7	39.3
Motor vehicles and accessories retailing, and filling stations	433	407	26	1.0	1.4	0.2	94.0	6.0
Other retail trade	2,929	1,970	959	7.0	6.8	7.7	67.3	32.7
Finance, insurance, and real estate	1,031	659	372	2.5	2.3	3.0	63.9	36.1
Business and repair services	780	693	87	1.9	2.4	0.7	88.8	11.2
Automobile storage, rental, and repair services	420	413	7	1.0	1.4	0.1	98.3	1.7
Business and repair services, except automobile	360	280	80	0.9	1.0	0.6	77.8	22.2
Personal services	2,855	960	1,895	6.9	3.3	15.2	33.6	66.4
Domestic service	1,359	72	1,287	3.3	0.2	10.3	5.3	94.7
Hotels and lodging places	317	155	162	0.8	0.5	1.3	48.9	51.1
Laundering, cleaning, and dyeing services	413	241	172	1.0	0.8	1.4	58.4	41.6
Miscellaneous personal services	766	492	274	1.8	1.7	2.2	64.2	35.8
Amusement, recreation, and related services	266	220	46	0.6	0.8	0.4	82.7	17.3
Professional and related services	2,301	926	1,375	5.5	3.2	11.0	40.2	59.8
Government	1,312	1,078	234	3.2	3.7	1.9	82.2	17.8
Industry not reported	1,023	576	447	2.5	2.0	3.6	56.3	43.7

Table A-43.—PERSONS 14 YEARS OLD AND OVER IN THE LABOR FORCE, 1940, AND GAINFUL WORKERS 14 YEARS OLD AND OVER, 1930, BY RACE AND SEX, FOR THE CITY OF CAMDEN

[Totals for population and gainful workers for 1930 include "Unknown age." Figures for white population in 1930 have been revised to include Mexicans who were classified with "Other races" in the 1930 reports. Percent not shown where less than 0.1 or where base is less than 100]

CENSUS YEAR AND RACE	TOTAL					MALE					FEMALE				
	Population		Persons in the labor force, and gainful workers,[1] 14 years old and over			Population		Persons in the labor force, and gainful workers,[1] 14 years old and over			Population		Persons in the labor force, and gainful workers,[1] 14 years old and over		
	Total (all ages)	14 years old and over	Number	Per-cent of total popu-lation	Per-cent of popu-lation 14 yrs. and over	Total (all ages)	14 years old and over	Number	Per-cent of total popu-lation	Per-cent of popu-lation 14 yrs. and over	Total (all ages)	14 years old and over	Number	Per-cent of total popu-lation	Per-cent of popu-lation 14 yrs. and over
1940	117,536	93,463	54,105	46.0	57.9	58,802	46,542	38,306	65.1	82.3	58,734	46,921	15,799	26.9	33.7
White	104,995	84,170	48,661	46.3	57.8	52,574	41,969	34,647	65.9	82.6	52.421	42,201	14,014	26.7	33.2
Negro	12,478	9,238	5,403	43.3	58.5	6,182	4,531	3,622	58.6	79.9	6,296	4,707	1,781	28.3	37.8
Other races	63	55	41	-	-	46	42	37	-	-	17	13	4	-	-
1930	118,700	87,135	50,118	42.2	57.5	59,442	43,707	37,460	63.0	85.7	59,258	43,428	12,658	21.4	29.1
White	107,292	78,845	44,723	41.7	56.7	53,713	39,509	33,797	62.9	85.5	53,579	39,336	10,926	20.4	27.8
Negro	11,340	8,236	5,349	47.2	64.9	5,676	4,151	3,618	63.7	87.2	5,664	4,085	1,731	30.6	42.4
Other races	68	54	46	-	-	53	47	45	-	-	15	7	1	-	-

[1] Data for 1930 represent gainful workers 14 years old and over.

"Television Draws 1,700 to Theatre, Images Generally Clear," New York Times, October 23, 1931

"More than 1,700 persons visited the Broadway Theatre yesterday morning to see on a large screen television images flashed by wire lines from an improvised stage in the lobby of the Theatre Guild Playerhouse, a few hundred yards' distance. The audience displayed a keen interest in the demonstration. Except for bursts of spontaneous applause at the ends of the feature presentations, the spectators were completely absorbed in the mysteries of the new science of seeing by electrical means. For the most part, the images were clear enough to afford recognition of a well-known face.

Only once was it necessary to interrupt the show; the operator turned off the mechanism for a few minutes to allow the glow tube in the receiver to cool. During the lull in the scheduled program, Carveth Wells, who served as master of ceremonies, told about the television mechanism. He made it clear that while television is still in a process of development, the Broadway management desired to place on record its conviction that the new art has reached the point where it can command recognition from the theatres.

One feature presented was part of a scene from a current Broadway production. The players were Margaret Barker and Franchot Tone. The images flashed on a screen 10 feet square simultaneously with the sound of their voices reproduced by loudspeakers. Emily Day, formerly soprano of the National Grand Opera of Mexico, Carl Paul Ican, Indian baritone of the Philadelphia Grand Opera Company, and Ruth Burns, New York actress, did the singing...The system used was that developed by Ulisses A. Sanabria, chief engineer of Sanabria Television of Chicago."

Dr. C.B. Jolliffe, chief engineer of the Federal Radio Commission, 1931: "In the opinion of the engineers, television is still in an experimental stage. Every time you see anything about television in the papers today, something is bound to be said about 'great progress,' or 'revolutionary invention.' The greatest progress I have noticed in the past few months has been in publicity. The basic principles of present-day television were laid down several years ago, but progress seems faster now because engineers are making refinements to those basic principles. The progress of television is steady and normal, with nothing unusual about it, not even the statement that recognition (by the Federal Radio Commission) is just around the corner."

"Television, Is It Getting Anywhere?"
by George Tichenor, *The Forum,* October 1931

"A variety of programs are regularly broadcast, with sound accompaniment. There have been Helen Morgan, Vera Hurst, George Gershwin, Sigmund Spaeth, and others in individual appearances. Jimmy McLaunin, boxer, and Ray Steele, wrestler, were interviewed. A fashion show was staged by W2XCR, with six models parading before the camera. Boxing bouts, fencing, golf lessons, and even piano lessons have been scheduled. From its Passaic station, W2XCD, the DeForest Company conducted the first band concert by remote control. The concert was given by the police band at their headquarters. The Commissioner of Public Safety led the movements before the transmitter in the studio. His Lieutenant in the concert hall followed the directions as he viewed them in the receiver, and a sound radio hook-up brought the music back to the studio so the Commissioner could take up his lead.

The Jenkins studio once broadcast pictures that were received on the *Ile de France,* but the Shortwave and Television Corporation of Boston outshowmanshipped its rival by sending to the *Leviathan,* which is, of course, a larger boat. The Chicago Daily News station, W9XAP, claims to have broadcast the first sight and sound play, with WMAW as a sound outlet. The air talk was presented in movie style: close-ups, without a break in the dialogue. Station W2XCW, of Schenectady, New York, on 20,000 watts, has sent out images received in Germany."

How Wheaties Became "Breakfast of Champions"

Consumers of 1940 were tough customers, and decided they weren't ready for healthy, whole wheat flakes. Undaunted, Donald Davis used sophisticated consumer surveys and the immediacy of national radio to breathe new life into Wheaties breakfast cereal, creating a brand so popular, that children everywhere wanted to be a Wheaties champion.

Life at Home

- Donald Davis helped raise the visibility of both ready-to-eat Wheaties and the fledgling business of radio advertising.
- Wheaties started its life as the scattered droppings on a hot stove, when a Minneapolis health clinician stirred a batch of bran gruel a little too vigorously, resulting in the spill.
- The result was thin wafers of wheat bran, the first of many steps to a healthy, tasty breakfast food.
- It took two years, and 36 varieties of wheat, before the Washburn-Crosby Company, the forerunner to General Mills, discovered a flake that would not crumble in the box.
- The discovery came at a time when bran was being touted as ideal for digestion and an increasingly urban America was showing an interest in breakfast cereal that demanded less preparation.
- The wife of a Washburn-Crosby Company executive, who won a company-sponsored contest to name the new product, suggested Wheaties because "there's nothing as endearing as a nickname."
- Once on the grocery shelves, however, Wheaties was quickly termed "a slow mover."
- Company executive Donald Davis believed that the customer was not simply a sales report; but a human being with needs to be satisfied and tastes to be pleased.
- With an engineer's faith in numbers, Davis devised a plan to ask thousands of customers in every geographic area what they wished to eat, what products they liked best and what newspapers and magazines they read.
- His researchers rang doorbells, made phone calls and mailed out questionnaires, constantly on the prowl for data on the American housewife.
- What he discovered was that American women liked to be spoken to directly, frequently and intimately where matters of food were concerned.
- These preferences spawned the answer lady—Betty Crocker—as a way to give a personalized response to consumer questions.

Donald Davis made Wheaties visible through the media.

- Under the supervision of home economist and businesswoman Marjorie Child Husted, the image of Betty Crocker was transformed into an icon for General Mills, and received thousands of letters daily.
- In this environment, Donald proposed to operate the company's own radio station to promote Minneapolis-St. Paul and General Mills's products.
- "Let's walk around the idea," Donald told his staff.
- Radio was still in its infancy, viewed by most as a toy, but Donald saw it as a major force of communications, and was determined to make his company a pioneer in this new medium.
- Donald pulled together a group of Minneapolis-St. Paul businessmen to buy half of a failing radio station and its equipment, on the condition the Twin Cities would assume responsibility for the other half, and the stations call letters were changed to WCCO for Washburn-Crosby Company.
- Seven months later, WCCO made history in the Midwest by using its 5,000-watt voice to broadcast the inauguration of President Calvin Coolidge.
- Thus, the stage was set for Wheaties and radio to execute a decade-long two step that benefited both.

The first singing commercials were used to promote Wheaties.

Life at Work

- Donald Davis helped breathe new life into the flagging cereal brand Wheaties when Minnesota radio station WCCO formed a male quartet named The Gold Medal Four composed of a municipal court bailiff, printer, businessman, and undertaker, who were paid $24 a week for their work.
- Together, they produced the world's first singing commercial, sung to the tune of the popular song, "She's a Jazz Baby."
- "Have you tried Wheaties?/They're whole wheat with all the bran/Won't you try Wheaties?/For wheat is the best food of man."

"The Breakfast of Champions" slogan was first used by the Minneapolis Millers.

- Two years later, as pressure mounted to dump the lagging Wheaties brand at the newly named General Mills Company, research showed that of the 53,000 cases of Wheaties shipped annually, 30,000 cases were going to the Minneapolis-St. Paul area, where the commercials were being broadcast.
- The advertising was working, but a new national approach was needed to attain the company's goal to "develop services worthy of the American people."
- The management of General Mills, even before Donald became its president, believed that advertising copy must be "truthful, based on the concept of service, and must be designed to expand the market and not simply take business from the competitors."
- The answer to saving Wheaties was nationwide radio.
- If Wheaties was to be a national brand, Donald fully understood that radio advertising, featuring the Wheaties quartet on national hook-up, was a necessary gamble.
- The vehicle would be the sponsorship of half-hour music programs being created by an upstart company known as Columbia Broadcasting Company, and the message needed to be tailored to the right audience.
- The answer came in the form of *Skippy*, a popular comic strip with both the public and Donald personally, who could be transformed into a radio character.
- This gave General Mills a way to talk directly to children; an advertisement in *The Saturday Evening Post* reading "Make Your Child Love Whole Wheat" was clearly not working.
- Teamed with *Skippy*, Wheaties offered special treats like membership in a secret-society-of-the-air, unfiltered by parents, for the price of several box tops.
- To make sure mothers were not alienated, Donald's team worked with *Skippy* creator Percy Crosby to organize "no more arguments at breakfast" campaigns.
- When *Skippy*'s power to persuade began to fade, Jack Armstrong, the All-American Boy, became the next General Mills radio phenomenon, whose storylines centered around the globe-trotting adventures of Armstrong, a popular athlete at Hudson High School, his friends Billy Fairfield and Billy's sister Betty, and their "Uncle Jim," James Fairfield, an industrialist.
- "Uncle Jim" Fairfield's need to visit exotic parts of the world in connection with his business gave Jack Armstrong plenty of adventures.
- Sponsored throughout its run by Wheaties, the 15-minute serial often offered radio premiums, "souvenirs" of the various shows that usually related to Jack's adventures.
- The campaign to push ham and eggs off the breakfast table was further advanced when Donald launched the company into major radio sponsorship of baseball-the domain of men.
- Since Wheaties advertising appeared on a billboard at Nicollet Park, home of the Minneapolis Millers minor league baseball team, the slogan "The Breakfast of Champions," was created to meet the needs of billboard advertising, and then became as familiar as the famous athletes that gave testimonials for the cereal.
- Wheaties-sponsored baseball broadcasts began from one radio station in Minneapolis, Minnesota, initially covering the minor league Minneapolis Millers on station WCCO.
- This radio sponsorship of baseball games expanded to 95 other radio stations and professional teams throughout the country, and the sale of Wheaties followed, topping 1.5 million cases.

- The General Mills Company began including pictures of athletes on its Wheaties boxes, the first being baseball stars Lou Gehrig of the New York Yankees and Jimmie Foxx of the Philadelphia Athletics.
- They were followed by aviator Elinor Smith and tennis star Ellsworth Vines.
- Within a few years, the slogan "Breakfast of Champions" was so ingrained in the sports culture that athletes who struck out or missed an easy fly ball were accused of failing to "eat their Wheaties" that day.

Life in the Community: Minneapolis-Saint Paul, Minnesota

- Minneapolis-Saint Paul, the most populous urban area in the state of Minnesota, was built around the Mississippi, Minnesota and St. Croix rivers.
- Growth was fueled by agriculture, and the region became the acknowledged leader in the production of breadstuffs.
- Farmers found that hard red spring wheat was the answer to the harsh, physical conditions of the north central states, and the wheat's hardness resulted from a higher proportion of gluten to starch, giving it a special value as a bread flour.
- The area was nicknamed The Twin Cities for its two largest cities, Minneapolis and Saint Paul, the former the larger and the latter the state capital.
- Despite the Twin moniker, the two cities had independent municipalities with defined borders and were quite distinct from each other
- Minneapolis was influenced by its early Scandinavian/Lutheran heritage, while St. Paul was characterized by its early French, Irish and German Catholic roots.
- Minneapolis and St. Paul have competed against each other since they were founded.
- Both cities built campuses of the University of Minnesota, and competing cathedrals, and the rivalry even led to the two cities arresting and kidnapping each other's census takers in an attempt to keep either city from outgrowing the other.
- The situation occasionally erupted into inter-city violence, as happened at a game between the Minneapolis Millers and the St. Paul Saints, both baseball teams of the American Association.

Wheaties offered special membership for kids.

The nine tables that follow are reprinted from the actual 1940 census, for the city of Minneapolis. They include actual data on race, percentage of voting population, school attendance, number of school years completed, foreign born, and employment of workers 14 years and older by job, industry and race. In addition to being incredibly fascinating, these facts help to strengthen and visualize the actual environment in which Donald Davis lived and worked. Tables for St. Paul immediately follow those for Minneapolis.

Table B-35.—AGE, BY RACE AND SEX, FOR THE CITY OF MINNEAPOLIS: 1940 AND 1930

[Figures for white population in 1930 revised to include Mexicans classified with "Other races" in the 1930 reports. Percent not shown where less than 0.1 or where base is less than 100]

AGE AND CENSUS YEAR	ALL CLASSES			NATIVE WHITE			FOREIGN-BORN WHITE			NEGRO			OTHER RACES		
	Total	Male	Female	Total	Male	Female	Total	Male	Female	Total	Male	Female	Total	Male	Female
All ages: 1940	492,370	234,542	257,828	422,950	197,302	225,648	64,149	34,424	29,725	4,646	2,378	2,268	625	438	187
Under 5 years	31,116	15,942	15,174	30,783	15,788	14,995	16	8	8	255	115	140	62	31	31
5 to 9 years	29,456	14,873	14,583	29,065	14,676	14,389	42	23	19	303	152	151	46	22	24
10 to 14 years	33,850	16,915	16,935	33,369	16,667	16,702	110	49	61	327	171	156	44	28	16
15 to 19 years	40,812	19,425	21,387	39,947	18,996	20,951	474	236	238	339	165	174	52	28	24
20 to 24 years	46,532	20,355	26,177	45,407	19,825	25,582	753	348	405	332	157	175	40	25	15
25 to 29 years	42,876	19,341	23,535	40,941	18,396	22,545	1,479	708	771	372	172	200	84	65	19
30 to 34 years	39,675	18,201	21,474	36,734	16,626	20,108	2,477	1,302	1,175	375	204	171	85	69	20
35 to 39 years	38,048	17,425	20,623	33,655	15,092	18,563	3,981	2,096	1,885	365	199	166	47	38	9
40 to 44 years	38,020	17,900	20,120	32,341	14,875	17,466	5,252	2,811	2,441	390	185	205	37	29	8
45 to 49 years	37,231	18,166	19,065	29,371	13,673	15,698	7,411	4,242	3,169	413	223	190	36	28	8
50 to 54 years	33,218	16,826	16,392	23,721	11,272	12,449	9,114	5,340	3,774	349	187	162	34	27	7
55 to 59 years	25,150	12,746	12,404	16,336	7,754	8,582	8,517	4,825	3,692	280	153	127	17	14	3
60 to 64 years	18,920	9,134	9,786	11,434	5,159	6,275	7,270	3,849	3,421	205	115	90	11	11	-
65 to 69 years	14,648	6,916	7,732	8,468	3,707	4,761	5,996	3,110	2,886	173	90	83	11	9	2
70 to 74 years	10,633	4,908	5,725	5,590	2,399	3,191	4,954	2,456	2,498	83	47	36	6	6	-
75 years and over	12,185	5,469	6,716	5,788	2,397	3,391	6,303	3,021	3,282	85	43	42	9	8	1
Under 1 year	6,760	3,467	3,293	6,679	3,439	3,240	1	1	-	70	23	47	10	4	6
5 years	5,765	2,944	2,821	5,686	2,896	2,790	14	8	6	55	34	21	10	6	4
14 years	7,300	3,664	3,636	7,191	3,611	3,580	27	11	16	69	31	38	13	11	2
15 years	7,426	3,734	3,692	7,333	3,687	3,646	31	19	12	55	26	29	7	2	5
16 and 17 years	15,697	7,811	7,886	15,360	7,653	7,707	172	80	92	149	71	78	16	7	9
21 years and over	348,424	163,726	184,698	281,296	127,616	153,680	63,358	34,041	29,317	3,354	1,743	1,611	416	326	90
All ages: 1930	464,356	225,547	238,809	378,694	179,165	199,529	80,936	43,783	37,153	4,176	2,189	1,987	550	410	140
Under 5 years	34,177	17,322	16,855	33,800	17,130	16,670	55	23	32	286	150	136	36	19	17
5 to 9 years	38,685	19,689	18,996	37,923	19,313	18,610	420	204	216	299	150	149	43	22	21
10 to 14 years	36,986	18,489	18,497	36,149	18,072	18,077	556	273	283	250	129	121	31	15	16
15 to 19 years	37,008	17,172	19,836	35,475	16,409	19,066	1,248	609	639	233	110	123	52	44	8
20 to 24 years	43,308	18,831	24,477	40,244	17,219	23,025	2,640	1,373	1,267	314	148	166	110	91	19
25 to 29 years	40,926	18,216	22,710	36,336	15,850	20,486	4,173	2,133	2,040	339	169	170	78	64	14
30 to 34 years	40,926	19,036	21,890	35,048	15,994	19,054	5,413	2,791	2,622	434	227	207	31	24	7
35 to 39 years	41,803	20,642	21,161	32,875	15,546	17,329	8,394	4,803	3,591	494	265	229	40	28	12
40 to 44 years	36,469	18,803	17,666	26,050	12,720	13,330	9,971	5,820	4,151	407	229	178	41	34	7
45 to 49 years	29,864	15,410	14,454	19,306	9,347	9,959	10,144	5,836	4,308	379	201	178	35	26	9
50 to 54 years	23,446	11,817	11,629	14,256	6,832	7,424	8,903	4,816	4,087	266	153	113	21	16	5
55 to 59 years	18,192	9,267	8,925	10,560	5,069	5,491	7,421	4,069	3,352	198	117	81	13	12	1
60 to 64 years	15,020	7,444	7,576	7,799	3,668	4,131	7,094	3,707	3,387	117	60	57	10	9	1
65 to 69 years	12,132	6,037	6,095	5,762	2,735	3,027	6,284	3,248	3,036	81	50	31	5	4	1
70 to 74 years	8,026	4,003	4,023	3,780	1,816	1,964	4,215	2,177	2,038	30	10	20	1	-	1
75 years and over	7,185	3,286	3,899	3,165	1,384	1,781	3,974	1,884	2,090	44	17	27	2	1	1
Not reported	203	83	120	166	61	105	31	17	14	5	4	1	1	1	-
Under 1 year	6,377	3,310	3,067	6,326	3,283	3,043	2	1	1	43	23	20	6	3	3
5 years	7,604	3,931	3,673	7,511	3,881	3,630	30	16	14	54	28	26	9	6	3
14 years	7,573	3,711	3,862	7,377	3,617	3,760	141	66	75	47	22	25	8	6	2
15 years	7,292	3,582	3,710	7,057	3,456	3,601	174	90	84	56	31	25	5	5	-
16 and 17 years	14,063	6,804	7,259	13,531	6,548	6,983	431	211	220	84	33	51	17	12	5
21 years and over	308,983	149,381	159,602	227,344	105,003	122,341	78,224	42,462	35,762	3,052	1,626	1,426	363	290	73
Percent: 1940	100.0	100.0	100.0	100.0	100.0	100.0	100.0	100.0	100.0	100.0	100.0	100.0	100.0	100.0	100.0
Under 5 years	6.3	6.8	5.9	7.3	8.0	6.6	-	-	-	5.5	4.8	6.2	9.9	7.1	16.6
5 to 9 years	6.0	6.3	5.7	6.9	7.4	6.4	0.1	0.1	0.1	6.5	6.4	6.7	7.4	5.0	12.8
10 to 14 years	6.9	7.2	6.6	7.9	8.4	7.4	0.2	0.1	0.2	7.0	7.2	6.9	7.0	6.4	8.6
15 to 19 years	8.3	8.3	8.3	9.4	9.6	9.3	0.7	0.7	0.8	7.3	6.9	7.7	8.3	6.4	12.8
20 to 24 years	9.5	8.7	10.2	10.7	10.0	11.3	1.2	1.0	1.4	7.1	6.6	7.7	6.4	5.7	8.0
25 to 29 years	8.7	8.2	9.1	9.7	9.3	10.0	2.3	2.1	2.6	8.0	7.2	8.8	13.4	14.8	10.2
30 to 34 years	8.1	7.8	8.3	8.7	8.4	8.9	3.9	3.8	4.0	8.1	8.6	7.5	14.2	15.8	10.7
35 to 39 years	7.7	7.4	8.0	8.0	7.6	8.2	6.2	6.1	6.3	7.9	8.4	7.3	7.5	8.7	4.8
40 to 44 years	7.7	7.6	7.8	7.6	7.5	7.7	8.2	8.2	8.2	8.4	7.8	9.0	5.9	6.6	4.3
45 to 49 years	7.6	7.7	7.4	6.9	6.9	7.0	11.6	12.3	10.7	8.9	9.4	8.4	5.8	6.4	4.3
50 to 54 years	6.7	7.2	6.4	5.6	5.7	5.5	14.2	15.5	12.7	7.5	7.9	7.1	5.4	6.2	3.7
55 to 59 years	5.1	5.4	4.8	3.9	3.9	3.8	13.3	14.0	12.4	6.0	6.4	5.6	2.7	3.2	1.6
60 to 64 years	3.8	3.9	3.8	2.7	2.6	2.8	11.3	11.2	11.5	4.4	4.8	4.0	1.8	2.5	-
65 to 69 years	3.0	2.9	3.0	2.0	1.9	2.1	9.3	9.0	9.7	3.7	3.8	3.7	1.8	2.1	1.1
70 to 74 years	2.2	2.1	2.2	1.3	1.2	1.4	7.7	7.1	8.4	1.8	2.0	1.6	1.0	1.4	-
75 years and over	2.5	2.3	2.6	1.4	1.2	1.5	9.8	8.8	11.0	1.8	1.8	1.9	1.4	1.8	0.5
Under 1 year	1.4	1.5	1.3	1.6	1.7	1.4	-	-	-	1.5	1.0	2.1	1.6	0.9	3.2
5 years	1.2	1.3	1.1	1.3	1.5	1.2	-	-	-	1.2	1.4	0.9	1.6	1.4	2.1
14 years	1.5	1.6	1.4	1.7	1.8	1.6	-	-	0.1	1.5	1.3	1.7	2.1	2.5	1.1
15 years	1.5	1.6	1.4	1.7	1.9	1.6	-	0.1	-	1.2	1.1	1.3	1.1	0.5	2.7
16 and 17 years	3.2	3.3	3.1	3.6	3.9	3.4	0.3	0.2	0.3	3.2	3.0	3.4	2.6	1.6	4.8
21 years and over	70.8	69.8	71.6	66.5	64.7	68.1	98.8	98.9	98.6	72.2	73.3	71.0	66.6	74.4	48.1
Percent: 1930	100.0	100.0	100.0	100.0	100.0	100.0	100.0	100.0	100.0	100.0	100.0	100.0	100.0	100.0	100.0
Under 5 years	7.4	7.7	7.1	8.9	9.6	8.4	0.1	0.1	0.1	6.8	6.9	6.8	6.5	4.6	12.1
5 to 9 years	8.3	8.7	8.0	10.0	10.8	9.3	0.5	0.5	0.6	7.2	6.9	7.5	7.8	5.4	15.0
10 to 14 years	8.0	8.2	7.7	9.5	10.1	9.1	0.7	0.6	0.8	6.0	5.9	6.1	5.6	3.7	11.4
15 to 19 years	8.0	7.6	8.3	9.4	9.2	9.6	1.5	1.4	1.7	5.6	5.0	6.2	9.5	10.7	5.7
20 to 24 years	9.3	8.3	10.2	10.6	9.6	11.5	3.3	3.1	3.4	7.5	6.8	8.4	20.0	22.2	13.6
25 to 29 years	8.8	8.1	9.5	9.6	8.8	10.3	5.2	4.9	5.5	8.1	7.7	8.6	14.2	15.6	10.0
30 to 34 years	8.8	8.4	9.2	9.3	8.9	9.5	6.7	6.4	7.1	10.4	10.4	10.4	5.6	5.9	5.0
35 to 39 years	9.0	9.2	8.9	8.7	8.7	8.7	10.4	11.0	9.7	11.8	12.1	11.5	7.3	6.8	8.6
40 to 44 years	7.9	8.3	7.4	6.9	7.1	6.7	12.3	13.3	11.2	9.7	10.5	9.0	7.5	8.3	5.0
45 to 49 years	6.4	6.8	6.1	5.1	5.2	5.0	12.5	13.3	11.6	9.1	9.2	9.0	6.4	6.3	6.4
50 to 54 years	5.0	5.2	4.9	3.8	3.8	3.7	11.0	11.0	11.0	6.4	7.0	5.7	3.8	3.9	3.6
55 to 59 years	3.9	4.1	3.7	2.8	2.8	2.8	9.2	9.3	9.0	4.7	5.3	4.1	2.4	2.9	0.7
60 to 64 years	3.2	3.3	3.2	2.1	2.0	2.1	8.8	8.5	9.1	2.8	2.7	2.9	1.8	2.2	0.7
65 to 69 years	2.6	2.7	2.6	1.5	1.5	1.5	7.8	7.4	8.2	1.9	2.3	1.6	0.9	1.0	0.7
70 to 74 years	1.7	1.8	1.7	1.0	1.0	1.0	5.2	5.0	5.5	0.7	0.5	1.0	0.2	-	0.7
75 years and over	1.5	1.5	1.6	0.8	0.8	0.9	4.9	4.3	5.6	1.1	0.8	1.4	0.4	0.2	0.7
Not reported	-	-	0.1	-	-	0.1	-	-	-	0.1	0.2	0.1	0.2	0.2	-
Under 1 year	1.4	1.5	1.3	1.7	1.8	1.5	-	-	-	1.0	1.1	1.0	1.1	0.7	2.1
5 years	1.6	1.7	1.5	2.0	2.2	1.8	-	-	-	1.3	1.3	1.3	1.6	1.5	2.1
14 years	1.6	1.6	1.6	1.9	2.0	1.9	0.2	0.2	0.2	1.1	1.0	1.3	1.5	1.5	1.4
15 years	1.6	1.6	1.6	1.9	1.9	1.8	0.2	0.2	0.2	1.3	1.4	1.3	0.9	1.2	-
16 and 17 years	3.0	3.0	3.0	3.6	3.7	3.5	0.5	0.5	0.6	2.0	1.5	2.6	3.1	2.9	3.6
21 years and over	66.5	66.2	66.8	60.0	58.6	61.3	96.6	97.0	96.3	73.1	74.3	71.8	66.0	70.7	52.1

Table B-36.—RACE, BY NATIVITY AND SEX, FOR THE CITY OF MINNEAPOLIS: 1940 AND 1930

[Figures for white population in 1930 have been revised to include Mexicans who were classified with "Other races" in the 1930 reports. Percent not shown where less than 0.1 or where base is less than 100. Sex ratio not shown where number of females is less than 100]

SEX, NATIVITY, AND CENSUS YEAR	All classes	White	Negro	Other races	Other races: Indian	Other races: Chinese	Other races: Japanese	Other races: All other	Percent by race: All classes	Percent by race: White	Percent by race: Negro	Percent by race: Other races	Percent by nativity: All classes	Percent by nativity: White	Percent by nativity: Negro	Percent by nativity: Indian	Percent by nativity: Chinese	Percent by nativity: Japanese
TOTAL																		
1940	492,370	487,099	4,646	625	145	304	24	152	100.0	98.9	0.9	0.1	100.0	100.0	100.0	100.0	100.0	-
Native	428,006	422,950	4,617	439	136	137	14	152	100.0	98.8	1.1	0.1	86.9	86.8	99.4	93.8	45.1	-
Foreign born	64,364	64,149	29	186	9	167	10	-	100.0	99.7	-	0.3	13.1	13.2	0.6	6.2	54.9	-
1930	464,356	459,630	4,176	550	158	221	38	133	100.0	99.0	0.9	0.1	100.0	100.0	100.0	100.0	100.0	-
Native	383,233	378,694	4,148	391	152	91	15	133	100.0	98.8	1.1	0.1	82.5	82.4	99.3	96.2	41.2	-
Foreign born	81,123	80,936	28	159	6	130	23	-	100.0	99.8	-	0.2	17.5	17.6	0.7	3.8	58.8	-
MALE																		
1940	234,542	231,726	2,378	438	66	232	18	122	100.0	98.8	1.0	0.2	100.0	100.0	100.0	-	100.0	-
Native	199,942	197,302	2,360	280	62	86	10	122	100.0	98.7	1.2	0.1	85.2	85.1	99.2	-	37.1	-
Foreign born	34,600	34,424	18	158	4	146	8	-	100.0	99.5	0.1	0.5	14.8	14.9	0.8	-	62.9	-
1930	225,547	222,948	2,189	410	78	175	30	127	100.0	98.8	1.0	0.2	100.0	100.0	100.0	-	100.0	-
Native	181,605	179,165	2,170	270	75	60	8	127	100.0	98.7	1.2	0.1	80.5	80.4	99.1	-	37.1	-
Foreign born	43,942	43,783	19	140	3	115	22	-	100.0	99.6	-	0.3	19.5	19.6	0.9	-	62.9	-
FEMALE																		
1940	257,828	255,373	2,268	187	79	72	6	30	100.0	99.0	0.9	0.1	100.0	100.0	100.0	-	-	-
Native	228,064	225,648	2,257	159	74	51	4	30	100.0	98.9	1.0	0.1	88.5	88.4	99.5	-	-	-
Foreign born	29,764	29,725	11	28	5	21	2	-	100.0	99.9	-	0.1	11.5	11.6	0.5	-	-	-
1930	238,809	236,682	1,987	140	80	46	8	6	100.0	99.1	0.8	0.1	100.0	100.0	100.0	-	-	-
Native	201,628	199,529	1,978	121	77	31	7	6	100.0	99.0	1.0	0.1	84.4	84.3	99.5	-	-	-
Foreign born	37,181	37,153	9	19	3	15	1	-	100.0	99.9	-	0.1	15.6	15.7	0.5	-	-	-
MALES PER 100 FEMALES																		
1940	91.0	90.7	104.9	234.2	-	-	-	-	-	-	-	-	-	-	-	-	-	-
Native	87.7	87.4	104.6	176.1	-	-	-	-	-	-	-	-	-	-	-	-	-	-
Foreign born	116.2	115.8	-	-	-	-	-	-	-	-	-	-	-	-	-	-	-	-
1930	94.4	94.2	110.2	292.9	-	-	-	-	-	-	-	-	-	-	-	-	-	-
Native	90.1	89.8	109.7	223.1	-	-	-	-	-	-	-	-	-	-	-	-	-	-
Foreign born	118.2	117.8	-	-	-	-	-	-	-	-	-	-	-	-	-	-	-	-

Table B-37.—POTENTIAL VOTING POPULATION, BY CITIZENSHIP, RACE, NATIVITY, AND SEX, FOR THE CITY OF MINNEAPOLIS: 1940 AND 1930

[Figures for white population in 1930 have been revised to include Mexicans who were classified with "Other races" in the 1930 reports. Percent not shown where less than 0.1]

CITIZENSHIP, RACE, AND NATIVITY	Total population (all ages): Total number 1940	Total number 1930	Percent 1940	Percent 1930	Male 1940	Male 1930	Female 1940	Female 1930	Population 21 years old and over: Total number 1940	Total number 1930	Percent 1940	Percent 1930	Male 1940	Male 1930	Female 1940	Female 1930
Total	492,370	464,356	100.0	100.0	234,542	225,547	257,828	238,809	348,424	308,983	100.0	100.0	163,726	149,381	184,698	159,602
Percent citizen	-	-	97.2	96.0	-	-	-	-	-	-	96.1	94.4	-	-	-	-
Percent alien and citiz. not rptd.	-	-	2.8	4.0	-	-	-	-	-	-	3.9	5.6	-	-	-	-
Citizen	478,545	445,599	100.0	100.0	227,058	215,144	251,487	230,455	334,982	291,735	100.0	100.0	156,431	139,757	178,551	151,978
White—Native	422,950	378,694	88.4	85.0	197,302	179,165	225,648	199,529	281,296	227,344	84.0	77.9	127,616	105,003	153,680	122,341
Naturalized	50,515	62,349	10.6	14.0	27,102	33,528	23,413	28,821	50,089	61,127	15.0	21.0	26,892	32,970	23,197	28,157
Negro—Native	4,617	4,148	1.0	0.9	2,360	2,170	2,257	1,978	3,326	3,025	1.0	1.0	1,725	1,608	1,601	1,417
Naturalized	24	17	-	-	14	11	10	6	23	16	-	-	14	10	9	6
Other races—Native	439	391	0.1	0.1	280	270	159	121	248	223	0.1	0.1	184	166	64	57
Indian	136	152	-	-	62	75	74	77	62	81	-	-	27	35	35	46
Chinese	137	91	-	-	86	60	51	31	70	44	-	-	52	37	18	7
Japanese	14	15	-	-	10	8	4	7	9	4	-	-	8	3	1	1
Filipino	147	133	-	-	120	127	27	6	103	94	-	-	95	91	8	3
Hindu	1	-	-	-	1	-	-	-	1	-	-	-	1	-	-	-
All other	4	-	-	-	1	-	3	-	3	-	-	-	1	-	2	-
Alien	10,036	17,451	100.0	100.0	5,665	9,767	4,371	7,684	9,741	15,999	100.0	100.0	5,520	9,011	4,221	6,988
White—First papers	4,103	5,760	40.9	33.0	2,854	4,240	1,249	1,520	4,069	5,599	41.8	35.0	2,836	4,146	1,233	1,453
No papers	5,744	11,524	57.2	66.0	2,650	5,381	3,094	6,143	5,501	10,252	56.5	64.1	2,539	4,785	2,962	5,517
Negro—First papers	-	3	-	-	-	1	-	2	-	3	-	-	-	1	-	2
No papers	3	5	-	-	3	5	-	-	3	5	-	-	3	5	-	-
Other races—Foreign born	186	159	1.9	0.9	158	140	28	19	168	140	1.7	0.9	142	124	26	16
Indian	9	6	0.1	-	4	3	5	3	9	6	0.1	-	4	3	5	3
Chinese	167	130	1.7	0.7	146	115	21	15	149	111	1.5	0.7	130	99	19	12
Japanese	10	23	0.1	0.1	8	22	2	1	10	23	0.1	0.1	8	22	2	1
Filipino	-	-	-	-	-	-	-	-	-	-	-	-	-	-	-	-
Hindu	-	-	-	-	-	-	-	-	-	-	-	-	-	-	-	-
All other	-	-	-	-	-	-	-	-	-	-	-	-	-	-	-	-
Citizenship not reported	3,789	1,306	100.0	100.0	1,819	636	1,970	670	3,701	1,249	100.0	100.0	1,775	613	1,926	636
White	3,787	1,303	99.9	99.8	1,818	634	1,969	669	3,699	1,246	99.9	99.8	1,774	611	1,925	635
Negro	2	3	0.1	0.2	1	2	1	1	2	3	0.1	0.2	1	2	1	1

Table B-38.—SCHOOL ATTENDANCE, BY AGE, RACE, AND SEX, FOR THE CITY OF MINNEAPOLIS: 1940 AND 1930

[Figures for white population in 1930 revised to include Mexicans classified with "Other races" in the 1930 reports. Percent not shown where less than 0.1 or where base is less than 100]

AGE, SEX, AND CENSUS YEAR	ALL CLASSES			NATIVE WHITE			FOREIGN-BORN WHITE			NEGRO			OTHER RACES		
	Total number	Attending school		Total number	Attending school		Total number	Attending school		Total number	Attending school		Total number	Attending school	
		Number	Percent		Number	Percent		Number	Percent		Number	Percent		Number	Percent
1940															
Total, 5 to 24 years	150,650	92,949	61.7	147,788	91,478	61.9	1,379	518	37.6	1,301	837	64.3	182	116	63.7
5 years	5,765	3,821	66.3	5,686	3,780	66.5	14	6	-	55	29	-	10	6	-
6 years	5,497	5,226	95.1	5,421	5,154	95.1	5	4	-	62	60	-	9	8	-
7 to 9 years	18,194	17,838	98.0	17,958	17,609	98.1	23	20	-	186	182	97.8	27	27	-
10 to 13 years	26,550	26,061	98.2	26,178	25,700	98.2	83	79	-	258	252	97.7	31	30	-
14 years	7,300	7,123	97.6	7,191	7,015	97.6	27	26	-	69	69	-	13	13	-
15 years	7,426	7,234	97.4	7,333	7,147	97.5	31	29	-	55	51	-	7	7	-
16 and 17 years	15,697	13,404	85.4	15,360	13,126	85.5	172	144	83.7	149	123	82.6	16	11	-
18 and 19 years	17,689	6,706	37.9	17,254	6,529	37.8	271	118	43.5	135	50	37.0	29	9	-
20 years	8,712	1,821	20.9	8,490	1,791	21.1	149	26	17.4	68	3	-	5	1	-
21 to 24 years	37,820	3,715	9.8	36,917	3,627	9.8	604	66	10.9	264	18	6.8	35	4	-
Male, 5 to 24 years	71,568	47,053	65.7	70,164	46,291	66.0	656	278	42.4	645	419	65.0	103	65	63.1
5 years	2,944	1,935	65.7	2,896	1,909	65.9	8	4	-	34	18	-	6	4	-
6 years	2,777	2,623	94.5	2,738	2,585	94.4	3	2	-	32	32	-	4	4	-
7 to 9 years	9,152	8,965	98.0	9,042	8,858	98.0	12	10	-	86	85	-	12	12	-
10 to 13 years	13,251	13,019	98.2	13,056	12,826	98.2	38	38	-	140	138	98.6	17	17	-
14 years	3,664	3,576	97.6	3,611	3,523	97.6	11	11	-	31	31	-	11	11	-
15 years	3,734	3,639	97.5	3,687	3,595	97.5	19	18	-	26	24	-	2	2	-
16 and 17 years	7,811	6,675	85.5	7,653	6,547	85.5	80	67	-	71	56	-	7	5	-
18 and 19 years	7,880	3,454	43.8	7,656	3,351	43.8	137	68	49.6	68	28	-	19	7	-
20 years	3,661	938	25.6	3,559	919	25.8	67	17	-	32	1	-	3	1	-
21 to 24 years	16,694	2,229	13.4	16,266	2,178	13.4	281	43	15.3	125	6	4.8	22	2	-
Female, 5 to 24 years	79,082	45,896	58.0	77,624	45,187	58.2	723	240	33.2	656	418	63.7	79	51	-
5 years	2,821	1,886	66.9	2,790	1,871	67.1	6	2	-	21	11	-	4	2	-
6 years	2,720	2,603	95.7	2,683	2,569	95.8	2	2	-	30	28	-	5	4	-
7 to 9 years	9,042	8,873	98.1	8,916	8,751	98.1	11	10	-	100	97	97.0	15	15	-
10 to 13 years	13,299	13,042	98.1	13,122	12,874	98.1	45	41	-	118	114	96.6	14	13	-
14 years	3,636	3,547	97.6	3,580	3,492	97.5	16	15	-	38	38	-	2	2	-
15 years	3,692	3,595	97.4	3,646	3,552	97.4	12	11	-	29	27	-	5	5	-
16 and 17 years	7,886	6,729	85.3	7,707	6,579	85.4	92	77	-	78	67	-	9	6	-
18 and 19 years	9,809	3,252	33.2	9,598	3,178	33.1	134	50	37.3	67	22	-	10	2	-
20 years	5,051	883	17.5	4,931	872	17.7	82	9	-	36	2	-	2	-	-
21 to 24 years	21,126	1,486	7.0	20,651	1,449	7.0	323	23	7.1	139	12	8.6	13	2	-
1930															
Total, 5 to 24 years	155,987	101,132	64.8	149,791	98,295	65.6	4,864	2,009	41.3	1,096	693	63.2	236	135	57.2
5 years	7,604	5,141	67.6	7,511	5,084	67.7	30	17	-	54	35	-	9	5	-
6 years	7,535	7,136	94.7	7,425	7,032	94.7	48	45	-	54	53	-	8	6	-
7 to 9 years	23,546	23,055	97.9	22,987	22,509	97.9	342	331	96.8	191	190	99.5	26	25	-
10 to 13 years	29,413	29,187	99.2	28,772	28,552	99.2	415	411	99.0	203	201	99.0	23	23	-
14 years	7,578	7,470	98.6	7,377	7,275	98.6	141	140	99.3	47	47	-	8	8	-
15 years	7,292	7,139	97.9	7,057	6,914	98.0	174	169	97.1	56	51	-	5	5	-
16 and 17 years	14,063	9,953	70.8	13,531	9,584	70.8	431	298	69.1	84	58	-	17	13	-
18 and 19 years	15,653	5,469	34.9	14,887	5,203	34.9	643	223	34.7	93	33	-	30	10	-
20 years	8,517	1,975	23.2	8,003	1,869	23.4	433	89	20.6	56	8	-	25	9	-
21 to 24 years	34,791	4,607	13.2	32,241	4,273	13.3	2,207	286	13.0	258	17	6.6	85	31	-
Male, 5 to 24 years	74,181	50,718	68.4	71,013	49,219	69.3	2,459	1,060	43.1	537	346	64.4	172	93	54.1
5 years	3,931	2,638	67.1	3,881	2,610	67.3	16	8	-	28	18	-	6	2	-
6 years	3,871	3,674	94.9	3,816	3,621	94.9	22	22	-	29	28	-	4	3	-
7 to 9 years	11,887	11,637	97.9	11,616	11,372	97.9	166	161	97.0	93	92	-	12	12	-
10 to 13 years	14,778	14,655	99.2	14,455	14,334	99.2	207	205	99.0	107	107	100.0	9	9	-
14 years	3,711	3,659	98.6	3,617	3,566	98.6	66	65	-	22	22	-	6	6	-
15 years	3,582	3,509	98.0	3,456	3,389	98.1	90	88	-	31	27	-	5	5	-
16 and 17 years	6,804	4,798	70.5	6,548	4,628	70.7	211	142	67.3	33	20	-	12	8	-
18 and 19 years	6,786	2,589	38.2	6,405	2,435	38.0	308	126	40.9	46	18	-	27	10	-
20 years	3,494	971	27.8	3,238	905	27.9	212	52	24.5	24	5	-	20	9	-
21 to 24 years	15,337	2,588	16.9	13,981	2,359	16.9	1,161	191	16.5	124	9	7.3	71	29	-
Female, 5 to 24 years	81,806	50,414	61.6	78,778	49,076	62.3	2,405	949	39.5	559	347	62.1	64	42	-
5 years	3,673	2,503	68.1	3,630	2,474	68.2	14	9	-	26	17	-	3	3	-
6 years	3,664	3,462	94.5	3,609	3,411	94.5	26	23	-	25	25	-	4	3	-
7 to 9 years	11,659	11,418	97.9	11,371	11,137	97.9	176	170	96.6	98	98	-	14	13	-
10 to 13 years	14,635	14,532	99.3	14,317	14,218	99.3	208	206	99.0	96	94	-	14	14	-
14 years	3,862	3,811	98.7	3,760	3,709	98.6	75	75	-	25	25	-	2	2	-
15 years	3,710	3,630	97.8	3,601	3,525	97.9	84	81	-	25	24	-	-	-	-
16 and 17 years	7,259	5,155	71.0	6,983	4,956	71.0	220	156	70.9	51	38	-	5	5	-
18 and 19 years	8,867	2,880	32.5	8,482	2,768	32.6	335	97	29.0	47	15	-	3	-	-
20 years	5,023	1,004	20.0	4,765	964	20.2	221	37	16.7	32	3	-	5	-	-
21 to 24 years	19,454	2,019	10.4	18,260	1,914	10.5	1,046	95	9.1	134	8	6.0	14	2	-

Table B-39.—PERSONS 25 YEARS OLD AND OVER, BY YEARS OF SCHOOL COMPLETED, RACE, AND SEX, FOR THE CITY OF MINNEAPOLIS: 1940

[Percent not shown where less than 0.1; median and percent not shown where base is less than 100]

YEARS OF SCHOOL COMPLETED	ALL CLASSES			NATIVE WHITE			FOREIGN-BORN WHITE			NEGRO			OTHER RACES		
	Total	Male	Female	Total	Male	Female	Total	Male	Female	Total	Male	Female	Total	Male	Female
Persons 25 years old and over	310,604	147,032	163,572	244,379	111,350	133,029	62,754	33,760	28,994	3,090	1,618	1,472	381	304	77
No school years completed	3,139	1,567	1,572	667	335	332	2,331	1,145	1,186	95	49	46	46	38	8
Grade school: 1 to 4 years	11,763	6,314	5,449	5,356	2,827	2,529	6,011	3,255	2,756	349	192	157	47	40	7
5 or 6 years	20,095	10,296	9,799	11,223	5,567	5,656	8,444	4,488	3,956	389	213	176	39	28	11
7 or 8 years	111,703	55,405	56,298	77,906	37,119	40,787	32,779	17,705	15,074	957	532	425	61	49	12
High school: 1 to 3 years	49,382	22,411	26,971	44,429	19,881	24,548	4,275	2,210	2,065	622	277	345	56	43	13
4 years	67,476	26,970	40,506	61,495	23,968	37,527	5,493	2,758	2,735	429	198	231	59	46	13
College: 1 to 3 years	24,721	11,056	13,665	23,064	10,105	12,959	1,485	843	642	138	83	55	34	25	9
4 years or more	20,834	12,195	8,639	19,223	10,992	8,231	1,504	1,127	377	72	45	27	35	31	4
Not reported	1,491	818	673	1,016	556	460	432	229	203	39	29	10	4	4	-
Median school years completed	9.5	9.0	9.9	10.8	10.4	11.1	7.9	7.9	7.9	8.4	8.3	8.7	8.9	8.8	-
Percent less than 5 years completed	4.8	5.4	4.3	2.5	2.8	2.2	13.3	13.0	13.6	14.4	14.9	13.8	24.4	25.7	-
PERCENT DISTRIBUTION															
Persons 25 years old and over	100.0	100.0	100.0	100.0	100.0	100.0	100.0	100.0	100.0	100.0	100.0	100.0	100.0	100.0	-
No school years completed	1.0	1.1	1.0	0.3	0.3	0.2	3.7	3.4	4.1	3.1	3.0	3.1	12.1	12.5	-
Grade school: 1 to 4 years	3.8	4.3	3.3	2.2	2.5	1.9	9.6	9.6	9.5	11.3	11.9	10.7	12.3	13.2	-
5 or 6 years	6.5	7.0	6.0	4.6	5.0	4.3	13.5	13.3	13.6	12.6	13.2	12.0	10.2	9.2	-
7 or 8 years	36.0	37.7	34.4	31.9	33.3	30.7	52.2	52.4	52.0	31.0	32.9	28.9	16.0	16.1	-
High school: 1 to 3 years	15.9	15.2	16.5	18.2	17.9	18.5	6.8	6.5	7.1	20.1	17.1	23.4	14.7	14.1	-
4 years	21.7	18.3	24.8	25.2	21.5	28.2	8.8	8.2	9.4	13.9	12.2	15.7	15.5	15.1	-
College: 1 to 3 years	8.0	7.5	8.4	9.4	9.1	9.7	2.4	2.5	2.2	4.5	5.1	3.7	8.9	8.2	-
4 years or more	6.7	8.3	5.3	7.9	9.9	6.2	2.4	3.3	1.3	2.3	2.8	1.8	9.2	10.2	-
Not reported	0.5	0.6	0.4	0.4	0.5	0.3	0.7	0.7	0.7	1.3	1.8	0.7	1.0	1.3	-

Table B-40.—FOREIGN-BORN WHITE, BY COUNTRY OF BIRTH, BY SEX, FOR THE CITY OF MINNEAPOLIS: 1940 AND 1930

[Figures for white population in 1930 revised to include Mexicans classified with "Other races" in the 1930 reports. Percent not shown where less than 0.1 or where base is less than 100]

COUNTRY OF BIRTH	BOTH SEXES		PERCENT		MALE		FEMALE	
	1940	1930	1940	1930	1940	1930	1940	1930
All countries	64,149	80,936	100.0	100.0	34,424	43,783	29,725	37,153
England	1,868	2,453	2.9	3.0	978	1,310	890	1,143
Scotland	787	1,081	1.2	1.3	428	582	359	499
Wales	104	170	0.2	0.2	55	96	49	74
Northern Ireland	179	346	0.3	0.4	94	178	85	168
Irish Free State (Eire)	775	1,116	1.2	1.4	386	558	389	558
Norway	11,777	15,492	18.4	19.1	5,996	8,027	5,781	7,465
Sweden	19,244	24,866	30.0	30.7	10,584	13,843	8,660	11,023
Denmark	2,010	2,418	3.1	3.0	1,245	1,507	765	911
Netherlands	301	355	0.5	0.4	169	219	132	136
Belgium	85	114	0.1	0.1	45	61	40	53
Luxemburg	72	68	0.1	0.1	41	38	31	30
Switzerland	210	288	0.3	0.4	120	158	90	130
France	176	279	0.3	0.3	76	127	100	152
Germany	4,433	5,969	6.9	7.4	2,255	3,120	2,178	2,849
Poland	3,637	4,555	5.7	5.6	1,969	2,489	1,668	2,066
Czechoslovakia	1,503	2,308	2.3	2.9	813	1,257	690	1,051
Austria	1,564	1,292	2.4	1.6	854	703	710	589
Hungary	401	343	0.6	0.4	221	169	180	174
Yugoslavia	165	123	0.3	0.2	133	84	32	39
Russia (U. S. S. R.)	4,481	4,846	7.0	6.0	2,451	2,605	2,030	2,241
Lithuania	521	538	0.8	0.7	291	306	230	232
Latvia	80	119	0.1	0.1	46	60	34	59
Finland	917	1,154	1.4	1.4	462	581	455	573
Rumania	1,099	1,599	1.7	2.0	583	814	516	785
Bulgaria	77	81	0.1	0.1	72	75	5	6
Turkey in Europe	3	3	-	-	2	1	1	2
Greece	765	709	1.2	0.9	627	581	138	128
Italy	702	785	1.1	1.0	443	496	259	289
Spain	13	20	-	-	11	14	2	6
Portugal	1	1	-	-	-	1	1	-
Other Europe	71	86	0.1	0.1	37	45	34	41
Palestine and Syria	204	218	0.3	0.3	110	120	94	98
Turkey in Asia	40	27	0.1	-	29	17	11	10
Other Asia	61	94	0.1	0.1	36	60	25	34
Canada—French	836	1,373	1.3	1.7	400	672	436	701
Canada—Other	4,614	5,358	7.2	6.6	2,126	2,634	2,488	2,724
Newfoundland	18	12	-	-	10	6	8	6
Mexico	189	123	0.3	0.2	133	87	56	36
Cuba and other West Indies	19	13	-	-	12	7	7	6
Central and South America	59	42	0.1	0.1	31	21	28	21
Australia	21	28	-	-	14	16	7	12
Azores	1	-	-	-	1	-	-	-
All other and not reported	66	71	0.1	0.1	35	38	31	33

Table B-41.—PERSONS 14 YEARS OLD AND OVER, BY EMPLOYMENT STATUS, CLASS OF WORKER, RACE, AND SEX, FOR THE CITY OF MINNEAPOLIS: 1940

[Percent not shown where less than 0.1 or where base is less than 100]

EMPLOYMENT STATUS	ALL CLASSES			NATIVE WHITE			FOREIGN-BORN WHITE			NEGRO			OTHER RACES		
	Total	Male	Female	Total	Male	Female	Total	Male	Female	Total	Male	Female	Total	Male	Female
Total population (all ages)	492,370	234,542	257,828	422,950	197,302	225,648	64,149	34,424	29,725	4,646	2,378	2,268	625	438	187
Persons 14 years old and over	405,248	190,476	214,772	336,924	153,782	183,142	64,008	34,355	29,653	3,830	1,971	1,859	486	368	118
In labor force	222,955	149,679	73,276	189,581	122,176	67,405	30,845	25,649	5,196	2,181	1,547	634	348	307	41
Not in labor force	182,293	40,797	141,496	147,343	31,606	115,737	33,163	8,706	24,457	1,649	424	1,225	138	61	77
Engaged in own home housew'k	106,307	841	105,466	86,226	639	85,587	19,171	187	18,984	860	14	846	50	1	49
In school	37,657	19,397	18,260	36,887	18,995	17,892	411	222	189	309	147	162	50	33	17
Unable to work	23,224	12,618	10,606	13,420	6,859	6,561	9,460	5,553	3,907	323	188	135	21	18	3
In institutions	1,259	664	595	712	383	329	540	279	261	7	2	5	-	-	-
Other and not reported	13,846	7,277	6,569	10,098	4,730	5,368	3,581	2,465	1,116	150	73	77	17	9	8
LABOR FORCE BY EMPLOYMENT STATUS															
In labor force	222,955	149,679	73,276	189,581	122,176	67,405	30,845	25,649	5,196	2,181	1,547	634	348	307	41
Employed (exc. public emerg. work)	186,386	122,480	63,906	158,530	99,807	58,723	26,116	21,377	4,739	1,444	1,030	414	296	266	30
At work	180,942	118,681	62,261	154,126	96,900	57,226	25,142	20,534	4,608	1,385	987	398	289	260	29
With a job	5,444	3,799	1,645	4,404	2,907	1,497	974	843	131	59	43	16	7	6	1
On public emerg. work (WPA, etc.)	10,364	8,352	2,012	9,143	7,320	1,823	980	870	110	233	155	78	8	7	1
Seeking work	26,205	18,847	7,358	21,908	15,049	6,859	3,749	3,402	347	504	362	142	44	34	10
Experienced workers	22,105	16,513	5,592	17,925	12,783	5,142	3,684	3,364	320	461	337	124	35	29	6
New workers	4,100	2,334	1,766	3,983	2,266	1,717	65	38	27	43	25	18	9	5	4
PERCENT BY SEX															
In labor force	100.0	67.1	32.9	100.0	64.4	35.6	100.0	83.2	16.8	100.0	70.9	29.1	100.0	88.2	11.8
Employed (exc. public emerg.)	100.0	65.7	34.3	100.0	63.0	37.0	100.0	81.9	18.1	100.0	71.3	28.7	100.0	89.9	10.1
On pub. emerg. work (WPA, etc.)	100.0	80.6	19.4	100.0	80.1	19.9	100.0	88.8	11.2	100.0	66.5	33.5	-	-	-
Seeking work	100.0	71.9	28.1	100.0	68.7	31.3	100.0	90.7	9.3	100.0	71.8	28.2	-	-	-
Not in labor force	100.0	22.4	77.6	100.0	21.5	78.5	100.0	26.3	73.7	100.0	25.7	74.3	100.0	44.2	55.8
Engaged in own home housew'k	100.0	0.8	99.2	100.0	0.7	99.3	100.0	1.0	99.0	100.0	1.6	98.4	-	-	-
In school	100.0	51.5	48.5	100.0	51.5	48.5	100.0	54.0	46.0	100.0	47.6	52.4	-	-	-
Unable to work	100.0	54.3	45.7	100.0	51.1	48.9	100.0	58.7	41.3	100.0	58.2	41.8	-	-	-
In institutions	100.0	52.7	47.3	100.0	53.8	46.2	100.0	51.7	48.3	-	-	-	-	-	-
Other and not reported	100.0	52.6	47.4	100.0	46.8	53.2	100.0	68.8	31.2	100.0	48.7	51.3	-	-	-
EMPLOYED WORKERS BY CLASS OF WORKER															
Employed (exc. public emerg.)	186,386	122,480	63,906	158,530	99,807	58,723	26,116	21,377	4,739	1,444	1,030	414	296	266	30
Wage and salary workers	163,807	104,765	59,042	141,361	86,741	54,620	20,917	16,886	4,031	1,306	938	368	223	200	23
Employers and own-account workers	20,802	17,131	3,671	15,640	12,551	3,089	4,971	4,430	541	124	87	37	67	63	4
Unpaid family workers	1,061	213	848	908	203	705	144	7	137	4	1	3	5	2	3
Class of worker not reported	716	371	349	621	312	309	84	54	30	10	4	6	1	1	-
At work	180,942	118,681	62,261	154,126	96,900	57,226	25,142	20,534	4,608	1,385	987	398	289	260	29
Wage and salary workers	159,666	101,990	57,676	137,946	84,588	53,358	20,236	16,299	3,937	1,266	907	359	218	196	22
Employers and own-account workers	19,600	16,162	3,438	14,737	11,840	2,897	4,690	4,184	506	108	77	31	65	61	4
Unpaid family workers	1,035	204	831	883	194	689	143	7	136	4	1	3	5	2	3
Class of worker not reported	641	325	316	560	278	282	73	44	29	7	2	5	1	1	-
With a job	5,444	3,799	1,645	4,404	2,907	1,497	974	843	131	59	43	16	7	6	1
Wage and salary workers	4,141	2,775	1,366	3,415	2,153	1,262	681	587	94	40	31	9	5	4	1
Employers and own-account workers	1,202	969	233	903	711	192	281	246	35	16	10	6	2	2	-
Unpaid family workers	26	9	17	25	9	16	1	-	1	-	-	-	-	-	-
Class of worker not reported	75	46	29	61	34	27	11	10	1	3	2	1	-	-	-
PERCENT DISTRIBUTION															
Persons 14 years old and over	100.0	100.0	100.0	100.0	100.0	100.0	100.0	100.0	100.0	100.0	100.0	100.0	100.0	100.0	100.0
In labor force	55.0	78.6	34.1	56.3	79.4	36.8	48.2	74.7	17.5	56.9	78.5	34.1	71.6	83.4	34.7
Not in labor force	45.0	21.4	65.9	43.7	20.6	63.2	51.8	25.3	82.5	43.1	21.5	65.9	28.4	16.6	65.3
Engaged in own home housew'k	26.2	0.4	49.1	25.6	0.4	46.7	30.0	0.5	64.0	22.5	0.7	45.5	10.3	0.3	41.5
In school	9.3	10.2	8.5	10.9	12.4	9.8	0.6	0.6	0.6	8.1	7.5	8.7	10.3	9.0	14.4
Unable to work	5.7	6.6	4.9	4.0	4.5	3.6	14.8	16.2	13.2	8.4	9.5	7.3	4.3	4.9	2.5
In institutions	0.3	0.3	0.3	0.2	0.2	0.2	0.8	0.8	0.9	0.2	0.1	0.3	-	-	-
Other and not reported	3.4	3.8	3.1	3.0	3.1	2.9	5.6	7.2	3.8	3.9	3.7	4.1	3.5	2.4	6.8
LABOR FORCE BY EMPLOYMENT STATUS															
In labor force	100.0	100.0	100.0	100.0	100.0	100.0	100.0	100.0	100.0	100.0	100.0	100.0	100.0	100.0	-
Employed (exc. public emerg. work)	83.6	81.8	87.2	83.6	81.7	87.1	84.7	83.3	91.2	66.2	66.6	65.3	85.1	86.6	-
At work	81.2	79.3	85.0	81.3	79.3	84.9	81.5	80.1	88.7	63.5	63.8	62.8	83.0	84.7	-
With a job	2.4	2.5	2.2	2.3	2.4	2.2	3.2	3.3	2.5	2.7	2.8	2.5	2.0	2.0	-
On public emerg. work (WPA, etc.)	4.6	5.6	2.7	4.8	6.0	2.7	3.2	3.4	2.1	10.7	10.0	12.3	2.3	2.3	-
Seeking work	11.8	12.6	10.0	11.6	12.3	10.2	12.2	13.3	6.7	23.1	23.4	22.4	12.6	11.1	-
Experienced workers	9.9	11.0	7.6	9.5	10.5	7.6	11.9	13.1	6.2	21.1	21.8	19.6	10.1	9.4	-
New workers	1.8	1.6	2.4	2.1	1.9	2.5	0.2	0.1	0.5	2.0	1.6	2.8	2.6	1.6	-
EMPLOYED WORKERS BY CLASS OF WORKER															
Employed (exc. public emerg.)	100.0	100.0	100.0	100.0	100.0	100.0	100.0	100.0	100.0	100.0	100.0	100.0	100.0	100.0	-
Wage and salary workers	87.9	85.5	92.4	89.2	86.9	93.0	80.1	79.0	85.1	90.4	91.1	88.9	75.3	75.2	-
Employers and own-account workers	11.2	14.0	5.7	9.9	12.6	5.3	19.0	20.7	11.4	8.6	8.4	8.9	22.6	23.7	-
Unpaid family workers	0.6	0.2	1.3	0.6	0.2	1.2	0.6	-	2.9	0.3	0.1	0.7	1.7	0.8	-
Class of worker not reported	0.4	0.3	0.5	0.4	0.3	0.5	0.3	0.3	0.6	0.7	0.4	1.4	0.3	0.4	-
At work	100.0	100.0	100.0	100.0	100.0	100.0	100.0	100.0	100.0	100.0	100.0	100.0	100.0	100.0	-
Wage and salary workers	88.2	85.9	92.6	89.5	87.3	93.2	80.5	79.4	85.4	91.4	91.9	90.2	75.4	75.4	-
Employers and own-account workers	10.8	13.6	5.5	9.6	12.2	5.1	18.7	20.4	11.0	7.8	7.8	7.8	22.5	23.5	-
Unpaid family workers	0.6	0.2	1.3	0.6	0.2	1.2	0.6	-	3.0	0.3	0.1	0.8	1.7	0.8	-
Class of worker not reported	0.4	0.3	0.5	0.4	0.3	0.5	0.3	0.2	0.6	0.5	0.2	1.3	0.3	0.4	-
With a job	100.0	100.0	100.0	100.0	100.0	100.0	100.0	100.0	100.0	-	-	-	-	-	-
Wage and salary workers	76.1	73.0	83.0	77.5	74.1	84.3	69.9	69.6	71.8	-	-	-	-	-	-
Employers and own-account workers	22.1	25.5	14.2	20.5	24.5	12.8	28.9	29.2	26.7	-	-	-	-	-	-
Unpaid family workers	0.5	0.2	1.0	0.6	0.3	1.1	0.1	-	0.8	-	-	-	-	-	-
Class of worker not reported	1.4	1.2	1.8	1.4	1.2	1.8	1.1	1.2	0.8	-	-	-	-	-	-

Table B-42 —EMPLOYED WORKERS 14 YEARS OLD AND OVER, BY MAJOR OCCUPATION GROUP, INDUSTRY GROUP, AND SEX, FOR THE CITY OF MINNEAPOLIS: 1940

[Percent not shown where less than 0.1 or where base is less than 100]

MAJOR OCCUPATION GROUP AND INDUSTRY GROUP	Total	Male	Female	PERCENT BY OCCUPATION AND INDUSTRY			PERCENT BY SEX	
				Total	Male	Female	Male	Female
Total population (all ages)	492,870	234,542	257,828	-	-	-	47.6	52.4
All persons 14 years old and over	405,248	190,476	214,772	-	-	-	47.0	53.0
In labor force	222,955	149,679	73,276	100.0	100.0	100.0	67.1	32.9
Employed workers (except on public emergency work)	186,386	122,480	63,906	83.6	81.8	87.2	65.7	34.3
MAJOR OCCUPATION GROUP								
Employed (except on public emergency work)	186,386	122,480	63,906	100.0	100.0	100.0	65.7	34.3
Professional workers	15,396	7,747	7,649	8.3	6.3	12.0	50.3	49.7
Semiprofessional workers	2,900	2,101	799	1.6	1.7	1.3	72.4	27.6
Farmers and farm managers	104	98	6	0.1	0.1	-	94.2	5.8
Proprietors, managers, and officials, except farm	19,829	17,517	2,312	10.6	14.3	3.6	88.3	11.7
Clerical, sales, and kindred workers	56,073	30,533	25,540	30.1	24.9	40.0	54.5	45.5
Craftsmen, foremen, and kindred workers	24,839	24,147	692	13.3	19.7	1.1	97.2	2.8
Operatives and kindred workers	30,439	21,878	8,561	16.3	17.9	13.4	71.9	28.1
Domestic service workers	8,202	192	8,010	4.4	0.2	12.5	2.3	97.7
Service workers, except domestic	19,607	9,963	9,644	10.5	8.1	15.1	50.8	49.2
Farm laborers (wage workers) and farm foremen	249	237	12	0.1	0.2	-	95.2	4.8
Farm laborers, unpaid family workers	12	8	4	-	-	-	-	-
Laborers, except farm	7,553	7,355	198	4.1	6.0	0.3	97.4	2.6
Occupation not reported	1,183	704	479	0.6	0.6	0.7	59.5	40.5
INDUSTRY GROUP								
Employed (except on public emergency work)	186,386	122,480	63,906	100.0	100.0	100.0	65.7	34.3
Agriculture, forestry, and fishery	620	580	40	0.3	0.5	0.1	93.5	6.5
Agriculture	595	555	40	0.3	0.5	0.1	93.3	6.7
Forestry (except logging) and fishery	25	25	-	-	-	-	-	-
Mining	119	113	6	0.1	0.1	-	95.0	5.0
Coal mining	2	1	1	-	-	-	-	-
Crude petroleum and natural gas production	12	10	2	-	-	-	-	-
Other mines and quarries	105	102	3	0.1	0.1	-	97.1	2.9
Construction	8,817	8,581	236	4.7	7.0	0.4	97.3	2.7
Manufacturing	40,132	30,254	9,878	21.5	24.7	15.5	75.4	24.6
Food and kindred products	8,458	6,538	1,920	4.5	5.3	3.0	77.3	22.7
Textile-mill products	2,429	869	1,560	1.3	0.7	2.4	35.8	64.2
Apparel and other fabricated textile products	3,287	972	2,315	1.8	0.8	3.6	29.6	70.4
Logging	24	22	2	-	-	-	-	-
Sawmills and planing mills	1,008	950	58	0.5	0.8	0.1	94.2	5.8
Furniture, store fixtures, and miscellaneous wooden goods	1,679	1,511	168	0.9	1.2	0.3	90.0	10.0
Paper and allied products	923	703	220	0.5	0.6	0.3	76.2	23.8
Printing, publishing, and allied industries	4,586	3,546	1,040	2.5	2.9	1.6	77.3	22.7
Chemicals and allied products	1,504	1,216	288	0.8	1.0	0.5	80.9	19.1
Petroleum and coal products	344	314	30	0.2	0.3	-	91.3	8.7
Leather and leather products	244	187	57	0.1	0.2	0.1	76.6	23.4
Stone, clay, and glass products	551	500	51	0.3	0.4	0.1	90.7	9.3
Iron and steel and their products	4,236	3,557	679	2.3	2.9	1.1	84.0	16.0
Nonferrous metals and their products	760	701	59	0.4	0.6	0.1	92.2	7.8
Machinery	5,955	5,375	580	3.2	4.4	0.9	90.3	9.7
Automobiles and automobile equipment	1,304	1,204	100	0.7	1.0	0.2	92.3	7.7
Transportation equipment, except automobile	78	71	7	-	0.1	-	-	-
Other and not specified manufacturing industries	2,762	2,018	744	1.5	1.6	1.2	63.1	26.9
Transportation, communication, and other public utilities	18,015	15,898	2,117	9.7	13.0	3.3	88.2	11.8
Railroads (including railroad repair shops) and railway express service	8,071	7,669	402	4.3	6.3	0.6	95.0	5.0
Trucking service	1,885	1,778	107	1.0	1.5	0.2	94.3	5.7
Other transportation	3,087	2,869	218	1.7	2.3	0.3	92.9	7.1
Communication	2,276	1,169	1,107	1.2	1.0	1.7	51.4	48.6
Utilities	2,696	2,413	283	1.4	2.0	0.4	89.5	10.5
Wholesale and retail trade	50,612	33,359	17,253	27.2	27.2	27.0	65.9	34.1
Wholesale trade	12,603	9,941	2,662	6.8	8.1	4.2	78.9	21.1
Food and dairy products stores, and milk retailing	7,328	5,669	1,659	3.9	4.6	2.6	77.4	22.6
Eating and drinking places	7,139	3,249	3,890	3.8	2.7	6.1	45.5	54.5
Motor vehicles and accessories retailing, and filling stations	3,385	3,110	275	1.8	2.5	0.4	91.9	8.1
Other retail trade	20,157	11,390	8,767	10.8	9.3	13.7	56.5	43.5
Finance, insurance, and real estate	12,296	7,387	4,909	6.6	6.0	7.7	60.1	39.9
Business and repair services	5,098	4,357	741	2.7	3.6	1.2	85.5	14.5
Automobile storage, rental, and repair services	2,148	2,095	53	1.2	1.7	0.1	97.5	2.5
Business and repair services, except automobile	2,950	2,262	688	1.6	1.8	1.1	76.7	23.3
Personal services	19,155	5,028	14,127	10.3	4.1	22.1	26.2	73.8
Domestic service	8,892	432	8,460	4.8	0.4	13.2	4.9	95.1
Hotels and lodging places	3,631	1,641	1,990	1.9	1.3	3.1	45.2	54.8
Laundering, cleaning, and dyeing services	2,655	1,230	1,425	1.4	1.0	2.2	46.3	53.7
Miscellaneous personal services	3,977	1,725	2,252	2.1	1.4	3.5	43.4	56.6
Amusement, recreation, and related services	2,309	1,722	587	1.2	1.4	0.9	74.6	25.4
Professional and related services	18,979	7,787	11,192	10.2	6.4	17.5	41.0	59.0
Government	7,878	6,033	1,845	4.2	4.9	2.9	76.6	23.4
Industry not reported	2,356	1,381	975	1.3	1.1	1.5	58.6	41.4

Table B-43.—PERSONS 14 YEARS OLD AND OVER IN THE LABOR FORCE, 1940, AND GAINFUL WORKERS 14 YEARS OLD AND OVER, 1930, BY RACE AND SEX, FOR THE CITY OF MINNEAPOLIS

[Totals for population and gainful workers for 1930 include "Unknown age." Figures for white population in 1930 have been revised to include Mexicans who were classified with "Other races" in the 1930 reports. Percent not shown where less than 0.1 or where base is less than 100]

CENSUS YEAR AND RACE	TOTAL					MALE					FEMALE				
	Population		Persons in the labor force, and gainful workers,[1] 14 years old and over			Population		Persons in the labor force, and gainful workers,[1] 14 years old and over			Population		Persons in the labor force, and gainful workers,[1] 14 years old and over		
	Total (all ages)	14 years old and over	Number	Per-cent of total popu-lation	Per-cent of popu-lation 14 yrs. and over	Total (all ages)	14 years old and over	Number	Per-cent of total popu-lation	Per-cent of popu-lation 14 yrs. and over	Total (all ages)	14 years old and over	Number	Per-cent of total popu-lation	Per-cent of popu-lation 14 yrs. and over
1940	492,370	405,248	222,955	45.3	55.0	234,542	190,476	149,679	63.8	78.6	257,828	214,772	73,276	28.4	34.1
White	487,099	400,932	220,426	45.3	55.0	231,726	188,137	147,825	63.8	78.6	255,373	212,795	72,601	28.4	34.1
Negro	4,646	3,830	2,181	46.9	56.9	2,378	1,971	1,547	65.1	78.5	2,268	1,859	634	28.0	34.1
Other races	625	486	348	55.7	71.6	438	368	307	70.1	83.4	187	118	41	21.9	34.7
1930	464,356	362,081	211,799	45.6	58.5	225,547	173,758	147,387	65.3	84.8	238,809	188,323	64,412	27.0	34.2
White	459,630	358,245	209,255	45.5	58.4	222,948	171,616	145,487	65.3	84.8	236,682	186,629	63,768	26.9	34.2
Negro	4,176	3,388	2,226	53.3	65.7	2,189	1,782	1,608	73.5	90.2	1,987	1,606	618	31.1	38.5
Other races	550	448	318	57.8	71.0	410	360	292	71.2	81.1	140	88	26	18.6	-

[1] Data for 1930 represent gainful workers 14 years old and over.

The nine tables that follow are reprinted from the actual 1940 census, for the city of St. Paul. They include actual data on race, percentage of voting population, school attendance, number of school years completed, foreign born, and employment of workers 14 years and older by job, industry and race. Statistics for Minneapolis precede this section.

Table C-35.—AGE, BY RACE AND SEX, FOR THE CITY OF ST. PAUL: 1940 AND 1930

[Figures for white population in 1930 revised to include Mexicans classified with "Other races" in the 1930 reports. Percent not shown where less than 0.1 or where base is less than 100]

AGE AND CENSUS YEAR	ALL CLASSES			NATIVE WHITE			FOREIGN-BORN WHITE			NEGRO			OTHER RACES		
	Total	Male	Female	Total	Male	Female	Total	Male	Female	Total	Male	Female	Total	Male	Female
All ages: 1940	287,736	137,561	150,175	249,787	117,906	131,881	33,612	17,442	16,170	4,139	2,070	2,069	198	143	55
Under 5 years	20,308	10,436	9,872	20,044	10,306	9,738	5	5	-	244	117	127	15	8	7
5 to 9 years	18,847	9,581	9,266	18,555	9,448	9,107	26	9	17	254	114	140	12	10	2
10 to 14 years	21,193	10,721	10,472	20,809	10,528	10,281	55	28	27	311	152	159	18	13	5
15 to 19 years	24,088	11,418	12,670	23,511	11,145	12,366	263	130	133	293	131	162	21	12	9
20 to 24 years	26,390	11,774	14,616	25,676	11,434	14,242	442	196	246	259	136	123	13	8	5
25 to 29 years	25,317	11,545	13,772	24,061	10,992	13,069	944	410	534	277	119	158	35	24	11
30 to 34 years	22,782	10,632	12,150	21,037	9,741	11,296	1,384	714	670	335	155	180	26	22	4
35 to 39 years	21,753	10,035	11,718	19,314	8,817	10,497	2,108	1,049	1,059	316	157	159	15	12	3
40 to 44 years	21,248	10,045	11,203	18,440	8,554	9,886	2,452	1,310	1,142	343	170	173	13	11	2
45 to 49 years	21,177	10,282	10,895	17,408	8,187	9,221	3,395	1,894	1,501	369	197	172	5	4	1
50 to 54 years	18,524	9,199	9,325	13,737	6,524	7,213	4,433	2,473	1,960	343	193	150	11	9	2
55 to 59 years	14,014	7,070	6,944	9,364	4,447	4,917	4,407	2,486	1,921	238	133	105	5	4	1
60 to 64 years	10,804	5,288	5,516	6,659	3,124	3,535	3,916	2,030	1,886	224	130	94	5	4	1
65 to 69 years	8,288	3,715	4,573	4,828	2,050	2,778	3,307	1,584	1,723	152	80	72	1	1	-
70 to 74 years	6,006	2,718	3,288	3,146	1,331	1,815	2,776	1,346	1,430	83	40	43	1	1	-
75 years and over	6,997	3,102	3,895	3,198	1,278	1,920	3,699	1,778	1,921	98	46	52	2	-	2
Under 1 year	4,112	2,121	1,991	4,060	2,090	1,970	1	1	-	49	28	21	2	2	-
5 years	3,724	1,928	1,796	3,662	1,896	1,766	4	1	3	57	30	27	1	1	-
14 years	4,355	2,168	2,187	4,263	2,119	2,144	16	8	8	72	39	33	4	2	2
15 years	4,610	2,272	2,338	4,528	2,236	2,292	22	13	9	58	22	36	2	1	1
16 and 17 years	9,476	4,549	4,927	9,253	4,435	4,818	89	53	36	124	57	67	10	4	6
21 years and over	198,317	93,174	105,143	162,024	74,309	87,715	33,169	17,229	15,940	2,996	1,536	1,460	128	100	28
All ages: 1930	271,606	131,570	140,036	222,765	105,858	116,907	44,508	23,410	21,098	4,001	2,086	1,915	332	216	116
Under 5 years	21,673	10,999	10,674	21,359	10,836	10,523	29	17	12	249	128	121	36	18	18
5 to 9 years	23,580	11,743	11,837	23,069	11,490	11,579	214	109	105	274	128	146	23	16	7
10 to 14 years	22,317	11,254	11,063	21,720	10,947	10,773	299	148	151	272	145	127	26	14	12
15 to 19 years	22,818	10,655	12,163	21,665	10,146	11,519	834	361	473	273	120	153	46	28	18
20 to 24 years	24,223	10,648	13,575	22,395	9,793	12,602	1,516	705	811	267	123	144	45	27	18
25 to 29 years	23,773	10,788	12,985	21,132	9,467	11,665	2,323	1,158	1,165	287	144	143	31	19	12
30 to 34 years	22,986	10,937	12,049	19,909	9,275	10,634	2,710	1,459	1,251	341	181	160	26	22	4
35 to 39 years	23,652	11,546	12,106	19,394	9,141	10,253	3,788	2,162	1,626	447	225	222	23	18	5
40 to 44 years	20,552	10,355	10,197	15,291	7,394	7,897	4,867	2,737	2,130	374	209	165	20	15	5
45 to 49 years	16,748	8,534	8,214	10,957	5,296	5,661	5,395	3,017	2,378	376	208	168	20	13	7
50 to 54 years	13,376	6,781	6,595	8,119	3,949	4,170	4,934	2,632	2,302	310	191	119	13	9	4
55 to 59 years	10,357	4,996	5,361	5,992	2,778	3,214	4,158	2,100	2,058	196	110	86	11	8	3
60 to 64 years	8,880	4,304	4,576	4,575	2,119	2,456	4,177	2,111	2,066	122	69	53	6	5	1
65 to 69 years	7,335	3,546	3,789	3,358	1,526	1,832	3,871	1,966	1,905	104	52	52	2	2	-
70 to 74 years	5,077	2,552	2,525	2,284	1,050	1,284	2,746	1,476	1,270	45	25	20	2	1	1
75 years and over	4,196	1,900	2,296	1,501	630	871	2,633	1,244	1,389	60	25	35	2	1	1
Not reported	63	32	31	45	21	24	14	8	6	4	3	1	-	-	-
Under 1 year	4,264	2,220	2,044	4,209	2,191	2,018	1	-	1	48	25	23	6	4	2
5 years	4,712	2,341	2,371	4,643	2,310	2,333	16	7	9	49	21	28	4	3	1
14 years	4,460	2,213	2,247	4,329	2,141	2,188	73	40	33	53	29	24	5	3	2
15 years	4,444	2,208	2,236	4,288	2,138	2,150	104	45	59	48	23	25	4	2	2
16 and 17 years	8,868	4,252	4,616	8,433	4,068	4,365	316	131	185	102	40	62	17	13	4
21 years and over	176,435	84,890	91,545	130,494	60,550	69,944	42,873	22,666	20,207	2,877	1,537	1,340	191	137	54
Percent: 1940	100.0	100.0	100.0	100.0	100.0	100.0	100.0	100.0	100.0	100.0	100.0	100.0	100.0	100.0	-
Under 5 years	7.1	7.6	6.6	8.0	8.7	7.4	-	-	-	5.9	5.7	6.1	7.6	5.6	-
5 to 9 years	6.6	7.0	6.2	7.4	8.0	6.9	0.1	0.1	0.1	6.1	5.5	6.8	6.1	7.0	-
10 to 14 years	7.4	7.8	7.0	8.3	8.9	7.8	0.2	0.2	0.2	7.5	7.3	7.7	9.1	9.1	-
15 to 19 years	8.4	8.3	8.4	9.4	9.5	9.4	0.8	0.7	0.8	7.1	6.3	7.8	10.6	8.4	-
20 to 24 years	9.2	8.6	9.7	10.3	9.7	10.8	1.3	1.1	1.5	6.3	6.6	5.9	6.6	5.6	-
25 to 29 years	8.8	8.4	9.2	9.6	9.3	9.9	2.8	2.4	3.3	6.7	5.7	7.6	17.7	16.8	-
30 to 34 years	7.9	7.7	8.1	8.4	8.3	8.6	4.1	4.1	4.1	8.1	7.5	8.7	13.1	15.4	-
35 to 39 years	7.6	7.3	7.8	7.7	7.5	8.0	6.3	6.0	6.5	7.6	7.6	7.7	7.6	8.4	-
40 to 44 years	7.4	7.3	7.5	7.4	7.3	7.5	7.3	7.5	7.1	8.3	8.2	8.4	6.6	7.7	-
45 to 49 years	7.4	7.5	7.3	7.0	6.9	7.0	10.1	10.9	9.3	8.9	9.5	8.3	2.5	2.8	-
50 to 54 years	6.4	6.7	6.2	5.5	5.5	5.5	13.2	14.2	12.1	8.3	9.3	7.2	5.6	6.3	-
55 to 59 years	4.9	5.1	4.6	3.7	3.8	3.7	13.1	14.3	11.9	5.8	6.4	5.1	2.5	2.8	-
60 to 64 years	3.8	3.8	3.7	2.7	2.6	2.7	11.7	11.6	11.7	5.4	6.3	4.5	2.5	2.8	-
65 to 69 years	2.9	2.7	3.0	1.9	1.7	2.1	9.8	9.1	10.7	3.7	3.9	3.5	0.5	0.7	-
70 to 74 years	2.1	2.0	2.2	1.3	1.1	1.4	8.3	7.7	8.8	2.0	1.9	2.1	0.5	0.7	-
75 years and over	2.4	2.3	2.6	1.3	1.1	1.5	11.0	10.2	11.9	2.4	2.2	2.5	1.0	-	-
Under 1 year	1.4	1.5	1.3	1.6	1.8	1.5	-	-	-	1.2	1.4	1.0	1.0	1.4	-
5 years	1.3	1.4	1.2	1.5	1.6	1.3	-	-	-	1.4	1.4	1.3	0.5	0.7	-
14 years	1.5	1.6	1.5	1.7	1.8	1.6	-	-	-	1.7	1.9	1.6	2.0	1.4	-
15 years	1.6	1.7	1.6	1.8	1.9	1.7	0.1	0.1	0.1	1.4	1.1	1.7	1.0	0.7	-
16 and 17 years	3.2	3.3	3.3	3.7	3.8	3.7	0.3	0.3	0.2	3.0	2.8	3.2	5.1	2.8	-
21 years and over	68.9	67.7	70.0	64.9	63.0	66.5	98.7	98.8	98.6	72.4	74.2	70.6	64.6	69.9	-
Percent: 1930	100.0	100.0	100.0	100.0	100.0	100.0	100.0	100.0	100.0	100.0	100.0	100.0	100.0	100.0	100.0
Under 5 years	8.0	8.4	7.6	9.6	10.2	9.0	0.1	0.1	0.1	6.2	6.1	6.3	10.8	8.3	15.5
5 to 9 years	8.7	8.9	8.5	10.4	10.9	9.9	0.5	0.5	0.5	6.8	6.1	7.6	6.9	7.4	6.0
10 to 14 years	8.2	8.6	7.9	9.8	10.3	9.2	0.7	0.6	0.7	6.8	7.0	6.6	7.8	6.5	10.3
15 to 19 years	8.4	8.1	8.7	9.7	9.6	9.9	1.9	1.5	2.2	6.8	5.8	8.0	13.9	13.0	15.5
20 to 24 years	8.9	8.1	9.7	10.1	9.3	10.8	3.4	3.0	3.8	6.7	5.9	7.5	13.6	12.5	15.5
25 to 29 years	8.8	8.2	9.3	9.5	8.9	10.0	5.2	4.9	5.5	7.2	6.9	7.5	9.3	8.8	10.3
30 to 34 years	8.5	8.3	8.6	8.9	8.8	9.1	6.1	6.2	5.9	8.5	8.7	8.4	7.8	10.2	3.4
35 to 39 years	8.7	8.8	8.6	8.7	8.6	8.8	8.5	9.2	7.7	11.2	10.8	11.6	6.9	8.3	4.3
40 to 44 years	7.6	7.9	7.3	6.9	7.0	6.8	10.9	11.7	10.1	9.3	10.0	8.6	6.0	6.9	4.3
45 to 49 years	6.2	6.5	5.9	4.9	5.0	4.8	12.1	12.9	11.3	9.4	10.0	8.8	6.0	6.0	6.0
50 to 54 years	4.9	5.2	4.7	3.6	3.7	3.6	11.1	11.2	10.9	7.7	9.2	6.2	3.9	4.2	3.4
55 to 59 years	3.8	3.8	3.8	2.7	2.6	2.7	9.3	9.0	9.8	4.9	5.3	4.5	3.3	3.7	2.6
60 to 64 years	3.3	3.3	3.3	2.1	2.0	2.1	9.4	9.0	9.8	3.0	3.3	2.8	1.8	2.3	0.9
65 to 69 years	2.7	2.7	2.7	1.5	1.4	1.6	8.7	8.4	9.0	2.6	2.5	2.7	0.6	0.9	-
70 to 74 years	1.9	1.9	1.8	1.0	1.0	1.1	6.2	6.3	6.0	1.1	1.2	1.0	0.6	0.5	0.9
75 years and over	1.5	1.4	1.6	0.7	0.6	0.7	5.9	5.3	6.6	1.5	1.2	1.8	0.6	0.5	0.9
Not reported	-	-	-	-	-	-	-	-	-	0.1	0.1	0.1	-	-	-
Under 1 year	1.6	1.7	1.5	1.9	2.1	1.7	-	-	-	1.2	1.2	1.2	1.8	1.9	1.7
5 years	1.7	1.8	1.7	2.1	2.2	2.0	-	-	-	1.2	1.0	1.5	1.2	1.4	0.9
14 years	1.6	1.7	1.6	1.9	2.0	1.9	0.2	0.2	0.2	1.3	1.4	1.3	1.5	1.4	1.7
15 years	1.6	1.7	1.6	1.9	2.0	1.8	0.2	0.2	0.3	1.2	1.1	1.3	1.2	0.9	1.7
16 and 17 years	3.3	3.2	3.3	3.8	3.8	3.7	0.7	0.6	0.9	2.5	1.9	3.2	5.1	6.0	3.4
21 years and over	65.0	64.5	65.4	58.6	57.2	59.8	96.3	96.8	95.8	71.9	73.7	70.0	57.5	63.4	46.6

Table C-36.—RACE, BY NATIVITY AND SEX, FOR THE CITY OF ST. PAUL: 1940 AND 1930

[Figures for white population in 1930 have been revised to include Mexicans who were classified with "Other races" in the 1930 reports. Percent not shown where less than 0.1 or where base is less than 100. Sex ratio not shown where number of females is less than 100]

SEX, NATIVITY, AND CENSUS YEAR	All classes	White	Negro	Other races	OTHER RACES				PERCENT BY RACE				PERCENT BY NATIVITY					
					Indian	Chinese	Japanese	All other	All classes	White	Negro	Other races	All classes	White	Negro	Indian	Chinese	Japanese
TOTAL																		
1940	287,736	283,399	4,139	198	60	76	13	49	100.0	98.5	1.4	0.1	100.0	100.0	100.0	-	-	-
Native	254,020	249,787	4,093	140	58	28	6	48	100.0	98.3	1.6	0.1	88.3	88.1	98.9	-	-	-
Foreign born	33,716	33,612	46	58	2	48	7	1	100.0	99.7	0.1	0.2	11.7	11.9	1.1	-	-	-
1930	271,606	267,273	4,001	332	169	122	10	31	100.0	98.4	1.5	0.1	100.0	100.0	100.0	100.0	100.0	-
Native	226,954	222,765	3,950	239	167	40	2	30	100.0	98.2	1.7	0.1	83.6	83.3	98.7	98.8	32.8	-
Foreign born	44,652	44,508	51	93	2	82	8	1	100.0	99.7	0.1	0.2	16.4	16.7	1.3	1.2	67.2	-
MALE																		
1940	137,561	135,348	2,070	143	25	67	9	42	100.0	98.4	1.5	0.1	100.0	100.0	100.0	-	-	-
Native	120,045	117,906	2,047	92	24	25	2	41	100.0	98.2	1.7	0.1	87.3	87.1	98.9	-	-	-
Foreign born	17,516	17,442	23	51	1	42	7	1	100.0	99.6	0.1	0.3	12.7	12.9	1.1	-	-	-
1930	131,570	129,268	2,086	216	75	104	8	29	100.0	98.3	1.6	0.2	100.0	100.0	100.0	-	100.0	-
Native	108,057	105,858	2,064	135	74	31	2	28	100.0	98.0	1.9	0.1	82.1	81.9	98.9	-	29.8	-
Foreign born	23,513	23,410	22	81	1	73	6	1	100.0	99.6	0.1	0.3	17.9	18.1	1.1	-	70.2	-
FEMALE																		
1940	150,175	148,051	2,069	55	35	9	4	7	100.0	98.6	1.4	-	100.0	100.0	100.0	-	-	-
Native	133,975	131,881	2,046	48	34	3	4	7	100.0	98.4	1.5	-	89.2	89.1	98.9	-	-	-
Foreign born	16,200	16,170	23	7	1	6	-	-	100.0	99.8	0.1	-	10.8	10.9	1.1	-	-	-
1930	140,036	138,005	1,915	116	94	18	2	2	100.0	98.5	1.4	0.1	100.0	100.0	100.0	-	-	-
Native	118,897	116,907	1,886	104	93	9	-	2	100.0	98.3	1.6	0.1	84.9	84.7	98.5	-	-	-
Foreign born	21,139	21,098	29	12	1	9	2	-	100.0	99.8	0.1	0.1	15.1	15.3	1.5	-	-	-
MALES PER 100 FEMALES																		
1940	91.6	91.4	100.0	-	-	-	-	-	-	-	-	-	-	-	-	-	-	-
Native	89.6	89.4	100.0	-	-	-	-	-	-	-	-	-	-	-	-	-	-	-
Foreign born	108.1	107.9	-	-	-	-	-	-	-	-	-	-	-	-	-	-	-	-
1930	94.0	93.7	108.9	186.2	-	-	-	-	-	-	-	-	-	-	-	-	-	-
Native	90.9	90.5	109.4	129.8	-	-	-	-	-	-	-	-	-	-	-	-	-	-
Foreign born	111.2	111.0	-	-	-	-	-	-	-	-	-	-	-	-	-	-	-	-

Table C-37.—POTENTIAL VOTING POPULATION, BY CITIZENSHIP, RACE, NATIVITY, AND SEX, FOR THE CITY OF ST. PAUL: 1940 AND 1930

[Figures for white population in 1930 have been revised to include Mexicans who were classified with "Other races" in the 1930 reports. Percent not shown where less than 0.1]

CITIZENSHIP, RACE, AND NATIVITY	TOTAL POPULATION (ALL AGES)								POPULATION 21 YEARS OLD AND OVER							
	Total number		Percent		Male		Female		Total number		Percent		Male		Female	
	1940	1930	1940	1930	1940	1930	1940	1930	1940	1930	1940	1930	1940	1930	1940	1930
Total	287,736	271,606	100.0	100.0	137,561	131,570	150,175	140,036	198,317	176,435	100.0	100.0	93,174	84,890	105,143	91,545
Percent citizen	-	-	97.2	96.3	-	-	-	-	-	-	96.0	94.8	-	-	-	-
Percent alien and citiz. not rptd.	-	-	2.8	3.7	-	-	-	-	-	-	4.0	5.2	-	-	-	-
Citizen	279,565	261,605	100.0	100.0	133,565	126,153	146,000	135,452	190,390	167,301	100.0	100.0	89,306	79,885	101,084	87,416
White—Native	249,787	222,765	89.3	85.2	117,906	105,858	131,881	116,907	162,024	130,494	85.1	78.0	74,309	60,550	87,715	69,944
Naturalized	25,512	34,614	9.1	13.2	13,507	18,083	12,005	16,531	25,300	33,828	13.3	20.2	13,409	17,736	11,891	16,092
Negro—Native	4,093	3,950	1.5	1.5	2,047	2,064	2,046	1,886	2,957	2,827	1.6	1.7	1,519	1,516	1,438	1,311
Naturalized	33	37	-	-	13	13	20	24	28	36	-	-	9	12	19	24
Other races—Native	140	239	0.1	0.1	92	135	48	104	81	116	-	0.1	60	71	21	45
Indian	58	167	-	0.1	24	74	34	93	29	80	-	-	12	38	17	42
Chinese	28	40	-	-	25	31	3	9	17	16	-	-	16	15	1	1
Japanese	6	2	-	-	2	2	4	-	3	1	-	-	1	1	2	-
Filipino	48	30	-	-	41	28	7	2	32	19	-	-	31	17	1	2
Hindu	-	-	-	-	-	-	-	-	-	-	-	-	-	-	-	-
All other	-	-	-	-	-	-	-	-	-	-	-	-	-	-	-	-
Alien	4,956	9,258	100.0	100.0	2,569	5,075	2,387	4,183	4,799	8,428	100.0	100.0	2,481	4,684	2,318	3,744
White—First papers	2,008	3,267	40.5	35.3	1,351	2,418	657	849	1,994	3,182	41.6	37.8	1,341	2,376	653	806
No papers	2,886	5,887	58.2	63.6	1,164	2,568	1,722	3,319	2,755	5,160	57.4	61.2	1,098	2,234	1,657	2,926
Negro—First papers	1	2	-	-	1	2	-	-	1	2	-	-	1	2	-	-
No papers	3	9	0.1	0.1	2	6	1	3	2	9	-	0.1	1	6	1	3
Other races—Foreign born	58	93	1.2	1.0	51	81	7	12	47	75	1.0	0.9	40	66	7	9
Indian	2	2	-	-	1	1	1	1	2	-	-	-	1	-	1	-
Chinese	48	82	1.0	0.9	42	73	6	9	37	66	0.8	0.8	31	59	6	7
Japanese	7	8	0.1	0.1	7	6	-	2	7	8	0.1	0.1	7	6	-	2
Filipino	-	-	-	-	-	-	-	-	-	-	-	-	-	-	-	-
Hindu	1	1	-	-	1	1	-	-	1	1	-	-	1	1	-	-
All other	-	-	-	-	-	-	-	-	-	-	-	-	-	-	-	-
Citizenship not reported	3,215	743	100.0	100.0	1,427	342	1,788	401	3,128	706	100.0	100.0	1,387	321	1,741	385
White	3,206	740	99.7	99.6	1,420	341	1,786	399	3,120	703	99.7	99.6	1,381	320	1,739	383
Negro	9	3	0.3	0.4	7	1	2	2	8	3	0.3	0.4	6	1	2	2

Table C-38.—SCHOOL ATTENDANCE, BY AGE, RACE, AND SEX, FOR THE CITY OF ST. PAUL: 1940 AND 1930

[Figures for white population in 1930 revised to include Mexicans classified with "Other races" in the 1930 reports. Percent not shown where less than 0.1 or where base is less than 100]

AGE, SEX, AND CENSUS YEAR	ALL CLASSES			NATIVE WHITE			FOREIGN-BORN WHITE			NEGRO			OTHER RACES		
	Total number	Attending school		Total number	Attending school		Total number	Attending school		Total number	Attending school		Total number	Attending school	
		Number	Percent		Number	Percent		Number	Percent		Number	Percent		Number	Percent
1940															
Total, 5 to 24 years	90,518	56,157	62.0	88,551	55,076	62.2	786	269	34.2	1,117	773	69.2	64	39	-
5 years	3,724	1,873	50.3	3,662	1,838	50.2	4	3	-	57	31	-	1	1	-
6 years	3,548	3,318	93.5	3,494	3,266	93.5	4	2	-	47	47	-	3	3	-
7 to 9 years	11,575	11,342	98.0	11,399	11,172	98.0	18	16	-	150	147	98.0	8	7	-
10 to 13 years	16,838	16,587	98.5	16,546	16,299	98.5	39	39	-	239	236	98.7	14	13	-
14 years	4,355	4,262	97.9	4,263	4,172	97.9	16	14	-	72	72	-	4	4	-
15 years	4,610	4,448	96.5	4,528	4,366	96.4	22	22	-	58	58	-	2	2	-
16 and 17 years	9,476	7,793	82.2	9,253	7,616	82.3	89	71	-	124	102	82.3	10	4	-
18 and 19 years	10,002	3,719	37.2	9,730	3,617	37.2	152	51	33.6	111	48	43.2	9	3	-
20 years	4,983	960	19.3	4,844	933	19.3	94	20	-	41	7	-	4	-	-
21 to 24 years	21,407	1,855	8.7	20,832	1,797	8.6	348	31	8.9	218	25	11.5	9	2	-
Male, 5 to 24 years	43,494	28,647	65.9	42,555	28,103	66.0	363	153	42.1	533	362	67.9	43	29	-
5 years	1,928	947	49.1	1,896	927	48.9	1	1	-	30	18	-	1	1	-
6 years	1,776	1,641	92.4	1,758	1,624	92.4	2	1	-	14	14	-	2	2	-
7 to 9 years	5,877	5,767	98.1	5,794	5,685	98.1	6	6	-	70	70	-	7	6	-
10 to 13 years	8,553	8,424	98.5	8,409	8,284	98.5	20	20	-	113	110	97.3	11	10	-
14 years	2,168	2,133	98.4	2,119	2,085	98.4	8	7	-	39	39	-	2	2	-
15 years	2,272	2,203	97.0	2,236	2,167	96.9	13	13	-	22	22	-	1	1	-
16 and 17 years	4,549	3,756	82.6	4,435	3,664	82.6	53	43	-	57	47	-	4	2	-
18 and 19 years	4,597	2,035	44.3	4,474	1,982	44.3	64	28	-	52	22	-	7	3	-
20 years	2,231	566	25.4	2,170	550	25.3	41	13	-	20	3	-	-	-	-
21 to 24 years	9,543	1,175	12.3	9,264	1,135	12.3	155	21	13.5	116	17	14.7	8	2	-
Female, 5 to 24 years	47,024	27,510	58.5	45,996	26,973	58.6	423	116	27.4	584	411	70.4	21	10	-
5 years	1,796	926	51.6	1,766	911	51.6	3	2	-	27	13	-	-	-	-
6 years	1,772	1,677	94.6	1,736	1,642	94.6	2	1	-	33	33	-	1	1	-
7 to 9 years	5,698	5,575	97.8	5,605	5,487	97.9	12	10	-	80	77	-	1	1	-
10 to 13 years	8,285	8,163	98.5	8,137	8,015	98.5	19	19	-	126	126	100.0	3	3	-
14 years	2,187	2,129	97.3	2,144	2,087	97.3	8	7	-	33	33	-	2	2	-
15 years	2,338	2,245	96.0	2,292	2,199	95.9	9	9	-	36	36	-	1	1	-
16 and 17 years	4,927	4,037	81.9	4,818	3,952	82.0	36	28	-	67	55	-	6	2	-
18 and 19 years	5,405	1,684	31.2	5,256	1,635	31.1	88	23	-	59	26	-	2	-	-
20 years	2,752	394	14.3	2,674	383	14.3	53	7	-	21	4	-	4	-	-
21 to 24 years	11,864	680	5.7	11,568	662	5.7	193	10	5.2	102	8	7.8	1	-	-
1930															
Total, 5 to 24 years	92,938	58,719	63.2	88,849	56,923	64.1	2,863	1,037	36.2	1,086	680	62.6	140	79	56.4
5 years	4,712	2,907	61.7	4,643	2,872	61.9	16	4	-	49	29	-	4	2	-
6 years	4,728	4,372	92.5	4,638	4,288	92.5	24	21	-	61	59	-	5	4	-
7 to 9 years	14,140	13,842	97.9	13,788	13,501	97.9	174	168	96.6	164	159	97.0	14	14	-
10 to 13 years	17,857	17,709	99.2	17,391	17,251	99.2	226	222	98.2	219	215	98.2	21	21	-
14 years	4,460	4,360	97.8	4,329	4,232	97.8	73	72	-	53	51	-	5	5	-
15 years	4,444	4,096	92.2	4,288	3,955	92.2	104	94	90.4	48	43	-	4	4	-
16 and 17 years	8,868	5,385	60.7	8,433	5,136	60.9	316	179	56.6	102	61	59.8	17	9	-
18 and 19 years	9,506	2,871	30.2	8,944	2,716	30.4	414	110	26.6	123	36	29.3	25	9	-
20 years	4,783	935	19.5	4,458	892	20.0	259	33	12.7	56	8	-	10	2	-
21 to 24 years	19,440	2,242	11.5	17,937	2,080	11.6	1,257	134	10.7	211	19	9.0	35	9	-
Male, 5 to 24 years	44,300	29,497	66.6	42,376	28,580	67.4	1,323	539	40.7	516	325	63.0	85	53	-
5 years	2,341	1,461	62.4	2,310	1,446	62.6	7	1	-	21	12	-	3	2	-
6 years	2,276	2,087	91.7	2,231	2,046	91.7	12	11	-	28	26	-	5	4	-
7 to 9 years	7,126	6,972	97.8	6,949	6,803	97.9	90	86	-	79	75	-	8	8	-
10 to 13 years	9,041	8,968	99.2	8,806	8,736	99.2	108	107	99.1	116	114	98.3	11	11	-
14 years	2,213	2,180	98.5	2,141	2,110	98.6	40	39	-	29	28	-	3	3	-
15 years	2,208	2,083	94.3	2,138	2,019	94.4	45	43	-	23	19	-	2	2	-
16 and 17 years	4,252	2,700	63.5	4,068	2,585	63.5	131	80	61.1	40	26	-	13	9	-
18 and 19 years	4,195	1,369	32.6	3,940	1,282	32.5	185	65	35.1	57	16	-	13	6	-
20 years	2,029	427	21.0	1,889	403	21.3	109	19	17.4	28	3	-	3	2	-
21 to 24 years	8,619	1,250	14.5	7,904	1,150	14.5	596	88	14.8	95	6	-	24	6	-
Female, 5 to 24 years	48,638	29,222	60.1	46,473	28,343	61.0	1,540	498	32.3	570	355	62.3	55	26	-
5 years	2,371	1,446	61.0	2,333	1,426	61.1	9	3	-	28	17	-	1	-	-
6 years	2,452	2,285	93.2	2,407	2,242	93.1	12	10	-	33	33	-	-	-	-
7 to 9 years	7,014	6,870	97.9	6,839	6,698	97.9	84	82	-	85	84	-	6	6	-
10 to 13 years	8,816	8,741	99.1	8,585	8,515	99.2	118	115	97.5	103	101	98.1	10	10	-
14 years	2,247	2,180	97.0	2,188	2,122	97.0	33	33	-	24	23	-	2	2	-
15 years	2,236	2,013	90.0	2,150	1,936	90.0	59	51	-	25	24	-	2	2	-
16 and 17 years	4,616	2,685	58.2	4,365	2,551	58.4	185	99	53.5	62	35	-	4	-	-
18 and 19 years	5,311	1,502	28.3	5,004	1,434	28.7	229	45	19.7	66	20	-	12	3	-
20 years	2,754	508	18.4	2,569	489	19.0	150	14	9.3	28	5	-	7	-	-
21 to 24 years	10,821	992	9.2	10,033	930	9.3	661	46	7.0	116	13	11.2	11	3	-

Table C-39.—PERSONS 25 YEARS OLD AND OVER, BY YEARS OF SCHOOL COMPLETED, RACE, AND SEX, FOR THE CITY OF ST. PAUL: 1940

[Percent not shown where less than 0.1; median and percent not shown where base is less than 100]

YEARS OF SCHOOL COMPLETED	ALL CLASSES			NATIVE WHITE			FOREIGN-BORN WHITE			NEGRO			OTHER RACES		
	Total	Male	Female	Total	Male	Female	Total	Male	Female	Total	Male	Female	Total	Male	Female
Persons 25 years old and over	176,910	83,631	93,279	141,192	65,045	76,147	32,821	17,074	15,747	2,778	1,420	1,358	119	92	27
No school years completed	2,504	1,237	1,267	482	250	232	1,941	942	999	74	40	34	7	5	2
Grade school: 1 to 4 years	7,166	3,703	3,463	3,401	1,714	1,687	3,481	1,817	1,664	271	159	112	13	13	-
5 or 6 years	11,887	5,866	6,021	6,999	3,359	3,640	4,559	2,324	2,235	320	176	144	9	7	2
7 or 8 years	71,100	34,521	36,579	53,773	25,567	28,206	16,367	8,445	7,922	937	492	445	23	17	6
High school: 1 to 3 years	27,705	12,737	14,968	25,022	11,401	13,621	2,115	1,084	1,031	541	234	307	27	18	9
4 years	33,017	13,161	19,856	30,180	11,772	18,408	2,461	1,220	1,241	360	159	201	16	10	6
College: 1 to 3 years	11,772	5,291	6,481	10,831	4,753	6,078	763	434	329	168	95	73	10	9	1
4 years or more	10,687	6,585	4,102	9,767	5,886	3,881	809	628	181	98	59	39	13	12	1
Not reported	1,072	530	542	737	343	394	325	180	145	9	6	3	1	1	-
Median school years completed	8.9	8.8	8.9	9.7	9.4	9.9	7.8	7.8	7.7	8.5	8.3	8.7	9.8	-	-
Percent less than 5 years completed	5.5	5.9	5.1	2.8	3.0	2.5	16.5	16.2	16.9	12.4	14.0	10.8	16.8	-	-
PERCENT DISTRIBUTION															
Persons 25 years old and over	100.0	100.0	100.0	100.0	100.0	100.0	100.0	100.0	100.0	100.0	100.0	100.0	100.0	-	-
No school years completed	1.4	1.5	1.4	0.3	0.4	0.3	5.9	5.5	6.3	2.7	2.8	2.5	5.9	-	-
Grade school: 1 to 4 years	4.1	4.4	3.7	2.4	2.6	2.2	10.6	10.6	10.6	9.8	11.2	8.2	10.9	-	-
5 or 6 years	6.7	7.0	6.5	5.0	5.2	4.8	13.9	13.6	14.2	11.5	12.4	10.6	7.6	-	-
7 or 8 years	40.2	41.3	39.2	38.1	39.3	37.0	49.9	49.5	50.3	33.7	34.6	32.8	19.3	-	-
High school: 1 to 3 years	15.7	15.2	16.0	17.7	17.5	17.9	6.4	6.3	6.5	19.5	16.5	22.6	22.7	-	-
4 years	18.7	15.7	21.3	21.4	18.1	24.2	7.5	7.1	7.9	13.0	11.2	14.8	13.4	-	-
College: 1 to 3 years	6.7	6.3	6.9	7.7	7.3	8.0	2.3	2.5	2.1	6.0	6.7	5.4	8.4	-	-
4 years or more	6.0	7.9	4.4	6.9	9.0	5.1	2.5	3.7	1.1	3.5	4.2	2.9	10.9	-	-
Not reported	0.6	0.6	0.6	0.5	0.5	0.5	1.0	1.1	0.9	0.3	0.4	0.2	0.8	-	-

Table C-40.—FOREIGN-BORN WHITE, BY COUNTRY OF BIRTH, BY SEX, FOR THE CITY OF ST. PAUL: 1940 AND 1930

[Figures for white population in 1930 revised to include Mexicans classified with "Other races" in the 1930 reports. Percent not shown where less than 0.1 or where base is less than 100]

COUNTRY OF BIRTH	BOTH SEXES		PERCENT		MALE		FEMALE	
	1940	1930	1940	1930	1940	1930	1940	1930
All countries	33,612	44,508	100.0	100.0	17,442	23,410	16,170	21,098
England	1,094	1,497	3.3	3.4	585	813	509	684
Scotland	457	599	1.4	1.3	249	323	208	276
Wales	22	55	0.1	0.1	14	33	8	22
Northern Ireland	171	341	0.5	0.8	87	180	84	161
Irish Free State (Eire)	1,320	1,901	3.9	4.3	612	909	708	992
Norway	2,548	3,414	7.6	7.7	1,274	1,735	1,274	1,679
Sweden	6,100	8,404	18.1	18.9	3,206	4,537	2,894	3,867
Denmark	865	1,164	2.6	2.6	488	661	377	503
Netherlands	145	181	0.4	0.4	84	113	61	68
Belgium	49	63	0.1	0.1	21	32	28	31
Luxemburg	115	196	0.3	0.4	70	118	45	78
Switzerland	328	421	1.0	0.9	191	242	137	179
France	192	256	0.6	0.6	82	114	110	142
Germany	5,294	7,478	15.8	16.8	2,583	3,710	2,711	3,768
Poland	1,835	2,610	5.5	5.9	1,005	1,427	830	1,183
Czechoslovakia	906	1,513	2.7	3.4	434	733	472	780
Austria	2,046	2,536	6.1	5.7	1,040	1,304	1,006	1,232
Hungary	753	857	2.2	1.9	400	444	353	413
Yugoslavia	117	200	0.3	0.4	57	113	60	87
Russia (U. S. S. R.)	3,067	3,537	9.1	7.9	1,623	1,857	1,444	1,680
Lithuania	194	206	0.6	0.5	97	112	97	94
Latvia	43	61	0.1	0.1	22	33	21	28
Finland	86	87	0.3	0.2	44	48	42	39
Rumania	431	589	1.3	1.3	228	315	203	274
Bulgaria	9	10	-	-	8	10	1	-
Turkey in Europe	1	-	-	-	1	-	-	-
Greece	260	277	0.8	0.6	223	236	37	41
Italy	1,503	1,722	4.5	3.9	965	1,101	538	621
Spain	6	10	-	-	4	7	2	3
Portugal	-	1	-	-	-	1	-	-
Other Europe	28	50	0.1	0.1	8	27	20	23
Palestine and Syria	217	265	0.6	0.6	125	149	92	116
Turkey in Asia	32	24	0.1	0.1	24	18	8	6
Other Asia	58	53	0.2	0.1	30	29	28	24
Canada—French	491	720	1.5	1.6	219	371	272	349
Canada—Other	2,315	2,742	6.9	6.2	1,057	1,278	1,258	1,464
Newfoundland	12	4	-	-	5	2	7	2
Mexico	441	372	1.3	0.8	247	225	194	147
Cuba and other West Indies	5	5	-	-	4	3	1	2
Central and South America	19	18	0.1	-	11	10	8	8
Australia	14	12	-	-	6	7	8	5
Azores	-	-	-	-	-	-	-	-
All other and not reported	23	57	0.1	0.1	9	30	14	27

Table C-41.—PERSONS 14 YEARS OLD AND OVER, BY EMPLOYMENT STATUS, CLASS OF WORKER, RACE, AND SEX, FOR THE CITY OF ST. PAUL: 1940

[Percent not shown where less than 0.1 or where base is less than 100]

EMPLOYMENT STATUS	ALL CLASSES			NATIVE WHITE			FOREIGN-BORN WHITE			NEGRO			OTHER RACES		
	Total	Male	Female	Total	Male	Female	Total	Male	Female	Total	Male	Female	Total	Male	Female
Total population (all ages)	287,736	137,561	150,175	249,787	117,906	131,881	33,612	17,442	16,170	4,139	2,070	2,069	198	143	55
Persons 14 years old and over	231,743	108,991	122,752	194,642	89,743	104,899	33,542	17,408	16,134	3,402	1,726	1,676	157	114	43
In labor force	125,447	86,427	39,020	107,974	72,026	35,948	15,500	12,946	2,554	1,866	1,364	502	107	91	16
Not in labor force	106,296	22,564	83,732	86,668	17,717	68,951	18,042	4,462	13,580	1,536	362	1,174	50	23	27
Engaged in own home housew'k	63,821	455	63,366	52,244	356	51,888	10,724	85	10,639	836	14	822	17	-	17
In school	21,181	10,918	10,263	20,730	10,675	10,055	207	121	86	223	104	119	21	18	3
Unable to work	11,868	6,523	5,345	6,916	3,672	3,244	4,680	2,706	1,974	270	143	127	2	2	-
In institutions	949	383	566	575	223	352	352	148	204	16	12	4	6	-	6
Other and not reported	8,477	4,285	4,192	6,203	2,791	3,412	2,079	1,402	677	191	89	102	4	3	1
LABOR FORCE BY EMPLOYMENT STATUS															
In labor force	125,447	86,427	39,020	107,974	72,026	35,948	15,500	12,946	2,554	1,866	1,364	502	107	91	16
Employed (exc. public emerg. work)	104,216	70,637	33,579	89,695	58,726	30,969	13,146	10,854	2,292	1,283	976	307	92	81	11
At work	101,135	68,430	32,705	87,222	57,030	30,192	12,579	10,376	2,203	1,243	944	299	91	80	11
With a job	3,081	2,207	874	2,473	1,696	777	567	478	89	40	32	8	1	1	-
On public emerg. work (WPA, etc.)	5,716	4,454	1,262	4,947	3,855	1,092	522	450	72	242	147	95	5	2	3
Seeking work	15,515	11,336	4,179	13,332	9,445	3,887	1,832	1,642	190	341	241	100	10	8	2
Experienced workers	12,899	9,940	2,959	10,784	8,084	2,700	1,791	1,621	170	316	228	88	8	7	1
New workers	2,616	1,396	1,220	2,548	1,361	1,187	41	21	20	25	13	12	2	1	1
PERCENT BY SEX															
In labor force	100.0	68.9	31.1	100.0	66.7	33.3	100.0	83.5	16.5	100.0	73.1	26.9	100.0	85.0	15.0
Employed (exc. public emerg.)	100.0	67.8	32.2	100.0	65.5	34.5	100.0	82.6	17.4	100.0	76.1	23.9	-	-	-
On pub. emerg. work (WPA, etc.)	100.0	77.9	22.1	100.0	77.9	22.1	100.0	86.2	13.8	100.0	60.7	39.3	-	-	-
Seeking work	100.0	73.1	26.9	100.0	70.8	29.2	100.0	89.6	10.4	100.0	70.7	29.3	-	-	-
Not in labor force	100.0	21.2	78.8	100.0	20.4	79.6	100.0	24.7	75.3	100.0	23.6	76.4	-	-	-
Engaged in own home housew'k	100.0	0.7	99.3	100.0	0.7	99.3	100.0	0.8	99.2	100.0	1.7	98.3	-	-	-
In school	100.0	51.5	48.5	100.0	51.5	48.5	100.0	58.5	41.5	100.0	46.6	53.4	-	-	-
Unable to work	100.0	55.0	45.0	100.0	53.1	46.9	100.0	57.8	42.2	100.0	53.0	47.0	-	-	-
In institutions	100.0	40.4	59.6	100.0	38.8	61.2	100.0	42.0	58.0	-	-	-	-	-	-
Other and not reported	100.0	50.5	49.5	100.0	45.0	55.0	100.0	67.4	32.6	100.0	46.6	53.4	-	-	-
EMPLOYED WORKERS BY CLASS OF WORKER															
Employed (exc. public emerg.)	104,216	70,637	33,579	89,695	58,726	30,969	13,146	10,854	2,292	1,283	976	307	92	81	11
Wage and salary workers	92,530	61,174	31,356	80,799	51,677	29,122	10,483	8,527	1,956	1,173	905	268	75	65	10
Employers and own-account workers	10,639	9,085	1,554	7,995	6,704	1,291	2,527	2,300	227	102	67	35	15	14	1
Unpaid family workers	611	171	440	512	161	351	96	8	88	1	-	1	2	2	-
Class of worker not reported	436	207	229	389	184	205	40	19	21	7	4	3	-	-	-
At work	101,135	68,430	32,705	87,222	57,030	30,192	12,579	10,376	2,203	1,243	944	299	91	80	11
Wage and salary workers	90,244	59,599	30,645	78,881	50,400	28,481	10,154	8,260	1,894	1,135	875	260	74	64	10
Employers and own-account workers	9,909	8,482	1,427	7,498	6,311	1,187	2,296	2,092	204	100	65	35	15	14	1
Unpaid family workers	596	164	432	499	154	345	94	8	86	1	-	1	2	2	-
Class of worker not reported	386	185	201	344	165	179	35	16	19	7	4	3	-	-	-
With a job	3,081	2,207	874	2,473	1,696	777	567	478	89	40	32	8	1	1	-
Wage and salary workers	2,286	1,575	711	1,918	1,277	641	329	267	62	38	30	8	1	1	-
Employers and own-account workers	730	603	127	497	393	104	231	208	23	2	2	-	-	-	-
Unpaid family workers	15	7	8	13	7	6	2	-	2	-	-	-	-	-	-
Class of worker not reported	50	22	28	45	19	26	5	3	2	-	-	-	-	-	-
PERCENT DISTRIBUTION															
Persons 14 years old and over	100.0	100.0	100.0	100.0	100.0	100.0	100.0	100.0	100.0	100.0	100.0	100.0	100.0	100.0	-
In labor force	54.1	79.3	31.8	55.5	80.3	34.3	46.2	74.4	15.8	54.9	79.0	30.0	68.2	79.8	-
Not in labor force	45.9	20.7	68.2	44.5	19.7	65.7	53.8	25.6	84.2	45.1	21.0	70.0	31.8	20.2	-
Engaged in own home housew'k	27.5	0.4	51.6	26.8	0.4	49.5	32.0	0.5	65.9	24.6	0.8	49.0	10.8	-	-
In school	9.1	10.0	8.4	10.7	11.9	9.6	0.6	0.7	0.5	6.6	6.0	7.1	13.4	15.8	-
Unable to work	5.1	6.0	4.4	3.6	4.1	3.1	14.0	15.5	12.2	7.9	8.3	7.6	1.3	1.8	-
In institutions	0.4	0.4	0.4	0.3	0.2	0.3	1.0	0.9	1.3	0.5	0.7	0.2	3.8	-	-
Other and not reported	3.7	3.9	3.4	3.2	3.1	3.3	6.2	8.1	4.2	5.6	5.2	6.1	2.5	2.6	-
LABOR FORCE BY EMPLOYMENT STATUS															
In labor force	100.0	100.0	100.0	100.0	100.0	100.0	100.0	100.0	100.0	100.0	100.0	100.0	100.0	-	-
Employed (exc. public emerg. work)	83.1	81.7	86.1	83.1	81.5	86.1	84.8	83.8	89.7	68.8	71.6	61.2	86.0	-	-
At work	80.6	79.2	83.8	80.8	79.2	84.0	81.2	80.1	86.3	66.6	69.2	59.6	85.0	-	-
With a job	2.5	2.6	2.2	2.3	2.4	2.2	3.7	3.7	3.5	2.1	2.3	1.6	0.9	-	-
On public emerg. work (WPA, etc.)	4.6	5.2	3.2	4.6	5.4	3.0	3.4	3.5	2.8	13.0	10.8	18.9	4.7	-	-
Seeking work	12.4	13.1	10.7	12.3	13.1	10.8	11.8	12.7	7.4	18.3	17.7	19.9	9.3	-	-
Experienced workers	10.3	11.5	7.6	10.0	11.2	7.5	11.6	12.5	6.7	16.9	16.7	17.5	7.5	-	-
New workers	2.1	1.6	3.1	2.4	1.9	3.3	0.3	0.2	0.8	1.3	1.0	2.4	1.9	-	-
EMPLOYED WORKERS BY CLASS OF WORKER															
Employed (exc. public emerg.)	100.0	100.0	100.0	100.0	100.0	100.0	100.0	100.0	100.0	100.0	100.0	100.0	-	-	-
Wage and salary workers	88.8	86.6	93.4	90.1	88.0	94.0	79.7	78.6	85.3	91.4	92.7	87.3	-	-	-
Employers and own-account workers	10.2	12.9	4.6	8.9	11.4	4.2	19.2	21.2	9.9	8.0	6.9	11.4	-	-	-
Unpaid family workers	0.6	0.2	1.3	0.6	0.3	1.1	0.7	0.1	3.8	0.1	-	0.3	-	-	-
Class of worker not reported	0.4	0.3	0.7	0.4	0.3	0.7	0.3	0.2	0.9	0.5	0.4	1.0	-	-	-
At work	100.0	100.0	100.0	100.0	100.0	100.0	100.0	100.0	100.0	100.0	100.0	100.0	-	-	-
Wage and salary workers	89.2	87.1	93.7	90.4	88.4	94.3	80.7	79.6	86.0	91.3	92.7	87.0	-	-	-
Employers and own-account workers	9.8	12.4	4.4	8.6	11.1	3.9	18.3	20.2	9.3	8.0	6.9	11.7	-	-	-
Unpaid family workers	0.6	0.2	1.3	0.6	0.3	1.1	0.7	0.1	3.9	0.1	-	0.3	-	-	-
Class of worker not reported	0.4	0.3	0.6	0.4	0.3	0.6	0.3	0.2	0.9	0.6	0.4	1.0	-	-	-
With a job	100.0	100.0	100.0	100.0	100.0	100.0	100.0	100.0	-	-	-	-	-	-	-
Wage and salary workers	74.2	71.4	81.4	77.6	75.3	82.5	58.0	55.9	-	-	-	-	-	-	-
Employers and own-account workers	23.7	27.3	14.5	20.1	23.2	13.4	40.7	43.5	-	-	-	-	-	-	-
Unpaid family workers	0.5	0.3	0.9	0.5	0.4	0.8	0.4	-	-	-	-	-	-	-	-
Class of worker not reported	1.6	1.0	3.2	1.8	1.1	3.3	0.9	0.6	-	-	-	-	-	-	-

Table C-42.—EMPLOYED WORKERS 14 YEARS OLD AND OVER, BY MAJOR OCCUPATION GROUP, INDUSTRY GROUP, AND SEX, FOR THE CITY OF ST. PAUL: 1940

[Percent not shown where less than 0.1 or where base is less than 100]

MAJOR OCCUPATION GROUP AND INDUSTRY GROUP	Total	Male	Female	PERCENT BY OCCUPATION AND INDUSTRY			PERCENT BY SEX	
				Total	Male	Female	Male	Female
Total population (all ages)	287,736	137,561	150,175	-	-	-	47.8	52.2
All persons 14 years old and over	231,743	108,991	122,752	-	-	-	47.0	53.0
In labor force	125,447	86,427	39,020	100.0	100.0	100.0	68.9	31.1
Employed workers (except on public emergency work)	104,216	70,637	33,579	83.1	81.7	86.1	67.8	32.2
MAJOR OCCUPATION GROUP								
Employed (except on public emergency work)	104,216	70,637	33,579	100.0	100.0	100.0	67.8	32.2
Professional workers	8,764	4,474	4,290	8.4	6.3	12.8	51.0	49.0
Semiprofessional workers	1,644	1,015	629	1.6	1.4	1.9	61.7	38.3
Farmers and farm managers	96	92	4	0.1	0.1	-	-	-
Proprietors, managers, and officials, except farm	10,373	9,372	1,001	10.0	13.3	3.0	90.3	9.7
Clerical, sales, and kindred workers	30,858	16,906	13,952	29.6	23.9	41.5	54.8	45.2
Craftsmen, foremen, and kindred workers	13,230	12,804	426	12.7	18.1	1.3	96.8	3.2
Operatives and kindred workers	17,589	13,646	3,943	16.9	19.3	11.7	77.6	22.4
Domestic service workers	4,443	101	4,342	4.3	0.1	12.9	2.3	97.7
Service workers, except domestic	10,709	6,176	4,533	10.3	8.7	13.5	57.7	42.3
Farm laborers (wage workers) and farm foremen	154	152	2	0.1	0.2	-	98.7	1.3
Farm laborers, unpaid family workers	15	9	6	-	-	-	-	-
Laborers, except farm	5,675	5,523	152	5.4	7.8	0.5	97.3	2.7
Occupation not reported	666	367	299	0.6	0.5	0.9	55.1	44.9
INDUSTRY GROUP								
Employed (except on public emergency work)	104,216	70,637	33,579	100.0	100.0	100.0	67.8	32.2
Agriculture, forestry, and fishery	396	373	23	0.4	0.5	0.1	94.2	5.8
Agriculture	362	341	21	0.3	0.5	0.1	94.2	5.8
Forestry (except logging) and fishery	34	32	2	-	-	-	-	-
Mining	102	89	13	0.1	0.1	-	87.3	12.7
Coal mining	3	2	1	-	-	-	-	-
Crude petroleum and natural gas production	4	2	2	-	-	-	-	-
Other mines and quarries	95	85	10	0.1	0.1	-	-	-
Construction	4,647	4,525	122	4.5	6.4	0.4	97.4	2.6
Manufacturing	22,569	17,994	4,575	21.7	25.5	13.6	79.7	20.3
Food and kindred products	6,502	5,641	861	6.2	8.0	2.6	86.8	13.2
Textile-mill products	260	136	124	0.2	0.2	0.4	52.3	47.7
Apparel and other fabricated textile products	1,511	584	927	1.4	0.8	2.8	38.6	61.4
Logging	7	6	1	-	-	-	-	-
Sawmills and planing mills	200	176	24	0.2	0.2	0.1	88.0	12.0
Furniture, store fixtures, and miscellaneous wooden goods	632	572	60	0.6	0.8	0.2	90.5	9.5
Paper and allied products	927	682	245	0.9	1.0	0.7	73.6	26.4
Printing, publishing, and allied industries	3,553	2,502	1,051	3.4	3.5	3.1	70.4	29.6
Chemicals and allied products	625	451	174	0.6	0.6	0.5	72.2	27.8
Petroleum and coal products	238	235	3	0.2	0.3	-	98.7	1.3
Leather and leather products	203	143	60	0.2	0.2	0.2	70.4	29.6
Stone, clay, and glass products	1,253	1,059	194	1.2	1.5	0.6	84.5	15.5
Iron and steel and their products	1,578	1,410	168	1.5	2.0	0.5	89.4	10.6
Nonferrous metals and their products	384	361	23	0.4	0.5	0.1	94.0	6.0
Machinery	2,704	2,489	215	2.6	3.5	0.6	92.0	8.0
Automobiles and automobile equipment	614	580	34	0.6	0.8	0.1	94.5	5.5
Transportation equipment, except automobile	65	64	1	0.1	0.1	-	-	-
Other and not specified manufacturing industries	1,313	903	410	1.3	1.3	1.2	68.8	31.2
Transportation, communication, and other public utilities	13,022	11,419	1,603	12.5	16.2	4.8	87.7	12.3
Railroads (including railroad repair shops) and railway express service	7,902	7,235	667	7.6	10.2	2.0	91.6	8.4
Trucking service	1,090	1,022	68	1.0	1.4	0.2	93.8	6.2
Other transportation	1,578	1,478	100	1.5	2.1	0.3	93.7	6.3
Communication	1,246	623	623	1.2	0.9	1.9	50.0	50.0
Utilities	1,206	1,061	145	1.2	1.5	0.4	88.0	12.0
Wholesale and retail trade	26,777	17,777	9,000	25.7	25.2	26.8	66.4	33.6
Wholesale trade	5,899	4,597	1,302	5.7	6.5	3.9	77.9	22.1
Food and dairy products stores, and milk retailing	4,135	3,259	876	4.0	4.6	2.6	78.8	21.2
Eating and drinking places	3,635	1,907	1,728	3.5	2.7	5.1	52.5	47.5
Motor vehicles and accessories retailing, and filling stations	1,802	1,706	96	1.7	2.4	0.3	94.7	5.3
Other retail trade	11,306	6,308	4,998	10.8	8.9	14.9	55.8	44.2
Finance, insurance, and real estate	6,074	3,993	2,081	5.8	5.7	6.2	65.7	34.3
Business and repair services	2,388	1,993	395	2.3	2.8	1.2	83.5	16.5
Automobile storage, rental, and repair services	993	.969	24	1.0	1.4	0.1	97.6	2.4
Business and repair services, except automobile	1,395	1,024	371	1.3	1.4	1.1	73.4	26.6
Personal services	9,127	2,380	6,747	8.8	3.4	20.1	26.1	73.9
Domestic service	4,805	282	4,523	4.6	0.4	13.5	5.9	94.1
Hotels and lodging places	1,436	668	768	1.4	0.9	2.3	46.5	53.5
Laundering, cleaning, and dyeing services	1,060	497	563	1.0	0.7	1.7	46.9	53.1
Miscellaneous personal services	1,826	933	893	1.8	1.3	2.7	51.1	48.9
Amusement, recreation, and related services	996	796	200	1.0	1.1	0.6	79.9	20.1
Professional and related services	10,743	4,071	6,672	10.3	5.8	19.9	37.9	62.1
Government	6,318	4,616	1,702	6.1	6.5	5.1	73.1	26.9
Industry not reported	1,057	611	446	1.0	0.9	1.3	57.8	42.2

Table C-43.—PERSONS 14 YEARS OLD AND OVER IN THE LABOR FORCE, 1940, AND GAINFUL WORKERS 14 YEARS OLD AND OVER, 1930, BY RACE AND SEX, FOR THE CITY OF ST. PAUL

[Totals for population and gainful workers for 1930 include "Unknown age." Figures for white population in 1930 have been revised to include Mexicans who were classified with "Other races" in the 1930 reports. Percent not shown where less than 0.1 or where base is less than 100]

CENSUS YEAR AND RACE	TOTAL					MALE					FEMALE				
	Population		Persons in the labor force, and gainful workers,[1] 14 years old and over			Population		Persons in the labor force, and gainful workers,[1] 14 years old and over			Population		Persons in the labor force, and gainful workers,[1] 14 years old and over		
	Total (all ages)	14 years old and over	Number	Percent of total population	Percent of population 14 yrs. and over	Total (all ages)	14 years old and over	Number	Percent of total population	Percent of population 14 yrs. and over	Total (all ages)	14 years old and over	Number	Percent of total population	Percent of population 14 yrs. and over
1940	287,736	231,743	125,447	43.6	54.1	137,561	108,991	86,427	62.8	79.3	150,175	122,752	39,020	26.0	31.8
White	283,399	228,184	123,474	43.6	54.1	135,348	107,151	84,972	62.8	79.3	148,051	121,033	38,502	26.0	31.8
Negro	4,139	3,402	1,866	45.1	54.9	2,070	1,726	1,364	65.9	79.0	2,069	1,676	502	24.3	30.0
Other races	198	157	107	54.0	68.2	143	114	91	63.6	79.8	55	43	16	-	-
1930	271,606	208,496	117,733	43.3	56.5	131,570	99,787	83,828	63.7	84.0	140,036	108,709	33,905	24.2	31.2
White	267,273	204,985	115,543	43.2	56.4	129,268	97,902	82,161	63.6	83.9	138,005	107,083	33,382	24.2	31.2
Negro	4,001	3,259	2,020	50.5	62.0	2,086	1,714	1,522	73.0	88.8	1.915	1,545	498	26.0	32.2
Other races	332	252	170	51.2	67.5	216	171	145	67.1	84.8	116	81	25	21.6	-

[1] Data for 1930 represent gainful workers 14 years old and over.

"Harvard Palates Provide Problem, College Authorities Have Constant Task to Meet Food Likes and Dislikes," *The New York Times*, October 14, 1934

One of the big problems of Harvard College authorities is that of satisfying more than 3,000 healthy but widely varied student appetites. Harvard undergraduates, it appears, have very definite likes and dislikes when they sit down to meals in the undergraduate dining halls.

For example, they don't care for "New England boiled dinners" or "New England fish dinners," although a large percentage comes from homes in the section where these dishes were made famous, and curiously, they like spinach and eat plenty of it, but never have pie or doughnuts for breakfast.

Among the meals, steak ranks first in popularity, with chicken, lamb chops and roast beef following in that order.

A visiting committee of 20 women, mothers of students, is appointed by the Harvard Board of Overseers each year. These women inspect the menus, talk to the students, and eat in the dining halls about once a week, and offer suggestions to the management.

Menus are so diversified that there is no sense of sameness.

Typical menus are:

Breakfast: Sliced banana or preserved peaches; oatmeal, Wheat Krumbles, cornflakes, Post Toasties, puffed wheat, Shredded Wheat biscuits, Wheaties, Post bran flakes, Pep, puffed rice, rice flakes, Rice Krispies, All Bran, scrambled eggs with bacon, or boiled eggs; toast, rolls, muffins and grilled cakes, tea, coffee, cocoa, milk or buttermilk.

Luncheon: Hamburger steak with mushroom sauce, poached eggs, sautéed potatoes, buttered new cabbage, lettuce hearts with French dressing, cinnamon buns, sliced pineapple, apple pie, cherry cookie; coffee, cocoa, milk, buttermilk; choice of dry cereals, crackers and milk; ice cream or fruit served in the place of meat or dessert.

Dinner: Bisque of tomato; grilled lamb chop, sausage and bacon, French fried sweet potatoes, green string beans, Parker House rolls; pineapple and cream cheese salad; fudge spumoni ice cream, assorted cake and coffee.

Radio Timeline

1916: The first regular broadcasts on 9XM featured Wisconsin state weather, delivered in Morse Code.

1919: The first clear transmission of human speech occurred on 9XM after experiments with voice (1918) and music (1917).

1920: Regular wireless broadcasts for entertainment began in Argentina, pioneered by the group around Enrique Telémaco Susini; E.W. Scripps's WWJ in Detroit received its commercial broadcasting license and carried a regular schedule of programming.

August 31, 1920: The first known radio news program was broadcast by station 8MK, the unlicensed predecessor of WWJ (AM) in Detroit, Michigan.

October 1920: Westinghouse in Pittsburgh, Pennsylvania, became the first U.S. commercial broadcasting station to be licensed when it was granted call letters KDKA.

Mid-1920s: Amplifying vacuum tubes developed by Westinghouse engineers dramatically improved radio receivers and transmitters, replacing the crystal set receivers; Inventions of the triode amplifier, generator, and detector improved audio.

Early 1930s: Single sideband (SSB) and frequency modulation (FM) were invented by amateur radio operators; Westinghouse was brought into the patent allies group, General Electric, American Telephone and Telegraph, and Radio Corporation of America, and became a part owner of RCA.

1933: FM radio, which Edwin H. Armstrong invented, was patented; FM used frequency modulation of the radio wave to minimize static and interference from electrical equipment and the atmosphere in the audio program.

Wheaties advertisement featuring baseball great Lou Gehrig: I believe any man who wants to go places in any sport has to keep in good physical shape. I always watch my eating pretty closely and make it a point to put away a good breakfast in the morning. But I want my food to taste good, too. And there's nothing better than a big bowl of Wheaties with plenty of milk or cream and sugar. That's a "Breakfast of Champions" you want to try. You'll be glad you did. Because Wheaties sure taste great!

General Mills Timeline

1866: Cadwallader Washburn, owner of Minneapolis Milling Company, opened the first flour mill in Minneapolis.

1877: John Crosby entered into partnership with Washburn, whose company was then renamed the Washburn-Crosby Company.

1880: The Washburn-Crosby Company won a gold medal at the first International Millers' Exhibition, leading to the later creation of the Gold Medal brand.

1888: James S. Bell took over leadership of the Washburn-Crosby Company.

1921: The fictional Betty Crocker was created by Washburn-Crosby.

1924: Wheaties ready-to-eat cereal debuted.

1928: James S. Bell's son, James Ford, led the creation of General Mills through the merger of Washburn-Crosby with several other regional millers.

1931: Bisquick, the first baking mix, was introduced.

What To Do
About The Child Who "Hates" Cereals

And—A Way That Works Wonders In Getting Him To Eat A Big Breakfast

Try This Marvelous New Creation That Now Brings Whole Wheat in Flakes as Light as Snowflakes . . Crispy, Crunchy, Golden-brown Flakes with All the Gaiety, All the Allure of A French Confection

Yet

A Dish That With Milk or Cream and Sugar and Some Kind of Fruit Makes A Meal So Nourishing It's Called "The Breakfast of Champions"

Accepted by The Committee On Foods of The American Medical Association as a Pure Food, Honestly Advertised

NOW in answer to the question so many mothers are asking—"What Can I Do To Get My Child to Like Cereals?"—comes a very simple solution. And—one that is acceptable to leading child authorities.

They say that, due to the serious digestive disturbances often resulting from emotional "scenes," no child should ever be coaxed or forced to eat a cereal he "hates." Instead, a child should be served a cereal he will eat willingly.

If you agree with their thinking on this subject, then you are urged to try this amazing new whole wheat creation. For it brings whole wheat, at last, in a ready-to-serve form that children adore.

A new and unique form of the most basic of all cereals for human consumption. A form so marvelously delicious and enticing that children revel in it like a party dish—*will eat it absolutely without coaxing, commanding.*

It's whole wheat in flakes as light as snowflakes. Crispy, crunchy, golden-brown flakes having all the gaiety, all the allure of a French Confection.

Yet that, with abundant milk and sugar, makes a dish which, together with some kind of fruit, comprises a breakfast that builds strong bones, red blood, solid flesh. And—gives the energy the growing child needs for work or play.

In short, this new development of the millers of famous Gold Medal "Kitchen-tested" Flour is a simple transformation of the "necessary" food, whole wheat, into one that's marvelously light and tempting.

The name of this whole wheat creation is Wheaties. And it's supremely delicious, served with milk or cream and sugar.

If you believe in whole wheat for yourself and child—you are urged to try Wheaties.

All The Mineral, Vitamin Containing Elements Retained

In the manufacture of Wheaties, none of the bran, containing valuable phosphorus and iron, none of the germ (that part of the wheat berry where nature has stored up essential vitamins A, B, E, and G) has been removed. All the carbohydrates that provide energy, all the protein that builds healthy flesh, all these are retained in Wheaties.

Another point, accepted by the American Medical Association's Foods Committee, is that whole wheat, from which Wheaties are made, contains nearly *twice* the body-building protein and a greater percentage of minerals than even such commonly used foods as corn or rice.

Wheaties cost but [illegible] the package—enough for a week. Yet the special type of wheat they're made from is far superior to best grades of ordinary wheat. Do you wonder why millions of homes "switched" to Wheaties last year? Why this dish with some kind of fruit is called—by such stars of sport as Jimmy Foxx, Lou Gehrig and many others—"The Breakfast of Champions"?

Get Wheaties at your grocer's. Ask for by name—W-H-E-A-T-I-E-S. You'll be glad you did.

GOLD MEDAL FOODS, INCORPORATED of GENERAL MILLS, INC., MINNEAPOLIS, MINN.

WHEATIES *"The Breakfast of Champions"*

WITH ABUNDANT MILK OR CREAM, SUGAR AND SOME KIND OF FRUIT

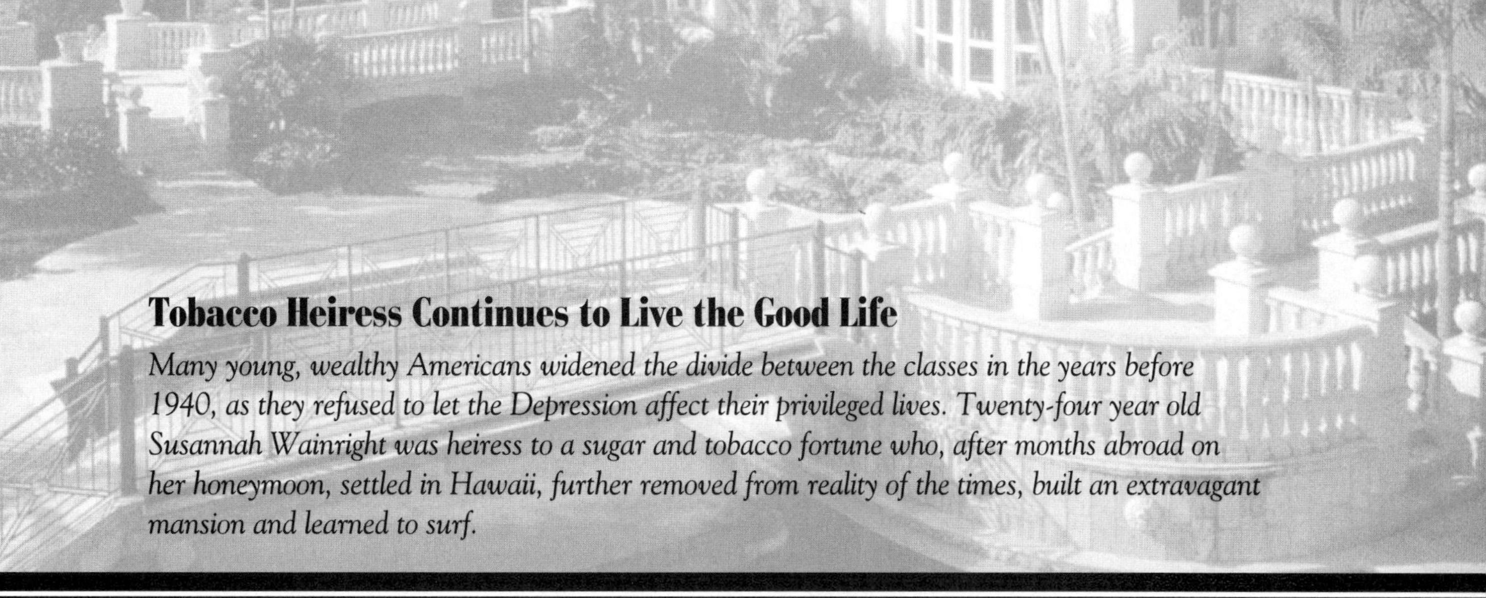

Tobacco Heiress Continues to Live the Good Life

Many young, wealthy Americans widened the divide between the classes in the years before 1940, as they refused to let the Depression affect their privileged lives. Twenty-four year old Susannah Wainright was heiress to a sugar and tobacco fortune who, after months abroad on her honeymoon, settled in Hawaii, further removed from reality of the times, built an extravagant mansion and learned to surf.

Life at Home

- Susannah Wainwright was the heiress to a sugar and tobacco fortune created during the days of the great trusts
- She was married when she was 22, and she and her husband, Edmund, built a home in Hawaii to escape the glaring eyes of the social set of Palm Beach, Florida, and Bar Harbor, Maine.
- She has already inherited more than $150 million, with more to come on her thirtieth birthday; Edmund lives on a small trust fund from his grandfather and an allowance from his wife.
- The couple was married by a Supreme Court Justice they had never met, in a ceremony that took place before a roaring fire in the spacious, heavily draped downstairs library of her New York mansion.
- She wore a simple blue crepe dress and hat for the wedding, which lasted five minutes and omitted the word "obey" from the vows.
- After the ceremony, two private chauffeurs, each driving Rolls-Royces, took the couple, a dozen suitcases and Susannah's personal maid to the awaiting honeymoon ship, the *Conti di Savoria*, which sailed for the Orient on a tour that included the Mediterranean, Egypt, Baghdad, India, Siam, Java, China, Japan, the Philippines and finally, Hawaii.
- Ten years older than Susannah, Edmund was the son of a wealthy Philadelphia family interested in making his name in politics; while on their honeymoon, he met a former girlfriend in Naples and had an affair while his new wife was shopping.
- During the trip, Susannah fell in love with the Taj Mahal and hired a Delhi architect to draw up plans in the style of a Mogul temple that included dozens of tessellated windows and doors inlaid with jade, agate, malachite, lapis lazuli and mother-of-pearl.

Susannah Wainwright was the heiress to a sugar and tobacco fortune.

- The construction in India of each door required six men working for three months, after which they were shipped, along with the windows and walls, to their new home in Hawaii.
- While in India, the couple took a 500-mile detour to Wardha where Mahatma Gandhi granted them an audience; Susannah was deeply impressed by the Holy One, especially his views on the emancipation of Indian women.
- During the fourth month of the honeymoon (scheduled for 24 months), when train travel became too grueling, she hired a private railroad car to calm her nerves; when the couple reached Singapore, she was admitted to the hospital for rest from "the fatigue of her honeymoon travels."
- Once discharged, she went on a shopping spree, spending $5,000 in a matter of hours on clothing, Chinese-style satin brocade pajamas, two-century-old Chinese ivory carvings, lingerie and jewelry.
- In Bangkok the couple purchased $20,000 in ancient rugs, in addition to nearly $300,000 in jade, a five-foot bronze monkey, a marble sunken bathtub and a huge ruby on a heavy gold chain.
- In Bali they hired a private yacht to take them to the Philippines, where the honeymooners were invited to tea with Mrs. Arthur Rubinstein, wife of the pianist.
- The couple next visited Japan and then, to end their 18,000-mile trek, sailed to Hawaii, where Susannah found freedom from the social expectations of the United States, and decided to go no further.
- In Hawaii, she took hula lessons and learned to surf from Duke Kahanamoku, Olympic swimming champion and sheriff in Honolulu, who introduced the flutter kick style of freestyle racing.
- When she wrote to her friends about the joys of surfing, they thought her silly; few on the East Coast of the United States thought standing on a board in the middle of a rushing tide sounded fun or stylish.
- Her wealth came from the tobacco and sugar businesses created at the turn of the century by her grandfather, who enjoyed a near monopoly for many years, and Susannah had no interest in the business or where her money came from.
- Her husband decided to return to the mainland to help President Roosevelt end the depression, as he considers himself an expert on economics.
- Before he left, he and Susannah went to the Big Island where they climbed to the top of Mauna Loa.
- Susannah and Edmund continue to travel, but separately; since the wedding, they have covered 500,000 miles, but seldom are both in the same city at the same time.
- The couple did attend the coronation of King George VI of Great Britain together, a grand royal spectacle, and enjoyed seats next to the royal family.
- In Palm Beach, rumors are rampant that the couple's marriage is over and divorce is imminent.

Life at Work

- Susannah put all her energy into building her new home in Hawaii
- They purchased a 4.5-acre plot for $100,000 in the residential section of Black Point near Diamond Head, on land formerly owned by Honolulu businessman Ernest H. Wodehouse, who had paid $16,000 for the land at the turn of the century.
- Hawaii was becoming the playground for American bluebloods, including railroad heir George Vanderbilt, tinplate heir Henry Topping, Pennsylvania steel magnate B. Barton Singer, Jr., and Fleishmann yeast heir Christian Holmes.
- Lavish cottages sprung up near Diamond Head, which was known as "Millionaire's Row."
- Publisher Roy Howard dubbed the Hawaiian islands "The American Riviera," and many of its wealthy live on fortunes created when monopolistic trusts were legal, even encouraged by government policy.
- In addition to elaborate homes, depression-era dollars were lavished on private zoos, tropical gardens, aviaries and glassed-in aquarium walls.
- Susannah loved the informality of the islands, and no one is scandalized when she wears pants to dinner.

- Edmund worked hard to incorporate the doors and designs she bought in India into their Hawaii palace and focused on his political career.
- To assist him in his effort to gain the attention of President Roosevelt, Susannah gave $50,000 to the Democratic Party.
- To improve his political network, the couple threw an elaborate dinner dance for 500 at a friend's townhouse on East 72nd Street in New York, where thousands of orchids and hundreds of palm trees were brought in from her grandfather's country estate as decoration for the event.
- Edmund was also working on an economics book which he believed Simon and Schuster would publish.
- One of his political advisors was William Randolph Hearst, whose California home resembled a Spanish castle, hung with seventeenth-century Flemish tapestries and occupying 350,000 acres, where Hearst raises American buffalo, giraffes, zebras, camels and ostriches on the grounds.
- The castle was often filled with the Hollywood set who come to party, and individual servants are assigned to guests once they arrive.

Life in the Community: Honolulu, Hawaii

- Despite a rising tide of tourism, the economy of the territory was still dependent on pineapples, sugar cane and fishing, and many Hawaiians gathered much of their food from the ocean.
- American law became definitive in Hawaii in 1900 under President William McKinley when he named Sanford B. Dole the first governor of the territory.
- A key element of Hawaiian society was the presence of approximately 20,000 American sailors stationed in Hawaii, making the military a key economic force on the islands.
- Building a dry dock at Pearl Harbor had a payroll of $60,000 a month for 10 years, and was an undertaking second in cost only to the Panama Canal.
- Small-business owners, from taxi operators to barbers, tattoo artists to nightclub owners, made a killing whenever the fleet is back from maneuvers or the enlisted men of Schofield come to town with their pay.
- Living in Honolulu required an understanding of the diverse Asian culture, with several dialects of Chinese spoken, and the distinction between Japanese from the southern area of Japan and the Okinawans from the Ryukyu Islands.
- Further, a Korean does not want to be mistaken for either a Chinese or a Japanese, and all wish to be distinguished from the late arrivals from the Philippines, who separate themselves into three divisions-Tagalog, Visayan and Ilocano.
- Despite years of discussions concerning statehood for Hawaii, the racial mix of the island is causing problems in Congress.

The Wainwrights were captivated by the beauty of Hawaii.

Towering Diamond Head loomed prominently over developing Honolulu.

Hawaiian Journey, "Hawaii Calls"

"There must be millions of Americans who, as children in the 1930s and 1940s, remember tuning in to a radio program called 'Hawaii Calls.' They would await that thrilling opening moment when the soft wash of the surf on the beach and the haunting sound of the conch-shell trumpet could be heard. The swaying palms, the sandy beach, the blue sky, and the colorfully costumed Hawaiian singers gathered on the shore could be seen in the mind, stimulated by the 'magic of radio.' More than anything else, 'Hawaii Calls' was responsible for popularizing Hawaiian music on the mainland and in other parts of the world, where it was heard by shortwave radio.

The music played on the program was known as 'hapa-haole,' or half-white, music. These songs sung in a Hawaiian style consisted of mostly English words with a few Hawaiian words thrown in for spice and color. Some, including 'Sweet Leilani' and 'My Little Grass Shack,' became world-famous. The program and its performers presented the kind of Hawaiian entertainment that they felt the outside world wanted to hear. Often the performers sang Hawaiian songs in the Hawaiian language, but the overall emphasis was on the hapa-haole music so popular at the time."

Frozen Food Innovator Focuses on Portable Food for Soldiers

As 1940 approached, it was obvious that America would be drawn into war, a sentiment strongly felt by Owen Verheil, who travelled extensively in Europe after selling his frozen food business. With more than 30 patents on food preservation, he turned his attention to nutritious, portable foods for soldiers.

Life at Home

- Owen Verheil sold his frozen food business for $22 million, receiving about $5 million profit for his life's work, including patents
- He has since devoted himself to improving science and his fellow man.
- Curious by nature and adventurous by habit, he traveled extensively in Alaska, Greenland and Sweden, mostly to talk with scientists about the preservative qualities of cold temperatures.
- His passion was objects made in jade; it delighted him that for centuries the Chinese used a single calligraphic character to denote both "jade" and "treasure" and carries a tiny carved figure in his pocket purchased from the Kowloon Jade Market in Hong Kong.
- He enjoyed cooking, gardening, inventing, playing Chinese checkers with his grandchildren and entertaining the smartest men and women in the world.
- He loved to experiment, even with the foods he cooks, recently serving his guests porpoise meat, whose flavor he compares to that of canvasback duck.
- He often went to the movies alone, enjoying the corny puns in shows like "No Snooze is Good Snooze"and his favorite actress, Claudette Colbert.
- Owen was born in on a farm in Long Island, New York, where he spent his summers enjoying countless hours tramping along the seashore.
- A loner by nature, Owen had little interest in organized sports and dropped out of Amherst College, due to shaky family finances.

Owen Verheil had a passion for objects made of jade.

- His first job was as a naturalist with the United States Department of Agriculture's Biological Survey, collecting specimens of the animal and bird life in New Mexico and Arizona.
- In 1912, he took a six-week cruise to Labrador with a medical missionary and stayed to trap and breed black foxes.

Emily devoted her time to their six grandchildren.

- During the trip he saw food frozen rapidly by extreme winter cold, noticing that duck and caribou meat preserved in this manner retained its taste, compared to food frozen during the warm spring, which was less smooth and less appetizing.
- He and his wife, Emily, returned to live in Labrador, where he put a barrel of cabbages outside in sea water, in temperatures of 10 degrees below zero; whenever the family wanted leafy vegetables, he went out and chopped loose a head of cabbage.
- The family moved outside Bangor, Maine, and bought a Georgian colonial-style country estate that includes 145 acres.
- The seven bedrooms gave them enough room for their six grandchildren, three boys and three girls, and the massive living room, anchored by a French 1760s white-limestone fireplace, was excellent for entertaining guests, arguing about science or solving the world's political problems with the best minds in the area.
- They took a two-day trip to the New York World's Fair, which made him excited about the progress under way; it was so large and sprawling they would have quickly become lost without their map.
- Despite their wealth, Emily was most comfortable in her traditional role as wife, mother and grandmother, occasionally skipping trips with her husband to stay home and quietly knit, decorate the house and entertain their grandchildren.
- It brought her great pleasure to make clothes for the grandchildren, as it did when she made clothing for her own children during the early years of her marriage.
- Owen purchased a Rolls-Royce large enough for all the grandchildren and hired a chauffeur, even though Emily is embarrassed by the mere thought of having a chauffeur, let alone to carry grandchildren around.

Life at Work

- Owen began his company with $7.00, with which he bought salt, ice and an electric fan, and worked out of a corner of the Clothel Refrigerating Company of New York.
- His goal was to create a fish-freezing plant and his first freezer consisted of a funnel-shaped can which was filled with food and then submerged in brine.
- Next, he developed a freezer using narrow cans equipped with automatic loaders, which could process 2.5- to 5 pound blocks of food by submerging the containers in a tank of frigid calcium chloride brine; unfortunately, when the finished frozen food was loaded into cans, producing airspace, it failed.
- He discovered that shipping frozen foods required special containers; balsa wood proved too expensive, so he turned to a fiberboard shipping carton that cost only $0.01 per pound.
- The patent for the new shipping container with good insulating quality was his first.
- After six years in business, about one million pounds of fruits and vegetables were frozen.
- He sold his company to the Postum Company for $22 million; $20 million was paid for his patents and only $2 million for other assets.
- Owen held more than 30 United States and foreign patents, mostly related to food preservation, and selling his business freed him to experiment with new ways to preserve food.
- He concentrated much of his effort on creating nutritious, portable foods for soldiers, as he thought it obvious that the European war will soon include the United States.

The Verheils' Georgian colonial-style home included 145 acres.

- During their last trip abroad, Owen and Emily attended a play in London, participated in a lecture at Oxford and then visited the Hague, Netherlands, for the celebration of the queen's fortieth anniversary of her coronation; Emily loved the white cape the queen was wearing during the parade.
- Owen's experiments with food preservation ranged from ways to more efficiently seal food and its flavors to methods of grinding up food for rapid freezing so it can be economically shipped in bulk.
- He was glad he remained in the industry, focused on perfecting the freezing of food-despite all the challenges; he often likens the frozen food industry to a small infant-plenty of noise at one end and an absolute lack of control on the other.
- The Postum Company began marketing frozen foods, based on Owen's patents, featuring frozen peas and spinach in their vegetable line and raspberries, loganberries and cherries in the fruit line.
- When the new frozen foods were offered, a salesman in Springfield, Massachusetts, said it was not an easy sell: "It took about five minutes to fast-talk a reluctant housewife into buying a package of peas at $0.35" because most housewives were more interested in price than in convenience.
- In the beginning, the main selling theme was "quick frozen versus cold storage."
- Many grocery stores were reluctant to spend large sums on expensive refrigerator capacity for an unproven product.
- An editorial in *Quick Frozen Foods*, a publication for the supermarket industry, campaigned for self-service cabinets, in which shoppers could select the frozen foods without the assistance of a clerk.
- Many in the industry were convinced that frozen foods were "a passing fad," that were "too expensive to handle."

- The principal brands of frozen food were Bird's Eye and Honor Brand, followed by Bodle, Little America, Hershey, Cedergreen, and Dulany Fairmont.
- To improve distribution, several major companies contracted with the American Radiator Company to manufacture boxes that can be placed in stores on a monthly payment basis.
- A shift took place within the frozen food industry toward retail-sized packages, and one third of the strawberries packed and sold went into consumer sizes.
- Strawberries, which once had been a bulk item used primarily by bakers and ice cream makers, have became a retail leader for ready-to-eat desserts in the home.
- The biggest pre-cooked innovations of the year came from the Postum Company, under the Bird's Eye label, featuring chicken fricassee and a cross-cut steak.
- Since the industry must sell a concept, not a price, a typical advertisement reads, "It's October. The fresh asparagus season closed months ago. Yet today we offer you quick frozen asparagus, actually field fresher than the king can get in the middle of the season. Here's why-asparagus changes fast after cutting. The sugars turn quickly to starch. Stringy fibers develop. Even in season, your average asparagus may take up to three days to reach your table. By that time it's but a dry copy of the green shoots the farmer cuts in the field."

Life in the Community: Bangor, Maine

- Bangor was the third largest city in Maine, nestled along the Penobscot River.
- Twenty-three miles from deep sea anchorage and at the head of the tidewater, Bangor established its place early on as the logging capital of America, where hard-drinking, deepwater sailormen mixed with the rough, backcountry loggers.
- Main (the Pine Tree State) has 39,000 farms, more than Connecticut, New Hampshire and Rhode Island combined.
- Potato farmers fought to maintain their position as the nation's top producer of potatoes, battling Alaska and Idaho.
- Owen and Emily's only son attended Bowdoin College in Brunswick; incorporated in 1794, the men-only institution is known nationally as a "Little Ivy League" school.

SECTION TWO: HISTORICAL SNAPSHOTS

The decade leading up to 1940 was full of fits and starts: Depression to stable economy; Stable economy to Depression; Joblessness to innovation; Male dominated careers to female workers; Homebaked cookies to Pepperidge Farm. These years represented huge shifts in just about every industry and every phase of life in America. These Historical Snapshots highlight significant "firsts" as America travelled toward 1940, ignoring the speed limit or the fasten your seatbelt light.

Early 1930s

- Unemployment passed four million
- More than 1,352 banks closed
- The first analog computer was placed in operation by Vannevar Bush
- U.S. had one passenger car per 5.5 persons
- Gasoline consumption rose to nearly 16 billion gallons
- Trousers became acceptable attire for women who played golf and rode horses
- Radio set sales increased to 13.5 million
- Advertisers spent $60 million on radio commercials
- Boeing hired eight nurses to act as flight attendants
- *Fortune Magazine* was launched by Henry R. Luce, costing $1.00 per issue
- The University of Southern California polo team refused to play against the University of California at Los Angeles until its one female member was replaced by a male
- Laurette Schimmoler of Ohio became the first woman airport manager, earning $510 a year
- The movie industry employed 100,000 people
- Alka-Seltzer was introduced by Miles Laboratories
- Clairol hair products were introduced by U.S. chemists
- Bird's Eye Frosted Foods were sold nationally for the first time
- The International Apple Shippers Association gave 6,000 jobless men surplus apples on credit to sell for $0.05 on street corners
- *The Big Trail*, starring John Wayne, *All Quiet on the Western Front*, *The Blue Angel*, *Monte Carlo*, and *Hell's Angels* all premiered
- Jean Harlow became a blonde for her role in *Hell's Angels*
- Hostess Twinkies, Snickers, sliced Wonder Bread, Jiffy biscuits, windshield wipers, Plexiglas and *Fortune* magazine all made their first appearance
- The Greta Garbo look was replacing the flapper style of Clara Bow
- *As I Lay Dying* by William Faulkner and *The 42nd Parallel* by John Dos Passos were published; *Lincoln* by Emil Ludwig was a bestseller
- The first all-air commercial New York-to-Los Angeles transport began by Transcontinental and West Airlines

- "Georgia on My Mind," "What Is This Thing Called Love?" and "On the Sunny Side of the Street" were all popular songs
- A *Literary Digest* poll showed that 40 percent of the U.S. population favored the repeal of Prohibition, while 29 percent wanted modification
- Tree sitting, contact bridge and knitting were current fads, along with playing backgammon and "Sorry"
- America's illiteracy rate fell to 4.3 percent
- Movies began projecting 24 frames per second to accommodate sound, up from 16 frames per second during the silent movie era.
- Movie attendance climbed to 90 million
- The proliferation of country clubs in New England professional journal, *Architectural Record*, to devote regular features to country club styles and influence.
- A clock using the natural vibration of a quartz crystal, subjected to an electrical current, produced accurate time within a thousandth of a second
- 3M engineer Richard Drew invented Scotch tape to seal the cellophane used to wrap foods such as bread and candy
- Pre-sliced bread, exceeded 50 percent of all bread sales across America.
- Public school children attended classes an average of 143 days a year
- The cyclotron was created as a means of accelerating particles by magnetic resonance for the purpose of splitting atoms
- WXBS, the CBS pioneer experimental television station, began operation with the premier telecast of *Felix the Cat*
- Rolex began selling the first waterproof watch, calling it the Oyster
- The film version of *Dracula* starring Bela Lugosi was released
- California received the go-ahead from Congress to build the San Francisco-Oakland Bay Bridge
- "The Star-Spangled Banner" was adopted as the United States' national anthem
- Nevada legalized both gambling and the six-month divorce
- The Scottsboro Boys were arrested in Alabama and falsely charged with rape
- Lucky Strike cigarettes outsold its rival, Camel
- Construction of the Empire State Building was completed in New York City
- Thomas Edison submitted his last patent application
- The National Education Association reported that 75 percent of all cities banned the employment of married women to protect jobs for men
- The Emerson iron lung was perfected
- Baseball player Pepper Martin of the St. Louis Cardinals batted .500 to lead the "Gashouse Gang" to a World Series championship over Philadelphia
- The comic strip detective character Dick Tracy was created by cartoonist Chester Gould debuting in the *Detroit Mirror* newspaper
- Gangster Al Capone was sentenced to 11 years in prison for tax evasion in Chicago, Illinois
- Popular books included *The Good Earth* by Pearle S. Buck, *Only Yesterday* by William Lewis Allen, *Sanctuary* by William Faulkner and *Dear Lovely Death* by Langston Hughes
- Jane Addams became the first American woman to be awarded the Nobel Peace Prize
- The National Committee for Modification of the Volstead Act was formed to work for the repeal of Prohibition in the United States
- Radio premieres included *The Ed Sullivan Show, The March of Time* and *The Eddie Cantor Show*
- The top one percent of Americans held a 44-percent share of all personal assets in America

- Inflation for the year was at a negative 4.4 percent
- Four men were killed during a bitter coal miners' strike in Harlan, Kentucky
- Safeway Stores reached their peak of expansion with 3,527 stores
- Silent film extra Clark Gable appeared in the movie *A Free Soul* and gained instant stardom
- A photoelectric cell was installed commercially for the first time
- Infrared photographs, air conditioners, the Schick electric dry shaver, Beech-Nut baby food, Alka Seltzer and stockings in transparent mesh all made their first appearance
- Lucky Luciano organized the Mafia into federated families
- The rate of admission to state mental hospitals for the past year was triple the rate from 1922 to 1930
- Nearly 6,000 cases of infantile paralysis struck New York
- Midwestern farmers were helpless as grasshoppers destroyed 160,000 miles of pristine farmland
- The New York Waldorf-Astoria Hotel opened
- Mrs. Hattie W. Caraway (D-Arkansas) became the first woman elected to the U.S. Senate
- President Herbert Hoover pushed through a dramatic tax increase
- Mobster Al Capone was sent to prison in Atlanta, Georgia, for tax evasion
- George Burns and Gracie Allen debuted as regulars on the *Guy Lombardo Show*
- Irving Berlin's musical *Face the Music* premiered in New York City
- The Purple Heart award was reinstituted
- The Glass-Steagall Act was passed, giving the Federal Reserve the right to expand credit in order to increase money circulation
- The infant son of Charles and Anne Lindbergh was kidnapped from his nursery at the family home near Princeton, New Jersey
- The executive committee of the Daughters of the American Revolution voted to exclude blacks from appearing at Constitution Hall
- The Ford Motor Company unveiled its V8 engine
- Vitamin C was isolated by C. C. King at the University of Pittsburgh
- The Royal Shakespeare Theatre opened at Stratford-on-Avon, replacing one built in 1879
- Texaco fire chief Ed Wynn premiered on *Texaco Star Theater* before a live radio audience
- The Pulitzer prize was awarded to Pearl S. Buck for *The Good Earth*
- The cartoon character Goofy first appeared in *Mickey's Revue* by Walt Disney
- Congress changed the name "Porto Rico" to "Puerto Rico"
- Drug Inc.; Procter & Gamble; Loew's; Nash Motors; Int'l Shoe; Int'l Business Machines; and Coca Cola were added to the Dow Jones Industrial Index
- World War I veterans marched on Washington, DC, to demand cash bonuses that weren't due for another 13 years
- A federal gas tax was enacted
- The George Washington quarter went into circulation to commemorate his 200th birthday
- Amelia Earhart became the first woman to fly nonstop across the United States, traveling from Los Angeles to Newark, New Jersey, in just over 19 hours
- A five-day work week was established for General Motors workers
- The FBI publicized a list of "Public Enemies"
- The Zippo lighter, the Mounds candy bar, Fritos corn chips and Skippy peanut butter all made their first appearance
- President Herbert Hoover reduced his own salary by 20 percent in response to the Depression

- The Dow Jones Industrial Average fell to 41.89, only one point above where the average began in 1896
- The discovery of the male hormone testosterone stimulated interest in animal gonad transplants
- Cole Porter's musical *The Gay Divorcee* premiered in New York City
- The Committee on Cost of Medical Care recommended socialized medicine in the United States
- German physicist Albert Einstein was granted a visa, making it possible for him to travel to the United States
- Fred Astaire and Ginger Rogers made *Flying Down to Rio* their first movie together
- Radio City Music Hall opened in New York City
- A new rule in basketball required that the ball be brought over the mid-court line in 10 seconds
- Construction of the Golden Gate Bridge began in San Francisco Bay
- *The Lone Ranger* debuted on American radio
- Unemployment reached 15 million
- The cost of a National Football League franchise topped $10,000
- In Miami, Florida, Giuseppe Zangara attempted to assassinate President-elect Franklin D. Roosevelt
- The magazine *Newsweek* was published for the first time
- Prohibition ended and beer was allowed to be sold nine months before liquor was
- The film version of *King Kong,* starring Fay Wray, premiered at Radio City Music Hall and the RKO Roxy Theatre in New York City
- The Mount Rushmore National Memorial was dedicated
- Newly elected president Franklin D. Roosevelt, proclaimed, "The only thing we have to fear is fear itself" in his inauguration speech
- Jews called for a boycott of German goods to protest Nazi oppression
- President Franklin D. Roosevelt issued Executive Order 6102, making it illegal for U.S. citizens to own gold
- The detection of radio waves from the center of the Milky Way Galaxy was reported in *The New York Times*
- Walt Disney's cartoon *The Three Little Pigs* was released
- *Miss Lonelyhearts* by Nathaniel West, *God's Little Acre* by Erskine Caldwell and *To a God Unknown* by John Steinbeck were all published
- The use of an electric shock to the heart to reverse potentially fatal ventricular fibrillation was developed
- Helen Wills Moody won her second straight Wimbledon title, her sixth overall
- In professional football the goal post was moved to the goal line
- The first drive-in theater opened in Camden, New Jersey
- The *American Totalisator Company* unveiled its first electronic pari-mutuel betting machine at the Arlington Park Racetrack near Chicago
- The first Major League Baseball All-Star Game was played at Comiskey Park in Chicago
- Wiley Post becomes the first person to fly solo around the world, traveling 15,596 miles in seven days, 18 hours, and 45 minutes
- The chocolate chip cookie was invented by Ruth Wakefield
- The Twentieth Amendment to the Constitution was declared in effect, changing the inauguration date of members of Congress from March 4 to January 3
- Blondie Boopadoop married Dagwood Bumstead in the comic strip *Blondie*
- Francis Perkins was appointed Secretary of Labor, the first woman in the Cabinet

- President Franklin D. Roosevelt ordered a four-day bank holiday to stop large amounts of money from being withdrawn
- George Darrow added some copyrighted art work to the board game Monopoly and began selling it commercially in Philadelphia
- President Roosevelt delivered the first of his radio "fireside chats"
- Congress authorized the Civilian Conservation Corps to relieve rampant unemployment
- The Tennessee Valley Authority Act was created to build dams in the Tennessee Valley
- Saudi Arabia gave Standard Oil of California exclusive rights to explore for oil
- The first issue of *Esquire* magazine was published
- Due to rising anti-Semitism and anti-intellectualism in Hitler's Germany, Albert Einstein immigrated to Princeton, New Jersey

Mid 1930s

- Leni Riefenstahl directed *Triumph of the Will*, documenting the rise of the Third Reich in Germany
- The Civil Works Administration provided employment for four million people
- Donald Duck, Walgreen's drugstores, Flash Gordon, Seagram's Seven Royal Crown and the term "hi-fi" all made their first appearance
- Ernest and Julio Gallo invested $5,900 in a wine company
- The ongoing drought reduced the national corn crop by nearly one billion bushels
- Edna St. Vincent Millay published *Wine from These Grapes*; F. Scott Fitzgerald completed *Tender Is the Night*
- Dicumarol, an anticoagulant, was developed from clover
- "Tumbling Tumbleweeds," "I Only Have Eyes for You" and "Honeysuckle Rose" were all popular songs
- The Securities and Exchange Commission was created
- The movie *It Happened One Night* won academy awards for Best Picture, Best Director (Frank Capra), Best Actress (Claudette Colbert) and Best Actor (Clark Gable)
- The U.S. Gold Reserve Act authorized the president to devalue the dollar
- Enrico Fermi suggested that neutrons and protons were the same fundamental particles in two different quantum states
- The FBI shot John Dillinger, Public Enemy No. I, generating a hail of publicity
- Greyhound bus lines cut its business fares in half to $8 between New York and Chicago to encourage more traffic
- On an island off the coast of San Francisco, Alcatraz prison was opened
- The comic *Flash Gordon* was published
- Published books included *Tender is the Night* by F. Scott Fitzgerald, *Murder on the Orient Express* by Agatha Christie, *The Postman Always Rings Twice* by James M. Cain, and *Fer-De-Lance* by Rex Stout, the last of which marked the debut of Stout's corpulent sleuth Nero Wolfe
- On top of Mt. Washington in New Hampshire, 231 mph wind was recorded, the strongest wind in the world
- The cartoon character Donald Duck debuted in *Silly Symphonies*
- Bank robbers Clyde Barrow and Bonnie Parker were killed in Louisiana, following an intensive hunt for them after they had shot two young highway patrolmen
- The U.S. unemployment rate was 24.9 percent

- The first All-American Soap Box Derby was held in Dayton, Ohio
- The Quality Network, a co-op radio network, was reorganized as the Mutual Broadcasting Network
- New music on the 78 rpm discs included "Autumn in New York," "Blue Moon," "For All We Know," "I Get a Kick Out of You," "You and the Night" and the Music," and "Winter Wonderland"
- Off the coast of New Jersey, 134 people died in a fire aboard the passenger liner *Morro Castle*
- Metro-Goldwyn-Mayer purchased the rights to *The Wonderful Wizard of Oz* from the estate of L. Frank Baum for $40,000
- California physician Francis Townsend's old-age pension plan proposed levying a two percent tax that would provide $200 a month to all Americans over 60, who would then be required to spend their allotment within a month, thus spurring the economy.
- Coca-Cola sales dropped with the repeal of Prohibition.
- The Sears & Roebuck catalog began listing contraceptive devices.
- U.S. physicist Isidor Isaac Rabi began his work on the atomic and molecular beam magnetic resonance method for observing spectra in the radio frequency range.
- The A&P grocery store chain controlled 11 percent of grocery sales.
- The fan club for Buck Jones, America's number one movie cowboy, grew to more than three million members.
- The Supreme Court declared the National Recovery Administration to be unconstitutional
- The word "boondoggling" came to refer to "busy work" created to find activities for the unemployed
- Congress authorized creation of the Works Progress Administration, the National Labor Relations Board and the Rural Electrification Administration
- Group sports in public areas gained in popularity, especially bicycling, skiing, golf and softball
- The average cost of advertising on NBC radio was $360 per minute
- Congress passed the Banking Act of 1935, the Emergency Relief Appropriation Act, the National Labor Relations Act, and the Social Security Act
- Despite the domination of automobiles, Americans still spent $1,000 a day on buggy whips
- Economic recovery had begun as unemployment fell to 20.1 percent
- Popularity of the board game Monopoly exploded, with 20 million sets sold in one week
- Mary McLeod Bethune organized the National Council of Negro Women as a lobbying coalition of black women's groups
- Alcoholics Anonymous was founded
- Average monthly sales of *True Confessions* magazine topped 7.3 million
- New York Attorney General Thomas Dewey gained national attention with the convictions of Lucky Luciano and 70 others for racketeering
- Making their first appearance were: a woman member of the stock exchange, beer in cans, Toyota, Jolly Green Giant, Gallup polls, hot meals served on airplanes and Kodachrome for 16 mm cameras
- Fashion for women featured a severe military look showcasing square, epaulette shoulders, low heels, plumed hats and gauntlet gloves
- Baseball star Babe Ruth was traded by the New York Yankees to the Boston Braves
- *Tortilla Flat* by John Steinbeck, *Taps at Reveille* by F. Scott Fitzgerald, *The Last Puritan* by George Santayana, and *Of Time and the River* by Thomas Wolfe were published
- The Wagner Act (National Labor Relations Act) established the first national labor policy to protect the rights of workers to organize and to elect their own representatives for collective bargaining
- The Guffey Act was passed to stabilize the coal industry and to improve labor conditions
- Andrew Mellon donated $10 million, plus a $25 million art collection, for the construction of the National Art Gallery in Washington, D.C., stipulating that no gallery be named for him

- Popular songs included "You Are My Lucky Star"; "I Loves You, Porgy"; "I Got Plenty o' Nuthin'"; "Stairway to the Stars" and "I'm in the Mood for Love"
- The Committee for Industrial Organization (CIO) formed within the AFL to foster industrial unionism
- Americans consumed 50 million chickens and the cost of poultry rose above red meat
- The first building to be completely covered in glass was built in Toledo, Ohio, for the Owens-Illinois Glass Company
- *The Green Hornet* radio show debuted
- John Maynard Keynes's book *The General Theory of Employment, Interest and Money* was published
- Radium E became the first radioactive element to be made synthetically
- The first superhero to wear a skin-tight costume and a mask, *The Phantom*, made his appearance in U.S. newspapers
- Construction of Hoover Dam was completed
- The Santa Fe Railroad inaugurated the all-Pullman *Super Chief* passenger train between Chicago, Illinois, and Los Angeles, California
- Margaret Mitchell's novel *Gone with the Wind* was published
- German Max Schmeling knocked out American Joe Louis in the twelfth round of their heavyweight boxing match at Yankee Stadium in New York City
- The 1936 Summer Olympics opened in Berlin, Germany, and marked the first live television coverage of a sports event in world history
- African-American athlete Jesse Owens won the 100-meter dash at the Berlin Olympics and Hitler, believing him to be of an inferior race, refused to shake his hand
- The sculpture of Thomas Jefferson's head at Mount Rushmore was dedicated
- H. R. Ekins, reporter for the *New York World-Telegram*, won a race around the world on commercial airline flights with a time of 18 and a half days, beating out Dorothy Kilgallen of the *New York Journal* and Leo Kieran of the *New York Times*
- In the U.S. presidential election, Franklin D. Roosevelt was reelected to a second term in a landslide victory over Alf Landon
- The first edition of *LIFE Magazine* was published
- Radio station WQXR was founded in New York City
- Polaroid sunglasses and Ambré Solaire sunblock were both marketed for the first time
- Approximately 38 percent of American families had an income of less than $1,000 a year
- Ford unveiled the V-8 engine
- Recent advances in photography, including the 35 mm camera and easy-to-use exposure meters, fueled a photography boom
- The population of America reached 127 million
- *Life* magazine began publication, claiming in an early issue that one in 10 Americans had a tattoo
- New York's Triborough Bridge opened, with a toll of $0.25
- The National Park Service created numerous federal parks and fish and game preserves; in all, 600,000 acres were added to state preserves
- Mercedes-Benz created the first diesel-fueled passenger car
- The WPA Federal Art Project employed 3,500 artists who produced 4,500 murals, 189,000 sculptures and 450,000 paintings
- A Colorado farmland survey showed that half of the 6,000 farmhouses in one area had been abandoned

- Dust storms denuded large portions of the farmland of Kansas, Oklahoma, Colorado, Nebraska and the Dakotas
- A sleeper berth from Newark to Los Angeles cost $150; the New York Fifth Avenue double-decker bus fare was between $0.05 and $0.10
- Margaret Mitchell's book, *Gone with the Wind*, sold a record one million copies in six months
- A *Fortune* magazine poll indicated that 67 percent of readers favored birth control
- Seven million women paid more than $2 billion for 35 million permanents
- The photo-finish camera, bicycle traffic court, screw-cap bottle with pour lip, the Presbyterian Church of America and Tampax all made their first appearance
- Congress passed the Neutrality Acts designed to keep America out of foreign wars
- A revolt against progressive education was led by Robert M. Hutchins, president of the University of Chicago
- Molly Dewson of the National Consumers' League led a fight to gain the appointment of more female postmasters
- The first successful helicopter flight was made
- The "Chase and Sanborn Hour," with Edgar Bergen and Charlie McCarthy, and "The Shadow," starring Robert Hardy Andrews, both premiered on radio

Late 1930s

- The U.S. economy plunged back into a deep recession; unemployment climbed to 14.3 percent
- Hugo L. Black's appointment to the U.S. Supreme Court raised controversy because of Black's youthful membership in the KKK
- A *Fortune* poll reported that 50 percent of all college men and 25 percent of all college women had had premarital sexual relations
- The principle of the minimum wage for women was upheld by the U.S. Supreme Court
- *Popular Photography* magazine began publication
- Spam was introduced by George A. Hormel & Company
- Icemen delivered to more than 50 percent of middle-class households
- Louis B. Mayer of Metro-Goldwyn-Mayer made $1.16 million, while Major Edward Bowes of the *Amateur Hour* on radio made $427,817
- An estimated 500,000 American students took part in a student strike against war, united in a pledge never to support any war declared by the United States
- General Motors introduced the automatic transmission
- Parkard Motor Car Company sold a record 109,000 cars, while Pierce-Arrow autos went out of business
- Spinach growers erected a statue of Popeye the Sailor Man in Wisconsin
- Americans spent 4.5 hours daily listening to the radio
- The restoration of Colonial Williamsburg, Virginia, was completed
- John D. Rockefeller, who died at 98, left an estate estimated at $1 billion
- The trampoline, skywriting at night, Pepperidge Farm, the shopping cart, and the Lincoln Tunnel all made their first appearances
- In Flint, Michigan, a sit-down strike against General Motors ended after 44 days, with the company agreeing to recognize the United Automobile Workers Union
- DuPont research chemist Wallace H. Carothers received a patent for nylon

- Jack S. Liebowitz and Harry Donenfeld published their first issue of *Detective Comics,* later known as *DC Comics*
- The radio show *Lorenzo Jones* starring Karl Swenson was first aired
- The first U.S. Social Security checks were distributed
- President Franklin Roosevelt signed an act of neutrality, keeping the United States out of World War II
- Margaret Mitchell won a Pulitzer Prize for her novel *Gone with the Wind*
- The *Hindenburg* burst into flames and crashed to the ground, killing 36, as it attempted to dock with a mooring mast at Lakehurst Naval Air Station in New Jersey
- New York City's Lincoln Tunnel opened to traffic
- Actress Mae West performed a skit featuring Adam and Eve that got her banned from NBC Radio
- The first Santa Claus Training School opened in Albion, New York
- President Franklin Roosevelt dedicated the WPA-constructed Timberline Lodge in Mt. Hood National Forest
- The U.S. House of Representatives passed the Marijuana Tax Act stipulating that pot could not be sold without a license and that no licenses would be issued
- The Pullman Company formally recognized the Brotherhood of Sleeping Car Porters
- Ernest Hemingway's novel *To Have and Have Not* was published
- NBC formed the first full-sized symphony orchestra exclusively for radio broadcasting for Arturo Toscanini
- The U.S. congressional session was air-conditioned for the first time
- Seeing eye dogs came into use for aiding the blind
- The Fair Labor Standards Act established the Minimum Hourly Rate at 25 cents
- The Federal National Mortgage Association known as Fannie Mae was established
- Aviator Howard Hughes established a new 'round-the-world record of three days, 19 hours
- The March of Dimes' Polio Foundation was created by Franklin Roosevelt
- A Gallup poll indicated that 58 percent of Americans believed that the United States would be drawn into war; 65 percent favored boycotting German goods
- Seabiscuit defeated War Admiral in their long-awaited race to decide the best horse in America
- Action comics issued the first *Superman* comic
- New York staged a World's Fair called "The World of Tomorrow" which was visited by 25 million people
- Fifty percent of Americans polled selected radio as the most reliable news medium; 17 percent chose newspapers
- Orson Welles's radio adaptation of *The War of the Worlds* was broadcast, causing mass panic in the eastern United States
- Adolf Hitler was named *Time* magazine's "Man of the Year"
- Kate Smith sang her rendition of Irvin Berlin's "God Bless America" for the first time during an Armistice Day radio broadcast
- Disney Studios released *Snow White and the Seven Dwarfs*
- Thornton Wilder's play *Our Town* was performed for the first time
- A toothbrush became the first commercial product to be made with nylon yarn, used for the bristles
- Heavyweight boxing champion Joe Louis knocked out Max Schmeling in the first round of their rematch at Yankee Stadium in New York City
- Movie box office receipts reached an all-time high and averaged $25 per family per year

- The Birth Control Federation of America began its "Negro Project" designed to control the population of people it deemed less fit to rear children
- The Social Security Act was amended to allow extended benefits to the aged, widows, minors, and parents of a deceased person
- After DAR denied her the chance to sing at Constitution Hall because of her race, Marian Anderson sang at the Lincoln Memorial in Washington, D.C., before a crowd of 75,000
- *Reader's Digest* reached a circulation of eight million, up from 250,000 10 years earlier
- Radio sales continued to rise so that 27.5 million families owned 45 million radio sets
- The Federal Theatre Project was disbanded after accusations of communist influence
- Movie box-office receipts reached an all-time high; 85 million Americans, or 65 percent of the total U.S. population, went to the movies at least once a week
- A Gallup poll showed that 58 percent of Americans believed the U.S. would be drawn into the war, while 65 percent favored boycotting Germany
- Hollywood production code restrictions were lifted to enable Clark Gable in *Gone with the Wind* to say, "Frankly, my dear, I don't give a damn."
- Newly emigrated Enrico Fermi and John R. Dunning of Columbia University used the cyclotron to split uranium and obtain a massive energy release, suggesting a "chain reaction"
- Paul Miller developed the insecticide DDT
- Gangster Louis Lepke surrendered to popular newspaper and radio columnist Walter Winchell, who handed him over to J. Edgar Hoover
- The U.S. Supreme Court ruled that sit-down strikes were illegal
- The federal budget topped $9 billion, supported by only four million taxpayers; America had 1.13 million federal civilian employees
- The first baseball game was televised
- The New York World's Fair's theme, "The World of Tomorrow," was attracting thousands
- General Motors controlled 42 percent of the United States market in cars and trucks; its 220,000 employees made an average of $1,500 annually
- Transatlantic airmail service, the marketing of nylon stockings, the use of fluorescent lighting, and Packard's air-conditioned automobile were all introduced
- The Sears, Roebuck catalogue still featured horse-drawn farm wagons, washing machines run by gasoline, and refrigerators designed to cool with a block of ice
- Zippers on men's trousers became standard equipment
- The Hewlett-Packard Company was founded
- Flier Amelia Earhart was officially declared dead after her disappearance during a flight two years earlier
- Students at Harvard University demonstrated the new fad of swallowing goldfish to reporters
- John Steinbeck's novel *The Grapes of Wrath* was first published
- Billie Holiday recorded "Strange Fruit," an anti-lynching song
- *Batman*, created by Bob Kane, made his first appearance in a comic book
- Major League Baseball's Lou Gehrig, the legendary Yankee first baseman known as "The Iron Horse," ended his 2,130-consecutive-game streak after contracting amyotrophic lateral sclerosis
- The *St. Louis*, a ship carrying a cargo of 907 Jewish refugees, was denied permission to land in Florida and forced to return to Europe, where many of its passengers later died in Nazi death camps during the Holocaust
- The National Baseball Hall of Fame and Museum was officially dedicated in Cooperstown, New York
- The First World Science Fiction Convention opened in New York City

- Albert Einstein wrote to President Franklin Roosevelt about developing the atomic bomb using uranium, which led to the creation of the Manhattan Project
- MGM's classic musical film *The Wizard of Oz*, based on L. Frank Baum's famous novel, premiered at Grauman's Chinese Theatre in Hollywood
- The Golden Gate International Exposition opened in San Francisco
- The sculpture of Theodore Roosevelt's head was dedicated at Mount Rushmore
- Gerald J. Cox, speaking at an American Water Works Association meeting, publicly proposed the fluoridation of public water supplies in the U.S.
- Nylon stockings went on sale for the first time
- *Hedda Hopper's Hollywood* premiered on radio with Hollywood gossip columnist Hedda Hopper as host
- La Guardia Airport opened for business in New York City
- General Motors introduced the Hydra-Matic drive, the first mass-produced, fully automatic transmission, as an option in 1940 model year Oldsmobiles

1940

- RKO released Walt Disney's second full-length animated film, Pinocchio and Tom and Jerry make their debut in Puss Gets the Boot
- Martin Kamen and Sam Ruben discovered Carbon-14, the basis of the radiocarbon dating method used to determine the age of archaeological and geological finds
- Truth or Consequences debuted on NBC Radio
- Booker T. Washington became the first African-American to be depicted on a U.S. postage stamp
- The first McDonald's restaurant opened in San Bernardino, California
- President Franklin D. Roosevelt asked Congress for approximately $900 million to construct 50,000 airplanes per year
- World War I General John J. Pershing, in a nationwide radio broadcast, urged all-out aid to Britain in order to defend America, while national hero Charles Lindbergh led an isolationist rally at Soldier Field in Chicago
- The U.S. told Great Britain that 50 U.S. destroyers needed for escort work would be transferred to Great Britain in return for 99-year leases on British bases in the North Atlantic, West Indies, and Bermuda
- The Selective Training and Service Act of 1940 created the first peacetime draft in U.S. history
- The United States imposed a total embargo on all scrap metal shipments to Japan
- Franklin D. Roosevelt defeated Republican challenger Wendell Willkie to become the first and only third-term president
- Agatha Christie's mystery novel *And Then There Were None* was published

SECTION THREE: ECONOMY OF THE TIMES

Prices in the decade leading up to 1940 did not fluctuate significantly. The valleys and peaks of the economy didn't allow for drastic, steady changes, whether to income, shaving cream or bicycles. The following tables show typical American incomes and prices of everyday items leading up to 1940. The last page of this section (page 266) is a Consumer Price Index that compares the value of a dollar in the decade covered in this book, and beyond, to the value of a dollar in 2010.

1930

Average Annual Income, Standard Jobs

All Industries w/Farm Labor	$1,388
Bituminous Coal Mining	$909
Building Trades	$1,233
Domestics	$676
Farm Labor	$444
Federal Civilian	$1,768
Gas and Electricity Workers	$1,603
Manufacturing, Durable Goods	$1,391
Manufacturing, Nondurable Goods	$1,425
Medical/Health Workers	$933
Motion Picture Services	$2,179
Nonprofit Organization Workers	$1,698
Passenger Transportation Workers	$1,587
Personal Services	$1,200
Public School Teachers	$1,455
Radio Broadcasting Workers	$2,624
Railroads	$1,717
State and Government Workers	$1,517
Telephone/Telegraph Workers	$1,410
Wholesale/Retail Trade Workers	$1,569

Selected Prices

A.C. Spark Plug	$0.60
Airway Lightfood Shoes	$0.75
Cheviot Trousers	$2.89
Dunlap Hat for Men	$5
Gasoline Iron	$3.98
Golden Crest Hosier	$0.89
Goodyear Firestone Goodrich Tire	$2.95
J.C. Higgins Baseball	$0.95
Juniper Windsor Cook Stove	$21.50

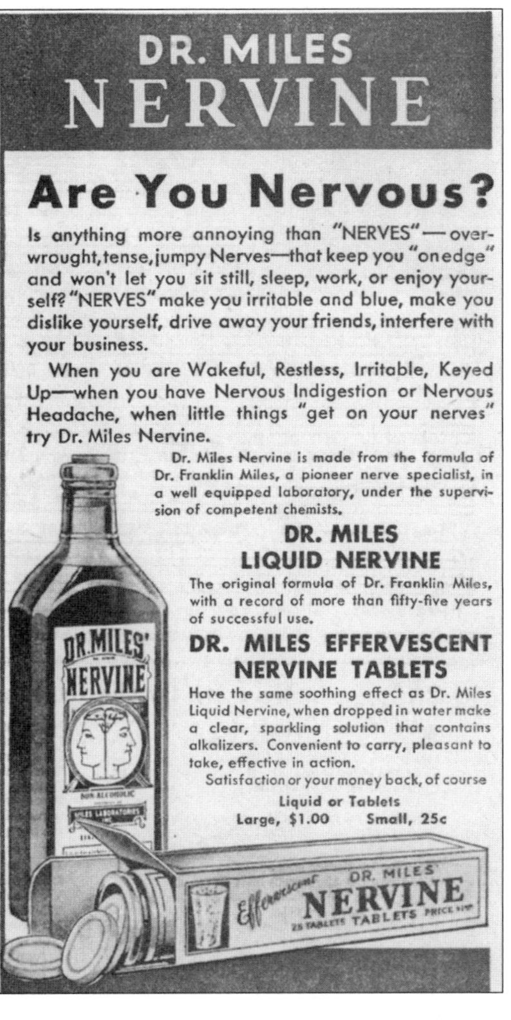

Kool Mild Menthol Cigarettes, Pack $0.15
Kraft Marshmallows, Box of 200. . . . . $0.65
Lady Elgin Wristwatch $25
Lakeside Lawnmower $5.49
Light Bulbs, 40-Watt, Pkg of Eight. $1
Pepperell Blanket. $0.31
Petroleum Vaseline Jelly, 4 oz $0.13
Rogers Silver Plate Flatware, 26-Piece $28.45
Tobrin Screwdriver, per Dozen. $10
Underwood Typewriter $49.50
Winnerset Microscope $6
Borax, Muleteam. $0.14
Candy Bar, Hershey's Almond. $0.05
Chifforobe $18.95
Cold Cream $0.49
Dress, Ladies' Silk Crepe. $2.98
Galoshes, Child's. $0.98
Radio, Philco $20
Tent, Boy's Camp $4.95
Thermometer, Fever $0.79
Tulip Bulbs, 20. . . . . $1.10
Valentines, 16 Cards $0.25
Washing Machine $57.95
Wristwatch, Man's Elgin, Gold $33.25

1931

Average Annual Income, Standard Jobs

All Industries, w/o Farm Labor	$1,406
All Industries, w/Farm Labor	$1,298
Bituminous Coal Mining	$723
Building Trades	$907
Domestics	$584
Farm Labor	$355
Federal Civilian	$1,895
Federal Employees, Exec Depts	$1,549
Federal Military	$1,164
Finance, Insurance and Real Estate	$1,858
Gas and Electricity Workers	$1,600
Mnfg, Durable Goods	$1,127
Mnfg, Nondurable Goods	$1,352
Medical/Health Services Workers	$919
Miscellaneous Manufacturing	$1,230
Motion Picture Services	$2,175
Nonprofit Organization Workers	$1,653
Passenger Trans, Local/Highway	$1,500
Personal Services	$1,136
Public School Teachers	$1,463
Radio Broadcasting /TV Workers	$2,732
Railroad Workers	$1,661
State/Local Government Workers	$1,497
Telephone/Telegraph Workers	$1,436
Wholesale/Retail Trade Workers	$1,495

Selected Prices

Automobile, REO	$795
Binoculars	$33.48
Camera, Kodak 6-20	$20
Clock, Gilbert	$5.95
Croquet Set	$3.98
Dinner Plates, Semi-Porcelain, dz.	$0.84
Flowers, 20 Tulips	$1.10
Girdle, Woman's	$1.74
Hair Color Treatment, Bottle	$1.29
Light Bulbs, Package of Eight	$1
Monthly, Popular Mechanics,	$0.25
Marshmallows, Kraft, Box of 200	$0.65
Radio, Philco	$20
Rug, 9' x 12' Velvet	$14.95
Shave Cream, Colgate	$0.25
Valentines, 16 Cards	$0.25
Washing Machine	$57.95
Wristwatch, Lady Elgin	$25
Cream Separator	$69.95

27 W. COLLEGE ST. PHONES 48 and 49

Wright & Parsons

Established in 1900

Glenn Valley Peas, very tender, 2 for 23c.

1 Pkg Yummy .... 49c. and 1 free

Edwards' Bartlett Pears, per can ...... 25c.

Pink Salmon, per can .... 15c.

Brer Rabbit Molasses, Gold Label per can .... 30c.

Brer Rabbit Molasses, Green Label per can .... 25c.

California Lima Beans, 13c. lb; 2 for 25c.

Lipton's Tea, ¼ lb. 25c; ½ lb. 47c; 1 lb. 90c.

First Prize Jelly, large jar .... 15c.

Cream Cornstarch .... 10c. pkg.

Wesson Oil: pts 30c; qts 52c; gal. $1.60

Storage Eggs -- our own storing, 23c. doz.

SATURDAY SPECIALS

Head Lettuce .... 10c.

10 lbs Sugar .... 52c.

4 lbs. Bananas .... 25c.

Pk. Potatoes .... 35c.

Field Tiller $94.50
Hen. $25
Milker $42.50
Mixer $21
Pitchfork $1.35
Radio. $20
Screwdriver. $1
Seed, per Bushel $1
Tractor Tires $35.15

REDUCTION IN PRICES

THE FOLLOWING PRICES ARE EFFECTIVE
MONDAY, JANUARY 19, 1931

	New Price	Old Price	Reduction
DeLuxe Roadster	$475	$520	$45
DeLuxe Phaeton	580	625	45
Phaeton	435	440	5
Roadster	430	435	5
Sport Coupe	500	525	25
Coupe	490	495	5
DeLuxe Coupe	525	545	20
Tudor Sedan	490	495	5
Fordor Sedan	590	600	10
Town Sedan	630	660	30
Cabriolet	595	625	30
Victoria	580	625	45
DeLuxe Sedan	630	640	10
Station Wagon	625	640	15
Model A Chassis	340	345	5
Model AA Truck Chassis 131½-INCH WHEELBASE	495	510	15
Model AA Truck Chassis 157-INCH WHEELBASE	525	535	10

(All Prices F. O. B. Detroit, Mich.)

You may purchase a Ford car or truck on convenient, economical terms through the authorized Ford Finance Plans of the Universal Credit Company

H. G. KLERMUND

PHONE 512 FORD DEALER Open Evenings

ASK ABOUT OUR 7 FOR 6

1932

Selected Prices

Baby Powder, Two Cans..................$0.29
Bed Sheet $0.65
Electric Washer.......................$79.85
Home Egg Hatcher $39.95
Ice Box..............................$18.75
Lawn Mower $5.49
Marshmallows, Box of 200 ....$0.65
Mattress.............................$4.65
Microphone $1
Towels, Cannon, 12 ....$1
Baby's Rubber Pants, Three Pairs $0.22
Camera, Kodak..........................$20
Coal, per Half Ton $4
Electric Iron $1
Hair Cut, Barber Shop $0.20
Motor Oil, Gallon $0.49
Rug, 9' x 12'.........................$14.95
Sewing Machine $19.95
Shotgun, Double Barrel $36.98
Towels, Six...........................$0.65
Baby Powder, Johnson & Johnson..........$0.29
Bicycle $17.50
Clock, Mahogany Finish.................$5.95
Hair Color Treatment, Slate Color.........$1.29
Highway Flare Torches, per Dozen $24
Hog Trough, 20-Gauge Steel, Lot of Six.....$0.48
Iron, Electric.............................$1
Marshmallows, Kraft Box of 200...........$0.65
Pocket Watch, Ingersoll Mickey Mouse $1.50
Shaving Cream, Colgate Rapid............$0.25
Shoes, Man's Oxford....................$2.48
Telephone Call, New York to London,
Three Minutes..........................$30
Tent, 5' x 7' $4.95
Valentines, 16 Cards $0.25
Wrenches, Complete Set $15

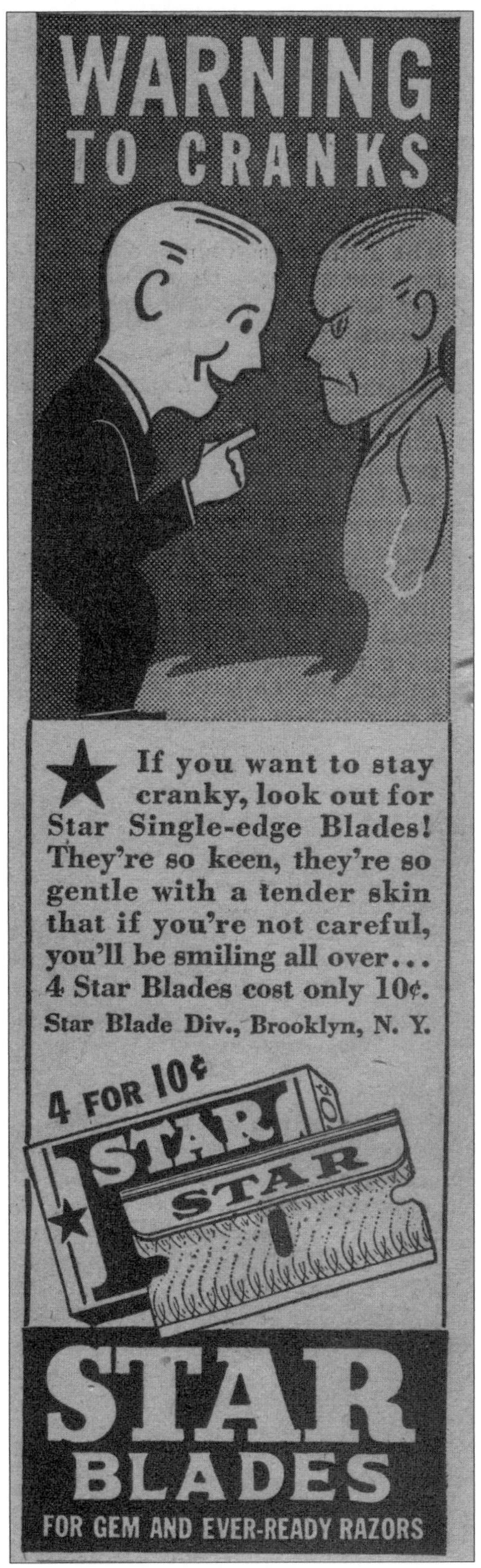

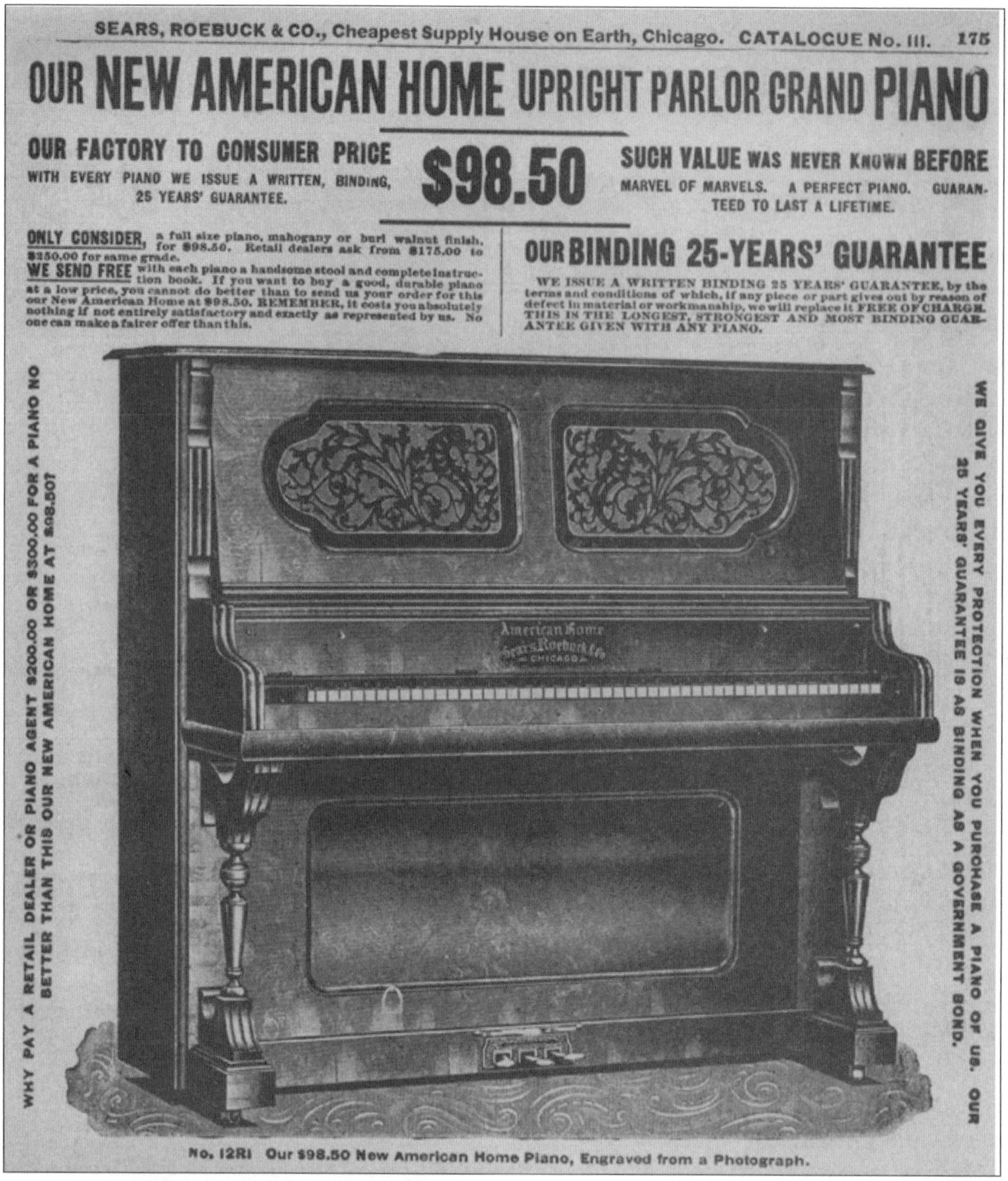

SEARS, ROEBUCK & CO., Cheapest Supply House on Earth, Chicago. CATALOGUE No. 111. 175

OUR NEW AMERICAN HOME UPRIGHT PARLOR GRAND PIANO

OUR FACTORY TO CONSUMER PRICE
WITH EVERY PIANO WE ISSUE A WRITTEN, BINDING, 25 YEARS' GUARANTEE.

$98.50

SUCH VALUE WAS NEVER KNOWN BEFORE
MARVEL OF MARVELS. A PERFECT PIANO. GUARANTEED TO LAST A LIFETIME.

ONLY CONSIDER, a full size piano, mahogany or burl walnut finish, for $98.50. Retail dealers ask from $175.00 to $250.00 for same grade.
WE SEND FREE with each piano a handsome stool and complete instruction book. If you want to buy a good, durable piano at a low price, you cannot do better than to send us your order for this our New American Home at $98.50. REMEMBER, it costs you absolutely nothing if not entirely satisfactory and exactly as represented by us. No one can make a fairer offer than this.

OUR BINDING 25-YEARS' GUARANTEE
WE ISSUE A WRITTEN BINDING 25 YEARS' GUARANTEE, by the terms and conditions of which, if any piece or part gives out by reason of defect in material or workmanship, we will replace it FREE OF CHARGE. THIS IS THE LONGEST, STRONGEST AND MOST BINDING GUARANTEE GIVEN WITH ANY PIANO.

WHY PAY A RETAIL DEALER OR PIANO AGENT $200.00 OR $300.00 FOR A PIANO NO BETTER THAN THIS OUR NEW AMERICAN HOME AT $98.50?

WE GIVE YOU EVERY PROTECTION WHEN YOU PURCHASE A PIANO OF US. OUR 25 YEARS' GUARANTEE IS AS BINDING AS A GOVERNMENT BOND.

American Home
Sears, Roebuck & Co.
CHICAGO

No. 12R1 Our $98.50 New American Home Piano, Engraved from a Photograph.

1933

Selected Prices

Brace and Bit Set	$2.80
Chifforobe	$18.95
Electric Iron	$1.00
Lathe	$340
Radio	$39.85
Sewing Machine	$19.95
Shave Cream	$0.25
Shortwave Receiver	$14.70
Soda	$0.39
Ad in Ladies' Home Journal, Full-page	$12,500
Babies' Rubber Pants, Three Pairs	$0.22
Boys' Knickers	$0.77
Cedar Chest	$12.95
Cod Liver Oil, Gallon, for Livestock	$1.79
Model Airplane	$6.50
Movie Ticket, Adult	$0.25
Phonograph Records, Five	$0.29
Silk Hosiery	$0.89

Fewer Colds *for* Children

Listerine gargle kills germs associated with colds and sore throat

Now parents everywhere realize that it is easier to prevent colds than to cure them. In every home fight against this destructive infection, which undermines health, proceeds with new vigor.

In view of medical evidence that colds are of germ origin, the wisdom of using a germ-killing mouth wash at least twice a day becomes more and more apparent. The mouth and throat must be kept clean and healthy.

Listerine is trustworthy

And for this purpose, no mouth wash is as trustworthy as Listerine—now at new low prices. Behind Listerine lies more than 50 years of use by noted physicians, by hospitals, and by the public. Its germicidal power, its safe action, are a matter of record.

Used regularly as a mouth wash, it has proved itself an effective aid in preventing colds. And in checking their course, once started.

Fewer colds for garglers

Controlled tests on several hundred individuals, indicate that regular twice-a-day users of Listerine contracted fewer colds than those who did not gargle with it. When Listerine users did contract colds, the colds were less severe than those of non-garglers.

Such results are to be expected. Millions of germs breed in the mouth and throat. Among them the bacteria associated with common cold and sore throat.

99% reduction of germs

The moment Listerine enters the mouth it begins to kill these germs. Hour after hour its effect continues.

Actual tests five minutes after the Listerine gargle have shown reductions as high as 99% in the number of germs. And four hours after gargling, reductions of as high as 64% have been noted. No wonder Listerine is preferred above all antiseptics.

Get the habit

Get your children and yourself into the habit of gargling every morning and night with Listerine. It is non-poisonous, *its action is safe*—and its effect cleansing and stimulating.

This pleasant precaution may forestall a trying sore throat, a serious cold, even bronchitis, influenza, and pneumonia.

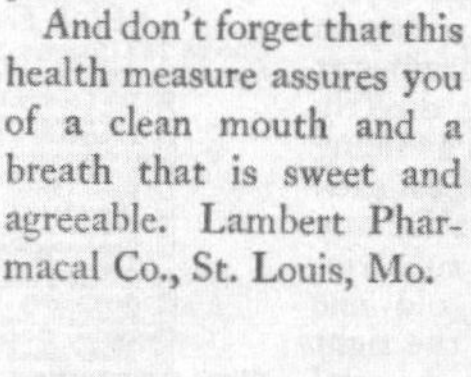

And don't forget that this health measure assures you of a clean mouth and a breath that is sweet and agreeable. Lambert Pharmacal Co., St. Louis, Mo.

and for Sore Throat

LISTERINE

the safe antiseptic

1934

Selected Prices

Apples, Box of 100	$3.25
Baby Powder, Johnson & Johnson	$0.29
Binoculars	$33.48
Cloth, Silk and Cotton Crepe, Yard	$0.35
Cook Stove, Cast Iron	$21.50
Croquet Set	$3.98
Gum, Wrigley's Spearmint	$0.37
Hair Clipper	$3.87
Hog Troughs, Steel	$0.48
Iron, Electric	$1.00
Light Bulbs, Eight, 40-Watt	$1.00
Mattress, 54"	$4.65
Phonograph Record	$0.29
Saw, 3.5'	$1.48
Shampoo, Coconut Oil	$0.49
Buck Rogers Pocket Watch	$0.75
Buster Brown Hose Supporter	$0.24
Canoe	$68.00
Eggs, Dozen	$0.38
Electric Washer	$79.85
Girdle	$1.74
Ice Box	$18.75
Kraft Marshmallows, Box of 200	$0.65
Microphone	$1.00
Portable Typewriter	$49.50

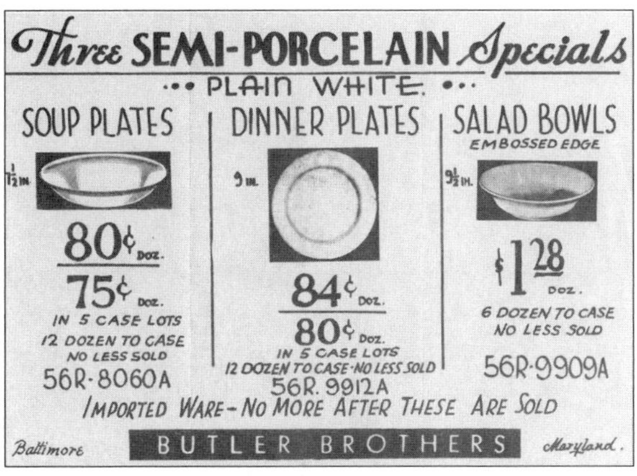

Now 25¢ 10¢
JUNIOR HOME
for
MAR. 1934
Parent and Child
NOW ONLY 10¢
STORIES
POSTERS
THINGS TO DO
CLUBS TO JOIN
EASTER SURPRISES
ARTICLES FOR PARENTS

1935

Annual Average Income, Standard Jobs

All Industries, w/Farm Labor $1,115
Bituminous Coal Mining $957
Building Trades $1,027
Domestics $485
Farm Labor $324
Federal Civilian $1,759
Federal Military $1,154
Gas and Electricity Workers $1,589
Manufacturing, Durable Goods $1,264
Manufacturing, Nondurable Goods $1,178
Medical/Health Services Workers $829
Motion Picture Services $1,892
Passenger Transportation Workers $1,361
Personal Services $915
Public School Teachers $1,293
Radio Broadcasting $2,089
Railroads $1,645
State and Local Government Workers $1,361
Telephone and Telegraph Workers $1,378
Wholesale and Retail Trade Workers $1,279

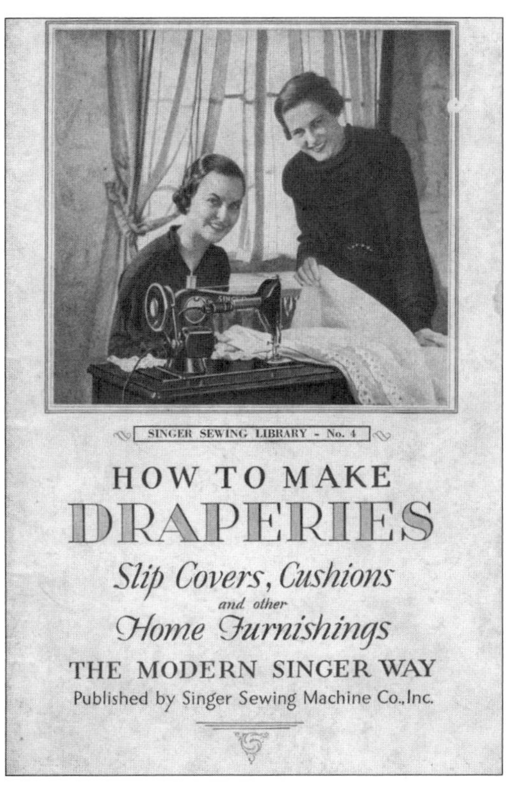

SINGER SEWING LIBRARY - No. 4
HOW TO MAKE
DRAPERIES
Slip Covers, Cushions
and other
Home Furnishings
THE MODERN SINGER WAY
Published by Singer Sewing Machine Co., Inc.

Selected Prices

Baby Seat, Loom Woven Cotton Lined $12.98
Birdbath, Sandstone $50.00
Broiler Pan, Oval Aluminum $0.75
Charcoal Grill $1.95
China Cabinet, Pine, Extra Width $32.50
Dinnerware, Semi-Porcelain, for Six. $4.98
Fishing Reel $8.25
Flashlight $1.39
Garden Tractor, Handiman, 4-HP Motor $242
Gun Case, Lined with Lambskin $3.00
Jergens Lotion $0.69
Olive Oil $0.39
Paper Pattern for Dress $0.15
Pocket Radio $2.90
Pressure Cooker, Eight-Quart $7.45
Razor Blade $1.00
Shotgun, Double Barrel $30.00
Sportman's Encyclopedia $1.00
Tire, Goodyear All Weather $15.55
Waterhose, 25' Green 5/8" $3.00
Broiler Pan $0.75
Camera, Kodak Bantam $22.50
China Cabinet $32.50
Cocktail Glasses, Set of Seven $0.79

Flatware, Service for Six $29.75
Garden Tractor $242
Hamburger, Half-pound $0.12
Hotel Room, New York Commodore $4.00
Radio $49.50
Refrigerator $169.50
Sofa and Chair $66.85
Typewriter $54.50

1936

National Consumer Expenditures (per capita)

Auto Parts	$3.12
Auto Usage	$39.01
Clothing	$42.13
Dentists	$2.34
Furniture	$6.24
Gas and Oil	$14.82
Health Insurance	$0.78
Housing	$63.97
Intercity Transport...	$2.34
Local Transport	$6.24
New Auto Purchase	$14.82
Personal Business	$24.18
Personal Care	$7.02
Physicians	$5.43
Private Education and Research	$3.90
Recreation	$23.40
Religion/Welfare Activities	$7.02
Telephone and Telegraph	$3.90
Tobacco	$11.70
Utilities	$23.40
Per Capita Consumption	$483.69

Annual Income, Standard Jobs

All Industries, w/o Farm Labor	$1,226
All Industries, w/Farm Labor	$1,146
Bituminous Coal Mining	$1,103
Building Trades	$1,178
Domestics	$506
Farm Labor	$351
Federal Civilian	$1,896
Federal Employees, Executive Departments	$1,112
Federal Military	$1,152
Finance, Insurance and Real Estate	$1,713
Gas and Electricity Workers	$1,615
Manufacturing, Durable Goods	$1,376
Manufacturing, Nondurable Goods	$1,210
Medical/Health Services Workers	$851
Miscellaneous Manufacturing	$1,298
Motion Picture Services	$1,896
Nonprofit Organization Workers	$1,465
Passenger TransportationWorkers, Local and Highway	$1,433

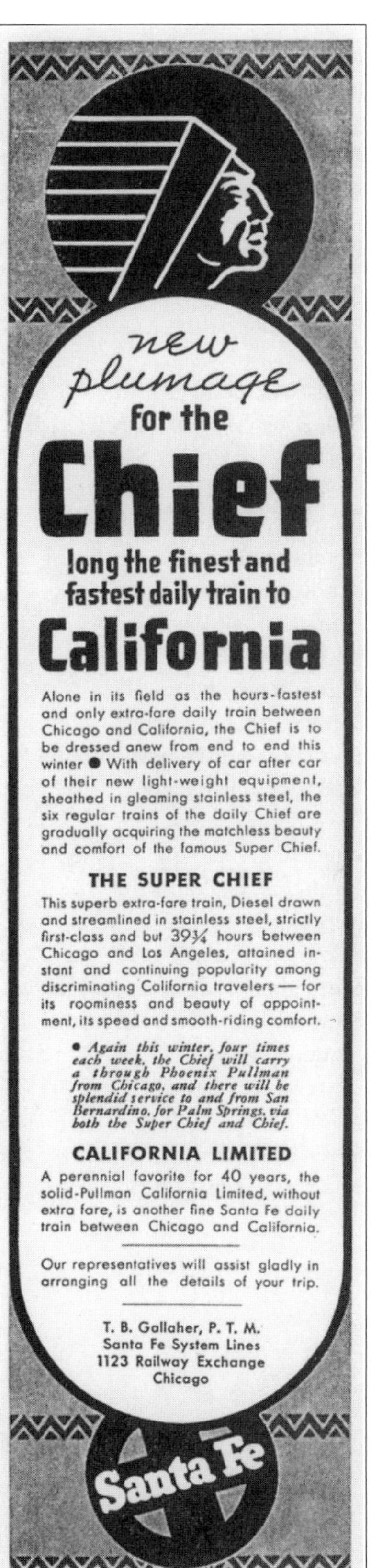

Personal Services $940
Public School Teachers... . . . . $1,329
Radio Broadcasting and
Television Workers $2,223
Railroad Workers. $1,724
State and Local Government Workers $1,433
Telephone and Telegraph Workers $1,420
Wholesale and Retail Trade Workers $1,295

Selected Prices

Airline Fare, New York to Chicago. $44.95
Automobile Battery. $16.95
Basketball $3.59
Bath Salts, Elizabeth Arden $4.50
Bed, Louis XIV w/Mattress $345.00
Dog, English Cocker Spaniel. $50.00
Dress, Maternity... . . . . $2.98
Guitar. $8.45
Hotel Room, Boston, per Night $4.00
Itch Relief, Absorbine Jr $1.25
Man's Suit, all Wool $13.95
Paintbrush, 4" $0.90
Pocket Telescope $1.00
Refrigerator, Cold Spot $169.50
Sausage, Country Style, Pound. $0.20
Wall Clock, Regulator. $6.98
Water Hose, 25'. $3.00
Windows, Andersen Casement. $10.03
Antifreeze, Gallon. $1.00
Baby Carriage $12.98
Electric Coffee Mill $9.75
Flashlight. $0.55
Fountain Pen $1.00
Garden Tractor $242.00
Lawn Mower, Power $69.50
Motor Yacht $26,300.00
Seat Covers, Sedan $5.85
Sofa and Chair. $66.85

1937

Average Annual Income, Standard Jobs

All Industries, w/Farm Labor	$1,259
Bituminous Coal Mining	$1,170
Building Trades	$1,278
Domestics	$588
Farm Labor	$407
Federal Civilian	$1,797
Federal Military	$1,132
Gas and Electricity Workers	$1,705
Manufacturing, Durable Goods	$1,491
Mnsg, Nondurable Goods	$1,267
Medical/Health Services Workers	$876
Motion Picture Services	$1,972
Passenger Transportation Workers	$1,505
Personal Services	$978
Public School Teachers	$1,367
Radio Broadcasting	$2,361
Railroads	$1,774
State/Local Government Workers	$1,505
Telephone and Telegraph Workers	$1,481
Wholesale/Retail Trade Workers	$1,352

Selected Prices

Chesterfield Pipe, 5" Size	$0.39
Cold Wave Fan, Oscillating	$5.50
Eileen Drury Women's Frock	$1.98
Florsheim Men's Shoes	$8.75
Goodyear Double Eagle Car Battery	$16.95
Goodyear Wings Deluxe-8 Radio	$38.50
Hercules Pitchfork	$1.35
J.C. Higgins Basketball	$3.59
Kenmore Deluxe Vacuum Cleaner	$31.45
Kodak Bantam Camera	$22.50
Lifetime Steel Bed, Complete	$16.50
Lysol Disinfectant, Large Size	$0.83
Maternity Corset	$2.98
Merit Ax	$0.98
Morninglow Bath Towels, Four	$0.79
Nestlé's Baby Hair Treatment	$0.83
Polar Air Refrigerator	$22.98
Sir Walter Raleigh Smoking Tobacco	$0.15
Supertone Gene Autry Guitar	$8.45
Velflor Rug, 9' x 12'	$8.75
Wildroot Hair Tonic	$0.47
Windex Window Cleaner	$0.39
Airline Fare, Los Angeles to New York	$149.95
Automobile, Plymouth Sedan	$685.00

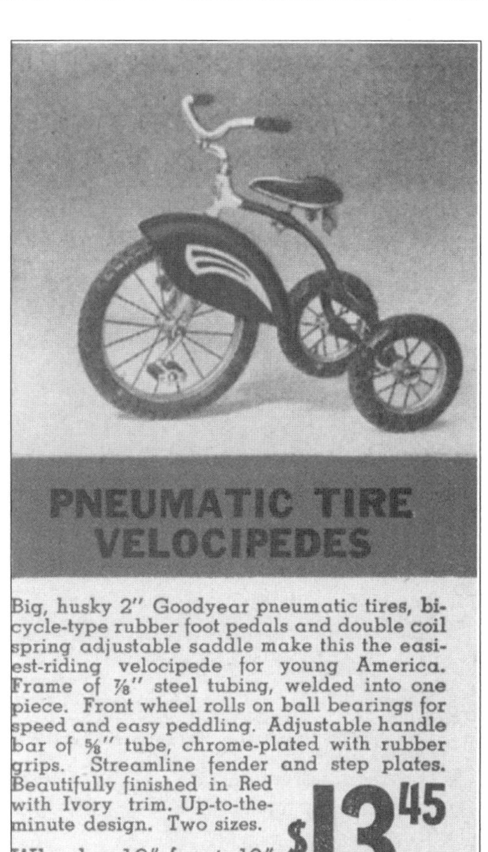

Baby Carriage	$12.98
Bicycle	$43.95
Cocktail Glasses and Shaker	$0.79
Cow Milker	$42.50
Kitchen Range	$76.95
Movie Camera	$49.50
Shotgun	$30.00
Tire, Goodyear	$18.75

TREASURY DEPARTMENT

WASHINGTON

The United States Treasury Department is enclosing for your information a booklet describing UNITED STATES SAVINGS BONDS.

These bonds increase in cash surrender value every year for ten years, when they mature with a guaranteed cash value 33-1/3% greater than the purchase price. They may be redeemed at any time after 60 days from date of purchase.

These securities, which are direct obligations of the United States Government, are an excellent medium of investment for those who wish to save their money for future use or as gifts to others.

Your Postmaster will be pleased to furnish you with full information and assistance in making purchases of these bonds or, if you prefer, you may order direct by mail from the Treasurer of the United States, Washington, D. C.

Sincerely,
HENRY MORGENTHAU, JR.
Secretary of the Treasury.

1938

Selected Prices

Basketball	$3.59
Bicycle Tires	$1.90
Camera, Kodak	$22.50
Compass	$1.95
Hotel Room, New York	$4.00
Laxative, Ex-Lax, Chocolate	$0.19
Radio	$17.95
Saddle	$27.95
Sun Lamp	$6.75
Target Pistol	$20.00

1939

National Consumer Expenditures (per capita)

Auto Parts	$3.82
Auto Usage	$39.69
Clothing	$45.03
Dentists	$3.05
Furniture	$6.87
Gas and Oil	$16.79
Health Insurance	$1.53
Housing	$71.74
Intercity Transport	$3.05
Local Transport	$6.87
New Auto Purchase	$12.21
Personal Business	$24.42
Personal Care	$13.74
Physicians	$6.87
Private Education and Research	$4.58
Recreation	$26.71
Religion/Welfare Activities	$7.63
Telephone and Telegraph	$4.58
Tobacco	$13.74
Utilities	$23.66
Per Capita Consumption	$511.34

Annual Income, Standard Jobs

All Industries, w/o Farm Labor	$1,346
All Industries, w/Farm Labor	$1,266
Bituminous Coal Mining	$1,197
Building Trades, Union Workers	$1,268
Domestics	$544
Farm Labor	$436
Federal Civilian	$1,843
Federal Employees, Executive Departments	$1,137
Federal Military	$1,134

Finance, Insurance and Real Estate	$1,729
Gas and Electricity Workers	$1,766
Manufacturing, Durable Goods	$1,479
Manufacturing, Nondurable Goods	$1,263
Medical/Health Services Workers	$908
Miscellaneous Manufacturing	$1,337
Motion Picture Services	$1,971
Nonprofit Organization Workers	$1,546
Passenger Transportation Workers, Local and Highway	$1,569
Personal Services	$1,034
Public School Teachers	$1,403
Radio Broadcasting and Television Workers	$2,427
Railroad Workers	$1,877
State and Local Government Workers	$1,569
Telephone and Telegraph Workers	$1,600
Wholesale and Retail Trade Workers	$1,360

Selected Prices

Carbon Arc Sunlamp	$6.75
Challenge Flashlight	$0.55
Cold Wave Oscillating Fan	$5.50
Copley Plaza Luxury Hotel Room, per Night	$4.00
Ex-Lax Laxative	$0.19
Giralda Farms English Cocker Spaniel Pups	$50.00
Hammacher Schlemmer Dining Table	$10.50
Hammacher Schlemmer Wrought Iron Table	$56.00
Hercules Pitchfork	$1.35
Ingraham Regulator Wall Clock	$6.98
Kodak Bantam Camera	$22.50
Kook-Kwick Pressure Cooker	$7.45
Listerine Mouthwash, 14 Ounces	$0.59
Lombard & Co. English Sandstone Birdbath	$50.00
Milk of Magnesia	$0.08
Prima Milker	$42.50
Same Sex Life, by H.W. Long, M.D.	$1.85
Simmons Beautyrest Box Spring and Mattress	$345.00
Sta-Sharp Pocketknife	$0.95
Velflor Rug, 9' x 12'	$8.75
Coca-Cola	$0.25
Home Movie, 16 mm	$8.75
Movie Camera	$49.50
Movie Ticket	$0.25

SWEET and LOW

YOU CAN COMPARE a bowl of Kellogg's Corn Flakes to a lullaby. These crisp, delicious flakes are an excellent sleep-inducer these warm evenings. They're satisfying and easily digested. Result — you sleep sweetly and arise cheerfully.

Try a bowl of Kellogg's after that late party. They're sold every place where you can buy food.

Nothing takes the place of

Kellogg's

CORN FLAKES

Nylons $1.95
Pocket Telescope $1.00
Seat Covers, Sedan $5.85
Toothpaste $0.25

1940

Selected Prices

Alka Seltzer, Eight Tablets $0.24
Cheese Slicer $0.10
Coffee, Pound $0.33
Lincoln Continental Coupe $2,783.00
Lipstick $1.00
Paper Shelving, Nine Feet $0.05
Radio/Phonograph Cabinet $185.00
Tattoo $0.25
Tea Kettle, Copper $3.49
Varnish, Quart $1.43

Value of a Dollar Index 1860-2010
2010=$1.00

Year	Amount	Year	Amount	Year	Amount	Year	Amount
1860	$26.32	1898	$26.32	1936	$15.69	1974	$4.42
1861	$25.00	1899	$26.32	1937	$15.15	1975	$4.05
1862	$21.74	1900	$25.64	1938	$15.47	1976	$3.83
1863	$17.24	1901	$25.64	1939	$15.69	1977	$3.60
1864	$13.89	1902	$25.64	1940	$15.58	1978	$3.35
1865	$13.33	1903	$25.00	1941	$14.84	1979	$3.00
1866	$13.70	1904	$24.39	1942	$13.38	1980	$2.65
1867	$14.71	1905	$25.00	1943	$12.61	1981	$2.40
1868	$15.38	1906	$24.39	1944	$12.39	1982	$2.26
1869	$16.13	1907	$23.26	1945	$12.12	1983	$2.19
1870	$16.67	1908	$23.81	1946	$11.18	1984	$2.10
1871	$17.86	1909	$23.81	1947	$9.78	1985	$2.03
1872	$17.86	1910	$22.73	1948	$9.09	1986	$1.99
1873	$18.18	1911	$22.73	1949	$9.16	1987	$1.92
1874	$19.23	1912	$22.73	1950	$9.05	1988	$1.84
1875	$20.00	1913	$22.03	1951	$8.39	1989	$1.76
1876	$20.41	1914	$21.81	1952	$8.20	1990	$1.67
1877	$20.83	1915	$21.59	1953	$8.14	1991	$1.60
1878	$21.74	1916	$20.01	1954	$8.11	1992	$1.55
1879	$21.74	1917	$17.04	1955	$8.14	1993	$1.51
1880	$21.28	1918	$14.54	1956	$8.02	1994	$1.47
1881	$21.28	1919	$12.61	1957	$7.76	1995	$1.43
1882	$21.28	1920	$10.91	1958	$7.55	1996	$1.39
1883	$21.74	1921	$12.18	1959	$7.47	1997	$1.34
1884	$22.22	1922	$12.98	1960	$7.37	1998	$1.31
1885	$22.73	1923	$12.75	1961	$7.29	1999	$1.27
1886	$23.26	1924	$12.75	1962	$7.20	2000	$1.27
1887	$22.73	1925	$12.46	1963	$7.13	2001	$1.23
1888	$22.73	1926	$12.32	1964	$7.04	2002	$1.21
1889	$23.81	1927	$12.53	1965	$6.92	2003	$1.19
1890	$23.81	1928	$12.68	1966	$6.71	2004	$1.15
1891	$23.81	1929	$12.68	1967	$6.53	2005	$1.12
1892	$23.81	1930	$13.06	1968	$6.27	2006	$1.08
1893	$24.39	1931	$14.35	1969	$5.94	2007	$1.05
1894	$25.64	1932	$16.04	1970	$5.62	2008	$1.01
1895	$25.64	1933	$16.91	1971	$5.39	2009	$1.02
1896	$25.64	1934	$16.28	1972	$5.22	2010	$1.00
1897	$26.32	1935	$15.92	1973	$4.91		

SECTION FOUR: ALL AROUND US— WHAT WE SAW, WROTE, READ & LISTENED TO

To quote the US Census Bureau, "The 1940 Census came at a momentous time in our nation's history—as we recovered from the Great Depression and not long before our entry into World War II." This section provides a first hand look at exactly what was on the minds of the American people in the decade leading up to 1940. You will find reprints of newspaper and magazine articles, quotes, letters, even comic strips. These pieces appear in chronological order, showing how opinions may have changed throughout the decade, and how they shaped the thoughts of Americans living in 1940.

"Looking down on the World from the Tallest Skyscraper," *Popular Mechanics*, January 1930:
"Workmen have laid the last piece of steel framework for the Chrysler building in New York, which, when completed, will be the tallest habitable structure in the world at present. It rises for more than 800 feet, overtopping the 792 feet of the Woolworth building. From the dome of the $15 million structure, every point on Manhattan can be seen. One of the unusual sights is the Chanin building nearby which, when viewed from the Chrysler building, has a startling modernistic effect, which is hardly to be expected in a skyscraper."

"How Safe Is Flying?" by John Draper,
***Popular Mechanics*, January 1930**

"Hitherto unwritten stories of heroism, of singlehanded battles against the forces of nature and of the thrills of flying, have been brought to light by a questionnaire sent by *Popular Mechanics* magazine to more than 8,000 licensed pilots to learn their actual experience with lightning.

Many of the pilots contended that lightning could not strike an airplane in flight, although it is positively known that eight balloons have been destroyed by lightning in the past nine years. While Zeppelins have been struck more than 100 times, none has been wrecked in this way, the nature of their metal framework probably being responsible for their immunity.

In all the history of aviation, the only verified case of lightning striking an airplane in flight was reported as follows: 'While flying from Paris to London with 14 passengers, Mr. F. L. Barnard had an alarming experience. He ran into a thunderstorm over Picardy, between Beauvais and Poix. Suddenly there was a loud report as a flash of lightning struck the machine. A large piece of fabric on the lower plane was burnt, the compass was put out of action, and one engine started to miss, as apparently the permanent field of one of the magnets had been upset. On examination, it was found that, in addition to the hole in the fabric, one of the main spars was scorched, all of the bonding was fused and one of the ailerons damaged.'

There have been other, although not verified, cases of crashes attributed to lightning. In 1928 the deaths of Capt. Emil Carranza, Mexican flying ace, and Morris M. Titterington, inventor of the earth-inductor compass, were believed due to bolts. In the same year a mail plane plunged to earth with its motor wide open during an electrical disturbance. Although no positive proof that this was due to lightning could be obtained, observers believe the pilot was stunned by a bolt. The same is true of a navy plane which plunged into lower Chesapeake Bay in 1927. The naval board which investigated the crash reported 'its belief that the lightning flash stunned both pilots in the ship to such a degree that they could not recover in time to save the plane and that it went in uncontrolled.'

With mail and passenger planes now covering 84,656 miles daily, C. M. Keys, president of the Transcontinental Air Transport, recently quoted figures showing that there were 6,500 persons killed in 1928 as a result of the operation of the railways, or one fatality for 172,768 train miles. In the same year, there were 368 persons killed in civil aviation or one fatality for 191,800 plane miles, a slightly better record than was made by the railways. The Actuary Society of America, insurance risk experts, reported that there is only a 4,000-to-one chance of an accident when riding with a licensed pilot over a scheduled passenger route. They found that in 1928 only 13 passengers were killed out of the 50,000 carried in such flights.

'The forces of nature cannot be eliminated, but they may be balanced, one against another,' Count Zeppelin once said. Mr. Keys now declares that 'aeronautical science has progressed to the point where the only uncontrollable factor is weather, which in final analysis remains the major cause of interrupted transportation both on land and sea.' "

Editorial, "What Do You Think of This Plan for Discussing the Eighteenth Amendment?" *Oberlin News Tribune*, January 1, 1931

"Whenever an important issue confronts the country, every community includes two classes: those who do care and those who don't care how it is decided.

Just now the prohibition issue is regarded by many as the most vital question before the American people, and the conviction is generally that it will be decided within the next two years. How many are there in Oberlin who don't care how it is settled?

Those who do care include wets, drys and doubters. While the wets comprise a large number of persons with whom personal appetite, social standing or financial advantage outweigh every other consideration, there are many having no axe to grind, who favor the repeal or modification of the Eighteenth Amendment from the most unselfish motives, being persuaded that some other plan will produce better results for the people as a whole. Such persons-and their number seems to have been increasing within the last few weeks-are just as anxious to get and circulate the facts in the case as are the most ardent drys. Then why cannot these two groups in Oberlin join hands with the honest doubters in an intensive scrutiny of the arguments for and against the Eighteenth Amendment? Not the arguments of the brewers and bootleggers, not those of lawless society leaders, nor yet those of bigoted dyedin-the-wool drys, but of thoughtful, unselfish, patriotic students of history both ancient and modern as it is related to this problem.

It seems as if some plan should be found for community co-operation in our search for the truth about prohibition. When we read an article of special merit we wish that everybody else might read it too, but to hand or mail a single copy to one person after another is a discouragingly slow process, and to persuade all our fellow townspeople to subscribe to our favorite journals is impossible, even if desirable. The question has arisen whether it would not be practicable to have a representative committee of capable and patriotic citizens which would receive such articles from anyone finding them and condense them for our own local paper, as articles are condensed for the *Readers' Digest*, or at least skim the cream of them for us by at least mentioning, of course, where the whole article could be found.Would such a plan be feasible? Would it help us to an intelligent decision on this issue?

W.T.C.U. Committee"

Advertisement: "The Endless Chain of Credit," *Oberlin News Tribune*, September 1931: "Credit is an endless chain needed in modern business. If those who owe the retailer fail to pay, how can the retailer pay the wholesaler and how can the wholesaler pay the manufacturer? The bills you owe when paid become rent and wages and shoes and other essentials. An invoice is a reminder of your promise to pay. It is not to be held as an unfriendly act warranting your taking your trade to another store. If requests for payment at the time promised are offensive to you, relieve your temper by keeping your word and paying. Credit is an impetus to business when its terms are met. It becomes a drag on progress when promises are broken. The Oberlin Credit Association"

"Studio Test for Details of Opening,"
***The Raleigh Times* (North Carolina), April 11, 1931**

Possibilities of studio television are to be investigated when New York gets on the air with its first combined sight and sound broadcast.

Program plans are not complete, but the intention is to put on illustrated news items, stock reports, illustrated talks, drama, dancing lessons, vaudeville artists, costumed singers, and other types of entertainment suitable for sight as well as sound.

Following somewhat in the footsteps of Chicago, where "talking movies" of studio presentations have been on the air for some time via the WMAQ and the WIBO and their associated short-wave television stations, the metropolitan area business will have a chance to tune in for visual and aural entertainment coming from the same studio. Tests of equipment already are under way, with hope that the opening will be presented about April 15, or shortly thereafter.

A broadcasting station, WGBS on 254 meters, is to deliver the sound parts of the program, while W2XCR, Jenkins experimental television transmitter on 147 meters, will deliver the sight. Two receivers will be necessary to bring in the synchronized programs, a broadcast set for sound and the short-wave receiver for television.

The studios are located on the sixth floor of the Fifth Avenue building, not far from the site of the proposed Radio City. They consist of a large room, 14 x 25 feet, the studio proper, or session room, and the control room in the television room.

The studio is fitted acoustically like any broadcast room. At one side is an open window through which the lens of his television "camera" points. In the studio is a portable bank for photoelectric cells, the "microphone" for television.

The camera will use what is known as the "flying spot." That is, a sitter in a darkened room will be bathed with a beam of light directed by scanning disk. The light then is reflected to the photo cells.

"Thousands in One Music Class: Piano Instruction Is Latest Form of Radio Activities," ***The Raleigh Times*****, April 11, 1931**

Fifty thousand piano pupils in one class! Impossible? No, indeed, for the radio has stepped from its role as entertainer and turned instructor. Last week Dr. Sigmund Spaeth stepped before the microphone at 11:30 in the morning and informed listeners on the WEAF network that learning to play the piano was not the long, weary task that we had been led to believe in our youth, but really quite simple if you wanted to try it. Then he proceeded to prove his point by showing the few chords that are necessary to provide a satisfactory accompaniment for many well-known songs.

On Tuesday-on the WJZ network, 3 p.m.-Osbourne McConathy demonstrated the ease with which a simple melody may be played on the piano. And in doing this, he proved two things: that it is not hard for the allegedly unmusical to learn to play, and that the radio can be effective as a medium for teaching, even in the case of such an ephemeral subject as music.

And this last point is highly important; it may answer many questions skeptics have been asking for several years. Radio, you know, has been something of a black sheep in certain circles, especially among musicians. Many unkind things have been said about it, chiefly to the effect that it's been freezing American people into passive listeners, making them content to sit back and listen (or talk) while others do their playing and singing for them. It is one of the evils of the machine age, some said, for it stifles all desire to learn to do things for ourselves.

Who will play the piano in the future if we don't have to do it in order to hear music? they asked. And it has required pretty stout-hearted enthusiasts to keep courage, under the fire of such comments, not to admit that the doubters were probably right.

"Ruth Is Ready," ***The Raleigh Times*** **(North Carolina), April 11, 1931:** Babe Ruth has served notice on Hank Wilson and other aspirants to homerun honors that he will be very much in the limelight again this year. He has found the range and cracked out three homers during the past three days to tell the fans that he is ready for battle. The doubters every spring come forth with a suggestion that the Babe cannot be as good as last year. But he continues to harass hurlers and please the fans with his long wallops over the fences.

"Feeding Methods," by H.C. Knandel,
***Comfort Magazine,* April 1932**

There are many methods of feeding hens for egg production. Whatever system is used, it should be so designed that maximum net returns will result. The two methods of feeding quite generally employed by poultry men are the hand and hopper method. Whichever method is adopted, it is imperative to supply the fowls with all the necessary ingredients which will not only produce a good supply of eggs but at the same time will keep the fowls in good physical condition. When the hand method is used, the mash is usually placed in hoppers so that the fowls have access to it throughout the day. The grain is fed by hand both morning and evening and is scattered in the litter. In the morning, to each 100 birds, two pounds of scratch grain are fed in the litter. At night, the birds are given all they will consume. When fowls are in heavy production, it is essential that they be fed quite heavily on scratch grain in an effort to maintain body weight so they will be able to stand up under the strain of heavy egg production.

Leghorn pullets and hens laying 50 percent or more should be fed at least 12 pounds of scratch grain per day per 100 fowls...

Fowls not only require scratch grain and mash but grit, oyster shell and perhaps green food as well. Grit and oyster shell should be placed in hoppers and kept constantly before the birds. Hens, lacking teeth, must grind their food in their gizzard. Grit is the grinding machinery and should be supplied in unlimited quantities.

"Hoover Favors Change in Prohibition and an Attack on Depression," *The Washington Post,* August 11, 1932: President Hoover declared tonight, in accepting renomination to the presidency, that he believed a change in national prohibition is necessary "to remedy present evils" that have grown up under it.

As to the economic situation, he spoke of new plans looking into a movement "from defense to a powerful attack upon the depression," an assertion that was said in high quarters to embrace the carrying out of his recently enunciated nine-point program as well as other propositions not ready for announcement.

"Orders Widen Fight for Negro's Rights, Conference Adopts Margold Plan to Begin 100 Cases in South Against Discrimination," *The New York Times*, May 21, 1932

WASHINGTON—A legal campaign planned by Nathan R. Margold of New York to defend Negroes against every form of discrimination was adopted here today by the National Association for the Advancement of Colored People.

Dr. Robert R. Moton, head of Tuskegee Institute, endorsed the plan as one likely to obtain for Negroes "a reasonable certainty of justice nowhere assured to them at present in this country." The plan is to be carried out under the direction of Mr. Margold.

The plan involves bringing simultaneously more than 100 cases in as many communities to test the right of states or of individuals "to infringe" on the social as well as the civic rights of Negroes.

"We plan a flood of litigation in all of the Southern states," he said, "asserting the right of the Negro to equality of treatment, and striking at the heart of the situation by challenging the principle of segregation which is the backbone of the whole Negro problem. "In the case of schools, the segregation issue will be the legal weapon employed to secure equality in the form of more and better schools for Negro children. "Jim Crow laws will be the subject of direct attack on a new front..."

The Scottsboro case was cited by Dr. Moton as an instance in which Negroes had been condemned on testimony which, he asserted, would have led to the acquittal of white men.

"Immigrants," *The New York Times*, December 24, 1932: The Secretary of State has reported to the President of the United States the number of quota immigrants has fallen during the last fiscal year to little more than 10,000 persons (12,697), which is only 8 percent of the total annual quotas. This marked reduction is due to the restrictive policy that has been followed during the years of the Depression. The estimate is that 500,000 aliens who would normally have emigrated to the United States have been refused visas by their consular officers abroad, chiefly on the grounds that the applications are unable to give the necessary assurance that they are not likely to become public charges. Had they come they would have swollen the numbers of the unemployed. No one can question the wisdom of this policy in general.

There is also a marked decrease in the non-quota immigration, barely a fifth of what it was in 1930, the total number of visas granted to them being 24,040.

"Talks with Girls," by Cousin Marion, *Comfort Magazine*, January 1932

Last spring I asked what made a girl popular, and the men fell all over themselves to tell me their ideas on the subject.

When the girls were given the same opportunity to express their ideas on what made a man popular I naturally expected to receive as many letters...Weeks passed and not a single letter! I was beginning to think it was a case of women being satisfied with anything masculine and no questions asked when the letters began to straggle in. Finally there were almost as many as the men wrote, but the evident delay in writing them made me wonder if that "putting off" was responsible for the fact that men go ahead and do important things in the world while women waste their time and energy in doing the inessentials first with the result that they never do accomplish big things in life. Of course some women do, we all know that, but I wonder if it's not because some of them learned the wisdom of conserving their strength for something important instead of doing something first that could have been done later just as well or left undone entirely.

The average woman, when faced with a piece of writing, something that requires concentration and thought, is likely to put the room in which she is to work in order before sitting down to her desk; she may even put the entire house in order, stopping to wash and iron a few silk things and cleaning the refrigerator before she finally gets down to work. By that time she is too tired to think.

A man wouldn't do that. If his desk wasn't in order he'd push things back to make room for his paper and go to work. The silk things and the refrigerator, or whatever is the masculine equivalent for these things, could go unwashed and uncleaned. They would cease to exist until such time as he had finished the writing he wanted to do.

A woman would suddenly, and for no reason, decide that it was time the closets were cleaned and sprayed in case there should be a moth, or that her hair needed an oil shampoo before she had another permanent, or that she ought to find the poem Cousin Emma wanted.

After the closets were cleaned and sprayed she'd give herself an oil shampoo, and while her hair was drying she'd hunt through scrapbooks and envelopes of poems in an effort to find the particular poem Cousin Emma had mentioned.

A man wouldn't know a moth if he saw one and he'd let the barber worry about his hair, and as for Cousin Emma and her poem, he just couldn't be bothered looking for it. (Let her remember her own poems. Probably it didn't amount to anything anyway, and she'd only lose it again if she had it.)

If I have mentioned any of my outstanding failings in the matter of getting to work, it is because I want to make dilatory women see the error of their ways and to urge upon them the necessity of making a New Year resolution to do the important things first.

That's a fine resolution to make, short, concise and to the point. I ought to know. It's one of my favorite resolutions.

Now we'll find out what makes men popular. (I've always wondered.)

A Georgia girl writes: "I think manners and appearance should come first. Girls admire a boy with nice manners. Be a gentleman at all times. Wear neatly pressed and wellfitting clothes. Nothing is more horrible than saggy clothes. A girl wants a man for a pal and not for an affectionate flatterer. Of course a little praise now and then is appreciated, but be reasonable about it. A girl likes to be proud of the man she goes out with. He should be able to carry on a decent conversation."

Compared with a saggy chin muscle, saggy clothes are things of beauty but girl-from-Georgia is too young to know anything about saggy muscles.

A freshman from the Ohio State University expresses herself very ably. "Cleanliness and good health always help to make a man popular. I like men who are amusing, men who can talk on any and every subject. Men who are always serious are frightfully boresome. A sense of humor is a requisite. Most girls like to have their boyfriends know what to do and when to do it. They needn't follow Emily Post in every detail, but they should observe the most important rules. Few things embarrass me as much as walking with a fellow who doesn't know enough to walk along the outside of the sidewalk and gracefully keep there despite crossing streets. Being polite goes a long way with girls. There may be a few who like the cave-man type, but I think they are in the minority; however, I think fellows should have some will power. . . . When a fellow asks me for a date I like to have him know where we are going, not only so I'll know how to dress, but to save the fuss when we start of, 'Where shall we go?' 'Anywhere you say.' 'No, you decide'. . . . And there's that little something called personality. In short, it's personality combined with a sense of humor, good manners, ability to talk and be a good listener, neatness and cleanliness, and ability to plan a good time which makes a man popular with girls. Good looks? They help, but are not absolutely essential."

Economic Problems of the Family, by Hazel Kyrk, 1933: "In her book, *Successful Family Life on a Moderate Income*, Mrs. Abel lays down as her first principle for success-the money income of the family tolerably certain and earned wholly or chiefly by the man. Is the latter one of the requirements that should be set up? There is no doubt that the ideal home as many would picture it is one in which the whole of the money income is furnished by the husband and father. The reasons presented for taking this position would, it is believed, be of very diverse character.

There are those who view with complacence the gainful employment of working class wives and mothers but object to it in the case of women in their own family or class. No concern may be felt over the wide-spread practice of employment outside the home by Negro women but a similar condition among White women, especially the native-born, may be considered most alarming. This dual standard suggests the basis for certain of the objections to the wife as a contributor to the money income."

"Crisis Threatens Alabama Schools, Shortage of Funds Has Closed 85 Percent, with Remainder on Part Time," *The New York Times*, April 21, 1933:

MONTGOMERY, Ala.—The State of Alabama is confronted with a financial crisis which threatens the very life of its free public schools. With 85 percent of its elementary schools closed already, the people of the state are facing the prospect of utter collapse of their educational system or, at best, a drastic curtailment of its functions.

This is a serious prospect for any state. It is especially so for Alabama, which has the fifth largest number of illiterates in the United States and which is struggling to keep a respectable number of pupils in its classrooms beyond the lower grades of grammar school. Yet three and a half years of economic depression have brought its school system, geared as it was to a $28 million operating fund in 1929, to a point where it must continue to function, if at all, on less than half that amount unless new revenues are found in sources yet untapped...

Discussing the situation in an interview with *The New York Times* correspondent today, Dr. A. F. Harmon, State Superintendent of Education, made no attempt to disguise or minimize the gravity of the conditions threatening his department and the 5,688 schools over which it exercises supervisory control.

"As far as education is concerned," said Dr. Harmon, "we are facing the worst situation that has confronted us since the Reconstruction period. "Our school system is in the throes of an agony induced by the statewide, nationwide and worldwide financial panic. The shafts of light which have begun to shine through the nation's financial clouds have not reached the doors of the schools of this state. The sacrifices made by teachers, though great, have not been sufficient, nor can they ever be sufficient, to carry through the complete school program without help."

Today, Sherwood Anderson, "I Want to Work," April, 1934

"The New Deal has cracked something open. In the South and pretty much all over the United States there was, before Roosevelt came, a feeling that to have anything to do with a union meant a certain social blight…in reality, half of it is resistance to change, any kind of change. The President's job isn't just to get people back to work, get higher prices for farm products. There is a higher job he has already begun, a kind of striking down into men's imaginations. It has already gone pretty far.

I went to a meeting of Negro workers. Even the illiterate ones can listen to the radio. Just because a man can't read or write doesn't necessarily mean that he hasn't a mind. I have found that out myself, living these last five years among mountain men in southwest Virginia . . . the Negroes were at their meeting discussing the same things I had heard discussed in a Sunday school class…labor, the yellow dog contract, the lockout, advisability of labor getting itself intelligently organized…'If a man like President Roosevelt thinks labor should organize, why shouldn't I think so?' That is the notion.

At the meeting of Negroes a Black man got up and proposed that at the next meeting to be held, he bring his preacher.

There were objections, apologetic but determined objections. 'I believe in God and His son, Jesus Christ, but there is the carnal and the uncarnal. We have come here to talk about the carnal. We have to talk among ourselves.'"

"Safe Relief from Nervous Tension," Dr. Miles New Weather Almanac and Handbook of Valuable information, 1934

America lives on its nerves. The machine age has lightened physical labor, but has made nerve strain infinitely more severe. As a result, more people than ever before are suffering from diseases caused or made worse by overtaxed nerves. Never before have so many people needed the relief, poise, relaxation and rest that comes from using a good nerve sedative such as Dr. Miles Nervine.

When you feel tense and keyed up; when you are irritable, restless and blue; when you can't sleep, worry over trifles, want to avoid social gatherings; have nervous headaches, nervous indigestion, a bottle of Dr. Miles Nervine will bring about a wonderful change for the better.

Buying Drapery Fabrics, How to Make Draperies, Slip Covers, Cushions and Other Home Furnishings the Modern Singer Way, 1934: Drapery fabrics rather than dress fabrics are invariably better suited to draperies, especially in texture and color. Fabrics of similar weight and texture often cost less in the drapery department than in the dress fabric department, and the designs are usually more suitable. There are, however, many fabrics obtainable in the dress fabric department that are desirable to use, such as calico, gingham, unbleached muslin and organdie. On the other hand, dotted Swiss, silks for draperies, cretonne and casement cloths should be purchased in the drapery department.

"From Inner Tubes to Rubber Dollies," by Mabel Dunlap, Junior Home for Parent and Child, March 1934:

Do you remember the little girl who sang, "My mother told me that she would buy me a rubber dollie if I'd be good"? Well, you can make these rubber dolls yourself. And you can wash them and dress them as well!

Get a worn-out inner tube and wash it well so that you will not soil your dress while working on it. A light-colored tube makes Suki and Eva; and a black one, Mammy and Topsy. The big picture of Eva, Figure 1, may be used as an idea for each doll. And each doll has a front and back just alike. Fill the inside with cotton or cloth and sew the doll together with a rather large needle and strong thread. The hair and features of Suki and Eva may be drawn with India ink. The lips, of course, are made with red ink. The dotted lines give you an idea for the dress. You can, of course, make changes for the different dolls. Suki's and Mammy's dress will be longer than the other two. Mammy's head kerchief is a triangle of bright cloth, three by five inches. Her shawl collar is a bigger square of white cloth, and her apron is just a rectangle of white cotton. Sew this into a long, narrow strip that serves as the ties. Her dress might be bright red. Make her two little earrings of bright-colored paper and attach them to her kerchief.

For the black faces, cut the eyes and mouths from the light-colored rubber. (Color the mouths red with white centers, and eyes are shown in Figures 4 and 5). Glue them to the black faces. Topsy's pigtails should be cut in one piece with the head, and little red string bows form her ribbons. Her dress might be dark blue, with several bright patches on it. And her belt might be just a string.

Suki, the little Japanese doll, might be dressed in yellow with a bright-colored sash tied at the back. With Crayolas or ink, make a circle on the front and back of her dress, something like the one shown in Figure 3.

In making the dresses for Topsy and Eva, simply cut the sleeves shorter. Highlights on the faces of Topsy and Mammy may be made with white ink, or you can cut small pieces from the light-colored rubber and glue them on. Make Eva's dress from any pretty material you may have. If you have some narrow lace, you might put that around the neck, sleeves and bottom of the skirt. All the dresses will have openings in order to get them on the dollies!

The Plight of the Bituminous Coal Miner, by Homer Lawrence Morris, Ph.D.: "I ain't had a regular job for four years and I've only been able to pick up odd jobs on the road. I've only had 11 days' work, and that on the road, during the past year. I own a four-room house and lot but I gotta pay $9.00 taxes on it and I ain't got the money to pay it. When a man has been out of work as long as I have, he loses his heart to do anything." West Virginia Coal Miner, 1934.

GRIT
HE'LL NEVER HATCH THAT EGG
SIT-DOWNS
PROSPERITY
PRODUCTION
THE WRONG BIRD FOR THE JOB
U.S.
HOW'D YA LIKE TO LIVE WITH ME RIGHT ALONG?
PLANS FOR PERMANENT ADOPTION
C.C.C.
UNCLE'S TAKEN A LIKIN' TO THE BOY
COM'ON, SAM, JUS' ONE LIL' DRINK
WAR SPIRITS
XX
PEACE HOPES
EUROPE
NEUTRALITY
WILL HE STAY ON THE WATER WAGON?
VACATION THOUGHTS
IN THE SPRING A YOUNG MAN'S FANCY
E. Ziegler
RANDOM SHOTS AT CURRENT EVENTS

"Gleams From Film Capital, Burlington," *Daily Times News* (North Carolina), December 27, 1934

Children will take over the household of many Hollywood couples. Although too young to clamor for toys, three children of the Bing Crosbys will blink their delight at an immense lighted Christmas tree. Gene Markey and Joan Bennett have prepared a gay party for their two young daughters. There'll be a reunion at the home of Will Rogers. Will, Jr., has come home from Stanford, Jimmy from Pomona College and Mary from the East where she is working with a stock company.

Contrary to expectations, Mary Pickford and Douglas Fairbanks will exchange the season's greetings at Pickfair. Fairbanks rushed home from New York but if it augered reconciliation, neither will tell.

Happy in ignorance of what awaits her, Mrs. Nicholas Columbo proudly exhibited a cablegram simulating Christmas greetings from her son, Russ Columbo, popular crooner who was killed accidentally early last fall.

"With love, from Russ" the message read, and the mother was unaware that her other children were still practicing the merciful hoax they carried out since Russ died. She believes he is in Europe, too busy making a motion picture to return for the holidays. Physicians say she may have recovered sufficiently from a heart attack to be told of his death within a week or so.

The Editor Looks On: Food from Everywhere," Household Magazine, May 1934: Nothing shows the cosmopolitan character of the average American home more than our names for food. Hardly an important language in the world is unrepresented in the names of common articles of diet in the United States. Chocolate is Mexican Spanish; coffee from Arabic; tea from the Amoy dialect of Chinese. The word mutton has a French origin, while lamb comes from the Anglo-Saxon of our forefathers. Orange is of Persian derivation, and so is lemon. Peach goes back to classical Greek, as does cherry. Potato is one of the few English words with a Haitian origin, and the Haitians were talking of the sweet potato rather than the Irish potato. Marmalade is a slightly changed Portuguese word, but jam, to professors of language, is merely a variant of champ, which means bite and comes from a Swedish dialect…

One could go on and on. The names of our foods bear witness to a variety of diet unknown in ancient or even modern times. The Venerable Bede, when about to die, gave his associates a little pepper as a prized treasure. Queen Margaret of Navarre nibbled sugar as a royal delicacy while she composed her love stories. (The sugar, appropriately enough, was unrefined.) Many persons living today can recall a time when oranges were sold only in our largest cities. Now the world is our source of food.

"4,000 in CWA Put on Short Week; Supply Purchases Hauled by Low Funds," January 19, 1935

With its $400 million fund of emergency reemployment rapidly nearing exhaustion, [the Civil Works Administration] today placed four million workers now carried on its rolls to a 24-hour week in cities of more than 2,500 population, and 15 hours a week for smaller communities and rural districts. Instructions to this effect were sent to all state directors by Harry L. Hopkins, head of the CWA

The action of Director Hopkins today thus put squarely before Congress the need for deciding in the near future whether the civil works program is to continue. The $400 million fund originally made available for the work was expected to carry it through February 15 on a full operating schedule. The proposed addition of $350 million is intended to continue the program to May 1.

"Pay-As-You-Listen Is a Riddle of the Age," by Orin E. Dunlap Jr., *The New York Times*, January 14, 1935

How to levy a fee on millions of unseen listeners is a riddle that has caused more than one economist hours of concentration during the past decade. Recently, several of the calculators have reached what they consider to be practical conclusions, and they presented their suggestions to Uncle Sam for possible use in the "New Deal."

Generally, they open the discussion by calling attention to the fact that automobiles are taxed for their right to use the highways and they display license plates as proof; the driver pays his license fee and pays a tax on gasoline and oil. The railroad is taxed for its right of way across the countryside and ships pay a fee for entering ports. The long distance telephone call is taxed.

So is the radio set in many foreign lands, but not in the United States. That is why twentieth century physiocrats have caught the idea that broadcasters and listeners should assist in meeting expenses. In the President's budget recommendations, the authorized obligation for the Radio Commission for 1934 was listed at $640,000, and the budget estimate for 1935 at $668,885.

Mindful of the revenue collected on radio receivers in foreign countries-for example, in England, there are approximately eight million outfits, the owners of which pay an annual tax of $2.50—the economists are wondering if radio on this side of the sea has reached an age where it can be called upon to pay its own way. They point to the fact that a property rental is generally paid for billboards erected along the highways or signs painted on barns. Why, then, they ask, should not Uncle Sam collect an annual toll on each wave length? Another argument, frequently expounded, is that circulars going through the mail add to the government's revenue by carrying a postage stamp, but an hour radio program is criss-crossed through space without Uncle Sam deriving any revenue, although he controls the channels. A ship passing through a canal usually pays a toll, but a broadcast flashes across the entire continent without paying "a continental."

All of these factors have Caused the economists to scratch their heads and turn toward radio as a source of income.

"We Are much Cleverer. Topic of The Times," *The New York Times*, January 19, 1935: Easily the best news of the day is the report that we are no longer a people with the average mental age of a 12-year-old child; our mental age is nearly 18 years. That is the finding of an expert who writes in School Life, the official publication of the Federal Office of Education in Washington.

...This tremendous improvement in American intelligence is not credited to the administration or the New Deal or anything governmental. The Washington specialist simply finds that the celebrated army intelligence test upon which the 12-year-old mentality of the American was alleged do not justify such a condition. This point is essentially the same made by critics like Dr. Fabian Franklin at the time. The speed of a person's response to a specific mechanical stimulus does not measure his intelligence, which is his total response in his own way and his own time to the whole world in which he lives. We are now told that the capacity to learn may continue indefinitely. At any rate, it is good to hear that there are no less than 10 million Americans with a mental age of 23 and over, and there are only three million of us with a mental age of 12.

"Children in Gainful Occupations," *Needlecraft Magazine,* March 1935

No one who has ever seen a child made prematurely old and careworn by the unrelenting taskmaster, hard work, can fail to sympathize with the efforts which have been put forth from time to time in an attempt to limit the age at which children may be employed in gainful occupations. In his recent message to Congress, President Roosevelt commented upon child labor, stating that it had been "for the moment outlawed" under the various codes of fair competition. For years the question of an amendment to our constitution restricting the labor of children has been agitated. Away back in June 1924, this amendment was first proposed and it has been ratified by 20 states. The resolution reads: "The Congress shall have power to limit, regulate and prohibit the labor of persons under 18 years of age."

Much controversy has been waged over the advisability of ratifying this amendment. Its foes point out that it involves a question which should be determined by each state individually; that climatic conditions have much to do with the age at which young people should be permitted to go to work; and that there is danger in permitting Congress power to absolutely control the life of young people throughout the nation, where conditions-vary. so decidedly in the various sections of the country. There have always been a considerable number of sincerely minded individuals who believe the principle of "States' Rights" should not be violated, and that to as great an extent as is practicable all, questions should be decided and adjusted by the individual states; and that the federal government should handle only such as require a central administrative power.

The American Farm Bureau Federation has been, until recently, opposed to the Child Labor Amendment, but of late they have reversed their, opinion, and are now lined up with the advocates of the amendment. The American Federation of Labor has always been one of the amendment's warmest friends and defenders, and they are now calling upon the state federations of 28 states to make the passage of the amendment their chief legislative objective this winter.

You and I will probably be called upon later to vote to either ratify or defeat this resolution; so it is not too soon to be thinking the matter over, that we may make up our minds on which side of the controversy we choose to be found. In any event, we can all undoubtedly agree that every child has an inalienable right to leisure, wholesome recreation, opportunity for education, and freedom from adult cares while he is growing, and before he has reached his maturity. It is not only for his welfare but for the future welfare of the nation in which he lives, that this should be possible. That is a consideration we should not overlook.

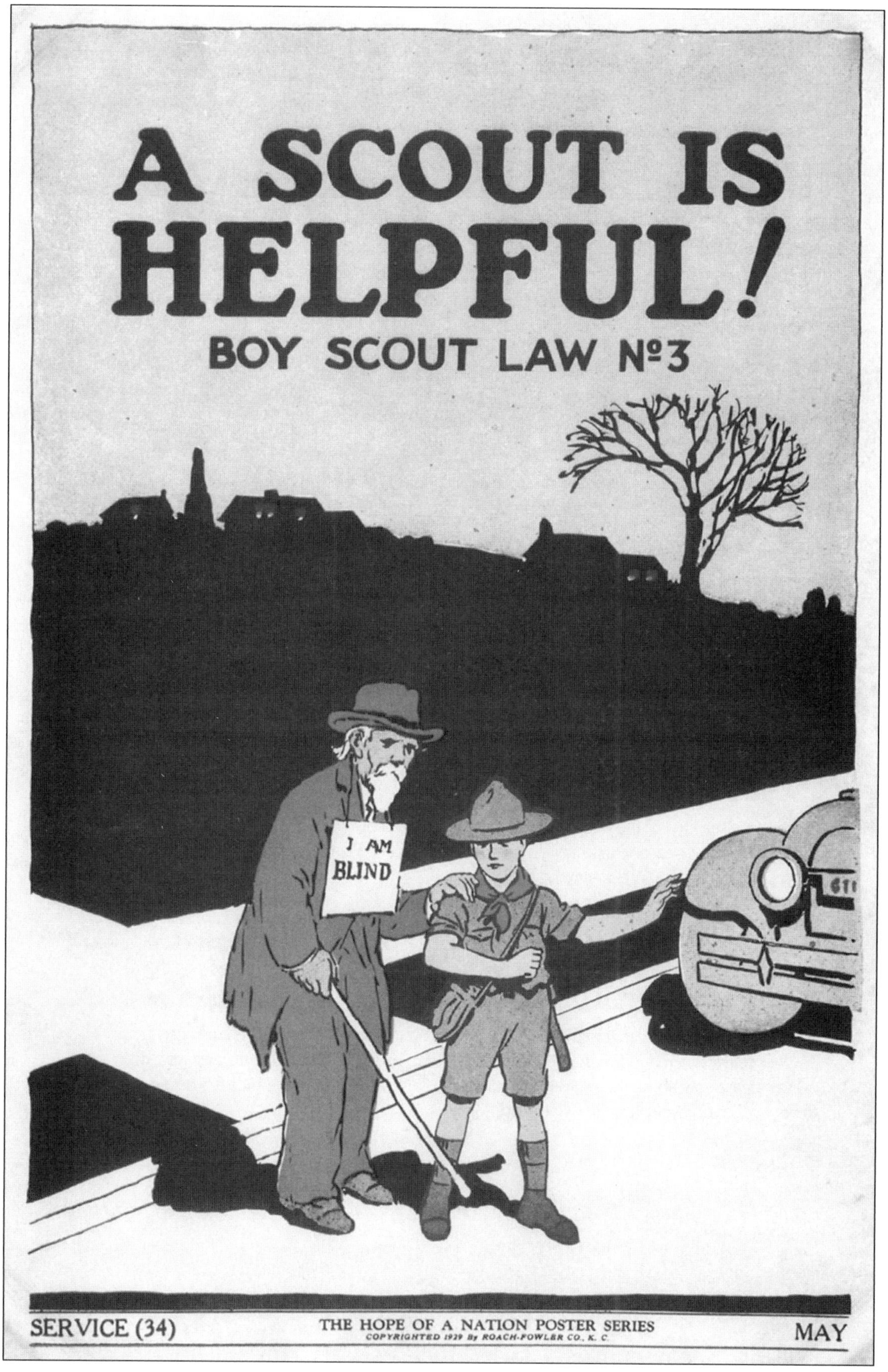
A SCOUT IS HELPFUL!
BOY SCOUT LAW №3
I AM BLIND
SERVICE (34)
THE HOPE OF A NATION POSTER SERIES
COPYRIGHTED 1929 By ROACH-FOWLER CO., K. C.
MAY

"Ask Birth Control at House Hearing,"
***The New York Times*, January 19, 1935**

Amendment to the penal laws to permit medically supervised dissemination of birth control information and advice to overburdened parents of "unwarrantably" large families in their own interest and those of taxpayers who are staggering under the "greatest relief load in history" was urged today on moral, economic and scientific grounds at a crowded hearing before the House Judiciary Committee.

Mrs. Thomas N . Hepburn of Hartford remarked in concluding the pleas for birth control that she had six children. One of her children is Katherine Hepburn, the actress. More than 500 men and women who overflowed the caucus room of the House building applauded the assertion of Dr. Joseph J. Spengler of the University of Arizona that "without birth control the New Deal will be a frizzle."

Margaret Sanger declared "the forgotten women of the nation, including more than 32 million child-bearing mothers, sought not to bring into the world more, children than they could care for."

"We are engaged today, publicly, in the greatest relief job in history," Dr. James H. S. Bossard declared. "If it is to mean nothing more than giving out money and more money, then we have learned nothing since the days of the Roman Empire."

Father Charles E. Coughlin of Detroit spoke for half an hour in opposition to the birth control bill pending in Congress, declaring that America's problem was not one of reproduction but of "control of money in the hands of the Reserve Banks."

"We had better turn our minds to the solution of the problem of how to prevent our billions from going into the pockets of a few men and how to get a few more hundred into the pockets of our farmers and workers…"

Representative Pierce, former Governor of Oregon and sponsor in the House of the amendments to the Comstock Law, declared the present law "absolutely unenforceable and in that respect on all fours with the prohibition Amendment."

The three sections of the criminal code from which exemption is sought forbid possession or transmission by mail or express of anything relating to contraception, under penalty of $2,000 fine or five years' imprisonment; or both.

The result, according to Representative Pierce and the medical experts who appeared on behalf of this bill, is the "bootlegging" of contraceptive devices often to the injury of those most in need of help from qualified physicians who are prevented by law from supplying them, or from sending the desired information or advice.

"We want to bring these things out in the open so that legally licensed physicians can give authoritative information to the people who need it," Representative Pierce declared. "No one need worry about race suicide. What we seek is protection of the race from suicidal effects of the present conditions of things."

***New York Times,* June 7, 1935:** "Supreme Court Justice Charles C. Lockwood, who was born in the Williamsburg section of Brooklyn, upheld yesterday the city's action in acquiring, over property owners' objections, 12 square blocks of land for the Williamsburg low-cost housing project.

He ruled that the condemnation proceeding whereby the city took the land from the former owners was legal in every respect. He also observed that in days past minority groups in Williamsburg had opposed the substitution of trolley cars for horse cars, and the building of the Williamsburg Bridge.

The housing project is intended to provide homes for persons of small means and is to be financed by federal funds. One of the objections to the city's method of taking the land through its right of eminent domain was that the project was to benefit only a single class of persons and not the public as a whole."

Augusta Swanson, Telling Memories among Southern Women

"I had two sisters and one brother, all half-sisters and a half-brother. Everyone had different fathers. My mother, she was not married. My father was White and brother's father was White, but the others were Colored. Because, see in the country, they didn't have no money, and the only way you could get it was to go with these White men to get a little change. And that's why so many of them had these babies with White men. Because they'd offer them a little change where Colored didn't have nothing to give them. Nothing to help them get along-no money, nothing.

And when she'd tell me my daddy was White and was coming to see me, if I had listened to her, I probably would have had money. But I couldn't stand him. It made me mad when she told me that. He owned a grocery store. And when she'd tell me he was coming over and wanted to talk to me, I wouldn't even come out to see him. I didn't want to see no White man.

The other thing they could do on the plantation to get by was to put the children out to work. And so when I was eight years old, my mother sent me to live with a lady. Her name was Miz May. She wanted someone to keep her company.

At first, I wasn't big enough to do anything, but she taught me how to read and write, crochet, knit, cook, and how to housekeep. She used to fool me to death. She'd come tell me that the fairy had hid a present, a big surprise, and she'd say, 'Augusta, the only way you can find that surprise, you have to move everything, and make sure you general clean, because if you don't, you'll never find that surprise.' And so, here I am working myself to death, just moving and dusting, moving trying to find it. And I never did find it. But I sat right by her and slept right in her room on a cot, right by her just like I was her daughter. And all I learned was through her, 'cause she would teach me everything right there. That's why I never did go to school."

"Sex Not Enough in Marriage," ***Sexology, The Magazine of Sex Science,*** **December 1936:** "Romantic youth has been educated to the idea that love conquers everything; true love triumphs over every obstacle, and so forth, and so forth. It is disquieting, therefore, to discover in later life that love alone is no guarantee of a happy marriage. It is, of course, a help where men and women understand the cultivation of love through day-by-day mutual adjustments and modifications of individual habits and tastes to provide opportunity for the maximum growth of two personalities. But, even in the narrow field of sexual relations, love alone is inadequate. Knowledge of technique is perhaps the first requisite and this, very frequently, is lacking. Premarital experience of the man does not, as a rule, furnish the requisite knowledge. Indeed, quite the contrary can be the case, for such experience has usually been with prostitutes, in which case the responsibility of facilitating relations rests with the woman, whereas in marriage it rests with the man, in the beginning at least. French prostitutes during the war commented on the lack of finesse in approach exhibited by the American soldiers, contrasting them in this respect with the French. It would appear from this that possibly the untaught youth of America has less artistry in such matters than the more sophisticated youth of Europe. In this country, the Puritan tradition has exalted romantic love, while condemning all consideration of the more intimate details of this expression. The result is men, however capable of romantic love they may be, often enter marriage and even go through life in most appalling ignorance of the physiological and psychological nature of their partners. The Puritan tradition has created an altogether false and extremely restricted view of the wife's possible participation in sexual pleasure, in regard to both its possibility and its seemliness. The result is, often, complete lack of cooperation between partners in any attempt to arrive at a beautiful and mutually satisfactory sex expression. There are very frequent cases of men seeking outside of marriage those satisfactions which should be found within marriage. As long as such conduct is limited to prostitutes, since there is no competition in the field of love, the wife often condones it because of her own mistaken idea of the scope of marriage relationships. The motive for marriage should be what natural law makes it, the desire for personal satisfaction, complete sexual and psychological development, and a more abundant emotional life. We are not preparing our youth for marriage until we teach them to attain first all of these fundamentals."

"Social Security Betrayed," by Abraham Epstein,
***The Nation,* October 10, 1936**

"Far from being a rational social measure, the New Deal Social Security Act is the most reactionary social-insurance plan in existence. Its major features are neither social nor conducive to security. In a world ruled by slogans, it is not surprising, however, to find American liberals ensnared into unquestioning acceptance of the act. The promise of security is most alluring. The slogan of 'social security' encompasses all fond hopes and pious wishes. Even enemies of social legislation insist they favor the idea of social security.

The vast range and complexity of the act has served to obscure its social limitations and sinister implications. The combination of 10 different insurance and relief programs, based on three different philosophies of governmental operation, has made understanding well-nigh impossible. The embodiment of good, bad, and indifferent plans in one measure has impeded critical discussion of the socially questionable features.

Sooner or later, the American people are bound to realize that, despite its glittering title, the act does not solve the problems of insecurity. The law does not even attempt to meet the major ills of present-day society. The great modern hazards afflicting millions of wage and salaried earners are sickness and invalidity, unemployment, old-age dependency, industrial accidents, death, widowhood, and orphanage. Although illness is one of the major causes of economic insecurity, threatening workers in good times as in bad and accounting for nearly half of all dependency in normal times, the act completely ignores this problem. It does not touch upon accident compensation, which is still non-existent in two states and extremely inadequate in most others, nor does it make burial provisions. Except for the destitute blind, it fails to provide for the invalid. Its chief concern is with unemployment and old-age dependency."

Franklin D. Roosevelt, campaign speech, presidential election, 1936: "For 12 years this nation was afflicted with hear-nothing, see-nothing, do-nothing government. Never before in our history have these forces been so united against one candidate as they stand today. They are unanimous in their hatred of me-and I welcome their hatred."

"What Sort of People Are Getting Divorces?"
by Farnsworth Crowder, *McCall's,* February 1936

"The obvious and easy answer is-all sorts of people. The butcher, the baker, the candlestick maker, the banker, the broker, the slavey and stoker, all rub shoulders in the echoing halls of the divorce courts. The fellowship of disillusion knows no class lines. But an easy answer is not always correct, and a sweeping cynicism is almost sure to be wrong. All sorts of people, it is pleasant to report authoritatively, are not getting divorces; it only seems so.

The names on the casualty lists are drawn, to be sure, from every profession and every social stratum, but there is a telltale family resemblance among most of the unhappy wights who cannot stay put in marriage.

It is only recently that case histories have been examined scientifically to determine why American husbands and wives do not continue as husbands and wives. From these examinations there emerges, illuminatively, a composite picture of the individual who is a likely candidate for divorce.

Let's describe him. He is a native-born Protestant, childless and without property. He lives in a furnished house or flat in the western part of the United States. He is below par in health. He is contemptuous of old-fashioned standards. He (or she) is inclined to be bossy, uncooperative, self-centered, conscious of his own ego and indifferent to his partner's. His conception of love is immature. He has not been able to progress beyond the heated lightning of romance to an affectionate sharing of common destinies.

This, sketched in roughly, is the picture of the man or woman who keeps Reno alive. True, it is a synthetic portrait, but it is built up from the researches of two men who, without theses to prove or causes to advocate, have sought to isolate the realities of divorce. One is Dr. Paul Popenoe, who directs the trail-blazing Institute of Domestic Relations in the domestically restless city of Los Angeles. The other is Professor William Ogburn, the University of Chicago's renowned student of social trends and the problems of the American family.

Dr. Popenoe acts as father confessor to thousands who have become shoaled on marital reefs, and it was to bring sense out of confusion that he posed the question: What sort of people are getting divorces? He began to query his consultants and then, as the mass of information grew, to codify the answers.

From the answers collected, however diverse and contradictory, there emerges not only the picture of the dissatisfied husband and wife, but also a pretty definite map of the hazards of the marriage partnership. The whirlpools, the rapids, the shallows are all marked out on the blueprint-here, plotted out, are the dangers a wary couple may avoid. It is difficult to give specific advice on marriage, but this sweeping injunction seems reasonable enough: Consider the divorced, and then go thou not and do likewise! Don't live as they do, don't be what they are.

From the way they live and the way they are, emerges a decalogue for youth at the altar, a Ten Commandments of Marriage. No one can keep all these commandments, but everyone can keep some of them. There is nothing adamant about the code. Marriage is a patchwork of compromises and concessions at best. To those who avoid divorce and separation I say-edit the decalogue to fit your own ground rules.

1. Stay out of the West: This is not a warning to shy clear of Nevada. Reno's notoriety has bred a fallacy: that people in large numbers rush to the lax-law state to file for divorce decrees. Well, they don't. The number who do so is negligible. Eight in every 10 decrees are issued to couples who were married in the very state they are seeking divorce. So Reno (with less than three decrees out of every 100 granted) bulks far larger in the news than it does in the statistics.

But the West appears, nevertheless, to be rough on matrimony. The famous sun that's a little brighter, the ready smile that's a trifle wider and the larger heart that's a trifle warmer do not, in fact, make marriage even a little solider. On the contrary. The riskiest place, geographically, to contract a marriage is on the Pacific slope; the safest place, the middle Atlantic seaboard...

2. Don't live in a metropolis. Marriage flourishes better in the smaller city, in the towns and the country. In 1930, in Chicago, separation and divorce were twice as fatal as death to family unity...

3. Don't be childless. When a man and a woman hold hands, we call it romance. When that linkage, with its mutual self-absorption, is broken and a child enters the chain, we have a family and its strongest link is likely to be that smallest mortal. Professor Ogburn makes the statement that 'Families without children may almost be classed as a different type of family. Such situations affect the activity of wives in and out of the home and have a bearing on the stability of the marriage.' How much of a bearing may be judged from the fact that from 1900 to 1930, the percentage of broken homes among families without children was nearly three times as large as the percentage with children.

4. Own things. Possessions—furniture, a house, land—are mooring posts. Couples adrift, unattached to material things, are in danger of drifting apart.

5. Don't scorn to do the things your grandparents did. That may seem futile advice, because it is impossible to battle or decry the influence of a mechanical civilization. The home as a factory vanished because it could not meet the stiff competition from the outside. Industry clamors for

the chance to do for you what grandma did for herself-knead the bread, do the laundry, bake the beans, churn the butter, sew the clothing and put up the pickles.

6. Avoid being bossy. A short time ago Dr. Popenoe conducted a study of 2,600 marriages that had stood the test for five years. One thing he wanted to know about was this matter of who wears the pants. Can a family have two heads? He found that it not only can but does 'in more than one third of the educated families in America; and such families are happier than any other kind.' The figures leave no doubt 'that a democratic co-partnership is associated with the greatest happiness; that man-dominated marriages come next in this respect; and that marriages dominated by the wife show a definitely smaller percentage of happiness than do the other two.'

7. Give your partner's ego room to breathe.

There is a jingle that runs:
Though in wedlock
He and she go
Each maintains
A separate ego

8. Keep biologically up to par. Dr. Popenoe is the authority for the statement that 'divorcés are, on the whole, biologically inferior to the happily married part of the population.' What does he mean? For one thing, that they show a higher frequency to nervous breakdown. For another, that they are more temperamentally unstable. For a third, that they have a shorter life expectancy…

9. Don't be a matrimonial illiterate. Most people are still married by ministers who pronounce the state 'holy' and solicit God's blessing upon it. A pastor who averages over a hundred marriage services a year says that they fill him with melancholy forebodings, that time and again he wanted to stand with his fingers crossed in his prayer book 'for the union won't be holy and the prayer won't be holy and the prayer won't help much. The eager kids don't know what it's all about. They are matrimonial illiterates.'

10. Love your mate. Love, like Life, like Spirit, is impossible to define. 'Life is one damned thing after another; love is two damned things after each other.' "

"Woman Runs Signal Tower; Handles It 'Like a Man,'" *Grit,* April 18, 1937

If a woman takes a man's job, she must be able to handle it like a man, contends Mrs. Ella Bower, who, as adeptly as a man, pulls switches and signal levers in the Pennsylvania and Lehigh Valley Railroad's joint signal tower near Stanley, NY.

Nearly three decades of service at a railroad job, held by few women, have made her as efficient as any male tower operator, her fellow workmen say.

Mrs. Bower in her 29 years of service has worked at nearly every tower in the Williamsport (Pa.) Division of the Pennsylvania Railroad.

"I've climbed semaphore poles 35 feet high to display signals," she says. "I have always contended that, if a woman is to take a man's job, she must be ready and capable of doing what is expected of the position when if is filled by the man."

Her hobby is knitting, but there is little time for knitting during working hours, she has discovered.

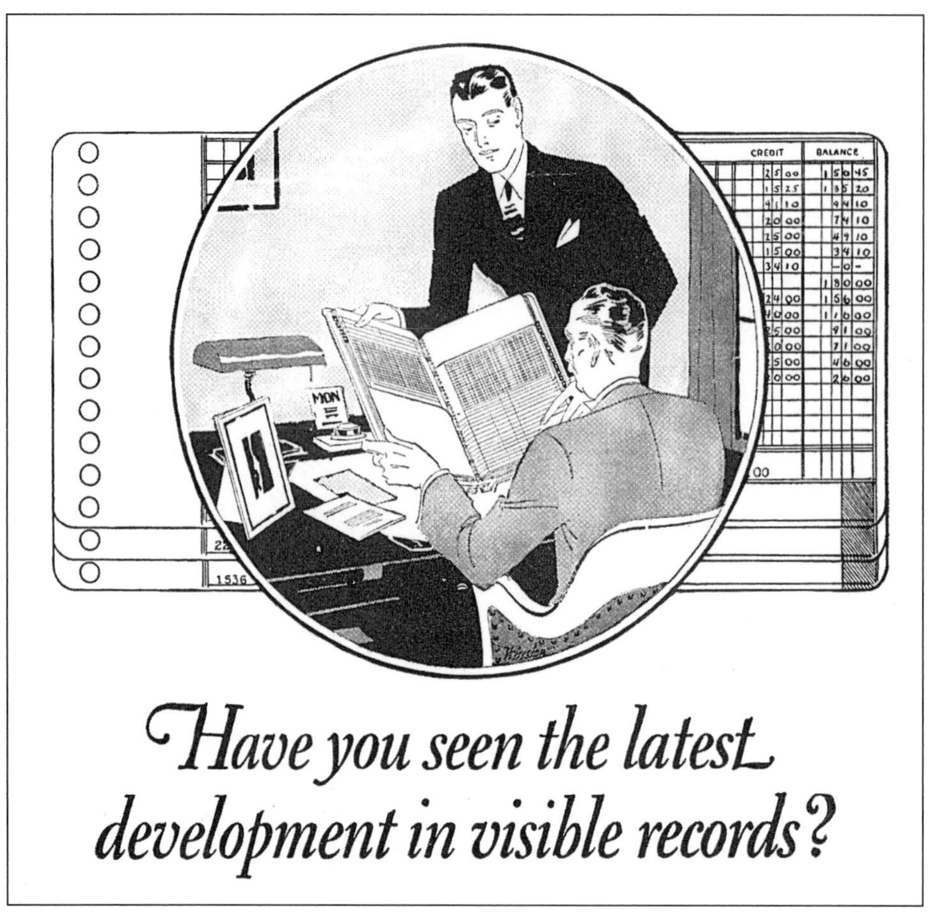

Have you seen the latest development in visible records?

"Twenty Years When Nothing Stood Still,"
***Forbes Magazine*, December 15, 1937**

"Twenty years ago-remember back to 1917?

People used shoe buttons then, and buckles, and the zipper was a new kind of haircut. Detroit and Cleveland went on daylight-saving time in the summer, and farmers fanatically opposed the idea elsewhere. Stainless steels, small diesel engines, radio broadcasting-thousands of things we now take for granted were unborn in 1917.

We yelled "sissy" at anyone who wanted too much comfort. Now we demand comfort in offices, factories, homes, cabs of motor trucks, airplanes-everywhere.

The first beauty shop was yet to be born. First, permanent waves cost $60 each. Now 65,000 beauty shops do over a $200 million business each year, spend over $60 million for wages, and support 85 exclusive manufacturers. And there is an additional beauty bill of $125 million for lipsticks and other supplies the girls use themselves.

The men aren't so choosy.

They go to any old barbershop, so there are twice as many shops to serve them, but the income per average shop is less. The girls buy from their shops fifteen cents' worth of supplies for every $1.00 in service; the men seldom buy supplies from barbers.

But the safety razor has zoomed to almost universal use since 1917. Now it is challenged by electric shavers. Shaving soap- and cream-makers watch with bated breath, but they are developing beard stiffeners to make the electrics work better. The art of shaving is now the subject of industrial research-with the Mellon Institute spending five years to study it.

We admired blind believing then. Now we get the facts on everything. Statistics are gathered by the government, colleges and universities, and the National Industrial Conference Board, thousands of trade associations, labor unions, and so many 'foundations' that it takes a thick book to catalog them.

Foreign nations had holds on our machinery, dyes, ball bearings, and lots of others. Now we lead in this production.

We have become 'clothes conscious.' Rayon consumption is up 3,500 percent since 1920, but cotton is up also. We wear more of more kinds of clothes specially designed for individual activities.

The war brought the vogue for streamlined figures. Waistlines and skirt lengths have gone up and down amazingly.

We eat drugstore lunches, and our national dietary habits have changed. The California Fruit Growers' Exchange had been going strong on orange juice for 10 years by 1917. Now vitamins have come in. Tomato juice, sauerkraut juice, and others have joined the parade. Baby diets have changed so much for the better that dentists and doctors are doomed to less work per thousand of population.

Mazda lamps were then just replacing carbon arcs in silent movie projectors. Now three-dimensional pictures in full colors with sounds are just around the corner.

Fountain pens with iridium-tipped gold points were cheap at $5. Now electric welding makes stainless steel iridium-tipped points in good pens for $0.50 or less.

Screwdrivers have safe plastic handles. They can be hammered on like chisels, do not conduct electricity, and at last the tips are nonskid. Shoelace tips are of plastic instead of metal.

And drugs have improved. The morphine habit was the terror of all who needed drugs for pain. Now, synthetic drugs-at one-thirtieth of the price-are non-habit-forming.

Three-day drying periods for Portland cement were taken for granted. Now a day is enough for some kinds. Night photography was largely by flash powder. There were some floodlights, but they were not as good as the present ones. Now we have developed photo floodlights, flash powders which are not fire hazards nor dangerous to the eyes-and even flash bulbs which do not burn out with one exposure.

More than 1,500 industrial laboratories spend $300 million per year to develop new things-a major industry all by itself-with over 40,000 research men employed.

Technical improvements are legion. The cotton mill work week was 66 hours. Now it's 40 hours, with two shifts. The result: Mills then needed five spindles in place for each bale of cotton used. Now they need only three and one half. Modernization has helped. Cigarettes dropped on rugs were hotel keepers' horror. Now rugs are fireproofed. Moths did heartbreaking damage. Now fabrics are mothproofed. Even wood is fireproofed.

Book pages were reduced to postage-stamp size and projected on screens for reading. A library used to be a space-consuming luxury, but now a five-foot shelf can contain thousands of volumes. Books may even become talking affairs which are read aloud to listeners.

In radio, talking pictures, and even in ordinary business, voice training is now as important as appropriate dress was in 1917."

"First Woman Inventor in U.S. Is Attractive Beulah Henry," *GRIT,* April 18, 1937

Speak of inventors, and most folks will conjure up a picture of test tubes, electrical whatnots, littered rooms, soiled smocks, and men or women with a far-off look in their eyes.

Quite the opposite of this picture, however, is blonde Beulah Louise Henry, the "Lady Edison" of inventors, who has received patents for 52 inventions in the last 15 years. Her "laboratory" is a modern hotel room. She is vivacious, cultured, and attractive. She is an artist of considerable ability and, feminine-like, very proud of her cooking.

The secret of her inventive ability, Miss Henry says, is spiritual. Inventions just come to her out of the air, "finished and in color, just like a picture." She had no mechanical training to prepare for the life of an inventor. But at the age of nine, ideas for improvements began coming to her almost like visions. When these visions come, she goes to her mechanic and describes them, and work. Sometimes she has to work as long as four years on one invention before it is perfect.

Miss Henry's newest invention is an office equipment device which she asserts will save time, money, and trouble for the employer and worker. It is called a "protograph" and is an attachment which can be adjusted to any standard typewriter and make from one to four copies, all-in-one writing, without the use of carbon paper. Additional copies are made by the use of typewriter ribbons which are fed from side to side automatically, as the original ribbon. The protograph may be released from operating position by pressing a button.

Among her other inventions for parasols, toys, bathing slippers with high heels, football valves, water bottle stoppers, many mechanical devices which hardly seem possible for a woman to have devised, and the "Radio Rose."

The last is a life-size, lifelike doll, dainty and attractive, with a seven-tube radio concealed in its body.

"Home Under the Seats," *Pathfinder,* August 27, 1938

At Columbus, Ohio, Ohio State University's million-dollar stadium-13th largest in the country-seats 75,000 spectators. Distinguished with the fact that it won an important architectural prize when completed in 1921, it is outstanding for yet another reason-eventually, beneath its 75,000 seats, it will house as many as 2,400 students.

This prospect moved closer to reality last week as WPA workers went ahead in making a dormitory out of a third section of the U-shaped stadium's huge understructure. Designed to provide living quarters for 120 young men, the project meant that the number of below-seat residents at Ohio State soon would reach total of 440.

The idea had its birth in the depression year of 1933. At that time, anxious to help needy students remain in school, university officials decided to provide cheap housing for 75 undergraduates by building a dormitory in the fourth floor tower at the stadium's southwest corner. Promptly named the "Tower Club" by those who moved in, the new residential unit was no less successful than it was unique. Accordingly, a year later, the university won the help of the Federal Public Works Administration in making a similar unit out of a section of the underside itself-thus providing a home for 105 additional students. Then, early this year, with the aid of the Works Progress Administration, a second under-section became the home of 140 more. With last week's project, the total expenditure on the "Tower Club" to date was estimated at $172,500, about half of which represented federal funds.

"Gomez and Ruffing Get Demands, Opening Way to Final Agreements with Gehrig, DiMaggio, Crosetti, Rolfe, and Others," *Lowell Sun* (Massachusetts), March 1, 1938

Owner Jack Ruppert of the New York Yankees today is committed to an expenditure of a reported $37,000 for next season for the salaries of two players, namely Lefty Gomez and Red Ruffing, who signed yesterday, but his troubles are not over by any means. In fact, owner Ruppert has about $100,000 go to satisfy all hands.

Having corralled his two best pitchers at what was said to be salaries of $18,500 each, representing a raise of $3,500 a piece, he now is confronted by the task of signing first baseman Lou Gehrig, outfielder Joe DiMaggio, shortstop Frank Crosetti, third baseman Ed Rolfe and pitcher Spud Chandler. Putting it another way, he has everything except a baseball team.

The advance guard started workout yesterday at St. Petersburg in preparation for a quest of a third straight American League pennant and world championship, with the rest of the hands to report the next few days, but two or three of the aforementioned recalcitrants may not be there.

DiMaggio and Gehrig between them are asking about $75,000, and the rest are just as generous as possible with owner Rupert's money in their own behalf, with the result that there may be some absentees when the general spring sessions finally get underway.

"Rate Budge Number 1 in Tennis Event," *Piqua Daily Call* (Ohio), September 1, 1938

Don Budge, who already has won the Australian, French and Wimbledon tennis titles this year, will be seeded number one for the U.S. Championships September 8-17 at Forest Hills, New York, when the draw is made today.

Budge stands out like a skyscraper in a wheat field. Yet in spite of his eminence, and in spite of the fact that he is the odds-on favorite to win his second straight national singles title, the tournament promises the best that the United States has to offer, which is considerable.

Heading the invaders will be the Australians, opponents of Budge and Co. in the Davis Cup challenge round...

Since she is ranked number one nationally and has been more active than Helen Jacobs, Alice Marble appears due for the top ranking in the women's single field, which also will have a strong international group.

"Business and Finance," *Time*, April 3, 1939: "Manhattan reporters last week journeyed to the docks to count cases of gold being unloaded from the *Queen Mary*. They counted 355 cases, thus estimating that the *Queen* brought in some $20 million. This was presently dwarfed by a shipment on the *Manhattan* estimated at $56 million, the largest ever. At the week's end, four other liners were on the way from frightened Europe with $75 million more to add to the $15,007,517,132.83 (57 percent of the world's monetary supply) in gold already admittedly in the U.S. Treasury's hands.

As usual when the golden tide laps high on U.S. shores, reporters went to see Secretary of the Treasury Morgenthau. As usual, he poohpoohed the idea of inflation. But though he said the gold was not affecting U.S. economy, it was amply clear that the continued European crisis was. Markets are nervous. Businessmen cut their buying for the future so low that three new indexes of inventories published by the National Industrial Conference Board touched the lowest point since May 1937. Most cheerful fact of the week (to businessmen): the sales ratio of twin beds to double beds was up from one-to-10 in 1936 to one-to-five.""

Ready for New Clothes for School," by Marilyn Madison, *Home Arts-Needlecraft,* September 1938

"Begin today to plan what the children will have new for school. Be practical in your selections, and plan a wardrobe that will not need to have consideration from you every school morning

A thrifty mother of my acquaintance says, 'I buy shoes first, then socks right for the shoes. Then I buy sweaters and berets or caps. Next, I select the material for skirts or buy shorts or pants to go with the sweaters. Then I choose fabrics for dresses and blouses to give desired variety. Of course, I do all this to a planned color scheme so that each child looks as though thought has been given to his or her clothing.

'For the girls and the boys, when I have chosen styles in dresses and blouses right for them, I plan to make at least three garments in each style, varying the fabric and trimming so that each has individuality. I cut all garments one day, do my machine work all in one day, and then take my time with the finishing. There is less of this to do since I use slide fasteners in every garment I make. The children like them and they cut dressing time in half '

In making clothes to fit, 'I'd like to say a word about clothing for the 10- to 14-year-olds. By all means plan for becomingness in sewing for girls of these ages. No set rule can be put down, because some girls are chubby, some lanky, some large or small for their ages; so consider well the style and the fabric. Strive for simplicity. Tailored effects are safest, usually. Remember that bright, attractive clothes prove a real stimulus to a girl's pride, and, when sewing for these ages, listen to their whims and try to please them. The sooner a girl begins to know what she wants in a dress, the sooner she will express individuality and good taste. Dresses for a 10- to 14-year-old girl are no more difficult to make than for a two to six, but they do need more consideration as to individual becomingness'

'Hand embroidery is being emphasized this season, also bias-binding trims, loads of rickrack in all widths and colors, and colored and plain slide fasteners. Cotton having dark backgrounds and bright designs is as popular for winter as are the wool crepes and challis. Novelty plaids go in many of the pleated skirts."

Writer Norman Cousins' panacea to unemployment, "Will Women Lose Their Jobs?," 1939:
"There are approximately 10 million people out of work in the United States today; there are also 10 million or more women, married and single, who are job holders. Simply fire the women, who shouldn't be working anyway, and hire the men. Presto! No unemployment. No relief rolls. No Depression."

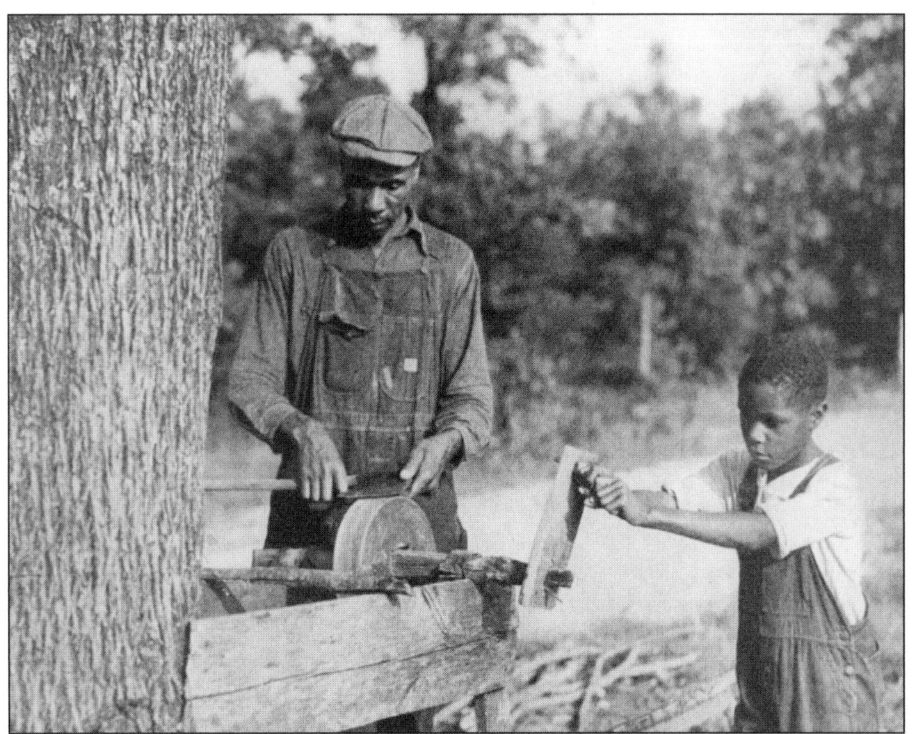

Willson Whitman's God's Valley, 1939: A lot has been said about the sharecropping system and you could say a lot more without explaining just how bad it is. You have to see it, and you have to think about it. A lot of Southerners see it without thinking, because the people it produces are such sorry-looking folks that it is taken for granted that such people would be in trouble anyhow. But there are more of these people than there used to be. Just in the last few years it's got so that more than half the farmers work for other men, and in the cotton country 60 out of a hundred do."

"Town of Tomorrow," by Dorothy Ducas and Elizabeth Gordon, *The New York Herald Tribune* World's Fair Section, April 30, 1939

"The 15 demonstration houses which make up the Town of Tomorrow at the New York World's Fair bear a marked resemblance to the Town of Today. This is no accident. Housing prophets at the Fair apparently believe there is nothing very startling in the immediate future of home building, nothing to dazzle the eye and confound the mind. If these 15 houses are an indication, good houses, compact and well-made and containing all the conveniences and comforts of present-day living, will be the order of a New Day, probably at a lower cost than all these things have been possible before.

Making no attempt to present 'trick' houses, created to wrest 'ohs' and 'ahs' from a newly house-conscious public, World's Fair architects have given us 15 houses such as everyone yearns to own today. There are houses done in the modern style, of course-six of them, five with attractively arranged flat roofs-but traditional Colonial, Georgian, Swedish, and Rural French, too. There is an increased use of glass, in sliding wall panels and glass/brick sections of walls. There is one new-fangled entrance to a home through the garage, which is wallpapered and windowed so it merits the name 'motor room.' And utility rooms galore, to house heating equipment, replacing traditional basements. But none of these things is exactly unheralded, as a look at a new building in any up-and-coming city will convince you…

In general, they are small houses, ranging in price from $2,500 to $35,000, depending upon where they would be built and how much special equipment you put into them…They show definite trends, such as the elimination of dining rooms, increased attention to fire safety, more garden space, lots of built-in shelving and cabinet work, definite recreation space, outdoor decks and terraces. And here's an interesting detail: only two houses eliminate fireplaces. The future, like the present, will preserve a sentimental attachment to the family hearth."

"Cabarets to Pay City Sales Tax by the Month," New York Herald Tribune, April 30, 1939: "Because many fly-by-night cabarets have swindled the city of the sales tax they collected from patrons by closing up after only a few weeks' existence, Comptroller Joseph D. McGoldrick issued a new rule yesterday requiring all-night clubs and cabarets to pay the sales tax monthly instead of quarterly…'Numerous fly-by-night cabarets have been able to avoid any sales tax whatsoever by the simple process of going out of business,' said Mr. McGoldrick. 'Despite the fact that the patrons have paid the tax to the clubs, the city has never received it.'"

The Risks and Rewards of 1939—A Financial Review of the Year, Federal Reserve Bank of New York

January to April

In the first few weeks of the year, the inflow of capital from abroad, which had diminished considerably following the Munich Agreement in September 1938, remained at a relatively low level. The inward movement increased in March, when a new crisis was precipitated by German demands on Czechoslovakia, and continued in heavy volume for several weeks after the occupation and dismemberment of that country by Germany. As a result of the increased transfers of capital into this country, together with payments due on the continued excess of merchant exports over imports to the United States, heavy pressure was put on European exchanges, especially sterling. At the same time, large transfers of funds in United States paper currency were demanded for shipment to Europe, presumably for hoarding. In March and April, shipments of U.S. currency to Europe reached record levels; total shipments topped $73 million during the two months.

The influence of European demands tended to check requirements for bank credit by industrial and commercial concerns; the U.S. Treasury found it unnecessary to borrow on the usual Treasury financing date. In the absence of these opportunities or the possibility of employing its funds, New York City banks added to their holdings of outstanding government bonds. Prices of high-grade securities rose, and yields declined further.

Despite the accentuation of easy money conditions, there was no evidence of a stimulating effect on business activity.

May to July

As the disquieting effects of the dismemberment of Czechoslovakia subsided, there was a temporary respite from disturbances in Europe. The movement of capital from Europe to America ceased; the foreign demand for United States currency subsided. Gold imports continued in large volume during May and were sizable during June and July. Only a part of the gold was sold to obtain dollars; the remainder was earmarked for foreign central banks; this reflected a tendency of European countries to transfer part of their gold reserves to the United States for safekeeping. At the end of July the total amount of gold held under earmark for foreign accounts at the Federal Reserve Bank of New York reached the unprecedented figure of $1.3 billion. The accumulation of idle funds continued to have a stimulating effect on prices of high-grade securities and a depressing influence on money rates. Prices on government and other prime bonds reached new high levels, and bond yields corresponding declined to new low levels. New security flotations increased considerably, most for refunding purposes. Business activity remained at a relatively low level in May and there was little demand for business loans or for loans to finance security trading. In June, there was an abrupt increase in business activity, reflecting the temporary relief from disturbing developments in Europe.

August and September
The lull between the crises in Europe proved to be of short duration. An increasingly critical situation in the relations between Germany and Poland led in August to the third major European crisis within a year. Germany invaded Poland on September 1; shortly thereafter, England and France declared war against Germany. This resulted in an accelerated flow of capital from Europe to the United States, chiefly by way of London; this produced heavy pressure against the sterling exchange and required the British authorities to provide support to maintain the value of the sterling against the dollar.

The decision of the British authorities to suspend official support of sterling on August 25 resulted in a sharp drop in the pound from $4.68 to $4.12; this action abruptly checked the flow of capital to the United States."

The Great Leap, Before and After, by John Brooks: "A nationwide survey of 1,400 husbands and wives made by the American Association of University Women resulted in the conclusion that children of middle-class families were more apt to suffer from their mothers' over-conscientiousness than from neglect. The same survey showed that among the educated couples under consideration, 92 percent handled their money jointly, 80 percent took joint responsibility for the upbringing of their children, 60 percent of the husbands regularly took a hand in the cooking. Incidentally, two-thirds of the husbands in the survey earned under $5,000 a year, and almost one-third of the families-presumably the other third-had full-time domestic help."

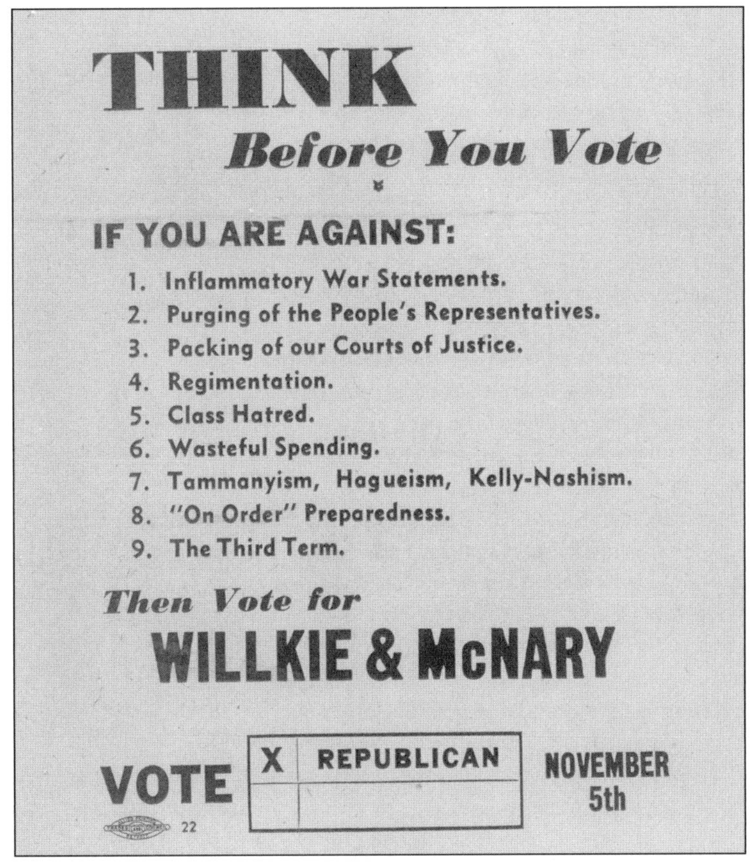

"The New York World's Fair Music Festival," Olin Downes, *Etude Music Magazine*, May 1939

A visitor from Cape Town, South Africa, who was taken for a preview through the New York World's Fair grounds, was heard to exclaim in a kind of neo-Mayfair accent, "My word, one couldn't begin to see all this in a lifetime." The reason for this, doubtless, is that highly experienced and energetic men behind the huge project realized that Canadians who will visit the World's Fair would be presented with an enormous variety of appeals-high-brow, low-brow, broad-brow and narrow-brow-something representative of everything under the sun, for everyone under the sun.

One might say that the same dimensions and characteristics apply to the music programs arranged and still being arranged for the World's Fair. In fact, these dimensions are so extensive that, even though I have been surrounded with them since the beginning, I'm still bewildered by their size. They've long since left the boundaries of the Fair itself.

This reminds me of the story of a colored man named Esau, who worked upon the campus of a little Southern college in a town invisible upon the map. At the time of the Chicago Fair, he was enraptured by the posters in the railroad station so as to take his savings to venture upon the long trip. Practically none of the colored folks had ever been more than three miles from town. When he left, every worker from the neighboring plantations was at the station to see him off. He was gone a month. Colored picture postcards of the Fair thrilled his friends. When he came back, an anxious and excited crowd was on hand to greet him. The president of the college asked the traveler what he liked best at the Fair. Esau scratched his head, meditated, and then said, "Well, Massa Boss, you see when I got to Chicago I just got so busy I never did get time to get to the fairgrounds."

As a matter of fact, the plans for the music of the Fair, as now outlined, will very properly be devoted to concerts and operas in New York City itself. About one-half of the celebrations will be upon Manhattan Island and one half at the fairgrounds. As projected, the first six months of the fair season (May 1 to November 1) will include so many important occasions that one can confidently predict that it will be the most significant musical festival the world has ever known…

We have given a suggestion as to the participation of some foreign governments. It may be interesting to know that several countries overseas recognize the importance of music as a glorified expression of national ideals, and therefore these countries have arranged to engage great American symphony orchestras to play the music of their famous composers at a distinguished series of concerts given under the auspices of these countries. The plans are so far-reaching that I can give here only a sketch. Two performances of the New York Philharmonic Symphony Orchestra are certain, and six to 10 are possible. Poland has engaged this great orchestra for a Polish program Monday third; and Roumania has engaged it for May 5. Roumania has also engaged the Philadelphia Orchestra from May 14 to 16, to be conducted by the eminent Roumanian composer George Enesco. Czechoslovakia, Brazil, Switzerland, Finland, Argentina, and other nations are now negotiating for similar engagements with American orchestras. Practically all of the leading American orchestras have been invited to come to the Fair, and many have accepted.

SECTION FIVE: 1940 CENSUS SUMMARY & COMPARISON DATA

Refers to numbers at bottom of the page

MAP OF THE UNITED STATES SHOWING POPULATION PER SQUARE MILE BY COUNTIES: 1940

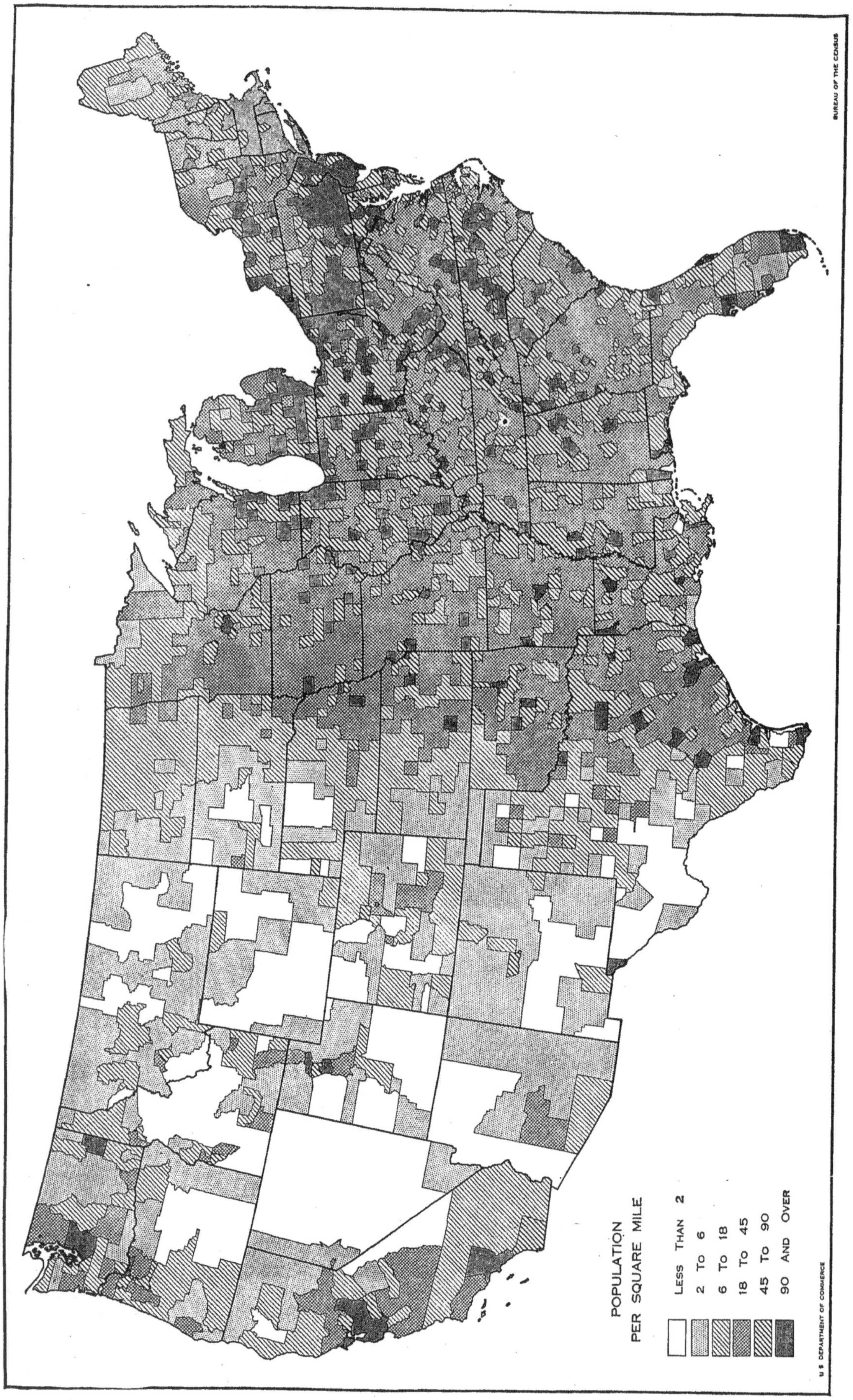

POPULATION PER SQUARE MILE

LESS THAN 2
2 TO 6
6 TO 18
18 TO 45
45 TO 90
90 AND OVER

U S DEPARTMENT OF COMMERCE

BUREAU OF THE CENSUS

4

UNITED STATES SUMMARY

NUMBER OF INHABITANTS

INTRODUCTION

This section summarizes the statistics relating to the number of inhabitants of the United States as returned in the 1940 census, presenting the total population of the various areas, without classification by race, sex, age, or any other characteristics, such classification being reserved for other volumes of the census reports. The population is shown for States, for cities and other urban places arranged in groups according to size, for metropolitan districts, and for incorporated places having from 1,000 to 2,500 inhabitants. Comparative figures are presented for the States and for cities of 100,000 or more for all censuses, beginning with the first in which the area was separately enumerated. For smaller incorporated places, and metropolitan districts, comparative figures are given for at least one earlier census wherever available. The population of the minor civil divisions (townships, etc.), of the counties in the several States, of incorporated places having fewer than 1,000 inhabitants, of wards of incorporated places of 5,000 or more inhabitants, and of census tracts, is given in the sections relating to the various States.

Population data in other census reports.—Data on the basic characteristics of the population, including urban, rural-nonfarm and rural-farm residence, sex, age, race, nativity, citizenship, country of birth, school attendance, highest grade of school completed, employment status, class of worker, occupation, and industry are presented in the Second Series of Population Bulletins. More detailed statistics on the labor force are shown in the Third Series of Population Bulletins which present data on employment status, occupation, and industry in combination with age, race, and other characteristics, as well as data on wage or salary income in 1939, hours worked in the census week, months worked in 1939, and duration of unemployment. A continuation of the statistics on the general characteristics of the population, begun in the Second Series, is presented in the Fourth Series of Population Bulletins, which include additional data on age, citizenship, school attendance, and highest grade of school completed, together with statistics on marital status and relationship to head of household. Statistics on internal migration and families, as well as detailed tabulations of sample data on the characteristics of the labor force and of the general population, will be presented in subsequent series of bulletins.

Unincorporated places.—The Census Bureau often receives requests for the population of villages or small towns that are not incorporated and therefore have no legally established boundaries. The publication of official population figures is necessarily limited to those places that have definite and well recognized boundaries—that is, to places incorporated as cities, boroughs, towns, or villages. Informal population counts are sometimes provided, however, for unincorporated places, where the enumerators have indicated the beginning and the ending of these places on their schedules. Record is made of all requests for the population of unincorporated places, and approximate figures will be sent, if and when available, to those who have made such request.

Enumeration at usual place of residence.—For the country as a whole, and for every State and every political subdivision within the State, the population reported is the resident or *de jure* population. The enumerators under the census law have been instructed to enumerate persons at their "usual place of residence" or "usual place of abode"—that is, at their permanent homes or regular lodging places. Hence persons were not in all cases counted in the places where they happened to be found by the enumerators; in particular, they were not always counted in the places where they worked or carried on their daily occupations. Thus it happens that the business or industrial population of any large city includes a considerable number of persons who are not counted as a part of the census population of the city. These persons carry on their business or perform their daily tasks, spend a considerable portion of their incomes, and perhaps eat all or part of their meals, in the city, but have their residences or lodging places outside the municipal limits.

Persons temporarily absent from their usual places of residence—for example, persons away from home on a visit or on business, traveling for pleasure, attending school or college, or sick in a hospital—were enumerated at their homes or the places where they usually live, information regarding them being obtained from some other member of their family or from relatives or acquaintances. Entire households away from home were enumerated where found, and the returns were allocated to their usual place of residence. Persons having no regular place of residence anywhere, however, were enumerated where they were found at the time of the enumeration and were counted as residents of that area.

Persons in the military service in the United States were enumerated as residents of the States, counties, and minor civil divisions in which their posts of duty were located, and members of their families were enumerated where they actually resided. The crews of vessels in the American merchant marine were enumerated as such and counted as a part of the population of the port from which the vessel operated.

United States and possessions.—Table 1 shows the population of the United States and its territories and possessions for 1940, 1930, and 1920. In the other tables of this section the figures are limited to the 48 States and the District of Columbia.

TABLE 1.—POPULATION OF THE UNITED STATES AND ITS TERRITORIES AND POSSESSIONS: 1940, 1930, AND 1920

AREA	Gross area (land and water) in square miles, 1940	POPULATION		
		1940	1930	1920
United States and all territories and possessions	3, 735, 223	150, 621, 231	[1] 138, 439, 069	[2] 118, 107, 150
Continental United States	3, 022, 387	131, 669, 275	122, 775, 046	105, 710, 620
Territories and possessions, exclusive of the Philippines	597, 236	2, 477, 023	2, 061, 570	1, 680, 292
Alaska	586, 400	[3] 72, 524	[3] 59, 278	55, 036
American Samoa	76	12, 908	10, 055	8, 056
Guam	206	22, 290	18, 509	13, 275
Hawaii [4]	6, 433	423, 330	368, 336	255, 912
Panama Canal Zone	553	51, 827	39, 467	22, 858
Puerto Rico	3, 435	1, 869, 255	1, 543, 913	1, 299, 809
Virgin Islands of the United States	133	24, 889	22, 012	[2] 25, 346
The Philippines	115, 600	[5] 16, 356, 000	[1] 13, 513, 000	[2] 10, 599, 000
Military and naval services, etc., abroad		118, 933	80, 453	117, 238

[1] Revised. Differs from figure published in 1930 census reports; revised figure for the Philippines is an estimate derived by interpolation between censuses of Dec. 31, 1918 (10,314,310), and Jan. 1, 1939 (16,000,303).

[2] Revised. Differs from figure published in 1930 census reports; revised figure for Virgin Islands is an estimate derived by interpolation between censuses of Nov. 1, 1917 (26,051), and April 1, 1930; revised figure for the Philippines estimated by interpolation between censuses of 1918 and 1939.

[3] Census taken as of Oct. 1 of the preceding year.

[4] Includes Baker, Canton, Enderbury, Howland, Jarvis, Johnston, and Midway Islands.

[5] Estimate derived by extrapolation from censuses of 1918 and 1939.

Population of continental United States from 1790.—The areas now forming the 48 States and the District of Columbia were first completely enumerated in 1890, and all areas, except what is now the State of Oklahoma, were included also in the censuses of 1860, 1870, and 1880. The gradual increase in the territory [1] covered by the census is indicated below.

The first census, taken in 1790, covered the area now occupied by the District of Columbia and the following States: Maine, New Hampshire, Vermont, Massachusetts, Rhode Island, Connecticut, New York, New Jersey, Pennsylvania, Delaware, Maryland, Virginia, West Virginia, North Carolina, South Carolina, Kentucky, Tennessee, and part of Georgia.

In 1800 the enumerated territory was extended to include the areas of the present States of Ohio, Indiana, Illinois, Michigan, Wisconsin, and all but the extreme northern and southern parts of Alabama and Mississippi.

In 1810 there were further additions, comprising the territory now forming the present State of Arkansas, all but the northwestern corner of Missouri, and all but the southwestern part of Louisiana. The extreme northern parts of Alabama and Mississippi were also first canvassed at this census.

In 1820 the southern tips of Alabama and Mississippi, the northwestern part of Georgia, and the southwestern part of Louisiana were covered. The territory was extended in 1830 to include Florida, and in 1840 to include Iowa, northeastern Minnesota, and the remaining part of Missouri.

In 1850 very sizable additions were made, comprising the territory that now forms Texas, Utah, Washington, Oregon, and California, and most of New Mexico.

In 1860 the area covered was brought up to its present extent, except for Oklahoma, which was first enumerated in 1890.

Table 2 shows the population of continental United States from 1790 to 1940, with the decennial increase, the land area included in the legal boundaries at each census, and the population per square mile.

TABLE 2.—POPULATION AND AREA OF CONTINENTAL UNITED STATES: 1790 TO 1940

CENSUS DATE	Population	INCREASE OVER PRECEDING CENSUS [1]		Land area in square miles [2]	Population per square mile
		Number	Percent		
1940 (Apr. 1)	131, 669, 275	8, 894, 229	7. 2	2, 977, 128	44. 2
1930 (Apr. 1)	122, 775, 046	17, 064, 426	16. 1	2, 977, 128	41. 2
1920 (Jan. 1)	105. 710, 620	13, 738, 354	14. 9	2, 973, 776	35. 5
1910 (Apr. 15)	91, 972, 266	15, 977, 691	21. 0	2, 973, 890	30. 9
1900 (June 1)	75, 994, 575	13, 046, 861	20. 7	2, 974, 159	25. 6
1890 (June 1)	62, 947, 714	12, 791, 931	25. 5	2, 973, 965	21. 2
1880 (June 1)	50, 155, 783	[3] 11, 597, 412	[3] 30. 1	2, 973, 965	16. 9
1870 (June 1) [3]	38, 558, 371	7, 115, 050	22. 6	2, 973, 965	13. 0
1860 (June 1)	31, 443, 321	8, 251, 445	35. 6	2, 973, 965	10. 6
1850 (June 1)	23, 191, 876	6, 122, 423	35. 9	2, 944, 337	7. 9
1840 (June 1)	17, 069, 453	4, 203, 433	32. 7	1, 753, 588	9. 7
1830 (June 1)	12, 866, 020	3, 227, 567	33. 5	1, 753, 588	7. 3
1820 (Aug. 7)	9, 638, 453	2, 398, 572	33. 1	1, 753, 588	5. 5
1810 (Aug. 6)	7, 239, 881	1, 931, 398	36. 4	1, 685, 865	4. 3
1800 (Aug. 4)	5, 308, 483	1, 379, 269	35. 1	867, 980	6. 1
1790 (Aug. 2)	3, 929, 214			867, 980	4. 5

[1] Percentage increases are computed on basis of change in population since preceding census date, and period covered therefore is not always exactly 10 years. Adjustments for differences in census date must be made if strictly comparable figures are desired for each decade.

[2] The figures given for the various census years represent the area of all the land within the present boundaries of continental United States which was under the jurisdiction of the United States on the date in question, including in some cases considerable areas of land not then organized or settled and not covered by the census.

[3] A revised figure of 39,818,449 for the 1870 population includes adjustments for underenumeration in the Southern States. Unadjusted data are used in this and subsequent tables because revised figures for States, urban-rural residence, etc., are not available.

Data corresponding to those in table 2 are given in tables 3 to 5, which deal with population, decennial rates of increase, and population density, respectively, for individual regions, divisions, and States.

Apportionment.—The primary reason for the establishment of the decennial census of population, as set forth in the Constitution, was to provide a basis for the

[1] The sum of the areas enumerated was not always identical with the area included within the legal boundaries of the United States at the respective dates, nor was it always possible to indicate the exact boundaries of the enumerated areas. In the earlier censuses not all of a State or territory was covered by the enumerators but only that part up to the "frontier line" and any large isolated settlements beyond. For example, Iowa Territory in 1840 included all of what is now Iowa and most of what is now Minnesota, but within the Territory the only substantial settlements were in the southeastern corner of what is now Iowa, and hence only this part was covered by the census of 1840. It is not feasible to make a more exact statement than that the area of what is now Iowa was added to the area of enumeration in 1840. The western part of what is now Minnesota, however, was not included until later.

apportionment of members of the House of Representatives among the several States. Such an apportionment has been made on the basis of every census from 1790 to 1940, except that of 1920. Prior to 1870, the population basis for apportionment was the total free population of the States, omitting Indians not taxed, plus three-fifths of the number of slaves. After the apportionment of 1860 the scaling down of the number of slaves, of course, disappeared from the procedure; and in 1940 it was determined that there were no longer any Indians who should be classed as "not taxed" under the terms of the apportionment laws. The last apportionment was therefore made on the basis of the entire population of the 48 States. All apportionments are made under the constitutional provision that each State should have at least one Representative, no matter how small its population.

The results of each apportionment, starting with the initial apportionment in 1789 and including those based on each census from 1790 to 1940, are shown, by States, in table 2A.

TABLE 2A.—NUMBER OF MEMBERS IN HOUSE OF REPRESENTATIVES UNDER EACH APPORTIONMENT, BY STATES: 1789 TO 1940

[Includes Representatives assigned to newly admitted States after the apportionment act, as follows: 1790, 1; 1800, 1; 1810, 5; 1830, 2; 1840, 9; 1850, 3; 1860, 2; 1870, 1; 1880, 7; 1890, 1; and 1900, 5]

REGION, DIVISION, AND STATE	1940	[1] 1930	[2] 1920	[2] 1910	1900	1890	1880	1870	1860	1850	1840	1830	1820	1810	1800	1790	1789
United States	435	435	435	435	391	357	332	293	243	237	232	242	213	186	142	106	65
REGIONS:																	
The North	251	259	266	266	244	227	212	193	162	151	144	144	124	105	77	57	35
The South	135	133	136	136	126	112	107	93	76	83	86	98	89	81	65	49	30
The West	49	43	33	33	21	18	13	7	5	3	2	-	-	-	-	-	-
THE NORTH:																	
New England	28	29	32	32	29	27	26	28	27	29	31	38	39	41	35	29	17
Middle Atlantic	92	93	91	91	79	72	69	67	60	63	63	74	66	56	41	28	18
East North Central	87	90	86	86	82	78	74	69	56	48	43	30	18	8	1	-	-
West North Central	44	47	57	57	54	50	43	29	19	11	7	2	1	-	-	-	-
THE SOUTH:																	
South Atlantic	56	54	56	56	53	50	49	43	36	43	47	61	61	62	56	46	30
East South Central	35	34	39	39	38	37	36	34	28	32	32	33	25	18	9	3	-
West South Central	44	45	41	41	35	25	22	16	12	8	7	4	3	1	-	-	-
THE WEST:																	
Mountain	16	14	14	14	8	7	5	2	1	-	-	-	-	-	-	-	-
Pacific	33	29	19	19	13	11	8	5	4	3	2	-	-	-	-	-	-
NEW ENGLAND:																	
Maine	3	3	4	4	4	4	4	5	5	6	7	8	7	-	-	-	-
New Hampshire	2	2	2	2	2	2	2	3	3	3	4	5	6	6	5	4	3
Vermont	1	1	2	2	2	2	2	3	3	3	4	5	5	6	4	2	-
Massachusetts	14	15	16	16	14	13	12	11	10	11	10	12	13	20	17	14	8
Rhode Island	2	2	3	3	2	2	2	2	2	2	2	2	2	2	2	2	1
Connecticut	6	6	5	5	5	4	4	4	4	4	4	6	6	7	7	7	5
MIDDLE ATLANTIC:																	
New York	45	45	43	43	37	34	34	33	31	33	34	40	34	27	17	10	6
New Jersey	14	14	12	12	10	8	7	7	5	5	5	6	6	6	6	5	4
Pennsylvania	33	34	36	36	32	30	28	27	24	25	24	28	26	23	18	13	8
EAST NORTH CENTRAL:																	
Ohio	23	24	22	22	21	21	21	20	19	21	21	19	14	6	1	-	-
Indiana	11	12	13	13	13	13	13	13	11	11	10	7	3	1	-	-	-
Illinois	26	27	27	27	25	22	20	19	14	9	7	3	1	1	-	-	-
Michigan	17	17	13	13	12	12	11	9	6	4	3	1	-	-	-	-	-
Wisconsin	10	10	11	11	11	10	9	8	6	3	2	-	-	-	-	-	-
WEST NORTH CENTRAL:																	
Minnesota	9	9	10	10	9	7	5	3	2	2	-	-	-	-	-	-	-
Iowa	8	9	11	11	11	11	11	9	6	2	2	-	-	-	-	-	-
Missouri	13	13	16	16	16	15	14	13	9	7	5	2	1	-	-	-	-
North Dakota	2	2	3	3	2	1	1	-	-	-	-	-	-	-	-	-	-
South Dakota	2	2	3	3	2	2	2	-	-	-	-	-	-	-	-	-	-
Nebraska	4	5	6	6	6	6	3	1	1	-	-	-	-	-	-	-	-
Kansas	6	7	8	8	8	8	7	3	1	-	-	-	-	-	-	-	-
SOUTH ATLANTIC:																	
Delaware	1	1	1	1	1	1	1	1	1	1	1	1	1	2	1	1	1
Maryland	6	6	6	6	6	6	6	6	5	6	6	8	9	9	9	8	6
Virginia	9	9	10	10	10	10	10	9	11	13	15	21	22	23	22	19	10
West Virginia	6	6	6	6	5	4	4	3	-	-	-	-	-	-	-	-	-
North Carolina	12	11	10	10	10	9	9	8	7	8	9	13	13	13	12	10	5
South Carolina	6	6	7	7	7	7	7	5	4	6	7	9	9	9	8	6	5
Georgia	10	10	12	12	11	11	10	9	7	8	8	9	7	6	4	2	3
Florida	6	5	4	4	3	2	2	2	1	1	1	-	-	-	-	-	-
EAST SOUTH CENTRAL:																	
Kentucky	9	9	11	11	11	11	11	10	9	10	10	13	12	10	6	2	-
Tennessee	10	9	10	10	10	10	10	10	8	10	11	13	9	6	3	1	-
Alabama	9	9	10	10	9	9	8	8	6	7	7	5	3	1	-	-	-
Mississippi	7	7	8	8	8	7	7	6	5	5	4	2	1	1	-	-	-
WEST SOUTH CENTRAL:																	
Arkansas	7	7	7	7	7	6	5	4	3	2	1	1	-	-	-	-	-
Louisiana	8	8	8	8	7	6	6	6	5	4	4	3	3	1	-	-	-
Oklahoma	8	9	8	8	5	-	-	-	-	-	-	-	-	-	-	-	-
Texas	21	21	18	18	16	13	11	6	4	2	2	-	-	-	-	-	-
MOUNTAIN:																	
Montana	2	2	2	2	1	1	1	-	-	-	-	-	-	-	-	-	-
Idaho	2	2	2	2	1	1	1	-	-	-	-	-	-	-	-	-	-
Wyoming	1	1	1	1	1	1	1	-	-	-	-	-	-	-	-	-	-
Colorado	4	4	4	4	3	2	1	1	-	-	-	-	-	-	-	-	-
New Mexico	2	1	1	1	-	-	-	-	-	-	-	-	-	-	-	-	-
Arizona	2	1	1	1	-	-	-	-	-	-	-	-	-	-	-	-	-
Utah	2	2	2	2	1	1	-	-	-	-	-	-	-	-	-	-	-
Nevada	1	1	1	1	1	1	1	1	1	-	-	-	-	-	-	-	-
PACIFIC:																	
Washington	6	6	5	5	3	2	1	-	-	-	-	-	-	-	-	-	-
Oregon	4	3	3	3	2	2	1	1	1	1	-	-	-	-	-	-	-
California	23	20	11	11	8	7	6	4	3	2	2	-	-	-	-	-	-

[1] Apportionment established for the Seventy-third Congress, elected in the fall of 1932.

[2] Apportionment established for the Sixty-third Congress, elected in the fall of 1912, and used for subsequent Congresses up to and including the Seventy-second.

The population base for apportionment and other significant items are shown in table 2B.

TABLE 2B.—POPULATION BASE FOR APPORTIONMENT AND THE NUMBER OF REPRESENTATIVES APPORTIONED: 1790 TO 1940

CENSUS YEAR	Population base for apportionment[1]	Number of Representatives[2]	Ratio of apportionment population to Representatives	Date of apportionment act
1940	131, 006, 184	435	301, 164	Nov. 15, 1941.
1930	122, 093, 455	435	280, 675	June 18, 1929.
1920	(3)	435	(3)	(3)
1910	91, 603, 772	435	210, 583	Aug. 8, 1911.
1900	74, 562, 608	386	193, 167	Jan. 16, 1901.
1890	61, 908, 906	356	173, 901	Feb. 7, 1891.
1880	49, 371, 340	325	151, 912	Feb. 25, 1882.
1870	38, 115, 641	292	130, 533	Feb. 2, 1872.[4]
1860	29, 550, 038	241	122, 614	May 23, 1850.[5]
1850	21, 766, 691	234	93, 020	May 23, 1850.[6]
1840	15, 908, 376	223	71, 338	June 25, 1842.
1830	11, 930, 987	240	49, 712	May 22, 1832.
1820	8, 972, 396	213	42, 124	Mar. 7, 1822.
1810	6, 584, 231	181	36, 377	Dec. 21, 1811.
1800	4, 879, 820	141	34, 609	Jan. 14, 1802.
1790	3, 615, 823	105	34, 436	Apr. 14, 1792.
----------	----------	65	[7] 30, 000	Constitution, 1789.

[1] Excludes the population of the District of Columbia, the population of the territories, the number of Indians not taxed, and (prior to 1870) two-fifths of the slave population.
[2] This number is the actual number apportioned at the beginning of the decade.
[3] No apportionment was made after the census of 1920.
[4] Amended by act of May 30, 1872.
[5] Amended by the act of Mar. 4, 1862.
[6] Amended by act of July 30, 1852.
[7] The minimum ratio of population to Representatives stated in the Constitution (art. 1, sec. 2).

The first attempt to make provision for automatic reapportionment was included in the act for the taking of the seventh and subsequent censuses (approved May 23, 1850). By specifying the number of Representatives to be assigned and the method to be used, it was hoped to eliminate the need for a new act of Congress every decade and assure an equitable distribution of Representatives. When this Census Act was superseded in 1879, the automatic feature was discontinued and the method of computing the apportionment was determined by Congress on each occasion up to 1910.

No apportionment was made after the census of 1920, the apportionment of 1910 remaining in effect. In 1929, when the act for the taking of the fifteenth and subsequent censuses was under consideration, it seemed desirable to incorporate some provision which might prevent the repetition of the 1920 experience. A section was, therefore, included in the act which provided, for the 1930 and subsequent censuses, that unless Congress within a specified time enacted legislation providing for apportionment on a different basis, the apportionment should be made automatically by the method last used. In accordance with this act, a report was submitted by the President to Congress on December 4, 1930, showing the apportionment computations both by the method of major fractions (which was the one used in 1910) and by the method of equal proportions. In 1931, in the absence of additional legislation, the automatically effective apportionment followed the method of major fractions.

The census of 1940 was taken under the same law as that of 1930, but in 1941 this law was amended to the effect that apportionments based on the 1940 and subsequent censuses should be made by the method of equal proportions. In the application of this method, the Representatives are so assigned that the average population per Representative has the least possible relative variation as between one State and any other.

Under this method, California gained three Representatives between 1930 and 1940 and six other States, namely, Arizona, Florida, New Mexico, North Carolina, Oregon, and Tennessee, each gained one. To balance these gains, since the number of Representatives in the

CENTER OF POPULATION: 1940 AND 1930

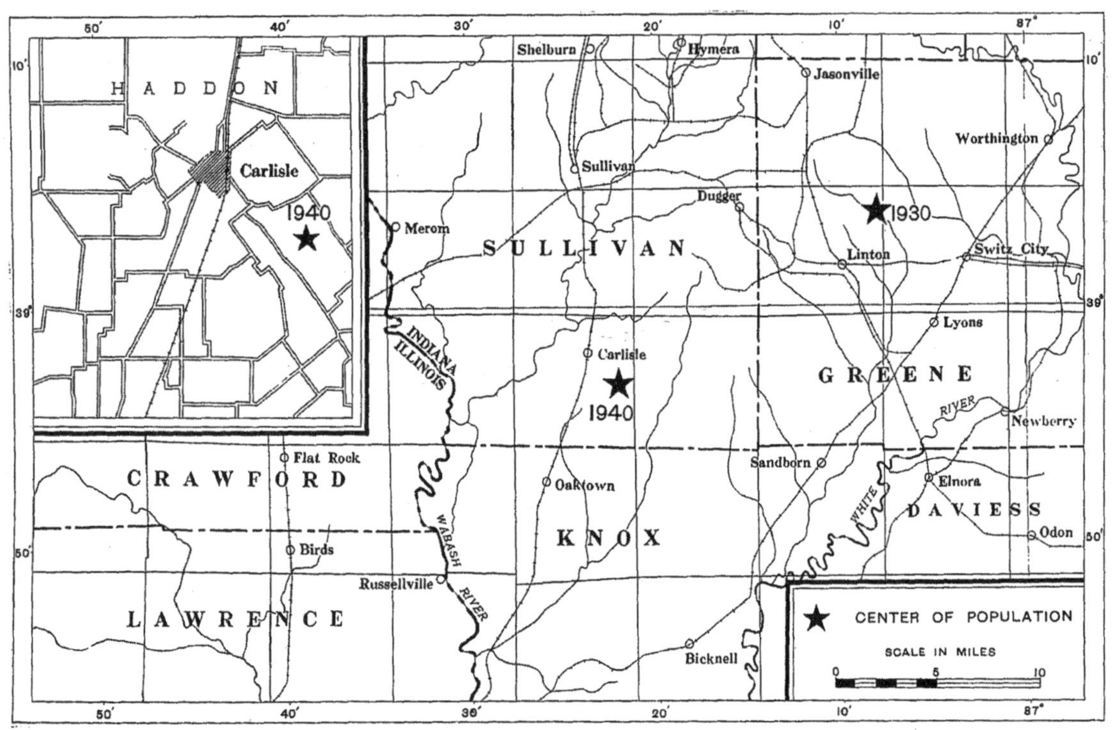

House was not changed, there were nine States which lost one Representative each, namely, Illinois, Indiana, Iowa, Kansas, Massachusetts, Nebraska, Ohio, Oklahoma, and Pennsylvania.

Center of population.—The "center of population," as defined by the Census Bureau, is that point which may be considered as the center of gravity of the United States; in other words, the point upon which the United States would balance, if it were a rigid plane without weight and the population distributed thereon, with each individual being assumed to have equal weight and to exert an influence on a central point proportional to his distance from the point.

The 1940 center of population is located 2.0 miles southeast by east of Carlisle, in Haddon township, Sullivan County, Indiana. This point is in southwestern Indiana, 36.0 miles south of Terre Haute and 20.0 miles north-northeast of Vincennes In terms of latitude and longitude, the 1940 center is located in latitude 38°56′54″ north, longitude 87°22′35″ west. During the decade from 1930 to 1940, the center of population moved 13.0 miles westward and 7.9 miles southward, reaching its most southerly point. The location of the center of population in 1940 and in 1930 is shown on the map on the opposite page.

The total westward movement from 1790 to 1940 was 602 miles. The greatest movement westward was during the decade from 1850 to 1860, when the center advanced 80.6 miles. The least movement westward was during the decade from 1910 to 1920, when it advanced only 9.8 miles. The point farthest north was the 1790 location, and the point farthest south, the 1940 location, but the difference was only 22.5 miles.

The table and map below give the approximate location of the center of population of the United States at each census from 1790 to 1940.

Table 2C.—LOCATION OF THE CENTER OF POPULATION OF THE UNITED STATES: 1790 TO 1940

YEAR	North latitude			West longitude			Approximate location
	°	′	″	°	′	″	
1790	39	16	30	76	11	12	23 miles east of Baltimore, Md.
1800	39	16	6	76	56	30	18 miles west of Baltimore, Md.
1810	39	11	30	77	37	12	40 miles northwest by west of Washington, D. C. (in Virginia).
1820	39	5	42	78	33	0	16 miles east of Moorefield, W. Va.[1]
1830	38	57	54	79	16	54	19 miles west-southwest of Moorefield, W. Va.[1]
1840	39	2	0	80	18	0	16 miles south of Clarksburg, W. Va.[1]
1850	38	59	0	81	19	0	23 miles southeast of Parkersburg, W. Va.[1]
1860	39	0	24	82	48	48	20 miles south by east of Chillicothe, Ohio.
1870	39	12	0	83	35	42	48 miles east by north of Cincinnati, Ohio.
1880	39	4	8	84	39	40	8 miles west by south of Cincinnati, Ohio (in Kentucky).
1890	39	11	56	85	32	53	20 miles east of Columbus, Ind.
1900	39	9	36	85	48	54	6 miles southeast of Columbus, Ind.
1910	39	10	12	86	32	20	In the city of Bloomington, Ind.
1920	39	10	21	86	43	15	8 miles south-southeast of Spencer, Owen County, Ind.
1930	39	3	45	87	8	6	3 miles northeast of Linton, Greene County, Ind.
1940	38	56	54	87	22	35	2 miles southeast by east of Carlisle, Haddon township, Sullivan County, Ind.

[1] West Virginia was set off from Virginia Dec. 31, 1862, and admitted as a State June 19, 1863.

CENTER OF POPULATION: 1790 TO 1940

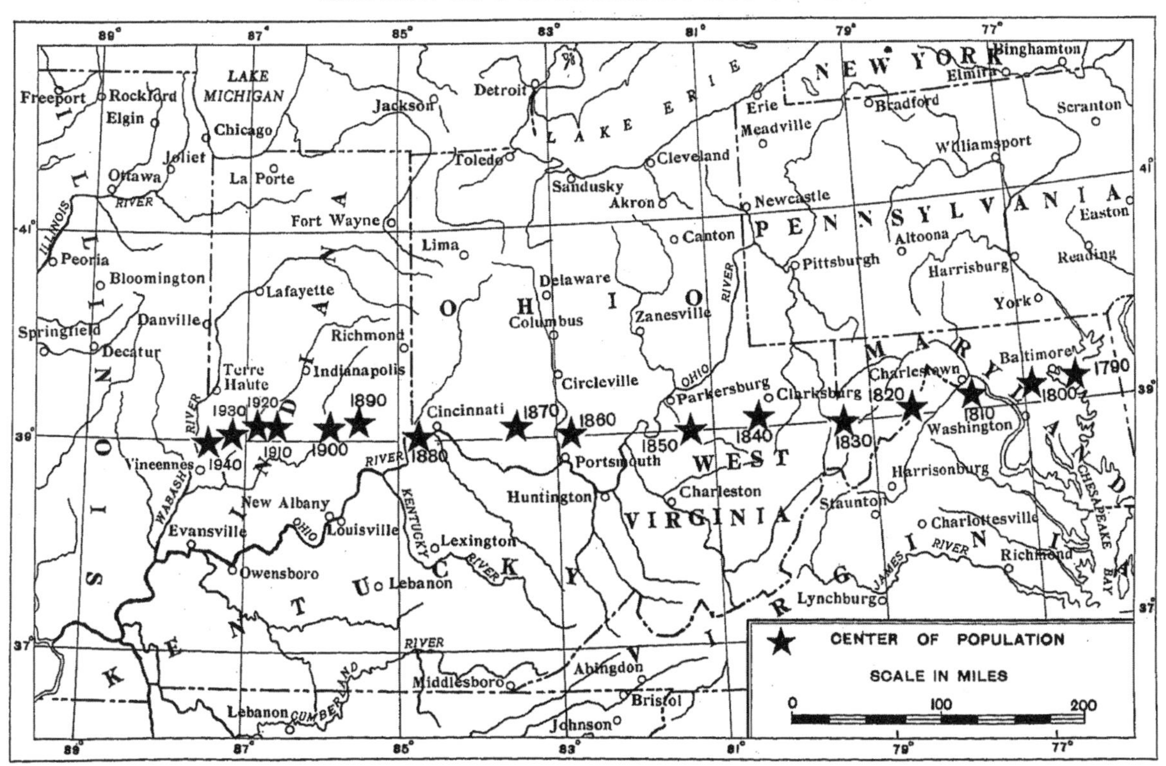

Urban and rural areas.—In the course of its history the census has employed several definitions of urban population. The current definition was adopted in substantially its present form at the time of the 1910 census and was slightly modified in 1920 and again in 1930. The present compilation, which has been extended back to 1790, is made on the basis of the definition of urban population employed in 1930 and 1940.

The urban area is made up for the most part of cities and other incorporated places having 2,500 inhabitants or more, places of this type constituting about 96 percent of the urban places in the United States. A second type is limited to the States of New Hampshire, Massachusetts, and Rhode Island, in which States it is not the practice to incorporate as municipalities places of less than 10,000. This type is made up of towns (townships) in which there is a village or thickly settled area having 2,500 inhabitants or more and comprising, either by itself or when combined with other villages within the same town, more than 50 percent of the total population of the town. This type of urban places comprised, in 1940, 7 towns in New Hampshire, 83 towns in Massachusetts, and 12 towns in Rhode Island. A third type of urban places is made up of townships and other political subdivisions (not incorporated as municipalities, nor containing any areas so incorporated) with a total population of 10,000 or more and a population density of 1,000 or more per square mile. Under the special rule establishing this type, urban classification was given in 1940 to places distributed as follows: 4 towns in Connecticut, 1 town in New York, 12 townships in New Jersey, 11 townships in Pennsylvania, 2 election districts in Maryland, 1 county (which had no minor civil divisions) in Virginia, 1 militia district in Georgia, and 1 township in California.

The individual places of types 2 and 3 that have been brought into the urban classification are included in the tables presenting the population of the various groups of urban places (tables 13 to 15) and marked with an asterisk (*).

The rural population is by no means identical with the farm population, that is, the population living on farms. (The rural-nonfarm population of the United States is now nearly as large as the rural-farm population.) Practically all of the farm population is rural, however. Statistics of the farm population are presented in the second and later series of Population bulletins, and in the volumes devoted to the detailed classification of the population data.

The total, urban, and rural population, and the decennial increase in each, are presented for all the census years from 1790 to 1940 for the United States as a whole in table 6, for regions, divisions, and States for 1940 and 1930 in some detail in table 7, and in less detail from 1790 to 1940 in table 8. The urban and rural population of the United States at each census is also shown graphically in the following chart.

Places grouped according to size.—For the convenience of those who are interested in places of various sizes, statistics are presented in tables 12 to 16 for the urban places arranged in groups according to size. In table 12 is presented the population of cities having 100,000 inhabitants or more in 1940, with comparative figures running back to the first census in which the city appears. Table 13 shows the population of urban places having 25,000 inhabitants or more in 1940, with comparative figures from 1910; table 14 shows the population for 1940, 1930, and 1920 of urban places having from 5,000 to 25,000 inhabitants; and table 15 presents similar figures for urban places having from 2,500 to 5,000 inhabitants. The places listed in these tables, taken together, comprise the urban classification in 1940.

Urban and Rural Population of the United States: 1790 to 1940

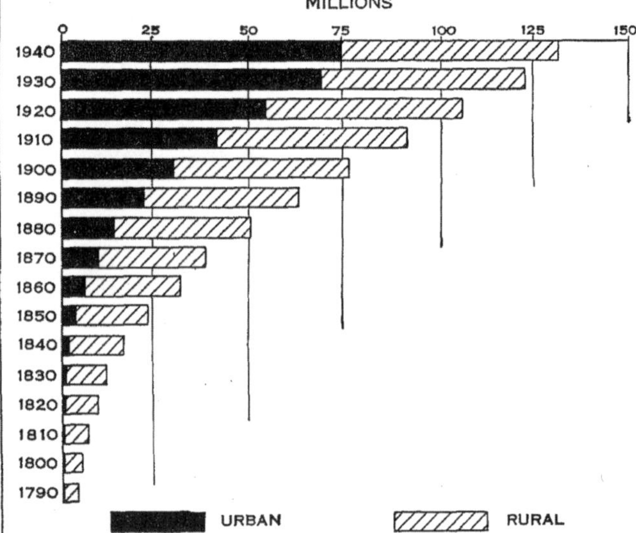

Table 16 shows the population of the larger incorporated places which are included in the rural classification, namely, those having from 1,000 to 2,500 inhabitants.[2]

The total population in each of the various size groups is summarized for the United States for 1940 and 1930 in table 9, which also indicates the changes in the number of places of each size between 1930 and 1940. Table 10 shows the total population in each of the groups for all the censuses from 1790 to 1940. Table 11 gives the number of places in each of the size groups, with their population, by regions, divisions, and States, for 1940 and 1930.

Counties.—The population is shown by counties, for 1940, 1930, and 1920, in table 3 in the sections for the States, together with the land area and the number of persons per square mile for 1940. The land areas

[2] The population of incorporated places having fewer than 1,000 inhabitants in any State is shown in table 5 in the section for that State.

given for 1940 are the results of the first complete remeasurement of the United States since 1881, rendered possible by greatly improved maps prepared during the last decade. These land areas, of course, differ somewhat from those published in earlier census reports. The urban and rural population of the counties is shown in table 3 of the sections for the respective States.

Maps.—The population density and the percentage change in population are shown graphically, by counties, on the maps on pages 2, 4, and 12, respectively.

The dot map, in which each dot represents 2,000 inhabitants, gives the most accurate picture of the distribution of population, since each dot has been placed with extreme care, using large scale county maps and State minor civil division outline maps for reference. In placing these dots, consideration was given to the location of cities and the course followed by railroads, highways, and rivers. On this map population densities are suggested by the variation in spacing between dots. The dots are piled up to form black patches for cities, and in the sparsely settled lands of the West, a population thinly distributed over a large area may be represented by a single dot at one central point.

The shaded density map shows population per square mile by counties. Of necessity, it generalizes the material shown, for individual county densities give way to class intervals, and individual variations of density cannot be distinguished within the county average.

The population increase-decrease map shows an important aspect of population change. Care should be exercised in the use of this map, for, in addition to the data being necessarily generalized by county units, the percentage of increase or decrease in population is a relative measure which obscures absolute population changes. A 2 percent increase for a New York county may result from a much greater absolute change in the total population than a 25 percent increase in a county in the sparsely settled West.

Institutions.—The population of institutions and military posts is included as a part of the population of the city, township, or other political area in which the institution or post is located. This institutional population in some cases forms an appreciable fraction of the total population of the city or town; and sometimes it seriously affects the distribution of the total by sex, age, or other characteristics. It has not been found practicable, however, to make any general provision for showing separately the population of the institutions. Usually, the population of the institution is readily available, so that due allowance may be made for its inclusion. In fact, the Census Bureau is in a position to furnish the 1940 census population of many of the larger institutions on request.

Metropolitan districts.—A metropolitan district has been set up for use in the 1940 census of population in connection with each city of 50,000 or more, two or more such cities sometimes being in one district. The general plan is to include in the district, in addition to the central city or cities, all adjacent and contiguous minor civil divisions or incorporated places having a population of 150 or more per square mile. In some metropolitan districts, a few less densely populated contiguous divisions are included on the basis of special qualifications. Occasionally only a portion of a minor civil division is included if the minor civil division has a large area and the principal concentration of population is in a small section in or near the central city, with the more remote sections being sparsely settled. In such cases, the unit considered is not the minor civil division but component enumeration districts. A metropolitan district is thus not a political unit but rather an area including all of the thickly settled territory in and around a city or group of cities. It tends to be a more or less integrated area with common economic, social, and, often, administrative interests.

Table 17 presents the population, land area, and population per square mile for each metropolitan district in 1940 (see map on p. 13) and also separately for its central city or cities and the area within the metropolitan district but outside the city. Table 18 gives the population of the metropolitan districts in 1940 and, for all except the seven districts where complete figures are not available, the population in 1930, together with the increase or decrease during the decade. The same statistics are also given in this table for the central city (or cities) and the outside area. Maps of individual metropolitan districts appear at the end of the section for each State.

Census tracts.—Census tracts are small areas into which certain large cities and sometimes their adjacent areas are subdivided for statistical and local administrative purposes, through cooperation with a local committee in each case. In most cases the tracts are permanently established, so that comparisons may be made from census to census. The boundaries of tracts are established so as to include for the most part approximately equal numbers of inhabitants or equal areas; and each tract is designed to include an area fairly homogeneous in population characteristics. There are now 10,461 census tracts, in or adjacent to 60 cities, the list including all cities of 250,000 or more and a few smaller ones.

In table 19 is presented a list of the areas for which 1940 census tract statistics are available, together with an indication as to the availability of comparable 1930 figures. Table 8 in each State section gives, by tracts, the population of the tracted areas in that State.

POPULATION CHANGE FOR THE UNITED STATES (INCREASE OR DECREASE) BY COUNTIES: 1930 TO 1940

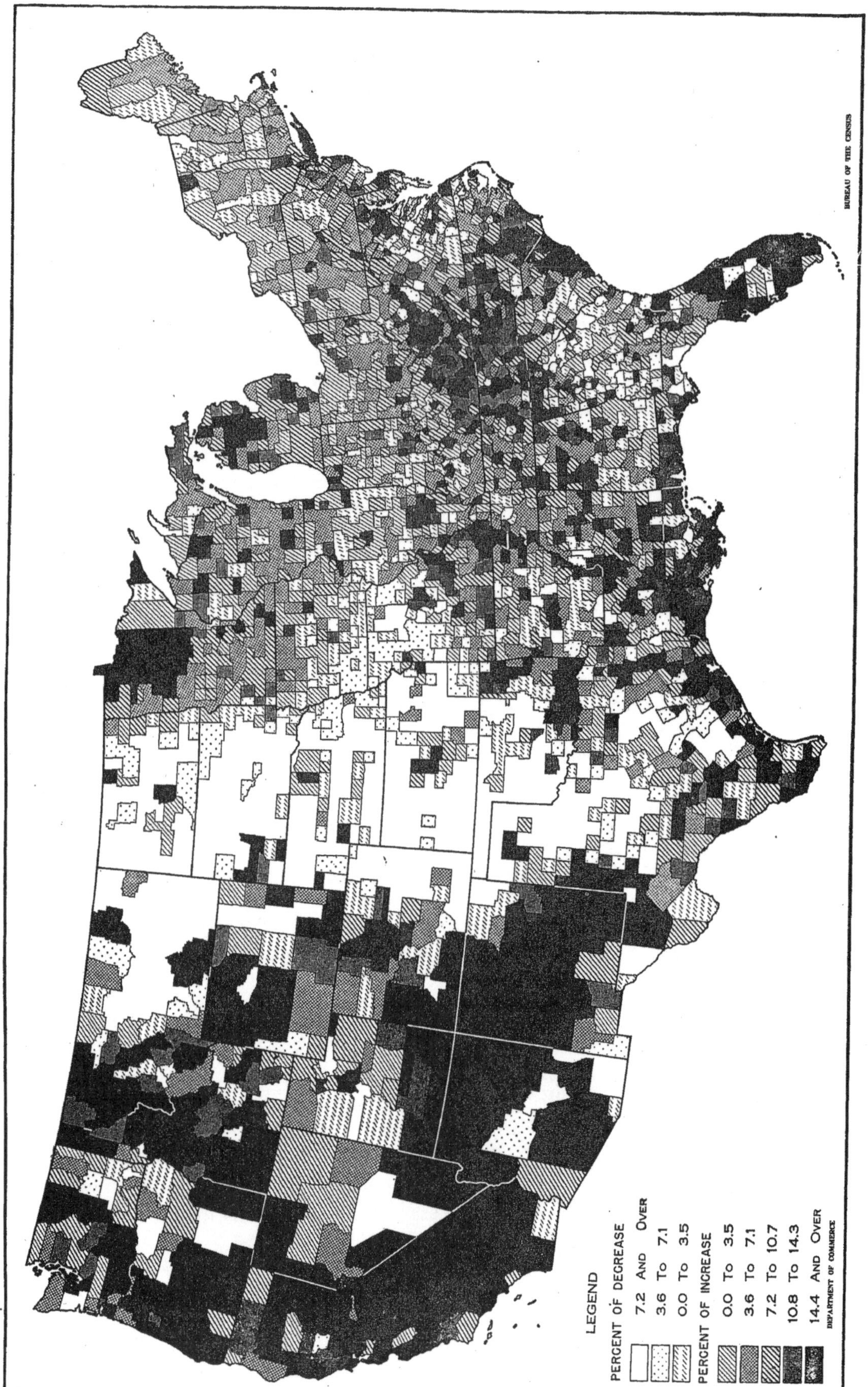

LEGEND

PERCENT OF DECREASE

- 7.2 AND OVER
- 3.6 TO 7.1
- 0.0 TO 3.5

PERCENT OF INCREASE

- 0.0 TO 3.5
- 3.6 TO 7.1
- 7.2 TO 10.7
- 10.8 TO 14.3
- 14.4 AND OVER

DEPARTMENT OF COMMERCE

BUREAU OF THE CENSUS

12

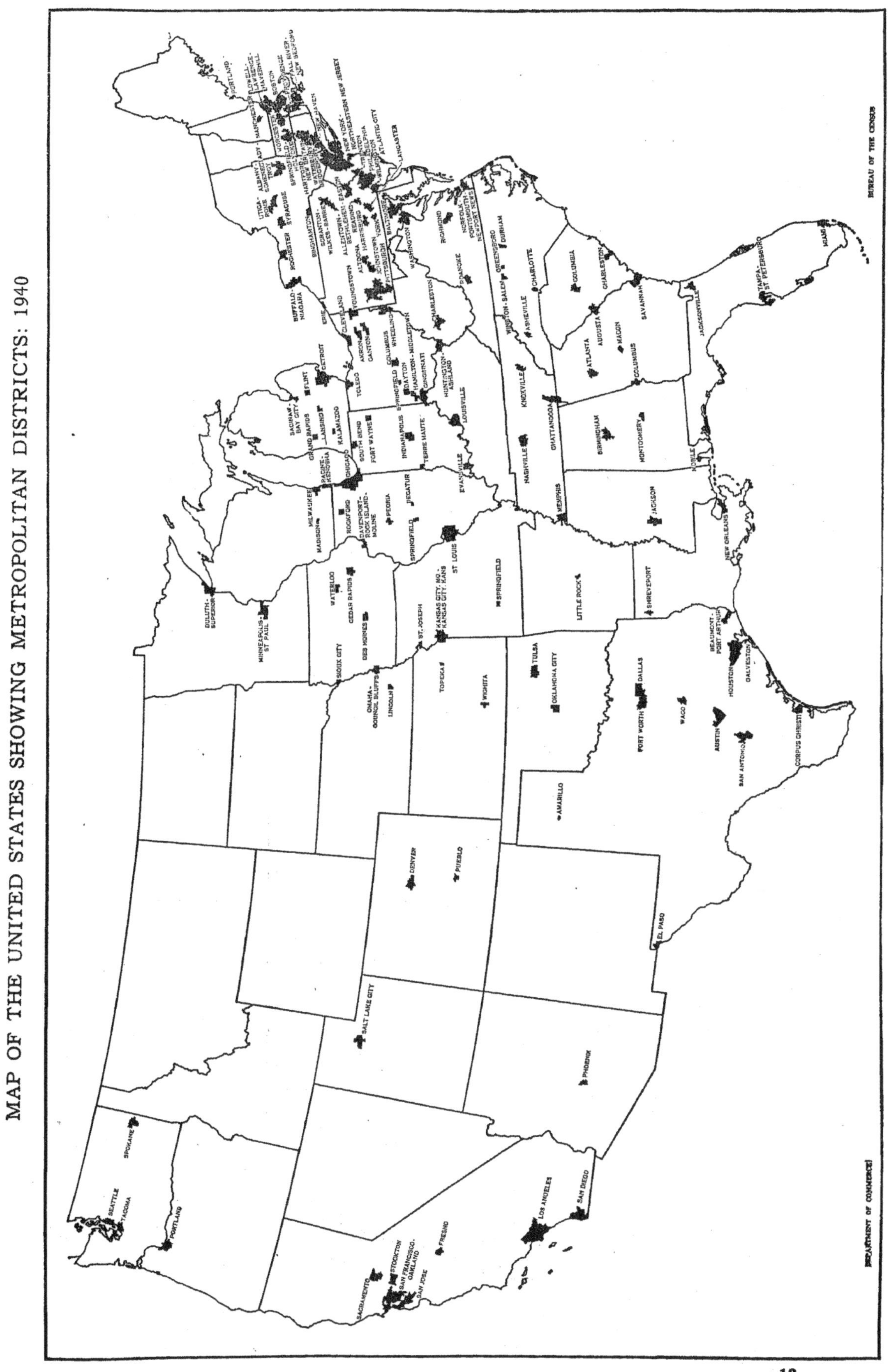
MAP OF THE UNITED STATES SHOWING METROPOLITAN DISTRICTS: 1940
SEATTLE
TACOMA
SPOKANE
PORTLAND
SACRAMENTO
STOCKTON
SAN FRANCISCO-OAKLAND
SAN JOSE
FRESNO
LOS ANGELES
SAN DIEGO
PHOENIX
SALT LAKE CITY
DENVER
PUEBLO
EL PASO
AMARILLO
FORT WORTH
DALLAS
WACO
AUSTIN
SAN ANTONIO
CORPUS CHRISTI
HOUSTON
GALVESTON
BEAUMONT-PORT ARTHUR
SHREVEPORT
NEW ORLEANS
TULSA
OKLAHOMA CITY
WICHITA
TOPEKA
LINCOLN
OMAHA-COUNCIL BLUFFS
SIOUX CITY
DES MOINES
CEDAR RAPIDS
WATERLOO
DULUTH-SUPERIOR
MINNEAPOLIS-ST PAUL
ST. JOSEPH
KANSAS CITY, MO-KANSAS CITY, KANS
SPRINGFIELD
LITTLE ROCK
ST LOUIS
MEMPHIS
JACKSON
MOBILE
MONTGOMERY
BIRMINGHAM
CHATTANOOGA
NASHVILLE
KNOXVILLE
ATLANTA
MACON
COLUMBUS
AUGUSTA
SAVANNAH
JACKSONVILLE
TAMPA-ST PETERSBURG
MIAMI
CHARLESTON
COLUMBIA
CHARLOTTE
ASHEVILLE
DURHAM
ROANOKE
RICHMOND
LOUISVILLE
EVANSVILLE
TERRE HAUTE
INDIANAPOLIS
DECATUR
PEORIA
ROCKFORD
MADISON
MILWAUKEE
CHICAGO
SOUTH BEND
FORT WAYNE
KALAMAZOO
GRAND RAPIDS
LANSING
FLINT
DETROIT
TOLEDO
CINCINNATI
DAYTON
COLUMBUS
WHEELING
CANTON
AKRON
CLEVELAND
YOUNGSTOWN
ERIE
PITTSBURGH
JOHNSTOWN
ALTOONA
BUFFALO-NIAGARA
ROCHESTER
SYRACUSE
BINGHAMTON
WASHINGTON
BALTIMORE
LANCASTER
ATLANTIC CITY
PORTLAND
BUREAU OF THE CENSUS
DEPARTMENT OF COMMERCE

13

TABLE 3.—POPULATION OF THE UNITED STATES.

	REGION, DIVISION, AND STATE	1940	1930	1920	1910	1900	1890 [1]	1880
1	United States	131, 669, 275	122, 775, 046	105, 710, 620	91, 972, 266	75, 994, 575	62, 947, 714	50, 155, 783
	REGIONS:							
2	The North	76, 120, 109	73, 021, 191	63, 681, 845	55, 757, 115	47, 379, 699	39, 817, 386	31, 871, 518
3	The South	41, 665, 901	37, 857, 633	33, 125, 803	29, 389, 330	24, 523, 527	20, 028, 059	16, 516, 568
4	The West	13, 883, 265	11, 896, 222	8, 902, 972	6, 825, 821	4, 091, 349	3, 102, 269	1, 767, 697
	THE NORTH:							
5	New England	8, 437, 290	8, 166, 341	7, 400, 909	6, 552, 681	5, 592, 017	4, 700, 749	4, 010, 529
6	Middle Atlantic	27, 539, 487	26, 260, 750	22, 261, 144	19, 315, 892	15, 454, 678	12, 706, 220	10, 496, 878
7	East North Central	26, 626, 342	25, 297, 185	21, 475, 543	18, 250, 621	15, 985, 581	13, 478, 305	11, 206, 668
8	West North Central	13, 516, 990	13, 296, 915	12, 544, 249	11, 637, 921	10, 347, 423	8, 932, 112	6, 157, 443
	THE SOUTH:							
9	South Atlantic	17, 823, 151	15, 793, 589	13, 990, 272	12, 194, 895	10, 443, 480	8, 857, 922	7, 597, 197
10	East South Central	10, 778, 225	9, 887, 214	8, 893, 307	8, 409, 901	7, 547, 757	6, 429, 154	5, 585, 151
11	West South Central	13, 064, 525	12, 176, 830	10, 242, 224	8, 784, 534	6, 532, 290	4, 740, 983	3, 334, 220
	THE WEST:							
12	Mountain	4, 150, 003	3, 701, 789	3, 336, 101	2, 633, 517	1, 674, 657	1, 213, 935	653, 119
13	Pacific	9, 733, 262	8, 194, 433	5, 566, 871	4, 192, 304	2, 416, 692	1, 888, 334	1, 114, 578
	NEW ENGLAND:							
14	Maine	847, 226	797, 423	768, 014	742, 371	694, 466	661, 086	648, 936
15	New Hampshire	491, 524	465, 293	443, 083	430, 572	411, 588	376, 530	346, 991
16	Vermont	359, 231	359, 611	352, 428	355, 956	343, 641	332, 422	332, 286
17	Massachusetts	4, 316, 721	4, 249, 614	3, 852, 356	3, 366, 416	2, 805, 346	2, 238, 947	1, 783, 085
18	Rhode Island	713, 346	687, 497	604, 397	542, 610	428, 556	345, 506	276, 531
19	Connecticut	1, 709, 242	1, 606, 903	1, 380, 631	1, 114, 756	908, 420	746, 258	622, 700
	MIDDLE ATLANTIC:							
20	New York	13, 479, 142	12, 588, 066	10, 385, 227	9, 113, 614	7, 268, 894	6, 003, 174	5, 082, 871
21	New Jersey	4, 160, 165	4, 041, 334	3, 155, 900	2, 537, 167	1, 883, 669	1, 444, 933	1, 131, 116
22	Pennsylvania	9, 900, 180	9, 631, 350	8, 720, 017	7, 665, 111	6, 302, 115	5, 258, 113	4, 282, 891
	EAST NORTH CENTRAL:							
23	Ohio	6, 907, 612	6, 646, 697	5, 759, 394	4, 767, 121	4, 157, 545	3, 672, 329	3, 198, 062
24	Indiana	3, 427, 796	3, 238, 503	2, 930, 390	2, 700, 876	2, 516, 462	2, 192, 404	1, 978, 301
25	Illinois	7, 897, 241	7, 630, 654	6, 485, 280	5, 638, 591	4, 821, 550	3, 826, 352	3, 077, 871
26	Michigan	5, 256, 106	4, 842, 325	3, 668, 412	2, 810, 173	2, 420, 982	2, 093, 890	1, 636, 937
27	Wisconsin	3, 137, 587	2, 939, 006	2, 632, 067	2, 333, 860	2, 069, 042	1, 693, 330	1, 315, 497
	WEST NORTH CENTRAL:							
28	Minnesota	2, 792, 300	2, 563, 953	2, 387, 125	2, 075, 708	1, 751, 394	1, 310, 283	780, 773
29	Iowa	2, 538, 268	2, 470, 939	2, 404, 021	2, 224, 771	2, 231, 853	1, 912, 297	1, 624, 615
30	Missouri	3, 784, 664	3, 629, 367	3, 404, 055	3, 293, 335	3, 106, 665	2, 679, 185	2, 168, 380
31	North Dakota	641, 935	680, 845	646, 872	577, 056	319, 146	190, 983	[3] 36, 909
32	South Dakota	642, 961	692, 849	636, 547	583, 888	401, 570	348, 600	[3] 98, 268
33	Nebraska	1, 315, 834	1, 377, 963	1, 296, 372	1, 192, 214	1, 066, 300	1, 062, 656	452, 402
34	Kansas	1, 801, 028	1, 880, 999	1, 769, 257	1, 690, 949	1, 470, 495	1, 428; 108	996, 096
	SOUTH ATLANTIC:							
35	Delaware	266, 505	238, 380	223, 003	202, 322	184, 735	168, 493	146, 608
36	Maryland	1, 821, 244	1, 631, 526	1, 449, 661	1, 295, 346	1, 188, 044	1, 042, 390	934, 943
37	District of Columbia	663, 091	486, 869	437, 571	331, 069	278, 718	230, 392	177, 624
38	Virginia	2, 677, 773	2, 421, 851	2, 309, 187	2, 061, 612	1, 854, 184	1, 655, 980	1, 512, 565
39	West Virginia	1, 901, 974	1, 729, 205	1, 463, 701	1, 221, 119	958, 800	762, 794	618, 457
40	North Carolina	3, 571, 623	3, 170, 276	2, 559, 123	2, 206, 287	1, 893, 810	1, 617, 949	1, 399, 750
41	South Carolina	1, 899, 804	1, 738, 765	1, 683, 724	1, 515, 400	1, 340, 316	1, 151, 149	995, 577
42	Georgia	3, 123, 723	2, 908, 506	2, 895, 832	2, 609, 121	2, 216, 331	1, 837, 353	1, 542, 180
43	Florida	1, 897, 414	1, 468, 211	968, 470	752, 619	528, 542	391, 422	269, 493
	EAST SOUTH CENTRAL:							
44	Kentucky	2, 845, 627	2, 614, 589	2, 416, 630	2, 289, 905	2, 147, 174	1, 858, 635	1, 648, 690
45	Tennessee	2, 915, 841	2, 616, 556	2, 337, 885	2, 184, 789	2, 020, 616	1, 767, 518	1, 542, 359
46	Alabama	2, 832, 961	2, 646, 248	2, 348, 174	2, 138, 093	1, 828, 697	1, 513, 401	1, 262, 505
47	Mississippi	2, 183, 796	2, 009, 821	1, 790, 618	1, 797, 114	1, 551, 270	1, 289, 600	1, 131, 597
	WEST SOUTH CENTRAL:							
48	Arkansas	1, 949, 387	1, 854, 482	1, 752, 204	1, 574, 449	1, 311, 564	1, 128, 211	802, 525
49	Louisiana	2, 363, 880	2, 101, 593	1, 798, 509	1, 656, 388	1, 381, 625	1, 118, 588	939, 946
50	Oklahoma	2, 336, 434	2, 396, 040	2, 028, 283	1, 657, 155	[4] 790, 391	[4] 258, 657	----------
51	Texas	6, 414, 824	5, 824, 715	4, 663, 228	3, 896, 542	3, 048, 710	2, 235, 527	1, 591, 749
	MOUNTAIN:							
52	Montana	559, 456	537, 606	548, 889	376, 053	243, 329	142, 924	39, 159
53	Idaho	524, 873	445, 032	431, 866	325, 594	161, 772	88, 548	32, 610
54	Wyoming	250, 742	225, 565	194, 402	145, 965	92, 531	62, 555	20, 789
55	Colorado	1, 123, 296	1, 035, 791	939, 629	799, 024	539, 700	413, 249	194, 327
56	New Mexico	531, 818	423, 317	360, 350	327, 301	195, 310	160, 282	119, 565
57	Arizona	499, 261	435, 573	334, 162	204, 354	122, 931	88, 243	40, 440
58	Utah	550, 310	507, 847	449, 396	373, 351	276, 749	210, 779	143, 963
59	Nevada	110, 247	91, 058	77, 407	81, 875	42, 335	47, 355	62, 266
	PACIFIC:							
60	Washington	1, 736, 191	1, 563, 396	1, 356, 621	1, 141, 990	518, 103	357, 232	75, 116
61	Oregon	1, 089, 684	953, 786	783, 389	672, 765	413, 536	317, 704	174, 768
62	California	6, 907, 387	5, 677, 251	3, 426, 861	2, 377, 549	1, 485, 053	1, 213, 398	864, 694

[1] Includes population (325,464) of Indian Territory and Indian reservations, specially enumerated in 1890, but not included in the general report on population for 1890.
[2] Includes persons (6,100 in 1840 and 5,318 in 1830) on public ships in the service of the United States, not credited to any region, division, or State.

UNITED STATES SUMMARY

BY DIVISIONS AND STATES: 1790 TO 1940

1870	1860	1850	1840	1830	1820	1810	1800	1790	
38, 558, 371	31, 443, 321	23, 191, 876	[2] 17, 069, 453	[2] 12, 866, 020	9, 638, 453	7, 239, 881	5, 308, 483	3, 929, 214	1
25, 279, 841	19, 690, 984	14, 030, 446	10, 112, 624	7, 152, 854	5, 219, 221	3, 778, 782	2, 686, 582	1, 968, 040	2
12, 288, 020	11, 133, 361	8, 982, 612	6, 950, 729	5, 707, 848	4, 419, 232	3, 461, 099	2, 621, 901	1, 961, 174	3
990, 510	618, 976	178, 818	—	—	—	—	—	—	4
3, 487, 924	3, 135, 283	2, 728, 116	2, 234, 822	1, 954, 717	1, 660, 071	1, 471, 973	1, 233, 011	1, 009, 408	5
8, 810, 806	7, 458, 985	5, 898, 735	4, 526, 260	3, 587, 664	2, 699, 845	2, 014, 702	1, 402, 565	958, 632	6
9, 124, 517	6, 926, 884	4, 523, 260	2, 924, 728	1, 470, 018	792, 719	272, 324	51, 006	—	7
3, 856, 594	2, 169, 832	880, 335	426, 814	140, 455	66, 586	19, 783	—	—	8
5, 853, 610	5, 364, 703	4, 679, 090	3, 925, 299	3, 645, 752	3, 061, 063	2, 674, 891	2, 286, 494	1, 851, 806	9
4, 404, 445	4, 020, 991	3, 363, 271	2, 575, 445	1, 815, 969	1, 190, 489	708, 590	335, 407	109, 368	10
2, 029, 965	1, 747, 667	940, 251	449, 985	246, 127	167, 680	77, 618	—	—	11
315, 385	174, 923	72, 927	—	—	—	—	—	—	12
675, 125	444, 053	105, 891	—	—	—	—	—	—	13
626, 915	628, 279	583, 169	501, 793	399, 455	298, 335	228, 705	151, 719	96, 540	14
318, 300	326, 073	317, 976	284, 574	269, 328	244, 161	214, 460	183, 858	141, 885	15
330, 551	315, 098	314, 120	291, 948	280, 652	235, 981	217, 895	154, 465	85, 425	16
1, 457, 351	1, 231, 066	994, 514	737, 699	610, 408	523, 287	472, 040	422, 845	378, 787	17
217, 353	174, 620	147, 545	108, 830	97, 199	83, 059	76, 931	69, 122	68, 825	18
537, 454	460, 147	370, 792	309, 978	297, 675	275, 248	261, 942	251, 002	237, 946	19
4, 382, 759	3, 880, 735	3, 097, 394	2, 428, 921	1, 918, 608	1, 372, 812	959, 049	589, 051	340, 120	20
906, 096	672, 035	489, 555	373, 306	320, 823	277, 575	245, 562	211, 149	184, 139	21
3, 521, 951	2, 906, 215	2, 311, 786	1, 724, 033	1, 348, 233	1, 049, 458	810, 091	602, 365	434, 373	22
2, 665, 260	2, 339, 511	1, 980, 329	1, 519, 467	937, 903	581, 434	230, 760	45, 365	—	23
1, 680, 637	1, 350, 428	988, 416	685, 866	343, 031	147, 178	24, 520	5, 641	—	24
2, 539, 891	1, 711, 951	851, 470	476, 183	157, 445	55, 211	12, 282	—	—	25
1, 184, 059	749, 113	397, 654	212, 267	31, 639	8, 896	4, 762	—	—	26
1, 054, 670	775, 881	305, 391	30, 945	—	—	—	—	—	27
439, 706	172, 023	6, 077	—	—	—	—	—	—	28
1, 194, 020	674, 913	192, 214	43, 112	—	—	—	—	—	29
1, 721, 295	1, 182, 012	682, 044	383, 702	140, 455	66, 586	19, 783	—	—	30
[3] 2, 405	[3] 4, 837	—	—	—	—	—	—	—	31
[3] 11, 776		—	—	—	—	—	—	—	32
122, 993	28, 841	—	—	—	—	—	—	—	33
364, 399	107, 206	—	—	—	—	—	—	—	34
125, 015	112, 216	91, 532	78, 085	76, 748	72, 749	72, 674	64, 273	59, 096	35
780, 894	687, 049	583, 034	470, 019	447, 040	407, 350	380, 546	341, 548	319, 728	36
131, 700	75, 080	51, 687	43, 712	39, 834	33, 039	24, 023	14, 093	—	37
1, 225, 163	1, 596, 318	1, 421, 661	1, 239, 797	1, 211, 405	1, 065, 366	974, 600	880, 200	747, 610	38
442, 014	—	—	—	—	—	—	—	—	39
1, 071, 361	992, 622	869, 039	753, 419	737, 987	638, 829	555, 500	478, 103	393, 751	40
705, 606	703, 708	668, 507	594, 398	581, 185	502, 741	415, 115	345, 591	249, 073	41
1, 184, 109	1, 057, 286	906, 185	691, 392	516, 823	340, 989	252, 433	162, 686	82, 548	42
187, 748	140, 424	87, 445	54, 477	34, 730	—	—	—	—	43
1, 321, 011	1, 155, 684	982, 405	779, 828	687, 917	564, 317	406, 511	220, 955	73, 677	44
1, 258, 520	1, 109, 801	1, 002, 717	829, 210	681, 904	422, 823	261, 727	105, 602	35, 691	45
996, 992	964, 201	771, 623	590, 756	309, 527	127, 901	—	—	—	46
827, 922	791, 305	606, 526	375, 651	136, 621	75, 448	40, 352	8, 850	—	47
484, 471	435, 450	209, 897	97, 574	30, 388	14, 273	1, 062	—	—	48
726, 915	708, 002	517, 762	352, 411	215, 739	153, 407	76, 556	—	—	49
—	—	—	—	—	—	—	—	—	50
818, 579	604, 215	212, 592	—	—	—	—	—	—	51
20, 595	—	—	—	—	—	—	—	—	52
14, 999	—	—	—	—	—	—	—	—	53
9, 118	—	—	—	—	—	—	—	—	54
39, 864	34, 277	—	—	—	—	—	—	—	55
91, 874	93, 516	61, 547	—	—	—	—	—	—	56
9, 658	—	—	—	—	—	—	—	—	57
86, 786	40, 273	11, 380	—	—	—	—	—	—	58
42, 491	6, 857	—	—	—	—	—	—	—	59
23, 955	11, 594	—	—	—	—	—	—	—	60
90, 923	52, 465	13, 294	—	—	—	—	—	—	61
560, 247	379, 994	92, 597	—	—	—	—	—	—	62

[3] 1860 figure is for Dakota Territory. Figures for 1870 and 1880 for North Dakota and South Dakota are for the parts of Dakota Territory which later constituted the respective States.

[4] Includes population of Indian Territory as follows: 1900, 392,060; 1890, 180,182.

NUMBER OF INHABITANTS

TABLE 4.—DECENNIAL RATES OF INCREASE IN POPULATION, BY DIVISIONS AND STATES: 1790 TO 1940

[A minus sign (—) denotes decrease. Percent not shown where less than 0.1]

REGION, DIVISION, AND STATE	INCREASE, 1930 TO 1940		PERCENT OF INCREASE													
	Number	Percent	1920 to 1930	1910 to 1920	1900 to 1910	1890 to 1900	1880 to 1890	1870 to 1880	1860 to 1870	1850 to 1860	1840 to 1850	1830 to 1840	1820 to 1830	1810 to 1820	1800 to 1810	1790 to 1800
United States	8, 894, 229	7. 2	16. 1	14. 9	21. 0	20. 7	25. 5	30. 1	22. 6	35. 6	35. 9	32. 7	33. 5	33. 1	36. 4	35. 1
REGIONS:																
The North	3, 098, 918	4. 2	14. 7	14. 2	17. 7	19. 0	24. 9	26. 1	28. 4	40. 3	38. 7	41. 4	37. 0	38. 1	40. 7	36. 5
The South	3, 808, 268	10. 1	14. 3	12. 7	19. 8	22. 4	21. 3	34. 4	10. 4	23. 9	29. 2	21. 8	29. 2	27. 7	32. 0	33. 7
The West	1, 987, 043	16. 7	33. 6	30. 4	66. 8	31. 9	75. 5	78. 5	60. 0	246. 1	-------	-------	-------	-------	-------	-------
THE NORTH:																
New England	270, 949	3. 3	10. 3	12. 9	17. 2	19. 0	17. 2	15. 0	11. 2	14. 9	22. 1	14. 3	17. 7	12. 8	19. 4	22. 2
Middle Atlantic	1, 278, 737	4. 9	18. 0	15. 2	25. 0	21. 6	21. 0	19. 1	18. 1	26. 5	30. 3	26. 2	32. 9	34. 0	43. 6	46. 3
East North Central	1, 329, 157	5. 3	17. 8	17. 7	14. 2	18. 6	20. 3	22. 8	31. 7	53. 1	54. 7	99. 0	85. 4	191. 1	433. 9	-------
West North Central	220, 075	1. 7	6. 0	7. 8	12. 5	15. 8	45. 1	59. 7	77. 7	146. 5	106. 3	203. 9	110. 9	236. 6	-------	-------
THE SOUTH:																
South Atlantic	2, 029, 562	12. 9	12. 9	14. 7	16. 8	17. 9	16. 6	29. 8	9. 1	14. 7	19. 2	7. 7	19. 1	14. 4	17. 0	23. 5
East South Central	891, 011	9. 0	11. 2	5. 7	11. 4	17. 4	15. 1	26. 8	9. 5	19. 6	30. 6	41. 8	52. 5	68. 0	111. 3	206. 7
West South Central	887, 695	7. 3	18. 9	16. 6	34. 5	37. 8	42. 2	64. 3	16. 2	85. 9	109. 0	82. 8	46. 8	116. 0	-------	-------
THE WEST:																
Mountain	448, 214	12. 1	11. 0	26. 7	57. 3	38. 0	85. 9	107. 1	80. 3	139. 9	-------	-------	-------	-------	-------	-------
Pacific	1, 538, 829	18. 8	47. 2	32. 8	73. 5	28. 0	69. 4	65. 1	52. 0	319. 3	-------	-------	-------	-------	-------	-------
NEW ENGLAND:																
Maine	49, 803	6. 2	3. 8	3. 5	6. 9	5. 0	1. 9	3. 5	—0. 2	7. 7	16. 2	25. 6	33. 9	30. 4	50. 7	57. 2
New Hampshire	26, 231	5. 6	5. 0	2. 9	4. 6	9. 3	8. 5	9. 0	—2. 4	2. 5	11. 7	5. 7	10. 3	13. 8	16. 6	29. 6
Vermont	—380	—0. 1	2. 0	—1. 0	3. 6	3. 4	-------	0. 5	4. 9	0. 3	7. 6	4. 0	18. 9	8. 3	41. 1	80. 8
Massachusetts	67, 107	1. 6	10. 3	14. 4	20. 0	25. 3	25. 6	22. 4	18. 4	23. 8	34. 8	20. 9	16. 6	10. 9	11. 6	11. 6
Rhode Island	25, 849	3. 8	13. 7	11. 4	26. 6	24. 0	24. 9	27. 2	24. 5	18. 4	35. 6	12. 0	17. 0	8. 0	11. 3	0. 4
Connecticut	102, 339	6. 4	16. 4	23. 9	22. 7	21. 7	19. 8	15. 9	16. 8	24. 1	19. 6	4. 1	8. 1	5. 1	4. 4	5. 5
MIDDLE ATLANTIC:																
New York	891, 076	7. 1	21. 2	14. 0	25. 4	21. 1	18. 1	16. 0	12. 9	25. 3	27. 5	26. 6	39. 8	43. 1	62. 8	73. 2
New Jersey	118, 831	2. 9	28. 1	24. 4	34. 7	30. 4	27. 7	24. 8	34. 8	37. 3	31. 1	16. 4	15. 6	13. 0	16. 3	14. 7
Pennsylvania	268, 830	2. 8	10. 5	13. 8	21. 6	19. 9	22. 8	21. 6	21. 2	25. 7	34. 1	27. 9	28. 5	29. 5	34. 5	38. 7
EAST NORTH CENTRAL:																
Ohio	260, 915	3. 9	15. 4	20. 8	14. 7	13. 2	14. 8	20. 0	13. 9	18. 1	30. 3	62. 0	61. 3	152. 0	408. 7	-------
Indiana	189, 293	5. 8	10. 5	8. 5	7. 3	14. 8	10. 8	17. 7	24. 5	36. 6	44. 1	99. 9	133. 1	500. 2	334. 7	-------
Illinois	266, 587	3. 5	17. 7	15. 0	16. 9	26. 0	24. 3	21. 2	48. 4	101. 1	78. 8	202. 4	185. 2	349. 5	-------	-------
Michigan	413, 781	8. 5	32. 0	30. 5	16. 1	15. 6	27. 9	38. 2	58. 1	88. 4	87. 3	570. 9	255. 7	86. 8	-------	-------
Wisconsin	198, 581	6. 8	11. 7	12. 8	12. 8	22. 2	28. 7	24. 7	35. 9	154. 1	886. 9	-------	-------	-------	-------	-------
WEST NORTH CENTRAL:																
Minnesota	228, 347	8. 9	7. 4	15. 0	18. 5	33. 7	67. 8	77. 6	155. 6	2,730.7	-------	-------	-------	-------	-------	-------
Iowa	67, 329	2. 7	2. 8	8. 1	—0. 3	16. 7	17. 7	36. 1	76. 9	251. 1	345. 8	-------	-------	-------	-------	-------
Missouri	155, 297	4. 3	6. 6	3. 4	6. 0	16. 0	23. 6	26. 0	45. 6	73. 3	77. 8	173. 2	110. 9	236. 6	-------	-------
North Dakota	—38, 910	—5. 7	5. 3	12. 1	80. 8	67. 1	[1] 417. 4	[1] 1, 434. 7	[1] 193.2							
South Dakota	—49, 888	—7. 2	8. 8	9. 0	45. 4	15. 2	[1] 254. 7	[1] 734. 5		-------	-------	-------	-------	-------	-------	-------
Nebraska	—62, 129	—4. 5	6. 3	8. 7	11. 8	0. 3	134. 9	267. 8	326. 5	-------	-------	-------	-------	-------	-------	-------
Kansas	—79, 971	—4. 3	6. 3	4. 6	15. 0	3. 0	43. 4	173. 4	239. 9	-------	-------	-------	-------	-------	-------	-------
SOUTH ATLANTIC:																
Delaware	28, 125	11. 8	6. 9	10. 2	9. 5	9. 6	14. 9	17. 3	11. 4	22. 6	17. 2	1. 7	5. 5	0. 1	13. 1	8. 8
Maryland	189, 718	11. 6	12. 5	11. 9	9. 0	14. 0	11. 5	19. 7	13. 7	17. 8	24. 0	5. 1	9. 7	7. 0	11. 4	6. 8
District of Columbia	176, 222	36. 2	11. 3	32. 2	18. 8	21. 0	29. 7	34. 9	75. 4	45. 3	18. 2	9. 7	20. 6	37. 5	70. 5	-------
Virginia	255, 922	10. 6	4. 9	12. 0	11. 2	12. 0	9. 5	23. 5	[2] —23. 3	12. 3	14. 7	2. 3	13. 7	9. 3	10. 7	17. 7
West Virginia	172, 769	10. 0	18. 1	19. 9	27. 4	25. 7	23. 3	39. 9	-------	-------	-------	-------	-------	-------	-------	-------
North Carolina	401, 347	12. 7	23. 9	16. 0	16. 5	17. 1	15. 6	30. 7	7. 9	14. 2	15. 3	2. 1	15. 5	15. 0	16. 2	21. 4
South Carolina	161, 039	9. 3	3. 3	11. 1	13. 1	16. 4	15. 6	41. 1	0. 3	5. 3	12. 5	2. 3	15. 6	21. 1	20. 1	38. 8
Georgia	215, 217	7. 4	0. 4	11. 0	17. 7	20. 6	19. 1	30. 2	12. 0	16. 7	31. 1	33. 8	51. 6	35. 1	55. 2	97. 1
Florida	429, 203	29. 2	51. 6	28. 7	42. 4	35. 0	45. 2	43. 5	33. 7	60. 6	60. 5	56. 9	-------	-------	-------	-------
EAST SOUTH CENTRAL:																
Kentucky	231, 038	8. 8	8. 2	5. 5	6. 6	15. 5	12. 7	24. 8	14. 3	17. 6	26. 0	13. 4	21. 9	38. 8	84. 0	199. 9
Tennessee	299, 285	11. 4	11. 9	7. 0	8. 1	14. 3	14. 6	22. 6	13. 4	10. 7	20. 9	21. 6	61. 3	61. 6	147. 8	195. 9
Alabama	186, 713	7. 1	12. 7	9. 8	16. 9	20. 8	19. 9	26. 6	3. 4	25. 0	30. 6	90. 9	142. 0	-------	-------	-------
Mississippi	173, 975	8. 7	12. 2	—0. 4	15. 8	20. 3	14. 0	36. 7	4. 6	30. 5	61. 5	175. 0	81. 1	87. 0	356. 0	-------
WEST SOUTH CENTRAL:																
Arkansas	94, 905	5. 1	5. 8	11. 3	20. 0	16. 3	40. 6	65. 6	11. 3	107. 5	115. 1	221. 1	112. 9	1, 244. 0	-------	-------
Louisiana	262, 287	12. 5	16. 9	8. 6	19. 9	23. 5	19. 0	29. 3	2. 7	36. 7	46. 9	63. 4	40. 6	100. 4	-------	-------
Oklahoma	—59, 606	—2. 5	18. 1	22. 4	109. 7	205. 6	-------	-------	-------	-------	-------	-------	-------	-------	-------	-------
Texas	590, 109	10. 1	24. 9	19. 7	27. 8	36. 4	40. 4	94. 5	35. 5	184. 2	-------	-------	-------	-------	-------	-------
MOUNTAIN:																
Montana	21, 850	4. 1	—2. 1	46. 0	54. 5	70. 3	265. 0	90. 1	-------	-------	-------	-------	-------	-------	-------	-------
Idaho	79, 841	17. 9	3. 0	32. 6	101. 3	82. 7	171. 5	117. 4	-------	-------	-------	-------	-------	-------	-------	-------
Wyoming	25, 177	11. 2	16. 0	33. 2	57. 7	47. 9	200. 9	128. 0	-------	-------	-------	-------	-------	-------	-------	-------
Colorado	87, 505	8. 4	10. 2	17. 6	48. 0	30. 6	112. 7	387. 5	16. 3	-------	-------	-------	-------	-------	-------	-------
New Mexico	108, 501	25. 6	17. 5	10. 1	67. 6	21. 9	34. 1	30. 1	—1. 8	51. 9	-------	-------	-------	-------	-------	-------
Arizona	63, 688	14. 6	30. 3	63. 5	66. 2	39. 3	118. 2	318. 7	-------	-------	-------	-------	-------	-------	-------	-------
Utah	42, 463	8. 4	13. 0	20. 4	34. 9	31. 3	46. 4	65. 9	115. 5	253. 9	-------	-------	-------	-------	-------	-------
Nevada	19, 189	21. 1	17. 6	—5. 5	93. 4	—10. 6	—23. 9	46. 5	519. 7	-------	-------	-------	-------	-------	-------	-------
PACIFIC:																
Washington	172, 795	11. 1	15. 2	18. 8	120. 4	45. 0	375. 6	213. 6	106. 6	-------	-------	-------	-------	-------	-------	-------
Oregon	135, 898	14. 2	21. 8	16. 4	62. 7	30. 2	81. 8	92. 2	73. 3	294. 7	-------	-------	-------	-------	-------	-------
California	1, 230, 136	21. 7	65. 7	44. 1	60. 1	22. 4	40. 3	54. 3	47. 4	310. 4	-------	-------	-------	-------	-------	-------

[1] Percent of increase in population from 1860 to 1870 is for Dakota Territory; percents from 1870 to 1880 and from 1880 to 1890 are for the parts of Dakota Territory that later constituted the States of North and South Dakota.

[2] Decrease due to loss of territory, West Virginia having been detached from Virginia and admitted as a separate State in 1863, and two additional counties having been annexed to West Virginia in 1866.

POPULATION OF THE UNITED STATES AND REGIONS: 1790 TO 1940

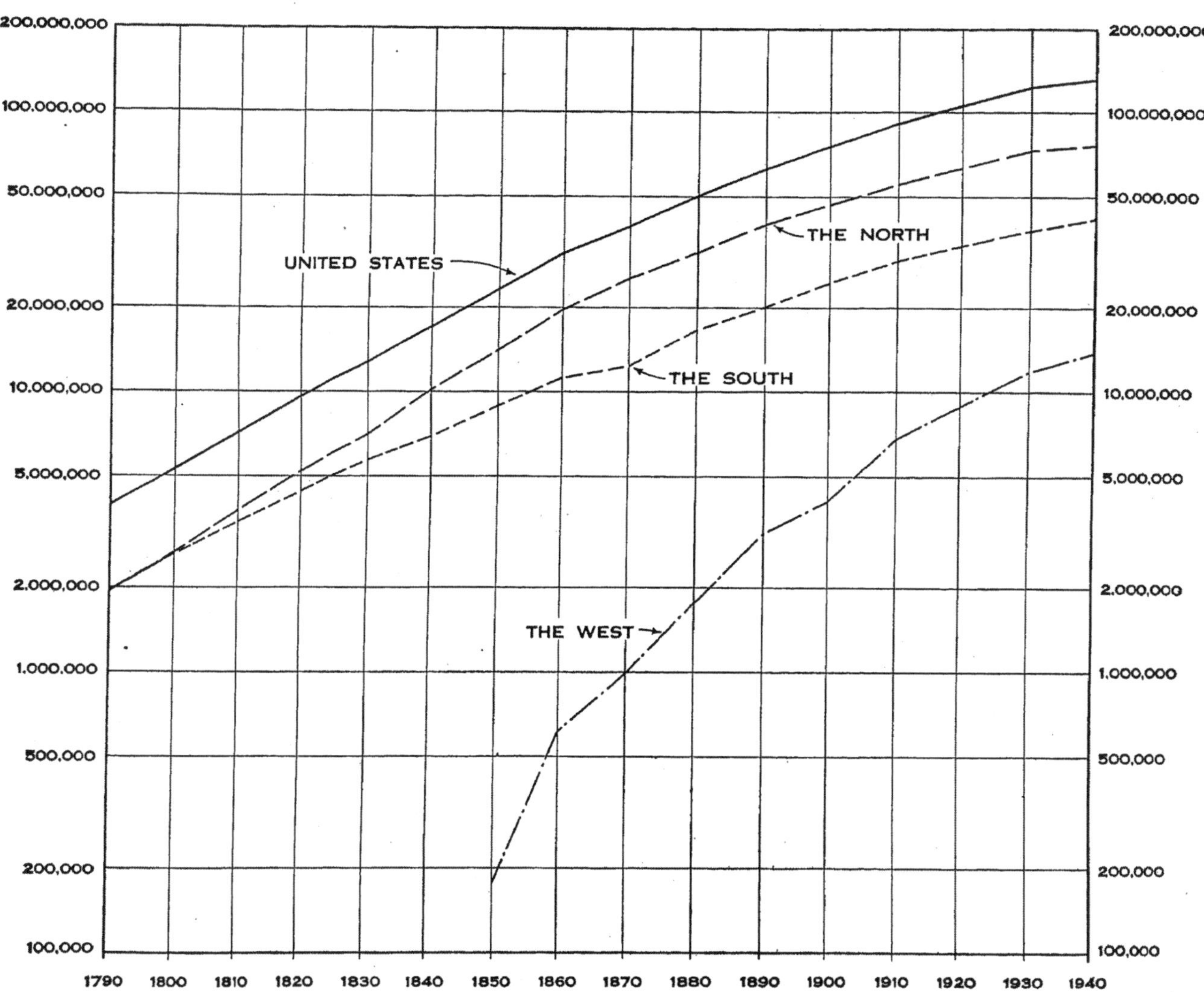

NUMBER OF INHABITANTS

TABLE 5.—POPULATION PER SQUARE MILE, BY DIVISIONS AND STATES: 1910 TO 1940

[The 1940 and 1930 densities are based on new measurements of land area, but the figures shown for 1920 and 1910 are based on the accepted land area figures of those dates]

REGION, DIVISION, AND STATE	Population, 1940	Land area in square miles, 1940	POPULATION PER SQUARE MILE			
			1940	1930	1920	1910
United States	131,669,275	2,977,128	44.2	41.2	35.5	30.9
REGIONS:						
The North	76,120,109	919,334	82.8	79.4	69.3	60.7
The South	41,665,901	879,828	47.4	43.0	37.7	33.5
The West	13,883,265	1,177,966	11.8	10.1	7.6	5.8
THE NORTH:						
New England	8,437,290	63,206	133.5	129.2	119.4	105.7
Middle Atlantic	27,539,487	100,496	274.0	261.3	222.6	193.2
East North Central	26,626,342	245,011	108.7	103.2	87.5	74.3
West North Central	13,516,990	510,621	26.5	26.0	24.6	22.8
THE SOUTH:						
South Atlantic	17,823,151	268,431	66.4	58.8	52.0	45.3
East South Central	10,778,225	180,568	59.7	54.8	49.5	46.8
West South Central	13,064,525	430,829	30.3	28.3	23.8	20.4
THE WEST:						
Mountain	4,150,003	857,836	4.8	4.3	3.9	3.1
Pacific	9,733,262	320,130	30.4	25.6	17.5	13.2
NEW ENGLAND:						
Maine	847,226	31,040	27.3	25.7	25.7	24.8
New Hampshire	491,524	9,024	54.5	51.6	49.1	47.7
Vermont	359,231	9,278	38.7	38.8	38.6	39.0
Massachusetts	4,316,721	7,907	545.9	537.4	479.2	418.8
Rhode Island	713,346	1,058	674.2	649.8	566.4	508.5
Connecticut	1,709,242	4,899	348.9	328.0	286.4	231.3
MIDDLE ATLANTIC:						
New York	13,479,142	47,929	281.2	262.6	217.9	191.2
New Jersey	4,160,165	7,522	553.1	537.3	420.0	337.7
Pennsylvania	9,900,180	45,045	219.8	213.8	194.5	171.0
EAST NORTH CENTRAL:						
Ohio	6,907,612	41,122	168.0	161.6	141.4	117.0
Indiana	3,427,796	36,205	94.7	89.4	81.3	74.9
Illinois	7,897,241	55,947	141.2	136.4	115.7	100.6
Michigan	5,256,106	57,022	92.2	84.9	63.8	48.9
Wisconsin	3,137,587	54,715	57.3	53.7	47.6	42.2
WEST NORTH CENTRAL:						
Minnesota	2,792,300	80,009	34.9	32.0	29.5	25.7
Iowa	2,538,268	55,986	45.3	44.1	43.2	40.0
WEST NORTH CENTRAL—Continued.						
Missouri	3,784,664	69,270	54.6	52.4	49.5	47.9
North Dakota	641,935	70,054	9.2	9.7	9.2	8.2
South Dakota	642,961	76,536	8.4	9.1	8.3	7.6
Nebraska	1,315,834	76,653	17.2	18.0	16.9	15.5
Kansas	1,801,028	82,113	21.9	22.9	21.6	20.7
SOUTH ATLANTIC:						
Delaware	266,505	1,978	134.7	120.5	113.5	103.0
Maryland	1,821,244	9,887	184.2	165.0	145.8	130.3
District of Columbia	663,091	61	10,870.3	7,981.5	7,292.9	5,517.8
Virginia	2,677,773	39,899	67.1	60.7	57.4	51.2
West Virginia	1,901,974	24,090	79.0	71.8	60.9	50.8
North Carolina	3,571,623	49,142	72.7	64.5	52.5	45.3
South Carolina	1,899,804	30,594	62.1	56.8	55.2	49.7
Georgia	3,123,723	58,518	53.4	49.7	49.3	44.4
Florida	1,897,414	54,262	35.0	27.1	17.7	13.7
EAST SOUTH CENTRAL:						
Kentucky	2,845,627	40,109	70.9	65.2	60.1	57.0
Tennessee	2,915,841	41,961	69.5	62.4	56.1	52.4
Alabama	2,832,961	51,078	55.5	51.8	45.8	41.7
Mississippi	2,183,796	47,420	46.1	42.4	38.6	38.8
WEST SOUTH CENTRAL:						
Arkansas	1,949,387	52,725	37.0	35.2	33.4	30.0
Louisiana	2,363,880	45,177	52.3	46.5	39.6	36.5
Oklahoma	2,336,434	69,283	33.7	34.6	20.2	23.9
Texas	6,414,824	263,644	24.3	22.1	17.8	14.8
MOUNTAIN:						
Montana	559,456	[1] 146,316	3.8	3.7	3.8	2.6
Idaho	524,873	[1] 82,808	6.3	5.4	5.2	3.9
Wyoming	250,742	[1] 97,506	2.6	2.3	2.0	1.5
Colorado	1,123,296	103,967	10.8	10.0	9.1	7.7
New Mexico	531,818	121,511	4.4	3.5	2.9	2.7
Arizona	499,261	113,580	4.4	3.8	2.9	1.8
Utah	550,310	82,346	6.7	6.2	5.5	4.5
Nevada	110,247	109,802	1.0	0.8	0.7	0.7
PACIFIC:						
Washington	1,736,191	66,977	25.9	23.3	20.3	17.1
Oregon	1,089,684	96,350	11.3	9.9	8.2	7.0
California	6,907,387	156,803	44.1	36.2	22.0	15.3

[1] Total land area includes part of Yellowstone National Park, geographically located in Montana (269 square miles), Idaho (58 square miles), and Wyoming (2,931 square miles). Total population of park returned as in Wyoming in years prior to 1930.

TABLE 6.—URBAN AND RURAL POPULATION OF THE UNITED STATES: 1790 TO 1940

[Urban-rural classification in accordance with 1940 definitions]

CENSUS YEAR	TOTAL			URBAN			RURAL			PERCENT OF TOTAL	
	Population	Increase over preceding census		Population	Increase over preceding census		Population	Increase over preceding census		Urban	Rural
		Number	Percent		Number	Percent		Number	Percent		
1940	131,669,275	8,894,229	7.2	74,423,702	5,468,879	7.9	57,245,573	3,425,350	6.4	56.5	43.5
1930	122,775,046	17,064,426	16.1	68,954,823	14,796,850	27.3	53,820,223	2,267,576	4.4	56.2	43.8
1920	105,710,620	13,738,354	14.9	54,157,973	12,159,041	29.0	51,552,647	1,579,313	3.2	51.2	48.8
1910	91,972,266	15,977,691	21.0	41,998,932	11,839,011	39.3	49,973,334	4,138,680	9.0	45.7	54.3
1900	75,994,575	13,046,861	20.7	30,159,921	8,053,656	36.4	45,834,654	4,993,205	12.2	39.7	60.3
1890	62,947,714	12,791,931	25.5	22,106,265	7,976,530	56.5	40,841,449	4,815,401	13.4	35.1	64.9
1880	50,155,783	11,597,412	30.1	14,129,735	4,227,374	42.7	36,026,048	7,370,038	25.7	28.2	71.8
1870	38,558,371	7,115,050	22.6	9,902,361	3,685,843	59.3	28,656,010	3,429,207	13.6	25.7	74.3
1860	31,443,321	8,251,445	35.6	6,216,518	2,672,802	75.4	25,226,803	5,578,643	28.4	19.8	80.2
1850	23,191,876	6,122,423	35.9	3,543,716	1,698,661	92.1	19,648,160	4,423,762	29.1	15.3	84.7
1840	17,069,453	4,203,433	32.7	1,845,055	717,808	63.7	15,224,398	3,485,625	29.7	10.8	89.2
1830	12,866,020	3,227,567	33.5	1,127,247	433,992	62.6	11,738,773	2,793,575	31.2	8.8	91.2
1820	9,638,453	2,398,572	33.1	693,255	167,796	31.9	8,945,198	2,230,776	33.2	7.2	92.8
1810	7,239,881	1,931,398	36.4	525,459	203,088	63.0	6,714,422	1,728,310	34.7	7.3	92.7
1800	5,308,483	1,379,269	35.1	322,371	120,716	59.9	4,986,112	1,258,553	33.8	6.1	93.9
1790	3,929,214			201,655			3,727,559			5.1	94.9

Table 7.—URBAN AND RURAL POPULATION, BY DIVISIONS AND STATES: 1940 AND 1930

[Urban-rural classification in accordance with 1940 definitions. A minus sign (—) denotes decrease]

REGION, DIVISION, AND STATE	TOTAL POPULATION 1940	TOTAL POPULATION 1930	TOTAL POPULATION Increase Number	TOTAL POPULATION Increase Per-cent	URBAN POPULATION 1940	URBAN POPULATION 1930	URBAN POPULATION Increase Number	URBAN POPULATION Increase Per-cent	RURAL POPULATION 1940	RURAL POPULATION 1930	RURAL POPULATION Increase Number	RURAL POPULATION Increase Per-cent	PERCENT OF TOTAL POPULATION Urban 1940	PERCENT OF TOTAL POPULATION Urban 1930	PERCENT OF TOTAL POPULATION Rural 1940	PERCENT OF TOTAL POPULATION Rural 1930
United States	131,669,275	122,775,046	8,894,229	7.2	74,423,702	68,954,823	5,468,879	7.9	57,245,573	53,820,223	3,425,350	6.4	56.5	56.2	43.5	43.8
REGIONS:																
The North	76,120,109	73,021,191	3,098,918	4.2	51,005,568	49,057,772	1,947,796	4.0	25,114,541	23,963,419	1,151,122	4.8	67.0	67.2	33.0	32.8
The South	41,665,901	37,857,633	3,808,268	10.1	15,290,483	12,904,248	2,386,235	18.5	26,375,418	24,953,385	1,422,033	5.7	36.7	34.1	63.3	65.9
The West	13,883,265	11,896,222	1,987,043	16.7	8,127,651	6,992,803	1,134,848	16.2	5,755,614	4,903,419	852,195	17.4	58.5	58.8	41.5	41.2
THE NORTH:																
New England	8,437,290	8,166,341	270,949	3.3	6,420,542	6,311,976	108,566	1.7	2,016,748	1,854,365	162,383	8.8	76.1	77.3	23.9	22.7
Middle Atlantic	27,539,487	26,260,750	1,278,737	4.9	21,147,543	20,394,707	752,836	3.7	6,391,944	5,866,043	525,901	9.0	76.8	77.7	23.2	22.3
East North Central	26,626,342	25,297,185	1,329,157	5.3	17,444,359	16,794,908	649,451	3.9	9,181,983	8,502,277	679,706	8.0	65.5	66.4	34.5	33.6
West North Central	13,516,990	13,296,915	220,075	1.7	5,993,124	5,556,181	436,943	7.9	7,523,866	7,740,734	−216,868	−2.8	44.3	41.8	55.7	58.2
THE SOUTH:																
South Atlantic	17,823,151	15,793,589	2,029,562	12.9	6,921,726	5,698,122	1,223,604	21.5	10,901,425	10,095,467	805,958	8.0	38.8	36.1	61.2	63.9
East South Central	10,778,225	9,887,214	891,011	9.0	3,165,356	2,778,687	386,669	13.9	7,612,869	7,108,527	504,342	7.1	29.4	28.1	70.6	71.9
West South Central	13,064,525	12,176,830	887,695	7.3	5,203,401	4,427,439	775,962	17.5	7,861,124	7,749,391	111,733	1.4	39.8	36.4	60.2	63.6
THE WEST:																
Mountain	4,150,003	3,701,789	448,214	12.1	1,771,742	1,457,922	313,820	21.5	2,378,261	2,243,867	134,394	6.0	42.7	39.4	57.3	60.6
Pacific	9,733,262	8,194,433	1,538,829	18.8	6,355,909	5,534,881	821,028	14.8	3,377,353	2,659,552	717,801	27.0	65.3	67.5	34.7	32.5
NEW ENGLAND:																
Maine	847,226	797,423	49,803	6.2	343,057	321,506	21,551	6.7	504,169	475,917	28,252	5.9	40.5	40.3	59.5	59.7
New Hampshire	491,524	465,293	26,231	5.6	283,225	273,079	10,146	3.7	208,299	192,214	16,085	8.4	57.6	58.7	42.4	41.3
Vermont	359,231	359,611	−380	−0.1	123,239	118,766	4,473	3.8	235,992	240,845	−4,853	−2.0	34.3	33.0	65.7	67.0
Massachusetts	4,316,721	4,249,614	67,107	1.6	3,859,476	3,831,426	28,050	0.7	457,245	418,188	39,057	9.3	89.4	90.2	10.6	9.8
Rhode Island	713,346	687,497	25,849	3.8	653,383	635,429	17,954	2.8	59,963	52,068	7,895	15.2	91.6	92.4	8.4	7.6
Connecticut	1,709,242	1,606,903	102,339	6.4	1,158,162	1,131,770	26,392	2.3	551,080	475,133	75,947	16.0	67.8	70.4	32.2	29.6
MIDDLE ATLANTIC:																
New York	13,479,142	12,588,066	891,076	7.1	11,165,893	10,521,952	643,941	6.1	2,313,249	2,066,114	247,135	12.0	82.8	83.6	17.2	16.4
New Jersey	4,160,165	4,041,334	118,831	2.9	3,394,773	3,339,244	55,529	1.7	765,392	702,090	63,302	9.0	81.6	82.6	18.4	17.4
Pennsylvania	9,900,180	9,631,350	268,830	2.8	6,586,877	6,533,511	53,366	0.8	3,313,303	3,097,839	215,464	7.0	66.5	67.8	33.5	32.2
EAST NORTH CENTRAL:																
Ohio	6,907,612	6,646,697	260,915	3.9	4,612,986	4,507,371	105,615	2.3	2,294,626	2,139,326	155,300	7.3	66.8	67.8	33.2	32.2
Indiana	3,427,796	3,238,503	189,293	5.8	1,887,712	1,795,892	91,820	5.1	1,540,084	1,442,611	97,473	6.8	55.1	55.5	44.9	44.5
Illinois	7,897,241	7,630,654	266,587	3.5	5,809,650	5,635,727	173,923	3.1	2,087,591	1,994,927	92,664	4.6	73.6	73.9	26.4	26.1
Michigan	5,256,106	4,842,325	413,781	8.5	3,454,867	3,302,075	152,792	4.6	1,801,239	1,540,250	260,989	16.9	65.7	68.2	34.3	31.8
Wisconsin	3,137,587	2,939,006	198,581	6.8	1,679,144	1,553,843	125,301	8.1	1,458,443	1,385,163	73,280	5.3	53.5	52.9	46.5	47.1
WEST NORTH CENTRAL:																
Minnesota	2,792,300	2,563,953	228,347	8.9	1,390,098	1,257,616	132,482	10.5	1,402,202	1,306,337	95,865	7.3	49.8	49.0	50.2	51.0
Iowa	2,538,268	2,470,939	67,329	2.7	1,084,231	979,292	104,939	10.7	1,454,037	1,491,647	−37,610	−2.5	42.7	39.6	57.3	60.4
Missouri	3,784,664	3,629,367	155,297	4.3	1,960,696	1,859,119	101,577	5.5	1,823,968	1,770,248	53,720	3.0	51.8	51.2	48.2	48.8
North Dakota	641,935	680,845	−38,910	−5.7	131,923	113,306	18,617	16.4	510,012	567,539	−57,527	−10.1	20.6	16.6	79.4	83.4
South Dakota	642,961	692,849	−49,888	−7.2	158,087	130,907	27,180	20.8	484,874	561,942	−77,068	−13.7	24.6	18.9	75.4	81.1
Nebraska	1,315,834	1,377,963	−62,129	−4.5	514,148	486,107	28,041	5.8	801,686	891,856	−90,170	−10.1	39.1	35.3	60.9	64.7
Kansas	1,801,028	1,880,999	−79,971	−4.3	753,941	729,834	24,107	3.3	1,047,087	1,151,165	−104,078	−9.0	41.9	38.8	58.1	61.2
SOUTH ATLANTIC:																
Delaware	266,505	238,380	28,125	11.8	139,432	123,146	16,286	13.2	127,073	115,234	11,839	10.3	52.3	51.7	47.7	48.3
Maryland	1,821,244	1,631,526	189,718	11.6	1,080,351	974,869	105,482	10.8	740,893	656,657	84,236	12.8	59.3	59.8	40.7	40.2
District of Columbia	663,091	486,869	176,222	36.2	663,091	486,869	176,222	36.2	----------	----------	----------	-----	100.0	100.0	-----	-----
Virginia	2,677,773	2,421,851	255,922	10.6	944,675	785,537	159,138	20.3	1,733,098	1,636,314	96,784	5.9	35.3	32.4	64.7	67.6
West Virginia	1,901,974	1,729,205	172,769	10.0	534,292	491,504	42,788	8.7	1,367,682	1,237,701	129,981	10.5	28.1	28.4	71.9	71.6
North Carolina	3,571,623	3,170,276	401,347	12.7	974,175	809,847	164,328	20.3	2,597,448	2,360,429	237,019	10.0	27.3	25.5	72.7	74.5
South Carolina	1,899,804	1,738,765	161,039	9.3	466,111	371,080	95,031	25.6	1,433,693	1,367,685	66,008	4.8	24.5	21.3	75.5	78.7
Georgia	3,123,723	2,908,506	215,217	7.4	1,073,808	895,492	178,316	19.9	2,049,915	2,013,014	36,901	1.8	34.4	30.8	65.6	69.2
Florida	1,897,414	1,468,211	429,203	29.2	1,045,791	759,778	286,013	37.6	851,623	708,433	143,190	20.2	55.1	51.7	44.9	48.3
EAST SOUTH CENTRAL:																
Kentucky	2,845,627	2,614,589	231,038	8.8	849,327	799,026	50,301	6.3	1,996,300	1,815,563	180,737	10.0	29.8	30.6	70.2	69.4
Tennessee	2,915,841	2,616,556	299,285	11.4	1,027,206	896,538	130,668	14.6	1,888,635	1,720,018	168,617	9.8	35.2	34.3	64.8	65.7
Alabama	2,832,961	2,646,248	186,713	7.1	855,941	744,273	111,668	15.0	1,977,020	1,901,975	75,045	3.9	30.2	28.1	69.8	71.9
Mississippi	2,183,796	2,009,821	173,975	8.7	432,882	338,850	94,032	27.8	1,750,914	1,670,971	79,943	4.8	19.8	16.9	80.2	83.1
WEST SOUTH CENTRAL:																
Arkansas	1,949,387	1,854,482	94,905	5.1	431,910	382,878	49,032	12.8	1,517,477	1,471,604	45,873	3.1	22.2	20.6	77.8	79.4
Louisiana	2,363,880	2,101,593	262,287	12.5	980,439	833,532	146,907	17.6	1,383,441	1,268,061	115,380	9.1	41.5	39.7	58.5	60.3
Oklahoma	2,336,434	2,396,040	−59,606	−2.5	879,663	821,681	57,982	7.1	1,456,771	1,574,359	−117,588	−7.5	37.6	34.3	62.4	65.7
Texas	6,414,824	5,824,715	590,109	10.1	2,911,389	2,389,348	522,041	21.8	3,503,435	3,435,367	68,068	2.0	45.4	41.0	54.6	59.0
MOUNTAIN:																
Montana	559,456	537,606	21,850	4.1	211,535	181,036	30,499	16.8	347,921	356,570	−8,649	−2.4	37.8	33.7	62.2	66.3
Idaho	524,873	445,032	79,841	17.9	176,708	129,507	47,201	36.4	348,165	315,525	32,640	10.3	33.7	29.1	66.3	70.9
Wyoming	250,742	225,565	25,177	11.2	93,577	70,097	23,480	33.5	157,165	155,468	1,697	1.1	37.3	31.1	62.7	68.9
Colorado	1,123,296	1,035,791	87,505	8.4	590,756	519,882	70,874	13.6	532,540	515,909	16,631	3.2	52.6	50.2	47.4	49.8
New Mexico	531,818	423,317	108,501	25.6	176,401	106,816	69,585	65.1	355,417	316,501	38,916	12.3	33.2	25.2	66.8	74.8
Arizona	499,261	435,573	63,688	14.6	173,981	149,856	24,125	16.1	325,280	285,717	39,563	13.8	34.8	34.4	65.2	65.6
Utah	550,310	507,847	42,463	8.4	305,493	266,264	39,229	14.7	244,817	241,583	3,234	1.3	55.5	52.4	44.5	47.6
Nevada	110,247	91,058	19,189	21.1	43,291	34,464	8,827	25.6	66,956	56,594	10,362	18.3	39.3	37.8	60.7	62.2
PACIFIC:																
Washington	1,736,191	1,563,396	172,795	11.1	921,969	884,539	37,430	4.2	814,222	678,857	135,365	19.9	53.1	56.6	46.9	43.4
Oregon	1,089,684	953,786	135,898	14.2	531,675	489,746	41,929	8.6	558,009	464,040	93,969	20.3	48.8	51.3	51.2	48.7
California	6,907,387	5,677,251	1,230,136	21.7	4,902,265	4,160,596	741,669	17.8	2,005,122	1,516,655	488,467	32.2	71.0	73.3	29.0	26.7

Table 8.—POPULATION OF THE UNITED STATES, URBAN AND RURAL, BY DIVISIONS AND STATES, 1790 TO 1940

[Urban-rural classification in accordance with 1940 definitions. A minus sign (—) denotes decrease. Percent not shown where less than 0.1]

CENSUS YEAR	Urban	Rural	PERCENT INCREASE OVER PRECEDING CENSUS		PERCENT	
			Urban	Rural	Urban	Rural
UNITED STATES:						
1940	74,423,702	57,245,573	7.9	6.4	56.5	43.5
1930	68,954,823	53,820,223	27.3	4.4	56.2	43.8
1920	54,157,973	51,552,647	29.0	3.2	51.2	48.8
1910	41,998,932	49,973,334	39.3	9.0	45.7	54.3
1900	30,159,921	45,834,654	36.4	12.2	39.7	60.3
1890	22,106,265	40,841,449	56.5	13.4	35.1	64.9
1880	14,129,735	36,026,048	42.7	25.7	28.2	71.8
1870	9,902,361	28,656,010	59.3	13.6	25.7	74.3
1860	6,216,518	25,226,803	75.4	28.4	19.8	80.2
1850	3,543,716	19,648,160	92.1	29.1	15.3	84.7
1840	1,845,055	15,224,398	63.7	29.7	10.8	89.2
1830	1,127,247	11,738,773	62.6	31.2	8.8	91.2
1820	693,255	8,945,198	31.9	33.2	7.2	92.8
1810	525,459	6,714,422	63.0	34.7	7.3	92.7
1800	322,371	4,986,112	59.9	33.8	6.1	93.9
1790	201,655	3,727,559	-------	-------	5.1	94.9
THE NORTH:						
1940	51,005,568	25,114,541	4.0	4.8	67.0	33.0
1930	49,057,772	23,963,419	22.1	2.0	67.2	32.8
1920	40,179,824	23,502,021	25.4	−0.9	63.1	36.9
1910	32,050,402	23,706,713	33.1	1.7	57.5	42.5
1900	24,076,196	23,303,503	36.1	5.3	50.8	49.2
1890	17,684,179	22,133,207	52.9	9.0	44.4	55.6
1880	11,568,656	20,302,862	41.9	18.5	36.3	63.7
1870	8,150,168	17,129,673	61.4	17.0	32.2	67.8
1860	5,050,579	14,640,405	81.1	30.2	25.6	74.4
1850	2,788,304	11,242,142	101.7	28.8	19.9	80.1
1840	1,382,117	8,730,507	67.2	38.0	13.7	86.3
1830	826,499	6,326,355	68.8	33.8	11.6	88.4
1820	489,545	4,729,676	28.0	39.3	9.4	90.6
1810	382,431	3,396,351	56.4	39.1	10.1	89.9
1800	244,529	2,442,053	53.3	35.0	9.1	90.9
1790	159,497	1,808,543	-------	-------	8.1	91.9
THE SOUTH:						
1940	15,290,483	26,375,418	18.5	5.7	36.7	63.3
1930	12,904,248	24,953,385	38.8	4.7	34.1	65.9
1920	9,300,055	23,825,748	40.4	4.7	28.1	71.9
1910	6,622,658	22,766,672	49.8	13.3	22.5	77.5
1900	4,420,885	20,102,642	35.6	19.9	18.0	82.0
1890	3,261,326	16,766,733	61.7	15.6	16.3	83.7
1880	2,016,735	14,499,833	34.8	34.4	12.2	87.8
1870	1,496,579	10,791,441	40.3	7.2	12.2	87.8
1860	1,066,794	10,066,567	43.4	22.2	9.6	90.4
1850	744,053	8,238,559	60.7	27.0	8.3	91.7
1840	462,938	6,487,791	53.9	20.0	6.7	93.3
1830	300,748	5,407,100	47.6	28.3	5.3	94.7
1820	203,710	4,215,522	42.4	27.0	4.6	95.4
1810	143,028	3,318,071	83.7	30.4	4.1	95.9
1800	77,842	2,544,059	84.6	32.6	3.0	97.0
1790	42,158	1,919,016	-------	-------	2.1	97.9
THE WEST:						
1940	8,127,651	5,755,614	16.2	17.4	58.5	41.5
1930	6,992,803	4,903,419	49.5	16.1	58.8	41.2
1920	4,678,094	4,224,878	40.7	20.7	52.5	47.5
1910	3,325,872	3,499,949	100.0	44.1	48.7	51.3
1900	1,662,840	2,428,509	43.3	25.1	40.6	59.4
1890	1,160,760	1,941,509	113.2	58.7	37.4	62.6
1880	544,344	1,223,353	113.0	66.5	30.8	69.2
1870	255,614	734,896	157.8	41.4	25.8	74.2
1860	99,145	519,831	772.8	210.4	16.0	84.0
1850	11,359	167,459	-------	-------	6.4	93.6
New England:						
1940	6,420,542	2,016,748	1.7	8.8	76.1	23.9
1930	6,311,976	1,854,365	12.3	4.1	77.3	22.7
1920	5,620,384	1,780,525	17.0	1.9	75.9	24.1
1910	4,805,791	1,746,890	25.3	−0.6	73.3	26.7
1900	3,835,001	1,757,016	32.5	−2.8	68.6	31.4
1890	2,893,860	1,806,889	37.6	−5.3	61.6	38.4
1880	2,102,996	1,907,533	35.7	−1.6	52.4	47.6
1870	1,549,501	1,938,423	34.9	−2.4	44.4	55.6
1860	1,148,489	1,986,794	46.4	2.2	36.6	63.4
1850	784,628	1,943,488	80.8	7.9	28.8	71.2
1840	433,941	1,800,881	58.4	7.1	19.4	80.6
1830	273,949	1,680,768	56.6	13.2	14.0	86.0
1820	174,985	1,485,086	17.7	12.2	10.5	89.5
1810	148,639	1,323,334	46.6	16.9	10.1	89.9
1800	101,418	1,131,593	33.1	21.3	8.2	91.8
1790	76,188	933,220	-------	-------	7.5	92.5
Middle Atlantic:						
1940	21,147,543	6,391,944	3.7	9.0	76.8	23.2
1930	20,394,707	5,866,043	21.5	7.1	77.7	22.3
1920	16,783,474	5,477,670	22.0	−1.5	75.4	24.6
1910	13,757,412	5,558,480	36.5	3.3	71.2	28.8
1900	10,075,883	5,378,795	36.7	0.8	65.2	34.8
1890	7,372,218	5,334,002	40.0	2.0	58.0	42.0
1880	5,267,218	5,229,660	35.1	6.5	50.2	49.8
1870	3,898,300	4,912,506	47.7	1.9	44.2	55.8
1860	2,638,848	4,820,137	75.4	9.7	35.4	64.6
1850	1,504,263	4,394,472	83.7	18.5	25.5	74.5
1840	818,791	3,707,469	60.3	20.5	18.1	81.9
1830	510,915	3,076,749	67.6	28.5	14.2	85.8
1820	304,918	2,394,927	31.9	34.3	11.3	88.7
1810	231,252	1,783,450	61.6	41.6	11.5	88.5
1800	143,111	1,259,454	71.8	43.9	10.2	89.8
1790	83,309	875,323	-------	-------	8.7	91.3
East North Central:						
1940	17,444,359	9,181,983	3.9	8.0	65.5	34.5
1930	16,794,908	8,502,277	28.7	0.9	66.4	33.6
1920	13,050,086	8,425,457	35.7	−2.4	60.8	39.2
1910	9,620,277	8,630,344	33.2	−1.5	52.7	47.3
1900	7,219,975	8,765,606	41.2	4.8	45.2	54.8
1890	5,111,944	8,366,361	66.0	3.0	37.9	62.1
1880	3,080,100	8,126,568	56.2	13.6	27.5	72.5
1870	1,971,705	7,152,812	102.5	20.1	21.6	78.4
1860	973,459	5,953,425	137.9	44.7	14.1	85.9
1850	409,125	4,114,135	262.3	46.3	9.0	91.0
1840	112,916	2,811,812	208.0	96.2	3.9	96.1
1830	36,658	1,433,360	280.2	83.0	2.5	97.5
1820	9,642	783,077	279.6	190.3	1.2	98.8
1810	2,540	269,784	-------	428.9	0.9	99.1
1800	-------	51,006	-------	-------	-------	100.0
1790	-------	-------	-------	-------	-------	-------
West North Central:						
1940	5,993,124	7,523,866	7.9	−2.8	44.3	55.7
1930	5,556,181	7,740,734	17.6	−1.0	41.8	58.2
1920	4,725,880	7,818,369	22.2	0.6	37.7	62.3
1910	3,866,922	7,770,999	31.3	5.0	33.2	66.8
1900	2,945,337	7,402,086	27.7	11.7	28.5	71.5
1890	2,306,157	6,625,955	106.2	31.5	25.8	74.2
1880	1,118,342	5,039,101	53.1	61.2	18.2	81.8
1870	730,662	3,125,932	152.1	66.3	18.9	81.1
1860	289,783	1,880,049	221.0	138.0	13.4	86.6
1850	90,288	790,047	448.2	92.5	10.3	89.7
1840	16,469	410,345	230.9	202.9	3.9	96.1
1830	4,977	135,478	-------	103.5	3.5	96.5
1820	-------	66,586	-------	236.6	-------	100.0
1810	-------	19,783	-------	-------	-------	100.0
South Atlantic:						
1940	6,921,726	10,901,425	21.5	8.0	38.8	61.2
1930	5,698,122	10,095,467	31.4	4.6	36.1	63.9
1920	4,336,482	9,653,790	40.2	6.1	31.0	69.0
1910	3,092,153	9,102,742	38.5	10.9	25.4	74.6
1900	2,232,632	8,210,848	29.2	15.2	21.4	78.6
1890	1,728,019	7,129,903	53.0	10.2	19.5	80.5
1880	1,129,524	6,467,673	34.3	29.0	14.9	85.1
1870	841,067	5,012,543	36.8	5.5	14.4	85.6
1860	614,671	4,750,032	33.6	12.6	11.5	88.5
1850	460,229	4,218,861	51.7	16.5	9.8	90.2
1840	303,377	3,621,922	33.8	5.9	7.7	92.3
1830	226,750	3,419,002	35.6	18.1	6.2	93.8
1820	167,243	2,893,820	37.7	13.3	5.5	94.5
1810	121,460	2,553,431	56.0	15.6	4.5	95.5
1800	77,842	2,208,652	84.6	22.0	3.4	96.6
1790	42,158	1,809,648	-------	-------	2.3	97.7
East South Central:						
1940	3,165,356	7,612,869	13.9	7.1	29.4	70.6
1930	2,778,687	7,108,527	39.3	3.0	28.1	71.9
1920	1,994,207	6,899,100	26.7	0.9	22.4	77.6
1910	1,574,229	6,835,672	39.2	6.5	18.7	81.3
1900	1,131,056	6,416,701	38.4	14.3	15.0	85.0
1890	817,308	5,611,846	74.3	9.7	12.7	87.3
1880	469,006	5,116,145	21.5	27.3	8.4	91.6
1870	386,088	4,018,357	63.1	6.2	8.8	91.2
1860	236,755	3,784,236	67.1	17.5	5.9	94.1
1850	141,689	3,221,582	161.6	27.8	4.2	95.8
1840	54,161	2,521,284	94.0	41.0	2.1	97.9
1830	27,916	1,788,053	200.5	51.4	1.5	98.5
1820	9,291	1,181,198	114.8	67.7	0.8	99.2
1810	4,326	704,264	-------	110.0	0.6	99.4
1800	-------	335,407	-------	206.7	-------	100.0
1790	-------	109,368	-------	-------	-------	100.0
West South Central:						
1940	5,203,401	7,861,124	17.5	1.4	39.8	60.2
1930	4,427,439	7,749,391	49.1	6.6	36.4	63.6
1920	2,969,366	7,272,858	51.8	6.5	29.0	71.0
1910	1,956,276	6,828,258	85.0	24.7	22.3	77.7
1900	1,057,197	5,475,093	47.7	36.0	16.2	83.8
1890	715,999	4,024,984	71.2	38.0	15.1	84.9
1880	418,205	2,916,015	55.2	65.6	12.5	87.5
1870	269,424	1,760,541	25.1	14.9	13.3	86.7
1860	215,368	1,532,299	51.5	92.0	12.3	87.7
1850	142,135	798,116	34.9	131.6	15.1	84.9
1840	105,400	344,585	128.7	72.3	23.4	76.6
1830	46,082	200,045	69.6	42.4	18.7	81.3
1820	27,176	140,504	57.6	132.7	16.2	83.8
1810	17,242	60,376	-------	-------	22.2	77.8
Mountain:						
1940	1,771,742	2,378,261	21.5	6.0	42.7	57.3
1930	1,457,922	2,243,867	19.7	5.9	39.4	60.6
1920	1,217,988	2,118,113	28.9	25.4	36.5	63.5
1910	944,863	1,688,654	74.5	49.0	35.9	64.1
1900	541,363	1,133,294	52.2	32.0	32.3	67.7
1890	355,627	858,308	152.6	67.5	29.3	70.7
1880	140,760	512,359	262.0	85.3	21.6	78.4
1870	38,883	276,502	120.7	75.8	12.3	87.7
1860	17,620	157,303	288.2	130.0	10.1	89.9
1850	4,539	68,388	-------	-------	6.2	93.8

TABLE 8.—POPULATION OF THE UNITED STATES, URBAN AND RURAL, BY DIVISIONS AND STATES: 1790 TO 1940—Continued

[Urban-rural classification in accordance with 1940 definitions. A minus sign (—) denotes decrease. Percent not shown where less than 0.1]

CENSUS YEAR	Urban	Rural	PERCENT INCREASE OVER PRECEDING CENSUS		PERCENT	
			Urban	Rural	Urban	Rural
Pacific:						
1940	6,355,909	3,377,353	14.8	27.0	65.3	34.7
1930	5,534,881	2,659,552	60.0	26.2	67.5	32.5
1920	3,460,106	2,106,765	45.3	16.3	62.2	37.8
1910	2,381,009	1,811,295	112.3	39.8	56.8	43.2
1900	1,121,477	1,295,215	39.3	19.6	46.4	53.6
1890	805,133	1,083,201	99.5	52.4	42.6	57.4
1880	403,584	710,994	86.2	55.1	36.2	63.8
1870	216,731	458,394	165.8	26.4	32.1	67.9
1860	81,525	362,528	1,095.4	265.9	18.4	81.6
1850	6,820	99,071	-------	-------	6.4	93.6
Maine:						
1940	343,057	504,169	6.7	5.9	40.5	59.5
1930	321,506	475,917	7.3	1.6	40.3	59.7
1920	299,569	468,445	14.2	−2.4	39.0	61.0
1910	262,248	480,123	12.6	4.0	35.3	64.7
1900	232,827	461,639	25.4	−2.9	33.5	66.5
1890	185,725	475,361	26.7	−5.4	28.1	71.9
1880	146,608	502,328	11.3	1.4	22.6	77.4
1870	131,744	495,171	26.2	−5.5	21.0	79.0
1860	104,373	523,906	32.2	3.9	16.6	83.4
1850	78,925	504,244	100.6	9.0	13.5	86.5
1840	39,342	462,451	212.3	19.5	7.8	92.2
1830	12,598	386,857	46.8	33.5	3.2	96.8
1820	8,581	289,754	19.7	30.8	2.9	97.1
1810	7,169	221,536	93.5	49.7	3.1	96.9
1800	3,704	148,015	-------	53.3	2.4	97.6
1790	-------	96,540	-------	-------	-------	100.0
New Hampshire:						
1940	283,225	208,299	3.7	8.4	57.6	42.4
1930	273,079	192,214	9.0	−0.2	58.7	41.3
1920	250,438	192,645	12.2	−7.1	56.5	43.5
1910	223,152	207,420	16.1	−5.4	51.8	48.2
1900	192,240	219,348	30.0	−4.1	46.7	53.3
1890	147,913	228,617	42.1	−5.9	39.3	60.7
1880	104,105	242,886	24.7	3.4	30.0	70.0
1870	83,456	234,844	15.8	−7.6	26.2	73.8
1860	72,038	254,035	32.6	−3.6	22.1	77.9
1850	54,327	263,649	90.4	3.0	17.1	82.9
1840	28,531	256,043	111.7	0.1	10.0	90.0
1830	13,475	255,853	83.9	8.0	5.0	95.0
1820	7,327	236,834	5.7	14.1	3.0	97.0
1810	6,934	207,526	29.9	16.2	3.2	96.8
1800	5,339	178,519	13.1	30.1	2.9	97.1
1790	4,720	137,165	-------	-------	3.3	96.7
Vermont:						
1940	123,239	235,992	3.8	−2.0	34.3	65.7
1930	118,766	240,845	8.0	−0.7	33.0	67.0
1920	109,976	242,452	11.2	−5.7	31.2	68.8
1910	98,917	257,039	30.4	−4.0	27.8	72.2
1900	75,831	267,810	49.8	−5.0	22.1	77.9
1890	50,638	281,784	51.8	−5.7	15.2	84.8
1880	33,367	298,919	45.3	−2.8	10.0	90.0
1870	22,960	307,591	269.5	−0.4	6.9	93.1
1860	6,213	308,885	1.7	0.3	2.0	98.0
1850	6,110	308,010	-------	5.5	1.9	98.1
1840	-------	291,948	-------	4.0	-------	100.0
1830	-------	280,652	-------	18.9	-------	100.0
1820	-------	235,981	-------	8.3	-------	100.0
1810	-------	217,895	-------	41.1	-------	100.0
1800	-------	154,465	-------	80.8	-------	100.0
1790	-------	85,425	-------	-------	-------	100.0
Massachusetts:						
1940	3,859,476	457,245	0.7	9.3	89.4	10.6
1930	3,831,426	418,188	10.5	9.1	90.2	9.8
1920	3,468,916	383,440	15.8	3.4	90.0	10.0
1910	2,995,739	370,677	24.2	−5.8	89.0	11.0
1900	2,411,877	393,469	31.4	−2.6	86.0	14.0
1890	1,834,888	404,059	37.8	−10.5	82.0	18.0
1880	1,331,580	451,505	37.0	−7.0	74.7	25.3
1870	972,081	485,270	32.6	−2.5	66.7	33.3
1860	733,209	497,857	45.5	1.5	59.6	40.4
1850	503,861	490,653	80.3	7.1	50.7	49.3
1840	279,454	458,245	47.3	8.9	37.9	62.1
1830	189,657	420,751	59.1	4.1	31.1	68.9
1820	119,187	404,100	18.5	8.8	22.8	77.2
1810	100,617	371,423	54.1	3.9	21.3	78.7
1800	65,300	357,545	27.5	9.1	15.4	84.6
1790	51,202	327,585	-------	-------	13.5	86.5
Rhode Island:						
1940	653,383	59,963	2.8	15.2	91.6	8.4
1930	635,429	52,068	14.5	5.7	92.4	7.6
1920	555,146	49,251	12.4	1.2	91.9	8.1
1910	493,938	48,672	30.5	−2.8	91.0	9.0
1900	378,471	50,085	28.4	−1.1	88.3	11.7
1890	294,843	50,663	30.1	1.5	85.3	14.7
1880	226,618	49,913	39.8	−9.7	82.0	18.0
1870	162,107	55,246	46.7	−13.8	74.6	25.4
1860	110,535	64,085	34.7	−2.1	63.3	36.7
1850	82,084	65,461	72.2	7.0	55.6	44.4
1840	47,662	61,168	56.9	−8.5	43.8	56.2
1830	30,372	66,827	59.1	4.5	31.2	68.8
1820	19,086	63,973	6.2	8.5	23.0	77.0
1810	17,978	58,953	25.3	7.6	23.4	76.6
1800	14,353	54,769	9.6	−1.7	20.8	79.2
1790	13,096	55,729	-------	-------	19.0	81.0
Connecticut:						
1940	1,158,162	551,080	2.3	16.0	67.8	32.2
1930	1,131,770	475,133	20.9	6.9	70.4	29.6
1920	930,339	444,292	28.0	16.0	67.8	32.2
1910	731,797	382,959	34.6	5.0	65.6	34.4
1900	543,755	364,665	43.1	−0.5	59.9	40.1
1890	379,853	366,405	45.7	1.2	50.9	49.1
1880	260,718	361,982	47.2	0.5	41.9	58.1
1870	177,153	360,301	45.1	6.6	33.0	67.0
1860	122,121	338,026	105.9	8.5	26.5	73.5
1850	59,321	311,471	52.3	14.9	16.0	84.0
1840	38,952	271,026	39.9	0.4	12.6	87.4
1830	27,847	269,828	33.9	6.0	9.4	90.6
1820	20,804	254,444	30.5	3.4	7.6	92.4
1810	15,941	246,001	25.3	3.2	6.1	93.9
1800	12,722	238,280	77.4	3.3	5.1	94.9
1790	7,170	230,776	-------	-------	3.0	97.0
New York:						
1940	11,165,893	2,313,249	6.1	12.0	82.8	17.2
1930	10,521,952	2,066,114	22.5	15.0	83.6	16.4
1920	8,588,586	1,796,641	19.5	−6.7	82.7	17.3
1910	7,188,131	1,925,483	35.7	−2.3	78.9	21.1
1900	5,298,111	1,970,783	35.5	−5.8	72.9	27.1
1890	3,910,278	2,092,896	36.3	−5.5	65.1	34.9
1880	2,868,529	2,214,342	31.0	1.0	56.4	43.6
1870	2,189,455	2,193,304	43.6	−6.9	50.0	50.0
1860	1,524,344	2,356,391	74.5	6.0	39.3	60.7
1850	873,414	2,223,980	85.3	13.6	28.2	71.8
1840	471,266	1,957,655	64.4	20.0	19.4	80.6
1830	286,618	1,631,990	78.0	34.7	14.9	85.1
1820	160,996	1,211,816	32.5	44.7	11.7	88.3
1810	121,488	837,561	62.5	62.9	12.7	87.3
1800	74,757	514,294	90.6	70.9	12.7	87.3
1790	39,213	300,907	-------	-------	11.5	88.5
New Jersey:						
1940	3,394,773	765,392	1.7	9.0	81.6	18.4
1930	3,339,244	702,090	32.4	10.8	82.6	17.4
1920	2,522,435	633,465	30.1	5.8	79.9	20.1
1910	1,938,612	598,555	45.9	7.9	76.4	23.6
1900	1,329,162	554,507	46.9	2.6	70.6	29.4
1890	904,543	540,390	47.0	4.8	62.6	37.4
1880	615,311	515,805	55.4	1.1	54.4	45.6
1870	396,012	510,084	80.2	12.8	43.7	56.3
1860	219,798	452,237	155.0	12.1	32.7	67.3
1850	86,195	403,300	118.0	20.9	17.6	82.4
1840	39,548	333,758	115.7	10.3	10.6	89.4
1830	18,333	302,490	145.8	12.0	5.7	94.3
1820	7,457	270,118	24.7	12.7	2.7	97.3
1810	5,979	239,583	-------	13.5	2.4	97.6
1800	-------	211,149	-------	14.7	-------	100.0
1790	-------	184,139	-------	-------	-------	100.0
Pennsylvania:						
1940	6,586,877	3,313,303	0.8	7.0	66.5	33.5
1930	6,533,511	3,097,839	15.2	1.6	67.8	32.2
1920	5,672,453	3,047,564	22.5	0.4	65.1	34.9
1910	4,630,669	3,034,442	34.3	6.3	60.4	39.6
1900	3,448,610	2,853,505	34.8	5.7	54.7	45.3
1890	2,557,397	2,700,716	43.4	8.0	48.6	51.4
1880	1,783,378	2,499,513	35.8	13.1	41.6	58.4
1870	1,312,833	2,209,118	46.7	9.8	37.3	62.7
1860	894,706	2,011,509	64.3	13.8	30.8	69.2
1850	544,654	1,767,132	76.8	24.8	23.6	76.4
1840	307,977	1,416,056	49.5	24.0	17.9	82.1
1830	205,964	1,142,269	50.9	25.1	15.3	84.7
1820	136,465	912,993	31.5	29.3	13.0	87.0
1810	103,785	706,306	51.8	32.3	12.8	87.2
1800	68,354	534,011	55.0	36.8	11.3	88.7
1790	44,096	390,277	-------	-------	10.2	89.8
Ohio:						
1940	4,612,986	2,294,626	2.3	7.3	66.8	33.2
1930	4,507,371	2,139,326	22.6	2.7	67.8	32.2
1920	3,677,136	2,082,258	38.0	−0.9	63.8	36.2
1910	2,665,143	2,101,978	33.4	−2.6	55.9	44.1
1900	1,998,382	2,159,163	32.3	−0.1	48.1	51.9
1890	1,510,153	2,162,176	46.5	−0.2	41.1	58.9
1880	1,030,769	2,167,293	50.9	9.3	32.2	67.8
1870	682,922	1,982,338	70.5	2.2	25.6	74.4
1860	400,435	1,939,076	65.2	11.6	17.1	82.9
1850	242,418	1,737,911	190.4	21.0	12.2	87.8
1840	83,491	1,435,976	127.8	59.3	5.5	94.5
1830	36,658	901,245	280.2	57.6	3.9	96.1
1820	9,642	571,792	279.6	150.5	1.7	98.3
1810	2,540	228,220	-------	403.1	1.1	98.9
1800	-------	45,365	-------	-------	-------	100.0
Indiana:						
1940	1,887,712	1,540,084	5.1	6.8	55.1	44.9
1930	1,795,892	1,442,611	21.1	−0.3	55.5	44.5
1920	1,482,855	1,447,535	29.6	−7.0	50.6	49.4
1910	1,143,835	1,557,041	32.6	−5.8	42.4	57.6
1900	862,689	1,653,773	46.2	3.2	34.3	65.7
1890	590,039	1,602,365	52.8	0.6	26.9	73.1
1880	386,211	1,592,090	55.9	11.1	19.5	80.5
1870	247,657	1,432,980	113.7	16.1	14.7	85.3

TABLE 8.—POPULATION OF THE UNITED STATES, URBAN AND RURAL, BY DIVISIONS AND STATES: 1790 TO 1940—Continued

[Urban-rural classification in accordance with 1940 definitions. A minus sign (—) denotes decrease. Percent not shown where less than 0.1]

CENSUS YEAR	Urban	Rural	PERCENT INCREASE OVER PRECEDING CENSUS: Urban	PERCENT INCREASE OVER PRECEDING CENSUS: Rural	PERCENT: Urban	PERCENT: Rural
Indiana—Continued.						
1860	115,904	1,234,524	159.7	30.8	8.6	91.4
1850	44,632	943,784	316.5	39.8	4.5	95.5
1840	10,716	675,150		96.8	1.6	98.4
1830		343,031		133.1		100.0
1820		147,178		500.2		100.0
1810		24,520		334.7		100.0
1800		5,641				100.0
Illinois:						
1940	5,809,650	2,087,591	3.1	4.6	73.6	26.4
1930	5,635,727	1,994,927	28.0	−4.2	73.9	26.1
1920	4,403,677	2,081,603	26.5	−3.6	67.9	32.1
1910	3,479,935	2,158,656	33.0	−2.1	61.7	38.3
1900	2,616,368	2,205,182	52.2	4.7	54.3	45.7
1890	1,719,172	2,107,180	82.8	−1.4	44.9	55.1
1880	940,504	2,137,367	57.8	10.0	30.6	69.4
1870	596,042	1,943,849	142.7	32.6	23.5	76.5
1860	245,545	1,466,406	281.1	86.3	14.3	85.7
1850	64,427	787,043	570.6	68.7	7.6	92.4
1840	9,607	466,576		196.3	2.0	98.0
1830		157,445		185.2		100.0
1820		55,211		349.5		100.0
1810		12,282				100.0
Michigan:						
1940	3,454,867	1,801,239	4.6	16.9	65.7	34.3
1930	3,302,075	1,540,250	47.3	7.9	68.2	31.8
1920	2,241,560	1,426,852	68.9	−3.8	61.1	38.9
1910	1,327,044	1,483,129	39.3	1.0	47.2	52.8
1900	952,323	1,468,659	30.4	7.7	39.3	60.7
1890	730,294	1,363,596	80.1	10.7	34.9	65.1
1880	405,412	1,231,525	70.4	30.2	24.8	75.2
1870	237,985	946,074	138.7	45.7	20.1	79.9
1860	99,701	649,412	243.5	76.2	13.3	86.7
1850	29,025	368,629	218.9	81.4	7.3	92.7
1840	9,102	203,165		542.1	4.3	95.7
1830		31,639		255.7		100.0
1820		8,896		86.8		100.0
1810		4,762				100.0
Wisconsin:						
1940	1,679,144	1,458,443	8.1	5.3	53.5	46.5
1930	1,553,843	1,385,163	24.8	−0.1	52.9	47.1
1920	1,244,858	1,387,209	24.0	4.3	47.3	52.7
1910	1,004,320	1,329,540	27.1	4.0	43.0	57.0
1900	790,213	1,278,829	40.5	13.1	38.2	61.8
1890	562,286	1,131,044	77.3	13.3	33.2	66.8
1880	317,204	998,293	53.2	17.8	24.1	75.9
1870	207,099	847,571	85.1	27.6	19.6	80.4
1860	111,874	664,007	290.9	139.9	14.4	85.6
1850	28,623	276,768		794.4	9.4	90.6
1840		30,945				100.0
Minnesota:						
1940	1,390,098	1,402,202	10.5	7.3	49.8	50.2
1930	1,257,616	1,306,337	19.6	−2.2	49.0	51.0
1920	1,051,593	1,335,532	23.7	9.0	44.1	55.9
1910	850,294	1,225,414	42.2	6.3	41.0	59.0
1900	598,100	1,153,294	35.0	33.0	34.1	65.9
1890	443,049	867,234	197.8	37.2	33.8	66.2
1880	148,758	632,015	110.2	71.3	19.1	80.9
1870	70,754	368,952	336.1	136.8	16.1	83.9
1860	16,223	155,800		2,463.8	9.4	90.6
1850		6,077				100.0
Iowa:						
1940	1,084,231	1,454,037	10.7	−2.5	42.7	57.3
1930	979,292	1,491,647	11.9	−2.4	39.6	60.4
1920	875,495	1,528,526	28.7	−1.0	36.4	63.6
1910	680,054	1,544,717	18.8	−6.9	30.6	69.4
1900	572,386	1,659,467	41.1	10.2	25.6	74.4
1890	405,764	1,506,533	64.0	9.4	21.2	78.8
1880	247,427	1,377,188	58.3	32.7	15.2	84.8
1870	156,327	1,037,693	160.4	68.8	13.1	86.9
1860	60,028	614,885	516.9	237.0	8.9	91.1
1850	9,730	182,484		323.3	5.1	94.9
1840		43,112				100.0
Missouri:						
1940	1,960,696	1,823,968	5.5	3.0	51.8	48.2
1930	1,859,119	1,770,248	17.2	−2.6	51.2	48.8
1920	1,586,903	1,817,152	13.9	−4.3	46.6	53.4
1910	1,393,705	1,899,630	23.5	−4.0	42.3	57.7
1900	1,128,104	1,978,561	31.6	8.6	36.3	63.7
1890	856,966	1,822,219	57.0	12.3	32.0	68.0
1880	545,993	1,622,387	27.1	25.6	25.2	74.8
1870	429,578	1,291,717	111.1	32.0	25.0	75.0
1860	203,487	978,525	152.6	62.7	17.2	82.8
1850	80,558	601,486	389.1	63.8	11.8	88.2
1840	16,469	367,233	230.9	171.1	4.3	95.7
1830	4,977	135,478		103.5	3.5	96.5
1820		66,586		236.6		100.0
1810		19,783				100.0
North Dakota:						
1940	131,923	510,012	16.4	−10.1	20.6	79.4
1930	113,306	567,539	28.4	1.6	16.6	83.4
1920	88,239	558,633	39.5	8.7	13.6	86.4
1910	63,236	513,820	170.1	73.7	11.0	89.0
1900	23,413	295,733	120.0	64.0	7.3	92.7
1890	10,643	180,340	295.2	427.1	5.6	94.4
1880 [1]	2,693	34,216		1,322.7	7.3	92.7
1870 [1]		2,405				100.0
1860 [1]		4,837				
South Dakota:						
1940	158,087	484,874	20.8	−13.7	24.6	75.4
1930	130,907	561,942	28.5	5.1	18.9	81.1
1920	101,872	534,675	33.2	5.4	16.0	84.0
1910	76,469	507,419	86.8	40.7	13.1	86.9
1900	40,936	360,634	43.4	12.7	10.2	89.8
1890	28,555	320,045	296.2	251.5	8.2	91.8
1880 [1]	7,208	91,060		673.3	7.3	92.7
1870 [1]		11,776				100.0
1860 [1]		4,837				
Nebraska:						
1940	514,148	801,686	5.8	−10.1	39.1	60.9
1930	486,107	891,856	19.9	0.1	35.3	64.7
1920	405,293	891,079	30.4	1.1	31.3	68.7
1910	310,852	881,362	23.0	8.3	26.1	73.9
1900	252,702	813,598	−13.4	5.5	23.7	76.3
1890	291,641	771,015	375.7	97.1	27.4	72.6
1880	61,307	391,095	177.0	287.8	13.6	86.4
1870	22,133	100,860		249.7	18.0	82.0
1860		28,841				100.0
Kansas:						
1940	753,941	1,047,087	3.3	−9.0	41.9	58.1
1930	729,834	1,151,165	18.4	−0.1	38.8	61.2
1920	616,485	1,152,772	25.2	−3.8	34.8	65.2
1910	492,312	1,198,637	49.3	5.1	29.1	70.9
1900	329,696	1,140,799	22.3	−1.5	22.4	77.6
1890	269,539	1,158,569	156.8	30.0	18.9	81.1
1880	104,956	891,140	102.3	185.1	10.5	89.5
1870	51,870	312,529	416.4	221.7	14.2	85.8
1860	10,045	97,161			9.4	90.6
Delaware:						
1940	139,432	127,073	13.2	10.3	52.3	47.7
1930	123,146	115,234	2.0	12.7	51.7	48.3
1920	120,767	102,236	24.4	−2.9	54.2	45.8
1910	97,085	105,237	13.3	6.3	48.0	52.0
1900	85,717	99,018	20.6	1.6	46.4	53.6
1890	71,067	97,426	45.1	−0.2	42.2	57.8
1880	48,989	97,619	58.8	3.7	33.4	66.6
1870	30,841	94,174	45.1	3.5	24.7	75.3
1860	21,258	90,958	52.1	17.3	18.9	81.1
1850	13,979	77,553	67.1	11.2	15.3	84.7
1840	8,367	69,718		−9.2	10.7	89.3
1830		76,748		5.5		100.0
1820		72,749		0.1		100.0
1810		72,674		13.1		100.0
1800		64,273		8.8		100.0
1790		59,096				100.0
Maryland:						
1940	1,080,351	740,893	10.8	12.8	59.3	40.7
1930	974,869	656,657	12.1	13.2	59.8	40.2
1920	869,422	580,239	32.1	−8.9	60.0	40.0
1910	658,192	637,154	11.3	6.8	50.8	49.2
1900	591,206	596,838	19.3	9.2	49.8	50.2
1890	495,702	546,688	31.9	−2.2	47.6	52.4
1880	375,843	559,100	27.2	15.2	40.2	59.8
1870	295,459	485,435	26.6	7.0	37.8	62.2
1860	233,300	453,749	24.1	14.9	34.0	66.0
1850	188,045	394,989	65.1	10.9	32.3	67.7
1840	113,912	356,107	25.1		24.2	75.8
1830	91,041	355,999	37.2	4.4	20.4	79.6
1820	66,378	340,972	42.6	2.1	16.3	83.7
1810	46,555	333,991	75.6	6.0	12.2	87.8
1800	26,514	315,034	96.4	2.9	7.8	92.2
1790	13,503	306,225			4.2	95.8
District of Columbia:						
1940	663,091		36.2		100.0	
1930	486,869		11.3		100.0	
1920	437,571		32.2		100.0	
1910	331,069		18.8		100.0	
1900	278,718		21.0		100.0	
1890	230,392		44.1		100.0	
1880	159,871	17,753	32.6	59.7	90.0	10.0
1870	120,583	11,117	72.6	112.8	91.6	8.4
1860	69,855	5,225	44.4	57.4	93.0	7.0
1850	48,367	3,320	23.6	−27.5	93.6	6.4
1840	39,135	4,577	10.2	5.8	89.5	10.5
1830	35,508	4,326	23.2	2.7	89.1	10.9
1820	28,825	4,214	41.4	15.8	87.2	12.8
1810	20,383	3,640	82.4	24.7	84.8	15.2
1800	11,174	2,919			79.3	20.7

[1] 1860 figure is for Dakota Territory. Figures for 1870 and 1880 for North Dakota and South Dakota are for the parts of Dakota Territory which later constituted the respective States.

Table 8.—POPULATION OF THE UNITED STATES, URBAN AND RURAL, BY DIVISIONS AND STATES: 1790 TO 1940—Continued

[Urban-rural classification in accordance with 1940 definitions. A minus sign (—) denotes decrease. Percent not shown where less than 0.1]

CENSUS YEAR	Urban	Rural	PERCENT INCREASE OVER PRECEDING CENSUS		PERCENT	
			Urban	Rural	Urban	Rural
Virginia:						
1940	944,675	1,733,098	20.3	5.9	35.3	64.7
1930	785,537	1,636,314	16.6	0.1	32.4	67.6
1920	673,984	1,635,203	41.4	3.2	29.2	70.8
1910	476,529	1,585,083	40.1	4.7	23.1	76.9
1900	340,067	1,514,117	20.3	10.3	18.3	81.7
1890	282,721	1,373,259	49.5	3.8	17.1	82.9
1880	189,079	1,323,486	29.8	22.6	12.5	87.5
1870	145,618	1,079,545	7.1	−26.1	11.9	88.1
1860	135,956	1,460,362	35.0	10.6	8.5	91.5
1850	100,690	1,320,971	43.0	13.0	7.1	92.9
1840	70,394	1,169,403	67.1	-------	5.7	94.3
1830	42,134	1,169,271	54.7	12.6	3.5	96.5
1820	27,235	1,038,131	10.7	9.3	2.6	97.4
1810	24,596	950,004	52.0	10.0	2.5	97.5
1800	16,184	864,016	31.6	17.5	1.8	98.2
1790	12,296	735,314	-------	-------	1.6	98.4
West Virginia: [1]						
1940	534,292	1,367,682	8.7	10.5	28.1	71.9
1930	491,504	1,237,701	33.2	13.1	28.4	71.6
1920	369,007	1,094,694	61.7	10.3	25.2	74.8
1910	228,242	992,877	81.9	19.1	18.7	81.3
1900	125,465	833,335	54.2	22.3	13.1	86.9
1890	81,365	681,429	50.5	20.7	10.7	89.3
1880	54,050	564,407	50.1	39.0	8.7	91.3
1870	36,009	406,005	-------	-------	8.1	91.9
North Carolina:						
1940	974,175	2,597,448	20.3	10.0	27.3	72.7
1930	809,847	2,360,429	65.2	14.1	25.5	74.5
1920	490,370	2,068,753	54.0	9.6	19.2	80.8
1910	318,474	1,887,813	70.5	10.6	14.4	85.6
1900	186,790	1,707,020	61.4	13.6	9.9	90.1
1890	115,759	1,502,190	110.0	11.7	7.2	92.8
1880	55,116	1,344,634	52.2	29.9	3.9	96.1
1870	36,218	1,035,143	47.5	6.9	3.4	96.6
1860	24,554	968,068	16.3	14.2	2.5	97.5
1850	21,109	847,930	58.6	14.6	2.4	97.6
1840	13,810	740,109	27.3	1.7	1.8	98.2
1830	10,455	727,532	−16.4	16.2	1.4	98.6
1820	12,502	626,327	-------	12.8	2.0	98.0
1810	-------	555,500	-------	16.2	-------	100.0
1800	-------	478,103	-------	21.4	-------	100.0
1790	-------	393,751	-------	-------	-------	100.0
South Carolina:						
1940	466,111	1,433,603	25.6	4.8	24.5	75.5
1930	371,080	1,367,685	26.2	−1.6	21.3	78.7
1920	293,987	1,389,737	30.8	7.7	17.5	82.5
1910	224,832	1,290,568	31.3	10.4	14.8	85.2
1900	171,256	1,169,060	47.4	13.0	12.8	87.2
1890	116,183	1,034,966	55.9	12.4	10.1	89.9
1880	74,539	921,038	22.2	42.9	7.5	92.5
1870	61,011	644,595	25.6	−1.6	8.6	91.4
1860	48,574	655,134	−1.0	5.8	6.9	93.1
1850	49,045	619,462	46.0	10.5	7.3	92.7
1840	33,601	560,797	-------	2.4	5.7	94.3
1830	33,599	547,586	35.6	14.6	5.8	94.2
1820	24,780	477,961	0.3	22.4	4.9	95.1
1810	24,711	390,404	31.3	19.5	6.0	94.0
1800	18,824	326,767	15.1	40.4	5.4	94.6
1790	16,359	232,714	-------	-------	6.6	93.4
Georgia:						
1940	1,073,808	2,049,915	19.9	1.8	34.4	65.6
1930	895,492	2,013,014	23.0	−7.1	30.8	69.2
1920	727,859	2,167,973	35.1	4.7	25.1	74.9
1910	538,650	2,070,471	55.5	10.7	20.6	79.4
1900	346,382	1,869,949	34.5	18.4	15.6	84.4
1890	257,472	1,579,881	77.5	13.1	14.0	86.0
1880	145,090	1,397,090	45.0	28.9	9.4	90.6
1870	100,053	1,084,056	32.6	10.4	8.4	91.6
1860	75,466	981,820	93.5	13.2	7.1	92.9
1850	38,994	867,191	58.1	30.1	4.3	95.7
1840	24,658	666,734	76.0	32.6	3.6	96.4
1830	14,013	502,810	86.3	50.8	2.7	97.3
1820	7,523	333,466	44.3	34.9	2.2	97.8
1810	5,215	247,218	1.3	56.9	2.1	97.9
1800	5,146	157,540	-------	90.8	3.2	96.8
1790	-------	82,548	-------	-------	-------	100.0
Florida:						
1940	1,045,791	851,623	37.6	20.2	55.1	44.9
1930	759,778	708,433	114.9	15.2	51.7	48.3
1920	353,515	614,955	61.4	15.3	36.5	63.5
1910	219,080	533,539	104.7	26.6	29.1	70.9
1900	107,031	421,511	38.4	34.2	20.3	79.7
1890	77,358	314,064	187.1	29.5	19.8	80.2
1880	26,947	242,546	76.4	40.6	10.0	90.0
1870	15,275	172,473	167.6	28.0	8.1	91.9
1860	5,708	134,716	-------	54.1	4.1	95.9
1850	-------	87,445	-------	60.5	-------	100.0
1840	-------	54,477	-------	56.9	-------	100.0
1830	-------	34,730	-------	-------	-------	100.0
Kentucky:						
1940	849,327	1,996,300	6.3	10.0	29.8	70.2
1930	799,026	1,815,563	26.1	1.8	30.6	69.4
1920	633,543	1,783,087	14.1	2.8	26.2	73.8
1910	555,442	1,734,463	18.8	3.3	24.3	75.7
1900	467,668	1,679,506	31.1	11.8	21.8	78.2
1890	356,713	1,501,922	42.7	7.4	19.2	80.8
1880	249,923	1,398,767	27.6	24.3	15.2	84.8
1870	195,896	1,125,115	62.4	8.7	14.8	85.2
1860	120,624	1,035,060	63.4	13.9	10.4	89.6
1850	73,804	908,601	138.5	21.3	7.5	92.5
1840	30,948	748,880	89.1	11.5	4.0	96.0
1830	16,367	671,550	76.2	21.0	2.4	97.6
1820	9,291	555,026	114.8	38.0	1.6	98.4
1810	4,326	402,185	-------	82.0	1.1	98.9
1800	-------	220,955	-------	199.9	-------	100.0
1790	-------	73,677	-------	-------	-------	100.0
Tennessee:						
1940	1,027,206	1,888,635	14.6	9.8	35.2	64.8
1930	896,538	1,720,018	46.7	−0.4	34.3	65.7
1920	611,226	1,726,659	38.6	−1.0	26.1	73.9
1910	441,045	1,743,744	35.0	2.9	20.2	79.8
1900	326,639	1,693,977	37.0	10.8	16.2	83.8
1890	238,394	1,529,124	105.5	7.2	13.5	86.5
1880	115,984	1,426,375	23.1	22.5	7.5	92.5
1870	94,237	1,164,283	102.5	9.5	7.5	92.5
1860	46,541	1,063,260	111.7	8.4	4.2	95.8
1850	21,983	980,734	217.3	19.3	2.2	97.8
1840	6,929	822,281	24.5	21.6	0.8	99.2
1830	5,566	676,338	-------	60.0	0.8	99.2
1820	-------	422,823	-------	61.6	-------	100.0
1810	-------	261,727	-------	147.8	-------	100.0
1800	-------	105,602	-------	195.9	-------	100.0
1790	-------	35,691	-------	-------	-------	100.0
Alabama:						
1940	855,941	1,977,020	15.0	3.9	30.2	69.8
1930	744,273	1,901,975	46.1	3.4	28.1	71.9
1920	509,317	1,838,857	37.5	4.0	21.7	78.3
1910	370,431	1,767,662	70.9	9.7	17.3	82.7
1900	216,714	1,611,983	42.4	18.4	11.9	88.1
1890	152,235	1,361,166	122.2	14.0	10.1	89.9
1880	68,518	1,193,987	9.3	27.8	5.4	94.6
1870	62,700	934,292	28.2	2.1	6.3	93.7
1860	48,901	915,300	39.0	24.3	5.1	94.9
1850	35,179	736,444	177.6	27.4	4.6	95.4
1840	12,672	578,084	296.7	88.7	2.1	97.9
1830	3,194	306,333	-------	139.5	1.0	99.0
1820	-------	127,901	-------	-------	-------	100.0
Mississippi:						
1940	432,882	1,750,914	27.8	4.8	19.8	80.2
1930	338,850	1,670,971	41.1	7.8	16.9	83.1
1920	240,121	1,550,497	15.8	−2.5	13.4	86.6
1910	207,311	1,589,803	72.7	11.1	11.5	88.5
1900	120,035	1,431,235	71.6	17.3	7.7	92.3
1890	69,966	1,219,634	102.3	11.2	5.4	94.6
1880	34,581	1,097,016	4.0	38.0	3.1	96.9
1870	33,255	794,667	60.7	3.1	4.0	96.0
1860	20,689	770,616	92.9	29.3	2.6	97.4
1850	10,723	595,803	196.9	60.1	1.8	98.2
1840	3,612	372,039	29.5	178.0	1.0	99.0
1830	2,789	133,832	-------	77.4	2.0	98.0
1820	-------	75,448	-------	87.0	-------	100.0
1810	-------	40,352	-------	356.0	-------	100.0
1800	-------	8,850	-------	-------	-------	100.0
Arkansas:						
1940	431,910	1,517,477	12.8	3.1	22.2	77.8
1930	382,878	1,471,604	31.8	0.7	20.6	79.4
1920	290,497	1,461,707	43.3	6.6	16.6	83.4
1910	202,681	1,371,768	81.4	14.3	12.9	87.1
1900	111,733	1,199,831	52.7	13.7	8.5	91.5
1890	73,159	1,055,052	128.5	36.9	6.5	93.5
1880	32,020	770,505	158.6	63.2	4.0	96.0
1870	12,380	472,091	232.2	9.4	2.6	97.4
1860	3,727	431,723	-------	105.7	0.9	99.1
1850	-------	209,897	-------	115.1	-------	100.0
1840	-------	97,574	-------	221.1	-------	100.0
1830	-------	30,388	-------	112.9	-------	100.0
1820	-------	14,273	-------	1,244.0	-------	100.0
1810	-------	1,062	-------	-------	-------	100.0
Louisiana:						
1940	980,439	1,383,441	17.6	9.1	41.5	58.5
1930	833,532	1,268,061	32.7	8.3	39.7	60.3
1920	628,163	1,170,346	26.5	0.9	34.9	65.1
1910	496,516	1,159,872	35.6	14.2	30.0	70.0
1900	366,288	1,015,337	29.0	21.6	26.5	73.5
1890	283,845	834,743	18.6	19.2	25.4	74.6
1880	239,390	700,556	18.2	33.6	25.5	74.5
1870	202,523	524,392	9.5	0.3	27.9	72.1
1860	185,026	522,976	37.6	36.4	26.1	73.9
1850	134,470	383,292	27.6	55.2	26.0	74.0

[1] The population at each census prior to 1870 of that part of Virginia which was later taken to form West Virginia was as follows: 1860, 376,688; 1850, 302,313; 1840, 224,537; 1830, 176.924: 1820, 136,808; 1810, 105,469; 1800, 78,592; 1790, 55,873.

24 NUMBER OF INHABITANTS

TABLE 8.—POPULATION OF THE UNITED STATES, URBAN AND RURAL, BY DIVISIONS AND STATES: 1790 TO 1940—Continued

[Urban-rural classification in accordance with 1940 definitions. A minus sign (—) denotes decrease. Percent not shown where less than 0.1]

CENSUS YEAR	Urban	Rural	PERCENT INCREASE OVER PRECEDING CENSUS		PERCENT	
			Urban	Rural	Urban	Rural
Louisiana—Continued.						
1840	105, 400	247, 011	128.7	45.6	29.9	70.1
1830	46, 082	169, 657	69.6	34.4	21.4	78.6
1820	27, 176	126, 231	57.6	112.8	17.7	82.3
1810	17, 242	59, 314	-------	-------	22.5	77.5
Oklahoma:						
1940	879, 663	1, 456, 771	7.1	—7.5	37.6	62.4
1930	821, 681	1, 574, 359	52.7	5.6	34.3	65.7
1920	538, 017	1, 490, 266	68.7	11.4	26.5	73.5
1910	318, 975	1, 338, 180	446.0	82.8	19.2	80.8
1900	58, 417	731, 974	516.0	193.8	7.4	92.6
1890	[3] 9, 484	[3] 249, 173	-------	-------	3.7	96.3
Texas:						
1940	2, 911, 389	3, 503, 435	21.8	2.0	45.4	54.6
1930	2, 389, 348	3, 435, 367	58.0	9.0	41.0	59.0
1920	1, 512, 689	3, 150, 539	61.2	6.5	32.4	67.6
1910	938, 104	2, 958, 438	80.1	17.0	24.1	75.9
1900	520, 759	2, 527, 951	49.0	34.0	17.1	82.9
1890	349, 511	1, 886, 016	138.1	30.5	15.6	84.4
1880	146, 795	1, 444, 954	169.2	89.1	9.2	90.8
1870	54, 521	764, 058	104.9	32.3	6.7	93.3
1860	26, 615	577, 600	247.2	181.9	4.4	95.6
1850	7, 665	204, 927	-------	-------	3.6	96.4
Montana:						
1940	211, 535	347, 921	16.8	—2.4	37.8	62.2
1930	181, 036	356, 570	5.2	—5.4	33.7	66.3
1920	172, 011	376, 878	28.9	55.3	31.3	68.7
1910	133, 420	242, 633	57.8	52.8	35.5	64.5
1900	84, 554	158, 775	118.0	52.5	34.7	65.3
1890	38, 787	104, 137	455.1	223.7	27.1	72.9
1880	6, 987	32, 172	125.0	84.0	17.8	82.2
1870	3, 106	17, 489	-------	-------	15.1	84.9
Idaho:						
1940	176, 708	348, 165	36.4	10.3	33.7	66.3
1930	129, 507	315, 525	8.8	0.9	29.1	70.9
1920	119, 037	312, 829	70.3	22.3	27.6	72.4
1910	69, 898	255, 696	598.8	68.5	21.5	78.5
1900	10, 003	151, 769	-------	71.4	6.2	93.8
1890	-----------	88, 548	-------	171.5	-------	100.0
1880	-----------	32, 610	-------	117.4	-------	100.0
1870	-----------	14, 999	-------	-------	-------	100.0
Wyoming.						
1940	93, 577	157, 165	33.5	1.1	37.3	62.7
1930	70, 097	155, 468	22.8	13.2	31.1	68.9
1920	57, 095	137, 307	32.1	33.6	29.4	70.6
1910	43, 221	102, 744	62.1	56.0	29.6	70.4
1900	26, 657	65, 874	24.1	60.4	28.8	71.2
1890	21, 484	41, 071	249.2	180.6	34.3	65.7
1880	6, 152	14, 637	-------	60.5	29.6	70.4
1870	-----------	9, 118	-------	-------	-------	100.0
Colorado:						
1940	590, 756	532, 540	13.6	3.2	52.6	47.4
1930	519, 882	515, 909	14.7	6.1	50.2	49.8
1920	453, 259	486, 370	12.7	22.6	48.2	51.8
1910	402, 192	396, 832	54.3	42.2	50.3	49.7
1900	260, 651	279, 049	40.2	22.7	48.3	51.7
1890	185, 905	227, 344	205.0	70.5	45.0	55.0
1880	60, 961	133, 366	1, 181.0	279.9	31.4	68.6
1870	4, 759	35, 105	0.2	18.9	11.9	88.1
1860	4, 749	29, 528	-------	-------	13.9	86.1
New Mexico:						
1940	176, 401	355, 417	65.1	12.3	33.2	66.8
1930	106, 816	316, 501	64.4	7.1	25.2	74.8
1920	64, 960	295, 390	39.5	5.2	18.0	82.0
1910	46, 571	280, 730	70.1	67.2	14.2	85.8
1900	27, 381	167, 929	174.6	11.7	14.0	86.0
New Mexico—Con.						
1890	9, 970	150, 312	50.3	33.1	6.2	93.8
1880	6, 635	112, 930	39.2	29.6	5.5	94.5
1870	4, 765	87, 109	2.8	—2.0	5.2	94.8
1860	4, 635	88, 881	2.1	55.9	5.0	95.0
1850	4, 539	57, 008	-------	-------	7.4	92.6
Arizona:						
1940	173, 981	325, 280	16.1	13.8	34.8	65.2
1930	149, 856	285, 717	24.1	33.9	34.4	65.6
1920	120, 788	213, 374	90.9	51.2	36.1	63.9
1910	63, 260	141, 094	224.5	36.4	31.0	69.0
1900	19, 495	103, 436	134.8	29.4	15.9	84.1
1890	8, 302	79, 941	18.5	139.1	9.4	90.6
1880	7, 007	33, 433	117.3	419.6	17.3	82.7
1870	3, 224	6, 434	-------	-------	33.4	66.6
Utah:						
1940	305, 493	244, 817	14.7	1.3	55.5	44.5
1930	266, 264	241, 583	23.5	3.3	52.4	47.6
1920	215, 584	233, 812	24.7	16.7	48.0	52.0
1910	172, 934	200, 417	64.0	17.0	46.3	53.7
1900	105, 427	171, 322	40.3	26.3	38.1	61.9
1890	75, 155	135, 624	123.2	23.0	35.7	64.3
1880	33, 665	110, 298	110.7	55.8	23.4	76.6
1870	15, 981	70, 805	94.0	121.0	18.4	81.6
1860	8, 236	32, 037	-------	181.5	20.5	79.5
1850	-----------	11, 380	-------	-------	-------	100.0
Nevada:						
1940	43, 291	66, 956	25.6	18.3	39.3	60.7
1930	34, 464	56, 594	125.9	—8.9	37.8	62.2
1920	15, 254	62, 153	14.1	—9.3	19.7	80.3
1910	13, 367	68, 508	85.8	95.0	16.3	83.7
1900	7, 195	35, 140	—55.1	12.2	17.0	83.0
1890	16, 024	31, 331	—17.2	—27.0	33.8	66.2
1880	19, 353	42, 913	174.6	21.1	31.1	68.9
1870	7, 048	35, 443	-------	416.9	16.6	83.4
1860	-----------	6, 857	-------	-------	-------	100.0
Washington:						
1940	921, 969	814, 222	4.2	19.9	53.1	46.9
1930	884, 539	678, 857	19.1	10.6	56.6	43.4
1920	742, 801	613, 820	22.7	14.4	54.8	45.2
1910	605, 530	536, 460	186.3	75.0	53.0	47.0
1900	211, 477	306, 626	66.3	33.3	40.8	59.2
1890	127, 178	230, 054	1, 686.0	238.3	35.6	64.4
1880	7, 121	67, 995	-------	183.8	9.5	90.5
1870	-----------	23, 955	-------	106.6	-------	100.0
1860	-----------	11, 594	-------	-------	-------	100.0
Oregon:						
1940	531, 675	558, 009	8.6	20.3	48.8	51.2
1930	489, 746	464, 040	25.5	18.1	51.3	48.7
1920	390, 346	393, 043	27.1	7.5	49.8	50.2
1910	307, 060	365, 705	130.6	30.4	45.6	54.4
1900	133, 180	280, 356	50.5	22.3	32.2	67.8
1890	88, 491	229, 213	242.3	53.9	27.9	72.1
1880	25, 852	148, 916	211.7	80.2	14.8	85.2
1870	8, 293	82, 630	188.6	66.6	9.1	90.9
1860	2, 874	49, 591	-------	273.0	5.5	94.5
1850	-----------	13, 294	-------	-------	-------	100.0
California:						
1940	4, 902, 265	2, 005, 122	17.8	32.2	71.0	29.0
1930	4, 160, 596	1, 516, 655	78.8	37.9	73.3	26.7
1920	2, 326, 959	1, 099, 902	58.5	21.0	67.9	32.1
1910	1, 468, 419	909, 130	89.0	28.4	61.8	38.2
1900	776, 820	708, 233	31.8	13.5	52.3	47.7
1890	589, 464	623, 934	59.1	26.3	48.6	51.4
1880	370, 611	494, 083	77.8	40.4	42.9	57.1
1870	208, 438	351, 809	165.0	16.7	37.2	62.8
1860	78, 651	301, 343	1, 053.2	251.3	20.7	79.3
1850	6, 820	85, 777	-------	-------	7.4	92.6

[3] Includes population of Indian Territory.

Table 9.—POPULATION IN GROUPS OF PLACES CLASSIFIED ACCORDING TO SIZE, WITH CHANGES IN NUMBER OF PLACES, FOR THE UNITED STATES: 1940 AND 1930

[A minus sign (—) denotes decrease in number of places]

AREA AND CLASS OF PLACES	1940			1930			CHANGE IN NUMBER OF PLACES, 1930-1940 [1]		
	Number of places [1]	Population	Percent of total population	Number of places [1]	Population	Percent of total population	Number added	Number taken out	Net change
United States	----------	**131, 669, 275**	**100. 0**	----------	**122, 775, 046**	**100. 0**	----------	----------	----------
Urban territory	**3, 464**	**74, 423, 702**	**56. 5**	**3, 165**	**68, 954, 823**	**56. 2**	**344**	**45**	**299**
Places of 1,000,000 or more	5	15, 910, 866	12. 1	5	15, 064, 555	12. 3	----------	----------	----------
Places of 500,000 to 1,000,000	9	6, 456, 959	4. 9	8	5, 763, 987	4. 7	1	----------	1
Places of 250,000 to 500,000	23	7, 827, 514	5. 9	24	7, 956, 228	6. 5	1	2	−1
Places of 100,000 to 250,000	55	7, 792, 650	5. 9	56	7, 540, 966	6. 1	3	4	−1
Places of 50,000 to 100,000	107	7, 343, 917	5. 6	98	6, 491, 448	5. 3	15	6	9
Places of 25,000 to 50,000	213	7, 417, 093	5. 6	185	6, 425, 693	5. 2	42	14	28
Places of 10,000 to 25,000	665	9, 966, 898	7. 6	606	9, 097, 200	7. 4	109	50	59
Places of 5,000 to 10,000	965	6, 681, 894	5. 1	851	5, 897, 156	4. 8	236	122	114
Places of 2,500 to 5,000	1, 422	5, 025, 911	3. 8	1, 332	4, 717, 590	3. 8	344	254	90
Rural territory	----------	**57, 245, 573**	**43. 5**	----------	**53, 820, 223**	**43. 8**	----------	----------	----------
Incorporated places of 1,000 to 2,500	3, 205	5, 026, 834	3. 8	3, 087	4, 820, 707	3. 9	561	443	118
Incorporated places under 1,000	10, 083	4, 315, 843	3. 3	10, 346	4, 362, 746	3. 6	566	829	−263
Unincorporated territory	----------	47, 902, 896	36. 4	----------	44, 636, 770	36. 4	----------	----------	----------
Cumulative summary:									
Places of 100,000 or more	92	37, 987, 989	28. 9	93	36, 325, 736	29. 6	2	3	−1
Places of 25,000 or more	412	52, 748, 999	40. 1	376	49, 242, 877	40. 1	39	3	36
Places of 10,000 or more	1, 077	62, 715, 897	47. 6	982	58, 340, 077	47. 5	108	13	95

[1] In 1940 Bluefield, Va., and Bluefield, W. Va.; Bristol, Tenn., and Bristol, Va.; Delmar, Del., and Delmar, Md.; Harrison, Ohio, and West Harrison, Ind.; Junction City, Ark., and Junction City, La.; Texarkana, Ark., and Texarkana, Tex.; Texhoma, Okla., and Texhoma, Tex.; and Union City, Ind., and Union City, Ohio, were counted as separate incorporated places, whereas in 1930 each pair was counted as a single place. If the 1930 treatment had been applied in 1940, there would have been three fewer urban places (two fewer in each of the groups 2,500 to 5,000 and 10,000 to 25,000, and one more in the group 25,000 to 50,000). There would also have been five fewer rural incorporated places (all in the group of less than 1,000 population).

TABLE 10.—POPULATION IN GROUPS OF PLACES CLASSIFIED ACCORDING TO SIZE, AND IN

	SUBJECT AND CLASS OF PLACES	1940	1930	1920	1910	1900	1890
	NUMBER OF PLACES[1]						
1	**Urban territory**	3,464	3,165	2,722	2,262	1,737	1,348
2	Places of 1,000,000 or more	5	5	3	3	3	3
3	Places of 500,000 to 1,000,000	9	8	9	5	3	1
4	Places of 250,000 to 500,000	23	24	13	11	9	7
5	Places of 100,000 to 250,000	55	56	43	31	23	17
6	Places of 50,000 to 100,000	107	98	76	59	40	30
7	Places of 25,000 to 50,000	213	185	143	119	82	66
8	Places of 10,000 to 25,000	665	606	465	369	280	230
9	Places of 5,000 to 10,000	965	851	715	605	465	340
10	Places of 2,500 to 5,000	1,422	1,332	1,255	1,000	832	654
11	**Incorporated rural territory**	13,288	13,433	12,857	11,832	8,930	6,490
12	Incorporated places of 1,000 to 2,500	3,205	3,087	3,032	2,720	2,128	1,603
13	Incorporated places under 1,000	10,083	10,346	9,825	9,112	6,802	4,887
	Cumulative summary:						
14	Places of 100,000 or more	92	93	68	50	38	28
15	Places of 25,000 or more	412	376	287	228	160	124
16	Places of 10,000 or more	1,077	982	752	597	440	354
	POPULATION						
17	**United States**	131,669,275	122,775,046	105,710,620	91,972,266	75,994,575	62,947,714
18	**Urban territory**	74,423,702	68,954,823	54,157,973	41,998,932	30,159,921	22,106,265
19	Places of 1,000,000 or more	15,910,866	15,064,555	10,145,532	8,501,174	6,429,474	3,662,115
20	Places of 500,000 to 1,000,000	6,456,959	5,763,987	6,223,769	3,010,667	1,645,087	806,343
21	Places of 250,000 to 500,000	7,827,514	7,956,228	4,540,838	3,949,839	2,861,296	2,447,608
22	Places of 100,000 to 250,000	7,792,650	7,540,966	6,519,187	4,840,458	3,272,490	2,781,894
23	Places of 50,000 to 100,000	7,343,917	6,491,448	5,265,408	4,178,915	2,709,338	2,027,569
24	Places of 25,000 to 50,000	7,417,093	6,425,693	5,075,041	4,023,397	2,800,627	2,268,786
25	Places of 10,000 to 25,000	9,966,898	9,097,200	7,034,668	5,548,868	4,338,250	3,451,258
26	Places of 5,000 to 10,000	6,681,894	5,897,156	4,967,625	4,217,420	3,204,195	2,383,685
27	Places of 2,500 to 5,000	5,025,911	4,717,590	4,385,905	3,728,194	2,899,164	2,277,007
28	**Rural territory**	57,245,573	53,820,223	51,552,647	49,973,334	45,834,654	40,841,449
	Incorporated places of 1,000 to 2,500	5,026,834	4,820,707	4,714,490	4,238,498	3,297,839	2,508,642
29	Incorporated places under 1,000	4,315,843	4,362,746	4,254,751	3,930,651	3,003,694	2,249,332
	Unincorporated territory	47,902,896	44,636,770	42,583,406	41,804,185	39,533,121	36,083,475
	Cumulative summary:						
30	Places of 100,000 or more	37,987,989	36,325,736	27,429,326	20,302,138	14,208,347	9,697,960
31	Places of 25,000 or more	52,748,999	49,242,877	37,769,775	28,504,450	19,718,312	13,994,315
32	Places of 10,000 or more	62,715,897	58,340,077	44,804,443	34,053,318	24,056,562	17,445,573
	PERCENT OF TOTAL POPULATION						
33	**United States**	100.0	100.0	100.0	100.0	100.0	100.0
34	**Urban territory**	56.5	56.2	51.2	45.7	39.7	35.1
35	Places of 1,000,000 or more	12.1	12.3	9.6	9.2	8.5	5.8
36	Places of 500,000 to 1,000,000	4.9	4.7	5.9	3.3	2.2	1.3
37	Places of 250,000 to 500,000	5.9	6.5	4.3	4.3	3.8	3.9
38	Places of 100,000 to 250,000	5.9	6.1	6.2	5.3	4.3	4.4
39	Places of 50,000 to 100,000	5.6	5.3	5.0	4.5	3.6	3.2
40	Places of 25,000 to 50,000	5.6	5.2	4.8	4.4	3.7	3.6
41	Places of 10,000 to 25,000	7.6	7.4	6.7	6.0	5.7	5.5
42	Places of 5,000 to 10,000	5.1	4.8	4.7	4.6	4.2	3.8
43	Places of 2,500 to 5,000	3.8	3.8	4.1	4.1	3.8	3.6
44	**Rural territory**	43.5	43.8	48.8	54.3	60.3	64.9
45	Incorporated places of 1,000 to 2,500	3.8	3.9	4.5	4.6	4.3	4.0
46	Incorporated places under 1,000	3.3	3.6	4.0	4.3	4.0	3.6
47	Unincorporated territory	36.4	36.4	40.3	45.5	52.0	57.3
	Cumulative summary:						
48	Places of 100,000 or more	28.9	29.6	25.9	22.1	18.7	15.4
49	Places of 25,000 or more	40.1	40.1	35.7	31.0	25.9	22.2
50	Places of 10,000 or more	47.6	47.5	42.4	37.0	31.7	27.7

[1] In 1940 Bluefield, Va., and Bluefield, W. Va.; Bristol, Tenn., and Bristol, Va.; Delmar, Del., and Delmar, Md.; Harrison, Ohio, and West Harrison, Ind.; Junction City, Ark., and Junction City, La.; Texarkana, Ark., and Texarkana, Tex.; Texhoma, Okla., and Texhoma, Tex.; and Union City, Ind., and Union City, Ohio, were counted as separate incorporated places, whereas in 1930 and earlier years each pair was counted as a single place. If the 1930 treatment had been applied in 1940 there would have been 3 fewer urban places (2 fewer in each of the groups 2,500 to 5,000 and 10,000 to 25,000, and 1 more in the group 25,000 to 50,000). There would also have been 5 fewer rural incorporated places (all in the group of less than 1,000 population).

[2] Not returned separately.

UNINCORPORATED RURAL TERRITORY, FOR THE UNITED STATES: 1790 TO 1940

1880	1870	1860	1850	1840	1830	1820	1810	1800	1790	
939	663	392	236	131	90	61	46	33	24	1
1	-	-	-	-	-	-	-	-	-	2
3	2	2	1	-	-	-	-	-	-	3
4	5	1	-	1	-	-	-	-	-	4
12	7	6	5	2	1	1	-	-	-	5
15	11	7	4	2	3	2	2	1	-	6
42	27	19	16	7	3	2	2	2	2	7
146	116	58	36	25	16	8	7	3	3	8
249	186	136	85	48	33	22	17	15	7	9
467	309	163	89	46	34	26	18	12	12	10
-	-	-	-	-	-	-	-	-	-	11
-	-	-	-	-	-	-	-	-	-	12
-	-	-	-	-	-	-	-	-	-	13
20	14	9	6	3	1	1	-	-	-	14
77	52	35	26	12	7	5	4	3	2	15
223	168	93	62	37	23	13	11	6	5	16
50, 155, 783	38, 558, 371	31, 443, 321	23, 191, 876	17, 069, 453	12, 866, 020	9, 638, 453	7, 239, 881	5, 308, 483	3, 929, 214	17
14, 129, 735	9, 902, 361	6, 216, 518	3, 543, 716	1, 845, 055	1, 127, 247	693, 255	525, 459	322, 371	201, 655	18
1, 206, 299	-	-	-	-	-	-	-	-	-	19
1, 917, 018	1, 616, 314	1, 379, 198	515, 547	-	-	-	-	-	-	20
1, 300, 809	1, 523, 820	266, 661	-	312, 710	-	-	-	-	-	21
1, 786, 783	989, 855	992, 922	659, 121	204, 506	202, 589	123, 706	-	-	-	22
947, 918	768, 238	452, 060	284, 355	187, 048	222, 474	126, 540	150, 095	60, 515	-	23
1, 446, 366	930, 119	670, 293	611, 328	235, 424	105, 243	70, 474	80, 342	67, 734	61, 653	24
2, 189, 447	1, 709, 541	884, 433	560, 783	404, 822	240, 371	121, 613	108, 980	54, 479	48, 182	25
1, 717, 146	1, 278, 145	976, 436	596, 086	328, 744	230, 859	155, 035	116, 271	94, 394	47, 569	26
1, 617, 949	1, 086, 329	594, 515	316, 496	171, 801	125, 711	95, 887	69, 771	45, 249	44, 251	27
36, 026, 048	28, 656, 010	25, 226, 803	19, 648, 160	15, 224, 398	11, 738, 773	8, 945, 198	6, 714, 422	4, 986, 112	3, 727, 559	28
(2)	(2)	(2)	(2)	(2)	(2)	(2)	(2)	(2)	(2)	29
6, 210, 909	4, 129, 989	2, 638, 781	1, 174, 668	517, 216	202, 589	123, 706	-	-	-	30
8, 605, 193	5, 828, 346	3, 761, 134	2, 070, 351	939, 688	530, 306	320, 720	230, 437	128, 249	61, 653	31
10, 794, 640	7, 537, 887	4, 645, 567	2, 631, 134	1, 344, 510	770, 677	442, 333	339, 417	182, 728	109, 835	32
100. 0	100. 0	100. 0	100. 0	100. 0	100. 0	100. 0	100. 0	100. 0	100. 0	33
28. 2	25. 7	19. 8	15. 3	10. 8	8. 8	7. 2	7. 3	6. 1	5. 1	34
2. 4	-	-	-	-	-	-	-	-	-	35
3. 8	4. 2	4. 4	2. 2	-	-	-	-	-	-	36
2. 6	4. 0	0. 8	-	1. 8	-	-	-	-	-	37
3. 6	2. 6	3. 2	2. 8	1. 2	1. 6	1. 3	-	-	-	38
1. 9	2. 0	1. 4	1. 2	1. 1	1. 7	1. 3	2. 1	1. 1	-	39
2. 9	2. 4	2. 1	2. 6	1. 4	0. 8	0. 7	1. 1	1. 3	1. 6	40
4. 4	4. 4	2. 8	2. 4	2. 4	1. 9	1. 3	1. 5	1. 0	1. 2	41
3. 4	3. 3	3. 1	2. 6	1. 9	1. 8	1. 6	1. 6	1. 8	1. 2	42
3. 2	2. 8	1. 9	1. 4	1. 0	1. 0	1. 0	1. 0	0. 9	1. 1	43
71. 8	74. 3	80. 2	84. 7	89. 2	91. 2	92. 8	92. 7	93. 9	94. 9	44
-	-	-	-	-	-	-	-	-	-	45
-	-	-	-	-	-	-	-	-	-	46
-	-	-	-	-	-	-	-	-	-	47
12. 4	10. 7	8. 4	5. 1	3. 0	1. 6	1. 3	-	-	-	48
17. 2	15. 1	12. 0	8. 9	5. 5	4. 1	3. 3	3. 2	2. 4	1. 6	49
21. 5	19. 5	14. 8	11. 3	7. 9	6. 0	4. 6	4. 7	3. 4	2. 8	50

[2] Not returned separately.

467750—42——3

TABLE 11.—POPULATION IN GROUPS OF PLACES CLASSIFIED ACCORDING TO SIZE, AND IN

CENSUS YEAR, AND REGION, DIVISION, AND STATE	URBAN TERRITORY							
	Places of 100,000 or more		Places of 50,000 to 100,000		Places of 25,000 to 50,000		Places of 10,000 to 25,000	
	Number of places	Population	Number of places	Population	Number of places [1]	Population	Number of places [1]	Population
UNITED STATES								
1940	92	37, 987, 989	107	7, 343, 917	213	7, 417, 093	665	9, 966, 898
1930	93	36, 325, 736	98	6, 491, 448	185	6, 425, 693	606	9, 097, 200
REGIONS:								
The North:								
1940	57	27, 628, 479	68	4, 699, 122	146	5, 180, 682	438	6, 677, 669
1930	59	27, 202, 977	67	4, 497, 466	129	4, 549, 550	423	6, 419, 340
The South:								
1940	23	6, 067, 513	30	2, 039, 870	43	1, 439, 138	154	2, 244, 976
1930	23	5, 358, 370	24	1, 519, 041	36	1, 199, 666	124	1, 829, 481
The West:								
1940	12	4, 291, 997	9	604, 925	24	797, 273	73	1, 044, 253
1930	11	3, 764, 389	7	474, 941	20	676, 477	59	848, 379
THE NORTH:								
New England:								
1940	12	2, 381, 775	13	960, 439	36	1, 298, 441	79	1, 218, 387
1930	13	2, 500, 799	12	853, 234	30	1, 103, 432	78	1, 242, 450
Middle Atlantic:								
1940	18	13, 129, 185	24	1, 637, 193	38	1, 327, 607	163	2, 553, 432
1930	18	12, 650, 337	23	1, 592, 351	35	1, 256, 970	162	2, 497, 660
East North Central:								
1940	18	9, 401, 035	23	1, 552, 458	60	2, 158, 647	128	1, 912, 698
1930	19	9, 403, 178	25	1, 577, 335	53	1, 830, 345	121	1, 788, 908
West North Central:								
1940	9	2, 716, 484	8	549, 032	12	395, 987	68	993, 152
1930	9	2, 648, 663	7	474, 546	11	358, 803	62	890, 322
THE SOUTH:								
South Atlantic:								
1940	10	2, 828, 884	17	1, 103, 103	20	684, 689	68	982, 924
1930	9	2, 322, 692	14	893, 634	18	609, 789	51	725, 071
East South Central:								
1940	6	1, 286, 747	4	280, 929	10	324, 286	31	477, 434
1930	6	1, 200, 032	3	109, 533	7	243, 411	32	478, 377
West South Central:								
1940	7	1, 951, 882	9	655, 838	13	430, 163	55	784, 618
1930	8	1, 835, 646	7	425, 874	11	346, 466	42	626, 033
THE WEST:								
Mountain:								
1940	2	472, 346	2	117, 576	7	245, 883	26	379, 771
1930	2	428, 128	1	50, 096	7	249, 057	17	239, 867
Pacific:								
1940	10	3, 819, 651	7	487, 349	17	551, 390	47	664, 482
1930	9	3, 336, 261	6	424, 845	13	427, 420	42	608, 512
NEW ENGLAND:								
Maine:								
1940	----	----	1	73, 643	2	68, 420	7	112, 758
1930	----	----	1	70, 810	2	63, 697	6	93, 503
New Hampshire:								
1940	----	----	1	77, 685	2	60, 098	7	100, 367
1930	----	----	1	76, 834	2	56, 691	7	96, 937
Vermont:								
1940	----	----	----	----	1	27, 686	2	27, 991
1930	----	----	----	----	----	----	3	53, 411
Massachusetts:								
1940	8	1, 654, 278	8	565, 315	16	623, 963	46	726, 127
1930	9	1, 774, 375	7	460, 411	14	576, 467	43	693, 428
Rhode Island:								
1940	1	253, 504	1	75, 797	6	213, 090	7	84, 576
1930	1	252, 981	1	77, 149	5	175, 792	7	95, 671
Connecticut:								
1940	3	473, 993	2	167, 999	9	305, 184	10	166, 568
1930	3	473, 443	2	168, 030	7	230, 785	12	209, 500
MIDDLE ATLANTIC:								
New York:								
1940	7	8, 935, 531	6	439, 961	10	365, 702	48	792, 092
1930	7	8, 404, 778	6	436, 076	10	364, 045	47	730, 349
New Jersey:								
1940	6	1, 222, 734	7	435, 247	16	557, 103	40	601, 872
1930	6	1, 254, 210	7	460, 809	13	475, 377	40	609, 321
Pennsylvania:								
1940	5	2, 970, 920	11	761, 985	12	404, 802	75	1, 159, 468
1930	5	2, 991, 349	10	695, 466	12	417, 548	75	1, 157, 990
EAST NORTH CENTRAL:								
Ohio:								
1940	8	2, 654, 012	4	245, 406	14	503, 237	33	542, 924
1930	8	2, 663, 801	4	242, 373	14	492, 591	33	517, 498
Indiana:								
1940	4	718, 369	4	284, 576	10	329, 421	17	235, 234
1930	5	785, 975	3	182, 154	9	292, 061	17	237, 807
Illinois:								
1940	2	3, 501, 895	7	491, 170	14	513, 383	36	551, 334
1930	2	3, 481, 407	7	483, 507	15	521, 527	34	482, 439
Michigan:								
1940	3	1, 939, 287	6	396, 664	9	356, 880	25	353, 400
1930	3	1, 893, 746	8	493, 598	6	218, 991	23	327, 343
Wisconsin:								
1940	1	587, 472	2	134, 642	13	455, 726	17	229, 806
1930	1	578, 249	3	175, 703	9	305, 175	14	223, 821
WEST NORTH CENTRAL:								
Minnesota:								
1940	3	881, 171	----	----	1	26, 312	11	170, 763
1930	3	837, 425	----	----	----	----	11	159, 580
Iowa:								
1940	1	159, 819	4	262, 266	6	196, 083	10	153, 165
1930	1	142, 559	3	196, 031	6	210, 474	11	167, 405

[1] In 1940 Bluefield, Va., and Bluefield, W. Va.; Bristol, Tenn., and Bristol, Va.; Delmar, Del., and Delmar, Md.; Harrison, Ohio, and West Harrison, Ind.; Junction City, Ark., and Junction City, La.; Texarkana, Ark., and Texarkana, Tex.; Texhoma, Okla., and Texhoma, Tex.; and Union City, Ind., and Union City, Ohio, were counted as separate incorporated places, whereas in 1930 each pair was counted as a single place. If the 1930 treatment had been applied in 1940 there would have been three fewer

UNINCORPORATED RURAL TERRITORY, BY DIVISIONS AND STATES: 1940 AND 1930

CENSUS YEAR, AND REGION, DIVISION, AND STATE	URBAN TERRITORY—continued				RURAL TERRITORY				
	Places of 5,000 to 10,000		Places of 2,500 to 5,000		Places of 1,000 to 2,500		Places under 1,000		Unincorporated territory
	Number of places	Population	Number of places [1]	Population	Number of places	Population	Number of places [1]	Population	Population
UNITED STATES									
1940	965	6,681,894	1,422	5,025,911	3,205	5,026,834	10,083	4,315,843	47,902,896
1930	851	5,897,156	1,332	4,717,590	3,087	4,820,707	10,346	4,362,746	44,636,770
REGIONS:									
The North:									
1940	588	4,097,647	765	2,721,969	1,772	2,774,281	6,173	2,606,424	19,733,836
1930	530	3,696,360	751	2,692,079	1,707	2,651,846	6,233	2,618,895	18,692,678
The South:									
1940	267	1,803,578	485	1,695,408	1,098	1,718,657	3,028	1,320,887	23,335,874
1930	221	1,499,625	427	1,498,065	1,068	1,684,059	3,231	1,371,030	21,898,296
The West:									
1940	110	780,669	172	608,534	335	533,896	882	388,532	4,833,186
1930	100	701,171	154	527,446	312	484,802	882	372,821	4,045,796
THE NORTH:									
New England:									
1940	65	463,460	26	98,040	27	44,758	44	19,225	1,952,765
1930	68	491,561	31	120,500	35	60,735	60	27,436	1,766,194
Middle Atlantic:									
1940	213	1,492,250	280	1,007,876	462	753,411	753	389,378	5,249,155
1930	194	1,363,751	287	1,033,638	447	727,558	765	382,897	4,755,588
East North Central:									
1940	204	1,431,546	277	987,975	704	1,093,265	2,115	991,483	7,097,235
1930	186	1,282,329	253	912,813	665	1,031,344	2,167	996,420	6,474,513
West North Central:									
1940	106	710,391	182	628,078	579	882,847	3,261	1,206,338	5,434,681
1930	82	558,719	180	625,128	560	832,209	3,241	1,212,142	5,696,383
THE SOUTH:									
South Atlantic:									
1940	97	651,299	193	670,827	447	702,201	1,370	568,612	9,630,612
1930	87	589,342	161	557,594	428	676,858	1,488	595,044	8,823,565
East South Central:									
1940	59	404,461	110	391,499	251	385,529	647	302,162	6,925,178
1930	45	304,737	100	352,597	242	376,610	776	337,891	6,394,026
West South Central:									
1940	111	747,818	182	633,082	400	630,927	1,011	450,113	6,780,084
1930	89	605,546	166	587,874	398	630,591	967	438,095	6,680,705
THE WEST:									
Mountain:									
1940	44	288,155	78	268,011	177	280,017	566	243,517	1,854,727
1930	39	269,556	64	221,218	164	251,571	546	227,093	1,765,203
Pacific:									
1940	66	492,514	94	340,523	158	253,879	316	145,015	2,978,459
1930	61	431,615	90	306,228	148	233,231	336	145,728	2,280,593
NEW ENGLAND:									
Maine:									
1940	10	69,379	6	18,857					504,169
1930	9	64,962	8	28,534	8	15,338	14	7,992	452,587
New Hampshire:									
1940	6	36,577	2	8,498					208,299
1930	4	24,460	4	18,157					192,214
Vermont:									
1940	7	51,948	4	15,614	20	32,836	41	17,310	185,846
1930	7	50,278	4	15,077	20	32,433	41	16,943	191,469
Massachusetts:									
1940	35	254,873	9	34,920					457,245
1930	39	287,939	10	38,806					418,188
Rhode Island:									
1940	3	22,574	1	3,842					59,963
1930	4	30,170	1	3,666					52,068
Connecticut:									
1940	4	28,109	4	16,309	7	11,922	3	1,915	537,243
1930	5	33,752	4	16,260	7	12,964	5	2,501	459,668
MIDDLE ATLANTIC:									
New York:									
1940	48	326,282	84	306,325	148	231,658	260	139,813	1,941,778
1930	41	277,831	85	308,873	146	228.791	254	135,139	1,702,184
NEW JERSEY:									
1940	53	380,281	56	197,536	84	143,840	83	42,260	579,292
1930	50	351,371	53	188,156	85	144,318	86	43,580	514,192
Pennsylvania:									
1940	112	785,687	140	504,015	230	377,913	410	207,305	2,728,085
1930	103	734,549	149	536,609	216	354,449	425	204,178	2,539,212
EAST NORTH CENTRAL:									
Ohio:									
1940	57	415,105	70	252,302	169	259,044	517	236,595	1,798,987
1930	51	359,925	64	231,183	160	247,358	528	236,786	1,655,182
Indiana:									
1940	32	205,537	31	114,575	104	166,949	327	153,854	1,219,281
1930	27	172,871	34	125,024	97	148,488	331	154,570	1,139,553
Illinois:									
1940	61	442,945	88	308,923	218	338,459	714	325,360	1,423,772
1930	56	393,926	78	272,921	211	327,745	726	323,523	1,343,659
Michigan:									
1940	35	240,333	47	168,303	118	182,242	232	116,250	1,502,747
1930	32	213,702	42	154,695	111	171,380	250	122.939	1,245,931
Wisconsin:									
1940	19	127,626	41	143,872	95	146,571	325	159,424	1,152,448
1930	20	141,905	36	128,990	87	136,373	332	158,602	1,090,188
WEST NORTH CENTRAL:									
Minnesota:									
1940	29	197,732	34	114,120	119	181,875	548	206,653	1,013,674
1930	18	123,500	41	137,111	93	135,139	562	205.208	965.990
Iowa:									
1940	23	149,498	45	163,400	127	191,549	715	279,500	982,988
1930	14	94,173	46	168,650	123	186,409	713	278,513	1,026,725

urban places (two fewer in each of the groups 2,500 to 5,000 and 10,000 to 25,000, and one more in the group 25,000 to 50,000). There would also have been five fewer rural incorporated places (all in the group of less than 1,000 population).

TABLE 11.—POPULATION IN GROUPS OF PLACES CLASSIFIED ACCORDING TO SIZE, AND IN

CENSUS YEAR, AND REGION, DIVISION, AND STATE	URBAN TERRITORY							
	Places of 100,000 or more		Places of 50,000 to 100,000		Places of 25,000 to 50,000		Places of 10,000 to 25,000	
	Number of places	Population	Number of places	Population	Number of places [1]	Population	Number of places [1]	Population
WEST NORTH CENTRAL—Continued.								
Missouri:								
1940	2	1, 215, 226	2	136, 949	2	70, 167	16	244, 275
1930	2	1, 221, 706	2	138, 462	2	59, 263	10	165, 060
North Dakota:								
1940					1	32, 580	3	52, 301
1930					1	28, 619	3	44, 301
South Dakota:								
1940					1	40, 832	5	62, 952
1930					1	33, 362	5	58, 971
Nebraska:								
1940	1	223, 844	1	81, 984			7	91, 996
1930	1	214, 006	1	75, 933			6	78, 013
Kansas:								
1940	2	236, 424	1	67, 833	1	30, 013	16	217, 700
1930	2	232, 967	1	64, 120	1	27, 085	16	216, 992
SOUTH ATLANTIC:								
Delaware:								
1940	1	112, 504						
1930	1	106, 597						
Maryland:								
1940	1	859, 100			2	71, 974	6	81, 088
1930	1	804, 874			2	68, 608	3	37, 962
District of Columbia:								
1940	1	663, 091						
1930	1	486, 869						
Virginia:								
1940	2	337, 374	3	177, 072	5	178, 511	6	76, 321
1930	2	312, 639	1	69, 206	4	149, 346	9	118, 830
West Virginia:								
1940			3	207, 849	2	60, 682	7	112, 861
1930			3	197, 639	2	58, 489	5	87, 952
North Carolina:								
1940	1	100, 899	4	250, 639	4	144, 367	17	244, 439
1930			5	313, 748	3	106, 394	13	172, 672
South Carolina:								
1940			2	133, 671	2	66, 983	6	89, 902
1930			2	113, 846	2	57, 877	5	63, 279
Georgia:								
1940	1	302, 288	4	273, 060	1	26, 282	14	206, 943
1930	1	270, 366	3	199, 195	1	43, 131	10	153, 017
Florida:								
1940	3	453, 628	1	60, 812	4	135, 890	12	171, 370
1930	3	341, 347			4	125, 944	7	91, 359
EAST SOUTH CENTRAL:								
Kentucky:								
1940	1	319, 077	1	62, 018	5	173, 482	6	73, 772
1930	1	307, 745	1	65, 252	4	138, 095	7	89, 511
Tennessee:								
1940	4	700, 087			1	25, 332	7	96, 535
1930	4	632, 609			1	25, 080	3	46, 091
Alabama:								
1940	1	267, 583	2	156, 804	3	89, 991	8	131, 605
1930	1	259, 678	2	134, 281			11	185, 622
Mississippi:								
1940			1	62, 107	1	35, 481	10	175, 522
1930					2	80, 236	11	157, 153
WEST SOUTH CENTRAL:								
Arkansas:								
1940			1	88, 039	1	36, 584	7	113, 857
1930			1	81, 679	2	42, 193	6	97, 261
Louisiana:								
1940	1	494, 537	1	98, 167	3	90, 094	5	79, 647
1930	1	458, 762	1	76, 655	2	56, 757	4	67, 480
Oklahoma:								
1940	2	346, 581			2	60, 413	17	233, 521
1930	2	326, 647			2	58, 425	12	168, 698
Texas:								
1940	4	1, 110, 764	7	469, 632	7	243, 072	26	357, 593
1930	5	1, 050, 237	5	267, 540	6	189, 091	20	292, 594
MOUNTAIN:								
Montana:								
1940					2	67, 009	4	67, 770
1930					2	68, 354	4	55, 334
Idaho:								
1940					1	26, 130	6	77, 754
1930							2	38, 015
Wyoming:								
1940							4	61, 594
1930							2	33, 980
Colorado:								
1940	1	322. 412	1	52, 162	1	36, 789	5	66, 906
1930	1	287, 861	1	50, 096	1	33, 237	5	56, 894
New Mexico:								
1940					1	35, 449	4	54, 491
1930					1	26, 570	2	22, 349
Arizona:								
1940			1	65, 414	1	36, 818		
1930					2	80. 624		
Utah:								
1940	1	149, 934			1	43, 688	2	29, 939
1930	1	140, 267			1	40, 272	1	14, 766
Nevada:								
1940							1	21, 317
1930							1	18, 529
PACIFIC:								
Washington:								
1940	3	599, 711			3	86, 759	8	118, 971
1930	3	587, 914			2	61, 390	10	142, 702
Oregon:								
1940	1	305, 394			1	30, 908	5	69, 026
1930	1	301, 815			1	26, 266	4	56, 350
California:								
1940	6	2, 914, 546	7	487, 349	13	433, 723	34	476, 485
1930	5	2, 446, 532	6	424, 845	10	339, 764	28	409, 460

[1] See note on page 28.

UNINCORPORATED RURAL TERRITORY, BY DIVISIONS AND STATES: 1940 AND 1930—Continued

CENSUS YEAR, AND REGION, DIVISION, AND STATE	URBAN TERRITORY—continued				RURAL TERRITORY				
	Places of 5,000 to 10,000		Places of 2,500 to 5,000		Places of 1,000 to 2,500		Places under 1,000		Unincorporated territory
	Number of places	Population	Number of places [1]	Population	Number of places	Population	Number of places [1]	Population	Population
WEST NORTH CENTRAL—Continued.									
Missouri:									
1940	24	155,927	41	138,152	113	178,384	593	202,827	1,442,757
1930	21	151,136	35	123,492	116	178,685	585	203,301	1,388,262
North Dakota:									
1940	6	39,225	2	7,817	36	49,861	285	97,930	362,221
1930	6	34,074	2	6,312	29	39,232	285	98,709	429,598
South Dakota:									
1940	4	24,682	9	29,621	37	53,942	247	88,433	342,499
1930	2	11,805	8	26,769	41	56,947	242	87,978	417,017
Nebraska:									
1940	8	54,912	19	61,412	69	105,997	426	158,042	537,647
1930	9	62,216	18	55,939	73	107,172	421	162,661	622,023
Kansas:									
1940	12	88,415	32	113,556	78	121,239	447	172,953	752,895
1930	12	81,815	30	106,855	85	128,625	433	175,772	846,768
SOUTH ATLANTIC:									
Delaware:									
1940	1	5,517	6	21,411	10	15,996	34	13,841	97,236
1930	---	---	4	16,549	11	17,744	36	14,050	83,440
Maryland:									
1940	3	23,172	12	45,017	29	44,573	92	45,304	651,016
1930	3	20,547	12	42,878	26	36,797	90	42,050	577,810
District of Columbia:									
1940									
1930	---	---	---	---	---	---	---	---	---
Virginia:									
1940	13	93,233	24	82,164	42	67,031	123	57,976	1,608,091
1930	10	68,993	19	66,523	42	69,099	128	57,653	1,500,562
West Virginia:									
1940	13	85,755	20	67,145	64	102,202	98	51,655	1,213,825
1930	12	85,750	17	61,674	62	98,609	107	53,583	1,085,509
North Carolina:									
1940	19	122,863	31	110,968	96	149,636	315	133,283	2,314,529
1930	17	113,093	30	103,340	91	141,572	339	134,346	2,084,511
South Carolina:									
1940	14	87,718	26	87,837	53	83,013	145	53,955	1,296,725
1930	12	73,855	19	62,223	54	88,114	171	62,129	1,217,442
Georgia:									
1940	19	129,552	39	135,683	94	146,357	419	148,830	1,754,728
1930	16	113,785	33	115,998	91	143,903	438	155,841	1,713,270
Florida:									
1940	15	103,489	35	120,602	59	93,393	144	63,768	694,462
1930	17	112,719	27	88,409	52	81,020	179	75,392	552,021
EAST SOUTH CENTRAL:									
Kentucky:									
1940	17	123,263	26	97,715	82	130,517	185	85,922	1,779,861
1930	16	112,451	24	85,972	74	117,656	242	97,497	1,600,410
Tennessee:									
1940	15	99,415	30	105,837	48	67,970	116	56,300	1,764,365
1930	14	99,184	26	93,574	49	72,008	136	63,828	1,584,182
Alabama:									
1940	16	107,803	29	102,155	63	99,237	157	75,793	1,801,990
1930	11	69,654	28	95,038	64	99,268	179	81,209	1,721,498
Mississippi:									
1940	11	73,980	25	85,792	58	87,805	189	84,147	1,578,962
1930	4	28,448	22	78,013	55	87,678	219	95,357	1,487,936
WEST SOUTH CENTRAL:									
Arkansas:									
1940	13	84,380	31	109,050	58	89,503	301	111,137	1,316,837
1930	9	56,416	31	105,329	58	89,513	282	106,577	1,275,514
Louisiana:									
1940	18	123,378	26	94,616	58	89,723	98	51,511	1,242,207
1930	11	72,564	29	101,314	53	78,415	109	55,639	1,134,007
Oklahoma:									
1940	22	139,226	31	99,922	88	139,005	357	141,538	1,176,228
1930	22	162,358	30	105,553	99	160,698	345	137,734	1,275,927
Texas:									
1940	58	400,834	94	329,494	196	312,696	255	145,927	3,044,812
1930	47	314,208	76	275,678	190	301,965	231	138,145	2,995,257
MOUNTAIN:									
Montana:									
1940	6	43,166	11	33,590	25	39,394	67	34,273	274,254
1930	6	38,245	6	19,103	24	36,270	74	34,109	286,191
Idaho:									
1940	3	18,615	16	54,209	25	36,941	100	42,425	268,799
1930	5	44,122	14	47,370	22	33,521	107	41,777	240,227
Wyoming:									
1940	2	15,358	6	16,625	18	32,050	58	17,179	107,936
1930	3	25,585	3	10,532	17	27,916	59	18,751	108,801
Colorado:									
1940	9	61,727	13	50,760	44	70,187	173	66,142	396,211
1930	10	60,916	9	30,878	42	60,826	172	60,839	394,244
New Mexico:									
1940	9	58,853	8	27,608	13	19,926	28	15,749	319,742
1930	4	25,920	9	31,977	11	17,458	29	15,335	283,708
Arizona:									
1940	8	49,399	6	22,350	10	15,301	8	6,778	303,201
1930	6	44,224	6	25,008	9	14,911	11	9,169	261,637
Utah:									
1940	5	27,297	16	54,635	38	58,050	129	58,345	128,422
1930	4	25,379	14	45,580	34	53,058	88	44,909	143,616
Nevada:									
1940	2	13,740	2	8,234	4	8,168	3	2,626	56,162
1930	1	5,165	3	10,770	5	7,611	6	2,204	46,779
PACIFIC:									
Washington:									
1940	6	43,280	20	73,248	45	70,674	137	66,931	676,617
1930	4	27,976	19	64,557	42	63,013	141	64,312	551,532
Oregon:									
1940	9	63,659	18	62,688	32	50,992	141	54,520	452,497
1930	9	61,218	13	44,097	29	46,354	147	50,996	366,690
California:									
1940	51	385,575	56	204,587	81	132,213	38	23,564	1,849,345
1930	48	342,421	58	197,574	77	123,864	48	30,420	1,362,371

TABLE 12.—POPULATION OF CITIES HAVING, IN 1940,

	CITY	1940	1930	1920	1910	1900	1890	1880
1	New York, N. Y.[1]	7,454,995	6,930,446	5,620,048	4,766,883	3,437,202	2,507,414	1,911,698
	Bronx Borough	1,394,711	1,265,258	732,016	430,980	200,507	88,908	51,980
	Brooklyn Borough	2,698,285	2,560,401	2,018,356	1,634,351	1,166,582	838,547	599,495
	Manhattan Borough	1,889,924	1,867,312	2,284,103	2,331,542	1,850,093	1,441,216	1,164,673
	Queens Borough	1,297,634	1,079,129	469,042	284,041	152,999	87,050	56,559
	Richmond Borough	174,441	158,346	116,531	85,969	67,021	51,693	38,991
2	Chicago, Ill	3,396,808	3,376,438	2,701,705	2,185,283	1,698,575	1,099,850	503,185
3	Philadelphia, Pa	1,931,334	1,950,961	1,823,779	1,549,008	1,293,697	1,046,964	847,170
4	Detroit, Mich	1,623,452	1,568,662	993,678	465,766	285,704	205,876	116,340
5	Los Angeles, Calif	1,504,277	1,238,048	576,673	319,198	102,479	50,395	11,183
6	Cleveland, Ohio	878,336	900,429	796,841	560,663	381,768	261,353	160,146
7	Baltimore, Md	859,100	804,874	733,826	558,485	508,957	434,439	332,313
8	St. Louis, Mo	816,048	821,960	772,897	687,029	575,238	451,770	350,518
9	Boston, Mass.[3]	770,816	781,188	748,060	670,585	560,892	448,477	362,839
10	Pittsburgh, Pa.[4]	671,659	669,817	588,343	533,905	451,512	343,904	235,071
11	Washington, D. C.[5]	663,091	486,869	437,571	331,069	278,718	188,932	147,293
12	San Francisco, Calif	634,536	634,394	506,676	416,912	342,782	298,997	233,959
13	Milwaukee, Wis	587,472	578,249	457,147	373,857	285,315	204,468	115,587
14	Buffalo, N. Y	575,901	573,076	506,775	423,715	352,387	255,664	155,134
15	New Orleans, La	494,537	458,762	387,219	339,075	287,104	242,039	216,090
16	Minneapolis, Minn	492,370	464,356	380,582	301,408	202,718	164,738	46,887
17	Cincinnati, Ohio	455,610	451,160	401,247	363,591	325,902	296,908	255,139
18	Newark, N. J	429,760	442,337	414,524	347,469	246,070	181,830	136,508
19	Kansas City, Mo	399,178	399,746	324,410	248,381	163,752	132,716	55,785
20	Indianapolis, Ind	386,972	364,161	314,194	233,650	169,164	105,436	75,056
21	Houston, Tex	384,514	292,352	138,276	78,800	44,633	27,557	16,513
22	Seattle, Wash	368,302	365,583	315,312	237,194	80,671	42,837	3,533
23	Rochester, N. Y	324,975	328,132	295,750	218,149	162,608	133,896	89,366
24	Denver, Colo	322,412	287,861	256,491	213,381	133,859	106,713	35,629
25	Louisville, Ky	319,077	307,745	234,891	223,928	204,731	161,129	123,758
26	Columbus, Ohio	306,087	290,564	237,031	181,511	125,560	88,150	51,647
27	Portland, Oreg	305,394	301,815	258,288	207,214	90,426	46,385	17,577
28	Atlanta, Ga	302,288	270,366	200,616	154,839	89,872	65.533	37,409
29	Oakland, Calif	302,163	284,063	216,261	150,174	66,960	48,682	34,555
30	Jersey City, N. J	301,173	316,715	298,103	267,779	206,433	163,003	120,722
31	Dallas, Tex	294,734	260,475	158,976	92,104	42,638	38,067	10,358
32	Memphis, Tenn	292,942	253,143	162,351	131,105	102,320	64,495	33,592
33	St. Paul, Minn	287,736	271,606	234,698	214,744	163,065	133,156	41,473
34	Toledo, Ohio	282,349	290,718	243,164	168,497	131,822	81,434	50,137
35	Birmingham, Ala	267,583	259,678	178,806	132,685	38,415	26,178	3,086
36	San Antonio, Tex	253,854	231,542	161,379	96,614	53,321	37,673	20,550
37	Providence, R. I	253,504	252,981	237.595	224,326	175,597	132,146	104,857
38	Akron, Ohio	244,791	255,040	208,435	69,067	42,728	27,601	16,512
39	Omaha, Nebr.[8]	223,844	214,006	191,601	124,096	102,555	140,452	30,518
40	Dayton, Ohio	210,718	200,982	152,559	116,577	85,333	61,220	38,678
41	Syracuse, N. Y	205,967	209,326	171,717	137,249	108,374	88,143	51,792
42	Oklahoma City, Okla	204,424	185,389	91,295	64,205	10,037	4,151	-----
43	San Diego, Calif	203,341	147,995	74.361	39,578	17,700	16,159	2,637
44	Worcester, Mass	193,694	195,311	179,754	145,986	118,421	84,655	58,291
45	Richmond, Va	193,042	182,929	171,667	127,628	85,050	81,388	63,600
46	Fort Worth, Tex	177,662	163,447	106,482	73,312	26,688	23,076	6,663
47	Jacksonville, Fla	173,065	129,549	91,558	57,699	28,429	17,201	7,650
48	Miami, Fla	172,172	110,637	29,571	5,471	1,681	-----	-----
49	Youngstown, Ohio	167,720	170,002	132,358	79,066	44,885	33,220	15,435
50	Nashville, Tenn	167,402	153,866	118,342	110,364	80,865	76,168	43,350
51	Hartford, Conn	166,267	164,072	138,036	98,915	79,850	53,230	42,015
52	Grand Rapids, Mich	164,292	168,592	137,634	112,571	87,565	60,278	32,016
53	Long Beach, Calif	164,271	142.032	55,593	17,809	2,252	564	-----
54	New Haven, Conn	160,605	162,655	162,537	133,605	108,027	[2] 86,045	62,882
55	Des Moines, Iowa	159,819	142,559	126,468	86,368	62,139	50,093	22,408
56	Flint, Mich	151,543	156,492	91,599	38,550	13,103	9,803	8,409
57	Salt Lake City, Utah	149,934	140,267	118,110	92,777	53,531	44,843	20,768
58	Springfield, Mass	149,554	149,900	129,614	88,926	62,059	44,179	33.340
59	Bridgeport, Conn	147,121	146,716	143,555	102,054	70,996	48,866	27,643
60	Norfolk, Va	144,332	129,710	115,777	67,452	46,624	34,871	21,966
61	Yonkers, N. Y	142,598	134,646	100,176	79.803	47,931	32,033	18,892
62	Tulsa, Okla	142,157	141,258	72,075	18,182	1,390	-----	-----
63	Scranton, Pa	140,404	143,433	137,783	129,867	102,026	75,215	45,850
64	Paterson, N. J	139,656	138,513	135,875	125,600	105,171	78,347	51,031
65	Albany. N. Y	130,577	127,412	113,344	100,253	94,151	94,923	90,758
66	Chattanooga, Tenn	128,163	119,798	57,895	44,604	30,154	29,100	12,892
67	Trenton, N. J	124,697	123,356	119,289	96,815	73,307	57,458	29,910
68	Spokane, Wash	122,001	115,514	104,437	104,402	36,848	19,922	-----
69	Kansas City, Kans	121,458	121,857	101,177	82,331	51,418	38,316	3,200
70	Fort Wayne, Ind	118,410	114,946	86,549	63,933	45,115	35,393	26,880
71	Camden, N. J	117,536	118,700	116,309	94,538	75,935	58,313	41,659
72	Erie, Pa	116,955	115,967	93.372	66,525	52,733	40,634	27,737
73	Fall River, Mass	115,428	115,274	120,485	119,295	104,863	74,398	48,961
74	Wichita, Kans	114,966	111,110	72,217	52,450	24,671	23,853	4,911
75	Wilmington, Del	112,504	106,597	110,168	87,411	76,508	61,431	42,478
76	Gary, Ind	111,719	100,426	55,378	16,802	-----	-----	-----
77	Knoxville, Tenn	111,580	105,802	77,818	36,346	32,637	22,535	9,693
78	Cambridge, Mass	110,879	113,643	109,694	104,839	91,886	70,028	52,669
79	Reading, Pa	110,568	111,171	107,784	96,071	78,961	58,661	43,278
80	New Bedford, Mass	110,341	112,597	121,217	96,652	62,442	40,733	26,845
81	Elizabeth, N. J	109,912	114,589	95.783	73,409	52,130	37,764	28,229
82	Tacoma, Wash	109,408	106,817	96,965	83,743	37,714	36,006	-----
83	Canton, Ohio	108.401	104,906	87,091	50,217	30,667	26,189	12,258
84	Tampa, Fla	108.391	101,161	51,608	37,782	15,839	5,532	720
85	Sacramento, Calif	105,958	93,750	65.908	44,696	29,282	26,386	21,420
86	Peoria. Ill	105.087	104,969	76,121	66,950	56.100	41,024	29,259
87	Somerville, Mass	102,177	103,908	93,091	77,236	61,643	40,152	24,933
88	Lowell, Mass	101,389	100,234	112.759	106,294	94,969	77,696	59,475
89	South Bend, Ind	101,268	104,193	70.983	53,684	35,999	21,819	13,280
90	Duluth, Minn	101.065	101,463	98.917	78,466	52,969	33.115	3,483
91	Charlotte, N. C	100,899	82,675	46,338	34,014	18,091	11,557	7,094
92	Utica. N. Y	100,518	101,740	94.156	74,419	56.383	44.007	33,914

[1] Population shown for years prior to 1900 is for New York and its boroughs as constituted under the act of consolidation in 1898.

[2] Corrected since publication of vol. I, 1930.

[3] Hyde Park town annexed to Boston city between 1910 and 1920. Combined population: 1910, 686,092; 1900, 574,136; 1890, 458,670; 1880, 369,927; 1870, 254,362. Hyde Park town not returned separately at earlier censuses.

[4] Includes population of Allegheny city as follows: 1900, 129,896; 1890, 105,287; 1880, 78,682; 1870, 53,180; 1860, 28,702; 1850, 21,262; 1840, 10,089; and 1830, 2,801. Allegheny city not returned separately at earlier censuses.

[5] City has been coextensive with the District of Columbia since 1895.

100,000 INHABITANTS OR MORE: 1790 TO 1940

1870	1860	1850	1840	1830	1820	1810	1800	1790	
1,478,103	1,174,779	696,115	391,114	242,278	152,056	119,734	79,216	49,401	1
37,393	23,593	8,032	5,346	3,023	2,782	2,267	1,755	1,781	
419,921	279,122	138,882	47,613	20,535	11,187	8,303	5,740	4,495	
912,292	813,669	515,547	312,710	202,589	123,706	96,373	60,515	33,131	
45,468	32,903	18,593	14,480	9,049	8,246	7,444	6,642	6,159	
33,029	25,492	15,061	10,965	7,082	6,135	5,347	4,564	3,835	
298,977	[2]112,172	29,963	4,470						2
674,022	565,529	121,376	93,665	80,462	63,802	53,722	41,220	28,522	3
79,577	45,619	21,019	9,102	2,222	1,422				4
5,728	4,385	1,610							5
92,829	43,417	17,034	6,071	1,076	606				6
267,354	212,418	169,054	102,313	80,620	62,738	46,555	26,514	13,503	7
310,864	160,773	77,860	16,469	4,977					8
250,526	177,840	136,881	93,383	61,392	43,298	33,787	24,937	18,320	9
139,256	77,923	67,863	31,204	15,369	7,248	4,768	1,565		10
109,199	61,122	40,001	23,364	18,826	13,247	8,208	[6]3,210		11
149,473	56,802	(7)							12
71,440	45,246	20,061	1,712						13
117,714	81,129	42,261	18,213	8,668	2,095	1,508			14
191,418	168,675	116,375	102,193	46,082	27,176	17,242			15
13,066	2,564								16
216,239	161,044	115,435	46,338	24,831	9,642	2,540			17
105,059	71,941	38,894	17,290	[6]10,953					18
32,260	4,418								19
48,244	18,611	8,091	2,692						20
9,382	4,845	2,396							21
1,107									22
62,386	48,204	36,403	20,191	9,207					23
4,759	4,749								24
100,753	68,033	43,194	21,210	10,341	4,012	1,357	359	200	25
31,274	18,554	17,882	6,048	2,435					26
8,293	2,874								27
21,789	9,554	2,572							28
10,500	1,543								29
82,546	29,226	6,856	3,072						30
									31
40,226	22,623	8,841							32
20,030	10,401	1,112							33
31,584	13,768	3,829	1,222						34
									35
12,256	8,235	3,488							36
68,904	50,666	41,513	23,171	16,833	11,767	10,071	7,614	6,380	37
10,006	3,477	3,266							38
16,083	1,883								39
30,473	20,081	10,977	6,067	2,950	1,000	383			40
43,051	28,119	22,271							41
									42
2,300	731								43
41,105	24,960	17,049	7,497	4,173	2,962	2,577	2,411	2,095	44
51,038	37,910	27,570	20,153	16,060	12,067	9,735	5,737	3,761	45
									46
6,912	2,118	1,045							47
									48
8,075	2,759								49
25,865	16,988	10,165	6,929	5,566	(9)	(9)	345		50
37,180	[2]26,917	[2]13,555	9,468	7,074	4,726	3,955	[10]3,523	[10]2,683	51
16,507	8,085	2,686							52
									53
50,840	39,267	20,345	12,960	10,180	7,147	5,772	4,049	[2]4,487	54
12,035	3,965								55
5,386	2,950								56
12,854	8,236								57
26,703	15,199	11,766	10,985	6,784	3,914	2,767	2,312	1,574	58
18,969	[2]12,106	[2]6,080	3,294						59
19,229	14,620	14,326	10,920	9,814	8,478	9,193	6,926	2,959	60
12,733	[10]8,218								61
									62
35,092	9,223								63
33,579	19,586	[6]11,334	[6]7,596						64
69,422	62,367	50,763	33,721	24,209	12,630	10,762	[2]5,289	3,498	65
6,093									66
22,874	17,228	6,461	4,035	3,925	3,942	3,002			67
									68
									69
17,718	[10]9,121	4,282							70
20,045	14,358	9.479	3,371						71
19,646	9,419	5,858	3,412	1,465	635	394	81		72
26,766	14,026	11,524	6,738	4,158	1,594	1,296			73
									74
30,841	21,258	13,979	8,367						75
									76
8,682	(9)	2,076							77
39,634	26,060	15,215	8,409	6,072	3,295	2,323	2,453	2,115	78
33,930	23,162	15,743	8,410	5,856	4,332	3,462	2,386		79
21,320	22,300	16,443	12,087	7,592	3,947	5,651	4,361	3,313	80
20,832	11,567	5,583	4,184	3,455	3,515	2,977			81
									82
8,660	4,041	2,603	(9)	1,257					83
796									84
16,283	13,785	6,820							85
22,849	14,045	5,095	1,467						86
14,685	8,025	3,540							87
40,928	36,827	33,383	20,796	6,474					88
7,206	3,832	1,652							89
3,131	80								90
4,473	2,265	1,065							91
28,804	22.529	17,565	12,782	8,323	2,972				92

[6] Population prior to incorporation.

[7] Returns for 1850 for San Francisco were destroyed by fire; population in 1852 according to State census of that year, 34,776.

[8] Omaha and South Omaha cities consolidated between 1910 and 1920. Combined population: 1910, 150,355; 1900, 128,556; 1890, 148,514. South Omaha not returned separately at earlier censuses.

[9] Not returned separately.

[10] Estimated.

TABLE 13.—POPULATION OF URBAN PLACES HAVING, IN 1940, 25,000 INHABITANTS OR MORE: 1910 TO 1940

[Places marked with an asterisk (*) were classified as urban under special rule in 1940. A minus sign (—) denotes decrease. Percent not shown where less than 0.1]

URBAN PLACE	POPULATION				PERCENT OF INCREASE		
	1940	1930	1920	1910	1930 to 1940	1920 to 1930	1910 to 1920
Alabama							
Anniston	25,523	22,345	17,734	12,794	14.2	26.0	38.6
Birmingham	267,583	259,678	178,806	132,685	3.0	45.2	34.8
Gadsden	36,975	24,042	14,737	10,557	53.8	63.1	39.6
Mobile	78,720	68,202	60,777	51,521	15.4	12.2	18.0
Montgomery	78,084	66,079	43,464	38,136	18.2	52.0	14.0
Tuscaloosa	27,493	20,659	11,996	8,407	33.1	72.2	42.7
Arizona							
Phoenix	65,414	48,118	29,053	11,134	35.9	65.6	160.9
Tucson	[1] 36,818	32,506	20,292	13,193	13.3	60.2	53.8
Arkansas							
Fort Smith	36,584	31,429	28,870	23,975	16.4	8.9	20.4
Little Rock	88,039	81,679	65,142	45,941	7.8	25.4	41.8
California							
Alameda	36,256	35,033	28,806	23,383	3.5	21.6	23.2
Alhambra	38,935	29,472	9,096	5,021	32.1	224.0	81.2
Bakersfield	29,252	26,015	18,638	12,727	12.4	39.6	46.4
Belvedere township*	37,192	33,023	6,339	2,621	12.6	420.9	141.9
Berkeley	85,547	82,109	56,036	40,434	4.2	46.5	38.6
Beverly Hills	26,823	17,429	674	...	53.9	2,485.9	...
Burbank	34,337	16,662	2,913	...	106.1	472.0	...
Fresno	60,685	52,513	45,086	24,892	15.6	16.5	81.1
Glendale	82,582	62,736	13,536	2,746	31.6	363.5	392.9
Huntington Park	28,648	24,591	4,513	1,299	16.5	444.9	247.4
Inglewood	30,114	19,480	3,286	1,536	54.6	492.8	113.9
Long Beach	164,271	142,032	55,593	17,809	15.7	155.5	212.2
Los Angeles	1,504,277	1,238,048	576,673	319,198	21.5	114.7	80.7
Oakland	302,163	284,063	216,261	150,174	6.4	31.4	44.0
Pasadena	81,864	76,086	45,354	30,291	7.6	67.8	49.7
Riverside	34,696	29,696	19,341	15,212	16.8	53.5	27.1
Sacramento	105,958	93,750	65,908	44,696	13.0	42.2	47.5
San Bernardino	43,646	37,481	18,721	12,779	16.4	100.2	46.5
San Diego	203,341	147,995	74,361	39,578	37.4	99.0	87.9
San Francisco	634,536	634,394	506,676	416,912	...	25.2	21.5
San Jose [1a]	68,457	57,651	39,642	28,946	18.7	45.4	37.0
Santa Ana	31,921	30,322	15,485	8,429	5.3	95.8	83.7
Santa Barbara	34,958	33,613	19,441	11,659	4.0	72.9	66.7
Santa Monica	53,500	37,146	15,252	7,847	44.0	143.5	94.4
South Gate	26,945	19,632	...	...	37.3	...	...
Stockton	54,714	47,963	40,296	23,253	14.1	19.0	73.3
Colorado							
Colorado Springs [2]	36,789	33,237	30,105	29,078	10.7	10.4	3.5
Denver	322,412	287,861	256,491	213,381	12.0	12.2	20.2
Pueblo	52,162	50,096	43,050	41,747	4.1	16.4	3.1
Connecticut							
Bridgeport	147,121	146,716	143,555	102,054	0.3	2.2	40.7
Bristol	30,167	28,451	20,620	9,527	6.0	38.0	116.4
Hartford	166,267	164,072	138,036	98,915	1.3	18.9	39.6
Meriden	39,494	38,481	29,867	27,265	2.6	28.8	9.5
Middletown	26,495	24,554	13,638	11,851	7.9	80.0	15.1
New Britain	68,685	68,128	59,316	43,916	0.8	14.9	35.1
New Haven	160,605	162,655	162,537	133,605	−1.3	0.1	21.7
New London	30,456	29,640	25,688	19,659	2.8	15.4	30.7
Norwalk [3]	39,849	36,019	27,743	6,954	10.6	29.8	299.0
Stamford	47,938	46,346	35,096	25,138	3.4	32.1	39.6
Torrington	26,988	26,040	20,623	15,483	3.6	26.3	33.2
Waterbury	99,314	99,902	91,715	73,141	−0.6	8.9	25.4
West Hartford town*	33,776	24,941	8,854	4,808	35.4	181.7	84.2
West Haven town*	30,021	25,808	...	...	16.3	...	...
Delaware							
Wilmington	112,504	106,597	110,168	87,411	5.5	−3.2	26.0
District of Columbia							
Washington [4]	663,091	486,869	437,571	331,069	36.2	11.3	32.2
Florida							
Jacksonville	173,065	129,549	91,558	57,699	33.6	41.5	58.7
Miami	172,172	110,637	29,571	5,471	55.6	274.1	440.5
Miami Beach	28,012	6,494	644	...	331.4	908.4	...
Orlando	36,736	27,330	9,282	3,894	34.4	194.4	138.4
Pensacola	37,449	31,579	31,035	22,982	18.6	1.8	35.0
St. Petersburg	60,812	40,425	14,237	4,127	50.4	183.9	245.0
Tampa	108,391	101,161	51,608	37,782	7.1	96.0	36.6
West Palm Beach	33,693	26,610	8,659	1,743	26.6	207.3	396.8
Georgia							
Atlanta	302,288	270,366	200,616	154,839	11.8	34.8	29.6
Augusta	65,919	60,342	52,548	41,040	9.2	14.8	28.0
Columbus	53,280	43,131	31,125	20,554	23.5	38.6	51.4
Macon	57,865	53,829	52,995	40,665	7.5	1.6	30.3
Georgia—Continued							
Rome	26,282	21,843	13,252	12,099	20.3	64.8	9.5
Savannah	95,996	85,024	83,252	65,064	12.9	2.1	28.0
Idaho							
Boise City	26,130	21,544	21,393	17,358	21.3	0.7	23.2
Illinois							
Alton	31,255	30,151	24,682	17,528	3.7	22.2	40.8
Aurora	47,170	46,589	36,397	29,807	1.2	28.0	22.1
Belleville	28,405	28,425	24,823	21,122	−0.1	14.5	17.5
Berwyn	48,451	47,027	14,150	5,841	3.0	232.3	142.3
Bloomington	32,868	30,930	28,725	25,768	6.3	7.7	11.5
Chicago	3,396,808	3,376,438	2,701,705	2,185,283	0.6	25.0	23.6
Cicero	64,712	66,602	44,995	14,557	−2.8	48.0	209.1
Danville	36,919	36,765	33,776	27,871	0.4	8.8	21.2
Decatur	59,305	57,510	43,818	31,140	3.1	31.2	40.7
East St. Louis	75,609	74,347	66,767	58,547	1.7	11.4	14.0
Elgin	38,333	35,929	27,454	25,976	6.7	30.9	5.7
Evanston	65,389	63,338	37,234	24,978	3.2	70.1	49.1
Galesburg	28,876	28,830	23,834	22,089	0.2	21.0	7.9
Joliet	42,365	42,993	38,442	34,670	−1.5	11.8	10.9
Maywood	26,648	25,829	12,072	8,033	3.2	114.0	50.3
Moline	34,608	32,236	30,734	24,199	7.4	4.9	27.0
Oak Park	66,015	63,982	39,858	19,444	3.2	60.5	105.0
Peoria	105,087	104,969	76,121	66,950	0.1	37.9	13.7
Quincy	40,469	39,241	35,978	36,587	3.1	9.1	−1.7
Rockford	84,637	85,864	65,651	45,401	−1.4	30.8	44.6
Rock Island	42,775	37,953	35,177	24,335	12.7	7.9	44.6
Springfield	75,503	71,864	59,183	51,678	5.1	21.4	14.5
Waukegan	34,241	33,499	19,226	16,069	2.2	74.2	19.6
Indiana							
Anderson	41,572	39,804	29,767	22,476	4.4	33.7	32.4
East Chicago	54,637	54,784	35,967	19,098	−0.3	52.3	88.3
Elkhart	33,434	32,949	24,277	19,282	1.5	35.7	25.9
Evansville	97,062	102,249	85,264	69,647	−5.1	19.9	22.4
Fort Wayne	118,410	114,946	86,549	63,933	3.0	32.8	35.4
Gary	111,719	100,426	55,378	16,802	11.2	81.3	229.6
Hammond	70,184	64,560	36,004	20,925	8.7	79.3	72.1
Indianapolis	386,972	364,161	314,194	233,650	6.3	15.9	34.5
Kokomo	33,795	32,843	30,067	17,010	2.9	9.2	76.8
Lafayette	28,798	26,240	22,486	20,081	9.7	16.7	12.0
Marion	26,767	24,496	23,747	19,359	9.3	3.2	22.7
Michigan City	26,476	26,735	19,457	19,027	−1.0	37.4	2.3
Mishawaka	28,298	28,630	15,195	11,886	−1.2	88.4	27.8
Muncie	49,720	46,548	36,524	24,005	6.8	27.4	52.2
New Albany	25,414	25,819	22,992	20,629	−1.6	12.3	11.5
Richmond	35,147	32,493	26,765	22,324	8.2	21.4	19.9
South Bend	101,268	104,193	70,983	53,684	−2.8	46.8	32.2
Terre Haute	62,693	62,810	66,083	58,157	−0.2	−5.0	13.6
Iowa							
Burlington	25,832	26,755	24,057	24,324	−3.4	11.2	−1.1
Cedar Rapids	62,120	56,097	45,566	32,811	10.7	23.1	38.9
Clinton	26,270	25,726	24,151	25,577	2.1	6.5	−5.6
Council Bluffs	41,439	42,048	36,162	29,292	−1.4	16.3	23.5
Davenport	66,039	60,751	56,727	43,028	8.7	7.1	31.8
Des Moines	159,819	142,559	126,468	86,368	12.1	12.7	46.4
Dubuque	43,892	41,679	39,141	38,494	5.3	6.5	1.7
Mason City	27,080	23,304	20,065	11,230	16.2	16.1	78.7
Ottumwa	31,570	28,075	23,003	22,012	12.4	22.0	4.5
Sioux City	82,364	79,183	71,227	47,828	4.0	11.2	48.9
Waterloo	51,743	46,191	36,230	26,693	12.0	27.5	35.7
Kansas							
Hutchinson	30,013	27,085	23,298	16,364	10.8	16.3	42.4
Kansas City	121,458	121,857	101,177	82,331	−0.3	20.4	22.9
Topeka	67,833	64,120	50,022	43,684	5.8	28.2	14.5
Wichita	114,966	111,110	72,217	52,450	3.5	53.9	37.7
Kentucky							
Ashland	29,537	29,074	14,729	8,688	1.6	97.4	69.5
Covington	62,018	65,252	57,121	53,270	−5.0	14.2	7.2
Lexington	49,304	45,736	41,534	35,099	7.8	10.1	18.3
Louisville	319,077	307,745	234,891	223,928	3.7	31.0	4.9
Newport	30,631	29,744	29,317	30,309	3.0	1.5	−3.3
Owensboro	30,245	22,765	17,424	16,011	32.9	30.7	8.8
Paducah	33,765	33,541	24,735	22,760	0.7	35.6	8.7
Louisiana							
Alexandria	27,066	23,025	17,510	11,213	17.6	31.5	56.2
Baton Rouge	34,719	30,729	21,782	14,897	13.0	41.1	46.2
Monroe	28,309	26,028	12,675	10,209	8.8	105.3	24.2
New Orleans	494,537	458,762	387,219	339,075	7.8	18.5	14.2
Shreveport	98,167	76,655	43,874	28,015	28.1	74.7	56.6
Maine							
Bangor	29,822	28,749	25,978	24,803	3.7	10.7	4.7
Lewiston	38,598	34,948	31,791	26,247	10.4	9.9	21.1
Portland	73,643	70,810	69,272	58,571	4.0	2.2	18.3

[1] Includes population, 1,066, of South Tucson city, separately incorporated in 1939. Revised 1940 population figure for Tucson is 35,752. The urban-rural tabulations have not been adjusted for this correction.

[1a] Willow Glen city annexed in 1936; combined population in 1930, 61,818.

[2] Colorado City and Colorado Springs city consolidated as Colorado Springs city between 1910 and 1920; combined population in 1910, 33,411.

[3] Norwalk and South Norwalk cities consolidated and made coextensive with Norwalk town between 1910 and 1920; combined population in 1910, 15,922.

[4] Coextensive with the District of Columbia since 1895.

UNITED STATES SUMMARY

TABLE 13.—POPULATION OF URBAN PLACES HAVING, IN 1940, 25,000 INHABITANTS OR MORE: 1910 TO 1940—Con.

[Places marked with an asterisk (*) were classified as urban under special rule in 1940. A minus sign (—) denotes decrease. Percent not shown where less than 0.1]

URBAN PLACE	POPULATION				PERCENT OF INCREASE		
	1940	1930	1920	1910	1930 to 1940	1920 to 1930	1910 to 1920
Maryland							
Baltimore	859, 100	804, 874	733, 826	558, 485	6. 7	9. 7	31. 4
Cumberland	39, 483	37, 747	29, 837	21, 839	4. 6	26. 5	36. 6
Hagerstown	32, 491	30, 861	28, 064	16, 507	5. 3	10. 0	70. 0
Massachusetts							
Arlington town*	40, 013	36, 094	18, 665	11, 187	10. 9	93. 4	66. 8
Belmont town*	26, 867	21, 748	10, 749	5, 542	23. 5	102. 3	94. 0
Beverly	25, 537	25, 086	22, 561	18, 650	1. 8	11. 2	21. 0
Boston [5]	770, 816	781, 188	748, 060	670, 585	—1. 3	4. 4	11. 6
Brockton	62, 343	63, 797	66, 254	56, 878	—2. 3	—3. 7	16. 5
Brookline town*	49, 786	47, 490	37, 748	27, 792	4. 8	25. 8	35. 8
Cambridge	110, 879	113, 643	109, 694	104, 839	—2. 4	3. 6	4. 6
Chelsea	41, 259	45, 816	43, 184	32, 452	—9. 9	6. 1	33. 1
Chicopee	41, 664	43, 930	36, 214	25, 401	—5. 2	21. 3	42. 6
Everett	46, 784	48, 424	40, 120	33, 484	—3. 4	20. 7	19. 8
Fall River	115, 428	115, 274	120, 485	119, 295	0. 1	—4. 3	1. 0
Fitchburg	41, 824	40, 692	41, 029	37, 826	2. 8	—0. 8	8. 5
Haverhill	46, 752	48, 710	53, 884	44, 115	—4. 0	—9. 6	22. 1
Holyoke	53, 750	56, 537	60, 203	57, 730	—4. 9	—6. 1	4. 3
Lawrence	84, 323	85, 068	94, 270	85, 892	—0. 9	—9. 8	9. 8
Lowell	101, 389	100, 234	112, 759	106, 294	1. 2	—11. 1	6. 1
Lynn	98, 123	102, 320	99, 148	89, 336	—4. 1	3. 2	11. 0
Malden	58, 010	58, 036	49, 103	44, 404	----	18. 2	10. 6
Medford	63, 083	59, 714	39, 038	23, 150	5. 6	53. 0	68. 6
Melrose	25, 333	23, 170	18, 204	15, 715	9. 3	27. 3	15. 8
New Bedford	110, 341	112, 597	121, 217	96, 652	—2. 0	—7. 1	25. 4
Newton	69, 873	65, 276	46, 054	39, 806	7. 0	41. 7	15. 7
Pittsfield	49, 684	49, 677	41, 763	32, 121	----	18. 9	30. 0
Quincy	75, 810	71, 983	47, 876	32, 642	5. 3	50. 4	46. 7
Revere	34, 405	35, 680	28, 823	18, 219	—3. 6	23. 8	58. 2
Salem	41, 213	43, 353	42, 529	43, 697	—4. 9	1. 9	—2. 7
Somerville	102, 177	103. 908	93, 091	77, 236	—1. 7	11. 6	20. 5
Springfield	149, 554	149, 900	129, 614	88, 926	—0. 2	15. 7	45. 8
Taunton	37, 395	37, 355	37, 137	34, 259	0. 1	0. 6	8. 4
Waltham	40, 020	39, 247	30, 915	27, 834	2. 0	27. 0	11. 1
Watertown town*	35, 427	34, 913	21, 457	12, 875	1. 5	62. 7	66. 7
Worcester	193, 694	195, 311	179, 754	145, 986	—0. 8	8. 7	23. 1
Michigan							
Ann Arbor	29, 815	26, 944	19, 516	14, 817	10. 7	38. 1	31. 7
Battle Creek	43, 453	43, 573	36, 164	25, 267	—0. 3	20. 5	43. 1
Bay City	47, 956	47, 355	47, 554	45, 166	1. 3	—0. 4	5. 3
Dearborn	63, 584	50, 358	2, 470	911	26. 3	1, 938. 8	171. 1
Detroit	1, 623, 452	1, 568, 662	993, 678	465, 766	3. 5	57. 9	113. 3
Flint	151, 543	156, 492	91, 599	38, 550	—3. 2	70. 8	137. 6
Grand Rapids	164, 292	168, 592	137, 634	112, 571	—2. 6	22. 5	22. 3
Hamtramck	49, 839	56, 268	48, 615	3, 559	—11. 4	15. 7	1,266.0
Highland Park	50, 810	52, 959	46, 499	4, 120	—4. 1	13. 9	1,028.6
Jackson	49, 656	55, 187	48, 374	31, 433	—10. 0	14. 1	53. 9
Kalamazoo	54, 097	54, 786	48, 487	39, 437	—1. 3	13. 0	22. 9
Lansing	78, 753	78, 397	57, 327	31, 229	0. 5	36. 8	83. 6
Muskegon	47, 697	41, 390	36, 570	24, 062	15. 2	13. 2	52. 0
Pontiac	66, 626	64, 928	34, 273	14, 532	2. 6	89. 4	135. 8
Port Huron	32, 759	31, 361	25, 944	18, 863	4. 5	20. 9	37. 5
Royal Oak	25, 087	22, 904	6, 007	1, 071	9. 5	281. 3	460. 9
Saginaw	82, 794	80, 715	61, 903	50, 510	2. 6	30. 4	22. 6
Wyandotte	30, 618	28, 368	13, 851	8, 287	7. 9	104. 8	67. 1
Minnesota							
Duluth	101, 065	101, 463	98, 917	78, 466	—0. 4	2. 6	26. 1
Minneapolis	492, 370	464, 356	380, 582	301, 408	6. 0	22. 0	26. 3
Rochester	26, 312	20, 621	13, 722	7, 844	27. 6	50. 3	74. 9
St. Paul	287, 736	271, 606	234, 698	214, 744	5. 9	15. 7	9. 3
Mississippi							
Jackson	62, 107	48, 282	22, 817	21, 262	28. 6	111. 6	7. 3
Meridian	35, 481	31, 954	23, 399	23, 285	11. 0	36. 6	0. 5
Missouri							
Joplin	37, 144	33, 454	29, 902	32, 073	11. 0	11. 9	—6. 8
Kansas City	399, 178	399, 746	324, 410	248, 381	—0. 1	23. 2	30. 6
St. Joseph	75, 711	80, 935	77, 939	77, 403	—6. 5	3. 8	0. 7
St. Louis	816, 048	821, 960	772, 897	687, 029	—0. 7	6. 3	12. 5
Springfield	61, 238	57, 527	39, 631	35, 201	6. 5	45. 2	12. 6
University City	33, 023	25, 809	6, 792	2, 417	28. 0	280. 0	181. 0
Montana							
Butte	37, 081	39, 532	41, 611	39, 165	—6. 2	—5. 0	6. 2
Great Falls	29, 928	28, 822	24, 121	13, 948	3. 8	19. 5	72. 9
Nebraska							
Lincoln	81, 984	75, 933	54, 948	43, 973	8. 0	38. 2	25. 0
Omaha [6]	223, 844	214, 006	191, 601	124, 096	4. 6	11. 7	54. 4
New Hampshire							
Concord	27, 171	25, 228	22, 167	21, 497	7. 7	13. 8	3. 1
Manchester	77, 685	76, 834	78, 384	70, 063	1. 1	—2. 0	11. 9
Nashua	32, 927	31, 463	28, 379	26, 005	4. 7	10. 9	9. 1
New Jersey							
Atlantic City	64, 094	66, 198	50, 707	46, 150	—3. 2	30. 6	9. 9
Bayonne	79, 198	88, 979	76, 754	55, 545	—11. 0	15. 9	38. 2
Belleville	28, 167	26, 974	15, 660	--------	4. 4	72. 2	-----
Bloomfield	41, 623	38, 077	22, 019	15, 070	9. 3	72. 9	46. 1
Camden	117, 536	118, 700	116, 309	94, 538	—1. 0	2. 1	23. 0
Clifton	48, 827	46, 875	26, 470	--------	4. 2	77. 1	-----
East Orange	68, 945	68, 020	50, 710	34, 371	1. 4	34. 1	47. 5
Elizabeth	109, 912	114, 589	95, 783	73, 409	—4. 1	19. 6	30. 5
Garfield	28, 044	29, 739	19, 381	10, 213	—5. 7	53. 4	89. 8
Hackensack	26, 279	24, 568	17, 667	14, 050	7. 0	39. 1	25. 7
Hoboken	50, 115	59, 261	68, 166	70, 324	—15. 4	—13. 1	—3. 1
Irvington	55, 328	56, 733	25, 480	11, 877	—2. 5	122. 7	114. 5
Jersey City	301, 173	316, 715	298, 103	267, 779	—4. 9	6. 2	11. 3
Kearny	39, 467	40, 716	26, 724	18, 659	—3. 1	52. 4	43. 2
Montclair	39, 807	42, 017	28, 810	21, 550	—5. 3	45. 8	33. 7
Newark	429, 760	442, 337	414, 524	347, 469	—2. 8	6. 7	19. 3
New Brunswick	33, 180	34, 555	32, 779	23, 388	—4. 0	5. 4	40. 2
North Bergen township*	39, 714	40, 714	23, 344	15, 662	—2. 5	74. 4	49. 0
Orange	35, 717	35, 399	33, 268	29, 630	0. 9	6. 4	12. 3
Passaic	61, 394	62, 959	63, 841	54, 773	—2. 5	—1. 4	16. 6
Paterson	139, 656	138, 513	135, 875	125, 600	0. 8	1. 9	8. 2
Perth Amboy	41, 242	43, 516	41, 707	32, 121	—5. 2	4. 3	29. 8
Plainfield	37, 469	34, 422	27, 700	20, 550	8. 9	24. 3	34. 8
Teaneck township*	25, 275	16, 513	4, 192	2, 082	53. 1	293. 9	101. 3
Trenton	124, 697	123, 356	119, 289	96, 815	1. 1	3. 4	23. 2
Union City [7]	56, 173	58, 659	20, 651	21, 023	—4. 2	184. 0	—1. 8
West New York	39, 439	37, 107	29, 926	13, 560	6. 3	24. 0	120. 7
West Orange	25, 662	24, 327	15, 573	10, 980	5. 5	56. 2	41. 8
Woodbridge township*	27, 191	25, 266	13, 423	8, 949	7. 6	88. 2	50. 0
New Mexico							
Albuquerque	35, 449	26, 570	15, 157	11, 020	33. 4	75. 3	37. 5
New York							
Albany	130, 577	127, 412	113, 344	100, 253	2. 5	12. 4	13. 1
Amsterdam	33, 329	34, 817	33, 524	31, 267	—4. 3	3. 9	7. 2
Auburn	35, 753	36, 652	36, 192	34, 668	—2. 5	1. 3	4. 4
Binghamton	78, 309	76, 662	66, 800	48, 443	2. 1	14. 8	37. 9
Buffalo	575, 901	573, 076	506, 775	423, 715	0. 5	13. 1	19. 6
Elmira	45, 106	47, 397	45, 393	37, 170	—4. 8	4. 4	22. 1
Jamestown	42, 638	45, 155	38, 917	31, 297	—5. 6	16. 0	24. 3
Kingston	28, 589	28, 088	26, 688	25, 908	1. 8	5. 2	3. 0
Mount Vernon	67, 362	61, 499	42, 726	30, 919	9. 5	43. 9	38. 2
Newburgh	31, 883	31, 275	30, 366	27, 805	1. 9	3. 0	9. 2
New Rochelle	58, 408	54, 000	36, 213	28, 867	8. 2	49. 1	25. 4
New York City	7, 454, 995	6, 930, 446	5, 620, 048	4, 766, 883	7. 6	23. 3	17. 9
Bronx Borough	1, 394, 711	1, 265, 258	732, 016	430, 980	10. 2	72. 8	69. 8
Brooklyn Borough	2, 698, 285	2, 560, 401	2, 018, 356	1, 634, 351	5. 4	26. 9	23. 5
Manhattan Borough	1, 889, 924	1, 867, 312	2, 284, 103	2, 331, 542	1. 2	—18. 2	—2. 0
Queens Borough	1, 297, 634	1, 079, 129	469, 042	284, 041	20. 2	130. 1	65. 1
Richmond Borough	174, 441	158, 346	116, 531	85, 969	10. 2	35. 9	35. 6
Niagara Falls	78, 029	75, 460	50, 760	30, 445	3. 4	48. 7	66. 7
Poughkeepsie	40, 478	40, 288	35, 000	27, 936	0. 5	15. 1	25. 3
Rochester	324, 975	328, 132	295, 750	218, 149	—1. 0	10. 9	35. 6
Rome	34, 214	32, 338	26, 341	20, 497	5. 8	22. 8	28. 5
Schenectady	87, 549	95, 692	88, 723	72, 826	—8. 5	7. 9	21. 8
Syracuse	205, 967	209, 326	171, 717	137, 249	—1. 6	21. 9	25. 1
Troy	70, 304	72, 763	71, 996	76, 813	—3. 4	1. 1	—6. 3
Utica	100, 518	101, 740	94, 156	74, 419	—1. 2	8. 1	26. 5
Watertown	33, 385	32, 205	31, 285	26, 730	3. 7	2. 9	17. 0
White Plains	40. 327	35, 830	21, 031	[8] 15, 949	12. 6	70. 4	31. 9
Yonkers	142, 598	134, 646	100, 176	79, 803	5. 9	34. 4	25. 5
North Carolina							
Asheville	51, 310	50, 193	28, 504	18, 762	2. 2	76. 1	51. 9
Charlotte	100, 899	82, 675	46, 338	34, 014	22. 0	78. 4	36. 2
Durham	60, 195	52, 037	21, 719	18, 241	15. 7	139. 6	19. 1
Greensboro	59, 319	53, 569	19, 861	15, 895	10. 7	169. 7	25. 0
High Point	38, 495	36, 745	14, 302	9, 525	4. 8	156. 9	50. 2
Raleigh	46, 897	37, 379	24, 418	19, 218	25. 5	53. 1	27. 1
Rocky Mount	25, 568	21, 412	12, 742	8, 051	19. 4	68. 0	58. 3
Wilmington	33, 407	32, 270	33, 372	25, 748	3. 5	—3. 3	29. 6
Winston-Salem [9]	79, 815	75, 274	48, 395	22, 700	6. 0	55. 5	113. 2
North Dakota							
Fargo	32, 580	28, 619	21, 961	14, 331	13. 8	30. 3	53. 2
Ohio							
Akron	244, 791	255, 040	208, 435	69, 067	—4. 0	22. 4	201. 8
Canton	108, 401	104, 906	87, 091	50, 217	3. 3	20. 5	73. 4
Cincinnati	455, 610	451, 160	401, 247	363, 591	1. 0	12. 4	10. 4
Cleveland	878, 336	900, 429	796, 841	560, 663	—2. 5	13. 0	42. 1
Cleveland Heights	54, 992	50, 945	15, 236	2, 955	7. 9	234. 4	415. 6
Columbus	306, 087	290, 564	237, 031	181, 511	5. 3	22. 6	30. 6
Dayton	210, 718	200, 982	152, 559	116, 577	4. 8	31. 7	30. 9
East Cleveland	39, 495	39, 667	27, 292	9, 179	—0. 4	45. 3	197. 3

[5] Hyde Park town annexed to Boston city in 1912; combined population in 1910, 686,092.
[6] Omaha and South Omaha cities consolidated as Omaha city between 1910 and 1920; combined population in 1910, 150,355.
[7] Union and West Hoboken towns consolidated as Union City in 1925; combined population in 1920, 60,725; in 1910, 56,426.
[8] Population of White Plains village before its consolidation with White-Plains town as White Plains city.
[9] Winston city and Salem town consolidated as Winston-Salem city between 1910 and 1920. Figure shown for 1910 represents combined population of Winston and Salem.

467750—42——4

TABLE 13.—POPULATION OF URBAN PLACES HAVING, IN 1940, 25,000 INHABITANTS OR MORE: 1910 TO 1940—Con.

[Places marked with an asterisk (*) were classified as urban under special rule in 1940. A minus sign (—) denotes decrease. Percent not shown where less than 0.1]

URBAN PLACE	POPULATION				PERCENT OF INCREASE		
	1940	193	1920	1910	1930 to 1940	1920 to 1930	1910 to 1920
Ohio—Continued							
Elyria	25, 120	25, 633	20, 474	14, 825	−2. 0	25. 2	38. 1
Hamilton	50, 592	52, 176	39, 675	35, 279	−3. 0	31. 5	12. 5
Lakewood	69, 160	70, 509	41, 732	15, 181	−1. 9	69. 0	174. 9
Lima	44, 711	42, 287	41, 326	30, 508	5. 7	2. 3	35. 5
Lorain	44, 125	44, 512	37, 295	28, 883	−0. 9	19. 4	29. 1
Mansfield	37, 154	33, 525	27, 824	20, 768	10. 8	20. 5	34. 0
Marion	30, 817	31, 084	27, 891	18, 232	−0. 9	11. 4	53. 0
Massillon	26, 644	26, 400	17, 428	13, 879	0. 9	51. 5	25. 6
Middletown	31, 220	29, 992	23, 594	13, 152	4. 1	27. 1	79. 4
Newark	31, 487	30, 596	26, 718	25, 404	2. 9	14. 5	5. 2
Norwood	34, 010	33, 411	24, 966	16, 185	1. 8	33. 8	54. 3
Portsmouth	40, 466	42, 560	33, 011	23, 481	−4. 9	28. 9	40. 6
Springfield	70, 662	68, 743	60, 840	46, 921	2. 8	13. 0	29. 7
Steubenville	37, 651	35, 422	28, 508	22, 391	6. 3	24. 3	27. 3
Toledo	282, 349	290, 718	243, 164	168, 497	−2. 9	19. 6	44. 3
Warren	42, 837	41, 062	27, 050	11, 081	4. 3	51. 8	144. 1
Youngstown	167, 720	170, 002	132, 358	79, 066	−1. 3	28. 4	67. 4
Zanesville	37, 500	36, 440	29, 569	28, 026	2. 9	23. 2	5. 5
Oklahoma							
Enid	28, 081	26, 399	16, 576	13, 799	6. 4	59. 3	20. 1
Muskogee	32, 332	32, 026	30, 277	25, 278	1. 0	5. 8	19. 8
Oklahoma City	204, 424	185, 389	91, 295	64, 205	10. 3	103. 1	42. 2
Tulsa	142, 157	141, 258	72, 075	18, 182	0. 6	96. 0	296. 4
Oregon							
Portland	305, 394	301, 815	258, 288	207, 214	1. 2	16. 9	24. 6
Salem	30, 908	26, 266	17, 679	14, 094	17. 7	48. 6	25. 4
Pennsylvania							
Aliquippa [10]	27, 023	27, 116	2, 931	1, 743	−0. 3	825. 1	68. 2
Allentown	96, 904	92, 563	73, 502	51, 913	4. 7	25. 9	41. 6
Altoona	80, 214	82, 054	60, 331	52, 127	−2. 2	36. 0	15. 7
Bethlehem [11]	58, 490	57, 892	50, 358	12, 837	1. 0	15. 0	292. 3
Chester	59, 285	59, 164	58, 030	38, 537	0. 2	2. 0	50. 6
Easton	33, 589	34, 468	33, 813	28, 523	−2. 6	1. 9	18. 5
Erie	116, 955	115, 967	93, 372	66, 525	0. 9	24. 2	40. 4
Harrisburg	83, 893	80, 339	75, 917	64, 186	4. 4	5. 8	18. 3
Haverford township*	27, 594	21, 362	6, 631	3, 989	29. 2	222. 2	66. 2
Hazleton	38, 009	36, 765	32, 277	25, 452	3. 4	13. 9	26. 8
Johnstown	66, 668	66, 993	67, 327	55, 482	−0. 5	−0. 5	21. 3
Lancaster	61, 345	59, 949	53, 150	47, 227	2. 3	12. 8	12. 5
Lebanon	27, 206	25, 561	24, 643	19, 240	6. 4	3. 7	28. 1
Lower Merion township*	39, 566	35, 166	23, 866	17, 671	12. 5	47. 3	35. 1
McKeesport	55, 355	54, 632	46, 781	42, 694	1. 3	16. 8	9. 6
New Castle	47, 638	48, 674	44, 938	36, 280	−2. 1	8. 3	23. 9
Norristown	38, 181	35, 853	32, 319	27, 875	6. 5	10. 9	15. 9
Philadelphia	1, 931, 334	1, 950, 961	1, 823, 779	1, 549, 008	−1. 0	7. 0	17. 7
Pittsburgh	671, 659	669, 817	588, 343	533, 905	0. 3	13. 8	10. 2
Reading	110, 568	111, 171	107, 784	96, 071	−0. 5	3. 1	12. 2
Scranton	140, 404	143, 433	137, 783	129, 867	−2. 1	4. 1	6. 1
Sharon	25, 622	25, 908	21, 747	15, 270	−1. 1	19. 1	42. 4
Upper Darby township*	56, 883	[12] 47, 145	8, 956	5, 385	20. 7	426. 4	66. 3
Washington	26, 166	24, 545	21, 480	18, 778	6. 6	14. 3	14. 4
Wilkes-Barre	86, 236	86, 626	73, 833	67, 105	−0. 5	17. 3	10. 0
Wilkinsburg	29, 853	29, 639	24, 403	18, 924	0. 7	21. 5	29. 0
Williamsport	44, 355	45, 729	36, 198	31, 860	−3. 0	26. 3	13. 6
York	56, 712	55, 254	47, 512	44, 750	2. 6	16. 3	6. 2
Rhode Island							
Central Falls	25, 248	25, 898	24, 174	22, 754	−2. 5	7. 1	6. 2
Cranston	47, 085	42, 911	29, 407	21, 107	9. 7	45. 9	39. 3
East Providence town*	32, 165	29, 995	21, 793	15, 808	7. 2	37. 6	37. 9
Newport	30, 532	27, 612	30, 255	27, 149	10. 6	−8. 7	11. 4
Pawtucket	75, 797	77, 149	64, 248	51, 622	−1. 8	20. 1	24. 5
Providence	253, 504	252, 981	237, 595	224, 326	0. 2	6. 5	5. 9
Warwick	28, 757	23, 196	13, 481	26, 629	24. 0	72. 1	−49. 4
Woonsocket	49, 303	49, 376	43, 496	38, 125	−0. 1	13. 5	14. 1
South Carolina							
Charleston	71, 275	62, 265	67, 957	58, 833	14. 5	−8. 4	15. 5
Columbia	62, 396	51, 581	37, 524	26, 319	21. 0	37. 5	42. 6
Greenville	34, 734	29, 154	23, 127	15, 741	19. 1	26. 1	46. 9
Spartanburg	32, 249	28, 723	22, 638	17, 517	12. 3	26. 9	29. 2
South Dakota							
Sioux Falls	40, 832	33, 362	25, 202	14, 094	22. 4	32. 4	78. 8

URBAN PLACE	POPULATION				PERCENT OF INCREASE		
	1940	1930	1920	1910	1930 to 1940	1920 to 1930	1910 to 1920
Tennessee							
Chattanooga	128, 163	119, 798	57, 895	44, 604	7. 0	106. 9	29. 8
Johnson City	25, 332	25, 080	12, 442	8, 502	1. 0	101. 6	46. 3
Knoxville	111, 580	105, 802	77, 818	36, 346	5. 5	36. 0	114. 1
Memphis	292, 942	253, 143	162, 351	131, 105	15. 7	55. 9	23. 8
Nashville	167, 402	153, 866	118, 342	110, 364	8. 8	30. 0	7. 2
Texas							
Abilene	26, 612	23, 175	10, 274	9, 204	14. 8	125. 6	11. 6
Amarillo	51, 686	43, 132	15, 494	9, 957	19. 8	178. 4	55. 6
Austin	87, 930	53, 120	34, 876	29, 860	65. 5	52. 3	16. 8
Beaumont	59, 061	57, 732	40, 422	20, 640	2. 3	42. 8	95. 8
Corpus Christi	57, 301	27, 741	10, 522	8, 222	106. 6	163. 6	28. 0
Dallas	294, 734	260, 475	158, 976	92, 104	13. 2	63. 8	72. 6
El Paso	96, 810	102, 421	77, 560	39, 279	−5. 5	32. 1	97. 5
Fort Worth	177, 662	163, 447	106, 482	73, 312	8. 7	53. 5	45. 2
Galveston	60, 862	52, 938	44, 255	36, 981	15. 0	19. 6	19. 7
Houston	384, 514	292, 352	138, 276	78. 800	31. 5	111. 4	75. 5
Laredo	39, 274	32, 618	22, 710	14, 855	20. 4	43. 6	52. 9
Lubbock	31, 853	20, 520	4, 051	1, 938	55. 2	406. 5	109. 0
Port Arthur	46, 140	50, 902	22, 251	7, 663	−9. 4	128. 8	190. 4
San Angelo	25, 802	25, 308	10, 050	10, 321	2. 0	151. 8	−2. 6
San Antonio	253, 854	231, 542	161, 379	96, 614	9. 6	43. 5	67. 0
Tyler	28, 279	17, 113	12, 085	10, 400	65. 2	41. 6	16. 2
Waco	55, 982	52, 848	38, 500	26, 425	5. 9	37. 3	45. 7
Wichita Falls	45, 112	43, 690	40, 079	8, 200	3. 3	9. 0	388. 8
Utah							
Ogden	43, 688	40, 272	32, 804	25, 580	8. 5	22. 8	28. 2
Salt Lake City	149, 934	140, 267	118, 110	92, 777	6. 9	18. 8	27. 3
Vermont							
Burlington	27, 686	24, 789	22, 779	20, 468	11. 7	8. 8	11. 3
Virginia							
Alexandria	33, 523	24, 149	18, 060	15, 329	38. 8	33. 7	17. 8
Arlington County*	57, 040	26, 615	16, 040	10, 231	114. 3	65. 9	56. 8
Danville	32, 749	22, 247	21, 539	19, 020	47. 2	3. 3	13. 2
Lynchburg	44, 541	40, 661	30, 070	29, 494	9. 5	35. 2	2. 0
Newport News	37, 067	34, 417	35, 596	20, 205	7. 7	−3. 3	76. 2
Norfolk	144, 332	129, 710	115, 777	67, 452	11. 3	12. 0	71. 6
Petersburg	30, 631	28, 564	31, 012	24, 127	7. 2	−7. 9	28. 5
Portsmouth	50, 745	45, 704	54. 387	33, 190	11. 0	−16. 0	63. 9
Richmond	193, 042	182, 929	171, 667	127, 628	5. 5	6. 6	34. 5
Roanoke	69, 287	69, 206	50, 842	34, 874	0. 1	36. 1	45. 8
Washington							
Bellingham	29, 314	30, 823	25, 585	24, 298	−4. 9	20. 5	5. 3
Everett	30, 224	30, 567	27, 644	24, 814	−1. 1	10. 6	11. 4
Seattle	368, 302	365, 583	315, 312	237, 194	0. 7	15. 9	32. 9
Spokane	122. 001	115, 514	104, 437	104, 402	5. 6	10. 6	-----
Tacoma	109, 408	106, 817	96, 965	83, 743	2. 4	10. 2	15. 8
Yakima	27, 221	22, 101	18, 539	14, 082	23. 2	19. 2	31. 7
West Virginia							
Charleston	67, 914	60, 408	39, 608	22, 996	12. 4	52. 5	72. 2
Clarksburg	30, 579	28, 866	27, 869	9, 201	5. 9	3. 6	202. 9
Huntington	78, 836	75, 572	50, 177	31, 161	4. 3	50. 6	61. 0
Parkersburg	30, 103	29, 623	20, 050	17, 842	1. 6	47. 7	12. 4
Wheeling	61, 099	61, 659	56, 208	41, 641	−0. 9	9. 7	35. 0
Wisconsin							
Appleton	28, 436	25, 267	19, 561	16, 773	12. 5	29. 2	16. 6
Beloit	25, 365	23, 611	21, 284	15, 125	7. 4	10. 9	40. 7
Eau Claire	30, 745	26, 287	20, 906	18, 310	17. 0	25. 7	14. 2
Fond du Lac	27, 209	26, 449	23, 427	18, 797	2. 9	12. 9	24. 6
Green Bay	46, 235	37, 415	31, 017	25, 236	23. 6	20. 6	22. 9
Kenosha	48, 765	50, 262	40, 472	21, 371	−3. 0	24. 2	89. 4
La Crosse	42, 707	39, 614	30, 421	30, 417	7. 8	30. 2	-----
Madison	67, 447	57, 899	38, 378	25, 531	16. 5	50. 9	50. 3
Milwaukee	587, 472	578, 249	457, 147	373, 857	1. 6	26. 5	22. 3
Oshkosh	39, 089	40. 108	33, 162	33, 062	−2. 5	20. 9	0. 3
Racine	67, 195	67, 542	58, 593	38, 002	−0. 5	15. 3	54. 2
Sheboygan	40, 638	39, 251	30, 955	26, 398	3. 5	26. 8	17. 3
Superior	35, 136	36, 113	39, 671	40, 384	−2. 7	−9. 0	−1. 8
Wausau	27, 268	23, 758	18, 951	16, 560	14. 8	25. 4	14. 4
Wauwatosa	27, 769	21, 194	5, 818	3, 346	31. 0	264. 3	73. 9
West Allis	36, 364	34, 671	13, 745	6, 645	4. 9	152. 2	106. 8

[10] Aliquippa and Woodlawn boroughs consolidated as Aliquippa borough in 1928; combined population in 1920, 15,426; in 1910, 3,139.
[11] Bethlehem and South Bethlehem boroughs consolidated as Bethlehem city between 1910 and 1920; combined population in 1910, 32,810.
[12] Corrected figure.

Table 14.—POPULATION OF URBAN PLACES HAVING, IN 1940, FROM 5,000 TO 25,000 INHABITANTS: 1920 TO 1940

[Places marked with an asterisk (*) were classified as urban under special rule in 1940]

URBAN PLACE	1940	1930	1920
Alabama			
Alexander City	6,640	4,519	2,293
Andalusia	6,886	5,154	4,023
Bessemer	22,826	20,721	18,674
Cullman	5,074	2,786	2,467
Decatur [1]	16,604	15,593	4,752
Dothan	17,194	16,046	10,034
Eufaula	6,269	5,208	4,939
Fairfield	11,703	11,059	5,003
Florence	15,043	11,729	10,529
Greenville	5,075	3,985	3,471
Homewood	7,397	6,103	------
Huntsville	13,050	11,554	8,018
Jasper	6,847	5,313	3,246
Lanett	6,141	5,204	4,976
Opelika	8,487	6,156	4,960
Phenix City [2]	15,351	13,862	5,432
Prichard	6,084	4,580	------
Selma	19,834	18,012	15,589
Sheffield	7,933	6,221	6,682
Sylacauga	6,269	4,115	2,141
Talladega	9,298	7,596	6,546
Tarrant City	6,833	7,341	734
Troy	7,055	6,814	5,696
Tuscumbia	5,515	4,533	3,855
Arizona			
Bisbee	5,853	8,023	9,205
Douglas	8,623	9,828	9,916
Flagstaff	5,080	3,891	3,186
Globe	6,141	7,157	7,044
Mesa	7,224	3,711	3,036
Nogales	5,135	6,006	8,460
Prescott	6,018	5,517	5,010
Yuma	5,325	4,892	4,237
Arkansas			
Arkadelphia	5,078	3,380	3,311
Batesville	5,267	4,484	4,299
Blytheville	10,652	10,098	6,447
Camden	8,975	7,273	3,238
Conway	5,782	5,534	4,564
El Dorado	15,858	16,421	3,887
Fayetteville	8,212	7,394	5,362
Forrest City	5,699	4,594	3,377
Helena	8,546	8,316	9,112
Hope	7,475	6,008	4,790
Hot Springs	21,370	20,238	11,695
Jonesboro	11,729	10,326	9,384
Malvern	5,290	5,115	3,864
North Little Rock	21,137	19,418	14,048
Paragould	7,079	5,966	6,306
Pine Bluff	21,290	20,760	19,280
Russellville	5,927	5,628	4,505
Stuttgart	5,628	4,927	4,522
Texarkana	11,821	10,764	8,257
Van Buren	5,422	5,182	5,224
California			
Albany	11,493	8,569	2,462
Anaheim	11,031	10,995	5,526
Antioch	5,106	3,563	1,936
Arcadia	9,122	5,216	2,239
Azusa	5,209	4,808	2,460
Bell	11,264	7,884	------
Brawley	11,718	10,439	5,389
Burlingame	15,940	13,270	4,107
Calexico	5,415	6,299	6,223
Chico	9,287	7,961	9,339
Chula Vista	5,138	3,869	1,718
Coalinga	5,026	2,851	2,934
Colton	9,686	8,014	4,282
Compton	16,198	12,516	1,478
Corona	8,764	7,018	4,129
Coronado	6,932	5,425	3,289
Culver City	8,976	5,669	503
Daly City	9,625	7,838	3,779
El Centro	10,017	8,434	5,464
El Cerrito	6,137	3,870	1,505
Eureka	17,055	15,752	12,923
Fullerton	10,442	10,860	4,415
Gardena	5,909	------	------
Grass Valley	5,701	3,817	4,006
Hanford	8,234	7,028	5,888
Hawthorne	8,263	6,596	------
Hayward	6,736	5,530	3,487
Hermosa Beach	7,197	4,796	2,327
Lodi	11,079	6,788	4,850
Lynwood	10,982	7,323	------
Madera	6,457	4,665	3,444
Manhattan Beach	6,398	1,891	859
Martinez	7,381	6,569	3,858
Marysville	6,646	5,763	5,461
California—Continued			
Maywood	10,731	6,794	------
Merced	10,135	7,066	3,974
Modesto	16,379	13,842	9,241
Monrovia	12,807	10,890	5,480
Montebello	8,016	5,498	------
Monterey	10,084	9,141	5,479
Monterey Park	8,531	6,406	4,108
Napa	7,740	6,437	6,757
National City	10,344	7,301	3,116
Ontario	14,197	13,583	7,280
Orange	7,901	8,066	4,884
Oxnard	8,519	6,285	4,417
Pacific Grove	6,249	5,558	2,974
Palo Alto	16,774	13,652	5,900
Petaluma	8,034	8,245	6,226
Piedmont	9,866	9,333	4,282
Pittsburg	9,520	9,610	4,715
Pomona	23,539	20,804	13,505
Porterville	6,270	5,303	4,097
Redding	8,109	4,188	2,962
Redlands	14,324	14,177	9,571
Redondo Beach	13,092	9,347	4,913
Redwood City	12,453	8,962	4,020
Richmond	23,642	20,093	16,843
Roseville	6,653	6,425	4,477
Salinas	11,586	10,263	4,308
San Anselmo	5,790	4,650	2,475
San Bruno	6,519	3,610	1,562
San Buenaventura	13,264	11,603	4,156
San Fernando	9,094	7,567	3,204
San Gabriel	11,867	7,224	2,640
San Leandro	14,601	11,455	5,703
San Luis Obispo	8,881	8,276	5,895
San Marino	8,175	3,730	584
San Mateo	19,403	13,444	5,979
San Rafael	8,573	8,022	5,512
Santa Clara	6,650	6,302	5,220
Santa Cruz	16,896	14,395	10,917
Santa Maria	8,522	7,057	3,943
Santa Paula	8,986	7,452	3,967
Santa Rosa	12,605	10,636	8,758
South Pasadena	14,356	13,730	7,652
South San Francisco	6,629	6,193	4,411
Torrance	9,950	7,271	------
Tulare	8,259	6,207	3,539
Upland	6,316	4,713	2,912
Vallejo	20,072	[3] 16,072	[3] 21,107
Visalia	8,904	7,263	5,753
Watsonville	8,937	8,344	5,013
Whittier	16,115	14,822	7,997
Woodland	6,637	5,542	4,147
Colorado			
Alamosa	5,613	5,107	3,171
Boulder	12,958	11,223	11,006
Canon City	6,690	5,938	4,551
Durango	5,887	5,400	4,116
Englewood	9,680	7,980	4,356
Fort Collins	12,251	11,489	8,755
Grand Junction	12,479	10,247	8,665
Greeley	15,995	12,203	10,958
La Junta	7,040	7,193	4,964
Longmont	7,406	6,029	5,848
Loveland	6,145	5,506	5,065
Sterling	7,411	7,195	6,415
Trinidad	13,223	11,732	10,906
Walsenburg	5,855	5,503	3,565
Connecticut			
Ansonia	19,210	19,898	17,643
Danbury	22,339	22,261	18,943
Derby	10,287	10,788	11,238
East Hartford town*	18,615	17,125	11,648
Naugatuck	15,388	14,315	15,051
Norwich	23,652	23,021	22,304
Putnam	7,775	7,318	7,711
Rockville	7,572	7,445	7,726
Shelton	10,971	10,113	9,475
Southington	5,088	5,125	5,085
Stratford town*	22,580	19,212	12,347
Wallingford	11,425	11,170	9,648
Willimantic	12,101	12,102	12,330
Winsted	7,674	7,883	8,248
Delaware			
Dover	5,517	4,800	4,042
Florida			
Bartow	6,158	5,269	4,203
Bradenton	7,444	5,986	3,868
Clearwater	10,136	7,607	2,427
Florida—Continued			
Coral Gables	8,294	5,697	------
Daytona Beach [4]	22,584	16,598	825
De Land	7,041	5,246	3,324
Fort Lauderdale	17,996	8,666	2,065
Fort Myers	10,604	9,082	3,678
Fort Pierce	8,040	4,803	2,115
Gainesville	13,757	10,465	6,860
Hollywood	6,239	2,869	------
Key West	12,927	12,831	18,749
Lake City	5,836	4,416	3,341
Lakeland	22,068	18,554	7,062
Lake Wales	5,024	3,401	796
Lake Worth	7,408	5,940	1,106
Marianna	5,079	3,372	2,499
Ocala	8,986	7,281	4,914
Palatka	7,140	6,500	5,102
Panama City	11,610	5,402	1,722
Plant City	7,491	6,800	3,729
River Junction	7,110	5,624	------
St. Augustine	12,090	12,111	6,192
Sanford	10,217	10,100	5,588
Sarasota	11,141	8,398	2,149
Tallahassee	16,240	10,700	5,637
Winter Haven	6,199	7,130	1,597
Georgia			
Albany	19,055	14,507	11,555
Americus	9,281	8,760	9,010
Athens	20,650	18,192	16,748
Bainbridge	6,352	6,141	4,792
Brunswick	15,035	14,022	14,413
Carrollton	6,214	5,052	4,363
Cartersville	6,141	5,250	4,350
Cedartown	9,025	8,124	4,053
College Park	8,213	6,604	3,622
Cordele	7,929	6,880	6,538
Dalton	10,448	8,160	5,222
Decatur	16,561	13,276	6,150
Dist. 1511 (Fulton County)*	12,155	8,460	1,494
Douglas	5,175	4,206	3,401
Dublin	7,814	6,681	7,707
East Point	12,403	9,512	5,241
Elberton	6,188	4,650	6,475
Fitzgerald	7,388	6,412	6,870
Gainesville	10,243	8,624	6,272
Griffin	13,222	10,321	8,240
Hapeville	5,059	4,224	1,631
La Grange	21,983	20,131	17,038
Marietta	8,667	7,638	6,190
Milledgeville	6,778	5,534	4,619
Moultrie	10,147	8,027	6,789
Newnan	7,182	6,386	7,037
Statesboro	5,028	3,996	3,807
Thomaston	6,396	4,922	2,502
Thomasville	12,683	11,733	8,196
Tifton	5,228	3,390	3,005
Toccoa	5,494	4,602	3,567
Valdosta	15,595	13,482	10,783
Waycross	16,763	15,510	18,068
Idaho			
Burley	5,329	3,826	5,408
Caldwell	7,272	4,974	5,106
Coeur d'Alene	10,049	8,297	6,447
Idaho Falls	15,024	9,429	8,064
Lewiston	10,548	9,403	6,574
Moscow	6,014	4,476	3,956
Nampa	12,149	8,206	7,621
Pocatello	18,133	16,471	15,001
Twin Falls	11,851	8,787	8,324
Illinois			
Arlington Heights	5,668	4,997	2,250
Batavia	5,101	5,045	4,395
Beardstown	6,505	6,344	7,111
Bellwood	5,220	4,991	1,881
Belvidere	8,094	8,123	7,804
Benton	7,372	8,219	7,201
Blue Island	16,638	16,534	11,424
Brookfield	10,817	10,035	3,589
Cairo	14,407	13,532	15,203
Calumet City	13,241	12,298	7,492
Canton	11,577	11,718	10,928
Carbondale	8,550	7,528	6,267
Centralia	16,343	12,583	12,491
Champaign	23,302	20,348	15,873
Charleston	8,197	8,012	6,615
Chester	5,110	3,922	2,904
Chicago Heights	22,461	22,321	19,653
Clinton	6,331	5,920	5,898
Collinsville	9,767	9,235	9,753
De Kalb	9,146	8,545	7,871

[1] Albany and Decatur cities and Fairview town consolidated as Decatur city in 1927; combined population in 1920, 12,772.
[2] Girard city and Phenix City consolidated as Phenix City in 1923; combined population in 1920, 10,374.
[3] Corrected figure.
[4] Daytona, Daytona Beach, and Seabreeze cities consolidated as Daytona Beach city in 1925; combined population in 1920, 6,841.

NUMBER OF INHABITANTS

TABLE 14.—POPULATION OF URBAN PLACES HAVING, IN 1940, FROM 5,000 TO 25,000 INHABITANTS: 1920 TO 1940—Continued

[Places marked with an asterisk (*) were classified as urban under special rule in 1940]

URBAN PLACE	1940	1930	1920
Illinois—Continued			
Des Plaines	9,518	8,798	3,451
Dixon	10,671	9,908	8,191
Downers Grove	9,526	8,977	3,543
Du Quoin	7,515	7,593	7,285
East Moline	12,359	10,107	8,675
East Peoria	6,806	5,027	2,214
Edwardsville	8,008	6,235	5,336
Effingham	6,180	4,978	4,024
Elmhurst	15,458	14,055	4,594
Elmwood Park	13,689	11,270	1,380
Flora	5,474	4,393	3,558
Forest Park	14,840	14,555	10,768
Freeport	22,366	22,045	19,669
Glencoe	6,825	6,295	3,381
Glen Ellyn	8,055	7,680	2,851
Granite City	22,974	25,130	14,757
Harrisburg	11,453	11,625	7,125
Harvey	17,878	16,374	9,216
Herrin	9,352	9,708	10,986
Highland Park	14,476	12,203	6,167
Hinsdale	7,336	6,923	4,042
Hoopeston	5,381	5,613	5,451
Jacksonville	19,844	17,747	15,713
Johnston City	5,418	5,955	7,137
Kankakee	22,241	20,620	16,753
Kewanee	16,901	17,093	16,026
La Grange	10,479	10,103	6,525
Lake Forest	6,885	6,554	3,657
La Salle	12,812	13,149	13,050
Lawrenceville	6,213	6,303	5,080
Lincoln	12,752	12,855	11,882
Litchfield	7,048	6,612	6,215
Lombard	7,075	6,197	1,331
Macomb	8,764	8,509	6,714
Madison	7,782	7,661	4,996
Marion	9,251	9,033	9,582
Mattoon	15,827	14,631	13,552
Melrose Park	10,933	10,741	7,147
Metropolis	6,287	5,573	5,055
Monmouth	9,096	8,666	8,116
Morris	6,145	5,568	4,505
Mount Carmel	6,987	7,132	7,456
Mt. Vernon	14,724	12,375	9,815
Murphysboro	8,976	8,182	10,703
Naperville	5,272	5,118	3,830
Niles Center	7,172	5,007	763
Normal	6,983	6,768	5,143
North Chicago	8,465	8,466	5,839
Olney	7,831	6,140	4,491
Ottawa	16,005	15,094	10,816
Pana	5,966	5,835	6,122
Paris	9,281	8,781	7,985
Park Ridge	12,063	10,417	3,383
Pekin	19,407	16,129	12,086
Peru	8,983	9,121	8,869
Pontiac	9,585	8,272	6,664
Princeton	5,224	4,762	4,126
River Forest	9,487	8,829	4,358
Riverside	7,935	6,770	2,532
St. Charles	5,870	5,377	4,099
Salem	7,319	4,420	3.457
Spring Valley	5,010	5,270	6,493
Sterling	11,363	10,012	8,182
Streator	14,930	14,728	14,779
Summit	7,043	6,548	4,019
Taylorville	8,313	7,316	5,806
Urbana	14,064	13,060	10,244
Vandalia	5,288	4,342	3,316
Venice	5,454	5,362	3,895
Villa Park	7,236	6,220	854
West Frankfort	12,383	14,683	8,478
Wheaton	7,389	7,258	4,137
Wilmette	17,226	15,233	7,814
Winnetka	12,430	12,166	6,694
Wood River	8,197	8,136	3,476
Woodstock	6,123	5,471	5,523
Zion	6,555	5,991	5,580
Indiana			
Auburn	5,415	5,088	4,650
Bedford	12,514	13,208	9,076
Bicknell	5,110	5,212	7,635
Bloomington	20,870	18,227	11,595
Bluffton	5,417	5,074	5,391
Brazil	8,126	8,744	9,293
Clinton	7,092	7,936	10,962
Columbus	11,738	9,935	8,990
Connersville	12,898	12,795	9,901
Crawfordsville	11,089	10,355	10,139
Indiana—Continued			
Decatur	5,861	5,156	4,762
Elwood	10,913	10,685	10,790
Frankfort	13,706	12,196	11,585
Franklin	6,264	5,682	4,909
Goshen	11,375	10,397	9,525
Greensburg	6,065	5,702	5,345
Hartford City	6,946	6,613	6,183
Hobart	7,166	5,787	3,450
Huntington	13,903	13,420	14,000
Jasper	5,041	3,905	2,539
Jeffersonville	11,493	11,946	10,098
Kendallville	5,431	5,439	5,273
La Porte	16,180	15,755	15,158
Lebanon	6,529	6,445	6,257
Linton	6,263	5,085	5,856
Logansport	20,177	18,508	21,626
Madison	6,923	6,530	6,711
Martinsville	5,009	4,962	4,895
Mount Vernon	5,638	5,035	5,284
New Castle	16,620	14,027	14,458
Noblesville	5,575	4,811	4,758
Peru	12,432	12,730	12,410
Plymouth	5,713	5,290	4,338
Portland	6,362	5,276	5,958
Princeton	7,786	7,505	7,132
Rushville	5,960	5,709	5,498
Seymour	8,620	7,508	7,348
Shelbyville	10,791	10,618	9,701
Sullivan	5,077	5,306	4,489
Tell City	5,395	4,873	4,086
Tipton	5,101	4,861	4,507
Valparaiso	8,736	8,079	6,518
Vincennes	18,228	17,564	17,160
Wabash	9,653	8,840	9,872
Warsaw	6,378	5,730	5,478
Washington	9,312	9,070	8,743
West Lafayette	6,270	5,095	3,830
Whiting	10,307	10,880	10,145
Winchester	5,303	4,487	4,021
Iowa			
Albia	5,157	4,425	5,067
Ames	12,555	10,261	6,270
Atlantic	5,802	5,585	5,329
Boone	12,373	11,886	12,451
Carroll	5,389	4,691	4,254
Cedar Falls	9,349	7,362	6,316
Centerville	8,413	8,147	8,486
Chariton	5,754	5,365	5,175
Charles City	8,681	8,039	7,350
Cherokee	7,469	6,443	5,824
Creston	8,033	8,615	8,034
Decorah	5,303	4,581	4,039
Estherville	5,651	4,940	4,699
Fairfield	6,773	6,619	5,948
Fort Dodge	22,904	21,895	19,347
Fort Madison	14,063	13,779	12,066
Grinnell	5,210	4,949	5,362
Iowa City	17,182	15,340	11,267
Keokuk	15,076	15,106	14,423
Knoxville	6,936	4,697	3,523
Le Mars	5,353	4,788	4,683
Marshalltown	19,240	17,373	15,731
Muscatine	18,286	16,778	16,068
Newton	10,462	11,560	6,627
Oelwein	7,801	7,794	7,455
Oskaloosa	11,024	10,123	9,427
Perry	5,977	5,881	5,642
Red Oak	5,763	5,778	5,578
Shenandoah	6,846	6,502	5,255
Spencer	6,599	5,019	4,599
Storm Lake	5,274	4,157	3,658
Washington	5,227	4,814	4,697
Webster City	6,738	7,024	5,657
Kansas			
Abilene	5,671	5,658	4,895
Arkansas City	12,752	13,946	11,253
Atchison	12,648	13,024	12,630
Chanute	10,142	10,277	10,286
Coffeyville	17,355	16,198	13,452
Concordia	6,255	5,792	4,705
Dodge City	8,487	10,059	5,061
El Dorado	10,045	10,311	10,995
Emporia	13,188	14,067	11,273
Fort Scott	10,557	10,763	10,693
Garden City	6,285	6,121	3,848
Great Bend	9,044	5,548	4,460
Hays	6,385	4,618	3,165
Kansas—Continued			
Independence	11,565	12,782	11,920
Iola	7,244	7,160	8,513
Junction City	8,507	7,407	7,533
Lawrence	14,390	13,726	12,456
Leavenworth	19,220	17,466	16,912
McPherson	7,194	6,147	4,595
Manhattan	11,659	10,136	7,989
Newton	11,048	11,034	9,781
Ottawa	10,193	9,563	9,018
Parsons	14,294	14,903	16,028
Pittsburg	17,571	18,145	18,052
Pratt	6,591	6,322	5,183
Salina	21,073	20,155	15,085
Wellington	7,246	7,405	7,048
Winfield	9,506	9,398	7,933
Kentucky			
Bellevue	8,741	8,497	7,379
Bowling Green	14,585	12,348	9,638
Corbin	7,893	8,036	3,406
Danville	6,734	6,729	5,099
Dayton	8,379	9,071	7,646
Fort Thomas	11,034	10,008	5,028
Frankfort	11,492	11,626	9,805
Glasgow	5,815	5,042	2,559
Harlan	5,122	4,327	2,647
Hazard	7,397	7,021	4,348
Henderson	13,160	11,668	12,169
Hopkinsville	11,724	10,746	9,696
Jenkins	9,428	8,465	4,707
Ludlow	6,185	6,485	4,582
Madisonville	8,209	6,908	5,030
Mayfield	8,619	8,177	6,583
Maysville	6,572	6,557	6,107
Middlesborough	11,777	10,350	8,041
Paris	6,697	6,204	6,310
Princeton	5,389	4,764	3,689
Richmond	7,335	6,495	5,622
Somerset	6,154	5,506	4,672
Winchester	8,594	8,233	8,333
Louisiana			
Abbeville	6,672	4,356	3,461
Bastrop	6,626	5,121	1,216
Bogalusa	14,604	14,029	8,245
Bossier City	5,786	4,003	1,094
Crowley	9,523	7,656	6,108
Eunice	5,242	3,597	3,272
Gretna	10,879	9,584	7,197
Hammond	6,033	6,072	3,855
Houma	9,052	6,531	5,160
Jackson	5,384	3,966	2,320
Jennings	7,343	4,036	3,824
Lafayette	19,210	14,635	7,855
Lake Charles	21,207	15,791	13,088
Minden	6,677	5,623	6,105
Morgan City	6,969	5,985	5,429
Natchitoches	6,812	4,547	3,388
New Iberia	13,747	8,003	6,278
Opelousas	8,980	6,299	4,437
Plaquemine	5,049	5,124	4,632
Ruston	7,107	4,400	3,389
Tallulah	5,712	3,332	1,316
Thibodaux	5,851	4,442	3,526
West Monroe	8,560	6,566	2,240
Maine			
Auburn	19,817	18,571	16,985
Augusta	19,360	17,198	14,114
Bath	10,235	9,110	14,731
Belfast	5,540	4,993	5,083
Biddeford	19,790	17,633	18,008
Brewer	6.510	6,329	6,064
Brunswick*	7,003	6,144	5,784
Calais	5,161	5,470	6,084
Gardiner	6,044	5,609	5,475
Old Town	7,688	7,266	6,956
Presque Isle [5]	7,939	6,965	5,581
Rockland	8,899	9,075	8,109
Rumford Falls*	8,447	8,726	7,016
Saco	8,631	7,233	6,817
South Portland	15,781	13,840	9,254
Waterville	16,688	15,454	13,351
Westbrook	11,087	10,807	9,453
Maryland			
Annapolis	13,069	12,531	11,214
Cambridge	10,102	8,544	7,467

[5] Presque Isle town incorporated as a city Jan. 1, 1940. As the information concerning this incorporation was received subsequent to the urban tabulations, the population of the village alone (5,456), rather than that of the whole town, has been included in urban totals and in totals for urban places of 5,000 to 25,000.

TABLE 14.—POPULATION OF URBAN PLACES HAVING, IN 1940, FROM 5,000 TO 25,000 INHABITANTS: 1920 TO 1940—Continued

[Places marked with an asterisk (*) were classified as urban under special rule in 1940]

URBAN PLACE	1940	1930	1920
Maryland—Continued			
Frederick	15,802	14,434	11,066
Frostburg	7,659	5,588	6,017
Hyattsville	6,575	4,264	2,675
Salisbury	13,313	10,997	7,553
Takoma Park	8,938	6,415	3,168
Dist. 12 (Baltimore County)*	15,436	11,556	4,162
Dist. 13 (Baltimore County)*	13,366	10,466	4,588
Massachusetts			
Abington town*	5,708	5,872	5,787
Adams town*	12,608	12,697	12,967
Amesbury town*	10,862	11,899	10,036
Amherst town*	6,410	5,888	5,550
Andover town*	11,122	9,969	8,268
Athol town*	11,180	10,677	9,792
Attleboro	22,071	21,769	19,731
Auburn town*	6,629	6,147	3,891
Barnstable town*	8,333	7,271	4,836
Braintree town*	16,378	15,712	10,580
Bridgewater town*	8,902	9,055	8,438
Canton town*	6,381	5,816	5,945
Clinton town*	12,440	12,817	12,979
Concord town*	7,972	7,477	6,461
Danvers town*	14,179	12,957	11,108
Dartmouth town*	9,011	8,778	6,493
Dedham town*	15,508	15,136	10,792
Dracut town*	7,339	6,912	5,280
Easthampton town*	10,316	11,323	11,261
Fairhaven town*	10,938	10,951	7,291
Framingham town*	23,214	22,210	17,033
Franklin town*	7,303	7,028	6,497
Gardner	20,206	19,399	16,971
Gloucester	24,046	24,204	22,947
Great Barrington town*	5,824	5,934	6,315
Greenfield town*	15,672	15,500	15,462
Hingham town*	8,003	6,657	5,604
Hudson town*	8,042	8,469	7,607
Ipswich town*	6,348	5,599	6,201
Leominster	22,226	21,810	19,744
Lexington town*	13,187	9,467	6,350
Longmeadow town*	5,790	4,437	2,618
Ludlow town*	8,181	8,876	7,470
Mansfield town*	6,530	6,364	6,255
Marblehead town*	10,856	8,668	7,324
Marlborough	15,154	15,587	15,028
Maynard town*	6,812	7,156	7,086
Methuen town*	21,880	21,069	15,189
Middleborough town*	9,032	8,608	8,453
Milford town*	15,388	14,741	13,471
Millbury town*	6,983	6,957	5,653
Milton town*	18,708	16,434	9,382
Montague town*	7,582	8,081	7,675
Natick town*	13,851	13,589	10,907
Needham town*	12,445	10,845	7,012
Newburyport	13,916	15,084	15,618
North Adams	22,213	21,621	22,282
Northampton	24,794	24,381	21,951
North Andover town*	7,524	6,961	6,265
North Attleborough town*	10,359	10,197	9,238
Northbridge town*	10,242	9,713	10,174
Norwood town*	15,383	15,049	12,627
Orange town*	5,611	5,365	5,393
Palmer town*	9,149	9,577	9,896
Peabody	21,711	21,345	19,552
Plymouth town*	13,100	13,042	13,045
Randolph town*	7,634	6,553	4,756
Reading town*	10,866	9,767	7,439
Rockland town*	8,087	7,524	7,544
Saugus town*	14,825	14,700	10,874
Somerset town*	5,873	5,398	3,520
Southbridge town*	16,825	14,264	14,245
South Hadley town*	6,856	6,773	5,527
Spencer town*	6,641	6,272	5,930
Stoneham town*	10,765	10,060	7,873
Stoughton town*	8,632	8,204	6,865
Swampscott town*	10,761	10,346	8,101
Uxbridge town*	6,417	6,285	5,384
Wakefield town*	16,223	16,318	13,025
Walpole town*	7,443	7,273	5,446
Ware town*	7,557	7,385	8,525
Webster town*	13,186	12,992	13,258
Wellesley town*	15,127	11,439	6,224
Westfield	18,793	19,775	18,604
West Springfield town*	17,135	16,684	13,443
Weymouth town*	23,868	20,882	15,057
Whitman town*	7,759	7,638	7,147
Winchendon town*	6,575	6,202	5,904
Winchester town*	15,081	12,719	10,485
Winthrop town*	16,768	16,852	15,455
Woburn	19,751	19,434	16,574
Michigan			
Adrian	14,230	13,064	11,878
Albion	8,345	8,324	8,354
Alma	7,202	6,734	7,542
Alpena	12,808	12,166	11,101
Benton Harbor	16,668	15,434	12,233
Berkley	6,406	5,571	-------
Birmingham	11,196	9,539	3,694
Cadillac	9,855	9,570	9,750
Charlotte	5,544	5,307	5,126
Cheboygan	5,673	4,923	5,642
Coldwater	7,343	6,735	6,114
Dowagiac	5,007	5,550	5,440
East Detroit	8,584	5,955	-------
East Lansing	5,839	4,389	1,889
Ecorse	13,209	12,716	4,394
Escanaba	14,830	14,524	13,103
Ferndale	22,523	20,855	2,640
Grand Haven	8,799	8,345	7,205
Greenville	5,321	4,730	4,304
Grosse Pointe	6,179	5,173	2,084
Grosse Pointe Farms	7,217	3,533	1,649
Grosse Pointe Park	12,646	11,174	1,355
Hancock	5,554	5,795	7,527
Hastings	5,175	5,227	5,132
Hillsdale	6,381	5,896	5,476
Holland	14,616	14,346	12,183
Inkster	7,044	4,440	-------
Ionia	6,392	6,562	6,935
Iron Mountain	11,080	11,652	8,251
Ironwood	13,369	14,299	15,739
Ishpeming	9,491	9,238	10,500
Kingsford	5,771	5,526	-------
Lapeer	5,365	5,008	4,723
Lincoln Park	15,236	12,336	-------
Ludington	8,701	8,898	8,810
Manistee	8,694	8,078	9,694
Manistique	5,399	5,198	6,380
Marquette	15,928	14,789	12,718
Marshall	5,253	5,019	4,270
Menominee	10,230	10,320	8,907
Midland	10,329	8,038	5,483
Monroe	18,478	18,110	11,573
Mount Clemens	14,389	13,497	9,488
Mount Pleasant	8,413	5,211	4,819
Muskegon Heights	16,047	15,584	9,514
Negaunee	6,813	6,552	7,419
Niles	11,328	11,326	7,311
Owosso	14,424	14,496	12,575
Petoskey	6,019	5,740	5,064
Plymouth	5,360	4,484	2,857
River Rouge	17,008	17,314	9,822
Roseville	9,023	6,836	-------
St. Clair Shores	10,405	6,745	-------
St. Joseph	8,963	8,349	7,251
Sault Ste. Marie	15,847	13,755	12,096
Sturgis	7,214	6,950	5,995
Three Rivers	6,710	6,863	5,209
Traverse City	14,455	12,539	10,925
Trenton	5,284	4,022	1,682
Ypsilanti	12,121	10,143	7,413
Minnesota			
Albert Lea	12,200	10,169	8,056
Alexandria	5,051	3,876	3,388
Anoka	6,426	4,851	4,287
Austin	18,307	12,276	10,118
Bemidji	9,427	7,202	7,086
Brainerd	12,071	10,221	9,591
Chisholm	7,487	8,308	9,039
Cloquet	7,304	6,782	5,127
Columbia Heights	6,035	5,613	2,968
Crookston	7,161	6,321	6,825
Detroit Lakes	5,015	3,675	3,426
Edina	5,855	3,138	1,833
Ely	5,970	6,156	4,902
Eveleth	6,887	7,484	7,205
Fairmont	6,988	5,521	4,630
Faribault	14,527	12,767	11,089
Fergus Falls	10,848	9,389	7,581
Hastings	5,662	5,086	4,571
Hibbing	16,385	15,666	15,089
International Falls	5,626	5,036	3,448
Little Falls	6,047	5,014	5,500
Mankato	15,654	14,038	12,469
Montevideo	5,220	4,319	4,419
Moorhead	9,491	7,651	5,720
New Ulm	8,743	7,308	6,745
Owatonna	8,694	7,654	7,252
Red Wing	9,962	9,629	8,637
Richfield	6,750	3,344	2,411
Minnesota—Continued			
Robbinsdale	6,018	4,427	1,369
St. Cloud	24,173	21,000	15,873
St. Louis Park	7,737	4,710	2,281
St. Peter	5,870	4,811	4,335
South St. Paul	11,844	10,009	6,860
Stillwater	7,013	7,173	7,735
Thief River Falls	6,019	4,268	4,685
Virginia	12,264	11,963	14,022
West St. Paul	5,733	4,463	2,962
Willmar	7,623	6,173	5,892
Winona	22,490	20,850	19,143
Worthington	5,918	3,878	3,481
Mississippi			
Biloxi	17,475	14,850	10,937
Brookhaven	6,232	5,288	4,706
Canton	6,011	4,725	3,252
Clarksdale	12,168	10,043	7,552
Columbia	6,064	4,833	2,826
Columbus	13,645	10,743	10,501
Corinth	7,818	6,220	5,498
Greenville	20,892	14,807	11,560
Greenwood	14,767	11,123	7,793
Grenada	5,831	4,349	3,402
Gulfport	15,195	12,547	8,157
Hattiesburg	21,026	18,601	13,270
Laurel	20,598	18,017	13,037
McComb	9,898	10,057	7,775
Natchez	15,296	18,422	12,608
Pascagoula	5,900	4,339	6,082
Picayune	5,129	4,698	2,479
Tupelo	8,212	6,361	5,055
Vicksburg	24,460	22,943	18,072
West Point	5,627	4,677	4,400
Yazoo City	7,258	5,579	5,244
Missouri			
Boonville	6,089	6,435	4,665
Brookfield	6,174	6,428	6,304
Cape Girardeau	19,426	16,227	10,252
Carthage	10,585	9,736	10,068
Caruthersville	6,612	4,781	4,750
Charleston	5,182	3,357	3,410
Chillicothe	8,012	8,177	6,772
Clayton	13,069	9,613	3,028
Clinton	6,041	5,744	5,098
Columbia	18,399	14,967	10,392
De Soto	5,121	5,069	5,003
Ferguson	5,724	3,798	1,874
Flat River	5,401	-------	-------
Fulton	8,207	6,105	5,595
Hannibal	20,865	22,761	19,306
Independence	16,066	15,296	11,686
Jefferson City	24,268	21,596	14,490
Kennett	6,335	4,128	3,622
Kirksville	10,080	8,293	7,213
Kirkwood	12,132	9,169	4,422
Lebanon	5,025	3,562	2,848
Lexington	5,341	4,595	4,695
Maplewood	12,875	12,657	7,431
Marshall	8,533	8,103	5,200
Maryville	5,700	5,217	4,711
Mexico	9,053	8,290	6,013
Moberly	12,920	13,772	12,808
Neosho	5,318	4,485	3,968
Nevada	8,181	7,448	7,139
Poplar Bluff	11,163	7,551	8,042
Richmond Heights	12,802	9,150	2,136
Rolla	5,141	3,670	2,077
St. Charles	10,803	10,491	8,503
Sedalia	20,428	20,806	21,144
Sikeston	7,944	5,676	3,613
Trenton	7,046	6,992	6,951
Warrensburg	5,868	5,146	4,811
Washington	6,756	5,918	3,132
Webb City	7,033	6,876	7,807
Webster Groves	18,394	16,487	9,474
Montana			
Anaconda	11,004	12,494	11,668
Billings	23,261	16,380	15,100
Bozeman	8,665	6,855	6,183
Havre	6,427	6,372	5,429
Helena	15,056	11,803	12,037
Kalispell	8,245	6,094	5,147
Lewistown	5,874	5,358	6,120
Livingston	6,642	6,391	6,311
Miles City	7,313	7,175	7,937
Missoula	18,449	14,657	12,668

TABLE 14.—POPULATION OF URBAN PLACES HAVING, IN 1940, FROM 5,000 TO 25,000 INHABITANTS: 1920 TO 1940—Continued

[Places marked with an asterisk (*) were classified as urban under special rule in 1940]

URBAN PLACE	1940	1930	1920
Nebraska			
Alliance	6,253	6,669	4,591
Beatrice	10,883	10,297	9,664
Columbus	7,632	6,898	5,410
Fairbury	6,304	6,192	5,454
Falls City	6,146	5,787	4,930
Fremont	11,862	11,407	9,592
Grand Island	19,130	18,041	13,947
Hastings	15,145	15,490	11,647
Kearney	9,643	8,575	7,702
McCook	6,212	6,688	4,303
Nebraska City	7,339	7,230	6,279
Norfolk	10,490	10,717	8,634
North Platte	12,429	12,061	10,466
Scottsbluff	12,057	8,465	6,912
York	5,383	5,712	5,388
Nevada			
Las Vegas	8,422	5,165	2,304
Reno	21,317	18,529	12,016
Sparks	5,318	4,508	3,238
New Hampshire			
Berlin	19,084	20,018	16,104
Claremont town*	12,144	12,377	9,524
Derry town*	5,400	5,131	5,382
Dover	14,990	13,573	13,029
Exeter town*	5,398	4,872	4,604
Franklin	6,749	6,576	6,318
Keene	13,832	13,794	11,210
Laconia	13,484	12,471	10,897
Lebanon town*	7,590	7,073	6,162
Newport town*	5,304	4,659	4,109
Portsmouth	14,821	14,495	13,569
Rochester	12,012	10,209	9,673
Somersworth	6,136	5,680	6,688
New Jersey			
Asbury Park	14,617	14,981	12,400
Audubon	8,906	8,904	4,740
Bergenfield	10,275	8,816	3,667
Bogota	7,346	7,341	3,906
Boonton	6,739	6,866	5,372
Bound Brook	7,616	7,372	5,906
Bridgeton	15,992	15,699	14,323
Burlington	10,905	10,844	9,049
Carlstadt	5,644	5,425	4,472
Carteret	11,976	13,339	11,047
Cliffside Park	16,892	15,267	5,709
Collingswood	12,685	12,723	8,714
Cranford township*	12,860	11,126	6,001
Dover	10,491	10,031	9,803
Dumont	7,556	5,861	2,537
Dunellen	5,360	5,148	3,394
East Rutherford	7,268	7,080	5,463
Englewood	18,966	17,805	11,627
Fair Lawn	9,017	5,990	-------
Fairview	8,770	9,067	4,882
Fort Lee	9,468	8,759	5,761
Freehold	6,952	6,894	4,768
Glen Ridge	7,331	7,365	4,620
Glen Rock	5,177	4,369	2,181
Gloucester City	13,692	13,796	12,162
Guttenberg	6,200	6,535	6,726
Haddonfield	9,742	8,857	5,646
Haddon Heights	5,555	5,394	2,950
Haledon	5,303	4,812	3,435
Hammonton	7,668	7,656	6,417
Harrison	14,171	15,601	15,721
Hasbrouck Heights	6,716	5,658	2,895
Hawthorne	12,610	11,868	5,135
Highland Park	9,002	8,691	4,866
Hillside township*	18,556	17,601	5,267
Keyport	5,147	4,940	4,415
Leonia	5,763	5,350	2,979
Linden [6]	24,115	21,206	1,756
Lodi	11,552	11,549	8,175
Long Branch	17,408	18,399	13,521
Lyndhurst township*	17,454	17,362	9,515
Madison	7,944	7,481	5,523
Manville	6,065	5,441	-------
Maplewood township*	23,139	21,321	5,283
Metuchen	6,557	5,748	3,334
Millburn township*	11,652	8,602	4,633
Millville	14,806	14,705	14,691
Morristown	15,270	15,197	12,548
Neptune township*	10,207	10,625	6,470
Newton	5,533	5,401	4,125
North Arlington	9,904	8,263	1,767
North Plainfield	10,586	9,760	6,916
Nutley	21,954	20,572	9,421
New Jersey—Continued			
Palisades Park	8,141	7,065	2,633
Palmyra	5,178	4,968	-------
Paulsboro	7,011	7,121	4,352
Pennsauken township*	17,745	16,915	6,474
Penns Grove	6,488	5,895	6,060
Phillipsburg	18,314	19,255	16,923
Pitman	5,507	5,411	3,385
Pleasantville	11,050	11,580	5,887
Princeton	7,719	6,992	5,917
Prospect Park	5,714	5,909	4,292
Rahway	17,498	16,011	11,042
Red Bank	10,974	11,622	9,251
Ridgefield	5,271	4,671	1,560
Ridgefield Park	11,277	10,764	8,575
Ridgewood	14,948	12,188	7,580
Roselle	13,597	13,021	5,737
Roselle Park	9,661	8,969	5,438
Rutherford	15,466	14,915	9,497
Salem	8,618	8,047	7,435
Sayreville	8,186	8,658	7,181
Secaucus	9,754	8,950	5,423
Somerville	8,720	8,255	6,718
South Amboy	7,802	8,476	7,897
South Orange	13,742	13,630	7,274
South Plainfield	5,379	5,047	-------
South River	10,714	10,759	6,596
Summit	16,165	14,556	10,174
Tenafly	7,413	5,669	3,585
Totowa	5,130	4,600	1,864
Union township*	24,730	16,472	3,962
Ventnor City	7,905	6,674	2,193
Verona	8,957	7,161	3,039
Vineland	7,914	7,556	6,432
Wallington	8,981	9,063	5,715
Weehauken township*	14,363	14,807	14,485
Westfield	18,458	15,801	9,063
Westwood	5,388	4,861	2,597
Wildwood	5,150	5,330	2,790
Woodbury	8,306	8,172	5,801
Wood-Ridge	5,739	5,159	1,923
New Mexico			
Carlsbad	7,116	3,708	2,205
Clovis	10,065	8,027	4,904
Gallup	7,041	5,992	3,920
Hobbs	10,619	598	-------
Las Cruces	8,385	5,811	3,969
Las Vegas (city)	5,941	4,719	4,304
Las Vegas (town)	6,421	4,378	3,902
Portales	5,104	2,519	1,154
Raton	7,607	6,090	5,544
Roswell	13,482	11,173	7,033
Santa Fe	20,325	11,176	7,236
Silver City	5,044	3,519	2,662
Tucumcari	6,194	4,143	3,117
New York			
Amityville	5,058	4,437	3,265
Batavia	17,267	17,375	13,541
Beacon	12,572	11,933	10,996
Bronxville	6,888	6,387	3,055
Canandaigua	8,321	7,541	7,299
Catskill	5,429	5,082	4,728
Cedarhurst	5,463	5,065	2,838
Cohoes	21,955	23,226	22,987
Corning	16,212	15,777	15,820
Cortland	15,881	15,043	13,294
Depew	6,084	6,536	5,850
Dobbs Ferry	5,883	5,741	4,401
Dunkirk	17,713	17,802	19,336
East Aurora	5,253	4,815	3,703
East Rochester	6,691	6,627	3,901
East Rockaway	5,610	4,340	2,005
Endicott [7]	17,702	16,231	9,500
Floral Park	12,950	10,016	2,097
Fredonia	5,738	5,814	6,051
Freeport	20,410	15,467	8,599
Fulton	13,362	12,462	13,043
Garden City	11,223	7,180	2,420
Geneva	15,555	16,053	14,648
Glen Cove	12,415	11,430	8,664
Glens Falls	18,836	18,531	16,638
Gloversville	23,329	23,099	22,075
Great Neck	6,167	4,010	-------
Hamburg	5,467	4,731	3,185
Hastings-on-Hudson	7,057	7,097	5,526
Haverstraw	5,909	5,621	5,226
Hempstead	20,856	12,650	6,382
Herkimer	9,617	10,446	10,453
Hornell	15,649	16,250	15,025
New York—Continued			
Hudson	11,517	12,337	11,745
Hudson Falls	6,654	6,449	5,761
Ilion	8,927	9,890	10,169
Irondequoit town*	23,376	18,024	5,123
Ithaca	19,730	20,708	17,004
Johnson City	18,039	13,567	8,587
Johnstown	10,666	10,801	10,908
Kenmore	18,612	16,482	3,160
Lackawanna	24,058	23,948	17,918
Lancaster	7,236	7,040	6,059
Larchmont	5,970	5,282	2,468
Little Falls	10,163	11,105	13,029
Lockport	24,379	23,160	21,308
Long Beach	9,036	5,817	282
Lynbrook	14,557	11,993	4,371
Malone	8,743	8,657	7,556
Malverne	5,153	2,256	-------
Mamaroneck	13,034	11,766	6,571
Massena	11,328	10,637	5,993
Mechanicville	7,449	7,924	8,166
Medina	5,871	6,071	6,011
Middletown	21,908	21,276	18,420
Mineola	10,064	8,155	3,016
Mount Kisco	5,941	5,127	3,944
Newark	9,646	7,649	6,964
North Pelham	5,052	4,890	2,385
North Tarrytown	8,804	7,417	5,927
North Tonawanda	20,254	19,019	15,482
Norwich	8,694	8,378	8,268
Nyack	5,206	5,392	4,444
Ogdensburg	16,346	16,915	14,609
Olean	21,506	21,790	20,506
Oneida	10,291	10,558	10,541
Oneonta	11,731	12,536	11,582
Ossining	15,996	15,241	10,739
Oswego	22,062	22,652	23,626
Owego	5,068	4,742	4,147
Patchogue	7,181	6,860	4,031
Peekskill	17,311	17,125	15,868
Pelham Manor	5,302	4,908	1,754
Penn Yan	5,308	5,329	4,517
Plattsburgh	16,351	13,349	10,909
Port Chester	23,073	22,662	16,573
Port Jervis	9,749	10,243	10,171
Rensselaer	10,768	11,223	10,823
Rockville Centre	18,613	13,718	6,262
Rye	9,865	8,712	5,308
Salamanca	9,011	9,577	9,276
Saranac Lake	7,138	8,020	5,174
Saratoga Springs	13,705	13,169	13,181
Scarsdale	12,966	9,690	3,506
Scotia	7,960	7,437	4,358
Seneca Falls	6,452	6,443	6,389
Solvay	8,201	7,986	7,352
Tarrytown	6,874	6,841	5,807
Tonawanda	13,008	12,681	10,068
Tuckahoe	6,563	6,138	3,509
Tupper Lake	5,451	5,271	2,508
Valley Stream	16,679	11,790	-------
Watervliet	16,114	16,083	16,073
Waverly	5,450	5,662	5,270
Wellsville	5,942	5,674	4,996
Williston Park	5,750	4,427	-------
North Carolina			
Asheboro	6,981	5,021	2,559
Burlington	12,198	9,737	5,952
Canton	5,037	5,117	2,584
Concord	15,572	11,820	9,903
Dunn	5,256	4,558	2,805
Elizabeth City	11,564	10,037	8,925
Fayetteville	17,428	13,049	8,877
Forest City	5,035	4,069	2,312
Gastonia	21,313	17,093	12,871
Goldsboro	17,274	14,985	11,296
Greenville	12,674	9,194	5,772
Hamlet	5,111	4,801	3,808
Henderson	7,647	6,345	5,222
Hendersonville	5,381	5,070	3,720
Hickory	13,487	7,363	5,076
Kings Mountain	6,547	5,632	2,800
Kinston	15,388	11,362	9,771
Laurinburg	5,685	3,312	2,643
Lenoir	7,598	6,532	3,718
Lexington	10,550	9,652	5,254
Lumberton	5,803	4,140	2,691
Monroe	6,475	6,100	4,084
Mooresville	6,682	5,619	4,315
Morganton	7,670	6,001	2,867
Mount Airy	6,286	6,045	4,752
New Bern	11,815	11,981	12,198

[6] Linden borough and Linden township consolidated as Linden city in 1925; combined population in 1920, 8,368.
[7] Endicott and Union villages consolidated as Endicott village in 1921; combined population in 1920, 12,803.

TABLE 14.—POPULATION OF URBAN PLACES HAVING, IN 1940, FROM 5,000 TO 25,000 INHABITANTS: 1920 TO 1940—Continued

[Places marked with an asterisk (*) were classified as urban under special rule in 1940]

URBAN PLACE	1940	1930	1920
North Carolina—Continued			
Newton	5,407	4,394	3,021
Reidsville	10,387	6,851	5,333
Roanoke Rapids	8,545	3,404	3,369
Salisbury	19,037	16,951	13,884
Shelby	14,037	10,789	3,609
Statesville	11,440	10,490	7,895
Tarboro	7,148	6,379	4,568
Thomasville	11,041	10,090	5,676
Washington	8,569	7,035	6,314
Wilson	19,234	12,613	10,612
North Dakota			
Bismarck	15,496	11,090	7,122
Devils Lake	6,204	[3] 5,519	[3] 5,140
Dickinson	5,839	5,025	4,122
Grand Forks	20,228	17,112	14,010
Jamestown	8,790	8,187	6,627
Mandan	6,685	5,037	4,336
Minot	16,577	16,099	10,476
Valley City	5,917	5,268	4,686
Williston	5,790	5,106	4,178
Ohio			
Alliance	22,405	23,047	21,603
Ashland	12,453	11,141	9,249
Ashtabula	21,405	23,301	22,082
Athens	7,696	7,252	6,418
Barberton	24,028	23,934	18,811
Barnesville	5,002	4,602	4,865
Bedford	7,390	6,814	2,677
Bellaire	13,799	13,327	15,061
Bellefontaine	9,808	9,543	9,336
Bellevue	6,127	6,256	5,776
Berea	6,025	5,697	2,959
Bexley	8,705	7,396	1,342
Bowling Green	7,190	6,688	5,788
Bryan	5,404	4,689	4,252
Bucyrus	9,727	10,027	10,425
Cambridge	15,044	16,129	13,104
Campbell	13,785	14,673	11,237
Cheviot	9,043	8,046	4,108
Chillicothe	20,129	18,340	15,831
Circleville	7,982	7,369	7,049
Conneaut	9,355	9,691	9,343
Coshocton	11,509	10,908	10,847
Cuyahoga Falls	20,546	19,797	10,200
Defiance	9,744	8,818	8,876
Delaware	8,944	8,675	8,756
Delphos	5,746	5,672	5,745
Dover (Tuscarawas County)	9,691	9,716	8,101
East Liverpool	23,555	23,329	21,411
East Palestine	5,123	5,215	5,750
Euclid	17,866	12,751	3,363
Findlay	20,228	19,363	17,021
Fostoria	13,453	12,790	9,987
Fremont	14,710	13,422	12,468
Galion	8,685	7,674	7,374
Gallipolis	7,832	7,106	6,070
Garfield Heights	16,989	15,589	2,550
Girard	9,805	9,859	6,556
Grandview Heights	6,960	6,358	1,185
Greenville	7,745	7,036	7,104
Ironton	15,851	16,621	14,007
Jackson	6,295	5,922	5,842
Kent	8,581	8,375	7,070
Kenton	7,593	7,069	7,690
Lancaster	21,940	18,716	14,706
Lockland	5,601	5,703	4,007
Logan	6,177	6,080	5,493
Maple Heights	6,728	5,950	1,732
Marietta	14,543	14,285	15,140
Martins Ferry	14,729	14,524	11,634
Miamisburg	5,544	5,518	4,383
Mingo Junction	5,192	5,030	4,616
Mount Vernon	10,122	9,370	9,237
Nelsonville	5,368	5,322	6,440
New Boston	6,024	5,931	4,817
New Philadelphia	12,328	12,365	10,718
Niles	16,273	16,314	13,080
North College Hill	5,231	4,139	1,104
Norwalk	8,211	7,776	7,379
Oakwood	7,652	6,494	1,473
Painesville	12,235	10,944	7,272
Parma	16,365	13,899	------
Piqua	16,049	16,009	15,044
Ravenna	8,538	8,019	7,219
Reading	6,079	5,723	4,540
Rocky River	8,291	5,632	1,861
St. Bernard	7,387	7,487	6,312
Ohio—Continued			
St. Marys	5,532	5,433	5,679
Salem	12,301	10,622	10,305
Sandusky	24,874	24,622	22,897
Shaker Heights	23,393	17,783	1,616
Shelby	6,643	6,198	5,578
Sidney	9,790	9,301	8,590
South Euclid	6,146	4,399	1,605
Struthers	11,739	11,249	5,847
Tiffin	16,102	16,428	14,375
Toronto	7,426	7,044	4,684
Troy	9,697	8,675	7,260
Uhrichsville	6,435	6,437	6,428
University Heights	5,981	2,237	131
Upper Arlington	5,370	3,059	620
Urbana	8,335	7,742	7,621
Van Wert	9,227	8,472	8,100
Wadsworth	6,495	5,930	4,742
Wapakoneta	5,225	5,378	5,295
Washington Court House	9,402	8,426	7,962
Wellston	5,537	5,319	6,687
Wellsville	7,672	7,956	8,849
Wilmington	5,971	5,332	5,037
Wooster	11,543	10,742	8,204
Xenia	10,633	10,507	9,110
Oklahoma			
Ada	15,143	11,261	8,012
Altus	8,593	8,439	4,522
Alva	5,055	5,121	3,913
Anadarko	5,579	5,036	3,116
Ardmore	16,886	15,741	14,181
Bartlesville	16,267	14,763	14,417
Blackwell	8,537	9,521	7,174
Bristow	6,050	6,619	3,460
Chickasha	14,111	14,099	10,179
Clinton	6,736	7,512	2,596
Cushing	7,703	9,301	6,326
Duncan	9,207	8,363	3,463
Durant	10,027	7,463	7,340
Elk City	5,021	5,666	2,814
El Reno	10,078	9,384	7,737
Frederick	5,109	4,568	3,822
Guthrie	10,018	9,582	11,757
Henryetta	6,905	7,694	5,889
Hobart	5,177	4,982	2,936
Holdenville	6,632	7,268	2,932
Hugo	5,909	5,272	6,368
Lawton	18,055	12,121	8,930
McAlester	12,401	11,804	10,632
Miami	8,345	8,064	6,802
Norman	11,429	9,603	5,004
Okmulgee	16,051	17,097	17,430
Pauls Valley	5,104	4,235	3,694
Pawhuska	5,443	5,931	6,414
Perry	5,045	4,206	3,154
Picher	5,848	7,773	9,676
Ponca City	16,794	16,136	7,051
Sand Springs	6,137	6,674	4,076
Sapulpa	12,249	10,533	11,634
Seminole	11,547	11,459	854
Shawnee	22,053	23,283	15,348
Stillwater	10,097	7,016	4,701
Vinita	5,685	4,263	5,010
Wewoka	10,315	10,401	1,520
Woodward	5,406	5,056	3,849
Oregon			
Albany	5,654	5,325	4,840
Astoria	10,389	10,349	14,027
Baker	9,342	7,858	7,729
Bend	10,021	8,848	5,415
Corvallis	8,392	7,585	5,752
Eugene	20,838	18,901	10,593
Grants Pass	6,028	4,666	3,151
Klamath Falls	16,497	16,093	4,801
La Grande	7,747	8,050	6,913
Marshfield	5,259	5,287	4,034
Medford	11,281	11,007	5,756
Oregon City	6,124	5,761	5,686
Pendleton	8,847	6,621	6,837
The Dalles	6,266	5,883	5,807
Pennsylvania			
Abington township*	20,857	18,648	8,684
Ambridge	18,968	20,227	12,730
Archbald	8,296	9,587	8,603
Arnold	10,898	10,575	6,120
Ashland	7,045	7,164	6,666
Ashley	6,371	7,093	6,520
Avalon	6,155	5,940	5,277
Pennsylvania—Continued			
Bangor	5,687	5,824	5,402
Beaver	5,641	5,665	4,135
Beaver Falls [8]	17,098	17,147	12,802
Bellefonte	5,304	4,804	3,996
Bellevue	10,488	10,252	8,198
Berwick	13,181	12,660	12,181
Blairsville	5,002	5,296	4,391
Blakely	8,106	8,260	6,564
Bloomsburg	9,799	9,093	7,819
Brackenridge	6,400	6,250	4,987
Braddock	18,326	19,329	20,879
Bradford	17,691	19,306	15,525
Brentwood	7,552	5,381	1,695
Bridgeport	5,904	5,595	4,680
Bristol	11,895	11,799	10,273
Brownsville [9]	8,015	2,869	2,502
Butler	24,477	23,568	23,778
Canonsburg	12,599	12,558	10,632
Carbondale	19,371	20,061	18,640
Carlisle	13,984	12,596	10,916
Carnegie	12,663	12,497	11,516
Centerville	6,317	6,467	4,793
Chambersburg	14,852	13,788	13,171
Charleroi	10,784	11,260	11,516
Cheltenham township*	19,082	15,731	11,015
Clairton [10]	16,381	15,291	6,264
Clearfield	9,372	9,221	8,529
Coaldale	6,163	6,921	6,336
Coatesville	14,006	14,582	14,515
Collingdale (Darby P. O.)	8,162	7,857	3,834
Columbia	11,547	11,349	10,836
Connellsville	13,608	13,290	13,804
Conshohocken	10,776	10,815	8,481
Coraopolis	11,086	10,724	6,162
Corry	6,935	7,152	7,228
Crafton	7,163	7,004	5,954
Danville	7,122	7,185	6,952
Darby	10,334	9,899	7,922
Dickson City	11,548	12,395	11,049
Donora	13,180	13,905	14,131
Dormont	12,974	13,190	6,455
Du Bois	12,080	11,595	13,681
Dunmore	23,086	22,627	20,250
Dupont	5,278	5,161	4,576
Duquesne	20,693	21,396	19,011
Duryea	8,275	8,503	7,776
East Pittsburgh	6,079	6,214	6,527
East Stroudsburg	6,404	6,099	4,855
Edwardsville	7,998	8,847	9,027
Ellwood City	12,329	12,323	8,958
Emmaus	6,731	6,419	4,370
Ephrata	6,199	4,988	3,735
Etna	7,223	7,493	6,341
Exeter	5,802	5,724	4,176
Farrell	13,899	14,359	15,586
Ford City	5,795	6,127	5,605
Forest Hills	5,248	4,549	------
Forty Fort	6,293	6,224	3,389
Frackville	8,035	8,034	5,590
Franklin (Venango County)	9,948	10,254	9,970
Freeland	6,593	7,098	6,666
Gettysburg	5,916	5,584	4,439
Glassport	8,748	8,390	6,959
Greensburg	16,743	16,508	15,033
Greenville	8,149	8,628	8,101
Grove City	6,296	6,156	4,944
Hanover	13,076	11,805	8,664
Hanover township*	16,439	17,770	11,139
Harrison township*	13,161	12,387	9,389
Hollidaysburg [11]	5,910	5,969	4,071
Homestead	19,041	20,141	20,452
Honesdale	5,687	5,490	2,756
Huntingdon	7,170	7,558	7,051
Indiana	10,050	9,569	7,043
Jeannette	16,220	15,126	10,627
Jenkintown	5,024	4,797	3,366
Jersey Shore	5,432	5,781	6,103
Kane	6,133	6,232	7,283
Kingston [12]	20,679	21,600	8,952
Kittanning	7,550	7,808	7,153
Kulpmont	6,159	6,120	4,695
Lansdale	9,316	8,379	4,728
Lansdowne	10,837	[3] 9,023	4,797
Lansford	8,710	9,632	9,625
Larksville	8,467	9,322	9,438
Latrobe	11,111	10,644	9,484
Lehighton	6,615	6,490	6,102
Lewistown	13,017	13,357	9,849
Lock Haven	10,810	9,668	8,557

[3] Corrected figure.
[8] Beaver Falls and College Hill boroughs consolidated as Beaver Falls city in 1930; combined population in 1920, 15,445.
[9] Brownsville and South Brownsville boroughs consolidated as Brownsville borough in 1933; combined population in 1930, 8,183; in 1920, 7,177.
[10] Clairton, North Clairton, and Wilson boroughs consolidated as Clairton city in 1922; combined population in 1920, 10,777.
[11] Gaysport and Hollidaysburg boroughs consolidated as Hollidaysburg borough in 1924; combined population in 1920, 5,068.
[12] Dorranceton and Kingston boroughs consolidated as Kingston borough in 1922; combined population in 1920, 15,286.

Table 14.—POPULATION OF URBAN PLACES HAVING, IN 1940, FROM 5,000 TO 25,000 INHABITANTS: 1920 TO 1940—Continued

[Places marked with an asterisk (*) were classified as urban under special rule in 1940]

URBAN PLACE	1940	1930	1920
Pennsylvania—Continued			
Luzerne	7,082	6,950	5,998
McAdoo	5,127	5,239	4,674
McKees Rocks	17,021	18,116	16,713
Mahanoy City	13,442	14,784	15,599
Meadville	18,919	16,698	14,568
Mechanicsburg	5,709	5,647	4,688
Media	5,351	5,372	4,109
Middletown	7,046	6,085	5,920
Midland	6,373	6,007	5,452
Millvale	7,811	8,166	8,031
Milton	8,313	8,552	8,638
Minersville	8,686	9,392	7,845
Monaca	7,061	4,641	3,838
Monessen	20,257	20,268	18,179
Monongahela	8,825	8,675	8,688
Morrisville	5,493	5,368	3,639
Mount Carmel	17,780	17,967	17,469
Mount Lebanon township*	19,571	13,403	2,258
Mount Oliver	6,981	7,071	5,575
Mount Pleasant	5,824	5,869	5,862
Munhall	13,900	12,995	6,418
Nanticoke	24,387	26,043	22,614
Nanty-Glo	6,217	5,598	5,028
Narberth	5,217	4,669	3,704
Nazareth	5,721	5,505	4,288
New Brighton	9,630	9,950	9,361
New Kensington [13]	24,055	16,762	11,987
Northampton	9,622	9,839	9,349
North Braddock	15,679	16,782	14,928
Oakmont	6,260	6,027	4,512
Oil City	20,379	22,075	21,274
Old Forge	11,892	12,661	12,237
Olyphant	9,252	10,743	10,236
Palmerton	7,475	7,678	7,168
Palmyra	5,239	4,377	3,646
Phoenixville	12,282	12,029	10,484
Pitcairn	6,310	6,317	5,738
Pittston	17,828	18,246	18,497
Plains township*	15,621	16,044	13,986
Plymouth	15,507	16,543	16,500
Pottstown	20,194	19,430	17,431
Pottsville	24,530	24,300	21,876
Prospect Park	5,100	4,623	2,536
Punxsutawney	9,482	9,266	10,311
Quakertown	5,150	4,883	4,391
Rankin	7,470	7,956	7,301
Ridgway	6,253	6,313	6,037
Rochester	7,441	7,726	6,957
St. Clair	6,809	7,296	6,495
St. Marys	7,653	7,433	6,967
Sayre	7,569	7,902	8,078
Schuylkill Haven	6,518	6,514	5,437
Scottdale	6,493	6,714	5,768
Sewickley	5,614	5,599	4,955
Shaler township*	11,185	9,573	6,306
Shamokin	18,810	20,274	21,204
Sharpsburg	8,202	8,642	8,921
Sharpsville	5,129	5,194	4,674
Shenandoah	19,790	21,782	24,726
Shippensburg	5,244	4,345	4,372
Somerset	5,430	4,395	3,121
South Williamsport	6,033	6,058	4,341
State College	6,226	4,450	2,405
Steelton	13,115	13,291	13,428
Stowe township*	12,577	13,368	16,665
Stroudsburg	6,186	5,961	5,278
Summit Hill	5,406	5,567	5,499
Sunbury	15,462	15,626	15,721
Swissvale	15,919	16,029	10,908
Swoyerville	9,234	9,133	6,876
Tamaqua	12,486	12,936	12,363
Tarentum	9,846	9,551	8,925
Taylor	9,002	10,428	9,876
Throop	7,382	8,027	6,672
Titusville	8,126	8,055	8,432
Turtle Creek	9,805	10,690	8,138
Tyrone	8,845	9,042	9,084
Uniontown	21,819	19,544	15,692
Vandergrift	10,725	11,479	9,531
Warren	14,891	14,863	14,272
Waynesboro	10,231	10,167	9,720
West Chester	13,289	12,325	11,717
West Hazleton	7,523	7,310	5,854
West Pittston	7,943	7,940	6,968
West View	7,215	6,028	2,797
West York	5,590	5,381	3,320
Wilmerding	5,662	6,291	6,441
Pennsylvania—Continued			
Wilson	8,217	8,265	------
Windber	9,057	9,205	9,462
Winton	7,989	8,508	7,583
Yeadon	8,524	5,430	1,308
Rhode Island			
Barrington town*	6,231	5,162	3,897
Bristol town*	11,159	11,953	11,375
Burrillville town*	8,185	7,677	8,606
Cumberland town*	10,625	10,304	10,077
Johnston town*	10,672	9,357	6,855
Lincoln town*	10,577	10,421	9,543
North Providence town*	12,156	11,104	7,697
Warren town*	8,158	7,974	7,841
Westerly town*	11,199	10,997	9,952
West Warwick town*	18,188	17,696	15,461
South Carolina			
Aiken	6,168	6,033	4,103
Anderson	19,424	14,383	10,570
Camden	5,747	5,183	3,930
Chester	6,392	5,528	5,557
Clinton	5,704	5,643	3,767
Conway	5,066	3,011	1,969
Darlington	6,236	5,556	4,669
Easley	5,183	4,886	3,568
Florence	16,054	14,774	10,968
Gaffney	7,636	6,827	5,065
Georgetown	5,559	5,082	4,579
Greenwood	13,020	11,020	8,703
Hartsville	5,399	5,067	3,624
Laurens	6,894	5,443	4,629
Marion	5,746	4,921	3,892
Newberry	7,510	7,298	5,894
Orangeburg	10,521	8,776	7,290
Rock Hill	15,009	11,322	8,809
Sumter	15,874	11,780	9,508
Union	8,478	7,419	6,141
South Dakota			
Aberdeen	17,015	16,465	14,537
Brookings	5,346	4,376	3,924
Huron	10,843	10,946	8,302
Lead	7,520	5,733	5,013
Madison	5,018	4,289	4,144
Mitchell	10,633	10,942	8,478
Rapid City	13,844	10,404	5,777
Watertown	10,617	10,214	9,400
Yankton	6,798	6,072	5,024
Tennessee			
Alcoa	5,131	5,255	3,358
Athens	6,930	5,385	2,580
Bristol	14,004	12,005	8,047
Clarksville	11,831	9,242	8,110
Cleveland	11,351	9,136	6,522
Columbia	10,579	7,882	5,526
Dyersburg	10,034	8,733	6,444
Elizabethton	8,516	8,093	2,749
Greeneville	6,784	5,544	3,775
Harriman	5,620	4,588	4,019
Humboldt	5,160	4,613	3,913
Jackson	24,332	22,172	18,860
Kingsport	14,404	11,914	5,692
Lebanon	5,950	4,656	4,084
Maryville	5,609	4,958	3,739
Morristown	8,050	7,305	5,875
Murfreesboro	9,495	7,993	5,367
Paris	6,395	8,164	4,730
Pulaski	5,314	3,367	2,780
Shelbyville	6,537	5,010	2,912
Springfield	6,668	5,577	3,860
Union City	7,256	5,865	4,412
Texas			
Alamo Heights	5,700	3,874	------
Alice	7,792	4,239	1,880
Bay City	6,594	4,070	3,454
Beeville	6,789	4,806	3,063
Big Spring	12,604	13,735	4,273
Bonham	6,349	5,655	6,008
Borger	10,018	6,532	------
Brady	5,002	3,983	2,197
Breckenridge	5,826	7,569	1,846
Brenham	6,435	5,974	5,066
Brownsville	22,083	22,021	11,791
Brownwood	13,398	12,789	8,223
Bryan	11,842	7,814	6,307
Cameron	5,040	4,565	4,298
Texas—Continued			
Childress	6,464	7,163	5,003
Cleburne	10,558	11,539	12,820
Coleman	6,054	6,078	2,868
Colorado City	5,213	4,671	1,766
Corsicana	15,232	15,202	11,356
Crystal City	6,529	6,609	([14])
Cuero	5,474	4,672	3,671
Del Rio	13,343	11,693	10,589
Denison	15,581	13,850	17,065
Denton	11,192	9,587	7,626
Eagle Pass	6,459	5,059	5,765
Edinburg	8,718	4,821	1,406
Electra	5,588	6,712	4,744
Ennis	7,087	7,069	7,224
Gainesville	9,651	8,915	8,648
Goose Creek	6,929	5,208	------
Graham	5,175	4,981	2,544
Greenville	13,995	12,407	12,384
Harlingen	13,306	12,124	1,784
Henderson	6,437	2,932	2,273
Highland Park	10,288	8,422	2,321
Hillsboro	7,799	7,823	6,952
Huntsville	5,108	5,028	4,689
Jacksonville	7,213	6,748	3,723
Kerrville	5,572	4,546	2,353
Kilgore	6,708	------	------
Kingsville	7,782	6,815	4,770
Lamesa	6,038	3,528	1,188
Lockhart	5,018	4,367	3,731
Longview	13,758	5,036	5,713
Lufkin	9,567	7,311	4,878
McAllen	11,877	9,074	5,331
McKinney	8,555	7,307	6,677
Marlin	6,542	5,338	4,310
Marshall	18,410	16,203	14,271
Mercedes	7,624	6,608	3,414
Mexia	6,410	6,579	3,482
Midland	9,352	5,484	1,795
Mineral Wells	6,303	5,986	7,890
Mission	5,982	5,120	3,847
Nacogdoches	7,538	5,687	3,546
Navasota	6,138	5,128	5,060
New Braunfels	6,976	6,242	3,590
Odessa	9,573	2,407	------
Orange	7,472	7,913	9,212
Palestine	12,144	11,445	11,039
Pampa	12,895	10,470	987
Paris	18,678	15,649	15,040
Plainview	8,263	8,834	3,989
Robstown	6,780	4,183	948
Rusk	5,699	3,859	2,348
San Benito	9,501	10,753	5,070
San Marcos	6,006	5,134	4,527
Seguin	7,006	5,225	3,631
Sherman	17,156	15,713	15,031
Sulphur Springs	6,742	5,417	5,558
Sweetwater	10,367	10,848	4,307
Taylor	7,875	7,463	5,965
Temple	15,344	15,345	11,033
Terrell	10,481	8,795	8,349
Texarkana	17,019	16,602	11,480
Texas City	5,748	3,534	2,509
University Park	14,458	4,200	------
Uvalde	6,679	5,286	3,885
Vernon	9,277	9,137	5,142
Victoria	11,566	7,421	5,957
Waxahachie	8,655	8,042	7,958
Weatherford	5,924	4,912	6,203
Weslaco	6,883	4,879	------
West University Place	9,221	1,322	------
Utah			
Brigham	5,641	5,093	5,282
Logan	11,868	9,979	9,439
Murray	5,740	5,172	4,584
Price	5,214	4,084	2,364
Provo	18,071	14,766	10,303
South Salt Lake	5,701	------	------
Tooele	5,001	5,135	3,602
Vermont			
Barre	10,909	11,307	10,008
Bennington	7,628	7,390	7,230
Brattleboro*	9,622	8,709	7,324
Montpelier	8,006	7,837	7,125
Rutland	17,082	17,315	14,954
St. Albans	8,037	8,020	7,588
St. Johnsbury	7,437	7,920	7,164

[13] New Kensington and Parnassus boroughs consolidated as New Kensington borough in 1931; combined population in 1930, 23,002; in 1920, 15,803.
[14] Not returned separately.

TABLE 14.—POPULATION OF URBAN PLACES HAVING, IN 1940, FROM 5,000 TO 25,000 INHABITANTS: 1920 TO 1940—Continued

[Places marked with an asterisk (*) were classified as urban under special rule in 1940]

URBAN PLACE	1940	1930	1920
Vermont—Continued			
Springfield	5, 182	4, 943	5, 283
Winooski	6, 036	5, 308	4, 932
Virginia			
Bristol	9, 768	8, 840	6, 729
Charlottesville	19, 400	15, 245	10, 688
Clifton Forge	6, 461	6, 839	6, 164
Covington	6, 300	6, 538	5, 623
Fredericksburg	10, 066	6, 819	5, 882
Hampton	5, 898	6, 382	6, 138
Harrisonburg	8, 768	7, 232	5, 875
Hopewell	8, 679	11, 327	1, 397
Marion	5, 177	4, 156	3, 253
Martinsville	10, 080	7, 705	4, 075
Pulaski	8, 792	7, 168	5, 282
Radford	6, 990	6, 227	4, 627
Salem	5, 737	4, 833	4, 159
South Boston	5, 252	4, 841	4, 338
South Norfolk	8, 038	7, 857	7, 724
Staunton	13, 337	11, 990	10, 623
Suffolk	11, 343	10, 271	9, 123
Waynesboro [15]	7, 373	6, 226	1, 594
Winchester	12, 095	10, 855	6, 883
Washington			
Aberdeen	18, 846	21, 723	15, 337
Anacortes	5, 875	6, 564	5, 284
Bremerton [16]	15, 134	10, 170	8, 918
Centralia	7, 414	8, 058	7, 549
Ellensburg	5, 944	4, 621	3, 967
Hoquiam	10, 835	12, 766	10, 058
Kelso	6, 749	6, 260	2, 228
Longview	12, 385	10, 652	------
Olympia	13, 254	11, 733	7, 795
Port Angeles	9, 409	10, 188	5, 351
Puyallup	7, 889	7, 094	6, 323
Vancouver	18, 788	15, 766	12, 637

URBAN PLACE	1940	1930	1920
Washington—Continued			
Walla Walla	18, 109	15, 976	15, 503
Wenatchee	11, 620	11, 627	6, 324
West Virginia			
Beckley	12, 852	9, 357	4, 149
Bluefield	20, 641	19, 339	15, 282
Dunbar	5, 266	4, 189	------
Elkins	8, 133	7, 345	6, 788
Fairmont	23, 105	23, 159	17, 851
Grafton	7, 431	7, 737	8, 517
Hinton [17]	5, 815	6, 654	3, 912
Hollidays Cove	6, 137	4, 480	1, 213
Keyser	6, 177	6, 248	6, 003
Logan	5, 166	4, 396	2, 998
Martinsburg	15, 063	14, 857	12, 515
Morgantown	16, 655	16, 186	12, 127
Moundsville	14, 168	14, 411	10, 669
Princeton	7, 426	6, 955	6, 224
Richwood	5, 051	5, 720	4, 331
South Charleston	10, 377	5, 904	3, 650
Welch	6, 264	5, 376	3, 232
Wellsburg	6, 255	6, 398	4, 918
Weston	8, 268	8, 646	5, 701
Williamson	8, 366	9, 410	6, 819
Wisconsin			
Antigo	9, 495	8, 610	8, 451
Ashland	11, 101	10, 622	11, 334
Baraboo	6, 415	5, 545	5, 538
Beaver Dam	10, 356	9, 867	7, 992
Chippewa Falls	10, 368	9, 539	9, 130
Cudahy	10, 561	10, 631	6, 725
De Pere	6, 373	5, 521	5, 165
Fort Atkinson	6, 153	5, 793	4, 915
Janesville	22, 992	21, 628	18, 293
Kaukauna	7, 382	6, 581	5, 951

URBAN PLACE	1940	1930	1920
Wisconsin—Continued			
Manitowoc	24, 404	22, 963	17, 563
Marinette	14, 183	13, 734	13. 610
Marshfield	10, 359	8, 778	7, 394
Menasha	10, 481	9, 062	7, 214
Menomonie	6, 582	5, 595	5, 104
Merrill	8, 711	8, 458	8, 068
Monroe	6, 182	5, 015	4, 788
Neenah	10, 645	9, 151	7, 171
Oconto	5, 362	5, 030	4, 920
Portage	7, 016	6, 308	5, 582
Rhinelander	8, 501	8, 019	6, 654
Rice Lake	5, 719	5, 177	4, 457
Shawano	5, 565	4, 188	3, 544
Shorewood	15, 184	13, 479	2, 650
South Milwaukee	11, 134	10, 706	7, 598
Sparta	5, 820	4, 949	4, 466
Stevens Point	15, 777	13, 623	11. 371
Sturgeon Bay	5, 439	4, 983	4, 553
Two Rivers	10, 302	10, 083	7, 305
Watertown	11, 301	10, 613	9, 299
Waukesha	19, 242	17, 176	12, 558
Waupun	6, 798	5, 768	4, 440
West Bend	5, 452	4, 760	3, 378
West Milwaukee	5, 010	4, 168	2, 101
Whitefish Bay	9, 651	5, 362	882
Wisconsin Rapids	11, 416	8, 726	7, 243
Wyoming			
Casper	17, 964	16, 619	11, 447
Cheyenne	22, 474	17, 361	13, 829
Laramie	10, 627	8, 609	6, 301
Rawlins	5, 531	4, 868	3, 969
Rock Springs	9, 827	8, 440	6, 456
Sheridan	10, 529	8, 536	9, 175

[15] Basic City and Waynesboro towns consolidated as Waynesboro town in 1923; combined population in 1920, 3,806.
[16] Bremerton and Charleston cities consolidated as Bremerton city in 1928; combined population in 1920, 12,256.
[17] Avis town and Hinton city consolidated as Hinton city in 1927; combined population in 1920, 5,547.

TABLE 15.—POPULATION OF URBAN PLACES HAVING, IN 1940, FROM 2,500 TO 5,000 INHABITANTS: 1920 TO 1940

[Places marked with an asterisk (*) were classified as urban under special rule in 1940]

URBAN PLACE	1940	1930	1920
Alabama			
Albertville	3, 651	2, 716	1, 666
Athens	4, 342	4, 238	3, 323
Atmore	3, 200	3, 035	1, 775
Attalla	4, 885	4, 585	3, 462
Auburn	4, 652	2, 800	2, 143
Brewton	3, 323	2, 818	2, 682
Carbon Hill	2, 555	2, 519	2, 666
Clanton	3, 982	1, 847	1, 411
Demopolis	4, 137	4, 037	2, 779
Enterprise	4, 353	3, 702	3, 013
Fayette	2, 668	2, 109	1, 741
Florala	2, 999	2, 580	2, 633
Fort Payne	4, 424	3, 375	2, 025
Geneva	2, 803	1, 593	1, 581
Guntersville	4, 398	2, 826	1, 909
Hartselle	2, 584	2, 204	2, 009
Jacksonville	2, 995	2, 840	2, 395
Leeds	2, 910	2, 529	1, 600
Northport	3, 187	2, 173	1, 606
Opp	3, 178	2, 918	1, 556
Ozark	3, 601	3, 103	2, 518
Piedmont	4, 019	3, 668	2, 645
Prattville	2, 664	2, 331	2, 316
Roanoke	4, 168	4, 373	3, 841
Russellville	3, 510	3, 146	2, 269
Scottsboro	2, 834	2, 304	1, 417
Tuskegee	3, 937	3, 314	2, 475
Union Springs	3, 107	2, 875	4, 125
Wetumpka	3, 089	2, 357	1, 520
Arizona			
Clifton	2, 668	2, 305	4, 163
Glendale	4, 855	3, 665	2, 737
Miami	4, 722	7, 693	6, 689
Tempe	2, 906	2, 495	1, 963
Williams	2, 622	2, 166	1, 350
Winslow	4, 577	3, 917	3, 730
Arkansas			
Benton	3, 502	3, 445	2, 933
Brinkley	3, 409	3, 046	2, 714
Clarendon	2, 551	2, 149	2, 638

URBAN PLACE	1940	1930	1920
Arkansas—Continued			
Clarksville	3, 118	3, 031	2, 127
Crossett	4. 891	2, 811	2, 707
De Queen	3, 055	2, 938	2, 517
Dermott	3, 083	2, 942	2, 330
Fordyce	3, 429	3, 206	2, 996
Harrison	4, 238	3, 626	3, 477
McGehee	3, 663	3, 488	2, 368
Magnolia	4, 326	3, 008	2, 158
Marianna	4, 449	4, 314	5, 074
Marked Tree	2, 685	2, 276	1, 318
Mena	3, 510	3, 118	3, 441
Monticello	3, 650	3, 076	2, 378
Morrilton	4, 608	4, 043	3, 010
Nashville	2, 782	2, 469	2, 144
Newport	4, 321	4, 547	3, 771
Osceola	3, 226	2, 573	1, 755
Paris	3, 430	3, 234	1, 740
Pocahontas	3, 028	1, 896	1, 806
Prescott	3, 177	3, 033	2, 691
Rogers	3, 550	3, 554	3, 318
Searcy	3, 670	3, 387	2, 836
Siloam Springs	2, 764	2, 378	2, 569
Springdale	3, 319	2, 763	2, 263
Trumann	3, 381	2, 995	2, 598
Warren	2, 516	2, 523	2, 145
West Helena	4, 717	4, 489	6, 226
West Memphis	3, 369	895	------
Wynne	3, 633	3, 505	2, 933
California			
Auburn	4, 013	2, 661	2, 289
Banning	3, 874	2, 752	1, 810
Brea	2, 567	2, 435	1, 037
Carmel-by-the-Sea	2, 837	2, 260	638
Chino	4, 204	3, 118	2, 132
Claremont	3, 057	2, 719	1, 728
Covina	3. 049	2, 774	1, 999
Delano	4, 573	2, 632	805
Dinuba	3, 790	2, 968	3. 400
El Monte	4, 746	3, 479	1, 283
El Segundo	3, 738	3, 503	1, 563

URBAN PLACE	1940	1930	1920
California—Continued			
Emeryville	2, 521	2, 336	2, 390
Escondido	4, 560	3, 421	1, 789
Exeter	3, 883	2, 685	1, 862
Fillmore	3, 252	2, 893	1, 597
Fort Bragg	3, 235	3, 022	2, 616
Gilroy	3, 615	3, 502	2, 862
Glendora	2, 822	2, 761	2, 028
Healdsburg	2, 507	2, 296	2, 412
Hemet	2, 595	2, 235	1, 480
Hillsborough	2, 747	1, 891	931
Hollister	3, 881	3, 757	2, 781
Huntington Beach	3, 738	3, 690	1, 687
Laguna Beach	4, 460	1, 981	------
La Mesa	3, 925	2, 513	1, 004
La Verne	3, 092	2, 860	1, 698
Lindsay	4, 397	3, 878	2, 576
Livermore	2, 885	3, 119	1, 916
Lompoc	3, 379	2, 845	1, 876
Los Gatos	3, 597	3, 168	2, 317
Menlo Park	3, 258	2, 254	------
Mill Valley	4, 847	4, 164	2, 554
Mountain View	3, 946	3, 308	1, 888
Needles	3, 624	3, 144	2, 807
Newport Beach	4, 438	2, 203	894
North Sacramento	3, 053	2, 097	------
Oakdale	2, 592	2, 112	1, 745
Oceanside	4, 651	3, 508	1, 161
Oroville	4, 421	3, 698	3, 340
Palm Springs	3, 434	------	------
Paso Robles	3, 045	2, 573	1, 919
Placerville	3, 064	2, 322	1, 650
Red Bluff	3, 824	3, 517	3, 104
Reedley	3, 170	2, 589	2, 447
San Carlos	3, 520	1, 132	------
Sanger	4, 017	2, 967	2, 578
Sausalito	3, 540	3, 667	2, 790
Selma	3, 667	3, 047	3, 158
Sierra Madre	4, 581	3, 550	2, 026
Signal Hill	3, 184	2, 932	------
Sunnyvale	4, 373	3, 094	1, 675

TABLE 15.—POPULATION OF URBAN PLACES HAVING, IN 1940, FROM 2,500 TO 5,000 INHABITANTS: 1920 TO 1940—Continued

[Places marked with an asterisk (*) were classified as urban under special rule in 1940]

URBAN PLACE	1940	1930	1920
California—Continued			
Taft	3,205	3,442	3,317
Tracy	4,056	3,829	2,450
Turlock	4,839	4,276	3,394
Ukiah	3,731	3,124	2,305
Yuba City	4,968	3,605	1,708
Colorado			
Aurora	3,437	2,295	983
Brighton	4,029	3,394	2,715
Delta	3,717	2,938	2,623
Florence	2,632	2,475	2,629
Fort Morgan	4,884	4,423	3,818
Golden	3,175	2,426	2,135
Lamar	4,445	[1]4,165	2,512
Las Animas	3,232	2,517	2,252
Leadville	4,774	3,771	4,959
Monte Vista	3,208	2,610	2,484
Montrose	4,764	3,566	3,581
Rocky Ford	3,494	3,426	3,746
Salida	4,969	5,065	4,689
Connecticut			
Danielson	4,507	4,210	3,130
Groton	4,719	4,122	4,236
Jewett City	3,682	4,436	3,196
Stafford Springs	3,401	3,492	3,383
Delaware			
Bellefonte	2,503	761	291
Laurel	2,884	[1]2,542	2,253
Milford	4,214	3,719	2,703
Newark	4,502	3,899	2,183
New Castle	4,414	4,131	3,854
Seaford	2,804	2,468	2,141
Florida			
Apalachicola	3,268	3,150	3,066
Arcadia	4,055	4,082	3,479
Auburndale	2,723	1,849	715
Avon Park	3,125	3,355	890
Belle Glade	3,806	926	-------
Cocoa	3,098	2,164	1,445
Dade City	2,561	1,811	1,296
Dania	2,902	1,674	762
De Funiak Springs	2,570	2,636	2,097
Delray Beach	3,737	2,333	1,051
Eustis	2,930	2,835	1,193
Fernandina	3,492	3,023	3,147
Haines City	3,890	3,037	651
Hialeah	3,958	2,600	-------
Homestead	3,154	2,319	1,307
Jacksonville Beach	3,566	409	357
Kissimmee	3,225	3,163	2,722
Leesburg	4,687	4,113	1,835
Live Oak	3,427	2,734	3,103
Madison	2,730	2,189	1,952
Manatee	3,595	3,219	1,076
Melbourne	2,622	2,677	533
New Smyrna Beach	4,402	4,149	2,007
Pahokee	4,766	2,256	-----
Palm Beach	3,747	1,707	1,135
Palmetto	3,491	3,043	2,046
Perry	2,668	2,744	1,956
Pompano	4,427	2,614	636
Quincy	3,888	3,788	3,118
Sebring	3,155	2,912	812
Tarpon Springs	3,402	3,414	2,105
Vero Beach	3,050	2,268	793
Wauchula	2,710	2,574	2,081
Winter Garden	3,060	2,023	1,021
Winter Park	4,715	3,686	1,078
Georgia			
Barnesville	3,535	3,236	3,059
Baxley	2,916	2,122	1,142
Blakely	2,774	2,106	1,985
Buford	4,191	3,357	2,500
Cairo	4,653	3,169	1,908
Calhoun	2,955	2,371	1,955
Camilla	2,588	2,025	2,136
Canton	2,651	2,892	2,679
Commerce	3,294	3,002	2,459
Covington	3,900	3,203	3,203
Cuthbert	3,447	3,235	3,022
Dawson	3,681	3,827	3,504
Douglasville	2,555	2,316	2,159
Eastman	3,311	3,022	2,707
East Thomaston	3,590	3,061	1,058
Fort Valley	4,953	4,560	3,223
Hawkinsville	3,000	2,484	3,070
Hogansville	3,886	2,355	1,591
Jesup	2,903	2,303	1,941
Georgia—Continued			
Lafayette	3,509	2,811	2,104
Manchester	3,462	3,745	2,776
Millen	2,820	2,527	2,405
Monroe	4,168	3,706	3,211
Pelham	2,579	2,762	2,640
Porterdale	3,116	3,002	2,880
Quitman	4,450	4,149	4,393
Rockmart	3,764	3,264	1,400
Rossville	3,538	3,230	1,427
Sandersville	3,566	3,011	2,695
Silvertown	3,930	2,171	-------
Swainsboro	3,575	2,442	1,578
Sylvania	2,531	1,781	1,413
Thomson	3,088	1,914	2,140
Trion	3,800	3,289	1,588
Vidalia	4,109	3,585	2,860
Washington	3,537	3,158	4,208
Waynesboro	3,793	3,922	3,311
West Point	3,591	2,146	2,138
Winder	3,974	3,283	3,335
Idaho			
Alameda	2,691	1,885	-------
Blackfoot	3,681	3,199	3,937
Emmett	3,203	2,763	2,204
Gooding	2,568	1,592	1,843
Jerome	3,537	1,976	1,759
Kellogg	4,235	4,124	3,017
Malad City	2,731	2,535	2,598
Montpelier	2,824	2,436	2,984
Payette	3,322	2,618	2,433
Preston	4,236	3,381	3,235
Rexburg	3,437	3,048	3,569
Rupert	3,167	2,250	2,372
St. Anthony	2,719	2,778	2,957
Sandpoint	4,356	3,290	2,876
Wallace	3,839	3,634	2,816
Weiser	3,663	2,724	3,154
Illinois			
Abingdon	3,218	2,771	2,721
Aledo	2,593	2,203	2,231
Anna	4,092	3,436	3,019
Barrington	3,560	3,213	1,743
Bradley	3,689	3,048	2,128
Bushnell	2,906	2,850	2,716
Carlinville	4,965	4,144	5,212
Carlyle	2,591	2,078	2,027
Carmi	4,098	2,932	2,667
Carterville	2,893	2,866	3,404
Carthage	2,575	2,240	2,129
Casey	2,543	2,200	2,189
Christopher	3,833	4,244	3,830
Crevecoeur	3,535	350	-------
Crystal Lake	3,917	3,732	2,249
Dolton	3,068	2,923	2,076
East Alton	4,680	4,502	1,669
Eldorado	4,891	4,482	5,004
Evergreen Park	3,313	1,594	705
Fairfield	4,008	3,280	2,754
Franklin Park	3,007	2,425	914
Fulton	2,585	2,656	2,445
Galena	4,126	3,878	4,742
Galva	2,812	2,875	2,974
Geneseo	3,824	3,406	3,375
Geneva	4,101	4,607	3,327
Georgetown	3,235	3,407	3,061
Gillespie	4,440	5,111	4,063
Glenview	2,500	1,886	760
Greenville	3,391	3,233	3,091
Harvard	3,121	2,988	3,294
Havana	3,999	3,451	3,614
Highland	3,820	3,319	2,902
Highwood	3,707	3,590	1,446
Hillsboro	4,514	4,435	5,074
Homewood	4,078	3,227	1,389
Jerseyville	4,809	4,309	3,839
Kenilworth	2,935	2,501	1,188
La Grange Park	3,406	2,939	1,684
Lansing	4,462	3,378	1,409
Lemont	2,557	2,582	2,322
Libertyville	3,9[illegible]0	3,791	2,125
Lockport	3,475	3,383	2,684
Lyons	4,960	4,787	2,564
McLeansboro	2,528	2,162	1,927
Marseilles	4,455	4,292	3,391
Marshall	2,758	2,368	2,222
Mendota	4,215	4,008	3,9[illegible]4
Monticello	2,523	2,378	2,280
Morrison	3,187	3,067	3,000
Mount Olive	2,559	3,079	3,503
Nameoki	2,701	2,257	1,181
Illinois—Continued			
Nokomis	2,562	2,454	3,465
Oak Lawn	3,483	2,045	489
Oglesby	3,938	3,910	4,135
Oregon	2,825	2,376	2,227
Paxton	3,106	2,892	3,033
Peoria Heights	4,376	3,279	1,111
Petersburg	2,586	2,319	2,432
Phoenix	2,875	3,033	1,933
Pinckneyville	3,146	3,046	2,649
Pittsfield	2,884	2,356	2,129
Riverdale	2,865	2,504	1,166
River Grove	3,301	2,741	484
Robinson	4,311	3,668	3,375
Rochelle	4,200	3,785	3,310
Rock Falls	4,987	3,893	2,927
Roodhouse	2,557	2,621	2,928
Sandwich	2,608	2,611	2,409
Savanna	4,792	5,086	5,237
Shelbyville	4,092	3,491	3,568
Silvis	2,990	2,650	2,541
South Beloit	2,825	2,361	1,436
Sparta	3,664	3,385	3,340
Staunton	4,212	4,618	6,027
Steger	3,369	2,985	2,304
Sullivan	3,101	2,339	2,532
Sycamore	4,702	4,021	3,602
Tuscola	2,838	2,569	2,564
Virden	3,041	3,011	4,682
Washington Park	4,523	3,837	1,516
Watseka	3,744	3,144	2,817
West Chicago	3,355	3,477	2,594
Western Springs	4,856	3,894	1,258
Westmont	3,044	2,733	-------
Westville	3,446	3,901	4,241
White Hall	3,025	2,928	2,954
Zeigler	3,006	3,816	2,338
Indiana			
Alexandria	4,801	4,408	4,172
Angola	3,141	2,665	2,650
Attica	3,760	3,700	3,392
Aurora	4,828	4,386	4,299
Batesville	3,065	2,838	2,361
Beech Grove	3,907	3,552	1,459
Boonville	4,526	4,208	4,451
Columbia City	4,219	3,805	3,499
Crown Point	4,643	4,046	3,232
Dunkirk	2,942	2,583	2,532
East Gary	3,401	2,409	813
Garrett	4,285	4,428	4,796
Gas City	3,488	3,087	2,870
Greencastle	4,872	4,613	3,780
Greenfield	4,821	4,188	4,168
Highland	2,723	1,553	542
Huntingburg	3,816	3,440	3,261
Jasonville	3,418	3,536	4,461
Lawrenceburg	4,413	4,072	3,466
Mitchell	3,393	3,226	3,025
Monticello	3,153	2,331	2,536
Nappanee	3,028	2,957	2,678
North Manchester	3,170	2,765	2,711
North Vernon	3,112	2,989	3,084
Oakland City	3,068	2,842	2,270
Petersburg	3,075	2,609	2,367
Rensselaer	3,214	2,798	2,912
Rochester	3,835	3,518	3,720
Salem	3,194	3,194	2,836
Union City	3,535	3,084	3,406
West Terre Haute	3,729	3,588	4,310
Iowa			
Algona	4,954	3,985	3,724
Anamosa	4,069	3,579	2,881
Belle Plaine	3,202	3,239	3,887
Bettendorf	3,143	2,768	2,178
Bloomfield	2,732	2,226	2,064
Clarinda	4,905	4,962	4,511
Clarion	2,971	2,578	2,826
Clear Lake	3,764	3,066	2,804
Cresco	3,530	3,069	3,195
Denison	4,361	3,905	3,581
Eagle Grove	4,024	4,071	4,433
Eldora	3,553	3,200	3,189
Emmetsburg	3,374	2,865	2,762
Forest City	2,545	2,016	2,145
Glenwood	4,501	4,269	3,862
Hampton	4,006	3,473	2,992
Harlan	3,727	3,145	2,831
Hawarden	2,681	2,459	2,491
Humboldt	2,819	2,251	2,232
Independence	4,342	3,691	3,672
Indianola	4,123	3.488	3,628
Iowa Falls	4,425	4,112	3,954

[1] Corrected figure.

TABLE 15.—POPULATION OF URBAN PLACES HAVING, IN 1940, FROM 2,500 TO 5,000 INHABITANTS: 1920 TO 1940—Continued

[Places marked with an asterisk (*) were classified as urban under special rule in 1940]

URBAN PLACE	1940	1930	1920
Iowa—Continued			
Jefferson	4,088	3,431	3,416
Manchester	3,762	3,413	3,111
Maquoketa	4,076	3,595	3,626
Marion	4,721	4,348	4,138
Missouri Valley	3,994	4,230	3,985
Monticello	2,546	2,259	2,257
Mount Pleasant	4,610	3,743	3,987
Nevada	3,353	3,133	2,668
New Hampton	2,933	2,458	2,539
Onawa	3,438	2,538	2,256
Osage	3,196	2,964	2,878
Osceola	3,281	2,871	2,684
Pella	3,638	3,326	3,338
Rock Rapids	2,556	2,221	2,172
Sac City	3,165	2,854	2,630
Sheldon	3,768	3,320	3,488
Tama	2,832	2,626	2,601
Tipton	2,518	2,145	2,142
Vinton	4,163	3,372	3,381
Waukon	2,972	2,526	2,359
Waverly	4,156	3,652	3,352
West Des Moines [1]	4,252	4,280	3,631
Winterset	3,631	2,921	2,906
Kansas			
Anthony	2,873	2,947	2,740
Augusta	3,821	4,033	4,219
Baxter Springs	4,921	4,541	3,608
Belleville	2,580	2,383	2,254
Beloit	3,765	3,502	3,315
Caney	2,629	2,794	3,427
Cherryvale	3,185	4,251	4,698
Clay Center	4,518	4,386	3,715
Columbus	3,402	3,235	3,155
Council Grove	2,875	2,898	2,857
Eureka	3,803	3,698	2,606
Fredonia	3,524	3,446	3,954
Galena	4,375	4,736	4,712
Garnett	2,607	2,768	2,329
Girard	2,554	2,442	3,161
Goodland	3,306	3,626	2,664
Herington	3,804	4,519	4,065
Hiawatha	3,238	3,302	3,222
Hoisington	3,719	3,001	2,395
Holton	2,885	2,705	2,703
Horton	2,872	4,049	4,009
Kingman	3,213	2,752	2,407
Larned	3,533	3,532	3,139
Liberal	4,410	5,294	3,613
Lyons	4,497	2,939	2,516
Marysville	4,055	4,013	3,048
Neodesha	3,376	3,381	3,943
Norton	2,762	2,767	2,186
Olathe	3,979	3,656	3,268
Osawatomie	4,145	4,440	3,293
Paola	3,511	3,762	3,238
Russell	4,819	2,352	1,700
Kentucky			
Bardstown	3,152	1,767	1,717
Carrollton	2,910	2,409	2,281
Catlettsburg	4,524	5,025	4,183
Central City	4,199	4,321	3,108
Cumberland	4,149	2,639	300
Cynthiana	4,840	4,386	3,857
Dawson Springs	2,560	2,311	1,762
Earlington	2,858	3,309	3,652
Elizabethtown	3,667	2,590	2,530
Elsmere	2,885	2,917	919
Franklin	3,940	3,056	3,154
Fulton	3,308	3,502	3,415
Georgetown	4,420	4,229	3,903
Harrodsburg	4,673	4,029	3,765
Irvine	3,631	3,640	2,705
Lebanon	3,786	3,248	3,239
Morganfield	3,079	2,551	2,651
Mount Sterling	4,782	4,350	3,995
Murray	3,773	2,891	2,415
Nicholasville	3,192	3,128	2,786
Pikeville	4,185	3,376	2,110
Pineville	3,882	3,567	2,908
Providence	4,397	4,742	4,151
Russellville	3,983	3,297	3,124
Shelbyville	4,392	4,033	3,760
Versailles	2,548	2,244	2,061
Louisiana			
Bunkie	3,575	2,464	1,743
Covington	4,123	3,208	2,942
De Quincy	3,252	3,589	1,823
De Ridder	3,750	3,747	3,535
Donaldsonville	3,889	3,788	3,745
Louisiana—Continued			
Ferriday	2,857	2,502	1,044
Franklin	4,274	3,271	3,504
Homer	3,497	2,909	3,305
Jeanerette	3,362	2,228	2,512
Jonesboro	2,639	1,949	837
Kaplan	2,838	1,653	876
Lake Providence	3,711	2,867	1,917
Leesville	2,829	3,291	2,518
Mansfield	4,065	3,837	2,564
Oakdale	3,933	3,188	4,016
Pineville	4,297	3,612	2,188
Ponchatoula	4,001	2,898	955
Rayne	4,974	3,710	2,720
St. Martinville	3,501	2,455	2,465
Slidell	2,864	2,807	2,958
Springhill	2,822	1,546	748
Sulphur	3,504	1,888	1,714
Ville Platte	3,721	1,722	1,364
Westwego	4,992	3,987	[3]
Winnfield	4,512	3,721	2,975
Winnsboro	2,834	1,965	1,176
Maine			
Eastport	3,346	3,466	4,494
Ellsworth	3,911	3,557	3,058
Fairfield*	3,420	3,529	2,747
Fort Fairfield*	2,693	2,616	1,903
Hallowell	2,906	2,675	2,764
Madison*	2,581	3,036	2,729
Maryland			
Brunswick	3,856	3,671	3,905
Chestertown	2,760	2,809	2,537
Crisfield	3,908	3,850	4,116
Easton	4,528	4,092	3,442
Elkton	3,518	3,331	2,660
Greenbelt	2,831	----	----
Havre de Grace	4,967	3,985	4,377
Laurel	2,823	2,532	2,239
Mount Rainier	4,830	3,832	2,402
Pocomoke City	2,739	2,609	2,444
Westernport	3,565	3,440	3,977
Westminster	4,692	4,463	3,521
Massachusetts			
Ayer town*	3,572	3,060	3,052
Blackstone town*	4,566	4,674	4,299
Dalton town*	4,206	4,220	3,752
Dudley town*	4,616	4,265	3,701
Hopedale town*	3,113	2,973	2,777
Lee town*	4,222	4,061	4,085
Nantucket town*	3,401	3,678	2,797
Provincetown town*	3,668	3,808	4,246
Rockport town*	3,556	3,630	3,878
Michigan			
Allegan	4,526	3,941	3,637
Allen Park	3,487	944	----
Bad Axe	2,624	2,332	2,140
Belding	4,089	4,140	3,911
Bessemer	4,080	4,035	5,482
Big Rapids	4,987	4,671	4,558
Boyne City	2,904	2,650	4,284
Buchanan	4,056	3,922	3,187
Caro	3,070	2,554	2,704
Center Line	3,198	2,604	----
Clawson	4,006	3,377	----
Crystal Falls	2,641	2,995	3,394
Durand	3,127	3,081	2,672
East Grand Rapids	4,899	4,024	1,310
Eaton Rapids	3,060	2,822	2,379
Fenton	3,377	3,171	2,507
Fremont	2,520	2,157	2,180
Garden City	4,096	2,081	----
Gladstone	4,972	5,170	4,953
Grand Ledge	3,899	3,572	3,043
Grosse Pointe Woods [4]	2,805	961	----
Houghton	3,693	3,757	4,466
Howell	3,748	3,615	2,951
Iron River	4,416	4,665	4,295
L'Anse	2,564	2,421	1,013
Laurium	3,929	4,916	6,696
Marine City	3,633	3,462	3,731
Mason	2,867	2,575	1,879
Melvindale	4,764	4,053	----
Munising	4,409	3,956	5,037
Newberry	2,732	2,465	2,172
Northville	3,032	2,566	1,738
Norway	3,728	4,016	4,533
Otsego	3,428	3,245	3,168
Pleasant Ridge	3,391	2,885	472
Rochester	3,759	3,554	2,549
Rogers City	3,072	3,278	2,109
Michigan—Continued			
Romeo	2,627	2,283	2,102
St. Clair	3,471	3,389	3,204
St. Ignace	2,669	2,109	1,852
St. Johns	4,422	3,929	3,925
St. Louis	3,039	2,494	3,036
South Haven	4,745	4,804	3,829
Tecumseh	2,921	2,456	2,432
Wakefield	3,591	3,677	4,151
Wayne	4,223	3,423	1,891
Zeeland	3,007	2,850	2,275
Minnesota			
Bayport	2,633	2,590	1,936
Benson	2,729	2,095	2,111
Blue Earth	3,702	2,884	2,568
Breckenridge	2,745	2,264	2,401
Crosby	2,954	3,451	3,500
East Grand Forks	3,511	2,922	2,490
Gilbert	2,504	2,722	3,510
Glenwood	2,564	2,220	2,187
Grand Rapids	4,875	3,206	2,914
Hopkins	4,100	3,834	3,055
Hutchinson	3,887	3,406	3,379
Jackson	2,840	2,206	2,144
Lake City	3,204	3,210	2,846
Litchfield	3,920	2,880	2,790
Luverne	3,114	2,644	2,782
Marshall	4,590	3,250	3,092
Morris	3,214	2,474	2,320
Northfield	4,533	4,153	4,023
North Mankato	3,517	2,822	1,840
North St. Paul	3,135	2,915	1,979
Park Rapids	2,643	2,081	1,603
Pipestone	4,682	3,489	3,325
Redwood Falls	3,270	2,552	2,421
St. James	3,400	2,808	2,673
Sauk Center	3,016	2,716	2,699
Sauk Rapids	2,981	2,656	2,349
Sleepy Eye	2,923	2,576	2,449
Staples	2,952	2,667	2,570
Tracy	3,085	2,570	2,463
Two Harbors	4,046	4,425	4,546
Wadena	2,916	2,512	2,186
Waseca	4,270	3,815	3,908
White Bear Lake	2,858	2,600	2,022
Windom	2,807	2,123	2,123
Mississippi			
Aberdeen	4,746	3,925	4,071
Amory	3,727	3,214	2,861
Bay St. Louis	4,138	3,724	3,033
Belzoni	3,789	2,735	2,277
Cleveland	4,189	3,240	1,674
Crystal Springs	2,855	2,257	1,395
Durant	2,510	2,480	1,870
Ellisville	2,607	2,127	1,681
Forest	2,735	2,176	1,188
Hazlehurst	3,124	2,447	1,762
Holly Springs	2,750	2,271	2,113
Indianola	3,604	3,116	2,112
Kosciusko	4,291	3,237	2,258
Leland	3,700	2,426	2,003
Lexington	2,930	2,590	1,792
Louisville	3,451	3,013	1,777
Moss Point	3,042	2,453	3,340
New Albany	3,602	3,187	2,531
Oxford	3,433	2,890	2,150
Pass Christian	3,338	3,004	2,357
Philadelphia	3,711	2,560	1,669
Port Gibson	2,748	1,861	1,691
Starkville	4,900	3,612	2,596
Water Valley	3,340	3,738	4,315
Winona	2,532	2,607	2,572
Missouri			
Aurora	4,056	3,875	3,575
Berkeley	2,577	----	----
Bethany	2,682	2,209	2,080
Bolivar	2,636	2,256	1,980
Bonne Terre	3,730	4,021	3,815
Brentwood	4,383	2,819	----
Butler	2,958	2,706	2,702
California	2,525	2,384	2,218
Cameron	3,615	3,507	3,248
Carrollton	4,070	4,058	3,218
Chaffee	3,049	2,902	3,035
Crystal City	3,417	3,057	2,243
Dexter	3,108	2,714	2,635
Eldon	2,590	3,171	2,636
Excelsior Springs	4,864	4,565	4,165
Farmington	3,738	3,001	2,685
Fayette	2,608	2,630	2,318

[1] Name changed from Valley Junction in 1938.
[3] Not returned separately.
[4] Name changed from Lochmoor in 1939.

TABLE 15.—POPULATION OF URBAN PLACES HAVING, IN 1940, FROM 2,500 TO 5,000 INHABITANTS: 1920 TO 1940—Continued

[Places marked with an asterisk (*) were classified as urban under special rule in 1940]

URBAN PLACE	1940	1930	1920
Missouri—Continued			
Festus	4,620	4,085	3,348
Fredericktown	3,414	2,954	3,124
Glendale	2,526	1,451	749
Hayti	2,628	1,620	1,507
Higginsville	3,533	3,339	2,724
Jackson	3,113	2,465	2,114
Ladue [5]	3,981	780	------
Lamar	2,992	2,381	2,255
Liberty	3,598	3,516	3,097
Louisiana	4,669	[1] 3,746	4,060
Macon	4,206	3,851	3,549
Malden	2,673	2,025	2,098
Marceline	3,206	3,555	3,760
Monett	4,395	4,099	4,206
North Kansas City	2,688	2,574	870
Overland	2,934	------	------
Perryville	3,907	2,964	1,763
Richmond	4,240	4,129	4,409
Ste. Genevieve	2,787	2,662	2,046
Salem (Dent County)	3,151	2,250	1,771
Slater	3,070	3,478	3,797
Sullivan	2,517	2,013	909
Vandalia	2,672	2,450	2,158
West Plains	4,026	3,335	3,178
Montana			
Cut Bank	2,509	845	1,181
Deer Lodge	3,278	3,510	3,780
Dillon	3,014	2,422	2,701
Glasgow	3,799	2,216	2,059
Glendive	4,524	4,629	3,816
Laurel	2,754	2,558	2,239
Red Lodge	2,950	3,026	4,515
Roundup	2,644	2,577	2,434
Shelby	2,538	2,004	537
Sidney	2,978	2,010	1,400
Whitefish	2,602	2,803	2,867
Nebraska			
Auburn	3,639	3,068	2,863
Blair	3,289	2,791	2,702
Broken Bow	2,968	2,715	2,567
Chadron	4,262	4,606	4,412
Crete	3,038	2,865	2,445
Gering	3,104	2,531	2,508
Holdrege	3,360	3,263	3,108
Lexington	3,688	2,962	2,327
Ogallala	3,159	1,631	1,062
O'Neill	2,532	2,019	2,107
Plattsmouth	4,268	3,793	4,190
Schuyler	2,808	2,588	2,636
Seward	2,826	2,737	2,368
Sidney	3,388	3,306	2,852
South Sioux City	4,556	3,927	2,402
Superior	2,650	3,044	2,719
Wahoo	2,648	2,689	2,338
Wayne	2,719	2,381	2,115
West Point	2,510	2,225	2,002
Nevada			
Elko	4,094	3,217	2,173
Ely	4,140	3,045	2,090
New Hampshire			
Littleton town*	4,571	4,558	4,239
Milford town*	3,927	4,068	3,783
New Jersey			
Belmar	3,435	3,491	1,987
Bernardsville	3,405	3,336	------
Beverly	2,691	2,864	2,562
Bloomingdale	2,606	2,543	2,193
Bordentown	4,223	4,405	4,371
Bradley Beach	3,468	3,306	2,307
Butler	3,351	3,392	2,886
Caldwell	4,932	5,144	3,776
Cape May	2,583	2,637	2,999
Chatham	4,888	3,869	2,421
Clementon	2,866	2,605	------
Closter	2,603	2,502	1,840
East Paterson	4,937	4,779	2,441
Edgewater	4,028	4,089	3,530
Egg Harbor City	3,589	3,478	2,622
Flemington	2,617	2,729	2,590
Franklin	4,009	4,176	4,075
Garwood	3,622	3,344	2,084
Glassboro	4,925	4,799	------
Hackettstown	3,289	3,038	2,936
Hightstown	3,486	3,012	2,674
Hillsdale	3,438	2,959	------
Keansburg	2,904	2,190	1,321
Lambertville	4,447	4,518	4,660
Lindenwold	2,552	2,523	------
Little Ferry	4,545	4,155	2,715
New Jersey—Continued			
Margate City	3,266	2,913	249
Matawan	2,758	2,264	1,910
Maywood	4,052	3,398	1,618
Merchantville	3,679	3,592	2,749
Middlesex	3,763	3,504	1,852
Midland Park	4,525	3,638	2,243
Milltown	3,515	2,994	2,573
New Milford	3,215	2,556	------
Northfield	2,848	2,804	1,127
North Haledon	2,761	2,157	887
Oaklyn	3,869	3,843	1,148
Ocean City	4,672	5,525	2,512
Oceanport	3,159	1,872	------
Oradell	2,802	2,360	1,286
Paramus	3,688	2,649	------
Park Ridge	2,519	2,229	1,481
Pompton Lakes	3,189	3,104	2,008
Ramsey	3,566	3,258	2,090
Raritan	4,839	4,751	4,457
River Edge [6]	3,287	2,210	1,077
Rockaway	3,514	3,132	2,655
Rumson	2,926	2,073	1,658
Runnemede	2,835	2,436	------
Wanaque	3,143	3,119	2,916
Washington	4,643	4,410	3,341
West Caldwell	3,458	2,911	1,085
West Paterson	3,306	3,101	1,858
Westville	3,585	3,462	2,380
Wharton	3,854	3,683	2,877
Wood-Lynne	2,861	2,878	1,515
New Mexico			
Alamogordo	3,950	3,096	2,363
Artesia	4,071	2,427	1,115
Belen	3,038	2,116	1,306
Clayton	3,188	2,518	2,157
Deming	3,608	3,377	3,212
Hot Springs	2,940	1,336	455
Lordsburg	3,101	2,069	1,325
Socorro	3,712	2,058	1,256
New York			
Albion	4,660	4,878	4,683
Babylon	4,742	4,342	2,523
Baldwinsville	3,840	3,845	3,685
Ballston Spa	4,443	4,591	4,103
Bath	4,696	4,015	3,720
Brockport	3,590	3,511	2,980
Canajoharie	2,577	2,519	2,415
Canastota	4,150	4,235	3,995
Canisteo	2,550	2,548	2,201
Canton	3,018	2,822	2,522
Carthage	4,207	4,460	4,320
Cobleskill	2,617	2,594	2,410
Cooperstown	2,599	2,909	2,725
Corinth	3,054	2,613	2,576
Croton-on-Hudson	3,843	2,447	2,286
Dannemora	4,830	3,348	2,623
Dansville	4,976	4,928	4,631
Dolgeville	3,195	3,309	3,448
East Syracuse	4,520	4,646	4,106
Ellenville	4,000	3,280	3,116
Elmira Heights	4,829	5,061	4,188
Elmsford	3,078	2,935	1,535
Fairport	4,644	4,604	4,626
Falconer	3,222	3,579	2,742
Farmingdale	3,524	3,373	2,091
Fort Edward	3,620	3,850	3,871
Fort Plain	2,770	2,725	2,747
Frankfort	3,859	4,203	4,198
Goshen	3,073	2,891	2,843
Gouverneur	4,478	4,015	4,143
Gowanda	3,156	3,042	2,673
Granville	3,173	3,483	3,024
Green Island	3,988	4,331	4,411
Greenport	3,259	3,062	3,122
Highland Falls	3,711	2,910	2,588
Homer	2,928	3,195	2,356
Hoosick Falls	4,279	4,755	4,896
Horseheads	2,570	2,430	2,078
Irvington	3,272	3,067	2,701
Lake Placid	3,136	2,930	2,099
Lawrence	3,649	3,041	2,861
Le Roy	4,413	4,474	4,203
Liberty	3,788	3,427	2,459
Lindenhurst	4,756	4,040	------
Liverpool	2,500	2,244	1,831
Lowville	3,578	3,424	3,127
Lyons	3,863	3,956	4,253
Mohawk	2,882	2,835	2,919
Monticello	3,737	3,450	2,330
New York—Continued			
Mount Morris	3,530	3,238	3,312
New Hyde Park	4,691	3,314	------
New York Mills	3,628	4,006	------
Northport	3,093	2,528	1,977
Palmyra	2,709	2,592	2,480
Perry	4,468	4,231	4,717
Pleasantville	4,454	4,540	3,590
Potsdam	4,821	4,136	4,039
Sag Harbor	2,517	2,773	2,993
Saugerties	3,916	4,060	4,013
Sea Cliff	4,416	3,456	2,108
Sidney	3,012	2,444	2,670
Silver Creek	3,067	3,160	3,260
Sloan	3,836	3,482	1,791
Southampton	3,818	3,737	2,891
South Glens Falls	3,081	2,689	2,158
Spring Valley	4,308	3,948	3,818
Springville	2,849	2,540	2,331
Suffern	3,768	3,757	3,154
Ticonderoga	3,402	3,680	2,102
Walden	4,262	4,283	5,493
Walton	3,697	3,496	3,598
Wappingers Falls	3,427	3,336	3,235
Warsaw	3,554	3,477	3,622
Warwick	2,534	2,443	2,420
Waterford	2,903	2,921	2,637
Waterloo	4,010	4,047	3,809
Watkins Glen	2,913	2,956	2,785
Westbury	4,524	------	------
Westfield	3,434	3,466	3,413
West Haverstraw	2,533	2,834	2,018
Whitehall	4,851	5,191	5,258
Whitesboro	3,532	3,375	3,038
Williamsville	3,614	3,119	1,667
Yorkville	3,311	3,406	1,512
North Carolina			
Albemarle	4,060	3,493	2,691
Beaufort	3,272	2,957	2,968
Belmont	4,356	4,121	2,941
Bessemer City	3,567	3,739	2,176
Brevard	3,061	2,339	1,658
Chapel Hill	3,654	2,699	1,483
Cherryville	3,225	2,756	1,884
Clinton	3,557	2,712	2,110
Edenton	3,835	3,563	2,777
Elkin	2,734	2,357	1,195
Farmville	2,980	2,056	1,780
Graham	4,339	2,972	2,366
Lincolnton	4,525	3,781	3,390
Marion	2,889	2,467	1,784
Morehead City	3,695	3,483	2,958
Mount Olive	2,929	2,685	2,297
North Wilkesboro	4,478	3,668	2,363
Oxford	3,991	4,101	3,606
Rockingham	3,657	2,906	2,509
Roxboro	4,599	3,657	1,651
Sanford	4,960	4,253	2,977
Scotland Neck	2,559	2,339	2,061
Smithfield	3,678	2,543	1,895
Southern Pines	3,225	2,524	743
Spencer	3,072	3,128	2,510
Spindale	3,952	3,066	------
Valdese	2,615	1,816	------
Wadesboro	3,587	3,124	2,648
Waynesville	2,940	2,414	1,942
Whiteville	3,011	2,203	1,664
Williamston	3,966	2,731	1,800
North Dakota			
Grafton	4,070	3,136	2,512
Wahpeton	3,747	3,176	3,069
Ohio			
Amherst	2,896	2,844	2,485
Bay	3,356	2,294	751
Bridgeport	4,853	4,655	3,977
Cadiz	2,808	2,597	2,084
Carey	2,984	2,722	2,488
Carrollton	2,548	2,286	2,192
Celina	4,841	4,664	4,226
Chagrin Falls	2,505	2,739	2,237
Clyde	3,174	3,159	3,099
Columbiana	2,687	2,485	2,114
Crestline	4,337	4,425	4,313
Crooksville	2,890	3,251	3,311
Deer Park	3,510	2,642	824
Dennison	4,413	4,529	5,524
Dover (Cuyahoga County)	3,200	2,453	1,754
Eaton	3,552	3,347	3,210
Elmwood Place	4,248	4,562	3,990

[1] Corrected figure.
[5] Deer Creek, Ladue, and McKnight towns consolidated as Ladue city in 1936; combined population in 1930, 1,713.
[6] Name changed from Riverside in 1930.

TABLE 15.—POPULATION OF URBAN PLACES HAVING, IN 1940, FROM 2,500 TO 5,000 INHABITANTS: 1920 TO 1940—Continued

[Places marked with an asterisk (*) were classified as urban under special rule in 1940]

URBAN PLACE	1940	1930	1920
Ohio—Continued			
Fairfield [7]	------	------	------
Fairport	4,528	4,972	4,211
Fairview (Cuyahoga County)	4,700	3,689	642
Franklin	4,511	4,491	3,071
Geneva	4,171	3,791	3,081
Glouster	2,847	2,903	3,140
Greenfield	4,228	3,871	4,344
Greenhills	2,677	------	------
Hicksville	2,549	2,445	2,378
Hillsboro	4,713	4,040	4,356
Hubbard	4,189	4,080	3,320
Lebanon	3,890	3,222	3,396
Lisbon	3,379	3,405	3,113
London	4,697	4,141	4,080
Louisville	3,379	3,130	2,008
Marysville	4,037	3,639	3,635
Maumee	4,683	4,588	3,195
Mayfield Heights	2,696	2,612	------
Medina	4,359	4,071	3,430
Middleport	3,356	3,505	3,772
Minerva	2,937	2,675	2,261
Montpelier	3,703	3,677	3,052
Mount Healthy	3,997	3,530	2,255
Napoleon	4,825	4,545	4,143
Newburgh Heights	3,830	4,152	2,957
Newcomerstown	4,564	4,265	3,389
New Lexington	4,049	3,901	3,157
Newton Falls	3,120	3,458	1,100
North Baltimore	2,616	2,402	2,439
North Canton	2,988	2,648	1,597
North Olmsted	3,487	2,624	1,419
North Royalton	2,559	1,397	------
Oberlin	4,305	4,292	4,236
Orrville	4,484	4,427	4,107
Oxford	2,756	2,588	2,146
Perrysburg	3,457	3,182	2,429
Pomeroy	3,581	3,563	4,294
Port Clinton	4,505	4,408	3,928
Rittman	2,770	2,785	1,803
Rossford [8]	3,912	------	------
St. Clairsville	2,797	2,440	1,561
Sebring	3,902	3,949	3,541
Shadyside	4,048	4,098	3,084
Silverton	2,907	1,843	795
Tallmadge	3,452	------	------
Tippecanoe City	2,879	2,559	2,426
Upper Sandusky	3,907	3,889	3,708
Wauseon	3,016	2,889	3,035
Wellington	2,529	2,235	2,245
Westerville	3,146	2,879	2,480
Wickliffe	3,155	2,491	1,508
Willard	4,261	4,514	3,889
Willoughby	4,364	4,252	2,656
Wyoming	4,466	3,767	2,323
Oklahoma			
Antlers	3,254	2,246	1,842
Atoka	2,548	1,856	2,038
Bethany	2,590	2,032	485
Chandler	2,738	2,717	2,226
Cherokee	2,553	2,236	2,017
Claremore	4,134	3,720	3,435
Cleveland	2,510	2,959	2,717
Cordell	2,776	2,936	1,855
Drumright	4,303	4,972	6,460
Edmond	4,002	3,576	2,452
Hartshorne	2,596	3,587	3,480
Hollis	2,732	2,914	1,683
Hominy	3,267	3,485	2,875
Idabel	3,689	2,581	3,067
Kingfisher	3,352	2,726	2,447
Madill	2,594	2,203	2,717
Mangum	4,193	4,806	3,405
Marlow	2,899	3,084	2,276
Nowata	3,904	3,531	4,435
Okemah	3,811	4,002	2,162
Pawnee	2,742	2,562	2,418
Poteau	4,020	3,169	2,679
Pryor Creek	2,501	1,828	1,767
Purcell	3,116	2,817	2,938
Sayre	3,037	3,157	1,703
Sulphur	4,970	4,242	3,667
Tahlequah	3,027	2,495	2,271
Tonkawa	3,197	3,311	1,448
Wagoner	3,535	2,994	3,436
Watonga	2,828	2,228	1,678
Weatherford	2,504	2,417	1,929
Oregon			
Ashland	4,744	4,544	4,283
Burns	2,566	2,599	1,022
Coquille	3,327	2,732	1,642
Oregon—Continued			
Cottage Grove	2,626	2,473	1,919
Dallas	3,579	2,975	2,701
Hillsboro	3,747	3,039	2,468
Hood River	3,280	2,757	3,195
Lebanon	2,729	1,851	1,805
McMinnville	3,706	2,917	2,767
Newberg	2,960	2,951	2,566
North Bend	4,262	4,012	3,268
Ontario	3,551	1,941	2,039
Roseburg	4,924	4,362	4,258
St. Helens	4,304	3,994	2,220
Seaside	2,902	1,565	1,802
Silverton	2,925	2,462	2,251
Springfield	3,805	2,364	1,855
Tillamook	2,751	2,549	1,964
Pennsylvania			
Aldan	2,642	2,269	1,136
Ambler	3,953	3,944	3,094
Apollo	3,232	3,406	3,227
Aspinwall	4,716	4,263	3,170
Athens	4,215	4,372	4,384
Avoca	4,771	4,943	4,950
Barnesboro	3,831	3,506	4,183
Bedford	3,268	2,953	2,330
Bellewood	2,772	2,560	2,029
Ben Avon	2,516	2,472	2,198
Bentleyville	3,428	3,609	3,679
Birdsboro	3,313	3,542	3,299
Boyertown	3,983	3,943	3,189
Bridgeville	4,459	3,939	3,092
Brockway	2,709	2,690	2,369
Brookville	4,397	4,387	3,272
Burnham	2,997	3,089	2,765
California	2,614	2,362	2,480
Camp Hill	3,630	3,111	1,636
Castle Shannon	3,970	3,810	2,353
Catasauqua	4,764	4,851	4,714
Clarion	3,798	3,201	2,793
Clarks Summit	2,691	2,604	1,404
Clifton Heights	4,921	5,057	3,469
Clymer	3,082	2,672	2,867
Coplay	3,109	3,279	2,845
Coudersport	3,197	2,740	2,836
Cresson	2,500	2,317	2,170
Curwensville	3,422	3,140	2,973
Dale	3,291	3,364	3,115
Dallastown	2,917	2,849	2,124
Derry	3,003	3,046	2,889
Downingtown	4,645	4,548	4,024
Doylestown	4,976	4,577	3,837
East Conemaugh	4,810	4,979	5,256
East Lansdowne	3,323	3,168	1,561
East McKeesport	3,026	2,922	2,430
East Mauch Chunk	3,392	3,739	3,868
Ebensburg	3,719	3,063	2,179
Edgewood	4,697	4,821	3,181
Elizabeth	2,976	2,939	2,703
Elizabethtown	4,315	3,940	3,319
Emporium	3,775	2,929	3,036
Emsworth	2,765	2,709	2,165
Ferndale	2,740	2,742	1,450
Forest City	4,266	5,209	6,004
Fountain Hill	4,804	4,568	2,339
Freedom	3,227	3,227	3,452
Freeport	2,710	2,772	2,696
Gallitzin	3,618	3,458	3,580
Gilberton	3,710	4,227	4,766
Girardville	4,602	4,891	4,482
Glenolden	4,825	4,482	1,944
Greencastle	2,511	2,557	2,271
Hamburg	3,717	3,637	2,764
Hatboro	2,605	2,651	1,102
Hellertown	4,031	3,851	3,008
Hummelstown	3,264	3,036	2,654
Ingram	3,904	3,866	2,900
Irwin	3,441	3,443	3,235
Jermyn	3,238	3,519	3,326
Johnsonburg	4,955	4,737	5,400
Kennett Square	3,375	3,091	2,398
Kutztown	2,966	2,841	2,684
Laureldale	3,397	------	------
Leechburg	4,275	4,489	3,991
Lemoyne	4,358	4,171	1,939
Lewisburg	3,571	3,308	3,204
Lititz	4,840	4,368	3,680
Lykens	3,048	3,033	2,880
McDonald	3,530	3,281	2,751
Manheim	3,831	3,520	2,712
Marcus Hook	4,123	4,867	5,324
Masontown	3,721	3,873	1,525
Mauch Chunk	3,009	3,206	3,666
Pennsylvania—Continued			
Mayfield	3,172	3,774	3,832
Meyersdale	3,250	3,065	3,716
Millersburg	2,959	2,909	2,936
Montoursville	3,019	2,710	1,949
Moosic	4,568	4,557	4,364
Mount Joy	2,855	2,716	2,192
Mount Penn	3,654	3,017	1,370
Mount Union	4,763	4,892	4,744
Muncy	2,606	2,413	2,054
Myerstown	2,692	2,593	2,385
New Cumberland	4,525	4,283	1,577
North Bellevernon	3,022	3,072	2,605
North Catasauqua	2,530	2,700	2,321
North Charleroi	2,674	2,879	1,931
North East	3,704	[1] 3,710	3,481
Northumberland	4,469	4,483	4,061
Norwood	3,921	3,878	2,353
Oxford	2,723	2,606	2,093
Patton	3,085	2,988	3,628
Pen Argyl	4,059	4,310	4,096
Penbrook	3,627	3,567	2,072
Perkasie	4,121	3,463	3,150
Philipsburg	3,963	3,600	3,900
Polk	3,690	3,337	2,662
Portage	4,123	4,432	4,804
Port Carbon	3,279	3,225	2,882
Port Vue	3,001	3,510	2,538
Red Lion	4,891	4,757	3,198
Renovo	3,784	3,947	5,877
Reynoldsville	3,675	3,480	4,116
Ridley Park	3,887	3,356	2,313
Roaring Spring	2,724	2,724	2,379
Royersford	3,605	3,719	3,278
Selinsgrove	2,877	2,797	1,937
Sharon Hill	4,467	3,825	1,780
Shillington	4,932	4,401	2,175
Slatington	4,062	4,134	4,014
Souderton	4,036	3,857	3,125
South Connellsville	2,628	2,516	2,196
South Fork	3,023	3,227	4,239
South Greensburg	2,616	2,520	2,188
Southwest Greensburg	3,002	3,105	2,538
Spangler	3,201	2,761	3,035
Spring City	3,022	2,963	2,944
Springdale	4,989	4,781	2,929
Sugar Notch	2,505	2,768	2,612
Susquehanna Depot	2,740	3,203	3,764
Swarthmore	4,061	3,405	2,350
Towanda	4,154	4,104	4,269
Trafford	4,017	4,187	2,859
Union City	3,843	3,788	3,850
Verona	4,356	4,376	3,938
Waynesburg	4,891	4,915	3,332
Weatherly	2,754	2,531	2,356
Wellsboro	3,665	3,643	3,452
Wesleyville	2,918	2,854	1,457
West Homestead	3,526	3,552	3,435
Westmont	3,741	3,388	1,976
West Newton	2,765	2,953	2,645
West Reading	4,907	4,908	2,921
West Wyoming	2,992	2,769	1,938
Williamstown	2,769	2,958	2,878
Wyoming	4,728	4,648	3,582
Wyomissing	3,320	3,111	2,062
Youngwood	2,546	2,783	2,275
Rhode Island			
East Greenwich town*	3,842	3,666	3,290
South Carolina			
Abbeville	4,930	4,414	4,570
Bamberg	3,000	2,450	2,210
Batesburg	2,933	2,839	2,848
Beaufort	3,185	2,776	2,831
Bennettsville	4,895	3,667	3,197
Bishopville	2,995	2,249	2,090
Cheraw	4,497	3,573	3,150
Clover	3,067	3,111	1,608
Dillon	3,867	2,731	2,205
Eau Claire	3,508	2,915	2,566
Fort Mill	2,919	2,112	1,946
Greer	2,940	2,419	2,292
Honea Path	2,765	2,740	1,900
Kingstree	3,182	2,392	2,074
Lake City	2,522	1,942	1,606
Lancaster	4,430	3,545	3,032
Mullins	4,392	3,158	2,379
North Augusta	2,629	2,003	1,742
Summerville	3,023	2,579	2,550
Walhalla	2,820	2,388	2,068

[1] Corrected figure.

[7] Population for 1940 was originally reported as 2,549, a figure based on an erroneous inclusion of an area outside the village. This figure was later corrected to 1,409, the figure shown in table 16; but the original figure is included in urban totals and in totals for urban places of 2,500 to 5,000 shown in other tables.

[8] Information as to incorporation in 1939 received too late for inclusion of figures in urban totals and in totals for urban places of 2,500 to 5,000 shown in other tables.

TABLE 15.—POPULATION OF URBAN PLACES HAVING, IN 1940, FROM 2,500 TO 5,000 INHABITANTS: 1920 TO 1940—Continued

[Places marked with an asterisk (*) were classified as urban under special rule in 1940]

URBAN PLACE	1940	1930	1920
South Carolina—Continued			
Walterboro	3,373	2,592	1,853
Whitmire	3,272	2,763	1,955
Williamston	2,509	2,235	2,322
Winnsboro	3,181	2,344	1,822
Woodruff	3,508	3,175	2,396
York	3,495	2,827	2,731
South Dakota			
Canton	2,518	2,270	2,225
Deadwood	4,100	2,559	2,403
Hot Springs	4,083	[1] 3,486	[1] 2,141
Milbank	2,745	2,389	2,215
Mobridge	3,008	3,464	3,517
Pierre	4,322	3,659	3,209
Sisseton	2,513	1,569	1,431
Sturgis	3,008	1,747	1,250
Vermillion	3,324	2,850	2,590
Tennessee			
Brownsville	4,012	3,204	3,062
Clinton	2,761	1,927	1,409
Cookeville	4,364	3,738	2,395
Covington	3,513	3,397	3,410
Dickson	3,504	2,902	2,263
East Ridge	2,939	2,152	------
Erwin	3,350	3,623	2,965
Etowah	3,362	4,209	2,516
Fayetteville	4,684	3,822	3,629
Franklin	4,120	3,377	3,123
Gallatin	4,829	3,050	2,757
Jefferson City	2,576	1,898	1,414
La Follette	4,010	2,637	3,056
Lawrenceburg	3,807	3,102	2,461
Lenoir City	4,373	4,470	4,210
Lewisburg	3,582	3,112	2,711
Lexington	2,526	1,823	1,792
Loudon	3,017	2,578	------
McMinnville	4,649	3,914	2,814
Martin	3,587	3,300	2,837
Milan	3,035	3,155	2,057
Mount Pleasant	3,089	2,010	2,093
Newport	3,575	2,989	2,753
Ripley	2,784	2,330	2,070
Rockwood	3,981	3,898	4,652
Sparta	2,506	2,211	1,517
Sweetwater	2,593	2,271	1,972
Trenton	3,400	2,892	2,751
Tullahoma	4,549	4,023	3,479
Winchester	2,760	2,210	2,203
Texas			
Alpine	3,866	3,495	931
Alvin	3,087	1,511	1,519
Aransas Pass	4,095	2,482	1,569
Arlington	4,240	3,661	3,031
Athens	4,765	4,342	3,176
Ballinger	4,472	4,187	2,767
Belton	3,572	3,779	5,098
Benavides	3,081	------	------
Bowie	3,470	3,131	3,179
Brackettville	2,653	1,822	------
Brownfield	4,009	1,907	------
Burkburnett	2,814	3,281	5,300
Canyon	2,622	2,821	1,618
Center	3,010	2,510	1,838
Cisco	4,868	6,027	7,422
Clarksville	4,095	2,952	3,386
Comanche	3,209	2,435	3,524
Commerce	4,699	4,267	3,842
Conroe	4,624	2,457	1,858
Cooper	2,537	2,023	2,563
Cotulla	3,633	3,175	1,058
Crockett	4,536	4,441	3,061
Dalhart	4,682	4,691	2,676
Decatur	2,578	2,037	2,205
Donna	4,712	4,103	1,579
Dublin	2,546	2,271	3,229
Eastland	3,849	4,648	9,368
Edna	2,724	1,752	------
El Campo	3,906	2,034	1,766
Floydada	2,726	2,637	1,384
Fort Stockton	3,294	2,695	1,297
Fredericksburg	3,544	2,416	------
Freeport	2,579	3,162	1,798
Gatesville	3,177	2,601	2,499
Georgetown	3,682	3,583	2,871
Gilmer	3,138	1,963	2,268
Gladewater	4,454	------	------
Gonzales	4,722	3,859	3,128
Hamilton	2,716	2,084	2,018
Haskell	3,051	2,632	2,300

URBAN PLACE	1940	1930	1920
Texas—Continued			
Hearne	3,511	2,956	2,741
Hereford	2,584	2,458	1,696
Jasper	3,497	3,393	------
Jefferson	2,797	2,329	2,549
Kaufman	2,654	2,279	2,501
Kenedy	2,891	2,610	2,015
Kermit	2,584	------	------
La Grange	2,531	2,354	1,669
Lampasas	3,426	2,709	2,107
La Porte	3,072	1,280	889
Levelland	3,091	1,661	------
Liberty	3,087	2,187	1,117
Littlefield	3,817	3,218	------
Llano	2,658	2,124	1,645
Luling	4,437	5,970	1,502
McCamey	2,595	3,446	------
Marfa	3,805	3,909	3,553
Mart	2,856	2,853	3,105
Memphis	3,869	4,257	2,839
Mineola	3,223	3,304	2,299
Monahans	3,944	816	------
Mount Pleasant	4,528	3,541	4,099
Nocona	2,605	2,352	1,422
Olney	3,497	4,138	1,164
Paducah	2,677	2,802	1,357
Pasadena	3,436	1,647	------
Pearsall	3,164	2,536	2,161
Pecos	4,855	3,304	1,445
Pelly	3,712	3,452	------
Pharr	4,784	3,225	1,565
Pittsburg	2,916	2,640	2,540
Quanah	3,767	4,464	3,691
Ranger	4,553	6,208	16,205
Raymondville	4,050	2,050	------
Refugio	4,077	2,019	933
Rosenberg	3,457	1,941	1,279
San Diego	2,674	------	------
San Saba	2,927	2,240	2,011
Seagraves	3,225	505	------
Seymour	3,328	2,626	2,121
Shamrock	3,123	3,780	1,227
Silsbee	2,525	------	------
Sinton	3,770	1,852	1,058
Slaton	3,587	3,876	1,525
Smithville	3,100	3,296	3,204
Snyder	3,815	3,008	2,179
Sonora	2,528	1,942	1,009
Stamford	4,810	4,095	3,704
Stephenville	4,768	3,944	3,891
Taft	2,686	1,792	------
Teague	3,157	3,509	3,306
Wellington	3,308	3,570	1,968
Wharton	4,386	2,691	2,346
Yoakum	4,733	5,656	6,184
Utah			
American Fork	3,333	3,047	2,763
Bingham Canyon	2,834	3,248	2,676
Bountiful	3,357	2,571	2,063
Cedar City	4,695	3,615	2,462
Heber	2,748	2,477	1,931
Helper	2,843	2,707	1,606
Lehi	2,733	2,826	3,078
Midvale	2,875	2,451	2,209
Nephi	2,835	2,573	2,603
Orem	2,914	1,915	(2)
Park City	3,739	4,281	3,393
Payson	3,591	3,045	3,031
Richfield	3,584	3,067	3,262
St. George	3,591	2,434	2,215
Spanish Fork	4,167	3,727	4,036
Springville	4,796	3,748	3,010
Vermont			
Bellows Falls	4,236	3,930	4,860
Newport	4,902	5,094	4,976
Waterbury	3,074	[1] 2,858	[1] 2,365
Windsor	3,402	3,689	3,061
Virginia			
Abingdon	3,158	2,877	2,532
Altavista	2,919	2,367	1,206
Appalachia	3,010	3,595	2,036
Bedford	3,973	3,713	3,243
Big Stone Gap	4,331	3,908	3,009
Blackstone	2,699	1,772	1,497
Bluefield	3,921	3,906	2,752
Buena Vista	4,335	4,002	3,911
Colonial Heights	3,194	2,331	------
Emporia	2,735	2,144	1,869

URBAN PLACE	1940	1930	1920
Virginia—Continued			
Falls Church	2,576	2,019	1,659
Farmville	3,475	3,133	2,586
Franklin	3,466	2,930	2,363
Front Royal	3,831	2,424	1,404
Galax	3,195	2,544	1,250
Lexington	3,914	3,752	2,870
Norton	4,006	3,077	3,068
Phoebus	3,503	2,956	3,043
Pocahontas	2,623	2,293	2,591
Saltville	2,650	2,964	2,248
Vinton	3,455	3,610	2,770
Virginia Beach	2,600	1,719	846
Williamsburg	3,942	3,778	2,462
Wytheville	4,653	3,327	2,947
Washington			
Auburn	4,211	3,906	3,163
Camas	4,433	4,239	1,843
Chehalis	4,857	4,907	4,558
Clarkston	3,116	2,870	1,859
Colfax	2,853	2,782	3,027
Dayton	3,026	2,528	2,695
Enumclaw	2,627	2,084	1,378
Grand Coulee	3,659	------	------
Kent	2,586	2,320	2,282
Mount Vernon	4,278	3,690	3,341
Omak	2,918	2,547	525
Pasco	3,913	3,496	3,362
Port Townsend	4,683	3,979	2,847
Pullman	4,417	3,322	2,440
Raymond	4,045	3,828	4,260
Renton	4,488	4,062	3,301
Sedro-Woolley	2,954	2,719	2,379
Shelton	3,707	3,091	984
Snohomish	2,794	2,688	2,985
Toppenish	3,683	2,774	3,120
West Virginia			
Benwood	3,608	3,950	4,773
Buckhannon	4,450	4,374	3,785
Charles Town	2,926	2,434	2,527
Chester	3,805	3,701	3,283
Follansbee	4,834	4,841	3,135
Kenova	3,902	3,680	2,166
Keystone	2,942	1,897	1,839
McMechen	3,726	3,710	3,356
Mannington	3,145	3,261	3,673
Montgomery	3,231	2,906	2,130
Mullens	3,026	2,356	1,425
New Martinsville	3,491	2,814	2,341
Nitro	2,983	------	------
Oak Hill	3,213	2,076	1,037
Piedmont	2,677	2,241	2,835
Point Pleasant	3,538	3,301	3,059
St. Albans	3,558	3,254	2,825
Salem	2,571	2,943	2,920
Shinnston	2,817	2,802	1,679
Sistersville	2,702	3,072	3,238
Wisconsin			
Algoma	2,652	2,202	1,911
Berlin	4,247	4,106	4,400
Black River Falls	2,539	1,950	1,796
Burlington	4,414	4,114	3,626
Clintonville	4,134	3,572	3,275
Columbus	2,760	2,514	2,460
Delavan	3,444	3,301	3,016
Edgerton	3,266	2,906	2,688
Greendale	2,527	------	------
Hartford	3,910	3,754	4,515
Hudson	2,987	2,725	3,014
Hurley	3,375	3,264	3,188
Jefferson	3,059	2,639	2,572
Kewaunee	2,533	2,409	1,865
Kimberly	2,618	2,256	1,322
Ladysmith	3,671	3,493	3,581
Lake Geneva	3,238	3,073	2,632
Lancaster	2,963	2,432	2,485
Little Chute	3,360	2,833	2,017
Mauston	2,621	2,107	1,966
Mayville	2,754	2,521	3,011
Neillsville	2,562	2,118	2,160
New London	4,825	4,661	4,667
Oconomowoc	4,562	4,190	3,301
Park Falls	3,252	3,036	2,676
Platteville	4,762	4,047	4,353
Plymouth	4,170	3,882	3,415
Port Washington	4,046	3,693	3,340
Prairie du Chien	4,622	3,943	3,537
Reedsburg	3,608	2,967	2,997

[1] Corrected figure.

[2] Not returned separately.

TABLE 15.—POPULATION OF URBAN PLACES HAVING, IN 1940, FROM 2,500 TO 5,000 INHABITANTS: 1920 TO 1940—Continued

[Places marked with an asterisk (*) were classified as urban under special rule in 1940]

URBAN PLACE	1940	1930	1920
Wisconsin—Continued			
Richland Center	4,364	3,632	3,409
Ripon	4,566	3,984	3,929
River Falls	2,806	2,363	2,273
Sheboygan Falls	3,395	2,934	2,002
Spooner	2,639	2,426	2,293
Stoughton	4,743	4,497	5,101
Wisconsin—Continued			
Tomah	3,817	3,354	3,257
Tomahawk	3,365	2,919	2,898
Viroqua	3,549	2,792	2,574
Waupaca	3,458	3,131	2,839
Whitewater	3,689	3,465	3,215
Wyoming			
Cody	2,536	1,800	1,242
Evanston	3,605	3,075	3,226
Green River	2,640	2,589	2,140
Lander	2,594	1,826	2,133
Riverton	2,540	1,608	2,023
Worland	2,710	1,461	1,225

TABLE 16.—POPULATION OF INCORPORATED PLACES HAVING, IN 1940, FROM 1,000 TO 2,500 INHABITANTS: 1940 AND 1930

INCORPORATED PLACE	1940	1930
Alabama		
Abbeville	2,080	2,047
Aliceville	1,475	1,066
Ashford	1,224	920
Ashland	1,608	1,476
Bay Minette	1,763	1,545
Boaz	1,927	1,691
Brantley	1,126	1,053
Bridgeport	2,031	2,124
Brighton	1,377	1,708
Brundidge	1,909	1,434
Calera	1,092	975
Camp Hill	1,147	1,131
Centre	1,012	------
Chapman	1,167	1,189
Citronelle	1,057	1,082
Clayton	1,813	1,717
Columbiana	1,197	1,180
Cordova	[1] 1,881	1,830
Dadeville	2,025	1,549
Dora	1,032	1,143
East Brewton	1,340	1,002
Elba	2,363	2,523
Eutaw	1,895	1,721
Evergreen	2,216	2,007
Fairhope	1,845	1,549
Fort Deposit	1,351	1,092
Georgiana	1,627	1,480
Goodwater	1,028	996
Greensboro	2,034	1,795
Guin	1,175	1,099
Haleyville	2,427	2,115
Hamilton	1,002	695
Hartford	1,494	1,419
Headland	2,052	1,811
Heflin	1,684	1,231
Irondale	1,486	1,517
Jackson	2,039	1,828
Lafayette	2,138	2,119
Linden	1,203	982
Lineville	1,300	1,329
Lipscomb	1,740	1,774
Livingston	1,170	1,072
Luverne	2,243	1,874
Marion	2,382	2,141
Monroeville	1,724	1,355
Montevallo	1,490	1,245
Muscle Shoals	1,113	719
Oneonta	2,376	1,387
Oxford	1,393	1,206
Pleasant Grove	1,066	------
Ragland	1,070	981
Red Bay	1,560	1,297
Samson	2,182	1,656
Slocomb	1,041	964
Sulligent	1,287	1,078
Tallassee	1,011	849
Thomasville	2,000	1,504
Uniontown	1,869	1,424
Vincent	1,108	1,192
Warrior	1,008	646
West Blocton	1,317	1,070
Winfield	1,662	1,254
York	1,783	1,796
Arizona		
Buckeye	1,305	1,077
Casa Grande	1,545	1,351
Chandler	1,239	1,378
Florence	1,383	1,318
Holbrook	1,184	1,115
Jerome	2,295	4,932
Safford	2,266	1,706
Somerton	1,247	891
Thatcher	1,106	895
Tolleson	1,731	910
Arkansas		
Arkansas City	1,446	1,432
Ashdown	2,332	1,607
Atkins	1,322	1,364
Augusta	2,235	2,243
Bald Knob	1,445	1,273
Beebe	1,189	1,108
Bentonville	2,359	2,203
Berryville	1,482	1,286
Booneville	2,324	2,099
Carlisle	1,080	907
Coal Hill	1,040	1,169
Corning	1,619	1,550
Cotton Plant	1,778	1,689
Danville	1,010	761
Dardanelle	1,807	1,832
Des Arc	1,410	1,348
De Witt	2,498	1,853
Dierks	1,459	1,544
Dumas	2,323	1,669
Earle	1,872	2,062
England	2,027	2,130
Eudora	1,808	2,020
Eureka Springs	1,770	2,276
Forester	1,306	------
Greenwood	1,219	591
Gurdon	2,045	2,172
Hamburg	1,939	1,517
Harrisburg	1,193	1,111
Hartford	1,189	1,210
Heber Springs	1,656	1,401
Hoxie	1,466	1,448
Hughes	1,004	815
Huttig	1,379	1,386
Judsonia	1,011	1,123
Lake Village	2,045	1,582
Leachville	1,076	1,157
Lepanto	1,198	1,195
Levy	1,306	1,197
Lewisville	1,314	1,061
Lonoke	1,715	1,674
Luxora	1,258	1,074
McCrory	1,010	924
Manila	1,248	1,226
Mansfield	1,002	919
Monette	1,074	1,111
New Rocky Comfort (Foreman P. O.)	1,007	1,056
Ozark	1,402	1,564
Parkin	1,412	1,676
Piggott	2,034	1,885
Rector	1,736	1,617
Rison	1,005	876
Sheridan	1,338	1,590
Smackover	2,235	2,544
Stamps	2,405	2,705
Star City	1,090	932
Waldo	1,240	942
Waldron	1,298	1,077
Walnut Ridge	2,013	2,007
California		
Alturas	2,090	2,338
Angels	1,163	915
Arcata	1,855	1,709
Arroyo Grande	1,090	892
Atherton	1,908	[1] 1,242
Atwater	1,235	917
Avalon	1,637	1,897
Beaumont	2,208	1,332
Belmont	1,229	984
Benicia	2,419	2,913
Bishop	1,490	1,159
Blythe	2,355	1,020
Calipatria	1,799	1,554
Calistoga	1,124	1,000
California—Continued		
Ceres	1,332	981
Chowchilla	1,957	847
Clovis	1,626	1,316
Colusa	2,285	2,116
Concord	1,373	1,125
Corcoran	2,092	1,768
Corning	1,472	1,377
Corte Madera	1,098	1,027
Crescent City	1,363	1,720
Davis	1,672	1,243
Dixon	1,108	1,000
Dunsmuir	2,359	2,610
El Cajon	1,471	1,050
Elsinore	1,552	1,350
Fairfax	2,198	------
Fairfield	1,312	1,131
Fortuna	1,413	1,239
Fowler	1,531	1,171
Gridley	2,338	1,941
Gustine	1,355	1,016
Holtville	1,772	1,758
Imperial	1,493	1,943
Indio	2,296	------
Isleton	1,837	2,090
Jackson	2,024	2,005
King City	1,768	1,483
Kingsburg	1,504	1,322
La Habra	2,499	2,273
Lakeport	1,490	1,318
Larkspur	1,558	1,241
Lemoore	1,711	1,399
Lincoln	2,044	2,094
Los Banos	2,214	1,875
Manteca	1,981	1,614
Morgan Hill	1,014	908
Mount Shasta	1,618	1,009
Nevada City	2,445	1,701
Newman	1,214	1,269
Ojai	1,622	1,468
Orland	1,366	1,195
Patterson	1,109	905
Perris	1,011	763
Placentia	1,472	1,606
Pleasanton	1,278	1,237
Rialto	1,770	1,642
Rio Vista	1,666	1,309
Riverbank	1,130	803
Ross	1,751	1,355
St. Helena	1,758	1,582
San Jacinto	1,356	1,346
Seal Beach	1,553	1,156
Sebastopol	1,856	1,762
Shafter	1,258	------
Sonoma	1,158	980
Sonora	2,257	2,278
Susanville	1,575	1,358
Sutter Creek	1,134	1,013
Tehachapi	1,264	736
Vacaville	1,614	1,556
Walnut Creek	1,578	1,014
West Covina	1,072	769
Westmorland	1,010	------
Willits	1,625	1,424
Willows	2,215	2,024
Winters	1,133	896
Woodlake	1,146	------
Yreka City	2,485	2,126
Colorado		
Aguilar	1,397	1,383
Akron	1,417	1,135
Antonito	1,220	858
Arvada	1,482	1,276
Brush	2,481	2,312
Colorado—Continued		
Burlington	1,280	1,280
Center	1,515	1,011
Cortez	1,778	921
Craig	2,123	1,418
Crested Butte	1,145	1,251
Cripple Creek	2,358	1,427
Del Norte	1,923	1,410
Eaton	1,322	1,221
Edgewater	1,648	1,473
Erie	1,019	930
Fort Lupton	1,692	1,578
Fruita	1,466	1,053
Glenwood Springs	2,253	1,825
Gunnison	2,177	1,415
Holyoke	1,150	1,226
Idaho Springs	2,112	1,207
Julesburg	1,619	1,467
Lafayette	2,052	1,842
Limon	1,053	1,100
Littleton	2,244	2,019
Louisville	2,023	1,681
Manassa	1,008	953
Manitou Springs	1,462	1,205
Meeker	1,399	1,069
Oak Creek	1,769	1,211
Ordway	1,150	1,139
Pagosa Springs	1,591	804
Paonia	1,117	958
Rifle	1,373	1,287
Saguache	1,219	1,010
Silverton	1,127	1,301
South Canon	1,729	1,471
Springfield	1,082	1,393
Steamboat Springs	1,613	1,198
Telluride	1,337	512
Victor	1,784	1,291
Windsor	1,811	1,852
Wray	2,061	1,785
Yuma	1,606	1,360
Connecticut		
Branford	2,235	2,365
Colchester	1,234	937
Farmington	1,323	1,131
Guilford	1,986	1,880
Litchfield	1,234	1,075
Stonington	1,826	2,006
Unionville	2,084	2,135
Delaware		
Bridgeville	1,180	987
Delaware City	1,163	1,005
Elsmere	1,630	1,323
Georgetown	1,820	1,763
Harrington	2,113	1,812
Lewes	2,246	1,923
Middletown	1,529	1,247
Milton	1,198	1,130
Rehoboth	1,247	795
Smyrna	1,870	1,958
Florida		
Alachua	1,081	865
Apopka	1,312	1,134
Baldwin	1,002	749
Blountstown	1,931	1,270
Bonifay	1,924	1,292
Boynton	1,326	1,053
Brooksville	1,607	1,405
Bunnell	1,030	671
Carrabelle	1,019	920
Chipley	2,167	1,878
Clermont	1,631	1,086
Clewiston	1,338	------
Crescent City	1,124	955

[1] Corrected figure.

TABLE 16.—POPULATION OF INCORPORATED PLACES HAVING, IN 1940, FROM 1,000 TO 2,500 INHABITANTS: 1940 AND 1930—Continued

INCORPORATED PLACE	1940	1930
Florida—Continued		
Crestview	2,252	930
Cross City	1,869	1,071
Deerfield	1,850	1,483
Dunedin	1,758	1,435
Dunnellon	1,217	1,194
Fort Meade	1,992	1,981
Frostproof	1,704	1,406
Graceville	1,181	1,012
Green Cove Springs	1,752	1,719
Greenville	1,114	904
Gulfport	1,581	851
Hallandale	1,827	1,012
Hastings	1,035	673
Havana	1,221	1,169
High Springs	2,010	1,864
Holly Hill	1,665	1,146
Inverness	1,075	1,215
Jasper	1,722	1,748
Largo	1,031	1,429
Lynn Haven	1,246	928
Miami Shores	1,956	612
Milton	1,851	1,466
Monticello	2,042	1,901
Mount Dora	1,880	1,613
Mulberry	1,502	2,029
Naples	1,253	390
Neptune Beach	1,363	------
North Miami	1,973	------
Okeechobee	1,658	1,795
Ormond	1,914	1,517
Oviedo	1,356	1,042
Port St. Joe	2,393	851
Port Tampa	1,124	1,242
Punta Gorda	1,889	1,833
Riviera	1,981	811
St. Cloud	2,042	1,863
South Miami	2,408	1,160
Springfield	1,188	------
Starke	1,480	1,339
Stuart	2,438	1,924
Tavares	1,119	1,090
Titusville	2,220	2,089
Umatilla	1,149	907
Wewahitchka	1,022	584
Wildwood	1,346	1,409
Zephyrhills	1,252	748
Georgia		
Abbeville	1,010	1,018
Acworth	1,267	1,163
Adel	2,134	1,796
Alma	1,840	1,235
Arlington	1,337	1,232
Ashburn	2,266	2,073
Austell	1,229	963
Bibb City	1,631	1,707
Blackshear	2,010	1,817
Blue Ridge	1,362	1,190
Boston	1,099	1,243
Bowdon	1,024	1,024
Bremen	1,708	1,030
Buena Vista	1,161	1,097
Butler	1,093	857
Chamblee	1,081	893
Chatsworth	1,001	607
Chickamauga	1,665	1,715
Claxton	1,808	1,584
Clayton	1,088	798
Cochran	2,464	2,267
Colquitt	1,416	832
Conyers	1,619	1,495
Cornelia	1,808	1,542
Crawfordville	1,056	840
Dahlonega	1,294	905
Dallas	1,922	1,412
Darien	1,015	937
Donalsonville	1,718	1,183
Eatonton	2,399	1,876
Edison	1,241	1,321
Ellijay	1,497	657
Fairburn	1,502	1,372
Folkston	1,024	506
Forsyth	2,372	2,277
Fort Gaines	1,357	1,272
Glennville	1,674	1,503
Gordon	1,524	1,199
Grantville	1,267	1,346
Greensboro	2,459	2,125
Hartwell	2,372	2,048
Hazlehurst	1,732	1,378
Helena	1,073	963
Georgia—Continued		
Homerville	1,522	1,150
Jackson	1,917	1,776
Jefferson	1,839	1,869
Jonesboro	1,204	1,065
Lakeland	1,502	1,006
Lavonia	1,667	1,511
Lawrenceville	2,223	2,156
Lithonia	1,554	1,457
Louisville	1,803	1,650
Lumber City	1,044	1,043
Lumpkin	1,210	1,103
Lyons	1,900	1,445
McCaysville	1,832	1,969
McDonough	1,232	1,068
McRae	1,595	1,314
Madison	2,045	1,966
Metter	1,823	1,424
Montezuma	2,346	2,284
Monticello	1,746	1,593
Nashville	2,449	1,672
North Atlanta	1,365	[2]
Ocilla	2,124	2,034
Oglethorpe	1,048	953
Palmetto	1,029	964
Pearson	1,057	712
Pembroke	1,039	788
Perry	1,542	1,398
Richland	1,497	1,577
Rochelle	1,175	1,053
Roswell	1,622	1,432
Royston	1,549	1,447
Shellman	1,063	1,117
Smyrna	1,440	1,178
Social Circle	1,735	1,766
Soperton	1,339	1,081
Sparta	1,872	1,613
Stone Mountain	1,408	1,335
Summerville	1,358	933
Sylvester	2,191	1,984
Talbotton	1,060	1,064
Tallapoosa	2,338	2,417
Tennille	1,758	1,666
Twin City	1,019	901
Unadilla	1,137	1,203
Union Point	1,566	1,627
Vienna	2,063	1,832
Villa Rica	1,522	1,304
Wadley	1,133	1,055
Warrenton	1,284	1,289
Wrens	1,192	1,085
Wrightsville	1,760	1,741
Idaho		
Aberdeen	1,016	646
American Falls	1,439	1,280
Ashton	1,203	1,003
Bonners Ferry	1,345	1,418
Buhl	2,414	1,883
Cascade	1,029	726
Driggs	1,040	719
Filer	1,239	1,011
Glenns Ferry	1,290	1,414
Grangeville	1,929	1,360
Hailey	1,443	973
Meridian	1,465	1,004
Mountain Home	1,193	1,243
Mullan	2,291	1,891
Orofino	1,602	1,078
Parma	1,085	750
Priest River	1,056	949
Rigby	1,978	1,531
St. Maries	2,234	1,996
Salmon	2,439	1,371
Shelley	1,751	1,447
Shoshone	1,366	1,211
Soda Springs	1,087	831
Spirit Lake	1,006	1,241
Wendell	1,001	725
Illinois		
Albion	1,855	1,666
Altamont	2,111	1,225
Amboy	1,986	1,972
Antioch	1,098	1,101
Arcola	1,837	1,686
Arthur	1,405	1,361
Ashland	1,139	1,007
Assumption	1,561	1,554
Astoria	1,292	1,189
Athens	1,062	1,019
Illinois—Continued		
Atlanta	1,290	1,169
Auburn	1,952	2,242
Barry	1,545	1,506
Bartonville	1,879	1,886
Bement	1,466	1,517
Benld	2,444	2,980
Bensenville	1,869	1,680
Bethalto	1,207	687
Braidwood	1,354	1,161
Breese	2,206	1,957
Bridgeport	2,143	2,315
Broadview	1,457	2,334
Brooklyn	2,158	2,063
Brookport	1,247	1,336
Bunker Hill	1,082	947
Byron	1,113	915
Calumet Park	1,593	1,429
Cambridge	1,312	1,355
Camp Point	1,084	1,000
Carpentersville	1,289	1,461
Carrier Mills	2,360	2,140
Carrollton	2,285	2,075
Central City (Marion Co)	1,562	1,148
Cerro Gordo	1,016	965
Chatsworth	1,036	981
Chenoa	1,401	1,325
Chillicothe	2,303	1,978
Chrisman	1,112	1,092
Clarendon Hills	1,281	933
Clay City	1,136	707
Clayton	1,028	965
Coal City	1,852	1,637
Cobden	1,098	1,036
Colchester	1,426	1,342
Columbia	1,871	1,791
Coulterville	1,284	1,337
Crete	1,772	1,429
Crotty	1,235	1,185
Cuba	1,620	1,479
Dallas City	1,149	1,114
Deerfield	2,283	1,852
Delavan	1,181	1,084
Depue	2,296	2,200
Divernon	1,033	1,170
Dixmoor	1,022	944
Dupo	2,073	2,082
Dwight	2,499	2,534
Earlville	1,103	1,028
East Dubuque	1,475	1,395
East Dundee	1,306	1,341
Elmwood	1,348	1,166
El Paso	1,621	1,578
Erie	1,052	888
Eureka	1,714	1,534
Fairbury	2,300	2,310
Fairmont City	1,905	1,827
Farmer City	1,833	1,621
Farmington	2,225	2,269
Flossmoor	1,270	808
Fox Lake	1,110	880
Freeburg	1,507	1,434
Genoa	1,290	1,168
Gibson	2,401	2,163
Gilman	1,554	1,620
Girard	1,741	1,760
Glen Carbon	1,091	1,340
Golconda	1,301	1,184
Grafton	1,110	1,026
Grand Tower	1,043	953
Granville	1,038	949
Grays Lake	1,182	1,120
Grayville	2,240	1,904
Greenfield	1,006	1,038
Greenup	1,410	1,062
Griggsville	1,266	1,184
Hamilton	1,642	1,687
Hartford	1,842	1,566
Hazel Crest	1,299	1,162
Henry	1,877	1,658
Hillside	1,080	1,004
Hurst	1,012	1,123
Jonesboro	1,521	1,241
Keithsburg	1,130	1,081
Kincaid	1,749	1,583
Kinmundy	1,015	813
Knoxville	2,241	1,867
Lacon	1,627	1,548
Ladd	1,156	1,318
La Harpe	1,322	1,175
Lake Bluff	1,729	1,452
Illinois—Continued		
Lanark	1,292	1,208
Lebanon	1,867	1,828
Lena	1,169	1,145
Leroy	1,783	1,595
Lewistown	2,355	2,249
Lexington	1,284	1,292
Livingston	1,115	1,447
Lovington	1,215	1,121
McHenry	1,596	1,354
Manteno	1,537	1,149
Marengo	2,034	1,948
Marissa	1,657	1,630
Markham	1,388	349
Maroa	1,033	1,154
Martinsville	1,296	1,200
Mascoutah	2,294	2,311
Mason City	1,984	1,941
Midlothian	2,430	1,775
Milan	1,210	888
Milford	1,628	1,442
Millstadt	1,290	1,014
Minonk	1,897	1,910
Momence	2,425	2,236
Morrisonville	1,206	968
Morton	2,241	1,501
Morton Grove	2,010	1,974
Mound City	2,465	2,548
Mounds	2,144	2,129
Mt. Carroll	1,845	1,775
Mt. Morris	2,304	1,902
Mount Prospect	1,720	1,225
Mt. Pulaski	1,378	1,445
Mount Sterling	2,140	1,724
Moweaqua	1,366	1,478
Mundelein	1,328	1,011
Nashville	2,418	2,243
Nauvoo	1,088	966
Neoga	1,062	995
New Athens	1,355	1,269
New Baden	1,176	1,243
Newman	1,103	1,054
Newton	2,347	2,076
Niles	2,168	2,135
Norris City	1,295	1,109
Northbrook	1,265	1,193
North Chillicothe	1,216	1,004
North Riverside	1,036	969
North Utica	1,019	1,120
Oakland	1,131	1,036
Oblong	1,547	1,427
Odin	1,849	1,204
O'Fallon	2,407	2,373
Onarga	1,413	1,469
Palatine	2,222	2,118
Palestine	1,626	1,670
Pawnee	1,006	959
Pecatonica	1,302	1,152
Peotone	1,146	1,154
Plainfield	1,485	1,428
Plano	1,930	1,785
Polo	2,071	1,871
Posen	1,386	1,329
Prophetstown	1,469	1,353
Rantoul	2,367	1,555
Red Bud	1,302	1,208
Ridgway	1,167	930
Riverton	1,524	1,582
Roanoke	1,090	1,088
Robbins	1,349	753
Rockdale	1,532	1,701
Rockton	1,156	1,077
Roseville	1,061	975
Rosiclare	1,774	1,794
Rossville	1,428	1,453
Roxana	1,255	1,139
Royalton	1,772	2,108
Rushville	2,480	2,388
St. Anne	1,131	1,078
St. Elmo	2,290	1,329
St. Francisville	1,145	1,202
Sandoval	1,796	1,264
Sesser	2,117	2,315
Shawneetown	1,963	1,440
Sheldon	1,036	1,121
South Chicago Heights	1,837	1,691
South Holland	2,272	1,873
South Pekin	1,044	1,222
Steeleville	1,212	909
Stickney	2,446	2,005
Stockton	1,440	1,505

[2] Not returned separately.

TABLE 16.—POPULATION OF INCORPORATED PLACES HAVING, IN 1940, FROM 1,000 TO 2,500 INHABITANTS: 1940 AND 1930—Continued

INCORPORATED PLACE	1940	1930
Illinois—Continued		
Stonington	1,103	1,057
Sumner	1,070	967
Swansea	1,156	1,201
Thornton	1,101	1,012
Tilden	1,040	981
Tilton	1,486	1,394
Tinley Park	1,136	823
Toluca	1,433	1,413
Toulon	1,230	1,203
Trenton	1,316	1,271
Troy	1,154	1,122
Vienna	1,173	874
Villa Grove	2,072	2,001
Virginia	1,418	1,404
Wamac	1,432	1,232
Warren	1,119	1,179
Warsaw	1,895	1,866
Washington	2,456	1,741
Waterloo	2,361	2,239
Waverly	1,385	1,390
West City	1,017	1,091
West Dundee	1,831	1,697
Wilmington (Will Co.)	1,921	1,741
Winchester	1,651	1,532
Windsor (Shelby Co.)	1,005	927
Witt	1,490	1,516
Worden	1,264	1,111
Wyoming	1,360	1,408
Indiana		
Albany	1,623	1,413
Albion	1,234	1,108
Argos	1,190	1,211
Berne	2,075	1,883
Bloomfield	2,270	2,298
Bourbon	1,145	1,193
Bremen	2,179	2,105
Brookville	2,194	2,148
Brownsburg	1,136	1,042
Brownstown	1,860	1,758
Butler	1,794	1,643
Cambridge City	2,207	2,113
Cannelton	2,240	2,265
Cayuga	1,126	968
Centerville	1,162	993
Chesterton	2,470	2,231
Churubusco	1,122	1,095
Clarksville	2,386	2,243
Clay City	1,117	1,079
Corydon	1,865	2,009
Covington	2,096	2,008
Crothersville	1,169	979
Culver	1,605	1,502
Danville	2,093	1,930
Delphi	2,213	1,929
Dugger	1,406	1,383
Eaton	1,453	1,273
Edinburg	2,466	2,209
Fairmount	2,382	2,056
Fairview Park	1,074	1,106
Farmersburg	1,005	993
Flora	1,468	1,449
Fort Branch	1,552	1,341
Fortville	1,463	1,289
Fowler	1,903	1,564
French Lick	2,042	2,462
Goodland	1,097	978
Greendale	1,548	1,050
Greentown	1,060	1,021
Greenwood	2,499	2,377
Griffith	2,116	1,176
Hagerstown	1,638	1,262
Hope	1,046	1,085
Hymera	1,298	1,152
Jonesboro	1,791	1,496
Kentland	1,608	1,355
Knightstown	2,323	2,209
Knox	2,165	1,815
Lagrange	1,814	1,640
Lakeland	1,160	------
Lapel	1,146	1,140
Lawrence	1,087	840
Liberty	1,496	1,241
Ligonier	2,178	2,064
Loogootee	2,325	2,203
Lowell	1,448	1,274
Lynn	1,014	936
Middletown	1,520	1,348
Milan	1,000	877
Monon	1,262	1,374

INCORPORATED PLACE	1940	1930
Indiana—Continued		
Montezuma	1,366	1,292
Montpelier	1,800	1,859
Mooresville	1,979	1,910
Morocco	1,151	1,006
Munster	1,751	975
Newburg	1,374	1,262
New Harmony	1,390	1,022
New Haven	1,872	1,702
North Judson	1,408	1,348
Oolitic	1,186	1,210
Orleans	1,428	1,422
Osgood	1,198	1,173
Owensville	1,188	1,056
Paoli	2,218	2,016
Pendleton	1,681	1,538
Plainfield	1,811	1,617
Porter	1,190	805
Redkey	1,538	1,370
Ridgeville	1,003	909
Rising Sun	1,545	1,379
Rockport	2,421	2,396
Rockville	2,208	1,832
Scottsburg	2,189	1,702
Sellersburg	1,121	1,050
Shelburn	1,606	1,548
Sheridan	1,720	1,763
Shoals	1,031	1,128
South Whitley	1,118	1,102
Speedway	2,325	1,420
Spencer	2,375	2,179
Syracuse	1,346	1,190
Thorntown	1,226	1,325
Veedersburg	1,781	1,606
Vevay	1,209	1,183
Wakarusa	1,083	973
Walkerton	1,178	1,137
Warren	1,388	1,177
Waterloo	1,257	1,244
Williamsport	1,222	1,053
Winamac	1,835	1,679
Winslow	1,382	1,175
Woodruff Place	1,434	1,216
Worthington	1,729	1,687
Zionsville	1,314	1,131
Iowa		
Ackley	1,586	1,524
Adel	1,740	1,669
Akron	1,314	1,304
Alta	1,269	1,297
Alton	1,025	1,014
Anita	1,088	1,106
Audubon	2,409	2,255
Avoca	1,598	1,673
Bedford	2,151	2,100
Bellevue	1,771	1,717
Belmond	2,109	1,733
Britt	1,813	1,593
Brooklyn	1,408	1,345
Cascade	1,376	1,221
Clarksville	1,240	1,143
Colfax	2,252	2,213
Coon Rapids	1,533	1,303
Corning	2,162	2,026
Correctionville	1,151	1,058
Corydon	1,872	1,768
De Witt	2,205	2,041
Dunlap	1,550	1,522
Dyersville	2,138	2,046
Eldon	1,676	1,788
Elkader	1,556	1,382
Exira	1,046	937
Fayette	1,162	1,083
Fonda	1,188	1,027
Garner	1,549	1,241
George	1,107	907
Gowrie	1,028	1,059
Grand Junction	1,125	1,025
Greene	1,303	1,268
Greenfield	1,869	1,837
Griswold	1,132	1,139
Grundy Center	2,012	1,793
Guthrie Center	2,066	1,813
Guttenberg	1,860	1,918
Hamburg	2,187	2,103
Hartley	1,503	1,272

INCORPORATED PLACE	1940	1930
Iowa—Continued		
Holstein	1,296	1,300
Hull	1,072	905
Ida Grove	2,238	2,206
Jewell	1,051	950
Keosauqua	1,040	855
Keota	1,032	955
Kingsley	1,145	1,093
Lake City	2,216	2,012
Lake Mills	1,677	1,474
Lake View	1,082	993
Lamoni	1,567	1,739
Lansing	1,388	1,321
La Porte City	1,594	1,470
Laurens	1,304	1,071
Lehigh	1,004	996
Lenox	1,220	1,171
Leon	2,307	2,006
Logan	1,700	1,654
McGregor	1,309	1,299
Madrid	2,074	2,061
Malvern	1,325	1,320
Manilla	1,040	1,032
Manly	1,445	1,447
Manning	1,748	1,817
Manson	1,429	1,382
Mapleton	1,824	1,622
Marcus	1,206	1,138
Marengo	2,260	2,112
Melcher	1,290	1,673
Milford	1,202	1,062
Monona	1,191	1,163
Monroe	1,015	936
Montezuma	1,477	1,257
Moulton	1,181	1,476
Mount Ayr	1,930	1,704
Mount Vernon	1,489	1,441
Mystic	1,884	1,953
Nashua	1,439	1,363
New London	1,340	1,336
New Sharon	1,214	1,052
Nora Springs	1,198	1,070
Northwood	1,724	1,554
Oakland	1,317	1,181
Odebolt	1,350	1,388
Ogden	1,513	1,429
Orange City	1,920	1,727
Panora	1,169	1,014
Parkersburg	1,260	1,046
Paullina	1,230	1,013
Pocahontas	1,730	1,308
Postville	1,194	1,060
Primghar	1,081	962
Reinbeck	1,429	1,425
Remsen	1,196	1,181
Rockford	1,054	996
Rock Valley	1,507	1,204
Rockwell City	2,391	2,108
Rolfe	1,122	1,012
Sanborn	1,344	1,213
Scranton	1,014	1,058
Seymour	1,539	1,571
Sheffield	1,060	1,057
Sibley	2,356	1,870
Sidney	1,290	1,074
Sigourney	2,355	2,262
Sioux Center	1,680	1,497
Sioux Rapids	1,056	958
Spirit Lake	2,161	1,778
State Center	1,033	1,012
Story City	1,479	1,434
Strawberry Point	1,223	1,128
Stuart	1,611	1,626
Sumner	1,752	1,561
Toledo	2,073	1,825
Traer	1,493	1,417
Tripoli	1,001	891
Urbandale	1,083	596
Villisca	2,011	2,032
Wapello	1,603	1,502
Wellman	1,129	853
West Burlington	1,323	1,333
West Liberty	1,802	1,679
West Union	2,059	2,056
What Cheer	1,339	1,310
Williamsburg	1,308	1,219
Wilton	1,146	1,104
Woodbine	1,467	1,348

INCORPORATED PLACE	1940	1930
Kansas		
Arma	1,615	2,004
Ashland	1,186	1,232
Atwood	1,408	1,166
Baldwin City	1,096	1,127
Blue Rapids	1,433	1,465
Bonner Springs	1,837	1,837
Burlingame	1,019	1,127
Burlington	2,379	2,273
Caldwell	1,962	2,046
Cherokee	1,101	1,158
Chetopa	1,606	1,344
Cimarron	1,004	1,035
Clyde	1,060	1,174
Colby	2,458	2,153
Coldwater	1,214	1,296
Cottonwood Falls	1,078	963
Downs	1,219	1,383
Ellinwood	2,059	1,115
Ellis	2,042	1,957
Ellsworth	2,227	2,072
Elwood	1,014	849
Erie	1,286	1,184
Florence	1,329	1,493
Frankfort	1,243	1,346
Frontenac	1,766	2,085
Greensburg	1,417	1,338
Halstead	1,397	1,373
Harper	1,695	1,485
Hill City	1,115	1,027
Hillsboro	1,580	1,458
Howard	1,170	1,069
Hugoton	1,349	1,368
Humboldt	2,290	2,558
Kinsley	2,178	2,270
Kiowa	1,379	1,501
La Crosse	1,407	1,355
Lincoln	1,761	1,732
Lindsborg	1,913	2,016
Madison	1,198	1,488
Mankato	1,426	1,404
Marion	2,086	1,959
Meade	1,400	1,552
Medicine Lodge	1,870	1,655
Minneapolis	2,087	1,741
Mulberry	1,175	1,596
Ness City	1,355	1,509
Nickerson	1,052	1,052
Oakley	1,138	1,159
Oberlin	1,878	1,629
Osage City	2,079	2,402
Osborne	1,876	1,881
Oswego	1,953	1,845
Oxford	1,020	1,129
Peabody	1,367	1,491
Phillipsburg	2,109	1,543
Plainville	1,232	1,058
Pleasanton	1,227	1,214
Sabetha	2,241	2,332
St. Francis	1,041	944
St. John	1,735	1,552
St. Marys	1,132	1,304
Scott City	1,848	1,544
Sedan	1,948	1,776
Seneca	2,015	1,864
Smith Center	1,686	1,736
Stafford	2,011	1,614
Sterling	2,215	1,868
Stockton	1,418	1,201
Syracuse	1,226	1,383
Tonganoxie	1,114	1,109
Troy	1,049	1,042
Valley Falls	1,241	1,238
WaKeeney	1,852	1,408
Wamego	1,767	1,647
Washington	1,598	1,370
Weir	1,038	1,115
Wilson	1,068	1,038
Yates Center	2,176	2,013
Kentucky		
Albany	1,259	852
Augusta	1,701	1,675
Barbourville	2,420	2,380
Bardwell	1,218	1,139
Beattyville	1,012	906
Beaver Dam	1,166	1,036
Benton	1,906	1,021
Berea	2,176	1,827
Burkesville	1,092	886
Cadiz	1,228	1,114

TABLE 16.—POPULATION OF INCORPORATED PLACES HAVING, IN 1940, FROM 1,000 TO 2,500 INHABITANTS: 1940 AND 1930—Continued

INCORPORATED PLACE	1940	1930
Kentucky—Continued		
Campbellsville	2,488	1,923
Carlisle	1,414	1,469
Clay	1,429	1,551
Clinton	1,540	1,204
Cloverport	1,492	1,324
Columbia	1,372	1,195
Drakesboro	1,255	1,242
Eddyville	2,407	1,990
Elkhorn City	1,030	996
Elkton	1,214	951
Eminence	1,411	1,323
Erlanger	2,416	1,853
Evarts	1,642	1,438
Falmouth	2,099	1,876
Fleming	1,193	1,389
Flemingsburg	1,542	1,265
Grayson	1,176	1,022
Greensburg	1,176	770
Greenup	1,063	1,125
Greenville	2,347	2,451
Guthrie	1,253	1,272
Hartford	1,385	1,106
Hickman	2,268	2,321
Hodgenville	1,348	1,104
Horse Cave	1,278	1,259
Jackson	2,099	2,109
Kuttawa	1,125	883
La Grange	1,334	1,121
Lancaster	1,999	1,630
Lawrenceburg	2,046	1,763
Lebanon Junction	1,141	1,267
Leitchfield	1,146	950
Livermore	1,601	1,573
London	2,263	1,950
Louisa	2,023	1,961
Loyal	1,600	1,468
Manchester	1,509	(2)
Marion	2,163	1,892
Monticello	1,733	1,503
Morehead	1,901	825
Mortons Gap	1,072	1,068
Mount Vernon	1,100	939
Neon	1,187	1,077
Olive Hill	1,491	1,484
Owenton	1,190	975
Paintsville	2,324	2,411
Park Hills	1,615	1,275
Prestonsburg	2,328	2,105
Raceland	1,046	1,088
Ravenna	1,098	1,189
Russell	1,844	2,084
Salyersville	1,254	446
Scottsville	1,797	1,867
Sebree	1,109	940
Shively	1,273	-----
South Fort Mitchell	2,393	1,617
Southgate	1,841	1,735
Springfield	1,767	1,487
Stanford	1,940	1,544
Sturgis	2,321	2,154
Tompkinsville	1,438	850
Uniontown	1,327	1,235
Vanceburg	1,184	1,388
Van Lear	1,723	2,338
Wayland	1,950	2,436
Weeksbury	1,578	1,509
Wheelwright	2,027	1,822
Whitesburg	1,616	1,804
Wickliffe	1,039	1,108
Williamsburg	2,331	1,826
Williamstown	1,077	917
Wilmore	1,228	1,329
Louisiana		
Amite City	2,499	2,536
Arcadia	1,601	1,809
Basile	1,132	403
Bernice	1,071	965
Berwick	1,906	1,679
Breaux Bridge	1,668	1,399
Campti	1,004	999
Church Point	1,892	1,037
Colfax	1,354	1,141
Cottonport	1,196	1,015
Coushatta	1,289	959
Delcambre	1,255	640
Delhi	1,192	1,043
Denham Springs	1,233	1,002
Erath	1,408	895
Farmerville	1,428	1,137
Franklinton	1,579	963
Gibsland	1,023	1,090
Glenmora	1,452	1,875
Gueydan	1,506	1,313

INCORPORATED PLACE	1940	1930
Louisiana—Continued		
Harahan	1,082	892
Haynesville	2,418	2,541
Hodge	1,445	1,367
Independence	1,498	1,700
Iota	1,000	827
Jonesville	2,080	1,123
Kenner	2,375	2,440
Kentwood	1,854	1,726
Kinder	1,415	962
Lake Arthur	2,131	1,602
Lecompte	1,311	1,247
Logansport	1,222	1,040
Lutcher	2,167	1,481
Mamou	1,379	800
Mandeville	1,326	1,069
Mansura	1,138	1,067
Many	1,474	1,239
Marksville	1,811	1,527
Melville	1,828	1,541
Merryville	1,216	2,626
Napoleonville	1,301	1,180
New Roads	2,255	1,473
Oak Grove	1,654	1,241
Patterson	1,800	2,206
Plain Dealing	1,085	1,412
Port Allen	1,898	1,524
Rayville	2,412	2,076
Ringgold	1,006	618
St. Joseph	1,096	864
Simmesport	1,215	638
Tioga	1,300	522
Vidalia	1,318	1,141
Vinton	1,787	1,989
Vivian	2,460	1,646
Washington	1,264	1,004
Welsh	1,822	1,514
White Castle	1,692	1,499
Zwolle	1,500	1,264
Maryland		
Aberdeen	1,525	1,240
Bel Air	1,885	1,650
Berlin	1,435	1,480
Bladensburg	1,220	816
Brentwood	2,433	1,842
Capitol Heights	2,036	1,611
Centreville	1,141	1,291
Chesapeake City	1,094	1,016
Colmar Manor	1,480	1,225
Cottage City	1,044	938
Delmar	1,184	1,180
Denton	1,572	1,604
Emmitsburg	1,412	1,235
Fairmont Heights	1,391	1,218
Federalsburg	1,748	1,369
Gaithersburg	1,021	1,068
Indian Head	1,104	1,240
Lonaconing	2,429	2,426
Northeast [3]	1,328	1,412
Oakland	1,587	1,583
Ocean City	1,052	946
Riverdale	2,330	1,533
Rockville	2,047	[1] 1,460
St. Michaels	1,309	1,308
Seat Pleasant	1,553	-------
Snow Hill	1,926	1,604
Taneytown	1,208	938
Thurmont	1,307	1,185
Williamsport	1,772	1,775
Michigan		
Algonac	1,931	1,736
Bangor	1,409	1,274
Baraga	1,110	1,045
Belleville	1,286	758
Bellevue	1,011	1,029
Berrien Springs	1,510	1,413
Blissfield	2,144	2,103
Bloomfield Hills	1,281	1,127
Brighton	1,353	1,287
Bronson	1,871	1,651
Calumet	1,460	1,557
Carson City	1,112	972
Caspian	1,797	1,888
Cass City	1,362	1,261
Cassopolis	1,488	1,448
Cedar Springs	1,101	1,104
Charlevoix	2,299	2,247
Chelsea	2,246	2,268
Chesaning	1,807	1,594
Clare	1,844	1,491

INCORPORATED PLACE	1940	1930
Michigan—Continued		
Clinton	1,126	1,026
Clio	1,711	1,548
Constantine	1,384	1,259
Coopersville	1,083	1,004
Corunna	2,017	1,936
Croswell	1,381	1,470
Davison	1,397	1,298
Decatur	1,599	1,582
Dexter	1,087	894
Dundee	1,690	1,364
East Jordan	1,725	1,523
East Tawas	1,670	1,455
Essexville	2,390	1,864
Evart	1,335	1,301
Farmington	1,510	1,243
Flat Rock	1,467	1,231
Flushing	1,806	1,723
Fowlerville	1,118	1,141
Frankenmuth	1,100	925
Frankfort	1,642	1,468
Galesburg	1,040	936
Gaylord	2,055	1,627
Gladwin	1,600	1,248
Grand Blanc	1,012	917
Grandville	1,566	1,346
Grayling	2,124	1,073
Harbor Beach	2,186	1,802
Harbor Springs	1,423	1,429
Hart	1,922	1,690
Hartford	1,694	1,484
Holly	2,343	2,252
Homer	1,145	1,108
Hudson	2,426	2,361
Huntington Woods	1,705	655
Imlay City	1,446	1,495
Ithaca	2,000	1,780
Jonesville	1,302	1,316
Kalkaska	1,132	861
Lake Linden	1,631	1,714
Lake Odessa	1,417	1,220
Lake Orion	1,933	1,369
Lawton	1,134	1,164
Leslie	1,281	1,105
Lowell	1,944	1,919
Mancelona	1,173	1,143
Manchester	1,100	1,037
Manton	1,006	1,008
Marlette	1,161	990
Marysville	1,777	1,405
Milan	2,340	1,947
Milford	1,637	1,364
Montague	1,099	887
Morenci	1,845	1,773
Mount Morris	2,237	1,982
Nashville	1,279	1,249
Newaygo	1,282	1,227
New Baltimore	1,434	1,148
New Buffalo	1,190	1,051
North Muskegon	1,694	1,370
Oak Park	1,169	1,079
Onaway	1,449	1,492
Ontonagon	2,290	1,937
Ovid	1,248	1,131
Oxford	2,144	2,052
Paw Paw	1,910	1,684
Pinconning	1,027	826
Plainwell	2,424	2,279
Portland	2,247	1,902
Quincy	1,333	1,265
Reading	1,059	954
Reed City	1,845	1,792
Richmond	1,722	1,493
Rockford	1,773	1,613
Rockwood	1,147	953
St. Charles	1,300	1,463
Saline	1,227	1,009
Sandusky	1,512	1,305
Scottville	1,162	1,002
Sebewaing	1,598	1,441
Shelby	1,367	1,152
South Lyon	1,017	844
Sparta	1,945	1,939
Spring Lake	1,329	1,271
Stambaugh	2,081	2,400
Sylvan Lake	1,041	799
Tawas City	1,075	1,034
Three Oaks	1,351	1,336
Union City	1,339	1,104

INCORPORATED PLACE	1940	1930
Michigan—Continued		
Utica	1,022	873
Vassar	2,154	1,816
Vicksburg	1,774	1,735
Watervliet	1,193	1,207
Wayland	1,005	1,013
West Branch	1,962	1,164
Whitehall	1,407	1,394
White Pigeon	1,017	966
Williamston	1,704	1,458
Yale City	1,489	1,345
Minnesota		
Ada	1,638	1,285
Adrian	1,066	1,000
Aitkin	2,063	1,545
Appleton	1,877	1,625
Arlington	1,122	915
Aurora	1,528	1,463
Bagley	1,241	885
Barnesville	1,450	1,279
Baudette	1,017	822
Belle Plaine	1,407	1,246
Bird Island	1,201	1,004
Biwabik	1,304	1,383
Blooming Prairie	1,205	1,046
Bovey	1,355	1,248
Brooklyn Center	1,870	1,341
Browns Valley	1,075	981
Buffalo	1,695	1,109
Buhl	1,600	1,431
Caledonia	1,985	1,554
Cambridge	1,592	1,183
Canby	2,099	1,738
Cannon Falls	1,544	1,358
Cass Lake	1,904	1,409
Chaska	1,927	1,901
Chatfield	1,640	1,269
Cokato	1,175	1,125
Cold Spring	1,427	1,147
Coleraine	1,325	1,243
Crystal	2,373	1,865
Dawson	1,646	1,386
Deephaven	1,026	530
Delano	1,094	914
Dilworth	1,068	983
Dodge Center	1,029	854
Elbow Lake	1,150	903
Elk River	1,245	1,026
Excelsior	1,422	1,072
Fairfax	1,116	916
Farmington	1,580	1,342
Forest Lake	1,120	916
Fosston	1,271	978
Frazee	1,167	1,041
Gaylord	1,049	812
Glencoe	2,387	1,925
Golden Valley	2,048	1,326
Graceville	1,020	969
Granite Falls	2,388	1,791
Hallock	1,353	869
Hawley	1,122	958
Hector	1,044	864
Janesville	1,296	1,181
Jordan	1,422	1,119
Kasson	1,230	1,019
Keewatin	1,942	2,134
Kenyon	1,530	1,382
Lake Crystal	1,319	1,173
Lakefield	1,699	1,349
Lanesboro	1,100	1,011
Le Center [4]	1,232	948
Le Sueur	2,302	1,897
Long Prairie	2,311	1,854
Madelia	1,652	1,397
Madison	2,312	1,916
Mahnomen	1,429	989
Mapleton	1,070	862
Melrose	2,015	1,801
Milaca	1,627	1,318
Minneota	1,065	918
Montgomery	1,741	1,570
Monticello	1,076	921
Moose Lake	1,432	742
Mora	1,494	1,014
Morningside	1,282	903
Mound	1,189	668
Mountain Iron	1,492	1,349
Mountain Lake	1,745	1,388
Nashwauk	2,228	2,555
New Prague	1,645	1,543
Olivia	1,788	1,475
Ortonville	2,469	2,017

[1] Corrected figure.
[2] Not returned separately.
[3] Name changed from North East in 1938.
[4] Name changed from Le Sueur Center in 1931.

TABLE 16.—POPULATION OF INCORPORATED PLACES HAVING, IN 1940, FROM 1,000 TO 2,500 INHABITANTS: 1940 AND 1930—Continued

INCORPORATED PLACE	1940	1930
Minnesota—Con.		
Osakis	1,483	1,155
Paynesville	1,317	1,121
Pelican Rapids	1,560	1,365
Perham	1,534	1,411
Pine City	1,718	1,343
Pine Island	1,040	961
Plainview	1,500	1,233
Preston	1,447	1,214
Princeton	1,865	1,636
Proctor [5]	2,468	2,521
Red Lake Falls	1,530	1,386
Renville	1,256	1,064
Roseau	1,775	1,028
Rush City	1,020	908
Rushford (city)	1,182	1,125
St. Charles	1,507	1,311
St. Joseph	1,055	1,009
St. Paul Park	1,096	982
Sandstone	1,559	1,083
Shakopee	2,418	2,023
Sherburne	1,030	860
Slayton	1,587	1,102
South International Falls	1,299	939
Springfield	2,361	2,049
Spring Valley	2,133	1,712
Stewartville	1,025	793
Tyler	1,005	905
Wabasha	2,368	2,212
Waconia	1,315	1,291
Waite Park	1,427	1,318
Warren	1,639	1,472
Warroad	1,309	1,184
Waterville	1,600	1,419
Wayzata	1,473	1,100
Wells	2,217	1,795
Wheaton	1,700	1,279
Winnebago	1,992	1,701
Winthrop	1,195	1,037
Zumbrota	1,386	1,350
Mississippi		
Ackerman	1,528	1,169
Baldwyn	1,279	1,106
Batesville	1,815	1,062
Bay Springs	1,228	927
Booneville	1,893	1,703
Brandon	1,184	692
Bruce	1,385	946
Bude	1,207	1,378
Calhoun City	1,171	1,012
Carthage	1,766	998
Centreville	1,163	1,344
Charleston	2,100	2,014
Collins	1,100	935
Crosby [6]	1,489	715
Drew	1,579	1,373
East Tupelo	1,108	-------
Edwards	1,110	456
Electric Mills	1,205	1,084
Eupora	1,377	1,092
Fulton	1,154	927
Gloster	1,232	1,139
Hernando	1,072	938
Hollandale	1,606	1,211
Houston	1,729	1,477
Itta Bena	1,795	1,370
Iuka	1,664	1,441
Lambert	1,016	800
Long Beach	1,495	1,346
Lucedale	1,204	834
Lumberton	1,485	2,374
Macon	2,261	2,198
Magee	1,221	964
Magnolia	2,125	1,660
Marks	1,818	1,258
Mendenhall	1,282	919
Moorhead	1,504	1,553
Newton	1,800	2,011
Ocean Springs	1,881	1,663
Okolona	2,117	2,235
Pontotoc	1,832	2,018
Poplarville	1,664	1,498
Purvis	1,000	881
Quitman	1,471	1,872
Ripley	2,011	1,468
Rolling Fork	1,320	902
Rosedale	2,063	2,117
Ruleville	1,378	1,181
Sardis	2,022	1,298
Mississippi—Con.		
Senatobia	1,757	1,264
Shaw	1,669	1,612
Shelby	1,956	1,811
Summit	1,254	1,157
Tunica	1,322	1,043
Tylertown	1,376	1,102
Union	1,543	1,705
Waynesboro	1,445	1,120
Wiggins	1,141	1,074
Woodville	1,433	1,113
Missouri		
Albany	2,010	1,858
Appleton City	1,188	1,136
Ash Grove	1,101	1,107
Ava	1,393	1,041
Bernie	1,160	1,031
Bevier	1,105	1,229
Bismarck	1,302	1,185
Bloomfield	1,208	1,023
Bowling Green	1,975	1,855
Branson	1,011	958
Brunswick	1,749	1,715
Cabool	1,069	908
Campbell	1,786	1,592
Canton	2,125	2,044
Carl Junction	1,039	1,042
Carterville	1,582	1,600
Cassville	1,214	1,016
Centralia	1,996	2,009
Clarence	1,157	1,286
Concordia	1,077	1,140
Crane	1,013	1,030
Cuba	1,033	814
Doniphan	1,604	1,398
East Prairie	2,469	1,385
Edina	1,637	1,532
Eldorado Springs	2,342	1,917
Elsberry	1,548	1,204
Elvins	2,367	2,403
Fornfelt	1,504	1,500
Gallatin	1,642	1,504
Gideon	1,606	1,315
Glasgow	1,490	1,409
Granby	1,455	1,445
Grant City	1,209	1,126
Greenfield	1,353	1,304
Hamilton	1,655	1,572
Harrisonville	2,322	2,306
Hermann	2,308	2,063
Holden	1,818	1,807
Huntsville	1,739	1,897
Illmo	1,224	1,129
Ironton	1,083	974
Kahoka	1,781	1,507
King City	1,103	1,101
La Grange	1,222	1,160
La Plata	1,421	1,406
Lathrop	1,049	940
Lees Summit	2,263	2,035
Lilbourn	1,378	1,154
Marionville	1,127	1,227
Marshfield	1,764	1,378
Maysville	1,026	946
Memphis	1,935	1,728
Milan	2,016	2,002
Monroe City	1,978	1,820
Montgomery City	1,671	1,510
Morehouse	1,598	1,165
Mound City	1,606	1,525
Mountain Grove	2,431	2,229
Mount Vernon	1,982	1,342
Newburg	1,056	1,036
New Franklin	1,144	1,210
New Haven	1,002	876
New London	1,005	900
New Madrid	2,450	2,309
Norborne	1,239	1,190
Odessa	1,881	1,861
Oran	1,106	940
Osceola	1,190	1,043
Owensville	1,439	1,424
Pacific	1,687	1,456
Palmyra	2,285	1,967
Paris	1,473	1,367
Parma	1,187	1,051
Pattonsburg	1,017	1,009
Peirce City	1,208	1,135
Piedmont	1,177	916
Plattsburg	1,915	1,672
Pleasant Hill	2,118	2,330
Portageville	2,107	1,262
Missouri—Con.		
Potosi	2,017	1,279
Princeton	1,584	1,509
Rich Hill	1,994	2,118
Rock Hill	1,821	1,309
Rockport	1,406	1,162
St. Clair	1,410	1,135
St. Ferdinand	1,369	1,039
St. James	1,812	1,294
Salisbury	1,759	1,768
Sarcoxie	1,057	1,017
Savannah	2,108	1,888
Senath	1,261	1,086
Seneca	1,091	1,063
Shelbina	2,107	1,826
Shrewsbury	2,182	1,525
Stanberry	1,893	2,029
Steele	1,585	1,219
Steelville	1,013	854
Sugar Creek	1,638	1,657
Sweet Springs	1,413	1,641
Tarkio	2,114	2,016
Thayer	1,692	1,632
Tipton	1,219	1,067
Troy	1,493	1,419
Union	2,125	2,143
Unionville	2,052	1,811
Valley Park	2,091	1,772
Versailles	1,781	1,662
Warrenton	1,254	1,250
Wellsville	1,314	1,525
Weston	1,121	1,028
Willow Springs	1,530	1,430
Windsor	2,373	1,879
Montana		
Baker	1,304	1,212
Big Timber	1,533	1,224
Browning	1,825	1,172
Chinook	2,051	1,320
Choteau	1,181	926
Conrad	1,471	1,499
East Helena	1,143	1,039
Forsyth	1,696	1,591
Fort Benton	1,227	1,109
Hamilton	2,332	1,839
Hardin	1,886	1,169
Harlem	1,166	708
Harlowton	1,547	1,473
Libby	1,837	1,752
Malta	2,215	1,342
Philipsburg	1,304	1,300
Plentywood	1,574	1,226
Polson	2,156	1,455
Poplar	1,442	1,046
Ronan	1,032	537
Scobey	1,311	1,259
Terry	1,012	779
Townsend	1,309	735
Walkerville	1,880	2,052
Wolf Point	1,960	1,539
Nebraska		
Ainsworth	1,833	1,378
Albion	2,268	2,172
Alma	1,272	1,235
Arapahoe	1,002	1,017
Ashland	1,709	1,786
Atkinson	1,350	1,144
Aurora	2,419	2,715
Bayard	2,121	1,559
Beaver City	1,015	1,024
Bellevue	1,184	1,017
Benkelman	1,448	1,154
Bloomfield	1,467	1,435
Bridgeport	1,520	1,421
Burwell	1,412	1,156
Cambridge	1,084	1,203
Central City	2,460	2,474
Chappell	1,093	1,061
Cozad	2,156	1,813
Crawford	1,845	1,703
Creighton	1,272	1,388
David City	2,272	2,333
Deshler	1,037	1,177
Franklin	1,272	1,103
Friend	1,169	1,214
Fullerton	1,707	1,680
Geneva	1,888	1,662
Genoa	1,231	1,089
Gordon	1,967	1,958
Nebraska—Continued		
Gothenburg	2,330	2,322
Hartington	1,688	1,568
Hebron	1,909	1,804
Humboldt	1,386	1,435
Imperial	1,195	946
Kimball	1,725	1,711
Loup City	1,675	1,446
Lyons	1,033	985
Madison	1,812	1,842
Minatare	1,125	1,079
Minden	1,848	1,716
Mitchell	2,181	2,058
Neligh	1,796	1,649
Newman Grove	1,036	1,146
North Bend	1,003	1,108
Oakland	1,380	1,433
Ord	2,240	2,226
Osceola	1,039	1,054
Oxford	1,141	1,155
Pawnee City	1,647	1,573
Pender	1,135	1,006
Peru	1,024	835
Pierce	1,249	1,271
Plainview	1,411	1,216
Ponca	1,003	920
Randolph	1,094	1,145
Ravenna	1,429	1,559
Red Cloud	1,610	1,519
Rushville	1,125	1,006
St. Paul	1,571	1,621
Stanton	1,526	1,479
Stromsburg	1,127	1,320
Sutton	1,403	1,540
Tecumseh	2,104	1,829
Tekamah	1,925	1,804
Valentine	2,188	1,672
Walthill	1,204	1,162
Weeping Water	1,139	1,029
Wilber	1,355	1,352
Wisner	1,256	1,327
Wymore	2,457	2,680
Nevada		
Carson City	2,478	1,596
Fallon	1,911	1,758
Lovelock	1,294	1,263
Winnemucca	2,485	1,989
New Jersey		
Absecon	2,084	2,158
Allendale	2,058	1,730
Alpha	2,301	2,374
Atlantic Highlands	2,335	2,000
Avon-by-the-Sea	1,211	1,220
Barrington	2,329	2,252
Bellmawr	1,250	1,123
Belvidere	2,060	2,073
Berlin	1,753	1,955
Brooklawn	1,919	1,753
Clayton	2,320	2,351
Clinton	1,066	932
Cresskill	2,246	1,924
Demarest	1,165	1,013
East Newark	2,273	2,686
Eatontown	1,758	1,938
Elmer	1,344	1,219
Emerson	1,487	1,394
Essex Fells	1,466	1,115
Fair Haven	2,491	2,260
Fanwood	2,310	1,681
Florham Park	1,609	1,269
Franklin Lakes	1,203	893
Frenchtown	1,238	1,189
Hamburg	1,116	1,160
Harrington Park	1,389	1,251
Haworth	1,419	1,042
High Bridge	1,781	1,860
Highlands	2,076	1,877
Hohokus	1,626	925
Hopewell	1,678	1,467
Jamesburg	2,128	2,048
Kenilworth	2,451	2,243
Laurel Springs	1,344	1,343
Lawnside	1,270	1,379
Lincoln Park	2,186	1,831
Linwood	1,479	1,514
Little Silver	1,461	1,109
Magnolia	1,552	1,522
Manasquan	2,340	2,320

[5] Name changed from Proctorknott in 1939.
[6] Name changed from Stephenson in 1934.

TABLE 16.—POPULATION OF INCORPORATED PLACES HAVING, IN 1940, FROM 1,000 TO 2,500 INHABITANTS: 1940 AND 1930—Continued

INCORPORATED PLACE	1940	1930
New Jersey—Con.		
Mendham	1,343	1,278
Montvale	1,342	1,243
Moonachie	1,554	1,465
Morris Plains	2,018	1,713
Mountain Lakes	2,205	2,132
Mountainside	1,148	965
Mount Ephraim	2,282	2,319
National Park	1,977	1,828
Neptune City	2,392	2,258
Netcong	2,157	2,097
New Providence	2,374	1,918
North Caldwell	1,572	1,492
Northvale	1,159	1,144
North Wildwood	1,921	2,049
Norwood	1,512	1,358
Ogdensburg	1,165	1,138
Peapack-Gladstone	1,354	1,273
Pennington	1,492	1,335
Pine Hill	1,537	1,392
Point Pleasant	2,082	2,058
Point Pleasant Beach	2,059	1,844
Riverdale	1,110	1,052
Riverton	2,354	2,483
Roseland	1,556	1,058
Shrewsbury	1,058	857
Somerdale	1,170	1,151
Somers Point	1,992	2,073
South Bound Brook	1,928	1,763
Spotswood	1,201	921
Spring Lake	1,650	1,745
Spring Lake Heights	1,076	1,221
Stanhope	1,100	1,089
Sussex	1,478	1,415
Swedesboro	2,268	2,123
Tuckerton	1,320	1,429
Union Beach	2,076	1,893
Waldwick	2,475	1,728
Watchung	1,158	906
Wenonah	1,311	1,245
West Long Branch	2,030	1,686
Woodbine	2,111	2,164
Woodbury Heights	1,137	997
Woodcliff Lake	1,037	871
Woodstown	2,027	1,832
New Mexico		
Carrizozo	1,457	1,171
Eunice	1,227	------
Farmington	2,161	1,350
Fort Sumner	1,669	839
Jal	1,157	404
Lovington	1,916	961
Magdalena	1,323	1,371
Mountainair	1,477	1,027
Roy	1,138	713
Santa Rosa	2,310	1,127
Springer	1,314	957
Tularosa	1,446	1,406
Vaughn	1,331	968
New York		
Adams	1,594	1,613
Addison	1,617	1,538
Akron	2,263	2,188
Alexandria Bay	1,748	1,952
Allegany	1,436	1,411
Andover	1,290	1,241
Angola	1,663	1,543
Arcade	1,683	1,643
Ardsley	1,423	1,135
Athens	1,655	1,618
Attica	2,379	2,212
Avoca	1,006	940
Avon	2,339	2,403
Bainbridge	1,450	1,324
Bayville	1,516	1,042
Bellerose	1,317	1,202
Belmont	1,146	1,085
Blasdell	2,322	2,015
Bolivar	1,344	1,725
Boonville	2,076	2,090
Brewster	1,863	1,664
Briarcliff Manor	1,830	1,794
Brightwaters	1,562	1,061
Broadalbin	1,399	1,341
Brocton	1,293	1,301
Buchanan	1,600	1,346
Caledonia	1,226	1,487
Cambridge	1,572	1,762
Camden	2,021	1,912
Camillus	1,133	1,036
New York—Con.		
Castleton-on-Hudson	1,515	1,506
Cattaraugus	1,145	1,236
Cazenovia	1,689	1,788
Celoron	1,349	1,182
Champlain	1,354	1,197
Chateaugay	1,183	1,169
Chatham	2,254	2,424
Chester	1,140	1,154
Clayton	1,999	1,940
Clifton Springs	1,413	1,819
Clinton	1,478	1,475
Clyde	2,356	2,374
Cold Spring	1,897	1,784
Colonie	1,407	1,176
Cornwall	1,978	1,910
Coxsackie	2,352	2,195
Cuba	1,699	1,422
Delhi	1,841	1,840
Deposit	2,028	1,887
Dexter	1,109	1,020
Dundee	1,168	1,086
East Hampton	1,756	1,934
East Williston	1,152	493
Ellicottville	1,024	978
Fayetteville	2,172	2,008
Fonda	1,123	1,170
Franklinville	1,884	2,021
Friendship	1,148	1,154
Geneseo	2,144	2,261
Great Neck Estates	1,969	1,738
Great Neck Plaza	2,031	------
Greene	1,431	1,379
Greenwich	2,270	2,290
Groton	2,087	2,004
Hamilton	1,790	1,700
Hammondsport	1,112	1,063
Hancock	1,581	1,427
Hillburn	1,161	1,303
Holley	1,230	1,558
Honeoye Falls	1,274	1,187
Island Park	1,531	1,002
Jordan	1,115	1,145
Keeseville	1,921	1,794
Kings Point	1,247	1,294
Lakewood	2,314	1,837
Lewiston	1,280	1,013
Little Valley	1,234	1,196
McGraw	1,201	1,082
Manchester	1,330	1,429
Manlius	1,520	1,538
Marcellus	1,112	1,083
Maybrook	1,189	1,159
Mayville	1,354	1,273
Menands	1,764	1,522
Mexico	1,348	1,297
Middleburg	1,074	948
Middleport	1,575	1,596
Millbrook	1,340	1,296
Monroe	1,616	1,621
Montour Falls	1,345	1,489
Moravia	1,231	1,295
Munsey Park	1,456	411
Naples	1,152	1,070
New Hartford	1,914	1,885
New Paltz	1,492	1,362
North Collins	1,182	1,165
North Syracuse	2,083	1,766
Northville	1,111	1,250
Norwood	1,905	1,880
Nunda	1,077	1,085
Oakfield	1,876	1,919
Old Westbury	1,017	1,264
Orchard Park	1,304	1,144
Oriskany	1,115	1,142
Oxford	1,713	1,601
Painted Post	2,337	2,328
Pawling	1,446	1,204
Pelham	1,918	2,053
Phelps	1,499	1,397
Philmont	1,679	1,868
Phoenix	1,757	1,758
Piermont	1,876	1,765
Pittsford	1,544	1,460
Port Dickinson	2,436	1,902
Port Henry	1,935	2,040
Portville	1,018	969
Pulaski	1,895	2,046
Randolph	1,321	1,308
Ravena	1,810	1,963
Red Hook	1,056	996
New York—Con.		
Rhinebeck	1,697	1,569
Richfield Springs	1,209	1,333
Rouses Point	1,846	1,920
Sackets Harbor	1,962	[1] 1,680
St. Johnsville	2,283	2,273
Salem	1,034	1,081
Schuylerville	1,447	1,411
Sherburne	1,192	1,077
Sherrill	2,184	2,150
Shortsville	1,316	1,332
Skaneateles	1,949	1,882
Sloatsburg	1,771	1,623
Sodus	1,513	1,444
South Nyack	2,093	2,212
Spencerport	1,340	1,249
Stamford	1,088	1,103
Stewart Manor	1,625	1,291
Thomaston	1,159	------
Trumansburg	1,130	1,077
Unadilla	1,079	1,063
Valatie	1,208	1,246
Victor	1,111	1,042
Waterville	1,489	1,298
Wayland	1,795	1,814
Webster	1,680	1,552
Weedsport	1,341	1,325
West Carthage	1,767	1,722
Wolcott	1,326	1,260
North Carolina		
Aberdeen	1,076	1,382
Ahoskie	2,313	1,940
Andrews	1,520	1,748
Angier	1,028	760
Archdale	1,097	628
Aulander	1,057	1,041
Ayden	1,884	1,607
Belhaven	2,360	2,458
Benson	1,837	1,522
Bethel	1,333	1,149
Black Mountain	1,042	737
Boone	1,788	1,295
Bryson City	1,612	1,806
Burgaw	1,476	1,209
Carrboro	1,455	1,242
Carthage	1,381	1,129
Cary	1,141	909
Chadbourn	1,576	1,311
China Grove	1,567	1,258
Clayton	1,711	1,533
Columbia	1,090	864
Conover	1,195	973
Cornelius	1,195	1,230
Dallas	1,704	1,489
Davidson	1,550	1,445
East Bend	1,262	470
East Flat Rock	1,103	1,062
East Lumberton	1,039	1,111
East Spencer	2,181	2,098
Elizabethtown	1,123	765
Enfield	2,208	2,234
Fairmont	1,993	1,314
Franklin	1,249	1,094
Franklinton	1,273	1,320
Fremont	1,264	1,316
Fuquay Springs	1,323	963
Gibsonville	1,753	1,605
Granite Falls	1,873	2,147
Hazelwood	1,508	1,168
Hertford	1,959	1,914
Hillsboro	1,311	1,232
Jonesville	1,733	1,306
Kenly	1,095	965
Kernersville	2,103	1,754
La Grange	1,647	1,500
Landis	1,650	1,388
Lawndale	1,006	728
Leaksville	1,886	1,814
Littleton	1,200	1,133
Longview	1,489	1,262
Louisburg	2,309	2,182
Lowell	1,826	1,664
Madison	1,683	1,497
Maiden	1,803	1,628
Marshall	1,160	1,132
Marshville	1,007	933
Maxton	1,656	1,386
Mayodan	2,323	1,948
North Carolina—Con.		
Mebane	2,060	1,568
Mocksville	1,607	1,503
Mount Holly	2,055	2,254
Mount Pleasant	1,017	838
Murfreesboro	1,550	1,000
Murphy	1,873	1,612
Nashville	1,171	1,137
Norwood	1,515	1,452
Pineville	1,144	1,108
Plymouth	2,461	2,139
Raeford	1,628	1,303
Ramseur	1,220	1,220
Randleman	2,032	1,863
Red Springs	1,559	1,300
Robersonville	1,407	1,181
Rutherfordton	2,326	2,020
St. Pauls	1,923	2,080
Selma	2,007	1,857
Siler City	2,197	1,730
Southport	1,760	1,760
Spring Hope	1,222	1,222
Spruce Pine	1,968	1,546
Stanley	1,036	1,084
Sylva	1,409	1,340
Tabor	1,552	1,165
Taylorsville	1,122	926
Troy	1,861	1,522
Tryon	2,043	1,670
Wake Forest	1,562	1,536
Wallace	1,050	734
Walnut Cove	1,084	1,081
Warrenton	1,147	1,072
Warsaw	1,483	1,222
Weldon	2,341	2,323
Wendell	1,132	980
Wilkesboro	1,309	1,042
Windsor	1,747	1,425
Zebulon	1,070	860
North Dakota		
Ashley	1,345	1,033
Beach	1,178	1,263
Bottineau	1,739	1,322
Cando	1,282	1,164
Carrington	1,850	1,717
Casselton	1,358	1,253
Cavalier	1,105	850
Cooperstown	1,077	1,053
Crosby	1,404	1,271
Ellendale	1,517	1,264
Enderlin	1,593	1,839
Garrison	1,117	1,024
Hankinson	1,420	1,400
Harvey	1,851	2,157
Hebron	1,267	1,348
Hettinger	1,138	1,292
Hillsboro	1,338	1,317
Kenmare	1,528	1,494
Langdon	1,546	1,221
Larimore	1,222	979
Lidgerwood	1,042	1,029
Linton	1,602	1,192
Lisbon	1,997	1,650
Mayville	1,351	1,199
Mott	1,220	1,036
New Rockford	2,017	2,195
Northwood	1,063	971
Oakes	1,665	1,709
Park River	1,408	1,131
Rolla	1,008	852
Rugby	2,215	1,512
Stanley	1,058	936
Velva	1,017	870
Walhalla	1,138	700
Watford City	1,073	769
Wishek	1,112	1,146
Ohio		
Ada	2,368	2,499
Addyston	1,610	1,768
Adena	1,703	1,286
Amsterdam	1,177	1,171
Antwerp	1,086	1,024
Arcanum	1,188	1,149
Archbold	1,236	1,185
Arlington Heights	1,222	1,214
Ashville	1,101	1,085
Avon	2,118	1,826

[1] Corrected figure.

TABLE 16.—POPULATION OF INCORPORATED PLACES HAVING, IN 1940, FROM 1,000 TO 2,500 INHABITANTS: 1940 AND 1930—Continued

INCORPORATED PLACE	1940	1930
Ohio—Continued		
Avon Lake	2,274	1,610
Batavia	1,320	1,119
Bellville	1,199	987
Belpre	1,717	1,724
Bergholz	1,122	918
Bethel	1,604	1,312
Bethesda	1,127	1,159
Blanchester	1,785	1,597
Bluffton	2,077	2,035
Bradford	1,775	1,732
Bratenahl	1,350	1,308
Brecksville	1,900	1,308
Bremen	1,176	1,232
Brewster	1,534	1,464
Brilliant	1,683	1,682
Broadview Heights	1,141	689
Brooklyn	1,108	784
Brook Park	1,122	837
Brookville	1,653	1,403
Byesville	2,418	2,638
Caldwell	1,705	1,778
Canal Fulton	1,115	1,160
Canal Winchester	1,046	906
Canfield	1,141	1,015
Cardington	1,304	1,192
Cedarville	1,034	940
Chardon	2,001	1,818
Chauncey	1,234	1,269
Chesapeake	1,068	1,094
Cleves	1,871	1,711
Coal Grove	2,351	2,181
Coldwater	2,019	1,787
Columbus Grove	1,737	1,633
Continental	1,059	897
Corning	1,433	1,411
Cortland	1,014	940
Covington	1,945	1,807
Creston	1,110	1,029
Delta	1,773	1,778
Deshler	1,570	1,538
Dillonvale	1,652	1,434
Doylestown	1,259	1,150
Dresden	1,350	1,362
Edgerton	1,082	989
Elmore	1,103	1,107
Fairfield [7]	1,409	1,240
Flushing	1,217	1,119
Forest	1,083	1,103
Fort Recovery	1,123	1.118
Fredericktown	1,297	1,257
Garrettsville	1,264	1,179
Genoa	1,455	1,437
Georgetown	1,848	1,531
Germantown	2,095	2,029
Gibsonburg	2,169	2,129
Glendale	2,359	2,360
Granville	1,502	1,467
Grove City	1,787	1,546
Groveport	1,052	946
Harrison	1,656	1,449
Holgate	1,050	951
Hudson	1,417	1,324
Huron	1,827	1,699
Independence	1,815	1,525
Jamestown	1,079	944
Jefferson	1,676	1,601
Jewett	1,031	876
Johnstown	1,064	1,006
Lakemore	1,832	1,670
Leetonia	2,259	2,332
Leipsic	1,525	1,571
Lewisburg	1,126	936
Lodi	1,304	1,273
Loudonville	2,334	2,068
Loveland	1,904	1,954
Lowellville	2,359	2,550
Lyndhurst	2,391	1,922
McArthur	1,288	1,188
McConnelsville	1,895	1,754
McDonald	1,529	1,714
Madeira	1,384	1,162
Malvern	1,177	1,100
Manchester	2,163	2,009
Mechanicsburg	1,653	1,424
Mentor	1,827	1,589
Middleburgh Heights	1,225	874
Milford	2,139	1,915
Millersburg	2,239	2,203
Minster	1,504	1,381
Mogadore	1,616	1,502
Monroeville	1,173	1,080
Mount Gilead	2,008	1,871
Mount Sterling	1,115	1,090
Murray City	1,009	1,048
Navarre	1,703	1,593
New Bremen	1,484	1,485
New Carlisle	1,237	1,089
New Concord	1,067	1,087
New London	1,656	1,527
New Miami	1,443	1,289
New Richmond	1,767	1,830
New Straitsville	1,473	1,718
Newtown	1,146	939
Oak Harbor	1,925	1,849
Oak Hill	1,619	1,578
Osborn	1,705	1,271
Ottawa	2,342	2,169
Ottawa Hills	1,979	1,185
Parma Heights	1,330	960
Paulding	2,044	1,904
Payne	1,003	1,014
Peebles	1,356	1,235
Pemberville	1,036	960
Plain City	1,385	1,288
Plymouth	1,403	1,339
Poland	1,240	968
Powhatan Point	2,054	2,329
Richwood	1,628	1,573
Ripley	1,623	1,556
Rockford	1,066	887
Roseville	1,320	1,413
Sabina	1,525	1,296
Sagamore Hills	1,471	-------
St. Paris	1,308	1,177
Salineville	2,018	2,133
Scio	1,181	760
Sharonville	1,157	1.111
Shawnee	1,475	1,457
Sheffield Lake	1,099	1,256
Shreve	1,113	1,103
Smithfield	1,169	1,023
Solon	1,508	1,027
Somerset	1,352	1,297
South Charleston	1,198	1,208
South Zanesville	1,338	1,278
Spencerville	1,623	1,612
Strasburg	1,297	1,305
Strongsville	2,216	1,349
Swanton	1,594	1,505
Sylvania	2,199	2,106
Tiltonville	2,360	2,242
Union City	1,497	1.305
Utica	1,376	1,394
Vermilion	1,616	1,464
Versailles	1,711	1,465
Warrensville Heights	1,175	877
Waverly	1,757	1,603
Waynesburg	1,223	1,186
West Carrollton	2,176	2.101
West Jefferson	1,386	1,376
West Lafayette	1,152	1,106
West Liberty	1,228	1,248
West Milton	1,439	1,388
West Union	1,334	1,094
Williamsburg	1,194	1,147
Woodsfield	2,442	2,317
Woodville	1,219	1,151
Worthington	1,569	1,239
Yellow Springs	1,640	1,427
Yorkville	1,961	1,963
Oklahoma		
Afton	1,261	1,219
Allen	1,389	1,438
Apache	1,047	1,302
Barnsdall	1,831	2,001
Beaver City	1,166	1,028
Beggs	1,283	1,531
Bixby	1,291	1,251
Blanchard	1,139	1,040
Boise City	1,144	1,256
Britton	2.239	2,214
Broken Arrow	2,074	1,964
Broken Bow	2,367	2,291
Buffalo	1,209	990
Carnegie	1,740	2,063
Cement	1,039	1,117
Checotah	2,126	2,110
Chelsea	1,642	1,527
Cheyenne	1,070	826
Oklahoma—Continued		
Coalgate	2,118	2,064
Collinsville	1,927	2,249
Comanche	1,533	1,704
Commerce	2,422	2,608
Coweta	1,455	1,274
Crescent	1,301	1,190
Davis	1,698	1,705
Dawson	1,086	842
Dewey	2,114	2,095
Erick	1,591	2,231
Eufaula	2,355	2,073
Fairfax	2,327	2,134
Fairview	1,913	1,887
Fort Gibson	1,233	1,159
Garber City	1,086	1,356
Geary	1,634	1,892
Grandfield	1,116	1,416
Granite	1,058	1,341
Grove	1,093	804
Guymon	2,290	2,181
Haileyville	1,183	1,801
Haskell	1,572	1,682
Healdton	2,067	2,017
Heavener	2,215	2,269
Hennessey	1,342	1,271
Hooker	1,146	1,628
Jenks	1,026	1,110
Konawa	2,205	2,070
Krebs	1,436	1,375
Lexington	1,084	836
Lindsay	1,792	1,713
Marietta	1,837	1,505
Maud	2,036	4,326
Medford	1,121	1,084
Morris	1,197	1,706
Mountain View	1,075	1,025
Newkirk	2,283	2,135
Oilton	1,225	1,518
Okeene	1,079	1,035
Pond Creek	1,019	857
Prague	1,422	1,299
Quapaw	1,054	1,340
Quinton	1,245	1,804
Rush Springs	1,422	1,340
Ryan	1,115	1,258
Sallisaw	2,140	1,785
Sentinel	1,088	1,269
Shattuck	1,275	1,490
Skiatook	1,496	1,789
Snyder	1,278	1,195
Spiro	1,041	969
Stigler	1,861	1,517
Stilwell	1,717	1,366
Stroud	1,917	1,894
Talihina	1,057	1,032
Tecumseh	2,042	2,419
Temple	1,313	1,182
Thomas	1,220	1,256
Tipton	1,470	1,459
Tishomingo	1,951	1,281
Walters	2,238	2,262
Waurika	2,458	2,368
Waynoka	1,584	1,840
Weleetka	1,904	2,042
Wetumka	2,340	2,153
Wilburton	1,925	1,524
Wilson	1,700	2,517
Wynnewood	2,318	1,820
Yale	1,407	1,734
Yukon	1,660	1,455
Oregon		
Bandon	1,004	1,516
Beaverton	1,052	[1] 863
Enterprise	1,709	1,379
Forest Grove	2,449	1,859
Gladstone	1,629	1,348
Gresham	1,951	1,635
Heppner	1,140	1,190
Independence	1,372	1,248
Junction City	1,187	922
Lakeview	2,466	1,799
Milton	1,744	1,576
Milwaukie	1,871	1,767
Mount Angel	1,032	[1] 823
Myrtle Point	1,296	1,362
Newport	2,019	1,530
Nyssa	1,855	821
Oswego	1,726	1,285
Prineville	2,358	1,027
Oregon—Continued		
Rainier	1,183	1,353
Redmond	1,876	994
Reedsport	1,421	1,178
Sheridan	1,294	1,008
Stayton	1,085	797
Sweet Home	1,090	189
Toledo	2,288	2,137
Union	1,398	1,107
Vale	1,083	922
Vernonia	1,412	1,625
Warrenton	1,365	683
West Linn	2,165	1,956
West Salem	1,490	974
Woodburn	1,982	1,675
Pennsylvania		
Albion	1,604	1,681
Allenport	1,078	1,017
Austin	1,050	1,116
Avis	1,161	1,268
Avonmore	1,354	1,240
Baden	2,135	1,924
Bath	1,720	1,625
Beaver Meadow	2,030	1,890
Bellevernon	2,463	2,489
Berlin	1,602	1,393
Bessemer	1,635	2,001
Blawnox	2,162	2,186
Blossburg	1,955	1,696
Boswell	1,711	1,775
Bridgewater	1,621	1,792
Brownstown	1,598	1,586
Burgettstown	2,497	2,266
Cambridge Springs	1,807	1,665
Canton	2,040	1,904
Carrolltown	1,289	1,227
Catawissa	2,053	2,023
Central City	2,083	2,107
Centralia	2,449	2,446
Chalfant	1,372	1,192
Cheswick	1,241	1,053
Christiana	1,062	959
Cleona	1,108	968
Coalport	1,121	1,222
Cokeburg	1,415	1,550
Colwyn	2,202	2,064
Confluence	1,035	989
Conway	1,865	2,014
Coopersburg	1,193	1,057
Cornwall	1,680	1,837
Courtdale	1,039	1,007
Cressona	1,695	1,946
Dallas	1,484	1,188
Dalton	1,090	1,072
Denver	1,428	1,203
Dillsburg	1,054	983
Dravosburg	2,277	2,391
Duboistown	1,047	1,049
Dunbar	1,390	1,357
Duncannon	1,707	1,732
Duncansville	1,415	1,379
East Brady	1,427	1,563
East Greenville	1,776	1,749
East Vandergrift	2,005	2,441
East Washington	2,106	1,859
Eddystone	2,493	2,414
Edgeworth	1,696	1,679
Eldred	1,051	1,118
Elizabethville	1,410	1,341
Elkland	2,400	1,978
Ellsworth	1,975	2,274
Evansburg [Evans City P. O.]	1,604	1,561
Everett	2,425	1,874
Everson	1,809	1,900
Export	1,990	2,184
Fairchance	1,855	1,804
Falls Creek	1,258	1,231
Fayette City	1,598	1,594
Fleetwood	2,254	2,150
Flemington	1,301	1,191
Folcroft	1,592	1,432
Fox Chapel	1,080	-------
Franklin (Cambria County)	2,297	2,323
Freemansburg	1,728	1,777
Galeton	1,820	2,200
Geistown	1,037	871

[1] Corrected figure.
[7] Population for 1940 originally reported as 2,549 because of the erroneous inclusion of an area outside the village. Corrected figures were compiled too late to permit inclusion in totals for incorporated places of 1,000 to 2,500 in other tables. Original figure is included in urban totals and in totals for urban places of 2,500 to 5,000.

TABLE 16.—POPULATION OF INCORPORATED PLACES HAVING, IN 1940, FROM 1,000 TO 2,500 INHABITANTS: 1940 AND 1930—Continued

INCORPORATED PLACE	1940	1930
Pennsylvania—Con.		
Girard	1,732	1,554
Glen Rock	1,412	1,309
Gordon	1,062	1,069
Greentree	1,880	1,457
Hallstead	1,293	1,254
Hastings	2,105	2,011
Hatfield	1,301	1,149
Hawley	1,778	1,811
Heidelberg	2,239	2,130
Highspire	2,371	2,327
Homer City	2,078	2,004
Hooversville	1,364	1,448
Houston	1,610	1,742
Houtzdale	1,430	1,351
Hughestown	2,340	2,252
Hughesville	1,947	1,868
Hyndman	1,325	1,190
Irvona	1,049	1,213
Kenhorst	2,227	------
Knox [8]	1,098	1,037
Koppel	1,064	1,057
Langhorne	1,221	1,147
Laurel Run	1,057	944
Lebanon Independent	2,425	2,252
Leetsdale	2,332	2,774
Liberty (Allegheny County)	1,084	906
Ligonier	2,111	1,978
Lilly	2,282	2,162
Linesville	1,150	963
Littlestown	2,463	2,001
Lorain	1,373	1,360
McConnellsburg	1,055	768
McSherrystown	2,128	2,050
Malvern	1,680	1,551
Manchester	1,004	940
Manor	1,289	1,305
Mansfield	1,880	1,755
Marianna	1,493	1,762
Marietta	2,128	1,969
Marion Heights	2,068	2,001
Mars	1,318	1,302
Martinsburg	1,396	1,295
Marysville	1,882	1,922
Matamoras	1,735	1,784
Mercer	2,272	2,125
Mercersburg	1,763	1,634
Middleburg	1,124	1,024
Middleport	1,077	1,225
Mifflinburg	2,090	1,959
Mifflintown	1,097	1,027
Millersville	1,867	------
Mill Hall	1,513	1,421
Mohnton	1,853	1,824
Montgomery	1,893	1,903
Montrose	1,977	1,909
Morton	1,316	1,341
Moscow	1,097	892
Mount Holly Springs	1,260	1,140
Mount Jewett	1,445	1,379
Nescopeck	1,805	1,614
New Bethlehem	1,622	1,590
New Eagle	1,936	1,793
New Freedom	1,137	1,125
New Holland	2,153	1,725
New Hope	1,053	1,113
New Oxford	1,194	1,138
New Philadelphia	2,453	2,557
Newport	1,897	1,891
Newtown	2,009	1,824
Newville	1,758	1,482
New Wilmington	1,018	907
Nicholson	1,012	932
North Apollo	1,568	1,485
North Girard	1,108	1,077
North Irwin	1,153	1,064
North Wales	2,450	2,393
North York	2,416	2,416
Oakdale	1,766	1,703
Orwigsburg	2,182	2,031
Osceola	2,076	2,002
Paint	1,700	1,336
Palo Alto	1,934	1,908
Parkesburg	2,288	2,288
Parkside	1,579	1,497
Paxtang	1,707	1,594
Penn	1,081	926
Pennsburg	1,548	1,494
Pine Grove	2,239	2,257
Point Marion	2,068	2,039
Port Allegany	2,356	2,193
Pringle	2,000	2,372
Quarryville	1,120	1,028
Rimersburg	1,393	1,319
Robesonia	1,570	1,468
Rockledge	1,773	1,920
Rockwood	1,375	1,176
Roscoe	1,372	1,310
Roseto	1,778	1,746
Royalton	1,201	1,117
Saltsburg	1,097	1,035
Saxton	1,152	1,128
Scalp Level	1,950	1,875
Sellersville	2,115	2,063
Shickshinny	2,354	2,451
Shingle House	1,106	1,380
Shoemakersville	1,081	937
Sinking Spring	1,861	1,771
Slippery Rock	1,269	1,165
Smethport	1,840	1,733
South Coatesville	1,604	1,785
Southmont	2,146	1,925
South Renovo	1,018	1,054
South Waverly	1,212	1,336
Spring Grove	1,259	1,236
Stoneboro	1,194	1,189
Strasburg	1,048	975
Summerville	1,009	1,202
Sykesville	2,044	2,103
Telford [9]	1,747	412
Temple	1,408	1,378
Topton	1,568	[1]1,489
Tower City	2,221	2,482
Trainer	1,716	1,648
Tremont	2,314	2,304
Troy	1,228	1,190
Tunkhannock	2,161	1,973
Upland	2,431	2,500
Vanderbilt	1,063	994
Versailles	2,401	2,473
Vintondale	1,516	1,658
Wall	2,098	2,236
Walnutport	1,271	1,151
Wampum	1,061	883
Warrior Run	1,339	1,516
Watsontown	2,282	2,248
Waymart	1,095	902
Wernersville	1,160	1,096
West Brownsville	1,844	1,717
West Conshohocken	2,464	2,579
West Easton	1,159	1,564
West Elizabeth	1,297	1,074
West Fairview	1,820	1,794
Westfield	1,386	1,193
West Grove	1,357	1,375
West Kittanning	1,005	1,005
West Lawn	2,080	2,069
West Leechburg	1,123	1,044
West Middlesex	1,126	1,181
Wheatland	1,421	1,518
Whitaker	2,217	2,072
White Haven	1,528	1,537
Williamsburg	1,898	1,898
Wind Gap	1,377	1,388
Windsor	1,108	1,009
Womelsdorf	1,450	1,484
Wormleysburg	1,454	1,404
Wrightsville	2,120	2,247
Yardley	1,459	1,308
Youngsville	1,909	1,907
Zelienople	2,117	1,933
South Carolina		
Allendale	2,217	2,066
Andrews	2,008	1,712
Arden	1,187	987
Barnwell	1,922	1,834
Belton	2,119	1,765
Blacksburg	1,917	1,747
Blackville	1,456	1,284
Branchville	1,351	1,689
Calhoun Falls	1,832	1,759
Cayce	1,476	1,267
Central	1,496	1,440
Chesterfield	1,263	1,030
Cowpens	1,343	1,115
Denmark	2,056	1,713
Edgefield	2,119	2,132
Elloree	1,123	1,098
Estill	1,280	1,412
Fairfax	1,379	1,376
Fountain Inn	1,346	1,264
Hardeeville	1,361	728
South Carolina—Con.		
Holly Hill	1,062	702
Inman	1,115	969
Iva	1,285	1,273
Johnston	1,100	1,072
Jonesville	1,182	1,153
Kershaw	1,264	1,120
Landrum	1,289	1,212
Latta	1,334	1,166
Leesville	1,217	1,240
Lexington	1,033	1,152
Liberty	2,240	2,128
Loris	1,238	900
McColl	2,391	1,657
McCormick	1,456	1,304
Manning	2,381	1,884
Moncks Corner	1,165	623
Mount Pleasant	1,698	1,415
Myrtle Beach	1,597	------
Ninety-Six	1,453	1,381
Pendleton	1,278	1,035
Pickens	1,637	1,130
Ridgeland	1,021	715
St. George	1,908	1,639
St. Matthews	2,187	1,750
St. Stephens	1,185	911
Saluda	1,516	1,381
Seneca	2,155	1,929
Simpsonville	1,298	1,400
Timmonsville	1,979	1,919
West Columbia [10]	1,744	1,722
West Greenville	2,233	1,917
Westminster	2,014	1,774
Williston	1,107	1,024
South Dakota		
Arlington	1,157	1,020
Armour	1,013	1,009
Belle Fourche	2,496	2,032
Beresford	1,642	1,460
Britton	1,500	1,312
Centerville	1,046	1,169
Chamberlain	1,626	1,364
Clark	1,291	1,290
Custer	1,845	1,203
Dell Rapids	1,706	1,657
De Smet	1,016	1,017
Edgemont	1,002	1,103
Elk Point	1,483	1,294
Eureka	1,457	1,308
Flandreau	2,212	1,934
Gettysburg	1,324	1,400
Gregory	1,246	1,034
Highmore	1,136	1,034
Howard	1,193	1,224
Ipswich	1,002	913
Lemmon	1,781	1,508
Lennox	1,164	1,113
Martin	1,013	720
Miller	1,460	1,447
Parker	1,244	1,229
Parkston	1,305	1,336
Platte	1,017	1,207
Redfield	2,428	2,664
Salem	1,185	1,115
Scotland	1,204	1,163
Spearfish	2,139	1,577
Tyndall	1,289	1,287
Wagner	1,319	1,420
Webster	2,173	1,805
Wessington Springs	1,352	1,401
Winner	2,426	2,220
Woonsocket	1,050	1,108
Tennessee		
Alamo	1,137	907
Belle Meade	2,061	------
Bells	1,054	919
Bolivar	1,314	1,217
Bruceton	1,003	1,112
Carthage	1,512	1,068
Centerville	1,030	943
Collierville	1,042	1,008
Copperhill	1,005	1,050
Cowan	1,461	1,367
Crossville	1,511	1,128
Dayton	1,870	2,006
Dresden	1,115	1,047
Dyer	1,185	1,214
Englewood	1,342	1,471
Greenfield	1,509	1,429
Halls	1,511	1,474
Hartsville	1,095	1,015
Tennessee—Continued		
Henderson	1,771	1,503
Hohenwald	1,086	980
Huntingdon	1,432	1,286
Jamestown	1,230	857
Jellico	1,581	1,530
Lake City [11]	1,520	1,116
Livingston	1,527	1,526
Lookout Mountain	1,545	1,031
McKenzie	2,019	1,858
Manchester	1,715	1,227
Monterey	1,742	1,731
Mountain City	1,021	1,058
Newbern	1,740	1,621
Obion	1,151	1,100
Oneida	1,252	1,382
Palmer	1,228	1,158
Parsons	1,079	915
Portland	1,212	1,030
Richard City	1,008	522
Ridgely	1,068	979
Rogersville	2,018	1,590
Savannah	1,504	1,129
Sevierville	1,161	882
Signal Mountain	1,308	966
Somerville	1,570	1,333
South Fulton	2,050	1,988
South Pittsburg	2,285	2,103
Spring City	1,569	1,090
Tiptonville	1,503	1,359
Waverly	1,318	1,152
Texas		
Alamo	1,944	1,018
Albany	2,230	2,422
Alto	1,141	1,053
Alvarado	1,324	1,210
Angleton	1,763	1,229
Anson	2,338	2,093
Archer City	1,675	1,512
Arp	1,139	------
Asherton	1,538	1,858
Aspermont	1,041	769
Atlanta	2,453	1,685
Baird	1,810	1,905
Bartlett	1,668	1,873
Bastrop	1,976	1,895
Bellaire	1,124	390
Bellville	1,347	1,533
Bishop	1,329	953
Boerne	1,271	1,117
Bremond	1,106	------
Bridgeport	1,735	2,464
Burnet	1,945	1,055
Caldwell	2,165	1,724
Calvert	2,366	2,103
Canadian	2,151	2,068
Carrizo Springs	2,494	2,171
Carthage	2,178	1,651
Chillicothe	1,423	1,610
Clarendon	2,431	2,756
Cleveland	1,783	1,422
Clifton	1,732	1,367
Cockrell Hill	1,246	------
College Station	2,184	------
Columbus	2,422	2,054
Coolidge	1,102	1,169
Corrigan	1,402	------
Crane	1,420	------
Crosbyton	1,615	1,250
Cross Plains	1,229	1,507
Crowell	1,817	1,946
Daingerfield	1,032	818
Dawson	1,155	1,131
Dayton	1,279	1,207
De Kalb	1,287	1,023
De Leon	1,971	1,766
Detroit	1,064	------
Devine	1,398	1,093
Dilley	1,244	929
Dumas	2,117	------
Eagle Lake	2,124	2,343
Edcouch	1,758	914
Eden	1,603	1,194
Eldorado	1,530	1,404
Elgin	2,008	1,823
Elsa	1,006	------
Fairfield	1,047	------
Farmersville	2,206	1,878
Ferris	1,436	1,438
Flatonia	1,024	966
Floresville	1,708	1,581
Forney	1,295	1,216

[1] Corrected figure.
[8] Name changed from Edenburg in 1933.
[9] Telford and West Telford boroughs consolidated as Telford borough in 1935; combined population in 1930, 1,664.
[10] Name changed from Brookland in 1938.
[11] Name changed from Coal Creek in 1939.

TABLE 16.—POPULATION OF INCORPORATED PLACES HAVING, IN 1940, FROM 1,000 TO 2,500 INHABITANTS: 1940 AND 1930—Continued

INCORPORATED PLACE	1940	1930
Texas—Continued		
Franklin	1,087	961
Frankston	1,216	1,109
Freer	2,346	------
Galena Park	1,562	------
Garland	2,233	1,584
Giddings	2,166	1,835
Glen Rose	1,050	983
Goldthwaite	1,414	1,324
Goliad	1,446	1,424
Gorman	1,157	1,154
Granbury	1,166	996
Grand Prairie	1,595	1,529
Grand Saline	1,641	1,799
Granger	1,723	1,703
Grapeland	1,327	1,027
Grapevine	1,043	936
Griffing Park	1,344	(2)
Groesbeck	2,272	2,059
Hallettsville	1,581	1,406
Hamlin	2,406	2,328
Hempstead	1,674	------
Henrietta	2,391	2,020
Hico	1,242	1,463
Honey Grove	2,456	2,475
Hubbard	1,871	1,855
Humble	1,371	------
Iowa Park	1,980	2,009
Irving	1,089	731
Italy	1,224	1,230
Itasca	1,759	1,665
Jacksboro	2,368	1,837
Junction	2,086	1,415
Karnes City	1,571	1,141
Kemp	1,000	990
Kerens	1,287	1,435
Killeen	1,263	1,260
Kirbyville	1,088	1,184
Knox City	1,127	906
Ladonia	1,279	1,199
La Feria	1,644	1,594
Lancaster	1,151	1,133
Leonard	1,331	1,131
Linden	1,168	718
Livingston	1,851	1,165
Lockney	1,231	1,466
Lott	1,021	921
McGregor	2,062	2,041
McLean	1,489	1,521
Madisonville	2,095	1,294
Marble Falls	1,021	865
Matador	1,376	1,302
Mathis	1,950	------
Menard	2,375	1,969
Meridian	1,016	759
Merkel	2,005	1,848
Mesquite	1,045	729
Midlothian	1,027	1,168
Morton	1,137	------
Mount Vernon	1,443	1,222
Muleshoe	1,327	779
Munday	1,545	1,318
New Boston	1,111	949
New Castle	1,044	1,157
Nixon	1,835	1,037
Oakwood	1,086	888
Odem	1,147	842
O'Donnell	1,187	1,026
Olmos Park	1,822	------
Overton	2,313	426
Palacios	2,288	1,318
Pear Ridge	1,198	------
Perryton	2,325	2,824
Pilot Point	1,122	1,108
Plano	1,582	1,554
Pleasanton	2,074	1,154
Port Isabel	1,440	1,177
Port Lavaca	2,069	1,367
Port Neches	2,487	2,327
Post	2,046	1,668
Poteet	2,315	1,231
Premont	1,080	------
Ralls	1,512	1,365
Richmond	2,026	1,432
Rising Star	1,198	1,160
Rockdale	2,136	2,204
Rockport	1,729	1,140
Rocksprings	1,339	998
Rockwall	1,318	1,071
Roma-Los Saenz	1,414	------
Roscoe	1,166	1,250
Rosebud	1,842	1,565
Rotan	2,029	1,632
Round Rock	1,240	1,173
Royse City	1,190	1,128
Rule	1,195	1,094
Runge	1,001	1,136
Sabinal	1,768	1,586
St. Jo	1,010	960
San Augustine	1,516	1,247
Sanger	1,000	1,119
San Juan	2,264	1,615
Santa Anna	1,661	1,883
Schulenburg	1,970	1,604
Seminole	1,761	------
Shiner	1,520	1,372
Somerville	1,621	2,287
Sour Lake	1,504	------
Southside Place	1,263	------
Spearman	1,105	1,580
Spur	2,136	1,899
Stanton	1,245	1,384
Strawn	1,107	1,429
Tahoka	2,129	1,620
Terrell Hills	1,236	------
Three Rivers	1,337	1,275
Throckmorton	1,133	1,135
Timpson	1,494	1,545
Trinity	2,217	2,036
Troup	1,526	1,318
Tulia	2,055	2,202
Van Alstyne	1,650	1,453
Waelder	1,018	1,048
Weimar	1,353	1,256
West	1,979	1,807
West Columbia	1,573	------
Whitesboro	1,560	1,535
Whitewright	1,537	1,480
Wills Point	1,976	2,023
Wink	1,945	3,963
Winnsboro	2,092	1,905
Winters	2,335	2,423
Wolfe City	1,339	1,405
Woodsboro	1,426	1,286
Woodville	1,521	969
Wortham	1,267	1,404
Yorktown	2,081	1,882
Utah		
Beaver	1,808	1,673
Blanding	1,111	555
Clearfield	1,053	799
Delta	1,304	1,183
Ephraim	2,094	1,966
Escalante	1,106	862
Eureka	2,292	3,041
Fairview	1,314	1,120
Farmington	1,211	1,339
Fillmore	1,785	1,374
Grantsville	1,242	1,201
Gunnison	1,115	1,057
Hurricane	1,524	1,197
Hyrum	1,874	1,869
Kanab	1,365	1,195
Kaysville	1,211	992
Lewiston	1,804	1,783
Manti	2,268	2,200
Milford	1,393	1,517
Moab	1,084	853
Monroe	1,292	1,247
Morgan	1,078	953
Moroni	1,158	1,218
Mount Pleasant	2,382	2,284
Panguitch	1,979	1,541
Parowan	1,525	1,474
Pleasant Grove	1,941	1,754
Providence	1,110	1,088
Richmond	1,131	1,140
Roosevelt	1,264	1,051
Salina	1,616	1,383
Sandy	1,487	1,436
Santaquin	1,297	1,115
Smithfield	2,461	2,353
South Ogden	1,407	------
Tremonton	1,443	1,009
Vernal	2,119	1,744
Wellsville	1,402	1,270
Vermont		
Barton	1,262	1,363
Bristol	1,236	1,190
Enosburg Falls	1,168	1,195
Essex Junction	1,901	1,621
Vermont—Continued		
Fair Haven	1,968	2,289
Hardwick	1,607	1,667
Ludlow	1,780	1,642
Lyndonville	1,444	1,559
Middlebury	2,123	2,003
Morrisville	1,967	1,822
Northfield	2,129	2,075
North Troy	1,077	1,045
Orleans	1,332	1,301
Poultney	1,333	1,570
Proctor	2,184	2,515
Randolph	1,988	1,957
Richford	1,889	1,783
Swanton	1,461	1,558
Vergennes	1,662	1,705
Woodstock	1,325	1,312
Virginia		
Ashland	1,718	1,297
Berryville	1,262	1,094
Blacksburg	2,133	1,406
Cape Charles	2,299	2,527
Chase City	1,896	1,590
Chatham	1,230	1,143
Chincoteague	2,142	2,130
Christiansburg	2,299	1,970
Clintwood	1,106	729
Colonial Beach	1,105	928
Crewe	2,048	2,152
Culpeper	2,316	2,379
Damascus	1,441	1,610
Elkton	1,050	965
Fries	1,677	2,205
Gate City	1,565	1,216
Grundy	1,476	815
Herndon	1,046	887
Lawrenceville	1,703	1,629
Leesburg	1,698	1,640
Luray	1,511	1,459
Manassas	1,302	1,215
Narrows	1,489	1,345
Onancock	1,283	1,245
Orange	1,980	1,381
Pennington Gap	1,990	1,553
Quantico	1,139	538
Richlands	2,203	1,355
Rocky Mount	1,366	1,339
Shenandoah	1,829	1,980
Smithfield	1,178	1,179
South Hill	1,739	1,405
Strasburg	1,968	1,901
Tangier	1,020	1,120
Tazewell	1,374	1,211
Victoria	1,555	1,568
Vienna	1,237	903
Warrenton	1,651	1,450
Waverly	1,288	1,355
West Point	1,947	1,844
Wise	1,226	1,112
Woodstock	1,546	1,552
Washington		
Arlington	1,460	1,439
Blaine	1,524	1,642
Buckley	1,170	1,052
Burlington	1,632	1,407
Cashmere	1,465	1,473
Castle Rock	1,182	1,239
Chelan	1,738	1,403
Cheney	1,551	1,335
Chewelah	1,565	1,315
Cle Elum	2,230	2,508
Colville	2,418	1,803
Cosmopolis	1,207	1,493
Davenport	1,337	987
Deer Park	1,070	1,009
Edmonds	1,288	1,165
Elma	1,370	1,545
Goldendale	1,584	1,116
Grandview	1,449	1,085
Kalama	1,028	940
Kennewick	1,918	1,519
Kirkland	2,084	1,714
Leavenworth	1,608	1,415
Lynden	1,696	1,564
Marysville	1,748	1,354
Medical Lake	2,114	1,671
Monroe	1,590	1,570
Montesano	2,242	2,460
Newport	1,174	1,080
Okanogan	1,735	1,519
Oroville	1,206	800
Washington—Con.		
Orting	1,211	1,109
Palouse	1,028	1,151
Pomeroy	1,723	1,600
Port Orchard	1,566	1,145
Prosser	1,719	1,569
Ritzville	1,748	1,777
Roslyn	1,743	2,063
Selah	1,130	767
South Bend	1,771	1,798
Sumner	2,140	1,967
Sunnyside	2,368	2,113
Tekoa	1,383	1,408
Wapato	1,483	1,222
Washougal	1,267	1,206
Wilbur	1,011	737
West Virginia		
Addison	1,133	976
Alderson	1,493	1,458
Ansted	1,422	1,404
Barboursville	1,550	1,508
Belington	1,517	1,571
Berkeley Springs	1,145	1,039
Bramwell	1,494	1,574
Bridgeport	1,581	1,567
Cameron	1,908	2,281
Cedar Grove	1,411	1,110
Ceredo	1,212	1,164
Clendenin	1,200	1,217
Davis	1,454	1,656
East Rainelle	1,515	1,272
Fayetteville	1,347	1,143
Gassaway	1,429	1,618
Glendale	1,348	1,493
Grantsville	1,052	1,018
Harrisville	1,338	1,192
Hurricane	1,103	1,293
Kimball	1,580	1,467
Kingwood	1,676	1,709
Lewisburg	1,466	1,293
Lumberport	1,285	1,289
Mabscott	1,473	1,260
Madison	1,205	1,156
Man	1,342	835
Marlinton	1,644	1,586
Marmet	1,814	1,200
Milton	1,641	1,305
Monongah	1,790	1,909
Moorefield	1,291	734
Mount Hope	2,431	2,361
New Cumberland	2,098	2,300
Nutter Fort	1,803	1,825
Paden City	2,215	2,281
Parsons	2,077	2,012
Pennsboro	1,738	1,616
Petersburg	1,751	1,410
Philippi	1,955	1,767
Ranson	1,171	1,002
Ravenswood	1,061	1,189
Ridgeley	1,907	1,972
Riverside	1,043	940
Rivesville	1,552	1,700
Romney	2,013	1,441
Ronceverte	2,265	2,254
Rowlesburg	1,452	1,573
Sabraton	1,810	1,717
St. Marys	2,201	2,182
Smithers	2,232	------
Sophia	1,160	611
Spencer	2,497	2,493
Star City	1,175	1,121
Sutton	1,083	1,205
Terra Alta	1,471	1,474
Thomas	1,449	1,660
Vienna	2,338	------
War	1,277	1,392
Weirton Heights	2,476	------
Westover	1,752	1,633
West Union	1,020	984
White Sulphur Springs	2,093	1,484
Williamstown	1,687	1,657
Wisconsin		
Adams	1,310	1,231
Alma	1,139	1,009
Altoona	1,239	1,044
Amery	1,461	1,354
Arcadia	1,830	1,499
Augusta	1,519	1,359
Barron	2,059	1,863
Bayfield	1,212	1,195
Bloomer	2,204	1,365
Boscobel	2,008	1,762

[2] Not returned separately.

TABLE 16.—POPULATION OF INCORPORATED PLACES HAVING, IN 1940, FROM 1,000 TO 2,500 INHABITANTS: 1940 AND 1930—Continued

INCORPORATED PLACE	1940	1930
Wisconsin—Continued		
Brillion	1, 200	1, 167
Brodhead	1, 750	1, 533
Campbellsport	1, 094	789
Cedarburg	2, 245	2, 055
Chetek	1, 227	1, 076
Chilton	2, 203	1, 945
Cornell	1, 759	1, 510
Crandon	2, 000	1, 679
Cuba City	1, 259	1, 157
Cumberland	1, 539	1, 532
Darlington	2, 002	1, 764
Dodgeville	2, 269	1, 937
Durand	1, 858	1, 590
Eagle River	1, 491	1, 386
Elkhorn	2, 382	2, 340
Ellsworth	1, 340	1, 124
Elroy	1, 850	1, 546
Evansville	2, 321	2, 269
Fennimore	1, 592	1, 341
Fox Lake	1, 016	901
Fox Point	1, 180	474
Galesville	1, 147	1, 069
Gillett	1, 145	1, 076
Grafton	1, 150	1, 065
Hayward	1, 571	1, 207
Hillsboro	1, 146	972
Wisconsin—Continued		
Horicon	2, 253	2, 214
Independence	1, 036	866
Juneau	1, 301	1, 154
Kiel	1, 898	1, 803
Kohler	1, 789	1, 748
Lake Mills	2, 219	2, 007
Lodi	1, 116	1, 065
Marion	1, 034	992
Medford	2, 361	1, 918
Mellen	1, 598	1, 629
Menomonee Falls	1, 469	1, 291
Middleton	1, 358	983
Milton	1, 266	1, 128
Mineral Point	2, 275	2, 274
Mondovi	2, 077	1, 623
Monona	1, 323	------
Montello	1, 138	1, 245
Montreal	1, 700	1 819
Mosinee	1, 361	1, 229
Mount Horeb	1, 610	1, 425
Nekoosa	2, 212	2, 005
New Glarus	1, 068	1, 010
New Holstein	1, 502	1, 274
New Lisbon	1, 215	1, 076
New Richmond	2, 388	2, 112
Niagara	2, 266	2, 033
Wisconsin—Continued		
North Fond du Lac	2, 083	2, 244
Oconto Falls	1, 888	1, 921
Omro	1, 401	1, 255
Onalaska	1, 742	1, 408
Oregon	1, 005	857
Osseo	1, 105	933
Owen	1, 083	1, 102
Pardeeville	1, 001	873
Peshtigo	1, 947	1, 579
Pewaukee	1, 352	1, 067
Phillips	1, 915	1, 901
Port Edwards	1, 192	988
Prairie du Sac	1, 001	949
Princeton	1, 247	1, 183
Randolph	1, 146	1, 161
Rib Lake	1, 042	1, 180
St. Croix Falls	1, 007	952
Sauk City	1, 325	1, 137
Schofield	1, 536	1, 287
Seymour	1, 365	1, 201
Shorewood Hills	1, 064	347
Shullsburg	1, 197	1, 041
Stanley	2, 021	1, 988
Sun Prairie	1, 625	1, 337
Thorp	1, 052	892
Washburn	2, 363	2, 238
Wisconsin—Continued		
Waterloo	1, 474	1, 272
Wautoma	1, 180	1, 044
Westby	1, 438	1, 366
West Salem	1, 254	1, 011
Weyauwega	1, 173	1, 067
Whitehall	1, 035	915
Wisconsin Dells [12]	1, 762	1, 489
Wyoming		
Afton	1, 211	807
Basin	1, 099	903
Buffalo	2, 302	1, 749
Douglas	2, 205	1, 917
Gillette	2, 177	1, 340
Glenrock	1, 014	819
Greybull	1, 828	1, 806
Hanna	1, 127	------
Jackson	1, 046	533
Kemmerer	2, 026	1, 884
Lovell	2, 175	1, 857
Lusk	1, 814	1, 218
Newcastle	1, 962	1, 201
Powell	1, 948	1, 156
Superior	1, 240	1, 156
Thermopolis	2, 422	2, 129
Torrington	2, 344	1, 811
Wheatland	2, 110	1, 997

[12] Name changed from Kilbourn in 1931.

TABLE 17.—POPULATION, LAND AREA, AND POPULATION DENSITY OF METROPOLITAN DISTRICTS OF THE UNITED STATES: 1940

METROPOLITAN DISTRICT	Population	Land area in square miles	Population per square mile
Total (140 districts)	**62, 965, 773**	**44, 626. 0**	1, 411. 0
In central cities	42, 796, 170	5, 477. 5	7, 813. 1
Outside central cities	20, 169, 603	39, 148. 5	515. 2
Akron, Ohio	**349, 705**	**253. 3**	**1, 380. 6**
In central city	244, 791	53. 7	4, 558. 5
Outside central city	104, 914	199. 6	525. 6
Albany - Schenectady - Troy, N. Y.	**431, 575**	**463. 5**	**931. 1**
In central cities	288, 430	38. 5	7, 491. 7
Albany	130, 577	19. 0	6, 872. 5
Schenectady	87, 549	10. 2	8, 583. 2
Troy	70, 304	9. 3	7, 559. 6
Outside central cities	143, 145	425. 0	336. 8
Allentown - Bethlehem - Easton, Pa.	**325, 142**	**340. 6**	**954. 6**
In central cities	188, 983	36. 8	5, 135. 4
Allentown	96, 904	15. 7	6, 172. 2
Bethlehem	58, 490	17. 5	3, 342. 3
Easton	33, 589	3. 6	9, 330. 3
Outside central cities	136, 159	303. 8	448. 2
Altoona, Pa.	**114, 094**	**133. 5**	**854. 6**
In central city	80, 214	9. 0	8, 912. 7
Outside central city	33, 880	124. 5	272. 1
Amarillo, Tex.	**53, 463**	**33. 4**	**1, 600. 7**
In central city	51, 686	16. 4	3, 151. 6
Outside central city	1, 777	17. 0	104. 5
Asheville, N. C.	**76, 324**	**134. 0**	**569. 6**
In central city	51, 310	14. 5	3, 538. 6
Outside central city	25, 014	119. 5	209. 3
Atlanta, Ga.	**442, 294**	**257. 5**	**1, 717. 6**
In central city	302, 288	34. 7	8, 711. 5
Outside central city	140, 006	222. 8	628. 4
Atlantic City, N. J.	**100, 096**	**56. 2**	**1, 781. 1**
In central city	64, 094	11. 5	5, 573. 4
Outside central city	36, 002	44. 7	805. 4
Augusta, Ga.	**87, 809**	**187. 2**	**469. 1**
In central city	65, 919	9. 8	6, 726. 4
Outside central city	21, 890	177. 4	123. 4
Austin, Tex.	**106, 193**	**705. 2**	**150. 6**
In central city	87, 930	25. 1	3, 503. 2
Outside central city	18, 263	680. 1	26. 9
Baltimore, Md.	**1, 046, 692**	**577. 1**	**1, 813. 7**
In central city	859, 100	78. 7	10, 916. 1
Outside central city	187, 592	498. 4	376. 4
Beaumont-Port Arthur, Tex.	**138, 608**	**235. 9**	**587. 6**
In central cities	105, 201	19. 8	5, 313. 2
Beaumont	59, 061	10. 4	5, 678. 9
Port Arthur	46, 140	9. 4	4, 908. 5
Outside central cities	33, 407	216. 1	154. 6
Binghamton, N. Y.	**145, 156**	**182. 9**	**793. 6**
In central city	78, 309	10. 0	7, 830. 9
Outside central city	66, 847	172. 9	386. 6
Birmingham, Ala.	**407, 851**	**347. 6**	**1, 173. 3**
In central city	267, 583	50. 2	5, 330. 3
Outside central city	140, 268	297. 4	471. 6
Boston, Mass.	**2, 350, 514**	**1, 062. 3**	**2, 212. 7**
In central city	770, 816	46. 1	16, 720. 5
Outside central city	1, 579, 698	1, 016. 2	1, 554. 5
Bridgeport, Conn.	**216, 621**	**171. 5**	**1, 263. 1**
In central city	147, 121	14. 6	10, 076. 8
Outside central city	69. 500	156. 9	443. 0
Buffalo-Niagara, N. Y.	**857, 719**	**473. 4**	**1, 811. 8**
In central cities	653, 930	52. 1	12, 551. 4
Buffalo	575, 901	39. 4	14, 616. 8
Niagara Falls	78, 029	12. 7	6, 144. 0
Outside central cities	203, 789	421. 3	483. 7
Canton, Ohio	**200, 352**	**245. 7**	**815. 4**
In central city	108, 401	13. 9	7, 798. 6
Outside central city	91, 951	231. 8	396. 7
Cedar Rapids, Iowa	**73, 219**	**239. 0**	**306. 4**
In central city	62, 120	27. 1	2, 292. 3
Outside central city	11, 099	211. 9	52. 4
Charleston, S. C.	**98, 711**	**143. 3**	**688. 8**
In central city	71, 275	4. 5	15, 838. 9
Outside central city	27, 436	138. 8	197. 7
Charleston, W. Va.	**136, 332**	**281. 6**	**484. 1**
In central city	67, 914	7. 7	8, 820. 0
Outside central city	68, 418	273. 9	249. 8
Charlotte, N. C.	**112, 986**	**47. 0**	**2, 404. 0**
In central city	100, 899	19. 3	5, 227. 9
Outside central city	12, 087	27. 7	436. 4
Chattanooga, Tenn.	**193, 215**	**531. 8**	**363. 3**
In central city	128, 163	27. 4	4, 677. 5
Outside central city	65, 052	504. 4	129. 0
Chicago, Ill.	**4, 499, 126**	**1, 184. 2**	**3, 799. 3**
In central city	3, 396, 808	206. 7	16, 433. 5
Outside central city	1, 102, 318	977. 5	1, 127. 7
Cincinnati, Ohio	**789, 309**	**521. 9**	**1, 512. 4**
In central city	455, 610	72. 4	6, 293. 0
Outside central city	333, 699	449. 5	742. 4
Cleveland, Ohio	**1, 214, 943**	**336. 2**	**3, 613. 8**
In central city	878, 336	73. 1	12, 015. 5
Outside central city	336, 607	263. 1	1, 279. 4
Columbia, S. C.	**89, 555**	**123. 2**	**726. 9**
In central city	62, 396	8. 8	7, 090. 5
Outside central city	27, 159	114. 4	237. 4
Columbus, Ga.	**92, 478**	**185. 5**	**498. 5**
In central city	53, 280	6. 3	8, 457. 1
Outside central city	39, 198	179. 2	218. 7
Columbus, Ohio	**365, 796**	**219. 8**	**1, 664. 2**
In central city	306, 087	39. 0	7, 848. 4
Outside central city	59, 709	180. 8	330. 2
Corpus Christi, Tex.	**70, 677**	**295. 7**	**239. 0**
In central city	57, 301	9. 3	6, 161. 4
Outside central city	13, 376	286. 4	46. 7
Dallas, Tex.	**376, 548**	**549. 8**	**684. 9**
In central city	294, 734	40. 6	7, 259. 5
Outside central city	81, 814	509. 2	160. 7
Davenport, Iowa-Rock Island-Moline, Ill.	**174, 995**	**129. 2**	**1, 354. 5**
In central cities	143, 422	34. 1	4, 205. 9
Davenport, Iowa	66, 039	18. 1	3, 648. 6
Rock Island, Ill.	42, 775	9. 1	4, 700. 5
Moline, Ill.	34, 608	6. 9	5, 015. 7
Outside central cities	31, 573	95. 1	332. 0

TABLE 17.—POPULATION, LAND AREA, AND POPULATION DENSITY OF METROPOLITAN DISTRICTS OF THE UNITED STATES: 1940—Continued

METROPOLITAN DISTRICT	Population	Land area in square miles	Population per square mile
Dayton, Ohio	**271, 513**	**194. 8**	**1, 393. 8**
In central city	210, 718	23. 7	8, 891. 1
Outside central city	60, 795	171. 1	355. 3
Decatur, Ill	**65, 764**	**27. 5**	**2, 391. 4**
In central city	59, 305	9. 5	6, 242. 6
Outside central city	6, 459	18. 0	358. 8
Denver, Colo	**384, 372**	**341. 0**	**1, 127. 2**
In central city	322, 412	57. 9	5, 568. 4
Outside central city	61, 960	283. 1	218. 9
Des Moines, Iowa	**183, 973**	**210. 2**	**875. 2**
In central city	159, 819	53. 8	2, 970. 6
Outside central city	24, 154	156. 4	154. 4
Detroit, Mich	**2, 295, 867**	**856. 3**	**2, 681. 1**
In central city	1, 623, 452	137. 9	11, 772. 7
Outside central city	672, 415	718. 4	936. 0
Duluth, Minn.-Superior, Wis	**157, 098**	**458. 4**	**342. 7**
In central cities	136, 201	98. 9	1, 377. 2
Duluth, Minn	101, 065	62. 3	1, 622. 2
Superior, Wis	35, 136	36. 6	960. 0
Outside central cities	20, 897	359. 5	58. 1
Durham, N. C	**69, 683**	**106. 4**	**654. 9**
In central city	60, 195	13. 3	4, 525. 9
Outside central city	9, 488	93. 1	101. 9
El Paso, Tex	**115, 801**	**95. 1**	**1, 217. 7**
In central city	96, 810	13. 6	7, 118. 4
Outside central city	18, 991	81. 5	233. 0
Erie, Pa	**134, 039**	**88. 5**	**1, 514. 6**
In central city	116, 955	16. 2	7, 219. 4
Outside central city	17, 084	72. 3	236. 3
Evansville, Ind	**141, 614**	**176. 8**	**801. 0**
In central city	97, 062	9. 7	10, 006. 4
Outside central city	44, 552	167. 1	266. 6
Fall River-New Bedford, Mass	**272, 648**	**310. 3**	**878. 7**
In central cities	225, 769	53. 0	4, 259. 8
Fall River	115, 428	33. 9	3, 405. 0
New Bedford	110, 341	19. 1	5, 777. 0
Outside central cities	46, 879	257. 3	182. 2
Flint, Mich	**188, 554**	**144. 5**	**1, 304. 9**
In central city	151, 543	29. 3	5, 172. 1
Outside central city	37, 011	115. 2	321. 3
Fort Wayne, Ind	**134, 385**	**141. 1**	**952. 4**
In central city	118, 410	17. 1	6, 924. 6
Outside central city	15, 975	124. 0	128. 8
Fort Worth, Tex	**207, 677**	**287. 3**	**722. 9**
In central city	177, 662	49. 8	3, 567. 5
Outside central city	30, 015	237. 5	126. 4
Fresno, Calif	**97, 504**	**164. 6**	**592. 4**
In central city	60, 685	9. 9	6, 129. 8
Outside central city	36, 819	154. 7	238. 0
Galveston, Tex	**71, 677**	**130. 4**	**549. 7**
In central city	60, 862	8. 1	7, 513. 8
Outside central city	10, 815	122. 3	88. 4
Grand Rapids, Mich	**209, 873**	**142. 9**	**1, 468. 7**
In central city	164, 292	23. 0	7, 143. 1
Outside central city	45, 581	119. 9	380. 2
Greensboro, N. C	**73, 055**	**72. 2**	**1, 011. 8**
In central city	59, 319	18. 0	3, 295. 5
Outside central city	13, 736	54. 2	253. 4
Hamilton-Middletown, Ohio	**112, 686**	**225. 2**	**500. 4**
In central cities	81, 812	11. 9	6, 875. 0
Hamilton	50, 592	6. 6	7, 665. 5
Middletown	31, 220	5. 3	5, 890. 6
Outside central cities	30, 874	213. 3	144. 7
Harrisburg, Pa	**173, 367**	**130. 1**	**1, 332. 6**
In central city	83, 893	6. 2	13, 531. 1
Outside central city	89, 474	123. 9	722. 1
Hartford-New Britain, Conn	**502, 193**	**578. 6**	**867. 9**
In central cities	234, 952	31. 1	7, 554. 7
Hartford	166, 267	17. 4	9, 555. 6
New Britain	68, 685	13. 7	5, 013. 5
Outside central cities	267, 241	547. 5	488. 1
Houston, Tex	**510, 397**	**1, 024. 3**	**498. 3**
In central city	384, 514	72. 8	5, 281. 8
Outside central city	125, 883	951. 5	132. 3
Huntington, W. Va.-Ashland, Ky	**170, 979**	**255. 0**	**670. 5**
In central cities	108, 373	20. 6	5, 260. 8
Huntington, W. Va	78, 836	12. 6	6, 256. 8
Ashland, Ky	29, 537	8. 0	3, 692. 1
Outside central cities	62, 606	234. 4	267. 1
Indianapolis, Ind	**455, 357**	**315. 8**	**1, 441. 9**
In central city	386, 972	53. 6	7, 219. 6
Outside central city	68, 385	262. 2	260. 8
Jackson, Miss	**88, 003**	**436. 3**	**201. 7**
In central city	62, 107	16. 1	3, 857. 6
Outside central city	25, 896	420. 2	61. 6
Jacksonville, Fla	**195, 619**	**242. 2**	**807. 7**
In central city	173, 065	30. 2	5, 730. 6
Outside central city	22, 554	212. 0	106. 4
Johnstown, Pa	**151, 781**	**215. 7**	**703. 7**
In central city	66, 668	5. 6	11, 905. 0
Outside central city	85, 113	210. 1	405. 1
Kalamazoo, Mich	**77, 213**	**73. 3**	**1, 053. 4**
In central city	54, 097	8. 5	6, 364. 4
Outside central city	23, 116	64. 8	356. 7
Kansas City, Mo.-Kansas City, Kans	**634, 093**	**500. 4**	**1, 267. 2**
In central cities	520, 636	77. 8	6, 692. 0
Kansas City, Mo	399, 178	58. 6	6, 811. 9
Kansas City, Kans	121, 458	19. 2	6, 325. 9
Outside central cities	113, 457	422. 6	268. 5
Knoxville, Tenn	**151, 829**	**200. 9**	**755. 7**
In central city	111, 580	25. 4	4, 392. 9
Outside central city	40, 249	175. 5	229. 3
Lancaster, Pa	**132, 027**	**234. 0**	**564. 2**
In central city	61, 345	3. 9	15, 729. 5
Outside central city	70, 682	230. 1	307. 2
Lansing, Mich	**110, 356**	**108. 1**	**1, 020. 9**
In central city	78, 753	11. 6	6, 789. 1
Outside central city	31, 603	96. 5	327. 5
Lincoln, Nebr	**88, 191**	**110. 7**	**796. 7**
In central city	81, 984	24. 3	3, 373. 8
Outside central city	6, 207	86. 4	71. 8
Little Rock, Ark	**126, 724**	**114. 0**	**1, 111. 6**
In central city	88, 039	17. 9	4, 918. 4
Outside central city	38, 685	96. 1	402. 5
Los Angeles, Calif	**2, 904, 596**	**1, 540. 8**	**1, 885. 1**
In central city	1, 504, 277	448. 3	3, 355. 5
Outside central city	1, 400, 319	1, 092. 5	1, 281. 8
Louisville, Ky	**434, 408**	**454. 4**	**956. 0**
In central city	319, 077	37. 9	8, 418. 9
Outside central city	115, 331	416. 5	276. 9
Lowell-Lawrence-Haverhill, Mass	**334, 969**	**294. 0**	**1, 139. 4**
In central cities	232, 464	51. 6	4, 505. 1
Lowell	101, 389	12. 9	7, 859. 6
Lawrence	84, 323	6. 7	12, 585. 5
Haverhill	46, 752	32. 0	1, 461. 0
Outside central cities	102, 505	242. 4	422. 9
Macon, Ga	**74, 830**	**93. 4**	**801. 2**
In central city	57, 865	8. 0	7, 233. 1
Outside central city	16, 965	85. 4	198. 7
Madison, Wis	**78, 349**	**52. 7**	**1, 486. 7**
In central city	67, 447	8. 1	8, 326. 8
Outside central city	10, 902	44. 6	244. 4
Manchester, N. H	**81, 932**	**69. 7**	**1, 175. 5**
In central city	77, 685	32. 1	2, 420. 1
Outside central city	4, 247	37. 6	113. 0
Memphis, Tenn	**332, 477**	**288. 2**	**1, 153. 6**
In central city	292, 942	45. 6	6, 424. 2
Outside central city	39, 535	242. 6	163. 0
Miami, Fla	**250, 537**	**164. 0**	**1, 527. 7**
In central city	172, 172	30. 3	5, 682. 2
Outside central city	78, 365	133. 7	586. 1
Milwaukee, Wis	**790, 336**	**250. 3**	**3, 157. 6**
In central city	587, 472	43. 4	13, 536. 2
Outside central city	202, 864	206. 9	980. 5
Minneapolis-St. Paul, Minn	**911, 077**	**528. 0**	**1, 725. 5**
In central cities	780, 106	106. 0	7, 359. 5
Minneapolis	492, 370	53. 8	9, 151. 9
St. Paul	287, 736	52. 2	5, 512. 2
Outside central cities	130, 971	422. 0	310. 4
Mobile, Ala	**114, 906**	**88. 5**	**1, 298. 4**
In central city	78, 720	11. 7	6, 728. 2
Outside central city	36, 186	76. 8	471. 2
Montgomery, Ala	**93, 697**	**163. 2**	**574. 1**
In central city	78, 084	20. 3	3, 846. 5
Outside central city	15, 613	142. 9	109. 3
Nashville, Tenn	**241, 769**	**315. 9**	**765. 3**
In central city	167, 402	22. 0	7, 609. 2
Outside central city	74, 367	293. 9	253. 0
New Haven, Conn	**308, 228**	**242. 3**	**1, 272. 1**
In central city	160, 605	17. 9	8, 972. 3
Outside central city	147, 623	224. 4	657. 9
New Orleans, La	**540, 030**	**333. 8**	**1, 617. 8**
In central city	494, 537	199. 4	2, 480. 1
Outside central city	45, 493	134. 4	338. 5
New York-Northeastern New Jersey	**11, 690, 520**	**2, 560. 9**	**4, 565. 0**
In central cities	8, 435, 496	356. 7	23, 648. 7
Outside central cities	3, 255, 024	2, 204. 2	1, 476. 7
New York Division	8, 707, 666	1, 364. 6	6, 381. 1
New York	7, 454, 995	299. 0	24, 933. 1
Outside city	1, 252, 671	1, 065. 6	1, 175. 6
New Jersey Division	2, 982, 854	1, 196. 3	2, 493. 4
In central cities	980, 501	57. 7	16, 993. 1
Elizabeth	109, 912	11. 7	9, 394. 2
Jersey City	301, 173	14. 3	21, 061. 0
Newark	429, 760	23. 6	18, 210. 2
Paterson	139, 656	8. 1	17, 241. 5
Outside central cities	2, 002, 353	1, 138. 6	1, 758. 6

467750—42——5

TABLE 17.—POPULATION, LAND AREA, AND POPULATION DENSITY OF METROPOLITAN DISTRICTS OF THE UNITED STATES: 1940—Continued

METROPOLITAN DISTRICT	Population	Land area in square miles	Population per square mile
Norfolk-Portsmouth-Newport News, Va	330, 396	441. 9	747. 7
In central cities	232, 144	38. 1	6, 093. 0
Norfolk	144, 332	28. 2	5, 118. 2
Portsmouth	50, 745	6. 2	8, 184. 7
Newport News	37, 067	3. 7	10, 018. 1
Outside central cities	98, 252	403. 8	243. 3
Oklahoma City, Okla	221, 229	175. 9	1, 257. 7
In central city	204, 424	49. 8	4, 104. 9
Outside central city	16, 805	126. 1	133. 3
Omaha, Nebr.-Council Bluffs, Iowa	287, 698	199. 0	1, 445. 7
In central cities	265, 283	54. 2	4, 894. 5
Omaha, Nebr	223, 844	38. 9	5, 754. 3
Council Bluffs, Iowa	41, 439	15. 3	2, 708. 4
Outside central cities	22, 415	144. 8	154. 8
Peoria, Ill	162, 566	109. 0	1, 491. 4
In central city	105, 087	12. 4	8, 474. 8
Outside central city	57, 479	96. 6	595. 0
Philadelphia, Pa	2, 898, 644	1, 021. 3	2, 838. 2
In central city	1, 931, 334	127. 2	15, 183. 4
Outside central city	967, 310	894. 1	1, 081. 9
Phoenix, Ariz	121, 828	132. 1	922. 2
In central city	65, 414	9. 7	6, 743. 7
Outside central city	56, 414	122. 4	460. 9
Pittsburgh, Pa	1, 994, 060	1, 624. 5	1, 227. 5
In central city	671, 659	52. 1	12, 891. 7
Outside central city	1, 322, 401	1, 572. 4	841. 0
Portland, Maine	106, 566	95. 3	1, 118. 2
In central city	73, 643	21. 6	3, 409. 4
Outside central city	32, 923	73. 7	446. 7
Portland, Oreg	406, 406	307. 4	1, 322. 1
In central city	305, 394	63. 5	4, 809. 4
Outside central city	101, 012	243. 9	414. 2
Providence, R. I	711, 500	505. 3	1, 408. 1
In central city	253, 504	17. 9	14, 162. 2
Outside central city	457, 996	487. 4	939. 7
Pueblo, Colo	62, 039	71. 9	862. 9
In central city	52, 162	10. 0	5, 216. 2
Outside central city	9, 877	61. 9	159. 6
Racine-Kenosha, Wis	135, 075	188. 5	716. 6
In central cities	115, 960	16. 3	7, 114. 1
Racine	67, 195	8. 7	7, 723. 6
Kenosha	48, 765	7. 6	6, 416. 4
Outside central cities	19, 115	172. 2	111. 0
Reading, Pa	175, 355	162. 2	1, 081. 1
In central city	110, 568	8. 8	12, 564. 5
Outside central city	64, 787	153. 4	422. 3
Richmond, Va	245, 674	303. 9	808. 4
In central city	193, 042	21. 4	9, 020. 7
Outside central city	52, 632	282. 5	186. 3
Roanoke, Va	110, 593	240. 5	459. 8
In central city	69, 287	10. 7	6, 475. 4
Outside central city	41, 306	229. 8	179. 7
Rochester, N. Y	411, 970	305. 9	1, 346. 7
In central city	324, 975	34. 8	9, 338. 4
Outside central city	86, 995	271. 1	320. 9
Rockford, Ill	105, 259	143. 7	732. 5
In central city	84, 637	12. 0	7, 053. 1
Outside central city	20, 622	131. 7	156. 6
Sacramento, Calif	158, 999	469. 2	338. 9
In central city	105, 958	13. 7	7, 734. 2
Outside central city	53, 041	455. 5	116. 4
Saginaw-Bay City, Mich	153, 388	162. 1	946. 3
In central cities	130, 750	26. 2	4, 990. 5
Saginaw	82, 794	16. 6	4, 987. 6
Bay City	47, 956	9. 6	4, 995. 4
Outside central cities	22, 688	135. 9	166. 6
St. Joseph, Mo	86, 991	108. 8	799. 5
In central city	75, 711	14. 1	5, 369. 6
Outside central city	11, 280	94. 7	119. 1
St. Louis, Mo	1, 367, 977	956. 0	1, 430. 9
In central city	816, 048	61. 0	13, 377. 8
Outside central city	551, 929	895. 0	616. 7
Salt Lake City, Utah	204, 488	451. 0	453. 4
In central city	149, 934	52. 5	2, 855. 9
Outside central city	54, 554	398. 5	136. 9
San Antonio, Tex	319, 010	466. 3	684. 1
In central city	253, 854	35. 7	7, 110. 8
Outside central city	65, 156	430. 6	151. 3
San Diego, Calif	256, 368	520. 4	492. 6
In central city	203, 341	95. 3	2, 133. 7
Outside central city	53, 027	425. 1	124. 7
San Francisco-Oakland, Calif	1, 428, 525	1, 002. 9	1, 424. 4
In central cities	936, 699	97. 4	9, 617. 0
San Francisco	634, 536	44. 6	14, 227. 3
Oakland	302, 163	52. 8	5, 722. 8
Outside central cities	491, 826	905. 5	543. 2
San Jose, Calif	129, 367	242. 1	534. 4
In central city	68, 457	14. 8	4, 625. 5
Outside central city	60, 910	227. 3	268. 0
Savannah, Ga	117, 970	441. 1	267. 4
In central city	95, 996	11. 1	8, 648. 3
Outside central city	21, 974	430. 0	51. 1
Scranton-Wilkes-Barre, Pa	629, 581	385. 5	1, 633. 2
In central cities	226, 640	26. 3	8, 617. 5
Scranton	140, 404	19. 4	7, 237. 3
Wilkes-Barre	86, 236	6. 9	12, 498. 0
Outside central cities	402, 941	359. 2	1, 121. 8
Seattle, Wash	452, 639	216. 3	2, 092. 6
In central city	368, 302	68. 5	5, 376. 7
Outside central city	84, 337	147. 8	570. 6
Shreveport, La	112, 225	48. 4	2, 318. 7
In central city	98, 167	18. 7	5, 249. 6
Outside central city	14, 058	29. 7	473. 3
Sioux City, Iowa	87, 791	60. 8	1, 443. 9
In central city	82, 364	45. 0	1, 830. 3
Outside central city	5, 427	15. 8	343. 5
South Bend, Ind	147, 022	155. 6	944. 9
In central city	101, 268	19. 7	5, 140. 5
Outside central city	45, 754	135. 9	336. 7
Spokane, Wash	141, 370	278. 8	507. 1
In central city	122, 001	41. 5	2, 939. 8
Outside central city	19, 369	237. 3	81. 6
Springfield, Ill	89, 484	69. 2	1, 293. 1
In central city	75, 503	9. 5	7, 947. 7
Outside central city	13, 981	59. 7	234. 2
Springfield, Mo	70, 514	88. 2	799. 5
In central city	61, 238	13. 6	4, 502. 8
Outside central city	9, 276	74. 6	124. 3
Springfield, Ohio	77, 406	52. 8	1, 466. 0
In central city	70, 662	11. 8	5, 988. 3
Outside central city	6, 744	41. 0	164. 5
Springfield-Holyoke, Mass	394, 623	529. 2	745. 7
In central cities	203, 304	52. 7	3, 857. 8
Springfield	149, 554	31. 7	4, 717. 8
Holyoke	53, 750	21. 0	2, 559. 5
Outside central cities	191, 319	476. 5	401. 5
Stockton, Calif	79, 337	255. 7	310. 3
In central city	54, 714	9. 9	5, 526. 7
Outside central city	24, 623	245. 8	100. 2
Syracuse, N. Y	258, 352	226. 5	1, 140. 6
In central city	205, 967	25. 3	8, 141. 0
Outside central city	52, 385	201. 2	260. 4
Tacoma, Wash	156, 018	184. 2	847. 0
In central city	109, 408	46. 5	2, 352. 9
Outside central city	46, 610	137. 7	338. 5
Tampa-St. Petersburg, Fla	209, 693	262. 8	797. 9
In central cities	169, 203	71. 2	2, 376. 4
Tampa	108, 391	19. 0	5, 704. 8
St. Petersburg	60, 812	52. 2	1, 165. 0
Outside central cities	40, 490	191. 6	211. 3
Terre Haute, Ind	83, 370	104. 9	794. 8
In central city	62, 693	9. 8	6, 397. 2
Outside central city	20, 677	95. 1	217. 4
Toledo, Ohio	341, 663	204. 1	1, 674. 0
In central city	282, 349	37. 1	7, 610. 5
Outside central city	59, 314	167. 0	355. 2
Topeka, Kans	77, 749	43. 1	1, 803. 9
In central city	67, 833	11. 3	6, 002. 9
Outside central city	9, 916	31. 8	311. 8
Trenton, N. J	200, 128	159. 7	1, 253. 1
In central city	124, 697	7. 2	17, 319. 0
Outside central city	75, 431	152. 5	494. 6
Tulsa, Okla	188, 562	386. 4	488. 0
In central city	142, 157	21. 4	6, 642. 9
Outside central city	46, 405	365. 0	127. 1
Utica-Rome, N. Y	197, 128	394. 3	499. 9
In central cities	134, 732	92. 9	1, 450. 3
Utica	100, 518	15. 8	6, 361. 9
Rome	34, 214	77. 1	443. 8
Outside central cities	62, 396	301. 4	207. 0
Waco, Tex	71, 114	220. 5	322. 5
In central city	55, 982	12. 5	4, 478. 6
Outside central city	15, 132	208. 0	72. 8
Washington, D. C	907, 816	520. 0	1, 745. 8
In central city	663, 091	61. 4	10, 799. 5
Outside central city	244, 725	458. 6	533. 6
Waterbury, Conn	144, 822	203. 0	713. 4
In central city	99, 314	27. 6	3, 598. 3
Outside central city	45, 508	175. 4	259. 5
Waterloo, Iowa	67, 050	95. 5	702. 1
In central city	51, 743	13. 0	3, 980. 2
Outside central city	15, 307	82. 5	185. 5
Wheeling, W. Va	196, 340	420. 0	467. 5
In central city	61, 099	9. 6	6, 364. 5
Outside central city	135, 241	410. 4	329. 5
Wichita, Kans	127, 308	141. 8	897. 8
In central city	114, 966	21. 1	5, 448. 6
Outside central city	12, 342	120. 7	102. 3
Wilmington, Del	188, 974	248. 3	761. 1
In central city	112, 504	9. 8	11, 480. 0
Outside central city	76, 470	238. 5	320. 6
Winston-Salem, N. C	109, 833	177. 7	618. 1
In central city	79, 815	15. 1	5, 285. 8
Outside central city	30, 018	162. 6	184. 6
Worcester, Mass	306, 194	396. 2	772. 8
In central city	193, 694	37. 1	5, 220. 9
Outside central city	112, 500	359. 1	313. 3
York, Pa	92, 627	92. 6	1, 000. 3
In central city	56, 712	4. 1	13, 832. 2
Outside central city	35, 915	88. 5	405. 8
Youngstown, Ohio	372, 428	353. 7	1, 052. 9
In central city	167, 720	32. 8	5, 113. 4
Outside central city	204, 708	320. 9	637. 9

TABLE 18.—POPULATION OF METROPOLITAN DISTRICTS: 1940 AND 1930

[In the case of metropolitan districts defined in 1930, comparative figures for 1930 represent the population of the area as defined in 1930. Comparative figures are also shown for the metropolitan districts defined for the first time in 1940 if 1930 figures can be secured for exactly the same area. Such figures are obtainable for all but seven of the new metropolitan districts. For the areas included within each metropolitan district, see the reports for the individual States. A minus sign (—) denotes decrease]

METROPOLITAN DISTRICT	POPULATION		INCREASE	
	1940	1930	Number	Percent
Total (140 districts)	62,965,773	57,602,865	5,362,908	9.3
In central cities	42,796,170	40,343,442	2,452,728	6.1
Outside central cities	20,169,603	17,259,423	2,910,180	16.9
Percent outside central cities	32.0	30.0		
Akron, Ohio	349,705	346,681	3,024	0.9
In central city	244,791	255,040	−10,249	−4.0
Outside central city	104,914	91,641	13,273	14.5
Percent outside central city	30.0	26.4		
Albany-Schenectady-Troy, N. Y	431,575	425,259	6,316	1.5
In central cities	288,430	295,867	−7,437	−2.5
Outside central cities	143,145	129,392	13,753	10.6
Percent outside central cities	33.2	30.4		
Allentown-Bethlehem-Easton, Pa	325,142	322,172	2,970	0.9
In central cities	188,983	184,923	4,060	2.2
Outside central cities	136,159	137,249	−1,090	−0.8
Percent outside central cities	41.9	42.6		
Altoona, Pa	114,094	114,232	−138	−0.1
In central city	80,214	82,054	−1,840	−2.2
Outside central city	33,880	32,178	1,702	5.3
Percent outside central city	29.7	28.2		
Amarillo, Tex	53,463			
In central city	51,686			
Outside central city	1,777			
Percent outside central city	3.3			
Asheville, N. C	76,324	70,537	5,787	8.2
In central city	51,310	50,193	1,117	2.2
Outside central city	25,014	20,344	4,670	23.0
Percent outside central city	32.8	28.8		
Atlanta, Ga	442,294	370,920	71,374	19.2
In central city	302,288	270,366	31,922	11.8
Outside central city	140,006	100,554	39,452	39.2
Percent outside central city	31.7	27.1		
Atlantic City, N. J	100,096	102,024	−1,928	−1.9
In central city	64,094	66,198	−2,104	−3.2
Outside central city	36,002	35,826	176	0.5
Percent outside central city	36.0	35.1		
Augusta, Ga	87,809	77,431	10,378	13.4
In central city	65,919	60,342	5,577	9.2
Outside central city	21,890	17,089	4,801	28.1
Percent outside central city	24.9	22.1		
Austin, Tex	106,193			
In central city	87,930			
Outside central city	18,263			
Percent outside central city	17.2			
Baltimore, Md	1,046,692	949,247	97,445	10.3
In central city	859,100	804,874	54,226	6.7
Outside central city	187,592	144,373	43,219	29.9
Percent outside central city	17.9	15.2		
Beaumont-Port Arthur, Tex	138,608	127,849	10,759	8.4
In central cities	105,201	108,634	−3,433	−3.2
Outside central cities	33,407	19,215	14,192	73.9
Percent outside central cities	24.1	15.0		
Binghamton, N. Y	145,156	130,005	15,151	11.7
In central city	78,309	76,662	1,647	2.1
Outside central city	66,847	53,343	13,504	25.3
Percent outside central city	46.1	41.0		
Birmingham, Ala	407,851	382,792	25,059	6.5
In central city	267,583	259,678	7,905	3.0
Outside central city	140,268	123,114	17,154	13.9
Percent outside central city	34.4	32.2		
Boston, Mass	2,350,514	2,307,897	42,617	1.8
In central city	770.816	781,188	−10,372	−1.3
Outside central city	1,579,698	1,526,709	52,989	3.5
Percent outside central city	67.2	66.2		
Bridgeport, Conn	216,621	203,969	12,652	6.2
In central city	147,121	146,716	405	0.3
Outside central city	69,500	57,253	12,247	21.4
Percent outside central city	32.1	28.1		
Buffalo-Niagara, N. Y	857,719	820,573	37,146	4.5
In central cities	653,930	648,536	5,394	0.8
Outside central cities	203,789	172,037	31,752	18.5
Percent outside central cities	23.8	21.0		
Canton, Ohio	200,352	191,231	9,121	4.8
In central city	108,401	104,906	3,495	3.3
Outside central city	91,951	86,325	5,626	6.5
Percent outside central city	45.9	45.1		
Cedar Rapids, Iowa	73,219	66,591	6,628	10.0
In central city	62,120	56,097	6,023	10.7
Outside central city	11,099	10,494	605	5.8
Percent outside central city	15.2	15.8		
Charleston, S. C	98,711	79,760	18,951	23.8
In central city	71,275	62,265	9,010	14.5
Outside central city	27,436	17,495	9,941	56.8
Percent outside central city	27.8	21.9		
Charleston, W. Va	136,332	108,160	28,172	26.0
In central city	67,914	60,408	7,506	12.4
Outside central city	68,418	47,752	20,666	43.3
Percent outside central city	50.2	44.1		
Charlotte, N. C	112,986	91,264	21,722	23.8
In central city	100,899	82,675	18,224	22.0
Outside central city	12,087	8,589	3,498	40.7
Percent outside central city	10.7	9.4		
Chattanooga, Tenn	193,215	168,589	24,626	14.6
In central city	128,163	119,798	8,365	7.0
Outside central city	65,052	48,791	16,261	33.3
Percent outside central city	33.7	28.9		
Chicago, Ill	4,499,126	4,364,755	134,371	3.1
In central city	3,396,808	3,376,438	20,370	0.6
Outside central city	1,102,318	988,317	114,001	11.5
Percent outside central city	24.5	22.6		
Cincinnati, Ohio	789,309	759,464	29,845	3.9
In central city	455,610	451,160	4,450	1.0
Outside central city	333,699	308,304	25,395	8.2
Percent outside central city	42.3	40.6		
Cleveland, Ohio	1,214,943	1,194,989	19,954	1.7
In central city	878,336	900,429	−22,093	−2.5
Outside central city	336,607	294,560	42,047	14.3
Percent outside central city	27.7	24.6		
Columbia, S. C	89,555	73,963	15,592	21.1
In central city	62,396	51,581	10,815	21.0
Outside central city	27,159	22,382	4,777	21.3
Percent outside central city	30.3	30.3		
Columbus, Ga	92,478			
In central city	53,280			
Outside central city	39,198			
Percent outside central city	42.4			
Columbus, Ohio	365,796	340,400	25,396	7.5
In central city	306,087	290,564	15,523	5.3
Outside central city	59,709	49,836	9,873	19.8
Percent outside central city	16.3	14.6		
Corpus Christi, Tex	70,677	34,232	36,445	106.5
In central city	57,301	27,741	29,560	106.6
Outside central city	13,376	6,491	6,885	106.1
Percent outside central city	18.9	19.0		
Dallas, Tex	376,548	309,658	66,890	21.6
In central city	294,734	260,475	34,259	13.2
Outside central city	81,814	49,183	32,631	66.3
Percent outside central city	21.7	15.9		
Davenport (Iowa)-Rock Island-Moline (Ill.)	174,995	154,491	20,504	13.3
In central cities	143,422	130,940	12,482	9.5
Outside central cities	31,573	23,551	8,022	34.1
Percent outside central cities	18.0	15.2		
Dayton, Ohio	271,513	251,928	19,585	7.8
In central city	210,718	200,982	9,736	4.8
Outside central city	60,795	50,946	9,849	19.3
Percent outside central city	22.4	20.2		

Table 18.—POPULATION OF METROPOLITAN DISTRICTS: 1940 AND 1930—Continued

[In the case of metropolitan districts defined in 1930, comparative figures for 1930 represent the population of the area as defined in 1930. Comparative figures are also shown for the metropolitan districts defined for the first time in 1940 if 1930 figures can be secured for exactly the same area. Such figures are obtainable for all but seven of the new metropolitan districts. For the areas included within each metropolitan district, see the reports for the individual States. A minus sign (—) denotes decrease]

METROPOLITAN DISTRICT	POPULATION		INCREASE	
	1940	1930	Number	Percent
Decatur, Ill.	**65,764**	**62,867**	**2,897**	**4.6**
In central city	59,305	57,510	1,795	3.1
Outside central city	6,459	5,357	1,102	20.6
Percent outside central city	9.8	8.5		
Denver, Colo.	**384,372**	**330,761**	**53,611**	**16.2**
In central city	322,412	287,861	34,551	12.0
Outside central city	61,960	42,900	19,060	44.4
Percent outside central city	16.1	13.0		
Des Moines, Iowa	**183,973**	**160,963**	**23,010**	**14.3**
In central city	159,819	142,559	17,260	12.1
Outside central city	24,154	18,404	5,750	31.2
Percent outside central city	13.1	11.4		
Detroit, Mich.	**2,295,867**	**2,104,764**	**191,103**	**9.1**
In central city	1,623,452	1,568,662	54,790	3.5
Outside central city	672,415	536,102	136,313	25.4
Percent outside central city	29.3	25.5		
Duluth (Minn.)-Superior (Wis.)	**157,098**	**155,390**	**1,708**	**1.1**
In central cities	136,201	137,576	−1,375	−1.0
Outside central cities	20,897	17,814	3,083	17.3
Percent outside central cities	13.3	11.5		
Durham, N. C.	**69,683**	**58,525**	**11,158**	**19.1**
In central city	60,195	52,037	8,158	15.7
Outside central city	9,488	6,488	3,000	46.2
Percent outside central city	13.6	11.1		
El Paso, Tex.	**115,801**	**118,461**	**−2,660**	**−2.2**
In central city	96,810	102,421	−5,611	−5.5
Outside central city	18,991	16,040	2,951	18.4
Percent outside central city	16.4	13.5		
Erie, Pa.	**134,039**	**129,817**	**4,222**	**3.3**
In central city	116,955	115,967	988	0.9
Outside central city	17,084	13,850	3,234	23.4
Percent outside central city	12.7	10.7		
Evansville, Ind.	**141,614**	**123,130**	**18,484**	**15.0**
In central city	97,062	102,249	−5,187	−5.1
Outside central city	44,552	20,881	23,671	113.4
Percent outside central city	31.5	17.0		
Fall River-New Bedford, Mass.	**272,648**	**273,055**	**−407**	**−0.1**
In central cities	225,769	227,871	−2,102	−0.9
Outside central cities	46,879	45,184	1,695	3.8
Percent outside central cities	17.2	16.5		
Flint, Mich.	**188,554**	**179,939**	**8,615**	**4.8**
In central city	151,543	156,492	−4,949	−3.2
Outside central city	37,011	23,447	13,564	57.8
Percent outside central city	19.6	13.0		
Fort Wayne, Ind.	**134,385**	**126,558**	**7,827**	**6.2**
In central city	118,410	114,946	3,464	3.0
Outside central city	15,975	11,612	4,363	37.6
Percent outside central city	11.9	9.2		
Fort Worth, Tex.	**207,677**	**174,575**	**33,102**	**19.0**
In central city	177,662	163,447	14,215	8.7
Outside central city	30,015	11,128	18,887	169.7
Percent outside central city	14.5	6.4		
Fresno, Calif.	**97,504**	**78,118**	**19,386**	**24.8**
In central city	60,685	52,513	8,172	15.6
Outside central city	36,819	25,605	11,214	43.8
Percent outside central city	37.8	32.8		
Galveston, Tex.	**71,677**	**58,301**	**13,376**	**22.9**
In central city	60,862	52,938	7,924	15.0
Outside central city	10,815	5,363	5,452	101.7
Percent outside central city	15.1	9.2		
Grand Rapids, Mich.	**209,873**	**207,154**	**2,719**	**1.3**
In central city	164,292	168,592	−4,300	−2.6
Outside central city	45,581	38,562	7,019	18.2
Percent outside central city	21.7	18.6		
Greensboro, N. C.	**73,055**	**63,469**	**9,586**	**15.1**
In central city	59,319	53,569	5,750	10.7
Outside central city	13,736	9,900	3,836	38.7
Percent outside central city	18.8	15.6		
Hamilton-Middletown, Ohio	**112,686**	**106,989**	**5,697**	**5.3**
In central cities	81,812	82,168	−356	−0.4
Outside central cities	30,874	24,821	6,053	24.4
Percent outside central cities	27.4	23.2		
Harrisburg, Pa.	**173,367**	**161,672**	**11,695**	**7.2**
In central city	83,893	80,339	3,554	4.4
Outside central city	89,474	81,333	8,141	10.0
Percent outside central city	51.6	50.3		
Hartford-New Britain, Conn.	**502,193**	**471,185**	**31,008**	**6.6**
In central cities	234,952	232,200	2,752	1.2
Outside central cities	267,241	238,985	28,256	11.8
Percent outside central cities	53.2	50.7		
Houston, Tex.	**510,397**	**339,216**	**171,181**	**50.5**
In central city	384,514	292,352	92,162	31.5
Outside central city	125,883	46,864	79,019	168.6
Percent outside central city	24.7	13.8		
Huntington (W. Va.)-Ashland (Ky.)	**170,979**	**163,367**	**7,612**	**4.7**
In central cities	108,373	104,646	3,727	3.6
Outside central cities	62,606	58,721	3,885	6.6
Percent outside central cities	36.6	35.9		
Indianapolis, Ind.	**455,357**	**417,685**	**37,672**	**9.0**
In central city	386,972	364,161	22,811	6.3
Outside central city	68,385	53,524	14,861	27.8
Percent outside central city	15.0	12.8		
Jackson, Miss.	**88,003**	**68,252**	**19,751**	**28.9**
In central city	62,107	48,282	13,825	28.6
Outside central city	25,896	19,970	5,926	29.7
Percent outside central city	29.4	29.3		
Jacksonville, Fla.	**195,619**	**148,713**	**46,906**	**31.5**
In central city	173,065	129,549	43,516	33.6
Outside central city	22,554	19,164	3,390	17.7
Percent outside central city	11.5	12.9		
Johnstown, Pa.	**151,781**	**147,611**	**4,170**	**2.8**
In central city	66,668	66,993	−325	−0.5
Outside central city	85,113	80,618	4,495	5.6
Percent outside central city	56.1	54.6		
Kalamazoo, Mich.	**77,213**	**72,739**	**4,474**	**6.2**
In central city	54,097	54,786	−689	−1.3
Outside central city	23,116	17,953	5,163	28.8
Percent outside central city	29.9	24.7		
Kansas City (Mo.)-Kansas City (Kans.)	**634,093**	**608,186**	**25,907**	**4.3**
In central cities	520,636	521,603	−967	−0.2
Outside central cities	113,457	86,583	26,874	31.0
Percent outside central cities	17.9	14.2		
Knoxville, Tenn.	**151,829**	**135,714**	**16,115**	**11.9**
In central city	111,580	105,802	5,778	5.5
Outside central city	40,249	29,912	10,337	34.6
Percent outside central city	26.5	22.0		
Lancaster, Pa.	**132,027**	**123,156**	**8,871**	**7.2**
In central city	61,345	59,949	1,396	2.3
Outside central city	70,682	63,207	7,475	11.8
Percent outside central city	53.5	51.3		
Lansing, Mich.	**110,356**	**98,694**	**11,662**	**11.8**
In central city	78,753	78,397	356	0.5
Outside central city	31,603	20,297	11,306	55.7
Percent outside central city	28.6	20.6		
Lincoln, Nebr.	**88,191**	**85,840**	**2,351**	**2.7**
In central city	81,984	75,933	6,051	8.0
Outside central city	6,207	9,907	−3,700	−37.3
Percent outside central city	7.0	11.5		
Little Rock, Ark.	**126,724**	**113,137**	**13,587**	**12.0**
In central city	88,039	81,679	6,360	7.8
Outside central city	38,685	31,458	7,227	23.0
Percent outside central city	30.5	27.8		
Los Angeles, Calif.	**2,904,596**	**2,318,526**	**586,070**	**25.3**
In central city	1,504,277	1,238,048	266,229	21.5
Outside central city	1,400,319	1,080,478	319,841	29.6
Percent outside central city	48.2	46.6		

Table 18.—POPULATION OF METROPOLITAN DISTRICTS: 1940 AND 1930—Continued

[In the case of metropolitan districts defined in 1930, comparative figures for 1930 represent the population of the area as defined in 1930. Comparative figures are also shown for the metropolitan districts defined for the first time in 1940 if 1930 figures can be secured for exactly the same area. Such figures are obtainable for all but seven of the new metropolitan districts. For the areas included within each metropolitan district, see the reports for the individual States. A minus sign (—) denotes decrease]

METROPOLITAN DISTRICT	POPULATION		INCREASE	
	1940	1930	Number	Percent
Louisville, Ky.	434,408	404,396	30,012	7.4
In central city	319,077	307,745	11,332	3.7
Outside central city	115,331	96,651	18,680	19.3
Percent outside central city	26.5	23.9		
Lowell-Lawrence-Haverhill, Mass.	334,969	332,028	2,941	0.9
In central cities	232,464	234,012	—1,548	—0.7
Outside central cities	102,505	98,016	4,489	4.6
Percent outside central cities	30.6	29.5		
Macon, Ga.	74,830	67,227	7,603	11.3
In central city	57,865	53,829	4,036	7.5
Outside central city	16,965	13,398	3,567	26.6
Percent outside central city	22.7	19.9		
Madison, Wis.	78,349	64,350	13,999	21.8
In central city	67,447	57,899	9,548	16.5
Outside central city	10,902	6,451	4,451	69.0
Percent outside central city	13.9	10.0		
Manchester, N. H.	81,932	80,673	1,259	1.6
In central city	77,685	76,834	851	1.1
Outside central city	4,247	3,839	408	10.6
Percent outside central city	5.2	4.8		
Memphis, Tenn.	332,477	276,126	56,351	20.4
In central city	292,942	253,143	39,799	15.7
Outside central city	39,535	22,983	16,552	72.0
Percent outside central city	11.9	8.3		
Miami, Fla.	250,537	132,189	118,348	89.5
In central city	172,172	110,637	61,535	55.6
Outside central city	78,365	21,552	56,813	263.6
Percent outside central city	31.3	16.3		
Milwaukee, Wis.	790,336	743,414	46,922	6.3
In central city	587,472	578,249	9,223	1.6
Outside central city	202,864	165,165	37,699	22.8
Percent outside central city	25.7	22.2		
Minneapolis-St. Paul, Minn.	911,077	832,258	78,819	9.5
In central cities	780,106	735,962	44,144	6.0
Outside central cities	130,971	96,296	34,675	36.0
Percent outside central cities	14.4	11.6		
Mobile, Ala.	114,906			
In central city	78,720			
Outside central city	36,186			
Percent outside central city	31.5			
Montgomery, Ala.	93,697	78,389	15,308	19.5
In central city	78,084	66,079	12,005	18.2
Outside central city	15,613	12,310	3,303	26.8
Percent outside central city	16.7	15.7		
Nashville, Tenn.	241,769	209,422	32,347	15.4
In central city	167,402	153,866	13,536	8.8
Outside central city	74,367	55,556	18,811	33.9
Percent outside central city	30.8	26.5		
New Haven, Conn.	308,228	293,724	14,504	4.9
In central city	160,605	162,655	—2,050	—1.3
Outside central city	147,623	131,069	16,554	12.6
Percent outside central city	47.9	44.6		
New Orleans, La.	540,030	494,877	45,153	9.1
In central city	494,537	458,762	35,775	7.8
Outside central city	45,493	36,115	9,378	26.0
Percent outside central city	8.4	7.3		
New York-Northeastern New Jersey	11,690,520	10,901,424	789,096	7.2
In central cities	8,435,496	7,942,600	492,896	6.2
Outside central cities	3,255,024	2,958,824	296,200	10.0
Percent outside central cities	27.8	27.1		
Norfolk-Portsmouth-Newport News, Va.	330,396	273,233	57,163	20.9
In central cities	232,144	209,831	22,313	10.6
Outside central cities	98,252	63,402	34,850	55.0
Percent outside central cities	29.7	23.2		
Oklahoma City, Okla.	221,229	202,163	19,066	9.4
In central city	204,424	185,389	19,035	10.3
Outside central city	16,805	16,774	31	0.2
Percent outside central city	7.6	8.3		
Omaha (Nebr.)-Council Bluffs (Iowa)	287,698	273,851	13,847	5.1
In central cities	265,283	256,054	9,229	3.6
Outside central cities	22,415	17,797	4,618	25.9
Percent outside central cities	7.8	6.5		
Peoria, Ill.	162,566	144,732	17,834	12.3
In central city	105,087	104,969	118	0.1
Outside central city	57,479	39,763	17,716	44.6
Percent outside central city	35.4	27.5		
Philadelphia, Pa.	2,898,644	2,847,148	51,496	1.8
In central city	1,931,334	1,950,961	—19,627	—1.0
Outside central city	967,310	896,187	71,123	7.9
Percent outside central city	33.4	31.5		
Phoenix, Ariz.	121,828			
In central city	65,414			
Outside central city	56,414			
Percent outside central city	46.3			
Pittsburgh, Pa.	1,994,060	1,953,668	40,392	2.1
In central city	671,659	669,817	1,842	0.3
Outside central city	1,322,401	1,283,851	38,550	3.0
Percent outside central city	66.3	65.7		
Portland, Maine	106,566	99,874	6,692	6.7
In central city	73,643	70,810	2,833	4.0
Outside central city	32,923	29,064	3,859	13.3
Percent outside central city	30.9	29.1		
Portland, Oreg.	406,406	378,728	27,678	7.3
In central city	305,394	301,815	3,579	1.2
Outside central city	101,012	76,913	24,099	31.3
Percent outside central city	24.9	20.3		
Providence, R. I.	711,500	690,631	20,869	3.0
In central city	253,504	252,981	523	0.2
Outside central city	457,996	437,650	20,346	4.6
Percent outside central city	64.4	63.4		
Pueblo, Colo.	62,039			
In central city	52,162			
Outside central city	9,877			
Percent outside central city	15.9			
Racine-Kenosha, Wis.	135,075	133,463	1,612	1.2
In central cities	115,960	117,804	—1,844	—1.6
Outside central cities	19,115	15,659	3,456	22.1
Percent outside central cities	14.2	11.7		
Reading, Pa.	175,355	170,486	4,869	2.9
In central city	110,568	111,171	—603	—0.5
Outside central city	64,787	59,315	5,472	9.2
Percent outside central city	36.9	34.8		
Richmond, Va.	245,674	220,513	25,161	11.4
In central city	193,042	182,929	10,113	5.5
Outside central city	52,632	37,584	15,048	40.0
Percent outside central city	21.4	17.0		
Roanoke, Va.	110,593	103,120	7,473	7.2
In central city	69,287	69,206	81	0.1
Outside central city	41,306	33,914	7,392	21.8
Percent outside central city	37.3	32.9		
Rochester, N. Y.	411,970	398,591	13,379	3.4
In central city	324,975	328,132	—3,157	—1.0
Outside central city	86,995	70,459	16,536	23.5
Percent outside central city	21.1	17.7		
Rockford, Ill.	105,259	103,204	2,055	2.0
In central city	84,637	85,864	—1,227	—1.4
Outside central city	20,622	17,340	3,282	18.9
Percent outside central city	19.6	16.8		
Sacramento, Calif.	158,999	126,995	32,004	25.2
In central city	105,958	93,750	12,208	13.0
Outside central city	53,041	33,245	19,796	59.5
Percent outside central city	33.4	26.2		
Saginaw-Bay City, Mich.	153,388	144,647	8,741	6.0
In central cities	130,750	128,070	2,680	2.1
Outside central cities	22,638	16,577	6,061	36.6
Percent outside central cities	14.8	11.5		

TABLE 18.—POPULATION OF METROPOLITAN DISTRICTS: 1940 AND 1930—Continued

[In the case of metropolitan districts defined in 1930, comparative figures for 1930 represent the population of the area as defined in 1930. Comparative figures are also shown for the metropolitan districts defined for the first time in 1940 if 1930 figures can be secured for exactly the same area. Such figures are obtainable for all but seven of the new metropolitan districts. For the areas included within each metropolitan district, see the reports for the individual States. A minus sign (—) denotes decrease]

METROPOLITAN DISTRICT	POPULATION		INCREASE	
	1940	1930	Number	Percent
St. Joseph, Mo.	86,991	91,519	−4,528	−4.9
In central city	75,711	80,935	−5,224	−6.5
Outside central city	11,280	10,584	696	6.6
Percent outside central city	13.0	11.6		
St. Louis, Mo.	1,367,977	1,293,516	74,461	5.8
In central city	816,048	821,960	−5,912	−0.7
Outside central city	551,929	471,556	80,373	17.0
Percent outside central city	40.3	36.5		
Salt Lake City, Utah	204,488	184,451	20,037	10.9
In central city	149,934	140,267	9,667	6.9
Outside central city	54,554	44,184	10,370	23.5
Percent outside central city	26.7	24.0		
San Antonio, Tex.	319,010	279,271	39,739	14.2
In central city	253,854	231,542	22,312	9.6
Outside central city	65,156	47,729	17,427	36.5
Percent outside central city	20.4	17.1		
San Diego, Calif.	256,368	181,020	75,348	41.6
In central city	203,341	147,995	55,346	37.4
Outside central city	53,027	33,025	20,002	60.6
Percent outside central city	20.7	18.2		
San Francisco-Oakland, Calif.	1,428,525	1,290,094	138,431	10.7
In central cities	936,699	918,457	18,242	2.0
Outside central cities	491,826	371,637	120,189	32.3
Percent outside central cities	34.4	28.8		
San Jose, Calif.	129,367	103,428	25,939	25.1
In central city	68,457	57,651	10,806	18.7
Outside central city	60,910	45,777	15,133	33.1
Percent outside central city	47.1	44.3		
Savannah, Ga.	117,970	105,431	12,539	11.9
In central city	95,996	85,024	10,972	12,9
Outside central city	21,974	20,407	1,567	7.7
Percent outside central city	18.6	19.4		
Scranton-Wilkes-Barre, Pa.	629,581	652,312	−22,731	−3.5
In central cities	226,640	230,059	−3,419	−1.5
Outside central cities	402,941	422,253	−19,312	−4.6
Percent outside central cities	64.0	64.7		
Seattle, Wash.	452,639	420,663	31,976	7.6
In central city	368,302	365,583	2,719	0.7
Outside central city	84,337	55,080	29,257	53.1
Percent outside central city	18.6	13.1		
Shreveport, La.	112,225	86,066	26,159	30.4
In central city	98,167	76,655	21,512	28.1
Outside central city	14,058	9,411	4,647	49.4
Percent outside central city	12.5	10.9		
Sioux City, Iowa	87,791	83,775	4,016	4.8
In central city	82,364	79,183	3,181	4.0
Outside central city	5,427	4,592	835	18.2
Percent outside central city	6.2	5.5		
South Bend, Ind.	147,022	146,569	453	0.3
In central city	101,268	104,193	−2,925	−2.8
Outside central city	45,754	42,376	3,378	8.0
Percent outside central city	31.1	28.9		
Spokane, Wash.	141,370	128,798	12,572	9.8
In central city	122,001	115,514	6,487	5.6
Outside central city	19,369	13,284	6,085	45.8
Percent outside central city	13.7	10.3		
Springfield, Ill.	89,484	82,367	7,117	8.6
In central city	75,503	71,864	3,639	5.1
Outside central city	13,981	10,503	3,478	33.1
Percent outside central city	15.6	12.8		
Springfield, Mo.	70,514	63,663	6,851	10.8
In central city	61,238	57,527	3,711	6.5
Outside central city	9,276	6,136	3,140	51.2
Percent outside central city	13.2	9.6		
Springfield, Ohio	77,406	73,929	3,477	4.7
In central city	70,662	68,743	1,919	2.8
Outside central city	6,744	5,186	1,558	30.0
Percent outside central city	8.7	7.0		
Springfield-Holyoke, Mass.	394,623	398,991	−4,368	−1.1
In central cities	203,304	206,437	−3,133	−1.5
Outside central cities	191,319	192,554	−1,235	−0.6
Percent outside central cities	48.5	48.3		
Stockton, Calif.	79,337	61,880	17,457	28.2
In central city	54,714	47,963	6,751	14.1
Outside central city	24,623	13,917	10,706	76.9
Percent outside central city	31.0	22.5		
Syracuse, N. Y.	258,352	245,015	13,337	5.4
In central city	205,967	209,326	−3,359	−1.6
Outside central city	52,385	35,689	16,696	46.8
Percent outside central city	20.3	14.6		
Tacoma, Wash.	156,018	146,771	9,247	6.3
In central city	109,408	106,817	2,591	2.4
Outside central city	46,610	39,954	6,656	16.7
Percent outside central city	29.9	27.2		
Tampa-St. Petersburg, Fla.	209,693	169,010	40,683	24.1
In central cities	169,203	141,586	27,617	19.5
Outside central cities	40,490	27,424	13,066	47.6
Percent outside central cities	19.3	16.2		
Terre Haute, Ind.	83,370	82,240	1,130	1.4
In central city	62,693	62,810	−117	−0.2
Outside central city	20,677	19,430	1,247	6.4
Percent outside central city	24.8	23.6		
Toledo, Ohio	341,663	346,530	−4,867	−1.4
In central city	282,349	290,718	−8,369	−2.9
Outside central city	59,314	55,812	3,502	6.3
Percent outside central city	17.4	16.1		
Topeka, Kans.	77,749	71,679	6,070	8.5
In central city	67,833	64,120	3,713	5.8
Outside central city	9,916	7,559	2,357	31.2
Percent outside central city	12.8	10.5		
Trenton, N. J.	200,128	190,219	9,909	5.2
In central city	124,697	123,356	1,341	1.1
Outside central city	75,431	66,863	8,568	12.8
Percent outside central city	37.7	35.2		
Tulsa, Okla.	188,562	183,207	5,355	2.9
In central city	142,157	141,258	899	0.6
Outside central city	46,405	41,949	4,456	10.6
Percent outside central city	24.6	22.9		
Utica-Rome, N. Y.	197,128	190,918	6,210	3.3
In central cities	134,732	134,078	654	0.5
Outside central cities	62,396	56,840	5,556	9.8
Percent outside central cities	31.7	29.8		
Waco, Tex.	71,114			
In central city	55,982			
Outside central city	15,132			
Percent outside central city	21.3			
Washington, D. C.	907,816	621,059	286,757	46.2
In central city	663,091	486,869	176,222	36.2
Outside central city	244,725	134,190	110,535	82.4
Percent outside central city	27.0	21.6		
Waterbury, Conn.	144,822	140,575	4,247	3.0
In central city	99,314	99,902	−588	−0.6
Outside central city	45,508	40,673	4,835	11.9
Percent outside central city	31.4	28.9		
Waterloo, Iowa	67,050	57,052	9,998	17.5
In central city	51,743	46,191	5,552	12.0
Outside central city	15,307	10,861	4,446	40.9
Percent outside central city	22.8	19.0		
Wheeling, W. Va.	196,340	190,623	5,717	3.0
In central city	61,099	61,659	−560	−0.9
Outside central city	135,241	128,964	6,277	4.9
Percent outside central city	68.9	67.7		

Table 18.—POPULATION OF METROPOLITAN DISTRICTS: 1940 AND 1930—Continued

[In the case of metropolitan districts defined in 1930, comparative figures for 1930 represent the population of the area as defined in 1930. Comparative figures are also shown for the metropolitan districts defined for the first time in 1940 if 1930 figures can be secured for exactly the same area. Such figures are obtainable for all but seven of the new metropolitan districts. For the areas included within each metropolitan district, see the reports for the individual States. A minus sign (—) denotes decrease]

METROPOLITAN DISTRICT	POPULATION		INCREASE	
	1940	1930	Number	Percent
Wichita, Kans	127,308	119,174	8,134	6.8
In central city	114,966	111,110	3,856	3.5
Outside central city	12,342	8,064	4,278	53.1
Percent outside central city	9.7	6.8		
Wilmington, Del	188,974	163,592	25,382	15.5
In central city	112,504	106,597	5,907	5.5
Outside central city	76,470	56,995	19,475	34.2
Percent outside central city	40.5	34.8		
Winston-Salem, N. C	109,833	97,274	12,559	12.9
In central city	79,815	75,274	4,541	6.0
Outside central city	30,018	22,000	8,018	36.4
Percent outside central city	27.3	22.6		
Worcester, Mass	306,194	305,293	901	0.3
In central city	193,694	195,311	−1,617	−0.8
Outside central city	112,500	109,982	2,518	2.3
Percent outside central city	36.7	36.0		
York, Pa	92,627	87,195	5,432	6.2
In central city	56,712	55,254	1,458	2.6
Outside central city	35,915	31,941	3,974	12.4
Percent outside central city	38.8	36.6		
Youngstown, Ohio	372,428	364,560	7,868	2.2
In central city	167,720	170,002	−2,282	−1.3
Outside central city	204,708	194,558	10,150	5.2
Percent outside central city	55.0	53.4		

Table 19.—LIST OF CITIES FOR WHICH CENSUS TRACT DATA ARE PRESENTED IN THE STATE SECTIONS OR BULLETINS

TRACTED AREA	Number of tracts, 1940	1930 data tabulated
Akron, Ohio	57	Yes.
Adjacent areas	11	Yes.
Atlanta, Ga	75	No.
Adjacent areas	37	No.
Atlantic City, N. J	23	No.
Augusta, Ga	15	No.
Adjacent area	1	No.
Austin, Tex	14	No.
Baltimore, Md	157	Yes.
Berkeley, Calif	26	Yes.
Oakland, Calif	72	No.
Areas adjacent to Berkeley and Oakland	32	No.
Birmingham, Ala	52	No.
Boston, Mass	156	Yes.
Buffalo, N. Y	72	Yes.
Cambridge, Mass	30	No.
Camden, N. J	24	No.
Chicago, Ill	935	Yes.
Cincinnati, Ohio	107	Yes.
Adjacent areas	44	No.
Cleveland, Ohio	206	Yes.
Adjacent areas	142	Yes.
Columbus, Ohio	61	Yes.
Dallas, Tex	58	No.
Adjacent areas	6	No.
Dayton, Ohio	53	No.
Adjacent area	1	No.
Denver, Colo	44	No.
Des Moines, Iowa	44	No.
Detroit, Mich	369	No.
Adjacent areas	113	No.
Duluth, Minn	38	No.
Elizabeth, N. J	21	No.
Flint, Mich	41	No.
Adjacent area	23	No.
Hartford, Conn	41	No.
Adjacent areas	16	No.
Houston, Tex	50	No.
Indianapolis, Ind	107	Yes.
Adjacent areas	34	No.
Jersey City, N. J	63	No.
Adjacent areas	97	No.
Kansas City, Mo	92	No.
Long Beach, Calif	31	No.
Los Angeles, Calif	303	Yes.[1]
Areas adjacent to Long Beach and Los Angeles	255	No.
Louisville, Ky	89	No.
Adjacent area	12	No.
Macon, Ga	17	No.
Adjacent area	8	No.
Memphis, Tenn	75	Yes.[1]
Adjacent areas	9	No.
Milwaukee, Wis	153	No.
Minneapolis, Minn	121	No.
Adjacent areas	11	No.
Nashville, Tenn	40	Yes.
Newark, N. J	98	No.
New Haven, Conn	33	Yes.
New Orleans, La	133	No.
New York, N. Y.	3,343	Yes.[1]
Bronx Borough	493	Yes.[1]
Brooklyn Borough	925	Yes.[1]
Manhattan Borough	279	Yes.[1]
Queens Borough	1,334	Yes.[1]
Richmond Borough	312	Yes.[1]
Oakland, Calif	72	No.
Areas adjacent to Oakland and Berkeley	32	No.
Oklahoma City, Okla	60	No.
Adjacent areas	13	No.
Paterson, N. J	31	No.
Philadelphia, Pa	404	Yes.
Pittsburgh, Pa	194	Yes.
Adjacent areas	297	No.
Portland, Oreg	60	No.
Providence, R. I	49	Yes.
Richmond, Va	47	No.
Rochester, N. Y	88	No.
St. Louis, Mo	128	Yes.
Adjacent areas	119	No.
St. Paul, Minn	76	No.
Adjacent areas	4	No.
San Francisco, Calif	119	No.
Savannah, Ga	37	No.
Adjacent area	7	No.
Seattle, Wash	79	No.
Syracuse, N. Y	61	Yes.[1]
Toledo, Ohio	55	No.
Trenton, N. J	22	No.
Washington, D. C	96	Yes.
Yonkers, N. Y	24	Yes.[1]

[1] 1930 figures for tracts not presented in the section for the State for 1940, because of extensive changes in tract boundaries since 1930.

CHARACTERISTICS OF THE POPULATION

Table 49.—POPULATION BY RACE, WITH INDIVIDUAL MINOR RACES, FOR CITIES OF 100,000 OR MORE: 1940

City	All classes	White			Negro	Other races	Other races						
		Total	Native	Foreign born			Indian	Chinese	Japanes	Filipino	Hindu	Korean	All other
Akron, Ohio	244,791	232,482	207,062	25,42	12,260	49	10	34	[illegible]	3			
Albany, N. Y	130,577	127,564	112,386	15,17	2,929	84	13	68	[illegible]				
Atlanta, Ga	302,288	197,686	193,393	4,29	104,533	69	9	31	2	4	1		2
Baltimore, Md	859,100	692,705	631,736	60,96	165,843	552	28	379	2	114	8		2
Birmingham, Ala	267,583	158,622	154,197	4,42	108,938	23	3	19		1			
Boston, Mass	770,816	745,466	564,602	180,86	23,679	1,671	76	1,383	6	129	7	11	3
Bridgeport, Conn	147,121	143,314	109,883	33,43	3,767	40	16	24					
Buffalo, N. Y	575,901	557,618	465,829	91,78	17,694	589	487	75	1	7	7	1	
Cambridge, Mass	110,879	105,855	81,207	24,55	4,858	166	4	133	[illegible]	11	7		5
Camden, N. J	117,536	104,995	89,099	14,99	12,478	63	17	43		2	1		
Canton, Ohio	108,401	104,319	93,250	11,06	4,041	41		41					
Charlotte, N. C	100,899	69,475	68,583	89	31,403	21		21					
Chattanooga, Tenn	128,163	91,742	90,628	1,11	36,404	17	8	8				1	
Chicago, Ill	3,396,808	3,114,564	2,441,859	672,70	277,731	4,513	274	2,013	39[illegible]	1,740	38	39	19
Cincinnati, Ohio	455,610	399,853	374,063	25,79	55,593	164	21	108	1	12	2	2	1
Cleveland, Ohio	878,336	793,417	614,234	179,18	84,504	415	38	308	1	18	10	18	5
Columbus, Ohio	306,087	270,183	258,256	11,92	35,765	139	14	95	6	5	15		4
Dallas, Texas	294,734	244,246	236,891	7,35	50,407	81	28	21	19	13			
Dayton, Ohio	210,718	190,414	181,085	9,32	20,273	31	9	15	2	2	3		
Denver, Colo	322,412	313,810	289,053	24,75	7,836	766	195	110	323	128	1	9	
Des Moines, Iowa	159,819	153,426	145,952	7,474	6,360	33	8	16	2	7			
Detroit, Mich	1,623,452	1,472,662	1,151,998	320,664	149,119	1,671	434	583	63	435	94	61	1
Duluth, Minn	101,065	100,659	81,327	19,33	314	92	51	40					1
Elizabeth, N. J	109,912	104,910	82,305	22,60	4,941	61	2	39	1	19			
Erie, Pa	116,955	115,565	101,995	13,57	1,375	15	2	10		3			
Fall River, Mass	115,428	114,909	90,337	24,57	402	117	5	104		8			
Flint, Mich	151,543	144,858	129,013	15,84	6,599	86	43	30	11	1			1
Fort Wayne, Ind	118,410	115,877	111,468	4,40	2,517	16	1	3		12			
Fort Worth, Texas	177,662	152,345	148,805	3,54	25,254	63	33	23	1	6			
Gary, Ind	111,719	91,246	73,976	17,27	20,394	79	56	13	9		1		
Grand Rapids, Mich	164,292	161,567	141,220	20,34	2,660	65	51	5	1	5	2	1	
Hartford, Conn	166,267	159,119	122,514	36,60	7,090	58	10	32	8	8			
Houston, Texas	384,514	297,959	282,646	15,31	86,302	253	14	119	48	70	2		
Indianapolis, Ind	386,972	335,755	325,200	10,55	51,142	75	5	40	1	26	1	2	
Jacksonville, Fla	173,065	111,247	107,275	3,97	61,782	36	3	27	1	5			
Jersey City, N. J	301,173	287,598	234,438	53,16	13,416	159	22	112	1	10	13		1
Kansas City, Kans	121,458	100,390	93,818	6,57	21,033	35	23	1	6	1	4		
Kansas City, Mo	399,178	357,346	338,007	19,33	41,574	258	60	56	5	136	1		
Knoxville, Tenn	111,580	95,474	94,742	73	16,094	12	2	10					
Long Beach, Calif	164,271	162,582	150,150	12,43	610	1,079	52	80	696	241	4		6
Los Angeles, Calif	1,504,277	1,406,430	1,191,182	215,24	63,774	34,073	862	4,736	23,321	4,498	60	482	114
Louisville, Ky	319,077	271,867	265,666	6,20	47,158	52	6	36	1	8	1		
Lowell, Mass	101,389	101,252	81,834	19,41	94	43	1	35	7				
Memphis, Tenn	292,942	171,406	166,938	4,46	121,498	38	11	21	5	1			
Miami, Fla	172,172	135,192	122,675	12,51	36,857	123	5	37	31	49			1
Milwaukee, Wis	587,472	578,177	494,368	83,80	8,821	474	260	153	13	47	1		
Minneapolis, Minn	492,370	487,099	422,950	64,14	4,646	625	145	304	24	147	1		4
Nashville, Tenn	167,402	120,072	118,550	1,52	47,318	12	7	4	1				
Newark, N. J	429,760	383,534	293,188	90,34	45,760	466	24	250	12	169	2		
New Bedford, Mass	110,341	105,927	76,304	29,62	4,297	117	37	67		12			1
New Haven, Conn	160,605	154,262	121,872	32,39	6,235	108	11	71	22	2			2
New Orleans, La	494,537	344,775	330,080	14,69	149,034	728	37	230	22	424	12		3
New York, N. Y	7,454,995	6,977,501	4,897,481	2,080,02	458,444	19,050	1,064	12,753	2,087	2,727	213	102	104
Bronx Borough	1,394,711	1,370,319	909,843	460,47	23,529	863	62	597	86	92	18	4	4
Brooklyn Borough	2,698,285	2,587,951	1,820,313	767,63	107,263	3,071	463	1,251	174	1,097	26	16	44
Manhattan Borough	1,889,924	1,577,625	1,037,428	540,197	298,365	13,934	467	10,370	1,461	1,340	165	80	51
Queens Borough	1,297,634	1,270,731	994,143	276,58	25,890	1,013	66	465	347	126	3	1	5
Richmond Borough	174,441	170,875	135,754	35,121	3,397	169	6	70	19	72	1	1	
Norfolk, Va	144,332	98,248	94,591	3,657	45,893	191	3	80	20	88			
Oakland, Calif	302,163	287,936	245,275	42,661	8,462	5,765	121	3,201	1,790	627	3	17	6
Oklahoma City, Okla	204,424	184,715	181,897	2,818	19,344	365	303	34	8	7	1	12	
Omaha, Nebr	223,844	211,640	189,329	22,311	12,015	189	61	69	40	16	1	2	
Paterson, N. J	139,656	135,300	101,212	34,088	4,268	88	5	60	1	4	18		
Peoria, Ill	105,087	102,202	96,738	5,464	2,826	59	22	27		10			
Philadelphia, Pa	1,931,334	1,678,577	1,388,252	290,325	250,880	1,877	155	922	89	600	24	3	24
Pittsburgh, Pa	671,659	609,236	524,630	84,606	62,216	207	39	141	2	14	10	1	
Portland, Oreg	305,394	299,707	261,099	38,608	1,931	3,756	159	1,569	1,680	326	13	2	7
Providence, R. I	253,504	246,904	195,696	51,208	6,388	212	29	167		8	3		5
Reading, Pa	110,568	108,646	100,785	7,861	1,905	17		16	1				
Richmond, Va	193,042	131,706	128,293	3,413	61,251	85	23	60	2				
Rochester, N. Y	324,975	321,554	261,447	60,107	3,262	159	97	47	6	8	1		
Sacramento, Calif	105,958	99,808	87,664	12,144	1,468	4,682	81	1,508	2,879	152	17	34	11
St. Louis, Mo	816,048	706,794	647,388	59,406	108,765	489	60	236	24	148	4	15	2
St. Paul, Minn	287,736	283,399	249,787	33,612	4,139	198	60	76	13	48	1		
Salt Lake City, Utah	149,934	148,699	135,359	13,340	694	541	40	102	359	33		1	6
San Antonio, Tex	253,854	234,022	205,985	28,037	19,235	597	40	471	47	39			
San Diego, Calif	203,341	196,946	177,417	19,529	4,143	2,252	143	451	828	709	1	3	27
San Francisco, Calif	634,536	602,701	472,430	130,271	4,846	26,989	224	17,782	5,280	3,483	29	81	110
Scranton, Pa	140,404	139,647	121,267	18,380	754	3	2			1			
Seattle, Wash	368,302	354,101	294,489	59,612	3,789	10,412	222	1,781	6,975	1,392	9	6	27
Somerville, Mass	102,177	101,887	78,032	23,855	262	28	2	21	3	2			
South Bend, Ind	101,268	97,662	86,785	10,877	3,555	51	15	32	1	1		2	
Spokane, Wash	122,001	120,897	108,142	12,755	644	460	55	99	276	29	1		
Springfield, Mass	149,554	146,361	119,623	26,738	3,144	49	7	41				1	
Syracuse, N. Y	205,967	203,640	176,090	27,550	2,082	245	225	19	1				
Tacoma, Wash	109,408	107,611	91,757	15,854	650	1,147	188	48	877	31			3
Tampa, Fla	108,391	85,043	73,961	11,082	23,331	17	2	5	2	8			
Toledo, Ohio	282,349	267,589	242,842	24,747	14,597	163	22	90	30	18	3		
Trenton, N. J	124,697	115,357	93,501	21,856	9,308	32	6	24		2			
Tulsa, Okla	142,157	126,352	124,178	2,174	15,151	654	628	18	9	4			
Utica, N. Y	100,518	99,989	82,649	17,340	514	15	8	7					
Washington, D. C	663,091	474,326	440,312	34,014	187,266	1,499	190	656	68	567	4	3	11
Wichita, Kans	114,966	109,186	107,032	2,154	5,686	94	53	34	6	1			
Wilmington, Del	112,504	98,175	87,694	10,481	14,256	73	6	35	19	13			
Worcester, Mass	193,694	192,263	152,272	39,991	1,353	78	17	50	5	6			
Yonkers, N. Y	142,598	138,441	109,784	28,657	4,108	49		42	6	1			
Youngstown, Ohio	167,720	153,056	126,385	26,671	14,615	49	18	24		2	5		

TABLE 50.—RACE, BY SEX, FOR CITIES OF 100,000 OR MORE: 1940

CITY	ALL CLASSES			WHITE						NEGRO		OTHER RACES	
				Total		Native		Foreign born					
	Total	Male	Female	Male	Female	Male	Female	Male	Female	Male	Female	Male	Female
Akron, Ohio	244,701	121,529	123,262	115,436	117,046	101,686	105,376	13,750	11,670	6,065	6,195	28	21
Albany, N. Y	130,577	62,864	67,713	61,352	66,212	53,392	58,994	7,960	7,218	1,454	1,475	58	26
Atlanta, Ga	302,288	139,331	162,957	93,254	104,432	90,855	102,538	2,399	1,894	46,027	58,506	50	19
Baltimore, Md	859,100	422,916	436,184	341,806	350,899	310,249	321,487	31,557	29,412	80,683	85,160	427	125
Birmingham, Ala	267,583	127,420	140,163	76,916	81,706	74,439	79,758	2,477	1,948	50,493	58,445	11	12
Boston, Mass	770,816	373,147	397,669	360,552	384,014	274,671	289,931	85,881	94,983	11,305	12,374	1,290	381
Bridgeport, Conn	147,121	73,188	73,933	71,272	72,042	54,132	55,751	17,140	16,291	1,894	1,873	22	18
Buffalo, N. Y	575,901	283,767	292,134	274,633	282,985	226,924	238,905	47,709	44,080	8,813	8,881	321	268
Cambridge, Mass	110,879	52,479	58,400	50,076	55,779	38,751	42,546	11,325	13,233	2,280	2,578	123	43
Camden, N. J	117,536	58,802	58,734	52,574	52,421	44.817	45,182	7,757	7,239	6,182	6,296	46	17
Canton, Ohio	108,401	54,285	54,116	52,251	52,068	45,868	47,382	6,383	4,686	2,002	2,039	32	9
Charlotte, N. C	100,899	47,662	53,237	33,338	36,137	32,832	35,751	506	386	14,309	17,094	15	6
Chattanooga, Tenn	128,163	61,246	66,917	44,202	47,540	43,593	47,035	609	505	17,037	19,367	7	10
Chicago, Ill	3,396,808	1,681,665	1,715,143	1,547,490	1,567,074	1,192,833	1,249,026	354,657	318,048	130,588	147,143	3,587	926
Cincinnati, Ohio	455,610	217,082	238,528	190,388	209,465	177,184	196,879	13,204	12,586	26,584	29,009	110	54
Cleveland, Ohio	878,336	438,346	439,990	396,930	396,487	302,855	311,370	94,075	85,108	41,096	43,408	320	95
Columbus, Ohio	306,087	148,971	157,116	130,812	139,371	124,281	133,975	6,531	5,396	18,061	17,704	98	41
Dallas, Texas	294,734	139,759	154,975	116,450	127,796	112,457	124,434	3,993	3,362	23,254	27,153	55	26
Dayton, Ohio	210,718	103,358	107,360	93,370	97,044	88,347	92,738	5,023	4,306	9,970	10,303	18	13
Denver, Colo	322,412	155,635	166,777	151,582	162,228	138,577	150,476	13,005	11,752	3,612	4,224	441	325
Des Moines, Iowa	159,819	75,879	83,940	72,777	80,649	68,804	77,148	3,973	3,501	3,073	3,287	29	4
Detroit, Mich	1,623,452	827,499	795,953	751,817	720,845	579,520	572,478	172,297	148,367	74,485	74,634	1,197	474
Duluth, Minn	101,065	50,586	50,479	50,355	50,304	39,297	42,030	11,058	8,274	182	132	49	43
Elizabeth, N. J	109,912	54,878	55,034	52,390	52,520	40,601	41,704	11,789	10.816	2,437	2,504	51	10
Erie, Pa	116,955	58,082	58,873	57,372	58,193	49,902	52,093	7,470	6,100	701	674	9	6
Fall River, Mass	115,428	55,542	59,886	55,222	59,687	43,625	46,712	11,597	12,975	228	174	92	25
Flint, Mich	151,543	75,976	75,567	72,684	72,174	64,078	64,935	8,606	7,239	3,236	3,363	56	30
Fort Wayne, Ind	118,410	56,915	61,495	55,699	60,178	53,320	58,148	2,379	2,030	1,203	1,314	13	3
Fort Worth, Texas	177,662	85,061	92,601	73,234	79,111	71,336	77,469	1,898	1,642	11,781	13,473	46	17
Gary, Ind	111,719	58,075	53,644	47,916	43,330	37,641	36,335	10,275	6,995	10,116	10,278	43	36
Grand Rapids, Mich	164,292	79,418	84,874	78,085	83,482	67,454	73,766	10,631	9,716	1,297	1,363	36	29
Hartford, Conn	166,267	80,509	85,758	77,040	82,079	58,470	64,044	18,570	18,035	3,432	3,658	37	21
Houston, Texas	384,514	188,318	196,196	147,650	150,309	139,295	143,351	8,355	6,958	40,482	45,820	186	67
Indianapolis, Ind	386,972	185,461	201,511	161,046	174,709	155,492	169,708	5,554	5,001	24,356	26,786	59	16
Jacksonville, Fla	173,065	82,798	90,267	53,972	57,275	51,787	55,488	2,185	1,787	28,798	32,984	28	8
Jersey City, N. J	301,173	149,703	161,470	143,176	144,422	115,970	118,468	27,206	25,954	6,402	7,014	125	34
Kansas City, Kans	121,458	59,432	62,026	49,534	50,856	46,049	47,769	3,485	3,087	9,874	11,159	24	11
Kansas City, Mo	399,178	190,117	209,061	170,184	187,162	159,779	178,228	10,405	8,934	19,736	21,838	197	61
Knoxville, Tenn	111,580	52,708	58,872	45,263	50,211	44,852	49,890	411	321	7,436	8,658	9	3
Long Beach, Calif	164,271	77,593	86,678	76,619	85,963	70,752	79,398	5,867	6,565	293	317	681	398
Los Angeles, Calif	1,504,277	734,135	770,142	683,075	723,355	575,597	615,585	107,478	107,770	29,906	33,868	21,154	12,919
Louisville, Ky	319,077	152,267	166,810	129,971	141,896	126,769	138,897	3,202	2,999	22,264	24,894	32	20
Lowell, Mass	101,389	49,016	52,373	48,927	52,325	39,915	41,919	9,012	10,406	50	44	39	4
Memphis, Tenn	292,942	139,238	153,704	82,430	88,976	79,973	86,965	2,457	2,011	56,778	64,720	30	8
Miami, Fla	172,172	84,587	87,585	66,864	68,328	60,314	62,361	6,550	5,967	17,621	19,236	102	21
Milwaukee, Wis	587,472	289,118	298,354	284,340	293,837	238,925	255,443	45,415	38,394	4,486	4,335	292	182
Minneapolis, Minn	492,370	234,542	257,828	231,726	255,373	197,302	225,648	34,424	29,725	2,378	2,268	438	187
Nashville, Tenn	167,402	77,499	89,903	56,108	63,964	55,300	63,250	808	714	21,386	25,932	5	7
Newark, N. J	429,760	213,840	215,920	191,749	191,785	144,867	148,321	46,882	43,464	21,734	24,026	357	109
New Bedford, Mass	110,341	53,401	56,940	51,100	54,827	37,031	39,273	14,069	15,554	2,233	2,064	68	49
New Haven, Conn	160,605	78,333	82,272	75,285	78,977	58,824	63,048	16,461	15,929	2,978	3,257	70	38
New Orleans, La	494,537	234,277	260,260	164,966	179,809	156,642	173,438	8,324	6,371	68,820	80,205	482	246
New York, N. Y	7,454,995	3,676,293	3,778,702	3,455,003	3,522,498	2,397,164	2,500,317	1,057,839	1,022,181	205,727	252,717	15,563	3,487
Bronx Borough	1,394,711	689,327	705,384	677,620	692,699	447,519	462,324	230,101	230,375	11,048	12,481	659	204
Brooklyn Borough	2,698,285	1,332,545	1,365,740	1,282,485	1,305,466	891,768	928,545	390,717	376,921	47,744	59,519	2,316	755
Manhattan Borough	1,889,924	926,133	963,701	780,455	797,170	502,136	535,202	278,319	261,878	133,930	164,435	11,748	2,186
Queens Borough	1,297,634	638,605	659,029	626,382	644,349	486,379	507,764	140,003	136,585	11,525	14,365	698	315
Richmond Borough	174,441	89,683	84,758	88,061	82,814	69,362	66,392	18,699	16,422	1,480	1,917	142	27
Norfolk, Va	144,332	72,949	71,383	50,978	47,270	48,956	45,635	2,022	1,635	21,831	24,062	140	51
Oakland, Calif	302,163	149,227	152,936	141,584	146,352	119,211	126,064	22,373	20,288	4,200	4,262	3,443	2,322
Oklahoma City, Okla	204,424	98,774	105,650	89,418	95,297	87,832	94,065	1,586	1,232	9,173	10,171	183	182
Omaha, Nebr	223,844	108,750	115,094	102,712	108,928	91,044	98,285	11,668	10,643	5,920	6,095	118	71
Paterson, N. J	139,656	69,505	70,151	67,371	67,929	49,777	51,435	17,594	16,494	2,055	2,213	79	9
Peoria, Ill	105,087	51,832	53,255	50,360	51,842	47,413	49,325	2,947	2,517	1,434	1,302	38	21
Philadelphia, Pa	1,931,334	942,550	988,784	822,266	856,311	677,008	711,244	145,258	145,067	118,859	132,021	1,425	452
Pittsburgh, Pa	671,659	330,007	341,652	298,791	310,445	253,986	270,644	44,805	39,801	31,056	31,160	160	47
Portland, Oreg	305,394	149,135	156,259	145,776	153,931	124,932	136,167	20,844	17,764	1,025	906	2,334	1,422
Providence, R. I	253,504	121,797	131,707	118,555	128,349	93,583	102,113	24,972	26,236	3,060	3,328	182	30
Reading, Pa	110,568	53,954	56,614	52,969	55,677	48,691	52,094	4,278	3,583	969	936	16	1
Richmond, Va	193,042	90,220	102,822	62,032	69,674	60,203	68,090	1,829	1,584	28,125	33,126	63	22
Rochester, N. Y	324,975	157,574	167,401	155,867	165,687	125,293	136,154	30,574	29,533	1,620	1,642	87	72
Sacramento, Calif	105,958	53,496	52,462	50,130	49,678	43,014	44,650	7,116	5,028	773	695	2,593	2,089
St. Louis, Mo	816,048	391,798	424,250	339,697	367,097	308,306	330,082	31,391	28,015	51,762	57,003	339	150
St. Paul, Minn	287,736	137,561	150,175	135,348	148,051	117,906	131,881	17,442	16,170	2,070	2,069	143	55
Salt Lake City, Utah	149,934	73,229	76,705	72,511	76,188	66,016	69,343	6,495	6,845	374	320	344	197
San Antonio, Texas	253,854	123,508	130,346	114,441	119,581	101,357	104,628	13,084	14,953	8,680	10,555	387	210
San Diego, Calif	203,341	103,638	99,703	100,200	96,746	90,631	86,786	9,569	9,960	1,992	2,151	1,446	806
San Francisco, Calif	634,536	322,441	312,095	301,692	301,009	230,005	242,425	71,687	58,584	2,461	2,385	18,288	8,701
Scranton, Pa	140,404	68,593	71,811	68,184	71,463	58,634	62,633	9,550	8,830	407	347	2	1
Seattle, Wash	368,302	183,526	184,776	174,997	179,104	142,372	152,117	32,625	26,987	2,146	1,643	6,383	4,029
Somerville, Mass	102,177	49,332	52,845	49,184	52,703	37,859	40,173	11,325	12,530	123	139	25	3
South Bend, Ind	101,268	50,228	51,040	48,443	49,219	42,657	44,128	5,786	5,091	1,744	1,811	41	10
Spokane, Wash	122,001	60,416	61,585	59,809	61,088	52,611	55,531	7,198	5,557	329	315	278	182
Springfield, Mass	149,554	72,246	77,308	70,703	75,658	57,434	62,189	13,269	13,469	1,503	1,641	40	9
Syracuse, N. Y	205,967	100,296	105,671	99,182	104,458	84,843	91,247	14,339	13,211	997	1,085	117	128
Tacoma, Wash	109,408	55,038	54,370	54,078	53,533	45,343	46,414	8,735	7,119	342	308	618	529
Tampa, Fla	108,391	52,442	55,949	41,377	43,666	35,516	38,445	5,861	5,221	11,052	12,279	13	4
Toledo, Ohio	282,349	140,001	142,348	132,738	134,851	119,150	123,692	13,588	11,159	7,141	7,456	122	41
Trenton, N. J	124,697	62,175	62,522	57,452	57,905	46,115	47,386	11,337	10,519	4,703	4,605	20	12
Tulsa, Okla	142,157	68,187	73,970	60,925	65,427	59,704	64,474	1,221	953	6,961	8,190	301	353
Utica, N. Y	100,518	48,857	51,661	48,575	51,414	39,499	43,150	9,076	8,264	271	243	11	4
Washington, D. C	663,091	317,522	345,569	227,748	246,578	209,828	230,484	17,920	16,094	88,672	98,594	1,102	397
Wichita, Kans	114,966	54,996	59,970	52,199	56,987	51,052	55,980	1,147	1,007	2,725	2,961	72	22
Wilmington, Del	112,504	55,494	57,010	48,474	49,701	42,783	44,911	5,691	4,790	6,959	7,297	61	12
Worcester, Mass	193,694	94,455	99,239	93,753	98,510	73,884	78,388	19,869	20,122	646	707	56	22
Yonkers, N. Y	142,598	69,991	72,607	68,127	70,314	53,745	56,039	14,382	14,275	1,819	2,289	45	4
Youngstown, Ohio	167,720	84,652	83,068	77,223	75,833	62,377	64,008	14,846	11,825	7,307	7,218	32	17

524997 O - 43 - 9

CHARACTERISTICS OF THE POPULATION

TABLE 51.—PERCENT DISTRIBUTION BY RACE, FOR EACH SEX, AND NUMBER OF MALES PER 100 FEMALES, BY RACE, FOR CITIES OF 100,000 OR MORE: 1940

[Percent not shown where less than 0.1. Sex ratio not shown where number of females is less than 100]

CITY	PERCENT BY RACE												MALES PER 100 FEMALES					
	Both sexes				Male				Female				All classes	White			Negro	Other races
	Native white	Foreign-born white	Negro	Other races	Native white	Foreign-born white	Negro	Other races	Native white	Foreign-born white	Negro	Other races		Total	Native	Foreign-born		
Akron, Ohio	84.6	10.4	5.0	......	83.7	11.3	5.0	......	85.5	9.5	5.0	......	98.6	98.6	96.5	117.8	97.9	......
Albany, N. Y	86.1	11.6	2.2	0.1	84.9	12.7	2.3	0.1	87.1	10.7	2.2	......	92.8	92.7	90.5	110.3	98.6	......
Atlanta, Ga	64.0	1.4	34.6	......	65.2	1.7	33.0	......	62.9	1.2	35.9	......	85.5	89.3	88.6	126.7	78.7	......
Baltimore, Md	73.5	7.1	19.3	0.1	73.4	7.5	19.1	0.1	73.7	6.7	19.5	......	97.0	97.4	96.5	107.3	94.7	341.6
Birmingham, Ala	57.6	1.7	40.7	......	58.4	1.9	39.6	......	56.9	1.4	41.7	......	90.9	94.1	93.3	127.2	86.4	......
Boston, Mass	73.2	23.5	3.1	0.2	73.6	23.0	3.0	0.3	72.9	23.9	3.1	0.1	93.8	93.7	94.7	90.4	91.4	338.6
Bridgeport, Conn	74.7	22.7	2.6	......	74.0	23.4	2.6	......	75.4	22.0	2.5	......	90.0	98.9	97.1	105.2	101.1	......
Buffalo, N. Y	80.9	15.9	3.1	0.1	80.0	16.8	3.1	0.1	81.8	15.1	3.0	0.1	97.1	97.0	95.0	108.2	99.2	119.8
Cambridge, Mass	73.3	22.1	4.4	0.1	73.8	21.6	4.3	0.2	72.9	22.7	4.4	0.1	89.9	89.8	91.1	85.6	88.4	......
Camden, N. J	76.6	12.8	10.6	0.1	76.2	13.2	10.5	0.1	76.9	12.3	10.7	......	100.1	100.3	99.2	107.2	98.2	......
Canton, Ohio	86.0	10.2	3.7	......	84.5	11.8	3.7	0.1	87.6	8.7	3.8	......	100.3	100.4	96.8	136.2	98.2	......
Charlotte, N. C	68.0	0.9	31.1	......	68.9	1.1	30.0	......	67.2	0.7	32.1	......	89.5	92.3	91.8	131.1	83.7	......
Chattanooga, Tenn	70.7	0.9	28.4	......	71.2	1.0	27.8	......	70.3	0.8	28.9	......	91.5	93.0	92.7	120.6	88.0	......
Chicago, Ill	71.9	19.8	8.2	0.1	70.9	21.1	7.8	0.2	72.8	18.5	8.6	0.1	98.0	98.8	95.5	111.5	88.7	387.4
Cincinnati, Ohio	82.1	5.7	12.2	......	81.6	6.1	12.2	0.1	82.5	5.3	12.2	......	91.0	90.9	90.0	104.9	91.6	......
Cleveland, Ohio	69.0	20.4	9.6	......	69.1	21.5	9.4	0.1	70.8	19.3	9.9	......	99.6	100.1	97.3	110.5	94.7	......
Columbus, Ohio	84.4	3.9	11.7	......	83.4	4.4	12.1	0.1	85.3	3.4	11.3	......	94.8	93.9	92.8	121.0	102.0	......
Dallas, Tex	80.4	2.5	17.1	......	80.5	2.9	16.6	......	80.3	2.2	17.5	......	90.2	91.1	90.4	118.8	85.6	......
Dayton, Ohio	85.9	4.4	9.6	......	85.5	4.9	9.6	......	86.4	4.0	9.6	......	96.3	96.2	95.3	116.7	96.8	......
Denver, Colo	89.7	7.7	2.4	0.2	89.0	8.4	2.3	0.3	90.2	7.0	2.5	0.2	93.3	93.4	92.1	110.7	85.5	136.7
Des Moines, Iowa	91.3	4.7	4.0	......	90.7	5.2	4.0	......	91.9	4.2	3.9	......	90.4	90.2	89.2	113.5	93.5	......
Detroit, Mich	71.0	19.8	9.2	0.1	70.0	20.8	9.0	0.1	71.9	18.6	9.4	0.1	104.0	104.3	101.2	116.1	99.8	252.5
Duluth, Minn	80.5	19.1	0.3	0.1	77.7	21.9	0.4	0.1	83.3	16.4	0.3	0.1	100.2	100.1	93.5	133.6	137.9	......
Elizabeth, N. J	74.9	20.6	4.5	0.1	74.0	21.5	4.4	0.1	75.8	19.7	4.5	......	99.7	99.8	97.4	109.0	97.3	......
Erie, Pa	87.2	11.6	1.2	......	85.9	12.9	1.2	......	88.5	10.4	1.1	......	98.7	98.6	95.8	122.5	104.0	......
Fall River, Mass	78.3	21.3	0.3	0.1	78.5	20.9	0.4	0.2	78.0	21.7	0.3	......	92.7	92.5	93.4	89.4	131.0	......
Flint, Mich	85.1	10.5	4.4	0.1	84.3	11.3	4.3	0.1	85.9	9.6	4.5	......	100.5	100.7	98.7	118.9	96.2	......
Fort Wayne, Ind	94.1	3.7	2.1	......	93.7	4.2	2.1	......	94.6	3.3	2.1	......	92.6	92.6	91.7	117.2	91.6	......
Fort Worth, Tex	83.8	2.0	14.2	......	83.9	2.2	13.9	0.1	83.7	1.8	14.5	......	91.9	92.6	92.1	115.6	87.4	......
Gary, Ind	66.2	15.5	18.3	0.1	64.8	17.7	17.4	0.1	67.7	13.0	19.2	0.1	108.3	110.6	103.6	146.9	98.4	......
Grand Rapids, Mich	86.0	12.4	1.6	......	84.9	13.4	1.6	......	86.9	11.4	1.6	......	93.6	93.5	91.4	109.4	95.2	......
Hartford, Conn	73.7	22.0	4.3	......	72.6	23.1	4.3	......	74.7	21.0	4.3	......	93.9	93.9	91.3	103.0	93.8	......
Houston, Tex	73.5	4.0	22.4	0.1	74.0	4.4	21.5	0.1	73.1	3.5	23.4	......	96.0	98.2	97.2	120.1	88.4	......
Indianapolis, Ind	84.0	2.7	13.2	......	83.8	3.0	13.1	......	84.2	2.5	13.3	......	92.0	92.2	91.6	111.1	90.9	......
Jacksonville, Fla	62.0	2.3	35.7	......	62.5	2.6	34.8	......	61.5	2.0	36.5	......	91.7	94.2	93.3	122.3	87.3	......
Jersey City, N. J	77.8	17.7	4.5	0.1	77.5	18.2	4.3	0.1	78.2	17.1	4.6	......	98.8	99.1	97.9	104.8	91.3	......
Kansas City, Kans	77.2	5.4	17.3	......	77.5	5.9	16.6	......	77.0	5.0	18.0	......	95.8	97.4	96.4	112.9	88.5	......
Kansas City, Mo	84.7	4.8	10.4	0.1	84.0	5.5	10.4	0.1	85.3	4.3	10.4	......	90.9	90.9	89.6	116.5	90.4	......
Knoxville, Tenn	84.9	0.7	14.4	......	85.1	0.8	14.1	......	84.7	0.5	14.7	......	89.5	90.1	89.9	128.0	85.9	......
Long Beach, Calif	91.4	7.6	0.4	0.7	91.2	7.6	0.4	0.9	91.6	7.6	0.4	0.5	89.5	89.1	89.1	89.4	92.4	171.1
Los Angeles, Calif	79.2	14.3	4.2	2.3	78.4	14.6	4.1	2.9	79.9	14.0	4.4	1.7	95.3	94.4	93.5	99.7	88.3	163.7
Louisville, Ky	83.3	1.9	14.8	......	83.3	2.1	14.6	......	83.3	1.8	14.9	......	91.3	91.6	91.3	106.8	89.4	......
Lowell, Mass	80.7	19.2	0.1	......	81.4	18.4	0.1	0.1	80.0	19.9	0.1	......	93.6	93.5	95.2	86.6	......	......
Memphis, Tenn	57.0	1.5	41.5	......	57.4	1.8	40.8	......	56.6	1.3	42.1	......	90.6	92.6	92.0	122.2	87.7	......
Miami, Fla	71.3	7.3	21.4	0.1	71.3	7.7	20.8	0.1	71.2	6.8	22.0	......	96.6	97.9	96.7	109.8	91.6	......
Milwaukee, Wis	84.2	14.3	1.5	0.1	82.6	15.7	1.6	0.1	85.6	12.9	1.5	0.1	96.9	96.8	93.5	118.3	103.5	160.4
Minneapolis, Minn	85.9	13.0	0.9	0.1	84.1	14.7	1.0	0.2	87.5	11.5	0.9	0.1	91.0	90.7	87.4	115.8	104.9	234.2
Nashville, Tenn	70.8	0.9	28.3	......	71.4	1.0	27.6	......	70.4	0.8	28.8	......	86.2	87.7	87.4	113.2	82.5	......
Newark, N. J	68.2	21.0	10.6	0.1	67.7	21.9	10.2	0.2	68.7	20.1	11.1	0.1	99.0	100.0	97.7	107.9	90.5	327.5
New Bedford, Mass	69.2	26.8	3.9	0.1	69.3	26.3	4.2	0.1	69.0	27.3	3.6	0.1	93.8	93.2	94.3	90.5	108.2	......
New Haven, Conn	75.9	20.2	3.9	0.1	75.1	21.0	3.8	0.1	76.6	19.4	4.0	......	95.2	95.3	93.3	103.3	91.4	......
New Orleans, La	66.7	3.0	30.1	0.1	66.9	3.6	29.4	0.2	66.6	2.4	30.8	0.1	90.0	91.7	90.3	130.7	85.8	195.9
New York, N. Y	65.7	27.9	6.1	0.3	65.2	28.8	5.6	0.4	66.2	27.1	6.7	0.1	97.3	98.1	95.9	103.5	81.4	446.3
Bronx Borough	65.2	33.0	1.7	0.1	64.9	33.4	1.6	0.1	65.5	32.7	1.8	......	97.7	97.8	96.8	99.9	88.5	323.0
Brooklyn Borough	67.5	28.4	4.0	0.1	66.9	29.3	3.6	0.2	68.0	27.6	4.4	0.1	97.6	98.2	96.0	103.7	80.2	306.8
Manhattan Borough	54.9	28.6	15.8	0.7	54.2	30.1	14.5	1.3	55.5	27.2	17.1	0.2	96.1	97.9	93.8	106.3	81.4	537.4
Queens Borough	76.6	21.3	2.0	0.1	76.2	21.9	1.8	0.1	77.0	20.7	2.2	......	96.9	97.2	95.8	102.5	80.2	221.6
Richmond Borough	77.8	20.1	1.9	0.1	77.3	20.9	1.7	0.2	78.3	19.4	2.3	......	105.8	106.3	104.5	113.9	77.2	......
Norfolk, Va	65.5	2.5	31.8	0.1	67.1	2.8	29.9	0.2	63.9	2.3	33.7	0.1	102.2	107.8	107.3	123.7	90.7	......
Oakland, Calif	81.2	14.1	2.8	1.9	79.9	15.0	2.8	2.3	82.4	13.3	2.8	1.5	97.6	96.7	94.6	110.3	98.5	148.3
Oklahoma City, Okla	89.0	1.4	9.5	0.2	88.9	1.6	9.3	0.2	89.0	1.2	9.6	0.2	93.5	93.8	93.4	128.7	90.2	100.5
Omaha, Nebr	84.6	10.0	5.4	0.1	83.7	10.7	5.4	0.1	85.4	9.2	5.3	0.1	94.5	94.3	92.6	109.6	97.1	......
Paterson, N. J	72.5	24.4	3.1	0.1	71.6	25.3	3.0	0.1	73.3	23.5	3.2	......	99.1	99.2	96.8	106.7	92.9	......
Peoria, Ill	92.1	5.2	2.7	0.1	91.5	5.7	2.8	0.1	92.6	4.7	2.6	......	97.3	97.1	96.1	117.1	103.0	......
Philadelphia, Pa	71.9	15.0	13.0	0.1	71.8	15.4	12.6	0.2	71.9	14.7	13.4	......	95.3	96.0	95.2	100.1	90.0	315.3
Pittsburgh, Pa	78.1	12.6	9.3	......	77.0	13.6	9.4	......	79.2	11.6	9.1	......	96.6	96.2	93.8	112.6	99.7	......
Portland, Oreg	85.5	12.6	0.6	1.2	83.8	14.0	0.7	1.6	87.1	11.4	0.6	0.9	95.4	94.7	91.7	117.3	113.1	164.1
Providence, R. I	77.2	20.2	2.5	0.1	76.8	20.5	2.5	0.1	77.5	19.9	2.5	......	92.5	92.4	91.6	95.2	91.9	......
Reading, Pa	91.2	7.1	1.7	......	90.2	7.9	1.8	......	92.0	6.3	1.7	......	95.3	95.1	93.5	119.4	103.5	......
Richmond, Va	66.5	1.8	31.7	......	66.7	2.0	31.2	0.1	66.2	1.5	32.2	......	87.7	89.0	88.4	115.5	84.9	......
Rochester, N. Y	80.5	18.5	1.0	......	79.5	19.4	1.0	0.1	81.3	17.0	1.0	......	94.1	94.1	92.0	103.5	98.7	......
Sacramento, Calif	82.7	11.5	1.4	4.4	80.4	13.3	1.4	4.8	85.1	9.6	1.3	4.0	102.0	100.9	96.3	141.5	111.2	124.1
St. Louis, Mo	79.3	7.3	13.3	0.1	78.7	8.0	13.2	0.1	79.9	6.6	13.4	......	92.4	92.5	90.9	112.1	90.8	226.0
St. Paul, Minn	86.8	11.7	1.4	0.1	85.7	12.7	1.5	0.1	87.8	10.8	1.4	......	91.6	91.4	89.4	107.9	100.0	......
Salt Lake City, Utah	90.3	8.9	0.5	0.4	90.2	8.9	0.5	0.5	90.4	8.9	0.4	0.3	95.5	95.2	95.2	94.9	116.9	174.6
San Antonio, Tex	81.1	11.0	7.6	0.2	82.1	10.6	7.0	0.3	80.3	11.5	8.1	0.2	94.8	95.7	96.9	87.5	82.2	184.3
San Diego, Calif	87.3	9.6	2.0	1.1	87.4	9.2	1.9	1.4	87.0	10.0	2.2	0.8	103.9	103.6	104.4	96.1	92.6	179.4
San Francisco, Calif	74.5	20.5	0.8	4.3	71.3	22.2	0.8	5.7	77.7	18.8	0.8	2.8	103.3	100.2	94.9	122.4	103.2	210.2
Scranton, Pa	86.4	13.1	0.5	......	85.5	13.9	0.6	......	87.2	12.3	0.5	......	95.5	95.4	93.6	108.2	117.3	......
Seattle, Wash	80.0	16.2	1.0	2.8	77.6	17.8	1.2	3.5	82.3	14.6	0.9	2.2	99.3	97.7	93.6	120.9	130.6	158.4
Somerville, Mass	76.4	23.3	0.3	......	76.7	23.0	0.2	0.1	76.0	23.7	0.3	......	93.4	93.3	94.2	90.4	88.5	......
South Bend, Ind	85.7	10.7	3.5	0.1	84.9	11.5	3.5	0.1	86.5	10.0	3.5	......	98.4	98.4	96.7	113.7	96.3	......
Spokane, Wash	88.6	10.5	0.5	0.4	87.1	11.9	0.5	0.5	90.2	9.0	0.5	0.3	98.1	97.9	94.7	129.5	104.4	152.7
Springfield, Mass	80.0	17.9	2.1	......	79.5	18.4	2.1	0.1	80.4	17.4	2.1	......	93.5	93.5	92.4	98.5	91.6	......
Syracuse, N. Y	85.5	13.4	1.0	0.1	84.6	14.3	1.0	0.1	86.4	12.5	1.0	0.1	94.9	94.9	93.0	108.5	91.9	91.4
Tacoma, Wash	83.9	14.5	0.6	1.0	82.4	15.9	0.6	1.1	85.4	13.1	0.6	1.0	101.2	101.0	97.7	122.7	111.0	116.8
Tampa, Fla	68.2	10.2	21.5	......	67.7	11.2	21.1	......	68.7	9.3	21.9	......	93.7	94.8	92.4	112.3	90.0	......
Toledo, Ohio	86.0	8.8	5.2	0.1	85.1	9.7	5.1	0.1	86.9	7.8	5.2	......	98.4	98.4	96.3	121.8	95.8	......
Trenton, N. J	75.0	17.5	7.5	......	74.2	18.2	7.6	......	75.8	16.8	7.4	......	99.4	99.2	97.3	107.8	102.1	......
Tulsa, Okla	87.4	1.5	10.7	0.5	87.6	1.8	10.2	0.4	87.2	1.3	11.1	0.5	92.2	93.1	92.6	128.1	85.0	85.3
Utica, N. Y	82.2	17.3	0.5	......	80.8	18.6	0.6	......	83.5	16.0	0.5	......	94.6	94.5	91.5	109.8	111.5	......
Washington, D. C	66.4	5.1	28.2	0.2	66.1	5.6	27.9	0.3	66.7	4.7	28.5	0.1	91.9	92.4	91.0	111.3	89.9	277.6
Wichita, Kans	93.1	1.9	4.9	0.1	92.8	2.1	5.0	0.1	93.3	1.7	4.9	......	91.7	91.6	91.2	113.9	92.0	......
Wilmington, Del	77.9	9.3	12.7	0.1	77.1	10.3	12.5	0.1	78.8	8.4	12.8	......	97.3	97.5	95.3	118.8	95.4	......
Worcester, Mass	78.6	20.6	0.7	......	78.2	21.0	0.7	0.1	79.0	20.3	0.7	......	95.2	95.2	94.3	98.7	91.4	...
Yonkers, N. Y	77.0	20.1	2.9	......	76.8	20.5	2.6	0.1	77.2	19.7	3.2	......	96.4	96.9	95.0	100.7	79.5	...
Youngstown, Ohio	75.4	15.9	8.7	......	73.7	17.5	8.7	......	77.1	14.2	8.7	......	101.9	101.8	97.5	125.5	102.5	......

UNITED STATES SUMMARY—PRINCIPAL CITIES

Table 52.—RACE, BY SEX, FOR CITIES OF 50,000 TO 100,000: 1940

CITY	ALL CLASSES			WHITE									NEGRO			OTHER RACES		
				Total			Native			Foreign born								
	Total	Male	Female	Total	Male	Female	Total	Male	Female	Total	Male	Female	Total	Male	Female	Total	Male	Female
Allentown, Pa.	96,904	47,220	49,684	96,524	47,018	49,506	88,670	42,986	45,684	7,854	4,032	3,822	378	201	177	2	1	1
Altoona, Pa.	80,214	39,123	41,091	79,472	38,748	40,724	74,718	36,077	38,641	4,754	2,671	2,083	735	370	365	7	5	2
Amarillo, Tex.	51,686	25,329	26,357	48,900	23,986	24,914	48,251	23,645	24,606	649	341	308	2,761	1,327	1,434	25	16	9
Arlington County, Va.[1]	57,040	28,537	28,503	51,998	26,070	25,928	50,397	25,274	25,123	1,601	796	805	5,032	2,458	2,574	10	9	1
Asheville, N. C.	51,310	23,504	27,806	37,873	17,486	20,387	37,078	17,003	19,985	795	393	402	13,435	6,016	7,419	2	2	—
Atlantic City, N. J.	64,094	29,913	34,181	48,347	22,394	25,953	40,152	18,340	21,812	8,195	4,054	4,141	15,668	7,467	8,201	79	52	27
Augusta, Ga.	65,919	31,249	34,670	38,691	19,021	19,670	38,135	18,708	19,427	556	313	243	27,004	12,090	14,914	224	138	86
Austin, Texas	87,930	41,384	46,546	73,025	34,739	38,286	70,029	33,191	36,838	2,996	1,548	1,448	14,861	6,613	8,248	44	32	12
Bayonne, N. J.	79,198	40,330	38,868	77,419	39,455	37,964	60,213	30,571	29,642	17,206	8,884	8,322	1,754	859	895	25	16	9
Beaumont, Tex.	59,061	28,792	30,269	40,105	19,841	20,264	38,704	19,060	19,644	1,401	781	620	18,921	8,933	9,988	35	18	17
Berkeley, Calif.	85,547	39,912	45,635	80,267	37,257	43,010	69,510	32,001	37,509	10,757	5,256	5,501	3,395	1,577	1,818	1,885	1,078	807
Bethlehem, Pa.	58,490	29,289	29,201	57,841	28,967	28,874	49,674	24,595	25,079	8,167	4,372	3,795	638	315	323	11	7	4
Binghamton, N. Y.	78,309	37,950	40,359	77,559	37,553	40,006	68,569	32,728	35,841	8,990	4,825	4,165	740	389	351	10	8	2
Brockton, Mass.	62,343	30,307	32,036	61,705	30,038	31,757	50,281	24,377	25,904	11,514	5,661	5,853	596	240	356	42	29	13
Cedar Rapids, Iowa	62,120	29,737	32,383	61,452	29,416	32,036	57,583	27,409	30,174	3,869	2,007	1,862	663	318	345	5	3	2
Charleston, S. C.	71,275	32,774	38,501	39,488	18,833	20,655	38,189	18,117	20,072	1,299	716	583	31,765	13,929	17,836	22	12	10
Charleston, W. Va.	67,914	32,784	35,130	60,887	29,541	31,346	59,279	28,602	30,677	1,608	939	669	7,011	3,231	3,780	16	12	4
Chester, Pa.	59,285	29,739	29,546	49,102	24,742	24,360	42,563	21,236	21,327	6,539	3,506	3,033	10,162	4,979	5,183	21	18	3
Cicero, Ill.	64,712	32,676	32,036	64,698	32,668	32,030	49,332	24,642	24,690	15,366	8,026	7,340	7	3	4	7	5	2
Cleveland Heights, Ohio	54,992	24,910	30,082	54,458	24,776	29,682	46,524	20,895	25,629	7,934	3,881	4,053	511	120	391	23	14	9
Columbia, S. C.	62,396	29,318	33,078	40,191	19,096	21,095	39,683	18,822	20,861	508	274	234	22,195	10,214	11,981	10	8	2
Columbus, Ga.	53,280	24,561	28,719	35,804	17,032	18,772	35,518	16,866	18,652	286	166	120	17,453	7,518	9,935	23	11	12
Corpus Christi, Tex.	57,301	28,881	28,420	52,742	26,614	26,128	49,718	24,999	24,719	3,024	1,615	1,409	4,545	2,259	2,286	14	8	6
Covington, Ky.	62,018	29,624	32,394	58,858	28,093	30,765	57,692	27,474	30,218	1,166	619	547	3,154	1,526	1,628	6	5	1
Davenport, Iowa	66,039	32,227	33,812	65,235	31,814	33,421	61,058	29,640	31,418	4,177	2,174	2,003	801	411	390	3	2	1
Dearborn, Mich.	63,584	33,321	30,263	63,495	33,262	30,233	49,938	25,445	24,493	13,557	7,817	5,740	35	14	21	54	45	9
Decatur, Ill.	59,305	28,417	30,888	57,205	27,405	29,800	55,408	26,474	28,934	1,797	931	866	2,098	1,011	1,087	2	1	1
Durham, N. C.	60,195	27,905	32,290	36,840	17,496	19,344	36,436	17,265	19,171	404	231	173	23,347	10,401	12,946	8	8	—
East Chicago, Ind.	54,637	29,019	25,618	48,503	25,958	22,545	36,165	18,612	17,553	12,338	7,346	4,992	6,101	3,038	3,063	33	23	10
East Orange, N. J.	68,945	31,896	37,049	62,973	29,131	33,842	54,433	25,041	29,392	8,540	4,090	4,450	5,950	2,745	3,205	22	20	2
East St. Louis, Ill.	75,609	37,265	38,344	58,781	29,126	29,655	55,228	27,198	28,030	3,553	1,928	1,625	16,798	8,120	8,678	30	19	11
El Paso, Tex.	96,810	46,011	50,799	94,323	44,720	49,603	72,350	35,283	37,067	21,973	9,437	12,536	2,188	1,071	1,117	299	220	79
Evanston, Ill.	65,389	29,860	35,529	59,298	27,067	32,231	52,088	23,615	28,473	7,210	3,452	3,758	6,026	2,736	3,290	65	57	8
Evansville, Ind.	97,062	46,419	50,643	90,194	43,154	47,040	89,015	42,531	46,484	1,179	623	556	6,862	3,259	3,603	6	6	—
Fresno, Calif.	60,685	30,152	30,533	57,014	28,091	28,923	48,686	23,669	25,017	8,328	4,422	3,906	2,002	1,088	914	1,669	973	696
Galveston, Tex.	60,862	30,424	30,438	45,353	23,046	22,307	40,842	20,389	20,453	4,511	2,657	1,854	15,432	7,321	8,111	77	57	20
Glendale, Calif.	82,582	39,901	42,681	81,992	39,558	42,434	76,000	36,630	39,370	5,992	2,928	3,064	68	17	51	522	326	196
Greensboro, N. C.	59,319	28,104	31,215	42,968	20,470	22,498	42,468	20,181	22,287	500	289	211	16,343	7,628	8,715	8	6	2
Hamilton, Ohio	50,592	24,835	25,757	48,530	23,831	24,699	46,989	22,987	24,002	1,541	844	697	2,052	996	1,056	10	8	2
Hammond, Ind.	70,184	35,998	34,186	69,524	35,621	33,903	61,152	30,965	30,187	8,372	4,656	3,716	637	356	281	23	21	2
Harrisburg, Pa.	83,893	39,813	44,080	76,609	36,198	40,411	73,325	34,382	38,943	3,284	1,816	1,468	7,263	3,602	3,661	21	13	8
Highland Park, Mich.	50,810	25,288	25,522	49,475	24,620	24,855	38,706	19,006	19,700	10,769	5,614	5,155	1,292	641	651	43	27	16
Hoboken, N. J.	50,115	26,006	24,109	49,819	25,846	23,973	35,961	18,025	17,936	13,858	7,821	6,037	260	131	129	36	29	7
Holyoke, Mass.	53,750	25,831	27,919	53,646	25,779	27,867	41,579	20,182	21,397	12,067	5,597	6,470	94	45	49	10	7	3
Huntington, W. Va.	78,836	38,212	40,624	74,322	36,066	38,256	73,350	35,506	37,844	972	560	412	4,498	2,134	2,364	16	12	4
Irvington, N. J.	55,328	27,251	28,077	55,237	27,204	28,033	43,799	21,417	22,382	11,438	5,787	5,651	69	31	38	22	16	6
Jackson, Miss.	62,107	28,564	33,543	37,851	17,700	20,151	37,493	17,473	20,020	358	227	131	24,256	10,864	13,392	—	—	—
Johnstown, Pa.	66,668	33,206	33,462	65,093	32,401	32,692	57,803	28,297	29,506	7,290	4,104	3,186	1,560	794	766	15	11	4
Kalamazoo, Mich.	54,097	26,341	27,756	52,961	25,751	27,210	48,159	23,170	24,989	4,802	2,581	2,221	1,117	572	545	19	18	1
Lakewood, Ohio	69,160	32,283	36,877	69,041	32,241	36,800	61,398	28,539	32,859	7,643	3,702	3,941	91	19	72	28	23	5
Lancaster, Pa.	61,345	29,191	32,154	59,834	28,436	31,398	57,608	27,240	30,368	2,226	1,196	1,030	1,503	748	755	8	7	1
Lansing, Mich.	78,753	38,443	40,310	77,087	37,525	39,562	71,903	34,747	37,156	5,184	2,778	2,406	1,638	899	739	28	19	9
Lawrence, Mass.	84,323	41,555	42,768	84,173	41,459	42,714	61,234	30,155	31,079	22,939	11,304	11,635	122	68	54	28	28	—
Lincoln, Nebr.	81,984	38,209	43,775	81,163	37,824	43,339	76,099	35,289	40,810	5,064	2,535	2,529	794	368	426	27	17	10
Little Rock, Ark.	88,039	40,852	47,187	65,914	30,967	34,947	64,950	30,442	34,508	964	525	439	22,103	9,873	12,230	22	12	10
Lynn, Mass.	98,123	47,749	50,374	97,314	47,355	49,959	76,267	37,276	38,991	21,047	10,079	10,968	744	356	388	65	38	27
McKeesport, Pa.	55,355	28,140	27,215	53,155	27,036	26,119	44,427	22,144	22,283	8,728	4,892	3,836	2,184	1,091	1,093	16	13	3
Macon, Ga.	57,865	26,540	31,325	32,253	15,125	17,128	31,887	14,908	16,979	366	217	149	25,604	11,410	14,194	8	5	3
Madison, Wis.	67,447	31,363	36,084	67,047	31,154	35,893	62,519	28,766	33,753	4,528	2,388	2,140	365	185	180	35	24	11
Malden, Mass.	58,010	27,621	30,389	57,514	27,376	30,138	44,592	21,406	23,186	12,922	5,970	6,952	479	230	249	17	15	2
Manchester, N. H.	77,685	37,300	40,385	77,635	37,263	40,372	60,239	29,061	31,178	17,396	8,202	9,194	23	13	10	27	24	3
Medford, Mass.	63,083	30,405	32,678	62,420	30,100	32,320	50,654	24,480	26,174	11,766	5,620	6,146	648	293	355	15	12	3
Mobile, Ala.	78,720	37,168	41,552	49,606	23,898	25,708	48,134	23,001	25,133	1,472	897	575	29,046	13,224	15,822	68	46	22
Montgomery, Ala.	78,084	35,800	42,284	43,547	20,857	22,690	42,955	20,519	22,436	592	338	254	34,535	14,942	19,593	2	1	1
Mount Vernon, N. Y.	67,362	32,050	35,312	62,189	29,879	32,310	49,410	23,357	26,053	12,779	6,522	6,257	5,103	2,127	2,976	70	44	26
New Britain, Conn.	68,685	34,469	34,216	68,350	34,296	34,054	51,296	25,355	25,941	17,054	8,941	8,113	334	172	162	1	1	—
New Rochelle, N. Y.	58,408	28,634	29,774	52,107	25,954	26,153	41,156	20,542	20,614	10,951	5,412	5,539	6,228	2,633	3,595	73	47	26
Newton, Mass.	69,873	32,087	37,786	69,161	31,810	37,351	58,127	27,246	30,881	11,034	4,564	6,470	680	252	428	32	25	7
Niagara Falls, N. Y.	78,029	39,375	38,654	76,940	38,804	38,136	57,206	28,680	28,526	19,734	10,124	9,610	975	518	457	114	53	61
Oak Park, Ill.	66,015	30,313	35,702	65,875	30,247	35,628	59,578	27,226	32,352	6,297	3,021	3,276	98	30	68	42	36	6
Pasadena, Calif.	81,864	36,193	45,671	76,737	33,642	43,095	67,602	29,737	37,865	9,135	3,905	5,230	3,929	1,793	2,136	1,198	758	440
Passaic, N. J.	61,394	30,357	31,037	59,365	29,381	29,984	41,645	20,438	21,207	17,720	8,943	8,777	2,003	957	1,046	26	19	7
Pawtucket, R. I.	75,797	36,738	39,059	75,482	36,592	38,890	58,390	28,442	29,948	17,092	8,150	8,942	286	120	166	29	26	3
Phoenix, Ariz.	65,414	32,295	33,119	60,373	29,679	30,694	56,276	27,645	28,631	4,097	2,034	2,063	4,263	2,176	2,087	778	440	338
Pontiac, Mich.	66,626	34,220	32,406	63,788	32,791	30,997	57,158	29,113	28,045	6,630	3,678	2,952	2,794	1,398	1,396	44	31	13
Portland, Maine	73,643	35,164	38,479	73,269	34,950	38,319	63,425	30,287	33,138	9,844	4,663	5,181	325	182	143	49	32	17
Portsmouth, Va.	50,745	25,651	25,094	31,268	16,428	14,840	30,507	16,048	14,459	761	380	381	19,338	9,132	10,206	139	91	48
Pueblo, Colo.	52,162	25,864	26,298	50,659	25,090	25,569	46,315	22,690	23,625	4,344	2,400	1,944	1,381	685	696	122	89	33
Quincy, Mass.	75,810	36,986	38,824	75,765	36,960	38,805	61,078	29,929	31,149	14,687	7,031	7,656	17	6	11	28	20	8
Racine, Wis.	67,195	33,348	33,847	66,741	33,119	33,622	55,621	27,039	28,582	11,120	6,080	5,040	432	216	216	22	13	9

[1] Classified as urban under special rule.

TABLE 52.—RACE, BY SEX, FOR CITIES OF 50,000 TO 100,000: 1940—Continued

CITY	All classes Total	All classes Male	All classes Female	White Total Total	White Total Male	White Total Female	White Native Total	White Native Male	White Native Female	White Foreign born Total	White Foreign born Male	White Foreign born Female	Negro Total	Negro Male	Negro Female	Other races Total	Other races Male	Other races Female
Roanoke, Va	69, 287	32, 777	36, 510	56, 472	26, 854	29, 618	55, 766	26, 447	29, 319	706	407	299	12, 812	5, 920	6, 892	3	3	---
Rockford, Ill	84, 637	41, 883	42, 754	83, 426	41, 275	42, 151	69, 737	33, 720	36, 017	13, 689	7, 555	6, 134	1, 190	592	598	21	16	5
Saginaw, Mich	82, 794	41, 064	41, 730	79, 384	39, 259	40, 125	70, 896	34, 834	36, 062	8, 488	4, 425	4, 063	3, 315	1, 755	1, 560	95	50	45
St. Joseph, Mo	75, 711	36, 425	39, 286	72, 669	34, 906	37, 763	69, 914	33, 475	36, 439	2, 755	1, 431	1, 324	3, 029	1, 510	1, 519	13	9	4
St. Petersburg, Fla	60, 812	28, 019	32, 793	48, 794	22, 428	26, 366	45, 271	20, 739	24, 532	3, 523	1, 689	1, 834	11, 982	5, 560	6, 422	36	31	5
San Jose, Calif	68, 457	33, 240	35, 217	67, 406	32, 655	34, 751	58, 341	27, 775	30, 566	9, 065	4, 880	4, 185	291	133	158	760	452	308
Santa Monica, Calif	53, 500	26, 150	27, 350	51, 691	25, 210	26, 481	45, 299	22, 191	23, 108	6, 392	3, 019	3, 373	1, 265	600	665	544	340	204
Savannah, Ga	95, 996	44, 438	51, 558	52, 700	25, 124	27, 576	50, 844	24, 171	26, 673	1, 856	953	903	43, 237	19, 276	23, 961	59	38	21
Schenectady, N. Y	87, 549	43, 338	44, 211	86, 837	42, 964	43, 873	71, 423	34, 857	36, 566	15, 414	8, 107	7, 307	688	360	328	24	14	10
Shreveport, La	98, 167	46, 130	52, 037	62, 146	30, 148	31, 998	60, 686	29, 325	31, 361	1, 460	823	637	35, 975	15, 948	20, 027	46	34	12
Sioux City, Iowa	82, 364	39, 933	42, 431	81, 360	39, 402	41, 958	74, 773	35, 873	38, 900	6, 587	3, 529	3, 058	871	452	419	132	79	54
Springfield, Ill	75, 503	35, 846	39, 657	72, 122	34, 191	37, 931	67, 507	31, 709	35, 708	4, 615	2, 482	2, 133	3, 357	1, 635	1, 722	24	20	4
Springfield, Mo	61, 238	28, 922	32, 316	59, 432	28, 054	31, 378	58, 797	27, 733	31, 064	635	321	314	1, 804	868	936	2	---	2
Springfield, Ohio	70, 662	34, 631	36, 031	62, 352	30, 613	31, 739	60, 799	29, 768	31, 031	1, 553	845	708	8, 293	4, 009	4, 284	17	9	8
Stockton, Calif	54, 714	29, 372	25, 342	49, 632	25, 792	23, 840	42, 571	21, 417	21, 154	7, 061	4, 375	2, 686	875	509	366	4, 207	3, 071	1, 136
Terre Haute, Ind	62, 693	29, 965	32, 728	59, 292	28, 327	30, 965	57, 405	27, 318	30, 087	1, 887	1, 009	878	3, 398	1, 635	1, 763	3	3	---
Topeka, Kans	67, 833	31, 553	36, 280	62, 096	28, 853	33, 243	59, 809	27, 722	32, 087	2, 287	1, 131	1, 156	5, 679	2, 668	3, 011	58	32	26
Troy, N. Y	70, 304	33, 228	37, 076	69, 678	32, 906	36, 772	62, 124	29, 213	32, 911	7, 554	3, 693	3, 861	612	309	303	14	13	1
Union City, N. J	56, 173	27, 808	28, 365	56, 124	27, 781	28, 343	41, 976	20, 573	21, 403	14, 148	7, 208	6, 940	29	11	18	20	16	4
Upper Darby twp., Pa.[1]	56, 883	26, 887	29, 996	56, 446	26, 762	29, 684	52, 562	24, 867	27, 695	3, 884	1, 895	1, 989	413	112	301	24	13	11
Waco, Texas	55, 982	26, 295	29, 687	44, 944	21, 309	23, 635	43, 572	20, 582	22, 990	1, 372	727	645	11, 025	4, 974	6, 051	13	12	1
Waterbury, Conn	99, 314	49, 570	49, 744	97, 259	48, 544	48, 715	74, 944	36, 974	37, 970	22, 315	11, 570	10, 745	2, 015	995	1, 020	40	31	9
Waterloo, Iowa	51, 743	25, 274	26, 469	50, 237	24, 500	25, 737	48, 185	23, 394	24, 791	2, 052	1, 106	946	1, 498	768	730	8	6	2
Wheeling, W. Va	61, 099	29, 040	32, 059	59, 186	28, 138	31, 048	55, 183	25, 949	29, 234	4, 003	2, 189	1, 814	1, 897	890	1, 007	16	12	4
Wilkes-Barre, Pa	86, 236	42, 171	44, 065	85, 393	41, 733	43, 660	74, 464	35, 965	38, 499	10, 929	5, 768	5, 161	836	433	403	7	5	2
Winston-Salem, N. C	79, 815	37, 616	42, 199	43, 789	20, 904	22, 885	43, 431	20, 691	22, 740	358	213	145	36, 018	16, 704	19, 314	8	8	---
York, Pa	56, 712	27, 494	29, 218	54, 280	26, 265	28, 015	53, 292	25, 703	27, 589	988	562	426	2, 427	1, 224	1, 203	5	5	---

[1] Classified as urban under special rule.

TABLE 53.—AGE, BY RACE AND SEX, WITH PERCENT DISTRIBUTION BY AGE, FOR CITIES OF 100,000 OR MORE: 1940

[Percent not shown where less than 0.1 or where base is less than 100]

CITY AND AGE	NUMBER											PERCENT DISTRIBUTION										
	All classes			Native white		Foreign-born white		Negro		Other races		All classes			Native white		Foreign-born white		Negro		Other races	
	Total	Male	Female	Male	Female	Male	Female	Male	Female	Male	Female	Total	Male	Female	Male	Female	Male	Female	Male	Female	Male	Female
AKRON, OHIO																						
All ages	244,791	121,529	123,262	101,686	105,376	13,750	11,670	6,065	6,195	28	21	100.0	100.0	100.0	100.0	100.0	100.0	100.0	100.0	100.0	-	-
Under 5 years	16,366	8,312	8,054	7,791	7,540	8	8	511	503	2	3	6.7	6.8	6.5	7.7	7.2	0.1	0.1	8.4	8.1	-	-
5 to 9 years	17,026	8,613	8,413	8,047	7,828	20	25	542	558	4	2	7.0	7.1	6.8	7.9	7.4	0.1	0.2	8.9	9.0	-	-
10 to 14 years	21,072	10,586	10,486	9,980	9,766	48	47	558	668	-	5	8.6	8.7	8.5	9.8	9.3	0.3	0.4	9.2	10.8	-	-
15 to 19 years	24,395	11,893	12,502	11,153	11,659	173	186	563	654	4	3	10.0	9.8	10.1	11.0	11.1	1.3	1.6	9.3	10.6	-	-
20 to 24 years	22,198	10,432	11,766	9,850	11,040	166	200	416	523	-	3	9.1	8.6	9.5	9.7	10.5	1.2	1.7	6.9	8.4	-	-
25 to 29 years	20,146	9,406	10,740	8,473	9,571	490	564	442	605	1	-	8.2	7.7	8.7	8.3	9.1	3.6	4.8	7.3	9.8	-	-
30 to 34 years	19,850	9,379	10,471	8,142	9,080	754	861	481	530	2	-	8.1	7.7	8.5	8.0	8.6	5.5	7.4	7.9	8.6	-	-
35 to 39 years	19,896	9,569	10,327	7,897	8,387	1,074	1,283	597	655	1	2	8.1	7.9	8.4	7.8	8.0	7.8	11.0	9.8	10.6	-	-
40 to 44 years	20,263	10,371	9,892	7,988	7,767	1,736	1,617	645	505	2	3	8.3	8.5	8.0	7.9	7.4	12.6	13.9	10.6	8.2	-	-
45 to 49 years	19,030	10,142	8,888	7,207	6,683	2,442	1,869	487	336	6	-	7.8	8.3	7.2	7.1	6.3	17.8	16.0	8.0	5.4	-	-
50 to 54 years	14,990	8,242	6,748	5,340	4,876	2,579	1,649	321	223	2	-	6.1	6.8	5.5	5.3	4.6	18.8	14.1	5.3	3.6	-	-
55 to 59 years	10,324	5,492	4,832	3,549	3,549	1,725	1,137	216	146	2	-	4.2	4.5	3.9	3.5	3.4	12.5	9.7	3.6	2.4	-	-
60 to 64 years	7,526	3,783	3,743	2,521	2,836	1,146	814	115	93	1	-	3.1	3.1	3.0	2.5	2.7	8.3	7.0	1.9	1.5	-	-
65 to 69 years	5,188	2,472	2,716	1,752	2,039	639	572	81	105	-	-	2.1	2.0	2.2	1.7	1.9	4.6	4.9	1.3	1.7	-	-
70 to 74 years	3,306	1,458	1,848	1,032	1,391	383	410	42	47	1	-	1.4	1.2	1.5	1.0	1.3	2.8	3.5	0.7	0.8	-	-
75 years and over	3,215	1,379	1,836	964	1,364	367	428	48	44	-	-	1.3	1.1	1.5	0.9	1.3	2.7	3.7	0.8	0.7	-	-
Under 1 year	3,283	1,680	1,603	1,597	1,500	-	-	83	102	-	1	1.3	1.4	1.3	1.6	1.4	-	-	1.4	1.6	-	-
21 years and over	161,542	80,105	81,437	62,814	66,393	13,465	11,354	3,808	3,682	18	8	66.0	65.9	66.1	61.8	63.0	97.9	97.3	62.8	59.4	-	-
Median age	30.3	30.8	29.8	27.4	27.5	49.9	47.8	30.0	26.6	-	-	-	-	-	-	-	-	-	-	-	-	-
ALBANY, N. Y.																						
All ages	130,577	62,864	67,713	53,392	58,994	7,960	7,218	1,454	1,475	58	26	100.0	100.0	100.0	100.0	100.0	100.0	100.0	100.0	100.0	-	-
Under 5 years	7,416	3,839	3,577	3,729	3,469	4	4	105	102	1	2	5.7	6.1	5.3	7.0	5.9	0.1	0.1	7.2	6.9	-	-
5 to 9 years	7,778	3,953	3,825	3,825	3,689	9	13	119	120	-	3	6.0	6.3	5.6	7.2	6.3	0.1	0.2	8.2	8.1	-	-
10 to 14 years	8,903	4,542	4,361	4,408	4,197	29	50	100	109	5	5	6.8	7.2	6.4	8.3	7.1	0.4	0.7	6.9	7.4	-	-
15 to 19 years	9,915	4,798	5,117	4,589	4,880	120	128	86	108	3	1	7.6	7.6	7.6	8.6	8.3	1.5	1.8	5.9	7.3	-	-
20 to 24 years	10,977	5,035	5,942	4,788	5,676	145	144	100	117	2	5	8.4	8.0	8.8	9.0	9.6	1.8	2.0	6.9	7.9	-	-
25 to 29 years	10,902	5,104	5,798	4,697	5,252	279	363	126	182	2	1	8.3	8.1	8.6	8.8	8.9	3.5	5.0	8.7	12.3	-	-
30 to 34 years	10,746	5,122	5,624	4,529	4,968	460	486	129	168	4	2	8.2	8.1	8.3	8.5	8.4	5.8	6.7	8.9	11.4	-	-
35 to 39 years	10,656	5,204	5,452	4,242	4,622	760	664	194	164	8	2	8.2	8.3	8.1	7.9	7.8	9.5	9.2	13.3	11.1	-	-
40 to 44 years	10,180	5,009	5,171	3,920	4,247	939	818	144	105	6	1	7.8	8.0	7.6	7.3	7.2	11.8	11.3	9.9	7.1	-	-
45 to 49 years	10,070	4,956	5,114	3,609	4,037	1,228	981	114	94	5	2	7.7	7.9	7.6	6.8	6.8	15.4	13.6	7.8	6.4	-	-
50 to 54 years	9,204	4,603	4,601	3,276	3,620	1,233	897	87	84	7	-	7.0	7.3	6.8	6.1	6.1	15.5	12.4	6.0	5.7	-	-
55 to 59 years	7,240	3,452	3,788	2,434	2,975	945	775	68	38	5	-	5.5	5.5	5.6	4.6	5.0	11.9	10.7	4.7	2.6	-	-
60 to 64 years	6,072	2,850	3,222	2,108	2,546	708	634	32	41	2	1	4.7	4.5	4.8	3.9	4.3	8.9	8.8	2.2	2.8	-	-
65 to 69 years	4,674	2,086	2,588	1,573	2,041	483	525	28	21	2	1	3.6	3.3	3.8	2.9	3.5	6.1	7.3	1.9	1.4	-	-
70 to 74 years	2,888	1,185	1,703	875	1,359	294	336	12	8	4	-	2.2	1.9	2.5	1.6	2.3	3.7	4.7	0.8	0.5	-	-
75 years and over	2,956	1,126	1,830	790	1,416	324	400	10	14	2	-	2.3	1.8	2.7	1.5	2.4	4.1	5.5	0.7	0.9	-	-
Under 1 year	1,419	756	663	739	647	-	-	17	16	-	-	1.1	1.2	1.0	1.4	1.1	-	-	1.2	1.1	-	-
21 years and over	94,458	44,793	49,665	35,955	41,656	7,765	6,982	1,024	1,013	49	14	72.3	71.3	73.3	67.3	70.6	97.6	96.7	70.4	68.7	-	-
Median age	34.4	34.1	34.7	30.7	32.3	50.0	49.8	33.5	30.0	-	-	-	-	-	-	-	-	-	-	-	-	-
ATLANTA, GA.																						
All ages	302,288	139,331	162,957	90,855	102,538	2,399	1,894	46,027	58,506	50	19	100.0	100.0	100.0	100.0	100.0	100.0	100.0	100.0	100.0	-	-
Under 5 years	20,767	10,400	10,367	6,557	6,523	2	2	3,839	3,842	2	-	6.9	7.5	6.4	7.2	6.4	0.1	0.1	8.3	6.6	-	-
5 to 9 years	20,988	10,454	10,534	6,413	6,428	13	5	4,023	4,096	5	5	6.9	7.5	6.5	7.1	6.3	0.5	0.3	8.7	7.0	-	-
10 to 14 years	23,055	11,366	11,689	7,121	7,119	13	7	4,231	4,562	1	1	7.6	8.2	7.2	7.8	6.9	0.5	0.4	9.2	7.8	-	-
15 to 19 years	26,959	12,508	14,451	8,151	9,119	33	34	4,319	5,297	5	1	8.9	9.0	8.9	9.0	8.9	1.4	1.8	9.4	9.1	-	-
20 to 24 years	30,675	13,316	17,359	8,943	10,676	58	43	4,310	6,638	5	2	10.1	9.6	10.7	9.8	10.4	2.4	2.3	9.4	11.3	-	-
25 to 29 years	32,173	14,460	17,713	9,336	10,433	86	95	5,037	7,185	1	-	10.6	10.4	10.9	10.3	10.2	3.6	5.0	10.9	12.3	-	-
30 to 34 years	29,395	13,341	16,054	8,969	10,084	131	159	4,236	5,808	5	3	9.7	9.6	9.9	9.9	9.8	5.5	8.4	9.2	9.9	-	-
35 to 39 years	27,227	12,180	15,047	7,893	8,845	213	212	4,072	5,989	2	1	9.0	8.7	9.2	8.7	8.6	8.9	11.2	8.8	10.2	-	-
40 to 44 years	22,363	10,382	11,981	6,599	7,394	288	234	3,488	4,350	7	3	7.4	7.5	7.4	7.3	7.2	12.0	12.4	7.6	7.4	-	-
45 to 49 years	18,771	8,670	10,101	5,737	6,441	337	221	2,592	3,438	4	1	6.2	6.2	6.2	6.3	6.3	14.0	11.7	5.6	5.9	-	-

TABLE 53.—AGE, BY RACE AND SEX, WITH PERCENT DISTRIBUTION BY AGE, FOR CITIES OF 100,000 OR MORE: 1940—Continued

[Percent not shown where less than 0.1 or where base is less than 100]

CITY AND AGE	NUMBER											PERCENT DISTRIBUTION										
	All classes			Native white		Foreign-born white		Negro		Other races		All classes			Native white		Foreign-born white		Negro		Other races	
	Total	Male	Female	Male	Female	Male	Female	Male	Female	Male	Female	Total	Male	Female	Male	Female	Male	Female	Male	Female	Male	Female
ATLANTA, GA.—Con.																						
50 to 54 years	15,183	7,258	7,925	4,768	5,415	373	211	2,110	2,298	7	1	5.0	5.2	4.9	5.2	5.3	15.5	11.1	4.6	3.9		
55 to 59 years	11,365	5,202	6,163	3,635	4,388	265	170	1,298	1,605	4		3.8	3.7	3.8	4.0	4.3	11.0	9.0	2.8	2.7		
60 to 64 years	8,652	3,893	4,759	2,788	3,531	229	177	876	1,050		1	2.9	2.8	2.9	3.1	3.4	9.5	9.3	1.9	1.8		
65 to 69 years	6,960	2,945	4,015	1,937	2,742	147	139	861	1,134			2.3	2.1	2.5	2.1	2.7	6.1	7.3	1.9	1.9		
70 to 74 years	4,014	1,620	2,394	1,102	1,716	114	97	403	581	1		1.3	1.2	1.5	1.2	1.7	4.8	5.1	0.9	1.0		
75 years and over	3,741	1,336	2,405	906	1,684	97	88	332	633	1		1.2	1.0	1.5	1.0	1.6	4.0	4.6	0.7	1.1		
Under 1 year	4,260	2,138	2,122	1,399	1,387			739	735			1.4	1.5	1.3	1.5	1.4			1.6	1.3		
21 years and over	204,102	91,928	112,174	60,888	71,070	2,325	1,838	28,678	39,254	37	12	67.5	66.0	68.8	67.0	69.3	96.9	97.0	62.3	67.1		
Median age	29.5	29.0	29.8	29.4	30.5	50.3	48.5	27.3	28.4													
BALTIMORE, MD.																						
All ages	859,100	422,916	436,184	310,249	321,487	31,557	29,412	80,683	85,160	427	125	100.0	100.0	100.0	100.0	100.0	100.0	100.0	100.0	100.0	100.0	100.0
Under 5 years	56,153	28,519	27,634	21,861	21,027	33	26	6,605	6,556	20	25	6.5	6.7	6.3	7.0	6.5	0.1	0.1	8.2	7.7	4.7	20.0
5 to 9 years	58,692	29,489	29,203	22,468	21,864	68	57	6,936	7,268	17	14	6.8	7.0	6.7	7.2	6.8	0.2	0.2	8.6	8.5	4.0	11.2
10 to 14 years	67,928	34,099	33,829	26,861	26,087	132	140	7,087	7,581	19	21	7.9	8.1	7.8	8.7	8.1	0.4	0.5	8.8	8.9	4.4	16.8
15 to 19 years	75,684	36,968	38,716	30,075	30,678	377	329	6,491	7,690	25	19	8.8	8.7	8.9	9.7	9.5	1.2	1.1	8.0	9.0	5.9	15.2
20 to 24 years	79,961	38,862	41,099	31,988	32,736	405	456	6,454	7,898	15	9	9.3	9.2	9.4	10.3	10.2	1.3	1.6	8.0	9.3	3.5	7.2
25 to 29 years	78,774	39,112	39,662	30,611	29,908	969	1,101	7,502	8,646	30	7	9.2	9.2	9.1	9.9	9.3	3.1	3.7	9.3	10.2	7.0	5.6
30 to 34 years	73,752	36,546	37,206	27,415	27,428	1,657	1,712	7,433	8,062	41	4	8.6	8.6	8.5	8.8	8.5	5.3	5.8	9.2	9.5	9.6	3.2
35 to 39 years	70,403	35,290	35,113	24,518	24,315	2,791	2,637	7,915	8,157	66	4	8.2	8.3	8.1	7.9	7.6	8.8	9.0	9.8	9.6	15.5	3.2
40 to 44 years	65,089	32,961	32,128	22,211	22,513	3,724	3,246	6,973	6,364	53	5	7.6	7.8	7.4	7.2	7.0	11.8	11.0	8.6	7.5	12.4	4.0
45 to 49 years	58,417	29,467	28,950	19,433	20,170	4,480	3,787	5,516	4,984	38	9	6.8	7.0	6.6	6.3	6.3	14.2	12.9	6.8	5.9	8.9	7.2
50 to 54 years	49,948	25,187	24,761	16,095	17,126	4,807	3,750	4,255	3,880	30	5	5.8	6.0	5.7	5.2	5.3	15.2	12.7	5.3	4.6	7.0	4.0
55 to 59 years	38,206	18,475	19,731	11,930	13,756	3,830	3,370	2,698	2,603	17	2	4.4	4.4	4.5	3.8	4.3	12.1	11.5	3.3	3.1	4.0	1.6
60 to 64 years	30,675	14,224	16,451	9,271	11,568	3,093	2,992	1,832	1,890	28	1	3.6	3.4	3.8	3.0	3.6	9.8	10.2	2.3	2.2	6.6	0.8
65 to 69 years	23,963	10,720	13,243	6,928	9,126	2,234	2,399	1,541	1,718	17		2.8	2.5	3.0	2.2	2.8	7.1	8.2	1.9	2.0	4.0	
70 to 74 years	15,839	6,821	9,018	4,521	6,383	1,489	1,693	806	942	5		1.8	1.6	2.1	1.5	2.0	4.7	5.8	1.0	1.1	1.2	
75 years and over	15,616	6,176	9,440	4,063	6,802	1,468	1,717	639	921	6		1.8	1.5	2.2	1.3	2.1	4.7	5.8	0.8	1.1	1.4	
Under 1 year	10,217	5,182	5,035	3,996	3,867	1	2	1,178	1,163	7	3	1.2	1.2	1.2	1.3	1.2			1.5	1.4	1.6	2.4
21 years and over	584,776	286,271	298,505	202,740	215,229	30,851	28,760	52,335	54,471	345	45	68.1	67.7	68.4	65.3	66.9	97.8	97.8	64.9	64.0	80.8	36.0
Median age	30.8	30.6	31.1	28.6	29.7	51.2	51.6	29.5	28.2	38.5	15.7											
BIRMINGHAM, ALA.																						
All ages	267,583	127,420	140,163	74,439	79,758	2,477	1,948	50,493	58,445	11	12	100.0	100.0	100.0	100.0	100.0	100.0	100.0	100.0	100.0		
Under 5 years	19,223	9,583	9,640	5,366	5,175	1	1	4,215	4,461	1	3	7.2	7.5	6.9	7.2	6.5		0.1	8.3	7.6		
5 to 9 years	19,983	10,022	9,961	5,425	5,150	4	3	4,593	4,806		2	7.5	7.9	7.1	7.3	6.5	0.2	0.2	9.1	8.2		
10 to 14 years	23,362	11,629	11,733	6,589	6,489	9	6	5,031	5,237		1	8.7	9.1	8.4	8.9	8.1	0.4	0.3	10.0	9.0		
15 to 19 years	24,957	11,823	13,134	7,190	7,584	24	21	4,608	5,529	1		9.3	9.3	9.4	9.7	9.5	1.0	1.1	9.1	9.5		
20 to 24 years	25,646	11,333	14,313	7,086	8,245	31	26	4,216	6,041		1	9.6	8.9	10.2	9.5	10.3	1.3	1.3	8.3	10.3		
25 to 29 years	26,712	12,099	14,613	7,081	7,926	65	65	4,952	6,622	1		10.0	9.5	10.4	9.5	9.9	2.6	3.3	9.8	11.3		
30 to 34 years	24,688	11,262	13,426	6,652	7,543	110	99	4,500	5,782		2	9.2	8.8	9.6	8.9	9.5	4.4	5.1	8.9	9.9		
35 to 39 years	24,434	11,402	13,032	6,319	6,814	198	186	4,884	6,032	1		9.1	8.9	9.3	8.5	8.5	8.0	9.5	9.7	10.3		
40 to 44 years	20,115	9,832	10,283	5,534	5,869	237	175	4,060	4,237	1	2	7.5	7.7	7.3	7.4	7.4	9.6	9.0	8.0	7.2		
45 to 49 years	16,771	8,322	8,449	4,782	5,038	308	237	3,229	3,174	3		6.3	6.5	6.0	6.4	6.3	12.4	12.2	6.4	5.4		
50 to 54 years	13,259	6,712	6,547	4,093	4,172	369	246	2,247	2,128	3	1	5.0	5.3	4.7	5.5	5.2	14.9	12.6	4.4	3.6		
55 to 59 years	9,597	4,729	4,868	3,015	3,187	358	268	1,356	1,413			3.6	3.7	3.5	4.1	4.0	14.5	13.8	2.7	2.4		
60 to 64 years	7,326	3,525	3,801	2,357	2,539	268	204	900	1,058			2.7	2.8	2.7	3.2	3.2	10.8	10.5	1.8	1.8		
65 to 69 years	5,509	2,545	2,964	1,431	1,838	214	174	900	952			2.1	2.0	2.1	1.9	2.3	8.6	8.8	1.8	1.6		
70 to 74 years	3,132	1,447	1,685	845	1,068	140	105	462	512			1.2	1.1	1.2	1.1	1.3	5.7	5.4	0.9	0.9		
75 years and over	2,869	1,155	1,714	674	1,121	141	132	340	461			1.1	0.9	1.2	0.9	1.4	5.7	6.8	0.7	0.8		
Under 1 year	4,022	2,008	2,014	1,197	1,111			811	902		1	1.5	1.6	1.4	1.6	1.4			1.6	1.5		
21 years and over	174,787	82,161	92,626	48,517	53,550	2,432	1,913	31,203	37,157	9	6	65.3	64.5	66.1	65.2	67.1	98.2	98.2	61.8	63.6		
Median age	28.9	28.9	28.9	28.9	29.6	53.4	53.2	27.6	27.4													

UNITED STATES SUMMARY—PRINCIPAL CITIES

BOSTON, MASS.																						
All ages	770,816	373,147	397,669	274,671	289,931	85,881	94,983	11,305	12,374	1,290	381	100.0	100.0	100.0	100.0	100.0	100.0	100.0	100.0	100.0	100.0	100.0
Under 5 years	49,706	25,261	24,445	24,408	23,606	46	57	758	739	49	43	6.4	6.8	6.1	8.9	8.1	0.1	0.1	6.7	6.0	3.8	11.3
5 to 9 years	53,870	27,505	26,365	26,488	25,335	134	127	827	847	56	56	7.0	7.4	6.6	9.6	8.7	0.2	0.1	7.3	6.8	4.3	14.7
10 to 14 years	61,200	30,821	30,379	29,518	28,992	356	368	881	975	66	44	7.9	8.3	7.6	10.7	10.0	0.4	0.4	7.8	7.9	5.1	11.5
15 to 19 years	65,753	32,495	33,258	30,354	31,013	1,126	1,127	920	1,067	95	51	8.5	8.7	8.4	11.1	10.7	1.3	1.2	8.1	8.6	7.4	13.4
20 to 24 years	67,323	31,945	35,378	29,628	32,687	1,399	1,714	846	952	72	25	8.7	8.6	8.9	10.8	11.3	1.6	1.8	7.5	7.7	5.6	6.6
25 to 29 years	65,673	30,995	34,678	27,230	29,716	2,787	3,917	876	1,019	102	26	8.5	8.3	8.7	9.9	10.2	3.2	4.1	7.7	8.2	7.9	6.8
30 to 34 years	60,278	28,655	31,623	22,702	23,873	5.004	6,748	858	973	91	29	7.8	7.7	8.0	8.3	8.2	5.8	7.1	7.6	7.9	7.1	7.6
35 to 39 years	57,430	27,415	30,015	18,552	19,855	7,810	9,025	931	1,113	122	22	7.5	7.3	7.5	6.8	6.8	9.1	9.5	8.2	9.0	9.5	5.8
40 to 44 years	56,070	27,323	28,747	16,516	17,232	9,569	10,387	1,043	1,098	195	30	7.3	7.3	7.2	6.0	5.9	11.1	10.9	9.2	8.9	15.1	7.9
45 to 49 years	53,740	26,638	27,102	13,339	13,964	12,267	12,174	912	945	120	19	7.0	7.1	6.8	4.9	4.8	14.3	12.8	8.1	7.6	9.3	5.0
50 to 54 years	47,131	23,536	23,595	10,368	11,056	12,351	11,790	743	737	74	12	6.1	6.3	5.9	3.8	3.8	14.4	12.4	6.6	6.0	5.7	3.1
55 to 59 years	38,783	19,129	19,654	7,776	8,784	10,647	10,310	612	551	94	9	5.0	5.1	4.9	2.8	3.0	12.4	10.9	5.4	4.5	7.3	2.4
60 to 64 years	32,278	14,992	17,286	6,357	7,601	8,118	9,193	454	486	63	6	4.2	4.0	4.3	2.3	2.6	9.5	9.7	4.0	3.9	4.9	1.6
65 to 69 years	27,171	12,005	15,166	5,229	6,905	6,372	7.817	354	438	50	6	3.5	3.2	3.8	1.9	2.4	7.4	8.2	3.1	3.5	3.9	1.6
70 to 74 years	17,741	7,792	9,949	3,358	4,495	4,248	5,239	157	213	29	2	2.3	2.1	2.5	1.2	1.6	4.9	5.5	1.4	1.7	2.2	0.5
75 years and over	16.669	6,640	10,029	2,848	4,817	3,647	4,990	133	221	12	1	2.2	1.8	2.5	1.0	1.7	4.2	5.3	1.2	1.8	0.9	0.3
Under 1 year	9,322	4,669	4,653	4,528	4,504	2	5	132	138	7	6	1.2	1.3	1.2	1.6	1.6	---	---	1.2	1.1	0.5	1.6
21 years and over	526,925	250,689	276,236	158,030	174,520	83,896	92,963	7,754	8,574	1,009	179	68.4	67.2	69.5	57.5	60.2	97.7	97.9	68.6	69.3	78.2	47.0
Median age	31.8	31.3	32.3	24.5	25.6	51.0	50.8	33.2	33.0	39.7	19.7	---	---	---	---	---	---	---	---	---	---	---
BRIDGEPORT, CONN.																						
All ages	147,121	73,188	73,933	54,132	55,751	17,140	16,291	1,894	1,873	22	18	100.0	100.0	100.0	100.0	100.0	100.0	100.0	100.0	100.0	---	---
Under 5 years	9,067	4,659	4,408	4,481	4,225	12	12	165	169	1	2	6.2	6.4	6.0	8.3	7.6	0.1	0.1	8.7	9.0	---	---
5 to 9 years	9,463	4,795	4,668	4,549	4,455	35	25	210	185	1	3	6.4	6.6	6.3	8.4	8.0	0.2	0.2	11.1	9.9	---	---
10 to 14 years	11,546	5,828	5,718	5,557	5,456	95	85	176	175	---	2	7.8	8.0	7.7	10.3	9.8	0.6	0.5	9.3	9.3	---	---
15 to 19 years	13,375	6,635	6,740	6,259	6,337	226	217	150	184	---	2	9.1	9.1	9.1	11.6	11.4	1.3	1.3	7.9	9.8	---	---
20 to 24 years	15,095	7,347	7,748	7,019	7,359	215	251	111	138	2	---	10.3	10.0	10.5	13.0	13.2	1.3	1.5	5.9	7.4	---	---
25 to 29 years	14,126	7,110	7,016	6,387	6,221	554	616	168	176	1	3	9.6	9.7	9.5	11.8	11.2	3.2	3.8	8.9	9.4	---	---
30 to 34 years	11,550	5,741	5,809	4,693	4,664	913	974	135	170	---	1	7.9	7.8	7.9	8.7	8.4	5.3	6.0	7.1	9.1	---	---
35 to 39 years	10,081	4,860	5,221	3,384	3,626	1,287	1,424	185	169	4	2	6.9	6.6	7.1	6.3	6.5	7.5	8.7	9.8	9.0	---	---
40 to 44 years	10,284	4,986	5,298	2,867	3,103	1,959	2,072	158	121	2	2	7.0	6.8	7.2	5.3	5.6	11.4	12.7	8.3	6.5	---	---
45 to 49 years	10,661	5,430	5,231	2,561	2,699	2,728	2,432	139	100	2	---	7.2	7.4	7.1	4.7	4.8	15.9	14.9	7.3	5.3	---	---
50 to 54 years	9,644	5,022	4,622	1,951	2,075	2,950	2,454	118	93	3	---	6.6	6.9	6.3	3.6	3.7	17.2	15.1	6.2	5.0	---	---
55 to 59 years	6,978	3,649	3,329	1,379	1,549	2,195	1,715	73	65	2	---	4.7	5.0	4.5	2.5	2.8	12.8	10.5	3.9	3.5	---	---
60 to 64 years	5,488	2,709	2,779	1,079	1,295	1,589	1,439	39	45	2	---	3.7	3.7	3.8	2.0	2.3	9.3	8.8	2.1	2.4	---	---
65 to 69 years	4,318	2,027	2,291	850	1,110	1,144	1,132	32	48	1	1	2.9	2.8	3.1	1.6	2.0	6.7	6.9	1.7	2.6	---	---
70 to 74 years	2,852	1,289	1,563	559	770	707	772	23	21	---	---	1.9	1.8	2.1	1.0	1.4	4.1	4.7	1.2	1.1	---	---
75 years and over	2,593	1,101	1,492	557	807	531	671	12	14	1	---	1.8	1.5	2.0	1.0	1.4	3.1	4.1	0.6	0.7	---	---
Under 1 year	1,812	938	874	908	844	1	---	29	30	---	---	1.2	1.3	1.2	1.7	1.5	---	---	1.5	1.6	---	---
21 years and over	100,635	49,758	50,877	31,862	33,838	16,711	15,897	1,165	1,133	20	9	68.4	68.0	68.8	58.9	60.7	97.5	97.6	61.5	60.5	---	---
Median age	30.4	30.2	30.6	24.4	25.0	50.9	50.1	29.0	27.4	---	---	---	---	---	---	---	---	---	---	---	---	---
BUFFALO, N. Y.																						
All ages	575,901	283,767	292,134	226,924	238,905	47,709	44,080	8,813	8,881	321	268	100.0	100.0	100.0	100.0	100.0	100.0	100.0	100.0	100.0	100.0	100.0
Under 5 years	37,336	18,871	18,465	18,121	17,687	31	24	687	722	32	32	6.5	6.7	6.3	8.0	7.4	0.1	0.1	7.8	8.1	10.0	11.9
5 to 9 years	39,489	19,897	19,592	19,056	18,763	93	95	710	710	38	24	6.9	7.0	6.7	8.4	7.9	0.2	0.2	8.1	8.0	11.8	9.0
10 to 14 years	46,568	23,182	23,386	22,163	22,277	226	253	760	826	33	30	8.1	8.2	8.0	9.8	9.3	0.5	0.6	8.6	9.3	10.3	11.2
15 to 19 years	50,879	24,897	25,982	23,414	24,451	787	811	677	704	19	16	8.8	8.8	8.9	10.3	10.2	1.6	1.8	7.7	7.9	5.9	6.0
20 to 24 years	51,907	24,868	27,039	23,531	25,273	788	985	534	746	15	35	9.0	8.8	9.3	10.4	10.6	1.7	2.2	6.1	8.4	4.7	13.1
25 to 29 years	49,592	24,085	25,507	21,854	22,752	1,576	1,879	628	841	27	35	8.6	8.5	8.7	9.6	9.5	3.3	4.3	7.1	9.5	8.4	13.1
30 to 34 years	45,347	21,963	23,384	18,422	19,445	2,695	3,012	816	902	30	25	7.9	7.7	8.0	8.1	8.1	5.6	6.8	9.3	10.2	9.3	9.3
35 to 39 years	43,552	21,504	22,048	16,274	17,012	4,121	4,035	1,076	980	33	21	7.6	7.6	7.5	7.2	7.1	8.6	9.2	12.2	11.0	10.3	7.8
40 to 44 years	44,243	21,839	22,404	15,568	16,632	5,229	4,866	1,014	889	28	17	7.7	7.7	7.7	6.9	7.0	11.0	11.0	11.5	10.0	8.7	6.3
45 to 49 years	43,030	21,874	21,156	14,185	14,719	6,903	5,831	757	593	29	13	7.5	7.7	7.2	6.3	6.2	14.5	13.2	8.6	6.7	9.0	4.9
50 to 54 years	37,047	19,276	17,771	11,258	11,862	7,509	5,556	496	343	13	10	6.4	6.8	6.1	5.0	5.0	15.7	12.6	5.6	3.9	4.0	3.7
55 to 59 years	27,802	14,142	13,660	8,062	8,721	5,777	4,710	297	224	6	5	4.8	5.0	4.7	3.6	3.7	12.1	10.7	3.4	2.5	1.9	1.9
60 to 64 years	21,552	10,513	11,039	5,913	6,775	4,437	4,108	155	155	8	1	3.7	3.7	3.8	2.6	2.8	9.3	9.3	1.8	1.7	2.5	0.4
65 to 69 years	16,040	7,458	8,582	4,226	5,272	3,122	3,185	104	125	6	---	2.8	2.6	2.9	1.9	2.2	6.5	7.2	1.2	1.4	1.9	---
70 to 74 years	11,037	4,985	6,052	2,668	3,625	2,255	2,355	60	71	2	1	1.9	1.8	2.1	1.2	1.5	4.7	5.3	0.7	0.8	0.6	0.4
75 years and over	10,480	4,413	6,067	2,209	3,639	2,160	2,375	42	50	2	3	1.8	1.6	2.1	1.0	1.5	4.5	5.4	0.5	0.6	0.6	1.1
Under 1 year	7,314	3,664	3,650	3,533	3,503	---	2	126	138	5	7	1.3	1.3	1.2	1.6	1.5	---	---	1.4	1.6	1.6	2.6
21 years and over	391,200	191,961	199,239	139,498	150,634	46,389	42,679	5,877	5,766	197	160	67.9	67.6	68.2	61.5	63.1	97.2	96.8	66.7	64.9	61.4	59.7
Median age	31.3	31.4	31.3	26.6	27.4	50.9	50.2	32.5	29.4	29.4	24.6	---	---	---	---	---	---	---	---	---	---	---

CHARACTERISTICS OF THE POPULATION

TABLE 53.—AGE, BY RACE AND SEX, WITH PERCENT DISTRIBUTION BY AGE, FOR CITIES OF 100,000 OR MORE: 1940—Continued

[Percent not shown where less than 0.1 or where base is less than 100]

NUMBER

CITY AND AGE	All classes			Native white		Foreign-born white		Negro		Other races	
	Total	Male	Female	Male	Female	Male	Female	Male	Female	Male	Female
CAMBRIDGE, MASS.											
All ages	110,879	52,479	58,400	38,751	42,546	11,325	13,233	2,280	2,578	123	43
Under 5 years	7,374	3,718	3,656	3,541	3,474	13	17	160	160	4	5
5 to 9 years	7,726	3,839	3,887	3,628	3,680	20	23	187	178	4	6
10 to 14 years	8,776	4,437	4,339	4,103	4,030	79	46	248	257	7	6
15 to 19 years	9,651	4,730	4,921	4,203	4,388	231	225	279	301	17	7
20 to 24 years	10,029	4,852	5,177	4,285	4,610	322	368	216	197	29	2
25 to 29 years	10,061	4,816	5,245	4,134	4,341	526	732	142	167	14	5
30 to 34 years	8,964	4,226	4,738	3,353	3,478	726	1,082	135	175	12	3
35 to 39 years	8,138	3,896	4,242	2,685	2,785	1,079	1,278	120	176	12	3
40 to 44 years	7,807	3,617	4,190	2,170	2,484	1,269	1,500	170	205	8	1
45 to 49 years	7,161	3,378	3,783	1,715	2,008	1,503	1,595	154	178	6	2
50 to 54 years	6,454	3,057	3,397	1,351	1,736	1,569	1,491	135	168	2	2
55 to 59 years	5,388	2,429	2,959	1,120	1,440	1,198	1,374	107	144	4	1
60 to 64 years	4,634	2,059	2,575	907	1,371	1,051	1,106	97	98	4	
65 to 69 years	3,707	1,525	2,182	708	1,110	758	987	59	85		
70 to 74 years	2,568	1,011	1,557	456	772	521	744	34	41		
75 years and over	2,441	889	1,552	392	839	460	665	37	48		
Under 1 year	1,392	718	674	684	653	2	1	31	19	1	1
21 years and over	75,431	34,839	40,592	22,485	26,098	10,908	12,840	1,363	1,635	83	19
Median age	31.0	29.8	32.1	24.6	26.3	49.6	49.2	26.8	30.8	25.2	
CAMDEN, N. J.											
All ages	117,536	58,802	58,734	44,817	45,182	7,757	7,239	6,182	6,296	46	17
Under 5 years	7,965	4,100	3,865	3,544	3,294	1	3	554	567	1	1
5 to 9 years	8,189	4,185	4,004	3,586	3,453	6	10	592	540	1	1
10 to 14 years	10,078	5,045	5,033	4,378	4,388	32	24	632	619	3	2
15 to 19 years	11,158	5,537	5,621	4,873	4,952	92	92	565	575	7	2
20 to 24 years	11,795	5,693	6,102	5,097	5,429	113	98	481	574	2	1
25 to 29 years	10,563	5,244	5,319	4,568	4,556	212	235	461	526	3	2
30 to 34 years	8,872	4,484	4,388	3,691	3,493	364	397	423	498	6	
35 to 39 years	8,188	3,971	4,217	2,897	3,015	542	634	530	568	2	
40 to 44 years	8,315	4,117	4,198	2,703	2,742	937	950	471	499	6	7
45 to 49 years	8,441	4,326	4,115	2,523	2,520	1,360	1,195	441	399	2	1
50 to 54 years	7,197	3,783	3,414	2,107	2,058	1,336	1,071	331	285	9	
55 to 59 years	5,357	2,790	2,567	1,482	1,572	1,049	789	257	206	2	
60 to 64 years	4,300	2,200	2,100	1,314	1,327	705	625	181	148		
65 to 69 years	3,145	1,500	1,645	914	1,035	468	449	116	161	2	
70 to 74 years	2,053	962	1,091	580	688	307	343	75	60		
75 years and over	1,920	865	1,055	560	660	233	324	72	71		
Under 1 year	1,575	821	754	711	657			110	97		
21 years and over	77,743	38,817	38,926	27,440	27,953	7,598	7,087	3,745	3,875	34	11
Median age	29.5	29.6	29.5	26.0	26.2	50.8	49.9	27.9	27.6		
CANTON, OHIO											
All ages	108,401	54,285	54,116	45,868	47,382	6,383	4,686	2,002	2,039	32	9
Under 5 years	7,744	3,898	3,846	3,722	3,656	2	1	172	188	2	1
5 to 9 years	7,186	3,679	3,507	3,474	3,271	7	14	195	219	3	3
10 to 14 years	8,570	4,295	4,275	4,072	4,052	24	35	197	187	2	1
15 to 19 years	10,184	4,978	5,206	4,739	4,967	82	64	151	174	6	1
20 to 24 years	10,254	4,881	5,373	4,655	5,109	96	73	127	191	3	
25 to 29 years	9,353	4,532	4,821	4,181	4,378	201	246	147	195	3	2
30 to 34 years	8,256	4,054	4,202	3,609	3,655	277	346	168	201		
35 to 39 years	8,001	3,984	4,017	3,217	3,333	564	477	202	207	1	
40 to 44 years	7,992	4,151	3,841	3,039	3,072	885	616	222	152	5	1
45 to 49 years	7,939	4,250	3,689	2,853	2,854	1,217	721	175	114	5	
50 to 54 years	6,655	3,552	3,103	2,335	2,383	1,129	648	88	72		
55 to 59 years	5,254	2,766	2,488	1,906	1,960	787	471	72	57	1	
60 to 64 years	4,150	2,070	2,080	1,560	1,674	474	375	36	31		

PERCENT DISTRIBUTION

CITY AND AGE	All classes			Native white		Foreign-born white		Negro		Other races	
	Total	Male	Female	Male	Female	Male	Female	Male	Female	Male	Female
CAMBRIDGE, MASS.											
All ages	100.0	100.0	100.0	100.0	100.0	100.0	100.0	100.0	100.0	100.0	
Under 5 years	6.7	7.1	6.3	9.1	8.2	0.1	0.1	7.0	6.2	3.3	
5 to 9 years	7.0	7.3	6.7	9.4	8.6	0.2	0.2	8.2	6.9	3.3	
10 to 14 years	7.9	8.5	7.4	10.6	9.5	0.7	0.3	10.9	10.0	5.7	
15 to 19 years	8.7	9.0	8.4	10.8	10.3	2.0	1.7	12.2	11.7	13.8	
20 to 24 years	9.0	9.2	8.9	11.1	10.8	2.8	2.8	9.5	7.6	23.6	
25 to 29 years	9.1	9.2	9.0	10.7	10.2	4.6	5.5	6.2	6.5	11.4	
30 to 34 years	8.1	8.1	8.1	8.7	8.2	6.4	8.2	5.9	6.8	9.8	
35 to 39 years	7.3	7.4	7.3	6.9	6.5	9.5	9.7	5.3	6.8	9.8	
40 to 44 years	7.0	6.9	7.2	5.6	5.8	11.2	11.3	7.5	8.0	6.5	
45 to 49 years	6.5	6.4	6.5	4.4	4.7	13.3	12.1	6.8	6.9	4.9	
50 to 54 years	5.8	5.8	5.8	3.5	4.1	13.9	11.3	5.9	6.5	1.6	
55 to 59 years	4.9	4.6	5.1	2.9	3.4	10.6	10.4	4.7	5.3	3.3	
60 to 64 years	4.2	3.9	4.4	2.3	3.2	9.3	8.4	4.3	3.8	3.3	
65 to 69 years	3.3	2.9	3.7	1.8	2.6	6.7	7.5	2.6	3.3		
70 to 74 years	2.3	1.9	2.7	1.2	1.8	4.6	5.6	1.5	1.6		
75 years and over	2.2	1.7	2.7	1.0	2.0	4.1	5.0	1.6	1.9		
Under 1 year	1.3	1.4	1.2	1.8	1.5			1.4	0.7	0.8	
21 years and over	68.0	66.4	69.5	58.0	61.3	96.3	97.0	59.8	63.4	67.5	
Median age											
CAMDEN, N. J.											
All ages	100.0	100.0	100.0	100.0	100.0	100.0	100.0	100.0	100.0		
Under 5 years	6.8	7.0	6.6	7.9	7.3			9.0	9.0		
5 to 9 years	7.0	7.1	6.8	8.0	7.6	0.1	0.1	9.6	8.6		
10 to 14 years	8.6	8.6	8.6	9.8	9.7	0.4	0.3	10.2	9.8		
15 to 19 years	9.5	9.4	9.6	10.9	11.0	1.2	1.3	9.1	9.1		
20 to 24 years	10.0	9.7	10.4	11.4	12.0	1.5	1.4	7.8	9.1		
25 to 29 years	9.0	8.9	9.1	10.2	10.1	2.7	3.2	7.5	8.4		
30 to 34 years	7.5	7.6	7.5	8.2	7.7	4.7	5.5	6.8	7.9		
35 to 39 years	7.0	6.8	7.2	6.5	6.7	7.0	8.8	8.6	9.0		
40 to 44 years	7.1	7.0	7.1	6.0	6.1	12.1	13.1	7.6	7.9		
45 to 49 years	7.2	7.4	7.0	5.6	5.6	17.5	16.5	7.1	6.3		
50 to 54 years	6.1	6.4	5.8	4.7	4.6	17.2	14.8	5.4	4.5		
55 to 59 years	4.6	4.7	4.4	3.3	3.5	13.5	10.9	4.2	3.3		
60 to 64 years	3.7	3.7	3.6	2.9	2.9	9.1	8.6	2.9	2.4		
65 to 69 years	2.7	2.6	2.8	2.0	2.3	6.0	6.2	1.9	2.6		
70 to 74 years	1.7	1.6	1.9	1.3	1.5	4.0	4.7	1.2	1.0		
75 years and over	1.6	1.5	1.8	1.2	1.5	3.0	4.5	1.2	1.1		
Under 1 year	1.3	1.4	1.3	1.6	1.5			1.8	1.5		
21 years and over	66.1	66.0	66.3	61.2	61.9	98.0	97.9	60.6	61.5		
Median age											
CANTON, OHIO											
All ages	100.0	100.0	100.0	100.0	100.0	100.0	100.0	100.0	100.0		
Under 5 years	7.1	7.2	7.1	8.1	7.7			8.6	9.2		
5 to 9 years	6.6	6.8	6.5	7.6	6.9	0.1	0.3	9.7	10.7		
10 to 14 years	7.9	7.9	7.9	8.9	8.6	0.4	0.7	9.8	9.2		
15 to 19 years	9.4	9.2	9.6	10.3	10.5	1.3	1.4	7.5	8.5		
20 to 24 years	9.5	9.0	9.9	10.1	10.8	1.5	1.6	6.3	9.4		
25 to 29 years	8.6	8.3	8.9	9.1	9.2	3.1	5.2	7.3	9.6		
30 to 34 years	7.6	7.5	7.8	7.9	7.7	4.3	7.4	8.4	9.9		
35 to 39 years	7.4	7.3	7.4	7.0	7.0	8.8	10.2	10.1	10.2		
40 to 44 years	7.4	7.6	7.1	6.6	6.5	13.9	13.1	11.1	7.5		
45 to 49 years	7.3	7.8	6.8	6.2	6.0	19.1	15.4	8.7	5.6		
50 to 54 years	6.1	6.5	5.7	5.1	5.0	17.7	13.8	4.4	3.5		
55 to 59 years	4.8	5.1	4.6	4.2	4.1	12.3	10.1	3.6	2.8		
60 to 64 years	3.8	3.8	3.8	3.4	3.5	7.4	8.0	1.8	1.5		

65 to 69 years	2,985	1,430	1,555	1,106	1,293	292	238	32	24			2.8	2.6	2.9	2.4	2.7	4.6	5.1	1.6	1.2		
70 to 74 years	1,961	920	1,041	736	852	175	176	8	13	1		1.8	1.7	1.9	1.6	1.8	2.7	3.8	0.4	0.6		
75 years and over	1,917	845	1,072	664	873	171	185	10	14			1.8	1.6	2.0	1.4	1.8	2.7	3.9	0.5	0.7		
Under 1 year	1,501	767	734	733	693			34	41			1.4	1.4	1.4	1.6	1.5			1.7	2.0		
21 years and over	72,722	36,550	36,172	29,015	30,392	6,249	4,551	1,267	1,226	19	3	67.1	67.3	66.8	63.3	64.1	97.9	97.1	63.3	60.1		
Median age	30.6	31.1	30.0	27.7	28.0	49.3	48.3	30.4	26.6													
CHARLOTTE, N. C.																						
All ages	100,899	47,662	53,237	32,832	35,751	506	386	14,309	17,094	15	6	100.0	100.0	100.0	100.0	100.0	100.0	100.0	100.0	100.0		
Under 5 years	7,890	3,984	3,906	2,681	2,610	1	2	1,301	1,293	1	1	7.8	8.4	7.3	8.2	7.3	0.2	0.5	9.1	7.6		
5 to 9 years	7,568	3,784	3,784	2,519	2,495	3	2	1,262	1,286		1	7.5	7.9	7.1	7.7	7.0	0.6	0.5	8.8	7.5		
10 to 14 years	8,465	4,133	4,332	2,851	2,883	3	3	1,277	1,445	2	1	8.4	8.7	8.1	8.7	8.1	0.6	0.8	8.9	8.5		
15 to 19 years	9,756	4,438	5,318	3,005	3,583	11	11	1,417	1,724	5		9.7	9.3	10.0	9.2	10.0	2.2	2.8	9.9	10.1		
20 to 24 years	11,584	5,075	6,509	3,529	4,283	15	9	1,531	2,216		1	11.5	10.6	12.2	10.7	12.0	3.0	2.3	10.7	13.0		
25 to 29 years	11,366	5,257	6,109	3,537	3,886	26	26	1,693	2,197	1		11.3	11.0	11.5	10.8	10.9	5.1	6.7	11.8	12.9		
30 to 34 years	9,795	4,563	5,232	3,212	3,549	30	31	1,319	1,651	2	1	9.7	9.6	9.8	9.8	9.9	5.9	8.0	9.2	9.7		
35 to 39 years	9,087	4,295	4,792	2,905	3,089	63	47	1,326	1,655	1	1	9.0	9.0	9.0	8.8	8.6	12.5	12.2	9.3	9.7		
40 to 44 years	7,169	3,515	3,654	2,423	2,510	80	51	1,011	1,093	1		7.1	7.4	6.9	7.4	7.0	15.8	13.2	7.1	6.4		
45 to 49 years	5,477	2,751	2,726	1,976	1,875	68	37	706	814	1		5.4	5.8	5.1	6.0	5.2	13.4	9.6	4.9	4.8		
50 to 54 years	4,045	1,997	2,048	1,425	1,506	65	43	506	499	1		4.0	4.2	3.8	4.3	4.2	12.8	11.1	3.5	2.9		
55 to 59 years	3,071	1,454	1,617	1,093	1,200	46	32	315	385			3.0	3.1	3.0	3.3	3.4	9.1	8.3	2.2	2.3		
60 to 64 years	2,139	974	1,165	742	896	32	33	200	236			2.1	2.0	2.2	2.3	2.5	6.3	8.5	1.4	1.4		
65 to 69 years	1,749	757	992	462	636	30	28	265	328			1.7	1.6	1.9	1.4	1.8	5.9	7.3	1.9	1.9		
70 to 74 years	954	389	565	257	385	20	20	112	160			0.9	0.8	1.1	0.8	1.1	4.0	5.2	0.8	0.9		
75 years and over	784	296	488	215	365	13	11	68	112			0.8	0.6	0.9	0.7	1.0	2.6	2.8	0.5	0.7		
Under 1 year	1,651	865	786	588	559			277	226		1	1.6	1.8	1.5	1.8	1.6			1.9	1.3		
21 years and over	64,845	30,359	34,486	21,118	23,273	488	366	8,746	10,845	7	2	64.3	63.7	64.8	64.3	65.1	96.4	94.8	61.1	63.4		
Median age	27.3	27.3	27.3	27.6	27.6	46.5	46.5	26.1	26.3													
CHATTANOOGA, TENN.																						
All ages	128,163	61,246	66,917	43,593	47,035	609	505	17,037	19,367	7	10	100.0	100.0	100.0	100.0	100.0	100.0	100.0	100.0	100.0		
Under 5 years	9,801	4,884	4,917	3,563	3,528		1	1,320	1,387	1	1	7.6	8.0	7.3	8.2	7.5		0.2	7.7	7.2		
5 to 9 years	10,037	5,092	4,945	3,590	3,533	3	2	1,498	1,409	1	1	7.8	8.3	7.4	8.2	7.5	0.5	0.4	8.8	7.3		
10 to 14 years	11,092	5,540	5,552	4,021	3,899	8	1	1,510	1,652	1		8.7	9.0	8.3	9.2	8.3	1.3	0.2	8.9	8.5		
15 to 19 years	12,272	5,859	6,413	4,253	4,593	8	13	1,598	1,804		3	9.6	9.6	9.6	9.8	9.8	1.3	2.6	9.4	9.3		
20 to 24 years	12,520	5,637	6,883	4,094	4,812	17	17	1,526	2,053		1	9.8	9.2	10.3	9.4	10.2	2.8	3.4	9.0	10.6		
25 to 29 years	12,861	5,933	6,928	4,193	4,696	18	23	1,720	2,209	2		10.0	9.7	10.4	9.6	10.0	3.0	4.6	10.1	11.4		
30 to 34 years	11,964	5,633	6,331	4,094	4,364	27	26	1,512	1,941			9.3	9.2	9.5	9.4	9.3	4.4	5.1	8.9	10.0		
35 to 39 years	11,033	5,191	5,842	3,499	3,865	52	56	1,639	1,919	1	2	8.6	8.5	8.7	8.0	8.2	8.5	11.1	9.6	9.9		
40 to 44 years	9,031	4,352	4,679	2,954	3,175	60	61	1,338	1,443			7.0	7.1	7.0	6.8	6.8	9.9	12.1	7.9	7.5		
45 to 49 years	7,576	3,720	3,856	2,514	2,724	71	76	1,135	1,056			5.9	6.1	5.8	5.8	5.8	11.7	15.0	6.7	5.5		
50 to 54 years	6,084	3,016	3,068	2,114	2,231	95	52	807	785			4.7	4.9	4.6	4.8	4.7	15.6	10.3	4.7	4.1		
55 to 59 years	4,486	2,163	2,323	1,625	1,722	74	48	463	552	1	1	3.5	3.5	3.5	3.7	3.7	12.2	9.5	2.7	2.9		
60 to 64 years	3,446	1,619	1,827	1,233	1,423	63	35	318	369			2.7	2.6	2.7	2.8	3.0	10.3	6.9	1.9	1.9		
65 to 69 years	2,842	1,288	1,554	910	1,111	42	32	336	411			2.2	2.1	2.3	2.1	2.4	6.9	6.3	2.0	2.1		
70 to 74 years	1,666	734	932	523	686	30	33	181	212		1	1.3	1.2	1.4	1.2	1.5	4.9	6.5	1.1	1.1		
75 years and over	1,452	585	867	408	673	41	29	136	165			1.1	1.0	1.3	0.9	1.4	6.7	5.7	0.8	0.9		
Under 1 year	1,983	1,004	979	757	707			246	272	1		1.5	1.6	1.5	1.7	1.5			1.4	1.4		
21 years and over	82,413	38,779	43,634	27,361	30,484	588	482	10,826	12,663	4	5	64.3	63.3	65.2	62.8	64.8	96.5	95.4	63.5	65.4		
Median age	28.2	28.0	28.4	27.7	28.4	52.1	48.5	28.1	28.1													
CHICAGO, ILL.																						
All ages	3,396,808	1,681,665	1,715,143	1,192,533	1,249,026	354,657	318,048	130,588	147,143	3,587	928	100.0	100.0	100.0	100.0	100.0	100.0	100.0	100.0	100.0	100.0	100.0
Under 5 years	213,136	108,466	104,670	98,501	94,584	157	159	9,606	9,754	202	173	6.3	6.4	6.1	8.3	7.6			7.4	6.6	5.6	18.7
5 to 9 years	210,430	107,305	103,125	96,551	92,278	417	408	10,166	10,324	171	115	6.2	6.4	6.0	8.1	7.4	0.1	0.1	7.8	7.0	4.8	12.4
10 to 14 years	246,480	124,008	122,472	112,053	110,113	1,191	1,164	10,618	11,086	146	109	7.3	7.4	7.1	9.4	8.8	0.3	0.4	8.1	7.5	4.1	11.8
15 to 19 years	271,710	133,510	138,200	119,679	122,944	4,169	4,236	9,512	10,934	150	86	8.0	7.9	8.1	10.0	9.8	1.2	1.3	7.3	7.4	4.2	9.3
20 to 24 years	309,046	145,262	163,784	132,129	146,574	4,306	4,957	8,679	12,176	148	77	9.1	8.6	9.5	11.1	11.7	1.2	1.6	6.6	8.3	4.1	8.3
25 to 29 years	322,377	152,091	170,286	130,668	143,489	10,116	11,877	10,919	14,847	388	73	9.5	9.0	9.9	11.0	11.5	2.9	3.7	8.4	10.1	10.8	7.9
30 to 34 years	299,858	143,606	156,252	110,703	119,105	20,637	21,330	11,702	15,748	564	69	8.8	8.5	9.1	9.3	9.5	5.8	6.7	9.0	10.7	15.7	7.5
35 to 39 years	285,882	140,485	145,397	92,829	96,751	32,877	31,699	14,236	16,882	543	65	8.4	8.4	8.5	7.8	7.7	9.3	10.0	10.9	11.5	15.1	7.0
40 to 44 years	271,662	135,973	135,689	81,118	84,691	41,199	37,621	13,259	13,321	397	56	8.0	8.1	7.9	6.8	6.8	11.6	11.8	10.2	9.1	11.1	6.0
45 to 49 years	262,511	134,580	127,931	69,886	72,415	53,688	45,320	10,743	10,153	263	43	7.7	8.0	7.5	5.9	5.8	15.1	14.2	8.2	6.9	7.3	4.6
50 to 54 years	224,203	118,457	105,746	53,589	55,356	56,903	43,169	7,731	7,194	234	27	6.6	7.0	6.2	4.5	4.4	16.0	13.6	5.9	4.9	6.5	2.9
55 to 59 years	163,451	86,476	76,975	35,885	37,478	45,066	34,508	5,380	4,977	145	12	4.8	5.1	4.5	3.0	3.0	12.7	10.8	4.1	3.4	4.0	1.3
60 to 64 years	118,983	60,702	58,281	24,753	27,468	32,526	27,452	3,320	3,355	103	6	3.5	3.6	3.4	2.1	2.2	9.2	8.6	2.5	2.3	2.9	0.6
65 to 69 years	87,473	41,385	46,088	16,799	21,053	21,916	21,605	2,604	3,424	66	6	2.6	2.5	2.7	1.4	1.7	6.2	6.8	2.0	2.3	1.8	0.6
70 to 74 years	57,344	26,723	30,621	10,142	13,039	15,262	16,056	1,272	1,525	47	1	1.7	1.6	1.8	0.9	1.0	4.3	5.0	1.0	1.0	1.3	0.1
75 years and over	52,262	22,636	29,626	7,548	11,688	14,227	16,487	841	1,443	20	8	1.5	1.3	1.7	0.6	0.9	4.0	5.2	0.6	1.0	0.6	0.9
Under 1 year	40,939	20,728	20,211	18,759	18,342	6	11	1,926	1,819	37	39	1.2	1.2	1.2	1.6	1.5			1.5	1.2	1.0	4.2
21 years and over	2,397,392	1,181,374	1,216,018	741,819	802,061	347,599	310,879	89,060	102,658	2,896	420	70.6	70.2	70.9	62.2	64.2	98.0	97.7	68.2	70.0	80.7	45.4
Median age	32.1	32.4	31.8	26.4	27.0	50.8	50.0	32.5	31.4	35.2	18.8											

TABLE 53.—AGE, BY RACE AND SEX, WITH PERCENT DISTRIBUTION BY AGE, FOR CITIES OF 100,000 OR MORE: 1940—Continued

[Percent not shown where less than 0.1 or where base is less than 100]

NUMBER

CITY AND AGE	All classes			Native white		Foreign-born white		Negro		Other races	
	Total	Male	Female	Male	Female	Male	Female	Male	Female	Male	Female
CINCINNATI, OHIO											
All ages	455,610	217,082	238,528	177,184	196,879	13,204	12,586	26,584	29,009	110	54
Under 5 years	28,280	14,245	14,035	12,236	12,064	15	6	1,990	1,958	4	7
5 to 9 years	28,232	14,185	14,047	12,055	11,886	23	24	2,100	2,125	7	12
10 to 14 years	32,375	16,086	16,289	13,715	13,806	75	67	2,290	2,408	6	8
15 to 19 years	35,233	16,928	18,305	14,565	15,676	195	207	2,159	2,416	9	6
20 to 24 years	37,655	17,229	20,426	15,123	17,467	189	228	1,913	2,729	4	2
25 to 29 years	39,204	18,236	20,968	15,448	17,499	416	454	2,364	3,012	8	3
30 to 34 years	38,655	18,342	20,313	15,105	16,607	810	807	2,414	2,898	13	1
35 to 39 years	36,440	17,489	18,951	13,565	14,811	1,242	1,122	2,669	3,012	13	6
40 to 44 years	34,818	16,773	18,045	13,078	14,472	1,353	1,144	2,328	2,427	14	2
45 to 49 years	33,135	16,239	16,896	12,717	13,806	1,463	1,254	2,050	1,834	9	2
50 to 54 years	29,265	14,302	14,963	11,151	12,253	1,640	1,348	1,506	1,360	5	2
55 to 59 years	23,774	11,322	12,452	8,808	10,188	1,503	1,320	1,005	943	6	1
60 to 64 years	19,924	9,341	10,583	7,334	8,662	1,341	1,264	662	655	4	2
65 to 69 years	15,966	7,072	8,894	5,512	7,150	988	1,122	567	622	5	------
70 to 74 years	11,222	4,792	6,430	3,606	5,164	864	938	319	328	3	------
75 years and over	11,432	4,501	6,931	3,166	5,368	1,087	1,281	248	282	------	------
Under 1 year	5,287	2,672	2,615	2,313	2,266	------	------	358	348	1	1
21 years and over	324,276	152,374	171,902	121,767	140,082	12,843	12,223	17,680	19,576	84	21
Median age	33.5	33.2	33.7	31.8	33.0	52.5	53.6	31.0	29.8	36.5	------
CLEVELAND, OHIO											
All ages	878,336	438,346	439,990	302,855	311,379	94,075	85,108	41,096	43,408	320	95
Under 5 years	56,022	28,243	27,779	25,230	24,516	36	39	2,967	3,204	10	20
5 to 9 years	53,562	27,180	26,382	23,800	23,074	83	81	3,283	3,217	14	10
10 to 14 years	65,790	33,020	32,770	29,104	28,645	277	264	3,627	3,851	12	10
15 to 19 years	77,939	38,445	39,494	34,073	34,571	1,030	1,090	3,330	3,816	12	17
20 to 24 years	85,269	40,832	44,437	36,926	39,920	1,098	1,146	2,789	3,365	19	6
25 to 29 years	84,997	41,040	43,957	34,891	36,727	2,858	3,180	3,272	4,045	19	5
30 to 34 years	73,992	36,294	37,698	28,198	28,474	4,615	5,165	3,450	4,053	31	6
35 to 39 years	66,420	32,331	34,089	21,073	21,253	7,073	8,141	4,147	4,689	38	6
40 to 44 years	65,276	32,573	32,703	17,571	17,735	10,777	11,012	4,184	3,952	41	4
45 to 49 years	66,940	34,446	32,494	15,256	15,907	15,573	13,342	3,580	3,239	37	6
50 to 54 years	58,364	31,321	27,043	12,279	12,462	16,483	12,478	2,529	2,102	30	1
55 to 59 years	44,351	23,541	20,810	9,081	9,537	12,822	9,884	1,616	1,389	22	------
60 to 64 years	31,810	16,675	15,135	6,564	6,984	9,132	7,292	962	858	17	1
65 to 69 years	21,880	10,718	11,162	4,361	5,228	5,637	5,104	716	829	4	1
70 to 74 years	13,642	6,420	7,222	2,543	3,337	3,495	3,460	374	424	8	1
75 years and over	12,082	5,267	6,815	1,905	3,009	3,086	3,430	270	375	6	1
Under 1 year	11,299	5,719	5,580	5,183	4,934	3	5	532	635	1	6
21 years and over	609,125	303,803	305,322	183,911	193,299	92,326	83,334	27,295	28,651	271	38
Median age	31.1	31.4	30.7	25.3	25.7	51.1	49.7	31.9	30.3	40.6	------
COLUMBUS, OHIO											
All ages	306,087	148,971	157,116	124,281	133,975	6,531	5,396	18,061	17,704	98	41
Under 5 years	19,592	9,808	9,784	8,556	8,362	4	2	1,240	1,414	8	6
5 to 9 years	18,789	9,591	9,198	8,213	7,873	12	7	1,360	1,311	6	7
10 to 14 years	22,134	11,081	11,053	9,666	9,579	20	35	1,393	1,434	2	5
15 to 19 years	25,109	12,149	12,960	10,597	11,390	92	87	1,451	1,477	9	6
20 to 24 years	27,753	12,948	14,805	11,382	13,110	113	108	1,447	1,584	6	3
25 to 29 years	27,718	13,450	14,268	11,540	12,351	258	240	1,643	1,672	9	5
30 to 34 years	26,214	12,866	13,348	10,931	11,448	406	357	1,524	1,542	5	1
35 to 39 years	24,345	12,115	12,230	9,833	10,097	594	525	1,674	1,606	14	2
40 to 44 years	22,791	11,305	11,486	8,974	9,479	710	585	1,616	1,417	5	5
45 to 49 years	21,230	10,490	10,740	8,210	8,926	885	574	1,384	1,239	11	1
50 to 54 years	18,863	9,410	9,453	7,360	7,926	905	621	1,138	906	7	------
55 to 59 years	15,502	7,543	7,959	5,914	6,670	777	600	845	689	7	------
60 to 64 years	12,507	5,924	6,583	4,767	5,571	636	549	514	463	7	------

PERCENT DISTRIBUTION

CITY AND AGE	All classes			Native white		Foreign-born white		Negro		Other races	
	Total	Male	Female	Male	Female	Male	Female	Male	Female	Male	Female
CINCINNATI, OHIO											
All ages	100.0	100.0	100.0	100.0	100.0	100.0	100.0	100.0	100.0	100.0	------
Under 5 years	6.2	6.6	5.9	6.9	6.1	0.1	------	7.5	6.7	3.6	------
5 to 9 years	6.2	6.5	5.9	6.8	6.0	0.2	0.2	7.9	7.3	6.4	------
10 to 14 years	7.1	7.4	6.8	7.7	7.0	0.6	0.5	8.6	8.3	5.5	------
15 to 19 years	7.7	7.8	7.7	8.2	8.0	1.5	1.6	8.1	8.3	8.2	------
20 to 24 years	8.3	7.9	8.6	8.5	8.9	1.4	1.8	7.2	9.4	3.6	------
25 to 29 years	8.6	8.4	8.8	8.7	8.9	3.2	3.6	8.9	10.4	7.3	------
30 to 34 years	8.5	8.4	8.5	8.5	8.4	6.1	6.4	9.1	10.0	11.8	------
35 to 39 years	8.0	8.1	7.9	7.7	7.5	9.4	8.9	10.0	10.4	11.8	------
40 to 44 years	7.6	7.7	7.6	7.4	7.4	10.2	9.1	8.8	8.4	12.7	------
45 to 49 years	7.3	7.5	7.1	7.2	7.0	11.1	10.0	7.7	6.3	8.2	------
50 to 54 years	6.4	6.6	6.3	6.3	6.2	12.4	10.7	5.7	4.7	4.5	------
55 to 59 years	5.2	5.2	5.2	5.0	5.2	11.4	10.5	3.8	3.3	5.5	------
60 to 64 years	4.4	4.3	4.4	4.1	4.4	10.2	10.0	2.5	2.3	3.6	------
65 to 69 years	3.5	3.3	3.7	3.1	3.6	7.5	8.9	2.1	2.1	4.5	------
70 to 74 years	2.5	2.2	2.7	2.0	2.6	6.5	7.5	1.2	1.1	2.7	------
75 years and over	2.5	2.1	2.9	1.8	2.7	8.2	10.2	0.9	1.0	------	------
Under 1 year	1.2	1.2	1.1	1.3	1.2	------	------	1.3	1.2	0.9	------
21 years and over	71.2	70.2	72.1	68.7	71.2	97.3	97.1	66.5	67.5	76.4	------
Median age	------	------	------	------	------	------	------	------	------	------	------
CLEVELAND, OHIO											
All ages	100.0	100.0	100.0	100.0	100.0	100.0	100.0	100.0	100.0	100.0	------
Under 5 years	6.4	6.4	6.3	8.3	7.9	------	------	7.2	7.4	3.1	------
5 to 9 years	6.1	6.2	6.0	7.9	7.4	0.1	0.1	8.0	7.4	4.4	------
10 to 14 years	7.5	7.5	7.4	9.6	9.2	0.3	0.3	8.8	8.9	3.8	------
15 to 19 years	8.9	8.8	9.0	11.3	11.1	1.1	1.3	8.1	8.8	3.8	------
20 to 24 years	9.7	9.3	10.1	12.2	12.8	1.2	1.3	6.8	7.8	5.9	------
25 to 29 years	9.7	9.4	10.0	11.5	11.8	3.0	3.7	8.0	9.3	5.9	------
30 to 34 years	8.4	8.3	8.6	9.3	9.1	4.9	6.1	8.4	9.3	9.7	------
35 to 39 years	7.6	7.4	7.7	7.0	6.8	7.5	9.6	10.1	10.8	11.9	------
40 to 44 years	7.4	7.4	7.4	5.8	5.7	11.5	12.9	10.2	9.1	12.8	------
45 to 49 years	7.6	7.9	7.4	5.0	5.1	16.6	15.7	8.7	7.5	11.6	------
50 to 54 years	6.6	7.1	6.1	4.1	4.0	17.5	14.7	6.2	4.8	9.4	------
55 to 59 years	5.0	5.4	4.7	3.0	3.1	13.6	11.6	3.9	3.2	6.9	------
60 to 64 years	3.6	3.8	3.4	2.2	2.2	9.7	8.6	2.3	2.0	5.3	------
65 to 69 years	2.5	2.4	2.5	1.4	1.7	6.0	6.0	1.7	1.9	1.3	------
70 to 74 years	1.6	1.5	1.6	0.8	1.1	3.7	4.1	0.9	1.0	2.5	------
75 years and over	1.4	1.2	1.5	0.6	1.0	3.3	4.0	0.7	0.9	1.9	------
Under 1 year	1.3	1.3	1.3	1.7	1.6	------	------	1.3	1.5	0.3	------
21 years and over	69.3	69.3	69.4	60.7	62.1	98.1	97.9	66.4	66.0	84.7	------
Median age	------	------	------	------	------	------	------	------	------	------	------
COLUMBUS, OHIO											
All ages	100.0	100.0	100.0	100.0	100.0	100.0	100.0	100.0	100.0	------	------
Under 5 years	6.4	6.6	6.2	6.9	6.2	0.1	------	6.9	8.0	------	------
5 to 9 years	6.1	6.4	5.9	6.6	5.9	0.2	0.1	7.5	7.4	------	------
10 to 14 years	7.2	7.4	7.0	7.8	7.1	0.3	0.6	7.7	8.1	------	------
15 to 19 years	8.2	8.2	8.2	8.5	8.5	1.4	1.6	8.0	8.3	------	------
20 to 24 years	9.1	8.7	9.4	9.2	9.8	1.7	2.0	8.0	8.9	------	------
25 to 29 years	9.1	9.0	9.1	9.3	9.2	4.0	4.4	9.1	9.4	------	------
30 to 34 years	8.6	8.6	8.5	8.8	8.5	6.2	6.6	8.4	8.7	------	------
35 to 39 years	8.0	8.1	7.8	7.9	7.5	9.1	9.7	9.3	9.1	------	------
40 to 44 years	7.4	7.6	7.3	7.2	7.1	10.9	10.8	8.9	8.0	------	------
45 to 49 years	6.9	7.0	6.8	6.6	6.7	13.6	10.6	7.7	7.0	------	------
50 to 54 years	6.2	6.3	6.0	5.9	5.9	13.9	11.5	6.3	5.1	------	------
55 to 59 years	5.1	5.1	5.1	4.8	5.0	11.9	11.1	4.7	3.9	------	------
60 to 64 years	4.1	4.0	4.2	3.8	4.2	9.7	10.2	2.8	2.6	------	------

65 to 69 years	9,982	4,457	5,525	3,603	4,637	446	410	407	478	1	-	3.3	3.0	3.5	2.9	3.5	6.8	7.6	2.3	2.7	-	-
70 to 74 years	6,723	2,985	3,738	2,433	3,187	331	319	221	232	-	-	2.2	2.0	2.4	2.0	2.4	5.1	5.9	1.2	1.3	-	-
75 years and over	6,835	2,849	3,986	2,302	3,369	342	377	204	240	1	-	2.2	1.9	2.5	1.9	2.5	5.2	7.0	1.1	1.4	-	-
Under 1 year	3,898	1,957	1,941	1,710	1,667	-	-	246	273	1	1	1.3	1.3	1.2	1.4	1.2	-	-	1.4	1.5	-	-
21 years and over	215,157	104,023	111,134	85,214	94,164	6,369	5,237	12,368	11,717	72	16	70.3	69.8	70.7	68.6	70.3	97.5	97.1	68.5	66.2	-	-
Median age	32.3	32.1	32.4	31.0	31.9	50.9	51.4	31.6	29.9	-	-	-	-	-	-	-	-	-	-	-	-	-
DALLAS, TEX.																						
All ages	294,734	139,759	154,975	112,457	124,434	3,993	3,362	23,254	27,153	55	26	100.0	100.0	100.0	100.0	100.0	100.0	100.0	100.0	100.0	-	-
Under 5 years	19,029	9,606	9,423	8,084	7,785	4	4	1,517	1,632	1	2	6.5	6.9	6.1	7.2	6.3	0.1	0.1	6.5	6.0	-	-
5 to 9 years	18,972	9,522	9,450	7,767	7,593	19	5	1,732	1,848	4	4	6.4	6.8	6.1	6.9	6.1	0.5	0.1	7.4	6.8	-	-
10 to 14 years	21,719	10,750	10,969	8,802	8,887	14	18	1,933	2,063	1	1	7.4	7.7	7.1	7.8	7.1	0.4	0.5	8.3	7.6	-	-
15 to 19 years	25,099	11,761	13,338	9,768	10,915	68	55	1,924	2,367	1	1	8.5	8.4	8.6	8.7	8.8	1.7	1.6	8.3	8.7	-	-
20 to 24 years	28,380	12,651	15,729	10,675	12,917	96	99	1,878	2,711	2	2	9.6	9.1	10.1	9.5	10.4	2.4	2.9	8.1	10.0	-	-
25 to 29 years	30,682	14,001	16,681	11,482	13,206	199	238	2,306	3,234	14	3	10.4	10.0	10.8	10.2	10.6	5.0	7.1	9.9	11.9	-	-
30 to 34 years	29,529	13,674	15,855	11,022	12,448	342	284	2,305	3,121	5	2	10.0	9.8	10.2	9.8	10.0	8.6	8.4	9.9	11.5	-	-
35 to 39 years	27,842	13,031	14,811	10,015	11,414	457	363	2,552	3,032	7	2	9.4	9.3	9.6	8.9	9.2	11.4	10.8	11.0	11.2	-	-
40 to 44 years	23,252	11,342	11,910	8,747	9,371	425	329	2,165	2,207	5	3	7.9	8.1	7.7	7.8	7.5	10.6	9.8	9.3	8.1	-	-
45 to 49 years	19,718	9,857	9,861	7,633	7,893	512	370	1,709	1,597	3	1	6.7	7.1	6.4	6.8	6.3	12.8	11.0	7.3	5.9	-	-
50 to 54 years	15,610	7,720	7,890	6,100	6,437	513	363	1,105	1,089	2	1	5.3	5.5	5.1	5.4	5.2	12.8	10.8	4.8	4.0	-	-
55 to 59 years	11,076	5,273	5,803	4,131	4,785	431	306	708	711	3	1	3.8	3.8	3.7	3.7	3.8	10.8	9.1	3.0	2.6	-	-
60 to 64 years	8,556	3,917	4,639	3,161	3,872	289	289	466	478	1	-	2.9	2.8	3.0	2.8	3.1	7.2	8.6	2.0	1.8	-	-
65 to 69 years	6,895	3,080	3,815	2,331	3,036	253	241	496	537	-	1	2.3	2.2	2.5	2.1	2.4	6.3	7.2	2.1	2.0	-	-
70 to 74 years	4,227	1,861	2,366	1,425	1,912	174	169	259	285	3	-	1.4	1.3	1.5	1.3	1.5	4.4	5.0	1.1	1.0	-	-
75 years and over	4,148	1,713	2,435	1,314	1,963	197	229	199	241	3	2	1.4	1.2	1.6	1.2	1.6	4.9	6.8	0.9	0.9	-	-
Under 1 year	4,165	2,127	2,038	1,811	1,706	-	1	316	331	-	-	1.4	1.5	1.3	1.6	1.4	-	-	1.4	1.2	-	-
21 years and over	204,288	95,752	108,536	76,040	86,590	3,875	3,269	15,789	18,659	48	18	69.3	68.5	70.0	67.6	69.6	97.0	97.2	67.9	68.7	-	-
Median age	30.6	30.6	30.6	29.8	30.4	48.6	48.9	30.7	29.6	-	-	-	-	-	-	-	-	-	-	-	-	-
DAYTON, OHIO																						
All ages	210,718	103,358	107,360	88,347	92,738	5,023	4,306	9,970	10,303	18	13	100.0	100.0	100.0	100.0	100.0	100.0	100.0	100.0	100.0	-	-
Under 5 years	15,101	7,563	7,538	6,810	6,707	5	1	748	829	-	1	7.2	7.3	7.0	7.7	7.2	0.1	-	7.5	8.0	-	-
5 to 9 years	13,774	7,011	6,763	6,211	5,936	8	10	791	815	1	2	6.5	6.8	6.3	7.0	6.4	0.2	0.2	7.9	7.9	-	-
10 to 14 years	15,279	7,675	7,604	6,765	6,643	12	20	898	941	-	-	7.3	7.4	7.1	7.7	7.2	0.2	0.5	9.0	9.1	-	-
15 to 19 years	16,747	7,917	8,830	7,037	7,839	57	67	822	923	1	1	7.9	7.7	8.2	8.0	8.5	1.1	1.6	8.2	9.0	-	-
20 to 24 years	19,528	9,153	10,375	8,227	9,296	63	63	863	1,012	-	4	9.3	8.9	9.7	9.3	10.0	1.3	1.5	8.7	9.8	-	-
25 to 29 years	19,635	9,577	10,058	8,456	8,861	181	166	940	1,031	-	-	9.3	9.3	9.4	9.6	9.6	3.6	3.9	9.4	10.0	-	-
30 to 34 years	18,586	9,165	9,421	8,025	8,246	306	247	831	925	3	3	8.8	8.9	8.8	9.1	8.9	6.1	5.7	8.3	9.0	-	-
35 to 39 years	16,346	8,057	8,289	6,793	6,964	420	386	842	939	2	-	7.8	7.8	7.7	7.7	7.5	8.4	9.0	8.4	9.1	-	-
40 to 44 years	15,388	7,657	7,731	6,298	6,457	548	492	812	782	4	-	7.3	7.4	7.2	7.1	7.0	10.9	11.4	8.1	7.6	-	-
45 to 49 years	14,453	7,318	7,135	5,904	5,964	660	515	753	655	1	1	6.9	7.1	6.6	6.7	6.4	13.1	12.0	7.6	6.4	-	-
50 to 54 years	12,674	6,405	6,269	5,051	5,191	760	576	593	502	1	-	6.0	6.2	5.8	5.7	5.6	15.1	13.4	5.9	4.9	-	-
55 to 59 years	9,984	4,991	4,993	4,009	4,215	613	473	367	305	2	-	4.7	4.8	4.7	4.5	4.5	12.2	11.0	3.7	3.0	-	-
60 to 64 years	7,969	3,896	4,073	3,173	3,444	466	423	256	206	1	-	3.8	3.8	3.8	3.6	3.7	9.3	9.8	2.6	2.0	-	-
65 to 69 years	6,361	3,014	3,347	2,424	2,812	374	316	216	219	-	-	3.0	2.9	3.1	2.7	3.0	7.4	7.3	2.2	2.1	-	-
70 to 74 years	4,430	2,071	2,359	1,684	1,970	252	277	134	111	1	1	2.1	2.0	2.2	1.9	2.1	5.0	6.4	1.3	1.1	-	-
75 years and over	4,463	1,888	2,575	1,485	2,193	298	274	104	108	1	-	2.1	1.8	2.4	1.7	2.4	5.9	6.4	1.0	1.0	-	-
Under 1 year	3,015	1,514	1,501	1,388	1,355	-	-	126	146	-	-	1.4	1.5	1.4	1.6	1.5	-	-	1.3	1.4	-	-
21 years and over	146,135	71,500	74,635	60,015	63,828	4,924	4,191	6,545	6,608	16	8	69.3	69.2	69.5	67.9	68.8	98.0	97.3	65.6	64.1	-	-
Median age	31.4	31.5	31.3	30.4	30.7	51.7	51.6	29.6	28.1	-	-	-	-	-	-	-	-	-	-	-	-	-
DENVER, COLO.																						
All ages	322,412	155,635	166,777	138,577	150,476	13,005	11,752	3,612	4,224	441	325	100.0	100.0	100.0	100.0	100.0	100.0	100.0	100.0	100.0	100.0	100.0
Under 5 years	21,236	10,737	10,499	10,482	10,216	2	7	215	240	38	36	6.6	6.9	6.3	7.6	6.8	-	0.1	6.0	5.7	8.6	11.1
5 to 9 years	20,855	10,483	10,372	10,193	10,078	9	15	260	244	21	35	6.5	6.7	6.2	7.4	6.7	0.1	0.1	7.2	5.8	4.8	10.8
10 to 14 years	22,651	11,256	11,395	10,969	11,055	27	27	234	269	26	44	7.0	7.2	6.8	7.9	7.3	0.2	0.2	6.5	6.4	5.9	13.5
15 to 19 years	25,669	12,283	13,386	11,901	12,977	95	86	240	264	47	59	8.0	7.9	8.0	8.6	8.6	0.7	0.7	6.6	6.2	10.7	18.2
20 to 24 years	28,141	12,903	15,238	12,500	14,697	147	143	222	347	34	51	8.7	8.3	9.1	9.0	9.8	1.1	1.2	6.1	8.2	7.7	15.7
25 to 29 years	28,082	13,263	14,819	12,597	14,007	326	373	285	412	55	27	8.7	8.5	8.9	9.1	9.3	2.5	3.2	7.9	9.8	12.5	8.3
30 to 34 years	26,696	12,821	13,875	11,883	12,940	599	557	311	372	28	6	8.3	8.2	8.3	8.6	8.6	4.6	4.7	8.6	8.8	6.3	1.8
35 to 39 years	24,449	11,720	12,729	10,545	11,493	855	832	295	391	25	13	7.6	7.5	7.6	7.6	7.6	6.6	7.1	8.2	9.3	5.7	4.0
40 to 44 years	23,932	11,551	12,381	10,107	11,083	1,098	914	316	367	30	17	7.4	7.4	7.4	7.3	7.4	8.4	7.8	8.7	8.7	6.8	5.2
45 to 49 years	22,401	11,186	11,215	9,377	9,862	1,423	1,018	352	321	34	14	6.9	7.2	6.7	6.8	6.6	10.9	8.7	9.7	7.6	7.7	4.3
50 to 54 years	19,563	9,668	9,895	7,713	8,342	1,678	1,295	236	249	41	9	6.1	6.2	5.9	5.6	5.5	12.9	11.0	6.5	5.9	9.3	2.8
55 to 59 years	16,445	8,060	8,385	6,148	6,751	1,691	1,412	199	215	22	7	5.1	5.2	5.0	4.4	4.5	13.0	12.0	5.5	5.1	5.0	2.2
60 to 64 years	13,935	6,638	7,297	4,995	5,716	1,460	1,391	168	188	15	2	4.3	4.3	4.4	3.6	3.8	11.2	11.8	4.7	4.5	3.4	0.6
65 to 69 years	11,278	5,212	6,066	3,863	4,614	1,212	1,274	128	173	9	5	3.5	3.3	3.6	2.8	3.1	9.3	10.8	3.5	4.1	2.0	1.5
70 to 74 years	8,426	3,851	4,575	2,667	3,365	1,096	1,116	81	94	7	-	2.6	2.5	2.7	1.9	2.2	8.4	9.5	2.2	2.2	1.6	-
75 years and over	8,653	4,003	4,650	2,637	3,280	1,287	1,292	70	78	9	-	2.7	2.6	2.8	1.9	2.2	9.9	11.0	1.9	1.8	2.0	-
Under 1 year	4,337	2,207	2,130	2,150	2,080	-	-	49	46	8	4	1.3	1.4	1.3	1.6	1.4	-	-	1.4	1.1	1.8	1.2
21 years and over	226,511	108,372	118,139	92,619	103,274	12,842	11,582	2,614	3,145	297	138	70.3	69.6	70.8	66.8	68.6	98.7	98.6	72.4	74.5	67.3	42.5
Median age	32.7	32.7	32.8	30.3	30.9	55.7	57.2	35.7	34.5	30.0	19.0	-	-	-	-	-	-	-	-	-	-	-

TABLE 53.—AGE, BY RACE AND SEX, WITH PERCENT DISTRIBUTION BY AGE, FOR CITIES OF 100,000 OR MORE: 1940—Continued

[Percent not shown where less than 0.1 or where base is less than 100]

CITY AND AGE	NUMBER: All classes			Native white		Foreign-born white		Negro		Other races		PERCENT DISTRIBUTION: All classes			Native white		Foreign-born white		Negro		Other races	
	Total	Male	Female	Male	Female	Male	Female	Male	Female	Male	Female	Total	Male	Female	Male	Female	Male	Female	Male	Female	Male	Female
DES MOINES, IOWA																						
All ages	159,819	75,879	83,940	68,804	77,148	3,973	3,501	3,073	3,287	29	4	100.0	100.0	100.0	100.0	100.0	100.0	100.0	100.0	100.0	----	----
Under 5 years	11,483	5,892	5,591	5,640	5,348	2	----	250	243	----	----	7.2	7.8	6.7	8.2	6.9	0.1	----	8.1	7.4	----	----
5 to 9 years	10,577	5,310	5,267	5,057	4,971	4	9	248	287	1	----	6.6	7.0	6.2	7.3	6.4	0.1	0.3	8.1	8.7	----	----
10 to 14 years	11,624	5,871	5,753	5,596	5,463	11	11	262	279	2	----	7.3	7.7	6.9	8.1	7.1	0.3	0.3	8.5	8.5	----	----
15 to 19 years	13,644	6,417	7,227	6,107	6,909	46	40	262	278	2	----	8.5	8.5	8.6	8.9	9.0	1.2	1.1	8.5	8.5	----	----
20 to 24 years	14,949	6,435	8,514	6,123	8,188	51	51	258	275	3	----	9.4	8.5	10.1	8.9	10.6	1.3	1.5	8.4	8.4	----	----
25 to 29 years	14,194	6,427	7,767	6,096	7,361	95	127	235	279	1	----	8.9	8.5	9.3	8.9	9.5	2.4	3.6	7.6	8.5	----	----
30 to 34 years	12,896	6,006	6,890	5,620	6,482	169	154	214	252	3	2	8.1	7.9	8.2	8.2	8.4	4.3	4.4	7.0	7.7	----	----
35 to 39 years	12,249	5,636	6,613	5,177	6,114	252	246	204	252	3	1	7.7	7.4	7.9	7.5	7.9	6.3	7.0	6.6	7.7	----	----
40 to 44 years	11,523	5,483	6,040	4,880	5,512	399	308	199	219	5	1	7.2	7.2	7.2	7.1	7.1	10.0	8.8	6.5	6.7	----	----
45 to 49 years	10,974	5,395	5,579	4,697	4,991	487	355	206	233	5	----	6.9	7.1	6.6	6.8	6.5	12.3	10.1	6.7	7.1	----	----
50 to 54 years	9,481	4,704	4,777	3,940	4,165	551	425	212	187	1	----	5.9	6.2	5.7	5.7	5.4	13.9	12.1	6.9	5.7	----	----
55 to 59 years	7,920	3,773	4,147	3,093	3,576	513	413	164	158	3	----	5.0	5.0	4.9	4.5	4.6	12.9	11.8	5.3	4.8	----	----
60 to 64 years	6,261	3,042	3,219	2,475	2,722	436	383	131	114	----	----	3.9	4.0	3.8	3.6	3.5	11.0	10.9	4.3	3.5	----	----
65 to 69 years	4,949	2,340	2,609	1,896	2,189	351	307	93	113	----	----	3.1	3.1	3.1	2.8	2.8	8.8	8.8	3.0	3.4	----	----
70 to 74 years	3,483	1,621	1,862	1,267	1,516	282	288	72	58	----	----	2.2	2.1	2.2	1.8	2.0	7.1	8.2	2.3	1.8	----	----
75 years and over	3,612	1,527	2,085	1,140	1,641	324	384	63	60	----	----	2.3	2.0	2.5	1.7	2.1	8.2	11.0	2.1	1.8	----	----
Under 1 year	2,316	1,161	1,155	1,123	1,107	1	----	37	48	----	----	1.4	1.5	1.4	1.6	1.4	----	----	1.2	1.5	----	----
21 years and over	109,565	51,136	58,429	45,224	52,856	3,893	3,428	1,996	2,141	23	4	68.6	67.4	69.6	65.7	68.5	98.0	97.9	65.0	65.1	----	----
Median age	31.3	31.3	31.3	29.8	30.3	54.3	55.3	30.5	30.0	----	----	----	----	----	----	----	----	----	----	----	----	----
DETROIT, MICH.																						
All ages	1,623,452	827,499	795,953	579,520	5?2,478	172,297	148,367	74,485	74,634	1,197	474	100.0	100.0	100.0	100.0	100.0	100.0	100.0	100.0	100.0	100.0	100.0
Under 5 years	117,389	60,002	57,387	54,019	51,539	138	150	5,760	5,623	85	75	7.2	7.3	7.2	9.3	9.0	0.1	0.1	7.7	7.5	7.1	15.8
5 to 9 years	114,346	57,893	56,453	51,498	50,102	521	470	5,795	5,823	79	58	7.0	7.0	7.1	8.9	8.8	0.3	0.3	7.8	7.8	6.6	12.2
10 to 14 years	134,054	67,765	66,289	60,401	58,597	1,311	1,282	5,978	6,348	75	62	8.3	8.2	8.3	10.4	10.2	0.8	0.9	8.0	8.5	6.3	13.1
15 to 19 years	141,002	69,444	71,558	59,769	61,450	4,010	3,983	5,593	6,080	72	45	8.7	8.4	9.0	10.3	10.7	2.3	2.7	7.5	8.1	6.0	9.5
20 to 24 years	149,667	71,223	78,444	61,311	66,358	4,555	5,217	5,295	6,846	62	23	9.2	8.6	9.9	10.6	11.6	2.6	3.5	7.1	9.2	5.2	4.9
25 to 29 years	148,548	71,984	76,564	57,426	59,366	7,700	9,142	6,770	8,026	88	30	9.2	8.7	9.6	9.9	10.4	4.5	6.2	9.1	10.8	7.4	6.3
30 to 34 years	141,495	69,910	71,585	50,158	49,985	12,355	13,511	7,241	8,051	156	38	8.7	8.4	9.0	8.7	8.7	7.2	9.1	9.7	10.8	13.0	8.0
35 to 39 years	144,723	75,057	69,666	46,429	42,714	19,612	18,218	8,831	8,691	185	43	8.9	9.1	8.8	8.0	7.5	11.4	12.3	11.9	11.6	15.5	9.1
40 to 44 years	135,595	72,537	63,058	40,002	36,127	24,395	20,283	8,003	6,615	137	33	8.4	8.8	7.9	6.9	6.3	14.2	13.7	10.7	8.9	11.4	7.0
45 to 49 years	125,560	69,526	56,034	34,203	30,376	29,160	20,961	6,061	4,672	102	25	7.7	8.4	7.0	5.9	5.3	16.9	14.1	8.1	6.3	8.5	5.3
50 to 54 years	97,879	54,937	42,942	24,879	22,661	26,115	17,425	3,861	2,838	82	18	6.0	6.6	5.4	4.3	4.0	15.2	11.7	5.2	3.8	6.9	3.8
55 to 59 years	64,982	35,584	29,398	15,844	15,257	17,407	12,291	2,304	1,840	29	10	4.0	4.3	3.7	2.7	2.7	10.1	8.3	3.1	2.5	2.4	2.1
60 to 64 years	43,601	22,305	21,296	10,149	10,765	10,847	9,403	1,285	1,122	24	6	2.7	2.7	2.7	1.8	1.9	6.3	6.3	1.7	1.5	2.0	1.3
65 to 69 years	29,256	13,917	15,339	6,613	7,731	6,341	6,559	949	1,046	14	3	1.8	1.7	1.9	1.1	1.4	3.7	4.4	1.3	1.4	1.2	0.6
70 to 74 years	18,105	8,187	9,918	3,762	4,813	4,011	4,561	408	542	6	2	1.1	1.0	1.2	0.6	0.8	2.3	3.1	0.5	0.7	0.5	0.4
75 years and over	17,250	7,228	10,022	3,057	4,637	3,819	4,911	351	471	1	3	1.1	0.9	1.3	0.5	0.8	2.2	3.3	0.5	0.6	0.1	0.6
Under 1 year	23,478	12,022	11,456	10,784	10,258	12	9	1,211	1,164	15	25	1.4	1.5	1.4	1.9	1.8	----	----	1.6	1.6	1.3	5.3
21 years and over	1,088,739	559,292	529,447	342,696	338,412	165,315	141,343	50,408	49,462	873	230	67.1	67.6	66.5	59.1	59.1	95.9	95.3	67.7	66.3	72.9	48.5
Median age	30.2	31.1	29.4	25.2	24.9	47.0	45.5	31.4	29.1	34.4	19.7	----	----	----	----	----	----	----	----	----	----	----
DULUTH, MINN.																						
All ages	101,065	50,586	50,479	39,297	42,030	11,058	8,274	182	132	49	43	100.0	100.0	100.0	100.0	100.0	100.0	100.0	100.0	100.0	----	----
Under 5 years	6,910	3,560	3,350	3,545	3,345	4	----	9	4	2	1	6.8	7.0	6.6	9.0	8.0	----	----	4.9	3.0	----	----
5 to 9 years	6,426	3,327	3,099	3,303	3,081	7	6	12	8	5	4	6.4	6.6	6.1	8.4	7.3	0.1	0.1	6.6	6.1	----	----
10 to 14 years	7,945	3,990	3,955	3,962	3,925	13	12	12	12	3	6	7.9	7.9	7.8	10.1	9.3	0.1	0.1	6.6	9.1	----	----
15 to 19 years	8,996	4,394	4,602	4,312	4,513	56	65	20	13	6	11	8.9	8.7	9.1	11.0	10.7	0.5	0.8	11.0	9.8	----	----
20 to 24 years	9,035	4,129	4,906	4,042	4,794	75	94	8	15	4	3	8.9	8.2	9.7	10.3	11.4	0.7	1.1	4.4	11.4	----	----
25 to 29 years	8,392	3,993	4,399	3,829	4,207	147	186	14	5	3	1	8.3	7.9	8.7	9.7	10.0	1.3	2.2	7.7	3.8	----	----
30 to 34 years	7,520	3,488	4,032	3,153	3,717	317	305	14	7	4	3	7.4	6.9	8.0	8.0	8.8	2.9	3.7	7.7	5.3	----	----
35 to 39 years	7,225	3,384	3,841	2,875	3,329	497	497	9	11	3	4	7.1	6.7	7.6	7.3	7.9	4.5	6.0	4.9	8.3	----	----
40 to 44 years	7,311	3,518	3,793	2,760	3,155	747	631	9	6	2	1	7.2	7.0	7.5	7.0	7.5	6.8	7.6	4.9	4.5	----	----
45 to 49 years	7,265	3,693	3,572	2,377	2,655	1,298	903	12	10	6	4	7.2	7.3	7.1	6.0	6.3	11.7	10.9	6.6	7.6	----	----
50 to 54 years	6,824	3,651	3,173	1,814	1,918	1,814	1,242	18	11	5	2	6.8	7.2	6.3	4.6	4.6	16.4	15.0	9.9	8.3	----	----
55 to 59 years	5,426	3,081	2,345	1,258	1,219	1,807	1,115	14	11	2	----	5.4	6.1	4.6	3.2	2.9	16.3	13.5	7.7	8.3	----	----
60 to 64 years	3,990	2,149	1,841	792	826	1,343	1,005	13	10	1	----	3.9	4.2	3.6	2.0	2.0	12.1	12.1	7.1	7.6	----	----

UNITED STATES SUMMARY—PRINCIPAL CITIES 127

65 to 69 years	3,010	1,630	1,380	561	567	1,060	804	7	8	2	1	3.0	3.2	2.7	1.4	1.3	9.6	9.7	3.8	6.1		
70 to 74 years	2,249	1,247	1,002	354	374	885	627	7	1	1		2.2	2.5	2.0	0.9	0.9	8.0	7.6	3.8	0.8		
75 years and over	2,541	1,352	1,189	360	405	988	782	4			2	2.5	2.7	2.4	0.9	1.0	8.9	9.5	2.2			
Under 1 year	1,399	687	712	683	712			3		1		1.4	1.4	1.4	1.7	1.7			1.6			
21 years and over	68,983	34,493	34,490	23,370	26,203	10,964	8,172	126	94	33	21	68.3	68.2	68.3	59.5	62.3	99.1	98.8	69.2	71.2		
Median age	31.9	32.7	31.2	25.6	26.6	56.5	55.9	36.1	35.9													
ELIZABETH, N. J.																						
All ages	**109,912**	**54,878**	**55,034**	**40,601**	**41,704**	**11,789**	**10,816**	**2,437**	**2,504**	**51**	**10**	**100.0**	**100.0**	**100.0**	**100.0**	**100.0**	**100.0**	**100.0**	**100.0**	**100.0**		
Under 5 years	6,667	3,409	3,258	3,145	3,032	11	2	253	224			6.1	6.2	5.9	7.7	7.3	0.1		10.4	8.9		
5 to 9 years	7,141	3,578	3,563	3,288	3,271	24	24	265	265	1	3	6.5	6.5	6.5	8.1	7.8	0.2	0.2	10.9	10.6		
10 to 14 years	8,944	4,437	4,507	4,090	4,153	73	64	270	290	4		8.1	8.1	8.2	10.1	10.0	0.6	0.6	11.1	11.6		
15 to 19 years	10,258	5,047	5,211	4,655	4,775	174	203	212	231	6	2	9.3	9.2	9.5	11.5	11.4	1.5	1.9	8.7	9.2		
20 to 24 years	11,263	5,390	5,873	4,968	5,479	219	202	198	191	5	1	10.2	9.8	10.7	12.2	13.1	1.9	1.9	8.1	7.6		
25 to 29 years	10,451	5,157	5,294	4,604	4,607	367	456	183	231	3		9.5	9.4	9.6	11.3	11.0	3.1	4.2	7.5	9.2		
30 to 34 years	9,232	4,710	4,522	3,796	3,605	721	668	189	249	4		8.4	8.6	8.2	9.3	8.6	6.1	6.2	7.8	9.9		
35 to 39 years	8,161	4,156	4,005	2,790	2,730	1,086	1,023	274	251	6	1	7.4	7.6	7.3	6.9	6.5	9.2	9.5	11.2	10.0		
40 to 44 years	7,932	3,983	3,949	2,406	2,371	1,391	1,411	179	167	7		7.2	7.3	7.2	5.9	5.7	11.8	13.0	7.3	6.7		
45 to 49 years	7,804	3,947	3,857	1,975	2,042	1,828	1,693	135	120	9	2	7.1	7.2	7.0	4.9	4.9	15.5	15.7	5.5	4.8		
50 to 54 years	6,929	3,601	3,328	1,591	1,669	1,890	1,567	116	92	4		6.3	6.6	6.0	3.9	4.0	16.0	14.5	4.8	3.7		
55 to 59 years	5,124	2,673	2,451	1,134	1,225	1,487	1,146	51	79	1	1	4.7	4.9	4.5	2.8	2.9	12.6	10.6	2.1	3.2		
60 to 64 years	3,818	1,950	1,868	873	966	1,022	856	55	46			3.5	3.6	3.4	2.2	2.3	8.7	7.9	2.3	1.8		
65 to 69 years	2,823	1,352	1,471	598	789	724	644	29	38	1		2.6	2.5	2.7	1.5	1.9	6.1	6.0	1.2	1.5		
70 to 74 years	1,728	816	912	369	455	433	441	14	16			1.6	1.5	1.7	0.9	1.1	3.7	4.1	0.6	0.6		
75 years and over	1,637	672	965	319	535	339	416	14	14			1.5	1.2	1.8	0.8	1.3	2.9	3.8	0.6	0.6		
Under 1 year	1,343	684	659	638	613			46	46			1.2	1.2	1.2	1.6	1.5			1.9	1.8		
21 years and over	74,718	37,349	37,369	24,471	25,428	11,445	10,477	1,394	1,459	39	5	68.0	68.1	67.9	60.3	61.0	97.1	96.9	57.2	58.3		
Median age	30.1	30.4	29.8	25.2	25.2	50.0	49.0	25.6	26.1													
ERIE, PA.																						
All ages	**116,955**	**58,082**	**58,873**	**49,902**	**52,093**	**7,470**	**6,100**	**701**	**674**	**9**	**6**	**100.0**	**100.0**	**100.0**	**100.0**	**100.0**	**100.0**	**100.0**	**100.0**	**100.0**		
Under 5 years	8,399	4,261	4,138	4,217	4,081	2	2	42	55			7.2	7.3	7.0	8.5	7.8			6.0	8.2		
5 to 9 years	8,356	4,314	4,042	4,241	3,959	10	8	63	75			7.1	7.4	6.9	8.5	7.6	0.1	0.1	9.0	11.1		
10 to 14 years	10,183	5,189	4,994	5,099	4,890	26	32	63	70	1	2	8.7	8.9	8.5	10.2	9.4	0.3	0.5	9.0	10.4		
15 to 19 years	11,052	5,378	5,674	5,234	5,534	81	86	62	53	1	1	9.4	9.3	9.6	10.5	10.6	1.1	1.4	8.8	7.9		
20 to 24 years	11,237	5,421	5,816	5,301	5,709	75	63	45	44			9.6	9.3	9.9	10.6	11.0	1.0	1.0	6.4	6.5		
25 to 29 years	10,050	4,990	5,060	4,743	4,826	197	178	49	56	1		8.6	8.6	8.6	9.5	9.3	2.6	2.9	7.0	8.3		
30 to 34 years	8,742	4,259	4,483	3,872	4,106	318	307	68	70	1		7.5	7.3	7.6	7.8	7.9	4.3	5.0	9.7	10.4		
35 to 39 years	7,954	3,834	4,120	3,281	3,581	488	477	65	61		1	6.8	6.6	7.0	6.6	6.9	6.5	7.8	9.3	9.0		
40 to 44 years	8,039	4,006	4,033	3,159	3,251	776	728	69	54	2		6.9	6.9	6.9	6.3	6.2	10.4	11.9	9.8	8.0		
45 to 49 years	8,003	4,117	3,886	2,882	2,953	1,177	895	56	38	2		6.8	7.1	6.6	5.8	5.7	15.8	14.7	8.0	5.6		
50 to 54 years	7,185	3,760	3,425	2,374	2,451	1,347	939	39	34		1	6.1	6.5	5.8	4.8	4.7	18.0	15.4	5.6	5.0		
55 to 59 years	5,606	2,842	2,764	1,806	2,039	1,007	707	29	18			4.8	4.9	4.7	3.6	3.9	13.5	11.6	4.1	2.7		
60 to 64 years	4,336	2,079	2,257	1,358	1,683	698	555	22	19	1		3.7	3.6	3.8	2.7	3.2	9.3	9.1	3.1	2.8		
65 to 69 years	3,367	1,616	1,751	1,086	1,305	518	428	12	18			2.9	2.8	3.0	2.2	2.5	6.9	7.0	1.7	2.7		
70 to 74 years	2,273	1,079	1,194	667	861	400	328	12	4		1	1.9	1.9	2.0	1.3	1.7	5.4	5.4	1.7	0.6		
75 years and over	2,173	937	1,236	582	864	350	367	5	5			1.9	1.6	2.1	1.2	1.7	4.7	6.0	0.7	0.7		
Under 1 year	1,639	802	837	795	826			7	11			1.4	1.4	1.4	1.6	1.6			1.0	1.6		
21 years and over	76,737	37,880	38,857	30,071	32,481	7,335	5,960	467	413	7	3	65.6	65.2	66.0	60.3	62.4	98.2	97.7	66.6	61.3		
Median age	29.6	29.5	29.7	25.9	26.9	52.2	51.5	31.9	28.6													
FALL RIVER, MASS.																						
All ages	**115,428**	**55,542**	**59,886**	**43,625**	**46,712**	**11,597**	**12,975**	**228**	**174**	**92**	**25**	**100.0**	**100.0**	**100.0**	**100.0**	**100.0**	**100.0**	**100.0**	**100.0**	**100.0**		
Under 5 years	7,685	3,886	3,799	3,863	3,782	4	1	15	14	4	2	6.7	7.0	6.3	8.9	8.1			6.6	8.0		
5 to 9 years	8,388	4,239	4,149	4,203	4,119	19	10	15	18	2	2	7.3	7.6	6.9	9.6	8.8	0.2	0.1	6.6	10.3		
10 to 14 years	10,494	5,243	5,251	5,186	5,208	27	25	23	15	7	3	9.1	9.4	8.8	11.9	11.1	0.2	0.2	10.1	8.6		
15 to 19 years	12,017	5,900	6,117	5,801	5,998	68	86	19	24	12	9	10.4	10.6	10.2	13.3	12.8	0.6	0.7	8.3	13.8		
20 to 24 years	10,658	5,063	5,595	4,909	5,426	127	154	21	14	6	1	9.2	9.1	9.3	11.3	11.6	1.1	1.2	9.2	8.0		
25 to 29 years	9,743	4,742	5,001	4,433	4,620	288	369	13	10	8	2	8.4	8.5	8.4	10.2	9.9	2.5	2.8	5.7	5.7		
30 to 34 years	8,331	4,007	4,324	3,530	3,713	461	603	10	7	6	1	7.2	7.2	7.2	8.1	7.9	4.0	4.6	4.4	4.0		
35 to 39 years	8,061	3,770	4,291	2,830	3,278	905	1,001	25	9	10	3	7.0	6.8	7.2	6.5	7.0	7.8	7.7	11.0	5.2		
40 to 44 years	7,684	3,630	4,054	2,403	2,669	1,202	1,377	18	8	7		6.7	6.5	6.8	5.5	5.7	10.4	10.6	7.9	4.6		
45 to 49 years	7,298	3,492	3,806	1,887	2,117	1,578	1,673	19	16	8		6.3	6.3	6.4	4.3	4.5	13.6	12.9	8.3	9.2		
50 to 54 years	6,402	3,119	3,283	1,461	1,617	1,633	1,655	20	11	5		5.5	5.6	5.5	3.3	3.5	14.1	12.8	8.8	6.3		
55 to 59 years	5,310	2,473	2,837	1,038	1,266	1,419	1,565	7	4	9	2	4.6	4.5	4.7	2.4	2.7	12.2	12.1	3.1	2.3		
60 to 64 years	4,659	2,114	2,545	808	1,095	1,294	1,446	8	4	4		4.0	3.8	4.2	1.9	2.3	11.2	11.1	3.5	2.3		
65 to 69 years	3,755	1,746	2,009	614	833	1,130	1,166	2	10			3.3	3.1	3.4	1.4	1.8	9.7	9.0	0.9	5.7		
70 to 74 years	2,571	1,140	1,431	368	510	762	917	7	4	3		2.2	2.1	2.4	0.8	1.1	6.6	7.1	3.1	2.3		
75 years and over	2,372	978	1,394	291	461	680	927	6	6	1		2.1	1.8	2.3	0.7	1.0	5.9	7.1	2.6	3.4		
Under 1 year	1,440	727	713	724	708			2	5	1		1.2	1.3	1.2	1.7	1.5			0.9	2.9		
21 years and over	74,582	35,186	39,396	23,518	26,468	11,449	12,822	152	97	67	9	64.6	63.4	65.8	53.9	56.7	98.7	98.8	66.7	55.7		
Median age	29.3	28.6	30.0	22.8	23.9	53.4	53.6	34.0	26.0													

TABLE 53.—AGE, BY RACE AND SEX, WITH PERCENT DISTRIBUTION BY AGE, FOR CITIES OF 100,000 OR MORE: 1940—Continued

[Percent not shown where less than 0.1 or where base is less than 100]

CITY AND AGE	NUMBER											PERCENT DISTRIBUTION										
	All classes			Native white		Foreign-born white		Negro		Other races		All classes			Native white		Foreign-born white		Negro		Other races	
	Total	Male	Female	Male	Female	Male	Female	Male	Female	Male	Female	Total	Male	Female	Male	Female	Male	Female	Male	Female	Male	Female
FLINT, MICH.																						
All ages	151,543	75,976	75,567	64,078	64,935	8,606	7,239	3,236	3,363	58	30	100.0	100.0	100.0	100.0	100.0	100.0	100.0	100.0	100.0		
Under 5 years	12,729	6,414	6,315	6,141	6,023	1	4	270	284	2	4	8.4	8.4	8.4	9.6	9.3		0.1	8.3	8.4		
5 to 9 years	12,676	6,364	6,312	6,048	6,000	28	13	284	293	4	6	8.4	8.4	8.4	9.4	9.2	0.3	0.2	8.8	8.7		
10 to 14 years	13,955	7,015	6,940	6,642	6,535	72	56	297	345	4	4	9.2	9.2	9.2	10.4	10.1	0.8	0.8	9.2	10.3		
15 to 19 years	14,013	6,714	7,299	6,225	6,768	216	207	264	321	9	3	9.2	8.8	9.7	9.7	10.4	2.5	2.9	8.2	9.5		
20 to 24 years	13,301	6,035	7,266	5,592	6,708	238	269	203	288	2	1	8.8	7.9	9.6	8.7	10.3	2.8	3.7	6.3	8.6		
25 to 29 years	13,198	6,248	6,950	5,624	6,185	356	439	265	325	3	1	8.7	8.2	9.2	8.8	9.5	4.1	6.1	8.2	9.7		
30 to 34 years	13,279	6,623	6,656	5,673	5,703	643	602	301	349	6	2	8.8	8.7	8.8	8.9	8.8	7.5	8.3	9.3	10.4		
35 to 39 years	12,749	6,614	6,135	5,303	4,984	936	807	370	343	5	1	8.4	8.7	8.1	8.3	7.7	10.9	11.1	11.4	10.2		
40 to 44 years	11,432	6,044	5,388	4,590	4,197	1,100	936	349	251	5	4	7.5	8.0	7.1	7.2	6.5	12.8	12.9	10.8	7.5		
45 to 49 years	9,937	5,409	4,528	3,876	3,424	1,283	906	244	196	6	2	6.6	7.1	6.0	6.0	5.3	14.9	12.5	7.5	5.8		
50 to 54 years	7,944	4,330	3,614	2,956	2,716	1,205	774	167	123	2	1	5.2	5.7	4.8	4.6	4.2	14.0	10.7	5.2	3.7		
55 to 59 years	5,609	2,952	2,657	1,903	1,908	951	663	95	85	3	1	3.7	3.9	3.5	3.0	2.9	11.0	9.2	2.9	2.5		
60 to 64 years	4,108	2,064	2,044	1,397	1,443	619	543	46	58	2		2.7	2.7	2.7	2.2	2.2	7.2	7.5	1.4	1.7		
65 to 69 years	2,960	1,456	1,504	984	1,017	427	439	43	48	2		2.0	1.9	2.0	1.5	1.6	5.0	6.1	1.3	1.4		
70 to 74 years	1,768	843	925	581	635	242	256	20	34			1.2	1.1	1.2	0.9	1.0	2.8	3.5	0.6	1.0		
75 years and over	1,885	851	1,034	543	689	289	325	18	20	1		1.2	1.1	1.4	0.8	1.1	3.4	4.5	0.6	0.6		
Under 1 year	2,422	1,240	1,182	1,182	1,129			58	53			1.6	1.6	1.6	1.8	1.7			1.8	1.6		
21 years and over	95,573	48,336	47,237	37,992	38,254	8,234	6,904	2,074	2,066	36	13	63.1	63.6	62.5	59.3	58.9	95.7	95.4	64.1	61.4		
Median age	28.4	29.4	27.6	26.2	25.4	47.8	46.6	30.6	27.3													
FORT WAYNE, IND.																						
All ages	118,410	56,915	61,495	53,320	58,148	2,379	2,030	1,203	1,314	13	3	100.0	100.0	100.0	100.0	100.0	100.0	100.0	100.0	100.0		
Under 5 years	7,822	3,972	3,850	3,885	3,742	2	2	84	104	1	2	6.6	7.0	6.3	7.3	6.4	0.1	0.1	7.0	7.9		
5 to 9 years	7,997	4,040	3,957	3,952	3,827	5	5	83	125			6.8	7.1	6.4	7.4	6.6	0.2	0.2	6.9	9.5		
10 to 14 years	9,544	4,806	4,738	4,684	4,591	13	11	109	136			8.1	8.4	7.7	8.8	7.9	0.5	0.5	9.1	10.4		
15 to 19 years	10,286	4,953	5,333	4,798	5,182	29	31	126	120			8.7	8.7	8.7	9.0	8.9	1.2	1.5	10.5	9.1		
20 to 24 years	10,368	4,620	5,748	4,482	5,590	40	45	97	113	1		8.8	8.1	9.3	8.4	9.6	1.7	2.2	8.1	8.6		
25 to 29 years	10,286	4,774	5,512	4,589	5,313	80	80	102	118	3	1	8.7	8.4	9.0	8.6	9.1	3.4	3.9	8.5	9.0		
30 to 34 years	10,129	4,743	5,386	4,521	5,168	140	101	80	117	2		8.6	8.3	8.8	8.5	8.9	5.9	5.0	6.7	8.9		
35 to 39 years	9,767	4,820	4,947	4,497	4,646	217	181	103	120	3		8.2	8.5	8.0	8.4	8.0	9.1	8.9	8.6	9.1		
40 to 44 years	8,894	4,338	4,556	3,972	4,286	239	151	125	119	2		7.5	7.6	7.4	7.4	7.4	10.0	7.4	10.4	9.1		
45 to 46 years	7,977	3,927	4,050	3,585	3,766	255	207	86	77	1		6.7	6.9	6.6	6.7	6.5	10.7	10.2	7.1	5.9		
50 to 54 years	6,828	3,352	3,476	2,973	3,223	302	209	77	44			5.8	5.9	5.7	5.6	5.5	12.7	10.3	6.4	3.3		
55 to 59 years	5,740	2,781	2,959	2,466	2,725	270	190	45	44			4.8	4.9	4.8	4.6	4.7	11.3	9.4	3.7	3.3		
60 to 64 years	4,454	2,122	2,332	1,845	2,071	244	232	33	29			3.8	3.7	3.8	3.5	3.6	10.3	11.4	2.7	2.2		
65 to 69 years	3,399	1,524	1,875	1,331	1,643	173	202	20	30			2.9	2.7	3.0	2.5	2.8	7.3	10.0	1.7	2.3		
70 to 74 years	2,419	1,078	1,341	889	1,174	170	159	19	8			2.0	1.9	2.2	1.7	2.0	7.1	7.8	1.6	0.6		
75 years and over	2,500	1,065	1,435	851	1,201	200	224	14	10			2.1	1.9	2.3	1.6	2.1	8.4	11.0	1.2	0.8		
Under 1 year	1,505	752	753	738	735			14	17		1	1.3	1.3	1.2	1.4	1.3			1.2	1.3		
21 years and over	80,802	38,288	42,514	35,172	39,728	2,323	1,971	781	814	12	1	68.2	67.3	69.1	66.0	68.3	97.6	97.1	64.9	61.9		
Median age	31.4	31.4	31.5	30.3	30.8	52.8	54.8	30.0	27.5													
FORT WORTH, TEXAS																						
All ages	177,662	85,061	92,601	71,336	77,469	1,898	1,642	11,781	13,473	46	17	100.0	100.0	100.0	100.0	100.0	100.0	100.0	100.0	100.0		
Under 5 years	11,717	5,894	5,823	5,083	5,021	2		804	800	5	2	6.6	6.9	6.3	7.1	6.5	0.1		6.8	5.9		
5 to 9 years	11,951	5,964	5,987	5,109	5,095		5	852	885	3	2	6.7	7.0	6.5	7.2	6.6		0.3	7.2	6.6		
10 to 14 years	14,233	7,133	7,100	6,097	6,038	11	9	1,023	1,052	2	1	8.0	8.4	7.7	8.5	7.8	0.6	0.5	8.7	7.8		
15 to 19 years	16,106	7,674	8,432	6,622	7,230	34	17	1,015	1,185	3		9.1	9.0	9.1	9.3	9.3	1.8	1.0	8.6	8.8		
20 to 24 years	15,863	7,161	8,702	6,201	7,301	53	67	903	1,331	4	3	8.9	8.4	9.4	8.7	9.4	2.8	4.1	7.7	9.9		
25 to 29 years	16,517	7,514	9,003	6,375	7,421	107	110	1,029	1,472	3		9.3	8.8	9.7	8.9	9.6	5.6	6.7	8.7	10.9		
30 to 34 years	16,309	7,528	8,781	6,261	7,194	126	126	1,138	1,459	3	2	9.2	8.8	9.5	8.8	9.3	6.6	7.7	9.7	10.8		
35 to 39 years	15,472	7,198	8,274	5,855	6,640	163	170	1,177	1,462	3	2	8.7	8.5	8.9	8.2	8.6	8.6	10.4	10.0	10.9		
40 to 44 years	13,665	6,552	7,113	5,309	5,788	189	211	1,053	1,113	1	1	7.7	7.7	7.7	7.4	7.5	10.0	12.9	8.9	8.3		
45 to 49 years	12,167	6,003	6,164	4,866	5,074	247	184	885	905	5	1	6.8	7.1	6.7	6.8	6.5	13.0	11.2	7.5	6.7		
50 to 54 years	9,815	4,923	4,892	3,974	4,116	287	171	660	604	2	1	5.5	5.8	5.3	5.6	5.3	15.1	10.4	5.6	4.5		
55 to 59 years	7,533	3,796	3,737	3,179	3,216	172	129	438	392	7		4.2	4.5	4.0	4.5	4.2	9.1	7.9	3.7	2.9		
60 to 64 years	5,905	2,912	2,993	2,451	2,596	170	142	289	254	2	1	3.3	3.4	3.2	3.4	3.4	9.0	8.6	2.5	1.9		

65 to 69 years	4,745	2,201	2,544	1,811	2,141	119	120	270	283	1	--	2.7	2.6	2.7	2.5	2.8	6.3	7.3	2.3	2.1	--	--
70 to 74 years	2,894	1,373	1,521	1,125	1,301	102	89	146	130	--	1	1.6	1.6	1.6	1.6	1.7	5.4	5.4	1.2	1.0	--	--
75 years and over	2,770	1,235	1,535	1,018	1,297	116	92	99	146	2	--	1.6	1.5	1.7	1.4	1.7	6.1	5.6	0.8	1.1	--	--
Under 1 year	2,423	1,230	1,193	1,083	1,038	--	--	145	155	2	--	1.4	1.4	1.3	1.5	1.3	--	--	1.2	1.2	--	--
21 years and over	120,356	56,951	63,405	47,189	52,537	1,846	1,605	7,884	9,251	32	12	67.7	67.0	68.5	66.1	67.8	97.3	97.7	66.9	68.7	--	--
Median age	30.7	30.8	30.7	30.1	30.4	50.3	47.9	31.2	30.0	--	--	--	--	--	--	--	--	--	--	--	--	--
GARY, IND.																						
All ages	**111,719**	**58,075**	**53,644**	**37,641**	**36,335**	**10,275**	**6,995**	**10,116**	**10,278**	**43**	**36**	**100.0**	**100.0**	**100.0**	**100.0**	**100.0**	**100.0**	**100.0**	**100.0**	**100.0**	--	--
Under 5 years	8,536	4,277	4,259	3,443	3,456	2	9	823	789	9	5	7.6	7.4	7.9	9.1	9.5	--	0.1	8.1	7.7	--	--
5 to 9 years	8,194	4,110	4,084	3,261	3,144	27	19	815	911	7	10	7.3	7.1	7.6	8.7	8.7	0.3	0.3	8.1	8.9	--	--
10 to 14 years	9,398	4,667	4,731	3,627	3,719	59	53	980	953	1	6	8.4	8.0	8.8	9.6	10.2	0.6	0.8	9.7	9.3	--	--
15 to 19 years	10,106	4,875	5,231	3,883	4,133	167	167	824	930	1	1	9.0	8.4	9.8	10.3	11.4	1.6	2.4	8.1	9.0	--	--
20 to 24 years	11,287	5,476	5,811	4,504	4,722	183	172	787	916	2	1	10.1	9.4	10.8	12.0	13.0	1.8	2.5	7.8	8.9	--	--
25 to 29 years	11,236	5,584	5,652	4,416	4,289	342	345	828	1,015	4	3	10.1	9.6	10.5	11.7	11.8	3.3	4.9	8.2	9.9	--	--
30 to 34 years	9,602	4,944	4,658	3,510	3,158	590	514	843	982	1	4	8.6	8.5	8.7	9.3	8.7	5.7	7.3	8.3	9.6	--	--
35 to 39 years	9,184	4,763	4,421	2,849	2,525	931	797	977	1,097	6	2	8.2	8.2	8.2	7.6	6.9	9.1	11.4	9.7	10.7	--	--
40 to 44 years	8,421	4,547	3,874	2,255	2,047	1,336	985	951	841	5	1	7.5	7.8	7.2	6.0	5.6	13.0	14.1	9.4	8.2	--	--
45 to 49 years	8,142	4,609	3,533	1,937	1,706	1,890	1,175	781	652	1	--	7.3	7.9	6.6	5.1	4.7	18.4	16.8	7.7	6.3	--	--
50 to 54 years	6,732	4,029	2,703	1,489	1,208	1,966	1,067	573	426	1	2	6.0	6.9	5.0	4.0	3.3	19.1	15.3	5.7	4.1	--	--
55 to 59 years	4,620	2,738	1,882	1,007	876	1,310	729	418	276	3	1	4.1	4.7	3.5	2.7	2.4	12.7	10.4	4.1	2.7	--	--
60 to 64 years	2,832	1,661	1,171	676	581	757	439	228	151	--	--	2.5	2.9	2.2	1.8	1.6	7.4	6.3	2.3	1.5	--	--
65 to 69 years	1,710	957	753	404	357	397	228	155	168	1	--	1.5	1.6	1.4	1.1	1.0	3.9	3.3	1.5	1.6	--	--
70 to 74 years	954	498	456	240	212	185	153	72	91	1	--	0.9	0.9	0.9	0.6	0.6	1.8	2.2	0.7	0.9	--	--
75 years and over	765	340	425	146	202	133	143	61	80	--	--	0.7	0.6	0.8	0.4	0.6	1.3	2.0	0.6	0.8	--	--
Under 1 year	1,605	809	796	654	645	--	--	155	151	--	--	1.4	1.4	1.5	1.7	1.8	--	--	1.5	1.5	--	--
21 years and over	73,401	39,173	34,228	22,658	20,987	9,986	6,707	6,504	6,521	25	13	65.7	67.5	63.8	60.2	57.8	97.2	95.9	64.3	63.4	--	--
Median age	28.7	30.0	27.4	25.1	23.9	49.0	46.9	30.0	28.2	--	--	--	--	--	--	--	--	--	--	--	--	--
GRAND RAPIDS, MICH.																						
All ages	**164,292**	**79,418**	**84,874**	**67,454**	**73,766**	**10,631**	**9,716**	**1,297**	**1,363**	**36**	**29**	**100.0**	**100.0**	**100.0**	**100.0**	**100.0**	**100.0**	**100.0**	**100.0**	**100.0**	--	--
Under 5 years	11,866	6,008	5,858	5,903	5,753	2	1	99	99	4	5	7.2	7.6	6.9	8.8	7.8	--	--	7.6	7.3	--	--
5 to 9 years	11,683	5,908	5,775	5,794	5,638	5	10	108	125	1	2	7.1	7.4	6.8	8.6	7.6	--	0.1	8.3	9.2	--	--
10 to 14 years	13,321	6,700	6,621	6,569	6,465	22	29	105	124	4	3	8.1	8.4	7.8	9.7	8.8	0.2	0.3	8.1	9.1	--	--
15 to 19 years	14,501	6,818	7,683	6,634	7,459	85	103	96	118	3	3	8.8	8.6	9.1	9.8	10.1	0.8	1.1	7.4	8.7	--	--
20 to 24 years	14,500	6,720	7,780	6,465	7,539	147	131	104	108	4	2	8.8	8.5	9.2	9.6	10.2	1.4	1.3	8.0	7.9	--	--
25 to 29 years	13,794	6,626	7,168	6,264	6,776	260	268	100	122	2	2	8.4	8.3	8.4	9.3	9.2	2.4	2.8	7.7	9.0	--	--
30 to 34 years	12,527	6,003	6,524	5,438	5,958	438	457	127	106	--	3	7.6	7.6	7.7	8.1	8.1	4.1	4.7	9.8	7.8	--	--
35 to 39 years	11,852	5,690	6,162	4,885	5,344	699	698	101	115	5	5	7.2	7.2	7.3	7.2	7.2	6.6	7.2	7.8	8.4	--	--
40 to 44 years	10,973	5,392	5,581	4,378	4,664	899	791	111	123	4	3	6.7	6.8	6.6	6.5	6.3	8.5	8.1	8.6	9.0	--	--
45 to 49 years	11,167	5,471	5,696	4,021	4,507	1,346	1,102	102	87	2	--	6.8	6.9	6.7	6.0	6.1	12.7	11.3	7.9	6.4	--	--
50 to 54 years	10,003	4,939	5,064	3,328	3,807	1,534	1,187	74	69	3	1	6.1	6.2	6.0	4.9	5.2	14.4	12.2	5.7	5.1	--	--
55 to 59 years	7,935	3,877	4,058	2,503	2,917	1,309	1,083	65	58	--	--	4.8	4.9	4.8	3.7	4.0	12.3	11.1	5.0	4.3	--	--
60 to 64 years	6,730	3,222	3,508	1,946	2,348	1,238	1,128	36	32	2	--	4.1	4.1	4.1	2.9	3.2	11.6	11.6	2.8	2.3	--	--
65 to 69 years	5,166	2,321	2,845	1,370	1,877	920	932	31	36	--	--	3.1	2.9	3.4	2.0	2.5	8.7	9.6	2.4	2.6	--	--
70 to 74 years	3,917	1,782	2,135	956	1,301	805	816	21	18	--	--	2.4	2.2	2.5	1.4	1.8	7.6	8.4	1.6	1.3	--	--
75 years and over	4,357	1,941	2,416	1,000	1,413	922	980	17	23	2	--	2.7	2.4	2.8	1.5	1.9	8.7	10.1	1.3	1.7	--	--
Under 1 year	2,415	1,249	1,166	1,224	1,143	--	--	24	23	1	--	1.5	1.6	1.4	1.8	1.5	--	--	1.9	1.7	--	--
21 years and over	110,159	52,770	57,389	41,393	46,955	10,484	9,543	870	875	23	16	67.1	66.4	67.6	61.4	63.7	98.6	98.2	67.1	64.2	--	--
Median age	31.0	30.8	31.2	26.9	28.0	54.6	55.4	31.4	29.4	--	--	--	--	--	--	--	--	--	--	--	--	--
HARTFORD, CONN.																						
All ages	**166,267**	**80,509**	**85,758**	**58,470**	**64,044**	**18,570**	**18,035**	**3,432**	**3,658**	**37**	**21**	**100.0**	**100.0**	**100.0**	**100.0**	**100.0**	**100.0**	**100.0**	**100.0**	**100.0**	--	--
Under 5 years	10,104	5,181	4,923	4,864	4,591	14	13	302	317	1	2	6.1	6.4	5.7	8.3	7.2	0.1	0.1	8.8	8.7	--	--
5 to 9 years	10,330	5,223	5,107	4,815	4,731	40	42	367	332	1	2	6.2	6.5	6.0	8.2	7.4	0.2	0.2	10.7	9.1	--	--
10 to 14 years	12,530	6,264	6,266	5,798	5,801	105	88	355	375	6	2	7.5	7.8	7.3	9.9	9.1	0.6	0.5	10.3	10.3	--	--
15 to 19 years	14,910	7,059	7,851	6,462	7,180	277	316	315	352	5	3	9.0	8.8	9.2	11.1	11.2	1.5	1.8	9.2	9.6	--	--
20 to 24 years	16,708	7,748	8,960	7,089	8,227	370	422	288	308	1	3	10.0	9.6	10.4	12.1	12.8	2.0	2.3	8.4	8.4	--	--
25 to 29 years	15,857	7,516	8,341	6,489	7,146	742	896	284	298	1	1	9.5	9.3	9.7	11.1	11.2	4.0	5.0	8.3	8.1	--	--
30 to 34 years	14,063	6,667	7,396	5,235	5,705	1,172	1,392	257	299	3	--	8.5	8.3	8.6	9.0	8.9	6.3	7.7	7.5	8.2	--	--
35 to 39 years	12,899	6,221	6,678	4,142	4,512	1,784	1,833	293	332	2	1	7.8	7.7	7.8	7.1	7.0	9.6	10.2	8.5	9.1	--	--
40 to 44 years	12,372	6,046	6,326	3,496	3,821	2,257	2,217	284	288	9	--	7.4	7.5	7.4	6.0	6.0	12.2	12.3	8.3	7.9	--	--
45 to 49 years	11,750	5,836	5,914	2,777	3,118	2,838	2,587	219	207	2	2	7.1	7.2	6.9	4.7	4.9	15.3	14.3	6.4	5.7	--	--
50 to 54 years	10,034	5,245	4,789	2,300	2,329	2,787	2,294	155	165	3	1	6.0	6.5	5.6	3.9	3.6	15.0	12.7	4.5	4.5	--	--
55 to 59 years	7,548	3,712	3,836	1,542	1,883	2,063	1,827	107	125	--	1	4.5	4.6	4.5	2.6	2.9	11.1	10.1	3.1	3.4	--	--
60 to 64 years	6,304	2,959	3,345	1,272	1,667	1,617	1,589	69	89	1	--	3.8	3.7	3.9	2.2	2.6	8.7	8.8	2.0	2.4	--	--
65 to 69 years	4,840	2,173	2,667	971	1,378	1,134	1,190	67	98	1	1	2.9	2.7	3.1	1.7	2.2	6.1	6.6	2.0	2.7	--	--
70 to 74 years	3,166	1,465	1,701	628	930	802	735	35	36	--	--	1.9	1.8	2.0	1.1	1.5	4.3	4.1	1.0	1.0	--	--
75 years and over	2,852	1,194	1,658	590	1,025	568	594	35	37	1	2	1.7	1.5	1.9	1.0	1.6	3.1	3.3	1.0	1.0	--	--
Under 1 year	1,896	970	926	915	871	1	1	54	53	--	1	1.1	1.2	1.1	1.6	1.4	--	--	1.6	1.4	--	--
21 years and over	115,194	55,305	59,889	35,201	40,182	18,053	17,484	2,027	2,213	24	10	69.3	68.7	69.8	60.2	62.7	97.2	96.9	59.1	60.5	--	--
Median age	31.0	30.9	31.0	25.2	26.0	49.4	48.5	26.6	27.4	--	--	--	--	--	--	--	--	--	--	--	--	--

TABLE 53.—AGE, BY RACE AND SEX, WITH PERCENT DISTRIBUTION BY AGE, FOR CITIES OF 100,000 OR MORE: 1940—Continued

[Percent not shown where less than 0.1 or where base is less than 100]

CITY AND AGE	NUMBER											PERCENT DISTRIBUTION										
	All classes			Native white		Foreign-born white		Negro		Other races		All classes			Native white		Foreign-born white		Negro		Other races	
	Total	Male	Female	Male	Female	Male	Female	Male	Female	Male	Female	Total	Male	Female	Male	Female	Male	Female	Male	Female	Male	Female
HOUSTON, TEXAS																						
All ages	384,514	188,318	196,196	139,295	143,351	8,355	6,958	40,432	45,820	186	67	100.0	100.0	100.0	100.0	100.0	100.0	100.0	100.0	100.0	100.0	-
Under 5 years	26,834	13,383	13,451	10,610	10,544	12	13	2,754	2,880	7	14	7.0	7.1	6.9	7.6	7.4	0.1	0.2	6.8	6.3	3.8	-
5 to 9 years	25,763	12,851	12,912	9,989	9,802	28	28	2,824	3,079	10	3	6.7	6.8	6.6	7.2	6.8	0.3	0.4	7.0	6.7	5.4	-
10 to 14 years	28,191	13,974	14,217	10,851	10,739	47	55	3,070	3,414	6	9	7.3	7.4	7.2	7.8	7.5	0.6	0.8	7.6	7.5	3.2	-
15 to 19 years	31,988	14,753	17,235	11,400	13,097	125	150	3,217	3,983	11	5	8.3	7.8	8.8	8.2	9.1	1.5	2.2	7.9	8.7	5.9	-
20 to 24 years	38,575	17,519	21,056	13,643	15,730	226	291	3,639	5,033	11	2	10.0	9.3	10.7	9.8	11.0	2.7	4.2	9.0	11.0	5.9	-
25 to 29 years	43,568	20,753	22,815	15,639	16,263	428	519	4,668	6,027	18	6	11.3	11.0	11.6	11.2	11.3	5.1	7.5	11.5	13.2	9.7	-
30 to 34 years	40,440	19,716	20,724	14,483	14,696	715	616	4,486	5,400	32	12	10.5	10.5	10.6	10.4	10.3	8.6	8.9	11.1	11.8	17.2	-
35 to 39 years	37,329	18,526	18,803	12,939	12,829	1,017	833	4,549	5,136	21	5	9.7	9.8	9.6	9.3	8.9	12.2	12.0	11.2	11.2	11.3	-
40 to 44 years	30,074	15,637	14,437	10,971	10,221	1,041	831	3,597	3,384	28	1	7.8	8.3	7.4	7.9	7.1	12.5	11.9	8.9	7.4	15.1	-
45 to 49 years	24,125	12,666	11,459	8,723	8,143	1,096	747	2,835	2,565	12	4	6.3	6.7	5.8	6.3	5.7	13.1	10.7	7.0	5.6	6.5	-
50 to 54 years	18,384	9,714	8,670	6,891	6,337	1,048	732	1,762	1,598	13	3	4.8	5.2	4.4	4.9	4.4	12.5	10.5	4.4	3.5	7.0	-
55 to 59 years	13,089	6,682	6,407	4,750	4,761	855	593	1,071	1,051	6	2	3.4	3.5	3.3	3.4	3.3	10.2	8.5	2.6	2.3	3.2	-
60 to 64 years	9,695	4,686	5,009	3,367	3,806	599	501	713	702	7	-	2.5	2.5	2.6	2.4	2.7	7.2	7.2	1.8	1.5	3.8	-
65 to 69 years	7,551	3,522	4,029	2,378	2,792	475	408	668	828	1	1	2.0	1.9	2.1	1.7	1.9	5.7	5.9	1.7	1.8	0.5	-
70 to 74 years	4,523	2,054	2,469	1,419	1,750	283	311	352	408	-	-	1.2	1.1	1.3	1.0	1.2	3.4	4.5	0.9	0.9	-	-
75 years and over	4,385	1,882	2,503	1,242	1,841	360	330	277	332	3	-	1.1	1.0	1.3	0.9	1.3	4.3	4.7	0.7	0.7	1.6	-
Under 1 year	5,494	2,789	2,705	2,254	2,162	-	-	533	539	2	4	1.4	1.5	1.4	1.6	1.5	-	-	1.3	1.2	1.1	-
21 years and over	264,418	130,301	134,117	94,140	95,972	8,097	6,662	27,916	31,447	148	36	68.8	69.2	68.4	67.6	66.9	96.9	95.7	69.0	68.6	79.6	-
Median age	29.7	30.2	29.2	29.2	28.6	47.5	46.0	30.1	28.8	34.7	-	-	-	-	-	-	-	-	-	-	-	-
INDIANAPOLIS, IND.																						
All ages	386,972	185,461	201,511	155,492	169,708	5,554	5,001	24,356	26,786	59	16	100.0	100.0	100.0	100.0	100.0	100.0	100.0	100.0	100.0	-	-
Under 5 years	26,266	13,418	12,848	11,583	11,077	5	5	1,828	1,764	2	2	6.8	7.2	6.4	7.4	6.5	0.1	0.1	7.5	6.6	-	-
5 to 9 years	25,308	12,550	12,758	10,676	10,850	14	3	1,855	1,905	5	-	6.5	6.8	6.3	6.9	6.4	0.3	0.1	7.6	7.1	-	-
10 to 14 years	28,082	13,879	14,203	11,782	12,059	20	22	2,075	2,120	2	2	7.3	7.5	7.0	7.6	7.1	0.4	0.4	8.5	7.9	-	-
15 to 19 years	31,427	15,139	16,288	12,986	13,995	73	45	2,079	2,248	1	-	8.1	8.2	8.1	8.4	8.2	1.3	0.9	8.5	8.4	-	-
20 to 24 years	33,702	15,495	18,207	13,604	15,805	79	93	1,810	2,307	2	2	8.7	8.4	9.0	8.7	9.3	1.4	1.9	7.4	8.6	-	-
25 to 29 years	34,345	16,172	18,173	14,002	15,436	156	166	2,008	2,570	6	1	8.9	8.7	9.0	9.0	9.1	2.8	3.3	8.2	9.6	-	-
30 to 34 years	33,249	15,693	17,556	13,428	14,817	299	284	1,955	2,453	11	2	8.6	8.5	8.7	8.6	8.7	5.4	5.7	8.0	9.2	-	-
35 to 39 years	31,533	15,035	16,498	12,545	13,583	439	420	2,045	2,493	6	2	8.1	8.1	8.2	8.1	8.0	7.9	8.4	8.4	9.3	-	-
40 to 44 years	29,226	13,955	15,271	11,416	12,518	555	484	1,980	2,268	4	1	7.6	7.5	7.6	7.3	7.4	10.0	9.7	8.1	8.5	-	-
45 to 49 years	26,695	12,905	13,790	10,439	11,367	650	548	1,811	1,874	5	1	6.9	7.0	6.8	6.7	6.7	11.7	11.0	7.4	7.0	-	-
50 to 54 years	23,732	11,754	11,978	9,378	9,989	798	574	1,574	1,415	4	-	6.1	6.3	5.9	6.0	5.9	14.4	11.5	6.5	5.3	-	-
55 to 59 years	19,435	9,382	10,053	7,455	8,368	702	554	1,220	1,131	5	-	5.0	5.1	5.0	4.8	4.9	12.6	11.1	5.0	4.2	-	-
60 to 64 years	15,286	7,297	7,989	5,946	6,744	571	543	777	701	3	1	4.0	3.9	4.0	3.8	4.0	10.3	10.9	3.2	2.6	-	-
65 to 69 years	12,272	5,626	6,646	4,523	5,495	446	474	655	677	2	-	3.2	3.0	3.3	2.9	3.2	8.0	9.5	2.7	2.5	-	-
70 to 74 years	8,299	3,733	4,566	3,042	3,781	361	367	330	417	-	1	2.1	2.0	2.3	2.0	2.2	6.5	7.3	1.4	1.6	-	-
75 years and over	8,115	3,428	4,687	2,687	3,824	386	419	354	443	1	1	2.1	1.8	2.3	1.7	2.3	6.9	8.4	1.5	1.7	-	-
Under 1 year	5,214	2,695	2,519	2,312	2,154	1	-	381	365	1	-	1.3	1.5	1.3	1.5	1.3	-	-	1.6	1.4	-	-
21 years and over	269,452	127,629	141,823	105,994	118,649	5,426	4,911	16,160	18,253	49	10	69.6	68.8	70.4	68.2	69.9	97.7	98.2	66.3	68.1	-	-
Median age	32.2	31.9	32.4	31.2	31.9	53.1	53.8	31.3	31.0	-	-	-	-	-	-	-	-	-	-	-	-	-
JACKSONVILLE, FLA.																						
All ages	173,065	82,798	90,287	51,787	55,488	2,185	1,787	28,798	32,984	28	8	100.0	100.0	100.0	100.0	100.0	100.0	100.0	100.0	100.0	-	-
Under 5 years	11,922	5,980	5,942	3,937	3,787	4	4	2,036	2,150	3	1	6.9	7.2	6.6	7.6	6.8	0.2	0.2	7.1	6.5	-	-
5 to 9 years	12,527	6,260	6,267	3,923	3,746	4	3	2,331	2,517	2	1	7.2	7.6	6.9	7.6	6.8	0.2	0.2	8.1	7.6	-	-
10 to 14 years	14,137	7,016	7,121	4,404	4,423	8	11	2,601	2,686	3	1	8.2	8.5	7.9	8.5	8.0	0.4	0.6	9.0	8.1	-	-
15 to 19 years	15,121	6,833	8,288	4,295	5,096	22	16	2,516	3,175	-	1	8.7	8.3	9.2	8.3	9.2	1.0	0.9	8.7	9.6	-	-
20 to 24 years	16,799	7,282	9,517	4,729	5,843	33	39	2,518	3,634	2	1	9.7	8.8	10.5	9.1	10.5	1.5	2.2	8.7	11.0	-	-
25 to 29 years	17,699	8,067	9,632	5,082	5,765	60	90	2,924	3,777	1	-	10.2	9.7	10.7	9.8	10.4	2.7	5.0	10.2	11.5	-	-
30 to 34 years	16,551	7,733	8,818	4,839	5,351	114	125	2,776	3,341	4	1	9.6	9.3	9.8	9.3	9.6	5.2	7.0	9.6	10.1	-	-
35 to 39 years	15,999	7,696	8,303	4,591	4,708	194	166	2,908	3,429	3	-	9.2	9.3	9.2	8.9	8.5	8.9	9.3	10.1	10.4	-	-
40 to 44 years	13,189	6,572	6,617	3,925	3,944	270	193	2,376	2,478	1	2	7.6	7.9	7.3	7.6	7.1	12.4	10.8	8.3	7.5	-	-
45 to 49 years	10,790	5,472	5,318	3,377	3,284	244	179	1,849	1,855	2	-	6.2	6.6	5.9	6.5	5.9	11.2	10.0	6.4	5.6	-	-
50 to 54 years	8,526	4,460	4,066	2,721	2,638	287	205	1,450	1,223	2	-	4.9	5.4	4.5	5.3	4.8	13.1	11.5	5.0	3.7	-	-
55 to 59 years	6,365	3,182	3,183	2,020	2,116	309	212	852	855	1	-	3.7	3.8	3.5	3.9	3.8	14.1	11.9	3.0	2.6	-	-
60 to 64 years	4,851	2,336	2,515	1,525	1,726	216	181	592	608	3	-	2.8	2.8	2.8	2.9	3.1	9.9	10.1	2.1	1.8	-	-

65 to 69 years	4,052	1,918	2,134	1,158	1,316	179	162	581	656			2.3	2.3	2.4	2.2	2.4	8.2	9.1	2.0	2.0		
70 to 74 years	2,398	1,098	1,300	681	876	130	93	286	331	1		1.4	1.3	1.4	1.3	1.6	5.9	5.2	1.0	1.0		
75 years and over	2,139	893	1,246	580	869	111	108	202	269			1.2	1.1	1.4	1.1	1.6	5.1	6.0	0.7	0.8		
Under 1 year	2,190	1,083	1,107	761	740			322	367			1.3	1.3	1.2	1.5	1.3			1.1	1.1		
21 years and over	116,101	55,350	60,751	34,357	37,358	2,141	1,749	18,833	21,641	19	3	67.1	66.8	67.3	66.3	67.3	98.0	97.9	65.4	65.6		
Median age	29.5	30.0	29.2	29.5	29.2	52.4	51.6	29.1	28.1													
JERSEY CITY, N. J.																						
All ages	301,173	149,703	151,470	115,970	118,468	27,206	25,954	6,402	7,014	125	34	100.0	100.0	100.0	100.0	100.0	100.0	100.0	100.0	100.0	100.0	
Under 5 years	18,141	9,219	8,922	8,632	8,318	16	18	567	582	4	4	6.0	6.2	5.9	7.4	7.0	0.1	0.1	8.9	8.3	3.2	
5 to 9 years	20,198	10,300	9,898	9,675	9,214	53	52	567	629	5	3	6.7	6.9	6.5	8.3	7.8	0.2	0.2	8.9	9.0	4.0	
10 to 14 years	25,289	12,755	12,534	11,992	11,767	117	111	641	651	5	5	8.4	8.5	8.3	10.3	9.9	0.4	0.4	10.0	9.3	4.0	
15 to 19 years	28,552	14,259	14,293	13,324	13,276	370	371	558	640	7	6	9.5	9.5	9.4	11.5	11.2	1.4	1.4	8.7	9.1	5.6	
20 to 24 years	29,797	14,428	15,369	13,522	14,284	350	415	547	669	9	1	9.9	9.6	10.1	11.7	12.1	1.3	1.6	8.5	9.5	7.2	
25 to 29 years	27,848	13,588	14,260	12,309	12,676	755	888	518	691	6	5	9.2	9.1	9.4	10.6	10.7	2.8	3.4	8.1	9.9	4.8	
30 to 34 years	25,244	12,467	12,777	10,401	10,533	1,497	1,575	550	669	19		8.4	8.3	8.4	9.0	8.9	5.5	6.1	8.6	9.5	15.2	
35 to 39 years	23,228	11,593	11,635	8,601	8,610	2,380	2,347	591	676	21	2	7.7	7.7	7.7	7.4	7.3	8.7	9.0	9.2	9.6	16.8	
40 to 44 years	22,742	11,362	11,380	7,626	7,641	3,132	3,219	587	515	17	5	7.6	7.6	7.5	6.6	6.4	11.5	12.4	9.2	7.3	13.6	
45 to 49 years	21,021	10,536	10,485	5,998	6,183	4,124	3,920	407	381	7	1	7.0	7.0	6.9	5.2	5.2	15.2	15.1	6.4	5.4	5.6	
50 to 54 years	18,260	9,413	8,847	4,675	4,930	4,436	3,612	294	305	8		6.1	6.3	5.8	4.0	4.2	16.3	13.9	4.6	4.3	6.4	
55 to 59 years	13,514	6,859	6,655	3,206	3,578	3,435	2,878	208	198	10	1	4.5	4.6	4.4	2.8	3.0	12.6	11.1	3.2	2.8	8.0	
60 to 64 years	10,575	5,278	5,297	2,507	2,791	2,619	2,345	148	160	4	1	3.5	3.5	3.5	2.2	2.4	9.6	9.0	2.3	2.3	3.2	
65 to 69 years	7,633	3,623	4,010	1,739	2,117	1,761	1,780	121	113	2		2.5	2.4	2.6	1.5	1.8	6.5	6.9	1.9	1.6	1.6	
70 to 74 years	4,886	2,187	2,699	951	1,329	1,183	1,297	52	73	1		1.6	1.5	1.8	0.8	1.1	4.3	5.0	0.8	1.0	0.8	
75 years and over	4,245	1,836	2,409	812	1,221	978	1,126	46	62			1.4	1.2	1.6	0.7	1.0	3.6	4.3	0.7	0.9		
Under 1 year	3,355	1,744	1,611	1,616	1,507	2	1	126	103			1.1	1.2	1.1	1.4	1.3			2.0	1.5		
21 years and over	202,954	100,318	102,636	69,670	72,960	26,571	25,293	3,977	4,367	100	16	67.4	67.0	67.8	60.1	61.6	97.7	97.5	62.1	62.3	80.0	
Median age	30.2	30.1	30.2	25.3	25.9	50.9	50.1	28.1	27.4	36.8												
KANSAS CITY, KANS.																						
All ages	121,458	59,432	62,026	46,049	47,769	3,485	3,087	9,874	11,159	24	11	100 0	100.0	100.0	100.0	100.0	100.0	100.0	100.0	100.0		
Under 5 years	8,867	4,554	4,313	3,724	3,521	2	1	826	791	2		7.3	7.7	7.0	8.1	7.4	0.1		8.3	7.1		
5 to 9 years	9,116	4,591	4,525	3,777	3,691		1	812	833	2		7.5	7.7	7.3	8.2	7.7			8.2	7.5		
10 to 14 years	10,135	5,066	5,069	4,184	4,107	11	6	871	956			8.3	8.5	8.2	9.1	8.6	0.3	0.2	8.8	8.6		
15 to 19 years	11,429	5,621	5,808	4,716	4,805	22	27	880	974	3	2	9.4	9.5	9.4	10.2	10.1	0.6	0.9	8.9	8.7		
20 to 24 years	10,599	4,922	5,677	4,247	4 734	41	54	631	888	3	1	8.7	8.3	9.2	9.2	9.0	1.2	1.7	6.4	8.0		
25 to 29 years	10,075	4,878	5,197	4,074	4,255	111	104	691	837	2	1	8.3	8.2	8.4	8.8	8.9	3.2	3.4	7.0	7.5		
30 to 34 years	9,540	4,512	5,028	3,717	4,024	144	156	651	845		3	7.9	7.6	8.1	8.1	8.4	4.1	5.1	6.6	7.6		
35 to 39 years	9,193	4,345	4,848	3,376	3,577	220	252	749	1,017		2	7.6	7.3	7.8	7.3	7.5	6.3	8.2	7.6	9.1		
40 to 44 years	8,555	4,122	4,433	3,006	3,183	331	315	783	935	2		7.0	6.9	7.1	6.5	6.7	9.5	10.2	7.9	8.4		
45 to 49 years	8,345	4,166	4,179	2,905	2,914	502	431	757	833	2	1	6.9	7.0	6.7	6.3	6.1	14.4	14.0	7.7	7.5		
50 to 54 years	7,248	3,681	3,567	2,415	2,512	625	429	637	626	4		6.0	6.2	5.8	5.2	5.3	17.9	13.9	6.5	5.6		
55 to 59 years	5,737	2,928	2,809	1,934	1,923	453	359	540	526	1	1	4.7	4.9	4.5	4.2	4.0	13.0	11.6	5.5	4.7		
60 to 64 years	4,420	2,209	2,211	1,466	1,581	334	266	409	364			3.6	3.7	3.6	3.2	3.3	9.6	8.6	4.1	3.3		
65 to 69 years	3,537	1,677	1,860	1,086	1,278	268	230	322	352	1		2.9	2.8	3.0	2.4	2.7	7.7	7.5	3.3	3.2		
70 to 74 years	2,317	1,099	1,218	705	841	213	201	180	176	1		1.9	1.8	2.0	1.5	1.8	6.1	6.5	1.8	1.6		
75 years and over	2,345	1,061	1,284	717	823	208	255	135	206	1		1.9	1.8	2.1	1.6	1.7	6.0	8.3	1.4	1.8		
Under 1 year	1,725	885	840	716	685	1		167	155	1		1.4	1.5	1.4	1.6	1.4			1.7	1.4		
21 years and over	79,766	38,557	41,209	28,746	30,736	3,442	3,037	6,354	7,427	15	9	65.7	64.9	66.4	62.4	64.3	98.8	98.4	64.4	66.6		
Median age	30.3	30.1	30.4	27.9	28.6	52.9	52.3	31.7	31.8													
KANSAS CITY, MO.																						
All ages	399,178	190,117	209,061	159,779	178,228	10,405	8,934	19,736	21,838	197	61	100.0	100.0	100.0	100.0	100.0	100.0	100.0	100.0	100.0	100.0	
Under 5 years	23,123	11,805	11,318	10,571	10,062	12	8	1,211	1,239	11	9	5.8	6.2	5.4	6.6	5.6	0.1	0.1	6.1	5.7	5.6	
5 to 9 years	23,147	11,701	11,446	10,417	10,188	12	18	1,266	1,229	6	11	5.8	6.2	5.5	6.5	5.7	0.1	0.2	6.4	5.6	3.0	
10 to 14 years	25,333	12,666	12,667	11,376	11,335	39	27	1,249	1,304	2	1	6.3	6.7	6.1	7.1	6.4	0.4	0.3	6.3	6.0	1.0	
15 to 19 years	30,063	14,205	15,858	12,829	14,245	100	95	1,275	1,514	1	4	7.5	7.5	7.6	8.0	8.0	1.0	1.1	6.5	6.9	0.5	
20 to 24 years	33,883	14,873	19,010	13,498	17,029	124	134	1,245	1,841	6	6	8.5	7.8	9.1	8.4	9.6	1.2	1.5	6.3	8.4	3.0	
25 to 29 years	35,720	16,309	19,411	14,407	16,988	279	359	1,593	2,059	30	5	8.9	8.6	9.3	9.0	9.5	2.7	4.0	8.1	9.4	15.2	
30 to 34 years	35,117	16,152	18,965	13,927	16,344	559	556	1,628	2,062	38	3	8.8	8.5	9.1	8.7	9.2	5.4	6.2	8.2	9.4	19.3	
35 to 39 years	35,073	16,285	18,788	13,557	15,648	888	788	1,806	2,345	34	7	8.8	8.6	9.0	8.5	8.8	8.5	8.8	9.2	10.7	17.3	
40 to 44 years	32,510	15,651	16,859	12,691	13,892	1,011	888	1,924	2,074	25	5	8.1	8.2	8.1	7.9	7.8	9.7	9.9	9.7	9.5	12.7	
45 to 49 years	30,375	14,928	15,447	11,674	12,531	1,320	1,018	1,926	1,897	8	1	7.6	7.9	7.4	7.3	7.0	12.7	11.4	9.8	8.7	4.1	
50 to 54 years	26,235	13,129	13,106	10,105	10,723	1,511	1,031	1,503	1,348	10	4	6.6	6.9	6.3	6.3	6.0	14.5	11.5	7.6	6.2	5.1	
55 to 59 years	21,035	10,466	10,569	8,007	8,592	1,298	988	1,151	985	10	4	5.3	5.5	5.1	5.0	4.8	12.5	11.1	5.8	4.5	5.1	
60 to 64 years	16,220	7,875	8,345	6,049	6,821	1,052	863	770	660	4	1	4.1	4.1	4.0	3.8	3.8	10.1	9.7	3.9	3.0	2.0	
65 to 69 years	12,988	5,988	7,000	4,562	5,616	847	785	575	599	4		3.3	3.1	3.3	2.9	3.2	8.1	8.8	2.9	2.7	2.0	
70 to 74 years	8,823	4,045	4,778	3,073	3,881	630	572	337	325	5		2.2	2.1	2.3	1.9	2.2	6.1	6.4	1.7	1.5	2.5	
75 years and over	9,533	4,039	5,494	3,036	4,333	723	804	277	357	3		2.4	2.1	2.6	1.9	2.4	6.9	9.0	1.4	1.6	1.5	
Under 1 year	4,731	2,459	2,272	2,228	2,031	1		228	239	2	2	1.2	1.3	1.1	1.4	1.1			1.2	1.1	1.0	
21 years and over	291,001	136,949	154,052	112,073	129,071	10,224	8,763	14,476	16,184	176	34	72.9	72.0	73.7	70.1	72.4	98.3	98.1	73.3	74.1	89.3	
Median age	34.0	34.2	33.9	32.4	32.8	52.8	52.8	36.1	34.2	35.7												

524997 O - 43 - 10

TABLE 53.—AGE, BY RACE AND SEX, WITH PERCENT DISTRIBUTION BY AGE, FOR CITIES OF 100,000 OR MORE: 1940—Continued

[Percent not shown where less than 0.1 or where base is less than 100]

CITY AND AGE	NUMBER											PERCENT DISTRIBUTION										
	All classes			Native white		Foreign-born white		Negro		Other races		All classes			Native white		Foreign-born white		Negro		Other races	
	Total	Male	Female	Male	Female	Male	Female	Male	Female	Male	Female	Total	Male	Female	Male	Female	Male	Female	Male	Female	Male	Female
KNOXVILLE, TENN.																						
All ages	111,580	52,708	58,872	44,852	49,890	411	321	7,436	8,658	9	3	100.0	100.0	100.0	100.0	100.0	100.0	100.0	100.0	100.0	-	-
Under 5 years	8,846	4,451	4,395	3,950	3,839	-	3	500	551	1	2	7.9	8.4	7.5	8.8	7.7	-	0.9	6.7	6.4	-	-
5 to 9 years	9,120	4,618	4,502	3,994	3,923	2	-	622	579	-	-	8.2	8.8	7.6	8.9	7.9	0.5	-	8.4	6.7	-	-
10 to 14 years	9,846	4,965	4,881	4,277	4,176	2	2	686	703	-	-	8.8	9.4	8.3	9.5	8.4	0.5	0.6	9.2	8.1	-	-
15 to 19 years	10,458	4,926	5,532	4,248	4,667	7	2	671	863	-	-	9.4	9.3	9.4	9.5	9.4	1.7	0.6	9.0	10.0	-	-
20 to 24 years	10,714	4,721	5,993	4,054	5,108	8	4	659	881	-	-	9.6	9.0	10.2	9.0	10.2	1.9	1.2	8.9	10.2	-	-
25 to 29 years	10,708	4,870	5,838	4,168	4,925	20	20	680	893	2	-	9.6	9.2	9.9	9.3	9.9	4.9	6.2	9.1	10.3	-	-
30 to 34 years	10,092	4,657	5,435	3,998	4,566	17	24	641	845	1	-	9.0	8.8	9.2	8.9	9.2	4.1	7.5	8.6	9.8	-	-
35 to 39 years	9,179	4,251	4,928	3,572	4,047	40	30	636	851	3	-	8.2	8.1	8.4	8.0	8.1	9.7	9.3	8.6	9.8	-	-
40 to 44 years	7,613	3,628	3,985	2,978	3,309	50	32	598	643	2	1	6.8	6.9	6.8	6.6	6.6	12.2	10.0	8.0	7.4	-	-
45 to 49 years	6,395	2,998	3,397	2,410	2,816	60	30	528	551	-	-	5.7	5.7	5.8	5.4	5.6	14.6	9.3	7.1	6.4	-	-
50 to 54 years	5,527	2,648	2,879	2,198	2,418	49	34	401	427	-	-	5.0	5.0	4.9	4.9	4.8	11.9	10.6	5.4	4.9	-	-
55 to 59 years	4,242	2,029	2,213	1,695	1,872	49	42	285	299	-	-	3.8	3.8	3.8	3.8	3.8	11.9	13.1	3.8	3.5	-	-
60 to 64 years	3,281	1,542	1,739	1,305	1,515	28	28	209	196	-	-	2.9	2.9	3.0	2.9	3.0	6.8	8.7	2.8	2.3	-	-
65 to 69 years	2,684	1,200	1,484	988	1,268	26	28	186	188	-	-	2.4	2.3	2.5	2.2	2.5	6.3	8.7	2.5	2.2	-	-
70 to 74 years	1,613	672	941	565	818	34	17	73	106	-	-	1.4	1.3	1.6	1.3	1.6	8.3	5.3	1.0	1.2	-	-
75 years and over	1,262	532	780	452	623	19	25	61	82	-	-	1.1	1.0	1.2	1.0	1.2	4.6	7.8	0.8	0.9	-	-
Under 1 year	1,735	874	861	786	756	-	-	88	104	-	1	1.6	1.7	1.5	1.8	1.5	-	-	1.2	1.2	-	-
21 years and over	71,230	32,851	38,379	27,614	32,295	399	312	4,830	5,771	8	1	63.8	62.3	65.2	61.6	64.7	97.1	97.2	65.0	66.7	-	-
Median age	28.2	27.7	28, 5	27.3	28.3	50.0	52.0	29.3	29.2	-	-	-	-	-	-	-	-	-	-	-	-	-
LONG BEACH, CALIF.																						
All ages	164,271	77,593	86,678	70,752	79,398	5,867	6,565	293	317	681	398	100.0	100.0	100.0	100.0	100.0	100.0	100.0	100.0	100.0	100.0	100.0
Under 5 years	9,517	4,857	4,660	4,784	4,605	10	7	18	12	45	36	5.8	6.3	5.4	6.8	5.8	0.2	0.1	6.1	3.8	6.6	9.0
5 to 9 years	8,468	4,293	4,175	4,228	4,108	12	13	9	10	44	44	5.2	5.5	4.8	6.0	5.2	0.2	0.2	3.1	3.2	6.5	11.1
10 to 14 years	9,312	4,567	4,745	4,468	4,644	29	38	21	18	49	45	5.7	5.9	5.5	6.3	5.8	0.5	0.6	7.2	5.7	7.2	11.3
15 to 19 years	11,278	5,373	5,905	5,204	5,712	92	129	20	16	57	48	6.9	6.9	6.8	7.4	7.2	1.6	2.0	6.8	5.0	8.4	12.1
20 to 24 years	13,271	6,218	7,053	5,942	6,710	184	236	26	48	66	59	8.1	8.0	8.1	8.4	8.5	3.1	3.6	8.9	15.1	9.7	14.8
25 to 29 years	14,713	7,175	7,538	6,758	7,075	291	380	44	50	82	33	9.0	9.2	8.7	9.6	8.9	5.0	5.8	15.0	15.8	12.0	8.3
30 to 34 years	13,529	6,757	6,772	6,340	6,315	300	398	36	35	81	24	8.2	8.7	7.8	9.0	8.0	5.1	6.1	12.3	11.0	11.9	6.0
35 to 39 years	13,616	6,834	6,782	6,331	6,243	403	485	32	35	68	19	8.3	8.8	7.8	8.9	7.9	6.9	7.4	10.9	11.0	10.0	4.8
40 to 44 years	12,564	6,127	6,437	5,534	5,846	517	534	31	25	45	32	7.6	7.9	7.4	7.8	7.4	8.8	8.1	10.6	7.9	6.6	8.0
45 to 49 years	11,349	5,431	5,918	4,779	5,277	599	595	22	22	31	24	6.9	7.0	6.8	6.8	6.6	10.2	9.1	7.5	6.9	4.6	6.0
50 to 54 years	10,549	4,873	5,676	4,097	5,000	722	639	18	16	36	21	6.4	6.3	6.5	5.8	6.3	12.3	9.7	6.1	5.0	5.3	5.3
55 to 59 years	9,024	3,954	5,070	3,291	4,381	618	673	9	9	36	7	5.5	5.1	5.8	4.7	5.5	10.5	10.3	3.1	2.8	5.3	1.8
60 to 64 years	8,175	3,346	4,829	2,738	4,126	581	691	5	7	22	5	5.0	4.3	5.6	3.9	5.2	9.9	10.5	1.7	2.2	3.2	1.3
65 to 69 years	7,338	2,963	4,375	2,433	3,734	517	633	1	7	12	1	4.5	3.8	5.0	3.4	4.7	8.8	9.6	0.3	2.2	1.8	0.3
70 to 74 years	5,427	2,218	3,209	1,773	2,692	439	515	-	2	6	-	3.3	2.9	3.7	2.5	3.4	7.5	7.8	-	0.6	0.9	-
75 years and over	6,141	2,607	3,534	2,052	2,930	553	599	1	5	1	-	3.7	3.4	4.1	2.9	3.7	9.4	9.1	0.3	1.6	0.1	-
Under 1 year	2,015	1,064	951	1,048	941	-	3	4	2	12	5	1.2	1.4	1.1	1.5	1.2	-	-	1.4	0.6	1.8	1.3
21 years and over	123,380	57,434	65,046	51,047	59,137	5,692	6,338	223	255	472	216	75.1	74.0	76.1	72.1	74.5	97.0	96.5	76.1	80.4	69.3	54.3
Median age	35.8	34.7	36.8	33.1	35.4	53.4	53.7	31.2	30.6	29.8	22.2	-	-	-	-	-	-	-	-	-	-	-
LOS ANGELES, CALIF.																						
All ages	1,504,277	734,135	770,142	575,597	615,585	107,478	107,770	29,906	33,868	21,154	12,919	100.0	100.0	100.0	100.0	100.0	100.0	100.0	100.0	100.0	100.0	100.0
Under 5 years	83,973	42,929	41,044	39,607	37,871	125	120	1,926	1,858	1,271	1,195	5.6	5.8	5.3	6.9	6.2	0.1	0.1	6.4	5.5	6.0	9.2
5 to 9 years	80,162	40,197	39,965	36,953	36,637	226	254	1,813	1,931	1,205	1,143	5.3	5.5	5.2	6.4	6.0	0.2	0.2	6.1	5.7	5.7	8.8
10 to 14 years	90,088	45,455	44,633	41,376	40,763	579	577	1,958	1,918	1,542	1,375	6.0	6.2	5.8	7.2	6.6	0.5	0.5	6.5	5.7	7.3	10.6
15 to 19 years	104,139	51,135	53,004	45,119	47,016	1,917	2,039	2,136	2,174	1,963	1,775	6.9	7.0	6.9	7.8	7.6	1.8	1.9	7.1	6.4	9.3	13.7
20 to 24 years	124,750	61,182	63,568	53,442	55,169	3,301	3,785	2,409	2,848	2,030	1,766	8.3	8.3	8.3	9.3	9.0	3.1	3.5	8.1	8.4	9.6	13.7
25 to 29 years	141,813	70,315	71,498	59,254	59,942	5,569	6,551	3,249	3,817	2,243	1,188	9.4	9.6	9.3	10.3	9.7	5.2	6.1	10.9	11.3	10.6	9.2
30 to 34 years	134,451	66,962	67,489	53,755	54,446	7,838	8,501	3,062	3,777	2,307	765	8.9	9.1	8.8	9.3	8.8	7.3	7.9	10.2	11.2	10.9	5.9
35 to 39 years	131,273	65,571	65,702	49,297	49,632	11,203	11,388	2,958	3,718	2,113	964	8.7	8.9	8.5	8.6	8.1	10.4	10.6	9.9	11.0	10.0	7.5
40 to 44 years	121,214	60,554	60,660	44,172	45,087	12,106	11,717	2,633	2,891	1,643	965	8.1	8.2	7.9	7.7	7.3	11.3	10.9	8.8	8.5	7.8	7.5
45 to 49 years	111,092	54,736	56,356	38,100	41,074	13,344	12,054	2,262	2,483	1,030	745	7.4	7.5	7.3	6.6	6.7	12.4	11.2	7.6	7.3	4.9	5.8
50 to 54 years	100,990	49,638	51,352	32,348	36,888	14,034	12,048	1,825	1,950	1,431	466	6.7	6.8	6.7	5.6	6.0	13.1	11.2	6.1	5.8	6.8	3.6
55 to 59 years	83,794	40,266	43,528	25,826	30,872	12,142	10,916	1,247	1,473	1,051	267	5.6	5.5	5.7	4.5	5.0	11.3	10.1	4.2	4.3	5.0	2.1
60 to 64 years	69,084	31,488	37,596	20,709	27,025	9,089	9,339	932	1,069	758	163	4.6	4.3	4.9	3.6	4.4	8.5	8.7	3.1	3.2	3.6	1.3

UNITED STATES SUMMARY—PRINCIPAL CITIES

65 to 69 years	53,888	23,202	30,686	15,549	22,267	6,566	7,335	777	1,004	310	80	3.6	3.2	4.0	2.7	3.6	6.1	6.8	2.6	3.0	1.5	0.6
70 to 74 years	36,461	15,456	21,005	10,240	15,060	4,679	5,434	377	478	160	33	2.4	2.1	2.7	1.8	2.4	4.4	5.0	1.3	1.4	0.8	0.3
75 years and over	37,105	15,049	22,056	9,850	15,836	4,760	5,712	342	479	97	29	2.5	2.0	2.9	1.7	2.6	4.4	5.3	1.1	1.4	0.5	0.2
Under 1 year	17,488	9,018	8,470	8,381	7,809	5	4	379	387	253	270	1.2	1.2	1.1	1.5	1.3	-	-	1.3	1.1	1.2	2.1
21 years and over	1,123,485	543,610	579,875	403,206	443,302	104,022	104,113	21,636	25,450	14,746	7,010	74.7	74.0	75.3	70.1	72.0	96.8	96.6	72.3	75.1	69.7	54.3
Median age	34.7	34.2	35.3	31.1	32.8	49.1	48.7	32.4	33.2	30.7	22.8	-	-	-	-	-	-	-	-	-	-	-
LOUISVILLE, KY.																						
All ages	319,077	152,267	166,810	126,769	138,897	3,202	2,999	22,264	24,894	32	20	100.0	100.0	100.0	100.0	100.0	100.0	100.0	100.0	100.0	-	-
Under 5 years	21,960	11,078	10,882	9,704	9,483	4	6	1,370	1,391	-	2	6.9	7.3	6.5	7.7	6.8	0.1	0.2	6.2	5.6	-	-
5 to 9 years	21,761	10,993	10,768	9,431	9,186	9	13	1,550	1,564	3	5	6.8	7.2	6.5	7.4	6.6	0.3	0.4	7.0	6.3	-	-
10 to 14 years	25,037	12,396	12,641	10,640	10,804	16	19	1,736	1,815	4	3	7.8	8.1	7.6	8.4	7.8	0.5	0.6	7.8	7.3	-	-
15 to 19 years	26,671	12,788	13,883	10,961	11,869	36	31	1,790	1,979	1	4	8.4	8.4	8.3	8.6	8.5	1.1	1.0	8.0	7.9	-	-
20 to 24 years	27,281	12,444	14,837	10,814	12,783	44	49	1,585	2,005	1	-	8.5	8.2	8.9	8.5	9.2	1.4	1.6	7.1	8.1	-	-
25 to 29 years	28,762	13,521	15,241	11,601	12,832	90	89	1,828	2,319	2	1	9.0	8.9	9.1	9.2	9.2	2.8	3.0	8.2	9.3	-	-
30 to 34 years	27,966	13,073	14,893	11,098	12,388	150	140	1,820	2,365	5	-	8.8	8.6	8.9	8.8	8.9	4.7	4.7	8.2	9.5	-	-
35 to 39 years	26,478	12,652	13,826	10,369	11,095	221	198	2,054	2,530	8	3	8.3	8.3	8.3	8.2	8.0	6.9	6.6	9.2	10.2	-	-
40 to 44 years	23,590	11,462	12,128	9,204	9,821	287	216	1,968	2,091	3	-	7.4	7.5	7.3	7.3	7.1	9.0	7.2	8.8	8.4	-	-
45 to 49 years	21,254	10,426	10,828	8,230	8,613	323	263	1,870	1,952	3	-	6.7	6.8	6.5	6.5	6.2	10.1	8.8	8.4	7.8	-	-
50 to 54 years	18,243	8,895	9,348	7,018	7,558	386	285	1,490	1,505	1	-	5.7	5.8	5.6	5.5	5.4	12.1	9.5	6.7	6.0	-	-
55 to 59 years	14,679	6,994	7,685	5,562	6,320	366	345	1,065	1,019	1	1	4.6	4.6	4.6	4.4	4.6	11.4	11.5	4.8	4.1	-	-
60 to 64 years	12,070	5,534	6,536	4,420	5,406	343	341	774	789	-	-	3.8	3.6	3.9	3.5	3.9	10.7	11.4	3.5	3.2	-	-
65 to 69 years	10,052	4,519	5,533	3,553	4,465	281	344	685	724	-	-	3.2	3.0	3.3	2.8	3.2	8.8	11.5	3.1	2.9	-	-
70 to 74 years	6,595	2,883	3,712	2,236	3,044	283	287	364	380	-	1	2.1	1.9	2.2	1.8	2.2	8.8	9.6	1.6	1.5	-	-
75 years and over	6,678	2,609	4,069	1,928	3,230	363	373	318	466	-	-	2.1	1.7	2.4	1.5	2.3	11.3	12.4	1.4	1.9	-	-
Under 1 year	4,413	2,235	2,178	1,983	1,905	-	-	252	272	-	1	1.4	1.5	1.3	1.6	1.4	-	-	1.1	1.1	-	-
21 years and over	218,317	102,626	115,691	83,957	95,023	3,128	2,922	15,517	17,740	24	6	68.4	67.4	69.4	66.2	68.4	97.7	97.4	69.7	71.3	-	-
Median age	31.4	31.1	31.7	30.1	31.0	55.5	57.8	33.5	32.9	-	-	-	-	-	-	-	-	-	-	-	-	-
LOWELL, MASS.																						
All ages	101,389	49,016	52,373	39,915	41,919	9,012	10,406	50	44	39	4	100.0	100.0	100.0	100.0	100.0	100.0	100.0	-	-	-	-
Under 5 years	6,928	3,625	3,303	3,617	3,292	4	6	4	4	-	1	6.8	7.4	6.3	9.1	7.9	-	0.1	-	-	-	-
5 to 9 years	7,616	3,901	3,715	3,886	3,706	9	8	5	1	1	-	7.5	8.0	7.1	9.7	8.8	0.1	0.1	-	-	-	-
10 to 14 years	9,239	4,698	4,541	4,672	4,516	19	18	6	6	1	1	9.1	9.6	8.7	11.7	10.8	0.2	0.2	-	-	-	-
15 to 19 years	9,874	4,891	4,983	4,820	4,907	63	73	5	2	3	1	9.7	10.0	9.5	12.1	11.7	0.7	0.7	-	-	-	-
20 to 24 years	8,990	4,294	4,696	4,146	4,566	142	128	4	2	2	-	8.9	8.8	9.0	10.4	10.9	1.6	1.2	-	-	-	-
25 to 29 years	7,788	3,768	4,020	3,565	3,765	198	252	1	3	4	-	7.7	7.7	7.7	8.9	9.0	2.2	2.4	-	-	-	-
30 to 34 years	6,904	3,356	3,548	3,035	3,177	312	368	3	3	6	-	6.8	6.8	6.8	7.6	7.6	3.5	3.5	-	-	-	-
35 to 39 years	6,568	3,128	3,440	2,572	2,770	548	666	5	3	3	1	6.5	6.4	6.6	6.4	6.6	6.1	6.4	-	-	-	-
40 to 44 years	6,857	3,191	3,666	2,371	2,624	813	1,038	3	4	4	-	6.8	6.5	7.0	5.9	6.3	9.0	10.0	-	-	-	-
45 to 49 years	6,827	3,306	3,521	2,099	2,185	1,199	1,335	3	1	5	-	6.7	6.7	6.7	5.3	5.2	13.3	12.8	-	-	-	-
50 to 54 years	5,839	2,788	3,051	1,526	1,697	1,256	1,352	3	2	3	-	5.8	5.7	5.8	3.8	4.0	13.9	13.0	-	-	-	-
55 to 59 years	4,871	2,326	2,545	1,146	1,283	1,177	1,258	2	4	1	-	4.8	4.7	4.9	2.9	3.1	13.1	12.1	-	-	-	-
60 to 64 years	4,400	2,029	2,371	880	1,128	1,144	1,239	2	4	3	-	4.3	4.1	4.5	2.2	2.7	12.7	11.9	-	-	-	-
65 to 69 years	3,723	1,658	2,065	695	947	959	1,117	1	1	3	-	3.7	3.4	3.9	1.7	2.3	10.6	10.7	-	-	-	-
70 to 74 years	2,677	1,170	1,507	496	665	671	842	3	-	-	-	2.6	2.4	2.9	1.2	1.6	7.4	8.1	-	-	-	-
75 years and over	2,288	887	1,401	389	691	498	706	-	4	-	-	2.3	1.8	2.7	1.0	1.6	5.5	6.8	-	-	-	-
Under 1 year	1,258	666	592	664	592	1	-	1	-	-	-	1.2	1.4	1.1	1.7	1.4	-	-	-	-	-	-
21 years and over	65,739	30,990	34,749	22,046	24,448	8,881	10,269	29	31	34	1	64.8	63.2	66.3	55.2	58.3	98.5	98.7	-	-	-	-
Median age	30.2	29.1	31.3	23.6	25.0	54.8	54.8	-	-	-	-	-	-	-	-	-	-	-	-	-	-	-
MEMPHIS, TENN.																						
All ages	292,942	139,238	153,704	79,973	86,965	2,457	2,011	56,778	64,720	30	8	100.0	100.0	100.0	100.0	100.0	100.0	100.0	100.0	100.0	-	-
Under 5 years	19,752	10,054	9,698	5,727	5,340	2	4	4,324	4,354	1	-	6.7	7.2	6.3	7.2	6.1	0.1	0.2	7.6	6.7	-	-
5 to 9 years	19,553	9,595	9,958	5,370	5,487	2	4	4,223	4,467	-	-	6.7	6.9	6.5	6.7	6.3	0.1	0.2	7.4	6.9	-	-
10 to 14 years	22,010	10,927	11,083	6,426	6,178	8	8	4,492	4,896	1	1	7.5	7.8	7.2	8.0	7.1	0.3	0.4	7.9	7.6	-	-
15 to 19 years	23,995	10,974	13,021	6,730	7,623	18	32	4,226	5,365	-	1	8.2	7.9	8.5	8.4	8.8	0.7	1.6	7.4	8.3	-	-
20 to 24 years	27,604	12,223	15,381	7,778	9,045	41	31	4,399	6,305	5	-	9.4	8.8	10.0	9.7	10.4	1.7	1.5	7.7	9.7	-	-
25 to 29 years	29,808	13,485	16,323	7,896	8,804	68	82	5,519	7,435	2	2	10.2	9.7	10.6	9.9	10.1	2.8	4.1	9.7	11.5	-	-
30 to 34 years	28,727	13,330	15,397	7,639	8,555	149	131	5,537	6,711	5	-	9.8	9.6	10.0	9.6	9.8	6.1	6.5	9.8	10.4	-	-
35 to 39 years	27,366	12,851	14,515	6,785	7,452	204	188	5,858	6,874	4	1	9.3	9.2	9.4	8.5	8.6	8.3	9.3	10.3	10.6	-	-
40 to 44 years	22,373	10,977	11,396	5,995	6,293	253	213	4,728	4,890	1	-	7.6	7.9	7.4	7.5	7.2	10.3	10.6	8.3	7.6	-	-
45 to 49 years	19,376	9,833	9,543	5,368	5,462	331	235	4,130	3,845	4	1	6.6	7.1	6.2	6.7	6.3	13.5	11.7	7.3	5.9	-	-
50 to 54 years	15,574	7,797	7,777	4,439	4,706	337	243	3,019	2,827	2	1	5.3	5.6	5.1	5.6	5.4	13.7	12.1	5.3	4.4	-	-
55 to 59 years	11,811	5,847	5,964	3,378	3,624	293	230	2,173	2,110	3	-	4.0	4.2	3.9	4.2	4.2	11.9	11.4	3.8	3.3	-	-
60 to 64 years	8,978	4,281	4,697	2,595	3,022	247	231	1,438	1,444	1	-	3.1	3.1	3.1	3.2	3.5	10.1	11.5	2.5	2.2	-	-
65 to 69 years	7,687	3,523	4,164	1,869	2,385	202	150	1,452	1,628	-	1	2.6	2.5	2.7	2.3	2.7	8.2	7.5	2.6	2.5	-	-
70 to 74 years	4,418	1,962	2,456	1,092	1,517	143	100	726	839	1	-	1.5	1.4	1.6	1.4	1.7	5.8	5.0	1.3	1.3	-	-
75 years and over	3,910	1,579	2,331	886	1,472	159	129	534	730	-	-	1.3	1.1	1.5	1.1	1.7	6.4	6.4	0.9	1.1	-	-
Under 1 year	4,090	2,112	1,978	1,273	1,131	-	-	839	847	-	-	1.4	1.5	1.3	1.6	1.3	-	-	1.5	1.3	-	-
21 years and over	202,140	95,414	106,726	54,261	60,390	2,414	1,958	38,713	44,372	26	6	69.0	68.5	69.4	67.8	69.4	98.2	97.4	68.2	68.6	-	-
Median age	30.7	30.9	30.5	30.0	30.6	52.3	51.6	31.1	29.7	-	-	-	-	-	-	-	-	-	-	-	-	-

TABLE 53.—AGE, BY RACE AND SEX, WITH PERCENT DISTRIBUTION BY AGE, FOR CITIES OF 100,000 OR MORE: 1940—Continued

[Percent not shown where less than 0.1 or where base is less than 100]

NUMBER

CITY AND AGE	All classes: Total	All classes: Male	All classes: Female	Native white: Male	Native white: Female	Foreign-born white: Male	Foreign-born white: Female	Negro: Male	Negro: Female	Other races: Male	Other races: Female
MIAMI, FLA.											
All ages	172,172	84,587	87,585	60,314	62,361	6,550	5,967	17,621	19,236	102	21
Under 5 years	10,128	5,181	4,947	3,926	3,690	6	8	1,243	1,247	6	2
5 to 9 years	9,817	4,976	4,841	3,724	3,556	25	20	1,226	1,260	1	5
10 to 14 years	11,852	5,868	5,984	4,395	4,350	52	39	1,420	1,594	1	1
15 to 19 years	12,561	5,986	6,575	4,496	4,693	100	95	1,389	1,786	1	1
20 to 24 years	15,881	7,369	8,512	5,255	5,859	153	186	1,950	2,465	11	2
25 to 29 years	17,863	8,499	9,364	5,885	6,373	219	304	2,381	2,685	14	2
30 to 34 years	17,268	8,462	8,806	5,848	6,092	453	441	2,145	2,270	16	3
35 to 39 years	16,553	8,231	8,322	5,539	5,709	656	558	2,018	2,055	18	...
40 to 44 years	14,090	7,127	6,963	4,929	4,894	726	679	1,463	1,386	9	4
45 to 49 years	11,596	5,895	5,701	4,174	4,096	802	668	908	936	11	1
50 to 54 years	9,972	5,034	4,938	3,478	3,583	910	704	638	651	8	...
55 to 59 years	7,377	3,519	3,858	2,510	2,840	659	666	345	352	5	...
60 to 64 years	6,177	3,004	3,173	2,172	2,374	619	604	213	195	...	...
65 to 69 years	4,936	2,345	2,591	1,714	1,953	477	434	153	204	1	...
70 to 74 years	3,265	1,637	1,628	1,191	1,246	376	300	70	82	...	...
75 years and over	2,836	1,454	1,382	1,078	1,053	317	261	59	68	...	...
Under 1 year	2,030	1,021	1,009	773	765	...	2	247	242	1	...
21 years and over	124,939	61,304	63,635	42,855	44,995	6,341	5,771	12,017	12,858	91	11
Median age	32.3	32.6	32.0	32.1	32.2	50.5	49.9	28.3	27.4	35.3	...
MILWAUKEE, WIS.											
All ages	587,472	289,118	298,354	238,925	255,443	45,415	38,394	4,486	4,335	292	182
Under 5 years	39,494	20,055	19,439	19,685	19,055	20	23	331	338	19	23
5 to 9 years	39,811	20,074	19,737	19,685	19,327	40	38	331	350	18	22
10 to 14 years	44,820	22,517	22,303	22,023	21,810	157	135	315	345	22	13
15 to 19 years	48,155	23,212	24,943	22,367	23,977	541	560	288	379	16	27
20 to 24 years	51,452	23,804	27,648	23,040	26,721	469	530	274	377	21	20
25 to 29 years	52,473	24,789	27,684	23,207	25,926	1,218	1,313	331	424	33	21
30 to 34 years	49,735	23,918	25,817	20,830	23,030	2,653	2,342	403	430	32	15
35 to 39 years	47,322	23,222	24,100	18,851	20,069	3,887	3,530	458	487	26	14
40 to 44 years	44,922	22,815	22,107	17,887	18,045	4,412	3,707	486	349	30	6
45 to 49 years	43,099	22,267	20,832	15,845	16,101	5,952	4,435	449	289	21	7
50 to 54 years	37,819	19,887	17,932	12,358	12,981	7,153	4,727	362	217	14	7
55 to 59 years	28,833	14,716	14,117	8,723	9,570	5,774	4,410	202	134	17	3
60 to 64 years	22,089	10,958	11,131	6,031	7,111	4,811	3,929	104	88	12	3
65 to 69 years	15,894	7,526	8,368	4,161	5,205	3,267	3,087	94	76	4	...
70 to 74 years	10,746	4,812	5,934	2,341	3,268	2,432	2,641	34	25	5	...
75 years and over	10,808	4,546	6,262	1,891	3,247	2,629	2,987	24	27	2	1
Under 1 year	7,871	3,865	4,006	3,794	3,932	2	...	67	71	2	3
21 years and over	405,467	198,818	206,649	150,908	166,200	44,516	37,502	3,182	2,854	212	93
Median age	31.8	32.1	31.4	27.7	28.2	52.3	52.7	34.6	29.5	32.7	21.5
MINNEAPOLIS, MINN.											
All ages	492,370	234,542	257,828	197,302	225,648	34,424	29,725	2,378	2,268	438	187
Under 5 years	31,116	15,942	15,174	15,788	14,995	8	8	115	140	31	31
5 to 9 years	29,456	14,873	14,583	14,676	14,389	23	19	152	151	22	24
10 to 14 years	33,850	16,915	16,935	16,667	16,702	49	61	171	156	28	16
15 to 19 years	40,812	19,425	21,387	18,996	20,951	236	238	165	174	28	24
20 to 24 years	46,532	20,355	26,177	19,825	25,582	348	405	157	175	25	15
25 to 29 years	42,876	19,341	23,535	18,396	22,545	708	771	172	200	65	19
30 to 34 years	39,675	18,201	21,474	16,626	20,108	1,302	1,175	204	171	69	20
35 to 39 years	38,048	17,425	20,623	15,092	18,563	2,096	1,885	199	166	38	9
40 to 44 years	38,020	17,900	20,120	14,875	17,466	2,811	2,441	185	205	29	8
45 to 49 years	37,231	18,166	19,065	13,673	15,698	4,242	3,169	223	190	28	8
50 to 54 years	33,218	16,826	16,392	11,272	12,449	5,340	3,774	187	162	27	7
55 to 59 years	25,150	12,746	12,404	7,754	8,582	4,825	3,692	153	127	14	3
60 to 64 years	18,920	9,134	9,786	5,159	6,275	3,849	3,421	115	90	11	...

PERCENT DISTRIBUTION

CITY AND AGE	All classes: Total	All classes: Male	All classes: Female	Native white: Male	Native white: Female	Foreign-born white: Male	Foreign-born white: Female	Negro: Male	Negro: Female	Other races: Male	Other races: Female
MIAMI, FLA.											
All ages	100.0	100.0	100.0	100.0	100.0	100.0	100.0	100.0	100.0	100.0	...
Under 5 years	5.9	6.1	5.6	6.5	5.9	0.1	0.1	7.1	6.5	5.9	...
5 to 9 years	5.7	5.9	5.5	6.2	5.7	0.4	0.3	7.0	6.6	1.0	...
10 to 14 years	6.9	6.9	6.8	7.3	7.0	0.8	0.7	8.1	8.3	1.0	...
15 to 19 years	7.3	7.1	7.5	7.5	7.5	1.5	1.6	7.9	9.3	1.0	...
20 to 24 years	9.2	8.7	9.7	8.7	9.4	2.3	3.1	11.1	12.8	10.8	...
25 to 29 years	10.4	10.0	10.7	9.8	10.2	3.3	5.1	13.5	14.0	13.7	...
30 to 34 years	10.0	10.0	10.1	9.7	9.8	6.9	7.4	12.2	11.8	15.7	...
35 to 39 years	9.6	9.7	9.5	9.2	9.2	10.0	9.4	11.5	10.7	17.6	...
40 to 44 years	8.2	8.4	7.9	8.2	7.8	11.1	11.4	8.3	7.2	8.8	...
45 to 49 years	6.7	7.0	6.5	6.9	6.6	12.2	11.2	5.2	4.9	10.8	...
50 to 54 years	5.8	6.0	5.6	5.8	5.7	13.9	11.8	3.6	3.4	7.8	...
55 to 59 years	4.3	4.2	4.4	4.2	4.6	10.1	11.2	2.0	1.8	4.9	...
60 to 64 years	3.6	3.6	3.6	3.6	3.8	9.5	10.1	1.2	1.0	...	...
65 to 69 years	2.9	2.8	3.0	2.8	3.1	7.3	7.3	0.9	1.1	1.0	...
70 to 74 years	1.9	1.9	1.9	2.0	2.0	5.7	5.0	0.4	0.4	...	...
75 years and over	1.6	1.7	1.6	1.8	1.7	4.8	4.4	0.3	0.4	...	...
Under 1 year	1.2	1.2	1.2	1.3	1.2	...	...	1.4	1.3	1.0	...
21 years and over	72.6	72.5	72.7	71.0	72.1	96.8	96.7	68.2	66.8	89.2	...
Median age	...	...	...	...	...	...	...	...	...	...	...
MILWAUKEE, WIS.											
All ages	100.0	100.0	100.0	100.0	100.0	100.0	100.0	100.0	100.0	100.0	100.0
Under 5 years	6.7	6.9	6.5	8.2	7.5	...	0.1	7.4	7.8	6.5	12.6
5 to 9 years	6.8	6.9	6.6	8.2	7.6	0.1	0.1	7.4	8.1	6.2	12.1
10 to 14 years	7.6	7.8	7.5	9.2	8.5	0.3	0.4	7.0	8.0	7.5	7.1
15 to 19 years	8.2	8.0	8.4	9.4	9.4	1.2	1.5	6.4	8.7	5.5	14.8
20 to 24 years	8.8	8.2	9.3	9.6	10.5	1.0	1.4	6.1	8.7	7.2	11.0
25 to 29 years	8.9	8.6	9.3	9.7	10.1	2.7	3.4	7.4	9.8	11.3	11.5
30 to 34 years	8.5	8.3	8.7	8.7	9.0	5.8	6.1	9.0	9.9	11.0	8.2
35 to 39 years	8.1	8.0	8.1	7.9	7.9	8.6	9.2	10.2	11.2	8.9	7.7
40 to 44 years	7.6	7.9	7.4	7.5	7.1	9.7	9.7	10.8	8.1	10.3	3.3
45 to 49 years	7.3	7.7	7.0	6.6	6.3	13.1	11.6	10.0	6.7	7.2	3.8
50 to 54 years	6.4	6.9	6.0	5.2	5.1	15.8	12.3	8.1	5.0	4.8	3.8
55 to 59 years	4.9	5.1	4.7	3.7	3.7	12.7	11.5	4.5	3.1	5.8	1.6
60 to 64 years	3.8	3.8	3.7	2.5	2.8	10.6	10.2	2.3	2.0	4.1	1.6
65 to 69 years	2.7	2.6	2.8	1.7	2.0	7.2	8.0	2.1	1.8	1.4	...
70 to 74 years	1.8	1.7	2.0	1.0	1.3	5.4	6.9	0.8	0.6	1.7	...
75 years and over	1.8	1.6	2.1	0.8	1.3	5.8	7.8	0.5	0.6	0.7	0.5
Under 1 year	1.3	1.3	1.3	1.6	1.5	...	...	1.5	1.6	0.7	1.6
21 years and over	69.0	68.8	69.3	63.2	65.1	98.0	97.7	70.9	65.8	72.6	51.1
Median age	...	...	...	...	...	...	...	...	...	...	...
MINNEAPOLIS, MINN.											
All ages	100.0	100.0	100.0	100.0	100.0	100.0	100.0	100.0	100.0	100.0	100.0
Under 5 years	6.3	6.8	5.9	8.0	6.6	...	...	4.8	6.2	7.1	16.6
5 to 9 years	6.0	6.3	5.7	7.4	6.4	0.1	0.1	6.4	6.7	5.0	12.8
10 to 14 years	6.9	7.2	6.6	8.4	7.4	0.1	0.2	7.2	6.9	6.4	8.6
15 to 19 years	8.3	8.3	8.3	9.6	9.3	0.7	0.8	6.9	7.7	6.4	12.8
20 to 24 years	9.5	8.7	10.2	10.0	11.3	1.0	1.4	6.6	7.7	5.7	8.0
25 to 29 years	8.7	8.2	9.1	9.3	10.0	2.1	2.6	7.2	8.8	14.8	10.2
30 to 34 years	8.1	7.8	8.3	8.4	8.9	3.8	4.0	8.6	7.5	15.8	10.7
35 to 39 years	7.7	7.4	8.0	7.6	8.2	6.1	6.3	8.4	7.3	8.7	4.8
40 to 44 years	7.7	7.6	7.8	7.5	7.7	8.2	8.2	7.8	9.0	6.6	4.3
45 to 49 years	7.6	7.7	7.4	6.9	7.0	12.3	10.7	9.4	8.4	6.4	4.3
50 to 54 years	6.7	7.2	6.4	5.7	5.5	15.5	12.7	7.9	7.1	6.2	3.7
55 to 59 years	5.1	5.4	4.8	3.9	3.8	14.0	12.4	6.4	5.6	3.2	1.6
60 to 64 years	3.8	3.9	3.8	2.6	2.8	11.2	11.5	4.8	4.0	2.5	...

UNITED STATES SUMMARY—PRINCIPAL CITIES

65 to 69 years	14,648	6,916	7,732	3,707	4,761	3,110	2,886	90	83	9	2	3.0	2.9	3.0	1.9	2.1	9.0	9.7	3.8	3.7	2.1	1.1
70 to 74 years	10,633	4,908	5,725	2,399	3,191	2,456	2,498	47	36	6		2.2	2.1	2.2	1.2	1.4	7.1	8.4	2.0	1.6	1.4	
75 years and over	12,185	5,469	6,716	2,397	3,391	3,021	3,282	43	42	8	1	2.5	2.3	2.6	1.2	1.5	8.8	11.0	1.8	1.9	1.8	0.5
Under 1 year	6,760	3,467	3,293	3,439	3,240	1		23	47	4	6	1.4	1.5	1.3	1.7	1.4			1.0	2.1	0.9	3.2
21 years and over	348,424	163,726	184,698	127,616	153,680	34,041	29,317	1,743	1,611	326	90	70.8	69.8	71.6	64.7	68.1	98.9	98.6	73.3	71.0	74.4	48.1
Median age	32.7	32.9	32.6	28.5	29.5	55.1	56.2	36.3	34.0	31.4	19.7											
NASHVILLE, TENN.																						
All ages	167,402	77,499	89,903	55,300	63,250	808	714	21,386	25,932	5	7	100.0	100.0	100.0	100.0	100.0	100.0	100.0	100.0	100.0		
Under 5 years	11,804	5,972	5,832	4,409	4,304	1	2	1,562	1,525		1	7.1	7.7	6.5	8.0	6.8	0.1	0.3	7.3	5.9		
5 to 9 years	12,201	6,113	6,088	4,378	4,356	6	3	1,729	1,729			7.3	7.9	6.8	7.9	6.9	0.7	0.4	8.1	6.7		
10 to 14 years	13,168	6,477	6,691	4,653	4,841	6	4	1,818	1,845		1	7.9	8.4	7.4	8.4	7.7	0.7	0.6	8.5	7.1		
15 to 19 years	15,109	7,008	8,101	5,155	5,711	24	11	1,829	2,378		1	9.0	9.0	9.0	9.3	9.0	3.0	1.5	8.6	9.2		
20 to 24 years	16,277	7,141	9,136	5,207	6,531	11	15	1,922	2,589	1	1	9.7	9.2	10.2	9.4	10.3	1.4	2.1	9.0	10.0		
25 to 29 years	16,450	7,445	9,005	5,343	6,193	29	29	2,073	2,781		2	9.8	9.6	10.0	9.7	9.8	3.6	4.1	9.7	10.7		
30 to 34 years	15,116	6,845	8,271	4,920	5,747	35	46	1,889	2,478	1		9.0	8.8	9.2	8.9	9.1	4.3	6.4	8.8	9.6		
35 to 39 years	13,551	6,026	7,525	4,186	4,923	74	73	1,765	2,529	1		8.1	7.8	8.4	7.6	7.8	9.2	10.2	8.3	9.8		
40 to 44 years	11,399	5,203	6,196	3,553	4,166	92	73	1,556	1,957	2		6.8	6.7	6.9	6.4	6.6	11.4	10.2	7.3	7.5		
45 to 49 years	10,079	4,667	5,412	3,213	3,692	90	72	1,364	1,647		1	6.0	6.0	6.0	5.8	5.8	11.1	10.1	6.4	6.4		
50 to 54 years	8,752	4,080	4,672	2,841	3,278	100	72	1,139	1,322			5.2	5.3	5.2	5.1	5.2	12.4	10.1	5.3	5.1		
55 to 59 years	6,892	3,173	3,719	2,280	2,772	74	66	819	881			4.1	4.1	4.1	4.1	4.4	9.2	9.2	3.8	3.4		
60 to 64 years	5,503	2,533	2,970	1,834	2,233	77	72	622	665			3.3	3.3	3.3	3.3	3.5	9.5	10.1	2.9	2.6		
65 to 69 years	5,080	2,225	2,855	1,509	1,986	64	55	652	814			3.0	2.9	3.2	2.7	3.1	7.9	7.7	3.0	3.1		
70 to 74 years	3,072	1,375	1,697	961	1,277	56	50	358	370			1.8	1.8	1.9	1.7	2.0	6.9	7.0	1.7	1.4		
75 years and over	2,949	1,216	1,733	858	1,240	69	71	289	422			1.8	1.6	1.9	1.6	2.0	8.5	9.9	1.4	1.6		
Under 1 year	2,362	1,184	1,178	897	899			287	279			1.4	1.5	1.3	1.6	1.4			1.3	1.1		
21 years and over	111,853	50,512	61,341	35,695	42,703	768	693	14,044	17,941	5	4	66.8	65.2	68.2	64.5	67.5	95.0	97.1	65.7	69.2		
Median age	29.6	29.1	30.1	28.6	29.7	51.8	52.0	29.4	30.2													
NEWARK, N. J.																						
All ages	429,760	213,840	215,920	144,867	148,321	46,882	43,464	21,734	24,026	357	109	100.0	100.0	100.0	100.0	100.0	100.0	100.0	100.0	100.0	100.0	100.0
Under 5 years	25,988	13,169	12,819	11,181	10,911	34	28	1,936	1,864	18	16	6.0	6.2	5.9	7.7	7.4	0.1	0.1	8.9	7.8	5.0	14.7
5 to 9 years	29,262	14,832	14,430	12,606	12,205	100	90	2,102	2,116	24	19	6.8	6.9	6.7	8.7	8.2	0.2	0.2	9.7	8.8	6.7	17.4
10 to 14 years	35,489	17,886	17,603	15,527	15,091	246	256	2,096	2,234	17	22	8.3	8.4	8.2	10.7	10.2	0.5	0.6	9.6	9.3	4.8	20.2
15 to 19 years	40,061	19,659	20,402	17,144	17,540	637	671	1,851	2,180	27	11	9.3	9.2	9.4	11.8	11.8	1.4	1.5	8.5	9.1	7.6	10.1
20 to 24 years	41,282	19,824	21,458	17,408	18,470	752	796	1,654	2,187	10	5	9.6	9.3	9.9	12.0	12.5	1.6	1.8	7.6	9.1	2.8	4.6
25 to 29 years	40,825	19,587	21,238	16,166	16,885	1,596	1,812	1,808	2,536	17	5	9.5	9.2	9.8	11.2	11.4	3.4	4.2	8.3	10.6	4.8	4.6
30 to 34 years	36,531	17,899	18,632	13,026	13,101	2,811	3,032	2,021	2,489	41	10	8.5	8.4	8.6	9.0	8.8	6.0	7.0	9.3	10.4	11.5	9.2
35 to 39 years	33,770	16,793	16,977	9,983	10,079	4,563	4,374	2,194	2,519	53	5	7.9	7.9	7.9	6.9	6.8	9.7	10.1	10.1	10.5	14.8	4.6
40 to 44 years	32,445	16,410	16,035	8,515	8,401	6,001	5,685	1,838	1,941	56	8	7.5	7.7	7.4	5.9	5.7	12.8	13.1	8.5	8.1	15.7	7.3
45 to 49 years	29,722	15,219	14,503	6,744	6,800	6,959	6,385	1,487	1,314	29	4	6.9	7.1	6.7	4.7	4.6	14.8	14.7	6.8	5.5	8.1	3.7
50 to 54 years	25,686	13,496	12,190	5,182	5,357	7,247	5,917	1,044	905	23	1	6.0	6.3	5.6	3.6	3.6	15.5	13.6	4.8	3.8	6.4	0.9
55 to 59 years	19,325	10,121	9,204	3,741	3,998	5,699	4,608	670	596	11	2	4.5	4.7	4.3	2.6	2.7	12.2	10.6	3.1	2.5	3.1	1.8
60 to 64 years	15,140	7,609	7,531	3,024	3,351	4,129	3,722	439	457	17	1	3.5	3.6	3.5	2.1	2.3	8.8	8.6	2.0	1.9	4.8	0.9
65 to 69 years	10,958	5,370	5,588	2,172	2,560	2,883	2,700	307	328	8		2.5	2.5	2.6	1.5	1.7	6.1	6.2	1.4	1.4	2.2	
70 to 74 years	6,932	3,216	3,716	1,281	1,782	1,775	1,740	157	194	3		1.6	1.5	1.7	0.9	1.2	3.8	4.0	0.7	0.8	0.8	
75 years and over	6,344	2,750	3,594	1,167	1,780	1,450	1,648	130	166	3		1.5	1.3	1.7	0.8	1.2	3.1	3.8	0.6	0.7	0.8	
Under 1 year	4,655	2,395	2,260	2,056	1,941	4		334	317	1	2	1.1	1.1	1.0	1.4	1.3			1.5	1.3	0.3	1.8
21 years and over	290,703	144,374	146,329	85,036	88,902	45,659	42,222	13,411	15,164	268	41	67.6	67.5	67.8	58.7	59.9	97.4	97.1	61.7	63.1	75.1	37.6
Median age	30.3	30.5	30.0	24.6	25.0	49.8	48.9	28.4	27.8	37.3	14.4											
NEW BEDFORD, MASS.																						
All ages	110,341	53,401	56,940	37,031	39,273	14,069	15,554	2,233	2,064	68	49	100.0	100.0	100.0	100.0	100.0	100.0	100.0	100.0	100.0		
Under 5 years	6,610	3,309	3,301	3,121	3,085	6	4	179	210	3	2	6.0	6.2	5.8	8.4	7.9			8.0	10.2		
5 to 9 years	7,099	3,486	3,613	3,241	3,371	12	15	226	221	7	6	6.4	6.5	6.3	8.8	8.6	0.1	0.1	10.1	10.7		
10 to 14 years	8,906	4,562	4,344	4,286	4,053	18	24	256	254	2	13	8.1	8.5	7.6	11.6	10.3	0.1	0.2	11.5	12.3		
15 to 19 years	10,626	5,298	5,328	4,907	4,960	93	100	294	261	4	7	9.6	9.9	9.4	13.3	12.6	0.7	0.6	13.2	12.6		
20 to 24 years	9,907	4,842	5,065	4,432	4,629	200	236	205	198	5	2	9.0	9.1	8.9	12.0	11.8	1.4	1.5	9.2	9.6		
25 to 29 years	8,934	4,386	4,548	3,820	3,974	431	447	132	126	3	1	8.1	8.2	8.0	10.3	10.1	3.1	2.9	5.9	6.1		
30 to 34 years	7,767	3,670	4,097	2,868	3,158	709	839	85	97	8	3	7.0	6.9	7.2	7.7	8.0	5.0	5.4	3.8	4.7		
35 to 39 years	7,854	3,719	4,135	2,356	2,606	1,249	1,424	108	103	6	2	7.1	7.0	7.3	6.4	6.6	8.9	9.2	4.8	5.0		
40 to 44 years	8,034	3,775	4,259	2,079	2,339	1,553	1,807	134	109	9	4	7.3	7.1	7.5	5.6	6.0	11.0	11.6	6.0	5.3		
45 to 49 years	8,119	3,979	4,140	1,752	1,894	2,032	2,106	186	137	9	3	7.4	7.5	7.3	4.7	4.8	14.4	13.5	8.3	6.6		
50 to 54 years	7,243	3,445	3,798	1,232	1,474	2,074	2,210	135	113	4	1	6.6	6.5	6.7	3.3	3.8	14.7	14.2	6.0	5.5		
55 to 59 years	5,844	2,865	2,979	910	1,074	1,847	1,827	106	76	2	2	5.3	5.4	5.2	2.5	2.7	13.1	11.7	4.7	3.7		
60 to 64 years	4,618	2,191	2,427	701	813	1,403	1,563	86	51	1		4.2	4.1	4.3	1.9	2.1	10.0	10.0	3.9	2.5		
65 to 69 years	3,761	1,751	2,010	586	720	1,103	1,249	60	40	2	1	3.4	3.3	3.5	1.6	1.8	7.8	8.0	2.7	1.9		
70 to 74 years	2,452	1,090	1,362	354	513	711	830	24	17	1	2	2.2	2.0	2.4	1.0	1.3	5.1	5.3	1.1	1.8		
75 years and over	2,567	1,033	1,534	386	610	628	873	17	51	2		2.3	1.9	2.7	1.0	1.6	4.5	5.6	0.8	2.5		
Under 1 year	1,243	623	620	588	581	1		33	38	1	1	1.1	1.2	1.1	1.6	1.5			1.5	1.8		
21 years and over	75,009	35,684	39,325	20,522	22,876	13,893	15,368	1,219	1,061	50	20	68.0	66.8	69.1	55.4	58.2	98.7	98.8	54.6	51.4		
Median age	32.0	31.1	32.8	23.3	24.5	51.8	51.8	23.9	22.2													

TABLE 53.—AGE, BY RACE AND SEX, WITH PERCENT DISTRIBUTION BY AGE, FOR CITIES OF 100,000 OR MORE: 1940—Continued

[Percent not shown where less than 0.1 or where base is less than 100]

CITY AND AGE	NUMBER											PERCENT DISTRIBUTION										
	All classes			Native white		Foreign-born white		Negro		Other races		All classes			Native white		Foreign-born white		Negro		Other races	
	Total	Male	Female	Male	Female	Male	Female	Male	Female	Male	Female	Total	Male	Female	Male	Female	Male	Female	Male	Female	Male	Female
NEW HAVEN, CONN.																						
All ages	160,605	78,333	82,272	58,824	63,048	16,461	15,929	2,978	3,257	70	38	100.0	100.0	100.0	100.0	100.0	100.0	100.0	100.0	100.0	—	—
Under 5 years	9,581	4,891	4,690	4,629	4,409	4	11	257	266	1	4	6.0	6.2	5.7	7.9	7.0	—	0.1	8.6	8.2	—	—
5 to 9 years	10,409	5,236	5,173	4,958	4,872	18	19	258	276	2	6	6.5	6.7	6.3	8.4	7.7	0.1	0.1	8.7	8.5	—	—
10 to 14 years	13,094	6,600	6,494	6,256	6,123	41	52	298	311	5	8	8.2	8.4	7.9	10.6	9.7	0.2	0.3	10.0	9.5	—	—
15 to 19 years	14,899	7,412	7,487	6,939	7,070	170	128	294	284	9	5	9.3	9.5	9.1	11.8	11.2	1.0	0.8	9.9	8.7	—	—
20 to 24 years	15,883	7,630	8,253	7,270	7,795	159	191	197	265	4	2	9.9	9.7	10.0	12.4	12.4	1.0	1.2	6.6	8.1	—	—
25 to 29 years	14,636	7,060	7,576	6,403	6,747	425	566	229	261	3	2	9.1	9.0	9.2	10.9	10.7	2.6	3.6	7.7	8.0	—	—
30 to 34 years	12,404	5,858	6,546	4,914	5,366	763	933	179	245	2	2	7.7	7.5	8.0	8.4	8.5	4.6	5.9	6.0	7.5	—	—
35 to 39 years	11,349	5,358	5,991	3,825	4,340	1,281	1,381	248	269	4	1	7.1	6.8	7.3	6.5	6.9	7.8	8.7	8.3	8.3	—	—
40 to 44 years	11,112	5,426	5,686	3,291	3,597	1,902	1,845	220	241	13	3	6.9	6.9	6.9	5.6	5.7	11.6	11.6	7.4	7.4	—	—
45 to 49 years	10,915	5,352	5,563	2,611	3,010	2,512	2,330	219	223	10	—	6.8	6.8	6.8	4.4	4.8	15.3	14.6	7.4	6.8	—	—
50 to 54 years	9,761	4,915	4,846	2,071	2,363	2,653	2,298	186	182	5	3	6.1	6.3	5.9	3.5	3.7	16.1	14.4	6.2	5.6	—	—
55 to 59 years	7,609	3,890	3,719	1,597	1,899	2,156	1,690	133	129	4	1	4.7	5.0	4.5	2.7	3.0	13.1	10.6	4.5	4.0	—	—
60 to 64 years	6,613	3,149	3,464	1,433	1,739	1,614	1,624	98	101	4	—	4.1	4.0	4.2	2.4	2.8	9.8	10.2	3.3	3.1	—	—
65 to 69 years	5,375	2,524	2,851	1,163	1,517	1,265	1,237	92	96	4	1	3.3	3.2	3.5	2.0	2.4	7.7	7.8	3.1	2.9	—	—
70 to 74 years	3,474	1,578	1,896	740	1,022	802	822	36	52	—	—	2.2	2.0	2.3	1.3	1.6	4.9	5.2	1.2	1.6	—	—
75 years and over	3,491	1,454	2,037	724	1,179	696	802	34	56	—	—	2.2	1.9	2.5	1.2	1.9	4.2	5.0	1.1	1.7	—	—
Under 1 year	1,852	941	911	896	871	1	—	44	39	—	1	1.2	1.2	1.1	1.5	1.4	—	—	1.5	1.2	—	—
21 years and over	109,480	52,721	56,759	34,659	39,021	16,184	15,662	1,825	2,061	53	15	68.2	67.3	69.0	58.9	61.9	98.3	98.3	61.3	63.3	—	—
Median age	30.7	30.3	31.1	24.6	25.9	51.8	51.1	29.0	29.3	—	—	—	—	—	—	—	—	—	—	—	—	—
NEW ORLEANS, LA.																						
All ages	494,537	234,277	260,260	156,642	173,438	8,324	6,371	68,829	80,205	482	246	100.0	100.0	100.0	100.0	100.0	100.0	100.0	100.0	100.0	100.0	100.0
Under 5 years	33,084	16,697	16,387	10,633	10,463	6	9	6,017	5,864	41	51	6.7	7.1	6.3	6.8	6.0	0.1	0.1	8.7	7.3	8.5	20.7
5 to 9 years	34,297	17,286	17,011	11,085	10,711	14	14	6,160	6,251	27	35	6.9	7.4	6.5	7.1	6.2	0.2	0.2	8.9	7.8	5.6	14.2
10 to 14 years	41,335	20,650	20,685	13,846	13,693	46	46	6,721	6,918	37	28	8.4	8.8	7.9	8.8	7.9	0.6	0.7	9.8	8.6	7.7	11.4
15 to 19 years	45,686	22,144	23,542	15,435	16,032	108	96	6,563	7,380	38	34	9.2	9.5	9.0	9.9	9.2	1.3	1.5	9.5	9.2	7.9	13.8
20 to 24 years	41,997	19,089	22,908	13,822	15,702	139	150	5,113	7,033	15	23	8.5	8.1	8.8	8.8	9.1	1.7	2.4	7.4	8.8	3.1	9.3
25 to 29 years	45,747	20,947	24,800	14,747	16,398	212	244	5,951	8,142	37	16	9.3	8.9	9.5	9.4	9.5	2.5	3.8	8.6	10.2	7.7	6.5
30 to 34 years	45,165	20,760	24,405	14,235	16,094	366	352	6,103	7,947	56	12	9.1	8.9	9.4	9.1	9.3	4.4	5.5	8.9	9.9	11.6	4.9
35 to 39 years	43,704	20,572	23,132	13,627	14,620	637	553	6,245	7,947	63	12	8.8	8.8	8.9	8.7	8.4	7.7	8.7	9.1	9.9	13.1	4.9
40 to 44 years	38,268	18,697	19,571	12,286	12,931	926	594	5,431	5,982	54	14	7.7	8.0	7.5	7.8	7.5	11.1	9.3	7.9	7.5	11.2	5.7
45 to 49 years	33,194	16,218	16,976	10,429	11,289	1,043	688	4,710	4,992	36	7	6.7	6.9	6.5	6.7	6.5	12.5	10.8	6.8	6.2	7.5	2.8
50 to 54 years	26,417	12,891	13,526	8,244	9,222	1,182	763	3,446	3,536	19	5	5.3	5.5	5.2	5.3	5.3	14.2	12.0	5.0	4.4	3.9	2.0
55 to 59 years	20,556	9,724	10,832	6,236	7,519	1,061	757	2,413	2,555	14	1	4.2	4.2	4.2	4.0	4.3	12.7	11.9	3.5	3.2	2.9	0.4
60 to 64 years	16,094	7,220	8,874	4,880	6,363	846	644	1,478	1,863	16	4	3.3	3.1	3.4	3.1	3.7	10.2	10.1	2.1	2.3	3.3	1.6
65 to 69 years	13,359	5,547	7,812	3,446	5,424	697	540	1,390	1,845	14	3	2.7	2.4	3.0	2.2	3.1	8.4	8.5	2.0	2.3	2.9	1.2
70 to 74 years	8,205	3,333	4,872	2,167	3,488	535	415	620	968	11	1	1.7	1.4	1.9	1.4	2.0	6.4	6.5	0.9	1.2	2.3	0.4
75 years and over	7,429	2,502	4,927	1,524	3,439	506	506	468	982	4	—	1.5	1.1	1.9	1.0	2.0	6.1	7.9	0.7	1.2	0.8	—
Under 1 year	6,809	3,447	3,362	2,226	2,184	—	—	1,217	1,165	4	13	1.4	1.5	1.3	1.4	1.3	—	—	1.8	1.5	0.8	5.3
21 years and over	331,411	153,591	177,820	102,852	119,274	8,119	6,181	42,285	52,272	335	93	67.0	65.6	68.3	65.7	68.8	97.5	97.0	61.4	65.2	69.5	37.8
Median age	30.6	30.1	31.0	29.6	31.2	52.8	52.9	28.2	29.1	34.1	16.3	—	—	—	—	—	—	—	—	—	—	—
NEW YORK, N. Y.																						
All ages	7,454,995	3,676,293	3,778,702	2,397,164	2,500,317	1,057,839	1,022,181	205,727	252,717	15,563	3,487	100.0	100.0	100.0	100.0	100.0	100.0	100.0	100.0	100.0	100.0	100.0
Under 5 years	433,894	221,415	212,479	204,900	195,756	1,310	1,273	14,706	14,985	499	465	5.8	6.0	5.6	8.5	7.8	0.1	0.1	7.1	5.9	3.2	13.3
5 to 9 years	470,556	238,798	231,758	218,849	211,534	3,038	3,063	16,442	16,692	469	469	6.3	6.5	6.1	9.1	8.5	0.3	0.3	8.0	6.6	3.0	13.4
10 to 14 years	561,108	283,453	277,655	258,847	251,931	6,832	6,810	17,294	18,554	480	360	7.5	7.7	7.3	10.8	10.1	0.6	0.7	8.4	7.3	3.1	10.3
15 to 19 years	606,942	300,717	306,225	267,425	269,501	17,163	17,323	15,574	19,104	555	297	8.1	8.2	8.1	11.2	10.8	1.6	1.7	7.6	7.6	3.6	8.5
20 to 24 years	649,153	304,862	344,291	270,434	295,585	18,615	22,550	15,251	25,848	562	308	8.7	8.3	9.1	11.3	11.8	1.8	2.2	7.4	10.2	3.6	8.8
25 to 29 years	697,153	322,558	374,595	259,948	287,725	41,380	55,537	20,008	30,970	1,222	363	9.4	8.8	9.9	10.8	11.5	3.9	5.4	9.7	12.3	7.9	10.4
30 to 34 years	691,027	331,782	359,245	226,078	238,194	81,972	91,443	21,924	29,256	1,808	352	9.3	9.0	9.5	9.4	9.5	7.7	8.9	10.7	11.6	11.6	10.1
35 to 39 years	669,421	330,950	338,471	178,358	184,423	126,448	124,990	23,418	28,768	2,726	290	9.0	9.0	9.0	7.4	7.4	12.0	12.2	11.4	11.4	17.5	8.3
40 to 44 years	628,714	317,471	311,243	149,293	153,256	145,301	136,268	20,299	21,490	2,578	229	8.4	8.6	8.2	6.2	6.1	13.7	13.3	9.9	8.5	16.6	6.6
45 to 49 years	550,743	282,769	267,974	115,648	118,025	150,517	134,237	14,802	15,579	1,802	133	7.4	7.7	7.1	4.8	4.7	14.2	13.1	7.2	6.2	11.6	3.8
50 to 54 years	467,020	243,321	223,699	84,449	89,449	147,338	122,934	10,251	11,217	1,283	99	6.3	6.6	5.9	3.5	3.6	13.9	12.0	5.0	4.4	8.2	2.8
55 to 59 years	346,871	178,162	168,709	57,354	63,575	113,428	97,508	6,675	7,576	705	50	4.7	4.8	4.5	2.4	2.5	10.7	9.5	3.2	3.0	4.5	1.4
60 to 64 years	267,974	132,668	135,306	43,605	51,806	84,260	78,490	4,311	4,974	492	36	3.6	3.6	3.6	1.8	2.1	8.0	7.7	2.1	2.0	3.2	1.0

65 to 69 years	190,439	89,275	101,164	29,909	39,732	56,461	57,567	2,676	3,845	229	20	2.6	2.4	2.7	1.2	1.6	5.3	5.6	1.3	1.5	1.5	0.6
70 to 74 years	120,675	54,474	66,201	17,959	25,853	35,194	38,364	1,219	1,978	102	6	1.6	1.5	1.8	0.7	1.0	3.3	3.8	0.6	0.8	0.7	0.2
75 years and over	103,305	43,618	59,687	14,108	23,972	28,582	33,824	877	1,881	51	10	1.4	1.2	1.6	0.6	1.0	2.7	3.3	0.4	0.7	0.3	0.3
Under 1 year	81,889	41,795	40,094	38,897	37,109	57	66	2,748	2,828	93	91	1.1	1.1	1.1	1.6	1.5	---	---	1.3	1.1	0.6	2.6
21 years and over	5,254,633	2,570,647	2,683,986	1,393,545	1,515,100	1,024,793	988,556	138,864	178,491	13,445	1,839	70.5	69.9	71.0	58.1	60.6	96.9	96.7	67.5	70.6	86.4	52.7
Median age	32.2	32.5	32.0	24.6	25.4	47.9	46.9	30.8	30.0	39.0	22.5	---	---	---	---	---	---	---	---	---	---	---
BRONX BOROUGH																						
All ages	1,394,711	689,327	705,384	447,519	462,324	230,101	230,375	11,048	12,481	659	204	100.0	100.0	100.0	100.0	100.0	100.0	100.0	100.0	100.0	100.0	100.0
Under 5 years	84,598	43,070	41,528	42,098	40,507	211	184	737	818	24	19	6.1	6.2	5.9	9.4	8.8	0.1	0.1	6.7	6.6	3.6	9.3
5 to 9 years	91,667	46,721	44,946	45,180	43,448	587	524	938	947	16	27	6.6	6.8	6.4	10.1	9.4	0.3	0.2	8.5	7.6	2.4	13.2
10 to 14 years	110,253	55,627	54,626	53,069	52,022	1,366	1,389	1,167	1,193	25	22	7.9	8.1	7.7	11.9	11.3	0.6	0.6	10.6	9.6	3.8	10.8
15 to 19 years	117,378	58,357	59,021	53,757	54,006	3,585	3,704	976	1,292	39	19	8.4	8.5	8.4	12.0	11.7	1.6	1.6	8.8	10.4	5.9	9.3
20 to 24 years	120,681	57,427	63,254	52,852	57,060	3,631	4,668	916	1,507	28	19	8.7	8.3	9.0	11.8	12.3	1.6	2.0	8.3	12.1	4.2	9.3
25 to 29 years	130,082	60,115	69,967	50,254	55,985	8,864	12,695	941	1,271	56	16	9.3	8.7	9.9	11.2	12.1	3.9	5.5	8.5	10.2	8.5	7.8
30 to 34 years	129,526	62,603	66,923	42,222	43,996	19,266	21,691	1,037	1,216	78	20	9.3	9.1	9.5	9.4	9.5	8.4	9.4	9.4	9.7	11.8	9.8
35 to 39 years	124,739	61,327	63,412	30,967	31,616	29,092	30,508	1,170	1,266	98	22	8.9	8.9	9.0	6.9	6.8	12.6	13.2	10.6	10.1	14.9	10.8
40 to 44 years	117,451	58,867	58,584	24,947	25,442	32,798	32,204	1,002	922	120	16	8.4	8.5	8.3	5.6	5.5	14.3	14.0	9.1	7.4	18.2	7.8
45 to 49 years	103,925	53,505	50,420	18,729	18,678	33,899	31,023	789	706	88	13	7.5	7.8	7.1	4.2	4.0	14.7	13.5	7.1	5.7	13.4	6.4
50 to 54 years	86,439	45,428	41,011	12,559	12,958	32,273	27,594	568	455	28	4	6.2	6.6	5.8	2.8	2.8	14.0	12.0	5.1	3.6	4.2	2.0
55 to 59 years	62,367	32,119	30,248	7,781	8,657	23,984	21,238	326	349	28	4	4.5	4.7	4.3	1.7	1.9	10.4	9.2	3.0	2.8	4.2	2.0
60 to 64 years	46,227	23,174	23,053	5,614	6,626	17,312	16,212	230	214	18	1	3.3	3.4	3.3	1.3	1.4	7.5	7.0	2.1	1.7	2.7	0.5
65 to 69 years	32,170	15,033	17,137	3,772	5,059	11,108	11,942	143	135	10	1	2.3	2.2	2.4	0.8	1.1	4.8	5.2	1.3	1.1	1.5	0.5
70 to 74 years	20,258	8,869	11,389	2,092	3,198	6,718	8,105	57	86	2	---	1.5	1.3	1.6	0.5	0.7	2.9	3.5	0.5	0.7	0.3	---
75 years and over	16,950	7,085	9,865	1,626	3,066	5,407	6,694	51	104	1	1	1.2	1.0	1.4	0.4	0.7	2.3	2.9	0.5	0.8	0.2	0.5
Under 1 year	16,136	8,250	7,886	8,089	7,738	12	5	144	136	5	7	1.2	1.2	1.1	1.8	1.7	---	---	1.3	1.1	0.8	3.4
21 years and over	966,685	473,892	492,793	242,868	261,285	223,408	223,499	7,064	7,898	552	111	69.3	68.7	69.9	54.3	56.5	97.1	97.0	63.9	63.3	83.8	54.4
Median age	31.6	31.9	31.4	22.8	23.6	47.3	46.2	29.2	26.9	38.2	23.9	---	---	---	---	---	---	---	---	---	---	---
BROOKLYN BOROUGH																						
All ages	2,698,285	1,332,545	1,365,740	891,768	928,545	390,717	376,921	47,744	59,519	2,316	755	100.0	100.0	100.0	100.0	100.0	100.0	100.0	100.0	100.0	100.0	100.0
Under 5 years	168,829	86,455	82,374	81,573	77,461	366	362	4,396	4,435	120	116	6.3	6.5	6.0	9.1	8.3	0.1	0.1	9.2	7.5	5.2	15.4
5 to 9 years	183,251	92,878	90,373	87,268	84,833	808	812	4,682	4,594	120	134	6.8	7.0	6.6	9.8	9.1	0.2	0.2	9.8	7.7	5.2	17.7
10 to 14 years	222,302	112,669	109,633	105,774	102,495	2,033	1,947	4,749	5,106	113	85	8.2	8.5	8.0	11.9	11.0	0.5	0.5	9.9	8.6	4.9	11.3
15 to 19 years	241,176	119,608	121,568	109,682	110,723	5,732	5,669	4,093	5,093	101	83	8.9	9.0	8.9	12.3	11.9	1.5	1.5	8.6	8.6	4.4	11.0
20 to 24 years	250,217	117,971	132,246	107,414	117,299	6,768	7,976	3,693	6,919	96	52	9.3	8.9	9.7	12.0	12.6	1.7	2.1	7.7	11.6	4.1	6.9
25 to 29 years	258,285	120,243	138,042	100,337	110,760	15,205	19,948	4,545	7,279	156	55	9.6	9.0	10.1	11.3	11.9	3.9	5.3	9.5	12.2	6.7	7.3
30 to 34 years	241,824	116,826	124,998	83,789	87,083	28,063	31,541	4,729	6,323	245	51	9.0	8.8	9.2	9.4	9.4	7.2	8.4	9.9	10.6	10.6	6.8
35 to 39 years	223,449	110,443	113,006	60,496	62,423	44,810	44,639	4,729	5,893	408	51	8.3	8.3	8.3	6.8	6.7	11.5	11.8	9.9	9.9	17.6	6.8
40 to 44 years	209,508	105,297	104,211	47,692	49,174	53,284	50,634	3,946	4,354	375	49	7.8	7.9	7.6	5.3	5.3	13.6	13.4	8.3	7.3	16.2	6.5
45 to 49 years	183,759	93,920	89,839	34,602	36,042	56,166	50,732	2,901	3,039	251	26	6.8	7.0	6.6	3.9	3.9	14.4	13.5	6.1	5.1	10.8	3.4
50 to 54 years	157,401	81,657	75,744	24,478	26,849	55,068	46,631	1,948	2,243	163	21	5.8	6.1	5.5	2.7	2.9	14.1	12.4	4.1	3.8	7.0	2.8
55 to 59 years	119,469	61,117	58,352	16,527	19,088	43,237	37,751	1,280	1,500	73	13	4.4	4.6	4.3	1.9	2.1	11.1	10.0	2.7	2.5	3.2	1.7
60 to 64 years	93,761	46,607	47,154	12,789	15,746	32,845	30,364	924	1,037	49	7	3.5	3.5	3.5	1.4	1.7	8.4	8.1	1.9	1.7	2.1	0.9
65 to 69 years	67,171	32,093	35,078	9,171	12,324	22,310	21,912	582	835	30	7	2.5	2.4	2.6	1.0	1.3	5.7	5.8	1.2	1.4	1.3	0.9
70 to 74 years	41,973	19,380	22,593	5,603	8,282	13,447	13,867	324	444	6	---	1.6	1.5	1.7	0.6	0.9	3.4	3.7	0.7	0.7	0.3	---
75 years and over	35,910	15,381	20,529	4,573	7,963	10,575	12,136	223	425	10	5	1.3	1.2	1.5	0.5	0.9	2.7	3.2	0.5	0.7	0.4	0.7
Under 1 year	31,478	15,967	15,511	15,136	14,687	16	19	795	772	20	33	1.2	1.2	1.1	1.7	1.6	---	---	1.7	1.3	0.9	4.4
21 years and over	1,832,686	896,844	935,842	485,815	530,206	380,090	366,378	29,101	38,935	1,838	323	67.9	67.3	68.5	54.5	57.1	97.3	97.2	61.0	65.4	79.4	42.8
Median age	30.5	30.7	30.3	22.9	23.8	48.4	47.5	27.5	27.5	37.5	17.6	---	---	---	---	---	---	---	---	---	---	---
MANHATTAN BOROUGH																						
All ages	1,889,924	926,133	963,791	502,136	535,292	278,319	261,878	133,930	164,435	11,748	2,186	100.0	100.0	100.0	100.0	100.0	100.0	100.0	100.0	100.0	100.0	100.0
Under 5 years	88,850	45,003	43,847	35,604	34,198	519	545	8,579	8,827	301	277	4.7	4.9	4.5	7.1	6.4	0.2	0.2	6.4	5.4	2.6	12.7
5 to 9 years	97,670	49,286	48,384	38,020	36,829	1,228	1,264	9,758	10,024	280	267	5.2	5.3	5.0	7.6	6.9	0.4	0.5	7.3	6.1	2.4	12.2
10 to 14 years	114,161	57,283	56,878	44,494	43,354	2,332	2,348	10,156	10,958	301	218	6.0	6.2	5.9	8.9	8.1	0.8	0.9	7.6	6.7	2.6	10.0
15 to 19 years	129,209	63,064	66,145	48,227	49,683	5,044	5,003	9,430	11,288	363	171	6.8	6.8	6.9	9.6	9.3	1.8	1.9	7.0	6.9	3.1	7.8
20 to 24 years	158,152	71,838	86,314	56,273	63,705	5,551	6,828	9,603	15,570	411	211	8.4	7.8	9.0	11.2	11.9	2.0	2.6	7.2	9.5	3.5	9.7
25 to 29 years	178,462	81,344	97,118	55,538	61,044	11,532	15,349	13,335	20,479	939	246	9.4	8.8	10.1	11.1	11.4	4.1	5.9	10.0	12.5	8.0	11.3
30 to 34 years	181,251	85,702	95,549	47,766	51,169	21,587	24,064	14,948	20,080	1,401	236	9.6	9.3	9.9	9.5	9.6	7.8	9.2	11.2	12.2	11.9	10.8
35 to 39 years	186,173	92,035	94,138	41,202	42,712	32,435	31,215	16,281	20,011	2,117	200	9.9	9.9	9.8	8.2	8.0	11.7	11.9	12.2	12.2	18.0	9.1
40 to 44 years	174,962	89,625	85,337	35,563	36,364	37,882	33,914	14,228	14,913	1,952	146	9.3	9.7	8.9	7.1	6.8	13.6	13.0	10.6	9.1	16.6	6.7
45 to 49 years	153,273	79,022	74,251	28,276	29,499	39,145	33,847	10,229	10,828	1,372	77	8.1	8.5	7.7	5.6	5.5	14.1	12.9	7.6	6.6	11.7	3.5
50 to 54 years	132,697	69,637	63,060	22,700	24,176	38,914	31,079	6,985	7,739	1,037	66	7.0	7.5	6.5	4.5	4.5	14.0	11.9	5.2	4.7	8.8	3.0
55 to 59 years	98,996	51,309	47,687	16,346	18,376	29,790	24,052	4,598	5,220	575	29	5.2	5.5	4.9	3.3	3.4	10.7	9.2	3.4	3.2	4.9	1.3
60 to 64 years	77,105	37,982	39,123	13,134	16,152	21,639	19,589	2,816	3,359	393	23	4.1	4.1	4.1	2.6	3.0	7.8	7.5	2.1	2.0	3.3	1.1
65 to 69 years	54,965	25,368	29,597	9,022	12,446	14,413	14,512	1,754	2,627	179	12	2.9	2.7	3.1	1.8	2.3	5.2	5.5	1.3	1.6	1.5	0.5
70 to 74 years	34,623	15,488	19,135	5,676	8,183	9,007	9,655	715	1,292	90	5	1.8	1.7	2.0	1.1	1.5	3.2	3.7	0.5	0.8	0.8	0.2
75 years and over	29,375	12,147	17,228	4,295	7,402	7,301	8,604	514	1,220	37	2	1.6	1.8	1.8	0.9	1.4	2.6	3.3	0.4	0.7	0.3	0.1
Under 1 year	16,811	8,589	8,222	6,876	6,408	16	24	1,831	1,748	68	42	0.9	0.9	0.9	1.4	1.2	---	---	1.2	1.1	0.6	1.9
21 years and over	1,429,955	697,638	732,317	325,111	359,428	267,850	251,178	94,254	120,491	10,423	1,220	75.7	75.3	76.0	64.7	67.1	96.2	95.9	70.4	73.3	88.7	55.8
Median age	34.9	35.5	34.4	27.6	28.3	47.7	46.5	32.0	31.3	39.4	23.8	---	---	---	---	---	---	---	---	---	---	---

TABLE 53.—AGE, BY RACE AND SEX, WITH PERCENT DISTRIBUTION BY AGE, FOR CITIES OF 100,000 OR MORE: 1940—Continued

[Percent not shown where less than 0.1 or where base is less than 100]

CITY AND AGE	NUMBER											PERCENT DISTRIBUTION										
	All classes			Native white		Foreign-born white		Negro		Other races		All classes			Native white		Foreign-born white		Negro		Other races	
	Total	Male	Female	Male	Female	Male	Female	Male	Female	Male	Female	Total	Male	Female	Male	Female	Male	Female	Male	Female	Male	Female
NEW YORK, N. Y.																						
QUEENS BOROUGH																						
All ages	1,297,634	638,605	659,029	486,379	507,764	140,003	136,585	11,525	14,365	698	315	100.0	100.0	100.0	100.0	100.0	100.0	100.0	100.0	100.0	100.0	100.0
Under 5 years	80,640	41,286	39,354	40,167	38,362	206	178	863	765	50	49	6.2	6.5	6.0	8.3	7.6	0.1	0.1	7.5	5.3	7.2	15.6
5 to 9 years	85,282	43,451	41,831	42,075	40,392	388	425	939	977	49	37	6.6	6.8	6.3	8.7	8.0	0.3	0.3	8.1	6.8	7.0	11.7
10 to 14 years	99,097	50,009	49,088	47,876	46,892	989	1,009	1,109	1,157	35	30	7.6	7.8	7.4	9.8	9.2	0.7	0.7	9.6	8.1	5.0	9.5
15 to 19 years	102,824	51,233	51,591	47,768	47,620	2,475	2,658	951	1,292	39	21	7.9	8.0	7.8	9.8	9.4	1.8	1.9	8.3	9.0	5.6	6.7
20 to 24 years	104,142	49,225	54,917	45,931	50,490	2,363	2,783	905	1,619	26	25	8.0	7.7	8.3	9.4	9.9	1.7	2.0	7.9	11.3	3.7	7.9
25 to 29 years	115,621	53,532	62,089	47,156	53,409	5,278	6,978	1,041	1,659	57	43	8.9	8.4	9.4	9.7	10.5	3.8	5.1	9.0	11.5	8.2	13.7
30 to 34 years	124,442	59,656	64,786	46,475	50,208	12,048	13,105	1,067	1,429	66	44	9.6	9.3	9.8	9.6	9.9	8.6	9.6	9.3	9.9	9.5	14.0
35 to 39 years	121,793	60,419	61,374	40,760	42,911	18,478	17,028	1,090	1,419	91	16	9.4	9.5	9.3	8.4	8.5	13.2	12.5	9.5	9.9	13.0	5.1
40 to 44 years	113,847	57,119	56,728	36,818	38,058	19,194	17,475	1,001	1,181	106	14	8.8	8.9	8.6	7.6	7.5	13.7	12.8	8.7	8.2	15.2	4.4
45 to 49 years	97,851	50,184	47,667	30,501	30,403	18,810	16,333	800	914	73	17	7.5	7.9	7.2	6.3	6.0	13.4	12.0	6.9	6.4	10.5	5.4
50 to 54 years	80,272	41,224	39,048	22,136	22,923	18,364	15,429	678	689	46	7	6.2	6.5	5.9	4.6	4.5	13.1	11.3	5.9	4.8	6.6	2.2
55 to 59 years	57,965	29,377	28,588	14,782	15,515	14,149	12,607	426	462	20	4	4.5	4.6	4.3	3.0	3.1	10.1	9.2	3.7	3.2	2.9	1.3
60 to 64 years	44,392	21,476	22,916	10,464	11,777	10,681	10,820	305	314	26	5	3.4	3.4	3.5	2.2	2.3	7.6	7.9	2.6	2.2	3.7	1.6
65 to 69 years	31,301	14,273	17,028	6,790	8,645	7,307	8,155	169	228	7	-	2.4	2.2	2.6	1.4	1.7	5.2	6.0	1.5	1.6	1.0	-
70 to 74 years	20,466	8,941	11,525	3,816	5,390	5,013	5,993	108	141	4	1	1.6	1.4	1.7	0.8	1.1	3.6	4.4	0.9	1.0	0.6	0.3
75 years and over	17,699	7,200	10,499	2,864	4,769	4,260	5,609	73	119	3	2	1.4	1.1	1.6	0.6	0.9	3.0	4.1	0.6	0.8	0.4	0.6
Under 1 year	15,483	7,977	7,506	7,801	7,330	13	17	161	150	2	9	1.2	1.2	1.1	1.6	1.4	-	-	1.4	1.0	0.3	2.9
21 years and over	909,487	442,738	466,749	299,424	325,103	135,311	131,607	7,486	9,865	517	174	70.1	69.3	70.8	61.6	64.0	96.6	96.4	65.0	68.7	74.1	55.2
Median age	32.5	32.6	32.4	27.1	27.8	47.3	47.0	29.8	29.1	36.5	24.1	-	-	-	-	-	-	-	-	-	-	-
RICHMOND BOROUGH																						
All ages	174,441	89,683	84,758	69,362	66,392	18,699	16,422	1,480	1,917	142	27	100.0	100.0	100.0	100.0	100.0	100.0	100.0	100.0	100.0	100.0	-
Under 5 years	10,977	5,601	5,376	5,458	5,228	8	4	131	140	4	4	6.3	6.2	6.3	7.9	7.9	-	-	8.9	7.3	2.8	-
5 to 9 years	12,686	6,462	6,224	6,306	6,032	27	38	125	150	4	4	7.3	7.2	7.3	9.1	9.1	0.1	0.2	8.4	7.8	2.8	-
10 to 14 years	15,295	7,865	7,430	7,634	7,168	112	117	113	140	6	5	8.8	8.8	8.8	11.0	10.8	0.6	0.7	7.6	7.3	4.2	-
15 to 19 years	16,355	8,455	7,900	7,991	7,469	327	289	124	139	13	3	9.4	9.4	9.3	11.5	11.2	1.7	1.8	8.4	7.3	9.2	-
20 to 24 years	15,961	8,401	7,560	7,964	7,031	302	295	134	233	1	1	9.1	9.4	8.9	11.5	10.6	1.6	1.8	9.1	12.2	0.7	-
25 to 29 years	14,703	7,324	7,379	6,663	6,527	501	567	146	282	14	3	8.4	8.2	8.7	9.6	9.8	2.7	3.5	9.9	14.7	9.9	-
30 to 34 years	13,984	6,995	6,989	5,826	5,738	1,008	1,042	143	208	18	1	8.0	7.8	8.2	8.4	8.6	5.4	6.3	9.7	10.9	12.7	-
35 to 39 years	13,267	6,726	6,541	4,933	4,761	1,633	1,600	148	179	12	1	7.6	7.5	7.7	7.1	7.2	8.7	9.7	10.0	9.3	8.5	-
40 to 44 years	12,946	6,563	6,383	4,273	4,218	2,143	2,041	122	120	25	4	7.4	7.3	7.5	6.2	6.4	11.5	12.4	8.2	6.3	17.6	-
45 to 49 years	11,935	6,138	5,797	3,540	3,403	2,497	2,302	83	92	18	-	6.8	6.8	6.8	5.1	5.1	13.4	14.0	5.6	4.8	12.7	-
50 to 54 years	10,211	5,375	4,836	2,576	2,543	2,719	2,201	71	91	9	1	5.9	6.0	5.7	3.7	3.8	14.5	13.4	4.5	4.7	6.3	-
55 to 59 years	8,074	4,240	3,834	1,918	1,939	2,268	1,850	45	45	9	-	4.6	4.7	4.5	2.8	2.9	12.1	11.3	3.0	2.3	6.3	-
60 to 64 years	6,489	3,429	3,060	1,604	1,505	1,783	1,505	36	50	6	-	3.7	3.8	3.6	2.3	2.3	9.5	9.2	2.4	2.6	4.2	-
65 to 69 years	4,832	2,508	2,324	1,154	1,258	1,323	1,046	28	20	3	-	2.8	2.8	2.7	1.7	1.9	7.1	6.4	1.9	1.0	2.1	-
70 to 74 years	3,355	1,796	1,559	772	800	1,009	744	15	15	-	-	1.9	2.0	1.8	1.1	1.2	5.4	4.5	1.0	0.8	-	-
75 years and over	3,371	1,805	1,566	750	772	1,039	781	16	13	-	-	1.9	2.0	1.8	1.1	1.2	6.5	4.8	1.1	0.7	-	-
Under 1 year	1,981	1,012	969	995	946	-	1	17	22	-	-	1.1	1.1	1.1	1.4	1.4	-	-	1.1	1.1	-	-
21 years and over	115,820	59,535	56,285	40,327	39,078	18,134	15,894	959	1,302	115	11	66.4	66.4	66.4	58.1	58.9	97.0	96.8	64.8	67.9	81.0	-
Median age	30.4	30.5	30.4	24.6	25.2	51.5	49.8	28.9	27.8	39.6	-	-	-	-	-	-	-	-	-	-	-	-
NORFOLK, VA.																						
All ages	144,332	72,949	71,383	48,956	45,835	2,022	1,635	21,831	24,062	140	51	100.0	100.0	100.0	100.0	100.0	100.0	100.0	100.0	100.0	100.0	-
Under 5 years	9,507	4,889	4,618	3,245	2,950	4	4	1,631	1,657	9	7	6.6	6.7	6.5	6.6	6.5	0.2	0.2	7.5	6.9	6.4	-
5 to 9 years	9,753	4,848	4,905	3,064	3,107	12	7	1,760	1,782	12	9	6.8	6.6	6.9	6.3	6.8	0.6	0.4	8.1	7.4	8.6	-
10 to 14 years	10,777	5,348	5,429	3,399	3,326	7	16	1,935	2,082	7	5	7.5	7.3	7.6	6.9	7.3	0.3	1.0	8.9	8.7	5.0	-
15 to 19 years	14,442	8,161	6,281	5,944	4,050	34	15	2,175	2,208	8	8	10.0	11.2	8.8	12.1	8.9	1.7	0.9	10.0	9.2	5.7	-
20 to 24 years	15,451	8,409	7,042	6,384	4,678	45	51	1,978	2,308	2	5	10.7	11.5	9.9	13.0	10.3	2.2	3.1	9.1	9.6	1.4	-
25 to 29 years	13,958	6,896	7,062	4,882	4,640	76	88	1,926	2,329	12	5	9.7	9.5	9.9	10.0	10.2	3.8	5.4	8.8	9.7	8.6	-
30 to 34 years	12,691	6,302	6,389	4,472	4,095	114	115	1,700	2,177	16	2	8.8	8.6	8.9	9.1	9.0	5.6	7.0	7.8	9.0	11.4	-
35 to 39 years	12,313	5,947	6,366	3,815	3,830	190	182	1,926	2,351	16	3	8.5	8.2	8.9	7.8	8.4	9.4	11.1	8.8	9.8	11.4	-
40 to 44 years	11,084	5,525	5,559	3,452	3,398	242	215	1,806	1,943	25	3	7.7	7.6	7.8	7.1	7.4	12.0	13.1	8.3	8.1	17.9	-
45 to 49 years	9,467	4,667	4,800	2,836	2,953	311	192	1,508	1,652	12	3	6.6	6.4	6.7	5.8	6.5	15.4	11.7	6.9	6.9	8.6	-
50 to 54 years	7,739	3,925	3,814	2,390	2,374	293	204	1,236	1,236	6	-	5.4	5.4	5.3	4.9	5.2	14.5	12.5	5.7	5.1	4.3	-
55 to 59 years	5,506	2,710	2,796	1,726	1,900	246	154	731	741	7	1	3.8	3.7	3.9	3.5	4.2	12.2	9.4	3.3	3.1	5.0	-
60 to 64 years	4,348	2,052	2,296	1,311	1,598	160	155	577	543	4	-	3.0	2.8	3.2	2.7	3.5	7.9	9.5	2.6	2.3	2.9	-

65 to 69 years	3,420	1,608	1,812	970	1,195	129	107	506	510	3	-	2.4	2.2	2.5	2.0	2.6	6.4	6.5	2.3	2.1	2.1	-
70 to 74 years	2,035	928	1,107	574	757	93	66	260	284	1	-	1.4	1.3	1.6	1.2	1.7	4.6	4.0	1.2	1.2	0.7	-
75 years and over	1,841	734	1,107	492	784	66	64	176	259	-	-	1.3	1.0	1.6	1.0	1.7	3.3	3.9	0.8	1.1	-	-
Under 1 year	1,884	990	894	683	609	-	-	303	284	4	1	1.3	1.4	1.3	1.4	1.3	-	-	1.4	1.2	2.9	-
21 years and over	96,390	47,700	48,690	31,726	31,262	1,949	1,586	13,923	15,822	102	20	66.8	65.4	68.2	64.8	68.5	96.4	97.0	63.8	65.8	72.9	-
Median age	29.4	28.5	30.3	27.5	30.1	49.6	48.2	28.7	29.3	36.3	-	-	-	-	-	-	-	-	-	-	-	-
OAKLAND, CALIF.																						
All ages	302,163	149,227	152,936	119,211	126,064	22,373	20,288	4,200	4,262	3,443	2,322	100.0	100.0	100.0	100.0	100.0	100.0	100.0	100.0	100.0	100.0	100.0
Under 5 years	17,337	8,776	8,561	8,302	8,084	11	11	258	249	205	217	5.7	5.9	5.6	7.0	6.4	-	0.1	6.1	5.8	6.0	9.3
5 to 9 years	16,285	8,286	7,999	7,760	7,466	24	29	254	246	248	258	5.4	5.6	5.2	6.5	5.9	0.1	0.1	6.0	5.8	7.2	11.1
10 to 14 years	18,539	9,342	9,197	8,737	8,599	72	76	254	228	279	294	6.1	6.3	6.0	7.3	6.8	0.3	0.4	6.0	5.3	8.1	12.7
15 to 19 years	22,647	11,062	11,585	10,122	10,694	301	283	264	299	375	309	7.5	7.4	7.6	8.5	8.5	1.3	1.4	6.3	7.0	10.9	13.3
20 to 24 years	24,780	11,843	12,937	10,743	11,867	440	444	333	368	327	258	8.2	7.9	8.5	9.0	9.4	2.0	2.2	7.9	8.6	9.5	11.1
25 to 29 years	26,874	13,316	13,558	11,794	12,169	736	797	418	381	368	211	8.9	8.9	8.9	9.9	9.7	3.3	3.9	10.0	8.9	10.7	9.1
30 to 34 years	26,158	13,007	13,151	11,045	11,351	1,271	1,314	357	362	334	124	8.7	8.7	8.6	9.3	9.0	5.7	6.5	8.5	8.5	9.7	5.3
35 to 39 years	24,382	12,382	12,000	9,768	9,627	1,983	1,780	350	431	281	162	8.1	8.3	7.8	8.2	7.6	8.9	8.8	8.3	10.1	8.2	7.0
40 to 44 years	23,729	11,945	11,784	9,045	9,266	2,263	1,986	389	392	248	140	7.9	8.0	7.7	7.6	7.4	10.1	9.8	9.3	9.2	7.2	6.0
45 to 49 years	22,693	11,499	11,194	8,306	8,569	2,644	2,135	344	362	205	128	7.5	7.7	7.3	7.0	6.8	11.8	10.5	8.2	8.5	6.0	5.5
50 to 54 years	21,218	10,704	10,514	7,082	7,640	3,137	2,492	297	295	188	87	7.0	7.2	6.9	5.9	6.1	14.0	12.3	7.1	6.9	5.5	3.7
55 to 59 years	17,683	8,939	8,744	5,588	6,136	2,929	2,322	273	225	149	61	5.9	6.0	5.7	4.7	4.9	13.1	11.4	6.5	5.3	4.3	2.6
60 to 64 years	14,262	6,889	7,373	4,292	5,163	2,326	2,033	160	138	111	39	4.7	4.6	4.8	3.6	4.1	10.4	10.0	3.8	3.2	3.2	1.7
65 to 69 years	10,677	4,863	5,814	3,081	3,993	1,601	1,663	124	143	57	15	3.5	3.3	3.8	2.6	3.2	7.2	8.2	3.0	3.4	1.7	0.6
70 to 74 years	7,296	3,255	4,041	1,825	2,658	1,318	1,296	75	72	37	15	2.4	2.2	2.6	1.5	2.1	5.9	6.4	1.8	1.7	1.1	0.6
75 years and over	7,603	3,119	4,484	1,721	2,782	1,317	1,627	50	71	31	4	2.5	2.1	2.9	1.4	2.2	5.9	8.0	1.2	1.7	0.9	0.2
Under 1 year	3,573	1,834	1,739	1,750	1,664	-	1	48	46	36	28	1.2	1.2	1.1	1.5	1.3	-	-	1.1	1.1	1.0	1.2
21 years and over	222,497	109,485	113,012	82,224	88,836	21,879	19,798	3,111	3,187	2,271	1,191	73.6	73.4	73.9	69.0	70.5	97.8	97.6	74.1	74.8	66.0	51.3
Median age	34.7	34.6	34.8	31.0	31.8	52.3	52.6	34.5	35.0	28.9	21.6	-	-	-	-	-	-	-	-	-	-	-
OKLAHOMA CITY, OKLA.																						
All ages	204,424	98,774	105,650	87,832	94,065	1,586	1,232	9,173	10,171	183	182	100.0	100.0	100.0	100.0	100.0	100.0	100.0	100.0	100.0	100.0	100.0
Under 5 years	15,353	7,846	7,507	7,161	6,826	5	2	665	667	15	12	7.5	7.9	7.1	8.2	7.3	0.3	0.2	7.2	6.6	8.2	6.6
5 to 9 years	15,329	7,779	7,550	7,033	6,817	1	5	732	717	13	11	7.5	7.9	7.1	8.0	7.2	0.1	0.4	8.0	7.0	7.1	6.0
10 to 14 years	15,745	7,841	7,904	7,044	7,088	10	6	774	795	13	15	7.7	7.9	7.5	8.0	7.5	0.6	0.5	8.4	7.8	7.1	8.2
15 to 19 years	17,044	7,957	9,087	7,231	8,154	12	13	697	899	17	21	8.3	8.1	8.6	8.2	8.7	0.8	1.1	7.6	8.8	9.3	11.5
20 to 24 years	19,143	8,451	10,692	7,677	9,502	20	27	742	1,126	12	37	9.4	8.6	10.1	8.7	10.1	1.3	2.2	8.1	11.1	6.6	20.3
25 to 29 years	20,991	9,443	11,548	8,401	10,138	58	58	974	1,332	10	20	10.3	9.6	10.9	9.6	10.8	3.7	4.7	10.6	13.1	5.5	11.0
30 to 34 years	20,556	9,696	10,860	8,590	9,541	103	78	987	1,224	16	17	10.1	9.8	10.3	9.8	10.1	6.5	6.3	10.8	12.0	8.7	9.3
35 to 39 years	18,148	8,783	9,365	7,606	8,156	142	133	1,021	1,059	14	17	8.9	8.9	8.9	8.7	8.7	9.0	10.8	11.1	10.4	7.7	9.3
40 to 44 years	14,967	7,523	7,444	6,612	6,627	155	127	739	681	17	9	7.3	7.6	7.0	7.5	7.0	9.8	10.3	8.1	6.7	9.3	4.9
45 to 49 years	12,376	6,213	6,163	5,414	5,486	182	118	596	553	21	6	6.1	6.3	5.8	6.2	5.8	11.5	9.6	6.5	5.4	11.5	3.3
50 to 54 years	10,040	5,132	4,908	4,503	4,406	222	132	398	364	9	6	4.9	5.2	4.6	5.1	4.7	14.0	10.7	4.3	3.6	4.9	3.3
55 to 59 years	7,758	3,811	3,947	3,326	3,554	175	121	300	270	10	2	3.8	3.9	3.7	3.8	3.8	11.0	9.8	3.3	2.7	5.5	1.1
60 to 64 years	6,059	3,058	3,001	2,693	2,720	164	116	196	162	5	3	3.0	3.1	2.8	3.1	2.9	10.3	9.4	2.1	1.6	2.7	1.6
65 to 69 years	4,916	2,399	2,517	2,090	2,250	112	99	190	164	7	4	2.4	2.4	2.4	2.4	2.4	7.1	8.0	2.1	1.6	3.8	2.2
70 to 74 years	2,982	1,400	1,582	1,217	1,413	103	95	78	72	2	2	1.5	1.4	1.5	1.4	1.5	6.5	7.7	0.9	0.7	1.1	1.1
75 years and over	3,017	1,442	1,575	1,234	1,387	122	102	84	86	2	-	1.5	1.5	1.5	1.4	1.5	7.7	8.3	0.9	0.8	1.1	-
Under 1 year	3,110	1,583	1,527	1,442	1,405	-	-	139	118	2	4	1.5	1.6	1.4	1.6	1.5	-	-	1.5	1.2	1.1	2.2
21 years and over	137,229	65,828	71,401	57,971	63,225	1,556	1,203	6,179	6,861	122	112	67.1	66.6	67.6	66.0	67.2	98.1	97.6	67.4	67.5	66.7	61.5
Median age	29.7	30.0	29.4	29.6	29.3	52.4	51.9	30.0	28.3	33.6	24.3	-	-	-	-	-	-	-	-	-	-	-
OMAHA, NEBR.																						
All ages	223,844	108,750	115,094	91,044	98,285	11,668	10,643	5,920	6,095	118	71	100.0	100.0	100.0	100.0	100.0	100.0	100.0	100.0	100.0	100.0	-
Under 5 years	15,518	7,932	7,586	7,508	7,174	3	3	411	398	10	11	6.9	7.3	6.6	8.2	7.3	-	-	6.9	6.5	8.5	-
5 to 9 years	15,409	7,826	7,583	7,345	7,069	14	5	457	499	10	10	6.9	7.2	6.6	8.1	7.2	0.1	-	7.7	8.2	8.5	-
10 to 14 years	17,250	8,753	8,497	8,214	7,961	24	22	508	507	7	7	7.7	8.0	7.4	9.0	8.1	0.2	0.2	8.6	8.3	5.9	-
15 to 19 years	19,329	9,314	10,015	8,770	9,427	80	88	455	491	9	9	8.6	8.6	8.7	9.6	9.6	0.7	0.8	7.7	8.1	7.6	-
20 to 24 years	19,354	8,503	10,851	8,056	10,308	97	101	341	433	9	9	8.6	7.8	9.4	8.8	10.5	0.8	0.9	5.8	7.1	7.6	-
25 to 29 years	19,274	8,911	10,363	8,238	9,597	264	271	403	488	6	7	8.6	8.2	9.0	9.0	9.8	2.3	2.5	6.8	8.0	5.1	-
30 to 34 years	18,366	8,616	9,750	7,583	8,654	549	499	477	593	7	4	8.2	7.9	8.5	8.3	8.8	4.7	4.7	8.1	9.7	5.9	-
35 to 39 years	17,178	8,264	8,914	6,938	7,550	766	801	551	562	9	1	7.7	7.6	7.7	7.6	7.7	6.6	7.5	9.3	9.2	7.6	-
40 to 44 years	16,725	8,134	8,591	6,537	7,098	1,051	999	533	492	13	2	7.5	7.5	7.5	7.2	7.2	9.0	9.4	9.0	8.1	11.0	-
45 to 49 years	16,006	8,064	7,942	6,135	6,330	1,418	1,178	503	428	8	6	7.2	7.4	6.9	6.7	6.4	12.2	11.1	8.5	7.0	6.8	-
50 to 54 years	14,370	7,290	7,080	5,033	5,300	1,857	1,409	391	368	9	3	6.4	6.7	6.2	5.5	5.4	15.9	13.2	6.6	6.0	7.6	-
55 to 59 years	11,235	5,765	5,470	3,819	3,941	1,600	1,231	340	297	6	1	5.0	5.3	4.8	4.2	4.0	13.7	11.6	5.7	4.9	5.1	-
60 to 64 years	8,195	4,098	4,097	2,664	2,747	1,216	1,161	212	189	6	-	3.7	3.8	3.6	2.9	2.8	10.4	10.9	3.6	3.1	5.1	-
65 to 69 years	6,366	2,992	3,374	1,839	2,159	986	1,021	161	193	6	1	2.8	2.8	2.9	2.0	2.2	8.5	9.6	2.7	3.2	5.1	-
70 to 74 years	4,399	2,058	2,341	1,164	1,392	803	871	90	78	1	-	2.0	1.9	2.0	1.3	1.4	6.9	8.2	1.5	1.3	0.8	-
75 years and over	4,870	2,230	2,640	1,201	1,578	940	983	87	79	2	-	2.2	2.1	2.3	1.3	1.6	8.1	9.2	1.5	1.3	1.7	-
Under 1 year	3,007	1,523	1,484	1,440	1,399	1	-	77	85	5	-	1.3	1.4	1.3	1.6	1.4	-	-	1.3	1.4	4.2	-
21 years and over	152,620	73,293	79,327	57,669	64,686	11,523	10,498	4,020	4,111	81	32	68.2	67.4	68.9	63.3	65.8	98.8	98.6	67.9	67.4	68.6	-
Median age	31.6	31.8	31.4	28.4	28.8	54.2	54.8	34.0	32.0	35.6	-	-	-	-	-	-	-	-	-	-	-	-

TABLE 53.—AGE, BY RACE AND SEX, WITH PERCENT DISTRIBUTION BY AGE, FOR CITIES OF 100,000 OR MORE: 1940—Continued

[Percent not shown where less than 0.1 or where base is less than 100]

CITY AND AGE	NUMBER											PERCENT DISTRIBUTION										
	All classes			Native white		Foreign-born white		Negro		Other races		All classes			Native white		Foreign-born white		Negro		Other races	
	Total	Male	Female	Male	Female	Male	Female	Male	Female	Male	Female	Total	Male	Female	Male	Female	Male	Female	Male	Female	Male	Female
PATERSON, N. J.																						
All ages	139,656	69,505	70,151	49,777	51,435	17,594	16,494	2,055	2,213	79	9	100.0	100.0	100.0	100.0	100.0	100.0	100.0	100.0	100.0	---	---
Under 5 years	7,922	4,106	3,816	3,897	3,655	13	7	194	150	2	4	5.7	5.9	5.4	7.8	7.1	0.1	---	9.4	6.8	---	---
5 to 9 years	8,987	4,568	4,419	4,360	4,190	22	20	183	209	3	---	6.4	6.6	6.3	8.8	8.1	0.1	0.1	8.9	9.4	---	---
10 to 14 years	10,790	5,441	5,349	5,166	5,079	84	80	190	189	1	1	7.7	7.8	7.6	10.4	9.9	0.5	0.5	9.2	8.5	---	---
15 to 19 years	12,037	5,961	6,076	5,577	5,693	195	199	185	183	4	1	8.6	8.6	8.7	11.2	11.1	1.1	1.2	9.0	8.3	---	---
20 to 24 years	12,489	5,987	6,502	5,566	5,934	254	325	161	243	6	---	8.9	8.6	9.3	11.2	11.5	1.4	2.0	7.8	11.0	---	---
25 to 29 years	12,502	6,181	6,321	5,409	5,458	587	630	177	233	8	---	9.0	8.9	9.0	10.9	10.6	3.3	3.8	8.6	10.5	---	---
30 to 34 years	11,535	5,645	5,890	4,466	4,640	949	1,009	220	240	10	1	8.3	8.1	8.4	9.0	9.0	5.4	6.1	10.7	10.8	---	---
35 to 39 years	10,830	5,395	5,435	3,683	3,725	1,500	1,470	206	239	6	1	7.8	7.8	7.7	7.4	7.2	8.5	8.9	10.0	10.8	---	---
40 to 44 years	10,409	5,276	5,133	3,065	3,102	1,990	1,875	203	156	18	---	7.5	7.6	7.3	6.2	6.0	11.3	11.4	9.9	7.0	---	---
45 to 49 years	9,903	5,033	4,870	2,532	2,688	2,387	2,074	105	107	9	1	7.1	7.2	6.9	5.1	5.2	13.6	12.6	5.1	4.8	---	---
50 to 54 years	8,990	4,589	4,401	1,899	2,107	2,601	2,204	82	90	7	---	6.4	6.6	6.3	3.8	4.1	14.8	13.4	4.0	4.1	---	---
55 to 59 years	7,097	3,635	3,462	1,379	1,533	2,204	1,868	50	61	2	---	5.1	5.2	4.9	2.8	3.0	12.5	11.3	2.4	2.8	---	---
60 to 64 years	5,873	2,938	2,935	1,115	1,280	1,788	1,604	35	42	---	---	4.2	4.2	4.2	2.2	2.5	10.2	9.7	1.7	1.9	---	---
65 to 69 years	4,417	2,141	2,276	787	1,018	1,312	1,218	40	40	2	---	3.2	3.1	3.2	1.6	2.0	7.5	7.4	1.9	1.8	---	---
70 to 74 years	3,014	1,363	1,651	494	679	858	948	10	24	1	---	2.2	2.0	2.4	1.0	1.3	4.9	5.7	0.5	1.1	---	---
75 years and over	2,861	1,246	1,615	382	645	850	963	14	7	---	---	2.0	1.8	2.3	0.8	1.3	4.8	5.8	0.7	0.3	---	---
Under 1 year	1,484	761	723	734	700	2	---	24	22	1	1	1.1	1.1	1.0	1.5	1.4	---	---	1.2	1.0	---	---
21 years and over	97,387	48,221	49,166	29,667	31,619	17,213	16,114	1,272	1,430	69	3	69.7	69.4	70.1	59.6	61.5	97.8	97.7	61.9	64.6	---	---
Median age	32.2	32.2	32.2	25.3	26.1	51.6	51.3	28.2	27.8	---	---	---	---	---	---	---	---	---	---	---	---	---
PEORIA, ILL.																						
All ages	105,087	51,832	53,255	47,413	49,325	2,947	2,517	1,434	1,392	38	21	100.0	100.0	100.0	100.0	100.0	100.0	100.0	100.0	100.0	---	---
Under 5 years	6,935	3,631	3,304	3,523	3,200	---	---	103	99	5	5	6.6	7.0	6.2	7.4	6.5	---	---	7.2	7.1	---	---
5 to 9 years	6,516	3,217	3,299	3,130	3,190	2	1	81	105	4	3	6.2	6.2	6.2	6.6	6.5	0.1	---	5.6	7.5	---	---
10 to 14 years	6,869	3,464	3,405	3,367	3,289	5	12	88	99	4	5	6.5	6.7	6.4	7.1	6.7	0.2	0.5	6.1	7.1	---	---
15 to 19 years	8,025	3,788	4,237	3,643	4,096	35	41	109	99	1	1	7.6	7.3	8.0	7.7	8.3	1.2	1.6	7.6	7.1	---	---
20 to 24 years	9,652	4,460	5,192	4,295	5,000	55	55	109	136	1	1	9.2	8.6	9.7	9.1	10.1	1.9	2.2	7.6	9.8	---	---
25 to 29 years	9,987	4,974	5,013	4,747	4,795	86	79	135	139	6	---	9.5	9.6	9.4	10.0	9.7	2.9	3.1	9.4	10.0	---	---
30 to 34 years	9,421	4,776	4,645	4,489	4,379	159	136	126	129	2	1	9.0	9.2	8.7	9.5	8.9	5.4	5.4	8.8	9.3	---	---
35 to 39 years	8,561	4,330	4,231	3,930	3,911	253	180	140	139	7	1	8.1	8.4	7.9	8.3	7.9	8.6	7.2	9.8	10.0	---	---
40 to 44 years	7,885	3,981	3,904	3,567	3,586	283	205	128	112	3	1	7.5	7.7	7.3	7.5	7.3	9.6	8.1	8.9	8.0	---	---
45 to 49 years	7,240	3,667	3,573	3,241	3,261	318	225	105	85	3	2	6.9	7.1	6.7	6.8	6.6	10.8	8.9	7.3	6.1	---	---
50 to 54 years	6,520	3,242	3,278	2,743	2,897	400	299	98	82	1	---	6.2	6.3	6.2	5.8	5.9	13.6	11.9	6.8	5.9	---	---
55 to 59 years	5,315	2,679	2,636	2,237	2,275	367	289	75	72	---	---	5.1	5.2	4.9	4.7	4.6	12.5	11.5	5.2	5.2	---	---
60 to 64 years	4,146	2,004	2,142	1,628	1,822	318	287	57	33	1	---	3.9	3.9	4.0	3.4	3.7	10.8	11.4	4.0	2.4	---	---
65 to 69 years	3,240	1,534	1,706	1,242	1,460	248	216	44	30	---	---	3.1	3.0	3.2	2.6	3.0	8.4	8.6	3.1	2.2	---	---
70 to 74 years	2,388	1,040	1,348	841	1,106	179	226	20	16	---	---	2.3	2.0	2.5	1.8	2.2	6.1	9.0	1.4	1.1	---	---
75 years and over	2,387	1,045	1,342	790	1,058	239	266	16	17	---	1	2.3	2.0	2.5	1.7	2.1	8.1	10.6	1.1	1.2	---	---
Under 1 year	1,378	713	665	691	639	---	---	22	24	---	2	1.3	1.4	1.2	15	1.3	---	---	1.5	1.7	---	---
21 years and over	75,012	37,024	37,988	33,070	34,561	2,895	2,452	1,035	968	24	.7	71.4	71.4	71.3	69.7	70.1	98.2	97.4	72.2	69.5	---	---
Median age	32.4	32.5	32.3	31.1	31.2	53.5	55.4	33.7	30.7	---	---	---	---	---	---	---	---	---	---	---	---	---
PHILADELPHIA, PA.																						
All ages	1,931,334	942,550	988,784	877,008	711,244	145,258	145,067	118,859	132,021	1,425	452	100.0	100.0	100.0	100.0	100.0	100.0	100.0	100.0	100.0	100.0	100.0
Under 5 years	122,202	62,119	60,083	52,279	50,213	65	63	9,700	9,742	75	65	6.3	6.6	6.1	7.7	7.1	---	---	8.2	7.4	5.3	14.4
5 to 9 years	130,156	65,933	64,223	55,181	53,362	160	155	10,504	10,642	88	64	6.7	7.0	6.5	8.2	7.5	0.1	0.1	8.8	8.1	6.2	14.2
10 to 14 years	151,711	76,393	75,318	64,914	63,314	495	457	10,912	11,470	72	77	7.9	8.1	7.6	9.6	8.9	0.3	0.3	9.2	8.7	5.1	17.0
15 to 19 years	166,271	81,864	84,407	70,650	71,912	1,519	1,615	9,640	10,829	55	51	8.6	8.7	8.5	10.4	10.1	1.0	1.1	8.1	8.2	3.9	11.3
20 to 24 years	172,599	81,858	90,741	71,649	76,863	1,774	2,023	8,389	11,818	46	37	8.9	8.7	9.2	10.6	10.8	1.2	1.4	7.1	8.0	3.2	8.2
25 to 29 years	170,219	80,930	89,289	66,963	70,346	4,395	5,693	9,493	13,220	79	30	8.8	8.6	9.0	9.9	9.9	3.0	3.9	8.0	10.0	5.5	6.6
30 to 34 years	159,802	76,625	83,177	58,255	60,731	8,272	9,489	9,976	12,931	122	26	8.3	8.1	8.4	8.6	8.5	5.7	6.5	8.4	9.8	8.6	5.8
35 to 39 years	152,209	74,070	78,139	48,662	50,619	13,415	14,005	11,826	13,486	167	29	7.9	7.9	7.9	7.2	7.1	9.2	9.7	9.9	10.2	11.7	6.4
40 to 44 years	147,576	72,986	74,590	44,140	46,048	17,451	17,380	11,184	11,144	211	18	7.6	7.7	7.5	6.5	6.5	12.0	12.0	9.4	8.4	14.8	4.0
45 to 49 years	137,522	68,717	68,805	38,215	40,273	21,398	19,981	8,957	8,525	147	26	7.1	7.3	7.0	5.6	5.7	14.7	13.8	7.5	6.5	10.3	5.8
50 to 54 years	117,889	59,239	58,650	30,618	33,506	22,118	19,115	6,377	6,019	126	10	6.1	6.3	5.9	4.5	4.7	15.2	13.2	5.4	4.6	8.8	2.2
55 to 59 years	91,927	45,780	46,147	23,401	25,895	17,832	16,045	4,456	4,201	91	6	4.8	4.9	4.7	3.5	3.6	12.3	11.1	3.7	3.2	6.4	1.3
60 to 64 years	75,357	36,292	39,065	19,257	22,896	13,842	13,238	3,126	2,926	67	5	3.9	3.9	4.0	2.8	3.2	9.5	9.1	2.6	2.2	4.7	1.1

UNITED STATES SUMMARY—PRINCIPAL CITIES

65 to 69 years	58,397	26,841	31,556	14,819	18,435	9,820	10,855	2,160	2,262	42	4	3.0	2.8	3.2	2.2	2.6	6.8	7.5	1.8	1.7	2.9	0.9
70 to 74 years	40,306	17,818	22,488	9,827	13,188	6,749	7,798	1,221	1,499	21	3	2.1	1.9	2.3	1.5	1.9	4.6	5.4	1.0	1.1	1.5	0.7
75 years and over	37,191	15,085	22,106	8,178	13,643	5,953	7,155	938	1,307	16	1	1.9	1.6	2.2	1.2	1.9	4.1	4.9	0.8	1.0	1.1	0.2
Under 1 year	22,371	11,394	10,977	9,673	9,187	4	6	1,702	1,773	15	11	1.2	1.2	1.1	1.4	1.3			1.4	1.3	1.1	2.4
21 years and over	1,326,413	639,755	686,658	419,640	457,154	142,551	142,310	76,437	87,004	1,127	19.0	68.7	67.9	69.4	62.0	64.3	98.1	98.1	64.3	65.9	79.1	42.0
Median age	31.6	31.4	31.8	26.8	27.8	50.8	50.4	30.4	29.4	40.2	17.0											
PITTSBURGH, PA.																						
All ages	671,659	330,007	341,652	253,986	270,644	44,805	39,801	31,056	31,160	160	47	100.0	100.0	100.0	100.0	100.0	100.0	100.0	100.0	100.0	100.0	
Under 5 years	44,257	22,433	21,824	20,109	19,474	18	17	2,302	2,330	4	3	6.6	6.8	6.4	7.9	7.2			7.4	7.5	2.5	
5 to 9 years	45,253	22,630	22,623	20,066	20,026	58	51	2,498	2,535	8	11	6.7	6.9	6.6	7.9	7.4	0.1	0.1	8.0	8.1	5.0	
10 to 14 years	56,540	28,602	27,938	25,669	24,894	149	139	2,773	2,901	11	4	8.4	8.7	8.2	10.1	9.2	0.3	0.3	8.9	9.3	6.9	
15 to 19 years	61,473	29,871	31,602	26,911	28,410	482	454	2,466	2,733	12	5	9.2	9.1	9.2	10.6	10.5	1.1	1.1	7.9	8.8	7.5	
20 to 24 years	63,827	29,552	34,275	26,822	31,055	554	564	2,169	2,651	7	5	9.5	9.0	10.0	10.6	11.5	1.2	1.4	7.0	8.5	4.4	
25 to 29 years	61,037	29,157	31,880	25,498	27,553	1,187	1,418	2,457	2,908	15	1	9.1	8.8	9.3	10.0	10.2	2.6	3.6	7.9	9.3	9.4	
30 to 34 years	54,915	26,444	28,471	21,994	23,509	1,918	2,078	2,518	2,883	14	1	8.2	8.0	8.3	8.7	8.7	4.3	5.2	8.1	9.3	8.8	
35 to 39 years	50,788	24,707	26,081	18,379	19,561	3,238	3,426	3,074	3,091	16	3	7.6	7.5	7.6	7.2	7.2	7.2	8.6	9.9	9.9	10.0	
40 to 44 years	48,158	24,052	24,106	16,152	17,214	4,848	4,244	3,031	2,640	21	8	7.2	7.3	7.1	6.4	6.4	10.8	10.7	9.8	8.5	13.1	
45 to 49 years	46,080	23,522	22,558	14,312	14,991	6,598	5,502	2,595	2,063	17	2	6.9	7.1	6.6	5.6	5.5	14.7	13.8	8.4	6.6	10.6	
50 to 54 years	40,043	20,522	19,521	11,501	12,452	7,243	5,581	1,761	1,486	17	2	6.0	6.2	5.7	4.5	4.6	16.2	14.0	5.7	4.8	10.6	
55 to 59 years	31,791	16,337	15,454	8,959	9,565	6,073	4,853	1,298	1,036	7		4.7	5.0	4.5	3.5	3.5	13.6	12.2	4.2	3.3	4.4	
60 to 64 years	25,504	12,768	12,736	6,985	7,963	4,895	4,080	885	693	3		3.8	3.9	3.7	2.8	2.9	10.9	10.3	2.8	2.2	1.9	
65 to 69 years	18,849	9,057	9,792	5,078	6,145	3,319	3,049	658	596	2	2	2.8	2.7	2.9	2.0	2.3	7.4	7.7	2.1	1.9	1.3	
70 to 74 years	12,198	5,736	6,462	3,157	3,937	2,221	2,201	355	324	3		1.8	1.7	1.9	1.2	1.5	5.0	5.5	1.1	1.0	1.9	
75 years and over	10,946	4,617	6,329	2,394	3,895	2,004	2,144	216	290	3		1.6	1.4	1.9	0.9	1.4	4.5	5.4	0.7	0.9	1.9	
Under 1 year	8,393	4,311	4,082	3,880	3,631		1	429	450	2		1.2	1.3	1.2	1.5	1.3			1.4	1.4	1.3	
21 years and over	451,393	220,654	230,739	156,000	171,613	43,961	39,006	20,570	20,096	123	24	67.2	66.9	67.5	61.4	63.4	98.1	98.0	66.2	64.5	76.9	
Median age	30.3	30.5	30.1	26.5	27.1	52.3	51.8	31.7	29.2	37.8												
PORTLAND, OREG.																						
All ages	305,394	149,135	156,259	124,932	136,167	20,844	17,764	1,025	906	2,334	1,422	100.0	100.0	100.0	100.0	100.0	100.0	100.0	100.0	100.0	100.0	100.0
Under 5 years	15,990	8,128	7,862	7,955	7,716	13	7	58	45	102	94	5.2	5.5	5.0	6.4	5.7	0.1		5.7	5.0	4.4	6.6
5 to 9 years	14,877	7,395	7,482	7,211	7,270	37	31	41	54	106	127	4.9	5.0	4.8	5.8	5.3	0.2	0.2	4.0	6.0	4.5	8.9
10 to 14 years	17,674	8,865	8,809	8,559	8,532	63	54	62	56	181	167	5.8	5.9	5.6	6.9	6.3	0.3	0.3	6.0	6.2	7.8	11.7
15 to 19 years	23,082	10,969	12,113	10,390	11,504	282	315	57	66	240	228	7.6	7.4	7.8	8.3	8.4	1.4	1.8	5.6	7.3	10.3	16.0
20 to 24 years	25,583	11,669	13,914	10,958	13,130	432	553	73	63	206	168	8.4	7.8	8.9	8.8	9.6	2.1	3.1	7.1	7.0	8.8	11.8
25 to 29 years	26,792	12,855	13,937	11,836	12,935	744	805	88	86	187	111	8.8	8.6	8.9	9.5	9.5	3.6	4.5	8.6	9.5	8.0	7.8
30 to 34 years	24,666	12,000	12,666	10,711	11,489	1,010	1,024	78	72	201	81	8.1	8.0	8.1	8.6	8.4	4.8	5.8	7.6	7.9	8.6	5.7
35 to 39 years	23,301	11,120	12,181	9,448	10,582	1,384	1,404	94	88	194	107	7.6	7.5	7.8	7.6	7.8	6.6	7.9	9.2	9.7	8.3	7.5
40 to 44 years	23,430	11,459	11,971	9,390	10,232	1,799	1,557	92	75	178	107	7.7	7.7	7.7	7.5	7.5	8.6	8.8	9.0	8.3	7.6	7.5
45 to 49 years	24,071	11,994	12,077	9,345	10,095	2,387	1,809	105	77	157	96	7.9	8.0	7.7	7.5	7.4	11.5	10.2	10.2	8.5	6.7	6.8
50 to 54 years	22,829	11,753	11,076	8,391	8,777	3,100	2,172	72	67	190	60	7.5	7.9	7.1	6.7	6.4	14.9	12.2	7.0	7.4	8.1	4.2
55 to 59 years	19,241	10,015	9,226	6,937	7,074	2,859	2,069	72	50	147	33	6.3	6.7	5.9	5.6	5.2	13.7	11.6	7.0	5.5	6.3	2.3
60 to 64 years	15,218	7,610	7,608	5,188	5,776	2,265	1,776	55	38	102	18	5.0	5.1	4.9	4.2	4.2	10.9	10.0	5.4	4.2	4.4	1.3
65 to 69 years	11,575	5,483	6,092	3,704	4,540	1,684	1,507	36	31	59	14	3.8	3.7	3.9	3.0	3.3	8.1	8.5	3.5	3.4	2.5	1.0
70 to 74 years	8,198	3,828	4,370	2,459	3,116	1,317	1,233	19	18	33	3	2.7	2.6	2.8	2.0	2.3	6.3	6.9	1.9	2.0	1.4	0.2
75 years and over	8,867	3,992	4,875	2,450	3,399	1,468	1,448	23	20	51	8	2.9	2.7	3.1	2.0	2.5	7.0	8.2	2.2	2.2	2.2	0.6
Under 1 year	3,531	1,797	1,734	1,764	1,705	1	1	13	10	19	18	1.2	1.2	1.1	1.4	1.3			1.3	1.1	0.8	1.3
21 years and over	228,950	111,640	117,310	88,806	98,628	20,378	17,248	792	673	1,664	761	75.0	74.9	75.1	71.1	72.4	97.8	97.1	77.3	74.3	71.3	53.5
Median age	35.9	36.2	35.6	32.6	33.0	53.7	53.0	38.0	35.6	33.6	22.8											
PROVIDENCE, R. I.																						
All ages	253,504	121,797	131,707	93,583	102,113	24,972	26,236	3,060	3,328	182	30	100.0	100.0	100.0	100.0	100.0	100.0	100.0	100.0	100.0	100.0	
Under 5 years	15,651	7,891	7,760	7,569	7,408	11	15	310	336	1	1	6.2	6.5	5.9	8.1	7.3		0.1	10.1	10.1	0.5	
5 to 9 years	17,035	8,712	8,323	8,392	7,994	20	26	295	300	5	3	6.7	7.2	6.3	9.0	7.8	0.1	0.1	9.6	9.0	2.7	
10 to 14 years	20,867	10,519	10,348	10,098	9,916	82	68	334	360	5	4	8.2	8.6	7.9	10.8	9.7	0.3	0.3	10.9	10.8	2.7	
15 to 19 years	23,841	11,836	12,005	11,273	11,372	250	284	294	346	19	3	9.4	9.7	9.1	12.0	11.1	1.0	1.1	9.6	10.4	10.4	
20 to 24 years	23,003	11,041	11,962	10,424	11,315	338	358	264	289	15		9.1	9.1	9.1	11.1	11.1	1.4	1.4	8.6	8.7	8.2	
25 to 29 years	21,790	10,223	11,567	9,359	10,415	655	908	194	243	15	1	8.6	8.4	8.8	10.0	10.2	2.6	3.5	6.3	7.3	8.2	
30 to 34 years	19,415	9,061	10,354	7,664	8,631	1,221	1,534	157	186	19	3	7.7	7.4	7.9	8.2	8.5	4.9	5.8	5.1	5.8	10.4	
35 to 39 years	17,693	8,317	9,376	6,143	6,953	1,949	2,201	197	215	28	7	7.0	6.8	7.1	6.6	6.8	7.8	8.4	6.4	6.5	15.4	
40 to 44 years	17,648	8,408	9,240	5,354	6,104	2,841	2,910	197	224	16	2	7.0	6.9	7.0	5.7	6.0	11.4	11.1	6.4	6.7	8.8	
45 to 49 years	17,365	8,347	9,018	4,461	5,239	3,661	3,565	204	212	21	2	6.8	6.9	6.8	4.8	5.1	14.7	13.6	6.7	6.4	11.5	
50 to 54 years	15,757	7,666	8,091	3,582	4,307	3,880	3,608	192	176	12		6.2	6.3	6.1	3.8	4.2	15.5	13.8	6.3	5.3	6.6	
55 to 59 years	13,075	6,282	6,793	2,958	3,553	3,148	3,091	160	148	16	1	5.2	5.2	5.2	3.2	3.5	12.6	11.8	5.2	4.4	8.8	
60 to 64 years	10,638	4,926	5,712	2,272	2,984	2,535	2,621	113	106	6	1	4.2	4.0	4.3	2.4	2.9	10.2	10.0	3.7	3.2	3.3	
65 to 69 years	8,521	3,814	4,707	1,779	2,471	1,954	2,153	80	83	1		3.4	3.1	3.6	1.9	2.4	7.8	8.2	2.6	2.5	0.5	
70 to 74 years	5,829	2,560	3,269	1,171	1,716	1,352	1,498	36	55	1		2.3	2.1	2.5	1.3	1.7	5.4	5.7	1.2	1.7	0.5	
75 years and over	5,376	2,194	3,182	1,084	1,735	1,075	1,396	33	49	2	2	2.1	1.8	2.4	1.2	1.7	4.3	5.3	1.1	1.5	1.1	
Under 1 year	2,993	1,499	1,494	1,449	1,433			50	60		1	1.2	1.2	1.1	1.5	1.4			1.6	1.8		
21 years and over	171,449	80,549	90,900	54,095	63,175	24,529	25,771	1,776	1,935	149	19	67.6	66.1	69.0	57.8	61.9	98.2	98.2	58.0	58.1	81.9	
Median age	31.2	30.4	31.9	24.5	26.5	51.9	51.7	25.9	25.7	37.1												

TABLE 53.—AGE, BY RACE AND SEX, WITH PERCENT DISTRIBUTION BY AGE, FOR CITIES OF 100,000 OR MORE: 1940—Continued

[Percent not shown where less than 0.1 or where base is less than 100]

CITY AND AGE	NUMBER: All classes			Native white		Foreign-born white		Negro		Other races		PERCENT DISTRIBUTION: All classes			Native white		Foreign-born white		Negro		Other races	
	Total	Male	Female	Male	Female	Male	Female	Male	Female	Male	Female	Total	Male	Female	Male	Female	Male	Female	Male	Female	Male	Female
READING, PA.																						
All ages	110,568	53,954	56,614	48,691	52,094	4,278	3,583	969	936	16	1	100.0	100.0	100.0	100.0	100.0	100.0	100.0	100.0	100.0	-	-
Under 5 years	6,121	3,118	3,003	3,038	2,931	1	2	79	70	-	-	5.5	5.8	5.3	6.2	5.6	-	0.1	8.2	7.5	-	-
5 to 9 years	7,002	3,568	3,434	3,469	3,324	6	3	93	107	-	-	6.3	6.6	6.1	7.1	6.4	0.1	0.1	9.6	11.4	-	-
10 to 14 years	8,467	4,228	4,239	4,127	4,146	8	7	93	86	-	-	7.7	7.8	7.5	8.5	8.0	0.2	0.2	9.6	9.2	-	-
15 to 19 years	9,696	4,769	4,927	4,662	4,785	40	50	66	92	1	-	8.8	8.8	8.7	9.6	9.2	0.9	1.4	6.8	9.8	-	-
20 to 24 years	9,884	4,767	5,117	4,649	5,000	47	54	69	63	2	-	8.9	8.8	9.0	9.5	9.6	1.1	1.5	7.1	6.7	-	-
25 to 29 years	9,518	4,671	4,847	4,429	4,628	156	131	83	88	3	-	8.6	8.7	8.6	9.1	8.9	3.6	3.7	8.6	9.4	-	-
30 to 34 years	8,860	4,265	4,595	3,969	4,293	217	209	79	92	-	1	8.0	7.9	8.1	8.2	8.2	5.1	5.8	8.2	9.8	-	-
35 to 39 years	7,925	3,816	4,109	3,385	3,692	333	322	97	95	1	-	7.2	7.1	7.3	7.0	7.1	7.8	9.0	10.0	10.1	-	-
40 to 44 years	7,633	3,712	3,921	3,177	3,382	438	453	94	86	3	-	6.9	6.9	6.9	6.5	6.5	10.2	12.6	9.7	9.2	-	-
45 to 49 years	7,913	3,829	4,084	3,022	3,480	734	556	72	48	1	-	7.2	7.1	7.2	6.2	6.7	17.2	15.5	7.4	5.1	-	-
50 to 54 years	7,261	3,607	3,654	2,838	3,083	720	531	47	40	2	-	6.6	6.7	6.5	5.8	5.9	16.8	14.8	4.8	4.3	-	-
55 to 59 years	6,172	3,005	3,167	2,396	2,702	571	445	37	20	1	-	5.6	5.6	5.6	4.9	5.2	13.3	12.4	3.8	2.1	-	-
60 to 64 years	4,864	2,345	2,519	1,922	2,218	407	285	15	16	1	-	4.4	4.3	4.4	3.9	4.3	9.5	8.0	1.5	1.7	-	-
65 to 69 years	3,965	1,885	2,080	1,586	1,836	281	227	17	17	1	-	3.6	3.5	3.7	3.3	3.5	6.6	6.3	1.8	1.8	-	-
70 to 74 years	2,668	1,250	1,418	1,056	1,258	178	148	16	12	-	-	2.4	2.3	2.5	2.2	2.4	4.2	4.1	1.7	1.3	-	-
75 years and over	2,619	1,119	1,500	966	1,336	141	160	12	4	-	-	2.4	2.1	2.6	2.0	2.6	3.3	4.5	1.2	0.4	-	-
Under 1 year	1,135	563	572	553	558	-	-	10	14	-	-	1.0	1.0	1.0	1.1	1.1	-	-	1.0	1.5	-	-
21 years and over	77,304	37,350	39,954	32,500	35,874	4,212	3,511	623	568	15	1	69.9	69.2	70.6	66.7	68.9	98.5	98.0	64.3	60.7	-	-
Median age	32.6	32.2	33.0	30.0	31.4	50.0	49.1	30.1	27.8	-	-	-	-	-	-	-	-	-	-	-	-	-
RICHMOND, VA.																						
All ages	193,042	90,220	102,822	60,203	68,090	1,829	1,584	28,125	33,126	63	22	100.0	100.0	100.0	100.0	100.0	100.0	100.0	100.0	100.0	-	-
Under 5 years	11,258	5,613	5,645	3,483	3,440	2	3	2,123	2,198	5	4	5.8	6.2	5.5	5.8	5.1	0.1	0.2	7.5	6.6	-	-
5 to 9 years	12,341	6,239	6,102	3,778	3,620	10	8	2,446	2,474	5	-	6.4	6.9	5.9	6.3	5.3	0.5	0.5	8.7	7.5	-	-
10 to 14 years	14,518	7,124	7,394	4,582	4,567	7	12	2,530	2,812	5	3	7.5	7.9	7.2	7.6	6.7	0.4	0.8	9.0	8.5	-	-
15 to 19 years	17,404	8,169	9,235	5,524	5,944	19	18	2,621	3,270	5	3	9.0	9.1	9.0	9.2	8.7	1.0	1.1	9.3	9.9	-	-
20 to 24 years	19,766	8,979	10,787	6,206	7,047	31	23	2,738	3,715	4	2	10.2	10.0	10.5	10.3	10.3	1.7	1.5	9.7	11.2	-	-
25 to 29 years	19,817	9,377	10,440	6,468	6,806	73	70	2,833	3,563	3	1	10.3	10.4	10.2	10.7	10.0	4.0	4.4	10.1	10.8	-	-
30 to 34 years	17,347	8,101	9,246	5,581	6,283	102	136	2,414	2,825	4	2	9.0	9.0	9.0	9.3	9.2	5.6	8.6	8.6	8.5	-	-
35 to 39 years	16,302	7,530	8,772	4,889	5,611	186	161	2,448	2,998	7	2	8.4	8.3	8.5	8.1	8.2	10.2	10.2	8.7	9.1	-	-
40 to 44 years	14,375	6,688	7,687	4,350	5,028	248	180	2,078	2,478	12	1	7.4	7.4	7.5	7.2	7.4	13.6	11.4	7.4	7.5	-	-
45 to 49 years	12,730	5,895	6,835	3,924	4,541	258	219	1,708	2,073	5	2	6.6	6.5	6.6	6.5	6.7	14.1	13.8	6.1	6.3	-	-
55 to 54 years	10,644	5,018	5,626	3,324	3,924	245	174	1,445	1,526	4	2	5.5	5.6	5.5	5.5	5.8	13.4	11.0	5.1	4.6	-	-
55 to 59 years	8,305	3,815	4,490	2,649	3,238	194	176	969	1,076	3	-	4.3	4.2	4.4	4.4	4.8	10.6	11.1	3.4	3.2	-	-
60 to 64 years	6,785	3,003	3,782	2,131	2,897	150	136	722	749	-	-	3.5	3.3	3.7	3.5	4.3	8.2	8.6	2.6	2.3	-	-
65 to 69 years	5,141	2,186	2,955	1,492	2,219	131	95	562	641	1	-	2.7	2.4	2.9	2.5	3.3	7.2	6.0	2.0	1.9	-	-
70 to 74 years	3,321	1,353	1,968	1,014	1,505	77	78	262	385	-	-	1.7	1.5	1.9	1.7	2.2	4.2	4.9	0.9	1.2	-	-
75 years and over	2,988	1,130	1,858	808	1,420	96	95	226	343	-	-	1.5	1.3	1.8	1.3	2.1	5.2	6.0	0.8	1.0	-	-
Under 1 year	2,328	1,190	1,138	762	719	-	-	427	417	1	2	1.2	1.3	1.1	1.3	1.1	-	-	1.5	1.3	-	-
21 years and over	133,599	61,385	72,214	41,663	49,069	1,786	1,539	17,894	21,595	42	11	69.2	68.0	70.2	69.2	72.1	97.6	97.2	63.6	65.2	-	-
Median age	30.4	29.8	31.0	30.1	32.1	49.6	49.1	27.8	27.9	-	-	-	-	-	-	-	-	-	-	-	-	-
ROCHESTER, N. Y.																						
All ages	324,975	157,574	167,401	125,293	136,154	30,574	29,533	1,620	1,642	87	72	100.0	100.0	100.0	100.0	100.0	100.0	100.0	100.0	100.0	-	-
Under 5 years	18,058	9,232	8,826	9,114	8,700	19	13	93	111	6	2	5.6	5.9	5.3	7.3	6.4	0.1	-	5.7	6.8	-	-
5 to 9 years	19,217	9,666	9,551	9,493	9,398	47	55	120	90	6	8	5.9	6.1	5.7	7.6	6.9	0.2	0.2	7.4	5.5	-	-
10 to 14 years	23,262	11,707	11,555	11,429	11,263	130	141	138	147	10	4	7.2	7.4	6.9	9.1	8.3	0.4	0.5	8.5	9.0	-	-
15 to 19 years	27,494	13,371	14,123	12,784	13,523	446	460	130	134	11	6	8.5	8.5	8.4	10.2	9.9	1.5	1.6	8.0	8.2	-	-
20 to 24 years	30,437	14,466	15,971	13,777	15,226	547	596	136	134	6	15	9.4	9.2	9.5	11.0	11.2	1.8	2.0	8.4	8.2	-	-
25 to 29 years	28,103	13,598	14,505	12,464	13,081	1,009	1,285	124	130	1	9	8.6	8.6	8.7	9.9	9.6	3.3	4.4	7.7	7.9	-	-
30 to 34 years	24,621	11,778	12,843	9,780	10,542	1,874	2,126	112	172	12	3	7.6	7.5	7.7	7.8	7.7	6.1	7.2	6.9	10.5	-	-
35 to 39 years	23,395	11,267	12,128	8,265	8,962	2,807	2,983	188	176	7	7	7.2	7.2	7.2	6.6	6.6	9.2	10.1	11.6	10.7	-	-
40 to 44 years	24,077	11,551	12,526	7,872	8,840	3,496	3,531	176	150	7	5	7.4	7.3	7.5	6.3	6.5	11.4	12.0	10.9	9.1	-	-
45 to 49 years	24,211	11,884	12,327	7,402	8,304	4,357	3,906	121	112	4	5	7.4	7.5	7.4	5.9	6.1	14.3	13.2	7.5	6.8	-	-
50 to 54 years	22,513	11,304	11,209	6,584	7,347	4,615	3,767	102	90	3	5	6.9	7.2	6.7	5.3	5.4	15.1	12.8	6.3	5.5	-	-
55 to 59 years	18,426	9,211	9,215	5,309	6,053	3,830	3,093	64	67	8	2	5.7	5.8	5.5	4.2	4.4	12.5	10.5	4.0	4.1	-	-
60 to 64 years	14,540	6,946	7,594	4,095	5,050	2,797	2,500	50	44	4	-	4.5	4.4	4.5	3.3	3.7	9.1	8.5	3.1	2.7	-	-
65 to 69 years	10,966	5,039	5,927	3,137	3,942	1,870	1,945	30	39	2	1	3.4	3.2	3.5	2.5	2.9	6.1	6.6	1.9	2.4	-	-

UNITED STATES SUMMARY—PRINCIPAL CITIES

70 to 74 years	7,627	3,335	4,292	1,972	2,767	1,345	1,501	18	24	--	--	2.3	2.1	2.6	1.6	2.0	4.4	5.1	1.1	1.5	--	--
75 years and over	8,028	3,219	4,809	1,816	3,156	1,385	1,631	18	22	--	--	2.5	2.0	2.9	1.4	2.3	4.5	5.5	1.1	1.3	--	--
Under 1 year	3,427	1,758	1,669	1,729	1,640	--	--	29	28	--	1	1.1	1.1	1.0	1.4	1.2	--	--	1.8	1.7	--	--
21 years and over	231,234	110,942	120,292	79,965	90,400	29,811	28,717	1,112	1,124	54	51	71.2	70.4	71.9	63.8	66.4	97.5	97.2	68.6	68.5	--	--
Median age	33.2	32.9	33.6	27.4	28.8	50.6	49.6	33.1	32.2	--	--	--	--	--	--	--	--	--	--	--	--	--
SACRAMENTO, CALIF.																						
All ages	105,958	53,496	52,462	43,014	44,650	7,116	5,028	773	695	2,593	2,089	100.0	100.0	100.0	100.0	100.0	100.0	100.0	100.0	100.0	100.0	100.0
Under 5 years	5,878	2,960	2,918	2,721	2,697	3	4	54	38	182	179	5.5	5.5	5.6	6.3	6.0	--	0.1	7.0	5.5	7.0	8.6
5 to 9 years	5,584	2,752	2,832	2,490	2,545	8	7	45	43	209	237	5.3	5.1	5.4	5.8	5.7	0.1	0.1	5.8	6.2	8.1	11.3
10 to 14 years	6,707	3,291	3,416	2,979	3,048	15	23	49	56	248	289	6.3	6.2	6.5	6.9	6.8	0.2	0.5	6.3	8.1	9.0	13.8
15 to 19 years	8,250	4,034	4,216	3,557	3,783	64	86	62	55	351	292	7.8	7.5	8.0	8.3	8.5	0.9	1.7	8.0	7.9	13.5	14.0
20 to 24 years	9,752	4,437	5,315	3,971	4,809	152	177	59	61	255	268	9.2	8.3	9.8	9.2	10.8	2.1	3.5	7.6	8.8	9.8	12.8
25 to 29 years	10,062	4,921	5,141	4,389	4,633	255	283	69	66	208	159	9.5	9.2	9.8	10.2	10.4	3.6	5.6	8.9	9.5	8.0	7.6
30 to 34 years	9,217	4,651	4,566	3,962	4,048	439	342	79	71	171	105	8.7	8.7	8.7	9.2	9.1	6.2	6.8	10.2	10.2	6.6	5.0
35 to 39 years	8,805	4,507	4,298	3,586	3,561	653	534	77	81	191	122	8.3	8.4	8.2	8.3	8.0	9.2	10.6	10.0	11.7	7.4	5.8
40 to 44 years	8,341	4,370	3,971	3,398	3,291	741	500	67	48	164	132	7.9	8.2	7.6	7.9	7.4	10.4	9.9	8.7	6.9	6.3	6.3
45 to 49 years	7,644	4,056	3,588	2,992	2,844	900	562	59	54	105	128	7.2	7.6	6.8	7.0	6.4	12.6	11.2	7.6	7.7	4.0	6.1
50 to 54 years	7,215	3,975	3,240	2,613	2,491	1,146	611	45	40	171	98	6.8	7.4	6.2	6.1	5.6	16.1	12.2	5.8	5.8	6.6	4.7
55 to 59 years	5,916	3,203	2,713	2,115	2,113	899	542	37	21	152	37	5.6	6.0	5.2	4.9	4.7	12.6	10.8	4.8	3.0	5.9	1.8
60 to 64 years	4,533	2,428	2,105	1,605	1,604	689	457	31	23	103	21	4.3	4.5	4.0	3.7	3.6	9.7	9.1	4.0	3.3	4.0	1.0
65 to 69 years	3,459	1,721	1,738	1,174	1,342	476	360	17	20	54	16	3.3	3.2	3.3	2.7	3.0	6.7	7.2	2.2	2.9	2.1	0.8
70 to 74 years	2,276	1,128	1,148	760	885	340	248	12	12	16	3	2.1	2.1	2.2	1.8	2.0	4.8	4.9	1.6	1.7	0.6	0.1
75 years and over	2,319	1,062	1,257	702	956	336	292	11	6	13	3	2.2	2.0	2.4	1.6	2.1	4.7	5.8	1.4	0.9	0.5	0.1
Under 1 year	1,284	634	650	580	614	--	--	11	7	43	29	1.2	1.2	1.2	1.3	1.4	--	--	1.4	1.0	1.7	1.4
21 years and over	77,686	39,645	38,041	30,553	31,642	7,001	4,879	558	490	1,533	1,030	73.3	74.1	72.5	71.0	70.9	98.4	97.0	72.2	70.5	59.1	49.3
Median age	33.7	34.7	32.6	31.8	31.0	51.4	50.0	33.1	32.0	26.2	20.9	--	--	--	--	--	--	--	--	--	--	--
ST. LOUIS, MO.																						
All ages	816,048	391,798	424,250	308,306	339,082	31,391	28,015	51,762	57,003	339	150	100.0	100.0	100.0	100.0	100.0	100.0	100.0	100.0	100.0	100.0	100.0
Under 5 years	48,330	24,514	23,816	20,591	19,961	15	9	3,884	3,820	24	26	5.9	6.3	5.6	6.7	5.9	--	--	7.5	6.7	7.1	17.3
5 to 9 years	49,933	25,182	24,751	21,172	20,646	31	31	3,959	4,047	20	27	6.1	6.4	5.8	6.9	6.1	0.1	0.1	7.6	7.1	5.9	18.0
10 to 14 years	57,413	28,677	28,736	24,501	24,465	88	79	4,070	4,167	18	25	7.0	7.3	6.8	7.9	7.2	0.3	0.3	7.9	7.3	5.3	16.7
15 to 19 years	62,556	30,317	32,239	26,201	27,658	328	314	3,778	4,253	10	14	7.7	7.7	7.6	8.5	8.2	1.0	1.1	7.3	7.5	2.9	9.3
20 to 24 years	67,624	30,789	36,835	26,960	31,590	298	334	3,513	4,901	18	10	8.3	7.9	8.7	8.7	9.3	0.9	1.2	6.8	8.6	5.3	6.7
25 to 29 years	73,823	34,511	39,312	29,343	32,622	791	919	4,352	5,763	25	8	9.0	8.8	9.3	9.5	9.6	2.5	3.3	8.4	10.1	7.4	5.3
30 to 34 years	73,354	34,545	38,809	28,281	31,275	1,540	1,581	4,675	5,943	49	10	9.0	8.8	9.1	9.2	9.2	4.9	5.6	9.0	10.4	14.5	6.7
35 to 39 years	69,869	33,275	36,594	25,378	27,871	2,529	2,526	5,327	6,186	41	11	8.6	8.5	8.6	8.2	8.2	8.1	9.0	10.3	10.9	12.1	7.3
40 to 44 years	63,192	30,834	32,358	22,858	24,582	3,066	2,823	4,868	4,947	42	6	7.7	7.9	7.6	7.4	7.2	9.8	10.1	9.4	8.7	12.4	4.0
45 to 49 years	59,512	29,132	30,380	21,068	23,245	3,789	3,240	4,252	3,892	23	3	7.3	7.4	7.2	6.8	6.9	12.1	11.6	8.2	6.8	6.8	2.0
50 to 54 years	52,150	25,565	26,585	18,059	20,259	4,429	3,507	3,062	2,816	15	3	6.4	6.5	6.3	5.9	6.0	14.1	12.5	5.9	4.9	4.4	2.0
55 to 59 years	42,241	20,655	21,586	14,177	16,246	4,171	3,207	2,286	2,130	21	3	5.2	5.3	5.1	4.6	4.8	13.3	11.4	4.4	3.7	6.2	2.0
60 to 64 years	34,137	16,316	17,821	11,319	13,586	3,476	2,878	1,510	1,355	11	2	4.2	4.2	4.2	3.7	4.0	11.1	10.3	2.9	2.4	3.2	1.3
65 to 69 years	26,408	12,249	14,159	8,484	10,601	2,646	2,364	1,105	1,193	14	1	3.2	3.1	3.3	2.8	3.1	8.4	8.4	2.1	2.1	4.1	0.7
70 to 74 years	18,382	8,164	10,218	5,606	7,460	1,945	1,894	606	863	7	1	2.3	2.1	2.4	1.8	2.2	6.2	6.8	1.2	1.5	2.1	0.7
75 years and over	17,124	7,073	10,051	4,308	7,015	2,249	2,309	515	727	1	--	2.1	1.8	2.4	1.4	2.1	7.2	8.2	1.0	1.3	0.3	--
Under 1 year	9,529	4,807	4,722	4,140	4,013	--	--	666	704	1	5	1.2	1.2	1.1	1.3	1.2	--	--	1.3	1.2	0.3	3.3
21 years and over	585,074	277,471	307,603	210,939	240,305	30,856	27,504	35,411	39,739	265	55	71.7	70.8	72.5	68.4	70.9	98.3	98.2	68.4	69.7	78.2	36.7
Median age	33.3	33.2	33.4	31.0	32.0	53.6	53.1	32.5	31.3	35.7	14.4	--	--	--	--	--	--	--	--	--	--	--
ST. PAUL, MINN.																						
All ages	287,736	137,561	150,175	117,906	131,881	17,442	16,170	2,070	2,069	143	55	100.0	100.0	100.0	100.0	100.0	100.0	100.0	100.0	100.0	100.0	--
Under 5 years	20,308	10,436	9,872	10,306	9,738	5	--	117	127	8	7	7.1	7.6	6.6	8.7	7.4	--	--	5.7	6.1	5.6	--
5 to 9 years	18,847	9,581	9,266	9,448	9,107	9	17	114	140	10	2	6.6	7.0	6.2	8.0	6.9	0.1	0.1	5.5	6.8	7.0	--
10 to 14 years	21,193	10,721	10,472	10,528	10,281	28	27	152	159	13	5	7.4	7.8	7.0	8.9	7.8	0.2	0.2	7.3	7.7	9.1	--
15 to 19 years	24,088	11,418	12,670	11,145	12,366	130	133	131	162	12	9	8.4	8.3	8.4	9.5	9.4	0.7	0.8	6.3	7.8	8.4	--
20 to 24 years	26,390	11,774	14,616	11,434	14,242	196	246	136	123	8	5	9.2	8.6	9.7	9.7	10.8	1.1	1.5	6.6	5.9	5.6	--
25 to 29 years	25,317	11,545	13,772	10,992	13,069	410	534	119	158	24	11	8.8	8.4	9.2	9.3	9.9	2.4	3.3	5.7	7.6	16.8	--
30 to 34 years	22,782	10,632	12,150	9,741	11,296	714	670	155	180	22	4	7.9	7.7	8.1	8.3	8.6	4.1	4.1	7.5	8.7	15.4	--
35 to 39 years	21,753	10,035	11,718	8,817	10,497	1,049	1,059	157	159	12	3	7.6	7.3	7.8	7.5	8.0	6.0	6.5	7.6	7.7	8.4	--
40 to 44 years	21,248	10,045	11,203	8,554	9,886	1,310	1,142	170	173	11	2	7.4	7.3	7.5	7.3	7.5	7.5	7.1	8.2	8.4	7.7	--
45 to 49 years	21,177	10,282	10,895	8,187	9,221	1,894	1,501	197	172	4	1	7.4	7.5	7.3	6.9	7.0	10.9	9.3	9.5	8.3	2.8	--
50 to 54 years	18,524	9,199	9,325	6,524	7,213	2,473	1,960	193	150	9	2	6.4	6.7	6.2	5.5	5.5	14.2	12.1	9.3	7.2	6.3	--
55 to 59 years	14,014	7,070	6,944	4,447	4,917	2,486	1,921	133	105	4	1	4.9	5.1	4.6	3.8	3.7	14.3	11.9	6.4	5.1	2.8	--
60 to 64 years	10,804	5,288	5,516	3,124	3,535	2,030	1,886	130	94	4	1	3.8	3.8	3.7	2.6	2.7	11.6	11.7	6.3	4.5	2.8	--
65 to 69 years	8,288	3,715	4,573	2,050	2,778	1,584	1,723	80	72	1	--	2.9	2.7	3.0	1.7	2.1	9.1	10.7	3.9	3.5	0.7	--
70 to 74 years	6,006	2,718	3,288	1,331	1,815	1,346	1,430	40	43	1	--	2.1	2.0	2.2	1.1	1.4	7.7	8.8	1.9	2.1	0.7	--
75 years and over	6,997	3,102	3,895	1,278	1,920	1,778	1,921	46	52	--	2	2.4	2.3	2.6	1.1	1.5	10.2	11.9	2.2	2.5	--	--
Under 1 year	4,112	2,121	1,991	2,090	1,970	1	--	28	21	2	--	1.4	1.5	1.3	1.8	1.5	--	--	1.4	1.0	1.4	--
21 years and over	198,317	93,174	105,143	74,309	87,715	17,229	15,940	1,536	1,460	100	28	68.9	67.7	70.0	63.0	66.5	98.8	98.6	74.2	70.6	69.9	--
Median age	31.7	31.6	31.8	27.8	28.9	56.0	57.1	38.5	34.6	29.3	--	--	--	--	--	--	--	--	--	--	--	--

TABLE 53.—AGE, BY RACE AND SEX, WITH PERCENT DISTRIBUTION BY AGE, FOR CITIES OF 100,000 OR MORE: 1940—Continued

[Percent not shown where less than 0.1 or where base is less than 100]

CITY AND AGE	NUMBER											PERCENT DISTRIBUTION										
	All classes			Native white		Foreign-born white		Negro		Other races		All classes			Native white		Foreign-born white		Negro		Other races	
	Total	Male	Female	Male	Female	Male	Female	Male	Female	Male	Female	Total	Male	Female	Male	Female	Male	Female	Male	Female	Male	Female
SALT LAKE CITY, UTAH																						
All ages	149,934	73,229	76,705	66,016	69,343	6,495	6,845	374	320	344	197	100.0	100.0	100.0	100.0	100.0	100.0	100.0	100.0	100.0	100.0	100.0
Under 5 years	13,182	6,701	6,481	6,667	6,448	2	7	17	10	15	16	8.8	9.2	8.4	10.1	9.3		0.1	4.5	3.1	4.4	8.1
5 to 9 years	12,377	6,259	6,118	6,219	6,073	9	11	18	17	13	17	8.3	8.5	8.0	9.4	8.8	0.1	0.2	4.8	5.3	3.8	8.6
10 to 14 years	12,829	6,481	6,348	6,387	6,262	39	39	24	24	31	23	8.6	8.9	8.3	9.7	9.0	0.6	0.6	6.4	7.5	9.0	11.7
15 to 19 years	14,263	6,949	7,314	6,781	7,160	94	87	29	35	45	32	9.5	9.5	9.5	10.3	10.3	1.4	1.3	7.8	10.9	13.1	16.2
20 to 24 years	14,709	6,904	7,805	6,711	7,622	121	136	36	24	36	23	9.8	9.4	10.2	10.2	11.0	1.9	2.0	9.6	7.5	10.5	11.7
25 to 29 years	13,050	6,287	6,763	6,016	6,482	227	247	26	26	18	8	8.7	8.6	8.8	9.1	9.3	3.5	3.6	7.0	8.1	5.2	4.1
30 to 34 years	11,847	5,697	6,150	5,303	5,690	354	436	26	20	14	4	7.9	7.8	8.0	8.0	8.2	5.5	6.4	7.0	6.3	4.1	2.0
35 to 39 years	10,404	5,063	5,341	4,497	4,758	509	547	32	21	25	15	6.9	6.9	7.0	6.8	6.9	7.8	8.0	8.6	6.6	7.3	7.6
40 to 44 years	9,420	4,610	4,810	3,947	4,207	617	558	30	22	16	23	6.3	6.3	6.3	6.0	6.1	9.5	8.2	8.0	6.9	4.7	11.7
45 to 49 years	8,614	4,218	4,396	3,495	3,690	682	654	29	38	12	14	5.7	5.8	5.7	5.3	5.3	10.5	9.6	7.8	11.9	3.5	7.1
50 to 54 years	7,677	3,762	3,915	2,954	3,206	746	678	35	20	27	11	5.1	5.1	5.1	4.5	4.6	11.5	9.9	9.4	6.3	7.8	5.6
55 to 59 years	6,468	3,262	3,206	2,439	2,490	782	694	21	20	20	2	4.3	4.5	4.2	3.7	3.6	12.0	10.1	5.6	6.3	5.8	1.0
60 to 64 years	5,231	2,543	2,688	1,834	1,904	668	769	14	10	27	5	3.5	3.5	3.5	2.8	2.7	10.3	11.2	3.7	3.1	7.8	2.5
65 to 69 years	3,912	1,787	2,125	1,216	1,446	537	659	22	18	12	2	2.6	2.4	2.8	1.8	2.1	8.3	9.6	5.9	5.6	3.5	1.0
70 to 74 years	2,833	1,333	1,500	812	941	497	551	7	6	17	2	1.9	1.8	2.0	1.2	1.4	7.7	8.0	1.9	1.9	4.9	1.0
75 years and over	3,118	1,373	1,745	738	964	611	772	8	9	16		2.1	1.9	2.3	1.1	1.4	9.4	11.3	2.1	2.8	4.7	
Under 1 year	2,690	1,401	1,289	1,397	1,285			3		1	4	1.8	1.9	1.7	2.1	1.9			0.8		0.3	2.0
21 years and over	94,370	45,536	48,834	38,709	41,824	6,322	6,676	278	230	227	104	62.9	62.2	63.7	58.6	60.3	97.3	97.5	74.3	71.9	66.0	52.8
Median age	27.9	27.6	28.2	25.2	25.9	54.0	55.2	36.7	36.0	35.0	22.3											
SAN ANTONIO, TEX.																						
All ages	253,854	123,508	130,346	101,357	104,628	13,084	14,953	8,680	10,555	387	210	100.0	100.0	100.0	100.0	100.0	100.0	100.0	100.0	100.0	100.0	100.0
Under 5 years	20,983	10,441	10,542	9,825	9,928	12	11	570	573	34	30	8.3	8.5	8.1	9.7	9.5	0.1	0.1	6.6	5.4	8.8	14.3
5 to 9 years	20,737	10,432	10,305	9,771	9,646	18	27	613	595	30	37	8.2	8.4	7.9	9.6	9.2	0.1	0.2	7.1	5.6	7.8	17.6
10 to 14 years	22,236	11,099	11,137	10,330	10,273	100	110	631	724	38	30	8.8	9.0	8.5	10.2	9.8	0.8	0.7	7.3	6.9	9.8	14.3
15 to 19 years	25,127	12,430	12,697	11,300	11,435	340	379	750	854	40	29	9.9	10.1	9.7	11.1	10.9	2.6	2.5	8.6	8.1	10.3	13.8
20 to 24 years	24,797	12,615	12,182	11,228	10,488	591	663	767	1,018	29	18	9.8	10.2	9.3	11.1	10.0	4.5	4.4	8.8	9.6	7.5	8.6
25 to 29 years	22,934	11,263	11,671	9,405	9,229	1,020	1,293	809	1,137	29	12	9.0	9.1	9.0	9.3	8.8	7.8	8.6	9.3	10.8	7.5	5.7
30 to 34 years	21,091	10,057	11,034	7,834	8,336	1,396	1,650	801	1,038	26	10	8.3	8.1	8.5	7.7	8.0	10.7	11.0	9.2	9.8	6.7	4.8
35 to 39 years	19,717	9,297	10,420	6,823	7,269	1,663	2,014	780	1,123	31	14	7.8	7.5	8.0	6.7	6.9	12.7	13.5	9.0	10.6	8.0	6.7
40 to 44 years	17,037	8,103	8,934	5,852	6,276	1,438	1,666	787	981	26	11	6.7	6.6	6.9	5.8	6.0	11.0	11.1	9.1	9.3	6.7	5.2
45 to 49 years	15,116	7,279	7,837	5,021	5,449	1,510	1,612	708	766	40	10	6.0	5.9	6.0	5.0	5.2	11.5	10.8	8.2	7.3	10.3	4.8
50 to 54 years	12,234	5,891	6,343	4,132	4,462	1,249	1,356	483	522	27	3	4.8	4.8	4.9	4.1	4.3	9.5	9.1	5.6	4.9	7.0	1.4
55 to 59 years	9,789	4,707	5,082	3,156	3,450	1,206	1,264	331	366	14	2	3.9	3.8	3.9	3.1	3.3	9.2	8.5	3.8	3.5	3.6	1.0
60 to 64 years	7,692	3,552	4,140	2,527	2,926	800	975	215	237	10	2	3.0	2.9	3.2	2.5	2.8	6.1	6.5	2.5	2.2	2.6	1.0
65 to 69 years	6,161	2,741	3,420	1,847	2,358	684	758	204	303	6	1	2.4	2.2	2.6	1.8	2.3	5.2	5.1	2.4	2.9	1.6	0.5
70 to 74 years	4,020	1,797	2,223	1,179	1,502	490	559	125	162	3		1.6	1.5	1.7	1.2	1.4	3.7	3.7	1.4	1.5	0.8	
75 years and over	4,183	1,804	2,379	1,127	1,601	567	616	106	161	4	1	1.6	1.5	1.8	1.1	1.5	4.3	4.1	1.2	1.5	1.0	0.5
Under 1 year	4,387	2,162	2,225	2,031	2,113	2	2	121	108	8	2	1.7	1.8	1.7	2.0	2.0			1.4	1.0	2.1	1.0
21 years and over	159,332	76,352	82,980	57,634	60,980	12,504	14,319	5,975	7,604	239	77	62.8	61.8	63.7	56.9	58.3	95.6	95.8	68.8	72.0	61.8	36.7
Median age	27.8	27.1	28.6	24.2	25.3	44.9	44.0	31.2	31.8	28.9	16.4											
SAN DIEGO, CALIF.																						
All ages	203,341	103,638	99,703	90,631	88,786	9,589	9,960	1,992	2,151	1,446	806	100.0	100.0	100.0	100.0	100.0	100.0	100.0	100.0	100.0	100.0	100.0
Under 5 years	13,604	7,026	6,578	6,777	6,326	7	14	132	154	110	84	6.7	6.8	6.6	7.5	7.3	0.1	0.1	6.6	7.2	7.6	10.4
5 to 9 years	11,696	5,837	5,859	5,574	5,610	36	26	132	120	95	103	5.8	5.6	5.9	6.1	6.5	0.4	0.3	6.6	5.6	6.6	12.8
10 to 14 years	12,266	6,175	6,091	5,836	5,770	59	67	148	131	132	123	6.0	6.0	6.1	6.4	6.6	0.6	0.7	7.4	6.1	9.1	15.3
15 to 19 years	16,744	9,555	7,189	9,083	6,744	169	159	160	160	143	126	8.2	9.2	7.2	10.0	7.8	1.8	1.6	8.0	7.4	9.9	15.6
20 to 24 years	20,544	11,765	8,779	11,159	8,128	318	363	196	219	92	69	10.1	11.4	8.8	12.3	9.4	3.3	3.6	9.8	10.2	6.4	8.6
25 to 29 years	20,140	10,356	9,784	9,581	8,939	453	558	199	225	123	62	9.9	10.0	9.8	10.6	10.3	4.7	5.6	10.0	10.5	8.5	7.7
30 to 34 years	17,362	9,049	8,313	8,200	7,339	568	731	137	200	144	43	8.5	8.7	8.3	9.0	8.5	5.9	7.3	6.9	9.3	10.0	5.3
35 to 39 years	15,776	8,263	7,513	7,064	6,267	885	976	151	216	163	54	7.8	8.0	7.5	7.8	7.2	9.2	9.8	7.6	10.0	11.3	6.7
40 to 44 years	13,731	6,891	6,840	5,670	5,646	894	964	165	178	162	52	6.8	6.6	6.9	6.3	6.5	9.3	9.7	8.3	8.3	11.2	6.5
45 to 49 years	12,559	6,128	6,431	4,934	5,296	942	951	157	142	95	42	6.2	5.9	6.4	5.4	6.1	9.8	9.5	7.9	6.6	6.6	5.2
50 to 54 years	11,491	5,606	5,885	4,279	4,708	1,139	1,014	115	145	73	18	5.7	5.4	5.9	4.7	5.4	11.9	10.2	5.8	6.7	5.0	2.2
55 to 59 years	9,737	4,577	5,160	3,376	4,054	1,034	1,007	118	85	49	14	4.8	4.4	5.2	3.7	4.7	10.8	10.1	5.9	4.0	3.4	1.7
0 to 64 years	8,659	3,928	4,731	2,910	3,714	910	954	73	56	35	7	4.3	3.8	4.7	3.2	[illegible]	[illegible]	[illegible]	[illegible]	[illegible]	[illegible]	[illegible]

UNITED STATES SUMMARY—PRINCIPAL CITIES

65 to 69 years	7,241	3,162	4,079	2,381	3,242	711	771	54	62	16	4	3.6	3.1	4.1	2.6	3.7	7.4	7.7	2.7	2.9	1.1	0.5
70 to 74 years	5,626	2,521	3,105	1,806	2,424	681	647	26	30	8	4	2.8	2.4	3.1	2.0	2.8	7.1	6.5	1.3	1.4	0.6	0.5
75 years and over	6,165	2,799	3,366	2,001	2,579	763	758	29	28	6	1	3.0	2.7	3.4	2.2	3.0	8.0	7.6	1.5	1.3	0.4	0.1
Under 1 year	2,835	1,489	1,346	1,427	1,310			37	18	25	18	1.4	1.4	1.3	1.6	1.5			1.9	0.8	1.7	2.2
21 years and over	145,072	72,717	72,355	61,138	60,811	9,237	9,637	1,402	1,556	940	351	71.3	70.2	72.6	67.5	70.1	96.5	96.8	70.4	72.3	65.0	43.5
Median age	31.9	30.6	33.4	28.6	31.3	52.0	50.8	31.1	31.7	31.0	18.7											
SAN FRANCISCO, CALIF.																						
All ages	634,536	322,441	312,095	230,005	242,425	71,687	58,584	2,461	2,385	18,288	8,701	100.0	100.0	100.0	100.0	100.0	100.0	100.0	100.0	100.0	100.0	100.0
Under 5 years	30,333	15,452	14,881	14,513	13,994	40	69	109	98	790	720	4.8	4.8	4.8	6.3	5.8	0.1	0.1	4.4	4.1	4.3	8.3
5 to 9 years	28,255	14,352	13,903	13,113	12,805	148	131	85	90	1,006	877	4.5	4.5	4.5	5.7	5.3	0.2	0.2	3.5	3.8	5.5	10.1
10 to 14 years	32,825	16,463	16,362	14,810	14,818	289	333	95	116	1,269	1,095	5.2	5.1	5.2	6.4	6.1	0.4	0.6	3.9	4.9	6.9	12.6
15 to 19 years	41,015	20,290	20,725	17,563	18,490	908	947	126	135	1,693	1,153	6.5	6.3	6.6	7.6	7.6	1.3	1.6	5.1	5.7	9.3	13.3
20 to 24 years	49,254	24,005	25,249	21,360	22,579	1,256	1,531	147	165	1,242	974	7.8	7.4	8.1	9.3	9.3	1.8	2.6	6.0	6.9	6.8	11.2
25 to 29 years	57,355	28,406	28,949	24,056	25,004	2,495	2,932	216	284	1,639	729	9.0	8.8	9.3	10.5	10.3	3.5	5.0	8.8	11.9	9.0	8.4
30 to 34 years	58,766	29,423	29,343	22,861	24,002	4,374	4,507	248	244	1,940	590	9.3	9.1	9.4	9.9	9.9	6.1	7.7	10.1	10.2	10.6	6.8
35 to 39 years	57,984	29,890	28,094	20,507	20,934	7,087	6,208	314	288	1,982	664	9.1	9.3	9.0	8.9	8.6	9.9	10.6	12.8	12.1	10.8	7.6
40 to 44 years	55,716	29,377	26,339	18,566	18,869	8,638	6,615	302	275	1,871	580	8.8	9.1	8.4	8.1	7.8	12.0	11.3	12.3	11.5	10.2	6.7
45 to 49 years	52,254	27,447	24,807	16,575	17,214	9,132	6,917	245	196	1,495	480	8.2	8.5	7.9	7.2	7.1	12.7	11.8	10.0	8.2	8.2	5.5
50 to 54 years	47,662	25,477	22,185	13,876	14,660	10,268	7,007	203	178	1,130	340	7.5	7.9	7.1	6.0	6.0	14.3	12.0	8.2	7.5	6.2	3.9
55 to 59 years	39,248	21,190	18,058	11,007	11,615	9,209	6,133	134	113	840	197	6.2	6.6	5.8	4.8	4.8	12.8	10.5	5.4	4.7	4.6	2.3
60 to 64 years	32,162	16,510	15,652	8,866	10,224	6,868	5,193	101	77	675	158	5.1	5.1	5.0	3.9	4.2	9.6	8.9	4.1	3.2	3.7	1.8
65 to 69 years	23,128	11,145	11,983	6,033	7,790	4,628	4,053	77	67	407	73	3.6	3.5	3.8	2.6	3.2	6.5	6.9	3.1	2.8	2.2	0.8
70 to 74 years	15,051	7,098	7,953	3,602	4,948	3,277	2,930	34	32	185	43	2.4	2.2	2.5	1.6	2.0	4.6	5.0	1.4	1.3	1.0	0.5
75 years and over	13,528	5,916	7,612	2,697	4,479	3,070	3,078	25	27	124	28	2.1	1.8	2.4	1.2	1.8	4.3	5.3	1.0	1.1	0.7	0.3
Under 1 year	6,118	3,163	2,955	2,998	2,799		1	30	16	135	139	1.0	1.0	0.9	1.3	1.2			1.2	0.7	0.7	1.6
21 years and over	492,970	251,440	241,530	166,114	178,137	70,032	56,810	2,022	1,919	13,272	4,664	77.7	78.0	77.4	72.2	73.5	97.7	97.0	82.2	80.5	72.6	53.6
Median age	36.7	37.1	36.2	32.1	32.8	50.7	49.4	38.3	36.1	33.9	22.6											
SCRANTON, PA.																						
All ages	140,404	68,593	71,811	58,634	62,633	9,550	8,830	407	347	2	1	100.0	100.0	100.0	100.0	100.0	100.0	100.0	100.0	100.0		
Under 5 years	9,187	4,752	4,435	4,725	4,415	5	4	22	16			6.5	6.9	6.2	8.1	7.0	0.1		5.4	4.6		
5 to 9 years	10,027	5,051	4,976	5,010	4,938	7	14	34	24			7.1	7.4	6.9	8.5	7.9	0.1	0.2	8.4	6.9		
10 to 14 years	12,234	6,089	6,145	6,013	6,084	49	37	27	24			8.7	8.9	8.6	10.3	9.7	0.5	0.4	6.6	6.9		
15 to 19 years	13,736	6,652	7,084	6,495	6,945	132	111	25	28			9.8	9.7	9.9	11.1	11.1	1.4	1.3	6.1	8.1		
20 to 24 years	13,491	6,451	7,040	6,324	6,887	102	122	25	31			9.6	9.4	9.8	10.8	11.0	1.1	1.4	6.1	8.9		
25 to 29 years	12,294	5,883	6,411	5,675	6,169	178	218	30	24			8.8	8.6	8.9	9.7	9.8	1.9	2.5	7.4	6.9		
30 to 34 years	11,262	5,482	5,780	5,096	5,382	346	362	40	36			8.0	8.0	8.0	8.7	8.6	3.6	4.1	9.8	10.4		
35 to 39 years	10,216	4,966	5,250	4,333	4,580	596	640	31	30	1		7.3	7.2	7.3	7.4	7.3	6.2	7.2	7.6	8.6		
40 to 44 years	9,846	4,819	5,027	3,787	4,166	993	839	38	22	1		7.0	7.0	7.0	6.5	6.7	10.4	9.5	9.3	6.3		
45 to 49 years	9,589	4,733	4,856	3,218	3,553	1,483	1,277	32	26			6.8	6.9	6.8	5.5	5.7	15.5	14.5	7.9	7.5		
50 to 54 years	8,340	4,169	4,171	2,617	2,870	1,530	1,273	22	27		1	5.9	6.1	5.8	4.5	4.6	16.0	14.4	5.4	7.8		
55 to 59 years	6,431	3,182	3,249	1,807	2,083	1,342	1,145	33	21			4.6	4.6	4.5	3.1	3.3	14.1	13.0	8.1	6.1		
60 to 64 years	5,125	2,485	2,640	1,422	1,682	1,046	947	17	11			3.7	3.6	3.7	2.4	2.7	11.0	10.7	4.2	3.2		
65 to 69 years	3,862	1,785	2,077	1,014	1,334	762	732	9	11			2.8	2.6	2.9	1.7	2.1	8.0	8.3	2.2	3.2		
70 to 74 years	2,551	1,143	1,408	600	843	528	557	15	8			1.8	1.7	2.0	1.0	1.3	5.5	6.3	3.7	2.3		
75 years and over	2,213	951	1,262	493	702	451	552	7	8			1.6	1.4	1.8	0.8	1.1	4.7	6.3	1.7	2.3		
Under 1 year	1,857	965	892	960	889			5	3			1.3	1.4	1.2	1.6	1.4			1.2	0.9		
21 years and over	92,526	44,797	47,729	35,162	38,851	9,338	8,625	295	252	2	1	65.9	65.3	66.5	60.0	62.0	97.8	97.7	72.5	72.6		
Median age	29.7	29.5	29.9	25.7	26.7	52.9	53.1	35.1	33.7													
SEATTLE, WASH.																						
All ages	368,302	183,526	184,776	142,372	152,117	32,625	26,987	2,146	1,643	6,383	4,029	100.0	100.0	100.0	100.0	100.0	100.0	100.0	100.0	100.0	100.0	100.0
Under 5 years	19,633	10,008	9,625	9,631	9,240	24	15	71	80	282	290	5.3	5.5	5.2	6.8	6.1	0.1	0.1	3.3	4.9	4.4	7.2
5 to 9 years	18,870	9,361	9,509	8,896	9,044	35	41	107	92	323	332	5.1	5.1	5.1	6.2	5.9	0.1	0.2	5.0	5.6	5.1	8.2
10 to 14 years	21,364	10,614	10,750	9,913	10,051	125	129	95	99	481	471	5.8	5.8	5.8	7.0	6.6	0.4	0.5	4.4	6.0	7.5	11.7
15 to 19 years	27,408	13,186	14,222	11,787	12,906	448	521	94	123	857	672	7.4	7.2	7.7	8.3	8.5	1.4	1.9	4.4	7.5	13.4	16.7
20 to 24 years	31,505	14,794	16,711	13,309	15,176	771	895	136	109	578	531	8.6	8.1	9.0	9.3	10.0	2.4	3.3	6.3	6.6	9.1	13.2
25 to 29 years	32,012	15,418	16,594	13,598	14,874	1,119	1,299	173	146	528	275	8.7	8.4	9.0	9.6	9.8	3.4	4.8	8.1	8.9	8.3	6.8
30 to 34 years	30,124	14,785	15,339	12,466	13,402	1,538	1,602	170	147	611	188	8.2	8.1	8.3	8.8	8.8	4.7	5.9	7.9	8.9	9.6	4.7
35 to 39 years	29,239	14,615	14,624	11,505	11,974	2,394	2,287	187	121	529	242	7.9	8.0	7.9	8.1	7.9	7.3	8.5	8.7	7.4	8.3	6.0
40 to 44 years	28,264	13,837	14,427	10,444	11,406	2,771	2,534	229	140	393	347	7.7	7.5	7.8	7.3	7.5	8.5	9.4	10.7	8.5	6.2	8.6
45 to 49 years	28,602	14,505	14,097	10,131	10,754	3,810	2,904	194	121	370	318	7.8	7.9	7.6	7.1	7.1	11.7	10.8	9.0	7.4	5.8	7.9
50 to 54 years	27,669	14,680	12,989	8,969	9,277	4,955	3,411	185	126	571	175	7.5	8.0	7.0	6.3	6.1	15.2	12.6	8.6	7.7	8.9	4.3
55 to 59 years	23,214	12,422	10,792	7,246	7,509	4,599	3,081	170	106	407	96	6.3	6.8	5.8	5.1	4.9	14.1	11.4	7.9	6.5	6.4	2.4
60 to 64 years	18,155	9,429	8,726	5,483	5,840	3,562	2,734	112	91	272	61	4.9	5.1	4.7	3.9	3.8	10.9	10.1	5.2	5.5	4.3	1.5
65 to 69 years	13,208	6,584	6,624	3,830	4,454	2,533	2,078	118	71	103	21	3.6	3.6	3.6	2.7	2.9	7.8	7.7	5.5	4.3	1.6	0.5
70 to 74 years	9,511	4,717	4,794	2,666	3,055	1,935	1,693	68	40	48	6	2.6	2.6	2.6	1.9	2.0	5.9	6.3	3.2	2.4	0.8	0.1
75 years and over	9,524	4,571	4,953	2,498	3,155	2,006	1,763	37	31	30	4	2.6	2.5	2.7	1.8	2.1	6.1	6.5	1.7	1.9	0.5	0.1
Under 1 year	4,091	2,071	2,020	1,998	1,939		3	17	13	56	65	1.1	1.1	1.1	1.4	1.3			0.8	0.8	0.9	1.6
21 years and over	274,871	137,546	137,325	99,631	107,879	31,847	26,107	1,755	1,226	4,313	2,113	74.6	74.9	74.3	70.0	70.9	97.6	96.7	81.8	74.6	67.6	52.4
Median age	35.6	36.2	34.9	31.6	[illegible]	53.3	51.9	40.9	36.1	31.2	22.3											

TABLE 53.—AGE, BY RACE AND SEX, WITH PERCENT DISTRIBUTION BY AGE, FOR CITIES OF 100,000 OR MORE: 1940—Continued

[Percent not shown where less than 0.1 or where base is less than 100]

CITY AND AGE	NUMBER											PERCENT DISTRIBUTION										
	All classes			Native white		Foreign-born white		Negro		Other races		All classes			Native white		Foreign-born white		Negro		Other races	
	Total	Male	Female	Male	Female	Male	Female	Male	Female	Male	Female	Total	Male	Female	Male	Female	Male	Female	Male	Female	Male	Female
SOMERVILLE, MASS.																						
All ages	102,177	49,332	52,845	37,859	40,173	11,325	12,530	123	139	25	3	100.0	100.0	100.0	100.0	100.0	100.0	100.0	100.0	100.0		
Under 5 years	7,659	3,958	3,731	3,948	3,720	2	3	8	8			7.5	8.0	7.1	10.4	9.3			6.5	5.8		
5 to 9 years	7,923	4,010	3,913	3,985	3,874	17	30	8	9			7.8	8.1	7.4	10.5	9.6	0.2	0.2	6.5	6.5		
10 to 14 years	8,562	4,374	4,188	4,297	4,099	71	81	6	8			8.4	8.9	7.9	11.3	10.2	0.6	0.6	4.9	5.8		
15 to 19 years	8,755	4,376	4,379	4,157	4,146	210	216	9	16		1	8.6	8.9	8.3	11.0	10.3	1.9	1.7	7.3	11.5		
20 to 24 years	8,602	4,063	4,539	3,812	4,193	242	334	8	11	1	1	8.4	8.2	8.6	10.1	10.4	2.1	2.7	6.5	7.9		
25 to 29 years	8,621	4,029	4,592	3,573	3,951	446	629	8	12	2		8.4	8.2	8.7	9.4	9.8	3.9	5.0	6.5	8.6		
30 to 34 years	8,509	4,048	4,461	3,198	3,321	836	1,129	11	11	3		8.3	8.2	8.4	8.4	8.3	7.4	9.0	8.9	7.9		
35 to 39 years	7,727	3,775	3,952	2,488	2,651	1,279	1,295	7	6	1		7.6	7.7	7.5	6.6	6.6	11.3	10.3	5.7	4.3		
40 to 44 years	6,845	3,318	3,527	1,976	2,184	1,321	1,326	16	17	5		6.7	6.7	6.7	5.2	5.4	11.7	10.6	13.0	12.2		
45 to 49 years	6,254	3,045	3,209	1,693	1,819	1,343	1,384	8	6	1		6.1	6.2	6.1	4.5	4.5	11.9	11.0	6.5	4.3		
50 to 54 years	5,631	2,732	2,899	1,274	1,590	1,445	1,316	9	2	4	1	5.5	5.5	5.5	3.4	3.9	12.8	10.5	7.3	1.4		
55 to 59 years	4,789	2,261	2,528	1,042	1,208	1,214	1,313	5	7			4.7	4.6	4.8	2.8	3.0	10.7	10.5	4.1	5.0		
60 to 64 years	4,128	1,925	2,203	884	1,088	1,029	1,106	7	9	5		4.0	3.9	4.2	2.3	2.7	9.1	8.8	5.7	6.5		
65 to 69 years	3,388	1,476	1,912	669	933	795	969	9	10	3		3.3	3.0	3.6	1.8	2.3	7.0	7.7	7.3	7.2		
70 to 74 years	2,353	1,029	1,324	444	639	582	681	3	4			2.3	2.1	2.5	1.2	1.6	5.1	5.4	2.4	2.9		
75 years and over	2,401	913	1,488	419	767	493	718	1	3			2.3	1.9	2.8	1.1	1.9	4.4	5.7	0.8	2.2		
Under 1 year	1,453	752	701	751	698			1	3			1.4	1.5	1.3	2.0	1.7			0.8	2.2		
21 years and over	67,486	31,825	35,661	20,745	23,447	10,966	12,117	90	95	24	2	66.0	64.5	67.5	54.8	58.4	96.8	96.7	73.2	68.3		
Median age	30.6	29.8	31.2	23.3	25.1	49.6	49.4	37.5	32.5													
SOUTH BEND, IND.																						
All ages	101,268	50,228	51,040	42,657	44,128	5,786	5,091	1,744	1,811	41	10	100.0	100.0	100.0	100.0	100.0	100.0	100.0	100.0	100.0		
Under 5 years	6,792	3,531	3,261	3,361	3,117	4	2	164	142	2		6.7	7.0	6.4	7.9	7.1	0.1		9.4	7.8		
5 to 9 years	6,920	3,508	3,412	3,336	3,215	5	6	166	189	1	2	6.8	7.0	6.7	7.8	7.3	0.1	0.1	9.5	10.4		
10 to 14 years	8,616	4,407	4,209	4,234	4,013	17	12	155	181	1	3	8.5	8.8	8.2	9.9	9.1	0.3	0.2	8.9	10.0		
15 to 19 years	9,329	4,530	4,799	4,332	4,575	41	62	152	162	5		9.2	9.0	9.4	10.2	10.4	0.7	1.2	8.7	8.9		
20 to 24 years	9,066	4,258	4,808	4,122	4,581	45	75	90	151	1	1	9.0	8.5	9.4	9.7	10.4	0.8	1.5	5.2	8.3		
25 to 29 years	9,094	4,353	4,741	4,075	4,433	152	164	124	144	2		9.0	8.7	9.3	9.6	10.0	2.6	3.2	7.1	8.0		
30 to 34 years	8,546	4,167	4,379	3,770	3,957	274	285	119	136	4	1	8.4	8.3	8.6	8.8	9.0	4.7	5.6	6.8	7.5		
35 to 39 years	8,336	4,099	4,237	3,466	3,558	474	486	155	193	4		8.2	8.2	8.3	8.1	8.1	8.2	9.5	8.9	10.7		
40 to 44 years	7,539	3,888	3,651	3,107	2,957	602	565	174	128	5	1	7.4	7.7	7.2	7.3	6.7	10.4	11.1	10.0	7.1		
45 to 49 years	6,946	3,472	3,474	2,580	2,665	759	684	129	123	4	2	6.9	6.9	6.8	6.0	6.0	13.1	13.4	7.4	6.8		
50 to 54 years	6,010	3,108	2,902	2,000	2,097	976	707	127	98	5		5.9	6.2	5.7	4.7	4.8	16.9	13.9	7.3	5.4		
55 to 59 years	4,766	2,413	2,353	1,496	1,648	844	633	71	72	2		4.7	4.8	4.6	3.5	3.7	14.6	12.4	4.1	4.0		
60 to 64 years	3,503	1,751	1,752	1,078	1,230	619	496	51	26	3		3.5	3.5	3.4	2.5	2.8	10.7	9.7	2.9	1.4		
65 to 69 years	2,461	1,198	1,263	754	870	413	364	30	29	1		2.4	2.4	2.5	1.8	2.0	7.1	7.1	1.7	1.6		
70 to 74 years	1,650	787	863	479	575	285	271	23	17			1.6	1.6	1.7	1.1	1.3	4.9	5.3	1.3	0.9		
75 years and over	1,694	758	936	467	637	276	279	14	20	1		1.7	1.5	1.8	1.1	1.4	4.8	5.5	0.8	1.1		
Under 1 year	1,351	717	634	685	602			32	32			1.3	1.4	1.2	1.6	1.4			1.8	1.8		
21 years and over	67,835	33,455	34,380	26,625	28,285	5,707	4,992	1,091	1,099	32	4	67.0	66.6	67.4	62.4	64.1	98.6	98.1	62.6	60.7		
Median age	30.5	30.6	30.3	27.4	27.9	52.7	51.4	30.9	27.8													
SPOKANE, WASH.																						
All ages	122,001	60,416	61,585	52,611	55,531	7,198	5,557	329	315	278	182	100.0	100.0	100.0	100.0	100.0	100.0	100.0	100.0	100.0	100.0	100.0
Under 5 years	7,714	3,981	3,733	3,956	3,700	2	3	15	22	8	8	6.3	6.6	6.1	7.5	6.7		0.1	4.6	7.0	2.9	4.4
5 to 9 years	7,130	3,547	3,583	3,515	3,548	7	7	8	15	17	13	5.8	5.9	5.8	6.7	6.4	0.1	0.1	2.4	4.8	6.1	7.1
10 to 14 years	7,643	3,862	3,781	3,802	3,713	18	26	20	20	22	22	6.3	6.4	6.1	7.2	6.7	0.3	0.5	6.1	6.3	7.9	12.1
15 to 19 years	9,787	4,583	5,204	4,456	5,039	71	96	23	25	33	44	8.0	7.6	8.4	8.5	9.1	1.0	1.7	7.0	7.9	11.9	24.2
20 to 24 years	10,845	4,965	5,880	4,743	5,634	172	196	27	31	23	19	8.9	8.2	9.5	9.0	10.1	2.4	3.5	8.2	9.8	8.3	10.4
25 to 29 years	10,458	4,992	5,466	4,742	5,197	202	240	28	21	20	8	8.6	8.3	8.9	9.0	9.4	2.8	4.3	8.5	6.7	7.2	4.4
30 to 34 years	9,674	4,730	4,944	4,439	4,617	256	302	23	15	12	10	7.9	7.8	8.0	8.4	8.3	3.6	5.4	7.0	4.8	4.3	5.5
35 to 39 years	8,887	4,366	4,521	3,925	4,127	390	353	30	26	21	15	7.3	7.2	7.3	7.5	7.4	5.4	6.4	9.1	8.3	7.6	8.2
40 to 44 years	8,203	4,046	4,157	3,490	3,721	509	392	32	31	15	13	6.7	6.7	6.7	6.6	6.7	7.1	7.1	9.7	9.8	5.4	7.1
45 to 49 years	8,257	4,060	4,197	3,355	3,699	659	464	28	17	18	17	6.8	6.7	6.8	6.4	6.7	9.2	8.3	8.5	5.4	6.5	9.3
50 to 54 years	8,159	4,125	4,034	3,119	3,422	966	588	16	19	24	5	6.7	6.8	6.6	5.9	6.2	13.4	10.6	4.9	6.0	8.6	2.7
55 to 59 years	7,441	3,920	3,521	2,830	2,765	1,026	731	32	19	32	6	6.1	6.5	5.7	5.4	5.0	14.3	13.2	9.7	6.0	11.5	3.3
60 to 64 years	5,973	3,083	2,890	2,174	2,225	873	645	21	20	15		4.9	5.1	4.7	4.1	4.0	12.1	11.6	6.4	6.3	5.4	

65 to 69 years	4,708	2,452	2,256	1,724	1,675	706	561	13	18	9	2	3.9	4.1	3.7	3.3	3.0	9.8	10.1	4.0	5.7	3.2	1.1
70 to 74 years	3,421	1,822	1,599	1,144	1,176	667	417	6	6	5	-	2.8	3.0	2.6	2.2	2.1	9.3	7.5	1.8	1.9	1.8	-
75 years and over	3,701	1,882	1,819	1,197	1,273	674	536	7	10	4	-	3.0	3.1	3.0	2.3	2.3	9.4	9.6	2.1	3.2	1.4	-
Under 1 year	1,696	905	791	900	785	-	-	4	5	1	1	1.4	1.5	1.3	1.7	1.4	-	-	1.2	1.6	0.4	0.5
21 years and over	87,499	43,464	44,035	35,940	38,348	7,071	5,376	259	224	194	87	71.7	71.9	71.5	68.3	69.1	98.2	96.7	78.7	71.1	69.8	47.8
Median age	33.8	34.5	33.2	31.2	31.0	56.7	55.8	38.4	36.6	36.0	21.1	-	-	-	-	-	-	-	-	-	-	-
SPRINGFIELD, MASS.																						
All ages	149,554	72,246	77,308	57,434	62,189	13,289	13,469	1,503	1,641	40	9	100.0	100.0	100.0	100.0	100.0	100.0	100.0	100.0	100.0	-	-
Under 5 years	8,813	4,507	4,306	4,388	4,182	6	5	111	119	2	-	5.9	6.2	5.6	7.6	6.7	-	-	7.4	7.3	-	-
5 to 9 years	9,484	4,752	4,732	4,627	4,592	11	14	114	125	-	1	6.3	6.6	6.1	8.1	7.4	0.1	0.1	7.6	7.6	-	-
10 to 14 years	11,522	5,888	5,634	5,695	5,433	43	39	148	159	2	3	7.7	8.1	7.3	9.9	8.7	0.3	0.3	9.8	9.7	-	-
15 to 19 years	13,131	6,360	6,771	6,066	6,464	161	177	132	130	1	-	8.8	8.8	8.8	10.6	10.4	1.2	1.3	8.8	7.9	-	-
20 to 24 years	12,979	6,123	6,856	5,824	6,508	190	208	106	138	3	2	8.7	8.5	8.9	10.1	10.5	1.4	1.5	7.1	8.4	-	-
25 to 29 years	12,219	5,837	6,382	[illegible]	5,746	420	523	110	112	1	1	8.2	8.1	8.3	9.2	9.2	3.2	3.9	7.3	6.8	-	-
30 to 34 years	11,582	5,614	5,968	4,697	4,962	790	880	126	126	1	-	7.7	7.8	7.7	8.2	8.0	6.0	6.5	8.4	7.7	-	-
35 to 39 years	11,047	5,234	5,813	3,988	4,437	1,147	1,239	97	137	2	-	7.4	7.2	7.5	6.9	7.1	8.6	9.2	6.5	8.3	-	-
40 to 44 years	11,516	5,527	5,989	3,885	4,298	1,521	1,558	116	133	5	-	7.7	7.6	7.7	6.8	6.9	11.5	11.6	7.7	8.1	-	-
45 to 49 years	11,511	5,608	5,903	3,442	3,862	2,042	1,931	121	109	3	1	7.7	7.8	7.6	6.0	6.2	15.4	14.3	8.1	6.6	-	-
50 to 54 years	9,876	4,997	4,879	2,809	3,025	2,077	1,755	103	99	8	-	6.6	6.9	6.3	4.9	4.9	15.7	13.0	6.9	6.0	-	-
55 to 59 years	7,783	3,768	4,015	2,062	2,448	1,626	1,487	74	79	6	1	5.2	5.2	5.2	3.6	3.9	12.3	11.0	4.9	4.8	-	-
60 to 64 years	6,345	2,960	3,385	1,645	2,037	1,262	1,288	51	60	2	-	4.2	4.1	4.4	2.9	3.3	9.5	9.6	3.4	3.7	-	-
65 to 69 years	4,928	2,194	2,734	1,309	1,703	839	980	45	51	1	-	3.3	3.0	3.5	2.3	2.7	6.3	7.3	3.0	3.1	-	-
70 to 74 years	3,375	1,491	1,884	875	1,149	580	711	34	24	2	-	2.3	2.1	2.4	1.5	1.8	4.4	5.3	2.3	1.5	-	-
75 years and over	3,443	1,386	2,057	816	1,343	554	674	15	40	1	-	2.3	1.9	2.7	1.4	2.2	4.2	5.0	1.0	2.4	-	-
Under 1 year	1,704	848	856	824	831	1	-	23	25	-	-	1.1	1.2	1.1	1.4	1.3	-	-	1.5	1.5	-	-
21 years and over	103,961	49,513	54,448	35,502	40,181	13,006	13,182	970	1,080	35	5	69.5	68.5	70.4	61.8	64.6	98.0	97.9	64.5	65.8	-	-
Median age	32.9	32.4	33.3	27.0	28.4	50.7	50.5	31.2	31.5	-	-	-	-	-	-	-	-	-	-	-	-	-
SYRACUSE, N. Y.																						
All ages	205,967	100,296	105,671	84,843	91,247	14,339	13,211	997	1,085	117	128	100.0	100.0	100.0	100.0	100.0	100.0	100.0	100.0	100.0	100.0	100.0
Under 5 years	12,552	6,443	6,109	6,339	6,002	2	5	92	84	10	18	6.1	6.4	5.8	7.5	6.6	-	-	9.2	7.7	8.5	14.0
5 to 9 years	13,289	6,759	6,530	6,644	6,411	22	12	83	92	10	15	6.5	6.7	6.2	7.8	7.0	0.2	0.1	8.3	8.5	8.5	11.7
10 to 14 years	15,667	7,881	7,786	7,716	7,621	76	60	80	94	9	11	7.6	7.9	7.4	9.1	8.4	0.5	0.5	8.0	8.7	7.7	8.6
15 to 19 years	18,154	8,770	9,384	8,481	9,036	201	246	75	87	13	15	8.8	8.7	8.9	10.0	9.9	1.4	1.9	7.5	8.0	11.1	11.7
20 to 24 years	18,299	8,591	9,708	8,281	9,371	232	223	70	98	8	16	8.9	8.6	9.2	9.8	10.3	1.6	1.7	7.0	9.0	6.8	12.5
25 to 29 years	16,702	7,885	8,817	7,374	8,164	428	562	72	81	11	10	8.1	7.9	8.3	8.7	8.9	3.0	4.3	7.2	7.5	9.4	7.8
30 to 34 years	16,176	7,770	8,406	6,885	7,424	801	861	73	106	11	15	7.9	7.7	8.0	8.1	8.1	5.6	6.5	7.3	9.8	9.4	11.7
35 to 39 years	15,228	7,401	7,827	6,096	6,454	1,202	1,255	95	115	8	3	7.4	7.4	7.4	7.2	7.1	8.4	9.5	9.5	10.6	6.8	2.3
40 to 44 years	15,144	7,488	7,656	5,771	5,994	1,617	1,581	88	72	12	9	7.4	7.5	7.2	6.8	6.6	11.3	12.0	8.8	6.6	10.3	7.0
45 to 49 years	15,325	7,678	7,647	5,330	5,753	2,270	1,814	69	73	9	7	7.4	7.7	7.2	6.3	6.3	15.8	13.7	6.9	6.7	7.7	5.5
50 to 54 years	13,522	6,940	6,582	4,569	4,876	2,294	1,647	73	55	4	4	6.6	6.9	6.2	5.4	5.3	16.0	12.4	7.3	5.1	3.4	3.1
55 to 59 years	10,653	5,217	5,436	3,525	4,003	1,645	1,385	40	45	7	3	5.2	5.2	5.1	4.2	4.4	11.5	10.5	4.0	4.1	6.0	2.3
60 to 64 years	8,717	4,138	4,579	2,819	3,353	1,280	1,197	36	28	3	1	4.2	4.1	4.3	3.3	3.7	8.9	9.1	3.6	2.6	2.6	0.8
65 to 69 years	6,977	3,227	3,750	2,252	2,786	954	938	21	25	-	1	3.4	3.2	3.5	2.7	3.1	6.7	7.1	2.1	2.3	-	0.8
70 to 74 years	4,720	2,132	2,588	1,456	1,864	660	705	15	19	1	-	2.3	2.1	2.4	1.7	2.0	4.6	5.3	1.5	1.8	0.9	-
75 years and over	4,842	1,976	2,866	1,305	2,135	655	720	15	11	1	-	2.4	2.0	2.7	1.5	2.3	4.6	5.4	1.5	1.0	0.9	-
Under 1 year	2,482	1,305	1,177	1,285	1,156	-	1	17	16	3	4	1.2	1.3	1.1	1.5	1.3	-	-	1.7	1.5	2.6	3.1
21 years and over	142,640	68,768	73,872	54,046	60,251	13,995	12,847	653	708	74	66	69.3	68.6	69.9	63.7	66.0	97.6	97.2	65.5	65.3	63.2	51.6
Median age	32.6	32.5	32.7	28.4	29.4	50.7	50.0	31.8	30.3	28.9	21.6	-	-	-	-	-	-	-	-	-	-	-
TACOMA, WASH.																						
All ages	109,408	55,038	54,370	45,343	46,414	8,735	7,119	342	308	618	529	100.0	100.0	100.0	100.0	100.0	100.0	100.0	100.0	100.0	100.0	100.0
Under 5 years	6,657	3,433	3,224	3,380	3,155	6	5	9	14	38	50	6.1	6.2	5.9	7.5	6.8	0.1	0.1	2.6	4.5	6.1	9.5
5 to 9 years	6,473	3,324	3,149	3,259	3,073	10	6	15	20	40	50	5.9	6.0	5.8	7.2	6.6	0.1	0.1	4.4	6.5	6.5	9.5
10 to 14 years	7,774	3,910	3,864	3,798	3,773	23	26	20	18	69	47	7.1	7.1	7.1	8.4	8.1	0.3	0.4	5.8	5.8	11.2	8.9
15 to 19 years	8,925	4,376	4,549	4,153	4,334	101	102	25	26	97	87	8.2	8.0	8.4	9.2	9.3	1.2	1.4	7.3	8.4	15.7	16.4
20 to 24 years	9,002	4,236	4,766	3,983	4,476	170	206	21	24	62	60	8.2	7.7	8.8	8.8	9.6	1.9	2.9	6.1	7.8	10.0	11.3
25 to 29 years	8,960	4,356	4,604	4,052	4,243	251	298	15	17	38	46	8.2	7.9	8.5	8.9	9.1	2.9	4.2	4.4	5.5	6.1	8.7
30 to 34 years	8,514	4,229	4,285	3,788	3,888	390	363	24	17	27	17	7.8	7.7	7.9	8.4	8.4	4.5	5.1	7.0	5.5	4.4	3.2
35 to 39 years	7,982	4,010	3,972	3,404	3,403	549	519	20	19	37	31	7.3	7.3	7.3	7.5	7.3	6.3	7.3	5.8	6.2	6.0	5.9
40 to 44 years	7,944	3,947	3,997	3,188	3,326	696	589	28	25	35	57	7.3	7.2	7.4	7.0	7.2	8.0	8.3	8.2	8.1	5.7	10.8
45 to 49 years	7,705	3,927	3,778	2,987	3,018	886	703	23	25	31	32	7.0	7.1	6.9	6.6	6.5	10.1	9.9	6.7	8.1	5.0	6.0
50 to 54 years	7,477	3,884	3,593	2,605	2,696	1,187	846	32	29	60	22	6.8	7.1	6.6	5.7	5.8	13.6	11.9	9.4	9.4	9.7	4.2
55 to 59 years	6,503	3,494	3,009	2,158	2,119	1,260	855	31	21	45	14	5.9	6.3	5.5	4.0	4.6	14.4	12.0	9.1	6.8	7.3	2.6
60 to 64 years	5,234	2,751	2,483	1,721	1,677	973	785	31	11	26	10	4.8	5.0	4.6	3.8	3.6	11.1	11.0	9.1	3.6	4.2	1.9
65 to 69 years	3,928	1,977	1,951	1,173	1,285	774	646	22	18	8	2	3.6	3.6	3.6	2.6	2.8	8.9	9.1	6.4	5.8	1.3	0.4
70 to 74 years	3,061	1,566	1,495	879	936	673	545	10	13	4	1	2.8	2.8	2.7	1.9	2.0	7.7	7.7	2.9	4.2	0.6	0.2
75 years and over	3,269	1,618	1,651	815	1,012	786	625	16	11	1	3	3.0	2.9	3.0	1.8	2.2	9.0	8.8	4.7	3.6	0.2	0.6
Under 1 year	1,352	678	674	670	658	-	-	1	3	7	13	1.2	1.2	1.2	1.5	1.4	-	-	0.3	1.0	1.1	2.5
21 years and over	77,821	39,190	38,631	29,989	31,188	8,570	6,943	269	223	362	277	71.1	71.2	71.1	66.1	67.2	98.1	97.5	78.7	72.4	58.6	52.4
Median age	34.1	34.6	33.5	30.1	30.2	55.4	54.4	43.9	39.7	25.4	22.5	-	-	-	-	-	-	-	-	-	-	-

524097 O - 43 - 11

TABLE 53.—AGE, BY RACE AND SEX, WITH PERCENT DISTRIBUTION BY AGE, FOR CITIES OF 100,000 OR MORE: 1940—Continued

[Percent not shown where less than 0.1 or where base is less than 100]

NUMBER

CITY AND AGE	All classes			Native white		Foreign-born white		Negro		Other races	
	Total	Male	Female	Male	Female	Male	Female	Male	Female	Male	Female
TAMPA, FLA.											
All ages	108,391	52,442	55,949	35,516	38,445	5,861	5,221	11,052	12,279	13	4
Under 5 years	6,380	3,180	3,200	2,401	2,475	2	4	775	721	2	-
5 to 9 years	6,951	3,480	3,471	2,682	2,650	12	16	785	805	-	-
10 to 14 years	8,853	4,494	4,359	3,498	3,370	29	27	967	962	-	-
15 to 19 years	9,424	4,498	4,926	3,514	3,749	63	79	921	1,098	-	-
20 to 24 years	9,745	4,344	5,401	3,415	4,137	93	105	835	1,158	1	1
25 to 29 years	9,987	4,544	5,443	3,514	3,988	132	183	897	1,272	1	-
30 to 34 years	9,939	4,546	5,393	3,211	3,679	271	326	1,064	1,387	-	1
35 to 39 years	9,575	4,575	5,000	2,744	2,989	597	541	1,231	1,470	3	-
40 to 44 years	8,100	4,041	4,059	2,312	2,423	687	579	1,040	1,057	2	-
45 to 49 years	7,370	3,706	3,664	2,019	2,179	806	702	880	783	1	-
50 to 54 years	6,214	3,184	3,030	1,642	1,795	931	723	610	511	1	1
55 to 59 years	4,877	2,439	2,438	1,371	1,482	673	577	394	379	1	-
60 to 64 years	3,829	1,884	1,945	1,128	1,265	518	454	238	225	-	1
65 to 69 years	3,189	1,581	1,608	900	1,014	464	377	217	217	-	-
70 to 74 years	2,068	1,021	1,047	600	671	295	241	126	135	-	-
75 years and over	1,890	925	965	564	579	288	287	72	99	1	-
Under 1 year	1,309	657	652	490	500	-	-	167	152	-	-
21 years and over	74,832	35,964	38,868	22,779	25,352	5,738	5,075	7,436	8,437	11	4
Median age	31.4	31.8	31.1	28.2	28.6	51.3	50.3	31.6	30.4	-	-
TOLEDO, OHIO											
All ages	282,349	140,001	142,348	119,150	123,692	13,588	11,159	7,141	7,456	122	41
Under 5 years	18,427	9,428	8,999	8,879	8,434	6	4	537	558	6	3
5 to 9 years	17,884	9,026	8,858	8,480	8,251	13	11	524	592	9	4
10 to 14 years	21,380	10,765	10,615	10,130	9,939	34	35	593	632	8	9
15 to 19 years	23,903	11,465	12,438	10,805	11,647	117	129	535	657	8	5
20 to 24 years	24,080	11,367	12,713	10,738	11,949	138	136	486	624	5	4
25 to 29 years	23,714	11,430	12,284	10,491	11,205	377	374	549	703	13	2
30 to 34 years	22,743	11,168	11,575	9,971	10,219	601	612	587	743	9	1
35 to 39 years	22,404	11,181	11,223	9,494	9,573	939	914	739	734	9	2
40 to 44 years	21,203	10,712	10,491	8,646	8,776	1,378	1,074	671	638	17	3
45 to 49 years	21,582	11,283	10,299	8,456	8,324	2,146	1,432	674	540	7	3
50 to 54 years	18,260	9,306	8,954	6,740	7,093	2,125	1,497	432	363	9	1
55 to 59 years	14,611	7,527	7,084	5,487	5,581	1,714	1,234	319	268	7	1
60 to 64 years	11,488	5,660	5,828	4,143	4,543	1,323	1,142	189	142	5	1
65 to 69 years	8,802	4,191	4,611	2,990	3,574	1,032	905	163	131	6	1
70 to 74 years	5,981	2,848	3,133	1,980	2,308	778	753	87	71	3	1
75 years and over	5,887	2,644	3,243	1,720	2,276	867	907	56	60	1	-
Under 1 year	3,732	1,905	1,827	1,796	1,710	-	-	108	117	1	-
21 years and over	196,152	97,164	98,988	78,832	83,128	13,388	10,958	4,854	4,883	90	19
Median age	32.6	32.9	32.3	30.0	30.2	52.5	52.9	33.0	29.7	36.7	-
TRENTON, N. J.											
All ages	124,697	62,175	62,522	46,115	47,386	11,337	10,519	4,703	4,605	20	12
Under 5 years	7,111	3,699	3,412	3,292	3,023	2	1	404	386	1	2
5 to 9 years	7,872	3,954	3,918	3,574	3,463	10	8	367	445	3	2
10 to 14 years	10,152	5,073	5,079	4,563	4,515	33	34	476	527	1	3
15 to 19 years	12,140	5,918	6,222	5,338	5,518	126	116	454	586	-	2
20 to 24 years	12,336	6,025	6,311	5,548	5,795	110	121	367	394	-	1
25 to 29 years	11,365	5,874	5,491	5,054	4,779	356	333	463	379	1	-
30 to 34 years	9,594	4,878	4,716	3,917	3,796	566	553	393	367	2	-
35 to 39 years	8,931	4,432	4,499	3,077	3,177	871	910	484	411	-	1
40 to 44 years	9,104	4,536	4,568	2,777	2,865	1,331	1,336	426	367	2	-
45 to 49 years	9,080	4,566	4,514	2,500	2,585	1,746	1,690	318	238	2	1
50 to 54 years	8,107	4,219	3,888	2,000	2,120	2,014	1,600	203	168	2	-
55 to 59 years	6,205	3,208	2,997	1,472	1,633	1,585	1,254	147	110	4	-
60 to 64 years	4,554	2,270	2,284	1,128	1,303	1,067	909	75	72	-	-

PERCENT DISTRIBUTION

CITY AND AGE	All classes			Native white		Foreign-born white		Negro		Other races	
	Total	Male	Female	Male	Female	Male	Female	Male	Female	Male	Female
TAMPA, FLA.											
All ages	100.0	100.0	100.0	100.0	100.0	100.0	100.0	100.0	100.0	-	-
Under 5 years	5.9	6.1	5.7	6.8	6.4	-	0.1	7.0	5.9	-	-
5 to 9 years	6.4	6.6	6.2	7.6	6.9	0.2	0.3	7.1	6.6	-	-
10 to 14 years	8.2	8.6	7.8	9.8	8.8	0.5	0.5	8.7	7.8	-	-
15 to 19 years	8.7	8.6	8.8	9.9	9.8	1.1	1.5	8.3	8.9	-	-
20 to 24 years	9.0	8.3	9.7	9.6	10.8	1.6	2.0	7.6	9.4	-	-
25 to 29 years	9.2	8.7	9.7	9.9	10.4	2.3	3.5	8.1	10.4	-	-
30 to 34 years	9.2	8.7	9.6	9.0	9.6	4.6	6.2	9.6	11.3	-	-
35 to 39 years	8.8	8.7	8.9	7.7	7.8	10.2	10.4	11.1	12.0	-	-
40 to 44 years	7.5	7.7	7.3	6.5	6.3	11.7	11.1	9.4	8.6	-	-
45 to 49 years	6.8	7.1	6.5	5.7	5.7	13.8	13.4	8.0	6.4	-	-
50 to 54 years	5.7	6.1	5.4	4.6	4.7	15.9	13.8	5.5	4.2	-	-
55 to 59 years	4.5	4.7	4.4	3.9	3.9	11.5	11.1	3.6	3.1	-	-
60 to 64 years	3.5	3.6	3.5	3.2	3.3	8.8	8.7	2.2	1.8	-	-
65 to 69 years	2.9	3.0	2.9	2.5	2.6	7.9	7.2	2.0	1.8	-	-
70 to 74 years	1.9	1.9	1.9	1.7	1.7	5.0	4.6	1.1	1.1	-	-
75 years and over	1.7	1.8	1.7	1.6	1.5	4.9	5.5	0.7	0.8	-	-
Under 1 year	1.2	1.3	1.2	1.4	1.3	-	-	1.5	1.2	-	-
21 years and over	69.0	68.6	69.5	64.1	65.9	97.9	97.2	67.3	68.7	-	-
Median age	-	-	-	-	-	-	-	-	-	-	-
TOLEDO, OHIO											
All ages	100.0	100.0	100.0	100.0	100.0	100.0	100.0	100.0	100.0	100.0	-
Under 5 years	6.5	6.7	6.3	7.5	6.8	-	-	7.5	7.5	4.9	-
5 to 9 years	6.3	6.4	6.2	7.1	6.7	0.1	0.1	7.3	7.9	7.4	-
10 to 14 years	7.6	7.7	7.5	8.5	8.0	0.3	0.3	8.3	8.5	6.6	-
15 to 19 years	8.5	8.2	8.7	9.1	9.4	0.9	1.2	7.5	8.8	6.6	-
20 to 24 years	8.5	8.1	8.9	9.0	9.7	1.0	1.2	6.8	8.4	4.1	-
25 to 29 years	8.4	8.2	8.6	8.8	9.1	2.8	3.4	7.7	9.4	10.7	-
30 to 34 years	8.1	8.0	8.1	8.4	8.3	4.4	5.5	8.2	10.0	7.4	-
35 to 39 years	7.9	8.0	7.9	8.0	7.7	6.9	8.2	10.3	9.8	7.4	-
40 to 44 years	7.5	7.7	7.4	7.3	7.1	10.1	9.6	9.4	8.6	13.9	-
45 to 49 years	7.6	8.1	7.2	7.1	6.7	15.8	12.8	9.4	7.2	5.7	-
50 to 54 years	6.5	6.6	6.3	5.7	5.9	15.6	13.4	6.0	4.9	7.4	-
55 to 59 years	5.2	5.4	5.0	4.6	4.5	12.6	11.1	4.5	3.6	5.7	-
60 to 64 years	4.1	4.0	4.1	3.5	3.7	9.7	10.2	2.6	1.9	4.1	-
65 to 69 years	3.1	3.0	3.2	2.5	2.9	7.6	8.1	2.3	1.8	4.9	-
70 to 74 years	2.1	2.0	2.2	1.7	1.9	5.7	6.7	1.2	1.0	2.5	-
75 years and over	2.1	1.9	2.3	1.4	1.8	6.4	8.1	0.8	0.8	0.8	-
Under 1 year	1.3	1.4	1.3	1.5	1.4	-	-	1.5	1.6	0.8	-
21 years and over	69.5	69.4	69.5	66.2	67.2	98.5	98.2	68.0	65.5	73.8	-
Median age	-	-	-	-	-	-	-	-	-	-	-
TRENTON, N. J.											
All ages	100.0	100.0	100.0	100.0	100.0	100.0	100.0	100.0	100.0	-	-
Under 5 years	5.7	5.9	5.5	7.1	6.4	-	-	8.6	8.4	-	-
5 to 9 years	6.3	6.4	6.3	7.7	7.3	0.1	0.1	7.8	9.7	-	-
10 to 14 years	8.1	8.2	8.1	9.9	9.5	0.3	0.3	10.1	11.4	-	-
15 to 19 years	9.7	9.5	10.6	11.6	11.6	1.1	1.1	9.7	12.7	-	-
20 to 24 years	9.9	9.7	10.1	12.0	12.2	1.0	1.2	7.8	8.6	-	-
25 to 29 years	9.1	9.4	8.8	11.0	10.1	3.1	3.2	9.8	8.2	-	-
30 to 34 years	7.7	7.8	7.5	8.5	8.0	5.0	5.3	8.4	8.0	-	-
35 to 39 years	7.2	7.1	7.2	6.7	6.7	7.7	8.7	10.3	8.9	-	-
40 to 44 years	7.3	7.3	7.3	6.0	6.0	11.7	12.7	9.1	8.0	-	-
45 to 49 years	7.3	7.3	7.2	5.4	5.5	15.4	16.1	6.8	5.2	-	-
50 to 54 years	6.5	6.8	6.2	4.3	4.5	17.8	15.2	4.3	3.6	-	-
55 to 59 years	5.0	5.2	4.8	3.2	3.4	14.0	11.9	3.1	2.4	-	-
60 to 64 years	3.7	3.7	3.7	2.4	2.7	9.4	8.6	1.6	1.6	-	-

Age																						
65 to 69 years	3,410	1,507	1,903	773	1,150	672	691	62	62			2.7	2.4	3.0	1.7	2.4	5.9	6.6	1.3	1.3		
70 to 74 years	2,381	1,053	1,328	570	794	443	497	39	37	1		1.9	1.7	2.1	1.2	1.7	3.9	4.7	0.8	0.8		
75 years and over	2,355	963	1,392	532	870	405	466	25	56	1		1.9	1.5	2.2	1.2	1.8	3.6	4.4	0.5	1.2		
Under 1 year	1,356	739	617	643	550			95	67	1		1.1	1.2	1.0	1.4	1.2			2.0	1.5		
21 years and over	85,038	42,389	42,649	28,308	29,730	11,138	10,330	2,928	2,586	15	3	68.2	68.2	68.2	61.4	62.7	98.2	98.2	62.3	56.2		
Median age	30.7	30.6	30.9	25.7	26.4	51.3	50.5	28.1	24.5													
TULSA, OKLA.																						
All ages	142,157	68,187	73,970	59,704	64,474	1,221	953	6,961	8,190	301	353	100.0	100.0	100.0	100.0	100.0	100.0	100.0	100.0	100.0	100.0	100.0
Under 5 years	9,921	5,072	4,849	4,546	4,379		3	505	443	21	24	7.0	7.4	6.6	7.6	6.8		0.3	7.3	5.4	7.0	6.8
5 to 9 years	9,929	5,013	4,916	4,462	4,387	4	4	515	502	32	23	7.0	7.4	6.6	7.5	6.8	0.3	0.4	7.4	6.1	10.6	6.5
10 to 14 years	10,719	5,339	5,380	4,747	4,726	4	12	559	607	29	35	7.5	7.8	7.3	8.0	7.3	0.3	1.3	8.0	7.4	9.6	9.9
15 to 19 years	12,291	5,752	6,539	5,123	5,754	16	17	580	735	33	33	8.6	8.4	8.8	8.6	8.9	1.3	1.8	8.3	9.0	11.0	9.3
20 to 24 years	13,024	5,701	7,323	5,110	6,420	33	27	535	820	23	56	9.2	8.4	9.9	8.6	10.0	2.7	2.8	7.7	10.0	7.6	15.9
25 to 29 years	13,690	6,139	7,551	5,443	6,490	38	52	631	970	27	39	9.6	9.0	10.2	9.1	10.1	3.1	5.5	9.1	11.8	9.0	11.0
30 to 34 years	13,700	6,297	7,403	5,487	6,301	79	70	696	990	35	42	9.6	9.2	10.0	9.2	9.8	6.5	7.3	10.0	12.1	11.6	11.9
35 to 39 years	13,252	6,186	7,066	5,277	5,969	100	97	781	968	28	32	9.3	9.1	9.6	8.8	9.3	8.2	10.2	11.2	11.8	9.3	9.1
40 to 44 years	11,377	5,574	5,803	4,808	5,036	139	91	604	656	23	20	8.0	8.2	7.8	8.1	7.8	11.4	9.5	8.7	8.0	7.6	5.7
45 to 49 years	10,032	5,041	4,991	4,351	4,364	163	108	511	502	16	17	7.1	7.4	6.7	7.3	6.8	13.3	11.3	7.3	6.1	5.3	4.8
50 to 54 years	7,699	3,993	3,706	3,422	3,264	198	131	361	304	12	7	5.4	5.9	5.0	5.7	5.1	16.2	13.7	5.2	3.7	4.0	2.0
55 to 59 years	5,474	2,822	2,652	2,432	2,337	152	88	230	220	8	7	3.9	4.1	3.6	4.1	3.6	12.4	9.2	3.3	2.7	2.7	2.0
60 to 64 years	4,017	2,007	2,010	1,744	1,787	104	68	151	149	8	6	2.8	2.9	2.7	2.9	2.8	8.5	7.1	2.2	1.8	2.7	1.7
65 to 69 years	3,196	1,488	1,708	1,269	1,477	72	64	146	162	1	5	2.2	2.2	2.3	2.1	2.3	5.9	6.7	2.1	2.0	0.3	1.4
70 to 74 years	1,953	907	1,046	755	899	62	50	88	93	2	4	1.4	1.3	1.4	1.3	1.4	5.1	5.2	1.3	1.1	0.7	1.1
75 years and over	1,883	856	1,027	728	884	57	71	68	69	3	3	1.3	1.3	1.4	1.2	1.4	4.7	7.5	1.0	0.8	1.0	0.8
Under 1 year	2,095	1,075	1,020	936	912			132	104	7	4	1.5	1.6	1.4	1.6	1.4			1.9	1.3	2.3	1.1
21 years and over	96,726	45,927	50,799	39,871	43,921	1,190	908	4,684	5,745	182	225	68.0	67.4	68.7	66.8	68.1	97.5	95.3	67.3	70.1	60.5	63.7
Median age	30.5	30.9	30.3	30.4	30.1	50.9	49.8	31.1	30.1	27.3	25.7											
UTICA, N. Y.																						
All ages	100,518	48,857	51,661	39,499	43,150	9,076	8,264	271	243	11	4	100.0	100.0	100.0	100.0	100.0	100.0	100.0	100.0	100.0		
Under 5 years	6,386	3,270	3,116	3,255	3,104	1	3	14	9			6.4	6.7	6.0	8.2	7.2			5.2	3.7		
5 to 9 years	6,463	3,261	3,202	3,244	3,173	4	9	13	20			6.4	6.7	6.2	8.2	7.4		0.1	4.8	8.2		
10 to 14 years	7,543	3,765	3,778	3,735	3,732	16	23	14	23			7.5	7.7	7.3	9.5	8.6	0.2	0.3	5.2	9.5		
15 to 19 years	8,816	4,319	4,497	4,226	4,409	71	70	22	18			8.8	8.8	8.7	10.7	10.2	0.8	0.8	8.1	7.4		
20 to 24 years	8,952	4,156	4,796	4,062	4,690	81	92	12	14	1		8.9	8.5	9.3	10.3	10.9	0.9	1.1	4.4	5.8		
25 to 29 years	8,564	3,990	4,574	3,760	4,311	211	236	19	26		1	8.5	8.2	8.9	9.5	10.0	2.3	2.9	7.0	10.7		
30 to 34 years	7,717	3,757	3,960	3,326	3,497	398	438	32	24	1	1	7.7	7.7	7.7	8.4	8.1	4.4	5.3	11.8	9.9		
35 to 39 years	6,845	3,293	3,552	2,617	2,812	646	719	28	21	2		6.8	6.7	6.9	6.6	6.5	7.1	8.7	10.3	8.6		
40 to 44 years	7,010	3,380	3,630	2,307	2,476	1,038	1,135	31	19	4		7.0	6.9	7.0	5.8	5.7	11.4	13.7	11.4	7.8		
45 to 49 years	7,427	3,720	3,707	2,167	2,328	1,525	1,360	27	19	1		7.4	7.6	7.2	5.5	5.4	16.8	16.5	10.0	7.8		
50 to 54 years	6,701	3,392	3,309	1,772	2,085	1,595	1,207	23	16	2	1	6.7	6.9	6.4	4.5	4.8	17.6	14.6	8.5	6.6		
55 to 59 years	5,353	2,705	2,648	1,493	1,719	1,197	918	15	10		1	5.3	5.5	5.1	3.8	4.0	13.2	11.1	5.5	4.1		
60 to 64 years	4,320	2,099	2,221	1,283	1,550	807	662	9	9			4.3	4.3	4.3	3.2	3.6	8.9	8.0	3.3	3.7		
65 to 69 years	3,382	1,559	1,823	940	1,244	611	573	8	6			3.4	3.2	3.5	2.4	2.9	6.7	6.9	3.0	2.5		
70 to 74 years	2,405	1,068	1,337	646	946	420	385	2	6			2.4	2.2	2.6	1.6	2.2	4.6	4.7	0.7	2.5		
75 years and over	2,634	1,123	1,511	666	1,074	455	434	2	3			2.6	2.3	2.9	1.7	2.5	5.0	5.3	0.7	1.2		
Under 1 year	1,223	620	603	616	601			4	2			1.2	1.3	1.2	1.6	1.4			1.5	0.8		
21 years and over	69,547	33,423	36,124	24,248	27,808	8,958	8,141	206	171	11	4	69.2	68.4	69.9	61.4	64.4	98.7	98.5	76.0	70.4		
Median age	32.3	32.2	32.4	26.6	27.9	51.7	50.2	36.7	32.4													
WASHINGTON, D. C.																						
All ages	663,091	317,522	345,569	209,828	230,484	17,920	16,094	88,672	98,594	1,102	397	100.0	100.0	100.0	100.0	100.0	100.0	100.0	100.0	100.0	100.0	100.0
Under 5 years	39,851	20,054	19,797	12,850	12,651	19	17	7,126	7,067	59	62	6.0	6.3	5.7	6.1	5.5	0.1	0.1	8.0	7.2	5.4	15.6
5 to 9 years	37,245	18,643	18,602	11,713	11,565	54	40	6,824	6,959	52	38	5.6	5.9	5.4	5.6	5.0	0.3	0.2	7.7	7.1	4.7	9.6
10 to 14 years	41,089	20,549	20,540	13,460	13,368	82	88	6,963	7,050	44	34	6.2	6.5	5.9	6.4	5.8	0.5	0.5	7.9	7.2	4.0	8.6
15 to 19 years	48,680	23,588	25,092	16,444	16,792	266	250	6,835	8,014	43	36	7.3	7.4	7.3	7.8	7.3	1.5	1.6	7.7	8.1	3.9	9.1
20 to 24 years	65,483	31,247	34,236	23,256	23,403	407	389	7,542	10,393	42	51	9.9	9.8	9.9	11.1	10.2	2.3	2.4	8.5	10.5	3.8	12.8
25 to 29 years	74,346	35,783	38,563	24,846	25,582	809	910	10,004	12,027	124	44	11.2	11.3	11.2	11.8	11.1	4.5	5.7	11.3	12.2	11.3	11.1
30 to 34 years	65,768	31,826	33,942	20,916	22,260	1,268	1,359	9,471	10,293	171	30	9.9	10.0	9.8	10.0	9.7	7.1	8.4	10.7	10.4	15.5	7.6
35 to 39 years	58,348	28,183	30,165	17,471	19,009	1,899	1,888	8,652	9,243	161	25	8.8	8.9	8.7	8.3	8.2	10.6	11.7	9.8	9.4	14.6	6.3
40 to 44 years	53,889	25,853	28,036	16,331	18,749	2,416	2,060	6,967	7,202	139	25	8.1	8.1	8.1	7.8	8.1	13.5	12.8	7.9	7.3	12.6	6.3
45 to 49 years	46,641	22,630	24,011	14,389	16,157	2,594	2,045	5,559	5,786	88	23	7.0	7.1	6.9	6.9	7.0	14.5	12.7	6.3	5.9	8.0	5.8
50 to 54 years	37,918	18,268	19,650	11,496	13,412	2,540	1,829	4,168	4,399	64	10	5.7	5.8	5.7	5.5	5.8	14.2	11.4	4.7	4.5	5.8	2.5
55 to 59 years	28,870	13,436	15,434	8,508	10,649	1,890	1,522	2,996	3,255	42	8	4.4	4.2	4.5	4.1	4.6	10.5	9.5	3.4	3.3	3.8	2.0
60 to 64 years	23,757	10,772	12,985	7,041	9,239	1,430	1,269	2,265	2,470	36	7	3.6	3.4	3.8	3.4	4.0	8.0	7.9	2.6	2.5	3.3	1.8
65 to 69 years	18,309	7,730	10,579	5,050	7,472	966	1,019	1,694	2,087	20	1	2.8	2.4	3.1	2.4	3.2	5.4	6.3	1.9	2.1	1.8	0.3
70 to 74 years	11,651	4,777	6,874	3,245	5,095	655	676	871	1,103	6		1.8	1.5	2.0	1.5	2.2	3.7	4.2	1.0	1.1	0.5	
75 years and over	11,246	4,183	7,063	2,812	5,081	625	733	735	1,246	11	3	1.7	1.3	2.0	1.3	2.2	3.5	4.6	0.8	1.3	1.0	0.8
Under 1 year	8,422	4,255	4,167	2,805	2,717		1	1,441	1,432	9	17	1.3	1.3	1.2	1.3	1.2			1.6	1.5	0.8	4.3
21 years and over	484,738	229,341	255,397	151,450	172,034	17,429	15,610	59,565	67,535	897	218	73.1	72.2	73.9	72.2	74.6	97.3	97.0	67.2	68.5	81.4	54.9
Median age	31.9	31.4	32.4	30.6	32.7	48.4	47.6	29.5	29.1	35.5	22.8											

TABLE 53.—AGE, BY RACE AND SEX, WITH PERCENT DISTRIBUTION BY AGE, FOR CITIES OF 100,000 OR MORE: 1940—Continued

[Percent not shown where less than 0.1 or where base is less than 100]

CITY AND AGE	NUMBER											PERCENT DISTRIBUTION									
	All classes			Native white		Foreign-born white		Negro		Other races		All classes			Native white		Foreign-born white		Negro		Other races	
	Total	Male	Female	Male	Female	Male	Female	Male	Female	Male	Female	Total	Male	Female	Male	Female	Male	Female	Male	Female	Male	Female
WICHITA, KANS.																						
All ages	114,966	54,996	59,970	51,052	55,989	1,147	1,007	2,725	2,981	72	22	100.0	100.0	100.0	100.0	100.0	100.0	100.0	100.0	100.0	-	-
Under 5 years	8,269	4,284	3,985	4,081	3,791	2	2	199	189	2	3	7.2	7.8	6.6	8.0	6.8	0.2	0.2	7.3	6.4	-	-
5 to 9 years	7,755	3,982	3,773	3,738	3,560	7	4	233	209	4	-	6.7	7.2	6.3	7.3	6.4	0.6	0.4	8.6	7.1	-	-
10 to 14 years	8,298	4,249	4,049	3,967	3,801	1	3	276	244	5	1	7.2	7.7	6.8	7.8	6.8	0.1	0.3	10.1	8.2	-	-
15 to 19 years	9,918	4,545	5,373	4,295	5,081	11	11	232	276	7	5	8.6	8.3	9.0	8.4	9.1	1.0	1.1	8.5	9.3	-	-
20 to 24 years	10,760	4,902	5,858	4,650	5,573	33	20	210	261	9	4	9.4	8.9	9.8	9.1	10.0	2.9	2.0	7.7	8.8	-	-
25 to 29 years	10,746	4,917	5,829	4,613	5,483	64	51	233	294	7	1	9.3	8.9	9.7	9.0	9.8	5.6	5.1	8.6	9.9	-	-
30 to 34 years	10,094	4,803	5,291	4,510	4,982	73	60	214	249	6	-	8.8	8.7	8.8	8.8	8.9	6.4	6.0	7.9	8.4	-	-
35 to 39 years	9,152	4,304	4,848	3,968	4,457	99	88	230	301	7	2	8.0	7.8	8.1	7.8	8.0	8.6	8.7	8.4	10.2	-	-
40 to 44 years	8,231	3,893	4,338	3,582	4,007	107	91	198	238	6	2	7.2	7.1	7.2	7.0	7.2	9.3	9.0	7.3	8.0	-	-
45 to 49 years	7,495	3,619	3,876	3,243	3,567	132	102	236	204	8	3	6.5	6.6	6.5	6.4	6.4	11.5	10.1	8.7	6.9	-	-
50 to 54 years	6,519	3,101	3,418	2,822	3,150	135	101	140	166	4	1	5.7	5.6	5.7	5.5	5.6	11.8	10.0	5.1	5.6	-	-
55 to 59 years	5,192	2,509	2,683	2,280	2,484	119	95	104	104	6	-	4.5	4.6	4.5	4.5	4.4	10.4	9.4	3.8	3.5	-	-
60 to 64 years	4,273	1,997	2,276	1,810	2,096	103	95	83	85	1	-	3.7	3.6	3.8	3.5	3.7	9.0	9.4	3.0	2.9	-	-
65 to 69 years	3,311	1,570	1,741	1,412	1,570	89	97	69	74	-	-	2.9	2.9	2.9	2.8	2.8	7.8	9.6	2.5	2.5	-	-
70 to 74 years	2,320	1,101	1,219	993	1,113	73	73	35	33	-	-	2.0	2.0	2.0	1.9	2.0	6.4	7.2	1.3	1.1	-	-
75 years and over	2,633	1,220	1,413	1,088	1,265	99	114	33	34	-	-	2.3	2.2	2.4	2.1	2.3	8.6	11.3	1.2	1.1	-	-
Under 1 year	1,666	842	824	797	782	-	-	43	41	2	1	1.4	1.5	1.4	1.6	1.4	-	-	1.6	1.4	-	-
21 years and over	78,530	36,957	41,573	34,042	38,581	1,121	980	1,740	1,999	54	13	68.3	67.2	69.3	66.7	68.9	97.7	97.3	63.9	67.5	-	-
Median age	30.9	30.6	31.1	30.2	30.7	51.6	53.5	29.6	30.2	-	-	-	-	-	-	-	-	-	-	-	-	-
WILMINGTON, DEL.																						
All ages	112,504	55,494	57,010	42,783	44,911	5,691	4,790	8,959	7,297	61	12	100.0	100.0	100.0	100.0	100.0	100.0	100.0	100.0	100.0	-	-
Under 5 years	7,222	3,654	3,568	3,150	3,032	5	4	499	528	-	4	6.4	6.6	6.3	7.4	6.8	0.1	0.1	7.2	7.2	-	-
5 to 9 years	7,490	3,871	3,619	3,280	3,090	13	5	578	524	-	-	6.7	7.0	6.3	7.7	6.9	0.2	0.1	8.3	7.2	-	-
10 to 14 years	8,284	4,136	4,148	3,584	3,585	24	24	525	539	3	-	7.4	7.5	7.3	8.4	8.0	0.4	0.5	7.5	7.4	-	-
15 to 19 years	9,830	4,765	5,065	4,192	4,447	60	56	511	562	2	-	8.7	8.6	8.9	9.8	9.9	1.1	1.2	7.3	7.7	-	-
20 to 24 years	11,083	5,371	5,712	4,784	5,019	59	56	526	636	2	1	9.9	9.7	10.0	11.2	11.2	1.0	1.2	7.6	8.7	-	-
25 to 29 years	10,215	5,005	5,210	4,226	4,243	160	191	614	775	5	1	9.1	9.0	9.1	9.9	9.4	2.8	4.0	8.8	10.6	-	-
30 to 34 years	9,387	4,620	4,767	3,723	3,760	282	281	609	726	6	-	8.3	8.3	8.4	8.7	8.4	5.0	5.9	8.8	9.9	-	-
35 to 39 years	8,638	4,305	4,333	3,124	3,156	449	433	721	742	11	2	7.7	7.8	7.6	7.3	7.0	7.9	9.0	10.4	10.2	-	-
40 to 44 years	8,573	4,233	4,340	2,852	3,139	711	595	658	605	12	1	7.6	7.6	7.6	6.7	7.0	12.5	12.4	9.5	8.3	-	-
45 to 49 years	8,006	4,144	3,862	2,616	2,683	960	709	559	470	9	-	7.1	7.5	6.8	6.1	6.0	16.9	14.8	8.0	6.4	-	-
50 to 54 years	6,701	3,402	3,299	2,053	2,258	967	666	378	373	4	2	6.0	6.1	5.8	4.8	5.0	17.0	13.9	5.4	5.1	-	-
55 to 59 years	5,244	2,653	2,591	1,686	1,788	693	544	271	259	3	-	4.7	4.8	4.5	3.9	4.0	12.2	11.4	3.9	3.5	-	-
60 to 64 years	4,166	1,955	2,211	1,262	1,592	489	418	203	201	1	-	3.7	3.5	3.9	2.9	3.5	8.6	8.7	2.9	2.8	-	-
65 to 69 years	3,083	1,416	1,667	937	1,201	330	297	149	168	-	1	2.7	2.6	2.9	2.2	2.7	5.8	6.2	2.1	2.3	-	-
70 to 74 years	2,315	1,042	1,273	675	901	277	273	88	99	2	-	2.1	1.9	2.2	1.6	2.0	4.9	5.7	1.3	1.4	-	-
75 years and over	2,267	922	1,345	639	1,017	212	238	70	90	1	-	2.0	1.7	2.4	1.5	2.3	3.7	5.0	1.0	1.2	-	-
Under 1 year	1,366	675	691	575	601	-	-	100	90	-	-	1.2	1.2	1.2	1.3	1.3	-	-	1.4	1.2	-	-
21 years and over	77,445	38,002	39,443	27,625	29,725	5,575	4,688	4,746	5,022	56	8	68.8	68.5	69.2	64.6	66.2	98.0	97.9	68.2	68.8	-	-
Median age	31.1	31.0	31.2	27.8	28.9	50.6	50.3	31.9	30.6	-	-	-	-	-	-	-	-	-	-	-	-	-
WORCESTER, MASS.																						
All ages	193,694	94,455	99,239	73,884	78,388	19,869	20,122	646	707	58	22	100.0	100.0	100.0	100.0	100.0	100.0	100.0	100.0	100.0	-	-
Under 1 year	12,285	6,209	6,076	6,159	5,999	6	9	42	68	2	-	6.3	6.6	6.1	8.3	7.7	-	-	6.5	9.6	-	-
5 to 9 years	12,915	6,403	6,422	6,396	6,328	23	30	70	60	4	4	6.7	6.9	6.5	8.7	8.1	0.1	0.1	10.8	8.5	-	-
10 to 14 years	15,569	7,885	7,684	7,751	7,555	71	49	61	78	2	2	8.0	8.3	7.7	10.5	9.6	0.4	0.2	9.4	11.0	-	-
15 to 19 years	17,459	8,567	8,892	8,288	8,610	216	216	58	66	5	-	9.0	9.1	9.0	11.2	11.0	1.1	1.1	9.0	9.3	-	-
20 to 24 years	17,685	8,532	9,153	8,200	8,765	276	336	51	51	5	1	9.1	9.0	9.2	11.1	11.2	1.4	1.7	7.9	7.2	-	-
25 to 29 years	15,902	7,815	8,087	7,206	7,424	556	607	48	53	5	3	8.2	8.3	8.1	9.7	9.5	2.8	3.0	7.4	7.5	-	-
30 to 34 years	14,130	6,828	7,302	5,854	6,118	935	1,139	35	44	4	1	7.3	7.2	7.4	7.9	7.8	4.7	5.7	5.4	6.2	-	-
35 to 39 years	13,666	6,558	7,108	5,016	5,382	1,499	1,671	41	53	2	2	7.1	6.9	7.2	6.8	6.9	7.5	8.3	6.3	7.5	-	-
40 to 44 years	13,748	6,583	7,165	4,475	4,992	2,052	2,120	54	52	2	1	7.1	7.0	7.2	6.1	6.4	10.3	10.5	8.4	7.4	-	-
45 to 49 years	14,304	7,105	7,199	4,052	4,344	3,004	2,819	46	36	3	-	7.4	7.5	7.3	5.5	5.5	15.1	14.0	7.1	5.1	-	-

UNITED STATES SUMMARY—PRINCIPAL CITIES

50 to 54 years	12,161	6,198	5,963	3,122	3,309	3,029	2,615	36	37	11	2	6.3	6.6	6.0	4.2	4.2	15.2	13.0	5.6	5.2		
55 to 59 years	10,059	4,972	5,087	2,355	2,749	2,585	2,309	29	28	3	1	5.2	5.3	5.1	3.2	3.5	13.0	11.5	4.5	4.0		
60 to 64 years	8,034	3,763	4,271	1,779	2,169	1,954	2,074	28	28	2		4.1	4.0	4.3	2.4	2.8	9.8	10.3	4.3	4.0		
65 to 69 years	6,569	2,989	3,580	1,424	1,882	1,543	1,680	21	16	1	2	3.4	3.2	3.6	1.9	2.4	7.8	8.3	3.3	2.3		
70 to 74 years	4,499	2,041	2,458	916	1,279	1,115	1,159	7	18	3	2	2.3	2.2	2.5	1.2	1.6	5.6	5.8	1.1	2.5		
75 years and over	4,709	1,917	2,792	891	1,483	1,005	1,289	19	19	2	1	2.4	2.0	2.8	1.2	1.9	5.1	6.4	2.9	2.7		
Under 1 year	2,258	1,140	1,118	1,129	1,107	1		10	11			1.2	1.2	1.1	1.5	1.4			1.5	1.6		
21 years and over	131,947	63,642	68.305	43,703	48,115	19,491	19,753	406	421	42	16	68.1	67.4	68.8	59.1	61.4	98.1	98.2	62.8	60.0		
Median age	31.8	31.3	32.3	25.1	26.3	52.1	52.0	29.3	27.9													
YONKERS, N. Y.																						
All ages	142,598	69,991	72,607	53,745	56,039	14,382	14,275	1,819	2,289	45	4	100.0	100.0	100.0	100.0	100.0	100.0	100.0	100.0	100.0		
Under 5 years	8,855	4,555	4,300	4,389	4,147	22	10	143	143	1		6.2	6.5	5.9	8.2	7.4	0.2	0.1	7.9	6.2		
5 to 9 years	9,811	4,994	4,817	4.774	4,593	45	38	175	186			6.9	7.1	6.6	8.9	8.2	0.3	0.3	9.6	8.1		
10 to 14 years	11,765	6,006	5,759	5,721	5,483	112	86	171	190	2		8.3	8.6	7.9	10.6	9.8	0.8	0.6	9.4	8.3		
15 to 19 years	12,446	6,319	6.127	5,908	5,662	247	291	160	173	4	1	8.7	9.0	8.4	11.0	10.1	1.7	2.0	8.8	7.6		
20 to 24 years	12,074	5,791	6,283	5,392	5,746	254	303	142	234	3		8.5	8.3	8.7	10.0	10.3	1.8	2.1	7.8	10.2		
25 to 29 years	12,362	5,900	6,462	5,246	5,641	471	547	182	272	1	2	8.7	8.4	8.9	9.8	10.1	3.3	3.8	10.0	11.9		
30 to 34 years	12,295	5,835	6,460	4,768	5,201	906	1,032	153	227	8		8.6	8.3	8.9	8.9	9.3	6.3	7.2	8.4	9.9		
35 to 39 years	11,913	5,803	6,110	4,182	4,421	1,463	1,461	149	228	9		8.4	8.3	8.4	7.8	7.9	10.2	10.2	8.2	10.0		
40 to 44 years	11,484	5,671	5,813	3.721	3,896	1,808	1,742	136	175	6		8.1	8.1	8.0	6.9	7.0	12.6	12.2	7.5	7.6		
45 to 49 years	10,470	5,271	5,199	2,994	3.087	2,128	1,948	143	163	6	1	7.3	7.5	7.2	5.6	5.5	14.8	13.6	7.9	7.1		
50 to 54 years	8,842	4,404	4,438	2,199	2,433	2,110	1,879	93	126	2		6.2	6.3	6.1	4.1	4.3	14.7	13.2	5.1	5.5		
55 to 59 years	6,619	3,279	3,340	1,508	1,760	1,696	1,521	73	59	2		4.6	4.7	4.6	2.8	3.1	11.8	10.7	4.0	2.6		
60 to 64 years	5,168	2,440	2,728	1,184	1,401	1,222	1,274	34	53			3.6	3.5	3.8	2.2	2.5	8.5	8.9	1.9	2.3		
65 to 69 years	3,744	1,713	2,031	840	1,132	838	875	34	24	1		2.6	2.4	2.8	1.6	2.0	5.8	6.1	1.9	1.0		
70 to 74 years	2,461	1,083	1,378	506	720	558	638	19	20			1.7	1.5	1.9	0.9	1.3	3.9	4.5	1.0	0.9		
75 years and over	2,289	927	1,362	413	716	502	630	12	16			1.6	1.3	1.9	0.8	1.3	3.5	4.4	0.7	0.7		
Under 1 year	1,758	946	812	914	780	2		30	32			1.2	1.4	1.1	1.7	1.4			1.6	1.4		
21 years and over	97,305	46,963	50,342	31,896	35,017	13,886	13,772	1,143	1.550	38	3	68.2	67.1	69.3	59.3	62.5	96.6	96.5	62.8	67.7		
Median age	31.6	31.2	32.0	25.7	27.1	49.4	49.2	28.3	29.0													
YOUNGSTOWN, OHIO																						
All ages	167,720	84,652	83,068	62,377	64,008	14,846	11,825	7,397	7,218	32	17	100.0	100.0	100.0	100.0	100.0	100.0	100.0	100.0	100.0		
Under 5 years	11,103	5,713	5,390	5,141	4,830	3	6	568	553	1	1	6.6	6.7	6.5	8.2	7.5		0.1	7.7	7.7		
5 to 9 years	11,451	5,686	5,765	5,010	5,050	19	26	655	688	2	1	6.8	6.7	6.9	8.0	7.9	0.1	0.2	8.9	9.5		
10 to 14 years	14,915	7,408	7,507	6,585	6.619	48	50	772	834	3	4	8.9	8.8	9.0	10.6	10.3	0.3	0.4	10.4	11.6		
15 to 19 years	17,183	8,445	8,738	7,520	7.850	210	176	712	709	3	3	10.2	10.0	10.5	12.1	12.3	1.4	1.5	9.6	9.8		
20 to 24 years	17,301	8,544	8,757	7,844	7,979	198	186	501	592	1		10.3	10.1	10.5	12.6	12.5	1.3	1.6	6.8	8.2		
25 to 29 years	14,780	7,336	7,444	6,372	6,368	469	474	494	601	1	1	8.8	8.7	9.0	10.2	9.9	3.2	4.0	6.7	8.3		
30 to 34 years	12,331	6,084	6,247	4,901	4,959	663	706	520	582			7.4	7.2	7.5	7.9	7.7	4.5	6.0	7.0	8.1		
35 to 39 years	11,850	5,826	6,024	3,986	4,152	1,107	1,114	729	756	4	2	7.1	6.9	7.3	6.4	6.5	7.5	9.4	9.9	10.5		
40 to 44 years	11,829	6,040	5.789	3,524	3,652	1,752	1,508	759	629	5		7.1	7.1	7.0	5.6	5.7	11.8	12.8	10.3	8.7		
45 to 49 years	11,748	6,182	5,566	3,142	3,311	2,434	1,828	600	425	6	2	7.0	7.3	6.7	5.0	5.2	16.4	15.5	8.1	5.9		
50 to 54 years	10,700	5,776	4,924	2,673	2,784	2,667	1,837	431	302	5	1	6.4	6.8	5.9	4.3	4.3	18.0	15.5	5.8	4.2		
55 to 59 years	7,923	4,299	3,624	1,957	2,012	2,057	1,420	284	191	1	1	4.7	5.1	4.4	3.1	3.1	13.9	12.0	3.8	2.6		
60 to 64 years	5,911	3.093	2,818	1,498	1,694	1,417	988	178	136			3.5	3.7	3.4	2.4	2.6	9.5	8.4	2.4	1.9		
65 to 69 years	4,024	2,038	1,986	1,057	1,252	869	618	112	115		1	2.4	2.4	2.4	1.7	2.0	5.9	5.2	1.5	1.6		
70 to 74 years	2,425	1,218	1,207	685	715	490	447	43	45			1.4	1.4	1.5	1.1	1.1	3.3	3.8	0.6	0.6		
75 years and over	2,246	964	1,282	482	781	443	441	39	60			1.3	1.1	1.5	0.8	1.2	3.0	3.7	0.5	0.8		
Under 1 year	2,084	1,084	1,000	991	901			92	99	1		1.2	1.3	1.2	1.6	1.4			1.2	1.4		
21 years and over	109,583	55,684	53,899	36.563	38,062	14,514	11,512	4,584	4,317	23	8	65.3	65.8	64.9	58.6	59.5	97.8	97.4	62.0	59.8		
Median age	29.0	29.5	28.6	24.4	24.8	51.0	49.6	30.0	26.9													

TABLE 54.—POTENTIAL VOTING POPULATION, BY CITIZENSHIP, FOR CITIES OF 100,000 OR MORE: 1940

CITY	TOTAL POPULATION (ALL AGES)								POPULATION 21 YEARS AND OVER							
	Total (all ages)	Citizen				Alien		Citizenship not reported	Total 21 years and over	Citizen				Alien		Citizenship not reported
		Number	Percent	Native	Naturalized	First papers	No papers			Number	Percent	Native	Naturalized	First papers	No papers	
Akron, Ohio	244,791	235,433	96.2	219,313	16,120	2,761	4,761	1,836	161,542	152,477	94.4	136,665	15,812	2,747	4,552	1,786
Albany, N. Y	130,577	126,209	96.7	115,334	10.875	883	2,422	1,063	94,458	90,290	95.6	79,649	10,641	863	2,293	1,012
Atlanta, Ga	302,288	300,849	99.5	297,934	2,915	349	601	489	204,102	202,762	99.3	199,886	2,876	339	549	452
Baltimore, Md	859.100	833,625	97.0	797,402	36,223	5,518	13,750	6,207	584,776	560,251	95.8	524,450	35,801	5,397	13,234	5,894
Birmingham, Ala	267,583	266,093	99.4	263,127	2,966	328	577	585	174,787	173,358	99.2	170,411	2,947	321	557	551
Boston, Mass	770,816	700,160	90.8	586,736	113,424	14,523	44,143	11,990	526,925	458.700	87.1	346,943	111,757	14,325	42,329	11,571
Bridgeport, Conn	147,121	132,124	89.8	113,453	18,671	3,405	9,113	2,479	100,635	86,132	85.6	67,792	18,340	3,377	8,736	2,390
Buffalo, N. Y	575,901	550,780	95.6	483,500	67,280	6,792	13,124	5,205	391,200	367,369	93.9	301,628	65,741	6,685	12,183	4,963
Cambridge, Mass	110,879	99,258	89.5	85,313	13,945	2,224	7,009	2,388	75,431	64,380	85.3	50,723	13,657	2,200	6,591	2,260
Camden, N. J	117,536	112,374	95.6	102,471	9,903	925	3,019	1,218	77,743	72,719	93.5	62,991	9,728	913	2,933	1,178
Canton, Ohio	108,401	104,107	96.1	97,283	6,884	1,484	2,384	366	72,722	68,642	94.4	61,877	6,765	1,479	2,258	343
Charlotte, N. C	100,899	100,519	99.6	99,991	528	75	122	183	64,845	64,496	99.5	63,977	519	72	104	173
Chattanooga, Tenn	128,163	127,836	99.7	127,038	798	80	97	150	82,413	82,115	99.6	81,334	781	75	85	138
Chicago, Ill	3,396,808	3,204,008	94.3	2,721,661	482,347	56,364	118,100	18,336	2,397,392	2,212,128	92.3	1,736,583	475,545	55,559	112,095	17,610
Cincinnati, Ohio	455,610	448,150	98.4	429,712	18,438	1,905	2,618	2,937	324,276	317,258	97.8	299,108	18,150	1,830	2,364	2,824
Cleveland, Ohio	878,336	811,701	92.4	698,552	113,149	19,520	39,375	7,740	609,125	544,241	89.3	432,885	111,356	19,361	38,062	7,461
Columbus, Ohio	306,087	301,663	98.6	294,035	7,628	915	1,935	1,574	215,157	210,910	98.0	203,440	7,470	894	1,843	1,510
Dallas, Tex	294,734	291,004	98.8	287,339	3,755	559	2,262	819	204,288	200,824	98.3	197,108	3,716	546	2,140	778
Dayton, Ohio	210,718	207,855	98.6	201,357	6,498	870	1,202	791	146,135	143,380	98.1	136,993	6,387	861	1,131	763
Denver, Colo	322,412	314,511	97.5	297,430	17,081	1,739	4,160	2,002	226,511	218,807	96.6	201,868	16,939	1,723	4,037	1,944
Des Moines, Iowa	159,819	157,812	98.7	152,329	5,483	286	639	1,082	109,505	107,650	98.3	102,228	5,422	280	589	1,046
Detroit, Mich	1,623,452	1,498,555	92.3	1,300,764	197,791	36,204	79,584	9,109	1,088,739	971,301	89.2	780,184	191,117	35,596	73,432	8,410
Duluth, Minn	101,065	96,886	95.9	81,708	15,178	1,217	2,330	632	68,983	64,884	94.1	49,825	15,059	1,205	2,276	618
Elizabeth, N. J	109,912	100,828	91.7	87,249	13,579	1,906	4,919	2,259	74,718	65,998	88.3	52,732	13,266	1,879	4,707	2,134
Erie, Pa	116,955	112,473	96.2	103,366	9,107	1,330	2,284	868	76,737	72,391	94.3	63,425	8,966	1,320	2,196	830
Fall River, Mass	115,428	102,883	89.1	90,725	12,158	1,403	9,302	1,750	74,582	62,256	83.5	50,182	12,074	1,484	9,133	1,709
Flint, Mich	151,543	146,111	96.4	135,627	10,484	1,596	2,761	1,075	95,573	90,501	94.7	80,367	10.134	1,562	2,522	988
Fort Wayne, Ind	118,410	117,158	98.9	113,998	3,160	396	433	423	80,802	79,603	98.5	76,505	3,098	391	406	402
Fort Worth, Tex	177,662	175,780	98.9	174,098	1,682	224	1,363	295	120,356	118,551	98.5	116,883	1,668	220	1,305	280
Gary, Ind	111,719	105,607	94.6	94,374	11,233	1,022	3,834	596	73,401	67,591	92.1	56,635	10,956	1,604	3,663	543
Grand Rapids, Mich	164,292	157,758	96.0	143,918	13,840	1,533	3,078	1,923	110,159	103,797	94.2	90,106	13,691	1,521	2,951	1,890
Hartford, Conn	166,267	149,720	90.0	129,572	20,148	3,451	9,136	3,960	115,194	99,316	86.2	79,572	19,744	3,388	8,728	3,762
Houston, Tex	384,514	376,859	98.0	369,050	7,809	1,023	4,726	1,906	264,418	257,238	97.3	249,537	7,701	977	4,420	1,783
Indianapolis, Ind	386,972	383,736	99.2	376,344	7,392	844	1,149	1,243	269,452	266,347	98.8	259,045	7,302	826	1,063	1,216
Jacksonville, Fla	173,065	171,841	99.3	168,970	2,871	318	518	388	116,101	114,936	99.0	112,096	2,840	314	483	368
Jersey City, N. J	301,173	286,125	95.0	247,797	38,328	3,013	8,493	3,542	202,954	188,537	92.9	150,884	37,653	2,978	8,016	3,423
Kansas City, Kans	121,458	118,667	97.7	114,855	3,812	456	1,850	485	79,766	77,032	96.6	73,256	3,776	455	1,799	480
Kansas City, Mo	399,178	391,801	98.2	379,758	12,043	1,765	3,800	1,812	291,001	283.888	97.6	271,936	11,952	1,736	3,615	1,762
Knoxville, Tenn	111,580	111,324	99.8	110,837	487	38	82	136	71,230	70,989	99.7	70,508	481	37	79	125
Long Beach, Calif	164,271	160,017	97.4	151,542	8,475	1,060	2,115	1,079	123,380	119,366	96.7	111,057	8,309	1,040	1,962	1,012
Los Angeles, Calif	1,504,277	1,400,979	93.1	1 277,240	123,739	21,448	73,874	7,976	1,123,485	1,025,708	91.3	903,979	121,729	20,994	69,311	7,472
Louisville, Ky	319,077	317,369	99.5	312,832	4,537	402	565	741	218,317	216,718	99.3	212,223	4,495	385	498	716
Lowell, Mass	101,389	93,142	91.9	81,937	11,205	1,651	4,548	2,048	65,739	57,660	87.7	46,558	11,102	1,632	4,457	1,990
Memphis, Tenn	292,942	291,082	99.4	288,431	2,651	441	983	430	202,140	200,352	99.1	197,728	2,624	428	935	425
Miami, Fla	172,172	164,243	95.4	155,547	8,696	1,438	4,631	1,860	124,939	117,448	94.0	108,867	8,581	1,416	4,344	1,731
Milwaukee, Wis	587,472	565,485	96.3	503,531	61,954	7,016	12,238	2,733	405,467	384,274	94.8	323,328	60,946	6,945	11,632	2,616
Minneapolis, Minn	492,370	478,545	97.2	428,006	50,539	4,103	5,933	3,789	348,424	334,982	96.1	284,870	50,112	4,069	5,672	3,701
Nashville, Tenn	167,402	166,858	99.7	165,846	1,012	118	166	260	111,853	111,364	99.6	110,361	993	110	147	242
Newark, N. J	429,760	389,823	90.7	338,889	50,934	7,538	22,344	10,055	290,703	252,323	86.8	202,325	49,998	7,408	21,342	9,630
New Bedford, Mass	110,341	95,293	86.4	79,537	15,756	2,376	10,773	1,899	75,009	60,245	80.3	44,583	15,662	2,356	10,580	1,828
New Haven, Conn	160,605	146,887	91.5	127,882	19,005	2.509	9,066	2,143	109,480	96,067	87.7	77,310	18,757	2,484	8,846	2,083
New Orleans, La	494,537	489,721	99.0	479,334	10,387	1,108	3,063	645	331,411	326,837	98.6	316,620	10 217	1,093	2,867	614
New York, N. Y	7,454,995	6,632,398	89.0	5,316,338	1,316,060	194,634	511,382	116,681	5,254,633	4,474,689	85.2	3,184,429	1,290,260	190,022	480,119	109,803
Bronx Borough	1,394,711	1,241,269	89.0	931,258	310,011	36,551	96,218	20,673	966,685	820,888	84.9	516,925	303,958	35,761	90.564	19,477
Brooklyn Borough	2,698,285	2,407,484	89.2	1,920,231	487,253	55,105	183,915	51,781	1,832,686	1,554,080	84.8	1,076,150	477,930	54,115	175,345	49,146
Manhattan Borough	1,889,924	1,615,980	85.5	1,307,029	308,951	77.709	171,078	25,157	1,429,955	1,172,487	82.0	869,396	303,091	75,544	158,647	23,277
Queens Borough	1,297,634	1,203,752	92.8	1,018,697	185,055	23,155	53,929	16,798	909,487	821,425	90.3	640,354	181,071	22,625	49,671	15,766
Richmond Borough	174,441	163,913	94.0	139,123	24,790	2,014	6,242	2,272	115,820	105,814	91.4	81,604	24,210	1,977	5,892	2,137
Norfolk, Va	144,332	143,116	99.2	140,562	2,554	213	496	507	96,390	95,252	98.8	92,743	2,509	209	454	475
Oakland, Calif	302,163	284,545	94.2	257,622	26,923	4,002	10,815	2,711	222,497	205.581	92.4	179,063	26,518	4,048	10,301	2,567
Oklahoma City, Okla	204,424	203,356	99.5	201,573	1,783	211	461	396	137,229	136,201	99.3	134,437	1,764	208	440	380
Omaha, Nebr	223,844	218,015	97.4	201,455	16,560	1,426	2,894	1,509	152,620	146,971	96.3	130,526	16,445	1,412	2,769	1,468
Paterson, N. J	139,656	127,472	91.3	105,463	22,009	2,200	8.541	1.443	97,387	85,616	87.9	63.961	21,655	2,165	8,206	1,400
Peoria, Ill	105,087	103,696	98.7	99,605	4,091	433	470	488	75,012	73,676	98.2	69,647	4,029	427	429	480
Philadelphia, Pa	1,931,334	1,842,836	95.4	1,638,788	204,048	23,297	46,170	19,031	1,326,413	1,240,469	93.5	1,039,375	201,094	23,016	44,504	18,424
Pittsburgh, Pa	671,659	648,710	96.6	586,756	61,954	8,346	11,118	3,485	451,393	429,146	95.1	368,142	61,004	8,249	10,606	3,392
Portland, Oreg	305,394	291,032	95.3	265,389	25,643	3,963	7,746	2,653	228,950	215,199	94.0	189,992	25,207	3,918	7,319	2.514
Providence, R. I	253,504	235,138	92.8	201,655	33,483	3,469	11,121	3,776	171,449	153,573	89.6	120,517	33,056	3,632	10,584	3,660
Reading, Pa	110,568	107,268	97.0	102,688	4,580	1,022	1,681	597	77,304	74,080	95.8	69,563	4,517	1,009	1,638	577
Richmond, Va	193,042	191,732	99.3	189,555	2,177	313	615	382	133,599	132,359	99.1	130,206	2,153	308	568	364
Rochester, N. Y	324.975	307,770	94.7	264,737	43,033	3,634	9,303	4,268	231,234	214,739	92.9	172,593	42,146	3,578	8,799	4,118
Sacramento, Calif	105,958	98,838	93.3	92,238	6,600	1,104	4,917	1,099	77,686	70,811	91.2	64,314	6,497	1,095	4,741	1,039
St. Louis, Mo	816,048	794,609	97.4	756,401	38,208	5,597	10,911	4,931	585,074	564,257	96.4	526,483	37,774	5,535	10,481	4,801
St. Paul, Minn	287,736	279,565	97.2	254,020	25.545	2,009	2,947	3,215	198,317	190,390	96.0	165,062	25,328	1,995	2,804	3,128
Salt Lake City, Utah	149,934	146,186	97.5	136,374	9,812	852	1,831	1,065	94,370	90,757	96.2	81,160	9,597	837	1,746	1,030
San Antonio, Tex	253,854	232,960	91.8	225,558	7,402	1,325	18,570	999	159,332	139,534	87.6	132,272	7,262	1,288	17,593	917
San Diego, Calif	203,341	195,896	96.3	183,228	12,668	1.489	5,099	857	145,072	138,077	95.2	125,648	12,429	1,464	4,750	781
San Francisco, Calif	634,536	575,296	90.7	494,513	80,783	15,628	36,663	6,949	492,970	436,788	88.6	357,127	79,661	15,345	34,239	6,598
Scranton, Pa	140,404	133,837	95.3	122,015	11,822	1,701	2,494	2,372	92,526	86,149	93.1	74,554	11,595	1,680	2,379	2.318
Seattle, Wash	368,302	345,718	93.9	304,832	40,886	6,173	13,127	3,284	274,871	253,385	92.2	213,277	40,108	6,085	12,302	3,099
Somerville, Mass	102,177	93,638	91.6	78,278	15,360	1,831	5,754	954	67,486	59,370	88.0	44,360	15,010	1,809	5,434	873
South Bend, Ind	101,268	98,154	96.9	90,344	7,810	1,006	1,516	592	67,835	64,796	95.5	57,094	7,702	1,001	1,465	573
Spokane, Wash	122.001	118,059	96.8	109,046	9,013	1,065	1,917	960	87,499	83,740	95.7	74,863	8,877	1,053	1,796	910
Springfield, Mass	149,554	138,356	92.5	122,734	15,622	2,213	6.327	2,658	103,961	93,101	89.6	77,694	15,407	2,185	6,138	2,537
Syracuse, N. Y	205,967	196,541	95.4	178,335	18,206	1,582	5,407	2,347	142,640	133,555	93.6	115,736	17,819	1,561	5,276	2,248
Tacoma, Wash	109,408	104,295	95.3	93,178	11,117	1,544	2,702	867	77,821	72,900	93.7	61,942	10,958	1,530	2,589	802
Tampa, Fla	108,391	101,205	93.4	96,990	4,215	971	5,644	571	74,832	67.865	90.7	63,711	4,154	955	5.490	522
Toledo, Ohio	282,349	274,887	97.4	257,493	17,394	2,479	3,738	1,245	196,152	188,881	96.3	171,702	17,179	2,465	3,589	1,217
Trenton, N. J	124,697	117,281	94.1	102,790	14.491	1,355	4,425	1,636	85,038	77,797	91.5	63,519	14,278	1,338	4.313	1,590
Tulsa, Okla	142,157	141,373	99.4	139,963	1,410	206	314	264	96,726	96,001	99.3	94,609	1,392	202	280	243
Utica, N. Y	100,518	95,601	95.1	83,166	12,435	595	3,689	633	69,547	64,709	93.0	52,436	12,273	590	3,637	611
Washington, D. C	663,091	652.490	98.4	628,175	24,315	2,674	5,763	2,164	484,738	474,793	97.9	450,837	23,956	2,616	5,271	2,058
Wichita, Kans	114,966	114,094	99.2	112,774	1,320	159	398	315	78,530	77,703	98.9	76,399	1,304	156	368	303
Wilmington, Del	112,504	108,337	96.3	101,969	6,368	778	2,034	1,355	77,445	73,416	94.8	67,128	6,288	768	1,971	1,290
Worcester, Mass	193,694	175,950	90.8	153,634	22,316	2,945	10,148	4,651	131,947	114,660	86.9	92,636	22,024	2,928	9,854	4,505
Yonkers, N. Y	142,598	133,279	93.5	113,782	19,497	1,898	5,588	1,833	97,305	88,549	91.0	69,497	19,052	1,860	5,181	1,715
Youngstown, Ohio	167,720	158,518	94.5	141,002	17,516	2,433	5,146	1,623	109,583	100,657	91.9	83,510	17,147	2,416	4,983	1,627

UNITED STATES SUMMARY—PRINCIPAL CITIES

TABLE 55.—MALES IN THE POTENTIAL VOTING POPULATION, BY CITIZENSHIP, FOR CITIES OF 100,000 OR MORE: 1940

CITY	MALE POPULATION (ALL AGES)								MALE POPULATION 21 YEARS AND OVER							
	Males (all ages)	Citizen				Alien		Citizenship not reported	Males 21 years and over	Citizen				Alien		Citizenship not reported
		Number	Percent	Native	Naturalized	First papers	No papers			Number	Percent	Native	Naturalized	First papers	No papers	
Akron, Ohio	121, 520	117, 519	96. 7	107, 746	9, 773	1, 791	1, 294	925	80, 105	76, 226	95. 2	66, 607	9, 619	1, 785	1, 204	890
Albany, N. Y	62, 864	60, 782	96. 7	54, 863	5, 919	656	1, 057	469	44, 793	42, 793	95. 5	36, 988	5, 805	548	1, 005	447
Atlanta, Ga	139, 331	138, 613	99. 5	136, 884	1, 729	220	252	246	91, 928	91, 274	99. 3	89, 561	1, 713	215	216	223
Baltimore, Md	422, 916	410, 768	97. 1	390, 757	20, 011	3, 693	5, 559	2, 896	286, 271	274, 015	95. 9	254, 831	19, 784	3, 619	5, 296	2, 741
Birmingham, Ala	127, 420	126, 692	99. 4	124, 923	1, 769	230	206	292	82, 161	81, 467	99. 2	79, 709	1, 758	223	195	276
Boston, Mass	373, 147	345, 453	92. 6	285, 435	60, 018	8, 217	14, 456	5, 021	250, 689	224, 172	89. 4	165, 009	59, 163	8, 107	13, 595	4, 815
Bridgeport, Conn	73, 188	66, 630	91. 0	55, 859	10, 771	2, 346	3, 106	1, 106	49, 758	43, 454	87. 3	32, 858	10, 596	2, 330	2, 919	1, 055
Buffalo, N. Y	283, 767	272, 682	96. 1	235, 732	36, 950	4, 237	4, 448	2, 400	191, 961	181, 533	94. 6	145, 304	36, 229	4, 174	3, 980	2, 274
Cambridge, Mass	52, 479	47, 879	91. 2	40, 643	7, 236	1, 303	2, 350	947	34, 839	30, 536	87. 6	23, 454	7, 082	1, 290	2, 130	883
Camden, N. J	58, 802	56, 781	96. 6	50, 989	5, 792	577	942	502	38, 817	36, 870	95. 0	31, 165	5, 705	567	901	479
Canton, Ohio	54, 285	52, 134	96. 0	47, 859	4, 275	1, 038	906	207	36, 550	34, 471	94. 3	30, 261	4, 210	1, 038	846	195
Charlotte, N. C	47, 662	47, 459	99. 6	47, 142	317	47	56	100	30, 359	30, 171	99. 4	29, 859	312	46	48	94
Chattanooga, Tenn	61, 246	61, 076	99. 7	60, 631	445	51	38	81	38, 779	38, 625	99. 6	38, 186	439	50	31	73
Chicago, Ill	1, 681, 665	1, 599, 377	95. 1	1, 325, 165	274, 212	34, 752	38, 767	8, 769	1, 181, 374	1, 102, 841	93. 4	832, 018	270, 823	34, 363	35, 748	8, 422
Cincinnati, Ohio	217, 082	213, 708	98. 4	203, 798	9, 910	1, 091	919	1, 364	152, 374	149, 227	97. 9	139, 453	9, 774	1, 047	796	1, 304
Cleveland, Ohio	438, 346	409, 577	93. 4	343, 867	65, 710	13, 253	11, 848	3, 668	303, 803	275, 884	90. 8	211, 085	64, 799	13, 165	11, 208	3, 546
Columbus, Ohio	148, 971	146, 724	98. 5	142, 347	4, 377	592	843	812	104, 023	101, 866	97. 9	97, 570	4, 296	577	793	787
Dallas, Tex	139, 759	137, 841	98. 6	135, 740	2, 101	387	1, 109	422	95, 752	93, 932	98. 1	91, 851	2, 081	377	1, 045	398
Dayton, Ohio	103, 358	102, 007	98. 7	98, 312	3, 695	528	439	384	71, 500	70, 202	98. 2	66, 555	3, 647	522	403	373
Denver, Colo	155, 635	151, 564	97. 4	142, 471	9, 093	1, 169	1, 928	974	108, 372	104, 393	96. 3	95, 375	9, 018	1, 165	1, 873	941
Des Moines, Iowa	75, 879	74, 901	98. 7	71, 894	3, 007	189	288	501	51, 136	50, 207	98. 2	47, 231	2, 976	186	258	485
Detroit, Mich	827, 499	775, 011	93. 7	653, 994	121, 017	24, 753	23, 465	4, 270	559, 292	510, 475	91. 3	392, 848	117, 627	24, 428	20, 450	3, 939
Duluth, Minn	50, 586	47, 886	94. 7	39, 510	8, 376	921	1, 443	336	34, 493	31, 840	92. 3	23, 515	8, 325	914	1, 415	324
Elizabeth, N. J	54, 878	51, 128	93. 2	43, 050	8, 078	1, 258	1, 519	973	37, 349	33, 778	90. 4	25, 862	7, 916	1, 242	1, 415	914
Erie, Pa	58, 082	56, 067	96. 5	50, 604	5, 463	856	735	424	37, 880	35, 921	94. 8	30, 537	5, 384	850	701	408
Fall River, Mass	55, 542	50, 308	90. 6	43, 832	6, 476	964	3, 562	708	35, 186	30, 060	85. 4	23, 626	6, 434	958	3, 482	686
Flint, Mich	75, 976	73, 721	97. 0	67, 332	6, 389	1, 024	710	521	48, 336	46, 261	95. 7	40, 066	6, 195	1, 009	596	470
Fort Wayne, Ind	56, 915	56, 298	98. 9	54, 534	1, 764	245	148	224	38, 288	37, 697	98. 5	35, 963	1, 734	242	136	213
Fort Worth, Tex	85, 061	84, 081	98. 8	83, 143	938	138	677	165	56, 951	56, 016	94. 4	55, 087	929	136	645	154
Gary, Ind	58, 075	55, 261	95. 2	47, 752	7, 509	1, 124	1, 402	288	39, 173	36, 483	93. 1	29, 140	7, 343	1, 113	1, 315	262
Grand Rapids, Mich	79, 418	76, 459	96. 3	68, 770	7, 689	1, 096	993	870	52, 770	49, 885	94. 5	42, 269	7, 616	1, 094	935	856
Hartford, Conn	80, 509	73, 561	91. 4	61, 870	11, 691	2, 147	3, 102	1, 699	55, 305	48, 681	88. 0	37, 187	11, 494	2, 113	2, 012	1, 590
Houston, Tex	188, 318	184, 279	97. 9	179, 845	4, 434	664	2, 388	987	130, 301	126, 488	97. 1	122, 103	4, 385	640	2, 237	936
Indianapolis, Ind	185, 461	183, 881	99. 1	179, 859	4, 022	552	450	578	127, 629	126, 123	98. 8	122, 156	3, 967	543	402	561
Jacksonville, Fla	82, 798	82, 177	99. 2	80, 522	1, 655	190	232	199	55, 350	54, 763	98. 9	53, 122	1, 641	187	213	187
Jersey City, N. J	149, 703	143, 691	96. 0	122, 341	21, 350	1, 752	2, 636	1, 624	100, 318	94, 613	94. 3	73, 604	21, 009	1, 739	2, 396	1, 570
Kansas City, Kans	59, 432	58, 037	97. 7	55, 926	2, 111	313	858	224	38, 557	37, 186	96. 4	35, 094	2, 092	313	838	220
Kansas City, Mo	190, 117	186, 426	98. 1	179, 651	6, 775	1, 204	1, 618	869	136, 040	133, 387	97. 4	126, 665	6, 722	1, 192	1, 526	845
Knoxville, Tenn	52, 708	52, 572	99. 7	52, 287	285	28	33	75	32, 851	32, 724	99. 6	32, 442	282	27	32	68
Long Beach, Calif	77, 593	75, 644	97. 5	71, 531	4, 113	613	864	472	57, 434	55, 592	96. 8	51, 549	4, 043	600	801	441
Los Angeles, Calif	734, 135	684, 280	93. 2	618, 994	65, 286	12, 582	33, 409	3, 864	543, 610	496, 506	91. 3	432, 208	64, 298	12, 339	31, 158	3, 607
Louisville, Ky	152, 267	151, 438	99. 5	149, 031	2, 407	252	217	360	102, 626	101, 847	99. 2	99, 464	2, 383	239	192	348
Lowell, Mass	49, 016	45, 577	93. 0	39, 962	5, 615	953	1, 674	812	30, 990	27, 637	89. 2	22, 081	5, 556	943	1, 623	787
Memphis, Tenn	139, 238	138, 290	99. 3	136, 747	1, 543	305	410	233	95, 414	94, 500	99. 0	92, 969	1, 531	298	388	228
Miami, Fla	84, 587	80, 835	95. 6	76, 094	4, 741	868	2, 040	844	61, 304	57, 784	94. 3	53, 090	4, 694	855	1, 893	772
Milwaukee, Wis	289, 118	279, 384	96. 6	243, 595	35, 789	4, 435	3, 971	1, 328	198, 818	189, 487	95. 3	154, 201	35, 286	4, 394	3, 659	1, 278
Minneapolis, Minn	234, 542	227, 058	96. 8	199, 942	27, 116	2, 854	2, 811	1, 819	163, 726	156, 431	95. 5	129, 525	26, 906	2, 836	2, 684	1, 775
Nashville, Tenn	77, 490	77, 226	99. 6	76, 666	560	65	72	136	50, 512	50, 268	99. 5	49, 721	547	59	62	123
Newark, N. J	213, 840	196, 401	91. 8	166, 611	29, 790	4, 926	7, 965	4, 548	144, 374	127, 695	88. 4	98, 391	29, 304	4, 860	7, 485	4, 334
New Bedford, Mass	53, 401	46, 997	88. 0	38, 600	8, 397	1, 453	4, 205	746	35, 684	29, 414	82. 4	21, 068	8, 346	1, 445	4, 113	712
New Haven, Conn	78, 333	72, 525	92. 6	61, 654	10, 871	1, 549	3, 262	997	52, 721	47, 060	89. 3	36, 323	10, 737	1, 538	3, 153	970
New Orleans, La	234, 277	231, 813	98. 9	225, 581	6, 232	776	1, 340	348	153, 591	151, 260	98. 5	145, 109	6, 151	766	1, 229	336
New York, N. Y	3, 676, 293	3, 334, 268	90. 7	2, 585, 482	748, 786	109, 581	181, 304	51, 140	2, 570, 647	2, 240, 729	87. 5	1, 513, 830	735, 899	107, 288	165, 823	47, 807
Bronx Borough	689, 327	633, 191	91. 9	457, 606	175, 585	19, 816	27, 307	9, 013	473, 892	421, 402	88. 9	248, 929	172, 563	19, 416	24, 547	8, 437
Brooklyn Borough	1, 332, 545	1, 217, 598	91. 4	936, 164	281, 434	31, 985	60, 250	22, 712	896, 844	787, 968	87. 9	511, 277	276, 691	31, 458	55, 975	21, 443
Manhattan Borough	926, 133	796, 731	86. 0	623, 514	173, 217	43, 275	74, 682	11, 445	697, 638	576, 455	82. 6	406, 096	170, 359	42, 181	68, 461	10, 541
Queens Borough	638, 605	601, 487	94. 2	497, 331	104, 156	13, 253	16, 896	6, 969	442, 738	408, 445	92. 3	306, 236	102, 209	13, 002	14, 844	6, 447
Richmond Borough	89, 683	85, 261	95. 1	70, 867	14, 394	1, 252	2, 169	1, 001	59, 535	55, 369	93. 0	41, 292	14, 077	1, 231	1, 996	939
Norfolk, Va	72, 949	72, 341	99. 2	70, 833	1, 508	130	237	241	47, 700	47, 135	98. 8	45, 657	1, 478	127	217	221
Oakland, Calif	149, 227	140, 304	94. 0	125, 610	14, 694	2, 746	4, 847	1, 330	109, 485	100, 937	92. 2	86, 450	14, 487	2, 725	4, 565	1, 258
Oklahoma City, Okla	98, 774	98, 191	99. 4	97, 162	1, 029	151	223	209	65, 828	65, 268	99. 1	64, 246	1, 022	149	210	201
Omaha, Nebr	108, 750	106, 002	97. 5	97, 028	8, 974	987	1, 017	744	73, 293	70, 655	96. 4	61, 721	8, 934	977	942	719
Paterson, N. J	69, 505	64, 370	92. 6	51, 828	12, 542	1, 449	3, 076	610	48, 221	43, 291	89. 8	30, 930	12, 361	1, 427	2, 911	592
Peoria, Ill	51, 832	51, 108	98. 6	48, 871	2, 237	270	192	262	37, 024	36, 324	98. 1	34, 115	2, 209	268	175	257
Philadelphia, Pa	942, 550	908, 001	96. 3	795, 707	112, 294	12, 011	14, 089	8, 449	639, 755	606, 488	94. 8	495, 640	110, 848	11, 881	13, 234	8, 152
Pittsburgh, Pa	330, 007	319, 765	96. 9	284, 975	34, 790	4, 630	3, 956	1, 656	220, 654	210, 800	95. 5	176, 478	34, 322	4, 575	3, 076	1, 603
Portland, Oreg	149, 135	141, 305	94. 7	127, 318	13, 987	2, 741	3, 789	1, 300	111, 040	104, 128	93. 3	90, 340	13, 788	2, 709	3, 579	1, 224
Providence, R. I	121, 797	114, 314	93. 9	96, 368	17, 946	2, 160	3, 733	1, 590	80, 549	73, 524	91. 3	55, 782	17, 742	2, 127	3, 363	1, 535
Reading, Pa	53, 954	52, 462	97. 2	49, 657	2, 805	619	587	286	37, 350	35, 893	96. 1	33, 120	2, 773	613	566	278
Richmond, Va	90, 220	89, 570	99. 3	88, 336	1, 234	194	268	188	61, 385	60, 772	99. 0	59, 549	1, 223	190	247	176
Rochester, N. Y	157, 574	150, 640	95. 6	126, 925	23, 715	2, 017	2, 998	1, 919	110, 942	104, 353	94. 1	81, 071	23, 282	1, 988	2, 740	1, 801
Sacramento, Calif	53, 496	49, 276	92. 1	45, 408	3, 868	822	2, 817	581	39, 645	35, 563	89. 7	31, 735	3, 828	815	2, 711	556
St. Louis, Mo	391, 798	381, 786	97. 4	360, 227	21, 559	3, 763	3, 890	2, 359	277, 471	267, 775	96. 5	246, 443	21, 332	3, 735	3, 667	2, 294
St. Paul, Minn	137, 561	133, 565	97. 1	120, 045	13, 520	1, 352	1, 217	1, 427	93, 174	89, 306	95. 8	75, 888	13, 418	1, 342	1, 139	1, 387
Salt Lake City, Utah	73, 229	71, 430	97. 5	66, 574	4, 856	530	777	492	45, 536	43, 806	96. 2	39, 061	4, 745	524	732	474
San Antonio, Tex	123, 508	113, 877	92. 2	110, 234	3, 643	809	8, 427	395	76, 352	67, 258	88. 1	63, 676	3, 582	789	7, 952	353
San Diego, Calif	103, 638	100, 227	96. 7	93, 648	6, 579	884	2, 156	371	72, 717	69, 534	95. 6	63, 087	6, 447	870	1, 985	328
San Francisco, Calif	322, 441	290, 206	90. 0	243, 414	46, 792	10, 067	18, 742	3, 426	251, 440	220, 953	87. 9	174, 706	46, 247	9, 925	17, 304	3, 258
Scranton, Pa	68, 593	65, 645	95. 7	59, 038	6, 607	967	902	1, 079	44, 797	41, 940	93. 6	35, 454	6, 495	955	841	1, 052
Seattle, Wash	183, 526	170, 836	93. 1	148, 468	22, 368	4, 344	6, 713	1, 633	137, 546	125, 439	91. 2	103, 424	22, 015	4, 207	6, 260	1, 550
Somerville, Mass	49, 332	46, 152	93. 6	37, 977	8, 175	1, 086	1, 718	376	31, 825	28, 842	90. 6	20, 829	8, 013	1, 077	1, 563	343
South Bend, Ind	50, 228	48, 990	97. 5	44, 406	4, 584	568	375	295	33, 455	32, 255	96. 4	27, 717	4, 538	567	349	284
Spokane, Wash	60, 416	58, 076	96. 1	53, 074	5, 002	806	1, 057	477	43, 464	41, 205	94. 8	36, 259	4, 946	801	998	460
Springfield, Mass	72, 246	67, 670	93. 7	58, 913	8, 757	1, 325	2, 076	1, 175	49, 513	45, 100	91. 1	36, 445	8, 655	1, 309	1, 989	1, 115
Syracuse, N. Y	100, 296	96, 122	95. 8	85, 911	10, 211	1, 002	2, 071	1, 101	68, 708	64, 759	94. 2	54, 737	10, 022	992	1, 964	1, 053
Tacoma, Wash	55, 038	52, 246	94. 9	46, 078	6, 168	1, 183	1, 184	425	39, 190	36, 492	93. 1	30, 403	6, 089	1, 178	1, 127	393
Tampa, Fla	52, 442	48, 952	93. 3	46, 407	2, 545	696	2, 532	262	35, 964	32, 573	90. 6	30, 057	2, 516	688	2, 459	244
Toledo, Ohio	140, 001	136, 297	97. 4	126, 349	9, 948	1, 757	1, 273	674	97, 164	93, 556	96. 3	83, 715	9, 841	1, 749	1, 198	661
Trenton, N. J	62, 175	59, 211	95. 2	50, 801	8, 410	854	1, 362	748	42, 389	39, 522	93. 2	31, 214	8, 308	844	1, 302	721
Tulsa, Okla	68, 187	67, 752	99. 4	66, 951	801	143	151	141	45, 927	45, 516	99. 1	44, 722	794	141	137	133
Utica, N. Y	48, 857	46, 901	96. 0	39, 772	7, 129	352	1, 312	292	33, 423	31, 499	94. 2	24, 456	7, 043	351	1, 290	283
Washington, D. C	317, 522	312, 529	98. 4	298, 942	13, 587	1, 591	2, 315	1, 087	229, 341	224, 695	98. 0	211, 280	13, 415	1, 559	2, 061	1, 026
Wichita, Kans	54, 996	54, 524	99. 1	53, 817	707	111	216	145	36, 957	36, 509	98. 8	35, 812	697	109	198	141
Wilmington, Del	55, 494	53, 569	96. 5	49, 763	3, 806	555	745	625	38, 002	36, 149	95. 1	32, 387	3, 762	549	710	594
Worcester, Mass	94, 455	86, 945	92. 0	74, 538	12, 407	1, 983	3, 599	1, 928	63, 642	56, 361	88. 6	44, 104	12, 257	1, 972	3, 452	1, 857
Yonkers, N. Y	69, 991	66, 553	95. 1	55, 516	11, 037	1, 067	1, 593	778	46, 903	43, 799	93. 3	32, 989	10, 810	1, 054	1, 399	711
Youngstown, Ohio	84, 652	80, 531	95. 1	69, 773	10, 758	1, 567	1, 735	819	55, 684	51, 702	92. 8	41, 137	10, 565	1, 555	1, 659	768

CHARACTERISTICS OF THE POPULATION

TABLE 56.—FEMALES IN THE POTENTIAL VOTING POPULATION, BY CITIZENSHIP, FOR CITIES OF 100,000 OR MORE: 1940

CITY	FEMALE POPULATION (ALL AGES)								FEMALE POPULATION 21 YEARS AND OVER							
	Females (all ages)	Citizen				Alien		Citizenship not reported	Females 21 years and over	Citizen				Alien		Citizenship not reported
		Number	Percent	Native	Naturalized	First papers	No papers			Number	Percent	Native	Naturalized	First papers	No papers	
Akron, Ohio	123,262	117,914	95.7	111,567	6,347	970	3,467	911	81,437	76,251	93.6	70,058	6,193	962	3,348	876
Albany, N. Y	67,713	65,427	96.6	60,471	4,956	327	1,365	594	49,665	47,497	95.6	42,661	4,836	315	1,288	565
Atlanta, Ga	162,957	162,236	99.6	161,050	1,186	129	349	243	112,174	111,488	99.4	110,325	1,163	124	333	229
Baltimore, Md	436,184	422,857	96.9	406,645	16,212	1,825	8,191	3,311	298,505	285,636	95.7	269,619	16,017	1,778	7,938	3,153
Birmingham, Ala	140,163	139,401	99.5	138,204	1,197	98	371	293	92,626	91,891	99.2	90,702	1,189	98	362	275
Boston, Mass	397,669	354,707	89.2	301,301	53,406	6,306	29,687	6,969	276,236	234,528	84.9	181,934	52,594	6,218	28,734	6,756
Bridgeport, Conn	73,933	65,494	88.6	57,594	7,900	1,059	6,007	1,373	50,877	42,678	83.9	34,934	7,744	1,047	5,817	1,335
Buffalo, N. Y	292,134	278,098	95.2	247,768	30,330	2,555	8,676	2,805	199,239	185,836	93.3	156,324	29,512	2,511	8,203	2,689
Cambridge, Mass	58,400	51,379	88.0	44,670	6,709	921	4,659	1,441	40,592	33,844	83.4	27,269	6,575	910	4,461	1,377
Camden, N. J	58,734	55,593	94.7	51,482	4,111	348	2,077	716	38,926	35,849	92.1	31,826	4,023	346	2,032	699
Canton, Ohio	54,116	52,033	96.2	49,424	2,609	446	1,478	159	36,172	34,171	94.5	31,616	2,555	441	1,412	148
Charlotte, N. C	53,237	53,060	99.7	52,849	211	28	66	83	34,486	34,325	99.5	34,118	207	26	56	79
Chattanooga, Tenn	66,917	66,760	99.8	66,407	353	29	59	69	43,634	43,490	99.7	43,148	342	25	54	65
Chicago, Ill	1,715,143	1,604,631	93.6	1,396,496	208,135	21,612	79,333	9,567	1,216,018	1,109,287	91.2	904,565	204,722	21,196	76,347	9,188
Cincinnati, Ohio	238,528	234,442	98.3	225,914	8,528	814	1,699	1,573	171,902	168,031	97.7	159,655	8,376	783	1,568	1,520
Cleveland, Ohio	439,990	402,124	91.4	354,685	47,439	6,267	27,527	4,072	305,322	268,357	87.9	221,800	46,557	6,196	26,854	3,915
Columbus, Ohio	157,116	154,939	98.6	151,688	3,251	323	1,092	762	111,134	109,044	98.1	105,870	3,174	317	1,050	723
Dallas, Tex	154,975	153,253	98.9	151,599	1,654	172	1,153	397	108,536	106,892	98.5	105,257	1,635	169	1,095	380
Dayton, Ohio	107,360	105,848	98.6	103,045	2,803	342	763	407	74,635	73,178	98.0	70,438	2,740	339	728	390
Denver, Colo	166,777	162,947	97.7	154,959	7,988	570	2,232	1,028	118,139	114,414	96.8	106,493	7,921	558	2,164	1,003
Des Moines, Iowa	83,940	82,911	98.8	80,435	2,476	97	351	581	58,429	57,443	98.3	54,997	2,446	94	331	561
Detroit, Mich	795,953	723,544	90.9	646,770	76,774	11,451	56,119	4,839	529,447	460,826	87.0	387,336	73,490	11,168	52,982	4,471
Duluth, Minn	50,479	49,000	97.1	42,198	6,802	296	887	296	34,490	33,044	95.8	26,310	6,734	291	861	294
Elizabeth, N. J	55,034	49,700	90.3	44,199	5,501	648	3,400	1,286	37,369	32,220	86.2	26,870	5,350	637	3,292	1,220
Erie, Pa	58,873	56,406	95.8	52,762	3,644	474	1,549	444	38,857	36,470	93.9	32,888	3,582	470	1,495	422
Fall River, Mass	59,886	52,575	87.8	46,893	5,682	529	5,740	1,042	39,396	32,196	81.7	26,556	5,640	526	5,651	1,023
Flint, Mich	75,567	72,390	95.8	68,295	4,095	572	2,051	554	47,237	44,240	93.7	40,301	3,939	553	1,926	518
Fort Wayne, Ind	61,495	60,860	99.0	59,464	1,396	151	285	199	42,514	41,906	98.6	40,542	1,364	149	270	189
Fort Worth, Tex	92,601	91,699	99.0	90,955	744	86	686	130	63,405	62,535	98.6	61,796	739	84	660	126
Gary, Ind	53,644	50,406	94.0	46,622	3,784	498	2,432	308	34,228	31,108	90.9	27,495	3,613	491	2,348	281
Grand Rapids, Mich	84,874	81,299	95.8	75,148	6,151	437	2,085	1,053	57,389	53,912	93.9	47,837	6,075	427	2,016	1,034
Hartford, Conn	85,758	76,159	88.8	67,702	8,457	1,304	6,034	2,261	59,889	50,635	84.5	42,385	8,250	1,275	5,816	2,163
Houston, Tex	196,196	192,580	98.2	189,205	3,375	359	2,338	919	134,117	130,750	97.5	127,434	3,316	337	2,183	847
Indianapolis, Ind	201,511	199,855	99.2	196,485	3,370	292	699	665	141,823	140,224	98.9	136,889	3,335	283	661	655
Jacksonville, Fla	90,267	89,664	99.3	88,448	1,216	128	286	189	60,751	60,173	99.0	58,974	1,199	127	270	181
Jersey City, N. J	151,470	142,434	94.0	125,456	16,978	1,261	5,857	1,918	102,636	93,924	91.5	77,280	16,644	1,239	5,620	1,853
Kansas City, Kans	62,026	60,630	97.7	58,929	1,701	143	992	261	41,209	39,846	96.7	38,162	1,684	142	961	260
Kansas City, Mo	209,061	205,375	98.2	200,107	5,268	561	2,182	943	154,052	150,501	97.7	145,271	5,230	544	2,090	917
Knoxville, Tenn	58,872	58,752	99.8	58,550	202	10	49	61	38,379	38,265	99.7	38,066	199	10	47	57
Long Beach, Calif	86,678	84,373	97.3	80,011	4,362	447	1,251	607	65,946	63,774	96.7	59,508	4,266	440	1,161	571
Los Angeles, Calif	770,142	716,699	93.1	658,246	58,453	8,866	40,465	4,112	579,875	529,202	91.3	471,771	57,431	8,655	38,153	3,865
Louisville, Ky	166,810	165,931	99.5	163,801	2,130	150	348	381	115,691	114,871	99.3	112,759	2,112	146	306	368
Lowell, Mass	52,373	47,565	90.8	41,964	5,601	698	2,874	1,236	34,749	30,023	86.4	24,477	5,546	689	2,834	1,203
Memphis, Tenn	153,704	152,792	99.4	151,684	1,108	136	573	203	106,726	105,852	99.2	104,759	1,093	130	547	197
Miami, Fla	87,585	83,408	95.2	79,453	3,955	570	2,591	1,016	63,635	59,664	93.8	55,777	3,887	561	2,451	959
Milwaukee, Wis	298,354	286,101	95.9	259,936	26,165	2,581	8,267	1,405	206,649	194,787	94.3	169,127	25,660	2,551	7,973	1,338
Minneapolis, Minn	257,828	251,487	97.5	228,064	23,423	1,249	3,122	1,970	184,698	178,551	96.7	155,345	23,206	1,233	2,988	1,926
Nashville, Tenn	89,903	89,632	99.7	89,180	452	53	94	124	61,341	61,086	99.6	60,640	446	51	85	119
Newark, N. J	215,920	193,422	89.6	172,278	21,144	2,612	14,379	5,507	146,329	124,628	85.2	103,934	20,694	2,548	13,857	5,296
New Bedford, Mass	56,940	48,296	84.8	40,937	7,359	923	6,508	1,153	39,325	30,831	78.4	23,515	7,316	911	6,467	1,116
New Haven, Conn	82,272	74,362	90.4	66,228	8,134	960	5,804	1,146	56,759	49,007	86.3	40,987	8,020	946	5,693	1,113
New Orleans, La	260,260	257,908	99.1	253,753	4,155	332	1,723	297	177,820	175,577	98.7	171,511	4,066	327	1,638	278
New York, N. Y	3,778,702	3,298,130	87.3	2,730,856	567,274	84,953	330,078	65,541	2,683,986	2,224,960	82.9	1,670,599	554,361	82,734	314,296	61,996
Bronx Borough	705,384	608,078	86.2	473,652	134,426	16,735	68,911	11,660	492,793	399,391	81.0	267,996	131,395	16,345	66,017	11,040
Brooklyn Borough	1,365,740	1,189,886	87.1	984,067	205,819	23,120	123,666	29,060	935,842	766,112	81.9	564,873	201,239	22,657	119,370	27,703
Manhattan Borough	963,791	819,249	85.0	683,515	135,734	34,434	96,390	13,712	732,317	596,032	81.4	463,300	132,732	33,363	90,186	12,736
Queens Borough	659,029	602,265	91.4	521,366	80,899	9,902	37,033	9,829	466,749	412,980	88.5	334,118	78,862	9,023	34,827	9,319
Richmond Borough	84,758	78,652	92.8	68,256	10,396	762	4,073	1,271	56,285	50,445	89.6	40,312	10,133	746	3,896	1,198
Norfolk, Va	71,383	70,775	99.1	69,729	1,046	83	259	266	48,690	48,117	98.8	47,086	1,031	82	237	254
Oakland, Calif	152,936	144,241	94.3	132,012	12,229	1,346	5,968	1,381	113,012	104,644	92.6	92,613	12,031	1,323	5,736	1,309
Oklahoma City, Okla	105,650	105,165	99.5	104,411	754	60	238	187	71,401	70,933	99.3	70,191	742	59	230	179
Omaha, Nebr	115,094	112,013	97.3	104,427	7,586	439	1,877	765	79,327	76,316	96.2	68,805	7,511	435	1,827	749
Paterson, N. J	70,151	63,102	90.0	53,635	9,467	751	5,465	833	49,166	42,325	86.1	33,031	9,294	738	5,295	808
Peoria, Ill	53,255	52,588	98.7	50,734	1,854	163	278	226	37,988	37,352	98.3	35,532	1,820	159	264	223
Philadelphia, Pa	988,784	934,835	94.5	843,081	91,754	11,286	32,081	10,582	686,658	633,981	92.3	543,735	90,246	11,135	31,270	10,272
Pittsburgh, Pa	341,652	328,946	96.3	301,781	27,164	3,716	7,162	1,820	230,739	218,346	94.6	191,664	26,682	3,674	6,930	1,780
Portland, Oreg	156,259	149,727	95.8	138,071	11,656	1,222	3,957	1,353	117,310	111,071	94.7	99,652	11,419	1,209	3,740	1,290
Providence, R. I	131,707	120,824	91.7	105,287	15,537	1,309	7,388	2,180	90,900	80,049	88.1	64,735	15,314	1,505	7,221	2,125
Reading, Pa	56,614	54,806	96.8	53,031	1,775	403	1,094	311	39,954	38,187	95.6	36,443	1,744	396	1,072	209
Richmond, Va	102,822	102,162	99.4	101,219	943	119	347	194	72,214	71,587	99.1	70,657	930	118	321	188
Rochester, N. Y	167,401	157,130	93.9	137,812	19,318	1,617	6,305	2,349	120,292	110,386	91.8	91,522	18,864	1,590	6,059	2,257
Sacramento, Calif	52,462	49,562	94.5	46,830	2,732	282	2,100	518	38,041	35,248	92.7	32,570	2,678	280	2,030	483
St. Louis, Mo	424,250	412,823	97.3	396,174	16,649	1,834	7,021	2,572	307,603	296,482	96.4	280,040	16,442	1,800	6,814	2,507
St. Paul, Minn	150,175	146,000	97.2	133,975	12,025	657	1,730	1,788	105,143	101,084	96.1	89,174	11,910	653	1,665	1,741
Salt Lake City, Utah	76,705	74,756	97.5	69,800	4,956	322	1,054	573	48,834	46,951	96.1	42,099	4,852	313	1,014	556
San Antonio, Tex	130,346	119,083	91.4	115,324	3,759	516	10,143	604	82,980	72,270	87.1	68,590	3,680	499	9,641	564
San Diego, Calif	99,703	95,669	96.0	89,580	6,089	605	2,943	486	72,355	68,543	94.7	62,561	5,982	594	2,765	453
San Francisco, Calif	312,095	285,090	91.3	251,099	33,991	5,561	17,921	3,523	241,530	215,835	89.4	182,421	33,414	5,420	16,935	3,340
Scranton, Pa	71,811	68,192	95.0	62,977	5,215	734	1,592	1,293	47,729	44,200	92.6	39,100	5,100	725	1,538	1,266
Seattle, Wash	184,776	174,882	94.6	156,364	18,518	1,829	6,414	1,651	137,325	127,946	93.2	109,853	18,093	1,788	6,042	1,549
Somerville, Mass	52,845	47,486	89.9	40,301	7,185	745	4,036	578	35,661	30,528	85.6	23,531	6,997	732	3,871	530
South Bend, Ind	51,040	49,164	96.3	45,938	3,226	438	1,141	297	34,380	32,541	94.7	29,377	3,164	434	1,116	289
Spokane, Wash	61,585	59,983	97.4	55,972	4,011	259	860	483	44,035	42,535	96.6	38,604	3,931	252	798	450
Springfield, Mass	77,308	70,686	91.4	63,821	6,865	888	4,251	1,483	54,448	48,001	88.2	41,249	6,752	876	4,140	1,422
Syracuse, N. Y	105,671	100,419	95.0	92,424	7,995	580	3,426	1,246	73,872	68,796	93.1	60,999	7,797	569	3,312	1,195
Tacoma, Wash	54,370	52,049	95.7	47,100	4,949	361	1,518	442	38,631	36,408	94.2	31,539	4,869	352	1,462	409
Tampa, Fla	55,949	52,253	93.4	50,583	1,670	275	3,112	309	38,868	35,292	90.8	33,654	1,638	267	3,031	278
Toledo, Ohio	142,348	138,590	97.4	131,144	7,446	722	2,465	571	98,988	95,325	96.3	87,987	7,338	716	2,391	556
Trenton, N. J	62,522	58,070	92.9	51,989	6,081	501	3,063	888	42,649	38,275	89.7	32,305	5,970	494	3,011	869
Tulsa, Okla	73,970	73,621	99.5	73,012	609	63	163	123	50,799	50,485	99.4	49,887	598	61	143	110
Utica, N. Y	51,661	48,700	94.3	43,394	5,306	243	2,377	341	36,124	33,210	91.9	27,980	5,230	239	2,347	328
Washington, D. C	345,569	339,961	98.4	329,233	10,728	1,083	3,448	1,077	255,307	250,008	97.9	239,557	10,541	1,057	3,210	1,032
Wichita, Kans	59,970	59,570	99.3	58,957	613	48	182	170	41,573	41,194	99.1	40,587	607	47	170	162
Wilmington, Del	57,010	54,768	96.1	52,206	2,562	223	1,280	730	39,443	37,267	94.5	34,741	2,526	219	1,261	696
Worcester, Mass	99,239	89,005	89.7	79,096	9,909	962	6,549	2,723	68,305	58,299	85.4	48,532	9,767	950	6,402	2,648
Yonkers, N. Y	72,607	66,726	91.9	58,266	8,460	831	3,995	1,055	50,342	44,750	88.9	36,508	8,242	806	3,782	1,004
Youngstown, Ohio	83,068	77,987	93.9	71,229	6,758	866	3,411	804	53,899	48,955	90.8	42,373	6,582	861	3,324	759

TABLE 57.--SCHOOL ATTENDANCE BY AGE, FOR CITIES OF 100,000 OR MORE: 1940

CITY	TOTAL PERSONS 5 TO 24 YEARS OLD: Total number	TOTAL PERSONS 5 TO 24 YEARS OLD: Attending school: Number	TOTAL PERSONS 5 TO 24 YEARS OLD: Attending school: Percent	5 AND 6 YEARS OLD: Total number	5 AND 6 YEARS OLD: Attending school: Number	5 AND 6 YEARS OLD: Attending school: Percent	7 TO 13 YEARS OLD: Total number	7 TO 13 YEARS OLD: Attending school: Number	7 TO 13 YEARS OLD: Attending school: Percent	14 AND 15 YEARS OLD: Total number	14 AND 15 YEARS OLD: Attending school: Number	14 AND 15 YEARS OLD: Attending school: Percent	16 TO 20 YEARS OLD: Total number	16 TO 20 YEARS OLD: Attending school: Number	16 TO 20 YEARS OLD: Attending school: Percent	21 TO 24 YEARS OLD: Total number	21 TO 24 YEARS OLD: Attending school: Number	21 TO 24 YEARS OLD: Attending school: Percent
Akron, Ohio	84,691	52,813	62.4	6,401	2,679	41.9	27,308	26,751	98.0	9,039	8,789	97.2	24,135	13,389	55.5	17,808	1,205	6.8
Albany, N. Y	37,573	23,202	61.8	3,033	2,201	72.6	11,820	11,546	97.6	3,697	3,591	97.1	10,144	5,227	51.5	8,870	637	7.2
Atlanta, Ga	101,677	53,867	53.0	8,055	4,284	53.2	31,238	29,932	95.8	9,598	8,143	84.8	28,528	10,214	35.8	24,258	1,294	5.3
Baltimore, Md	282,265	152,797	54.1	22,918	11,184	48.8	89,594	86,962	97.1	28,356	26,265	92.6	77,303	25,276	32.7	64,094	3,110	4.9
Birmingham, Ala	93,948	52,662	56.1	7,682	2,560	33.3	30,915	29,870	96.6	9,521	8,700	92.3	25,455	10,540	41.4	20,375	893	4.4
Boston, Mass	248,146	154,515	62.3	20,461	14,644	71.6	82,186	80,709	98.2	25,054	24,353	97.2	66,484	30,767	46.3	53,961	4,042	7.5
Bridgeport, Conn	49,479	28,155	56.9	3,514	2,829	80.5	15,103	14,843	98.3	4,925	4,791	97.3	13,877	5,211	37.6	12,060	481	4.0
Buffalo, N. Y	188,843	112,688	59.7	15,243	10,160	66.7	61,031	59,125	96.9	19,482	18,706	96.0	51,609	22,563	43.7	41,478	2,134	5.1
Cambridge, Mass	36,182	22,566	62.4	2,847	2,171	76.3	11,903	11,655	97.9	3,614	3,489	96.5	9,710	4,494	46.3	8,108	757	9.3
Camden, N. J	41,220	21,745	52.8	3,055	1,470	48.1	13,053	12,549	96.1	4,190	3,999	95.2	11,521	3,456	30.0	9,392	271	2.9
Canton, Ohio	36,194	20,811	57.5	2,780	947	34.0	11,156	10,945	98.1	3,815	3,727	97.7	10,175	4,827	47.4	8,250	365	4.4
Charlotte, N. C	37,373	19,061	51.0	2,960	889	30.0	11,285	10,973	97.2	3,542	3,124	88.2	10,377	3,776	36.4	9,209	299	3.2
Chattanooga, Tenn	45,921	24,052	52.4	3,939	1,211	30.7	14,868	14,260	95.9	4,626	4,067	87.9	12,516	4,200	33.6	9,972	314	3.1
Chicago, Ill	1,037,666	600,426	57.9	80,929	45,733	56.5	325,414	317,932	97.7	101,816	98,454	96.7	278,121	123,208	44.3	251,386	15,099	6.0
Cincinnati, Ohio	133,495	78,426	58.7	10,782	4,961	46.0	43,291	42,260	97.6	13,203	12,713	96.3	35,778	16,046	44.8	30,441	2,446	8.0
Cleveland, Ohio	282,560	163,332	57.8	20,374	13,460	66.1	84,930	83,104	97.8	28,880	28,145	97.5	79,005	35,318	44.7	69,371	3,305	4.8
Columbus, Ohio	93,785	52,501	56.0	7,300	3,003	41.1	29,102	28,058	96.4	9,315	8,748	93.9	25,621	11,051	43.1	22,447	1,641	7.3
Dallas, Texas	94,170	48,215	51.2	7,525	1,650	21.9	28,606	27,396	95.8	9,237	8,353	90.4	26,049	9,784	37.6	22,753	1,032	4.5
Dayton, Ohio	65,328	35,896	54.9	5,428	1,715	31.6	20,498	19,960	97.4	6,199	5,930	95.8	17,357	7,584	43.7	15,846	698	4.4
Denver, Colo	97,316	58,684	60.3	8,164	5,301	64.9	30,733	29,635	96.4	9,331	8,757	93.8	26,437	12,893	48.8	22,651	2,098	9.3
Des Moines, Iowa	50,794	30,565	60.2	4,206	3,562	82.9	15,420	15,065	97.7	4,909	4,718	96.1	14,146	6,387	45.2	12,023	833	6.9
Detroit, Mich	539,069	323,891	60.1	43,252	31,230	72.2	177,667	173,836	97.8	55,341	53,583	96.8	141,064	59,457	42.1	121,745	5,785	4.8
Duluth, Minn	32,402	21,118	65.2	2,532	1,881	74.3	10,215	10,060	98.5	3,346	3,276	97.9	9,079	5,264	58.0	7,230	637	8.8
Elizabeth, N. J	37,606	21,315	56.7	2,642	1,764	66.8	11,598	11,264	97.1	3,781	3,638	96.2	10,506	4,224	40.2	9,079	425	4.7
Erie, Pa	40,828	24,136	59.1	3,177	1,390	43.8	13,275	12,886	97.1	4,305	4,175	97.0	11,062	5,252	47.5	9,000	433	4.8
Fall River, Mass	41,557	22,404	53.9	3,201	1,738	54.3	13,426	13,141	97.9	4,675	4,511	96.5	11,859	2,870	24.2	8,396	144	1.7
Flint, Mich	53,945	35,753	66.3	4,825	3,944	81.7	19,081	18,840	98.7	5,640	5,527	98.0	13,695	6,989	51.0	10,704	453	4.2
Fort Wayne, Ind	38,195	22,886	59.9	2,945	1,841	62.5	12,587	12,078	96.0	4,112	3,856	93.8	10,142	4,643	45.8	8,409	468	5.6
Fort Worth, Texas	58,153	32,723	56.3	4,533	1,648	36.4	18,637	18,101	97.1	6,070	5,492	90.5	16,349	6,717	41.1	12,564	765	6.1
Gary, Ind	38,985	23,208	59.5	3,154	1,695	53.7	12,565	12,242	97.4	3,843	3,754	97.7	10,220	5,124	50.1	9,203	393	4.3
Grand Rapids, Mich	54,005	33,941	62.8	4,434	3,371	76.0	17,783	17,369	97.7	5,652	5,481	97.0	14,398	7,032	48.8	11,738	688	5.9
Hartford, Conn	54,478	30,838	56.6	3,932	2,829	71.9	16,357	16,008	97.9	5,303	5,132	96.8	15,377	6,248	40.6	13,509	621	4.6
Houston, Texas	124,517	66,044	53.0	10,029	4,131	41.2	38,168	36,961	96.8	11,468	10,533	91.8	33,507	12,886	38.4	31,255	1,533	4.9
Indianapolis, Ind	118,519	67,449	56.9	9,650	3,841	39.8	38,036	37,097	97.5	11,689	11,226	96.0	31,870	13,618	42.7	27,265	1,667	6.1
Jacksonville, Fla	58,584	31,838	54.3	4,803	1,650	34.4	19,093	18,529	97.0	5,554	5,123	92.2	15,592	6,045	38.8	13,542	491	3.6
Jersey City, N. J	103,836	59,159	57.0	7,540	5,003	66.4	32,596	31,889	97.8	10,688	10,256	96.0	29,254	11,014	37.6	23,758	997	4.2
Kansas City, Kans	41,279	24,928	60.4	3,578	2,238	62.5	13,585	13,250	97.5	4,320	4,025	93.2	11,342	4,945	43.6	8,454	470	5.6
Kansas City, Mo	112,426	63,980	56.9	8,865	6,487	73.2	34,362	33,443	97.3	10,803	10,214	94.5	31,024	12,542	40.4	27,372	1,294	4.7
Knoxville, Tenn	40,138	21,955	54.7	3,635	1,006	27.7	13,353	12,947	97.0	3,914	3,523	90.0	10,602	3,949	37.2	8,634	530	6.1
Long Beach, Calif	42,329	26,091	61.6	3,354	2,509	74.8	12,351	12,069	97.7	4,300	4,171	97.0	11,369	6,482	57.0	10,955	860	7.9
Los Angeles, Calif	399,139	244,024	61.1	31,301	22,645	72.3	119,704	117,104	97.8	39,147	38,059	97.2	106,667	57,562	54.0	102,320	8,654	8.5
Louisville, Ky	100,750	56,995	56.6	8,429	4,161	49.4	33,247	32,202	96.9	10,243	9,598	93.7	26,881	9,870	36.7	21,950	1,164	5.3
Lowell, Mass	35,719	22,002	61.6	2,918	1,826	62.6	12,061	11,848	98.2	3,740	3,631	97.1	10,003	4,325	43.2	6,997	372	5.3
Memphis, Tenn	93,162	49,507	53.1	7,400	2,612	35.3	29,547	28,335	95.9	9,110	8,234	90.3	24,987	9,341	37.4	22,112	985	4.5
Miami, Fla	50,111	26,419	52.7	3,728	1,528	41.0	15,599	15,132	97.0	4,643	4,328	93.2	13,135	5,038	38.4	13,006	393	3.0
Milwaukee, Wis	184,238	120,043	65.2	15,141	11,548	76.3	60,470	59,617	98.6	18,507	18,201	98.3	48,393	27,443	56.7	41,727	3,234	7.8
Minneapolis, Minn	150,650	92,949	61.7	11,262	9,047	80.3	44,744	43,899	98.1	14,726	14,357	97.5	42,098	21,931	52.1	37,820	3,715	9.8
Nashville, Tenn	56,755	30,687	54.1	4,713	1,556	33.0	17,928	17,347	96.8	5,471	4,970	90.8	15,633	6,035	38.6	13,010	779	6.0
Newark, N. J	146,094	82,663	56.6	10,763	7,688	71.4	46,571	45,204	97.1	15,047	14,246	94.7	40,688	14,165	34.8	33,025	1,360	4.1
New Bedford, Mass	36,538	19,998	54.7	2,684	1,814	67.6	11,324	10,853	95.8	4,102	3,828	93.3	10,612	3,270	30.8	7,816	233	3.0
New Haven, Conn	54,285	32,408	59.7	3,964	3,107	78.4	16,715	16,321	97.6	5,654	5,502	97.3	15,211	6,632	43.6	12,741	846	6.6
New Orleans, La	163,315	95,138	58.3	12,918	8,314	64.4	54,054	52,392	96.9	17,448	15,785	90.5	45,622	16,988	37.2	33,273	1,659	5.0
New York, N. Y	2,287,759	1,350,041	59.0	177,086	102,925	58.1	741,268	718,336	96.9	228,199	219,882	96.4	619,915	276,644	44.6	521,291	32,254	6.2
Bronx Borough	439,979	267,230	60.7	34,229	20,319	59.4	145,580	141,506	97.2	44,739	43,293	96.8	118,880	55,856	47.0	96,551	6,265	6.5
Brooklyn Borough	896,946	530,075	59.1	69,164	40,503	58.6	291,032	282,723	97.1	91,100	87,928	96.5	245,474	106,561	43.4	200,176	12,360	6.2
Manhattan Borough	499,192	279,004	55.9	36,608	20,125	55.0	152,191	146,799	96.5	46,523	44,604	95.9	135,797	58,688	43.2	128,073	8,788	6.9
Queens Borough	391,345	236,831	60.5	32,351	18,986	58.7	132,304	127,539	96.4	39,596	37,975	95.9	103,256	48,083	46.6	83,838	4,248	5.1
Richmond Borough	60,297	36,892	61.2	4,734	2,992	63.2	20,161	19,769	98.1	6,241	6,082	97.5	16,508	7,456	45.2	12,653	593	4.7
Norfolk, Va	50,423	25,308	50.2	3,757	1,486	39.6	14,609	14,174	97.0	4,440	4,108	92.5	15,629	5,111	32.7	11,988	429	3.6
Oakland, Calif	82,251	50,677	61.6	6,447	4,098	63.6	24,401	23,820	97.6	8,152	7,949	97.5	23,329	13,018	55.8	19,922	1,792	9.0
Oklahoma City, Okla	67,261	40,326	60.0	6,157	3,907	63.5	21,709	21,110	97.3	6,362	5,966	93.8	17,614	8,210	46.7	15,419	1,115	7.2
Omaha, Nebr	71,342	45,803	64.2	5,930	4,969	83.8	23,141	22,738	98.3	7,260	7,067	97.3	19,375	9,878	51.0	15,636	1,151	7.4
Paterson, N. J	44,303	25,157	56.8	3,408	2,858	83.9	14,173	13,754	97.0	4,479	4,208	93.9	12,287	3,984	32.4	9,956	353	3.5
Peoria, Ill	31,062	16,744	53.9	2,499	1,334	53.4	9,503	9,234	97.2	2,900	2,716	93.7	8,238	3,116	37.8	7,922	344	4.3
Philadelphia, Pa	620,737	352,778	56.8	49,451	25,463	51.5	201,211	195,170	97.0	62,975	60,652	96.3	169,082	65,837	38.9	138,018	5,656	4.1
Pittsburgh, Pa	227,093	135,013	59.5	16,872	9,254	54.8	73,082	71,610	98.0	23,667	23,095	97.6	62,388	28,494	45.7	51,084	2,560	5.0
Portland, Oreg	81,216	47,567	58.6	5,780	2,926	50.6	22,915	22,301	97.3	7,882	7,582	96.2	23,877	12,669	53.1	20,762	2,089	10.1
Providence, R. I	84,746	49,706	58.7	6,429	4,405	68.5	27,015	26,474	98.0	9,049	8,784	97.1	23,911	8,980	37.6	18,342	1,063	5.8
Reading, Pa	35,049	19,471	55.6	2,669	1,388	52.0	11,038	10,770	97.6	3,617	3,501	96.8	9,819	3,589	36.6	7,906	223	2.8
Richmond, Va	64,029	34,009	53.1	4,618	2,223	48.1	19,139	18,586	97.1	6,342	5,774	91.0	18,086	6,662	36.8	15,844	764	4.8
Rochester, N. Y	100,410	60,441	60.2	7,325	5,012	68.4	30,258	29,372	97.1	10,136	9,784	96.5	27,964	14,314	51.2	24,727	1,959	7.9
Sacramento, Calif	30,293	18,757	61.9	2,158	1,441	66.8	8,720	8,532	97.8	2,902	2,825	97.3	8,614	5,237	60.8	7,899	722	9.1
St. Louis, Mo	237,526	135,467	57.0	19,259	14,509	75.3	76,309	74,353	97.4	23,617	21,755	92.1	63,459	22,574	35.6	54,882	2,276	4.1
St. Paul, Minn	90,518	56,157	62.0	7,272	5,191	71.4	28,413	27,929	98.3	8,965	8,710	97.2	24,461	12,472	51.0	21,407	1,855	8.7
Salt Lake City, Utah	54,178	34,402	63.5	4,844	2,941	60.7	17,702	17,366	98.1	5,450	5,318	97.6	14,386	7,630	53.0	11,796	1,147	9.7
San Antonio, Tex	92,897	47,308	50.9	8,208	1,959	23.9	30,255	28,584	94.5	9,022	7,580	84.0	26,054	8,480	32.5	19,358	705	3.6
San Diego, Calif	61,250	34,129	55.7	4,844	3,468	71.6	16,492	16,110	97.7	5,176	5,048	97.5	18,153	8,165	45.0	16,585	1,338	8.1
San Francisco, Calif	151,349	90,231	59.6	10,959	7,113	64.9	43,233	42,000	97.1	14,133	13,692	96.9	42,908	23,717	55.3	40,116	3,709	9.2
Scranton, Pa	49,488	28,812	58.2	3,837	2,328	60.7	15,741	15,380	97.7	5,359	5,161	96.3	13,754	5,549	40.3	10,797	394	3.6
Seattle, Wash	99,147	61,771	62.3	7,315	4,708	64.3	28,321	27,648	97.6	9,525	9,210	96.7	28,637	16,993	59.3	25,349	3,217	12.7
Somerville, Mass	33,842	21,309	63.0	3,106	1,924	61.9	11,686	11,457	98.0	3,449	3,364	97.5	8,761	4,203	48.0	6,840	361	5.3
South Bend, Ind	33,931	20,887	61.6	2,537	1,475	58.1	11,214	11,043	98.5	3,664	3,591	98.0	9,226	4,346	47.1	7,200	432	5.9
Spokane, Wash	35,405	20,853	58.9	2,796	1,159	41.5	10,326	10,112	97.9	3,349	3,251	97.1	10,317	5,487	53.2	8,617	844	9.8
Springfield, Mass	47,116	28,698	60.9	3,462	2,750	79.4	15,038	14,708	97.8	5,036	4,862	96.5	13,244	5,825	44.0	10,336	553	5.4
Syracuse, N. Y	65,409	41,121	62.9	4,906	3,955	80.6	20,762	20,188	97.2	6,746	6,485	96.1	18,361	9,331	50.8	14,634	1,162	7.9
Tacoma, Wash	32,174	19,263	59.9	2,520	763	30.3	10,110	9,753	96.5	3,399	3,242	95.4	8,901	4,877	54.8	7,244	628	8.7
Tampa, Fla	34,973	19,822	56.7	2,579	1,126	43.7	11,344	11,070	97.6	3,688	3,453	93.6	9,568	3,919	41.0	7,794	254	3.3
Toledo, Ohio	87,247	52,730	60.4	6,812	3,700	54.3	28,059	27,447	97.8	9,086	8,831	97.2	23,813	11,643	48.9	19,477	1,109	5.7
Trenton, N. J	42,500	24,098	56.7	2,949	2,106	71.4	12,939	12,641	97.7	4,454	4,162	93.4	12,206	4,744	38.9	9,952	445	4.5
Tulsa, Okla	45,963	27,896	60.7	3,849	2,462	64.0	14,473	14,085	97.3	4,647	4,441	95.6	12,541	6,229	49.7	10,453	679	6.5
Utica, N. Y	31,774	19,140	60.2	2,469	1,898	76.9	9,906	9,608	97.0	3,287	3,182	96.8	8,923	4,051	45.4	7,189	401	5.6
Washington, D. C	192,497	110,040	57.2	14,499	8,950	61.7	55,253	53,901	97.6	17,456	16,806	96.3	51,294	24,054	46.9	53,995	6,329	11.7
Wichita, Kans	36,731	22,118	60.2	3,053	2,020	66.2	11,267	11,038	98.0	3,550	3,363	94.7	10,297	4,990	48.5	8,564	707	8.3
Wilmington, Del	36,687	20,089	54.8	2,799	1,323	47.3	11,244	10,987	97.7	3,451	3,319	96.2	10,343	4,018	38.8	8,850	442	5.0
Worcester, Mass	63,628	38,789	61.0	4,874	3,581	73.5	20,403	19,686	96.5	6,530	6,235	95.5	17,655	8,295	47.0	14,166	992	7.0
Yonkers, N. Y	46,096	30,180	65.5	3,656	2,831	77.4	15,519	15,266	98.4	4,797	4,708	98.1	12,466	6,598	52.9	9,658	777	8.0
Youngstown, Ohio	60,850	35,664	58.6	4,218	1,642	38.9	18,977	18,568	97.8	6,516	6,304	97.7	17,323	8,388	48.4	13,816	702	5.1

TABLE 58.—PERSONS 25 YEARS OLD AND OVER, BY YEARS OF SCHOOL COMPLETED, FOR CITIES OF 100,000 OR MORE: 1940

CITY	Persons 25 years old and over	No school years completed	GRADE SCHOOL			HIGH SCHOOL		COLLEGE		Not reported	Median school years completed
			1 to 4 years	5 and 6 years	7 and 8 years	1 to 3 years	4 years	1 to 3 years	4 years or more		
Akron, Ohio	143, 734	3, 129	7, 739	12, 809	51, 644	20, 880	25, 903	7, 961	6, 838	831	8. 8
Albany, N. Y	85, 588	2, 198	4, 625	7, 728	30, 795	14, 068	16, 516	3, 629	5, 438	591	8. 8
Atlanta, Ga	179, 844	5, 309	25, 383	28, 008	37, 287	27, 921	30, 861	13, 191	10, 833	1, 051	8. 6
Baltimore, Md	520, 682	17, 675	65, 942	95, 266	163, 308	69, 439	58, 771	17, 568	22, 079	10, 634	7. 9
Birmingham, Ala	154, 412	6, 205	21, 926	21, 382	36, 769	23, 454	25, 314	10, 142	8, 221	900	8. 5
Boston, Mass	472, 964	24, 134	29, 153	34, 440	151, 645	78, 076	101, 945	21, 209	25, 110	7, 252	8. 9
Bridgeport, Conn	88, 575	4, 908	6, 145	9, 421	40, 206	10, 443	10, 485	2, 763	2, 832	1, 282	8. 1
Buffalo, N. Y	349, 722	11, 607	25, 118	35, 784	140, 176	63, 163	43, 042	11, 878	14, 756	4, 198	8. 4
Cambridge, Mass	67, 323	2, 293	3, 521	5, 027	21, 543	9, 370	13, 354	3, 260	6, 371	2, 578	9. 0
Camden, N. J	68, 351	3, 981	8, 156	11, 527	26, 074	9, 161	5, 300	1, 209	1, 356	1, 587	7. 7
Canton, Ohio	64, 463	2, 118	4, 174	6, 503	25, 063	11, 100	10, 261	2, 796	2, 225	223	8. 5
Charlotte, N. C	55, 636	2, 207	7, 430	7, 505	9, 727	8, 325	10, 101	5, 465	4, 488	388	9. 3
Chattanooga, Tenn	72, 441	2, 541	10, 309	12, 115	17, 891	10, 787	10, 876	3, 951	3, 129	842	8. 2
Chicago, Ill	2, 140, 006	88, 744	160, 019	185, 493	851, 311	327, 206	315, 844	108, 723	98, 901	9, 765	8. 5
Cincinnati, Ohio	293, 835	4, 134	24, 515	38, 714	103, 815	46, 138	40, 457	13, 742	17, 024	5, 296	8. 5
Cleveland, Ohio	539, 754	25, 880	54, 604	78, 206	170, 214	95, 050	75, 248	19, 188	17, 403	3, 961	8. 3
Columbus, Ohio	192, 710	2, 959	9, 689	18, 756	59, 243	35, 142	40, 894	11, 797	11, 870	2, 360	9. 4
Dallas, Texas	181, 535	3, 874	13, 300	19, 258	37, 447	35, 341	43, 531	16, 924	10, 736	1, 124	10. 4
Dayton, Ohio	130, 289	1, 325	6, 748	12, 689	47, 257	24, 964	24, 374	6, 396	5, 425	1, 111	8. 9
Denver, Colo	203, 860	3, 769	8, 803	12, 320	61, 584	33, 162	46, 196	18, 776	16, 621	2, 629	10. 3
Des Moines, Iowa	97, 542	858	3, 350	6, 016	26, 770	16, 934	25, 147	9, 437	7, 340	1, 690	10. 9
Detroit, Mich	966, 994	30, 424	86, 226	102, 645	314, 020	182, 265	160, 046	46, 310	41, 230	3, 828	8. 7
Duluth, Minn	61, 753	1, 376	3, 850	5, 382	22, 353	10, 060	10, 431	4, 036	3, 211	454	8. 8
Elizabeth, N. J	65, 639	4, 898	5, 436	6, 995	23, 534	9, 203	9, 029	2, 583	3, 077	884	8. 3
Erie, Pa	67, 728	2, 445	4, 995	6, 667	24, 320	11, 543	11, 328	2, 847	2, 891	692	8. 6
Fall River, Mass	66, 186	5, 687	8, 058	12, 515	22, 787	7, 091	5, 351	1, 621	1, 532	1, 544	7. 5
Flint, Mich	84, 869	1, 313	4, 708	7, 176	28, 464	10, 590	15, 118	4, 886	3, 063	551	9. 1
Fort Wayne, Ind	72, 393	449	2, 326	5, 399	20, 792	12, 213	13, 123	4, 413	3, 482	1, 106	8. 8
Fort Worth, Texas	107, 792	1, 879	8, 394	12, 824	23, 880	22, 628	21, 131	9, 961	6, 544	545	9. 9
Gary, Ind	64, 198	3, 094	7, 001	7, 061	20, 438	10, 562	10, 161	3, 123	2, 491	267	8. 4
Grand Rapids, Mich	98, 421	2, 209	4, 985	7, 800	34, 564	20, 421	16, 814	5, 787	4, 333	1, 508	8. 9
Hartford, Conn	101, 685	4, 604	6, 225	6, 954	36, 386	15, 777	16, 558	4, 223	4, 448	6, 510	8. 6
Houston, Texas	233, 163	5, 834	20, 365	29, 200	48, 635	43, 690	45, 490	19, 791	15, 939	4, 219	9. 7
Indianapolis, Ind	242, 187	3, 147	13, 009	19, 442	87, 256	42, 480	45, 187	15, 457	14, 282	1, 927	8. 9
Jacksonville, Fla	102, 559	2, 644	13, 487	15, 127	25, 823	15, 421	16, 932	6, 430	4, 673	2, 022	8. 5
Jersey City, N. J	179, 196	9, 931	13, 662	16, 767	82, 546	24, 015	18, 755	4, 904	5, 958	1, 968	8. 2
Kansas City, Kans	71, 312	1, 726	6, 239	8, 946	25, 797	12, 147	10, 045	3, 552	2, 475	385	8. 4
Kansas City, Mo	263, 629	4, 379	14, 352	20, 483	78, 404	44, 095	60, 076	23, 112	15, 947	2, 181	9. 9
Knoxville, Tenn	62, 596	1, 870	8, 212	10, 287	15, 253	9, 086	9, 377	4, 354	3, 898	259	8. 4
Long Beach, Calif	112, 425	572	2, 614	5, 210	31, 466	22, 757	29, 586	11, 708	7, 680	742	11. 1
Los Angeles, Calif	1, 021, 165	22, 115	47, 406	66, 712	265, 375	186, 113	255, 666	95, 417	72, 648	9, 653	10. 7
Louisville, Ky	196, 367	3, 602	17, 030	23, 355	78, 105	28, 718	25, 908	9, 665	8, 680	1, 164	8. 4
Lowell, Mass	58, 742	3, 023	4, 212	7, 502	20, 287	9, 585	9, 552	1, 805	1, 940	836	8. 4
Memphis, Tenn	180, 028	5, 708	24, 977	25, 973	43, 514	29, 160	29, 080	11, 169	8, 026	1, 821	8. 5
Miami, Fla	111, 933	1, 578	8, 515	11, 723	29, 108	19, 714	24, 090	8, 749	6, 470	1, 986	9. 6
Milwaukee, Wis	363, 740	7, 157	24, 646	43, 412	157, 723	48, 594	48, 674	16, 758	15, 127	1, 649	8. 3
Minneapolis, Minn	310, 604	3, 139	11, 763	20, 005	111, 703	49, 382	67, 476	24, 721	20, 834	1, 491	9. 5
Nashville, Tenn	98, 843	3, 185	11, 516	14, 377	28, 982	14, 888	14, 355	5, 873	4, 886	781	8. 4
Newark, N. J	257, 678	16, 506	24, 882	28, 778	101, 815	31, 967	25, 651	7, 707	8, 935	11, 437	8. 0
New Bedford, Mass	67, 193	7, 216	7, 409	11, 105	25, 339	6, 735	5, 306	1, 585	1, 328	1, 080	7. 6
New Haven, Conn	96, 739	5, 774	7, 137	8, 285	38, 430	11, 418	14, 639	4, 345	5, 400	1, 245	8. 4
New Orleans, La	298, 138	12, 023	48, 298	54, 980	84, 427	31, 292	38, 631	12, 486	14, 077	1, 915	7. 8
New York, N. Y	4, 733, 342	361, 184	340, 551	367, 288	1, 934, 829	600, 541	585, 923	174, 912	206, 091	102, 023	8. 3
Bronx Borough	870, 134	72, 504	66, 493	66, 219	367, 602	110, 602	103, 050	25, 165	39, 213	19, 286	8. 2
Brooklyn Borough	1, 632, 510	187, 044	129, 555	117, 509	649, 607	196, 718	177, 420	48, 883	73, 280	52, 344	8. 1
Manhattan Borough	1, 301, 882	78, 445	107, 290	126, 202	462, 355	154, 675	181, 578	67, 633	107, 182	16, 522	8. 4
Queens Borough	825, 649	19, 362	31, 967	50, 237	406, 605	123, 222	110, 738	29, 701	41, 095	12, 722	8. 5
Richmond Borough	103, 167	3, 829	5, 246	7, 031	48, 600	15, 324	13, 137	3, 530	5, 321	1, 149	8. 4
Norfolk, Va	84, 402	2, 886	11, 419	11, 654	19, 912	13, 455	14, 043	5, 675	4, 404	954	8. 6
Oakland, Calif	202, 575	4, 988	9, 532	13, 196	60, 388	35, 586	49, 927	14, 510	12, 334	2, 114	10. 0
Oklahoma City, Okla	121, 810	1, 303	6, 202	9, 055	30, 668	21, 875	26, 775	13, 457	9, 887	2, 588	10. 7
Omaha, Nebr	136, 984	2, 634	6, 578	8, 962	45, 505	23, 465	29, 808	10, 727	8, 141	1, 074	9. 5
Paterson, N. J	87, 431	6, 372	9, 887	11, 791	36, 372	9, 873	7, 027	2, 341	2, 748	1, 020	7. 8
Peoria, Ill	67, 090	538	3, 107	5, 706	26, 277	10, 821	12, 448	4, 227	3, 324	642	8. 8
Philadelphia, Pa	1, 188, 395	60, 923	96, 600	144, 893	474, 416	170, 118	144, 322	32, 527	44, 156	20, 440	8. 2
Pittsburgh, Pa	400, 309	16, 632	32, 197	48, 362	150, 633	53, 401	58, 295	16, 251	21, 830	2, 708	8. 3
Portland, Oreg	208, 188	2, 369	7, 458	10, 060	68, 384	36, 978	47, 181	19, 469	14, 651	1, 638	10. 2
Providence, R. I	153, 107	9, 455	12, 936	15, 122	56, 346	22, 270	22, 206	5, 625	8, 190	957	8. 4
Reading, Pa	69, 398	1, 739	7, 607	12, 831	25, 278	10, 528	7, 303	1, 493	1, 931	628	8. 0
Richmond, Va	117, 755	3, 333	14, 807	16, 610	26, 621	20, 863	20, 360	8, 128	6, 724	300	8. 8
Rochester, N. Y	206, 507	9, 458	13, 975	18, 057	75, 013	36, 683	29, 604	7, 602	9, 151	6, 964	8. 6
Sacramento, Calif	69, 787	1, 542	3, 588	4, 615	20, 487	12, 683	15, 565	6, 217	4, 789	301	10. 1
St. Louis, Mo	530, 192	11, 788	44, 305	66, 954	243, 125	65, 402	56, 277	18, 577	19, 465	4, 290	8. 2
St. Paul, Minn	176, 910	2, 504	7, 166	11, 887	71, 100	27, 706	33, 017	11, 772	10, 687	1, 072	8. 9
Salt Lake City, Utah	82, 574	800	2, 739	4, 515	21, 083	14, 755	20, 488	10, 130	7, 491	573	11. 4
San Antonio, Texas	139, 974	11, 388	22, 071	19, 674	28, 760	18, 759	21, 859	9, 282	7, 435	746	8. 1
San Diego, Calif	128, 487	1, 826	5, 451	7, 949	33, 800	26, 437	31, 121	12, 279	9, 051	573	10. 7
San Francisco, Calif	452, 854	9, 127	25, 200	30, 045	143, 563	73, 514	104, 564	30, 735	29, 542	6, 564	9. 6
Scranton, Pa	81, 729	5, 215	8, 801	9, 503	28, 647	10, 591	11, 342	2, 659	3, 324	1, 647	8. 2
Seattle, Wash	249, 522	3, 132	8, 969	12, 131	75, 166	40, 978	63, 173	23, 745	20, 774	1, 454	10. 8
Somerville, Mass	60, 646	1, 388	3, 205	5, 607	18, 773	13, 757	13, 090	2, 042	2, 225	559	9. 2
South Bend, Ind	60, 545	819	3, 077	7, 786	20, 245	10, 951	10, 077	3, 297	3, 055	338	8. 7
Spokane, Wash	78, 882	804	3, 223	4, 354	26, 008	13, 542	17, 887	7, 440	5, 097	518	10. 1
Springfield, Mass	93, 625	2, 459	5, 349	7, 988	24, 458	23, 157	20, 102	4, 673	4, 261	1, 178	9. 8
Syracuse, N. Y	128, 006	4, 669	6, 870	9, 298	44, 586	22, 203	24, 692	6, 112	8, 057	1, 459	8. 9
Tacoma, Wash	70, 577	819	2, 987	4, 696	25, 920	12, 867	14, 276	4, 997	3, 643	372	9. 2
Tampa, Fla	67, 038	2, 583	10, 782	10, 930	16, 115	10, 595	9, 645	3, 472	2, 684	232	8. 1
Toledo, Ohio	176, 675	2, 562	11, 805	19, 234	65, 576	29, 470	27, 996	8, 699	7, 801	3, 532	8. 6
Trenton, N. J	75, 086	4, 282	9, 554	12, 475	22, 377	10, 305	9, 385	2, 782	2, 828	1, 098	8. 0
Tulsa, Okla	86, 273	944	3, 947	6, 240	21, 465	15, 616	20, 737	9, 322	7, 518	484	11. 0
Utica, N. Y	62, 358	4, 447	4, 978	6, 488	22, 106	10, 106	8, 633	1, 933	2, 306	1, 361	8. 3
Washington, D. C	430, 743	6, 707	28, 405	41, 298	108, 258	65, 456	86, 840	41, 065	47, 252	5, 402	10. 3
Wichita, Kans	69, 966	531	2, 403	4, 288	21, 406	12, 406	15, 941	6, 998	5, 539	394	10. 5
Wilmington, Del	68, 595	2, 612	6, 065	7, 880	21, 075	12, 185	10, 430	2, 889	3, 734	1, 725	8. 6
Worcester, Mass	117, 781	7, 133	6, 044	9, 518	37, 980	21, 470	19, 588	5, 784	6, 437	3, 827	8. 8
Yonkers, N. Y	87, 647	3, 462	6, 300	7, 283	30, 401	12, 835	14, 456	4, 263	7, 353	1, 204	8. 7
Youngstown, Ohio	95, 767	4, 448	9, 553	11, 975	31, 953	15, 248	13, 688	4, 375	3, 716	811	8. 3

TABLE 59.—MALES 25 YEARS OLD AND OVER, BY YEARS OF SCHOOL COMPLETED, FOR CITIES OF 100,000 OR MORE: 1940

CITY	Males 25 years old and over	No school years completed	GRADE SCHOOL			HIGH SCHOOL		COLLEGE		Not reported	Median school years completed
			1 to 4 years	5 and 6 years	7 and 8 years	1 to 3 years	4 years	1 to 3 years	4 years or more		
Akron, Ohio	71,693	1,543	4,242	6,716	26,019	12,966	11,401	4,060	4,253	493	8.8
Albany, N. Y	40,697	1,211	2,503	3,846	14,854	6,299	6,700	1,745	3,255	275	8.7
Atlanta, Ga	81,287	2,537	12,262	12,444	16,885	12,073	12,533	6,009	5,992	552	8.6
Baltimore, Md	254,979	8,671	33,923	46,083	79,714	32,492	23,934	9,290	14,605	6,267	7.9
Birmingham, Ala	73,030	3,247	11,381	10,179	17,479	10,393	10,854	4,628	4,399	470	8.3
Boston, Mass	225,120	11,289	15,009	16,820	73,976	37,094	41,863	9.931	15,255	3,883	8.8
Bridgeport, Conn	43,924	2,292	3,154	4,651	19,884	5,259	4,641	1,325	1,965	753	8.2
Buffalo, N. Y	172,052	5,839	13,278	17,682	68,241	30,331	19,413	6,023	9,052	2,193	8.4
Cambridge, Mass	30,903	1,021	1,773	2,309	10,117	4,319	5,233	1,221	3,708	1,142	8.9
Camden, N. J	34,242	1,979	4,173	5,756	12,879	4,537	2,446	691	951	830	7.7
Canton, Ohio	32,554	1,162	2,407	3,429	12,756	5,409	4,497	1,321	1,443	130	8.4
Charlotte, N. C	26,248	1,084	3,036	3,423	4,635	3,917	4,480	2,492	2,382	199	9.2
Chattanooga, Tenn	34,234	1,343	5,271	5,645	8,394	4,866	4,652	1,726	1,843	494	8.1
Chicago, Ill	1,063,114	42,746	83,722	93,352	418,880	155,311	140,514	59,091	64,290	5,208	8.5
Cincinnati, Ohio	138,409	2,051	11,986	17,807	48,565	20,927	17,008	6,974	10,277	2,814	8.5
Cleveland, Ohio	270,626	12,444	28,994	39,534	85,213	47,010	34,334	10,082	10,796	2,219	8.2
Columbus, Ohio	93,394	1,657	5,102	9,497	29,432	16,611	16,709	5,920	7,120	1,256	9.1
Dallas, Texas	85,469	1,965	7,191	9,398	18,227	15,825	18,404	7,918	5,872	669	10.1
Dayton, Ohio	64,039	711	3,586	6,345	23,250	11,962	10,785	3,207	3,556	637	8.8
Denver, Colo	97,973	1,903	4,921	6,449	31,223	15,181	18,518	8,686	9,694	1,398	9.7
Des Moines, Iowa	45,954	478	1,992	3,219	13,327	7,758	9,845	4,150	4,263	922	10.4
Detroit, Mich	501,172	14,803	47,301	53,975	166,094	90,662	74,373	24,952	26,785	2,227	8.6
Duluth, Minn	31,186	855	2,444	3,011	11,747	5,073	4,453	1,586	1,745	272	8.6
Elizabeth, N. J	33,017	2,370	2,931	3,523	11,758	4,539	4,052	1,325	2,070	440	8.3
Erie, Pa	33,519	1,234	2,828	3,338	11,992	5,742	4,879	1,414	1,720	372	8.5
Fall River, Mass	31,211	2,603	3,891	5,855	10,898	3,447	2,277	577	915	748	7.5
Flint, Mich	43,434	712	2,697	3,976	15,163	9,597	6,985	2,136	1,810	340	8.9
Fort Wayne, Ind	34,524	245	1,202	2,666	14,140	5,664	5,807	2,179	2,218	394	8.8
Fort Worth, Tex	51,236	1,014	4,667	6,510	11,921	10,031	8,823	4,458	3,510	301	9.4
Gary, Ind	34,670	1,689	4,218	3,893	11,032	5,380	5,027	1,655	1,613	163	8.4
Grand Rapids, Mich	47,264	1,069	2,628	3,943	17,002	9,550	7,203	2,605	2,473	701	8.8
Hartford, Conn	49,034	2,190	3,304	3,554	17,887	7,391	6,729	1,791	2,780	3,408	8.5
Houston, Tex	115,838	2,837	10,835	14,871	24,904	20,432	19,974	10,064	9,546	2,375	9.5
Indianapolis, Ind	114,980	1,635	6,831	9,582	41,574	19,071	18,844	7,347	8,362	1,134	8.9
Jacksonville, Fla	49,427	1,387	7,175	7,324	12,576	6,807	7,237	3,042	2,716	1,163	8.3
Jersey city, N. J	88,742	4,685	7,127	8,304	40,759	11,936	8,402	2,540	3,918	1,011	8.2
Kansas City, Kans	34,678	876	3,407	4,562	12,757	5,527	4,222	1,704	1,400	223	8.3
Kansas City, Mo	124,867	2,332	7,991	10,495	38,412	20,027	24,217	10,623	9,596	1,174	9.4
Knoxville, Tenn	29,027	955	4,055	4,805	7,028	3,984	3,843	1,946	2,257	154	8.3
Long Beach, Calif	52,285	302	1,439	2,655	15,499	10,206	12,233	5,280	4,270	401	10.8
Los Angeles, Calif	493,237	10,495	24,820	34,305	131,710	86,121	108,806	47,614	42,780	6,577	10.5
Louisville, Ky	92,568	1,990	8,777	11,422	36,887	12,825	10,719	4,252	5,155	541	8.3
Lowell, Mass	27,607	1,393	2,025	3,457	9,572	4,730	4,097	790	1,126	417	8.4
Memphis, Tenn	85,465	2,934	13,136	12,643	20,853	12,606	12,336	5,094	4,640	1,223	8.3
Miami, Fla	55,207	840	4,722	5,936	14,812	9,071	10,430	4,524	3,740	1,132	9.2
Milwaukee, Wis	179,456	3,620	12,661	21,125	77,310	24,045	21,867	8,418	9,441	969	8.3
Minneapolis, Minn	147,032	1,567	6,314	10,296	55,405	22,411	26,070	11,056	12,195	818	9.0
Nashville, Tenn	44,788	1,696	5,972	6,737	13,303	6,139	5,695	2,341	2,536	369	8.2
Newark, N. J	128,470	7,538	12,768	14,350	40,929	15,632	11,576	4,348	6,354	5,975	8.1
New Bedford, Mass	31,904	3,315	3,724	5,355	12,099	3,244	2,178	619	802	568	7.5
New Haven, Conn	46,564	2,669	3,738	4,206	18,643	5,598	5,803	1,752	3,447	648	8.3
New Orleans, La	138,411	5,444	23,512	25,235	38,977	14,023	15,500	6,062	8,651	1,007	7.7
New York, N. Y	2,327,048	168,413	171,962	183,754	939,513	280,124	240,407	97,789	174,510	52,576	8.3
Bronx Borough	428,125	31,679	31,929	32,824	178,969	54,010	45,069	15,705	27,028	10,912	8.3
Brooklyn Borough	802,964	87,495	64,701	58,642	314,280	95,245	76,802	28,992	51,270	25,537	8.1
Manhattan Borough	639,069	38,675	56,341	64,190	227,237	72,673	71,927	33,801	65,401	9,414	8.4
Queens Borough	403,401	8,689	15,950	24,307	194,307	59,617	49,672	17,303	27,468	6,088	8.5
Richmond Borough	52,899	1,875	3,041	3,791	24,720	7,570	5,937	1,988	3,343	625	8.4
Norfolk, Va	41,294	1,497	5,803	5,828	10,037	6,520	6,114	2,326	2,645	524	8.4
Oakland, Calif	99,018	2,657	5,226	7,100	30,568	16,655	22,817	7,154	7,111	1,140	9.7
Oklahoma City, Okla	58,900	734	3,544	4,703	15,487	9,874	11,200	6,302	5,406	1,641	10.3
Omaha, Nebr	66,422	1,322	3,578	4,690	23,113	10,958	12,274	4,840	5,051	596	9.1
Paterson, N. J	43,442	2,920	5,096	5,848	17,926	5,086	3,103	1,072	1,817	475	7.8
Peoria, Ill	33,272	312	1,712	2,968	13,244	5,228	5,257	2,157	2,093	301	8.7
Philadelphia, Pa	574,383	28,634	48,871	70,493	226,028	80,878	61,337	17,194	30,357	10,591	8.2
Pittsburgh, Pa	196,919	8,466	17,290	24,081	73,214	25,253	24,839	8,642	13,669	1,450	8.3
Portland, Oreg	102,109	1,283	4,447	5,751	35,376	16,880	19,472	9,125	8,898	877	9.7
Providence, R. I	71,798	4,380	6,584	7,295	26,265	10,565	8,829	2,541	4,851	488	8.3
Reading, Pa	33,504	862	3,808	6,057	11,998	5,190	3,201	746	1,195	357	8.0
Richmond, Va	54,096	1,729	7,439	7,951	12,824	9,081	7,770	3,264	3,871	167	8.5
Rochester, N. Y	99,132	4,517	7,366	9,009	35,850	17,422	12,687	3,497	5,514	3,270	8.5
Sacramento, Calif	36,022	855	2,284	2,725	11,158	6,109	6,726	3,093	2,816	196	9.4
St. Louis, Mo	252,319	5,745	21,763	31,673	115,188	29,858	23,806	9,358	12,431	2,497	8.1
St. Paul, Minn	83,631	1,237	3,703	5,866	34,521	12,737	13,161	5,291	6,585	530	8.8
Salt Lake City, Utah	39,935	451	1,508	2,288	10,280	6,818	9,082	4,837	4,399	272	11.3
San Antonio, Tex	66,491	4,765	10,689	9,609	14,348	8,917	9,510	4,289	4,029	335	8.1
San Diego, Calif	63,280	1,015	2,997	4,238	17,608	12,828	13,686	5,540	5,041	327	10.3
San Francisco, Calif	231,879	4,738	15,487	18,096	75,144	35,832	44,804	15,440	18,140	4,108	9.0
Scranton, Pa	39,598	2,573	4,878	4,679	13,727	5,122	4,625	1,209	1,900	885	8.1
Seattle, Wash	125,563	1,923	5,726	7,279	40,270	19,584	26,762	11,227	12,017	775	10.1
Somerville, Mass	28,551	647	1,637	2,795	9,109	6,385	5,495	936	1,263	284	9.0
South Bend, Ind	29,994	425	2,063	4,012	10,063	5,357	4,322	1,553	1,994	205	8.7
Spokane, Wash	39,478	526	2,002	2,527	14,014	6,301	7,431	3,344	3,049	284	9.3
Springfield, Mass	44,616	1,120	2,692	3,964	12,096	11,069	8,348	2,056	2,674	597	9.6
Syracuse, N. Y	61,852	2,348	3,721	4,727	21,500	10,569	10,330	2,908	4,951	708	8.8
Tacoma, Wash	35,759	476	1,823	2,716	18,956	6,165	6,051	2,304	2,040	228	8.8
Tampa, Fla	32,446	1,137	5,598	5,418	8,048	4,826	4,126	1,709	1,455	129	8.0
Toledo, Ohio	87,950	1,368	6,482	9,851	32,844	14,244	11,979	4,444	4,833	1,905	8.5
Trenton, N. J	37,506	2,046	5,143	6,345	11,120	5,081	4,096	1,294	1,782	599	7.9
Tulsa, Okla	41,310	500	2,212	3,165	10,669	6,888	8,813	4,364	4,427	272	10.7
Utica, N. Y	30,086	2,043	2,746	3,287	10,452	4,855	3,717	884	1,373	729	8.3
Washington, D. C	203,441	3,300	15,301	20,768	52,496	29,221	31,605	17,815	30,029	2,906	9.9
Wichita, Kans	33,034	300	1,442	2,301	10,536	5,541	6,480	3,233	2,978	223	9.9
Wilmington, Del	33,697	1,279	3,188	4,042	10,583	5,651	4,185	1,416	2,451	902	8.5
Worcester, Mass	56,769	3,430	3,200	4,051	18,959	10,100	8,104	2,380	4,013	1,923	8.7
Yonkers, N. Y	42,326	1,575	3,269	3,525	14,436	6,098	6,231	2,137	4,442	613	8.7
Youngstown, Ohio	48,856	2,361	5,483	6,264	16,165	7,542	6,191	2,042	2,370	438	8.2

TABLE 60.—FEMALES 25 YEARS OLD AND OVER, BY YEARS OF SCHOOL COMPLETED, FOR CITIES OF 100,000 OR MORE: 1940

CITY	Females 25 years old and over	No school years completed	GRADE SCHOOL			HIGH SCHOOL		COLLEGE		Not reported	Median school years completed
			1 to 4 years	5 and 6 years	7 and 8 years	1 to 3 years	4 years	1 to 3 years	4 years or more		
Akron, Ohio	72,041	1,586	3,497	6,093	25,625	13,914	14,502	3,901	2,585	338	8.9
Albany, N. Y	44,891	987	2,122	3,882	15,941	7,769	9,807	1,884	2,183	316	8.9
Atlanta, Ga	98,557	2,772	13,121	15,564	20,402	15,848	18,328	7,182	4,841	499	8.7
Baltimore, Md	265,703	9,004	32,019	49,183	83,594	36,947	34,837	8,278	7,474	4,367	8.0
Birmingham, Ala	81,382	3,048	10,545	11,203	19,290	13,061	14,460	5,514	3,822	430	8.6
Boston, Mass	247,844	12,845	14,144	17,620	77,669	40,982	60,082	11,278	9,855	3,369	9.0
Bridgeport, Conn	44,651	2,706	2,991	4,770	20,322	5,184	5,844	1,438	867	520	8.1
Buffalo, N. Y	177,670	5,768	11,840	18,102	71,935	32,832	23,629	5,855	5,704	2,005	8.4
Cambridge, Mass	36,420	1,272	1,748	2,658	11,426	5,057	8,121	2,039	2,663	1,436	9.2
Camden, N. J	34,109	2,002	3,983	5,771	13,195	4,624	2,854	518	405	757	7.7
Canton, Ohio	31,909	956	1,767	3,074	12,307	5,691	5,764	1,475	782	93	8.6
Charlotte, N. C	29,388	1,123	3,794	4,082	5,092	4,408	5,621	2,973	2,106	189	9.3
Chattanooga, Tenn	38,207	1,198	5,038	6,470	9,497	5,921	6,224	2,225	1,286	348	8.3
Chicago, Ill	1,082,892	45,998	76,297	92,141	432,431	171,895	175,330	49,632	34,611	4,557	8.5
Cincinnati, Ohio	155,426	2,083	12,529	20,907	55,250	25,211	23,449	6,768	6,747	2,482	8.5
Cleveland, Ohio	269,128	13,436	25,610	38,672	85,001	48,040	40,914	9,106	6,607	1,742	8.3
Columbus, Ohio	99,316	1,302	4,587	9,259	29,811	18,531	24,095	5,877	4,750	1,104	9.7
Dallas, Texas	96,066	1,909	6,109	9,860	19,220	19,516	25,127	9,006	4,864	455	10.6
Dayton, Ohio	66,250	614	3,162	6,344	24,007	13,002	13,589	3,189	1,869	474	8.9
Denver, Colo	105,887	1,866	3,882	5,871	30,361	17,981	27,678	10,090	6,927	1,231	10.7
Des Moines, Iowa	51,588	380	1,358	2,707	13,443	9,176	15,302	5,287	3,077	768	11.4
Detroit, Mich	465,822	15,621	38,925	48,670	147,926	91,603	85,673	21,358	14,445	1,601	8.7
Duluth, Minn	30,567	521	1,406	2,371	10,606	5,587	5,978	2,450	1,466	182	9.2
Elizabeth, N. J	32,622	2,528	2,505	3,472	11,776	4,664	4,977	1,258	1,007	435	8.3
Erie, Pa	34,209	1,211	2,167	3,329	12,328	5,8[illegible]1	6,449	1,433	1,171	320	8.7
Fall River, Mass	34,975	3,084	4,167	6,660	11,889	3,644	3,074	1,044	617	796	7.5
Flint, Mich	41,435	601	2,011	3,200	13,301	9,993	8,133	2,750	1,244	202	9.5
Fort Wayne, Ind	37,869	204	1,124	2,733	15,643	6,549	7,316	2,234	1,264	802	8.9
Fort Worth, Tex	56,557	865	3,727	6,314	11,965	12,597	12,308	5,503	3,034	244	10.3
Gary, Ind	29,528	1,405	2,783	3,168	9,406	5,182	5,134	1,468	878	104	8.6
Grand Rapids, Mich	51,157	1,140	2,357	3,857	17,562	10,871	9,611	3,182	1,860	717	9.1
Hartford, Conn	52,651	2,414	2,921	3,400	18,490	8,386	9,829	2,432	1,668	3,102	8.7
Houston, Tex	117,325	2,997	9,530	14,329	23,731	23,258	25,516	9,727	6,393	1,844	9.9
Indianapolis, Ind	127,207	1,512	6,178	9,860	45,682	22,809	26,343	8,110	5,920	793	9.0
Jacksonville, Fla	53,132	1,257	6,312	7,803	13,247	8,614	9,095	3,388	1,957	859	8.6
Jersey City, N. J	90,454	5,246	6,535	8,463	41,787	12,679	10,293	2,454	2,040	957	8.2
Kansas City, Kans	36,634	850	2,832	4,384	13,040	6,620	5,823	1,848	1,075	162	8.6
Kansas City, Mo	138,762	2,047	6,361	9,988	39,992	24,668	35,859	12,480	6,351	1,007	10.3
Knoxville, Tenn	33,569	915	4,157	5,482	8,225	5,102	5,534	2,408	1,641	105	8.5
Long Beach, Calif	60,140	270	1,175	2,555	15,967	12,551	17,353	6,518	3,410	341	11.4
Los Angeles, Calif	527,928	11,620	22,646	32,407	133,656	90,992	146,860	47,803	29,868	3,076	10.9
Louisville, Ky	103,799	1,702	8,253	11,933	41,278	15,893	15,189	5,413	3,525	613	8.4
Lowell, Mass	31,135	1,630	2,187	4,045	10,715	4,855	5,455	1,015	814	419	8.4
Memphis, Tenn	94,503	2,774	11,841	13,330	22,661	16,554	17,344	6,075	3,386	598	8.7
Miami, Fla	56,726	738	3,793	5,787	14,296	10,643	13,660	4,225	2,730	854	9.9
Milwaukee, Wis	184,284	3,537	11,985	22,287	80,413	24,549	26,807	8,340	5,686	680	8.3
Minneapolis, Minn	163,572	1,572	5,449	9,799	56,298	20,971	40,506	13,665	8,639	673	9.9
Nashville, Tenn	54,055	1,489	5,544	7,640	15,679	8,740	8,660	3,532	2,350	412	8.5
Newark, N. J	129,208	8,968	12,114	14,428	51,886	16,335	14,075	3,359	2,581	5,462	8.0
New Bedford, Mass	35,289	3,901	3,775	5,750	13,240	3,491	3,128	966	526	512	7.6
New Haven, Conn	50,175	3,105	3,399	4,019	19,793	5,820	8,836	2,593	2,013	597	8.4
New Orleans, La	159,727	6,579	24,786	29,754	45,450	17,269	23,131	6,424	5,426	908	7.8
New York, N. Y	2,406,294	192,771	168,589	183,534	905,316	311,417	336,516	77,123	91,581	40,447	8.3
Bronx Borough	442,009	40,825	34,564	33,395	188,633	56,592	57,981	9,460	12,185	8,374	8.1
Brooklyn Borough	829,546	99,549	64,854	58,957	335,387	101,473	100,618	19,891	22,010	26,807	8.1
Manhattan Borough	662,223	39,770	50,949	62,012	235,118	82,002	109,651	33,832	41,781	7,108	8.5
Queens Borough	422,248	10,673	16,017	25,930	212,298	63,605	61,066	12,398	13,627	6,634	8.5
Richmond Borough	50,268	1,954	2,205	3,240	23,880	7,745	7,200	1,542	1,978	524	8.5
Norfolk, Va	43,108	1,389	5,616	5,826	9,875	6,935	7,929	3,349	1,759	430	8.7
Oakland, Calif	102,657	2,331	4,306	6,096	29,830	18,931	27,610	7,356	5,223	974	10.3
Oklahoma City, Okla	62,910	569	2,658	4,352	15,181	12,001	15,566	7,155	4,481	947	11.1
Omaha, Nebr	70,562	1,312	3,000	4,272	22,392	12,507	17,624	5,887	3,090	478	10.0
Paterson, N. J	43,989	3,443	4,791	5,943	18,446	4,787	3,834	1,269	931	545	7.8
Peoria, Ill	33,818	226	1,395	2,738	13,033	5,593	7,101	2,070	1,231	341	8.9
Philadelphia, Pa	614,012	32,289	47,729	74,400	248,388	80,240	82,985	15,383	13,799	9,849	8.2
Pittsburgh, Pa	203,390	8,166	14,898	24,281	77,419	28,148	33,456	7,609	8,161	1,252	8.4
Portland, Oreg	106,079	1,086	3,011	4,309	33,008	20,008	27,709	10,344	5,753	761	10.7
Providence, R. I	81,309	5,075	6,352	7,827	30,081	11,705	13,377	3,084	3,339	469	8.4
Reading, Pa	35,894	877	3,799	6,774	13,280	5,338	4,072	747	736	271	8.0
Richmond, Va	63,650	1,604	7,368	8,659	13,797	11,782	12,590	4,864	2,853	142	9.1
Rochester, N. Y	107,375	4,941	6,609	9,048	39,163	19,261	16,917	4,105	3,637	3,694	8.6
Sacramento, Calif	33,765	687	1,304	1,890	9,329	6,514	8,839	3,124	1,973	105	10.7
St. Louis, Mo	277,873	6,043	22,542	35,281	127,937	35,544	32,471	9,219	7,034	1,802	8.2
St. Paul, Minn	93,279	1,207	3,463	6,021	36,579	14,068	19,856	6,481	4,102	542	8.9
Salt Lake City, Utah	42,639	349	1,231	2,227	10,803	7,937	11,406	5,293	3,092	301	11.5
San Antonio, Tex	73,483	6,623	11,382	10,065	14,412	9,842	12,349	4,993	3,406	411	8.2
San Diego, Calif	65,207	811	2,454	3,711	16,192	13,609	17,435	6,730	4,010	246	11.1
San Francisco, Calif	220,975	4,389	9,713	11,949	68,419	37,682	59,670	15,295	11,402	2,456	10.2
Scranton, Pa	42,131	2,642	3,923	4,824	14,920	5,469	6,717	1,450	1,424	762	8.2
Seattle, Wash	123,959	1,209	3,243	4,852	34,896	21,394	36,411	12,518	8,757	679	11.4
Somerville, Mass	32,095	741	1,568	2,812	9,664	7,372	7,595	1,106	962	275	9.5
South Bend, Ind	30,551	394	1,914	3,774	10,182	5,594	5,755	1,744	1,061	133	8.8
Spokane, Wash	39,404	278	1,221	1,827	11,994	7,241	10,456	4,105	2,048	234	10.8
Springfield, Mass	49,009	1,339	2,657	4,024	12,362	12,088	11,754	2,617	1,587	581	10.0
Syracuse, N. Y	66,154	2,321	3,149	4,571	23,086	11,694	14,362	3,204	3,106	661	9.0
Tacoma, Wash	34,818	343	1,164	1,980	11,964	6,702	8,225	2,693	1,603	144	9.8
Tampa, Fla	34,592	1,446	5,184	5,512	8,067	5,769	5,519	1,763	1,229	103	8.3
Toledo, Ohio	88,725	1,194	5,323	9,383	32,732	15,226	16,017	4,255	2,968	1,627	8.7
Trenton, N. J	37,580	2,236	4,411	6,130	11,257	5,224	5,289	1,488	1,046	499	8.0
Tulsa, Okla	44,963	444	1,735	3,075	10,796	8,728	11,924	4,958	3,091	212	11.2
Utica, N. Y	32,272	2,404	2,232	3,201	11,654	5,251	4,916	1,049	933	632	8.4
Washington, D. C	227,302	3,407	13,104	20,530	55,762	36,235	55,235	23,250	17,223	2,496	10.6
Wichita, Kans	36,932	231	1,021	1,987	10,870	6,865	9,461	3,705	2,561	171	10.9
Wilmington, Del	34,898	1,333	2,877	3,838	10,492	6,534	6,245	1,473	1,283	823	8.7
Worcester, Mass	61,012	3,703	2,844	4,867	19,021	11,370	11,484	3,395	2,424	1,904	8.9
Yonkers, N. Y	45,321	1,887	3,121	3,758	15,965	6,737	8,226	2,126	2,911	591	8.7
Youngstown, Ohio	46,911	2,087	4,070	5,711	15,788	7,706	7,497	2,333	1,346	373	8.4

TABLE 61.—PERCENT DISTRIBUTION BY YEARS OF SCHOOL COMPLETED, FOR PERSONS 25 YEARS OLD AND OVER, FOR CITIES OF 100,000 OR MORE: 1940

CITY	Persons 25 years old and over	No school years completed	GRADE SCHOOL			HIGH SCHOOL		COLLEGE		Not reported	Less than 5 years completed
			1 to 4 years	5 and 6 years	7 and 8 years	1 to 3 years	4 years	1 to 3 years	4 years or more		
Akron, Ohio	100.0	2.2	5.4	8.9	35.0	18.7	18.0	5.5	4.8	0.6	7.6
Albany, N. Y	100.0	2.6	5.4	9.0	36.0	16.4	19.3	4.2	6.4	0.7	8.0
Atlanta, Ga	100.0	3.0	14.1	15.6	20.7	15.5	17.2	7.3	6.0	0.6	17.1
Baltimore, Md	100.0	3.4	12.7	18.3	31.4	13.3	11.3	3.4	4.2	2.0	16.1
Birmingham, Ala	100.0	4.1	14.2	13.8	23.8	15.2	16.4	6.6	5.3	0.6	18.3
Boston, Mass	100.0	5.1	6.2	7.3	32.1	16.5	21.6	4.5	5.3	1.5	11.3
Bridgeport, Conn	100.0	5.6	6.9	10.6	45.4	11.8	11.8	3.1	3.2	1.4	12.6
Buffalo, N. Y	100.0	3.3	7.2	10.2	40.1	18.1	12.3	3.4	4.2	1.2	10.5
Cambridge, Mass	100.0	3.4	5.2	7.5	32.0	13.9	19.8	4.8	9.5	3.8	8.6
Camden, N. J	100.0	5.8	11.9	16.9	38.1	13.4	7.8	1.8	2.0	2.3	17.8
Canton, Ohio	100.0	3.3	6.5	10.1	38.9	17.2	15.9	4.3	3.5	0.3	9.8
Charlotte, N. C	100.0	4.0	13.4	13.5	17.5	15.0	18.2	9.8	8.1	0.7	17.3
Chattanooga, Tenn	100.0	3.5	14.2	16.7	24.7	14.9	15.0	5.5	4.3	1.2	17.7
Chicago, Ill	100.0	4.1	7.5	8.6	39.7	15.2	14.7	5.1	4.6	0.5	11.6
Cincinnati, Ohio	100.0	1.4	8.3	13.2	35.3	15.7	13.8	4.7	5.8	1.8	9.8
Cleveland, Ohio	100.0	4.8	10.1	14.5	31.5	17.6	13.9	3.6	3.2	0.7	14.9
Columbus, Ohio	100.0	1.5	5.0	9.7	30.7	18.2	21.2	6.1	6.2	1.2	6.6
Dallas, Tex	100.0	2.1	7.3	10.6	20.6	19.5	24.0	9.3	5.9	0.6	9.5
Dayton, Ohio	100.0	1.0	5.2	9.7	36.3	19.2	18.7	4.9	4.2	0.9	6.2
Denver, Colo	100.0	1.8	4.3	6.0	30.2	16.3	22.7	9.2	8.2	1.3	6.2
Des Moines, Iowa	100.0	0.9	3.4	6.2	27.4	17.4	25.8	9.7	7.5	1.7	4.3
Detroit, Mich	100.0	3.1	8.9	10.6	32.5	18.8	16.6	4.8	4.3	0.4	12.1
Duluth, Minn	100.0	2.2	6.2	8.7	36.2	17.3	16.9	6.5	5.2	0.7	8.5
Elizabeth, N. J	100.0	7.5	8.3	10.7	35.9	14.0	13.8	3.9	4.7	1.3	15.7
Erie, Pa	100.0	3.6	7.4	9.8	35.9	17.0	16.7	4.2	4.3	1.0	11.0
Fall River, Mass	100.0	8.6	12.2	18.9	34.4	10.7	8.1	2.4	2.3	2.3	20.8
Flint, Mich	100.0	1.5	5.5	8.5	33.5	23.1	17.8	5.8	3.6	0.6	7.1
Fort Wayne, Ind	100.0	0.6	3.2	7.5	41.2	16.9	18.1	6.1	4.8	1.7	3.8
Fort Worth, Tex	100.0	1.7	7.8	11.9	22.2	21.0	19.6	9.2	6.1	0.5	9.5
Gary, Ind	100.0	4.8	10.9	11.0	31.8	16.5	15.8	4.9	3.9	0.4	15.7
Grand Rapids, Mich	100.0	2.2	5.1	7.9	35.1	20.7	17.1	5.9	4.4	1.5	7.3
Hartford, Conn	100.0	4.5	6.1	6.8	35.8	15.5	16.3	4.2	4.4	6.4	10.6
Houston, Tex	100.0	2.5	8.7	12.5	20.9	18.7	19.5	8.5	6.8	1.8	11.2
Indianapolis, Ind	100.0	1.3	5.4	8.0	36.0	17.5	18.7	6.4	5.9	0.8	6.7
Jacksonville, Fla	100.0	2.6	13.2	14.7	25.2	15.0	16.5	6.3	4.6	2.0	15.7
Jersey City, N. J	100.0	5.5	7.6	9.4	46.1	13.7	10.5	2.8	3.3	1.1	13.2
Kansas City, Kans	100.0	2.4	8.7	12.5	36.2	17.0	14.1	5.0	3.5	0.5	11.2
Kansas City, Mo	100.0	1.7	5.4	7.8	29.7	17.0	22.8	8.8	6.0	0.8	7.1
Knoxville, Tenn	100.0	3.0	13.1	16.4	24.4	14.5	15.0	7.0	6.2	0.4	16.1
Long Beach, Calif	100.0	0.5	2.3	4.6	28.0	20.2	26.3	10.5	6.8	0.7	2.8
Los Angeles, Calif	100.0	2.2	4.6	6.5	26.0	18.2	25.0	9.3	7.1	0.9	6.8
Louisville, Ky	100.0	1.9	8.7	11.9	30.8	14.6	13.2	4.9	4.4	0.6	10.6
Lowell, Mass	100.0	5.1	7.2	12.8	34.5	16.3	16.3	3.1	3.3	1.4	12.3
Memphis, Tenn	100.0	3.2	13.9	14.4	24.2	16.2	16.5	6.2	4.5	1.0	17.0
Miami, Fla	100.0	1.4	7.6	10.5	26.0	17.6	21.5	7.8	5.8	1.8	9.0
Milwaukee, Wis	100.0	2.0	6.8	11.9	43.4	13.4	13.4	4.6	4.2	0.5	8.7
Minneapolis, Minn	100.0	1.0	3.8	6.5	36.0	15.9	21.7	8.0	6.7	0.5	4.8
Nashville, Tenn	100.0	3.2	11.7	14.5	29.3	15.1	14.5	5.9	4.9	0.8	14.9
Newark, N. J	100.0	6.4	9.7	11.2	39.5	12.4	10.0	3.0	3.5	4.4	16.1
New Bedford, Mass	100.0	10.7	11.2	16.5	37.7	10.0	7.9	2.4	2.0	1.6	21.9
New Haven, Conn	100.0	6.0	7.4	8.6	30.7	11.8	15.1	4.5	5.6	1.3	13.3
New Orleans, La	100.0	4.0	16.2	18.4	28.3	10.5	13.0	4.2	4.7	0.6	20.2
New York, N. Y	100.0	7.6	7.2	7.8	40.9	12.7	12.4	3.7	5.6	2.2	14.8
Bronx Borough	100.0	8.3	7.6	7.6	42.2	12.7	11.8	2.9	4.5	2.2	16.0
Brooklyn Borough	100.0	11.5	7.9	7.2	30.8	12.0	10.9	3.0	4.5	3.2	19.4
Manhattan Borough	100.0	6.0	8.2	9.7	35.5	11.0	13.9	5.2	8.2	1.3	14.3
Queens Borough	100.0	2.3	3.9	6.1	49.2	14.9	13.4	3.6	5.0	1.5	6.2
Richmond Borough	100.0	3.7	5.1	6.8	47.1	14.9	12.7	3.4	5.2	1.1	8.8
Norfolk, Va	100.0	3.4	13.5	13.8	23.6	15.0	16.6	6.7	5.2	1.1	16.9
Oakland, Calif	100.0	2.5	4.7	6.5	20.8	17.6	24.6	7.2	6.1	1.0	7.2
Oklahoma City, Okla	100.0	1.1	5.1	7.4	25.2	18.0	22.0	11.0	8.1	2.1	6.2
Omaha, Nebr	100.0	1.9	4.8	6.5	33.2	17.1	21.8	7.8	5.9	0.8	6.7
Paterson, N. J	100.0	7.3	11.3	13.5	41.6	11.3	8.0	2.7	3.1	1.2	18.6
Peoria, Ill	100.0	0.8	4.6	8.5	30.2	16.1	18.6	6.3	5.0	1.0	5.4
Philadelphia, Pa	100.0	5.1	8.1	12.2	39.9	14.3	12.1	2.7	3.7	1.7	13.3
Pittsburgh, Pa	100.0	4.2	8.0	12.1	37.6	13.3	14.6	4.1	5.5	0.7	12.2
Portland, Oreg	100.0	1.1	3.6	4.8	32.8	17.8	22.7	9.4	7.0	0.8	4.7
Providence, R. I	100.0	6.2	8.4	9.9	36.8	14.5	14.5	3.7	5.3	0.6	14.6
Reading, Pa	100.0	2.5	11.0	18.5	36.4	15.2	10.6	2.2	2.8	0.9	13.5
Richmond, Va	100.0	2.8	12.6	14.1	22.6	17.7	17.3	6.9	5.7	0.3	15.4
Rochester, N. Y	100.0	4.6	6.8	8.7	36.3	17.8	14.3	3.7	4.4	3.4	11.3
Sacramento, Calif	100.0	2.2	5.1	6.6	29.4	18.2	22.3	8.0	6.9	0.4	7.4
St. Louis, Mo	100.0	2.2	8.4	12.6	45.9	12.3	10.6	3.5	3.7	0.8	10.6
St. Paul, Minn	100.0	1.4	4.1	6.7	40.2	15.7	18.7	6.7	6.0	0.6	5.5
Salt Lake City, Utah	100.0	1.0	3.3	5.5	25.5	17.9	24.8	12.3	9.1	0.7	4.3
San Antonio, Tex	100.0	8.1	15.8	14.1	20.5	13.4	15.6	6.6	5.3	0.5	23.9
San Diego, Calif	100.0	1.4	4.2	6.2	26.3	20.6	24.2	9.6	7.0	0.4	5.7
San Francisco, Calif	100.0	2.0	5.6	6.6	31.7	16.2	23.1	6.8	6.5	1.4	7.6
Scranton, Pa	100.0	6.4	10.8	11.6	35.1	13.0	13.9	3.3	4.1	2.0	17.1
Seattle, Wash	100.0	1.3	3.6	4.9	30.1	16.4	25.3	9.5	8.3	0.6	4.8
Somerville, Mass	100.0	2.3	5.3	9.2	31.0	22.7	21.6	3.4	3.7	0.9	7.6
South Bend, Ind	100.0	1.4	6.6	12.9	33.4	18.1	16.6	5.4	5.0	0.6	7.9
Spokane, Wash	100.0	1.0	4.1	5.5	33.0	17.2	22.7	9.4	6.5	0.7	5.1
Springfield, Mass	100.0	2.6	5.7	8.5	26.1	24.7	21.5	5.0	4.6	1.3	8.3
Syracuse, N. Y	100.0	3.6	5.4	7.3	34.8	17.4	19.3	4.8	6.3	1.1	9.0
Tacoma, Wash	100.0	1.2	4.2	6.7	36.7	18.2	20.2	7.1	5.2	0.5	5.4
Tampa, Fla	100.0	3.9	16.1	16.3	24.0	15.8	14.4	5.2	4.0	0.3	19.9
Toledo, Ohio	100.0	1.5	6.7	10.9	37.1	16.7	15.8	4.9	4.4	2.0	8.1
Trenton, N. J	100.0	5.7	12.7	16.6	29.8	13.7	12.5	3.7	3.8	1.5	18.4
Tulsa, Okla	100.0	1.1	4.6	7.2	24.9	18.1	24.0	10.8	8.7	0.6	5.7
Utica, N. Y	100.0	7.1	8.0	10.4	35.4	16.2	13.8	3.1	3.7	2.2	15.1
Washington, D. C	100.0	1.6	6.6	9.6	25.1	15.2	20.2	9.5	11.0	1.3	8.2
Wichita, Kans	100.0	0.8	3.5	6.1	30.6	17.7	22.8	10.0	7.9	0.6	4.3
Wilmington, Del	100.0	3.8	8.8	11.5	30.7	17.8	15.2	4.2	5.4	2.5	12.6
Worcester, Mass	100.0	6.1	5.1	8.1	32.2	18.2	16.6	4.9	5.5	3.2	11.2
Yonkers, N. Y	100.0	3.9	7.3	8.3	34.7	14.6	16.5	4.9	8.4	1.4	11.2
Youngstown, Ohio	100.0	4.6	10.0	12.5	33.4	15.9	14.3	4.6	3.9	0.8	14.6

TABLE 62.—PERCENT DISTRIBUTION BY YEARS OF SCHOOL COMPLETED, FOR MALES 25 YEARS OLD AND OVER, FOR CITIES OF 100,000 OR MORE: 1940

CITY	Males 25 years old and over	No school years completed	GRADE SCHOOL			HIGH SCHOOL		COLLEGE		Not reported	Less than 5 years completed
			1 to 4 years	5 and 6 years	7 and 8 years	1 to 3 years	4 years	1 to 3 years	4 years or more		
Akron, Ohio	100.0	2.2	5.9	9.4	36.3	18.1	15.9	5.7	5.9	0.7	8.1
Albany, N. Y.	100.0	3.0	6.2	9.5	36.5	15.5	16.5	4.3	8.0	0.7	9.1
Atlanta, Ga.	100.0	3.1	15.1	15.3	20.8	14.9	15.4	7.4	7.4	0.7	18.2
Baltimore, Md.	100.0	3.4	13.3	18.1	31.3	12.7	9.4	3.6	5.7	2.5	16.7
Birmingham, Ala.	100.0	4.4	15.6	13.9	23.9	14.2	14.9	6.3	6.0	0.6	20.0
Boston, Mass.	100.0	5.0	6.7	7.5	32.9	16.5	18.6	4.4	6.8	1.7	11.7
Bridgeport, Conn.	100.0	5.2	7.2	10.6	45.3	12.0	10.6	3.0	4.5	1.7	12.4
Buffalo, N. Y.	100.0	3.4	7.7	10.3	39.7	17.6	11.3	3.5	5.3	1.3	11.1
Cambridge, Mass.	100.0	3.3	5.7	7.7	32.7	14.0	16.9	4.0	12.0	3.7	9.0
Camden, N. J.	100.0	5.8	12.2	16.8	37.6	13.2	7.1	2.0	2.8	2.4	18.0
Canton, Ohio	100.0	3.6	7.4	10.5	39.2	16.6	13.8	4.1	4.4	0.4	11.0
Charlotte, N. C.	100.0	4.1	13.9	13.0	17.7	14.9	17.1	9.5	9.1	0.8	18.0
Chattanooga, Tenn.	100.0	3.9	15.4	16.5	24.5	14.2	13.6	5.0	5.4	1.4	19.3
Chicago, Ill.	100.0	4.0	7.9	8.8	39.4	14.6	13.2	5.6	6.0	0.5	11.9
Cincinnati, Ohio	100.0	1.5	8.7	12.9	35.1	15.1	12.3	5.0	7.4	2.0	10.1
Cleveland, Ohio	100.0	4.6	10.7	14.6	31.5	17.4	12.7	3.7	4.0	0.8	15.3
Columbus, Ohio	100.0	1.8	5.5	10.2	31.5	17.8	18.0	6.3	7.6	1.3	7.2
Dallas, Tex.	100.0	2.3	8.4	11.0	21.3	18.5	21.5	9.3	6.9	0.8	10.7
Dayton, Ohio	100.0	1.1	5.6	9.9	36.3	18.7	16.8	5.0	5.6	1.0	6.7
Denver, Colo.	100.0	1.9	5.0	6.6	31.9	15.5	18.9	8.9	9.9	1.4	7.0
Des Moines, Iowa	100.0	1.0	4.3	7.0	29.0	16.9	21.4	9.0	9.3	2.0	5.4
Detroit, Mich.	100.0	3.0	9.4	10.8	33.1	18.1	14.8	5.0	5.3	0.4	12.4
Duluth, Minn.	100.0	2.7	7.8	9.7	37.7	16.3	14.3	5.1	5.6	0.9	10.6
Elizabeth, N. J.	100.0	7.2	8.9	10.7	35.6	13.7	12.3	4.0	6.3	1.4	16.1
Erie, Pa.	100.0	3.7	8.4	10.0	35.8	17.1	14.6	4.2	5.1	1.1	12.1
Fall River, Mass.	100.0	8.3	12.5	18.8	34.9	11.0	7.3	1.8	2.9	2.4	20.8
Flint, Mich.	100.0	1.6	6.2	9.2	34.9	22.1	16.1	4.9	4.2	0.8	7.8
Fort Wayne, Ind.	100.0	0.7	3.5	7.7	41.0	16.4	16.8	6.3	6.4	1.1	4.2
Fort Worth, Tex.	100.0	2.0	9.1	12.7	23.3	19.6	17.2	8.7	6.9	0.6	11.1
Gary, Ind.	100.0	4.9	12.2	11.2	31.8	15.5	14.5	4.8	4.7	0.5	17.0
Grand Rapids, Mich.	100.0	2.3	5.6	8.3	36.0	20.2	15.2	5.5	5.2	1.7	7.8
Hartford, Conn.	100.0	4.5	6.7	7.2	36.5	15.1	13.7	3.7	5.7	7.0	11.2
Houston, Tex.	100.0	2.4	9.4	12.8	21.5	17.6	17.2	8.7	8.2	2.1	11.8
Indianapolis, Ind.	100.0	1.4	5.9	8.3	36.2	17.1	16.4	6.4	7.3	1.0	7.4
Jacksonville, Fla.	100.0	2.8	14.5	14.8	25.4	13.8	14.6	6.2	5.5	2.4	17.3
Jersey City, N. J.	100.0	5.3	8.0	9.4	45.9	13.4	9.5	2.9	4.4	1.1	13.3
Kansas City, Kans.	100.0	2.5	9.8	13.2	36.8	15.9	12.2	4.9	4.0	0.6	12.4
Kansas City, Mo.	100.0	1.9	6.4	8.4	30.8	16.0	19.4	8.5	7.7	0.9	8.3
Knoxville, Tenn.	100.0	3.3	14.0	16.6	24.2	13.7	13.2	6.7	7.8	0.5	17.3
Long Beach, Calif.	100.0	0.6	2.8	5.1	29.6	19.5	23.4	10.1	8.2	0.8	3.3
Los Angeles, Calif.	100.0	2.1	5.0	7.0	26.7	17.5	22.1	9.7	8.7	1.3	7.2
Louisville, Ky.	100.0	2.1	9.5	12.3	39.8	13.9	11.6	4.6	5.6	0.6	11.6
Lowell, Mass.	100.0	5.0	7.3	12.5	34.7	17.1	14.8	2.9	4.1	1.5	12.4
Memphis, Tenn.	100.0	3.4	15.4	14.8	24.4	14.7	14.4	6.0	5.4	1.4	18.8
Miami, Fla.	100.0	1.5	8.6	10.8	26.8	16.4	18.9	8.2	6.8	2.1	10.1
Milwaukee, Wis.	100.0	2.0	7.1	11.8	43.1	13.4	12.2	4.7	5.3	0.5	9.1
Minneapolis, Minn.	100.0	1.1	4.3	7.0	37.7	15.2	18.3	7.5	8.3	0.6	5.4
Nashville, Tenn.	100.0	3.8	13.3	15.0	29.7	13.7	12.7	5.2	5.7	0.8	17.1
Newark, N. J.	100.0	5.9	9.9	11.2	38.9	12.2	9.0	3.4	4.9	4.7	15.8
New Bedford, Mass.	100.0	10.4	11.7	16.8	37.9	10.2	6.8	1.9	2.5	1.8	22.1
New Haven, Conn.	100.0	5.7	8.0	9.2	40.0	12.0	12.5	3.8	7.4	1.4	13.8
New Orleans, La.	100.0	3.9	17.0	18.2	28.2	10.1	11.2	4.4	6.3	0.7	20.9
New York, N. Y.	100.0	7.2	7.4	7.9	40.4	12.4	10.7	4.2	7.5	2.3	14.6
Bronx Borough	100.0	7.4	7.5	7.7	41.8	12.6	10.5	3.7	6.3	2.5	14.9
Brooklyn Borough	100.0	10.9	8.1	7.3	39.1	11.9	9.6	3.6	6.4	3.2	19.0
Manhattan Borough	100.0	6.0	8.8	10.0	35.5	11.4	11.2	5.3	10.2	1.5	14.9
Queens Borough	100.0	2.2	4.0	6.0	48.2	14.8	12.3	4.3	6.8	1.5	6.1
Richmond Borough	100.0	3.5	5.7	7.2	46.7	14.3	11.2	3.8	6.3	1.2	9.3
Norfolk, Va.	100.0	3.6	14.1	14.1	24.3	15.8	14.8	5.6	6.4	1.3	17.7
Oakland, Calif.	100.0	2.7	5.2	7.1	30.6	16.7	22.3	7.2	7.1	1.1	7.9
Oklahoma City, Okla.	100.0	1.2	6.0	8.0	26.3	16.8	19.0	10.7	9.2	2.8	7.3
Omaha, Nebr.	100.0	2.0	5.4	7.1	34.8	16.5	18.5	7.3	7.6	0.9	7.4
Paterson, N. J.	100.0	6.7	11.7	13.5	41.3	11.7	7.3	2.5	4.2	1.1	18.5
Peoria, Ill.	100.0	0.9	5.1	8.9	39.8	15.7	15.8	6.5	6.3	0.9	6.1
Philadelphia, Pa.	100.0	5.0	8.5	12.3	39.3	14.1	10.7	3.0	5.3	1.8	13.5
Pittsburgh, Pa.	100.0	4.3	8.8	12.2	37.2	12.8	12.6	4.4	6.9	0.7	13.1
Portland, Oreg.	100.0	1.3	4.4	5.6	34.6	16.5	19.1	8.9	8.7	0.9	5.6
Providence, R. I.	100.0	6.1	9.2	10.2	36.6	14.7	12.3	3.5	6.8	0.7	15.3
Reading, Pa.	100.0	2.6	11.4	18.1	35.8	15.5	9.8	2.2	3.6	1.1	13.9
Richmond, Va.	100.0	3.2	13.8	14.7	23.7	16.8	14.4	6.0	7.2	0.3	16.9
Rochester, N. Y.	100.0	4.6	7.4	9.1	36.2	17.6	12.8	3.5	5.6	3.3	12.0
Sacramento, Calif.	100.0	2.4	6.3	7.6	31.0	17.1	18.7	8.6	7.8	0.5	8.7
St. Louis, Mo.	100.0	2.3	8.6	12.6	45.7	11.8	9.4	3.7	4.9	1.0	10.9
St. Paul, Minn.	100.0	1.5	4.4	7.0	41.3	15.2	15.7	6.3	7.9	0.6	5.9
Salt Lake City, Utah	100.0	1.1	3.8	5.7	25.7	17.1	22.7	12.1	11.0	0.7	4.9
San Antonio, Tex.	100.0	7.2	16.1	14.5	21.6	13.4	14.3	6.5	6.1	0.5	23.2
San Diego, Calif.	100.0	1.6	4.7	6.7	27.8	20.3	21.6	8.8	8.0	0.5	6.3
San Francisco, Calif.	100.0	2.0	6.7	7.8	32.4	15.5	19.4	6.7	7.8	1.8	8.7
Scranton, Pa.	100.0	6.5	12.3	11.8	34.7	12.9	11.7	3.1	4.8	2.2	18.8
Seattle, Wash.	100.0	1.5	4.6	5.8	32.1	15.6	21.3	8.9	9.6	0.6	6.1
Somerville, Mass.	100.0	2.3	5.7	9.8	31.9	22.4	19.2	3.3	4.4	1.0	8.0
South Bend, Ind.	100.0	1.4	6.9	13.4	33.6	17.9	14.4	5.2	6.6	0.7	8.3
Spokane, Wash.	100.0	1.3	5.1	6.4	35.5	16.0	18.8	8.5	7.7	0.7	6.4
Springfield, Mass.	100.0	2.5	6.0	8.9	27.1	24.8	18.7	4.6	6.0	1.3	8.5
Syracuse, N. Y.	100.0	3.8	6.0	7.6	34.8	17.1	16.7	4.7	8.0	1.3	9.8
Tacoma, Wash.	100.0	1.3	5.1	7.6	39.0	17.2	16.9	6.4	5.7	0.6	6.4
Tampa, Fla.	100.0	3.5	17.3	16.7	24.8	14.9	12.7	5.3	4.5	0.4	20.8
Toledo, Ohio	100.0	1.6	7.4	11.2	37.3	16.2	13.6	5.1	5.5	2.2	8.9
Trenton, N. J.	100.0	5.5	13.7	16.9	20.6	13.5	10.9	3.5	4.8	1.6	19.2
Tulsa, Okla.	100.0	1.2	5.4	7.7	25.8	16.7	21.3	10.6	10.7	0.7	6.6
Utica, N. Y.	100.0	6.8	9.1	10.9	34.7	16.1	12.4	2.9	4.6	2.4	15.9
Washington, D. C.	100.0	1.6	7.5	10.2	25.8	14.4	15.5	8.8	14.8	1.4	9.1
Wichita, Kans.	100.0	0.9	4.4	7.0	31.9	16.8	19.6	9.8	9.0	0.7	5.3
Wilmington, Del.	100.0	3.8	9.5	12.0	31.4	16.8	12.4	4.2	7.3	2.7	13.3
Worcester, Mass.	100.0	6.0	5.6	8.2	33.4	17.8	14.3	4.2	7.1	3.4	11.7
Yonkers, N. Y.	100.0	3.7	7.7	8.3	34.1	14.4	14.7	5.0	10.5	1.4	11.4
Youngstown, Ohio	100.0	4.8	11.2	12.8	33.1	15.4	12.7	4.2	4.9	0.9	16.1

Table 63.—PERCENT DISTRIBUTION BY YEARS OF SCHOOL COMPLETED, FOR FEMALES 25 YEARS OLD AND OVER, FOR CITIES OF 100,000 OR MORE: 1940

CITY	Females 25 years old and over	No school years completed	GRADE SCHOOL			HIGH SCHOOL		COLLEGE		Not reported	Less than 5 years completed
			1 to 4 years	5 and 6 years	7 and 8 years	1 to 3 years	4 years	1 to 3 years	4 years or more		
Akron, Ohio	100.0	2.2	4.9	8.5	35.6	19.3	20.1	5.4	3.6	0.5	7.1
Albany, N. Y	100.0	2.2	4.7	8.6	35.5	17.3	21.8	4.2	4.9	0.7	6.9
Atlanta, Ga	100.0	2.8	13.3	15.8	20.7	16.1	18.6	7.3	4.9	0.5	16.1
Baltimore, Md	100.0	3.4	12.1	18.5	31.5	13.9	13.1	3.1	2.8	1.6	15.4
Birmingham, Ala	100.0	3.7	13.0	13.8	23.7	16.0	17.8	6.8	4.7	0.5	16.7
Boston, Mass	100.0	5.2	5.7	7.1	31.3	16.5	24.2	4.6	4.0	1.4	10.9
Bridgeport, Conn	100.0	6.1	6.7	10.7	45.5	11.6	13.1	3.2	1.9	1.2	12.8
Buffalo, N. Y	100.0	3.2	6.7	10.2	40.5	18.5	13.3	3.3	3.2	1.1	9.9
Cambridge, Mass	100.0	3.5	4.8	7.3	31.4	13.9	22.3	5.6	7.3	3.9	8.3
Camden, N. J	100.0	5.9	11.7	16.0	38.7	13.6	8.4	1.5	1.2	2.2	17.5
Canton, Ohio	100.0	3.0	5.5	9.6	38.6	17.8	18.1	4.6	2.5	0.3	8.5
Charlotte, N. C	100.0	3.8	12.9	13.9	17.3	15.0	19.1	10.1	7.2	0.6	16.7
Chattanooga, Tenn	100.0	3.1	13.2	16.9	24.9	15.5	16.3	5.8	3.4	0.9	16.3
Chicago, Ill	100.0	4.2	7.0	8.5	39.9	15.9	16.2	4.6	3.2	0.4	11.3
Cincinnati, Ohio	100.0	1.3	8.1	13.5	35.5	16.2	15.1	4.4	4.3	1.6	9.4
Cleveland, Ohio	100.0	5.0	9.5	14.4	31.6	17.9	15.2	3.4	2.5	0.6	14.5
Columbus, Ohio	100.0	1.3	4.6	9.3	30.0	18.7	24.3	5.9	4.8	1.1	5.9
Dallas, Texs	100.0	2.0	6.4	10.3	20.0	20.3	26.2	9.4	5.1	0.5	8.3
Dayton Ohio	100.0	0.9	4.8	9.6	36.2	19.6	20.5	4.8	2.8	0.7	5.7
Denver, Colo	100.0	1.8	3.7	5.5	28.7	17.0	26.1	9.5	6.5	1.2	5.4
Des Moines, Iowa	100.0	0.7	2.6	5.4	26.1	17.8	29.7	10.2	6.0	1.5	3.4
Detroit, Mich	100.0	3.4	8.4	10.4	31.8	19.7	18.4	4.6	3.1	0.3	11.7
Duluth, Minn	100.0	1.7	4.6	7.8	34.7	18.3	19.6	8.0	4.8	0.6	6.3
Elizabeth, N. J	100.0	7.7	7.7	10.6	36.1	14.3	15.3	3.9	3.1	1.3	15.4
Erie, Pa	100.0	3.5	6.3	9.7	36.0	17.0	18.9	4.2	3.4	0.9	9.9
Fall River, Mass	100.0	8.8	11.9	19.0	34.0	10.4	8.8	3.0	1.8	2.3	20.7
Flint, Mich	100.0	1.5	4.9	7.7	32.1	24.1	19.6	6.6	3.0	0.5	6.3
Fort Wayne, Ind	100.0	0.5	3.0	7.2	41.3	17.3	19.3	5.9	3.3	2.1	3.5
Fort Worth, Tex	100.0	1.5	6.6	11.2	21.2	22.3	21.8	9.7	5.4	0.4	8.1
Gary, Ind	100.0	4.8	9.4	10.7	31.9	17.5	17.4	5.0	3.0	0.4	14.2
Grand Rapids, Mich	100.0	2.2	4.6	7.5	34.3	21.2	18.8	6.2	3.6	1.4	6.8
Hartford, Conn	100.0	4.6	5.5	6.5	35.1	15.9	18.7	4.6	3.2	5.9	10.1
Houston, Tex	100.0	2.6	8.1	12.2	20.2	19.8	21.7	8.3	5.4	1.6	10.7
Indianapolis, Ind	100.0	1.2	4.9	7.8	35.9	17.9	20.7	6.4	4.7	0.6	6.0
Jacksonville, Fla	100.0	2.4	11.9	14.7	24.9	16.2	18.2	6.4	3.7	1.6	14.2
Jersey City, N. J	100.0	5.8	7.2	9.4	46.2	14.0	11.4	2.7	2.3	1.1	13.0
Kansas City, Kans	100.0	2.3	7.7	12.0	35.6	18.1	15.9	5.0	2.9	0.4	10.1
Kansas City, Mo	100.0	1.5	4.6	7.2	28.8	17.8	25.8	9.0	4.6	0.7	6.1
Knoxville, Tenn	100.0	2.7	12.4	16.3	24.5	15.2	16.5	7.2	4.9	0.3	15.1
Long Beach, Calif	100.0	0.4	2.0	4.2	26.5	20.9	28.9	10.8	5.7	0.6	2.4
Los Angeles, Calif	100.0	2.2	4.3	6.1	25.3	18.9	27.8	9.1	5.7	0.6	6.5
Louisville, Ky	100.0	1.6	8.0	11.5	39.8	15.3	14.6	5.2	3.4	0.6	9.6
Lowell, Mass	100.0	5.2	7.0	13.0	34.4	15.6	17.5	3.3	2.6	1.3	12.3
Memphis, Tenn	100.0	2.9	12.5	14.1	24.0	17.5	18.3	6.4	3.6	0.6	15.5
Miami, Fla	100.0	1.3	6.7	10.2	25.2	18.8	24.1	7.4	4.8	1.5	8.0
Milwaukee, Wis	100.0	1.9	6.5	12.1	43.6	13.3	14.5	4.5	3.1	0.4	8.4
Minneapolis, Minn	100.0	1.0	3.3	6.0	34.4	16.5	24.8	8.4	5.3	0.4	4.3
Nashville, Tenn	100.0	2.8	10.3	14.1	29.0	16.2	16.0	6.5	4.3	0.8	13.0
Newark, N. J	100.0	6.9	9.4	11.2	40.2	12.6	10.9	2.6	2.0	4.2	16.3
New Bedford, Mass	100.0	11.1	10.7	16.3	37.5	9.9	8.9	2.7	1.5	1.5	21.8
New Haven, Conn	100.0	6.2	6.8	8.0	39.4	11.6	17.6	5.2	4.0	1.2	13.0
New Orleans, La	100.0	4.1	15.5	18.6	28.5	10.8	14.5	4.0	3.4	0.6	19.6
New York, N. Y	100.0	8.0	7.0	7.6	41.4	12.9	14.0	3.2	3.8	2.1	15.0
Bronx Borough	100.0	9.2	7.8	7.6	42.7	12.8	13.1	2.1	2.8	1.9	17.1
Brooklyn Borough	100.0	12.0	7.8	7.1	40.4	12.2	12.1	2.4	2.7	3.2	19.8
Manhattan Borough	100.0	6.0	7.7	9.4	35.5	12.4	16.6	5.1	6.3	1.1	13.7
Queens Borough	100.0	2.5	3.8	6.1	50.3	15.1	14.5	2.9	3.2	1.6	6.3
Richmond Borough	100.0	3.9	4.4	6.4	47.5	15.4	14.3	3.1	3.9	1.0	8.3
Norfolk, Va	100.0	3.2	13.0	13.5	22.9	16.1	18.4	7.8	4.1	1.0	16.2
Oakland, Calif	100.0	2.3	4.2	5.9	29.1	18.4	26.9	7.2	5.1	0.9	6.5
Oklahoma City, Okla	100.0	0.9	4.2	6.9	24.1	19.1	24.7	11.4	7.1	1.5	5.1
Omaha, Nebr	100.0	1.9	4.3	6.1	31.7	17.7	25.0	8.3	4.4	0.7	6.1
Paterson, N. J	100.0	7.8	10.9	13.5	41.9	10.9	8.7	2.9	2.1	1.2	18.7
Peoria, Ill	100.0	0.7	4.1	8.1	38.5	16.5	21.3	6.1	3.6	1.0	4.8
Philadelphia, Pa	100.0	5.3	7.8	12.1	40.5	14.5	13.5	2.5	2.2	1.6	13.0
Pittsburgh, Pa	100.0	4.0	7.3	11.9	38.1	13.8	16.4	3.7	4.0	0.6	11.3
Portland, Oreg	100.0	1.0	2.8	4.1	31.1	18.9	26.1	9.8	5.4	0.7	3.9
Providence, R. I	100.0	6.2	7.8	9.6	37.0	14.4	16.5	3.8	4.1	0.6	14.1
Reading, Pa	100.0	2.4	10.6	18.9	37.0	14.9	11.3	2.1	2.1	0.8	13.0
Richmond, Va	100.0	2.5	11.6	13.6	21.7	18.5	19.8	7.6	4.5	0.2	14.1
Rochester, N. Y	100.0	4.6	6.2	8.4	36.5	17.9	15.8	3.8	3.4	3.4	10.8
Sacramento, Calif	100.0	2.0	3.9	5.6	27.6	19.3	26.2	9.3	5.8	0.3	5.9
St. Louis, Mo	100.0	2.2	8.1	12.7	46.0	12.8	11.7	3.3	2.5	0.6	10.3
St. Paul, Minn	100.0	1.4	3.7	6.5	39.2	16.0	21.3	6.9	4.4	0.6	5.1
Salt Lake City, Utah	100.0	0.8	2.9	5.2	25.3	18.6	26.8	12.4	7.3	0.7	3.7
San Antonio, Tex	100.0	9.0	15.5	13.7	19.6	13.4	16.8	6.8	4.6	0.6	24.5
San Diego, Calif	100.0	1.2	3.8	5.7	24.8	20.9	26.7	10.3	6.1	0.4	5.0
San Francisco, Calif	100.0	2.0	4.4	5.4	31.0	17.1	27.0	6.9	5.2	1.1	6.4
Scranton, Pa	100.0	6.3	9.3	11.5	35.4	13.0	15.9	3.4	3.4	1.8	15.6
Seattle, Wash	100.0	1.0	2.6	3.9	28.2	17.3	29.4	10.1	7.1	0.5	3.6
Somerville, Mass	100.0	2.3	4.9	8.8	30.1	23.0	23.7	3.4	3.0	0.9	7.2
South Bend, Ind	100.0	1.3	6.3	12.4	33.3	18.3	18.8	5.7	3.5	0.4	7.6
Spokane, Wash	100.0	0.7	3.1	4.6	30.4	18.4	26.5	10.4	5.2	0.6	3.8
Springfield, Mass	100.0	2.7	5.4	8.2	25.2	24.7	24.0	5.3	3.2	1.2	8.2
Syracuse, N. Y	100.0	3.5	4.8	6.9	34.9	17.7	21.7	4.8	4.7	1.0	8.3
Tacoma, Wash	100.0	1.0	3.3	5.7	34.4	19.2	23.6	7.7	4.6	0.4	4.3
Tampa, Fla	100.0	4.2	15.0	15.9	23.3	16.7	16.0	5.1	3.6	0.3	19.2
Toledo, Ohio	100.0	1.3	6.0	10.6	36.9	17.2	18.1	4.8	3.3	1.8	7.3
Trenton, N. J	100.0	5.9	11.7	16.3	30.0	13.9	14.1	4.0	2.8	1.3	17.7
Tulsa, Okla	100.0	1.0	3.9	6.8	24.0	19.4	26.5	11.0	6.9	0.5	4.8
Utica, N. Y	100.0	7.4	6.9	9.9	36.1	16.3	15.2	3.3	2.9	2.0	14.4
Washington, D. C	100.0	1.5	5.8	9.0	24.5	15.9	24.3	10.2	7.6	1.1	7.3
Wichita, Kans	100.0	0.6	2.8	5.4	29.4	18.6	25.6	10.2	6.9	0.5	3.4
Wilmington, Del	100.0	3.8	8.2	11.0	30.1	18.7	17.9	4.2	3.7	2.4	12.1
Worcester, Mass	100.0	6.1	4.7	8.0	31.2	18.6	18.8	5.6	4.0	3.1	10.7
Yonkers, N. Y	100.0	4.2	6.9	8.3	35.2	14.9	18.1	4.7	6.4	1.3	11.1
Youngstown, Ohio	100.0	4.4	8.7	12.2	33.7	16.4	16.0	5.0	2.9	0.8	13.1

TABLE 64.—FOREIGN-BORN WHITE, BY COUNTRY OF BIRTH, FOR CITIES OF 100,000 OR MORE: 1940

COUNTRY OF BIRTH	AKRON, OHIO	ALBANY, N. Y.	ATLANTA, GA.	BALTIMORE, MD.	BIRMINGHAM, ALA.	BOSTON, MASS.	BRIDGEPORT, CONN.	BUFFALO, N. Y.	CAMBRIDGE, MASS.	CAMDEN, N. J.	CANTON, OHIO	CHARLOTTE, N. C.	CHATTANOOGA, TENN.	CHICAGO, ILL.
All countries	25, 420	15, 178	4, 293	60, 969	4, 425	180, 864	33, 431	91, 789	24, 558	14, 996	11, 069	892	1, 114	672, 705
England	1, 875	785	310	2, 355	482	7, 246	2, 020	5, 674	1, 018	963	518	123	100	19, 144
Scotland	1, 013	346	126	750	335	4, 143	785	2, 772	642	319	185	43	31	10, 314
Wales	206	48	8	95	40	98	26	159	17	25	163	5	8	807
Northern Ireland	70	312	24	228	24	2, 724	208	636	250	273	29	12	1	5, 152
Irish Free State (Eire)	353	1, 261	112	2, 159	74	34, 783	1, 957	3, 020	4, 744	477	77	22	23	35, 158
Norway	85	52	23	308	22	1, 079	103	341	95	107	14	6	5	14, 933
Sweden	440	139	57	331	55	3, 799	1, 274	776	466	101	68	14	16	46, 258
Denmark	113	78	12	183	17	493	252	238	58	26	52	4	5	8, 720
Netherlands	69	143	11	189	14	364	51	260	24	15	8	1	4	6, 784
Belgium	39	20	7	81	16	329	43	60	19	20	12	4	2	3, 504
Luxemburg	5	5	----	----	1	11	4	13	----	3	1	----	1	1, 290
Switzerland	220	59	28	200	23	228	80	331	32	37	205	8	19	2, 508
France	344	90	88	379	126	749	126	739	106	89	97	10	7	3, 237
Germany	1, 915	1, 687	386	9, 744	300	3, 851	1, 644	12, 483	376	1, 180	1, 074	91	133	83, 424
Poland	1, 260	1, 471	360	8, 662	210	6, 048	2, 899	20, 545	838	2, 785	515	25	120	119, 264
Czechoslovakia	1, 023	66	13	1, 816	9	198	2, 962	506	23	77	395	8	3	33, 596
Austria	1, 361	431	96	1, 984	72	1, 641	920	2, 374	142	529	544	17	19	26, 091
Hungary	3, 346	103	66	836	60	280	3, 810	1, 908	50	161	541	10	18	16, 020
Yugoslavia	2, 725	15	5	151	8	23	217	198	4	96	352	----	1	12, 059
Russia (U. S. S. R.)	1, 305	1, 729	1, 048	14, 670	395	28, 014	2, 249	4, 090	1, 079	1, 537	526	57	320	66, 950
Lithuania	208	156	62	2, 839	59	5, 076	698	269	891	255	38	9	26	26, 254
Latvia	16	11	29	358	10	795	39	43	33	18	11	3	7	1, 990
Finland	14	86	13	169	5	391	46	131	42	50	8	----	1	1, 733
Rumania	761	65	43	596	43	575	143	548	48	81	1, 052	1	7	8, 387
Bulgaria	78	16	2	8	3	22	7	54	1	6	41	----	----	427
Turkey in Europe	2	2	10	3	----	6	4	----	1	3	5	----	2	44
Greece	780	357	440	1, 193	382	3, 141	400	726	631	99	794	128	57	13, 972
Italy	3, 776	3, 836	179	8, 063	1, 130	31, 555	7, 879	17, 847	2, 991	4, 908	2, 214	34	35	66, 472
Spain	71	98	10	149	4	233	113	163	26	9	415	4	----	429
Portugal	4	4	3	29	----	855	175	16	1, 603	7	87	2	----	38
Other Europe	142	74	4	98	5	1, 095	321	84	80	16	21	3	5	731
Palestine and Syria	415	97	116	91	251	2, 018	162	284	61	11	303	66	12	827
Turkey in Asia	266	177	145	231	18	1, 136	161	121	254	95	367	17	----	1, 883
Other Asia	36	43	29	98	14	1, 068	53	81	191	66	27	11	7	2, 511
Canada—French	79	409	20	116	13	3, 098	656	788	1, 146	29	24	8	7	3, 115
Canada—Other	760	796	283	1, 153	146	30, 045	703	12, 947	5, 516	190	216	108	71	18, 463
Newfoundland	9	23	6	41	2	2, 150	25	157	746	227	2	1	1	210
Mexico	25	10	14	64	17	44	5	69	8	6	27	9	4	7, 132
Cuba and other West Indies	16	19	37	141	22	235	22	48	75	15	9	12	6	373
Central and South America	34	30	34	209	9	244	50	116	103	54	14	5	11	1, 062
Australia	14	8	7	39	2	63	6	37	20	19	2	4	----	300
Azores	----	1	1	----	----	62	10	2	65	----	----	----	----	7
All other and not reported	48	20	26	100	7	256	33	75	43	12	16	7	10	534

COUNTRY OF BIRTH	CINCINNATI, OHIO	CLEVELAND, OHIO	COLUMBUS, OHIO	DALLAS, TEX.	DAYTON, OHIO	DENVER, COLO.	DES MOINES, IOWA	DETROIT, MICH.	DULUTH, MINN.	ELIZABETH, N. J.	ERIE, PA.	FALL RIVER, MASS.	FLINT, MICH.	FORT WAYNE, IND.
All countries	26, 790	179, 183	11, 027	7, 355	9, 329	24, 757	7, 474	320, 664	19, 332	22, 605	13, 570	24, 572	15, 845	4, 409
England	950	6, 542	812	465	431	2, 001	765	21, 049	515	863	420	3, 640	2, 219	267
Scotland	319	3, 438	272	115	150	720	245	17, 061	267	968	230	244	939	58
Wales	43	584	138	13	13	164	109	691	13	26	21	17	61	21
Northern Ireland	114	825	48	27	32	168	24	2, 211	43	267	54	96	124	16
Irish Free State (Eire)	1, 271	5, 112	477	184	302	1, 207	207	4, 760	162	1, 544	272	1, 027	238	88
Norway	32	424	47	75	19	391	280	1, 137	3, 251	154	60	4	108	21
Sweden	109	1, 389	80	129	78	2, 427	1, 069	3, 185	5, 052	216	624	43	246	77
Denmark	66	355	30	81	22	669	370	1, 510	257	129	176	12	114	22
Netherlands	115	547	40	26	50	389	69	1, 711	24	37	24	2	72	29
Belgium	21	95	84	14	15	53	20	6, 890	70	21	9	9	83	13
Luxemburg	9	30	1	3	----	15	1	58	5	2	1	1	5	1
Switzerland	289	618	191	108	73	290	53	776	33	88	64	5	47	112
France	462	517	143	83	105	241	86	1, 639	35	125	76	72	74	81
Germany	3, 856	15, 427	2, 422	891	2, 639	2, 829	654	23, 785	767	2, 681	1, 867	90	868	1, 025
Poland	790	24, 771	329	400	486	1, 137	244	52, 235	936	3, 867	3, 325	1, 517	1, 224	237
Czechoslovakia	114	21, 066	122	240	139	255	56	4, 080	100	631	307	16	572	8
Austria	991	9, 931	504	143	441	956	146	7, 992	258	1, 271	678	312	277	73
Hungary	1, 213	20, 944	681	40	1, 248	316	24	11, 382	25	945	329	5	977	43
Yugoslavia	508	14, 103	255	25	366	252	88	6, 278	619	72	46	1	280	33
Russia (U. S. S. R.)	3, 317	11, 967	1, 154	744	735	3, 657	606	20, 252	678	1, 873	598	984	782	149
Lithuania	338	3, 890	85	47	265	123	241	4, 142	235	1, 211	87	12	42	22
Latvia	40	346	14	22	16	27	11	421	8	52	12	6	17	4
Finland	15	739	25	13	11	117	8	1, 944	2, 434	8	116	8	75	5
Rumania	1, 121	3, 907	176	83	162	222	43	5, 109	47	229	216	22	114	128
Bulgaria	55	186	31	10	26	46	----	702	11	----	1	----	43	24
Turkey in Europe	2	498	1	----	3	10	5	29	----	----	----	1	----	----
Greece	481	1, 891	415	176	306	418	157	5, 476	140	178	143	151	256	261
Italy	2, 722	20, 961	2, 451	423	553	2, 339	1, 130	26, 277	657	3, 790	2, 988	710	501	276
Spain	23	177	8	31	4	46	4	585	2	221	14	5	3	1
Portugal	14	22	----	1	----	3	----	50	----	384	91	4, 466	4	2
Other Europe	61	156	32	18	5	15	3	2, 412	27	12	17	11	23	6
Palestine and Syria	200	1, 068	59	83	52	51	57	2, 927	26	16	14	419	262	61
Turkey in Asia	156	40	42	9	103	30	1	2, 813	4	10	15	16	52	7
Other Asia	54	188	46	22	8	47	15	1, 864	5	57	30	14	232	9
Canada—French	77	551	55	23	38	159	30	9, 699	586	72	47	6, 027	591	25
Canada—Other	609	5, 110	540	294	378	1, 680	417	64, 438	1, 986	342	532	755	4, 148	280
Newfoundland	11	50	10	8	4	16	2	488	16	73	17	31	14	1
Mexico	20	162	16	2, 192	13	955	166	1, 505	8	5	15	1	103	6
Cuba and other West Indies	33	77	17	20	6	26	6	202	3	62	3	20	6	8
Central and South America	95	199	40	26	13	85	17	396	7	63	19	148	15	3
Australia	23	41	15	12	9	48	10	131	8	7	7	13	8	4
Azores	----	1	1	----	----	----	----	3	----	8	1	3, 505	----	----
All other and not reported	42	148	18	21	10	67	26	309	12	25	4	134	32	2

TABLE 64.—FOREIGN-BORN WHITE, BY COUNTRY OF BIRTH, FOR CITIES OF 100,000 OR MORE: 1940—Continued

COUNTRY OF BIRTH	FORT WORTH, TEX.	GARY, IND.	GRAND RAPIDS, MICH.	HARTFORD, CONN.	HOUSTON, TEX.	INDIANAPOLIS, IND.	JACKSONVILLE, FLA.	JERSEY CITY, N. J.	KANSAS CITY, KANS.	KANSAS CITY, MO.	KNOXVILLE, TENN.	LONG BEACH, CALIF.	LOS ANGELES, CALIF.	LOUISVILLE, KY.
All countries	3,540	17,270	20,347	36,605	15,313	10,555	3,972	53,160	6,572	19,339	732	12,432	215,248	6,201
England	210	495	602	1,296	845	734	515	1,855	235	1,067	86	2,539	19,713	335
Scotland	74	519	159	948	232	376	132	1,408	74	369	31	674	5,980	114
Wales	9	112	8	11	17	28	18	37	38	48	17	115	741	10
Northern Island	37	69	33	308	35	183	28	899	60	149	8	103	1,646	49
Irish Free State (Eire)	108	216	226	3,904	398	1,029	114	6,028	243	1,006	22	402	4,194	445
Norway	44	77	116	79	138	57	51	670	32	112	17	398	3,435	17
Sweden	114	445	638	1,452	269	145	126	501	353	1,124	8	572	7,844	52
Denmark	16	77	152	388	136	127	63	215	96	311	5	394	3,138	26
Netherlands	6	36	8,115	48	84	105	40	284	18	84	6	209	2,013	23
Belgium	6	21	53	30	35	17	12	94	77	266	1	46	816	6
Luxemburg	-------	4	2	7	3	4	-------	13	2	11	-------	5	95	4
Switzerland	32	14	39	62	110	105	34	226	41	210	29	120	1,940	299
France	40	58	50	154	195	155	46	292	43	232	8	125	3,196	136
Germany	330	694	1,423	1,528	1,702	2,571	453	6,206	673	2,701	58	1,120	17,528	1,953
Poland	185	2,201	3,583	3,733	720	387	121	8,847	638	1,358	44	136	7,448	350
Czechoslovakia	98	1,720	89	87	368	56	19	814	105	125	10	84	1,536	31
Austria	64	787	265	987	489	469	91	2,400	437	585	17	155	5,389	163
Hungary	15	1,027	101	196	127	212	52	950	44	176	37	72	3,978	52
Yugoslavia	23	2,095	11	50	29	312	2	99	1,435	165	4	59	3,441	14
Russia (U. S. S. R.)	302	806	449	5,484	1,129	763	320	3,711	405	2,800	69	419	25,595	845
Lithuania	19	473	1,034	1,283	55	114	56	326	83	222	10	26	1,158	68
Latvia	8	8	4	22	28	10	9	67	1	36	3	16	527	27
Finland	7	33	118	64	30	22	23	444	4	28	-------	68	1,049	17
Rumania	12	501	29	216	125	321	86	287	9	187	4	49	2,750	42
Bulgaria	2	91	3	2	4	73	-------	22	16	16	-------	14	221	-------
Turkey in Europe	-------	-------	3	6	3	1	-------	3	6	10	2	-------	17	-------
Greece	92	1,217	132	391	419	437	151	630	146	362	75	211	1,905	72
Italy	82	1,237	654	8,389	1,346	628	178	13,831	79	3,130	46	245	13,256	441
Spain	13	428	5	36	54	10	51	214	18	28	-------	18	1,154	8
Portugal	-------	4	1	252	5	2	3	105	-------	2	-------	12	197	1
Other Europe	2	105	13	25	23	27	12	72	6	17	4	24	253	9
Palestine and Syria	33	24	301	60	217	208	471	33	2	145	11	31	1,066	193
Turkey in Asia	23	131	47	203	65	106	27	231	3	20	2	64	1,931	15
Other Asia	16	182	51	179	48	34	26	93	9	28	3	86	1,685	14
Canada—French	20	110	119	2,541	29	49	33	121	21	73	4	163	2,159	13
Canada—Other	186	647	1,636	1,904	519	550	426	657	147	893	64	2,975	25,596	247
Newfoundland	2	18	12	107	18	4	9	76	-------	7	1	21	141	11
Mexico	1,274	517	35	6	5,035	31	10	42	947	1,012	2	445	36,840	16
Cuba and other West Indies	9	14	5	33	73	23	97	90	3	21	3	30	436	18
Central and South America	10	22	13	63	70	21	25	149	11	57	17	45	1,450	33
Australia	7	15	2	12	25	16	5	46	4	25	3	58	849	13
Azores	-------	-------	-------	24	-------	-------	1	5	-------	-------	-------	1	31	-------
All other and not reported	10	20	16	35	61	33	36	67	8	31	1	65	911	19

COUNTRY OF BIRTH	LOWELL, MASS.	MEMPHIS, TENN.	MIAMI, FLA.	MILWAUKEE, WIS.	MINNEAPOLIS, MINN.	NASHVILLE, TENN.	NEWARK, N. J.	NEW BEDFORD, MASS.	NEW HAVEN, CONN.	NEW ORLEANS, LA.	NEW YORK, N. Y.	BRONX BORO., N. Y.	BROOKLYN BORO., N. Y.	MANHATTAN BORO., N. Y.
All countries	19,418	4,468	12,517	83,809	64,149	1,522	90,346	29,623	32,390	14,695	2,080,020	460,476	767,638	540,197
England	1,784	287	1,446	1,414	1,868	114	2,986	6,136	1,108	731	63,115	10,570	19,216	18,833
Scotland	477	97	460	448	787	44	2,327	282	602	199	33,292	5,529	10,188	8,498
Wales	14	13	40	106	104	5	61	14	11	7	1,296	192	261	542
Northern Ireland	294	36	86	109	179	11	702	163	271	91	21,501	4,258	4,914	8,502
Irish Free State (Eire)	2,883	120	378	547	775	58	4,597	728	3,727	420	160,325	38,451	34,775	60,494
Norway	38	13	229	1,480	11,777	8	171	176	97	281	30,750	1,257	20,214	3,651
Sweden	244	79	454	934	19,244	13	385	159	710	162	28,881	3,644	11,241	7,792
Denmark	14	27	221	617	2,010	8	221	25	155	142	8,845	955	3,380	2,456
Netherlands	5	10	126	379	301	6	219	13	26	97	5,608	745	1,449	2,263
Belgium	52	8	59	121	85	3	56	74	77	68	3,888	481	831	1,705
Luxemburg	-------	-------	14	78	72	1	6	-------	3	2	340	47	38	128
Switzerland	8	34	110	866	210	20	280	36	56	101	8,551	1,209	1,100	3,621
France	51	64	224	218	176	29	469	228	116	1,113	19,696	2,366	2,814	9,865
Germany	109	552	1,433	28,085	4,433	242	7,813	266	1,554	1,403	224,749	40,803	42,111	72,785
Poland	1,352	467	350	14,695	3,637	142	10,376	1,925	2,772	355	194,163	52,409	87,980	38,446
Czechoslovakia	1	28	103	2,920	1,503	7	1,603	78	82	68	26,884	4,491	2,928	12,637
Austria	46	113	363	6,646	1,564	54	6,142	142	508	259	145,106	30,637	53,621	37,591
Hungary	12	55	317	3,521	401	53	2,564	28	271	65	62,588	20,985	12,010	19,472
Yugoslavia	-------	8	22	3,658	165	2	116	-------	13	178	6,475	815	1,090	2,619
Russia (U. S. S. R.)	531	650	1,191	6,606	4,481	299	14,538	735	4,586	811	395,696	115,050	201,961	59,335
Lithuania	434	30	74	520	521	14	1,124	83	664	36	15,089	2,495	7,944	2,270
Latvia	13	27	29	154	80	3	132	2	82	13	5,317	1,595	1,765	1,489
Finland	22	6	87	165	917	4	74	7	39	42	11,245	2,492	2,523	4,788
Rumania	14	48	181	527	1,099	25	1,014	9	142	84	40,655	14,109	16,349	7,602
Bulgaria	4	-------	5	67	77	-------	12	2	6	7	670	153	130	302
Turkey in Europe	-------	4	-------	8	3	4	1	-------	2	6	265	72	42	101
Greece	1,649	266	282	1,356	765	75	1,186	301	346	281	28,593	4,083	6,466	13,600
Italy	297	1,054	638	4,374	702	96	26,140	482	12,652	4,962	409,480	71,903	183,702	88,074
Spain	6	2	101	19	13	1	949	19	43	343	13,583	1,505	3,078	7,415
Portugal	921	-------	7	10	1	-------	1,452	4,794	134	18	2,676	376	870	908
Other Europe	16	11	30	106	71	2	51	56	11	33	5,757	923	1,063	2,851
Palestine and Syria	175	18	207	150	204	20	219	173	44	82	8,598	670	6,546	1,123
Turkey in Asia	155	13	95	125	40	1	172	28	120	47	17,398	5,096	3,722	6,066
Other Asia	216	7	49	62	61	15	122	16	60	29	5,107	918	859	2,878
Canada—French	5,516	17	175	338	836	3	233	5,677	336	80	6,270	872	1,558	2,530
Canada—Other	1,955	216	1,460	1,703	4,614	105	1,109	901	738	329	29,237	3,860	8,356	10,265
Newfoundland	19	4	19	22	18	1	48	134	55	9	4,838	400	3,089	531
Mexico	1	25	34	463	189	5	35	3	3	587	2,973	307	565	1,756
Cuba and other West Indies	6	19	1,124	24	19	4	131	46	28	238	13,344	2,109	2,589	6,903
Central and South America	17	11	86	77	59	11	337	153	96	818	12,429	1,876	2,770	6,203
Australia	2	4	30	27	21	1	45	2	11	27	987	92	210	464
Azores	33	-------	4	-------	1	-------	14	5,056	-------	-------	69	8	29	23
All other and not reported	32	25	75	64	66	4	114	471	33	71	3,682	518	1,282	1,320

524997 O - 43 - 12

TABLE 64.—FOREIGN-BORN WHITE, BY COUNTRY OF BIRTH, FOR CITIES OF 100,000 OR MORE: 1940—Continued

COUNTRY OF BIRTH	Queens Boro., N. Y.	Richmond Boro., N. Y.	Norfolk, Va.	Oakland, Calif.	Oklahoma City, Okla.	Omaha, Nebr.	Paterson, N. J.	Peoria, Ill.	Philadelphia, Pa.	Pittsburgh, Pa.	Portland, Oreg.	Providence, R. I.	Reading, Pa.	Richmond, Va.
All countries	276,588	35,121	3,657	42,661	2,818	22,311	34,088	5,464	290,325	84,606	38,608	51,208	7,861	3,413
England	12,632	1,864	316	4,021	221	687	1,779	496	17,063	4,211	3,128	4,735	209	306
Scotland	7,666	1,411	118	2,001	73	302	1,284	211	8,191	2,208	1,462	1,276	80	114
Wales	245	56	6	234	12	29	15	22	386	602	157	50	17	15
Northern Ireland	3,321	506	20	442	12	101	766	21	11,237	2,120	261	788	22	13
Irish Free State (Eire)	23,632	2,973	120	1,911	63	635	780	216	24,826	5,181	785	5,659	80	78
Norway	2,645	2.983	74	1,259	28	227	24	41	952	112	2,355	162	21	17
Sweden	5,107	1,097	55	2,562	89	2,183	80	360	1,592	665	3,622	1,629	23	25
Denmark	1,627	427	43	1,529	41	1,934	37	75	681	51	1,069	64	15	28
Netherlands	989	162	41	326	12	68	2,041	40	326	64	322	43	24	16
Belgium	771	100	11	150	13	224	558	82	356	90	191	115	5	7
Luxemburg	123	4	1	21	3	9	7	---	35	23	28	3	---	---
Switzerland	2,307	224	18	570	25	104	608	165	1,048	401	934	54	21	20
France	4,226	425	66	1,005	39	74	707	153	2,105	670	288	302	30	61
Germany	64,912	4,138	248	3,682	511	2,756	2,485	1,547	27,286	9,805	3,947	1,103	923	404
Poland	13,492	1,836	170	491	112	1,816	4,558	132	23,737	10,848	846	1,934	1,797	178
Czechoslovakia	6,593	235	18	190	208	2,816	151	39	2,150	3,673	363	66	289	24
Austria	13,364	893	44	847	66	570	666	156	10,501	6,102	1,009	716	491	103
Hungary	9,607	614	44	362	21	262	553	108	7,156	2,405	219	69	68	35
Yugoslavia	1,816	135	4	801	15	518	13	192	950	2,825	606	4	165	1
Russia (U. S. S. R.)	17,960	1,300	821	1,087	211	1,963	2,368	215	66,585	8,179	3,932	4,260	558	590
Lithuania	2,266	114	111	81	16	337	652	93	5,569	2,685	127	497	137	70
Latvia	415	53	42	60	2	26	56	7	683	60	63	30	7	21
Finland	1,078	364	21	359	5	11	10	6	304	81	1,078	60	3	5
Rumania	2,612	83	26	169	28	208	63	28	5,619	1,265	325	285	17	43
Bulgaria	75	10	---	23	3	20	1	23	52	54	112	12	1	2
Turkey in Europe	50	---	---	6	---	---	2	1	13	1	1	715	---	4
Greece	4,196	248	284	765	141	260	315	180	1,919	1,479	744	446	486	141
Italy	55,011	10,799	317	5,707	49	2,834	11,631	313	59,079	16,241	2,658	17,010	2,100	449
Spain	1,404	181	43	469	17	5	146	---	451	64	27	32	4	4
Portugal	467	46	18	3,240	---	---	34	2	175	12	21	1,145	7	2
Other Europe	854	66	10	48	5	14	16	4	675	80	72	31	8	8
Palestine and Syria	239	20	80	106	125	129	802	148	438	542	146	226	17	131
Turkey in Asia	2,447	67	38	163	11	31	216	13	1,530	125	128	25	59	129
Other Asia	907	45	37	296	21	21	158	5	1,066	95	109	1,023	8	90
Canada—French	1,188	122	17	341	36	68	69	21	528	96	416	2,886	25	44
Canada—Other	5,845	911	255	4,205	226	627	252	268	2,947	1,058	6,613	2,782	97	177
Newfoundland	636	122	9	36	2	11	8	3	378	61	32	86	2	4
Mexico	309	36	9	1,565	312	383	4	65	213	124	62	7	5	7
Cuba and other West Indies	1,602	141	31	57	15	2	12	5	456	30	29	57	10	21
Central and South America	1.456	124	28	316	8	13	116	9	615	103	65	179	7	12
Australia	193	28	12	381	7	12	7	6	171	43	113	21	5	3
Azores	4	5	---	418	---	---	---	---	3	---	3	525	2	---
All other and not reported	499	63	25	350	14	21	38	3	278	72	140	96	7	11

COUNTRY OF BIRTH	Rochester, N. Y.	Sacramento, Calif.	St. Louis, Mo.	St. Paul, Minn.	Salt Lake City, Utah	San Antonio, Tex.	San Diego, Calif.	San Francisco, Calif.	Scranton, Pa.	Seattle, Wash.	Somerville, Mass.	South Bend, Ind.	Spokane, Wash.	Springfield, Mass.
All countries	60,107	12,144	59,406	33,612	13,340	28,037	19,529	130,271	18,380	59,612	23,855	10,877	12,755	26,738
England	4,145	907	1,085	1,004	3,112	464	2,550	7,957	1,453	5,697	803	247	1,073	1,407
Scotland	1,387	306	508	457	548	84	700	3,519	486	2,420	796	95	308	1,408
Wales	72	32	53	22	112	6	85	287	1,164	368	12	4	59	12
Northern Ireland	348	76	355	171	51	20	162	1,778	103	532	459	19	102	248
Irish Free State (Eire)	2,376	479	3,217	1,320	186	355	552	10,271	1,125	1,482	4,372	98	306	3,547
Norway	84	165	119	2,548	599	32	426	2,951	7	8,436	78	44	1,154	63
Sweden	343	448	439	6,100	1,260	78	946	5,278	42	7,670	417	372	1,942	802
Denmark	152	220	207	865	971	44	391	2,760	11	1,514	67	66	322	50
Netherlands	1,418	58	162	145	979	35	202	882	13	438	5	69	129	21
Belgium	390	22	184	49	16	40	57	451	10	370	11	595	37	40
Luxemburg	10	1	27	115	3	4	9	66	---	40	---	7	18	3
Switzerland	294	338	937	328	444	91	103	2,620	105	392	11	31	134	42
France	378	123	657	192	58	201	301	4,868	48	421	89	55	82	116
Germany	7,302	931	14,120	5,294	2,053	1,427	1,815	14,977	1,321	3,581	206	1,063	1,303	1,032
Poland	3,737	148	4,187	1,835	71	260	279	2,441	3,115	858	218	2,948	142	2,285
Czechoslovakia	97	48	2,185	906	26	118	151	783	335	244	17	69	67	92
Austria	1,448	823	4,104	2,046	102	163	286	2,676	1,540	1,034	49	656	229	272
Hungary	291	67	2,434	753	41	66	158	1,016	304	229	15	2,530	45	57
Yugoslavia	173	493	1,795	117	49	19	164	1,821	12	627	12	279	164	3
Russia (U. S. S. R)	4,534	396	6,979	3,067	210	572	641	7,380	1,209	2,371	382	454	399	2,527
Lithuania	875	16	409	194	6	47	51	304	1,661	234	117	93	17	231
Latvia	60	18	51	43	5	10	35	299	8	151	24	5	5	34
Finland	44	102	26	86	50	10	84	1,620	5	1,740	14	5	150	129
Rumania	141	55	1,050	431	27	67	94	905	51	151	17	45	56	43
Bulgaria	25	7	84	9	5	---	8	103	4	50	2	21	21	7
Turkey in Europe	1	3	42	1	15	2	---	11	---	20	---	1	---	10
Greece	344	524	1,399	260	661	136	271	3,508	127	924	383	181	188	737
Italy	20,929	1,062	8,131	1,503	469	427	1,315	24,036	3,408	3,055	4,857	263	905	4,727
Spain	27	181	316	6	26	102	92	1,949	46	79	14	2	4	26
Portugal	125	522	4	---	2	2	504	605	61	15	1,102	6	2	43
Other Europe	78	20	381	28	15	3	39	924	30	315	209	11	11	23
Palestine and Syria	159	40	419	217	91	120	50	379	160	96	44	15	20	280
Turkey in Asia	238	36	176	32	1	21	57	809	14	492	456	22	4	323
Other Asia	59	105	74	58	22	30	107	1,601	11	274	198	7	18	108
Canada—French	462	67	173	491	30	31	240	721	15	851	613	53	248	3,500
Canada—Other	7,298	1,178	834	2,315	600	281	2,629	7,894	138	11,694	7,195	404	2,929	2,104
Newfoundland	35	6	8	12	1	9	25	79	7	121	440	4	9	75
Mexico	12	1,285	425	441	261	22,530	3,347	4,729	10	96	1	7	7	---
Cuba and other West Indies	33	11	41	5	3	48	50	222	5	31	26	5	10	45
Central and South America	89	61	109	19	18	58	151	2,684	18	119	29	8	11	55
Australia	19	53	46	14	64	11	80	1,088	14	201	9	4	13	10
Azores	1	153	---	---	1	1	81	143	---	3	64	---	---	6
All other and not reported	74	68	74	23	76	12	91	876	25	167	22	14	28	46

Table 64.—FOREIGN-BORN WHITE, BY COUNTRY OF BIRTH, FOR CITIES OF 100,000 OR MORE: 1940—Continued

COUNTRY OF BIRTH	SYRACUSE, N. Y.	TACOMA, WASH.	TAMPA, FLA.	TOLEDO, OHIO	TRENTON, N. J.	TULSA, OKLA.	UTICA, N. Y.	WASHINGTON, D. C.	WICHITA, KANS.	WILMINGTON DEL.	WORCESTER, MASS.	YONKERS, N. Y.	YOUNGSTOWN, OHIO
All countries	27,550	15,854	11,082	24,747	21,856	2,174	17,340	34,014	2,154	10,481	39,991	28,657	26,671
England	1,693	1,304	315	1,211	1,402	177	854	2,665	197	536	2,068	1,643	1,684
Scotland	587	495	92	442	479	76	183	942	65	270	859	2,336	954
Wales	71	74	14	38	13	21	800	71	14	8	16	33	696
Northern Ireland	133	122	22	131	112	20	85	432	6	239	378	446	127
Irish Free State (Eire)	2,017	325	73	617	736	53	593	2,326	65	987	4,991	2,802	678
Norway	67	2,701	33	105	15	28	15	264	22	67	233	231	37
Sweden	179	2,181	70	223	70	86	46	580	64	124	5,468	371	542
Denmark	66	427	47	127	35	24	49	259	31	48	165	135	24
Netherlands	59	61	31	59	31	23	27	203	23	14	55	118	24
Belgium	19	37	18	121	17	12	6	94	5	9	29	22	12
Luxemburg	1	9	3	12	2	-----	3	17	2	2	6	6	6
Switzerland	202	229	39	359	32	25	109	349	28	36	28	121	81
France	127	100	66	255	101	42	83	719	24	61	119	171	43
Germany	3,247	1,093	326	4,890	1,336	322	1,084	3,390	420	611	413	2,452	864
Poland	3,357	208	55	6,364	3,021	95	3,272	2,019	30	2,195	2,677	2,756	1,809
Czechoslovakia	119	239	26	493	1,283	20	31	265	25	24	22	1,390	3,468
Austria	716	500	64	515	553	58	233	879	57	331	159	2,328	1,008
Hungary	112	35	41	2,010	2,711	21	41	412	23	98	44	888	2,046
Yugoslavia	104	412	4	116	372	9	2	91	10	12	6	29	1,678
Russia (U. S. S. R.)	1,963	651	112	1,162	1,672	251	517	6,038	203	1,042	2,583	1,502	1,275
Lithuania	177	98	22	127	189	27	215	523	7	67	3,573	217	212
Latvia	20	16	7	15	47	60	2	209	1	31	21	35	21
Finland	39	253	8	22	14	2	11	138	3	18	1,300	57	44
Rumania	107	20	96	202	388	13	16	299	13	86	53	121	1,004
Bulgaria	26	13	-----	489	5	34	1	25	2	-----	8	12	63
Turkey in Europe	-----	1	-----	-----	6	5	2	9	1	21	25	-----	-----
Greece	367	214	70	674	173	125	74	1,863	61	276	487	153	656
Italy	7,833	1,016	2,684	859	6,582	50	7,092	4,913	22	2,805	4,069	6,408	6,243
Spain	36	4	2,600	7	19	3	8	167	2	54	15	117	167
Portugal	10	5	5	2	14	2	61	37	-----	19	59	212	3
Other Europe	37	12	2	20	9	2	6	86	4	9	791	18	33
Palestine and Syria	167	14	50	542	48	16	756	362	119	13	549	73	273
Turkey in Asia	274	81	9	187	18	2	28	356	3	17	637	84	115
Other Asia	105	27	5	34	15	6	20	156	11	15	830	275	29
Canada—French	638	195	44	324	76	18	242	276	24	64	3,387	115	25
Canada—Other	2,702	2,484	408	1,697	181	291	721	1,748	182	153	3,633	719	381
Newfoundland	18	10	5	17	4	3	12	58	-----	9	98	19	4
Mexico	21	10	95	196	11	125	2	94	343	16	4	8	86
Cuba and other West Indies	26	9	3,317	16	9	8	8	150	13	27	25	95	9
Central and South America	42	36	158	32	33	10	16	354	9	38	36	82	22
Australia	18	25	6	13	5	3	6	61	2	6	8	16	6
Azores	4	-----	-----	-----	-----	-----	2	6	-----	-----	9	3	-----
All other and not reported	44	18	40	22	17	6	6	109	9	23	55	38	39

TABLE 65.—PERSONS 14 YEARS OLD AND OVER BY EMPLOYMENT STATUS, FOR CITIES OF 100,000 OR MORE: 1940

CITY	Population 14 years old and over	IN LABOR FORCE: Total: Number	IN LABOR FORCE: Total: Percent of pop. 14 and over	Employed (except on emergency work): Number	Employed: Percent of labor force	On public emergency work: Number	On public emergency work: Percent of labor force	Seeking work: Number	Seeking work: Percent of labor force	Seeking work: Experienced workers	Seeking work: New workers	NOT IN LABOR FORCE: Total	Engaged in own home housework	In school	Unable to work	In institutions	Other and not reported
Akron, Ohio	194,716	103,461	53.1	82,558	79.8	9,701	9.4	11,202	10.8	8,258	2,944	91,255	55,626	22,165	8,560	382	4,522
Albany, N. Y.	108,299	61,184	56.5	52,580	85.9	1,790	2.9	6,814	11.1	5,846	968	47,115	28,791	8,935	5,382	663	3,344
Atlanta, Ga.	242,228	146,553	60.5	127,360	86.9	5,767	3.9	13,426	9.2	11,707	1,719	95,675	54,572	[illegible]624	14,278	1,105	8,096
Baltimore, Md.	690,435	388,417	56.3	348,358	89.7	7,362	1.9	32,697	8.4	26,623	6,074	302,018	179,478	45,760	37,449	5,928	30,403
Birmingham, Ala.	209,763	116,365	55.5	98,170	84.4	5,546	4.8	12,649	10.9	10,670	1,979	93,398	56,282	18,890	11,411	662	6,153
Boston, Mass.	618,463	337,817	54.6	270,666	80.1	22,283	6.6	44,868	13.3	35,412	9,456	280,646	157,152	54,119	36,895	6,206	26,274
Bridgeport, Conn.	119,437	71,041	59.5	62,266	87.6	2,238	3.2	6,537	9.2	5,260	1,277	48,396	29,627	9,846	5,059	269	3,595
Buffalo, N. Y.	462,291	247,385	53.5	196,054	79.2	8,500	3.4	42,831	17.3	34,362	8,469	214,906	132,364	39,913	23,092	3,233	16,304
Cambridge, Mass.	88,755	49,283	55.5	40,140	81.4	2,744	5.6	6,399	13.0	5,123	1,276	39,472	22,318	8,301	4,522	653	3,678
Camden, N. J.	93,463	54,105	57.9	41,588	76.9	4,103	7.6	8,414	15.6	6,350	2,064	39,358	24,396	7,576	5,301	65	2,020
Canton, Ohio	86,712	46,146	53.2	40,032	86.8	2,386	5.2	3,728	8.1	2,896	832	40,566	25,829	8,343	3,998	182	2,214
Charlotte, N. C.	78,764	49,221	62.5	45,325	92.1	1,001	2.2	2,805	5.7	2,455	350	29,543	16,885	6,750	3,448	191	2,269
Chattanooga, Tenn.	99,555	56,762	57.0	49,330	86.9	2,471	4.4	4,961	8.7	4,139	822	42,793	25,749	7,697	5,417	378	3,552
Chicago, Ill.	2,777,329	1,593,913	57.4	1,352,218	84.8	61,665	3.9	180,030	11.3	150,384	29,646	1,183,416	727,649	222,814	150,901	6,374	75,678
Cincinnati, Ohio	373,257	198,811	53.3	169,970	85.5	8,857	4.5	19,984	10.1	16,689	3,295	174,446	106,041	28,242	22,478	5,012	12,673
Cleveland, Ohio	717,010	400,204	55.8	319,582	79.2	29,966	7.5	50,656	12.7	39,742	10,914	316,806	195,222	61,927	37,726	3,891	18,040
Columbus, Ohio	250,093	130,117	52.0	112,447	86.4	6,446	5.0	11,224	8.6	9,586	1,638	119,976	66,092	19,080	14,413	8,973	11,418
Dallas, Tex.	239,574	143,195	59.8	125,475	87.6	3,630	2.5	14,090	9.8	12,432	1,658	96,379	58,825	18,620	11,926	603	6,405
Dayton, Ohio	169,691	92,712	54.6	81,616	88.0	4,728	5.1	6,368	6.9	5,355	1,013	76,979	46,874	12,109	9,925	1,994	6,077
Denver, Colo.	262,279	137,393	52.4	116,688	84.9	8,454	6.2	12,251	8.9	10,915	1,336	124,886	71,083	21,001	17,792	1,397	13,613
Des Moines, Iowa	128,620	69,515	54.0	58,261	83.8	5,185	7.5	6,069	8.7	5,341	728	59,105	35,187	10,295	6,809	306	6,508
Detroit, Mich.	1,285,144	733,632	57.1	625,456	85.3	29,458	4.0	78,718	10.7	61,404	17,314	551,512	360,893	110,488	50,853	1,785	27,493
Duluth, Minn.	81,408	42,838	52.6	32,584	76.1	2,804	6.5	7,450	17.4	6,477	973	38,570	22,338	8,597	4,336	886	2,413
Elizabeth, N. J.	89,005	51,367	57.7	44,681	87.0	1,525	3.0	5,161	10.0	4,305	856	37,638	23,375	7,190	3,158	204	3,711
Erie, Pa.	92,104	48,729	52.9	40,448	83.0	1,694	3.5	6,587	13.5	5,351	1,236	43,375	26,456	9,143	4,369	594	2,813
Fall River, Mass.	91,116	54,553	59.9	44,216	81.1	2,969	5.4	7,368	13.5	5,849	1,519	36,563	20,356	7,265	6,288	419	2,235
Flint, Mich.	114,908	62,904	54.7	55,305	87.9	2,519	4.0	5,080	8.1	4,025	1,055	52,004	32,997	11,365	4,620	144	2,878
Fort Wayne, Ind.	95,056	50,257	52.9	44,231	88.0	2,057	4.1	3,969	7.9	3,293	676	44,799	27,307	8,097	4,203	1,712	3,480
Fort Worth, Tex.	142,775	79,642	55.8	66,866	84.0	4,287	5.4	8,489	10.7	7,419	1,070	63,133	37,620	11,907	7,819	429	5,358
Gary, Ind.	87,464	46,839	53.6	40,626	86.7	1,709	3.6	4,504	9.6	3,774	730	40,625	26,683	8,937	3,056	25	1,924
Grand Rapids, Mich.	130,209	67,779	52.1	59,509	87.8	2,945	4.3	5,325	7.9	4,640	685	62,430	38,138	12,023	6,777	587	4,905
Hartford, Conn.	135,874	79,466	58.5	70,297	88.5	1,996	2.5	7,173	9.0	6,273	900	56,408	32,223	10,039	5,592	1,187	7,367
Houston, Tex.	309,483	181,311	58.6	163,161	90.0	3,383	1.9	14,767	8.1	13,317	1,450	128,172	79,429	21,854	13,333	565	12,991
Indianapolis, Ind.	313,020	171,476	54.8	148,132	86.4	7,554	4.4	15,790	9.2	13,725	2,065	141,544	86,635	23,683	17,554	3,195	10,477
Jacksonville, Fla.	137,247	79,398	57.9	67,540	85.1	4,694	5.9	7,164	9.0	6,461	703	57,849	32,573	10,646	7,314	502	6,814
Jersey City, N. J.	242,896	141,407	58.2	114,546	81.0	4,245	3.0	22,616	16.0	17,372	5,244	101,489	64,655	20,733	9,822	543	5,736
Kansas City, Kans.	95,428	50,745	53.2	40,551	79.9	2,768	5.5	7,426	14.6	6,020	1,406	44,683	27,303	9,020	5,519	80	2,761
Kansas City, Mo.	332,828	191,278	57.5	160,944	84.1	10,542	5.5	19,792	10.3	17,615	2,177	141,550	88,765	22,815	18,719	897	10,354
Knoxville, Tenn.	85,746	48,960	57.1	42,925	87.7	1,703	3.5	4,332	8.8	3,486	846	36,786	22,069	7,405	4,579	424	2,309
Long Beach, Calif.	139,049	66,420	47.8	57,747	86.9	2,233	3.4	6,440	9.7	5,895	545	72,629	43,254	10,696	7,581	110	10,988
Los Angeles, Calif.	1,269,299	686,756	54.1	586,897	85.5	18,551	2.7	81,308	11.8	75,035	6,273	582,543	334,979	98,521	72,946	6,771	69,326
Louisville, Ky.	255,441	141,736	55.5	121,709	85.9	3,682	2.6	16,345	11.5	13,489	2,856	113,705	70,249	18,837	14,359	1,431	8,829
Lowell, Mass.	79,482	43,130	54.3	33,546	77.8	3,973	9.2	5,611	13.0	4,437	1,174	36,352	19,656	7,804	6,042	502	2,348
Memphis, Tenn.	236,243	138,761	58.7	119,152	85.9	5,063	3.6	14,546	10.5	13,176	1,370	97,482	59,081	17,055	12,296	656	8,394
Miami, Fla.	142,717	83,989	58.9	75,321	89.7	901	1.1	7,767	9.2	7,521	246	58,728	33,859	8,258	6,223	431	9,957
Milwaukee, Wis.	472,307	258,274	54.7	212,313	82.2	14,746	5.7	31,215	12.1	24,725	6,490	214,093	132,650	45,217	19,696	3,107	13,423
Minneapolis, Minn.	405,248	222,955	55.0	186,386	83.6	10,364	4.6	26,205	11.8	22,105	4,100	182,293	106,307	37,657	23,224	1,259	13,846
Nashville, Tenn.	132,957	75,110	56.5	64,467	85.8	2,706	3.6	7,937	10.6	6,839	1,098	57,847	33,507	10,741	8,181	906	4,512
Newark, N. J.	346,438	198,817	57.4	158,764	79.9	8,660	4.4	31,393	15.8	27,450	3,943	147,621	84,845	23,475	17,890	907	20,504
New Bedford, Mass.	89,723	52,580	58.6	40,400	76.8	3,027	5.8	9,153	17.4	7,511	1,642	37,143	20,326	7,158	6,310	454	2,805
New Haven, Conn.	130,345	74,239	57.0	62,965	84.8	2,814	3.8	8,460	11.4	6,679	1,781	56,106	32,283	11,046	6,673	1,108	4,396
New Orleans, La.	394,481	218,793	55.5	177,312	81.0	15,884	7.3	25,597	11.7	21,376	4,221	175,688	102,533	33,071	26,598	3,144	10,342
New York, N. Y.	6,102,747	3,474,760	56.9	2,839,366	81.7	103,386	3.0	532,008	15.3	459,422	72,586	2,627,987	1,592,195	474,543	293,980	34,202	233,067
Bronx Borough	1,130,304	624,055	55.2	510,702	81.8	17,279	2.8	96,074	15.4	81,897	14,177	506,249	323,051	96,632	48,929	7,388	30,249
Brooklyn Borough	2,169,260	1,109,092	55.3	984,396	82.1	34,159	2.8	180,537	15.1	154,930	25,607	970,168	584,855	175,787	102,520	7,716	99,290
Manhattan Borough	1,612,275	993,545	61.6	783,564	78.9	38,744	3.9	171,237	17.2	152,680	18,557	618,730	340,431	105,219	96,739	11,044	64,697
Queens Borough	1,052,339	584,495	55.5	501,562	85.8	9,690	1.7	73,243	12.5	61,708	11,535	467,844	305,784	84,778	39,133	4,992	33,157
Richmond Borough	138,569	73,573	53.1	59,142	80.4	3,514	4.8	10,917	14.8	8,207	2,710	64,996	38,074	12,127	6,659	2,462	5,674
Norfolk, Va.	116,459	67,906	58.3	61,391	90.4	2,262	3.3	4,253	6.3	3,488	765	48,553	29,427	8,902	5,009	416	4,739
Oakland, Calif.	253,978	134,746	53.1	113,072	84.6	8,073	6.0	12,701	9.4	11,120	1,581	119,232	72,008	21,440	13,610	1,410	10,764
Oklahoma City, Okla.	161,205	89,175	55.3	76,146	85.4	2,941	3.3	10,088	11.3	9,275	813	72,030	42,679	13,597	7,534	504	7,716
Omaha, Nebr.	179,255	97,419	54.3	81,486	83.6	6,017	6.2	9,916	10.2	8,230	1,686	81,836	49,455	16,729	9,360	806	5,486
Paterson, N. J.	114,153	66,449	58.2	53,991	81.3	3,359	5.1	9,099	13.7	7,724	1,375	47,704	30,341	8,411	5,650	354	2,948
Peoria, Ill.	86,150	48,220	56.0	43,197	89.6	1,390	2.9	3,633	7.5	3,218	415	37,930	24,310	5,664	4,356	534	3,066
Philadelphia, Pa.	1,558,470	876,138	56.2	703,698	80.3	23,416	2.7	149,024	17.0	121,467	27,557	682,332	408,157	122,613	80,464	18,001	53,097
Pittsburgh, Pa.	537,448	286,615	53.3	223,056	77.8	13,215	4.6	50,344	17.6	38,760	11,584	250,833	155,044	51,480	27,055	3,025	14,229
Portland, Oreg.	260,709	142,167	54.5	120,639	84.9	5,845	4.1	15,683	11.0	14,177	1,506	118,542	70,327	20,291	15,516	949	11,459
Providence, R. I.	204,409	117,623	57.5	94,023	79.9	7,211	6.1	16,389	13.9	13,108	3,281	86,786	51,493	17,564	11,494	956	5,279
Reading, Pa.	90,740	53,119	58.5	44,351	83.5	2,948	5.5	5,820	11.0	4,996	824	37,621	23,194	6,770	4,597	244	2,816
Richmond, Va.	158,027	95,033	60.1	84,163	88.6	2,055	2.2	8,815	9.3	7,082	1,733	62,994	35,137	12,134	8,291	2,391	5,041
Rochester, N. Y.	269,334	147,576	54.8	125,852	85.3	3,942	2.7	17,782	12.0	14,465	3,317	121,758	68,751	24,013	14,877	4,161	9,956
Sacramento, Calif.	89,202	51,042	57.2	43,515	85.3	1,306	2.6	6,221	12.2	5,889	332	38,160	21,878	7,786	4,193	475	3,828
St. Louis, Mo.	672,150	381,801	56.8	323,563	84.7	14,639	3.8	43,599	11.4	36,286	7,313	290,349	185,326	44,020	34,094	7,319	19,590
St. Paul, Minn.	231,743	125,447	54.1	104,216	83.1	5,716	4.6	15,515	12.4	12,899	2,616	106,296	63,821	21,181	11,868	949	8,477
Salt Lake City, Utah	114,206	57,260	50.1	49,773	86.9	2,567	4.5	4,920	8.6	4,217	703	56,946	33,344	12,943	6,491	1,016	3,152
San Antonio, Tex.	194,408	106,014	54.5	87,586	82.6	5,801	5.5	12,627	11.9	10,785	1,842	88,394	54,576	16,114	10,046	419	7,239
San Diego, Calif.	168,401	88,140	52.3	78,275	88.8	3,539	4.0	6,326	7.2	5,855	471	80,261	46,948	12,366	9,294	413	11,240
San Francisco, Calif.	550,011	316,659	57.6	271,306	85.7	12,683	4.0	32,670	10.3	29,814	2,856	233,352	131,772	38,288	29,091	3,664	30,537
Scranton, Pa.	111,639	59,358	53.2	41,533	70.0	3,269	5.5	14,556	24.5	11,913	2,643	52,281	31,207	9,931	5,835	223	5,085
Seattle, Wash.	313,033	170,901	54.6	147,952	86.5	4,529	2.6	18,510	10.8	16,784	1,726	142,042	81,565	27,177	18,389	1,615	13,296
Somerville, Mass.	79,696	42,487	53.3	34,331	80.8	2,809	6.6	5,347	12.6	4,086	1,261	37,209	22,818	7,715	3,829	326	2,521
South Bend, Ind.	80,725	45,074	55.8	39,036	86.6	1,762	3.9	4,276	9.5	3,444	832	35,651	22,517	7,591	3,261	44	2,238
Spokane, Wash.	101,165	53,713	53.1	45,081	83.9	2,255	4.2	6,377	11.9	5,748	629	47,452	27,933	8,987	6,032	294	4,206
Springfield, Mass.	122,241	66,968	54.8	56,983	85.1	3,008	4.5	6,977	10.4	5,624	1,353	55,273	33,545	9,925	6,538	499	4,766
Syracuse, N. Y.	167,747	89,552	53.4	75,339	84.1	2,898	3.2	11,315	12.6	9,537	1,778	78,195	45,581	15,596	9,925	1,381	5,712
Tacoma, Wash.	90,121	46,364	51.4	38,573	83.2	3,045	6.6	4,746	10.2	4,054	692	43,757	26,388	8,143	5,652	210	3,364
Tampa, Fla.	88,088	52,359	59.4	42,159	80.5	4,414	8.4	5,786	11.1	5,003	783	35,729	19,857	7,497	5,010	389	2,976
Toledo, Ohio	229,051	123,092	53.7	99,209	80.6	8,840	7.2	15,043	12.2	12,562	2,481	105,959	63,191	20,215	11,568	3,359	7,626
Trenton, N. J.	101,698	57,139	56.2	47,916	83.9	2,574	4.5	6,649	11.6	5,422	1,227	44,559	23,871	8,476	4,891	4,229	3,092
Tulsa, Okla.	113,914	63,678	55.9	56,128	88.1	1,369	2.1	6,181	9.7	5,613	568	50,236	30,939	10,703	5,431	264	2,899
Utica, N. Y.	81,757	44,399	54.3	37,240	83.9	1,305	2.9	5,854	13.2	4,739	1,115	37,358	20,693	7,171	4,446	2,541	2,507
Washington, D. C.	553,488	344,033	62.2	308,900	89.8	10,417	3.0	24,716	7.2	21,005	3,711	209,455	111,620	42,346	22,103	9,516	23,870
Wichita, Kans.	92,377	48,530	52.5	43,166	88.9	1,677	3.5	3,687	7.6	3,244	443	43,847	25,948	8,460	5,924	409	3,106
Wilmington, Del.	91,239	52,689	57.7	46,096	87.5	1,600	3.0	4,993	9.5	4,333	660	38,550	22,807	6,816	4,375	344	4,208
Worcester, Mass.	156,132	81,440	52.2	68,886	84.6	3,846	4.7	8,708	10.7	7,435	1,273	74,692	41,104	12,672	7,628	3,419	9,869
Yonkers, N. Y.	114,568	63,642	55.5	53,176	83.6	2,344	3.7	8,122	12.8	6,538	1,584	50,926	31,107	11,234	5,102	393	3,090
Youngstown, Ohio	133,422	70,482	52.8	56,229	79.8	4,730	6.7	9,514	13.5	6,906	2,608	62,940	39,111	14,475	5,469	154	3,731

UNITED STATES SUMMARY—PRINCIPAL CITIES

TABLE 66.—MALES 14 YEARS OLD AND OVER BY EMPLOYMENT STATUS, FOR CITIES OF 100,000 OR MORE: 1940

CITY	Population 14 years old and over	IN LABOR FORCE										NOT IN LABOR FORCE					
		Total		Employed (except on emergency work)		On public emergency work		Seeking work				Total	Engaged in own home housework	In school	Unable to work	In institutions	Other and not reported
		Number	Percent of pop. 14 and over	Number	Percent of labor force	Number	Percent of labor force	Number	Percent of labor force	Experienced workers	New workers						
Akron, Ohio	96,170	77,154	80.2	61,021	79.1	7,943	10.3	8,190	10.6	6,411	1,779	19,016	586	11,321	4,594	255	2,260
Albany, N. Y	51,448	41,682	81.0	35,397	84.9	1,416	3.4	4,869	11.7	4,325	544	9,766	260	4,628	2,830	223	1,825
Atlanta, Ga	109,478	90,540	82.7	78,437	86.6	3,973	4.4	8,130	9.0	7,271	859	18,938	504	8,586	5,960	847	3,041
Baltimore, Md	337,951	272,231	80.6	243,348	89.4	6,220	2.3	22,663	8.3	19,210	3,453	65,720	1,763	25,492	10,072	3,907	15,426
Birmingham, Ala	98,531	80,729	81.9	68,348	84.7	4,008	5.0	8,373	10.4	7,226	1,147	17,802	468	9,409	4,943	513	2,469
Boston, Mass	295,782	228,263	77.2	179,010	78.4	17,439	7.6	31,814	13.9	26,268	5,546	67,519	2,268	27,914	20,257	3,395	13,685
Bridgeport, Conn	59,107	48,625	82.3	42,145	86.7	1,918	3.9	4,562	9.4	3,840	722	10,482	236	5,171	2,830	181	2,064
Buffalo, N. Y	226,704	180,503	79.6	141,377	78.3	7,017	3.9	32,109	17.8	27,498	4,611	46,201	1,652	20,725	13,783	1,221	8,820
Cambridge, Mass	41,374	32,152	77.7	25,247	78.5	2,392	7.4	4,513	14.0	3,762	751	9,222	408	4,469	2,220	364	1,761
Camden, N. J	46,542	38,306	82.3	29,081	75.9	3,460	9.0	5,765	15.0	4,572	1,193	8,236	287	4,014	2,804	55	1,076
Canton, Ohio	43,336	35,190	81.2	30,461	86.6	1,904	5.4	2,825	8.0	2,344	481	8,146	264	4,339	2,220	144	1,179
Charlotte, N. C	36,634	30,648	83.7	28,218	92.1	755	2.5	1,675	5.5	1,481	194	5,986	106	3,250	1,533	146	951
Chattanooga, Tenn	46,862	38,187	81.5	33,021	86.5	1,825	4.8	3,341	8.7	2,874	467	8,675	145	3,810	2,769	282	1,600
Chicago, Ill	1,367,260	1,121,618	82.0	942,365	84.0	49,949	4.5	129,304	11.5	112,636	16,668	245,642	7,296	113,660	78,768	3,650	30,268
Cincinnati, Ohio	175,794	139,878	79.6	118,590	84.8	6,922	4.9	14,366	10.3	12,420	1,946	35,916	1,085	14,527	11,332	2,420	6,552
Cleveland, Ohio	356,000	290,034	81.2	228,578	78.8	24,515	8.5	36,941	12.7	30,712	6,229	66,956	1,431	32,359	21,131	1,942	10,093
Columbus, Ohio	120,747	91,020	75.4	77,702	85.4	5,021	5.5	8,297	9.1	7,335	962	29,727	687	9,864	7,886	5,805	5,485
Dallas, Texas	112,103	93,122	83.1	81,612	87.6	2,383	2.6	9,127	9.8	8,251	876	18,981	489	9,525	5,806	421	2,740
Dayton, Ohio	82,736	66,974	80.9	58,500	87.3	3,781	5.6	4,693	7.0	4,049	644	15,762	433	6,025	5,469	1,004	2,831
Denver, Colo	125,457	96,230	76.7	80,547	83.7	6,642	6.9	9,041	9.4	8,259	782	29,227	637	10,797	9,951	819	7,023
Des Moines, Iowa	60,013	47,438	79.0	39,040	82.3	3,912	8.2	4,486	9.5	4,045	441	12,575	289	5,219	3,804	147	3,116
Detroit, Mich	655,722	555,539	84.7	474,250	85.4	24,102	4.3	57,187	10.3	47,192	9,995	100,183	3,502	56,510	26,052	899	13,220
Duluth, Minn	40,539	31,305	77.2	22,986	73.4	2,245	7.2	6,074	19.4	5,512	562	9,234	188	4,374	2,591	671	1,410
Elizabeth, N. J	44,381	36,531	82.3	31,414	86.0	1,258	3.4	3,859	10.6	3,310	549	7,850	369	3,779	1,726	154	1,822
Erie, Pa	45,384	36,126	79.6	29,980	83.0	1,163	3.2	4,983	13.8	4,285	698	9,258	268	4,725	2,422	307	1,446
Fall River, Mass	43,292	33,948	78.4	26,140	77.0	2,347	6.9	5,461	16.1	4,422	1,039	9,344	450	3,842	3,537	200	1,315
Flint, Mich	57,544	47,537	82.6	42,043	88.4	1,758	3.7	3,736	7.9	3,054	682	10,007	308	5,739	2,489	103	1,368
Fort Wayne, Ind	45,120	35,779	79.3	30,936	86.5	1,680	4.7	3,163	8.8	2,719	444	9,341	251	4,236	2,279	616	1,959
Fort Worth, Tex	67,604	54,618	80.8	46,001	84.2	2,865	5.2	5,752	10.5	5,179	573	12,986	265	6,012	4,111	281	2,317
Gary, Ind	45,941	38,460	83.7	33,552	87.2	1,362	3.5	3,546	9.2	3,068	478	7,481	261	4,546	1,696	16	962
Grand Rapids, Mich	62,201	48,824	78.5	42,377	86.8	2,359	4.8	4,088	8.4	3,650	438	13,377	433	6,076	3,996	283	2,589
Hartford, Conn	65,127	52,628	80.8	46,212	87.8	1,574	3.0	4,842	9.2	4,347	495	12,499	373	5,234	2,091	571	3,330
Houston, Tex	150,921	126,483	83.8	113,957	90.1	2,131	1.7	10,395	8.2	9,575	820	24,438	803	11,045	6,589	389	5,612
Indianapolis, Ind	148,426	120,072	80.9	102,747	85.6	5,741	4.8	11,584	9.6	10,345	1,239	28,354	665	12,036	9,031	1,485	5,137
Jacksonville, Fla	64,948	52,702	81.1	44,508	84.5	3,677	7.0	4,517	8.6	4,121	396	12,246	285	5,158	3,266	340	3,107
Jersey City, N. J	120,041	99,481	82.9	80,137	80.6	3,244	3.3	16,100	16.2	13,169	2,931	20,560	775	10,663	5,497	204	3,331
Kansas City, Kans	46,285	36,976	79.9	29,224	79.0	2,314	6.3	5,438	14.7	4,550	888	9,309	177	4,746	2,900	51	1,435
Kansas City, Mo	156,529	129,678	82.8	108,099	83.4	8,170	6.3	13,409	10.3	12,363	1,046	26,851	613	11,647	9,119	411	5,061
Knoxville, Tenn	39,615	32,079	81.0	27,637	86.2	1,338	4.2	3,104	9.7	2,570	534	7,536	155	3,714	2,358	246	1,063
Long Beach, Calif	64,908	48,874	75.3	42,596	87.2	1,650	3.4	4,628	9.5	4,348	280	16,034	348	5,300	4,012	72	6,212
Los Angeles, Calif	615,298	480,184	78.0	407,425	84.8	14,402	3.0	58,357	12.2	55,187	3,170	135,114	2,693	50,794	38,406	5,027	38,194
Louisville, Ky	120,333	98,059	81.5	84,183	85.8	2,646	2.7	11,230	11.5	9,618	1,612	22,274	666	9,520	7,197	670	4,221
Lowell, Mass	37,722	28,759	76.2	21,810	75.8	3,322	11.6	3,627	12.6	2,997	630	8,963	471	3,946	3,012	287	1,247
Memphis, Tenn	110,927	92,830	83.7	79,369	85.5	4,196	4.5	9,265	10.0	8,585	680	18,097	397	8,337	5,519	348	3,496
Miami, Fla	69,706	55,848	80.1	50,005	89.5	575	1.0	5,268	9.4	5,136	132	13,858	353	4,121	3,387	346	5,651
Milwaukee, Wis	231,008	186,135	80.6	149,939	80.6	12,000	6.4	24,196	13.0	20,289	3,907	44,873	893	23,139	10,683	2,352	7,806
Minneapolis, Minn	190,476	149,679	78.6	122,480	81.8	8,352	5.6	18,847	12.6	16,513	2,334	40,797	841	19,397	12,618	664	7,277
Nashville, Tenn	60,251	48,247	80.1	40,886	84.7	1,947	4.0	5,414	11.2	4,791	623	12,004	197	5,154	4,158	613	1,882
Newark, N. J	171,677	138,636	80.8	108,917	78.6	6,875	5.0	22,844	16.5	20,507	2,337	33,041	1,178	12,306	9,699	439	9,419
New Bedford, Mass	43,073	33,684	78.2	25,421	75.5	2,339	6.9	5,924	17.6	4,975	949	9,389	467	3,723	3,344	286	1,569
New Haven, Conn	62,972	49,973	79.4	41,527	83.1	2,337	4.7	6,109	12.2	5,055	1,054	12,999	350	5,963	3,756	720	2,201
New Orleans, La	183,990	148,958	81.0	119,518	80.2	12,133	8.1	17,307	11.6	15,097	2,210	35,032	704	16,631	11,572	1,841	4,284
New York, N. Y	2,989,576	2,424,740	81.1	1,964,346	81.0	86,845	3.6	373,549	15.4	335,922	37,627	561,836	20,265	248,124	162,619	18,746	115,082
Bronx Borough	555,013	450,350	81.1	368,191	81.8	14,291	3.2	67,868	15.1	60,934	6,934	104,663	3,769	50,975	28,652	5,359	15,908
Brooklyn Borough	1,063,403	852,218	80.1	694,090	81.4	29,538	3.5	128,590	15.1	115,110	13,480	211,185	8,112	93,053	60,176	3,479	46,365
Manhattan Borough	786,059	640,561	81.5	493,039	77.0	31,304	4.9	116,218	18.1	106,438	9,780	145,498	4,611	53,705	48,910	5,622	32,650
Queens Borough	513,780	426,087	82.9	364,547	85.6	8,626	2.0	52,914	12.4	46,910	6,004	87,693	3,441	44,103	20,914	2,204	17,031
Richmond Borough	71,321	55,524	77.9	44,479	80.1	3,086	5.6	7,959	14.3	6,530	1,429	15,797	332	6,288	3,967	2,082	3,128
Norfolk, Va	58,943	49,630	84.2	45,467	91.6	1,628	3.3	2,535	5.1	2,125	410	9,313	223	4,516	2,161	282	2,131
Oakland, Calif	124,795	98,581	79.0	83,493	84.7	5,937	6.0	9,151	9.3	8,253	898	26,214	715	10,874	7,546	823	6,256
Oklahoma City, Okla	76,870	61,023	79.4	51,982	85.2	1,807	3.0	7,234	11.9	6,775	459	15,847	296	6,807	4,243	433	4,069
Omaha, Nebr	86,012	68,630	79.8	56,554	82.4	5,042	7.3	7,034	10.2	6,154	880	17,382	317	8,708	5,127	350	2,880
Paterson, N. J	56,514	46,441	82.2	37,361	80.4	2,509	5.4	6,571	14.1	5,791	780	10,073	385	4,452	3,297	188	1,751
Peoria, Ill	42,190	34,833	82.6	30,946	88.8	1,079	3.1	2,808	8.1	2,549	259	7,357	226	2,889	2,450	161	1,631
Philadelphia, Pa	753,773	607,296	80.6	485,086	79.9	16,423	2.7	105,787	17.4	90,258	15,529	146,477	4,578	63,644	40,302	10,665	27,198
Pittsburgh, Pa	262,258	208,593	79.5	160,181	76.8	9,935	4.8	38,477	18.4	31,609	6,868	53,665	1,448	26,700	15,490	2,231	7,787
Portland, Oreg	126,683	100,176	79.1	83,802	83.7	4,499	4.5	11,875	11.9	11,060	815	26,507	538	10,418	8,897	508	6,146
Providence, R. I	96,946	77,792	80.2	60,847	78.2	5,609	7.2	11,336	14.6	9,331	2,005	10,154	418	9,115	6,252	357	3,012
Reading, Pa	43,931	35,732	81.3	29,052	81.3	2,440	6.8	4,240	11.9	3,777	463	8,199	226	3,546	2,572	20	1,835
Richmond, Va	72,782	58,996	81.1	52,330	88.7	1,226	2.1	5,431	9.2	4,537	894	13,786	261	6,012	3,716	1,832	1,065
Rochester, N. Y	129,405	100,470	77.6	84,202	83.8	3,091	3.1	13,177	13.1	11,286	1,891	28,935	874	12,313	8,691	1,927	5,130
Sacramento, Calif	45,162	35,994	79.7	30,228	84.0	974	2.7	4,792	13.3	4,604	188	9,168	199	3,953	2,375	353	2,288
St. Louis, Mo	319,271	264,010	82.7	221,421	83.9	11,788	4.5	30,801	11.7	26,687	4,114	55,261	1,359	22,602	17,421	3,594	10,285
St. Paul, Minn	108,991	86,427	79.3	70,637	81.7	4,454	5.2	11,336	13.1	9,940	1,396	22,564	455	10,918	6,523	383	4,285
Salt Lake City, Utah	55,134	41,988	76.2	36,004	85.7	2,139	5.1	3,845	9.2	3,407	438	13,146	163	6,874	3,602	809	1,698
San Antonio, Tex	93,815	75,488	80.5	62,152	82.3	4,097	5.4	9,239	12.2	8,094	1,145	18,327	519	8,342	5,484	327	3,655
San Diego, Calif	85,890	66,732	77.7	59,729	89.5	2,503	3.8	4,500	6.7	4,238	262	19,158	396	6,198	5,177	320	7,067
San Francisco, Calif	279,591	222,803	79.7	189,967	85.3	9,305	4.2	23,531	10.6	22,107	1,424	56,788	1,287	19,833	16,352	2,333	16,983
Scranton, Pa	54,046	42,648	78.9	28,755	67.4	2,328	5.5	11,565	27.1	9,939	1,626	11,398	392	5,085	3,408	155	2,358
Seattle, Wash	155,795	121,921	78.3	104,058	85.3	3,619	3.0	14,244	11.7	13,294	950	33,874	633	13,917	11,044	1,007	7,273
Somerville, Mass	37,851	30,135	79.6	23,952	79.5	2,392	7.9	3,791	12.6	3,056	735	7,716	315	3,904	2,033	154	1,310
South Bend, Ind	39,706	32,598	82.1	27,853	85.4	1,514	4.6	3,231	9.9	2,701	530	7,108	184	3,958	1,771	38	1,157
Spokane, Wash	49,856	38,797	77.8	32,005	82.5	1,764	4.5	5,028	13.0	4,703	325	11,059	176	4,658	3,566	145	2,514
Springfield, Mass	58,369	46,560	79.8	39,740	85.4	2,216	4.8	4,598	9.9	3,928	670	11,809	423	5,157	3,461	404	2,364
Syracuse, N. Y	80,847	63,102	78.1	52,535	83.3	2,174	3.4	8,393	13.3	7,392	1,001	17,745	649	7,918	5,567	666	2,945
Tacoma, Wash	45,177	35,274	78.1	29,183	82.7	2,453	7.0	3,638	10.3	3,221	417	9,903	125	4,132	3,556	127	1,903
Tampa, Fla	42,217	33,818	80.1	27,432	81.1	2,737	8.1	3,649	10.8	3,180	469	8,399	192	3,677	2,613	257	1,660
Toledo, Ohio	113,030	89,552	79.2	71,325	79.6	6,463	7.2	11,764	13.1	10,183	1,581	23,478	497	10,385	6,293	1,819	4,484
Trenton, N. J	50,513	38,733	76.7	31,790	82.1	2,123	5.5	4,820	12.4	4,065	755	11,780	287	4,560	2,704	2,594	1,635
Tulsa, Okla	53,947	43,872	81.3	38,835	88.5	680	1.5	4,357	9.9	4,051	306	10,075	236	5,369	2,873	244	1,353
Utica, N. Y	39,393	30,281	76.9	24,985	82.5	1,073	3.5	4,223	13.9	3,621	602	9,112	257	3,673	2,500	1,241	1,441
Washington, D. C	262,590	212,118	80.8	189,587	89.4	7,492	3.5	15,039	7.1	13,193	1,846	50,472	771	21,740	10,058	5,894	12,009
Wichita, Kans	43,368	33,941	78.3	29,964	88.3	1,333	3.9	2,644	7.8	2,381	263	9,427	144	4,209	3,273	242	1,559
Wilmington, Del	44,706	36,644	82.0	31,859	86.9	1,173	3.2	3,612	9.9	3,224	388	8,062	199	3,542	2,197	116	2,008
Worcester, Mass	75,444	57,341	76.0	48,288	84.2	2,875	5.0	6,178	10.8	5,411	767	18,103	654	6,605	4,456	1,837	4,551
Yonkers, N. Y	55,673	44,804	80.5	36,693	81.9	2,001	4.5	6,110	13.6	5,164	946	10,869	257	6,006	2,655	240	1,711
Youngstown, Ohio	67,463	54,289	80.5	43,594	80.3	3,644	6.7	7,045	13.0	5,563	1,482	13,180	474	7,537	3,165	126	1,878

CHARACTERISTICS OF THE POPULATION

Table 67.—FEMALES 14 YEARS OLD AND OVER BY EMPLOYMENT STATUS, FOR CITIES OF 100,000 OR MORE: 1940

CITY	Population 14 years old and over	IN LABOR FORCE: Total: Number	Total: Percent of pop. 14 and over	Employed (except on emergency work): Number	Employed: Percent of labor force	On public emergency work: Number	On public emergency work: Percent of labor force	Seeking work: Number	Seeking work: Percent of labor force	Seeking work: Experienced workers	Seeking work: New workers	NOT IN LABOR FORCE: Total	Engaged in own home housework	In school	Unable to work	In institutions	Other and not reported
Akron, Ohio	98,546	26,307	26.7	21,537	81.9	1,758	6.7	3,012	11.4	1,847	1,165	72,239	55,040	10,844	3,966	127	2,262
Albany, N. Y	56,851	19,502	34.3	17,183	88.1	374	1.9	1,945	10.0	1,521	424	37,349	28,531	4,307	2,552	440	1,519
Atlanta, Ga	132,750	56,013	42.2	48,923	87.3	1,794	3.2	5,296	9.5	4,436	860	76,737	54,068	9,038	8,318	258	5,055
Baltimore, Md	352,484	116,186	33.0	105,010	90.4	1,142	1.0	10,034	8.6	7,413	2,621	236,298	177,715	23,268	18,377	1,961	14,977
Birmingham, Ala	111,232	35,636	32.0	29,822	83.7	1,538	4.3	4,276	12.0	3,444	832	75,596	55,814	9,481	6,468	149	3,684
Boston, Mass	322,681	109,554	34.0	91,656	83.7	4,844	4.4	13,054	11.9	9,144	3,910	213,127	154,884	26,205	16,638	2,811	12,589
Bridgeport, Conn	60,330	22,416	37.2	20,121	89.8	320	1.4	1,975	8.8	1,420	555	37,914	29,391	4,675	2,229	88	1,531
Buffalo, N. Y	235,587	66,882	28.4	54,677	81.8	1,483	2.2	10,722	16.0	6,864	3,858	168,705	130,712	19,188	9,309	2,012	7,484
Cambridge, Mass	47,381	17,131	36.2	14,893	86.9	352	2.1	1,886	11.0	1,361	525	30,250	21,910	3,832	2,302	289	1,917
Camden, N. J	46,921	15,799	33.7	12,507	79.2	643	4.1	2,649	16.8	1,778	871	31,122	24,109	3,562	2,497	10	944
Canton, Ohio	43,376	10,956	25.3	9,571	87.4	482	4.4	903	8.2	552	351	32,420	25,565	4,004	1,778	38	1,035
Charlotte, N. C	42,130	18,573	44.1	17,107	92.1	336	1.8	1,130	6.1	974	156	23,557	16,779	3,500	1,915	45	1,318
Chattanooga, Tenn	52,693	18,575	35.3	16,309	87.8	646	3.5	1,620	8.7	1,265	355	34,118	25,604	3,887	2,648	96	1,883
Chicago, Ill	1,410,069	472,295	33.5	409,853	86.8	11,716	2.5	50,726	10.7	37,748	12,978	937,774	720,353	106,154	72,133	2,724	36,410
Cincinnati, Ohio	197,463	58,933	29.8	51,380	87.2	1,935	3.3	5,618	9.5	4,269	1,349	138,530	104,956	13,715	11,146	2,502	6,121
Cleveland, Ohio	360,020	110,170	30.6	91,004	82.6	5,451	4.9	13,715	12.4	9,030	4,685	249,850	193,791	29,568	16,595	1,949	7,947
Columbus, Ohio	129,346	39,097	30.2	34,745	88.9	1,425	3.6	2,927	7.5	2,251	676	90,249	65,405	9,216	6,527	3,168	5,933
Dallas, Tex	127,471	50,073	39.3	43,863	87.6	1,247	2.5	4,963	9.9	4,181	782	77,398	58,336	9,095	6,120	182	3,665
Dayton, Ohio	86,955	25,738	29.6	23,116	89.8	947	3.7	1,675	6.5	1,306	369	61,217	46,441	6,084	4,456	990	3,246
Denver, Colo	136,822	41,163	30.1	36,141	87.8	1,812	4.4	3,210	7.8	2,656	554	95,659	70,446	10,204	7,841	578	6,590
Des Moines, Iowa	68,607	22,077	32.2	19,221	87.1	1,273	5.8	1,583	7.2	1,296	287	46,530	34,898	5,076	3,005	159	3,392
Detroit, Mich	629,422	178,093	28.3	151,206	84.9	5,356	3.0	21,531	12.1	14,212	7,319	451,329	357,391	53,978	24,801	886	14,273
Duluth, Minn	40,869	11,533	28.2	9,598	83.2	559	4.8	1,376	11.9	965	411	29,336	22,150	4,223	1,745	215	1,003
Elizabeth, N. J	44,624	14,836	33.2	13,267	89.4	267	1.8	1,302	8.8	995	307	29,788	23,006	3,411	1,432	50	1,889
Erie, Pa	46,720	12,603	27.0	10,468	83.1	531	4.2	1,604	12.7	1,066	538	34,117	26,188	4,418	1,947	197	1,367
Fall River, Mass	47,824	20,605	43.1	18,076	87.7	622	3.0	1,907	9.3	1,427	480	27,219	19,906	3,423	2,751	219	920
Flint, Mich	57,364	15,367	26.8	13,262	86.3	761	5.0	1,344	8.7	971	373	41,997	32,689	5,626	2,131	41	1,510
Fort Wayne, Ind	49,936	14,478	29.0	13,295	91.8	377	2.6	806	5.6	574	232	35,458	27,056	3,861	1,924	1,096	1,521
Fort Worth, Tex	75,171	25,024	33.3	20,865	83.4	1,422	5.7	2,737	10.9	2,240	497	50,147	37,355	5,895	3,708	148	3,041
Gary, Ind	41,523	8,379	20.2	7,074	84.4	347	4.1	958	11.4	706	252	33,144	26,422	4,391	1,360	9	962
Grand Rapids, Mich	68,008	18,955	27.9	17,132	90.4	586	3.1	1,237	6.5	990	247	49,053	37,705	5,947	2,781	304	2,316
Hartford, Conn	70,747	26,838	37.9	24,085	89.7	422	1.6	2,331	8.7	1,926	405	43,909	31,850	4,805	2,601	616	4,037
Houston, Tex	158,562	54,828	34.6	49,204	89.7	1,252	2.3	4,372	8.0	3,742	630	103,734	78,626	10,809	6,744	176	7,379
Indianapolis, Ind	164,594	51,404	31.2	45,385	88.3	1,813	3.5	4,206	8.2	3,380	826	113,190	85,970	11,647	8,523	1,710	5,340
Jacksonville, Fla	72,299	26,696	36.9	23,032	86.3	1,017	3.8	2,647	9.9	2,340	307	45,603	32,288	5,488	4,048	162	3,617
Jersey City, N. J	122,855	41,926	34.1	34,409	82.1	1,001	2.4	6,516	15.5	4,203	2,313	80,929	63,880	10,070	4,325	249	2,405
Kansas City, Kans	49,143	13,769	28.0	11,327	82.3	454	3.3	1,988	14.4	1,470	518	35,374	27,126	4,274	2,619	29	1,326
Kansas City, Mo	176,299	61,600	34.9	52,845	85.8	2,372	3.9	6,383	10.4	5,252	1,131	114,699	88,152	11,168	9,600	486	5,203
Knoxville, Tenn	46,131	16,881	36.6	15,288	90.6	365	2.2	1,228	7.3	916	312	29,250	21,914	3,691	2,221	178	1,246
Long Beach, Calif	74,141	17,546	23.7	15,151	86.4	583	3.3	1,812	10.3	1,547	265	56,595	42,906	5,306	3,569	38	4,776
Los Angeles, Calif	654,001	206,572	31.6	179,472	86.9	4,149	2.0	22,951	11.1	19,848	3,103	447,429	332,286	47,727	34,540	1,744	31,132
Louisville, Ky	135,108	43,677	32.3	37,526	85.9	1,036	2.4	5,115	11.7	3,871	1,244	91,431	69,583	9,317	7,162	761	4,608
Lowell, Mass	41,760	14,371	34.4	11,736	81.7	651	4.5	1,984	13.8	1,440	544	27,389	19,185	3,858	3,030	215	1,101
Memphis, Tenn	125,316	45,931	36.7	39,783	86.6	867	1.9	5,281	11.5	4,591	690	79,385	58,684	8,718	6,777	308	4,898
Miami, Fla	73,011	28,141	38.5	25,316	90.0	326	1.2	2,499	8.9	2,385	114	44,870	33,506	4,137	2,836	85	4,306
Milwaukee, Wis	241,359	72,139	29.9	62,374	86.5	2,746	3.8	7,019	9.7	4,436	2,583	169,220	131,757	22,078	9,013	755	5,617
Minneapolis, Minn	214,772	73,276	34.1	63,906	87.2	2,012	2.7	7,358	10.0	5,592	1,766	141,496	105,466	18,260	10,606	595	6,569
Nashville, Tenn	72,706	26,863	36.9	23,581	87.8	759	2.8	2,523	9.4	2,048	475	45,843	33,310	5,587	4,023	293	2,630
Newark, N. J	174,761	60,181	34.4	49,847	82.8	1,785	3.0	8,549	14.2	6,943	1,606	114,580	83,667	11,169	8,191	468	11,085
New Bedford, Mass	46,650	18,896	40.5	14,970	79.3	688	3.6	3,229	17.1	2,536	693	27,754	19,859	3,435	2,966	168	1,326
New Haven, Conn	67,373	24,266	36.0	21,438	88.3	477	2.0	2,351	9.7	1,624	727	43,107	31,933	5,683	2,917	379	2,195
New Orleans, La	210,491	69,835	33.2	57,794	82.8	3,751	5.4	8,290	11.9	6,279	2,011	140,656	101,820	16,440	15,026	1,303	6,058
New York, N. Y	3,113,171	1,050,020	33.7	875,020	83.3	16,541	1.6	158,459	15.1	123,500	34,959	2,063,151	1,571,930	226,419	131,361	15,456	117,985
Bronx Borough	575,291	173,705	30.2	142,511	82.0	2,988	1.7	28,206	16.2	20,963	7,243	401,586	319,282	45,657	20,277	2,029	14,341
Brooklyn Borough	1,105,857	346,874	31.4	290,306	83.7	4,621	1.3	51,947	15.0	39,820	12,127	758,983	576,743	82,734	42,344	4,237	52,925
Manhattan Borough	826,216	352,984	42.7	290,525	82.3	7,440	2.1	55,019	15.6	46,242	8,777	473,232	335,820	51,514	47,829	6,022	32,047
Queens Borough	538,559	158,408	29.4	137,015	86.5	1,064	0.7	20,329	12.8	14,798	5,531	380,151	302,343	40,675	18,219	2,788	16,126
Richmond Borough	67,248	18,049	26.8	14,663	81.2	428	2.4	2,958	16.4	1,677	1,281	49,199	37,742	5,839	2,692	380	2,546
Norfolk, Va	57,516	18,276	31.8	15,924	87.1	634	3.5	1,718	9.4	1,363	355	39,240	29,204	4,446	2,848	134	2,608
Oakland, Calif	129,183	36,165	28.0	30,479	84.3	2,136	5.9	3,550	9.8	2,867	683	93,018	71,293	10,566	6,064	587	4,508
Oklahoma City, Okla	84,335	28,152	33.4	24,164	85.8	1,134	4.0	2,854	10.1	2,500	354	56,183	42,384	6,790	3,201	71	3,647
Omaha, Nebr	93,243	28,789	30.9	24,932	86.6	975	3.4	2,882	10.0	2,076	806	64,454	49,136	8,021	4,233	456	2,606
Paterson, N. J	57,639	20,008	34.7	16,630	83.1	850	4.2	2,528	12.6	1,933	595	37,631	29,956	3,959	2,353	166	1,197
Peoria, Ill	43,960	13,387	30.5	12,251	91.5	311	2.3	825	6.2	669	156	30,573	24,084	2,775	1,906	373	1,435
Philadelphia, Pa	804,697	268,842	33.4	218,612	81.3	6,993	2.6	43,237	16.1	31,209	12,028	535,855	403,579	58,969	40,072	7,426	25,809
Pittsburgh, Pa	275,190	78,022	28.4	62,875	80.6	3,280	4.2	11,867	15.2	7,151	4,716	197,168	153,596	24,780	11,556	794	6,442
Portland, Oreg	134,026	41,991	31.3	36,837	87.7	1,346	3.2	3,808	9.1	3,117	691	92,035	69,780	9,873	6,619	441	5,313
Providence, R. I	107,463	39,831	37.1	33,176	83.3	1,602	4.0	5,053	12.7	3,777	1,276	67,632	51,075	8,449	5,242	599	2,267
Reading, Pa	46,809	17,387	37.1	15,299	88.0	508	2.9	1,580	9.1	1,219	361	29,422	22,968	3,224	2,025	224	981
Richmond, Va	85,245	36,037	42.3	31,824	88.3	829	2.3	3,384	9.4	2,545	839	49,208	34,876	6,122	4,575	559	3,076
Rochester, N. Y	139,929	47,106	33.7	41,650	88.4	851	1.8	4,605	9.8	3,179	1,426	92,823	67,877	11,700	6,186	2,234	4,826
Sacramento, Calif	44,040	15,048	34.2	13,287	88.3	332	2.2	1,429	9.5	1,285	144	28,992	21,679	3,833	1,818	122	1,540
St. Louis, Mo	352,879	117,791	33.4	102,142	86.7	2,851	2.4	12,708	10.9	9,599	3,199	235,088	183,967	21,418	16,673	3,725	9,305
St. Paul, Minn	122,752	39,020	31.8	33,579	86.1	1,262	3.2	4,179	10.7	2,959	1,220	83,732	63,366	10,263	5,345	566	4,192
Salt Lake City, Utah	59,072	15,272	25.9	13,769	90.2	428	2.8	1,075	7.0	810	265	43,800	33,181	6,069	2,880	207	1,454
San Antonio, Tex	100,593	30,526	30.3	25,434	83.3	1,704	5.6	3,388	11.1	2,691	697	70,067	54,057	7,772	4,562	92	3,584
San Diego, Calif	82,511	21,408	25.9	18,546	86.6	1,036	4.8	1,826	8.5	1,617	209	61,103	46,552	6,168	4,117	93	4,173
San Francisco, Calif	270,420	93,856	34.7	81,339	86.7	3,378	3.6	9,139	9.7	7,707	1,432	176,564	130,485	18,455	12,739	1,331	13,554
Scranton, Pa	57,593	16,710	29.0	12,778	76.5	941	5.6	2,991	17.9	1,974	1,017	40,883	30,815	4,846	2,427	68	2,727
Seattle, Wash	157,238	49,070	31.2	43,894	89.5	910	1.9	4,266	8.7	3,490	776	108,168	80,932	13,260	7,345	608	6,023
Somerville, Mass	41,845	12,352	29.5	10,379	84.0	417	3.4	1,556	12.6	1,030	526	29,493	22,503	3,811	1,796	172	1,211
South Bend, Ind	41,019	12,476	30.4	11,183	89.6	248	2.0	1,045	8.4	743	302	28,543	22,333	3,633	1,490	6	1,081
Spokane, Wash	51,309	14,916	29.1	13,076	87.7	491	3.3	1,349	9.0	1,045	304	36,393	27,757	4,329	2,466	149	1,602
Springfield, Mass	63,872	20,408	32.0	17,237	84.5	792	3.9	2,379	11.7	1,696	683	43,464	33,122	4,768	3,077	95	2,402
Syracuse, N. Y	86,900	26,450	30.4	22,804	86.2	724	2.7	2,922	11.0	2,145	777	60,450	44,932	7,678	4,358	715	2,767
Tacoma, Wash	44,944	11,090	24.7	9,390	84.7	592	5.3	1,108	10.0	833	275	33,854	26,263	4,011	2,096	83	1,401
Tampa, Fla	45,871	18,541	40.4	14,727	79.4	1,677	9.0	2,137	11.5	1,823	314	27,330	19,665	3,820	2,397	132	1,316
Toledo, Ohio	116,021	33,540	28.9	27,884	83.1	2,377	7.1	3,279	9.8	2,379	900	82,481	62,694	9,830	5,275	1,540	3,142
Trenton, N. J	51,185	18,406	36.0	16,126	87.6	451	2.5	1,829	9.9	1,357	472	32,779	23,584	3,916	2,187	1,635	1,457
Tulsa, Okla	59,967	19,806	33.0	17,293	87.3	689	3.5	1,824	9.2	1,562	262	40,161	30,703	5,334	2,558	20	1,546
Utica, N. Y	42,364	14,118	33.3	12,255	86.8	232	1.6	1,631	11.6	1,118	513	28,246	20,436	3,498	1,946	1,300	1,066
Washington, D. C	290,898	131,915	45.3	119,313	90.4	2,925	2.2	9,677	7.3	7,812	1,865	158,983	110,849	20,606	12,045	3,622	11,861
Wichita, Kans	49,009	14,589	29.8	13,202	90.5	344	2.4	1,043	7.1	863	180	34,420	25,804	4,251	2,651	167	1,547
Wilmington, Del	46,533	16,045	34.5	14,237	88.7	427	2.7	1,381	8.6	1,109	272	30,488	22,608	3,274	2,178	228	2,200
Worcester, Mass	80,688	24,099	29.9	20,598	85.5	971	4.0	2,530	10.5	2,024	506	56,589	40,450	6,067	3,172	1,582	5,318
Yonkers, N. Y	58,895	18,838	32.0	16,483	87.5	343	1.8	2,012	10.7	1,374	638	40,057	30,850	5,228	2,447	153	1,379
Youngstown, Ohio	65,959	16,199	24.6	12,635	78.0	1,095	6.8	2,469	15.2	1,343	1,126	49,760	38,637	6,938	2,304	28	1,853

TABLE 68.—NONWHITE MALES AND FEMALES 14 YEARS OLD AND OVER BY EMPLOYMENT STATUS, FOR CITIES OF 100,000 OR MORE: 1940

[Percent not shown where less than 0.1]

CITY	MALE									FEMALE								
	Population 14 years and over	In labor force					Percent of male labor force			Population 14 years and over	In labor force					Percent of female labor force		
		Number	Per cent of pop. 14 yrs. and over	Employed (except on emerg. work)	On public emergency work	Seeking work	Employed (except on emerg. work)	On public emergency work	Seeking work		Number	Per cent of pop. 14 yrs. and over	Employed (except on emerg. work)	On public emergency work	Seeking work	Employed (except on emerg. work)	On public emergency work	Seeking work
Akron, Ohio	4, 576	3, 666	80. 1	1, 876	1, 236	554	51. 2	33. 7	15. 1	4, 631	1, 322	28. 5	771	325	220	58. 3	24. 6	17. 1
Albany, N. Y	1, 197	1, 032	86. 2	732	127	173	70. 9	12. 3	16. 8	1, 178	564	47. 9	455	24	85	80. 7	4. 3	15. 1
Atlanta, Ga	34, 832	28, 566	82. 0	22, 763	1, 824	3, 979	79. 7	6. 4	13. 0	46, 968	25, 532	54. 4	22, 116	449	2, 967	86. 6	1. 8	11. 6
Baltimore, Md	61, 831	49, 261	79. 7	39, 533	3, 261	6, 467	80. 3	6. 6	13. 1	65, 377	30, 602	46. 8	26, 908	393	3, 301	87. 9	1. 3	10. 8
Birmingham, Ala	37, 658	30, 891	82. 0	23, 802	2, 182	4, 907	77. 1	7. 1	15. 9	44, 999	17, 961	39. 9	14, 906	381	2, 674	83. 0	2. 1	14. 9
Boston, Mass	10, 169	7, 805	76. 8	6, 031	647	1, 127	77. 3	8. 3	14. 4	10, 260	3, 998	39. 0	3, 196	351	451	79. 9	8. 8	11. 3
Bridgeport, Conn	1, 394	1, 160	83. 2	833	149	178	71. 8	12. 8	15. 3	1, 397	539	38. 6	436	19	84	80. 9	3. 5	15. 6
Buffalo, N. Y	7, 048	5, 559	78. 9	3. 613	482	1, 464	65. 0	8. 7	26. 3	6, 980	1, 876	26. 9	1, 247	148	481	66. 5	7. 9	25. 6
Cambridge, Mass	1, 841	1, 358	73. 8	977	149	232	71. 9	11. 0	17. 1	2, 067	744	36. 0	614	25	105	82. 5	3. 4	14. 1
Camden, N. J	4, 573	3, 659	80. 0	1, 680	1, 059	920	45. 9	28. 9	25. 1	4, 720	1, 785	37. 8	1, 175	137	473	65. 8	7. 7	26. 5
Canton, Ohio	1, 500	1, 240	82. 7	793	288	159	64. 0	23. 2	12. 8	1, 489	519	34. 9	321	96	102	61. 8	18. 5	19. 7
Charlotte, N. C	10, 737	8, 997	83. 8	7, 809	403	785	86. 8	4. 5	8. 7	13, 361	7, 884	59. 0	7, 097	122	665	90. 0	1. 5	8. 4
Chattanooga, Tenn	13, 024	10, 660	81. 8	8, 652	731	1, 277	81. 2	6. 9	12. 0	15, 286	6, 689	43. 8	5, 925	97	667	88. 6	1. 5	10. 0
Chicago, Ill	105, 472	82, 329	78. 1	53, 309	15, 096	13, 924	64. 8	18. 3	16. 9	118, 878	42, 447	35. 7	27, 601	5, 013	9, 833	65. 0	11. 8	23. 2
Cincinnati, Ohio	20, 779	16, 266	78. 3	10, 409	2, 778	3, 079	64. 0	17. 1	18. 9	23, 032	8, 396	36. 5	5, 845	908	1, 643	69. 6	10. 8	19. 6
Cleveland, Ohio	32, 244	25, 651	79. 6	14, 991	6, 403	4, 257	58. 4	25. 0	16. 6	33, 976	11, 221	33. 0	7, 045	1, 661	2, 515	62. 8	14. 8	22. 4
Columbus, Ohio	14, 426	10, 202	70. 7	7, 077	1, 642	1, 483	69. 4	16. 1	14. 5	13, 829	4, 853	35. 1	3, 840	525	488	79. 1	10. 8	10. 1
Dallas, Tex	18, 511	15, 432	83. 4	11, 902	817	2, 713	77. 1	5. 3	17. 6	22, 090	13, 333	60. 4	11, 087	304	1, 942	83. 2	2. 3	14. 6
Dayton, Ohio	7, 750	6, 008	77. 5	3, 997	1, 220	791	66. 5	20. 3	13. 2	7, 935	2, 796	35. 2	2, 110	322	364	75. 5	11. 5	13. 0
Denver, Colo	3, 321	2, 503	75. 4	1, 883	362	258	75. 2	14. 5	10. 3	3, 745	1, 568	41. 9	1, 250	160	158	79. 7	10. 2	10. 1
Des Moines, Iowa	2, 395	1, 827	76. 3	1, 152	361	314	63. 1	19. 8	17. 2	2, 550	828	32. 5	540	172	116	65. 2	20. 8	14. 0
Detroit, Mich	59, 136	50, 089	84. 7	33, 582	8, 506	8, 001	67. 0	17. 0	16. 0	58, 440	17, 506	30. 0	12, 372	1, 753	3, 381	70. 7	10. 0	19. 3
Duluth, Minn	191	141	73. 8	105	11	25	74. 5	7. 8	17. 7	143	32	22. 4	22	6	4	-------	-------	-------
Elizabeth, N. J	1, 745	1, 437	82. 3	973	211	253	67. 7	14. 7	17. 6	1, 782	834	46. 8	698	27	109	83. 7	3. 2	13. 1
Erie, Pa	550	431	78. 4	228	64	139	52. 9	14. 8	32. 3	492	148	30. 1	85	21	42	57. 4	14. 2	28. 4
Fall River, Mass	260	206	79. 2	162	15	29	78. 6	7. 3	14. 1	150	51	34. 0	35	6	10	-------	-------	-------
Flint, Mich	2, 496	2, 041	81. 8	1, 409	253	319	72. 0	12. 4	15. 6	2, 525	718	28. 4	378	198	142	52. 6	27. 6	19. 8
Fort Wayne, Ind	960	747	77. 8	465	132	150	62. 2	17. 7	20. 1	973	364	37. 4	224	64	76	61. 5	17. 6	20. 9
Fort Worth, Tex	9, 360	7, 618	81. 4	5, 399	837	1, 382	70. 9	11. 0	18. 1	10, 976	5, 776	52. 6	4, 683	228	865	81. 1	3. 9	15. 0
Gary, Ind	7, 713	6, 285	81. 5	4, 300	913	1, 072	68. 4	14. 5	17. 1	7, 825	1, 488	19. 0	866	205	417	58. 2	13. 8	28. 0
Grand Rapids, Mich	1, 025	808	78. 8	539	132	137	66. 7	16. 3	17. 0	1, 065	301	28. 3	235	34	32	78. 1	11. 3	10. 6
Hartford, Conn	2, 517	1, 958	77. 8	1, 363	289	306	69. 6	14. 8	15. 6	2, 712	1, 089	40. 2	822	65	202	75. 5	6. 0	18. 5
Houston, Tex	32, 595	27, 380	84. 0	23, 511	605	3, 264	85. 9	2. 2	11. 9	37, 269	19, 990	53. 6	17, 778	271	1, 941	88. 9	1. 4	9. 7
Indianapolis, Ind	19, 074	15, 358	80. 5	10, 129	2, 250	2, 979	66. 0	14. 7	19. 4	21, 410	8, 122	37. 9	5, 880	762	1, 480	72. 4	9. 4	18. 2
Jacksonville, Fla	22, 354	18, 372	82. 2	14, 265	1, 742	2, 365	77. 6	9. 5	12. 9	26, 171	13, 041	49. 8	11, 115	189	1, 737	85. 2	1. 4	13. 3
Jersey City, N. J	4, 860	4, 053	83. 4	3, 026	208	819	74. 7	5. 1	20. 2	5, 306	2, 221	41. 9	1, 720	60	441	77. 4	2. 7	19. 9
Kansas City, Kans	7, 564	5, 979	79. 0	3, 642	877	1, 460	60. 9	14. 7	24. 4	8, 784	2, 662	30. 3	1, 673	172	817	62. 8	6. 5	30. 7
Kansas City, Mo	16, 428	13, 979	85. 1	9, 237	2, 379	2, 363	66. 1	17. 0	16. 9	18, 370	8, 674	47. 2	6, 338	601	1, 735	73. 1	6. 9	20. 0
Knoxville, Tenn	5, 776	4, 686	81. 1	3, 901	255	530	83. 2	5. 4	11. 3	7, 000	3, 657	52. 2	3, 340	45	272	91. 3	1. 2	7. 4
Long Beach, Calif	804	665	82. 7	612	12	41	92. 0	1. 8	6. 2	562	275	48. 9	240	9	26	87. 3	3. 3	9. 5
Los Angeles, Calif	42, 102	33, 409	79. 4	26, 614	2, 176	4, 619	79. 7	6. 5	13. 8	38, 082	16, 218	42. 6	13, 130	649	2, 439	81. 0	4. 0	15. 0
Louisville, Ky	17, 989	14, 349	79. 8	11, 091	742	2, 516	77. 3	5. 2	17. 5	20, 513	9, 370	45. 7	7, 293	332	1, 745	77. 8	3. 5	18. 6
Lowell, Mass	75	58	-------	48	9	1	-------	-------	-------	35	12	-------	10	1	1	-------	-------	-------
Memphis, Tenn	44, 685	38, 161	85. 4	29, 979	2, 637	5, 545	78. 6	6. 9	14. 5	52, 063	23, 320	44. 8	19, 460	247	3, 613	83. 4	1. 1	15. 5
Miami, Fla	14, 130	12, 426	87. 9	10, 962	105	1, 359	88. 2	0. 8	10. 9	15, 494	10, 863	70. 1	9, 570	51	1, 242	88. 1	0. 5	11. 4
Milwaukee, Wis	3, 810	3, 029	79 5	1, 547	625	857	51. 1	20. 6	28. 3	3, 509	1, 146	32. 7	560	235	351	48. 9	20. 5	30. 6
Minneapolis, Minn	2, 339	1, 854	79. 3	1, 296	162	396	69. 9	8. 7	21. 4	1, 977	675	34. 1	444	79	152	65. 8	11. 7	22. 5
Nashville, Tenn	16, 681	13, 334	79. 9	10, 626	537	2, 171	79. 7	4. 0	16. 3	21, 219	10, 411	49. 1	8, 946	165	1, 300	85. 9	1. 6	12. 5
Newark, N. J	16, 309	13, 091	80. 2	7, 900	1, 971	3, 120	61. 1	15. 1	23. 9	18, 305	7, 294	39. 8	5, 260	615	1, 419	72. 1	8. 4	19. 5
New Bedford, Mass	1, 686	1, 292	76. 6	718	157	417	55. 6	12. 2	32. 3	1, 466	521	35. 5	317	68	136	60. 8	13. 1	26. 1
New Haven, Conn	2, 286	1, 776	77. 7	1, 243	220	313	70. 0	12. 4	17. 6	2, 494	1, 099	44. 1	914	31	154	83. 2	2. 8	14. 0
New Orleans, La	51, 661	41, 686	80. 7	28, 639	6, 702	6, 345	68. 7	16. 1	15. 2	62, 745	27, 185	43. 3	22, 026	1, 029	4, 130	81. 0	3. 8	15. 2
New York, N. Y	174, 877	142, 149	81. 3	99, 166	15, 531	27, 452	69. 8	10. 9	19. 3	208, 430	105, 098	50. 4	81, 624	4, 520	18, 954	77. 7	4. 3	18. 0
Bronx Borough	9, 045	6, 140	67. 9	4, 593	556	991	74. 8	9. 1	16. 1	9, 910	4, 504	45. 4	3, 708	171	625	82. 3	3. 8	13. 9
Brooklyn Borough	36, 833	29, 411	79. 8	19, 982	3, 429	6, 000	67. 9	11. 7	20. 4	46, 839	21, 407	45. 7	17, 813	763	2, 831	83. 2	3. 6	13. 2
Manhattan Borough	118, 365	98, 064	82. 8	68, 310	10, 729	19, 025	69. 7	10. 9	19. 4	138, 264	72, 407	52. 4	54, 163	3, 466	14, 778	74. 8	4. 8	20. 4
Queens Borough	9, 370	7, 692	82. 1	5, 790	628	1, 274	75. 3	8. 2	16. 6	11, 885	6, 014	50. 6	5, 285	93	636	87. 9	1. 5	10. 0
Richmond Borough	1, 264	842	66. 6	491	189	162	58. 3	22. 4	19. 2	1, 532	766	50. 0	655	27	84	85. 5	3. 5	11. 0
Norfolk, Va	17, 000	13, 914	81. 8	11, 679	908	1, 327	83. 9	6. 5	9. 5	18, 987	9, 270	48. 9	7, 758	367	1, 154	83. 6	4. 0	12. 4
Oakland, Calif	6, 253	4, 767	76. 2	3, 411	910	446	71. 6	19. 1	9. 4	5, 214	1, 777	34. 1	1, 128	417	232	63. 5	23. 5	13. 1
Oklahoma City, Okla	7, 296	5, 872	80. 5	4, 385	265	1, 222	74. 7	4. 5	20. 8	8, 313	4, 862	58. 5	3, 971	197	694	81. 7	4. 1	14. 3
Omaha, Nebr	4, 737	3, 821	80. 7	2, 440	787	594	63. 9	20. 6	15. 5	4, 843	1, 530	31. 6	1, 024	113	393	66. 9	7. 4	25. 7
Paterson, N. J	1, 592	1, 320	82. 9	835	185	300	63. 3	14. 0	22. 7	1, 706	989	58. 0	819	70	100	82. 8	7. 1	10. 1
Peoria, Ill	1, 206	999	82. 8	736	103	160	73. 7	10. 3	16. 0	1, 118	425	38. 0	319	29	77	75. 1	6. 8	18. 1
Philadelphia, Pa	91, 038	71, 546	78. 6	43, 419	4, 698	23, 420	60. 7	6. 6	32. 7	102, 718	44, 735	43 6	31, 031	3, 112	10, 592	69. 4	7. 0	23. 7
Pittsburgh, Pa	24, 164	19, 253	79. 7	11, 086	2, 164	6, 003	57. 6	11. 2	31. 2	24, 005	7, 126	29. 7	4, 392	884	1, 850	61. 6	12. 4	26. 0
Portland, Oreg	2, 851	2, 217	77. 8	1, 796	45	376	81. 0	2. 0	17. 0	1, 847	626	33. 9	540	21	65	86. 3	3. 4	10. 4
Providence, R. I	2, 365	1, 920	81. 2	1, 172	448	300	61. 0	23. 3	15. 6	2, 418	991	41. 0	670	196	125	67. 6	19. 8	12. 6
Reading, Pa	735	629	85. 6	369	166	94	58. 7	26. 4	14. 9	687	255	37. 1	168	46	41	65. 9	18. 0	16. 1
Richmond, Va	21, 605	17, 187	79. 6	14, 020	509	2, 658	81. 6	3. 0	15. 5	26, 232	14, 724	56. 1	12, 589	202	1, 933	85. 5	1. 4	13. 1
Rochester, N. Y	1, 363	1, 049	77. 0	731	77	241	69. 7	7. 3	23. 0	1, 383	584	42. 2	495	13	76	84. 8	2. 2	13. 0
Sacramento, Calif	2, 637	1, 925	73. 0	1, 570	62	293	81. 6	3. 2	15. 2	2, 028	769	37. 9	593	20	156	77. 1	2. 6	20. 3
St. Louis, Mo	40, 936	33, 402	81. 6	22, 589	4, 307	6, 506	67. 6	12. 9	19. 5	45, 914	17, 186	37. 4	12, 684	1, 003	3, 499	73. 8	5. 8	20. 4
St. Paul, Minn	1, 840	1, 455	79. 1	1, 057	149	249	72. 6	10. 2	17. 1	1, 719	518	30. 1	318	98	102	61. 4	18. 9	19. 7
Salt Lake City, Utah	614	419	68. 2	349	23	47	83. 3	5. 5	11. 2	420	141	33. 6	125	3	13	88. 7	2. 1	9. 2
San Antonio, Tex	7, 303	6, 038	82. 7	4, 909	338	791	81. 3	5. 6	13. 1	8, 944	4, 894	54. 7	4, 194	155	545	85. 7	3. 2	11. 1
San Diego, Calif	2, 738	2, 136	78. 0	1, 667	255	214	78. 0	11. 9	10. 0	2, 294	919	40. 1	725	96	98	78. 9	10. 4	10. 7
San Francisco, Calif	17, 723	13, 528	76. 3	10, 873	726	1, 929	80. 4	5. 4	14. 3	8, 314	3, 061	36. 8	2, 592	172	297	84. 7	5. 6	9. 7
Scranton, Pa	329	265	80. 5	164	12	89	61. 9	4. 5	33. 6	288	112	38. 9	67	12	33	59. 8	10. 7	29. 5
Seattle, Wash	7, 205	5, 430	74. 4	4, 135	154	1, 141	76. 2	2. 8	21. 0	4, 447	1, 670	37. 6	1, 532	27	111	91. 7	1. 6	6. 6
Somerville, Mass	127	109	85. 8	86	9	14	78. 9	8. 3	12. 8	119	37	31. 1	31	-------	6	-------	-------	-------
South Bend, Ind	1, 327	1, 083	81. 6	610	282	191	56. 3	26. 0	17. 6	1, 330	404	30. 4	276	38	90	68. 3	9. 4	22. 3
Spokane, Wash	531	399	75. 1	338	15	46	84. 7	3. 8	11. 5	408	162	39. 7	132	11	19	81. 5	6. 8	11. 7
Springfield, Mass	1, 198	957	79. 9	665	131	161	69. 5	13. 7	16. 8	1, 278	489	38. 3	355	45	89	72. 6	9. 2	18. 2
Syracuse, N. Y	851	663	77. 9	408	76	179	61. 5	11. 5	27. 0	924	339	36. 7	250	26	63	73. 7	7. 7	18. 6
Tacoma, Wash	789	581	73. 6	446	49	86	76. 8	8. 4	14. 8	651	227	34. 9	206	6	15	90. 7	2. 6	6. 6
Tampa, Fla	8, 733	7, 381	84. 5	5, 808	663	910	78. 7	9. 0	12. 3	10. 002	5, 485	54. 8	4, 482	219	784	81. 7	4. 0	14. 3
Toledo, Ohio	5, 694	4, 550	79. 9	2, 496	981	1, 073	54. 9	21. 6	23. 6	5, 815	2, 084	35. 8	1, 025	642	417	49. 2	30. 8	20. 0
Trenton, N. J	3, 574	2, 407	67. 3	1, 416	515	476	58. 8	21. 4	19. 8	3, 380	1, 236	36. 6	932	78	226	75. 4	6. 3	18. 3
Tulsa, Okla	5, 713	4, 409	77. 2	3, 374	155	880	76. 5	3. 5	20. 0	7, 051	4, 215	59. 8	3, 490	159	566	82. 8	3. 8	13. 4
Utica, N. Y	244	190	77. 9	154	7	29	81. 1	3. 7	15. 3	200	90	45. 0	67	4	19	-------	-------	-------
Washington, D. C	70, 117	56, 752	80. 9	45, 909	4, 802	5, 951	81. 1	8. 5	10. 5	79, 284	40, 912	51. 6	34, 645	1, 373	4, 894	84. 7	3. 4	12. 0
Wichita, Kans	2, 135	1, 617	75. 7	1, 204	177	236	74. 5	10. 9	14. 6	2, 385	889	37. 3	716	42	131	80. 5	4. 7	14. 7
Wilmington, Del	5, 514	4, 651	84. 3	3, 395	400	856	73. 0	8. 6	18. 4	5, 828	3, 192	54. 8	2, 686	97	409	84. 1	3. 0	12. 8
Worcester, Mass	533	302	73. 5	297	39	56	75. 8	9. 9	14. 3	535	204	38. 1	145	28	31	71. 1	13. 7	15. 2
Yonkers, N. Y	1, 400	1, 129	80. 6	731	181	217	64. 7	16. 0	19. 2	1, 819	940	51. 7	834	38	68	88. 7	4. 0	7. 2
Youngstown, Ohio	5, 583	4, 520	81. 0	2, 582	1, 134	804	57. 1	25. 1	17. 8	5, 308	1, 394	26. 3	623	392	370	44. 7	28. 1	27. 2

TABLE 69.—MALES AND FEMALES 14 YEARS OLD AND OVER IN THE LABOR FORCE, 1940, AND MALE AND FEMALE GAINFUL WORKERS 14 YEARS OLD AND OVER, 1930, BY COLOR, FOR CITIES OF 100,000 OR MORE

[Figures for nonwhite gainful workers in 1930 have been revised to exclude Mexicans who were classified with "Other Races" in the 1930 Census Reports. Percent not shown where less than 0.1]

CITY	ALL CLASSES								NONWHITE							
	Male				Female				Male				Female			
	In labor force, 1940		Gainful workers, 1930		In labor force, 1940		Gainful workers, 1930		In labor force, 1940		Gainful workers, 1930		In labor force, 1940		Gainful workers, 1930	
	Number	Percent of pop. 14 yrs. and over	Number	Percent of pop. 14 yrs. and over	Number	Percent of pop. 14 yrs. and over	Number	Percent of pop. 14 yrs. and over	Number	Percent of pop. 14 yrs. and over	Number	Percent of pop. 14 yrs. and over	Number	Percent of pop. 14 yrs. and over	Number	Percent of pop. 14 yrs. and over
Akron, Ohio	77,154	80.2	82,512	86.3	26,307	26.7	23,806	26.3	3,666	80.1	3,948	89.4	1,322	28.5	1,145	30.0
Albany, N. Y	41,682	81.0	42,590	87.0	19,502	34.3	16,497	31.1	1,032	86.2	983	93.4	564	47.9	434	45.4
Atlanta, Ga	90,540	82.7	82,790	87.3	56,013	42.2	47,053	42.1	28,566	82.0	26,178	89.9	25,532	54.4	24,222	62.5
Baltimore, Md	272,231	80.6	260,855	87.3	116,186	33.0	101,088	32.3	49,261	79.7	49,318	91.2	30,602	46.8	29,919	54.8
Birmingham, Ala	80,720	81.9	80,976	87.1	35,636	32.0	32,168	31.8	30,891	82.0	30,915	89.7	17,961	39.9	18,039	45.2
Boston, Mass	228,263	77.2	246,880	84.4	109,554	34.0	108,367	35.2	7,805	76.8	8,274	87.7	3,998	39.0	4,055	49.0
Bridgeport, Conn	48,625	82.3	46,684	86.4	22,416	37.2	17,357	31.6	1,160	83.2	1,226	90.3	539	38.6	458	39.0
Buffalo, N. Y	180,503	79.6	180,926	84.6	66,882	28.4	58,235	26.7	5,559	78.9	5,304	91.7	1,876	26.9	1,662	32.9
Cambridge, Mass	32,152	77.7	34,154	84.4	17,131	36.2	17,102	37.0	1,358	73.8	1,585	82.9	744	36.0	838	40.5
Camden, N. J	38,306	82.3	37,460	85.7	15,799	33.7	12,658	29.1	3,650	80.0	3,663	87.3	1,785	37.8	1,732	42.3
Canton, Ohio	35,190	81.2	33,717	85.3	10,956	25.3	8,539	22.3	1,240	82.7	1,080	85.7	519	34.9	228	21.0
Charlotte, N. C	30,648	83.7	25,008	87.3	18,573	44.1	13,089	40.7	8,997	83.8	7,463	89.6	7,884	59.0	6,224	59.9
Chattanooga, Tenn	38,187	81.5	30,817	86.9	18,575	35.3	15,673	33.8	10,660	81.8	10,515	88.9	6,689	43.8	6,218	46.1
Chicago, Ill	1,121,618	82.0	1,151,922	86.6	472,205	33.5	406,670	31.5	82,320	78.1	88,805	91.2	42,447	35.7	44,541	46.7
Cincinnati, Ohio	139,878	79.6	147,344	85.7	58,933	29.8	55,588	29.9	16,266	78.3	16,657	89.1	8,396	36.5	7,936	43.1
Cleveland, Ohio	290,034	81.2	295,691	85.5	110,170	30.6	98,938	29.6	25,651	79.6	25,650	90.3	11,221	33.0	10,975	40.4
Columbus, Ohio	91,020	75.4	93,711	83.9	30,007	30.2	35,367	30.4	10,202	70.7	11,639	85.6	4,853	35.1	5,088	42.6
Dallas, Tex	93,122	83.1	84,556	87.7	50,073	39.3	38,155	36.4	15,432	83.4	12,919	90.9	13,333	60.4	10,363	62.3
Dayton, Ohio	66,974	80.9	66,335	86.2	25,738	29.6	22,854	29.1	6,008	77.5	5,754	88.3	2,796	35.2	2,560	41.0
Denver, Colo	96,230	76.7	92,612	84.4	41,103	30.1	37,686	31.9	2,503	75.4	2,831	88.3	1,568	41.9	1,649	49.3
Des Moines, Iowa	47,438	79.0	43,817	84.5	22,077	32.2	18,322	31.6	1,827	76.3	1,707	85.2	828	32.5	784	37.2
Detroit, Mich	555,530	84.7	548,371	88.6	178,093	28.3	140,826	25.7	50,080	84.7	46,213	92.0	17,506	30.0	15,435	34.7
Duluth, Minn	31,305	77.2	32,205	83.8	11,533	28.2	10,755	28.5	141	73.8	204	94.9	32	22.4	70	35.2
Elizabeth, N. J	36,531	82.3	38,102	87.3	14,836	33.2	11,828	28.6	1,437	82.3	1,679	92.0	834	46.8	614	37.0
Erie, Pa	36,126	79.6	34,849	83.9	12,603	27.0	10,579	24.7	431	78.4	473	89.4	148	30.1	114	27.0
Fall River, Mass	33,948	78.4	33,056	84.8	20,605	43.1	17,493	39.8	206	79.2	220	90.9	51	34.0	68	47.9
Flint, Mich	47,537	82.6	52,552	87.8	15,367	26.8	12,277	23.2	2,041	81.8	2,200	90.6	718	28.4	472	24.2
Fort Wayne, Ind	35,779	79.3	36,852	86.0	14,478	29.0	12,958	28.6	747	77.8	868	87.8	364	37.4	270	32.4
Fort Worth, Tex	54,618	80.8	52,508	86.9	25,024	33.3	19,268	30.1	7,618	81.4	7,481	89.7	5,776	52.6	4,999	54.0
Gary, Ind	38,460	83.7	36,328	88.6	8,379	20.2	6,174	19.1	6,285	81.5	6,515	90.5	1,488	19.0	1,246	19.6
Grand Rapids, Mich	48,824	78.5	51,752	83.8	18,955	27.9	18,053	27.5	808	78.8	1,031	88.1	301	28.3	418	38.0
Hartford, Conn	52,628	80.8	52,200	86.3	26,838	37.9	23,602	36.6	1,058	77.8	2,052	80.8	1,089	40.2	1,194	50.4
Houston, Tex	126,483	83.8	90,588	88.5	54,828	34.6	37,664	33.3	27,380	84.0	21,635	90.7	19,990	53.6	14,392	54.3
Indianapolis, Ind	120,072	80.9	118,143	86.4	51,404	31.2	46,094	31.2	15,358	80.5	14,427	87.9	8,122	37.9	7,686	43.7
Jacksonville, Fla	52,702	81.1	40,138	85.9	26,696	36.9	19,042	36.6	18,372	82.2	14,717	87.0	13,041	49.8	10,657	52.4
Jersey City, N. J	90,481	82.9	104,037	87.8	41,926	34.1	35,852	30.6	4,053	83.4	4,472	91.8	2,221	41.9	1,997	42.4
Kansas City, Kans	36,976	79.9	38,544	86.2	13,769	28.0	12,885	28.3	5,979	70.0	6,375	86.8	2,662	30.3	2,836	36.0
Kansas City, Mo	120,678	82.8	137,689	88.1	61,600	34.9	56,968	34.1	13,979	85.1	14,471	91.4	8,674	47.2	8,721	51.8
Knoxville, Tenn	32,079	81.0	31,766	86.0	16,881	36.6	13,323	32.5	4,686	81.1	5,448	87.5	3,657	52.2	3,583	51.7
Long Beach, Calif	48,874	75.3	43,365	78.3	17,546	23.7	14,710	24.1	665	82.7	485	88.3	275	48.9	146	44.6
Los Angeles, Calif	480,184	78.0	417,067	84.1	206,572	31.6	163,342	31.7	33,409	79.4	25,543	88.4	16,218	42.6	9,899	43.3
Louisville, Ky	98,059	81.5	98,304	87.2	43,677	32.3	39,797	31.8	14,349	79.8	16,394	90.2	9,370	45.7	10,696	53.4
Lowell, Mass	28,759	76.2	28,689	83.8	14,371	34.4	13,970	35.2	58	------	74	------	12	------	17	------
Memphis, Tenn	92,830	83.7	81,010	87.3	45,931	36.7	37,300	35.6	38,161	85.4	31,769	90.3	23,320	44.8	20,234	48.6
Miami, Fla	55,848	80.1	35,255	84.6	28,141	38.5	15,555	36.0	12,426	87.9	7,835	91.9	10,863	70.1	7,409	77.2
Milwaukee, Wis	186,135	80.6	100,880	85.5	72,139	29.9	63,326	28.6	3,020	79.5	3,022	87.4	1,146	32.7	874	32.3
Minneapolis, Minn	149,679	78.6	147,387	84.8	73,276	34.1	64,412	34.2	1,854	79.3	1,900	88.7	675	34.1	644	38.0
Nashville, Tenn	48,247	80.1	46,402	85.9	26,863	36.9	22,269	35.0	13,334	79.9	13,072	88.0	10,411	49.1	9,775	52.8
Newark, N. J	138,636	80.8	145,819	86.7	60,181	34.4	53,200	32.4	13,081	80.2	13,985	92.5	7,294	39.8	7,166	49.0
New Bedford, Mass	33,684	78.2	33,651	85.0	18,806	40.5	18,457	41.7	1,292	76.6	989	83.8	521	35.5	357	31.9
New Haven, Conn	49,973	79.4	49,179	83.8	24,266	36.0	20,040	32.0	1,776	77.7	1,799	88.2	1,099	44.1	900	44.8
New Orleans, La	148,958	81.0	143,189	87.7	60,835	33.2	61,047	33.2	41,686	80.7	39,858	89.8	27,185	43.3	27,506	51.3
New York, N. Y	2,424,740	81.1	2,322,296	86.9	1,050,020	33.7	862,662	32.2	142,149	81.3	124,674	92.3	105,098	50.4	79,505	57.6
Bronx Borough	450,350	81.1	412,535	86.1	173,705	30.2	137,299	28.1	6,140	67.9	4,028	81.7	4,504	45.4	2,331	47.1
Brooklyn Borough	852,218	80.1	828,407	86.0	346,874	31.4	280,703	29.1	29,411	79.8	24,590	91.9	21,407	45.7	13,888	49.7
Manhattan Borough	640,561	81.5	675,041	88.3	352,084	42.7	319,826	42.3	98,064	82.8	89,091	93.1	72,407	52.4	58,741	61.0
Queens Borough	426,087	82.9	358,040	88.0	158,408	29.4	110,926	26.8	7,692	82.1	6,064	90.8	6,014	50.6	4,171	52.7
Richmond Borough	55,524	77.9	50,273	82.9	18,049	26.8	13,908	25.0	842	66.6	901	84.6	766	50.0	374	39.2
Norfolk, Va	49,630	84.2	43,533	87.2	18,276	31.8	16,745	33.7	13,914	81.8	13,809	87.7	9,279	48.0	9,553	53.7
Oakland, Calif	98,581	79.0	95,078	83.5	30,165	28.0	30,943	27.2	4,767	76.2	5,030	83.0	1,777	34.1	1,496	34.2
Oklahoma City, Okla	61,023	79.4	62,540	87.0	28,152	33.4	21,581	30.8	5,872	80.5	5,222	87.4	4,862	58.5	3,400	55.1
Omaha, Nebr	68,630	79.8	67,444	84.0	28,789	30.9	25,791	30.9	3,821	80.7	4,035	88.1	1,530	31.6	1,929	43.7
Paterson, N. J	46,441	82.2	45,850	86.8	20,008	34.7	16,984	31.7	1,320	82.9	1,113	92.5	389	58.0	647	55.0
Peoria, Ill	34,833	82.6	36,040	86.8	13,387	30.5	12,769	30.6	999	82.8	1,204	90.1	425	38.0	583	52.8
Philadelphia, Pa	607,296	80.6	643,621	87.0	268,842	33.4	246,050	32.5	71,546	78.6	78,060	91.3	44,735	43.6	42,752	49.9
Pittsburgh, Pa	208,593	79.5	208,636	84.2	78,022	28.4	69,915	27.6	19,253	79.7	19,456	89.3	7,126	29.7	6,931	34.2
Portland, Oreg	100,176	79.1	105,425	86.2	41,991	31.3	39,710	32.1	2,217	77.8	2,478	88.8	626	33.9	506	35.5
Providence, R. I	77,792	80.2	76,460	85.4	39,831	37.1	35,843	35.6	1,920	81.2	1,805	89.4	991	41.0	1,008	48.6
Reading, Pa	35,732	81.3	36,622	87.7	17,387	37.1	14,284	32.5	629	85.6	778	88.9	255	37.1	239	35.5
Richmond, Va	58,996	81.1	55,478	86.1	36,037	42.3	28,275	37.4	17,187	79.6	15,382	86.9	14,724	56.1	11,314	52.5
Rochester, N. Y	100,470	77.6	102,851	83.3	47,100	33.7	41,989	31.9	1,049	77.0	991	88.3	584	42.2	561	49.6
Sacramento, Calif	35,994	79.7	34,850	86.3	15,048	34.2	10,670	30.7	1,925	73.0	2,169	85.4	769	37.9	444	29.3
St. Louis, Mo	264,010	82.7	279,431	88.0	117,791	33.4	106,549	31.6	33,402	81.6	33,545	90.4	17,186	37.4	17,444	45.2
St. Paul, Minn	86,427	79.3	83,828	84.0	39,020	31.8	33,905	31.2	1,455	79.1	1,667	88.4	518	30.1	523	32.2
Salt Lake City, Utah	41,988	76.2	40,348	81.4	15,272	25.9	13,679	26.3	419	68.2	591	83.8	141	23.6	118	32.0
San Antonio, Tex	75,488	80.5	71,720	86.0	30,526	30.3	25,908	29.6	6,038	82.7	5,925	89.1	4,894	54.7	4,556	56.7
San Diego, Calif	66,732	77.7	47,615	80.2	21,408	25.9	16,285	27.6	2,136	78.0	1,771	88.0	919	40.1	605	47.1
San Francisco, Calif	222,803	79.7	249,140	86.5	93,856	34.7	84,328	34.1	13,528	76.3	16,604	87.8	3,061	36.8	1,891	31.7
Scranton, Pa	42,648	78.9	42,323	83.3	16,710	29.0	14,358	26.5	265	80.5	297	89.5	112	38.9	89	32.1
Seattle, Wash	121,921	78.3	130,068	85.7	49,070	31.2	45,354	31.2	5,430	74.4	6,226	87.3	1,670	37.6	1,169	32.1
Somerville, Mass	30,135	79.6	31,751	85.3	12,352	29.5	12,514	30.3	109	85.8	126	85.7	37	31.1	32	30.2
South Bend, Ind	32,598	82.1	33,455	85.8	12,476	30.4	10,976	28.6	1,083	81.6	1,312	90.9	404	30.4	421	34.2
Spokane, Wash	38,797	77.8	38,508	84.0	14,916	29.1	13,495	29.4	399	75.1	485	89.5	162	39.7	121	34.6
Springfield, Mass	46,560	79.8	46,981	85.4	20,408	32.0	19,564	32.8	957	79.9	1,105	87.8	480	38.3	548	45.3
Syracuse, N. Y	63,102	78.1	67,157	84.6	26,450	30.4	23,870	29.2	663	77.9	797	86.5	339	36.7	276	38.0
Tacoma, Wash	35,274	78.1	35,709	84.8	11,090	24.7	10,525	25.7	581	73.6	835	89.0	227	34.9	218	34.8
Tampa, Fla	33,818	80.1	30,645	82.7	18,541	40.4	15,437	39.6	7,381	84.5	6,835	88.9	5,485	54.8	5,403	61.9
Toledo, Ohio	89,552	79.2	97,936	85.7	33,540	28.9	29,249	26.6	4,550	79.9	5,144	91.3	2,084	35.8	1,670	34.4
Trenton, N. J	38,733	76.7	37,627	81.4	18,406	36.0	13,347	29.0	2,407	67.3	2,463	77.9	1,236	36.6	971	36.4
Tulsa, Okla	43,872	81.3	46,809	88.3	19,806	33.0	17,821	32.7	4,409	77.2	5,755	89.8	4,215	59.8	4,206	59.1
Utica, N. Y	30,281	76.9	30,672	83.2	14,118	33.3	12,995	32.3	190	77.9	207	92.0	90	45.0	95	51.1
Washington, D. C	212,118	80.8	154,874	83.8	131,915	45.3	88,803	42.7	56,752	80.9	42,256	86.4	40,912	51.6	31,330	56.6
Wichita, Kans	33,941	78.3	34,788	84.8	14,589	29.8	13,126	29.7	1,617	75.7	1,895	88.9	889	37.3	1,001	45.7
Wilmington, Del	36,644	82.0	35,183	86.6	16,045	34.5	12,082	29.8	4,651	84.3	4,458	91.7	3,192	54.8	2,424	50.7
Worcester, Mass	57,341	76.0	59,551	83.7	24,090	29.9	23,364	30.9	392	73.5	458	86.1	204	38.1	225	40.9
Yonkers, N. Y	44,804	80.5	42,055	85.0	18,838	32.0	15,877	30.8	1,129	80.6	1,122	90.4	940	51.7	810	57.8
Youngstown, Ohio	54,283	80.5	51,901	83.4	16,109	24.6	12,114	20.5	4,520	81.0	4,934	87.7	1,394	26.3	958	19.8

Table 70.—MALE EMPLOYED WORKERS 14 YEARS OLD AND OVER, BY MAJOR OCCUPATION GROUP, FOR CITIES OF 100,000 OR MORE: 1940

CITY	Total employed (except on public emergency work)	Professional workers	Semiprofessional workers	Farmers and farm managers	Proprietors, managers, and officials, except farm	Clerical, sales, and kindred workers	Craftsmen, foremen, and kindred workers	Operatives and kindred workers	Domestic service workers	Service workers, except domestic	Farm laborers (wage workers) and farm foremen	Farm laborers, unpaid family workers	Laborers, except farm	Occupation not reported
Akron, Ohio	61,021	3,179	926	60	5,934	9,859	11,290	20,131	106	4,647	87	7	4,236	559
Albany, N. Y	35,397	2,368	535	37	4,833	8,238	6,544	5,835	93	3,805	60	-	2,766	193
Atlanta, Ga	78,437	3,999	1,016	54	9,358	18,638	12,347	14,217	1,224	10,067	73	2	6,972	470
Baltimore, Md	243,348	11,560	3,477	100	25,439	46,378	47,997	50,458	1,426	21,674	387	10	32,450	1,992
Birmingham, Ala	68,348	3,043	752	52	7,068	12,305	13,188	16,349	759	5,386	100	6	8,945	395
Boston, Mass	179,010	10,926	2,506	42	18,586	37,867	33,102	34,531	685	25,618	113	-	13,709	1,325
Bridgeport, Conn	42,145	1,570	619	23	3,782	6,290	9,950	12,341	66	3,080	50	2	4,147	225
Buffalo, N. Y	141,377	7,390	2,183	29	15,340	24,385	32,370	33,068	245	11,761	56	1	13,444	1,009
Cambridge, Mass	25,247	2,415	326	7	2,249	4,531	4,261	5,547	89	3,154	23	2	2,344	299
Camden, N. J	29,081	897	384	9	2,405	4,048	7,098	7,864	33	2,309	21	1	3,635	287
Canton, Ohio	30,461	1,288	442	14	3,034	4,624	6,747	8,548	47	1,906	23	-	3,573	215
Charlotte, N. C	28,218	1,331	357	30	3,631	6,481	4,290	6,026	471	2,556	68	2	2,823	152
Chattanooga, Tenn	33,021	1,558	399	39	3,393	5,280	6,142	8,374	412	3,074	40	2	4,088	214
Chicago, Ill	942,365	49,529	14,267	280	96,584	203,275	185,472	208,361	1,774	95,705	458	43	82,372	4,245
Cincinnati, Ohio	118,590	7,449	1,895	166	14,583	23,563	23,411	25,443	704	11,216	158	20	9,317	665
Cleveland, Ohio	228,578	8,944	3,118	101	18,832	37,836	53,101	61,250	354	10,180	197	7	24,813	845
Columbus, Ohio	77,702	4,877	1,114	92	9,511	16,149	15,883	15,967	271	7,684	150	-	5,212	702
Dallas, Tex	81,612	4,063	1,185	117	12,366	21,207	13,624	13,577	1,280	8,610	175	5	4,987	416
Dayton, Ohio	58,500	2,938	1,218	29	5,357	9,805	13,664	16,524	177	4,649	98	-	3,395	646
Denver, Colo	80,547	6,342	1,462	248	11,864	18,751	13,817	12,312	277	8,784	397	13	5,043	737
Des Moines, Iowa	39,040	2,650	475	132	6,016	10,194	6,467	6,749	119	3,457	111	7	2,192	471
Detroit, Mich	474,250	21,219	7,619	114	41,346	77,910	106,854	141,926	708	35,903	234	23	37,543	851
Duluth, Minn	22,986	1,338	328	66	3,506	4,955	4,268	4,172	30	2,042	102	8	2,070	101
Elizabeth, N. J	31,414	1,842	568	9	3,060	5,073	7,147	7,535	52	2,230	12	1	3,530	355
Erie, Pa	29,980	1,275	453	22	2,976	4,735	6,287	6,587	45	1,815	43	4	5,520	218
Fall River, Mass	26,140	798	221	34	2,254	3,230	4,132	11,317	24	2,032	136	5	1,842	115
Flint, Mich	42,043	1,541	551	28	3,276	5,607	8,916	14,531	51	2,429	51	9	4,608	355
Fort Wayne, Ind	30,936	1,700	668	26	3,749	6,530	6,490	7,535	39	2,002	41	3	1,884	269
Fort Worth, Tex	46,001	2,733	739	133	7,405	10,507	7,261	7,694	697	4,654	183	10	3,720	265
Gary, Ind	33,552	1,307	428	20	2,028	4,162	9,037	7,716	24	1,677	9	-	6,933	211
Grand Rapids, Mich	42,377	1,909	653	46	4,958	8,166	9,187	11,887	52	2,664	97	1	2,347	410
Hartford, Conn	46,212	2,075	687	19	4,482	9,431	10,067	10,985	107	4,613	110	-	3,042	594
Houston, Tex	113,957	6,524	1,669	138	15,284	24,025	19,821	20,141	1,760	10,625	225	5	12,665	1,066
Indianapolis, Ind	102,747	6,158	1,481	69	12,283	21,887	20,526	20,710	495	8,982	146	2	9,193	815
Jacksonville, Fla	44,508	1,805	504	74	5,985	9,041	7,154	8,085	552	4,549	83	1	6,395	280
Jersey City, N. J	80,137	3,224	910	12	7,147	16,573	15,140	17,392	93	7,838	32	-	11,280	496
Kansas City, Kans	29,224	1,210	301	37	2,657	4,895	5,877	6,635	89	2,511	61	1	4,757	193
Kansas City, Mo	108,099	6,461	1,451	151	15,749	28,336	17,053	18,236	593	11,705	237	11	7,497	619
Knoxville, Tenn	27,637	1,811	316	56	3,241	5,207	4,980	6,460	294	2,756	63	3	2,309	132
Long Beach, Calif	42,596	2,618	891	94	6,926	7,724	8,564	7,934	82	5,168	118	22	2,160	295
Los Angeles, Calif	407,425	31,166	9,772	2,073	57,056	80,096	73,761	68,554	2,416	42,254	3,231	163	28,672	2,211
Louisville, Ky	84,183	3,881	1,122	69	9,130	15,721	16,486	18,969	682	7,716	113	3	9,798	493
Lowell, Mass	21,810	881	203	26	2,008	2,991	4,048	7,903	31	1,794	63	-	1,664	198
Memphis, Tenn	79,369	3,385	843	225	9,203	15,093	12,947	15,665	1,110	8,114	293	8	11,985	498
Miami, Fla	50,005	2,463	970	156	6,841	9,892	8,149	7,112	646	7,425	285	1	5,595	470
Milwaukee, Wis	149,939	7,732	2,595	40	15,295	26,982	35,582	38,253	153	11,105	139	-	11,495	568
Minneapolis, Minn	122,480	7,747	2,101	98	17,517	30,533	24,147	21,878	192	9,963	237	8	7,355	704
Nashville, Tenn	40,886	2,092	509	37	4,181	8,035	7,483	8,168	862	4,593	93	-	4,596	237
Newark, N. J	108,917	5,380	1,470	21	10,907	19,245	21,315	27,142	271	10,622	54	3	10,870	1,608
New Bedford, Mass	25,421	818	240	53	2,145	3,194	4,521	9,722	49	2,182	90	9	2,168	221
New Haven, Conn	41,527	2,441	558	29	4,857	7,160	7,918	10,160	152	4,214	80	9	3,580	369
New Orleans, La	119,518	6,061	1,472	334	14,697	25,668	17,845	21,565	750	13,362	315	43	17,045	361
New York, N. Y	1,964,346	126,887	30,052	519	259,075	446,199	319,308	388,788	6,976	256,696	914	50	111,567	17,315
Bronx Borough	368,191	19,220	5,367	67	48,690	90,241	68,369	79,191	412	39,112	74	7	14,810	2,631
Brooklyn Borough	694,090	38,073	9,071	115	92,305	162,733	117,777	156,536	1,176	62,884	167	7	45,349	7,897
Manhattan Borough	493,039	45,660	7,756	75	69,509	95,853	51,618	79,562	4,467	105,690	133	2	29,293	3,421
Queens Borough	364,547	21,285	6,982	181	43,394	89,395	73,134	65,845	837	41,958	400	15	18,035	3,086
Richmond Borough	44,479	2,649	876	81	5,177	7,977	8,410	7,654	84	7,052	140	19	4,080	280
Norfolk, Va	45,467	1,620	730	58	5,687	6,696	7,782	7,022	220	9,730	122	1	5,576	223
Oakland, Calif	83,493	4,420	1,435	151	11,464	17,697	17,143	15,154	262	7,252	168	6	7,717	624
Oklahoma City, Okla	51,082	3,463	744	185	8,333	12,415	8,145	9,753	509	4,824	210	12	2,894	495
Omaha, Nebr	56,554	3,273	720	90	8,147	14,484	9,223	9,136	114	5,620	103	6	5,356	282
Paterson, N. J	37,361	1,638	546	12	3,926	5,861	6,815	12,840	99	3,104	79	-	2,244	197
Peoria, Ill	30,946	1,516	472	33	3,723	6,174	6,727	6,400	68	2,621	62	-	2,857	293
Philadelphia, Pa	485,086	23,244	7,172	228	50,963	92,971	90,002	117,878	1,931	48,762	499	34	35,698	3,704
Pittsburgh, Pa	160,181	9,138	2,374	40	15,495	33,573	28,237	29,030	552	16,082	127	6	24,865	662
Portland, Oreg	83,802	5,462	1,542	237	13,280	18,434	15,336	14,202	161	7,069	313	12	7,008	746
Providence, R. I	60,847	3,330	913	16	7,366	10,700	11,585	16,896	125	5,826	79	-	3,822	189
Reading, Pa	29,052	983	297	15	2,477	4,362	5,563	9,391	47	2,295	33	1	3,427	161
Richmond, Va	52,339	2,580	676	18	6,178	11,331	8,719	11,118	469	5,510	60	2	5,484	185
Rochester, N. Y	84,202	4,815	1,644	63	7,976	14,391	20,258	22,116	167	6,727	163	3	4,741	1,138
Sacramento, Calif	30,228	2,078	619	106	4,352	7,026	5,386	4,623	87	3,015	597	3	2,160	176
St. Louis, Mo	221,421	9,509	2,762	97	21,738	48,497	40,806	51,331	853	23,345	134	4	21,332	1,013
St. Paul, Minn	70,637	4,474	1,015	92	9,372	16,906	12,804	13,646	101	6,176	152	9	5,523	367
Salt Lake City, Utah	36,004	2,786	587	125	5,634	8,927	6,563	5,779	59	2,951	110	4	2,235	244
San Antonio, Tex	62,152	2,639	901	144	8,205	11,583	9,584	9,177	889	13,510	394	16	4,747	363
San Diego, Calif	59,729	3,311	1,676	215	7,162	8,855	11,993	7,276	179	14,737	315	12	3,682	316
San Francisco, Calif	189,967	10,917	2,990	256	24,922	43,397	28,853	20,395	1,918	30,843	341	11	14,839	1,285
Scranton, Pa	28,755	1,288	358	10	2,992	5,506	4,771	9,098	45	2,215	18	1	2,048	405
Seattle, Wash	104,058	6,892	1,702	152	16,697	21,866	20,297	16,507	314	9,600	280	15	8,992	645
Somerville, Mass	23,952	985	260	3	2,114	5,014	5,083	6,066	20	2,442	14	-	1,812	139
South Bend, Ind	27,853	1,438	482	17	2,930	5,020	5,630	8,386	45	1,848	33	-	1,839	185
Spokane, Wash	32,005	1,829	476	116	5,233	7,205	6,381	5,240	35	2,046	184	4	2,460	196
Springfield, Mass	39,746	2,031	659	44	4,513	7,807	9,399	9,043	57	3,535	63	4	2,284	307
Syracuse, N. Y	52,535	3,485	893	60	6,587	10,598	10,757	11,178	118	4,388	77	6	3,830	549
Tacoma, Wash	29,183	1,356	340	62	3,925	4,450	6,311	6,126	29	2,112	85	3	4,221	163
Tampa, Fla	27,432	1,019	298	62	3,464	5,112	4,007	6,831	297	2,620	135	2	3,486	99
Toledo, Ohio	71,325	3,672	1,075	48	8,548	13,563	15,601	17,258	107	5,567	114	5	5,466	301
Trenton, N. J	31,790	1,459	407	11	3,468	4,756	5,176	8,866	96	2,066	99	-	4,127	359
Tulsa, Okla	38,835	3,173	829	60	6,095	10,060	6,328	6,121	421	3,388	77	2	2,002	279
Utica, N. Y	24,985	1,036	275	34	3,202	4,640	4,627	6,612	59	2,275	81	3	1,993	148
Washington, D. C	189,587	19,078	3,797	60	19,046	47,637	28,547	25,872	1,420	26,789	186	3	16,077	1,075
Wichita, Kans	29,964	1,888	422	89	4,995	7,045	5,647	5,186	104	2,342	84	1	1,933	228
Wilmington, Del	31,859	1,925	582	12	3,425	5,280	6,400	7,066	213	2,512	46	-	4,123	275
Worcester, Mass	48,288	2,646	786	46	4,651	8,200	10,827	13,271	63	3,770	110	1	3,280	637
Yonkers, N. Y	36,693	3,044	688	28	5,475	8,063	6,108	7,178	175	2,604	101	1	2,990	238
Youngstown, Ohio	43,594	1,763	558	25	3,905	6,505	10,106	10,623	60	2,587	25	3	7,086	348

CHARACTERISTICS OF THE POPULATION

TABLE 71.—FEMALE EMPLOYED WORKERS 14 YEARS OLD AND OVER, BY MAJOR OCCUPATION GROUP, FOR CITIES OF 100,000 OR MORE: 1940

CITY	Total employed (except on public emergency work)	Professional workers	Semiprofessional workers	Farmers and farm managers	Proprietors, managers, and officials, except farm	Clerical, sales, and kindred workers	Craftsmen, foremen, and kindred workers	Operatives and kindred workers	Domestic service workers	Service workers, except domestic	Farm laborers (wage workers) and farm foremen	Farm laborers, unpaid family workers	Laborers, except farm	Occupation not reported
Akron, Ohio	21,537	2,460	132	2	560	7,585	258	4,306	2,734	2,721	1	3	491	284
Albany, N. Y	17,183	2,218	325	1	613	7,225	100	2,043	2,077	2,323	1	1	50	146
Atlanta, Ga	48,923	3,891	325	3	1,277	14,684	368	6,755	15,248	5,844	1	-	224	303
Baltimore, Md	105,010	10,356	890	3	3,171	31,348	1,606	21,725	21,241	12,385	20	5	1,038	1,213
Birmingham, Ala	29,822	3,374	175	5	791	7,973	164	2,733	10,367	3,865	8	4	111	252
Boston, Mass	91,656	12,945	1,285	3	2,202	35,090	1,306	16,007	7,936	13,710	8	-	363	801
Bridgeport, Conn	20,121	1,871	137	2	404	5,531	340	8,846	1,353	1,307	-	-	208	122
Buffalo, N. Y	54,677	7,490	686	1	2,162	19,556	800	8,901	6,747	7,273	1	-	423	637
Cambridge, Mass	14,893	2,191	164	-	368	4,848	204	2,918	1,886	1,982	-	-	127	205
Camden, N. J	12,507	1,006	84	-	348	3,049	195	4,865	1,246	1,123	-	-	442	149
Canton, Ohio	9,571	1,141	77	-	371	3,378	108	1,713	1,292	1,251	-	-	107	133
Charlotte, N. C	17,107	1,421	93	1	351	4,168	137	3,697	5,333	1,731	-	-	87	88
Chattanooga, Tenn	16,309	1,494	61	2	452	3,468	132	4,322	4,277	1,909	1	1	78	112
Chicago, Ill	409,853	35,636	4,523	28	13,773	168,222	5,927	88,666	33,674	51,485	21	14	5,436	2,448
Cincinnati, Ohio	51,380	6,298	460	6	1,724	16,630	1,168	9,245	8,377	6,817	6	16	215	409
Cleveland, Ohio	91,004	8,717	931	5	2,895	31,767	1,263	20,487	9,854	13,793	14	3	728	547
Columbus, Ohio	34,745	3,905	310	4	1,224	13,517	470	5,142	4,305	5,227	3	-	200	432
Dallas, Tex	43,863	3,786	450	13	1,841	15,318	490	6,299	9,359	5,906	6	4	114	277
Dayton, Ohio	23,116	2,357	169	1	662	7,888	360	4,983	2,873	3,336	4	1	134	839
Denver, Colo	36,141	4,928	475	14	2,247	13,837	394	3,366	4,735	5,481	27	4	182	451
Des Moines, Iowa	19,221	2,311	168	6	700	8,639	179	1,865	2,281	2,603	2	4	69	304
Detroit, Mich	151,206	15,485	1,648	14	4,839	57,649	2,295	25,606	17,991	22,841	7	1	1,680	1,150
Duluth, Minn	9,598	1,546	117	6	429	3,600	103	726	1,438	1,541	1	2	25	64
Elizabeth, N. J	13,267	1,337	76	2	344	4,311	149	4,513	1,330	886	-	-	154	165
Erie, Pa	10,468	1,352	119	-	335	3,645	108	1,800	1,289	1,395	2	2	256	165
Fall River, Mass	18,076	1,469	80	-	221	2,375	270	11,906	843	692	1	1	115	103
Flint, Mich	13,262	1,779	73	1	387	4,257	168	2,293	1,070	1,773	1	2	416	142
Fort Wayne, Ind	13,295	1,384	113	-	385	4,591	181	3,530	1,216	1,557	4	2	145	187
Fort Worth, Tex	20,865	2,249	160	11	1,078	6,694	167	2,780	4,288	3,130	3	5	149	151
Gary, Ind	7,074	990	71	-	297	2,417	40	1,220	750	1,128	-	-	72	89
Grand Rapids, Mich	17,132	2,125	209	1	521	6,068	233	3,348	1,966	2,214	3	-	101	253
Hartford, Conn	24,085	2,946	298	3	575	9,876	304	4,882	2,309	2,398	-	-	154	340
Houston, Tex	49,204	4,529	553	17	1,836	14,480	362	4,141	14,923	7,521	17	4	333	488
Indianapolis, Ind	45,385	4,864	421	5	1,567	16,846	607	7,658	6,215	6,204	5	2	520	471
Jacksonville, Fla	23,032	2,035	117	11	680	5,627	122	3,173	7,693	3,248	7	2	142	176
Jersey City, N. J	34,409	3,608	323	-	797	13,482	417	9,388	2,007	3,445	1	-	665	276
Kansas City, Kans	11,327	1,328	119	2	472	3,362	134	2,640	1,410	1,435	-	1	314	110
Kansas City, Mo	52,845	5,082	723	11	2,851	20,727	666	7,250	7,313	7,620	12	4	197	380
Knoxville, Tenn	15,288	1,390	77	5	446	3,496	152	4,737	3,116	1,730	1	1	48	89
Long Beach, Calif	15,151	2,105	223	4	1,613	5,076	115	1,034	1,869	2,848	6	23	38	197
Los Angeles, Calif	179,472	21,844	3,234	202	12,436	64,356	2,045	25,065	22,136	26,006	161	219	635	1,133
Louisville, Ky	37,526	3,630	336	4	1,191	11,748	520	7,703	6,950	4,602	1	-	480	352
Lowell, Mass	11,736	1,446	69	4	225	2,807	134	4,967	921	945	1	-	105	112
Memphis, Tenn	39,783	3,525	316	23	1,202	10,593	348	4,198	13,058	5,773	42	8	415	282
Miami, Fla	25,316	2,199	292	13	1,326	6,513	143	2,154	7,112	5,223	14	3	86	238
Milwaukee, Wis	62,374	6,932	693	10	2,182	24,090	753	12,958	5,613	8,308	5	1	352	387
Minneapolis, Minn	63,906	7,649	799	6	2,312	25,540	692	8,561	8,010	9,644	12	4	198	479
Nashville, Tenn	23,581	2,378	174	1	572	6,286	204	4,404	6,328	2,845	6	-	175	208
Newark, N. J	49,847	4,096	424	-	1,308	16,225	855	15,222	5,682	4,386	-	-	601	958
New Bedford, Mass	14,979	1,125	97	3	202	2,698	195	8,427	1,168	830	6	1	108	119
New Haven, Conn	21,438	2,743	227	1	546	6,225	247	6,695	2,510	1,763	6	-	255	220
New Orleans, La	57,794	5,904	603	18	1,909	16,580	461	8,793	15,780	6,973	58	15	460	240
New York, N. Y	875,020	90,145	12,146	30	20,077	324,605	10,171	191,265	116,226	89,508	46	10	2,601	9,121
Bronx Borough	142,511	11,630	1,528	1	4,910	66,205	1,778	32,949	9,183	12,587	-	2	293	1,355
Brooklyn Borough	290,306	25,076	2,698	4	8,166	114,303	3,794	81,217	29,205	20,384	6	1	1,359	4,003
Manhattan Borough	290,525	38,892	6,035	12	11,725	73,213	2,590	48,691	63,662	43,173	6	-	576	1,941
Queens Borough	137,015	12,264	1,043	18	3,816	64,524	1,874	26,116	12,607	12,153	17	2	331	1,590
Richmond Borough	14,663	2,283	242	4	460	6,270	126	2,292	1,509	1,271	17	5	42	142
Norfolk, Va	15,924	1,670	101	2	420	4,050	107	1,581	5,483	2,183	90	1	131	105
Oakland, Calif	30,479	3,914	496	9	2,094	12,768	335	3,718	2,537	4,056	6	13	219	314
Oklahoma City, Okla	24,164	2,689	272	16	1,384	9,000	202	1,708	4,805	3,721	6	3	84	274
Omaha, Nebr	24,932	3,148	374	6	1,011	10,257	198	2,209	3,385	3,642	5	1	497	199
Paterson, N. J	16,630	1,799	104	-	452	4,388	198	6,648	1,730	1,096	2	-	116	97
Peoria, Ill	12,251	1,499	181	-	490	4,355	146	1,901	1,552	1,888	-	-	95	144
Philadelphia, Pa	218,612	20,632	2,785	15	6,385	67,348	3,662	61,633	28,472	24,431	16	4	1,065	2,164
Pittsburgh, Pa	62,875	8,780	541	3	1,680	24,222	601	6,388	9,706	9,878	2	2	575	407
Portland, Oreg	36,837	4,811	570	24	2,458	14,312	400	4,003	3,906	5,813	13	13	153	352
Providence, R. I	33,176	3,777	228	1	826	9,746	638	11,395	3,209	3,084	-	1	146	125
Reading, Pa	15,290	1,026	209	1	365	3,219	177	7,355	1,225	1,522	1	1	74	124
Richmond, Va	31,824	3,129	248	4	818	9,002	234	7,362	6,978	3,600	1	-	332	116
Rochester, N. Y	41,650	4,776	421	7	1,111	14,044	1,951	11,105	3,278	4,110	4	-	173	670
Sacramento, Calif	13,287	1,740	189	12	659	6,544	111	1,003	1,056	1,753	15	4	69	132
St. Louis, Mo	102,142	8,810	1,109	3	3,105	34,190	1,207	25,096	13,141	13,780	1	5	937	668
St. Paul, Minn	33,579	4,290	629	4	1,001	13,952	426	3,943	4,342	4,533	2	6	152	299
Salt Lake City, Utah	13,769	2,251	151	6	661	6,065	136	1,238	1,200	1,863	4	1	50	143
San Antonio, Tex	25,434	3,044	296	15	1,340	6,830	212	3,610	5,930	3,859	33	10	63	183
San Diego, Calif	18,646	2,793	209	25	1,568	5,670	154	2,018	2,563	3,250	14	12	55	155
San Francisco, Calif	81,339	10,082	1,364	10	5,047	36,035	922	10,139	6,833	9,811	15	7	346	728
Scranton, Pa	12,778	1,742	104	1	311	4,127	146	3,395	1,363	1,292	-	-	55	242
Seattle, Wash	43,894	5,480	603	21	2,997	17,433	460	4,500	4,597	7,181	5	19	118	390
Somerville, Mass	10,379	1,107	71	1	192	4,569	201	2,392	590	1,093	-	-	82	81
South Bend, Ind	11,183	1,077	79	2	323	3,886	164	2,912	1,202	1,236	2	2	188	110
Spokane, Wash	13,076	1,902	154	7	837	4,987	132	1,108	1,497	2,253	13	9	55	122
Springfield, Mass	17,237	2,162	276	3	493	6,916	232	3,026	1,859	1,938	-	1	83	248
Syracuse, N. Y	22,804	3,358	215	7	770	8,313	425	3,513	2,640	2,966	1	2	248	346
Tacoma, Wash	9,390	1,422	117	13	682	3,393	92	1,028	1,072	1,409	2	6	72	82
Tampa, Fla	14,727	1,212	110	1	504	2,952	78	4,530	3,359	1,838	6	2	48	87
Toledo, Ohio	27,884	3,717	264	5	1,012	9,523	313	5,350	3,467	3,801	25	1	245	161
Trenton, N. J	16,126	1,634	85	2	473	4,206	157	5,739	1,644	1,469	11	-	436	180
Tulsa, Okla	17,293	1,665	178	5	936	6,296	147	1,094	3,869	2,919	2	1	45	136
Utica, N. Y	12,255	1,457	104	1	318	3,211	213	4,099	1,383	1,245	1	1	126	96
Washington, D. C	119,313	11,116	909	4	3,190	56,355	631	6,738	23,960	15,385	2	-	312	711
Wichita, Kans	13,202	1,842	152	11	819	4,879	103	1,078	1,898	2,214	5	2	56	143
Wilmington, Del	14,237	1,590	149	-	435	4,815	134	2,294	2,949	1,597	2	-	90	182
Worcester, Mass	20,598	2,931	300	1	436	7,114	264	4,693	2,088	2,213	-	-	162	396
Yonkers, N. Y	16,483	2,254	214	3	446	5,664	130	3,746	2,486	1,207	4	-	182	116
Youngstown, Ohio	12,635	1,797	106	1	438	4,835	144	1,398	1,987	1,735	1	-	77	147

TABLE 72.—PERCENT DISTRIBUTION BY MAJOR OCCUPATION GROUP, FOR MALE EMPLOYED WORKERS 14 YEARS OLD AND OVER, FOR CITIES OF 100,000 OR MORE: 1940

[Percent not shown where less than 0.1]

CITY	Total employed (except on public emergency work)	Professional workers	Semiprofessional workers	Farmers and farm managers	Proprietors, managers, and officials, except farm	Clerical, sales, and kindred workers	Craftsmen, foremen, and kindred workers	Operatives and kindred workers	Domestic service workers	Service workers, except domestic	Farm laborers (wage workers) and farm foremen	Farm laborers, unpaid family workers	Laborers, except farm	Occupation not reported
Akron, Ohio	100.0	5.2	1.5	0.1	9.7	16.2	18.5	33.0	0.2	7.6	0.1		6.9	0.9
Albany, N. Y	100.0	6.7	1.5	0.1	13.7	23.3	18.5	16.5	0.3	11.0	0.2		7.8	0.5
Atlanta, Ga	100.0	5.1	1.3	0.1	11.9	23.8	15.7	18.1	1.6	12.8	0.1		8.9	0.6
Baltimore, Md	100.0	4.8	1.4		10.5	19.1	19.7	20.7	0.6	8.9	0.2		13.3	0.8
Birmingham, Ala	100.0	4.5	1.1	0.1	10.3	18.0	19.3	23.9	1.1	7.9	0.1		13.1	0.6
Boston, Mass	100.0	6.1	1.4		10.4	21.2	18.5	19.3	0.4	14.3	0.1		7.7	0.7
Bridgeport, Conn	100.0	3.7	1.5	0.1	9.0	14.9	23.6	29.3	0.2	7.3	0.1		9.8	0.5
Buffalo, N. Y	100.0	5.2	1.5		10.9	17.2	22.9	23.4	0.2	8.3			9.5	0.8
Cambridge, Mass	100.0	9.6	1.3		8.9	17.9	16.9	22.0	0.4	12.5	0.1		9.3	1.2
Camden, N. J	100.0	3.1	1.3		8.3	13.9	24.4	27.0	0.1	8.2	0.1		12.5	1.0
Canton, Ohio	100.0	4.2	1.5		10.0	15.2	22.1	28.1	0.2	6.3	0.1		11.7	0.7
Charlotte, N. C	100.0	4.7	1.3	0.1	12.9	23.0	15.2	21.4	1.7	9.1	0.2		10.0	0.5
Chattanooga, Tenn	100.0	4.7	1.2	0.1	10.3	16.0	18.6	25.4	1.2	9.3	0.1		12.4	0.6
Chicago, Ill	100.0	5.3	1.5		10.2	21.6	19.7	22.1	0.2	10.2			8.7	0.5
Cincinnati, Ohio	100.0	6.3	1.6	0.1	12.3	19.9	19.7	21.5	0.6	9.5	0.1		7.9	0.6
Cleveland, Ohio	100.0	3.9	1.4		8.2	16.6	23.2	26.8	0.2	8.4	0.1		10.9	0.4
Columbus, Ohio	100.0	6.3	1.4	0.1	12.2	20.8	20.4	20.5	0.3	9.9	0.2		6.7	1.0
Dallas, Tex	100.0	5.0	1.5	0.1	15.2	26.0	16.7	16.6	1.6	10.5	0.2		6.1	0.5
Dayton, Ohio	100.0	5.0	2.1		9.2	16.8	23.4	28.2	0.3	7.9	0.2		5.8	1.1
Denver, Colo	100.0	7.9	1.8	0.3	14.7	23.3	17.2	15.9	0.3	10.9	0.5		6.3	0.9
Des Moines, Iowa	100.0	6.8	1.2	0.3	15.4	26.1	16.6	17.3	0.3	8.9	0.3		5.6	1.2
Detroit, Mich	100.0	4.5	1.6		8.7	16.4	22.5	29.9	0.1	7.6			7.9	0.6
Duluth, Minn	100.0	5.8	1.4	0.3	15.3	21.6	18.6	18.1	0.1	8.9	0.4		9.0	0.4
Elizabeth, N. J	100.0	5.9	1.8		9.7	16.1	22.8	24.0	0.2	7.1			11.2	1.1
Erie, Pa	100.0	4.3	1.5	0.1	9.9	15.8	21.0	22.0	0.2	6.1	0.1		18.4	0.7
Fall River, Mass	100.0	3.1	0.8	0.1	8.6	12.4	15.8	43.3	0.1	7.8	0.5		7.0	0.4
Flint, Mich	100.0	3.7	1.3	0.1	7.8	13.3	21.2	34.6	0.1	5.8	0.1		11.2	0.8
Fort Wayne, Ind	100.0	5.5	2.2	0.1	12.1	21.1	21.0	24.4	0.1	6.5	0.1		6.1	0.9
Fort Worth, Tex	100.0	5.9	1.6	0.3	16.1	22.8	15.8	16.7	1.5	10.1	0.4		8.1	0.6
Gary, Ind	100.0	3.9	1.3	0.1	6.0	12.4	26.9	23.0	0.1	5.0			20.7	0.6
Grand Rapids, Mich	100.0	4.5	1.5	0.1	11.7	19.3	21.7	28.1	0.1	6.3	0.2		5.5	1.0
Hartford, Conn	100.0	4.5	1.5		9.7	20.4	21.8	23.8	0.2	10.0	0.2		6.6	1.3
Houston, Tex	100.0	5.7	1.5	0.1	13.4	21.1	17.4	17.7	1.6	9.3	0.2		11.1	0.9
Indianapolis, Ind	100.0	6.0	1.4	0.1	12.0	21.3	20.0	20.2	0.5	8.7	0.1		8.9	0.8
Jacksonville, Fla	100.0	4.1	1.1	0.2	13.4	20.3	16.1	18.2	1.2	10.2	0.2		14.4	0.6
Jersey City, N. J	100.0	4.0	1.1		8.9	20.7	18.9	21.7	0.1	9.8			14.1	0.6
Kansas City, Kans	100.0	4.1	1.0	0.1	9.1	16.7	20.1	22.7	0.3	8.6	0.2		16.3	0.7
Kansas City, Mo	100.0	6.0	1.3	0.1	14.6	26.2	15.8	16.9	0.5	10.8	0.2		6.9	0.6
Knoxville, Tenn	100.0	6.6	1.1	0.2	11.7	18.8	18.0	23.4	1.1	10.0	0.2		8.4	0.5
Long Beach, Calif	100.0	6.1	2.1	0.2	16.3	18.1	20.1	18.6	0.2	12.1	0.3	0.1	5.1	0.7
Los Angeles, Calif	100.0	7.6	2.4	0.5	14.0	21.1	18.1	16.8	0.6	10.4	0.8		7.0	0.5
Louisville, Ky	100.0	4.6	1.3	0.1	10.8	18.7	19.6	22.5	0.8	9.2	0.1		11.6	0.6
Lowell, Mass	100.0	4.0	0.9	0.1	9.2	13.7	18.6	36.2	0.1	8.2	0.3		7.6	0.9
Memphis, Tenn	100.0	4.3	1.1	0.3	11.6	19.0	16.3	19.7	1.4	10.2	0.4		15.1	0.6
Miami, Fla	100.0	4.9	1.9	0.3	13.7	19.8	16.3	14.2	1.3	14.8	0.6		11.2	0.9
Milwaukee, Wis	100.0	5.2	1.7		10.2	18.0	23.7	25.5	0.1	7.4	0.1		7.7	0.4
Minneapolis, Minn	100.0	6.3	1.7	0.1	14.3	24.9	19.7	17.9	0.2	8.1	0.2		6.0	0.6
Nashville, Tenn	100.0	5.1	1.2	0.1	10.2	19.7	18.3	20.0	2.1	11.2	0.2		11.2	0.6
Newark, N. J	100.0	4.9	1.3		10.0	17.7	19.6	24.9	0.2	9.8			10.0	1.5
New Bedford, Mass	100.0	3.2	0.9	0.2	8.4	12.6	17.8	38.2	0.2	8.6	0.4		8.5	0.9
New Haven, Conn	100.0	5.9	1.3	0.1	11.7	17.2	19.1	24.5	0.4	10.1	0.2		8.6	0.9
New Orleans, La	100.0	5.1	1.2	0.3	12.3	21.5	14.9	18.0	0.6	11.2	0.3		14.3	0.3
New York, N. Y	100.0	6.5	1.5		13.2	22.7	16.3	19.8	0.4	13.1			5.7	0.9
Bronx Borough	100.0	5.2	1.5		13.2	24.5	18.6	21.5	0.1	10.6			4.0	0.7
Brooklyn Borough	100.0	5.5	1.3		13.3	23.4	17.0	22.6	0.2	9.1			6.5	1.1
Manhattan Borough	100.0	9.3	1.6		14.1	19.4	10.5	16.1	0.9	21.4			5.9	0.7
Queens Borough	100.0	5.8	1.9		11.9	24.5	20.1	18.1	0.2	11.5	0.1		4.9	0.8
Richmond Borough	100.0	6.0	2.0	0.2	11.6	17.9	18.9	17.2	0.2	15.9	0.3		9.2	0.6
Norfolk, Va	100.0	3.6	1.6	0.1	12.5	14.7	17.1	15.4	0.5	21.4	0.3		12.3	0.5
Oakland, Calif	100.0	5.3	1.7	0.2	13.7	21.2	20.5	18.1	0.3	8.7	0.2		9.2	0.7
Oklahoma City, Okla	100.0	6.7	1.4	0.4	16.0	23.9	15.7	18.8	1.0	9.3	0.4		5.6	1.0
Omaha, Nebr	100.0	5.8	1.3	0.2	14.4	25.6	16.3	16.2	0.2	9.9	0.2		9.5	0.5
Paterson, N. J	100.0	4.4	1.5		10.5	15.7	18.2	34.4	0.3	8.3	0.2		6.0	0.5
Peoria, Ill	100.0	4.9	1.5	0.1	12.0	20.0	21.7	20.7	0.2	8.5	0.2		9.2	0.9
Philadelphia, Pa	100.0	4.8	1.5		10.5	19.2	20.4	24.3	0.4	10.1	0.1		8.0	0.8
Pittsburgh, Pa	100.0	5.7	1.5		9.7	21.0	17.6	18.1	0.3	10.0	0.1		15.5	0.4
Portland, Oreg	100.0	6.5	1.8	0.3	15.8	22.0	18.3	16.9	0.2	8.4	0.4		8.4	0.9
Providence, R. I	100.0	5.5	1.5		12.1	17.6	19.0	27.8	0.2	9.6	0.1		6.3	0.3
Reading, Pa	100.0	3.4	1.0	0.1	8.5	15.0	19.1	32.3	0.2	7.9	0.1		11.8	0.6
Richmond, Va	100.0	4.9	1.3		11.8	21.6	16.7	21.2	0.9	10.5	0.1		10.5	0.4
Rochester, N. Y	100.0	5.7	2.0	0.1	9.5	17.1	24.1	20.3	0.2	8.0	0.2		5.6	1.4
Sacramento, Calif	100.0	6.9	2.0	0.4	14.4	23.2	17.8	15.3	0.3	10.0	2.0		7.1	0.6
St. Louis, Mo	100.0	4.3	1.2		9.8	21.9	18.4	23.2	0.4	10.5	0.1		9.6	0.5
St. Paul, Minn	100.0	6.3	1.4	0.1	13.3	23.9	18.1	19.3	0.1	8.7	0.2		7.8	0.5
Salt Lake City, Utah	100.0	7.7	1.6	0.3	15.6	24.8	18.2	16.1	0.2	8.2	0.3		6.2	0.7
San Antonio, Tex	100.0	4.2	1.4	0.2	13.2	18.6	15.4	14.8	1.4	21.7	0.6		7.6	0.6
San Diego, Calif	100.0	5.5	2.8	0.4	12.0	14.8	20.1	12.2	0.3	24.7	0.5		6.2	0.5
San Francisco, Calif	100.0	5.7	1.6	0.1	13.1	22.8	15.2	15.5	1.0	16.2	0.2		7.8	0.7
Scranton, Pa	100.0	4.5	1.2		10.4	19.1	16.6	31.6	0.2	7.7	0.1		7.1	1.4
Seattle, Wash	100.0	6.6	1.6	0.1	16.0	21.0	19.5	15.9	0.3	9.3	0.3		8.6	0.6
Somerville, Mass	100.0	4.1	1.1		8.8	20.9	21.2	25.3	0.1	10.2	0.1		7.6	0.6
South Bend, Ind	100.0	5.2	1.7	0.1	10.5	18.0	20.2	30.1	0.2	6.6	0.1		6.6	0.7
Spokane, Wash	100.0	5.7	1.5	0.4	16.4	22.5	19.9	16.4	0.1	8.3	0.6		7.7	0.6
Springfield, Mass	100.0	5.1	1.7	0.1	11.4	19.6	23.6	22.8	0.1	8.9	0.2		5.7	0.8
Syracuse, N. Y	100.0	6.6	1.7	0.1	12.5	20.2	20.5	21.3	0.2	8.4	0.1		7.3	1.0
Tacoma, Wash	100.0	4.6	1.2	0.2	13.4	15.2	21.6	21.0	0.1	7.2	0.3		14.5	0.6
Tampa, Fla	100.0	3.7	1.1	0.2	12.6	18.6	14.6	24.9	1.1	9.6	0.5		12.7	0.4
Toledo, Ohio	100.0	5.1	1.5	0.1	12.0	19.0	21.9	24.2	0.2	7.8	0.2		7.7	0.4
Trenton, N. J	100.0	4.6	1.3		10.9	15.0	16.3	27.9	0.3	9.3	0.3		13.0	1.1
Tulsa, Okla	100.0	8.2	2.1	0.2	15.7	25.9	16.3	15.8	1.1	8.7	0.2		5.2	0.7
Utica, N. Y	100.0	4.1	1.1	0.1	12.8	18.6	18.5	26.5	0.2	9.1			8.0	0.6
Washington, D. C	100.0	10.1	2.0		10.0	25.1	15.1	13.6	0.7	14.1	0.1		8.5	0.6
Wichita, Kans	100.0	6.3	1.4	0.3	16.7	23.5	18.8	17.3	0.3	7.8	0.3		6.5	0.8
Wilmington, Del	100.0	6.0	1.8		10.8	16.6	20.1	22.2	0.7	7.9	0.1		12.9	0.9
Worcester, Mass	100.0	5.5	1.6	0.1	9.6	17.0	22.4	27.5	0.1	7.8	0.2		6.8	1.3
Yonkers, N. Y	100.0	8.3	1.9	0.1	14.9	22.0	16.6	19.6	0.5	7.1	0.3		8.1	0.6
Youngstown, Ohio	100.0	4.0	1.3	0.1	9.0	14.9	23.2	24.4	0.1	5.9	0.1		16.3	0.8

TABLE 73.—PERCENT DISTRIBUTION BY MAJOR OCCUPATION GROUP, FOR FEMALE EMPLOYED WORKERS 14 YEARS OLD AND OVER, FOR CITIES OF 100,000 OR MORE: 1940

[Percent not shown where less than 0.1]

CITY	Total employed (except on public emergency work)	Professional workers	Semiprofessional workers	Farmers and farm managers	Proprietors, managers, and officials, except farm	Clerical, sales, and kindred workers	Craftsmen, foremen, and kindred workers	Operatives and kindred workers	Domestic service workers	Service workers, except domestic	Farm laborers (wage workers) and farm foremen	Farm laborers, unpaid family workers	Laborers, except farm	Occupation not reported
Akron, Ohio	100.0	11.4	0.6		2.6	35.2	1.2	20.0	12.7	12.6			2.3	1.3
Albany, N. Y	100.0	12.9	1.9		3.6	42.0	0.9	11.9	12.1	13.5			0.3	0.8
Atlanta, Ga	100.0	8.0	0.7		2.6	30.0	0.8	13.8	31.2	11.9			0.5	0.6
Baltimore, Md	100.0	9.9	0.9		3.0	29.9	1.5	20.7	20.2	11.8			1.0	1.2
Birmingham, Ala	100.0	11.3	0.6		2.7	26.7	0.5	9.2	34.8	13.0			0.4	0.8
Boston, Mass	100.0	14.1	1.4		2.4	38.3	1.4	17.5	8.7	15.0			0.4	0.9
Bridgeport, Conn	100.0	9.3	0.7		2.0	27.5	1.7	44.0	6.7	6.5			1.0	0.6
Buffalo, N. Y	100.0	13.7	1.3		4.0	35.8	1.5	16.3	12.3	13.3			0.8	1.2
Cambridge, Mass	100.0	14.7	1.1		2.5	32.6	1.4	19.6	12.7	13.3			0.9	1.4
Camden, N. J	100.0	8.0	0.7		2.8	24.4	1.6	38.9	10.0	9.0			3.5	1.2
Canton, Ohio	100.0	11.9	0.8		3.9	35.3	1.1	17.9	13.5	13.1			1.1	1.4
Charlotte, N. C	100.0	8.3	0.5		2.1	24.4	0.8	21.6	31.2	10.1			0.5	0.5
Chattanooga, Tenn	100.0	9.2	0.4		2.8	21.3	0.8	26.5	26.2	11.7			0.5	0.7
Chicago, Ill	100.0	8.7	1.1		3.4	41.0	1.4	21.6	8.2	12.6			1.3	0.6
Cincinnati, Ohio	100.0	12.3	0.9		3.4	32.4	2.3	18.0	16.3	13.3			0.4	0.8
Cleveland, Ohio	100.0	9.6	1.0		3.2	34.9	1.4	22.5	10.8	15.2			0.8	0.6
Columbus, Ohio	100.0	11.2	0.9		3.5	38.9	1.4	14.8	12.4	15.0			0.6	1.2
Dallas, Tex	100.0	8.6	1.0		4.2	34.9	1.1	14.4	21.3	13.5			0.3	0.6
Dayton, Ohio	100.0	10.2	0.7		2.9	34.1	1.6	21.6	12.4	14.4			0.6	1.5
Denver, Colo	100.0	13.6	1.3		6.2	38.3	1.1	9.3	13.1	15.2	0.1		0.5	1.2
Des Moines, Iowa	100.0	12.0	0.9		4.1	44.9	0.9	9.7	11.9	13.5			0.4	1.6
Detroit, Mich	100.0	10.2	1.1		3.2	38.1	1.5	16.9	11.9	15.1			1.1	0.8
Duluth, Minn	100.0	16.1	1.2	0.1	4.5	37.5	1.1	7.6	15.0	16.1			0.3	0.7
Elizabeth, N. J	100.0	10.1	0.6		2.6	32.5	1.1	34.0	10.0	6.7			1.2	1.2
Erie, Pa	100.0	12.9	1.1		3.2	34.8	1.0	17.2	12.3	13.3			2.4	1.6
Fall River, Mass	100.0	8.1	0.4		1.2	13.1	1.5	65.9	4.7	3.8			0.6	0.6
Flint, Mich	100.0	13.4	0.6		2.9	32.1	1.3	17.3	14.9	13.4			3.1	1.1
Fort Wayne, Ind	100.0	10.4	0.8		2.9	34.5	1.4	26.6	9.1	11.7			1.1	1.4
Fort Worth, Tex	100.0	10.8	0.8	0.1	5.2	32.1	0.8	13.3	20.6	15.0			0.7	0.7
Gary, Ind	100.0	14.0	1.0		4.2	34.2	0.7	17.3	10.7	15.9			1.0	1.0
Grand Rapids, Mich	100.0	12.4	1.2		3.0	35.4	1.4	19.5	11.5	12.9			1.1	1.5
Hartford, Conn	100.0	12.2	1.2		2.4	41.0	1.3	20.3	9.6	10.0			0.6	1.4
Houston, Tex	100.0	9.2	1.1		3.7	29.4	0.7	8.4	30.3	15.3			0.7	1.0
Indianapolis, Ind	100.0	10.7	0.9		3.5	37.1	1.3	16.9	13.7	13.7			1.1	1.0
Jacksonville, Fla	100.0	8.8	0.5		3.0	24.4	0.5	13.8	33.4	14.1			0.6	0.8
Jersey City, N. J	100.0	10.5	0.9		2.3	39.2	1.2	27.3	5.8	10.0			1.9	0.8
Kansas City, Kans	100.0	11.7	1.1		4.2	29.7	1.2	23.3	12.4	12.7			2.8	1.0
Kansas City, Mo	100.0	9.6	1.4		5.4	39.2	1.3	13.7	13.8	14.4			0.4	0.7
Knoxville, Tenn	100.0	9.1	0.5		2.9	22.9	1.0	31.0	20.4	11.3			0.3	0.6
Long Beach, Calif	100.0	13.9	1.5		10.6	33.5	0.8	6.8	12.3	18.8		0.2	0.3	1.3
Los Angeles, Calif	100.0	12.2	1.8	0.1	6.9	35.9	1.1	14.0	12.3	14.5	0.1	0.1	0.4	0.6
Louisville, Ky	100.0	9.7	0.9		3.2	31.3	1.4	20.5	18.5	12.3			1.3	0.9
Lowell, Mass	100.0	12.3	0.6		1.9	23.9	1.1	42.3	7.8	8.1			0.9	1.0
Memphis, Tenn	100.0	8.9	0.8	0.1	3.0	26.6	0.9	10.6	32.8	14.5	0.1		1.0	0.7
Miami, Fla	100.0	8.7	1.2	0.1	5.2	25.7	0.6	8.5	28.1	20.6	0.1		0.3	0.9
Milwaukee, Wis	100.0	11.1	1.1		3.5	38.6	1.2	20.8	9.0	13.5			0.6	0.6
Minneapolis, Minn	100.0	12.0	1.3		3.6	40.0	1.1	13.4	12.5	15.1			0.3	0.7
Nashville, Tenn	100.0	10.1	0.7		2.4	26.7	0.9	18.7	26.8	12.1			0.7	0.9
Newark, N. J	100.0	8.2	0.9		2.8	32.5	1.7	30.5	11.4	8.8			1.2	1.9
New Bedford, Mass	100.0	7.5	0.6		1.3	18.0	1.3	56.3	7.8	5.5			0.7	0.8
New Haven, Conn	100.0	12.8	1.1		2.5	29.0	1.2	31.2	11.7	8.2			1.2	1.0
New Orleans, La	100.0	10.2	1.0		3.3	28.7	0.8	15.2	27.3	12.1	0.1		0.8	0.4
New York, N. Y	100.0	10.3	1.4		3.3	37.1	1.2	21.9	13.3	10.2			0.3	1.0
Bronx Borough	100.0	8.2	1.1		3.4	46.5	1.2	23.1	6.4	8.8			0.2	1.0
Brooklyn Borough	100.0	8.6	0.9		2.8	39.4	1.3	28.0	10.1	7.0			0.5	1.4
Manhattan Borough	100.0	13.4	2.1		4.0	25.2	0.9	16.8	21.9	14.9			0.2	0.7
Queens Borough	100.0	9.0	1.2		2.8	47.1	1.4	19.1	9.2	8.9			0.2	1.2
Richmond Borough	100.0	15.6	1.7		3.1	42.8	0.9	15.6	10.3	8.7	0.1		0.3	1.0
Norfolk, Va	100.0	10.5	0.6		2.6	25.4	0.7	9.9	34.4	13.7	0.6		0.8	0.7
Oakland, Calif	100.0	12.8	1.6		6.9	41.9	1.1	12.2	8.3	13.3			0.7	1.0
Oklahoma City, Okla	100.0	11.1	1.1	0.1	5.7	37.2	0.8	7.1	19.9	15.4			0.3	1.1
Omaha, Nebr	100.0	12.6	1.5		4.1	41.1	0.8	8.9	13.6	14.6			2.0	0.8
Paterson, N. J	100.0	10.8	0.6		2.7	26.4	1.2	40.0	10.4	6.6			0.7	0.6
Peoria, Ill	100.0	12.2	1.5		4.0	35.5	1.2	15.5	12.7	15.4			0.8	1.2
Philadelphia, Pa	100.0	9.4	1.3		2.9	30.8	1.7	28.2	13.0	11.2			0.5	1.0
Pittsburgh, Pa	100.0	14.0	0.9		2.7	38.5	1.0	10.2	15.6	15.7			0.9	0.6
Portland, Oreg	100.0	13.1	1.5	0.1	6.7	38.9	1.1	10.9	10.6	15.8			0.4	1.0
Providence, R. I	100.0	11.4	0.7		2.5	29.4	1.9	34.3	9.7	9.3			0.4	0.4
Reading, Pa	100.0	6.7	1.4		2.4	21.0	1.2	48.1	8.0	9.9			0.5	0.8
Richmond, Va	100.0	9.8	0.8		2.6	28.3	0.7	23.1	21.9	11.3			1.0	0.4
Rochester, N. Y	100.0	11.5	1.0		2.7	33.7	4.7	26.7	7.9	9.9			0.4	1.6
Sacramento, Calif	100.0	13.1	1.4	0.1	5.0	49.3	0.8	7.5	7.9	13.2	0.1		0.5	1.0
St. Louis, Mo	100.0	8.6	1.1		3.0	33.5	1.3	24.6	12.9	13.5			0.9	0.7
St. Paul, Minn	100.0	12.8	1.9		3.0	41.5	1.3	11.7	12.9	13.5			0.5	0.9
Salt Lake City, Utah	100.0	16.3	1.1		4.8	44.0	1.0	9.0	8.7	13.5			0.4	1.0
San Antonio, Tex	100.0	12.0	1.2	0.1	5.3	26.9	0.8	14.2	23.3	15.2	0.1		0.2	0.7
San Diego, Calif	100.0	15.1	1.5	0.1	8.5	30.6	0.8	10.9	13.8	17.5	0.1	0.1	0.3	0.8
San Francisco, Calif	100.0	12.4	1.7		6.2	44.3	1.1	12.5	8.4	12.1			0.4	0.9
Scranton, Pa	100.0	13.6	0.8		2.4	32.3	1.1	26.6	10.7	10.1			0.4	1.9
Seattle, Wash	100.0	12.5	1.6		6.8	39.7	1.0	10.3	10.5	16.4			0.3	0.9
Somerville, Mass	100.0	10.7	0.7		1.8	44.0	1.9	23.0	5.7	10.5			0.8	0.8
South Bend, Ind	100.0	9.6	0.7		2.9	34.7	1.5	26.0	10.7	11.1			1.7	1.0
Spokane, Wash	100.0	14.5	1.2	0.1	6.4	38.1	1.0	8.5	11.4	17.2	0.1	0.1	0.4	0.9
Springfield, Mass	100.0	12.5	1.6		2.9	40.1	1.3	17.6	10.8	11.2			0.5	1.4
Syracuse, N. Y	100.0	14.7	0.9		3.4	36.5	1.9	15.4	11.6	13.0			1.1	1.5
Tacoma, Wash	100.0	15.1	1.2	0.1	7.3	36.1	1.0	10.9	11.4	15.0		0.1	0.8	0.9
Tampa, Fla	100.0	8.2	0.7		3.4	20.0	0.5	30.8	22.8	12.5			0.3	0.6
Toledo, Ohio	100.0	13.3	0.9		3.6	34.2	1.1	19.2	12.4	13.6	0.1		0.9	0.6
Trenton, N. J	100.0	10.1	0.5		2.9	26.6	1.0	35.6	10.2	9.1	0.1		2.7	1.1
Tulsa, Okla	100.0	9.6	1.0		5.4	36.4	0.9	6.3	22.4	16.9			0.3	0.8
Utica, N. Y	100.0	11.9	0.8		2.6	26.2	1.7	33.4	11.3	10.2			1.0	0.8
Washington, D. C	100.0	9.3	0.8		2.7	47.2	0.5	5.6	20.1	12.9			0.3	0.6
Wichita, Kans	100.0	14.0	1.2	0.1	6.2	37.0	0.8	8.2	14.4	16.8			0.4	1.1
Wilmington, Del	100.0	11.2	1.0		3.1	33.8	0.9	16.1	20.7	11.2			0.6	1.3
Worcester, Mass	100.0	14.2	1.5		2.1	34.5	1.3	22.8	10.1	10.7			0.8	1.9
Yonkers, N. Y	100.0	13.7	1.3		2.7	34.4	0.8	22.7	15.1	7.3			1.1	0.9
Youngstown, Ohio	100.0	14.2	0.8		3.5	38.3	1.1	11.1	15.7	13.7			0.6	0.9

TABLE 74.—MALE AND FEMALE EMPLOYED WORKERS 14 YEARS OLD AND OVER, BY INDUSTRY GROUP, FOR CITIES OF 100,000 OR MORE: 1940

INDUSTRY GROUP	AKRON, OHIO		ALBANY, N. Y.		ATLANTA, GA.		BALTIMORE, MD.		BIRMINGHAM, ALA.		BOSTON, MASS.		BRIDGEPORT, CONN.	
	Male	Female	Male	Female	Male	Female	Male	Female	Male	Female	Male	Female	Male	Female
Employed (exc. on public emergency work)	61,021	21,537	35,397	17,183	78,437	48,923	243,348	105,010	66,348	29,822	179,010	91,656	42,145	20,121
Agriculture, forestry, and fishery	235	11	139	8	365	26	787	38	282	28	1,365	44	203	4
Agriculture	229	10	137	8	315	16	737	36	274	28	362	26	134	3
Forestry (except logging) and fishery	6	1	2	-	50	10	50	2	8	-	1,003	18	69	1
Mining	112	5	25	-	26	3	249	4	3,942	32	73	13	13	2
Coal mining	48	3	-	-	1	-	12	-	3,572	29	8	3	2	-
Crude petroleum and natural gas production	6	2	1	-	2	-	6	-	11	-	4	-	1	-
Other mines and quarries	58	-	24	-	23	3	231	4	359	3	61	10	10	2
Construction	2,430	59	2,393	55	7,235	196	16,437	335	4,358	96	11,938	370	2,636	82
Manufacturing	32,989	6,906	5,783	2,124	16,857	6,144	86,758	23,435	22,910	2,274	41,418	16,003	22,529	10,925
Food and kindred products	1,693	272	1,276	206	3,134	862	11,200	3,228	2,224	501	6,419	2,059	1,011	206
Textile-mill products	31	17	392	285	2,232	1,272	1,135	1,022	324	255	1,936	1,424	399	308
Apparel and other fabricated textile products	42	36	108	406	480	1,499	6,465	10,508	116	303	3,097	4,947	685	3,265
Logging	1	-	53	-	2	-	15	2	10	2	21	1	8	-
Sawmills and planing mills	95	5	33	5	248	9	485	32	191	8	108	18	72	8
Furniture, store fixtures, and miscellaneous wooden goods	346	188	179	32	975	147	2,304	320	428	61	1,460	200	271	59
Paper and allied products	125	66	392	178	534	211	1,519	763	196	39	1,096	721	161	126
Printing, publishing, and allied industries	915	215	1,212	288	1,975	511	6,038	1,009	1,137	263	5,019	1,804	641	162
Chemicals and allied products	517	54	448	258	923	291	5,062	725	654	79	1,560	722	897	484
Petroleum and coal products	58	1	44	3	295	62	1,967	190	544	11	255	63	86	9
Leather and leather products	44	5	8	1	279	217	892	423	33	7	2,901	1,356	139	318
Stone, clay, and glass products	418	73	152	17	316	39	2,639	450	847	40	490	137	260	38
Iron and steel and their products	1,950	81	451	44	1,560	97	21,336	1,998	14,080	527	3,682	733	4,041	1,203
Nonferrous metals and their products	239	32	71	6	225	31	3,361	162	177	10	857	114	2,870	347
Machinery	1,613	117	467	88	1,489	212	4,644	788	981	60	4,418	932	6,865	2,656
Automobiles and automobile equipment	151	9	91	7	1,213	100	2,100	122	129	7	750	215	511	138
Transportation equipment, except automobile	125	4	29	1	144	8	11,950	162	140	8	3,478	62	758	21
Other and not specified manufacturing industries	24,626	5,731	377	299	833	576	3,586	1,531	699	75	3,862	1,895	2,845	1,577
Transportation, communication, and other public utilities	4,348	533	6,959	911	10,383	2,165	31,075	3,585	8,783	853	21,045	3,867	2,390	326
Railroads (incl. railroad repair shops) and railway express service	1,025	42	3,990	140	4,625	493	8,986	556	5,027	100	5,063	284	509	14
Trucking service	1,562	58	678	34	1,456	74	3,271	108	933	37	2,970	117	613	21
Other transportation	662	35	1,064	35	1,439	79	12,106	405	1,024	38	8,649	411	583	24
Communication	272	291	503	574	1,238	1,249	1,348	1,977	556	428	1,607	2,505	143	214
Utilities	827	107	724	128	1,625	270	5,364	539	1,243	250	2,756	550	542	53
Wholesale and retail trade	10,686	4,578	8,741	3,272	20,814	8,887	49,504	21,096	14,145	5,795	47,841	20,643	7,690	2,705
Wholesale trade	1,331	207	1,634	267	4,583	973	9,069	1,638	3,177	469	8,833	2,270	1,016	177
Food and dairy products, stores, and milk retailing	2,498	584	1,791	417	3,783	659	11,759	2,911	2,741	630	10,041	1,099	2,100	380
Eating and drinking places	1,548	1,072	1,487	589	2,170	1,970	5,849	4,476	1,121	1,406	8,083	4,661	1,055	352
Motor vehicles and accessories retailing, and filling stations	1,475	87	652	65	2,505	208	3,510	228	1,878	148	2,568	288	671	61
Other retail trade	3,784	2,628	3,177	1,934	7,773	5,077	19,317	11,843	5,228	3,142	18,316	11,425	2,848	1,735
Finance, insurance, and real estate	1,495	635	1,488	877	4,532	2,625	10,279	4,880	2,901	1,308	8,681	5,805	792	443
Business and repair services	1,540	147	990	99	2,255	395	5,629	626	1,434	167	5,356	869	788	87
Automobile storage, rental, and repair service	960	29	600	22	1,152	43	3,043	74	814	19	2,807	105	463	11
Business and repair services, except automobile	580	118	390	77	1,10[illegible]	352	2,586	552	620	148	2,549	764	325	76
Personal services	1,987	4,352	1,709	3,456	6,083	20,698	10,222	29,096	3,428	13,606	10,530	17,038	1,492	2,410
Domestic service	211	2,852	215	2,203	1,94	15,694	2,848	22,008	1,090	10,647	1,780	8,675	211	1,450
Hotels and lodging places	481	427	654	576	1,455	1,609	1,892	1,800	667	889	3,546	3,963	209	317
Laundering, cleaning, and dyeing services	526	416	274	297	1,407	1,920	2,312	2,443	704	1,118	2,147	2,200	388	359
Miscellaneous personal services	769	657	566	380	1,277	1,475	3,170	2,845	877	952	3,057	2,191	599	284
Amusement, recreation, and related services	625	131	482	150	1,045	342	3,099	669	545	135	2,585	852	334	78
Professional and related services	2,400	3,275	1,977	3,054	3,751	5,536	10,926	15,309	2,527	4,522	11,578	18,608	1,383	2,349
Government	1,640	526	4,354	2,906	4,209	1,429	14,420	3,463	2,196	483	13,714	3,448	1,412	354
Industry not reported	584	379	357	271	882	477	3,963	2,474	897	433	2,886	2,096	483	356

TABLE 74.—MALE AND FEMALE EMPLOYED WORKERS 14 YEARS OLD AND OVER, BY INDUSTRY GROUP, FOR CITIES OF 100,000 OR MORE: 1940—Continued

INDUSTRY GROUP	BUFFALO, N. Y.		CAMBRIDGE, MASS.		CAMDEN, N. J.		CANTON, OHIO		CHARLOTTE, N. C.		CHATTANOOGA, TENN.		CHICAGO, ILL.	
	Male	Female	Male	Female	Male	Female	Male	Female	Male	Female	Male	Female	Male	Female
Employed (exc. on public emergency work)	141,377	54,677	25,247	14,893	29,081	12,507	30,461	9,571	28,218	17,107	33,021	16,309	942,365	409,853
Agriculture, forestry, and fishery	248	14	167	4	55	2	88	2	192	8	138	8	1,425	142
Agriculture	217	9	113	3	48	2	85	2	190	7	128	7	1,252	120
Forestry (except logging) and fishery	31	5	54	1	7	...	3	...	2	1	10	1	173	22
Mining	111	13	12	1	9	1	128	1	30	2	64	...	427	79
Coal mining	8	1	1	...	...	...	91	1	1	...	14	...	122	33
Crude petroleum and natural gas production	10	1	...	...	2	...	16	...	1	...	2	...	76	3
Other mines and quarries	93	11	11	1	7	1	21	...	28	2	48	...	220	43
Construction	6,982	196	1,676	57	1,809	34	1,348	30	2,709	96	2,895	41	50,568	1,[illegible]39
Manufacturing	56,826	11,109	7,864	3,684	14,168	5,905	16,549	2,364	7,483	3,499	12,672	4,339	345,421	115,436
Food and kindred products	7,173	1,285	1,719	784	1,740	752	670	180	1,261	444	1,038	187	51,485	19,990
Textile-mill products	626	898	181	130	558	339	10	12	2,415	2,345	2,605	3,087	3,795	2,929
Apparel and other fabricated textile products	820	1,553	127	348	337	909	19	78	79	137	65	325	12,306	20,325
Logging	3	...	4	...	2	...	2	1	5	...	6	...	22	6
Sawmills and planing mills	275	18	16	3	19	1	44	3	86	8	276	6	1,434	138
Furniture, store fixtures, and miscellaneous wooden goods	1,220	194	347	36	389	39	162	13	221	33	1,131	115	17,345	3,003
Paper and allied products	896	736	187	139	489	74	68	67	203	57	255	54	8,254	5,005
Printing, publishing, and allied industries	2,908	617	854	411	939	251	438	82	619	115	509	113	37,989	11,919
Chemicals and allied products	3,898	733	924	359	606	119	130	26	625	101	370	112	12,448	4,638
Petroleum and coal products	1,023	65	48	7	401	10	57	3	58	8	210	20	3,748	722
Leather and leather products	291	72	351	426	791	173	8	...	21	9	268	42	7,901	3,641
Stone, clay, and glass products	875	464	162	17	184	10	318	48	257	66	531	33	5,213	1,371
Iron and steel and their products	14,225	534	540	64	749	94	11,949	1,158	485	13	4,247	120	66,072	7,800
Nonferrous metals and their products	1,677	207	98	14	96	16	166	29	58	1	70	3	10,233	1,921
Machinery	6,213	1,493	738	238	2,290	1,340	1,539	303	635	80	571	35	65,189	17,463
Automobiles and automobile equipment	4,890	920	129	16	166	25	193	24	160	22	32	3	7,458	1,452
Transportation equipment, except automobile	5,356	194	193	6	3,173	40	21	...	12	...	47	1	6,288	598
Other and not specified manufacturing industries	4,448	1,126	1,236	686	1,239	1,704	755	337	283	60	441	83	28,241	12,515
Transportation, communication, and other public utilities	18,890	2,039	9,303	541	2,638	283	2,370	243	3,264	591	3,467	340	114,817	20,900
Railroads (inc. railroad repair shops) and railway express service	9,664	524	430	36	962	26	1,105	23	813	38	1,626	73	44,607	4,247
Trucking service	2,177	98	517	19	273	5	374	10	805	54	429	10	16,694	856
Other transportation	3,636	212	706	59	793	20	266	14	598	39	465	17	30,825	1,985
Communication	826	862	160	332	124	211	129	127	385	379	215	132	7,917	11,750
Utilities	2,587	343	430	95	486	21	496	69	663	81	732	99	14,774	2,062
Wholesale and retail trade	28,411	13,695	5,031	2,321	5,290	1,826	5,189	2,479	7,595	2,791	6,725	2,561	208,258	102,028
Wholesale trade	5,483	1,221	832	244	693	100	1,058	127	2,022	385	1,132	172	42,750	11,516
Food and dairy products stores, and milk retailing	6,865	2,426	1,115	250	1,468	254	1,123	447	1,111	162	1,512	276	41,678	13,600
Eating and drinking places	3,704	2,262	884	615	752	487	622	648	760	656	734	724	29,482	19,614
Motor vehicles and accessories retailing, and filling stations	2,512	109	376	39	407	26	607	29	1,125	88	790	49	13,088	1,110
Other retail trade	9,847	7,587	1,824	1,173	1,970	959	1,779	1,228	2,577	1,500	2,557	1,340	81,260	56,188
Finance, insurance, and real estate	4,432	2,189	1,186	729	659	372	759	313	1,451	601	1,225	528	48,628	24,220
Business and repair services	3,295	389	755	141	693	87	772	75	805	96	744	94	28,853	5,629
Automobile storage, rental, and repair services	1,734	40	444	11	413	7	447	10	397	14	435	14	12,599	343
Business and repair services, except automobile	1,561	349	311	130	280	80	325	65	408	82	309	80	16,254	5,286
Personal services	5,152	11,195	1,128	3,164	960	1,895	911	2,126	1,913	6,999	1,861	5,881	43,077	71,702
Domestic service	626	7,076	266	2,058	72	1,287	76	1,356	718	5,438	594	4,431	3,960	35,545
Hotels and lodging places	1,379	1,439	247	450	155	162	190	193	350	511	425	523	14,341	13,703
Laundering, cleaning, and dyeing services	1,251	1,184	239	391	241	172	255	294	432	656	339	511	12,019	11,003
Miscellaneous personal services	1,896	1,496	376	265	492	274	390	283	413	394	503	416	12,757	11,451
Amusement, recreation, and related services	1,459	515	251	79	220	46	229	67	487	201	321	51	11,395	3,776
Professional and related services	6,846	10,286	2,690	3,283	926	1,375	1,093	1,488	1,093	1,831	1,253	1,981	41,685	50,498
Government	6,653	1,592	1,681	465	1,078	234	750	189	869	224	1,313	328	40,089	7,617
Industry not reported	2,072	1,445	513	424	576	447	275	194	327	168	343	157	7,722	6,327

TABLE 74.—MALE AND FEMALE EMPLOYED WORKERS 14 YEARS OLD AND OVER, BY INDUSTRY GROUP, FOR CITIES OF 100,000 OR MORE: 1940—Continued

INDUSTRY GROUP	CINCINNATI, OHIO		CLEVELAND, OHIO		COLUMBUS, OHIO		DALLAS, TEX.		DAYTON, OHIO		DENVER, COLO.		DES MOINES, IOWA	
	Male	Female	Male	Female	Male	Female	Male	Female	Male	Female	Male	Female	Male	Female
Employed (exc. on public emergency work)	**118, 590**	**51, 380**	**228, 578**	**91, 004**	**77, 702**	**34, 745**	**81, 612**	**43, 863**	**58, 500**	**23, 116**	**80, 547**	**36, 141**	**39, 040**	**19, 221**
Agriculture, forestry, and fishery	**634**	**41**	**760**	**43**	**488**	**29**	**644**	**38**	**254**	**10**	**1, 041**	**69**	**354**	**23**
Agriculture	612	40	721	41	475	25	631	38	252	10	944	61	353	23
Forestry (except logging) and fishery	22	1	39	2	13	4	13	--------	2	--------	97	8	1	--------
Mining	**98**	**8**	**141**	**20**	**173**	**16**	**470**	**77**	**38**	**1**	**635**	**42**	**675**	**6**
Coal mining	26	3	30	11	15	2	--------	1	6	--------	157	7	046	4
Crude petroleum and natural gas production	11	--------	28	4	24	3	411	73	5	--------	73	3	3	--------
Other mines and quarries	61	5	83	5	134	11	59	3	27	1	405	32	26	2
Construction	**8, 226**	**201**	**12, 533**	**268**	**5, 775**	**136**	**8, 075**	**175**	**3, 076**	**80**	**6, 125**	**122**	**2, 749**	**78**
Manufacturing	**42, 819**	**11, 822**	**104, 828**	**24, 598**	**20, 965**	**5, 989**	**14, 843**	**5, 839**	**29, 818**	**6, 761**	**14, 104**	**3, 261**	**7, 902**	**2, 261**
Food and kindred products	5, 486	1, 365	6, 026	1, 669	3, 498	937	3, 268	835	1, 858	650	3, 706	988	2, 200	403
Textile-mill products	348	162	1, 377	2, 155	651	157	542	324	23	16	80	35	366	477
Apparel and other fabricated textile products	1, 864	2, 896	2, 284	5, 761	325	496	851	2, 749	71	238	190	367	83	144
Logging	2	--------	6	--------	1	--------	3	--------	2	--------	18	--------	5	--------
Sawmills and planing mills	379	41	281	22	189	10	217	9	85	7	106	6	97	3
Furniture, store fixtures, and miscellaneous wooden goods	1, 684	384	2, 071	383	791	173	962	138	268	26	424	82	229	31
Paper and allied products	1, 116	610	1, 030	608	426	164	519	172	725	450	239	88	77	31
Printing, publishing, and allied industries	4, 081	1, 190	5, 136	1, 375	2, 003	504	2, 196	512	2, 048	719	1, 919	362	1, 662	606
Chemicals and allied products	3, 384	1, 004	4, 211	1, 193	706	146	598	196	658	230	551	93	359	188
Petroleum and coal products	528	63	1, 275	193	112	9	787	248	71	4	334	64	45	9
Leather and leather products	1, 494	947	226	40	1, 450	1, 517	165	28	17	8	253	87	97	28
Stone, clay, and glass products	812	160	1, 009	166	1, 294	447	420	31	177	18	619	60	355	21
Iron and steel and their products	5, 162	420	36, 596	2, 749	3, 407	310	633	84	2, 523	116	1, 456	81	626	42
Nonferrous metals and their products	2, 312	407	5, 831	504	415	40	275	30	335	28	551	27	110	9
Machinery	9, 435	930	20, 778	4, 601	3, 385	611	1, 523	220	14, 558	2, 812	1, 298	144	611	58
Automobiles and automobile equipment	1, 297	128	9, 815	1, 458	624	87	1, 123	49	3, 184	587	302	33	186	7
Transportation equipment, except automobile	138	22	2, 451	301	275	10	43	2	484	56	38	2	10	2
Other and not specified manufacturing industries	3, 297	1, 084	4, 425	1, 420	1, 314	371	709	212	2, 731	796	2, 020	742	784	202
Transportation, communication, and other public utilities	**12, 427**	**1, 611**	**23, 340**	**2, 932**	**11, 183**	**1, 059**	**9, 347**	**1, 950**	**3, 311**	**564**	**11, 289**	**1, 497**	**4, 199**	**623**
Railroads (inc. railroad repair shops) and railway express service	4, 653	203	8, 693	454	6, 324	84	2, 179	220	707	17	5, 546	239	1, 412	38
Trucking service	1, 825	85	3, 506	135	1, 366	58	1, 716	69	665	29	1, 464	70	889	48
Other transportation	2, 636	101	5, 552	326	1, 253	69	2, 137	150	675	52	1, 641	136	724	28
Communication	929	908	1, 288	1, 603	666	589	1, 230	1, 128	342	274	1, 232	017	572	448
Utilities	2, 384	314	4, 301	414	1, 574	259	2, 085	374	922	192	1, 406	135	602	61
Wholesale and retail trade	**24, 884**	**10, 494**	**43, 637**	**22, 292**	**17, 182**	**8, 177**	**24, 685**	**10, 480**	**10, 136**	**5, 226**	**21, 005**	**9, 311**	**10, 454**	**4, 333**
Wholesale trade	5, 031	1, 083	7, 095	1, 036	3, 204	732	6, 428	1, 635	1, 612	270	5, 170	1, 151	2, 342	417
Food and dairy products stores, and milk retailing	5, 326	1, 444	10, 402	3, 484	3, 664	965	3, 736	790	2, 164	501	3, 392	817	1, 786	439
Eating and drinking places	3, 392	2, 354	6, 196	5, 487	2, 184	2, 175	2, 700	2, 336	1, 368	1, 405	2, 115	2, 056	1, 060	1, 005
Motor vehicles and accessories retailing, and filling stations	2, 131	155	4, 081	313	2, 072	156	3, 462	267	1, 219	72	2, 501	194	1, 458	94
Other retail trade	9, 004	5, 458	14, 963	11, 072	6, 058	4, 149	8, 359	5, 452	3, 773	2, 978	7, 827	5, 003	3, 808	2, 378
Finance, insurance, and real estate	**5, 518**	**2, 604**	**6, 841**	**4, 084**	**3, 404**	**1, 766**	**5, 722**	**3, 398**	**1, 647**	**625**	**4, 567**	**2, 696**	**2, 919**	**2, 270**
Business and repair services	**3, 288**	**493**	**6, 277**	**842**	**2, 324**	**271**	**3, 059**	**466**	**1, 406**	**210**	**2, 991**	**374**	**1, 423**	**238**
Automobile storage, rental, and repair services	1, 540	47	3, 228	54	1, 233	28	1, 593	52	735	23	1, 688	37	691	26
Business and repair services, except automobile	1, 748	446	3, 049	788	1, 091	243	1, 466	414	671	187	1, 303	337	732	212
Personal services	**5, 641**	**12, 411**	**8, 837**	**17, 611**	**3, 473**	**7, 757**	**5, 883**	**14, 506**	**1, 974**	**4, 833**	**4, 098**	**8, 877**	**1, 780**	**4, 220**
Domestic service	1, 480	8, 812	1, 175	10, 254	472	4, 533	1, 789	9, 745	280	2, 997	549	5, 038	198	2, 428
Hotels and lodging places	1, 424	1, 215	2, 436	2, 470	1, 107	1, 372	1, 436	1, 438	560	596	1, 325	1, 519	576	704
Laundering, cleaning, and dyeing services	1, 201	1, 174	2, 155	2, 227	841	850	1, 266	1, 354	450	515	964	1, 115	381	416
Miscellaneous personal services	1, 536	1, 210	3, 071	2, 660	1, 053	1, 002	1, 392	1, 969	684	725	1, 260	1, 205	625	672
Amusement, recreation, and related services	**1, 488**	**412**	**2, 419**	**686**	**1, 127**	**274**	**1, 451**	**457**	**552**	**195**	**963**	**302**	**524**	**223**
Professional and related services	**6, 989**	**9, 452**	**8, 303**	**13, 968**	**4, 591**	**5, 863**	**3, 601**	**5, 294**	**2, 436**	**3, 357**	**5, 263**	**7, 116**	**2, 467**	**3, 105**
Government	**5, 184**	**929**	**8, 602**	**2, 195**	**5, 689**	**2, 573**	**3, 044**	**799**	**3, 052**	**786**	**6, 952**	**1, 506**	**2, 567**	**1, 152**
Industry not reported	**1, 394**	**902**	**2, 060**	**1, 465**	**1, 328**	**835**	**788**	**384**	**800**	**468**	**1, 514**	**968**	**1, 027**	**689**

TABLE 74.—MALE AND FEMALE EMPLOYED WORKERS 14 YEARS OLD AND OVER, BY INDUSTRY GROUP, FOR CITIES OF 100,000 OR MORE: 1940—Continued

INDUSTRY GROUP	DETROIT, MICH.		DULUTH, MINN.		ELIZABETH, N. J.		ERIE, PA.		FALL RIVER, MASS.		FLINT, MICH.		FORT WAYNE, IND.		FORT WORTH, TEX.	
	Male	Female	Male	Female	Male	Female	Male	Female	Male	Female	Male	Female	Male	Female	Male	Female
Employed (exc. on public emergency work)	474, 250	151, 206	22, 986	9, 598	31, 414	13, 267	29, 980	10, 468	26, 140	18, 076	42, 043	13, 262	30, 936	13, 295	46, 001	20, 865
Agriculture, forestry, and fishery	793	59	253	11	87	6	104	6	260	4	123	5	126	13	460	32
Agriculture	745	54	220	11	77	6	104	6	237	3	117	5	126	13	451	32
Forestry (except logging) and fishery	48	5	33	-------	10	-------	90	-------	23	1	6	-------	-------	-------	9	-------
Mining	198	20	212	45	10	1	23	2	10	2	16	1	16	3	592	87
Coal mining	17	3	1	-------	1	1	7	-------	-------	-------	3	-------	4	-------	2	1
Crude petroleum and natural gas production	25	-------	2	-------	2	-------	4	1	-------	-------	6	-------	3	2	526	86
Other mines and quarries	156	17	209	45	7	-------	12	1	10	2	7	1	9	1	64	-------
Construction	23, 497	602	1, 491	38	1, 560	36	1, 206	27	1, 336	17	1, 482	34	1, 768	44	3, 665	82
Manufacturing	260, 132	34, 991	4, 805	648	15, 804	5, 757	15, 685	2, 672	13, 829	12, 504	26, 636	3, 585	12, 104	4, 253	9, 552	2, 403
Food and kindred products	11, 594	2, 665	838	199	707	184	694	94	546	51	614	89	1, 544	286	4, 068	893
Textile-mill products	718	329	130	100	324	127	15	5	9, 568	5, 866	57	8	639	792	169	125
Apparel and other fabricated textile products	893	1, 529	38	47	505	2, 292	50	107	1, 222	6, 035	18	11	153	578	230	707
Logging	18	-------	100	-------	1	-------	4	-------	9	-------	-------	-------	1	-------	2	-------
Sawmills and planing mills	520	28	99	7	46	3	50	2	32	2	32	1	34	3	136	8
Furniture, store fixtures, and miscellaneous wooden goods	2, 034	499	401	56	705	156	204	42	142	29	57	19	121	23	418	36
Paper and allied products	1, 274	503	32	10	202	152	1, 316	270	205	47	8	-------	171	93	41	4
Printing, publishing, and allied industries	8, 188	2, 147	547	112	514	195	567	116	257	55	473	104	710	142	1, 078	210
Chemicals and allied products	4, 373	1, 540	96	18	1, 873	212	137	8	85	17	207	29	144	41	354	47
Petroleum and coal products	972	131	46	6	2, 140	156	80	5	56	7	13	-------	32	-------	988	199
Leather and leather products	367	183	2	-------	174	60	15	2	147	33	3	2	22	1	113	28
Stone, clay, and glass products	2, 361	425	185	10	67	7	80	10	39	1	32	4	69	5	196	9
Iron and steel and their products	17, 254	2, 246	1, 921	44	1, 529	115	4, 703	288	486	33	158	13	706	41	625	20
Nonferrous metals and their products	5, 363	615	41	3	582	63	470	41	32	4	28	-------	113	9	116	6
Machinery	20, 617	3, 670	151	13	4, 247	1, 521	5, 112	775	332	26	607	504	5, 707	2, 112	471	29
Automobile and automobile equipment	171, 988	15, 540	23	-------	496	47	50	8	19	1	23, 775	2, 690	1, 623	46	238	14
Transportation equipment, except automobile	1, 620	81	49	2	378	10	125	17	37	-------	8	1	15	1	101	5
Other and not specified manufacturing industries	9, 978	2, 860	107	21	1, 224	457	1, 935	792	615	297	456	110	300	80	208	54
Transportation, communication, and other public utilities	31, 176	5, 145	3, 928	547	3, 159	381	2, 623	251	1, 499	242	1, 802	300	4, 129	345	6, 085	704
Railroads (inc. railroad repair shops) and railway express service	7, 515	961	1, 833	83	1, 270	47	1, 123	27	149	6	292	12	2, 137	24	2, 778	99
Trucking service	5, 352	303	265	9	334	17	336	10	328	8	626	33	567	39	710	43
Other transportation	8, 416	494	1, 006	30	680	33	434	18	520	15	273	17	429	38	1, 291	141
Communication	2, 450	2, 327	220	352	211	219	162	149	64	158	177	139	246	158	443	338
Utilities	7, 443	1, 060	604	73	664	65	568	47	438	55	434	99	750	86	854	83
Wholesale and retail trade	78, 960	37, 770	6, 599	2, 692	5, 020	1, 595	5, 344	2, 529	5, 018	1, 533	6, 521	2, 883	6, 721	3, 050	12, 755	5, 421
Wholesale trade	13, 667	2, 807	2, 288	395	704	128	991	121	751	108	849	104	1, 374	252	3, 250	585
Food and dairy products stores, and milk retailing	17, 031	6, 118	1, 138	369	1, 333	275	1, 423	412	1, 382	209	1, 465	389	1, 369	318	1, 971	472
Eating and drinking places	11, 565	8, 478	522	588	774	235	470	542	560	174	673	757	615	598	1, 302	1, 313
Motor vehicles and accessories retailing, and filling stations	8, 827	595	607	43	443	29	605	46	393	28	1, 056	61	962	47	1, 914	91
Other retail trade	27, 870	19, 772	2, 044	1, 297	1, 766	928	1, 846	1, 408	1, 923	1, 014	2, 478	1, 572	2, 401	1, 835	4, 309	2, 960
Finance, insurance, and real estate	14, 707	8, 522	965	425	1, 128	815	778	319	573	153	865	451	1, 219	743	2, 238	940
Business and repair services	10, 644	2, 030	654	75	617	80	603	48	432	18	695	72	830	93	1, 599	163
Automobile storage, rental, and repair services	5, 003	169	396	9	327	5	382	8	249	6	411	13	428	16	902	25
Business and repair services, except automobile	5, 641	1, 861	258	66	290	75	221	40	183	12	284	59	402	77	697	138
Personal services	14, 392	32, 578	920	2, 462	900	2, 108	864	2, 122	862	1, 312	934	2, 952	927	2, 241	3, 129	7, 051
Domestic service	1, 476	18, 649	105	1, 504	104	1, 404	107	1, 353	103	884	87	2, 047	82	1, 288	905	4, 529
Hotels and lodging places	3, 696	4, 840	373	466	129	180	211	295	62	75	147	247	260	286	735	669
Laundering, cleaning, and dyeing services	3, 974	4, 225	130	217	256	269	187	216	293	168	249	197	218	249	653	759
Miscellaneous personal services	5, 246	4, 864	312	275	411	255	359	258	404	185	451	461	367	418	836	1, 094
Amusement, recreation, and related services	4, 759	1, 468	213	67	199	45	301	74	211	31	393	129	248	68	613	116
Professional and related services	16, 017	21, 405	1, 373	2, 142	1, 332	1, 790	1, 203	1, 993	927	1, 882	1, 300	2, 333	1, 431	1, 950	2, 540	3, 222
Government	15, 640	3, 977	1, 420	353	1, 006	206	837	257	972	179	913	299	909	220	2, 329	431
Industry not reported	8, 335	2, 639	153	93	592	447	319	238	211	199	363	218	508	272	444	213

TABLE 74.—MALE AND FEMALE EMPLOYED WORKERS 14 YEARS OLD AND OVER, BY INDUSTRY GROUP, FOR CITIES OF 100,000 OR MORE: 1940—Continued

INDUSTRY GROUP	GARY, IND.		GRAND RAPIDS, MICH.		HARTFORD, CONN.		HOUSTON, TEX.		INDIANAPOLIS, IND.		JACKSONVILLE, FLA.		JERSEY CITY, N. J.		KANSAS CITY, KANS.	
	Male	Female	Male	Female	Male	Female	Male	Female	Male	Female	Male	Female	Male	Female	Male	Female
Employed (exc. on public emergency work)	33,552	7,074	42,377	17,132	46,212	24,085	113,957	49,204	102,747	45,385	44,508	23,032	80,137	34,400	29,224	11,327
Agriculture, forestry, and fishery	38	-	242	20	247	7	778	70	461	23	354	31	101	4	153	6
Agriculture	35	-	236	18	235	6	753	70	437	23	257	20	96	4	151	6
Forestry (except logging) and fishery	3	-	6	2	12	1	25	-	24	-	97	2	5	-	2	-
Mining	1	-	363	7	35	-	3,261	360	101	10	23	2	26	3	68	2
Coal mining	-	-	1	-	-	-	-	-	18	5	1	-	5	-	-	1
Crude petroleum and natural gas production	-	-	273	7	-	-	3,180	353	8	-	5	-	4	-	3	-
Other mines and quarries	1	-	89	-	35	-	81	7	75	5	17	2	17	3	65	1
Construction	1,035	24	2,391	51	3,049	72	10,925	227	6,796	184	4,058	90	4,259	122	1,762	24
Manufacturing	23,108	1,466	18,104	4,194	17,339	5,333	26,292	4,094	33,625	9,533	7,044	2,479	25,683	11,442	9,349	2,875
Food and kindred products	506	61	1,167	394	1,064	147	4,090	619	5,659	918	1,719	307	2,859	1,055	4,481	1,047
Textile-mill products	153	588	355	630	135	85	412	209	1,405	1,772	45	25	612	501	18	9
Apparel and other fabricated textile products	17	51	59	97	98	419	314	681	526	1,197	58	87	865	2,405	196	1,007
Logging	-	-	5	-	9	-	39	-	7	-	107	1	1	-	3	-
Sawmills and planing mills	5	1	147	14	32	6	415	13	419	25	463	1[illegible]	80	9	64	4
Furniture, store fixtures, and miscellaneous wooden goods	22	5	5,578	537	301	27	995	123	1,054	158	447	89	650	124	309	56
Paper and allied products	5	1	455	157	145	91	427	72	900	487	487	37	793	513	307	137
Printing, publishing, and allied industries	189	36	1,168	317	789	185	2,193	478	2,767	751	720	137	1,776	490	570	179
Chemicals and allied products	76	8	278	50	200	68	836	100	1,734	783	904	78	3,084	1,341	840	175
Petroleum and coal products	325	8	101	8	21	3	5,045	1,082	257	49	96	13	1,369	107	804	33
Leather and leather products	3	-	191	72	34	13	52	7	149	32	11	-	429	552	33	24
Stone, clay, and glass products	72	5	261	21	140	28	697	33	894	95	242	11	446	96	87	4
Iron and steel and their products	21,546	507	1,627	516	2,704	518	2,461	188	4,805	510	289	17	3,151	754	733	30
Nonferrous metals and their products	19	1	569	193	149	159	342	33	682	123	52	4	494	167	86	6
Machinery	31	5	2,575	222	5,536	2,152	6,648	279	5,595	1,503	296	22	2,494	972	276	48
Automobiles and automobile equipment	63	46	2,196	394	105	20	310	24	2,931	210	181	7	605	29	298	26
Transportation equipment, except automobile	30	5	78	5	2,000	223	262	13	1,277	46	234	5	3,196	68	83	4
Other and not specified manufacturing industries	46	48	1,294	567	3,268	1,189	754	140	2,564	874	693	1,623	2,770	2,250	161	77
Transportation, communication, and other public utilities	2,065	157	3,915	657	2,701	471	16,890	1,778	12,494	1,539	9,270	891	15,920	1,874	6,187	431
Railroads (inc. railroad repair shops) and railway express service	1,331	17	1,521	30	521	21	5,636	372	5,271	143	3,888	96	7,774	274	3,901	67
Trucking service	104	2	836	86	540	36	2,012	72	2,112	115	784	65	1,740	84	559	15
Other transportation	257	19	421	46	651	44	6,135	263	2,190	114	3,442	129	4,146	213	800	86
Communication	79	62	390	335	267	266	874	772	922	907	490	565	691	1,111	178	201
Utilities	294	57	747	160	722	104	2,233	299	1,999	260	606	26	1,569	192	749	62
Wholesale and retail trade	3,650	2,002	8,998	3,863	10,055	4,259	28,244	10,853	22,716	10,358	12,692	4,221	14,794	4,869	5,887	2,597
Wholesale trade	329	39	2,143	366	1,581	374	6,148	1,038	4,866	929	3,423	546	2,451	816	1,388	354
Food and dairy products stores, and milk retailing	882	403	1,954	460	2,085	359	5,126	1,206	4,591	999	2,280	492	4,184	855	1,217	355
Eating and drinking places	624	529	681	822	1,493	543	3,384	3,349	2,129	2,410	1,173	1,248	2,310	878	558	620
Motor vehicles and accessories retailing, and filling stations	451	41	1,026	66	866	87	4,378	288	2,657	198	1,633	123	804	59	812	75
Other retail trade	1,364	990	3,194	2,149	4,030	2,806	9,208	4,972	8,473	5,822	4,113	1,812	5,045	2,261	1,912	1,193
Finance, insurance, and real estate	619	258	1,547	802	3,907	3,878	5,447	2,365	5,487	2,739	2,018	1,023	4,838	3,738	994	500
Business and repair services	437	48	1,232	191	1,194	114	3,597	337	3,004	392	1,247	114	1,758	312	759	88
Automobile storage, rental, and repair services	274	11	611	19	652	13	2,028	50	1,575	31	766	11	890	16	452	11
Business and repair services, except automobile	163	37	621	172	542	101	1,569	287	1,429	361	481	103	868	296	307	77
Personal services	590	1,430	1,521	3,498	1,969	4,013	7,445	20,933	4,649	10,346	3,065	10,612	2,859	4,574	1,038	2,452
Domestic service	34	787	171	2,108	345	2,434	2,760	15,505	771	6,504	830	7,913	227	2,126	143	1,457
Hotels and lodging places	162	200	477	437	471	554	1,371	1,578	1,301	1,161	921	1,195	308	419	202	236
Laundering, cleaning, and dyeing services	152	190	332	437	468	603	1,634	1,792	1,211	1,214	666	801	1,142	1,472	267	378
Miscellaneous personal services	242	253	541	516	685	422	1,080	2,058	1,366	1,467	648	703	1,182	557	426	381
Amusement, recreation, and related services	301	46	406	94	378	98	1,276	344	1,368	392	455	103	527	151	242	74
Professional and related services	827	1,330	1,756	3,005	2,130	4,190	5,035	6,594	5,599	6,988	1,692	2,683	3,826	5,456	1,264	1,844
Government	696	212	1,341	333	2,169	964	3,029	572	4,741	1,918	2,178	553	3,900	593	1,242	238
Industry not reported	185	101	561	417	1,039	686	1,738	677	1,706	963	482	240	1,646	1,271	279	196

524997 O - 43 - 13

TABLE 74.—MALE AND FEMALE EMPLOYED WORKERS 14 YEARS OLD AND OVER, BY INDUSTRY GROUP, FOR CITIES OF 100,000 OR MORE: 1940—Continued

INDUSTRY GROUP	KANSAS CITY, MO.		KNOXVILLE, TENN.		LONG BEACH, CALIF.		LOS ANGELES, CALIF.		LOUISVILLE, KY.		LOWELL, MASS.		MEMPHIS, TENN.		MIAMI, FLA.	
	Male	Female	Male	Female	Male	Female	Male	Female	Male	Female	Male	Female	Male	Female	Male	Female
Employed (exc. on public emergency work)	108,099	52,845	27,637	15,288	42,596	15,151	407,425	179,472	84,183	37,526	21,810	11,736	79,369	39,783	50,005	25,316
Agriculture, forestry, and fishery	630	41	168	15	521	49	10,821	743	285	16	144	9	802	100	1,065	46
Agriculture	619	41	158	15	416	46	8,822	712	267	14	124	8	771	99	936	43
Forestry (except logging) and fishery	11	-------	10	-------	105	3	1,999	31	18	2	20	1	31	1	129	3
Mining	248	8	178	9	3,797	97	2,645	275	136	8	127	2	78	-------	62	1
Coal mining	26	-------	30	5	3	-------	23	-------	19	-------	2	-------	4	-------	3	-------
Crude petroleum and natural gas production	54	3	1	-------	3,713	95	1,696	237	10	-------	1	-------	3	-------	12	-------
Other mines and quarries	168	5	147	4	81	2	926	38	107	8	124	2	71	-------	47	1
Construction	6,591	223	2,187	50	3,395	64	32,899	820	6,808	156	1,148	27	7,444	124	6,755	140
Manufacturing	23,748	7,909	7,507	4,537	6,952	816	82,671	23,943	26,461	8,404	10,017	5,420	19,850	3,127	4,667	624
Food and kindred products	5,573	1,159	1,188	119	821	233	11,708	3,881	5,352	1,885	728	261	3,174	635	1,340	151
Textile-mill products	112	76	2,229	2,799	29	14	1,286	1,069	562	557	5,377	3,384	759	161	28	16
Apparel and other fabricated textile products	926	3,117	265	1,199	43	151	3,994	9,440	332	866	74	228	322	486	101	74
Logging	9	1	11	-------	4	-------	27	1	14	1	13	-------	53	1	2	-------
Sawmills and planing mills	283	30	400	9	108	4	981	58	891	43	29	1	2,594	61	144	4
Furniture, stove fixtures, and miscellaneous wooden goods	801	133	350	35	154	13	5,737	633	3,049	261	236	40	2,074	225	437	52
Paper and allied products	557	262	84	11	38	9	1,460	530	128	85	179	70	404	126	18	8
Printing, publishing, and allied industries	3,152	1,124	495	81	739	103	9,385	2,152	2,257	565	542	131	1,210	225	1,027	152
Chemicals and allied products	1,327	530	114	18	540	46	2,828	853	1,008	189	252	90	2,054	572	153	28
Petroleum and coal products	799	187	27	2	1,625	57	2,860	594	509	75	35	3	173	13	30	4
Leather and leather products	176	69	18	6	15	5	801	422	136	10	1,430	896	51	4	16	12
Stone, clay, and glass products	416	64	767	133	179	32	2,553	414	494	65	26	4	404	28	258	15
Iron and steel and their products	3,214	258	809	40	351	10	6,707	464	4,112	556	206	27	927	71	266	12
Nonferrous metals and their products	478	27	159	4	97	4	2,593	225	702	88	35	10	121	15	76	5
Machinery	1,725	275	295	18	473	18	7,894	851	2,002	152	458	162	827	104	167	11
Automobiles and automobile equipment	2,892	166	15	1	536	10	2,790	226	1,137	42	44	10	1,808	50	75	2
Transportation equipment, except automobile	195	18	11	-------	968	53	13,572	551	94	3	98	1	37	-------	252	8
Other and not specified manufacturing industries	1,113	413	270	62	232	45	5,405	1,570	3,563	2,961	255	102	2,798	350	277	70
Transportation, communication, and other public utilities	15,238	2,057	3,505	266	3,300	515	37,882	6,581	13,051	1,399	1,988	255	11,277	1,249	5,532	660
Railroads (inc. railroad repair shops) and railway express service	6,077	270	1,974	36	227	6	8,728	340	7,721	374	823	29	4,623	156	1,044	41
Trucking service	2,325	138	407	17	402	16	4,500	204	1,438	64	247	6	1,443	65	373	16
Other transportation	3,410	389	411	22	1,633	70	11,765	654	1,755	77	311	23	3,046	134	2,552	124
Communication	1,198	886	232	133	234	342	3,970	4,279	596	773	138	122	644	781	570	382
Utilities	2,228	374	481	58	804	81	8,919	1,104	1,541	111	469	75	1,521	113	993	97
Wholesale and retail trade	30,318	14,410	7,055	2,633	9,744	4,512	104,191	44,917	18,507	7,710	4,216	1,794	20,867	8,675	14,632	6,174
Wholesale trade	7,983	2,155	1,464	200	1,752	197	22,233	5,575	4,608	1,143	500	67	5,760	1,116	2,384	304
Food and dairy products stores, and milk retailing	4,809	1,033	1,433	248	1,787	592	18,257	4,501	3,717	999	1,100	219	3,493	613	2,613	491
Eating and drinking places	3,395	3,119	683	614	1,341	1,480	16,185	11,123	2,006	1,565	614	320	1,739	1,919	2,846	2,123
Motor vehicles and accessories retailing, and filling stations	3,260	518	796	41	1,505	80	13,355	947	1,553	124	325	15	2,177	179	1,747	127
Other retail trade	10,871	7,585	2,679	1,530	3,350	2,163	34,161	22,771	6,563	3,879	1,077	1,173	7,698	4,848	5,042	3,129
Finance, insurance, and real estate	7,698	4,262	1,031	334	2,047	1,291	23,301	14,172	3,596	1,808	581	232	3,560	1,639	2,574	1,490
Business and repair services	3,775	609	732	51	1,765	155	16,353	2,292	2,176	265	380	37	2,060	246	1,929	208
Automobile storage, rental, and repair services	1,918	48	452	2	958	20	8,477	191	1,226	44	222	11	1,043	32	1,205	26
Business and repair services, except automobile	1,857	561	280	49	807	135	7,876	2,101	950	221	158	26	1,017	214	724	182
Personal services	6,142	13,554	1,616	4,651	1,689	3,797	23,607	42,579	4,210	10,603	678	1,507	5,186	18,256	5,970	11,844
Domestic service	934	7.753	421	3,264	232	2,203	6,235	24,622	1,124	7,239	121	966	1,717	13,503	1,788	7,398
Hotels and lodging places	1,930	2,035	395	443	410	409	5,578	5,693	1,041	1,030	96	167	1,192	1,664	2,091	1,977
Laundering, cleaning, and dyeing services	1,535	1,749	355	503	427	343	5,652	4,835	1,032	1,290	148	184	1,080	1,531	1,100	1,424
Miscellaneous personal services	1,743	2,017	445	441	620	842	6,142	7,429	1,013	1,044	313	190	1,197	1,558	991	1,045
Amusement, recreation, and related services	1,265	503	258	61	772	201	24,238	6,476	1,082	167	211	54	753	261	1,773	313
Professional and related services	5,897	7,449	1,549	2,007	2,152	2,858	24,687	28,191	3,748	5,527	980	1,862	3,357	5,054	2,137	2,984
Government	5,336	1,141	1,642	533	6,070	522	20,443	6,059	3,219	938	996	296	3,039	600	2,071	367
Industry not reported	1,213	679	209	141	392	274	3,687	2,424	904	525	344	241	1,096	452	836	466

UNITED STATES SUMMARY—PRINCIPAL CITIES 181

TABLE 74.—MALE AND FEMALE EMPLOYED WORKERS 14 YEARS OLD AND OVER, BY INDUSTRY GROUP, FOR CITIES OF 100,000 OR MORE: 1940—Continued

INDUSTRY GROUP	MILWAUKEE, WIS.		MINNEAPOLIS, MINN.		NASHVILLE, TENN.		NEWARK, N. J.		NEW BEDFORD, MASS.		NEW HAVEN, CONN.		NEW ORLEANS, LA.	
	Male	Female	Male	Female	Male	Female	Male	Female	Male	Female	Male	Female	Male	Female
Employed (exc. on public emergency work)	149, 939	62, 374	122, 480	68, 906	40, 886	23, 581	108, 917	49, 847	25, 421	14, 979	41, 527	21, 438	119, 518	57, 794
Agriculture, forestry, and fishery	481	38	580	40	197	13	194	5	573	18	295	18	1, 480	133
Agriculture	359	28	555	40	193	13	177	5	222	12	202	16	1, 076	119
Forestry (except logging) and fishery	122	10	25	-	4	-	17	-	351	6	93	2	404	14
Mining	109	7	113	6	96	-	29	2	16	1	45	-	190	15
Coal mining	12	2	1	1	5	-	5	-	1	-	3	-	2	-
Crude petroleum and natural gas production	2	-	10	2	2	-	7	-	-	-	-	-	144	4
Other mines and quarries	95	5	102	3	89	-	17	2	15	1	42	-	44	11
Construction	8, 671	248	8, 581	236	3, 867	67	6, 758	149	1, 209	34	2, 652	73	10, 626	197
Manufacturing	65, 484	16, 155	30, 254	9, 878	10, 020	4, 172	40, 632	17, 494	12, 595	8, 987	13, 914	7, 513	21, 604	7, 394
Food and kindred products	8, 052	1, 746	6, 538	1, 920	1, 794	418	4, 847	792	657	63	1, 121	209	6, 675	1, 404
Textile-mill products	1, 954	3, 043	869	1, 500	662	1, 053	1, 166	760	7, 721	5, 229	205	66	1, 165	1, 075
Apparel and other fabricated textile products	789	1, 603	972	2, 315	426	954	2, 100	4, 649	324	1, 880	751	3, 487	1, 025	2, 364
Logging	6	1	22	2	8	-	5	-	9	-	5	1	17	1
Sawmills and planing mills	437	29	950	58	311	9	216	15	83	7	26	2	513	35
Furniture, store fixtures, and miscellaneous wooden goods	1, 741	388	1, 511	168	529	44	1, 003	176	102	11	276	50	1, 600	174
Paper and allied products	1, 245	630	703	220	220	52	714	531	166	77	702	257	440	121
Printing, publishing, and allied industries	4, 099	1, 118	3, 546	1, 040	1, 370	559	1, 636	354	253	63	811	230	2, 203	350
Chemicals and allied products	1, 250	277	1, 216	288	986	100	3, 241	814	54	14	574	200	875	158
Petroleum and coal products	353	16	314	30	53	8	441	90	9	-	171	4	1, 026	196
Leather and leather products	4, 507	2, 651	187	57	763	549	1, 893	411	307	468	26	8	60	8
Stone, clay, and glass products	730	82	500	51	478	12	392	61	109	26	185	13	864	63
Iron and steel and their products	11, 075	1, 091	3, 557	679	1, 318	42	5, 260	561	725	168	4, 936	1, 248	1, 400	155
Nonferrous metals and their products	1, 103	122	701	59	72	3	1, 528	476	407	23	942	465	412	22
Machinery	18, 594	2, 139	5, 375	580	252	18	6, 694	3, 755	1, 006	576	857	143	859	107
Automobiles and automobile equipment	5, 308	489	1, 204	100	70	2	1, 193	117	12	1	152	32	200	7
Transportation equipment, except automobile	960	65	71	7	27	1	1, 761	65	144	9	136	6	1, 282	14
Other and not specified manufacturing industries	2, 612	665	2, 018	744	681	348	6, 482	3, 867	507	372	1, 948	1, 092	970	1, 140
Transportation, communication, and other public utilities	14, 814	2, 418	15, 898	2, 117	5, 211	714	9, 015	1, 471	1, 565	281	4, 557	903	22, 534	2, 016
Railroads (inc. railroad repair shops) and railway express service	5, 743	142	7, 069	402	2, 687	98	1, 727	54	138	5	2, 299	313	4, 735	146
Trucking service	1, 954	97	1, 778	107	711	30	2, 114	63	295	15	742	31	1, 715	54
Other transportation	3, 043	169	2, 869	218	609	38	2, 383	106	670	18	675	33	12, 758	474
Communication	1, 122	1, 638	1, 169	1, 107	383	470	632	940	110	191	338	460	1, 176	1, 208
Utilities	2, 952	372	2, 413	283	821	78	2, 159	308	352	52	503	66	2, 150	134
Wholesale and retail trade	30, 245	15, 273	33, 359	17, 253	9, 805	3, 553	24, 883	8, 334	4, 910	1, 732	9, 693	3, 120	30, 301	12, 234
Wholesale trade	6, 010	1, 279	9, 941	2, 662	1, 737	312	3, 577	595	617	85	1, 565	301	7, 436	1, 442
Food and dairy products stores, and milk retailing	6, 571	2, 439	5, 669	1, 659	1, 925	333	6, 368	1, 165	1, 457	253	2, 323	425	6, 360	1, 886
Eating and drinking places	4, 182	2, 660	3, 249	3, 890	1, 096	903	4, 047	1, 502	542	231	1, 430	436	4, 065	2, 511
Motor vehicles and accessories retailing, and filling stations	2, 633	202	3, 110	275	1, 073	63	1, 446	123	448	24	810	78	2, 409	181
Other retail trade	10, 849	8, 693	11, 390	8, 767	3, 974	1, 942	9, 445	4, 949	1, 846	1, 139	3, 565	1, 885	10, 031	6, 214
Finance, insurance, and real estate	5, 322	3, 615	7, 387	4, 909	1, 841	1, 118	4, 822	3, 671	484	200	1, 327	600	5, 924	2, 342
Business and repair services	3, 905	574	4, 357	741	1, 285	128	3, 222	329	545	26	1, 133	89	3, 518	336
Automobile storage, rental, and repair services	1, 888	48	2, 095	53	737	20	1, 741	58	349	8	656	15	1, 701	45
Business and repair services, except automobile	2, 017	526	2, 262	688	548	108	1, 481	271	196	18	477	74	1, 817	291
Personal services	4, 458	10, 490	5, 028	14, 127	2, 973	8, 932	4, 293	9, 066	988	1, 821	1, 902	3, 995	6, 466	21, 519
Domestic service	408	5, 882	432	8, 460	1, 135	6, 610	516	5, 895	159	1, 253	350	2, 687	1, 515	16, 288
Hotels and lodging places	1, 239	1, 720	1, 641	1, 990	522	576	526	896	132	132	348	385	1, 414	1, 413
Laundering, cleaning, and dyeing services	1, 040	1, 223	1, 230	1, 425	628	1, 039	1, 250	1, 209	269	197	517	551	1, 807	1, 742
Miscellaneous personal services	1, 771	1, 665	1, 725	2, 252	688	707	2, 001	1, 066	428	239	687	372	1, 840	2, 076
Amusement, recreation, and related services	1, 493	451	1, 722	587	462	108	1, 042	306	229	29	451	123	2, 228	671
Professional and related services	6, 858	10, 591	7, 787	11, 192	2, 347	3, 610	5, 186	5, 707	854	1, 496	3, 095	4, 078	6, 355	8, 899
Government	6, 817	1, 459	6, 033	1, 845	2, 247	839	5, 197	1, 101	1, 168	166	1, 807	442	6, 782	1, 485
Industry not reported	1, 282	1, 055	1, 381	975	535	327	3, 644	2, 212	290	188	656	484	1, 510	553

CHARACTERISTICS OF THE POPULATION

TABLE 74.—MALE AND FEMALE EMPLOYED WORKERS 14 YEARS OLD AND OVER, BY INDUSTRY GROUP, FOR CITIES OF 100,000 OR MORE: 1940—Continued

INDUSTRY GROUP	NEW YORK, N. Y.		BRONX BORO., N. Y.		BROOKLYN, BORO., N. Y.		MANHATTAN, BORO., N. Y.		QUEENS BORO., N. Y.		RICHMOND BORO., N. Y.		NORFOLK, VA.	
	Male	Female	Male	Female	Male	Female	Male	Female	Male	Female	Male	Female	Male	Female
Employed (exc. on public emergency work)	1,964,346	875,020	368,191	142,511	694,090	290,306	493,039	290,525	364,547	137,015	44,479	14,663	45,467	15,924
Agriculture, forestry, and fishery	3,229	239	305	17	1,024	46	438	56	1,141	88	321	32	317	103
Agriculture	2,599	214	262	15	636	36	336	49	1,085	84	280	30	265	102
Forestry (except logging) and fishery	630	25	43	2	388	10	102	7	56	4	41	2	52	1
Mining	822	174	130	17	191	58	274	56	209	39	18	4	20	1
Coal mining	82	11	7	--------	20	4	36	4	19	3	--------	--------	--------	--------
Crude petroleum and natural gas production	66	12	7	--------	17	9	29	1	11	2	2	--------	4	--------
Other mines and quarries	674	151	116	17	154	45	209	51	179	34	16	4	16	1
Construction	127,880	3,719	27,553	971	45,185	1,188	23,223	731	28,551	775	3,368	54	2,711	73
Manufacturing	504,413	242,053	94,977	46,653	214,563	101,173	91,749	55,314	92,602	36,960	10,522	2,953	7,874	1,180
Food and kindred products	54,260	13,388	9,518	1,843	20,277	5,538	10,341	2,512	13,204	3,341	920	154	1,229	220
Textile-mill products	26,440	15,641	4,770	2,814	10,963	6,618	5,903	2,874	4,550	3,236	254	99	195	222
Apparel and other fabricated textile products	121,618	114,936	34,261	24,505	59,742	51,112	20,026	26,853	7,206	11,359	383	1,157	190	313
Logging	44	6	9	2	16	2	11	2	6	--------	2	--------	7	--------
Sawmills and planing mills	1,291	116	126	27	608	46	135	18	401	25	21	--------	175	7
Furniture, store fixtures, and miscellaneous wooden goods	18,415	2,689	3,213	457	8,304	1,269	3,180	459	3,505	481	213	23	346	42
Paper and allied products	12,610	7,439	1,633	1,036	5,859	3,585	2,352	1,279	2,533	1,454	233	85	31	11
Printing, publishing, and allied industries	62,074	19,454	10,950	3,727	21,818	5,634	13,660	6,021	14,840	3,827	806	245	488	83
Chemicals and allied products	19,973	10,427	2,423	1,733	7,413	3,405	3,994	2,690	4,709	2,282	1,434	317	654	89
Petroleum and coal products	6,371	1,703	565	219	1,987	504	1,072	435	2,024	471	723	74	83	9
Leather and leather products	18,936	7,766	3,686	1,552	10,108	3,690	3,092	1,502	1,967	962	83	60	7	2
Stone, clay, and glass products	6,960	1,406	1,051	236	2,564	579	1,180	278	1,687	280	478	24	140	7
Iron and steel and their products	20,387	3,945	2,801	538	8,849	1,943	3,347	518	5,025	880	365	57	183	11
Nonferrous metals and their products	17,314	3,785	3,159	754	6,848	1,383	3,060	725	3,833	880	414	43	146	13
Machinery	36,106	8,353	5,429	1,256	14,040	3,730	6,071	1,429	9,934	1,820	632	118	165	8
Automobiles and automobile equipment	4,421	835	731	112	1,428	339	821	128	1,339	249	102	7	666	14
Transportation equipment, except automobile	21,163	822	1,659	98	10,958	363	1,842	131	4,279	199	2,425	31	2,884	77
Other and not specified manufacturing industries	56,030	29,292	8,993	4,744	22,781	11,433	11,662	7,460	11,560	5,196	1,034	459	276	52
Transportation, communication, and other public utilities	220,359	31,057	39,839	5,753	74,577	10,416	52,300	5,684	46,818	8,344	6,825	860	7,758	576
Railroads (inc. railroad repair shops) and railway express service	31,130	1,649	6,996	296	6,288	500	8,841	399	7,880	392	1,125	62	2,321	181
Trucking service	27,352	995	4,558	200	10,726	366	6,560	196	5,012	209	487	24	465	15
Other transportation	98,192	4,494	16,542	566	35,431	1,683	27,807	1,015	15,145	1,117	3,267	113	3,985	129
Communication	18,340	18,067	2,072	3,545	5,865	5,729	3,344	3,317	5,624	4,956	535	520	274	208
Utilities	45,345	5,852	8,771	1,146	16,267	2,138	5,730	757	13,157	1,670	1,411	141	713	43
Wholesale and retail trade	470,614	151,143	94,468	30,307	165,495	49,650	127,069	44,029	76,314	24,977	7,268	2,180	8,751	3,426
Wholesale trade	79,079	20,581	15,895	4,025	29,512	7,100	19,551	5,309	13,032	3,220	1,089	327	1,947	381
Food and dairy products stores, and milk retailing	114,878	18,863	26,296	4,048	43,236	7,198	23,018	3,893	20,066	3,314	2,262	410	2,143	438
Eating and drinking places	86,611	26,211	12,708	3,782	20,506	6,453	40,705	11,472	11,728	4,189	964	315	667	726
Motor vehicles and accessories retailing, and filling stations	15,837	1,462	3,047	305	5,431	498	2,437	273	4,442	359	480	27	800	59
Other retail trade	174,200	84,026	36,522	17,547	66,810	28,401	41,358	23,082	27,046	13,895	2,473	1,101	3,104	1,822
Finance, insurance, and real estate	162,199	62,261	28,041	10,472	43,885	18,727	54,178	17,079	33,033	14,201	3,062	1,782	1,529	494
Business and repair services	61,177	12,956	11,884	2,257	19,640	3,326	16,804	5,018	11,938	2,204	911	151	815	60
Automobile storage, rental, and repair services	25,214	524	4,973	131	8,424	163	6,518	133	4,878	88	421	9	468	7
Business and repair services, except automobile	35,963	12,432	6,911	2,126	11,216	3,163	10,286	4,885	7,060	2,116	490	142	347	53
Personal services	109,819	184,068	17,088	17,851	30,817	46,143	43,331	96,000	16,322	21,753	1,361	2,321	1,706	7,145
Domestic service	13,752	122,036	1,092	9,801	2,592	30,527	7,900	66,751	1,933	13,363	235	1,594	388	5,659
Hotels and lodging places	31,981	23,851	4,194	2,823	4,249	3,813	18,011	14,604	5,317	2,451	210	160	348	454
Laundering, cleaning, and dyeing services	28,394	16,747	6,022	1,039	10,658	6,189	7,871	6,004	3,549	2,359	294	256	440	486
Miscellaneous personal services	35,692	21,434	6,680	3,288	13,318	5,614	9,549	8,641	5,523	3,580	622	311	530	546
Amusement, recreation, and related services	31,610	11,386	4,839	1,509	8,277	2,419	12,138	5,703	5,958	1,672	398	83	403	122
Professional and related services	122,769	125,047	21,171	18,670	38,391	36,684	42,484	48,503	17,375	17,821	3,348	3,369	1,402	2,210
Government	108,811	17,922	21,295	3,661	34,481	6,092	19,871	4,910	26,725	2,764	6,439	495	11,726	339
Industry not reported	40,644	32,995	5,701	5,373	17,564	14,384	9,180	7,442	7,561	5,417	638	379	455	195

TABLE 74.—MALE AND FEMALE EMPLOYED WORKERS 14 YEARS OLD AND OVER, BY INDUSTRY GROUP, FOR CITIES OF 100,000 OR MORE: 1940—Continued

INDUSTRY GROUP	OAKLAND, CALIF.		OKLAHOMA CITY, OKLA.		OMAHA, NEBR.		PATERSON, N. J.		PEORIA, ILL.		PHILADELPHIA, PA.		PITTSBURGH, PA.	
	Male	Female	Male	Female	Male	Female	Male	Female	Male	Female	Male	Female	Male	Female
Employed (exc. on public emergency work)	83, 493	30, 479	51, 982	24, 164	56, 554	24, 932	37, 361	16, 630	30, 946	12, 251	485, 086	218, 612	160, 181	62, 875
Agriculture, forestry, and fishery	746	56	521	35	347	22	146	7	167	7	1, 525	93	438	21
Agriculture	669	51	511	34	330	22	139	7	148	6	1, 472	83	426	19
Forestry (except logging) and fishery	77	5	10	1	17		7		19	1	53	10	12	2
Mining	208	12	2, 782	169	39	4	34	1	288	6	413	47	620	57
Coal mining	2		2		2		1		275	4	131	25	403	33
Crude petroleum and natural gas production	56	4	2, 746	169	9	1			2		29	1	83	11
Other mines and quarries	150	8	34		28	3	33	1	11	2	253	21	134	13
Construction	7, 280	130	3, 829	78	3, 431	96	2, 065	30	2, 246	48	32, 830	917	11, 087	273
Manufacturing	22, 417	4, 046	8, 269	1, 304	12, 236	2, 455	16, 742	7, 062	12, 316	2, 486	177, 907	70, 400	52, 040	7, 921
Food and kindred products	3, 436	1, 112	3, 282	609	7, 034	1, 251	868	73	2, 542	981	17, 725	4, 053	7, 044	1, 980
Textile-mill products	366	178	21	8	41	14	8, 427	4, 058	52	22	23, 527	16, 870	293	227
Apparel and other fabricated textile products	186	383	78	77	139	238	516	1, 752	107	358	13, 959	19, 384	335	504
Logging	13		5		1	1	1	1			13	2	3	
Sawmills and planing mills	388	21	94	3	76	5	22	5	86	7	718	55	180	17
Furniture, store fixtures, and miscellaneous wooden goods	983	111	527	82	313	44	183	22	251	25	4, 456	427	1, 365	508
Paper and allied products	458	233	54	28	194	66	212	129	278	93	5, 422	2, 658	604	305
Printing, publishing, and allied industries	1, 985	425	1, 344	296	1, 347	264	489	127	718	181	13, 908	4, 082	3, 513	645
Chemicals and allied products	1, 173	208	284	23	334	67	297	160	422	62	7, 343	1, 554	1, 084	251
Petroleum and coal products	1, 172	110	352	23	125	19	104	14	41	9	5, 423	520	1, 043	183
Leather and leather products	100	24	29	2	101	23	66	79	21	3	5, 698	1, 868	170	42
Stone, clay, and glass products	919	144	250	15	197	15	193	116	96	12	2, 584	420	1, 419	232
Iron and steel and their products	2, 801	195	687	31	706	39	545	35	1, 206	116	19, 324	2, 457	24, 520	1, 450
Nonferrous metals and their products	422	47	85	2	316	14	85	5	178	18	2, 673	378	1, 043	119
Machinery	2, 770	302	715	39	655	84	952	84	5, 781	481	21, 609	4, 111	6, 053	724
Automobiles and automobile equipment	2, 276	143	162	6	166	33	106	7	75	8	6, 688	378	518	80
Transportation equipment, except automobiles	1, 750	35	16	2	20	1	3, 030	145	12		13, 748	374	775	24
Other and not specified manufacturing industries	1, 219	285	284	58	471	277	646	250	450	110	13, 089	9, 909	2, 078	630
Transportation, communication, and other public utilities	12, 887	1, 970	5, 192	880	10, 268	1, 634	2, 903	420	2, 923	365	45, 074	6, 257	18, 952	2, 731
Railroads (inc. railroad repair shops) and railway express service	5, 365	282	1, 038	37	5, 523	517	869	35	1, 139	51	12, 904	663	7, 099	303
Trucking service	1, 031	67	1, 317	64	808	40	629	39	431	15	6, 382	209	2, 543	97
Other transportation	3, 623	197	1, 310	48	1, 870	146	593	21	536	20	16, 202	1, 036	3, 536	195
Communication	882	1, 142	681	615	930	785	201	283	240	204	2, 824	3, 484	1, 085	1, 546
Utilities	1, 986	282	846	116	1, 068	146	611	42	577	75	6, 762	865	3, 789	590
Wholesale and retail trade	19, 160	8, 128	15, 036	5, 930	14, 216	5, 814	8, 213	2, 622	6, 653	3, 009	108, 933	42, 205	37, 168	16, 803
Wholesale trade	3, 836	796	4, 008	624	3, 864	879	1, 183	148	1, 268	229	16, 510	3, 442	7, 579	1, 470
Food and dairy products stores, and milk retailing	3, 877	1, 194	2, 329	645	2, 358	566	2, 271	540	1, 290	375	27, 717	5, 294	8, 582	2, 615
Eating and drinking places	2, 530	1, 475	1, 343	1, 576	1, 636	1, 314	1, 174	374	1, 047	731	14, 745	8, 841	4, 193	3, 443
Motor vehicles and accessories retailing, and filling stations	2, 220	162	2, 366	170	1, 500	135	724	53	832	71	5, 909	510	2, 882	256
Other retail trade	6, 697	4, 501	4, 990	2, 915	4, 858	2, 920	2, 861	1, 507	2, 216	1, 603	44, 052	24, 118	13, 932	9, 019
Finance, insurance, and real estate	4, 369	2, 389	3, 301	1, 732	3, 796	2, 786	1, 043	400	1, 165	612	20, 779	10, 254	7, 517	3, 311
Business and repair services	2, 942	374	2, 086	280	1, 873	255	947	49	900	117	13, 760	1, 627	4, 440	579
Automobile storage, rental, and repair services	1, 539	46	1, 204	27	1, 004	20	567	6	494	23	7, 168	174	2, 312	61
Business and repair services, except automobile	1, 403	328	882	253	869	235	380	43	406	94	6, 592	1, 453	2, 128	518
Personal services	3, 739	5, 957	3, 185	7, 706	2, 639	5, 960	1, 569	3, 130	1, 183	2, 850	21, 588	43, 708	7, 152	15, 089
Domestic service	544	2, 942	683	4, 999	220	3, 509	213	1, 834	137	1, 610	4, 522	29, 586	1, 399	10, 139
Hotels and lodging places	830	761	915	829	976	856	146	224	389	456	4, 115	3, 642	1, 917	1, 888
Laundering, cleaning, and dyeing services	1, 154	1, 046	656	712	602	725	535	740	267	326	4, 953	4, 733	1, 571	1, 502
Miscellaneous personal services	1, 211	1, 208	931	1, 166	841	870	675	332	390	458	7, 998	5, 747	2, 265	1, 560
Amusement, recreation, and related services	995	509	778	266	742	220	265	54	354	98	5, 020	1, 447	1, 987	565
Professional and related services	4, 061	5, 349	2, 967	3, 839	2, 810	4, 575	1, 825	2, 303	1, 286	2, 196	23, 930	30, 986	9, 151	12, 497
Government	3, 619	890	2, 989	1, 523	3, 485	720	1, 184	254	1, 046	217	24, 624	3, 967	8, 098	1, 976
Industry not reported	1, 070	669	1, 047	422	672	391	425	298	419	240	8, 703	6, 704	1, 531	1, 052

TABLE 74.—MALE AND FEMALE EMPLOYED WORKERS 14 YEARS OLD AND OVER, BY INDUSTRY GROUP, FOR CITIES OF 100,000 OR MORE: 1940—Continued

INDUSTRY GROUP	PORTLAND, OREG.		PROVIDENCE, R. I.		READING, PA.		RICHMOND, VA.		ROCHESTER, N. Y.		SACRAMENTO, CALIF.		ST. LOUIS, MO.	
	Male	Female	Male	Female	Male	Female	Male	Female	Male	Female	Male	Female	Male	Female
Employed (exc. on public emergency work)	83,802	36,837	60,847	33,176	29,052	15,299	52,339	31,824	84,202	41,650	30,228	13,287	221,421	102,142
Agriculture, forestry, and fishery	1,255	117	231	6	86	3	196	13	404	33	869	46	594	31
Agriculture	995	82	185	3	80	3	191	13	395	33	848	45	545	27
Forestry (except logging) and fishery	260	35	46	3	6	...	5	...	9	...	21	1	49	4
Mining	177	11	25	1	24	1	44	2	43	5	153	2	266	20
Coal mining	5	...	3	1	10	...	2	...	2	...	...	...	30	2
Crude petroleum and natural gas production	14	1	4	...	...	...	1	...	1	...	7	...	39	4
Other mines and quarries	158	10	18	...	14	1	41	2	40	5	146	2	197	14
Construction	6,098	128	4,124	96	1,428	26	4,632	105	5,136	103	2,417	57	13,647	256
Manufacturing	18,858	3,875	23,398	13,286	13,604	7,880	14,118	7,676	37,868	16,140	3,281	708	77,627	29,225
Food and kindred products	2,959	764	1,416	274	1,266	407	1,805	510	2,868	885	1,406	467	12,621	3,023
Textile-mill products	734	689	4,593	3,635	5,317	5,756	217	73	381	405	7	3	789	522
Apparel and other fabricated textile products	304	719	118	275	225	690	398	732	3,909	4,910	18	21	3,191	8,030
Logging	667	25	6	...	2	...	9	...	4	...	21	...	22	6
Saw mills and planing mills	2,980	114	30	1	46	3	380	10	90	13	135	1	1,117	42
Furniture, store fixtures, and miscellaneous wooden goods	2,346	254	343	73	73	10	394	39	1,004	180	207	14	3,165	400
Paper and allied products	322	96	182	164	282	135	1,304	494	744	549	11	3	1,915	1,200
Printing, publishing, and allied industries	2,138	445	1,066	321	409	47	1,203	431	2,176	532	682	141	5,901	1,530
Chemicals and allied products	492	84	410	136	307	42	1,874	365	494	204	70	10	4,232	1,640
Petroleum and coal products	148	21	109	24	50	3	44	7	67	4	47	1	780	251
Leather and leather products	146	40	135	80	272	214	106	15	1,488	1,110	6	1	7,746	5,681
Stone, clay, and glass products	242	17	191	22	118	9	316	17	599	59	49	3	2,233	117
Iron and steel and their products	1,967	159	3,925	741	2,980	191	898	107	1,467	114	194	4	10,340	890
Nonferrous metals and their products	408	25	1,420	625	256	5	173	13	430	60	65	5	2,090	217
Machinery	1,261	120	3,710	559	1,119	38	429	44	5,754	977	158	13	10,525	2,567
Automobiles and automobile equipment	340	34	59	8	205	4	87	22	671	199	84	7	3,795	395
Transportation equipment, except automobile	284	2	52	1	67	1	113	5	139	10	18	...	2,242	93
Other and not specified manufacturing industries	1,021	267	5,534	6,347	610	325	4,308	4,792	15,454	5,929	103	14	4,923	2,507
Transportation, communication, and other public utilities	12,786	1,559	4,615	851	3,568	242	7,045	919	6,206	1,371	5,761	872	26,078	3,828
Railroads (inc. railroad repair shops) and railway express service	4,294	175	952	31	2,154	41	3,611	262	1,726	69	3,788	50	11,116	959
Trucking service	1,599	132	729	32	376	4	803	39	888	31	286	17	4,624	210
Other transportation	4,047	225	1,375	65	392	17	1,146	63	1,293	75	601	33	5,499	377
Communication	931	736	341	551	113	96	473	479	490	930	418	671	1,082	1,900
Utilities	1,915	291	1,218	172	533	84	1,012	76	1,809	257	668	101	3,157	382
Wholesale and retail trade	21,911	10,787	14,455	5,378	5,113	2,412	12,758	5,376	16,143	7,066	7,980	2,828	50,688	22,212
Wholesale trade	6,078	1,280	2,652	488	788	127	3,073	650	2,255	452	1,907	351	12,246	3,679
Food and dairy products stores, and milk retailing	3,684	1,201	3,209	610	1,290	357	2,840	640	3,876	938	1,307	251	10,321	2,764
Eating and drinking places	2,175	2,607	1,789	787	566	573	865	948	2,205	1,199	1,303	675	6,250	4,474
Motor vehicles and accessories retailing, and filling stations	2,608	251	1,230	83	502	42	1,419	95	1,658	102	910	70	4,408	315
Other retail trade	7,366	5,442	5,575	3,410	1,967	1,313	4,552	3,043	6,149	4,375	2,553	1,481	17,454	10,980
Finance, insurance, and real estate	4,186	2,820	2,163	1,239	791	371	3,037	1,760	2,720	1,310	1,393	700	10,456	4,661
Business and repair services	3,109	426	1,505	155	673	65	1,097	120	2,148	255	940	126	6,254	844
Automobile storage, rental, and repair service	1,572	47	798	17	359	11	579	20	1,200	23	520	26	2,997	53
Business and repair service, except automobile	1,537	379	707	138	314	57	518	100	948	232	420	100	3,257	791
Personal services	3,507	7,814	3,025	5,596	1,214	2,204	3,169	9,897	3,212	5,853	1,465	2,448	10,987	23,712
Domestic service	336	4,222	471	3,423	146	1,291	823	7,270	455	3,529	172	1,165	2,078	13,623
Hotels and lodging places	1,125	1,230	675	711	437	350	776	859	845	678	472	524	3,313	3,437
Laundering, cleaning, and dyeing service	762	1,041	740	895	204	220	757	948	721	705	338	360	2,359	3,373
Miscellaneous personal services	1,284	1,321	1,139	567	427	343	813	820	1,191	941	483	399	3,237	3,279
Amusement, recreation, and related services	1,113	409	531	103	250	95	557	137	819	198	402	191	2,436	651
Professional and related services	4,920	6,854	3,477	5,384	1,193	1,615	2,332	4,278	4,229	6,854	1,521	2,222	9,845	13,696
Government	4,642	1,310	2,926	842	874	198	3,000	1,377	3,509	954	3,765	2,897	9,804	1,562
Industry not reported	1,240	727	372	239	234	184	354	164	1,765	1,508	281	190	2,739	1,454

TABLE 74.—MALE AND FEMALE EMPLOYED WORKERS 14 YEARS OLD AND OVER, BY INDUSTRY GROUP, FOR CITIES OF 100,000 OR MORE: 1940—Continued

INDUS RY GROUP	St. Paul, Minn.		Salt Lake City, Utah		San Antonio, Tex.		San Diego, Calif.		San Francisco, Calif.		Scranton, Pa.	
	Male	Female	Male	Female	Male	Female	Male	Female	Male	Female	Male	Female
Employed (exc. on public emergency work)	70,637	33,579	36,004	13,769	62,152	25,434	59,729	18,546	189,967	81,339	28,755	12,778
Agriculture, forestry, and fishery	373	23	379	25	737	66	1,924	85	1,627	77	77	3
Agriculture	341	21	353	23	730	66	845	69	987	63	59	3
Forestry (except logging) and fishery	32	2	26	2	7	—	1,079	16	640	14	18	—
Mining	89	13	903	45	544	48	90	—	387	81	5,128	88
Coal mining	2	1	28	1	2	—	1	—	5	—	5,117	87
Crude petroleum and natural gas production	2	2	17	1	475	48	21	—	72	15	1	1
Other mines and quarries	85	10	858	43	67	—	68	—	310	66	10	—
Construction	4,525	122	2,687	34	5,267	77	3,822	73	13,377	374	1,340	39
Manufacturing	17,994	4,575	5,414	1,050	7,684	2,149	9,092	1,384	34,004	11,049	4,341	3,407
Food and kindred products	5,641	861	1,150	312	2,880	488	1,607	944	7,388	2,437	1,124	223
Textile-mill products	136	124	93	118	32	13	16	10	518	393	906	1,416
Apparel and other fabricated textile products	584	927	79	171	210	802	31	50	1,260	2,603	300	1,113
Logging	6	1	8	—	38	—	9	—	21	—	2	—
Sawmills and planing mills	176	24	70	—	315	2	158	6	435	20	23	3
Furniture, store fixtures, and miscellaneous wooden goods	572	60	171	32	344	51	156	14	1,830	306	120	31
Paper and allied products	682	245	70	31	58	25	23	8	815	505	23	11
Printing, publishing, and allied industries	2,502	1,051	989	147	1,157	106	874	142	5,697	1,424	644	146
Chemicals and allied products	451	174	218	41	239	34	115	16	1,456	477	109	27
Petroleum and coal products	235	3	322	35	198	25	20	—	1,040	336	28	2
Leather and leather products	143	60	20	2	84	12	3	3	657	155	40	46
Stone, clay, and glass products	1,059	194	224	10	346	27	105	9	764	136	73	6
Iron and steel and their products	1,410	168	296	14	459	29	154	8	4,004	588	175	7
Nonferrous metals and their products	361	23	1,026	28	152	10	91	3	1,053	102	29	4
Machinery	2,489	215	335	39	601	38	187	17	2,583	408	256	47
Automobiles and automobile equipment	580	34	40	6	131	10	81	6	707	88	9	1
Transportation equipment, except automobile	64	1	14	2	21	1	5,305	84	1,498	24	15	—
Other and not specified manufacturing industries	903	410	289	62	419	296	157	64	2,269	1,047	465	324
Transportation, communication, and other public utilities	11,419	1,603	5,908	922	5,309	534	3,046	454	26,007	4,842	4,503	410
Railroads (inc. railroad repair shops) and railway express service	7,235	667	2,858	68	2,216	48	313	12	4,554	569	2,695	121
Trucking service	1,022	68	573	23	757	26	323	14	2,470	168	586	18
Other transportation	1,478	100	894	61	1,014	35	969	42	14,392	758	624	31
Communication	623	623	617	693	417	341	317	289	1,949	2,803	150	139
Utilities	1,061	145	966	77	905	84	1,124	97	2,642	544	548	101
Wholesale and retail trade	17,777	9,000	9,866	3,813	16,760	6,384	11,331	4,825	48,864	19,725	6,621	2,616
Wholesale trade	4,597	1,302	2,536	460	3,302	900	1,938	241	10,719	3,621	1,115	174
Food and dairy products stores, and milk retailing	3,259	876	1,414	335	3,663	637	2,252	586	8,682	1,961	1,738	372
Eating and drinking places	1,907	1,728	840	644	2,057	1,710	1,597	1,401	10,518	3,642	607	303
Motor vehicles and accessories retailing, and filling stations	1,706	96	1,364	99	2,179	137	1,034	85	3,377	345	632	54
Other retail trade	6,308	4,998	3,712	2,275	5,559	3,000	3,010	2,512	15,568	10,156	2,520	1,023
Finance, insurance, and real estate	3,993	2,081	2,045	850	2,648	1,193	2,062	1,167	12,919	8,379	928	452
Business and repair services	1,993	395	1,317	116	2,270	195	1,595	190	6,534	1,134	682	47
Automobile storage, rental, and repair services	969	24	742	11	1,382	27	888	22	2,962	81	396	8
Business and repair services, except automobile	1,024	371	575	105	888	168	707	168	3,572	1,053	286	39
Personal services	2,380	6,747	1,483	2,702	4,499	9,182	2,633	5,282	13,416	15,816	1,159	2,137
Domestic service	282	4,523	118	1,280	1,362	6,225	523	2,045	2,577	7,820	140	1,405
Hotels and lodging places	668	768	449	472	999	791	805	896	4,700	3,027	351	224
Laundering, cleaning, and dyeing services	497	563	405	487	784	900	586	609	3,082	2,306	208	254
Miscellaneous personal services	933	893	511	463	1,354	1,266	719	832	3,067	2,663	460	254
Amusement, recreation, and related services	796	200	517	181	891	204	799	226	3,028	1,165	322	82
Professional and related services	4,071	6,672	2,352	2,990	2,601	4,312	2,921	3,800	10,405	13,347	1,578	2,622
Government	4,616	1,702	2,637	756	12,012	830	19,968	773	16,133	3,166	1,210	365
Industry not reported	611	446	496	285	930	260	446	287	3,266	2,184	866	510

CHARACTERISTICS OF THE POPULATION

TABLE 74.—MALE AND FEMALE EMPLOYED WORKERS 14 YEARS OLD AND OVER, BY INDUSTRY GROUP, FOR CITIES OF 100,000 OR MORE: 1940—Continued

INDUSTRY GROUP	SEATTLE, WASH.		SOMERVILLE, MASS.		SOUTH BEND, IND.		SPOKANE, WASH.		SPRINGFIELD, MASS.		SYRACUSE, N. Y.	
	Male	Female	Male	Female	Male	Female	Male	Female	Male	Female	Male	Female
Employed (exc. on public emergency work)	**104,058**	**43,894**	**23,952**	**10,379**	**27,853**	**11,183**	**32,005**	**13,076**	**39,746**	**17,237**	**52,535**	**22,804**
Agriculture, forestry, and fishery	**2,279**	**73**	**176**	**6**	**79**	**8**	**478**	**40**	**220**	**8**	**205**	**15**
Agriculture	901	57	49	3	75	8	388	36	203	8	197	14
Forestry (except logging) and fishery	1,378	16	127	3	4	...	90	4	17	...	8	1
Mining	**451**	**23**	**14**	**4**	**11**	**2**	**199**	**17**	**20**	**1**	**38**	...
Coal mining	160	12	1	1	2	...	...	1	2	...	1	...
Crude petroleum and natural gas production	16	1	1	...	3	...	5	...	...	...	1	...
Other mines and quarries	275	10	12	3	6	2	194	16	18	1	36	...
Construction	**7,871**	**185**	**1,613**	**47**	**1,063**	**32**	**2,620**	**53**	**2,316**	**61**	**2,297**	**76**
Manufacturing	**24,325**	**4,329**	**6,983**	**2,783**	**14,805**	**3,855**	**5,627**	**901**	**15,948**	**4,005**	**19,710**	**4,771**
Food and kindred products	3,840	1,145	1,944	697	743	98	1,511	322	1,105	209	1,732	273
Textile-mill products	176	126	148	98	37	93	20	4	464	427	67	22
Apparel and other fabricated textile products	415	1,149	145	392	308	1,499	31	55	213	410	378	657
Logging	573	22	...	...	...	...	188	5	12	...	4	...
Sawmills and planing mills	2,134	80	41	7	51	3	1,307	49	42	9	65	4
Furniture, store fixtures, and miscellaneous wooden goods	905	106	387	36	208	18	430	120	511	146	549	99
Paper and allied products	297	129	272	178	182	79	87	14	636	438	288	164
Printing, publishing, and allied industries	2,517	501	596	240	531	73	761	211	1,229	392	1,254	311
Chemicals and allied products	574	164	445	173	136	28	117	9	763	141	1,499	270
Petroleum and coal products	119	12	85	22	116	4	96	4	51	2	43	5
Leather and leather products	129	43	313	323	8	4	16	3	96	119	385	600
Stone, clay, and glass products	453	34	104	16	58	10	116	5	125	6	643	373
Iron and steel and their products	2,690	201	458	64	540	36	204	12	2,606	205	4,185	309
Nonferrous metals and their products	474	34	143	25	50	3	72	3	263	27	723	117
Machinery	1,414	161	482	121	3,450	382	348	38	5,000	891	5,107	1,038
Automobiles and automobile equipment	437	49	259	17	7,094	1,005	89	8	188	31	1,660	236
Transportation equipment, except automobile	6,286	148	487	9	642	68	35	5	941	36	155	17
Other and not specified manufacturing industries	892	225	674	305	651	452	199	34	1,613	516	964	276
Transportation, communication, and other public utilities	**14,204**	**2,107**	**3,370**	**580**	**1,955**	**251**	**5,363**	**627**	**3,446**	**621**	**5,530**	**851**
Railroads (inc. railroad repair shops) and railway express service	2,615	164	929	53	298	5	2,819	87	1,241	28	2,082	47
Trucking service	1,328	135	773	21	642	22	634	38	628	26	865	44
Other transportation	6,892	343	1,070	83	276	12	728	46	490	40	897	77
Communication	1,237	1,230	225	375	127	95	384	363	358	402	448	486
Utilities	2,132	235	373	57	612	117	798	93	729	125	1,238	197
Wholesale and retail trade	**25,632**	**13,038**	**6,233**	**2,363**	**4,959**	**2,169**	**8,585**	**3,810**	**8,740**	**3,867**	**12,023**	**4,965**
Wholesale trade	6,997	1,839	1,283	321	892	110	1,939	357	1,522	352	2,475	470
Food and dairy products stores, and milk retailing	4,358	1,470	1,840	391	992	337	1,456	447	2,104	473	2,631	557
Eating and drinking places	3,146	3,121	865	402	523	386	871	1,031	972	633	1,552	924
Motor vehicles and accessories retailing, and filling stations	2,675	233	374	29	634	34	1,106	79	908	90	1,199	105
Other retail trade	8,456	6,375	1,871	1,130	1,918	1,302	3,213	1,896	3,234	2,319	4,166	2,909
Finance, insurance, and real estate	**6,048**	**3,909**	**1,024**	**893**	**928**	**650**	**1,952**	**1,062**	**1,906**	**1,297**	**2,255**	**1,244**
Business and repair services	**3,336**	**589**	**694**	**97**	**607**	**86**	**1,226**	**168**	**1,066**	**141**	**1,418**	**176**
Automobile storage, rental, and repair services	1,726	56	415	7	315	11	704	21	564	25	768	26
Business and repair services, except automobile	1,610	533	279	90	292	75	522	147	502	116	650	150
Personal services	**4,722**	**9,178**	**1,022**	**1,437**	**861**	**2,108**	**1,524**	**3,150**	**1,559**	**3,286**	**2,052**	**4,625**
Domestic service	509	5,019	76	670	80	1,250	121	1,623	203	1,990	279	2,819
Hotels and lodging places	1,537	1,670	255	178	233	259	602	638	532	400	613	723
Laundering, cleaning, and dyeing services	1,062	1,015	319	324	217	246	297	374	298	369	415	495
Miscellaneous personal services	1,524	1,474	372	265	331	353	504	515	526	428	745	588
Amusement, recreation, and related services	**1,293**	**550**	**197**	**76**	**230**	**60**	**425**	**127**	**405**	**73**	**585**	**142**
Professional and related services	**6,254**	**7,855**	**1,020**	**1,497**	**1,369**	**1,593**	**1,803**	**2,565**	**1,700**	**3,048**	**3,024**	**4,595**
Government	**6,529**	**1,266**	**1,351**	**338**	**694**	**182**	**1,783**	**326**	**1,978**	**429**	**2,555**	**677**
Industry not reported	**1,114**	**792**	**255**	**249**	**292**	**187**	**420**	**230**	**442**	**400**	**843**	**667**

UNITED STATES SUMMARY—PRINCIPAL CITIES 187

TABLE 74.—MALE AND FEMALE EMPLOYED WORKERS 14 YEARS OLD AND OVER, BY INDUSTRY GROUP, FOR CITIES OF 100,000 OR MORE: 1940—Continued

INDUSTRY GROUP	TACOMA, WASH.		TAMPA, FLA.		TOLEDO, OHIO		TRENTON, N. J.		TULSA, OKLA.		UTICA, N. Y.	
	Male	Female	Male	Female	Male	Female	Male	Female	Male	Female	Male	Female
Employed (exc. on public emergency work)	29,183	9,390	27,432	14,727	71,325	27,884	31,790	16,126	38,835	17,293	24,985	12,255
Agriculture, forestry, and fishery	432	30	329	12	329	40	150	19	209	17	141	4
Agriculture	245	29	284	12	310	40	140	19	206	17	138	4
Forestry (except logging) and fishery	187	1	45		19		10		3		3	
Mining	72	2	20		46	3	28	5	4,021	1,046	12	6
Coal mining	21	1			6		2		39		2	
Crude petroleum and natural gas production	3		2		15	1			3,946	1,044		
Other mines and quarries	48	1	18		25	2	26	5	36	2	10	6
Construction	2,325	30	1,953	35	3,880	113	1,910	35	3,087	89	1,332	33
Manufacturing	10,048	1,044	7,474	4,154	28,733	6,938	13,590	6,431	7,463	847	9,121	4,393
Food and kindred products	1,182	248	1,414	255	2,202	442	870	147	960	112	1,041	122
Textile-mill products	8	6	5	4	306	76	635	283	77	51	2,609	3,065
Apparel and other fabricated textile products	41	110	28	163	375	850	247	972	28	47	208	232
Logging	349	22	22		3		2				31	
Sawmills and planing mills	3,608	131	150	10	133	7	37	5	52	1	44	1
Furniture, store-fixtures, and miscellaneous wooden goods	937	298	373	163	378	50	150	42	118	14	274	36
Paper and allied products	426	22	18	7	326	171	139	55	33	3	334	118
Printing, publishing, and allied industries	567	85	493	86	1,147	224	395	81	910	179	412	66
Chemicals and allied products	289	31	312	20	643	93	181	28	212	26	348	109
Petroleum and coal products	27	2	30		1,364	138	39	3	1,941	180	34	4
Leather and leather products	35	11	7		128	12	111	125	7		55	22
Stone, clay, and glass products	90	3	267	8	3,479	800	2,214	1,003	148	11	71	16
Iron and steel and their products	395	13	180	15	3,490	352	3,446	372	1,045	40	2,045	173
Nonferrous metals and their products	1,138	16	35	1	833	85	145	54	122	5	251	10
Machinery	162	9	122	7	4,976	1,182	1,296	385	1,353	135	482	34
Automobiles and automobile equipment	20	1	22	2	7,058	1,760	842	536	94	1	178	12
Transportation equipment, except automobile	571	10	1,048	4	398	19	134	30	110	9	40	3
Other and not specified manufacturing industries	203	26	2,948	3,409	1,434	668	2,707	2,310	253	33	664	370
Transportation, communication, and other public utilities	4,130	419	3,528	281	9,657	915	2,493	275	3,631	595	2,939	316
Railroads (inc. railroad repair shops) and railway express service	2,093	75	1,121	24	5,231	126	1,190	33	808	29	1,484	80
Trucking service	251	16	281	20	1,228	69	328	22	679	35	446	11
Other transportation	1,099	54	1,439	50	1,412	66	322	29	1,208	89	319	24
Communication	223	243	210	146	393	519	130	161	387	318	127	130
Utilities	464	31	477	41	1,393	135	523	30	549	124	563	71
Wholesale and retail trade	5,875	2,650	8,012	2,584	15,309	6,689	6,053	2,253	9,923	4,210	5,912	1,957
Wholesale trade	1,158	211	2,149	297	3,149	555	778	129	2,485	359	1,017	143
Food and dairy products stores, and milk retailing	1,203	469	1,656	310	3,177	859	1,672	375	1,643	392	1,308	266
Eating and drinking places	634	577	1,018	709	1,932	1,565	831	435	1,015	1,168	785	265
Motor vehicles and accessories retailing, and filling stations	799	66	898	60	1,761	118	514	46	1,631	86	564	50
Other retail trade	2,081	1,327	2,291	1,208	5,290	3,592	2,258	1,268	3,149	2,205	2,148	1,233
Finance, insurance, and real estate	1,010	556	828	449	2,317	1,086	810	346	2,314	1,118	913	504
Business and repair services	870	70	818	74	1,743	211	715	53	1,469	135	653	64
Automobile storage, rental, and repair services	523	13	520	6	916	25	439	10	813	17	370	9
Business and repair services, except automobile	347	57	298	68	827	186	276	43	656	118	274	55
Personal services	929	1,979	1,771	5,046	2,539	5,767	1,275	2,673	2,340	6,059	1,028	2,300
Domestic service	86	1,171	430	3,503	276	3,607	183	1,712	566	4,076	126	1,474
Hotels and lodging places	219	240	440	629	751	704	233	214	639	644	288	308
Laundering, cleaning, and dyeing services	197	221	393	456	551	557	287	394	494	506	201	235
Miscellaneous personal services	427	347	508	458	961	899	572	353	641	833	413	283
Amusement, recreation, and related services	262	85	463	125	738	150	279	52	514	100	263	57
Professional and related services	1,519	2,014	1,067	1,628	3,097	5,129	1,709	2,289	2,144	2,450	1,294	2,086
Government	1,461	388	927	214	2,495	579	2,310	1,344	1,257	292	1,096	247
Industry not reported	250	123	242	125	442	264	468	351	463	385	281	288

TABLE 74.—MALE AND FEMALE EMPLOYED WORKERS 14 YEARS OLD AND OVER, BY INDUSTRY GROUP, FOR CITIES OF 100,000 OR MORE: 1940—Continued

INDUSTRY GROUP	WASHINGTON, D. C.		WICHITA, KANS.		WILMINGTON, DEL.		WORCESTER, MASS.		YONKERS, N. Y.		YOUNGSTOWN, OHIO	
	Male	Female	Male	Female	Male	Female	Male	Female	Male	Female	Male	Female
Employed (exc. on public emergency work)	189,587	119,313	29,964	13,202	31,859	14,237	48,288	20,598	36,693	16,483	43,594	12,635
Agriculture, forestry, and fishery	558	20	289	26	136	7	261	8	278	15	97	3
Agriculture	519	18	282	25	118	5	214	6	262	15	92	3
Forestry (except logging) and fishery	39	2	7	1	18	2	47	2	16	-	5	-
Mining	123	2	670	66	44	3	22	-	60	2	52	1
Coal mining	11	-	2	-	2	-	1	-	3	-	39	-
Crude petroleum and natural gas production	10	1	650	65	8	-	1	-	-	-	5	-
Other mines and quarries	102	1	18	1	34	3	20	-	57	2	8	1
Construction	19,379	351	2,342	47	2,943	71	2,379	72	3,172	78	2,062	57
Manufacturing	19,210	3,028	6,744	1,009	11,981	3,755	23,087	6,151	10,350	4,568	24,400	1,910
Food and kindred products	2,846	326	1,978	333	780	124	1,189	170	973	91	998	130
Textile-mill products	40	17	12	3	1,433	540	1,392	958	3,535	2,069	12	16
Apparel and other fabricated textile products	78	79	57	76	101	800	275	870	628	1,335	64	214
Logging	3	-	2	-	2	-	10	-	1	-	-	-
Sawmills and planing mills	100	13	118	9	16	5	35	2	35	3	13	2
Furniture, store fixtures, and miscellaneous wooden goods	241	26	103	16	270	71	285	37	106	6	363	50
Paper and allied products	208	108	46	15	58	21	519	492	94	35	11	4
Printing, publishing, and allied industries	7,560	1,941	904	218	427	106	933	272	918	277	372	72
Chemicals and allied products	258	64	138	15	3,464	1,322	209	54	385	211	136	9
Petroleum and coal products	59	3	409	83	164	7	52	4	127	18	55	1
Leather and leather products	31	14	22	7	1,726	449	1,954	1,298	48	4	81	25
Stone, clay, and glass products	542	32	93	9	92	4	1,808	245	90	17	166	25
Iron and steel and their products	5,880	210	621	64	923	83	7,131	663	327	45	20,437	647
Nonferrous metals and their products	207	20	149	29	172	2	256	36	98	15	105	34
Machinery	538	51	510	53	361	14	4,854	410	2,017	293	771	445
Automobiles and automobile equipment	84	8	72	8	71	4	90	15	448	36	50	21
Transportation equipment, except automobile	121	12	1,204	42	1,337	40	331	23	92	-	14	-
Other and not specified manufacturing industries	405	95	216	29	584	163	1,674	602	428	113	752	215
Transportation, communication, and other public utilities	17,798	3,334	3,486	439	4,657	300	3,321	484	4,091	806	3,527	425
Railroads (inc. railroad repair shops) and railway express service	4,287	272	1,122	27	2,400	19	824	21	966	91	1,835	63
Trucking service	1,446	63	608	30	193	8	625	16	376	15	512	15
Other transportation	6,828	275	755	59	1,277	34	694	37	806	34	440	36
Communication	1,644	2,385	296	225	121	156	282	298	460	433	175	193
Utilities	3,593	339	705	98	666	83	896	112	1,483	233	565	118
Wholesale and retail trade	36,776	15,805	8,315	3,653	5,332	2,465	9,111	3,723	7,767	2,176	6,924	3,584
Wholesale trade	4,864	760	2,321	397	713	103	1,478	251	1,578	308	1,085	150
Food and dairy product stores, and milk retailing	7,269	1,376	1,297	347	1,353	385	2,165	488	2,122	336	1,652	667
Eating and drinking places	6,120	4,387	718	1,069	559	611	1,167	658	774	257	770	686
Motor vehicles and accessories retailing, and filling stations	3,700	249	1,333	84	546	41	883	70	588	37	861	66
Other retail trade	14,823	9,033	2,646	1,756	2,161	1,325	3,418	2,256	2,705	1,238	2,556	2,006
Finance, insurance, and real estate	9,558	5,062	1,839	1,097	1,121	594	1,361	879	2,709	1,124	982	480
Business and repair services	4,539	739	1,112	114	643	93	962	89	1,179	207	948	99
Automobile storage, rental, and repair services	2,596	55	642	19	329	9	549	22	557	6	521	12
Business and repair services, except automobile	1,943	684	470	95	314	84	413	67	622	201	427	87
Personal services	11,670	35,180	1,384	3,508	1,461	4,063	1,555	3,526	1,552	3,511	1,186	3,059
Domestic service	2,592	24,825	178	1,998	531	3,068	224	2,229	445	2,604	116	2,068
Hotels and lodging places	3,802	4,706	345	430	262	336	340	465	153	137	298	300
Laundering, cleaning, and dyeing services	2,608	2,894	365	407	230	286	365	405	447	403	261	300
Miscellaneous personal services	2,668	2,755	496	673	438	373	626	427	507	367	511	391
Amusement, recreation, and related services	2,066	644	435	88	314	54	363	87	453	127	385	104
Professional and related services	13,997	15,830	1,658	2,545	1,197	2,089	2,739	4,191	2,631	3,167	1,499	2,413
Government	51,677	37,822	1,265	349	1,146	245	1,861	497	1,942	338	1,103	258
Industry not reported	2,236	1,496	425	261	884	498	1,266	891	509	364	429	248

TABLE 75.—PERCENT DISTRIBUTION BY INDUSTRY GROUP, FOR MALE AND FEMALE EMPLOYED WORKERS 14 YEARS OLD AND OVER, FOR CITIES OF 100,000 OR MORE: 1940

[Percent not shown where less than 0.1]

INDUSTRY GROUP	AKRON, OHIO		ALBANY, N. Y.		ATLANTA, GA.		BALTIMORE, MD.		BIRMINGHAM, ALA.		BOSTON, MASS.		BRIDGEPORT, CONN.		BUFFALO, N. Y.	
	Male	Female	Male	Female	Male	Female	Male	Female	Male	Female	Male	Female	Male	Female	Male	Female
Employed (exc. on public emergency work)	100.0	100.0	100.0	100.0	100.0	100.0	100.0	100.0	100.0	100.0	100.0	100.0	100.0	100.0	100.0	100.0
Agriculture, forestry, and fishery	0.4	0.1	0.4		0.5	0.1	0.3		0.4	0.1	0.8		0.5		0.2	
Agriculture	0.4		0.4		0.4		0.3		0.4	0.1	0.2		0.3		0.2	
Forestry (except logging) and fishery					0.1						0.6		0.2			
Mining	0.2		0.1				0.1		5.8	0.1					0.1	
Coal mining	0.1								5.2	0.1						
Crude petroleum and natural gas production																
Other mines and quarries	0.1		0.1				0.1		0.5						0.1	
Construction	4.0	0.3	6.8	0.3	9.2	0.4	6.8	0.3	6.4	0.3	6.7	0.4	6.3	0.4	4.9	0.4
Manufacturing	54.1	32.1	16.3	12.4	21.5	12.6	35.7	22.3	33.5	7.6	23.1	19.6	53.5	54.3	40.2	20.3
Food and kindred products	2.8	1.3	3.6	1.2	4.0	1.8	4.6	3.1	3.3	1.7	3.6	2.9	2.4	1.0	5.1	2.4
Textile-mill products	0.1	0.1	1.1	1.7	2.8	2.6	0.5	1.0	0.5	0.9	1.1	1.6	0.9	1.5	0.4	1.6
Apparel and other fabricated textile products	0.1	0.2	0.3	2.4	0.6	3.1	2.7	10.0	0.2	1.0	1.7	5.4	1.6	16.2	0.6	2.8
Logging			0.1													
Sawmills and planing mills	0.2		0.1		0.3		0.2		0.3		0.1		0.2		0.2	
Furniture, store fixtures, and miscellaneous wooden goods	0.6	0.9	0.5	0.2	1.2	0.3	1.0	0.3	0.6	0.2	0.8	0.2	0.6	0.3	0.9	0.4
Paper and allied products	0.2	0.3	1.1	1.0	0.7	0.4	0.6	0.7	0.3	0.1	0.6	0.8	0.4	0.6	0.6	1.3
Printing, publishing, and allied industries	1.5	1.0	3.4	1.7	2.5	1.0	2.5	1.0	1.7	0.9	2.8	2.0	1.5	0.8	2.1	1.1
Chemicals and allied products	0.8	0.3	1.3	1.5	1.2	0.6	2.1	0.7	1.0	0.3	0.9	0.8	2.1	2.4	2.8	1.3
Petroleum and coal products	0.1		0.1		0.4	0.1	0.8	0.2	0.8		0.1	0.1	0.2		0.7	0.1
Leather and leather products	0.1				0.4	0.4	0.4	0.4			1.6	1.5	0.3	1.6	0.2	0.1
Stone, clay, and glass products	0.7	0.3	0.4	0.1	0.4	0.1	1.1	0.4	1.2	0.2	0.3	0.1	0.6	0.2	0.6	0.8
Iron and steel and their products	3.2	0.4	1.3	0.3	2.0	0.2	8.8	1.9	20.6	1.8	2.1	0.8	9.6	6.0	10.1	1.0
Nonferrous metals and their products	0.4	0.1	0.2		0.3	0.1	1.4	0.2	0.3		0.5	0.1	6.8	1.7	1.2	0.4
Machinery	2.6	0.5	1.3	0.5	1.9	0.4	1.9	0.8	1.4	0.2	2.5	1.0	16.3	13.2	4.4	2.7
Automobiles and automobile equipment	0.2		0.3		1.5	0.2	0.9	0.1	0.2		0.4	0.2	1.2	0.7	3.5	1.7
Transportation equipment, except automobile	0.2		0.1		0.2		4.9	0.2	0.2		1.9	0.1	1.8	0.1	3.8	0.4
Other and not specified manufacturing industries	40.4	26.6	1.1	1.7	1.1	1.2	1.5	1.5	1.0	0.3	2.2	2.1	6.8	7.8	3.1	2.1
Transportation, communication, and other public utilities	7.1	2.5	19.7	5.3	13.2	4.4	12.8	3.4	12.9	2.9	11.8	4.2	5.7	1.6	13.4	3.7
Railroads (inc. railroad repair shops) and railway express service	1.7	0.2	11.3	0.8	5.9	1.0	3.7	0.5	7.4	0.3	2.8	0.3	1.2	0.1	6.8	1.0
Trucking service	2.6	0.3	1.9	0.2	1.9	0.2	1.3	0.1	1.4	0.1	1.7	0.1	1.5	0.1	1.5	0.2
Other transportation	1.1	0.2	3.0	0.2	1.8	0.2	5.0	0.4	1.5	0.1	4.8	0.4	1.4	0.1	2.6	0.4
Communication	0.4	1.4	1.4	3.3	1.6	2.6	0.6	1.9	0.8	1.4	0.9	2.7	0.3	1.1	0.6	1.6
Utilities	1.4	0.5	2.0	0.7	2.1	0.6	2.2	0.5	1.8	0.8	1.5	0.6	1.3	0.3	1.8	0.6
Wholesale and retail trade	17.4	21.3	24.7	19.0	26.5	18.2	20.3	20.1	20.7	19.4	26.7	22.5	18.2	13.4	20.1	25.0
Wholesale trade	2.2	1.0	4.6	1.6	5.8	2.0	3.7	1.6	4.6	1.6	4.9	2.5	2.4	0.9	3.9	2.2
Food and dairy products stores, and milk retailing	4.1	2.7	5.1	2.4	4.8	1.3	4.8	2.8	4.0	2.1	5.6	2.2	5.0	1.9	4.9	4.4
Eating and drinking places	2.5	5.0	4.2	3.4	2.8	4.0	2.4	4.3	1.6	4.7	4.5	5.1	2.5	1.7	2.6	4.1
Motor vehicles and accessories retailing, and filling stations	2.4	0.4	1.8	0.4	3.2	0.4	1.4	0.2	2.7	0.5	1.4	0.3	1.6	0.3	1.8	0.4
Other retail trade	6.2	12.2	9.0	11.3	9.9	10.4	7.9	11.3	7.6	10.5	10.2	12.5	6.8	8.6	7.0	13.9
Finance insurance, and real estate	2.4	2.9	4.2	5.1	5.8	5.4	4.2	4.6	4.2	4.7	4.8	6.3	1.9	2.2	3.1	4.0
Business and repair services	2.5	0.7	2.8	0.6	2.9	0.8	2.3	0.6	2.1	0.6	3.0	0.9	1.9	0.4	2.3	0.7
Automobile storage, rental, and repair services	1.6	0.1	1.7	0.1	1.5	0.1	1.3	0.1	1.2	0.1	1.6	0.1	1.1	0.1	1.2	0.1
Business and repair services, except automobile	1.0	0.5	1.1	0.4	1.4	0.7	1.1	0.5	0.9	0.5	1.4	0.8	0.8	0.4	1.1	0.6
Personal services	3.3	20.2	4.8	20.1	7.8	42.3	4.2	27.7	5.0	45.6	5.9	18.6	3.5	12.0	3.6	20.5
Domestic service	0.3	13.2	0.6	12.8	2.5	32.1	1.2	21.0	1.6	35.7	1.0	9.5	0.5	7.2	0.4	12.9
Hotels and lodging places	0.8	2.0	1.8	3.4	1.9	3.3	0.8	1.7	1.0	3.0	2.0	4.3	0.7	1.6	1.0	2.6
Laundering, cleaning, and dyeing services	0.9	1.9	0.8	1.7	1.8	3.9	1.0	2.3	1.2	3.7	1.2	2.4	0.9	1.8	0.9	2.2
Miscellaneous personal services	1.3	3.1	1.6	2.2	1.6	3.0	1.3	2.7	1.3	3.2	1.7	2.4	1.4	1.4	1.3	2.7
Amusement, recreation, and related services	1.0	0.6	1.4	0.9	1.3	0.7	1.3	0.6	0.8	0.5	1.4	0.9	0.8	0.4	1.0	0.9
Professional and related services	3.9	15.2	5.6	17.8	4.8	11.3	4.5	14.6	3.7	15.2	6.5	20.3	3.3	11.7	4.8	18.8
Government	2.7	2.4	12.3	16.9	5.4	2.9	5.9	3.3	3.2	1.6	7.7	3.8	3.4	1.8	4.7	2.9
Industry not reported	1.0	1.8	1.0	1.6	1.1	1.0	1.6	2.4	1.3	1.5	1.6	2.3	1.1	1.8	1.5	2.6

TABLE 75.—PERCENT DISTRIBUTION BY INDUSTRY GROUP, FOR MALE AND FEMALE EMPLOYED WORKERS 14 YEARS OLD AND OVER, FOR CITIES OF 100,000 OR MORE: 1940—Continued

[Percent not shown where less than 0.1]

INDUSTRY GROUP	CAMBRIDGE, MASS.		CAMDEN, N. J.		CANTON, OHIO		CHARLOTTE, N. C.		CHATTANOOGA, TENN.		CHICAGO, ILL.		CINCINNATI, OHIO	
	Male	Female	Male	Female	Male	Female	Male	Female	Male	Female	Male	Female	Male	Female
Employed (exc. on public emergency work)	100.0	100.0	100.0	100.0	100.0	100.0	100.0	100.0	100.0	100.0	100.0	100.0	100.0	100.0
Agriculture, forestry and fishery	0.7		0.2		0.3		0.7		0.4		0.2		0.5	0.1
Agriculture	0.4		0.2		0.3		0.7		0.4		0.1		0.5	0.1
Forestry (except logging) and fishery	0.2													
Mining					0.4		0.1		0.2				0.1	
Coal mining					0.3									
Crude petroleum and natural gas production					0.1									
Other mines and quarries					0.1		0.1		0.1				0.1	
Construction	6.6	0.4	6.2	0.3	4.4	0.3	9.6	0.6	8.8	0.3	5.4	0.4	6.9	0.4
Manufacturing	31.1	24.7	48.7	47.2	54.3	24.7	26.5	20.5	38.4	26.6	36.7	28.2	36.1	23.0
Food and kindred products	6.8	5.3	6.0	6.0	2.2	1.9	4.5	2.6	3.1	1.1	5.5	4.0	4.6	2.7
Textile-mill products	0.7	0.9	1.9	2.7		0.1	8.6	13.7	7.9	18.9	0.4	0.7	0.3	0.3
Apparel and other fabricated textile products	0.5	2.3	1.2	7.3	0.1	0.8	0.3	0.8	0.2	2.0	1.3	5.0	1.6	5.6
Logging														
Sawmills and planing mills	0.1		0.1		0.1		0.3		0.8		0.2		0.3	0.1
Furniture, store fixtures, and miscellaneous wooden goods	1.4	0.2	1.3	0.3	0.5	0.1	0.8	0.2	3.4	0.7	1.8	0.7	1.4	0.7
Paper and allied products	0.7	0.9	1.7	0.6	0.2	0.7	0.7	0.3	0.8	0.3	0.9	1.2	0.9	1.2
Printing, publishing, and allied industries	3.4	2.8	3.2	2.0	1.4	0.9	2.2	0.7	1.5	0.7	4.0	2.9	3.4	2.3
Chemicals and allied products	3.7	2.4	2.1	1.0	0.4	0.3	2.2	0.6	1.1	0.7	1.3	1.1	2.9	2.0
Petroleum and coal products	0.2		1.4	0.1	0.2		0.2		0.6	0.1	0.4	0.2	0.4	0.1
Leather and leather products	1.4	2.9	2.7	1.4			0.1	0.1	0.8	0.3	0.8	0.9	1.3	1.8
Stone, clay, and glass products	0.6	0.1	0.6	0.1	1.0	0.5	0.9	0.4	1.6	0.2	0.6	0.3	0.7	0.3
Iron and steel and their products	2.1	0.4	2.6	0.8	39.2	12.1	1.7	0.1	12.9	0.7	7.0	1.9	4.4	0.8
Nonferrous metals and their products	0.4	0.1	0.3	0.1	0.5	0.3	0.2		0.2		1.1	0.5	1.9	0.8
Machinery	2.9	1.6	7.9	10.7	5.1	3.2	2.3	0.5	1.7	0.2	6.9	4.3	8.0	1.8
Automobiles and automobile equipment	0.5	0.1	0.6	0.2	0.6	0.3	0.6	0.1	0.1		0.8	0.4	1.1	0.2
Transportation equipment, except automobiles	0.8		10.9	0.4	0.1				0.1		0.7	0.1	0.1	
Other and not specified manufacturing industries	4.9	4.6	4.3	13.6	2.5	3.5	1.0	0.4	1.3	0.5	3.0	3.1	2.8	2.1
Transport., commun., and other public utilities	9.1	3.6	9.1	2.3	7.8	2.5	11.6	3.5	10.5	2.1	12.2	5.1	10.5	3.1
Railroads (inc. railroad repair shops) and railway express service	1.7	0.2	3.3	0.2	3.6	0.2	2.0	0.2	4.9	0.4	4.7	1.0	3.9	0.4
Trucking service	2.0	0.1	0.9		1.2	0.1	2.9	0.3	1.3	0.1	1.8	0.2	1.5	0.2
Other transportation	3.0	0.4	2.7	0.2	0.9	0.1	2.1	0.2	1.4	0.1	3.3	0.5	2.2	0.2
Communication	0.6	2.2	0.4	1.7	0.4	1.3	1.4	2.2	0.7	0.8	0.8	2.9	0.8	1.8
Utilities	1.7	0.6	1.7	0.2	1.6	0.7	2.3	0.5	2.2	0.6	1.6	0.5	2.0	0.6
Wholesale and retail trade	19.9	15.6	18.2	14.6	17.0	25.9	26.9	16.3	20.4	15.7	22.1	24.9	21.0	20.4
Wholesale trade	3.3	1.6	2.4	0.8	3.5	1.3	7.2	2.3	3.4	1.1	4.5	2.8	4.2	2.1
Food and dairy products stores, and milk retailing	4.4	1.7	5.0	2.0	3.7	4.7	3.9	0.9	4.6	1.7	4.4	3.3	4.5	2.8
Eating and drinking places	3.5	4.1	2.6	3.9	2.0	6.8	2.7	3.8	2.2	4.4	3.1	4.8	2.9	4.6
Motor vehicles and accessories retailing, and filling stations	1.5	0.3	1.4	0.2	2.0	0.3	4.0	0.5	2.4	0.3	1.4	0.3	1.8	0.3
Other retail trade	7.2	7.9	6.8	7.7	5.8	12.8	9.1	8.8	7.7	8.2	8.6	13.7	7.6	10.6
Finance, insurance, and real estate	4.7	4.9	2.3	3.0	2.5	3.3	5.1	3.5	3.7	3.2	5.2	5.9	4.7	5.1
Business and repair services	3.0	0.9	2.4	0.7	2.5	0.8	2.9	0.6	2.3	0.6	3.1	1.4	2.8	1.0
Automobile storage, rental, and repair services	1.8	0.1	1.4	0.1	1.5	0.1	1.4	0.1	1.3	0.1	1.3	0.1	1.3	0.1
Business and repair services, except automobile	1.2	0.9	1.0	0.6	1.1	0.7	1.4	0.5	0.9	0.5	1.7	1.3	1.5	0.9
Personal services	4.5	21.2	3.3	15.2	3.0	22.2	6.8	40.9	5.6	36.1	4.6	17.5	4.8	24.2
Domestic service	1.1	13.8	0.2	10.3	0.2	14.2	2.5	31.8	1.8	27.2	0.4	8.7	1.2	17.1
Hotels and lodging places	1.0	3.0	0.5	1.3	0.6	2.0	1.2	3.0	1.3	3.2	1.5	3.3	1.2	2.4
Laundering, cleaning, and dyeing services	0.9	2.6	0.8	1.4	0.8	3.1	1.5	3.8	1.0	3.1	1.3	2.7	1.0	2.3
Miscellaneous personal services	1.5	1.8	1.7	2.2	1.3	3.0	1.5	2.3	1.5	2.6	1.4	2.8	1.3	2.4
Amusement, recreation, and related services	1.0	0.5	0.8	0.4	0.8	0.7	1.7	1.2	1.0	0.3	1.2	0.9	1.3	0.8
Professional and related services	10.7	22.0	3.2	11.0	3.6	15.5	3.9	10.7	3.8	12.1	4.4	12.3	5.9	18.4
Government	6.7	3.1	3.7	1.9	2.5	2.0	3.1	1.3	4.0	2.0	4.3	1.9	4.4	1.8
Industry not reported	2.0	2.8	2.0	3.6	0.9	2.0	1.2	1.0	1.0	1.0	0.8	1.5	1.2	1.8

TABLE 75.—PERCENT DISTRIBUTION BY INDUSTRY GROUP, FOR MALE AND FEMALE EMPLOYED WORKERS 14 YEARS OLD AND OVER, FOR CITIES OF 100,000 OR MORE: 1940—Continued

[Percent not shown where less than 0.1]

INDUSTRY GROUP	CLEVELAND, OHIO		COLUMBUS, OHIO		DALLAS, TEX.		DAYTON, OHIO		DENVER, COLO.		DES MOINES, IOWA		DETROIT, MICH.		DULUTH, MINN.	
	Male	Female	Male	Female	Male	Female	Male	Female	Male	Female	Male	Female	Male	Female	Male	Female
Employed (exc. on public emergency work)	100.0	100.0	100.0	100.0	100.0	100.0	100.0	100.0	100.0	100.0	100.0	100.0	100.0	100.0	100.0	100.0
Agriculture, forestry, and fishery	0.3	......	0.6	0.1	0.8	0.1	0.4	......	1.3	0.2	0.9	0.1	0.2	......	1.1	0.1
Agriculture	0.3	......	0.6	0.1	0.8	0.1	0.4	......	1.2	0.2	0.9	0.1	0.2	......	1.0	0.1
Forestry (except logging) and fishery	......	......	......	......	......	......	......	......	0.1	......	......	......	......	......	0.1	......
Mining	0.1	......	0.2	......	0.6	0.2	0.1	......	0.8	0.1	1.7	......	......	......	0.9	0.5
Coal mining	......	......	......	......	......	......	......	......	0.2	......	1.7	......	......	......	......	......
Crude petroleum and natural gas production	......	......	......	......	0.5	0.2	......	......	0.1	......	......	......	......	......	......	......
Other mines and quarries	......	......	0.2	......	0.1	......	......	......	0.5	0.1	0.1	......	......	......	0.9	0.5
Construction	5.5	0.3	7.4	0.4	9.9	0.4	5.3	0.3	7.6	0.3	7.0	0.4	5.0	0.4	6.5	0.4
Manufacturing	45.9	27.0	27.0	17.2	18.2	13.3	51.0	29.2	17.5	9.0	20.2	11.8	54.9	23.1	20.9	6.8
Food and kindred products	2.6	1.8	4.5	2.7	4.0	1.9	3.2	2.8	4.6	2.7	5.6	2.1	2.4	1.8	3.6	2.1
Textile-mills products	0.6	2.4	0.8	0.5	0.7	0.7	......	0.1	0.1	0.1	0.9	2.5	0.2	0.2	0.6	1.0
Apparel and other fabricated textile products	1.0	6.3	0.4	1.4	1.0	6.3	0.1	1.0	0.2	1.0	0.2	0.7	0.2	1.0	0.2	0.5
Logging	......	......	......	......	......	......	......	......	......	......	......	......	......	......	0.4	......
Sawmills and planing mills	0.1	......	0.2	......	0.3	......	0.1	......	0.1	......	0.2	......	0.1	......	0.4	0.1
Furniture, store fixtures, and miscellaneous wooden goods	0.9	0.4	1.0	0.5	1.2	0.3	0.5	0.1	0.5	0.2	0.6	0.2	0.4	0.3	1.7	0.6
Paper and allied products	0.5	0.7	0.5	0.5	0.6	0.4	1.2	1.9	0.3	0.2	0.2	0.2	0.3	0.3	0.1	0.1
Printing, publishing, and allied industries	2.2	1.5	2.6	1.5	2.7	1.2	3.5	3.1	2.4	1.0	4.3	3.2	1.7	1.4	2.4	1.2
Chemicals and allied products	1.8	1.3	0.9	0.4	0.7	0.4	1.1	1.0	0.7	0.3	0.9	1.0	0.9	1.0	0.4	0.2
Petroleum and coal products	0.6	0.2	0.1	......	1.0	0.6	0.1	......	0.4	0.2	0.1	......	0.2	0.1	0.2	0.1
Leather and leather products	0.1	......	1.9	4.4	0.2	0.1	......	......	0.3	0.2	0.2	0.1	0.1	0.1	......	......
Stone, clay, and glass products	0.4	0.2	1.7	1.3	0.5	0.1	0.3	0.1	0.8	0.2	0.9	0.1	0.5	0.3	0.8	0.1
Iron and steel and their products	16.0	3.0	4.5	0.9	0.8	0.2	4.3	0.5	1.8	0.2	1.6	0.2	3.6	1.5	8.4	0.5
Nonferrous metals and their products	2.6	0.6	0.5	0.1	0.3	0.1	0.6	0.1	0.7	0.1	0.3	......	1.1	0.4	0.2	......
Machinery	9.1	5.1	4.4	1.8	1.9	0.5	24.9	12.2	1.6	0.4	1.6	0.3	4.3	2.4	0.7	0.1
Automobiles and automobile equipment	4.3	1.6	0.8	0.3	1.4	0.1	5.4	2.5	0.4	0.1	0.5	......	36.3	10.3	0.1	......
Transportation equipment, except automobile	1.1	0.3	0.4	......	0.1	......	0.8	0.2	......	......	......	......	0.3	0.1	0.2	......
Other and not specified manufacturing industries	1.9	1.6	1.7	1.1	0.9	0.5	4.7	3.4	2.5	2.1	2.0	1.1	2.1	1.9	0.5	0.2
Transportation, communication, and other public utilities	10.2	3.2	14.4	3.0	11.5	4.4	5.7	2.4	14.0	4.1	10.8	3.2	6.6	3.4	17.1	5.7
Railroads (inc. railroad repair shops) and railway express service	3.8	0.5	8.1	0.2	2.7	0.5	1.2	0.1	6.9	0.7	3.6	0.2	1.6	0.6	8.0	0.9
Trucking service	1.5	0.1	1.8	0.2	2.1	0.2	1.1	0.1	1.8	0.2	2.3	0.2	1.1	0.2	1.2	0.1
Other transportation	2.4	0.4	1.6	0.2	2.6	0.3	1.2	0.2	2.0	0.4	1.9	0.1	1.8	0.3	4.4	0.3
Communication	0.6	1.8	0.9	1.7	1.5	2.6	0.6	1.2	1.5	2.5	1.5	2.3	0.5	1.5	1.0	3.7
Utilities	1.9	0.5	2.0	0.7	2.6	0.9	1.6	0.8	1.7	0.4	1.5	0.3	1.6	0.7	2.6	0.8
Wholesale and retail trade	19.1	24.5	22.1	23.5	30.2	28.9	17.3	22.6	26.1	25.8	26.8	22.5	16.7	25.0	28.7	28.0
Wholesale trade	3.5	2.1	4.1	2.1	7.9	3.7	2.8	1.2	6.4	3.2	6.0	2.2	2.9	1.9	10.0	4.1
Food and dairy products stores, and milk retailing	4.6	3.8	4.7	2.8	4.6	1.8	3.7	2.2	4.2	2.3	4.6	2.3	3.6	4.0	5.0	3.8
Eating and drinking places	2.7	6.0	2.8	6.3	3.3	5.3	2.3	6.1	2.6	5.7	2.7	5.2	2.4	5.6	2.3	6.1
Motor vehicles and accessories retailing, and filling stations	1.8	0.3	2.7	0.4	4.2	0.6	2.1	0.3	3.1	0.5	3.7	0.5	1.9	0.4	2.6	0.4
Other retail trade	6.5	12.2	7.8	11.9	10.2	12.4	6.4	12.9	9.7	14.1	9.8	12.4	5.9	13.1	8.9	13.5
Finance, insurance, and real estate	3.0	4.5	4.4	5.1	7.0	7.7	2.8	2.7	5.7	7.5	7.5	11.8	3.1	5.6	4.2	4.4
Business and repair services	2.7	0.9	3.0	0.8	3.7	1.1	2.4	0.9	3.7	1.0	3.6	1.2	2.2	1.3	2.8	0.8
Automobile storage, rental, and repair services	1.4	0.1	1.6	0.1	2.0	0.1	1.3	0.1	2.1	0.1	1.8	0.1	1.1	0.1	1.7	0.1
Business and repair services, except automobile	1.3	0.9	1.4	0.7	1.8	0.9	1.1	0.8	1.6	0.9	1.9	1.1	1.2	1.2	1.1	0.7
Personal services	3.9	19.4	4.5	22.3	7.2	33.1	3.4	20.9	5.1	24.6	4.6	23.0	3.0	21.5	4.0	25.7
Domestic service	0.5	11.3	0.6	13.0	2.2	22.2	0.5	13.0	0.7	13.9	0.5	12.6	0.3	12.3	0.5	15.7
Hotels and lodging places	1.1	2.7	1.4	3.9	1.8	3.3	1.0	2.6	1.6	4.2	1.5	3.7	0.8	3.2	1.6	4.9
Laundering, cleaning, and dyeing services	0.9	2.4	1.1	2.4	1.6	3.1	0.8	2.2	1.2	3.1	1.0	2.2	0.8	2.8	0.6	2.3
Miscellaneous personal services	1.3	2.9	1.4	2.9	1.7	4.5	1.2	3.1	1.6	3.3	1.6	3.5	1.1	3.2	1.4	2.9
Amusement, recreation, and related services	1.1	0.8	1.5	0.8	1.8	1.0	0.9	0.8	1.2	0.8	1.3	1.2	1.0	1.0	0.9	0.7
Professional and related services	3.6	15.3	5.9	16.9	4.4	12.1	4.2	14.5	6.5	19.7	6.3	16.2	3.4	14.2	6.0	22.3
Government	3.8	2.4	7.3	7.4	3.7	1.8	5.2	3.4	8.6	4.2	6.6	6.0	3.3	2.6	6.2	3.7
Industry not reported	0.9	1.6	1.7	2.4	1.0	0.9	1.4	2.0	1.9	2.7	2.6	3.6	0.7	1.7	0.7	1.0

TABLE 75.—PERCENT DISTRIBUTION BY INDUSTRY GROUP, FOR MALE AND FEMALE EMPLOYED WORKERS 14 YEARS OLD AND OVER, FOR CITIES OF 100,000 OR MORE: 1940—Continued

[Percent not shown where less than 0.1]

INDUSTRY GROUP	ELIZABETH, N. J.		ERIE, PA.		FALL RIVER, MASS.		FLINT, MICH.		FORT WAYNE, IND.		FORT WORTH, TEX.		GARY, IND.	
	Male	Female	Male	Female	Male	Female	Male	Female	Male	Female	Male	Female	Male	Female
Employed (exc. on public emergency work)	100.0	100.0	100.0	100.0	100.0	100.0	100.0	100.0	100.0	100.0	100.0	100.0	100.0	100.0
Agriculture, forestry, and fishery	0.3		0.6	0.1	1.0		0.3		0.4	0.1	1.0	0.2	0.1	
Agriculture	0.2		0.3	0.1	0.9		0.3		0.4	0.1	1.0	0.2	0.1	
Forestry (except logging) and fishery			0.3		0.1									
Mining			0.1						0.1		1.3	0.4		
Coal mining														
Crude petroleum and natural gas production											1.1	0.4		
Other mines and quarries											0.1			
Construction	5.0	0.3	4.0	0.3	5.1	0.1	3.5	0.3	5.7	0.3	8.0	0.4	3.1	0.3
Manufacturing	50.3	43.4	52.3	25.5	52.9	69.2	63.4	27.0	39.1	32.0	20.8	11.5	68.9	20.7
Food and kindred products	2.3	1.4	2.3	0.9	2.1	0.3	1.5	0.7	5.0	2.2	8.8	4.3	1.5	0.9
Textile-mill products	1.0	1.0	0.1		36.6	32.5	0.1	0.1	2.1	6.0	0.4	0.6	0.5	8.3
Apparel and other fabricated textile products	1.6	17.3	0.2	1.9	4.7	33.4		0.1	0.5	4.3	0.5	3.4	0.1	0.7
Logging														
Sawmills and planing mills	0.1		0.2		0.1		0.1		0.1		0.3			
Furniture, store fixtures, and miscellaneous wooden goods	2.2	1.2	0.7	0.4	0.5	0.2	0.1	0.1	0.4	0.2	0.9	0.2	0.1	0.1
Paper and allied products	0.9	1.1	4.4	2.6	0.8	0.3			0.6	0.7	0.1			
Printing, publishing, and allied industries	1.6	1.5	1.9	1.1	1.0	0.3	1.1	0.8	2.3	1.1	2.3	1.0	0.6	0.5
Chemicals and allied products	6.0	1.6	0.5	0.1	0.3	0.1	0.5	0.2	0.5	0.3	0.8	0.2	0.2	0.1
Petroleum and coal products	6.8	1.2	0.3		0.2				0.1		2.1	1.0	1.0	0.1
Leather and leather products	0.6	0.5	0.1		0.6	0.2			0.1		0.2	0.1		
Stone, clay, and glass products	0.2	0.1	0.3	0.1	0.1		0.1		0.2		0.4		0.2	0.1
Iron and steel and their products	4.9	0.9	15.9	2.8	1.9	0.2	0.4	0.1	2.3	0.3	1.4	0.1	64.2	8.4
Nonferrous metals and their products	1.9	0.5	1.6	0.4	0.1		0.1		0.4	0.1	0.3		0.1	
Machinery	13.5	11.5	17.1	7.4	1.3	0.1	1.7	3.8	18.4	15.9	1.0	0.1	0.1	0.1
Automobiles and automobile equipment	1.6	0.4	0.2	0.1	0.1		56.5	20.3	5.2	0.3	0.5	0.1	0.2	0.7
Transportation equipment, except automobile	1.2	0.1	0.4	0.2	0.1						0.2		0.1	0.1
Other and not specified manufacturing industries	3.9	3.4	6.5	7.6	2.4	1.6	1.1	0.8	1.0	0.6	0.5	0.3	0.1	0.7
Transport., commun., and other public utilities	10.1	2.9	8.7	2.4	5.7	1.3	14.3	2.3	13.3	2.6	13.2	3.4	6.2	2.2
Railroads (inc. railroad repair shops) and railway express service	4.0	0.4	3.7	0.3	0.6		0.7	0.1	6.9	0.2	6.0	0.5	4.0	0.2
Trucking service	1.1	0.1	1.1	0.1	1.3		1.5	0.2	1.8	0.3	1.6	0.2	0.3	
Other transportation	2.2	0.2	1.4	0.2	2.0	0.1	0.6	0.1	1.4	0.3	2.8	0.7	0.8	0.3
Communication	0.7	1.7	0.5	1.4	0.2	0.9	0.4	1.0	0.8	1.2	1.0	1.6	0.2	0.9
Utilities	2.1	0.5	1.9	0.4	1.7	0.3	1.0	0.7	2.4	0.6	1.9	0.4	0.9	0.8
Wholesale and retail trade	16.0	12.0	17.8	24.2	19.2	8.5	15.5	21.7	21.7	22.9	27.7	26.0	10.9	28.3
Wholesale trade	2.2	1.0	3.3	1.2	2.9	0.6	2.0	0.8	4.4	1.9	7.1	2.8	1.0	0.6
Food and dairy products stores, and milk retailing	4.2	2.1	4.7	3.9	5.3	1.2	3.5	2.9	4.4	2.4	4.3	2.3	2.6	5.7
Eating and drinking places	2.5	1.8	1.6	5.2	2.2	1.0	1.6	5.7	2.0	4.5	2.8	6.3	1.9	7.5
Motor vehicle and accessories retailing, and filling stations	1.4	0.2	2.0	0.4	1.5	0.2	2.5	0.5	3.1	0.4	4.2	0.4	1.3	0.6
Other retail trade	5.6	7.0	6.2	13.5	7.4	5.6	5.9	11.9	7.8	13.8	9.4	14.2	4.1	14.0
Finance, insurance, and real estate	3.6	6.1	2.6	3.0	2.2	0.8	2.1	3.4	3.9	5.6	4.9	4.5	1.8	3.6
Business and repair services	2.0	0.6	2.0	0.5	1.7	0.1	1.7	0.5	2.7	0.7	3.5	0.8	1.3	0.7
Automobile storage, rental, and repair services	1.0		1.3	0.1	1.0		1.0	0.1	1.4	0.1	2.0	0.1	0.8	0.2
Business and repair services, except automobile	0.9	0.6	0.7	0.4	0.7	0.1	0.7	0.4	1.3	0.6	1.5	0.7	0.5	0.5
Personal services	2.9	15.9	2.9	20.3	3.3	7.3	2.2	22.3	3.0	16.9	6.8	33.8	1.8	20.2
Domestic service	0.3	10.6	0.4	12.9	0.4	4.9	0.2	15.4	0.3	9.7	2.0	21.7	0.1	11.1
Hotels and lodging places	0.4	1.4	0.7	2.8	0.2	0.4	0.3	1.9	0.8	2.2	1.6	3.2	0.5	2.8
Laundering, cleaning, and dyeing services	0.8	2.0	0.6	2.1	1.1	0.9	0.6	1.5	0.7	1.9	1.4	3.6	0.5	2.7
Miscellaneous personal services	1.3	1.9	1.2	2.5	1.5	1.0	1.1	3.5	1.2	3.1	1.8	5.2	0.7	3.6
Amusement, recreation, and related services	0.6	0.3	1.0	0.7	0.8	0.2	0.9	1.0	0.8	0.5	1.3	0.6	0.9	0.7
Professional and related services	4.2	13.5	4.0	18.4	3.5	10.4	3.1	17.6	4.6	14.7	5.5	15.4	2.5	18.8
Government	3.2	1.6	2.8	2.5	3.7	1.0	2.2	2.3	2.9	1.7	5.1	2.1	2.1	3.0
Industry not reported	1.9	3.4	1.1	2.3	0.8	1.1	0.9	1.6	1.6	2.0	1.0	1.0	0.6	1.4

TABLE 75.—PERCENT DISTRIBUTION BY INDUSTRY GROUP, FOR MALE AND FEMALE EMPLOYED WORKERS 14 YEARS OLD AND OVER, FOR CITIES OF 100,000 OR MORE: 1940—Continued

[Percent not shown where less than 0.1]

INDUSTRY GROUP	GRAND RAPIDS, MICH.		HARTFORD, CONN.		HOUSTON, TEX.		INDIANAPOLIS, IND.		JACKSONVILLE, FLA.		JERSEY CITY, N. J.		KANSAS CITY, KANS.		KANSAS CITY, MO.	
	Male	Female	Male	Female	Male	Female	Male	Female	Male	Female	Male	Female	Male	Female	Male	Female
Employed (exc. on public emergency work)	100.0	100.0	100.0	100.0	100.0	100.0	100.0	100.0	100.0	100.0	100.0	100.0	100.0	100.0	100.0	100.0
Agriculture, forestry, and fishery	0.6	0.1	0.5	......	0.7	0.1	0.4	0.1	0.8	0.1	0.1	......	0.5	0.1	0.6	0.1
Agriculture	0.6	0.1	0.5	......	0.7	0.1	0.4	0.1	0.6	0.1	0.1	......	0.5	0.1	0.6	0.1
Forestry (except logging) and fishery	......	......	......	......	......	......	......	......	0.2	......	......	......	......	......	......	......
Mining	0.9	......	0.1	......	2.9	0.7	0.1	......	0.1	......	......	......	0.2	......	0.2	......
Coal mining	......	......	......	......	......	......	......	......	......	......	......	......	......	......	......	......
Crude petroleum and natural gas production	0.6	......	......	......	2.8	0.7	......	......	......	......	......	......	......	......	......	......
Other mines and quarries	0.2	......	0.1	......	0.1	......	0.1	......	......	......	......	......	0.2	......	0.2	......
Construction	5.6	0.3	6.6	0.3	9.6	0.5	6.6	0.4	9.1	0.4	5.3	0.4	6.0	0.2	6.1	0.4
Manufacturing	42.7	24.5	37.5	22.1	23.1	8.3	32.7	21.0	15.8	10.8	32.0	33.3	32.0	25.4	22.0	15.0
Food and kindred products	2.8	2.3	2.3	0.6	3.6	1.3	5.5	2.0	3.9	1.3	3.6	3.1	15.3	9.2	5.2	2.2
Textile-mill products	0.8	3.7	0.3	0.4	0.4	0.4	1.4	3.9	0.1	0.1	0.8	1.5	0.1	0.1	0.1	0.1
Apparel and other fabricated textile products	0.1	0.6	0.2	1.7	0.3	1.4	0.5	2.6	0.1	0.4	1.1	7.0	0.7	8.9	0.9	5.9
Logging	......	......	......	......	......	......	......	......	0.2	......	......	......	......	......	......	......
Sawmills and planing mills	0.3	0.1	0.1	......	0.4	......	0.4	0.1	1.0	0.1	0.1	......	0.2	......	0.3	0.1
Furniture, store fixtures, and miscellaneous wooden goods	13.2	3.1	0.7	0.1	0.9	0.2	1.0	0.3	1.0	0.4	0.8	0.4	1.1	0.5	0.7	0.3
Paper and allied products	1.1	0.9	0.3	0.4	0.4	0.1	0.9	1.1	1.1	0.2	1.0	1.5	1.1	1.2	0.5	0.5
Printing, publishing, and allied industries	2.8	1.9	1.7	0.8	1.9	1.0	2.7	1.7	1.6	0.6	2.2	1.5	2.0	1.6	2.9	2.1
Chemicals and allied products	0.7	0.3	0.5	0.3	0.7	0.2	1.7	1.7	2.0	0.3	3.8	3.9	2.9	1.5	1.2	1.0
Petroleum and coal products	0.2	......	......	......	4.4	2.2	0.3	0.1	0.2	0.1	1.7	0.3	2.8	0.3	0.7	0.4
Leather and leather products	0.5	0.4	0.1	0.1	......	......	0.1	0.1	......	......	0.5	1.6	0.1	0.2	0.2	0.1
Stone, clay, and glass products	0.6	0.1	0.3	0.1	0.6	0.1	0.9	0.2	0.5	......	0.6	0.3	0.3	......	0.4	0.1
Iron and steel and their products	3.8	3.0	5.9	2.2	2.2	0.4	4.7	1.1	0.6	0.1	3.9	2.2	2.5	0.3	3.0	0.5
Nonferrous metals and their products	1.3	1.1	0.3	0.7	0.3	0.1	0.7	0.3	0.1	......	0.6	0.5	0.3	0.1	0.4	0.1
Machinery	6.1	1.3	12.0	8.9	5.8	0.6	5.4	3.3	0.7	0.1	3.1	2.8	0.9	0.4	1.6	0.5
Automobiles and automobile equipment	5.2	2.3	0.2	0.1	0.3	......	2.9	0.5	0.4	......	0.8	0.1	1.0	0.2	2.7	0.3
Transportation equipment, except automobile	0.2	......	5.6	0.9	0.2	......	1.2	0.1	0.5	......	4.0	0.2	0.3	......	0.2	......
Other and not specified manufacturing industries	3.1	3.3	7.1	4.9	0.7	0.3	2.5	1.9	1.6	7.0	3.5	6.5	0.6	0.7	1.0	0.8
Transport., commun., and other public utilities	9.2	3.8	5.8	2.0	14.8	3.6	12.2	3.4	20.8	3.8	19.9	5.4	21.2	3.8	14.1	3.9
Railroads (inc. railroad repair shops) and railway express service	3.6	0.2	1.1	0.1	4.9	0.8	5.1	0.3	8.7	0.4	9.7	0.8	13.3	0.6	5.6	0.5
Trucking service	2.0	0.5	1.2	0.1	1.8	0.1	2.1	0.3	1.8	0.3	2.2	0.2	1.9	0.1	2.2	0.3
Other transportation	1.0	0.3	1.4	0.2	5.4	0.5	2.1	0.3	7.7	0.6	5.2	0.6	2.7	0.8	3.2	0.7
Communication	0.9	2.0	0.6	1.1	0.8	1.6	0.9	2.0	1.1	2.5	0.9	3.2	0.6	1.8	1.1	1.7
Utilities	1.8	0.9	1.6	0.4	2.0	0.6	1.9	0.6	1.5	0.1	2.0	0.6	2.6	0.5	2.1	0.7
Wholesale and retail trade	21.2	22.5	21.8	17.7	24.8	22.1	22.1	22.8	28.4	18.3	18.5	14.2	20.1	22.9	28.0	27.3
Wholesale trade	5.1	2.1	3.4	1.6	5.4	2.1	4.7	2.0	7.7	2.4	3.1	2.4	4.7	3.1	7.4	4.1
Food and dairy products stores, and milk retailing	4.6	2.7	4.5	1.5	4.5	2.5	4.5	2.2	5.1	2.1	5.2	2.5	4.2	3.1	4.4	2.0
Eating and drinking places	1.6	4.8	3.2	2.3	3.0	6.8	2.1	5.3	2.6	5.4	2.9	2.6	1.9	5.5	3.1	5.9
Motor vehicles and accessories retailing, and filling stations	2.4	0.4	1.9	0.4	3.8	0.6	2.6	0.4	3.7	0.5	1.0	0.2	2.8	0.7	3.0	1.0
Other retail trade	7.5	12.5	8.7	12.0	8.1	10.1	8.2	12.8	9.2	7.9	6.3	6.6	6.5	10.5	10.1	14.4
Finance, insurance, and real estate	3.7	4.7	8.5	16.1	4.8	4.8	5.3	6.0	4.5	4.4	6.0	10.9	3.4	4.4	7.1	8.1
Business and repair services	2.9	1.1	2.6	0.5	3.2	0.7	2.9	0.9	2.8	0.5	2.2	0.9	2.6	0.8	3.5	1.2
Automobile storage, rental, and repair services	1.4	0.1	1.4	0.1	1.8	0.1	1.5	0.1	1.7	......	1.1	......	1.5	0.1	1.8	0.1
Business and repair services, except automobile	1.5	1.0	1.2	0.4	1.4	0.6	1.4	0.8	1.1	0.4	1.1	0.9	1.1	0.7	1.7	1.1
Personal services	3.6	20.4	4.3	16.7	6.5	42.5	4.5	22.8	6.9	46.1	3.6	13.3	3.6	21.6	5.7	25.6
Domestic service	0.4	12.3	0.7	10.1	2.4	31.5	0.8	14.3	1.9	34.4	0.3	6.2	0.5	12.9	0.9	14.7
Hotels and lodging places	1.1	2.6	1.0	2.3	1.2	3.2	1.3	2.6	2.1	5.2	0.4	1.2	0.7	2.1	1.8	3.9
Laundering, cleaning, and dyeing services	0.8	2.6	1.0	2.5	1.4	3.6	1.2	2.7	1.5	3.5	1.4	4.3	0.9	3.3	1.4	3.3
Miscellaneous personal services	1.3	3.0	1.5	1.8	1.5	4.2	1.3	3.2	1.5	3.1	1.5	1.6	1.5	3.4	1.6	3.8
Amusement, recreation, and related services	1.0	0.5	0.8	0.4	1.1	0.7	1.3	0.9	1.0	0.4	0.7	0.4	0.8	0.7	1.2	1.0
Professional and related services	4.1	17.5	4.6	17.4	4.4	13.4	5.4	15.4	3.8	11.6	4.8	15.9	4.3	16.3	5.5	14.1
Government	3.2	1.9	4.7	4.0	2.7	1.2	4.6	4.2	4.9	2.4	4.9	1.7	4.2	2.1	4.9	2.2
Industry not reported	1.3	2.4	2.2	2.8	1.5	1.4	1.7	2.1	1.1	1.0	2.1	3.7	1.0	1.7	1.1	1.3

TABLE 75.—PERCENT DISTRIBUTION BY INDUSTRY GROUP, FOR MALE AND FEMALE EMPLOYED WORKERS 14 YEARS OLD AND OVER, FOR CITIES OF 100,000 OR MORE: 1940—Continued

[Percent not shown where less than 0.1]

INDUSTRY GROUP	KNOXVILLE, TENN.		LONG BEACH, CALIF.		LOS ANGELES, CALIF.		LOUISVILLE, KY.		LOWELL, MASS.		MEMPHIS, TENN.		MIAMI, FLA.	
	Male	Female	Male	Female	Male	Female	Male	Female	Male	Female	Male	Female	Male	Female
Employed (exc. on public emergency work)	100.0	100.0	100.0	100.0	100.0	100.0	100.0	100.0	100.0	100.0	100.0	100.0	100.0	100.0
Agriculture, forestry, and fishery	0.6	0.1	1.2	0.3	2.7	0.4	0.3	-	0.7	0.1	1.0	0.3	2.1	0.2
Agriculture	0.6	0.1	1.0	0.3	2.2	0.4	0.3	-	0.6	0.1	1.0	0.2	1.9	0.2
Forestry (except logging) and fishery	-	-	0.2	-	0.5	-	-	-	0.1	-	-	-	0.3	-
Mining	0.6	0.1	8.9	0.6	0.6	0.2	0.2	-	0.6	-	0.1	-	0.1	-
Coal mining	0.1	-	-	-	-	-	-	-	-	-	-	-	-	-
Crude petroleum and natural gas production	-	-	8.7	0.6	0.4	0.1	-	-	-	-	-	-	-	-
Other mines and quarries	0.5	-	0.2	-	0.2	-	0.1	-	0.6	-	0.1	-	0.1	-
Construction	7.9	0.3	8.0	0.4	8.1	0.5	8.1	0.4	5.3	0.2	9.4	0.3	13.5	0.6
Manufacturing	27.2	29.7	16.3	5.4	20.3	13.3	31.4	22.4	45.9	46.2	25.0	7.9	9.3	2.5
Food and kindred products	4.3	0.8	1.9	1.5	2.9	2.2	6.4	5.0	3.3	2.2	4.0	1.6	2.7	0.6
Textile-mill products	8.1	18.3	0.1	0.1	0.3	0.6	0.7	1.5	24.7	28.8	1.0	0.4	0.1	0.1
Apparel and other fabricated textile products	1.0	7.8	0.1	1.0	1.0	5.3	0.4	2.3	0.3	1.9	0.4	1.2	0.2	0.3
Logging	-	-	-	-	-	-	-	-	0.1	-	0.1	-	-	-
Sawmills and planing mills	1.4	0.1	0.3	-	0.2	-	1.1	0.1	0.1	-	3.3	0.2	0.3	-
Furniture, store fixtures, and miscellaneous wooden goods	1.3	0.2	0.4	0.1	1.4	0.4	3.6	0.7	1.1	0.3	2.6	0.6	0.9	0.2
Paper and allied products	0.3	0.1	0.1	0.1	0.4	0.3	0.2	0.2	0.8	0.6	0.6	0.3	-	-
Printing, publishing, and allied industries	1.8	0.5	1.7	0.7	2.3	1.2	2.7	1.5	2.5	1.1	1.5	0.6	2.1	0.6
Chemicals and allied products	0.4	0.1	1.3	0.3	0.7	0.5	1.3	0.5	1.2	0.8	2.6	1.4	0.3	0.1
Petroleum and coal products	0.1	-	3.8	0.4	0.7	0.3	0.7	0.2	0.2	-	0.2	-	0.1	-
Leather and leather products	0.1	-	-	-	0.2	0.2	0.2	-	6.6	7.6	0.1	-	-	-
Stone, clay, and glass products	2.8	0.9	0.4	0.2	0.6	0.2	0.6	0.2	0.1	-	0.5	0.1	0.5	0.1
Iron and steel and their products	2.9	0.3	0.8	0.1	1.6	0.3	4.9	1.5	0.9	0.2	1.2	0.2	0.5	-
Nonferrous metals and their products	0.6	-	0.2	-	0.6	0.1	0.8	0.2	0.2	0.1	0.2	-	0.2	-
Machinery	1.1	0.1	1.1	0.1	1.9	0.5	2.4	0.4	2.1	1.4	1.0	0.3	0.3	-
Automobiles and automobile equipment	0.1	-	1.3	0.1	0.7	0.1	1.4	0.1	0.2	0.1	2.3	0.1	0.1	-
Transportation equipment, except automobile	-	-	2.3	0.3	3.3	0.3	0.1	-	0.4	-	-	-	0.5	-
Other and not specified manufacturing industries	1.0	0.4	0.5	0.3	1.3	0.9	4.2	7.9	1.2	0.9	3.5	0.9	0.6	0.3
Transport., commun., and other public utilities	12.7	1.7	7.7	3.4	9.3	3.7	15.5	3.7	9.1	2.2	14.2	3.1	11.1	2.6
Railroads (inc. railroad repair shops) and railway express service	7.1	0.2	0.5	-	2.1	0.2	9.2	1.0	3.8	0.2	5.8	0.4	2.1	0.2
Trucking service	1.5	0.1	0.9	0.1	1.1	0.1	1.7	0.2	1.1	0.1	1.8	0.2	0.7	0.1
Other transportation	1.5	0.1	3.8	0.5	2.9	0.4	2.1	0.2	1.4	0.2	3.8	0.3	5.1	0.5
Communication	0.8	0.9	0.5	2.3	1.0	2.4	0.7	2.1	0.6	1.0	0.8	2.0	1.1	1.5
Utilities	1.7	0.4	1.9	0.5	2.2	0.6	1.8	0.3	2.2	0.6	1.9	0.3	2.0	0.4
Wholesale and retail trade	25.5	17.2	22.9	29.8	25.8	25.0	22.0	20.5	19.3	15.3	26.3	21.8	29.3	24.4
Wholesale trade	5.3	1.3	4.1	1.3	5.5	3.1	5.5	3.0	2.3	0.6	7.3	2.8	4.8	1.2
Food and dairy products stores, and milk retailing	5.2	1.6	4.2	3.9	4.5	2.5	4.4	2.7	5.0	1.9	4.4	1.5	5.2	1.9
Eating and drinking places	2.5	4.0	3.1	9.8	4.0	6.2	2.4	4.2	2.8	2.7	2.2	4.8	5.7	8.4
Motor vehicles and accessories retailing, and filling stations	2.9	0.3	3.5	0.5	3.3	0.5	1.8	0.3	1.5	0.1	2.7	0.4	3.5	0.5
Other retail trade	9.7	10.0	7.9	14.3	8.4	12.7	7.8	10.3	7.7	10.0	9.7	12.2	10.1	12.4
Finance insurance and real estate	3.7	2.2	4.8	8.5	5.7	7.9	4.3	4.8	2.7	2.0	4.5	4.1	5.1	5.9
Business and repair services	2.6	0.3	4.1	1.0	4.0	1.3	2.6	0.7	1.7	0.3	2.6	0.6	3.9	0.8
Automobile storage, rental, and repair services	1.6	-	2.2	0.1	2.1	0.1	1.5	0.1	1.0	0.1	1.3	0.1	2.4	0.1
Business and repair services, except automobile	1.0	0.3	1.9	0.9	1.9	1.2	1.1	0.6	0.7	0.2	1.3	0.5	1.4	0.7
Personal services	5.8	30.4	4.0	25.1	5.8	23.7	5.0	28.3	3.1	12.8	6.5	45.9	11.9	46.8
Domestic service	1.5	21.3	0.5	14.5	1.5	13.7	1.3	19.3	0.6	8.2	2.2	33.9	3.6	29.2
Hotels and lodging places	1.4	2.9	1.0	2.7	1.4	3.2	1.2	2.7	0.4	1.4	1.5	4.2	4.2	7.8
Laundering, cleaning, and dyeing services	1.3	3.3	1.0	2.3	1.4	2.7	1.2	3.4	0.7	1.6	1.4	3.8	2.2	5.6
Miscellaneous personal services	1.6	2.9	1.5	5.6	1.5	4.1	1.2	2.8	1.4	1.6	1.5	3.9	2.0	4.1
Amusement, recreation, and related services	0.9	0.4	1.8	1.3	5.9	3.6	1.3	0.4	1.0	0.5	0.9	0.7	3.5	1.2
Professional and related services	5.6	13.1	5.1	18.9	6.1	15.7	4.5	14.7	4.5	15.9	4.2	13.7	4.3	11.8
Government	5.9	3.5	14.2	3.4	5.0	3.4	3.8	2.5	4.6	2.5	3.8	1.5	4.1	1.4
Industry not reported	0.8	0.9	0.9	1.8	0.9	1.4	1.1	1.4	1.6	2.1	1.4	1.1	1.7	1.8

TABLE 75.—PERCENT DISTRIBUTION BY INDUSTRY GROUP, FOR MALE AND FEMALE EMPLOYED WORKERS 14 YEARS OLD AND OVER, FOR CITIES OF 100,000 OR MORE: 1940—Continued

[Percent not shown where less than 0.1]

INDUSTRY GROUP	MILWAUKEE, WIS.		MINNEAPOLIS, MINN.		NASHVILLE, TENN.		NEWARK, N. J.		NEW BEDFORD, MASS.		NEW HAVEN, CONN.		NEW ORLEANS, LA.	
	Male	Female	Male	Female	Male	Female	Male	Female	Male	Female	Male	Female	Male	Female
Employed (exc. on public emergency work)	100.0	100.0	100.0	100.0	100.0	100.0	100.0	100.0	100.0	100.0	100.0	100.0	100.0	100.0
Agriculture, forestry, and fishery	0.3	0.1	0.5	0.1	0.5	0.1	0.2		2.3	0.1	0.7	0.1	1.2	0.2
Agriculture	0.2		0.5	0.1	0.5	0.1	0.2		0.9	0.1	0.5	0.1	0.9	0.2
Forestry (except logging) and fishery	0.1								1.4		0.2		0.3	
Mining	0.1		0.1		0.2				0.1		0.1		0.2	
Coal mining														
Crude petroleum and natural gas production													0.1	
Other mines and quarries	0.1		0.1		0.2				0.1		0.1			
Construction	5.8	0.4	7.0	0.4	9.5	0.3	6.2	0.3	4.8	0.2	6.4	0.3	8.9	0.3
Manufacturing	43.7	25.9	24.7	15.5	24.5	17.7	37.3	35.1	49.5	60.0	33.5	35.0	18.1	12.8
Food and kindred products	5.4	2.8	5.3	3.0	4.4	1.8	4.5	1.6	2.6	0.4	2.7	1.0	5.6	2.4
Textile-mill products	1.3	4.9	0.7	2.4	1.6	4.5	1.1	1.5	30.4	34.9	0.5	0.3	1.0	1.9
Apparel and other fabricated textile products	0.5	2.6	0.8	3.6	1.0	4.0	2.0	9.3	1.3	12.6	1.8	16.3	0.9	4.1
Logging														
Sawmills and planing mills	0.3		0.8	0.1	0.8		0.2		0.3		0.1		0.4	0.1
Furniture, store fixtures, and miscellaneous wooden goods	1.2	0.6	1.2	0.3	1.3	0.2	0.9	0.4	0.4	0.1	0.7	0.2	1.3	0.3
Paper and allied products	0.8	1.0	0.6	0.3	0.5	0.2	0.7	1.1	0.7	0.5	1.9	1.2	0.4	0.2
Printing, publishing, and allied industries	2.7	1.8	2.9	1.6	3.4	2.4	1.5	0.7	1.0	0.4	2.0	1.1	1.8	0.6
Chemicals and allied products	0.8	0.4	1.0	0.5	2.4	0.4	3.0	1.6	0.2	0.1	1.4	0.9	0.7	0.3
Petroleum and coal products	0.2		0.3		0.1		0.4	0.2			0.4		0.9	0.3
Leather and leather goods	3.0	4.3	0.2	0.1	1.9	2.3	1.7	0.8	1.2	3.1	0.1		0.1	
Stone, clay, and glass products	0.5	0.1	0.4	0.1	1.2	0.1	0.4	0.1	0.4	0.2	0.4	0.1	0.7	0.1
Iron and steel and their products	7.8	1.7	2.9	1.1	3.2	0.2	4.8	1.1	2.9	1.1	11.9	5.8	1.2	0.3
Nonferrous metals and their products	0.7	0.2	0.6	0.1	0.2		1.4	1.0	1.6	0.2	2.3	2.2	0.3	
Machinery	12.4	3.4	4.4	0.9	0.6	0.1	6.1	7.5	4.0	3.8	2.1	0.7	0.7	0.2
Automobiles and automobile equipment	3.6	0.8	1.0	0.2	0.2		1.1	0.2			0.4	0.1	0.2	
Transportation equipment, except automobile	0.6	0.1	0.1		0.1		1.6	0.1	0.6	0.1	0.3		1.1	
Other and not specified manufacturing industries	1.7	1.1	1.6	1.2	1.7	1.5	6.0	7.8	2.0	2.5	4.7	5.1	0.8	2.0
Transport., commun., and other public utilities	9.9	3.9	13.0	3.3	12.7	3.0	8.3	3.0	6.2	1.9	11.0	4.2	18.9	3.5
Railroads (inc. railroad repair shops) and railway express service	3.8	0.2	6.3	0.6	6.6	0.4	1.6	0.1	0.5		5.5	1.5	4.0	0.3
Trucking service	1.3	0.2	1.5	0.2	1.7	0.1	1.9	0.1	1.2	0.1	1.8	0.1	1.4	0.1
Other transportation	2.0	0.3	2.3	0.3	1.5	0.2	2.2	0.2	2.6	0.1	1.6	0.2	10.7	0.8
Communication	0.7	2.6	1.0	1.7	0.9	2.0	0.6	1.9	0.4	1.3	0.8	2.1	1.0	2.1
Utilities	2.0	0.6	2.0	0.4	2.0	0.3	2.0	0.6	1.4	0.3	1.2	0.3	1.8	0.2
Wholesale and retail trade	20.2	24.5	27.2	27.0	24.0	15.1	22.8	16.7	19.3	11.6	23.3	14.6	25.4	21.2
Wholesale trade	4.0	2.1	8.1	4.2	4.2	1.3	3.3	1.2	2.4	0.6	3.8	1.4	6.2	2.5
Food and dairy products stores, and milk retailing	4.4	3.9	4.6	2.6	4.7	1.4	5.8	2.3	5.7	1.7	5.6	2.0	5.3	3.3
Eating and drinking places	2.8	4.3	2.7	6.1	2.7	3.8	3.7	3.0	2.1	1.5	3.4	2.0	3.4	4.3
Motor vehicles and accessories retailing, and filling stations	1.8	0.3	2.5	0.4	2.6	0.3	1.3	0.2	1.8	0.2	2.0	0.3	2.0	0.3
Other retail trade	7.2	13.9	9.3	13.7	9.7	8.2	8.7	9.9	7.3	7.6	8.6	8.8	8.4	10.8
Finance, insurance, and real estate	3.5	5.8	6.0	7.7	4.5	4.7	4.4	7.4	1.9	1.3	3.2	2.8	5.0	4.1
Business and repair services	2.6	0.9	3.6	1.2	3.1	0.5	3.0	0.7	2.1	0.2	2.7	0.4	2.9	0.6
Automobile storage, rental, and repair services	1.3	0.1	1.7	0.1	1.8	0.1	1.6	0.1	1.4	0.1	1.6	0.1	1.4	0.1
Business and repair services, except automobile	1.3	0.8	1.8	1.1	1.3	0.5	1.4	0.5	0.8	0.1	1.1	0.3	1.5	0.5
Personal services	3.0	16.8	4.1	22.1	7.3	37.9	3.9	18.2	3.9	12.2	4.6	18.6	5.4	37.2
Domestic service	0.3	9.4	0.4	13.2	2.8	28.0	0.5	11.8	0.6	8.4	0.8	12.5	1.3	28.2
Hotels and lodging places	0.8	2.8	1.3	3.1	1.3	2.4	0.5	1.8	0.5	0.9	0.8	1.8	1.2	2.4
Laundering, cleaning, and dyeing services	0.7	2.0	1.0	2.2	1.5	4.4	1.1	2.4	1.1	1.3	1.2	2.6	1.4	3.0
Miscellaneous personal services	1.2	2.7	1.4	3.5	1.7	3.0	1.8	2.1	1.7	1.6	1.7	1.7	1.5	3.6
Amusement, recreation, and related services	1.0	0.7	1.4	0.9	1.1	0.5	1.0	0.6	0.9	0.2	1.1	0.6	1.9	1.2
Professional and related services	4.6	17.0	6.4	17.5	5.7	15.3	4.8	11.4	3.4	10.0	7.5	19.0	5.3	15.4
Government	4.5	2.3	4.9	2.9	5.5	3.6	4.8	2.2	4.6	1.1	4.4	2.1	5.7	2.6
Industry not reported	0.9	1.7	1.1	1.5	1.3	1.4	3.3	4.4	1.1	1.3	1.6	2.3	1.3	1.0

524997 O - 43 - 14

TABLE 75.—PERCENT DISTRIBUTION BY INDUSTRY GROUP, FOR MALE AND FEMALE EMPLOYED WORKERS 14 YEARS OLD AND OVER, FOR CITIES OF 100,000 OR MORE: 1940—Continued

[Percent not shown where less than 0.1]

INDUSTRY GROUP	NEW YORK, N. Y.		BRONX BORO., N. Y.		BROOKLYN BORO., N. Y.		MANHATTAN BORO., N. Y.		QUEENS BORO., N. Y.		RICHMOND BORO., N. Y.		NORFOLK, VA.		OAKLAND, CALIF.	
	Male	Female	Male	Female	Male	Female	Male	Female	Male	Female	Male	Female	Male	Female	Male	Female
Employed (exc. on public emergency work)	100.0	100.0	100.0	100.0	100.0	100.0	100.0	100.0	100.0	100.0	100.0	100.0	100.0	100.0	100.0	100.0
Agriculture, forestry, and fishery	0.2	-	0.1	-	0.1	-	0.1	-	0.3	0.1	0.7	0.2	0.7	0.6	0.9	0.2
Agriculture	0.1	-	0.1	-	0.1	-	0.1	-	0.3	0.1	0.6	0.2	0.6	0.6	0.8	0.2
Forestry (except logging) and fishery	-	-	-	-	0.1	-	-	-	-	-	0.1	-	0.1	-	0.1	-
Mining	-	-	-	-	-	-	0.1	-	0.1	-	-	-	-	-	0.2	-
Coal mining	-	-	-	-	-	-	-	-	-	-	-	-	-	-	0.1	-
Crude petroleum and natural gas production	-	-	-	-	-	-	-	-	-	-	-	-	-	-	0.2	-
Other mines and quarries	-	-	-	-	-	-	-	-	-	-	-	-	-	-	-	-
Construction	6.5	0.4	7.5	0.7	6.5	0.4	4.7	0.3	7.8	0.6	7.6	0.4	6.0	0.5	8.7	0.4
Manufacturing	25.7	27.7	25.8	32.0	30.9	34.9	18.6	19.0	25.4	27.0	23.7	20.1	17.3	7.4	26.8	13.3
Food and kindred products	2.8	1.5	2.6	1.3	2.9	1.9	2.1	0.9	3.6	2.4	2.1	1.1	2.7	1.4	4.1	3.6
Textile mill products	1.3	1.8	1.3	2.0	1.6	2.3	1.2	1.0	1.2	2.4	0.6	0.7	0.4	1.4	0.4	0.6
Apparel and other fabricated textile products	6.2	13.1	9.3	17.2	8.6	17.6	4.1	9.2	2.0	8.3	0.9	7.9	0.4	2.0	0.2	1.3
Logging	-	-	-	-	-	-	-	-	0.1	-	-	-	0.4	-	0.5	0.1
Sawmills and planing mills	0.1	-	-	-	0.1	-	-	-	-	-	-	-	-	-	-	-
Furniture, store fixtures, and miscellaneous wooden goods	0.9	0.3	0.9	0.3	1.2	0.4	0.6	0.2	1.0	0.4	0.5	0.2	0.8	0.3	1.2	0.4
Paper and allied products	0.6	0.9	0.4	0.7	0.8	1.2	0.5	0.4	0.7	1.1	0.5	0.6	0.1	0.1	0.5	0.8
Printing, publishing and allied industries	3.2	2.2	3.0	2.6	3.1	1.9	2.8	2.1	4.1	2.8	1.8	1.7	1.1	0.5	2.4	1.4
Chemicals and allied products	1.0	1.2	0.7	1.2	1.1	1.2	0.8	0.9	1.3	1.7	3.2	2.2	1.4	0.6	1.4	0.7
Petroleum and coal products	0.3	0.2	0.2	0.2	0.3	0.2	0.2	0.1	0.6	0.3	1.6	0.5	0.2	0.1	1.4	0.4
Leather and leather products	1.0	0.9	1.0	1.1	1.5	1.3	0.6	0.5	0.5	0.7	0.2	0.4	-	-	0.1	0.1
Stone, clay, and glass products	0.4	0.2	0.3	0.2	0.4	0.2	0.2	0.1	0.5	0.2	1.1	0.2	0.3	-	1.1	0.5
Iron and steel and their products	1.0	0.5	0.8	0.4	1.3	0.7	0.7	0.2	1.4	0.6	0.8	0.4	0.4	0.1	3.4	0.6
Nonferrous metals and their products	0.9	0.4	0.9	0.5	1.0	0.5	0.6	0.2	1.1	0.6	0.9	0.3	0.3	0.1	0.5	0.2
Machinery	1.8	1.0	1.5	0.9	2.0	1.3	1.2	0.5	2.7	1.3	1.4	0.8	0.4	0.1	3.3	1.3
Automobiles and automobile equipment	0.2	0.1	0.2	0.1	0.2	0.1	0.2	-	0.4	0.2	0.2	-	1.5	0.1	2.7	0.5
Transportation equipment, except automobile	1.1	0.1	0.5	0.1	1.6	0.1	0.4	-	1.2	0.1	5.5	0.2	6.3	0.5	2.1	0.1
Other and not specified manufacturing industries	2.9	3.3	2.4	3.3	3.3	3.9	2.4	2.6	3.2	3.8	2.3	3.1	0.6	0.3	1.5	0.9
Transportation, communication, and other public utilities	11.2	3.5	10.8	4.0	10.7	3.8	10.6	2.0	12.8	6.1	15.3	5.9	17.1	3.6	15.4	6.5
Railroads (inc. railroad repair shops) and railway express service	1.6	0.2	1.9	0.2	0.9	0.2	1.8	0.1	2.2	0.3	2.5	0.4	5.1	1.1	6.4	0.9
Trucking service	1.4	0.1	1.2	0.1	1.5	0.1	1.3	0.1	1.4	0.2	1.1	0.2	1.0	0.1	1.2	0.2
Other transportation	5.0	0.5	4.5	0.4	5.1	0.6	5.6	0.3	4.2	0.8	7.3	0.8	8.8	0.8	4.3	0.6
Communication	0.9	2.1	0.8	2.5	0.8	2.0	0.7	1.1	1.5	3.6	1.2	3.5	0.6	1.3	1.1	3.7
Utilities	2.3	0.7	2.4	0.8	2.3	0.7	1.2	0.3	3.6	1.2	3.2	1.0	1.6	0.3	2.4	0.9
Wholesale and retail trade	24.0	17.3	25.7	21.3	23.8	17.1	25.8	15.2	20.9	18.2	16.3	14.9	19.2	21.5	22.9	26.7
Wholesale trade	4.0	2.4	4.3	3.2	4.3	2.4	4.0	1.8	3.6	2.4	2.4	2.2	4.3	2.4	4.6	2.6
Food and dairy products stores, and milk retailing	5.8	2.2	7.1	2.8	6.2	2.5	4.7	1.3	5.5	2.4	5.1	2.8	4.7	2.8	4.6	3.9
Eating and drinking places	4.4	3.0	3.5	2.7	3.0	2.2	8.3	3.9	3.2	3.1	2.2	2.1	1.5	4.6	3.0	4.8
Motor vehicles and accessories retailing, and filling stations	0.8	0.2	0.8	0.2	0.8	0.2	0.5	0.1	1.2	0.3	1.1	0.2	1.8	0.4	2.7	0.5
Other retail trade	8.9	9.6	9.9	12.3	9.6	9.8	8.4	7.9	7.4	10.1	5.6	7.5	7.0	11.4	8.0	14.8
Finance, insurance, and real estate	8.3	7.1	7.6	7.3	6.3	6.5	11.0	5.9	9.1	10.4	6.9	12.2	3.4	3.1	5.2	7.8
Business and repair services	3.1	1.5	3.2	1.6	2.8	1.1	3.4	1.7	3.3	1.6	2.0	1.0	1.8	0.4	3.5	1.2
Automobile storage, rental, and repair services	1.3	0.1	1.4	0.1	1.2	0.1	1.3	-	1.3	0.1	0.9	0.1	1.0	-	1.8	0.2
Business and repair services, except automobile	1.8	1.4	1.9	1.5	1.6	1.1	2.1	1.7	1.9	1.5	1.1	1.0	0.8	0.3	1.7	1.1
Personal services	5.6	21.0	4.9	12.5	4.4	15.9	8.8	33.0	4.5	15.9	3.1	15.8	3.8	44.9	4.5	19.5
Domestic service	0.7	13.9	0.3	6.9	0.4	10.5	1.6	23.0	0.5	9.8	0.5	10.9	0.9	35.5	0.7	9.7
Hotels and lodging places	1.6	2.7	1.1	2.0	0.6	1.3	3.7	5.0	1.5	1.8	0.5	1.1	0.8	2.9	1.0	2.5
Laundering, cleaning, and dyeing services	1.4	1.9	1.6	1.4	1.5	2.1	1.6	2.1	1.0	1.7	0.7	1.7	1.0	3.1	1.4	3.4
Miscellaneous personal services	1.8	2.4	1.8	2.3	1.9	1.9	1.9	3.0	1.5	2.6	1.4	2.1	1.2	3.4	1.5	4.0
Amusement, recreation, and related services	1.6	1.3	1.3	1.1	1.2	0.8	2.5	2.0	1.6	1.2	0.9	0.6	0.9	0.8	1.2	1.7
Professional and related services	6.2	14.3	5.7	13.1	5.5	12.6	8.6	16.7	4.8	13.0	7.5	23.0	3.1	13.9	4.9	17.5
Government	5.5	2.0	5.8	2.6	5.0	2.1	4.0	1.7	7.3	2.0	14.5	3.4	25.8	2.1	4.3	2.9
Industry not reported	2.1	3.8	1.5	3.8	2.5	5.0	1.9	2.6	2.1	4.0	1.4	2.6	1.0	1.2	1.3	2.2

TABLE 75.—PERCENT DISTRIBUTION BY INDUSTRY GROUP, FOR MALE AND FEMALE EMPLOYED WORKERS 14 YEARS OLD AND OVER, FOR CITIES OF 100,000 OR MORE: 1940—Continued

[Percent not shown where less than 0.1]

INDUSTRY GROUP	OKLAHOMA CITY, OKLA.		OMAHA, NEBR.		PATERSON, N. J.		PEORIA, ILL.		PHILADELPHIA, PA.		PITTSBURGH, PA.		PORTLAND, OREG.		PROVIDENCE, R. I.	
	Male	Female	Male	Female	Male	Female	Male	Female	Male	Female	Male	Female	Male	Female	Male	Female
Employed (exc. on public emergency work)	100.0	100.0	100.0	100.0	100.0	100.0	100.0	100.0	100.0	100.0	100.0	100.0	100.0	100.0	100.0	100.0
Agriculture, forestry, and fishery	1.0	0.1	0.8	0.1	0.4	-	0.5	0.1	0.3	-	0.3	-	1.5	0.3	0.4	-
Agriculture	1.0	0.1	0.6	0.1	0.4	-	0.5	-	0.3	-	0.3	-	1.2	0.2	0.3	-
Forestry (except logging) and fishery	-	-	-	-	-	-	0.1	-	-	-	-	-	0.3	0.1	0.1	-
Mining	5.4	0.7	0.1	-	0.1	-	0.9	-	0.1	-	0.4	0.1	0.2	-	-	-
Coal mining	-	-	-	-	-	-	0.9	-	-	-	0.3	0.1	-	-	-	-
Crude petroleum and natural gas production	5.3	0.7	-	-	-	-	-	-	-	-	0.1	-	-	-	-	-
Other mines and quarries	0.1	-	-	-	0.1	-	-	-	0.1	-	0.1	-	0.2	-	-	-
Construction	7.4	0.3	6.1	0.4	5.5	0.2	7.8	0.4	6.8	0.4	6.9	0.4	7.3	0.3	6.8	0.3
Manufacturing	15.9	5.4	21.6	9.8	44.8	42.5	39.8	20.3	36.7	32.2	32.5	12.6	22.5	10.5	38.5	40.0
Food and kindred products	6.3	2.5	12.4	5.0	2.3	0.4	8.2	8.0	3.7	2.3	4.4	3.1	3.5	2.1	2.3	0.8
Textile-mill products	-	-	0.1	0.1	22.6	24.4	0.2	0.2	4.9	7.7	0.2	0.4	0.9	1.9	7.5	11.0
Apparel and other fabricated textile products	0.2	0.3	0.2	1.0	1.4	10.5	0.3	2.9	2.9	8.9	0.2	0.8	0.5	2.0	0.2	0.8
Logging	-	-	-	-	-	-	-	-	-	-	-	-	0.8	0.1	-	-
Sawmills and planing mills	0.2	-	0.1	-	0.1	-	0.3	0.1	0.1	-	0.1	-	3.6	0.3	-	-
Furniture, store fixtures, and miscellaneous wooden goods	1.0	0.3	0.6	0.2	0.5	0.1	0.8	0.2	0.9	0.2	0.9	0.8	2.8	0.7	0.6	0.2
Paper and allied products	0.1	0.1	0.3	0.3	0.6	0.8	0.9	0.8	1.1	1.2	0.4	0.5	0.4	0.3	0.3	0.5
Printing, publishing, and allied industries	2.6	1.2	2.4	1.1	1.3	0.8	2.3	1.5	2.9	1.9	2.2	1.0	2.6	1.2	1.8	1.0
Chemicals and allied products	0.5	0.1	0.6	0.3	0.8	1.0	1.4	0.5	1.5	0.7	0.7	0.4	0.6	0.2	0.7	0.4
Petroleum and coal products	0.7	0.1	0.2	0.1	0.3	0.1	0.1	0.1	1.1	0.2	0.7	0.3	0.2	0.1	0.3	0.1
Leather and leather products	0.1	-	0.2	0.1	0.2	0.5	0.1	-	1.2	0.9	0.1	0.1	0.2	0.1	0.2	0.2
Stone, clay, and glass products	0.5	0.1	0.3	0.1	0.5	0.7	0.3	0.1	0.5	0.2	0.9	0.4	0.3	-	0.3	0.1
Iron and steel and their products	1.3	0.1	1.2	0.2	1.5	0.2	3.9	0.9	4.0	1.1	15.3	2.3	2.3	0.4	6.5	2.2
Nonferrous metals and their products	0.2	-	0.6	0.1	0.2	-	0.6	0.1	0.6	0.2	0.7	0.2	0.5	0.1	2.3	1.9
Machinery	1.4	0.2	1.2	0.3	2.5	0.5	18.7	3.9	4.5	1.9	3.8	1.2	1.5	0.3	6.1	1.7
Automobiles and automobile equipment	0.3	-	0.3	0.1	0.3	-	0.2	0.1	1.4	0.2	0.3	0.1	0.4	0.1	0.1	-
Transportation equipment, except automobile	-	-	-	-	8.1	0.9	-	-	2.8	0.2	0.5	-	0.3	-	0.1	-
Other and not specified manufacturing industries	0.5	0.2	0.8	1.1	1.7	1.5	1.5	0.9	2.7	4.5	1.3	1.0	1.2	0.7	9.1	19.1
Transportation, communication, and other public utilities	10.0	3.6	18.2	6.6	7.8	2.5	9.4	3.0	9.3	2.9	11.8	4.3	15.3	4.2	7.6	2.6
Railroads (incl. railroad repair shops) and railway express service	2.0	0.2	9.8	2.1	2.3	0.2	3.7	0.4	2.7	0.3	5.0	0.5	5.1	0.5	1.6	0.1
Trucking service	2.5	0.3	1.5	0.2	1.7	0.2	1.4	0.1	1.3	0.1	1.6	0.2	1.9	0.4	1.2	0.1
Other transportation	2.5	0.2	3.3	0.6	1.6	0.1	1.7	0.2	3.3	0.5	2.2	0.3	4.8	0.6	2.3	0.2
Communication	1.3	2.5	1.7	3.1	0.5	1.7	0.8	1.7	0.6	1.6	0.7	2.5	1.1	2.0	0.6	1.7
Utilities	1.6	0.5	1.9	0.6	1.6	0.3	1.9	0.6	1.4	0.4	2.4	0.9	2.3	0.8	2.0	0.5
Wholesale and retail trade	28.9	24.5	25.1	23.3	22.0	15.8	21.5	24.6	22.5	19.3	23.2	26.7	26.1	29.3	23.8	16.2
Wholesale trade	7.7	2.6	6.8	3.5	3.2	0.9	4.1	1.9	3.4	1.6	4.7	2.3	7.3	3.5	4.4	1.5
Food and dairy products stores, and milk retailing	4.5	2.7	4.2	2.3	6.1	3.2	4.2	3.1	5.7	2.4	5.4	4.2	4.4	3.3	5.3	1.8
Eating and drinking places	2.6	6.5	2.9	5.3	3.1	2.2	3.4	6.0	3.0	4.0	2.6	5.5	2.6	7.1	2.9	2.4
Motor vehicles and accessories retailing, and filling stations	4.6	0.7	2.7	0.5	1.9	0.3	2.7	0.6	1.2	0.2	1.8	0.4	3.1	0.7	2.0	0.3
Other retail trade	9.6	12.1	8.6	11.7	7.7	9.1	7.2	13.1	9.1	11.0	8.7	14.3	8.8	14.8	9.2	10.3
Finance, insurance, and real estate	6.4	7.2	6.7	11.2	2.8	2.4	3.8	5.0	4.3	4.7	4.7	5.3	5.0	7.7	3.6	3.7
Business and repair services	4.0	1.2	3.3	1.0	2.5	0.3	2.9	1.0	2.8	0.7	2.8	0.9	3.7	1.2	2.5	0.5
Automobile storage, rental, and repair services	2.3	0.1	1.8	0.1	1.5	-	1.6	0.2	1.5	0.1	1.4	0.1	1.9	0.1	1.3	0.1
Business and repair services, except automobile	1.7	1.0	1.5	0.9	1.0	0.3	1.3	0.8	1.4	0.7	1.3	0.8	1.8	1.0	1.2	0.4
Personal services	6.1	31.9	4.7	23.9	4.2	18.8	3.8	23.3	4.5	20.0	4.5	24.0	4.2	21.2	5.0	16.9
Domestic service	1.3	20.7	0.4	14.1	0.6	11.0	0.4	13.1	0.9	13.5	0.9	16.1	0.4	11.5	0.8	10.3
Hotels and lodging places	1.8	3.4	1.7	3.4	0.4	1.3	1.3	3.7	0.8	1.7	1.2	3.0	1.3	3.3	1.1	2.1
Laundering, cleaning, and dyeing services	1.3	2.9	1.1	2.9	1.4	4.4	0.9	2.7	1.0	2.2	1.0	2.4	0.9	2.8	1.2	2.7
Miscellaneous personal services	1.8	4.8	1.5	3.5	1.8	2.0	1.3	3.7	1.6	2.6	1.4	2.5	1.5	3.6	1.9	1.7
Amusement, recreation, and related services	1.5	1.1	1.3	0.9	0.7	0.3	1.1	0.8	1.0	0.7	1.2	0.9	1.3	1.1	0.9	0.3
Professional and related services	5.7	15.9	5.0	18.3	4.9	13.8	4.2	17.9	4.9	14.2	5.7	19.9	5.9	18.6	5.7	16.2
Government	5.8	6.3	6.2	2.9	3.2	1.5	3.4	1.6	5.1	1.8	5.1	3.1	5.5	3.6	4.8	2.5
Industry not reported	2.0	1.7	1.2	1.6	1.1	1.8	1.4	2.0	1.8	3.1	1.0	1.7	1.5	2.0	0.6	0.7

TABLE 75.—PERCENT DISTRIBUTION BY INDUSTRY GROUP, FOR MALE AND FEMALE EMPLOYED WORKERS 14 YEARS OLD AND OVER, FOR CITIES OF 100,000 OR MORE: 1940—Continued

[Percent not shown where less than 0.1]

INDUSTRY GROUP	READING, PA.		RICHMOND, VA.		ROCHESTER, N. Y.		SACRAMENTO, CALIF.		ST. LOUIS, MO.		ST. PAUL, MINN.		SALT LAKE CITY, UTAH	
	Male	Female	Male	Female	Male	Female	Male	Female	Male	Female	Male	Female	Male	Female
Employed (exc. on public emergency work)	100.0	100.0	100.0	100.0	100.0	100.0	100.0	100.0	100.0	100.0	100.0	100.0	100.0	100.0
Agriculture, forestry, and fishery	0.3	....	0.4	....	0.5	0.1	2.9	0.3	0.3	....	0.5	0.1	1.1	0.2
Agriculture	0.3	....	0.4	....	0.5	0.1	2.8	0.3	0.2	....	0.5	0.1	1.0	0.2
Forestry (except logging) and fishery	....	....	....	....	....	....	0.1	....	....	....	....	....	0.1	....
Mining	0.1	....	0.1	....	0.1	....	0.5	....	0.1	....	0.1	....	2.5	0.3
Coal mining	....	....	....	....	....	....	....	....	....	....	....	....	0.1	....
Crude petroleum and natural gas production	....	....	....	....	....	....	....	....	....	....	....	....	....	....
Other mines and quarries	....	....	0.1	....	....	....	0.5	....	0.1	....	0.1	....	2.4	0.3
Construction	4.9	0.2	8.8	0.3	6.1	0.2	8.0	0.4	6.2	0.3	6.4	0.4	7.5	0.2
Manufacturing	46.8	51.5	27.0	24.1	45.0	38.8	10.9	5.3	35.1	28.6	25.5	13.6	15.0	7.6
Food and kindred products	4.4	2.7	3.4	1.6	3.4	2.1	4.7	3.5	5.7	3.0	8.0	2.6	3.2	2.3
Textile-mill products	18.3	37 6	0.4	0.2	0.5	1.0	....	....	0.4	0.5	0.2	0.4	0.3	0.9
Apparel and other fabricated textile products	0.8	4.5	0.8	2.3	4.7	11.8	0.1	0.2	1.4	7.9	0.8	2.8	0.2	1.2
Logging	....	....	....	....	....	....	0.1	....	....	....	....	....	....	....
Sawmills and planing mills	0.2	....	0.7	....	0.1	....	0.4	....	0.5	....	0.2	0.1	0.2	....
Furniture, store fixtures, and miscellaneous wooden goods	0.3	0.1	0.8	0.1	1.3	0.4	0.7	0.1	1.4	0.5	0.8	0.2	0.5	0.2
Paper and allied products	1.0	0.9	2.5	1.6	0.9	1.3	....	....	0.9	1.2	1.0	0.7	0.2	0.2
Printing, publishing, and allied industries	1.4	0.3	2.3	1.4	2.6	1.3	2.3	1.1	2.7	1.5	3.5	3.1	2.7	1.1
Chemicals and allied products	1.1	0.3	3.6	1.1	0.6	0.5	0.2	0.1	1.0	1.6	0.6	0.5	0.6	0.3
Petroleum and coal products	0.2	....	0.1	....	0.1	....	0.2	....	0.4	0.2	0.3	....	0.9	0.3
Leather and leather products	0.9	1.4	0.2	....	1.8	2.7	....	....	3.5	5.6	0.2	0.2	0.1	....
Stone, clay, and glass products	0.4	0.1	0.6	0.1	0.7	0.1	0.2	....	1.0	0.1	1.5	0.6	0.6	0.1
Iron and steel and their products	10.3	1.2	1.7	0.3	1.7	0.3	0.6	....	4.7	0.9	2.0	0.5	0.8	0.1
Nonferrous metals and their products	0.9	....	0.3	....	0.5	0.1	0.2	....	0.9	0.2	0.5	0.1	2.8	0.2
Machinery	3.9	0.2	0.8	0.1	6.8	2.3	0.5	0.1	4.8	2.5	3.5	0.6	0.9	0.3
Automobiles and automobile equipment	0.7	....	0.2	0.1	0.8	0.5	0.3	0.1	1.7	0.4	0.8	0.1	0.1	....
Transportation equipment, except automobile	0.2	....	0.2	....	0.2	....	0.1	....	1.0	0.1	0.1	....	....	....
Other and not specified manufacturing industries	2.1	2.1	8.3	15.1	18.4	14.2	0.3	0.1	2.2	2.5	1.3	1.2	0.8	0.5
Transport., commun., and other public utilities	12.3	1.6	13.5	2.9	7.4	3.3	19.1	6.6	11.8	3.7	16.2	4.8	16.4	6.7
Railroads (inc. railroad repair shops) and railway express service	7.4	0.3	6.9	0.8	2.0	0.2	12.5	0.4	5.0	0.9	10.2	2.0	7.9	0.5
Trucking service	1.3	....	1.5	0.1	1.1	0.1	0.9	0.1	2.1	0.2	1.4	0.2	1.6	0.2
Other transportation	1.3	0.1	2.2	0.2	1.5	0.2	2.0	0.2	2.5	0.4	2.1	0.3	2.5	0.4
Communication	0.4	0.6	0.9	1.5	0.6	2.3	1.4	5.1	0.8	1.9	0.9	1.9	1.7	5.0
Utilities	1.8	0.5	1.9	0.2	2.1	0.6	2.2	0.8	1.4	0.4	1.5	0.4	2.7	0.6
Wholesale and retail trade	17.6	15.8	24.4	16.9	19.2	17.0	26.4	21.3	22.9	21.7	25.2	26.8	27.4	27.7
Wholesale trade	2.7	0.8	5.9	2.0	2.7	1.1	6.3	2.6	5.5	3.6	6.5	3.9	7.0	3.3
Food and dairy products stores, and milk retailing	4.4	2.3	5.4	2.0	4.6	2.3	4.3	1.9	4.7	2.7	4.6	2.6	3.9	2.4
Eating and drinking places	1.9	3.7	1.7	3.0	2.6	2.9	4.3	5.1	2.8	4.4	2.7	5.1	2.3	4.7
Motor vehicles and accessories retailing, and filling stations	1.7	0.3	2.7	0.3	2.0	0.2	3.0	0.5	2.0	0.3	2.4	0.3	3.8	0.7
Other retail trade	6.8	8.6	8.7	9.6	7.3	10.5	8.4	11.1	7.9	10.7	8.9	14.9	10.3	16.5
Finance, insurance, and real estate	2.7	2.4	5.8	5.5	3.2	3.1	4.6	5.3	4.7	4.6	5.7	6.2	5.7	6.2
Business and repair services	2.3	0.4	2.1	0.4	2.6	0.6	3.1	0.9	2.8	0.8	2.8	1.2	3.7	0.8
Automobile storage, rental, and repair services	1.2	0.1	1.1	0.1	1.4	0.1	1.7	0.2	1.4	0.1	1.4	0.1	2.1	0.1
Business and repair services, except automobile	1.1	0.4	1.0	0.3	1.1	0.6	1.4	0.8	1.5	0.8	1.4	1.1	1.6	0.8
Personal services	4.2	14.4	6.1	31.1	3.8	14.1	4.8	18.4	5.0	23.2	3.4	20.1	4.1	19.6
Domestic service	0.5	8.4	1.6	22.8	0.5	8.5	0.6	8.8	0.9	13.3	0.4	13.5	0.3	9.3
Hotels and lodging places	1.5	2.3	1.5	2.7	1.0	1.6	1.6	3.9	1.5	3.4	0.9	2.3	1.2	3.4
Laundering, cleaning, and dyeing services	0.7	1.4	1.4	3.0	0.9	1.7	1.1	2.7	1.1	3.3	0.7	1.7	1.1	3.5
Miscellaneous personal services	1.5	2.2	1.6	2.6	1.4	2.3	1.6	3.0	1.5	3.2	1.3	2.7	1.4	3.4
Amusement, recreation, and related services	0.9	0.6	1.1	0.4	1.0	0.5	1.3	1.4	1.1	0.6	1.1	0.6	1.4	1.3
Professional and related services	4.1	10.6	4.5	13.4	5.0	16.5	5.0	16.7	4.4	13.4	5.8	19.9	6.5	21.7
Government	3.0	1.3	5.7	4.3	4.2	2.3	12.5	21.8	4.4	1.5	6.5	5.1	7.3	5.5
Industry not reported	0.8	1.2	0.7	0.5	2.1	3.6	0.9	1.4	1.2	1.4	0.9	1.3	1.4	2.1

TABLE 75.—PERCENT DISTRIBUTION BY INDUSTRY GROUP, FOR MALE AND FEMALE EMPLOYED WORKERS 14 YEARS OLD AND OVER, FOR CITIES OF 100,000 OR MORE: 1940—Continued

[Percent not shown where less than 0.1]

INDUSTRY GROUP	SAN ANTONIO, TEX.		SAN DIEGO, CALIF.		SAN FRANCISCO, CALIF.		SCRANTON, PA.		SEATTLE, WASH.		SOMERVILLE, MASS.		SOUTH BEND, IND.		SPOKANE, WASH.	
	Male	Female	Male	Female	Male	Female	Male	Female	Male	Female	Male	Female	Male	Female	Male	Female
Employed (exc. on public emergency work)	100.0	100.0	100.0	100.0	100.0	100.0	100.0	100.0	100.0	100.0	100.0	100.0	100.0	100.0	100.0	100.0
Agriculture, forestry, and fishery	1.2	0.3	3.2	0.5	0.9	0.1	0.3	......	2.2	0.2	0.7	0.1	0.3	0.1	1.5	0.3
Agriculture	1.2	0.3	1.4	0.4	0.5	0.1	0.2	......	0.9	0.1	0.2	......	0.3	0.1	1.2	0.3
Forestry (except logging) and fishery	......	......	1.8	0.1	0.3	......	0.1	......	1.3	......	0.5	......	......	......	0.3	......
Mining	0.9	0.2	0.2	......	0.2	0.1	17.8	0.7	0.4	0.1	0.1	......	......	......	0.6	0.1
Coal mining	......	......	......	......	......	......	17.8	0.7	0.2	......	......	......	......	......	......	......
Crude petroleum and natural gas production	0.8	0.2	......	......	......	......	......	......	......	......	......	......	......	......	......	......
Other mines and quarries	0.1	......	0.1	......	0.2	0.1	......	......	0.3	......	0.1	......	......	......	0.6	0.1
Construction	8.5	0.3	6.4	0.4	7.0	0.5	4.7	0.3	7.6	0.4	6.7	0.5	3.8	0.3	8.2	0.4
Manufacturing	12.4	8.4	15.2	7.5	17.9	13.6	15.1	26.7	23.4	9.9	29.2	26.8	53.2	34.5	17.6	6.9
Food and kindred products	4.6	1.9	2.7	5.1	3.9	3.0	3.9	1.7	3.7	2.6	8.1	6.7	2.7	0.9	4.7	2.5
Textile-mill products	0.1	0.1	......	0.1	0.3	0.5	3.2	11.1	0.2	0.3	0.6	0.9	0.1	0.8	0.1	......
Apparel and other fabricated textile products	0.3	3.5	0.1	0.3	0.7	3.2	1.0	8.7	0.4	2.6	0.6	3.8	1.1	13.4	0.1	0.4
Logging	0.1	......	......	......	......	......	......	......	0.6	0.1	......	......	......	......	0.6	......
Sawmills and planing mills	0.5	......	0.3	......	0.2	......	0.1	......	2.1	0.2	0.2	0.1	0.2	......	4.1	0.4
Furniture, store fixtures, and miscellaneous wooden goods	0.6	0.2	0.3	0.1	1.0	0.4	0.4	0.2	0.9	0.2	1.6	0.3	0.7	0.2	1.3	0.9
Paper and allied products	0.1	0.1	......	......	0.4	0.6	0.1	0.1	0.3	0.3	1.1	1.7	0.7	0.7	0.3	0.1
Printing, publishing, and allied industries	1.9	0.8	1.5	0.8	3.0	1.8	2.2	1.1	2.4	1.1	2.5	2.3	1.0	0.7	2.4	1.6
Chemicals and allied products	0.4	0.1	0.2	0.1	0.8	0.6	0.4	0.2	0.6	0.4	1.9	1.7	0.5	0.3	0.4	0.1
Petroleum and coal products	0.3	0.1	......	......	0.5	0.4	0.1	......	0.1	......	0.4	0.2	0.4	......	0.3	......
Leather and leather products	0.1	......	......	......	0.3	0.2	0.1	0.4	0.1	0.1	1.3	3.1	......	......	......	......
Stone, clay, and glass products	0.6	0.1	0.2	......	0.4	0.2	0.3	......	0.4	0.1	0.4	0.2	0.2	0.1	0.4	......
Iron and steel and their products	0.7	0.1	0.3	......	2.1	0.7	0.6	0.1	2.6	0.5	1.9	0.6	1.9	0.3	0.6	0.1
Nonferrous metals and their products	0.2	......	0.2	......	0.6	0.1	0.1	......	0.5	0.1	0.6	0.2	0.2	......	0.2	......
Machinery	1.0	0.1	0.3	0.1	1.4	0.5	0.9	0.4	1.4	0.4	2.0	1.2	12.4	3.4	1.1	0.3
Automobiles and automobile equipment	0.2	......	0.1	......	0.4	0.1	......	......	0.4	0.1	1.1	0.2	25.5	9.0	0.3	0.1
Transportation equipment, except automobile	......	......	8.9	0.5	0.8	......	0.1	......	6.0	0.3	2.0	0.1	2.3	0.6	0.1	......
Other and not specified manufacturing industries	0.7	1.2	0.3	0.3	1.2	1.3	1.6	2.5	0.9	0.5	2.8	3.5	2.3	4.0	0.6	0.3
Transport., commun., and other public utilities	8.5	2.1	5.1	2.4	13.7	6.0	15.7	3.2	13.7	4.8	14.1	5.7	7.0	2.2	16.8	4.8
Railroads (inc. railroad repair shops) and railway express service	3.0	0.2	0.5	0.1	2.4	0.7	9.4	0.9	2.5	0.4	3.9	0.5	1.1	......	8.8	0.7
Trucking service	1.2	0.1	0.5	0.1	1.3	0.2	2.0	0.1	1.3	0.3	3.2	0.2	2.3	0.2	2.0	0.3
Other transportation	1.6	0.1	1.6	0.2	7.6	0.9	1.8	0.2	6.6	0.8	4.5	0.8	1.0	0.1	2.3	0.4
Communication	0.7	1.3	0.5	1.6	1.0	3.4	0.5	1.1	1.2	2.8	0.9	3.6	0.5	0.8	1.2	2.8
Utilities	1.5	0.3	1.9	0.5	1.4	0.7	1.9	0.8	2.0	0.5	1.0	0.5	2.2	1.0	2.5	0.7
Wholesale and retail trade	27.0	25.1	19.0	26.0	25.7	24.2	23.0	20.5	24.6	29.7	26.0	22.8	17.8	19.4	26.8	29.1
Wholesale trade	5.3	3.5	3.2	1.3	5.6	4.5	3.0	1.4	6.7	4.2	5.4	3.1	3.2	1.0	6.1	2.7
Food and dairy products stores, and milk retailing	5.9	2.5	3.8	3.2	4.6	2.4	6.0	2.9	4.2	3.3	7.7	3.8	3.6	3.0	4.5	3.4
Eating and drinking places	3.3	6.7	2.7	7.6	5.5	4.5	2.1	3.1	3.0	7.1	3.6	4.7	1.9	3.5	2.7	7.9
Motor vehicles and accessories retailing, and filling stations	3.5	0.5	2.7	0.5	1.8	0.4	2.2	0.4	2.6	0.5	1.6	0.3	2.3	0.3	3.5	0.6
Other retail trade	8.9	11.8	6.5	13.5	8.2	12.5	8.8	12.7	8.1	14.5	7.8	10.9	6.9	11.6	10.0	14.5
Finance, insurance, and real estate	4.3	4.7	3.5	6.3	6.8	10.3	3.2	3.5	5.8	8.9	4.3	8.6	3.3	5.8	6.1	8.1
Business and repair services	3.7	0.8	2.7	1.0	3.4	1.4	2.4	0.4	3.2	1.3	2.9	0.9	2.2	0.8	3.8	1.3
Automobile storage, rental, and repair services	2.2	0.1	1.5	0.1	1.6	0.1	1.4	0.1	1.7	0.1	1.7	0.1	1.1	0.1	2.2	0.2
Business and repair services, except automobile	1.4	0.7	1.2	0.9	1.9	1.3	1.0	0.3	1.5	1.2	1.2	0.9	1.0	0.7	1.6	1.1
Personal services	7.2	36.1	4.4	28.5	7.1	19.4	4.0	16.7	4.5	20.9	4.3	13.8	3.1	18.8	4.8	24.1
Domestic service	2.2	24.5	0.9	15.9	1.4	9.6	0.5	11.0	0.6	11.4	0.3	6.5	0.3	11.2	0.4	12.4
Hotels and lodging places	1.6	3.1	1.3	4.8	2.5	3.7	1.2	1.8	1.5	3.8	1.1	1.7	0.8	2.3	1.9	4.9
Laundering, cleaning, and dyeing services	1.3	3.5	1.0	3.3	1.6	2.8	0.7	2.0	1.0	2.3	1.3	3.1	0.8	2.2	0.9	2.9
Miscellaneous personal services	2.2	5.0	1.2	4.5	1.6	3.3	1.0	2.0	1.5	3.4	1.6	2.6	1.2	3.2	1.6	3.9
Amusement, recreation, and related services	1.4	0.8	1.3	1.2	1.6	1.4	1.1	0.6	1.2	1.3	0.8	0.7	0.8	0.5	1.3	1.0
Professional and related services	4.2	17.0	4.9	20.5	5.5	16.4	5.5	20.5	6.0	17.9	4.3	14.4	4.9	14.2	5.6	19.6
Government	19.3	3.3	33.4	4.2	8.5	3.9	4.2	2.9	6.3	2.9	5.6	3.3	2.5	1.6	5.6	2.5
Industry not reported	1.5	1.0	0.7	1.5	1.7	2.7	3.0	4.0	1.1	1.8	1.1	2.4	1.0	1.7	1.3	1.8

TABLE 75.—PERCENT DISTRIBUTION BY INDUSTRY GROUP, FOR MALE AND FEMALE EMPLOYED WORKERS 14 YEARS OLD AND OVER, FOR CITIES OF 100,000 OR MORE: 1940—Continued

[Percent not shown where less than 0.1]

INDUSTRY GROUP	SPRINGFIELD, MASS.		SYRACUSE, N. Y.		TACOMA, WASH.		TAMPA, FLA.		TOLEDO, OHIO		TRENTON, N. J.		TULSA, OKLA.	
	Male	Female	Male	Female	Male	Female	Male	Female	Male	Female	Male	Female	Male	Female
Employed (exc. on public emergency work)	100.0	100.0	100.0	100.0	100.0	100.0	100.0	100.0	100.0	100.0	100.0	100.0	100.0	100.0
Agriculture, forestry, and fishery	0.6	—	0.4	0.1	1.5	0.3	1.2	0.1	0.5	0.1	0.5	0.1	0.5	0.1
Agriculture	0.5	—	0.4	0.1	0.8	0.3	1.0	0.1	0.4	0.1	0.4	0.1	0.5	0.1
Forestry (except logging) and fishery	—	—	—	—	0.6	—	0.2	—	—	—	—	—	—	—
Mining	0.1	—	0.1	—	0.2	—	0.1	—	0.1	—	0.1	—	10.4	6.0
Coal mining	—	—	—	—	0.1	—	—	—	—	—	—	—	0.1	—
Crude petroleum and natural gas production	—	—	—	—	—	—	—	—	—	—	—	—	10.2	6.0
Other mines and quarries	—	—	0.1	—	0.2	—	0.1	—	—	—	0.1	—	0.1	—
Construction	5.8	0.4	4.4	0.3	8.0	0.3	7.1	0.2	5.4	0.4	6.0	0.2	7.9	0.5
Manufacturing	40.1	23.2	37.5	20.9	34.4	11.1	27.2	28.2	40.3	24.9	42.7	39.9	19.2	4.9
Food and kindred products	2.8	1.2	3.3	1.2	4.1	2.6	5.2	1.7	3.1	1.6	2.7	0.9	2.5	0.6
Textile-mill products	1.2	2.5	0.1	0.1	—	0.1	—	—	0.5	0.3	2.0	1.8	0.2	0.3
Apparel and other fabricated textile products	0.5	2.4	0.7	2.9	0.1	1.2	0.1	1.1	0.5	3.0	0.8	6.0	0.1	0.3
Logging	—	—	—	—	1.2	0.2	0.1	—	—	—	—	—	—	—
Sawmills and planing mills	0.1	0.1	0.1	—	12.4	1.4	0.5	0.1	0.2	—	0.1	—	0.1	—
Furniture, store fixtures, and miscellaneous wooden goods	1.3	0.8	1.0	0.4	3.2	3.2	1.4	1.1	0.5	0.2	0.5	0.3	0.3	0.1
Paper and allied products	1.6	2.5	0.5	0.7	1.5	0.2	0.1	—	0.5	0.6	0.4	0.3	0.1	—
Printing, publishing, and allied industries	3.1	2.3	2.4	1.4	1.9	0.9	1.8	0.6	1.6	0.8	1.2	0.5	2.3	1.0
Chemicals and allied products	1.9	0.8	2.9	1.2	1.0	0.3	1.1	0.1	0.9	0.3	0.6	0.2	0.5	0.2
Petroleum and coal products	0.1	—	0.1	—	0.1	—	0.1	—	1.9	0.5	0.1	—	5.0	1.0
Leather and leather products	0.2	0.7	0.7	2.6	0.1	0.1	—	—	0.2	—	0.3	0.8	—	—
Stone, clay, and glass products	0.3	—	1.2	1.6	0.3	—	1.0	0.1	4.9	2.9	7.0	6.2	0.4	0.1
Iron and steel and their products	6.8	1.2	8.0	1.4	1.4	0.1	0.7	0.1	4.9	1.3	10.8	2.3	2.7	0.2
Nonferrous metals and their products	0.7	0.2	1.4	0.5	3.9	0.2	0.1	—	1.2	0.3	0.5	0.3	0.3	—
Machinery	12.6	5.2	9.7	4.6	0.6	0.1	0.4	—	7.0	4.2	4.1	2.4	3.5	0.8
Automobiles and automobile equipment	0.5	0.2	3.2	1.0	0.1	—	0.1	—	9.9	6.3	2.6	3.3	0.2	—
Transportation equipment, except automobile	2.4	0.2	0.3	0.1	2.0	0.1	3.8	—	0.6	0.1	0.4	0.2	0.3	0.1
Other and not specified manufacturing industries	4.1	3.0	1.8	1.2	0.7	0.3	10.7	23.1	2.0	2.4	8.5	14.3	0.7	0.2
Transport., commun., and other public utilities	8.7	3.6	10.5	3.7	14.2	4.5	12.9	1.9	13.5	3.3	7.8	1.7	9.3	3.4
Railroads (inc. railroad repair shops) and railway express service	3.1	0.2	4.0	0.2	7.2	0.8	4.1	0.2	7.3	0.5	3.7	0.2	2.1	0.2
Trucking service	1.6	0.2	1.6	0.2	0.9	0.2	1.0	0.1	1.7	0.2	1.0	0.1	1.7	0.2
Other transportation	1.2	0.2	1.7	0.3	3.8	0.6	5.2	0.3	2.0	0.2	1.0	0.2	3.1	0.5
Communication	0.9	2.3	0.9	2.1	0.8	2.6	0.8	1.0	0.6	1.9	0.4	1.0	1.0	1.8
Utilities	1.8	0.7	2.4	0.9	1.6	0.3	1.7	0.3	2.0	0.5	1.6	0.2	1.4	0.7
Wholesale and retail trade	22.0	22.4	22.9	21.8	20.1	28.2	29.2	17.5	21.5	24.0	19.0	14.0	25.6	24.3
Wholesale trade	3.8	2.0	4.7	2.1	4.0	2.2	7.8	2.0	4.4	2.0	2.4	0.8	6.4	2.1
Food and dairy products stores, and milk retailing	5.3	2.7	5.0	2.4	4.1	5.0	6.0	2.1	4.5	3.1	5.3	2.3	4.2	2.3
Eating and drinking places	2.4	3.7	3.0	4.1	2.2	6.1	3.7	4.8	2.7	5.6	2.6	2.7	2.6	6.8
Motor vehicles and accessories retailing, and filling stations	2.3	0.5	2.3	0.5	2.7	0.7	3.3	0.4	2.5	0.4	1.6	0.3	4.2	0.5
Other retail trade	8.1	13.5	7.9	12.8	7.1	14.1	8.4	8.2	7.4	12.9	7.1	7.9	8.1	12.8
Finance, insurance, and real estate	4.8	7.5	4.3	5.5	3.5	5.9	3.0	3.0	3.2	3.9	2.5	2.1	6.0	6.5
Business and repair services	2.7	0.8	2.7	0.8	3.0	0.7	3.0	0.5	2.4	0.8	2.2	0.3	3.8	0.8
Automobile storage, rental, and repair services	1.4	0.1	1.5	0.1	1.8	0.1	1.9	—	1.3	0.1	1.4	0.1	2.1	0.1
Business and repair services, except automobile	1.3	0.7	1.2	0.7	1.2	0.6	1.1	0.5	1.2	0.7	0.9	0.3	1.7	0.7
Personal services	3.9	19.1	3.9	20.3	3.2	21.1	6.5	34.3	3.6	20.7	4.0	16.6	6.0	35.0
Domestic service	0.5	11.6	0.5	12.4	0.3	12.5	1.6	23.8	0.4	12.9	0.6	10.6	1.5	23.6
Hotels and lodging places	1.3	2.8	1.2	3.2	0.8	2.6	1.6	4.3	1.1	2.5	0.7	1.3	1.6	3.7
Laundering, cleaning, and dyeing services	0.7	2.1	0.8	2.2	0.7	2.4	1.4	3.1	0.8	2.0	0.9	2.4	1.3	2.9
Miscellaneous personal services	1.3	2.5	1.4	2.6	1.5	3.7	1.9	3.1	1.3	3.2	1.8	2.2	1.7	4.8
Amusement, recreation, and related services	1.0	0.4	1.1	0.6	0.9	0.9	1.7	0.6	1.0	0.5	0.9	0.3	1.3	0.6
Professional and related services	4.3	17.7	5.8	20.1	5.2	21.4	3.9	11.1	4.3	18.4	5.4	14.2	5.5	14.2
Government	5.0	2.5	4.9	3.0	5.0	4.1	3.4	1.5	3.5	2.1	7.3	8.3	3.2	1.7
Industry not reported	1.1	2.3	1.6	2.9	0.9	1.3	0.9	0.8	0.6	0.9	1.5	2.2	1.2	1.9

TABLE 75.—PERCENT DISTRIBUTION BY INDUSTRY GROUP, FOR MALE AND FEMALE EMPLOYED WORKERS 14 YEARS OLD AND OVER, FOR CITIES OF 100,000 OR MORE: 1940—Continued

[Percent not shown where less than 0.1]

INDUSTRY GROUP	UTICA, N. Y.		WASHINGTON, D. C.		WICHITA, KANS.		WILMINGTON, DEL.		WORCESTER, MASS.		YONKERS, N. Y.		YOUNGSTOWN, OHIO	
	Male	Female	Male	Female	Male	Female	Male	Female	Male	Female	Male	Female	Male	Female
Employed (etc. on public emergency work)	100.0	100.0	100.0	100.0	100.0	100.0	100.0	100.0	1000.0	100.0	100.0	100.0	100.0	100.0
Agriculture, forestry, and fishery	0.6		0.3		1.0	0.2	0.4		0.5		0.8	0.1	0.2	
Agriculture	0.6		0.3		0.9	0.2	0.4		0.4		0.7	0.1	0.2	
Forestry (except logging) and fishery							0.1		0.1					
Mining			0.1		2.2	0.5	0.1				0.2		0.1	
Coal mining													0.1	
Crude petroleum and natural gas production					2.2	0.5								
Other mines and quarries			0.1		0.1		01				0.2			
Construction	5.3	0.3	10.2	0.3	7.8	0.4	9.2	0.5	4.9	0.3	8.6	0.5	4.7	0.5
Manufacturing	36.5	35.8	10.1	2.5	22.5	7.6	37.6	26.4	47.8	29.9	28.2	27.7	56.0	15.1
Food and kindred products	4.2	1.0	1.5	0.3	0.6	2.5	2.4	0.9	2.5	0.8	2.7	0.6	2.3	1.0
Textile-mill products	10.4	25.0					4.5	3.8	2.9	4.7	9.6	12.6		0.1
Apparel and other fabricated textile products	0.8	1.9		0.1	0.2	0.6	0.3	5.6	0.6	4.2	1.7	8.1	0.1	1.7
Logging	0.1													
Sawmills and planing mills	0.2		0.1		0.4	0.1	0.1		0.1		0.1			
Furniture, store fixtures, and miscellaneous wooden goods	1.1	0.3	0.1		0.3	0.1	0.8	0.5	0.6	0.2	0.3		0.8	0.4
Paper and allied products	0.3	1.0	0.1	0.1	0.2	0.1	0.2	0.1	1.1	2.4	0.3	0.2		
Printing, publishing, and allied industries	1.6	0.5	4.0	1.6	3.0	1.7	1.3	0.7	1.9	1.3	2.5	1.7	0.9	0.6
Chemicals and allied products	1.4	0.9	0.1	0.1	0.5	0.1	10.9	9.3	0.4	0.3	1.0	1.3	0.3	0.1
Petroleum and coal products	0.1				1.4	0.6	0.5		0.1		0.3	0.1	0.1	
Leather and leather products	0.2	0.2			0.1	0.1	5.4	3.2	4.0	6.3	0.1		0.2	0.2
Stone, clay, and glass products	0.3	0.1	0.3		0.3	0.1	0.3		3.9	1.2	0.2	0.1	0.4	0.2
Iron and steel and their products	8.2	1.4	3.1	0.2	2.1	0.5	2.9	0.6	14.8	3.2	0.9	0.3	46.9	5.1
Nonferrous metals and their products	1.0	0.1	0.1		0.5	0.2	0.5		.0.5	0.2	0.3	0.1	0.2	0.3
Machinery	1.9	0.3	0.3		1.7	0.4	1.1	0.1	10.1	2.0	5.5	1.8	1.8	3.5
Automobiles and automobile equipment	0.7	0.1			0.2	0.1	0.2		0.2	0.1	1.2	0.2	0.1	0.2
Transportation equipment, except automobile	0.2		0.1		4.3	0.3	4.2	0.3	0.7	0.1	0.3			
Other and not specified manufacturing industries	2.7	3.0	0.2	0.1	0.7	0.2	1.8	1.1	3.5	2.9	1.2	0.7	1.7	1.7
Transport., commun., and other public utilities	11.8	2.6	9.4	2.8	11.6	3.3	14.6	2.1	6.9	2.3	11.1	4.9	8.1	3.4
Railroads, (inc. railroad repair shops) and railway express service	5.9	0.7	2.3	0.2	3.7	0.2	7.5	0.1	1.7	0.1	2.6	0.6	4.2	0.5
Trucking service	1.8	0.1	0.8	0.1	2.0	0.2	0.6	0.1	1.3	0.1	1.0	0.1	1.2	0.1
Other transportation	1.3	0.2	3.6	0.2	2.5	0.4	4.0	0.2	1.4	0.2	2.2	0.2	1.0	0.3
Communication	0.5	1.1	0.9	2.0	1.0	1.7	0.4	1.1	0.6	1.4	1.3	2.6	0.4	1.5
Utilities	2.3	0.6	1.9	0.3	2.4	0.7	2.1	0.6	1.9	0.5	4.0	1.4	1.3	0.9
Wholesale and retail trade	23.7	16.0	19.4	13.2	27.7	27.7	16.7	17.3	18.9	18.1	21.2	13.2	15.9	28.4
Wholesale trade	4.1	1.2	2.6	0.6	7.7	3.0	2.2	0.7	3.1	1.2	4.3	1.9	2.5	1.3
Food and dairy products stores, and milk retailing	5.6	2.2	3.8	1.2	4.3	2.6	4.2	2.7	4.5	2.4	5.8	2.0	3.8	5.3
Eating and drinking places	3.1	2.2	3.2	3.7	2.4	8.1	1.8	4.3	2.4	3.2	2.1	1.6	1.8	5.4
Motor vehicles and accessories retailing, and filling stations	2.3	0.4	2.0	0.2	4.4	0.6	1.7	0.3	1.8	0.3	1.6	0.2	2.0	0.5
Other retail trade	8.6	10.1	7.8	7 6	8.8	13.3	6.8	9.3	7.1	11.0	7.4	7.5	5.9	15.9
Finance, insurance, and real estate	3.7	4.1	5.0	4.2	6.1	8.3	3.5	4.2	2.8	4.3	7.4	6.8	2.3	3.8
Business and repair services	2.6	0.5	2.4	0.6	3.7	0.9	2.0	0.7	2.0	0.4	3.2	1.3	2.2	0.8
Automobile storage, rental, and repair services	1.5	0.1	1.4		2.1	0.1	1.0	0.1	1.1	0.1	1.5		1.2	0.1
Business and repair services, except automobile	1.1	0.4	1.0	0.6	1.6	0.7	1.0	0.6	0.9	0.3	1.7	1.2	1.0	0.7
Personal services	4.1	18.8	6.2	29.5	4.6	26.6	4.6	28.5	3.2	17.1	4.2	21.3	2.7	24.2
Domestic service	0.5	12.0	1.4	20.8	0.6	15.1	1.7	21.5	0.5	10.8	1.2	15.8	0.3	16.4
Hotels and lodging places	1.2	2.5	2.0	3.9	1.2	3.3	0.8	2.4	0.7	2.3	0.4	0.8	0.7	2.4
Laundering, cleaning, and dyeing services	0.8	1.9	1.4	2.4	1.2	3.1	0.7	2.0	0.8	2.0	1.2	2.4	0.6	2.4
Miscellaneous personal services	1.7	2.3	1.4	2.3	1.6	5.1	1.4	2.6	1.3	2.1	1.4	2.2	1.2	3.1
Amusement, recreation, and related services	1.1	0.5	1.1	0.5	1.5	0.7	1.0	0.4	0.8	0.4	1.2	0.8	0.9	0.8
Professional and related services	5.2	17.0	7.4	13.3	5.5	19.3	3.8	14.7	5.7	20.3	7.2	19.2	3.4	19.1
Government	4.4	2.0	27.3	31.7	4.2	2.6	3.6	1.7	3.9	2.4	5.3	2.1	2.5	2.0
Industry not reported	1.1	2.4	1.2	1.3	1.4	2.0	2.8	3.5	2.6	4.3	1.4	2.2	1.0	1.9

INDEX

A

Bold face numbers indicate original 1940 Census documents and refer to numbers at the bottom of the page.

Bold face numbers indicate original 1940 Census documents and refer to numbers at the bottom of the page.

D

Bold face numbers indicate original 1940 Census documents and refer to numbers at the bottom of the page.

Bold face numbers indicate original 1940 Census documents and refer to numbers at the bottom of the page.

H

I

J

K

L

Bold face numbers indicate original 1940 Census documents and refer to numbers at the bottom of the page.

Bold face numbers indicate original 1940 Census documents and refer to numbers at the bottom of the page.

Bold face numbers indicate original 1940 Census documents and refer to numbers at the bottom of the page.

Q

R

S

Bold face numbers indicate original 1940 Census documents and refer to numbers at the bottom of the page.

Bold face numbers indicate original 1940 Census documents and refer to numbers at the bottom of the page.

V

W

Y

Z

Bold face numbers indicate original 1940 Census documents and refer to numbers at the bottom of the page.